MW01602333

UNITED STATES CODE
TITLE 18
CRIMES AND CRIMINAL PROCEDURE
(2/3)
2018 EDITION

Updated as of April 23, 2018

THE LAW LIBRARY

TABLE OF CONTENTS

CHAPTER 102 - RIOTS

Amendments
1968—Pub. L. 90–284, title I, §104(a), Apr. 11, 1968, 82 Stat. 75, added chapter 102 and items 2101 and 2102.

§2101. Riots
(a) Whoever travels in interstate or foreign commerce or uses any facility of interstate or foreign commerce, including, but not limited to, the mail, telegraph, telephone, radio, or television, with intent—

(1) to incite a riot; or

(2) to organize, promote, encourage, participate in, or carry on a riot; or

(3) to commit any act of violence in furtherance of a riot; or

(4) to aid or abet any person in inciting or participating in or carrying on a riot or committing any act of violence in furtherance of a riot;

and who either during the course of any such travel or use or thereafter performs or attempts to perform any other overt act for any purpose specified in subparagraph (A), (B), (C), or (D) of this paragraph— 1

Shall be fined under this title, or imprisoned not more than five years, or both.

(b) In any prosecution under this section, proof that a defendant engaged or attempted to engage in one or more of the overt acts described in subparagraph (A), (B), (C), or (D) of paragraph (1) of subsection (a) 2 and (1) has traveled in interstate or foreign commerce, or (2) has use of or used any facility of interstate or foreign commerce, including but not limited to, mail, telegraph, telephone, radio, or television, to communicate with or broadcast to any person or group of persons prior to such overt acts, such travel or use shall be admissible proof to establish that such defendant traveled in or used such facility of interstate or foreign commerce.

(c) A judgment of conviction or acquittal on the merits under the laws of any State shall be a bar to any prosecution hereunder for the same act or acts.

(d) Whenever, in the opinion of the Attorney General or of the appropriate officer of the Department of Justice charged by law or under the instructions of the Attorney General with authority to act, any person shall have violated this chapter, the Department shall proceed as speedily as possible with a prosecution of such person hereunder and with any appeal which may lie from any decision adverse to the Government resulting from such prosecution.

(e) Nothing contained in this section shall be construed to make it unlawful for any person to travel in, or use any facility of, interstate or foreign commerce for the purpose of pursuing the legitimate objectives of organized labor, through orderly and lawful means.

(f) Nothing in this section shall be construed as indicating an intent on the part of Congress to prevent any State, any possession or Commonwealth of the United States, or the District of Columbia, from exercising jurisdiction over any offense over which it would have jurisdiction in the absence of this section; nor shall anything in this section be construed as depriving State and local law enforcement authorities of responsibility for prosecuting acts that may be violations of this section and that are violations of State and local law.

(Added Pub. L. 90–284, title I, §104(a), Apr. 11, 1968, 82 Stat. 75; amended Pub. L. 99–386, title I, §106, Aug. 22, 1986, 100 Stat. 822; Pub. L. 103–322, title XXXIII, §330016(1)(L), Sept. 13, 1994, 108 Stat. 2147; Pub. L. 104–294, title VI, §601(f)(15), Oct. 11, 1996, 110 Stat. 3500.)

Amendments

1996—Subsec. (a). Pub. L. 104–294 struck out par. (1) designation and redesignated subpars. (A) to (D) as pars. (1) to (4), respectively.

1994—Subsec. (a)(1). Pub. L. 103–322 substituted "fined under this title" for "fined not more than $10,000".

1986—Subsec. (d). Pub. L. 99–386 struck out "; or in the alternative shall report in writing, to the respective Houses of the Congress, the Department's reason for not so proceeding" after "such prosecution".

§2102. Definitions

(a) As used in this chapter, the term "riot" means a public disturbance involving (1) an act or acts of violence by one or more persons part of an assemblage of three or more persons, which act or acts shall constitute a clear and present danger of, or shall result in, damage or injury to the property of any other person or to the person of any other individual or (2) a threat or threats of the commission of an act or acts of violence by one or more persons part of an assemblage of three or more persons having, individually or collectively, the ability of immediate execution of such threat or threats, where the performance of the threatened act or acts of violence would constitute a clear and present danger of, or would result in, damage or injury to the property of any other person or to the person of any other individual.

(b) As used in this chapter, the term "to incite a riot", or "to organize, promote, encourage, participate in, or carry on a riot", includes, but is not limited to, urging or instigating other persons to riot, but shall not be deemed to mean the mere oral or written (1) advocacy of ideas or (2) expression of belief, not involving advocacy of any act or acts of violence or assertion of the rightness of, or the right to commit, any such act or acts.

(Added Pub. L. 90–284, title I, §104(a), Apr. 11, 1968, 82 Stat. 76.)

CHAPTER 103 - ROBBERY AND BURGLARY

Amendments

1992—Pub. L. 102–519, title I, §101(c), Oct. 25, 1992, 106 Stat. 3384, added item 2119.

1984—Pub. L. 98–305, §3, May 31, 1984, 98 Stat. 222, added item 2118.

1966—Pub. L. 89–654, §2(d), Oct. 14, 1966, 80 Stat. 904, substituted "Breaking or entering carrier facilities" for "Railroad car entered or seal broken" in item 2117.

§2111. Special maritime and territorial jurisdiction

Whoever, within the special maritime and territorial jurisdiction of the United States, by force and violence, or by intimidation, takes or attempts to take from the person or presence of another anything of value, shall be imprisoned not more than fifteen years.

(June 25, 1948, ch. 645, 62 Stat. 796; Pub. L. 103–322, title XXXII, §320903(a)(1), Sept. 13, 1994, 108 Stat. 2124.)

Historical and Revision Notes

Based on title 18, U.S.C., 1940 ed., §463 (Mar. 4, 1909, ch. 321, §284, 35 Stat. 1144).

Words "within the special maritime and territorial jurisdiction of the United States" were added to restrict the place of the offense to those places described in section 451 of title 18, U.S.C., 1940 ed., now section 7 of this title.

Minor changes were made in phraseology.

Amendments

1994—Pub. L. 103–322 inserted "or attempts to take" after "takes".

Short Title of 1996 Amendment

Pub. L. 104–217, §1, Oct. 1, 1996, 110 Stat. 3020, provided that: "This Act [amending section 2119 of this title] may be cited as the 'Carjacking Correction Act of 1996'."

§2112. Personal property of United States

Whoever robs or attempts to rob another of any kind or description of personal property belonging to the United States, shall be imprisoned not more than fifteen years.

(June 25, 1948, ch. 645, 62 Stat. 796; Pub. L. 103–322, title XXXII, §320903(a)(2), Sept. 13, 1994, 108 Stat. 2124.)

Historical and Revision Notes

Based on title 18, U.S.C., 1940 ed., §99 (Mar. 4, 1909, ch. 321, §46, 35 Stat. 1097).

That portion of said section 99 relating to felonious taking was omitted as covered by section 641 of this title.

The punishment by fine of not more than $5,000 or imprisoned not more than 10 years, or both, was changed to harmonize with section 2111 of this title. The 15–year penalty is not excessive for an offense of this type.

Minor verbal change was made.

Amendments

1994—Pub. L. 103–322 inserted "or attempts to rob" after "robs".

§2113. Bank robbery and incidental crimes

(a) Whoever, by force and violence, or by intimidation, takes, or attempts to take, from the person or presence of another, or obtains or attempts to obtain by extortion any property or money or any other thing of value belonging to, or in the care, custody, control, management, or possession of, any bank, credit union, or any savings and loan association; or

Whoever enters or attempts to enter any bank, credit union, or any savings and loan association, or any building used in whole or in part as a bank, credit union, or as a savings and loan association, with intent to commit in such bank, credit union, or in such savings and loan association, or building, or part thereof, so used, any felony affecting such bank, credit union, or such savings and loan association and in violation of any statute of the United States, or any larceny—

Shall be fined under this title or imprisoned not more than twenty years, or both.

(b) Whoever takes and carries away, with intent to steal or purloin, any property or money or any other thing of value exceeding $1,000 belonging to, or in the care, custody, control, management, or possession of any bank, credit union, or any savings and loan association, shall be fined under this title or imprisoned not more than ten years, or both; or

Whoever takes and carries away, with intent to steal or purloin, any property or money or any other thing of value not exceeding $1,000 belonging to, or in the care, custody, control, management, or possession of any bank, credit union, or any savings and loan association, shall be fined under this title or imprisoned not more than one year, or both.

(c) Whoever receives, possesses, conceals, stores, barters, sells, or disposes of, any property or money or other thing of value which has been taken or stolen from a bank, credit union, or savings and loan association in violation of subsection (b), knowing the same to be property which has been stolen shall be subject to the punishment provided in subsection (b) for the taker.

(d) Whoever, in committing, or in attempting to commit, any offense defined in subsections (a) and (b) of this section, assaults any person, or puts in jeopardy the life of any person by the use of a dangerous weapon or device, shall be fined under this title or imprisoned not more than twenty-five years, or both.

(e) Whoever, in committing any offense defined in this section, or in avoiding or attempting to avoid apprehension for the commission of such offense, or in freeing himself or attempting to free himself from arrest or confinement for such offense, kills any person, or forces any person to accompany him without the consent of such person, shall be imprisoned not less than ten years, or if death results shall be punished by death or life imprisonment.

(f) As used in this section the term "bank" means any member bank of the Federal Reserve System, and any bank, banking association, trust company, savings bank, or other banking institution organized or operating under the laws of the United States, including a branch or agency of a foreign bank (as such terms are defined in paragraphs (1) and (3) of section 1(b) of the International Banking Act of 1978), and any institution the deposits of which are insured by the Federal Deposit Insurance Corporation.

(g) As used in this section the term "credit union" means any Federal credit union and any State-chartered credit union the accounts of which are insured by the National Credit Union Administration Board, and any "Federal credit union" as defined in section 2 of the Federal Credit Union Act. The term "State-chartered credit union" includes a credit union chartered under the laws of a State of the United States, the District of Columbia, or any commonwealth, territory, or possession of the United States.

(h) As used in this section, the term "savings and loan association" means—

(1) a Federal savings association or State savings association (as defined in section 3(b) of the Federal Deposit Insurance Act (12 U.S.C. 1813(b))) having accounts insured by the Federal Deposit Insurance Corporation; and

(2) a corporation described in section 3(b)(1)(C) of the Federal Deposit Insurance Act (12 U.S.C. 1813(b)(1)(C)) that is operating under the laws of the United States.

(June 25, 1948, ch. 645, 62 Stat. 796; Aug. 3, 1950, ch. 516, 64 Stat. 394; Apr. 8, 1952, ch. 164, 66 Stat. 46; Pub. L. 86–354, §2, Sept. 22, 1959, 73 Stat. 639; Pub. L. 91–468, §8, Oct. 19, 1970, 84 Stat. 1017; Pub. L. 98–473, title II, §1106, Oct. 12, 1984, 98 Stat. 2145; Pub. L. 99–646, §68, Nov. 10, 1986, 100 Stat. 3616; Pub. L. 101–73, title IX, §962(a)(7), (d), Aug. 9, 1989, 103 Stat. 502, 503; Pub. L. 101–647, title XXV, §2597(l), Nov. 29, 1990, 104 Stat. 4911; Pub. L. 103–322, title VI, §60003(a)(9), title XXXII, §320608, title XXXIII, §330016(1)(K), (L), Sept. 13, 1994, 108 Stat. 1969, 2120, 2147; Pub. L. 104–294, title VI, §§606(a), 607(d), Oct. 11, 1996, 110 Stat. 3511; Pub. L. 107–273, div. B, title IV, §4002(d)(1)(C)(ii), Nov. 2, 2002, 116 Stat. 1809.)

Historical and Revision Notes

Based on sections 588a, 588b, 588c, of title 12, U.S.C., 1940 ed., Banks and Banking (May 18, 1934, ch. 304, §§1, 2, 3, 48 Stat. 783; Aug. 23, 1935, ch. 614, §333, 49 Stat. 720; Aug. 24, 1937, ch. 747, 50 Stat. 749; June 29, 1940, ch. 455, 54 Stat. 695).

Section consolidates sections 588a, 588b, and 588c of title 12, U.S.C., 1940 ed., Banks and Banking, as suggested by United States Attorney Clyde O. Eastus, of Fort Worth, Tex.

Words "felony or larceny" in subsection (a) were changed to "felony affecting such bank and in violation of any statute of the United States, or any larceny".

Use of term "felony" without limitation caused confusion as to whether a common law, State, or Federal felony was intended. Change conforms with Jerome v. U.S. (1943, 63 S. Ct. 483, 318 U.S. 101, 87 L. Ed. 640): "§2(a) [§588b(a) of title 12, U.S.C., 1940 ed., Banks and Banking] is not deprived of vitality if it is interpreted to exclude State felonies and to include only those Federal felonies which affect banks protected by the Act."

Minimum punishment provisions were omitted from subsection (c). (See reviser's note under section 203 of this title.) Also the provisions of subsection (b) measuring the punishment by the amount involved were extended and made applicable to the receiver as well as the thief. There seems no good reason why the thief of less than $100 should be liable to a maximum of imprisonment for one year and the receiver subject to 10 years.

The figures "100" were substituted for "50" in view of the fact that the present worth of $100 is less than the value of $50 when that sum was fixed as the dividing line between petit larceny and grand larceny.

The attention of Congress is directed to the mandatory minimum punishment provisions of sections 2113(e) and 2114 of this title. These were left unchanged because of the controversial question involved. Such legislative attempts to control the discretion of the sentencing judge are contrary to the opinions of experienced criminologists and criminal law experts. They are calculated to work manifest injustice in many cases.

Necessary minor translations of section references, and changes in phraseology, were made.

References in Text

Section 1(b) of the International Banking Act of 1978, referred to in subsec. (f), is classified to section 3101 of Title 12, Banks and Banking.

Section 2 of the Federal Credit Union Act, referred to in subsec. (g), is classified to section 1752 of Title 12.

Amendments

2002—Subsec. (b). Pub. L. 107–273 substituted "under this title" for "not more than $1,000" in last par.

1996—Subsec. (b). Pub. L. 104–294, §606(a), substituted "exceeding $1,000" for "exceeding $100" in two places.

Subsec. (g). Pub. L. 104–294, §607(d), inserted at end "The term 'State-chartered credit union' includes a credit union chartered under the laws of a State of the United States, the District of Columbia, or any commonwealth, territory, or possession of the United States."

1994—Subsecs. (a), (b). Pub. L. 103–322, §330016(1)(K), substituted "fined under this title" for "fined not more than $5,000" in last par. of subsec. (a) and first par. of subsec. (b).

Subsec. (d). Pub. L. 103–322, §330016(1)(L), substituted "fined under this title" for "fined not more than $10,000".

Subsec. (e). Pub. L. 103–322, §60003(a)(9), substituted "or if death results shall be punished by death or life imprisonment" for "or punished by death if the verdict of the jury shall so direct".

Subsec. (h). Pub. L. 103–322, §320608, added subsec. (h).

1990—Subsec. (f). Pub. L. 101–647 inserted "including a branch or agency of a foreign bank (as such terms are defined in paragraphs (1) and (3) of section 1(b) of the International Banking Act of 1978)," after "operating under the laws of the United States,".

1989—Subsec. (f). Pub. L. 101–73, §962(d)(1), substituted "any institution the deposits of which" for "any bank the deposits of which".

Subsecs. (g), (h). Pub. L. 101–73, §962(a)(7), (d)(2), (3), redesignated subsec. (h) as (g), substituted "National Credit Union Administration Board, and any 'Federal credit union' as defined in section 2 of the Federal Credit Union Act" for "Administrator of the National Credit Union Administration", and struck out former subsec. (g) which read as follows: "As used in this section the term 'savings and loan association' means any Federal savings and loan association and any 'insured institution' as defined in section 401 of the National Housing Act, as amended, and any 'Federal credit union' as defined in section 2 of the Federal Credit Union Act."

1986—Subsec. (a). Pub. L. 99–646 inserted ", or obtains or attempts to obtain by extortion" after "presence of another" in first par.

1984—Subsec. (c). Pub. L. 98–473 amended subsec. (c) generally, substituting "which has been taken or stolen from a bank, credit union, or savings and loan association in violation of subsection (b), knowing the same to be property which has been stolen" for "knowing the same to have been taken from a bank, credit union, or a savings and loan association, in violation of subsection (b) of this section".

1970—Subsecs. (a) to (c). Pub. L. 91–468, §8(1), inserted reference to "credit union" after "bank," each place it appears.

Subsec. (h). Pub. L. 91–468, §8(2), added subsec. (h).

1959—Subsec. (g). Pub. L. 86–354 included Federal credit unions in definition of "savings and loan association".

1952—Subsec. (g). Act Apr. 8, 1952, broadened definition of "savings and loan association" by including any insured institution as defined in section 401 of the National Housing Act, as amended.

1950—Act Aug. 3, 1950, brought within section State-chartered savings and loan associations whose accounts are insured by the Federal Savings and Loan Insurance Corporation.

§2114. Mail, money, or other property of United States

(a) Assault.—A person who assaults any person having lawful charge, control, or custody of any mail matter or of any money or other property of the United States, with intent to rob, steal, or purloin such mail matter, money, or other property of the United States, or robs or attempts to rob any such person of mail matter, or of any money, or other property of the United States, shall, for the first offense, be imprisoned not more than ten years; and if in effecting or attempting to effect such robbery he wounds the person having custody of such mail, money, or other property of the United States, or puts his life in jeopardy by the use of a dangerous weapon, or for a subsequent offense, shall be imprisoned not more than twenty-five years.

(b) Receipt, Possession, Concealment, or Disposal of Property.—A person who receives, possesses, conceals, or disposes of any money or other property that has been obtained in violation of this section, knowing the same to have been unlawfully obtained, shall be imprisoned not more than 10 years, fined under this title, or both.

(June 25, 1948, ch. 645, 62 Stat. 797; Pub. L. 98–473, title II, §223(d), Oct. 12, 1984, 98 Stat. 2028; Pub. L. 101–647, title XXXV, §3562, Nov. 29, 1990, 104 Stat. 4927; Pub. L. 103–322, title XXXII, §§320602, 320903(a)(3), Sept. 13, 1994, 108 Stat. 2115, 2124; Pub. L. 104–294, title VI, §604(b)(17), Oct. 11, 1996, 110 Stat. 3507.)

Historical and Revision Notes

Based on title 18, U.S.C., 1940 ed., §320 (Mar. 4, 1909, ch. 321, §197, 35 Stat. 1126; Aug. 26, 1935, ch. 694, 49 Stat. 867).

The attention of Congress is directed to the mandatory minimum punishment provisions of sections 2113(e) and 2114 of this title. These were left unchanged because of the controversial question involved. Such legislative attempts to control the discretion of the sentencing judge are contrary to the opinions of experienced criminologists and criminal law experts. They are calculated to work manifest injustice in many cases.

Minor changes were made in phraseology.

Amendments

1996—Pub. L. 104–294 amended Pub. L. 103–322, §320602. See 1994 Amendment note below.

1994—Pub. L. 103–322, §320903(a)(3), inserted "or attempts to rob" after "robs" in subsec. (a).

Pub. L. 103–322, §320602, as amended by Pub. L. 104–294, §604(b)(17), designated existing provisions as subsec. (a), inserted heading, substituted "A person who" for "Whoever", and added subsec. (b).

1990—Pub. L. 101–647 inserted a comma after "money" in section catchline.

1984—Pub. L. 98–473, which directed insertion of "not more than" after "imprisoned", was executed by making the insertion after "imprisoned" the second time appearing.

Effective Date of 1996 Amendment
Amendment by Pub. L. 104–294 effective Sept. 13, 1994, see section 604(d) of Pub. L. 104–294, set out as a note under section 13 of this title.

Effective Date of 1984 Amendment
Amendment by Pub. L. 98–473 effective Nov. 1, 1987, and applicable only to offenses committed after the taking effect of such amendment, see section 235(a)(1) of Pub. L. 98–473, set out as an Effective Date note under section 3551 of this title.

§2115. Post office
Whoever forcibly breaks into or attempts to break into any post office, or any building used in whole or in part as a post office, with intent to commit in such post office, or building or part thereof, so used, any larceny or other depredation, shall be fined under this title or imprisoned not more than five years, or both.
(June 25, 1948, ch. 645, 62 Stat. 797; Pub. L. 104–294, title VI, §601(a)(8), Oct. 11, 1996, 110 Stat. 3498.)

Historical and Revision Notes
Based on title 18, U.S.C., 1940 ed., §315 (Mar. 4, 1909, ch. 321, §192, 335 Stat. 1125).
Mandatory punishment provisions were rephrased in the alternative.
Minor change in phraseology was made.

Amendments
1996—Pub. L. 104–294 substituted "fined under this title" for "fined not more than $1,000".

§2116. Railway or steamboat post office
Whoever, by violence, enters a post-office car, or any part of any car, steamboat, or vessel, assigned to the use of the mail service, or willfully or maliciously assaults or interferes with any postal clerk in the discharge of his duties in connection with such car, steamboat, vessel, or apartment thereof, shall be fined under this title or imprisoned not more than three years, or both.
(June 25, 1948, ch. 645, 62 Stat. 797; Pub. L. 104–294, title VI, §601(a)(8), Oct. 11, 1996, 110 Stat. 3498.)

Historical and Revision Notes
Based on title 18, U.S.C., 1940 ed., §316 (Mar. 4, 1909, ch. 321, §193, 35 Stat. 1125).
Reference to persons aiding or assisting was deleted as unnecessary because such persons are made principals by section 2 of this title.
Minor changes were made in phraseology.

Amendments
1996—Pub. L. 104–294 substituted "fined under this title" for "fined not more than $1,000".

§2117. Breaking or entering carrier facilities
Whoever breaks the seal or lock of any railroad car, vessel, aircraft, motortruck, wagon or other vehicle or of any pipeline system, containing interstate or foreign shipments of freight or express or other property, or enters any such vehicle or pipeline system with intent in either case to commit larceny therein, shall be fined under this title or imprisoned not more than ten years, or both. If the offense involves a pre-retail medical product (as defined in section 670) the punishment for the offense shall be the same as the punishment for an offense under section 670

unless the punishment under this section is greater.

A judgment of conviction or acquittal on the merits under the laws of any State shall be a bar to any prosecution under this section for the same act or acts. Nothing contained in this section shall be construed as indicating an intent on the part of Congress to occupy the field in which provisions of this section operate to the exclusion of State laws on the same subject matter, nor shall any provision of this section be construed as invalidating any provision of State law unless such provision is inconsistent with any of the purposes of this section or any provision thereof.

(June 25, 1948, ch. 645, 62 Stat. 797; May 24, 1949, ch. 139, §44, 63 Stat. 96; Pub. L. 89–654, §2(a)–(c), Oct. 14, 1966, 80 Stat. 904; Pub. L. 103–322, title XXXIII, §330016(1)(K), Sept. 13, 1994, 108 Stat. 2147; Pub. L. 112–186, §4(c), Oct. 5, 2012, 126 Stat. 1429.)

Historical and Revision Notes

1948 Act

Based on title 18, U.S.C., 1940 ed., §409 (Feb. 13, 1913, ch. 50, §1, 37 Stat. 670; Jan. 28, 1925, ch. 102, 43 Stat. 793; Jan. 21, 1933, ch. 16, 47 Stat. 773; July 24, 1946, ch. 606, 60 Stat. 656). Other provisions of section 409 of title 18, U.S.C., 1940 ed., were incorporated in sections 659 and 660 of this title.

Minor changes were made in phraseology.

1949 Act

This section [section 44] conforms section 2117 of title 18, U.S.C., more closely with the original law from which it was derived, and with section 659 of such title.

Amendments

2012—Pub. L. 112–186 inserted at end of first par. "If the offense involves a pre-retail medical product (as defined in section 670) the punishment for the offense shall be the same as the punishment for an offense under section 670 unless the punishment under this section is greater."

1994—Pub. L. 103–322, which directed the amendment of section 2217 of this title by substituting "under this title" for "not more than $5,000", was executed by making the substitution in the first par. of this section, to reflect the probable intent of Congress, because this title does not contain a section 2217.

1966—Pub. L. 89–654 substituted "Breaking or entering carrier facilities" for "Railroad car entered or seal broken" as section catchline, inserted reference to "pipeline system", substituted "freight or express or other property" for "freight or express", and prohibited any construction which might indicate a Congressional intent to occupy the field or invalidate State law.

1949—Act May 24, 1949, inserted last par.

Executive Order No. 11836

Ex. Ord. No. 11836, Jan. 27, 1975, 40 F.R. 4255, which assigned responsibilities to Federal departments and agencies with respect to the National Cargo Security Program, was revoked by Ex. Ord. No. 12553, Feb. 25, 1986, 51 F.R. 7237.

§2118. Robberies and burglaries involving controlled substances

(a) Whoever takes or attempts to take from the person or presence of another by force or violence or by intimidation any material or compound containing any quantity of a controlled substance belonging to or in the care, custody, control, or possession of a person registered with the Drug Enforcement Administration under section 302 of the Controlled Substances Act (21 U.S.C. 822) shall, except as provided in subsection (c), be fined under this title or imprisoned not more than twenty years, or both, if (1) the replacement cost of the material or compound to the registrant was not less than $500, (2) the person who engaged in such taking or attempted such taking traveled in interstate or foreign commerce or used any facility in interstate or foreign commerce to facilitate such taking or attempt, or (3) another person was killed or suffered significant bodily injury as a result of such taking or attempt.

(b) Whoever, without authority, enters or attempts to enter, or remains in, the business premises or property of a person registered with the Drug Enforcement Administration under section 302 of the Controlled Substances Act (21 U.S.C. 822) with the intent to steal any material or compound containing any quantity of a controlled substance shall, except as provided in subsection (c), be fined under this title or imprisoned not more than twenty years, or both, if (1) the replacement cost of the controlled substance to the registrant was not less than $500, (2) the person who engaged in such entry or attempted such entry or who remained in such premises or property traveled in interstate or foreign commerce or used any facility in interstate or foreign commerce to facilitate such entry or attempt or to facilitate remaining in such premises or property, or (3) another person was killed or suffered significant bodily injury as a result of such entry or attempt.

(c)(1) Whoever in committing any offense under subsection (a) or (b) assaults any person, or puts in jeopardy the life of any person, by the use of a dangerous weapon or device shall be fined under this title and imprisoned for not more than twenty-five years.

(2) Whoever in committing any offense under subsection (a) or (b) kills any person shall be fined under this title or imprisoned for any term of years or life, or both.

(d) If two or more persons conspire to violate subsection (a) or (b) of this section and one or more of such persons do any overt act to effect the object of the conspiracy, each shall be fined under this title or imprisoned not more than ten years or both.

(e) For purposes of this section—

(1) the term "controlled substance" has the meaning prescribed for that term by section 102 of the Controlled Substances Act;

(2) the term "business premises or property" includes conveyances and storage facilities; and

(3) the term "significant bodily injury" means bodily injury which involves a risk of death, significant physical pain, protracted and obvious disfigurement, or a protracted loss or impairment of the function of a bodily member, organ, or mental or sensory faculty.

(Added Pub. L. 98–305, §2, May 31, 1984, 98 Stat. 221; amended Pub. L. 103–322, title XXXIII, §330016(1)(O)–(Q), Sept. 13, 1994, 108 Stat. 2148.)

References in Text

Section 102 of the Controlled Substances Act, referred to in subsec. (e)(1), is classified to section 802 of Title 21, Food and Drugs.

Amendments

1994—Subsecs. (a), (b). Pub. L. 103–322, §330016(1)(O), substituted "fined under this title" for "fined not more than $25,000".

Subsec. (c)(1). Pub. L. 103–322, §330016(1)(P), substituted "fined under this title" for "fined not more than $35,000".

Subsec. (c)(2). Pub. L. 103–322, §330016(1)(Q), substituted "fined under this title" for "fined not more than $50,000".

Subsec. (d). Pub. L. 103–322, §330016(1)(O), substituted "fined under this title" for "fined not more than $25,000".

Short Title

Pub. L. 98–305, §1, May 31, 1984, 98 Stat. 221, provided: "That this Act [enacting this section and provisions set out as a note under section 522 of Title 28, Judiciary and Judicial Procedure] may be cited as the 'Controlled Substance Registrant Protection Act of 1984'."

Report to Congress

Attorney General, for first three years after May 31, 1984, to submit to Congress an annual report with respect to enforcement activities relating to offenses under this section, see section 4 of Pub. L. 98–305, set out as a note under section 522 of Title 28, Judiciary and Judicial Procedure.

§2119. Motor vehicles

Whoever, with the intent to cause death or serious bodily harm 1 takes a motor vehicle that has been transported, shipped, or received in interstate or foreign commerce from the person or presence of another by force and violence or by intimidation, or attempts to do so, shall—

(1) be fined under this title or imprisoned not more than 15 years, or both,

(2) if serious bodily injury (as defined in section 1365 of this title, including any conduct that, if the conduct occurred in the special maritime and territorial jurisdiction of the United States, would violate section 2241 or 2242 of this title) results, be fined under this title or imprisoned not more than 25 years, or both, and

(3) if death results, be fined under this title or imprisoned for any number of years up to life, or both, or sentenced to death.

(Added Pub. L. 102–519, title I, §101(a), Oct. 25, 1992, 106 Stat. 3384; amended Pub. L. 103–322, title VI, §60003(a)(14), Sept. 13, 1994, 108 Stat. 1970; Pub. L. 104–217, §2, Oct. 1, 1996, 110 Stat. 3020.)

Amendments

1996—Par. (2). Pub. L. 104–217 inserted ", including any conduct that, if the conduct occurred in the special maritime and territorial jurisdiction of the United States, would violate section 2241 or 2242 of this title" after "section 1365 of this title".

1994—Pub. L. 103–322, §60003(a)(14), which directed the amendment of section 2119(3) of title 18 by substituting ", with the intent to cause death or serious bodily harm" for ", possessing a firearm as defined in section 921 of this title,", was executed by making the substitution in introductory provisions rather than in par. (3), to reflect the probable intent of Congress.

Par. (3). Pub. L. 103–322, §60003(a)(14), inserted before period at end ", or sentenced to death".

Federal Cooperation To Prevent "Carjacking" and Motor Vehicle Theft

Pub. L. 102–519, title I, §101(b), Oct. 25, 1992, 106 Stat. 3384, provided that: "In view of the increase of motor vehicle theft with its growing threat to human life and to the economic well-being of the Nation, the Attorney General, acting through the Federal Bureau of Investigation and the United States Attorneys, is urged to work with State and local officials to investigate car thefts, including violations of section 2119 of title 18, United States Code, for armed carjacking, and as appropriate and consistent with prosecutorial discretion, prosecute persons who allegedly violate such law and other relevant Federal statutes."

CHAPTER 105 - SABOTAGE

Amendments

§2151. Definitions

As used in this chapter:

The words "war material" include arms, armament, ammunition, livestock, forage, forest products and standing timber, stores of clothing, air, water, food, foodstuffs, fuel, supplies, munitions, and all articles, parts or ingredients, intended for, adapted to, or suitable for the use of the United States or any associate nation, in connection with the conduct of war or defense activities.

The words "war premises" include all buildings, grounds, mines, or other places wherein such war material is being produced, manufactured, repaired, stored, mined, extracted, distributed, loaded, unloaded, or transported, together with all machinery and appliances therein contained; and all forts, arsenals, navy yards, camps, prisons, or other installations of the Armed Forces of the United States, or any associate nation.

The words "war utilities" include all railroads, railways, electric lines, roads of whatever description, any railroad or railway fixture, canal, lock, dam, wharf, pier, dock, bridge, building, structure, engine, machine, mechanical contrivance, car, vehicle, boat, aircraft, airfields, air lanes, and fixtures or appurtenances thereof, or any other means of transportation whatsoever, whereon or whereby such war material or any troops of the United States, or of any associate nation, are being or may be transported either within the limits of the United States or upon the high seas or elsewhere; and all air-conditioning systems, dams, reservoirs, aqueducts, water and gas mains and pipes, structures and buildings, whereby or in connection with which air, water or gas is being furnished, or may be furnished, to any war premises or to the Armed Forces of the United States, or any associate nation, and all electric light and power, steam or pneumatic power, telephone and telegraph plants, poles, wires, and fixtures, and wireless stations, and the buildings connected with the maintenance and operation thereof used to supply air, water, light, heat, power, or facilities of communication to any war premises or to the Armed Forces of the United States, or any associate nation.

The words "associate nation" mean any nation at war with any nation with which the United States is at war.

The words "national-defense material" include arms, armament, ammunition, livestock, forage, forest products and standing timber, stores of clothing, air, water, food, foodstuffs, fuel, supplies, munitions, and all other articles of whatever description and any part or ingredient thereof, intended for, adapted to, or suitable for the use of the United States in connection with the national defense or for use in or in connection with the producing, manufacturing, repairing, storing, mining, extracting, distributing, loading, unloading, or transporting of any of the materials or other articles hereinbefore mentioned or any part or ingredient thereof.

The words "national-defense premises" include all buildings, grounds, mines, or other places wherein such national-defense material is being produced, manufactured, repaired, stored, mined, extracted, distributed, loaded, unloaded, or transported, together with all machinery and appliances therein contained; and all forts, arsenals, navy yards, camps, prisons, or other installations of the Armed Forces of the United States.

The words "national-defense utilities" include all railroads, railways, electric lines, roads of whatever description, railroad or railway fixture, canal, lock, dam, wharf, pier, dock, bridge, building, structure, engine, machine, mechanical contrivance, car, vehicle, boat, aircraft, airfields, air lanes, and fixtures or appurtenances thereof, or any other means of transportation whatsoever, whereon or whereby such national-defense material, or any troops of the United States, are being or may be transported either within the limits of the United States or upon the high seas or elsewhere; and all air-conditioning systems, dams, reservoirs, aqueducts, water and gas mains and pipes, structures, and buildings, whereby or in connection with which air, water, or gas may be furnished to any national-defense premises or to the Armed Forces of the United States, and all electric light and power, steam or pneumatic power, telephone and telegraph plants, poles, wires, and fixtures and wireless stations, and the buildings connected with the maintenance and operation thereof used to supply air, water, light, heat, power, or facilities of communication to any national-defense premises or to the Armed Forces of the United States.

(June 25, 1948, ch. 645, 62 Stat. 798; June 30, 1953, ch. 175, §2, 67 Stat. 133; Sept. 3, 1954, ch. 1261, title I, §101, 68 Stat. 1216.)

Historical and Revision Notes

Based on sections 101, 104, of title 50, U.S.C., 1940 ed., War and National Defense (Apr. 20, 1918, ch. 59, §§1, 4, 40 Stat. 533; Nov. 30, 1940, ch. 926, 54 Stat. 1220; Aug. 21, 1941, ch. 388, 55 Stat. 655; Dec. 24, 1942, ch. 824, 56 Stat. 1087).

Section consolidated definitive sections 101 and 104 of title 50, U.S.C., 1940 ed., War and National Defense.

Words "As used in this chapter" were inserted at beginning for brevity.

Definition of "United States", was omitted as covered by section 5 of this title.

Minor changes were made in phraseology and translations.

Amendments

1954—Act Sept. 3, 1954, redefined and enlarged definitions.

1953—Act June 30, 1953, inserted "or defense activities" after "conduct of war" in definition of "war material".

Short Title

Act Sept. 3, 1954, ch. 1261, §1, 68 Stat. 1216, provided that: "This Act [amending this section and sections 794 and 2153 to 2156 of this title] may be cited as the 'Espionage and Sabotage Act of 1954'."

Repeals

Section 7 of act June 30, 1953, ch. 175, 67 Stat. 134, repealed Joint Res. July 3, 1952, ch. 570, §1(a)(29), 66 Stat. 333; Joint Res. Mar. 31, 1953, ch. 13, §1, 67 Stat. 18, formerly cited as credits to this section and also formerly set out as a note under this section.

§2152. Fortifications, harbor defenses, or defensive sea areas

Whoever willfully trespasses upon, injures, or destroys any of the works or property or material of any submarine mine or torpedo or fortification or harbor-defense system owned or constructed or in process of construction by the United States; or

Whoever willfully interferes with the operation or use of any such submarine mine, torpedo, fortification, or harbor-defense system; or

Whoever knowingly, willfully, or wantonly violates any duly authorized and promulgated order or regulation of the President governing persons or vessels within the limits of defensive sea areas, which the President, for purposes of national defense, may from time to time establish by executive order—

Shall be fined under this title or imprisoned not more than five years, or both.

(June 25, 1948, ch. 645, 62 Stat. 799; Pub. L. 103–322, title XXXIII, §330016(1)(K), Sept. 13, 1994, 108 Stat. 2147.)

Historical and Revision Notes

Based on title 18, U.S.C., 1940 ed., §96 (Mar. 4, 1909, ch. 321, §44, 35 Stat. 1097; Mar. 4, 1917, ch. 180, 39 Stat. 1194; May 22, 1917, ch. 20, §19, 40 Stat. 89).

Jurisdiction and venue provisions were omitted as unnecessary and inconsistent with Rule 18 of the Federal Rules of Criminal Procedure providing for prosecution where the offense is committed, and section 3238 of this title providing that trial of offenses committed outside any district shall be in the district where the offender is found, or into which he is first brought. Words "on conviction thereof" were omitted as surplusage as punishment cannot be imposed until conviction is had.

Minor changes were made in phraseology.

Amendments

1994—Pub. L. 103–322 substituted "fined under this title" for "fined not more than $5,000" in last par.

Executive Order No. 10361

Ex. Ord. No. 10361, June 12, 1952, 17 F.R. 5357, formerly set out under this section, which established the Whittier Defensive Sea Area, Alaska, was revoked by Ex. Ord. No. 11549, July 28, 1970, 35 F.R. 12191.

§2153. Destruction of war material, war premises, or war utilities

(a) Whoever, when the United States is at war, or in times of national emergency as declared by the President or by the Congress, with intent to injure, interfere with, or obstruct the United States or any associate nation in preparing for or carrying on the war or defense activities, or, with reason to believe that his act may injure, interfere with, or obstruct the United States or any associate nation in preparing for or carrying on the war or defense activities, willfully injures, destroys, contaminates or infects, or attempts to so injure, destroy, contaminate or infect any war material, war premises, or war utilities, shall be fined under this title or imprisoned not more than thirty years, or both.

(b) If two or more persons conspire to violate this section, and one or more of such persons do any act to effect the object of the conspiracy, each of the parties to such conspiracy shall be punished as provided in subsection (a) of this section.

(June 25, 1948, ch. 645, 62 Stat. 799; June 30, 1953, ch. 175, §2, 67 Stat. 133; Sept. 3, 1954, ch. 1261, title I, §102, 68 Stat. 1217; Pub. L. 103–322, title XXXIII, §330016(1)(L), Sept. 13, 1994, 108 Stat. 2147.)

Historical and Revision Notes

Based on section 102 of title 50, U.S.C., 1940 ed., War and National Defense (Apr. 20, 1918, ch. 59, §2, 40 Stat. 534).

"As herein defined" was deleted as surplusage.

The conspiracy provisions are new. Their addition to the section was strongly urged by the Criminal Division of the Department of Justice, considering the gravity of the substantive offense as evidenced by the prescribed punishment therefor. The punishment provisions of the general conspiracy statute, section 371 of this title, are inadequate.

Words "upon conviction thereof" were omitted as unnecessary since punishment cannot be imposed until a conviction is secured.

Minor changes were made in phraseology.

Amendments

1994—Subsec. (a). Pub. L. 103–322 substituted "fined under this title" for "fined not more than $10,000".

1954—Act Sept. 3, 1954, made section applicable in time of national emergency as well as war, and recognized the possibility of bacteriological warfare by making "contamination" a crime.

1953—Subsec. (a). Act June 30, 1953, inserted "or defense activities" after "carrying on the war".

Repeals

Section 7 of act June 30, 1953, ch. 175, 67 Stat. 134, repealed Joint Res. July 3, 1952, ch. 570, §1(a)(29), 66 Stat. 333; Joint Res. Mar. 31, 1953, ch. 13, §1, 67 Stat. 18, formerly cited as credits to this section and also formerly set out as a note under this section.

§2154. Production of defective war material, war premises, or war utilities

(a) Whoever, when the United States is at war, or in times of national emergency as declared by the President or by the Congress, with intent to injure, interfere with, or obstruct the United States or any associate nation in preparing for or carrying on the war or defense activities, or, with reason to believe that his act may injure, interfere with, or obstruct the United States or any associate nation in preparing for or carrying on the war or defense activities, willfully makes, constructs, or causes to be made or constructed in a defective manner, or attempts to make, construct, or cause to be made or constructed in a defective manner any war material, war premises or war utilities, or any tool, implement, machine, utensil, or receptacle used or employed in making, producing, manufacturing, or repairing any such war material, war premises or war utilities, shall be fined under this title or imprisoned not more than thirty years, or both.

(b) If two or more persons conspire to violate this section, and one or more of such persons do any act to effect the object of the conspiracy, each of the parties to such conspiracy shall be punished as provided in subsection (a) of this section.

(June 25, 1948, ch. 645, 62 Stat. 799; June 30, 1953, ch. 175, §2, 67 Stat. 133; Sept. 3, 1954, ch. 1261, title I, §103, 68 Stat. 1218; Pub. L. 103–322, title XXXIII, §330016(1)(L), Sept. 13, 1994, 108 Stat. 2147.)

Historical and Revision Notes

Based on section 103 of title 50, U.S.C., 1940 ed., War and National Defense (Apr. 20, 1918, ch. 59, §3, 40 Stat. 534).

The conspiracy provisions are new. Their addition to the section was strongly urged by the Criminal Division of the Department of Justice, considering the gravity of the substantive offense as evidenced by the prescribed punishment therefor. The punishment provisions of the general conspiracy statute, section 371 of this title, are inadequate.

Words "upon conviction thereof" were omitted as unnecessary, since punishment cannot be imposed until a conviction is secured.

Minor changes were made in phraseology.

Amendments

1994—Subsec. (a). Pub. L. 103–322 substituted "fined under this title" for "fined not more than $10,000".

1954—Act Sept. 3, 1954, made section applicable in time of national emergency, and enlarged its scope by bringing "war premises, or war utilities" within jurisdiction of section.

1953—Subsec. (a). Act June 30, 1953, inserted "or defense activities" after "carrying on the war".

Repeals

Section 7 of act June 30, 1953, ch. 175, 67 Stat. 134, repealed Joint Res. July 3, 1952, ch. 570, §1(a)(29), 66 Stat. 333; Joint Res. Mar. 31, 1953, ch. 13, §1, 67 Stat. 18, formerly cited as credits to this section and also formerly set out as a note under this section.

§2155. Destruction of national-defense materials, national-defense premises, or national-defense utilities

(a) Whoever, with intent to injure, interfere with, or obstruct the national defense of the United States, willfully injures, destroys, contaminates or infects, or attempts to so injure, destroy, contaminate or infect any national-defense material, national-defense premises, or national-defense utilities, shall be fined under this title or imprisoned not more than 20 years, or both, and, if death results to any person, shall be imprisoned for any term of years or for life.

(b) If two or more persons conspire to violate this section, and one or more of such persons do any act to effect the object of the conspiracy, each of the parties to such conspiracy shall be punished as provided in subsection (a) of this section.

(June 25, 1948, ch. 645, 62 Stat. 799; Sept. 3, 1954, ch. 1261, title I, §104, 68 Stat. 1218; Pub. L. 103–322, title XXXIII, §330016(1)(L), Sept. 13, 1994, 108 Stat. 2147; Pub. L. 104–294, title VI, §601(f)(12), Oct. 11, 1996, 110 Stat. 3500; Pub. L. 107–56, title VIII, §810(e), Oct. 26, 2001, 115 Stat. 380.)

Historical and Revision Notes

Based on section 105 of title 50, U.S.C., 1940 ed., War and National Defense (Apr. 20, 1918, ch. 59, §5, as added Nov. 30, 1940, ch. 926, 54 Stat. 1221).

Words "upon conviction thereof" were omitted as unnecessary, since punishment cannot be imposed until a conviction is secured.

Minor changes were made in phraseology.

Amendments

2001—Subsec. (a). Pub. L. 107–56 substituted "20 years" for "ten years" and inserted ", and, if death results to any person, shall be imprisoned for any term of years or for life" before period at end.

1996—Pub. L. 104–294 substituted ", or" for "or" in section catchline.

1994—Subsec. (a). Pub. L. 103–322 substituted "fined under this title" for "fined not more than $10,000".

1954—Act Sept. 3, 1954, inserted conspiracy provisions.

§2156. Production of defective national-defense material, national-defense premises, or national-defense utilities

(a) Whoever, with intent to injure, interfere with, or obstruct the national defense of the United States, willfully makes, constructs, or attempts to make or construct in a defective manner, any national-defense material, national-defense premises or national-defense utilities, or any tool, implement, machine, utensil, or receptacle used or employed in making, producing, manufacturing, or repairing any such national-defense material, national-defense premises or national-defense utilities, shall be fined under this title or imprisoned not more than ten years, or both.

(b) If two or more persons conspire to violate this section, and one or more of such persons do any act to effect the object of the conspiracy, each of the parties to such conspiracy shall be punished as provided in subsection (a) of this section.

(June 25, 1948, ch. 645, 62 Stat. 800; Sept. 3, 1954, ch. 1261, title I, §105, 68 Stat. 1218; Pub. L. 103–322, title XXXIII, §330016(1)(L), Sept. 13, 1994, 108 Stat. 2147; Pub. L. 104–294, title VI, §601(f)(12), Oct. 11, 1996, 110 Stat. 3500.)

Historical and Revision Notes

Based on section 106 of title 50, U.S.C., 1940 ed., War and National Defense (Apr. 20, 1918, ch. 59, §6, as added Nov. 30, 1940, ch. 926, 54 Stat. 1221).

Reference to persons causing or procuring was omitted as unnecessary in view of definition of "principal" in section 2 of this title.

Words "upon conviction thereof" were omitted as unnecessary, since punishment cannot be imposed until a conviction is secured.

Minor changes were made in phraseology.

Amendments

1996—Pub. L. 104–294 substituted ", or" for "or" in section catchline.
1994—Subsec. (a). Pub. L. 103–322 substituted "fined under this title" for "fined not more than $10,000".
1954—Act Sept. 3, 1954, inserted conspiracy provisions.

[§2157. Repealed. Pub. L. 103–322, title XXXIII, §330004(13), Sept. 13, 1994, 108 Stat. 2142]

Section, added June 30, 1953, ch. 175, §2, 67 Stat. 133, related to temporary extension of sections 2153 and 2154 of this title.

CHAPTER 107 - SEAMEN AND STOWAWAYS

Amendments

1990—Pub. L. 101–647, title XII, §1207(b), Nov. 29, 1990, 104 Stat. 4832, struck out item 2198 "Seduction of female passenger".

§2191. Cruelty to seamen

Whoever, being the master or officer of a vessel of the United States, on the high seas, or on any other waters within the admiralty and maritime jurisdiction of the United States, flogs, beats, wounds, or without justifiable cause, imprisons any of the crew of such vessel, or withholds from them suitable food and nourishment, or inflicts upon them any corporal or other cruel and unusual punishment, shall be fined under this title or imprisoned not more than five years, or both.
(June 25, 1948, ch. 645, 62 Stat. 800; Pub. L. 104–294, title VI, §601(a)(8), Oct. 11, 1996, 110 Stat. 3498.)

Historical and Revision Notes

Based on title 18, U.S.C., 1940 ed., §482 and section 712 of title 46, U.S.C., 1940 ed., Shipping (Dec. 21, 1898, ch. 28, §22, 30 Stat. 761; Mar. 4, 1909, ch. 321, §291, 35 Stat. 1145).
Section consolidates section 482 of title 18, U.S.C., 1940 ed., and the following language from section 712 of title 46, U.S.C., 1940 ed., Shipping, prohibiting flogging and corporal punishment: "and any master or other officer thereof who shall violate the aforesaid provisions of this section, or either thereof, shall be deemed guilty of a misdemeanor, punishable by imprisonment for not less than three months nor more than two years." That language was the basis for the addition of the word "flogs" and the words "any corporal or other" for the word "any." The punishment imposed by section 482 was adopted as that was the later statute as incorporated in 1909 Criminal Code.
Words "shall be deemed guilty of a misdemeanor," contained in said section 712 of title 46, were omitted in view of definitive section 1 of this title.
Minor changes were made in phraseology.

Amendments

1996—Pub. L. 104–294 substituted "fined under this title" for "fined not more than $1,000".

§2192. Incitation of seamen to revolt or mutiny

Whoever, being of the crew of a vessel of the United States, on the high seas, or on any other waters within the admiralty and maritime jurisdiction of the United States, endeavors to make a revolt or mutiny on board such vessel, or combines, conspires, or confederates with any other person on board to make such revolt or mutiny, or solicits, incites, or stirs up any other of the crew to disobey or resist the lawful orders of the master or other officer of such vessel, or to refuse or neglect his proper duty on board thereof, or to betray his proper trust, or assembles with others in a tumultuous and mutinous manner, or makes a riot on board thereof, or unlawfully confines the master or other commanding officer thereof, shall be fined under this title or imprisoned not more than five years, or both.

(June 25, 1948, ch. 645, 62 Stat. 800; Pub. L. 104–294, title VI, §601(a)(8), Oct. 11, 1996, 110 Stat. 3498.)

Historical and Revision Notes

Based on title 18, U.S.C., 1940 ed., §483 (Mar. 4, 1909, ch. 321, §292, 35 Stat. 1146). Minor changes were made in phraseology.

Amendments

1996—Pub. L. 104–294 substituted "fined under this title" for "fined not more than $1,000".

§2193. Revolt or mutiny of seamen

Whoever, being of the crew of a vessel of the United States, on the high seas, or on any other waters within the admiralty and maritime jurisdiction of the United States, unlawfully and with force, or by fraud, or intimidation, usurps the command of such vessel from the master or other lawful officer in command thereof, or deprives him of authority and command on board, or resists or prevents him in the free and lawful exercise thereof, or transfers such authority and command to another not lawfully entitled thereto, is guilty of a revolt and mutiny, and shall be fined under this title or imprisoned not more than ten years, or both.

(June 25, 1948, ch. 645, 62 Stat. 800; Pub. L. 103–322, title XXXIII, §330016(1)(I), Sept. 13, 1994, 108 Stat. 2147.)

Historical and Revision Notes

Based on title 18, U.S.C., 1940 ed., §484 (Mar. 4, 1909, ch. 321, §293, 35 Stat. 1146). Punishment provision for mandatory fine and imprisonment was rephrased in the alternative so as to vest power in the court to impose either a fine, or imprisonment, or both, in its discretion.

Amendments

1994—Pub. L. 103–322 substituted "fined under this title" for "fined not more than $2,000".

§2194. Shanghaiing sailors

Whoever, with intent that any person shall perform service or labor of any kind on board of any vessel engaged in trade and commerce among the several States or with foreign nations, or on board of any vessel of the United States engaged in navigating the high seas or any navigable water of the United States, procures or induces, or attempts to procure or induce, another, by force or threats or by representations which he knows or believes to be untrue, or while the person so procured or induced is intoxicated or under the influence of any drug, to go on board of any such vessel, or to sign or in anywise enter into any agreement to go on board of any such vessel to perform service or labor thereon; or

Whoever knowingly detains on board of any such vessel any person so procured or induced to go on board, or to enter into any agreement to go on board, by any means herein defined—

Shall be fined under this title or imprisoned not more than one year, or both.

(June 25, 1948, ch. 645, 62 Stat. 800; Pub. L. 104–294, title VI, §601(a)(8), Oct. 11, 1996, 110 Stat. 3498.)

Historical and Revision Notes

Based on title 18, U.S.C., 1940 ed., §144 (Mar. 4, 1909, ch. 321, §82, 35 Stat. 1103).

Reference to persons aiding or abetting was omitted as unnecessary as such persons are made principals by section 2 of this title.

Minor changes were made in phraseology and arrangement.

Amendments

1996—Pub. L. 104–294 substituted "fined under this title" for "fined not more than $1,000" in last par.

§2195. Abandonment of sailors

Whoever, being master or commander of a vessel of the United States, while abroad, maliciously and without justifiable cause forces any officer or mariner of such vessel on shore, in order to leave him behind in any foreign port or place, or refuses to bring home again all such officers and mariners of such vessel whom he carried out with him, as are in a condition to return and willing to return, when he is ready to proceed on his homeward voyage, shall be fined under this title or imprisoned not more than six months, or both.

(June 25, 1948, ch. 645, 62 Stat. 801; Pub. L. 103–322, title XXXIII, §330016(1)(G), Sept. 13, 1994, 108 Stat. 2147.)

Historical and Revision Notes

Based on title 18, U.S.C., 1940 ed., §486 (Mar. 4, 1909, ch. 321, §295, 35 Stat. 1146).

Amendments

1994—Pub. L. 103–322 substituted "fined under this title" for "fined not more than $500".

§2196. Drunkenness or neglect of duty by seamen

Whoever, being a master, officer, radio operator, seaman, apprentice or other person employed on any merchant vessel, by willful breach of duty, or by reason of drunkenness, does any act tending to the immediate loss or destruction of, or serious damage to, such vessel, or tending immediately to endanger the life or limb of any person belonging to or on board of such vessel; or, by willful breach of duty or by neglect of duty or by reason of drunkenness, refuses or omits to do any lawful act proper and requisite to be done by him for preserving such vessel from immediate loss, destruction, or serious damage, or for preserving any person belonging to or on board of such ship from immediate danger to life or limb, shall be imprisoned not more than one year.

(June 25, 1948, ch. 645, 62 Stat. 801.)

Historical and Revision Notes

Based on section 704 of title 46, U.S.C., 1940 ed., Shipping (R.S. §4602).

Words "officer, radio operator," and "or other person employed on" were inserted at beginning of section to insure clarity and scope of section. Section 701 of title 46, U.S.C., 1940 ed., Shipping, is very similar to this section as revised, and has been applied to mates [Morris v. Cornell, D.C. Mass. 1843, Fed. Cas. No. 9,829; Gladding v. Constant, D.C. Mass. 1844, Fed. Cas. No. 5,468; Foye v. Dabney, D.C. Mass. 1853, Fed. Cas. No. 5,022; Foye v. Lickie, D.C. Mass. 1853, Fed.

Cas. No. 5,023; The Sylvia De Grasse, D.C.N.Y. 1843, Fed. Cas. No. 12,676; The Sadie C. Sumner, D.C. Mass. 1905, 142 F. 611], as well as engineers, assistant engineers and cooks. (See notes of decisions under section 701, of title 46, U.S.C., Shipping.)

Words "be guilty of a misdemeanor" were omitted as unnecessary in view of general definition of "misdemeanor" in section 1 of this title.

Minor changes were made in phraseology including substitution of "one year" for "twelve months" at end of section.

§2197. Misuse of Federal certificate, license or document

Whoever, not being lawfully entitled thereto, uses, exhibits, or attempts to use or exhibit, or, with intent unlawfully to use the same, receives or possesses any certificate, license, or document issued to vessels, or officers or seamen by any officer or employee of the United States authorized by law to issue the same; or

Whoever, without authority, alters or attempts to alter any such certificate, license, or document by addition, interpolation, deletion, or erasure; or

Whoever forges, counterfeits, or steals, or attempts to forge, counterfeit, or steal, any such certificate, license, or document; or unlawfully possesses or knowingly uses any such altered, changed, forged, counterfeit, or stolen certificate, license, or document; or

Whoever, without authority, prints or manufactures any blank form of such certificate, license, or document, or

Whoever possesses without lawful excuse, and with intent unlawfully to use the same, any blank form of such certificate, license, or document; or

Whoever, in any manner, transfers or negotiates such transfer of, any blank form of such certificate, license, or document, or any such altered, forged, counterfeit, or stolen certificate, license, or document, or any such certificate, license, or document to which the party transferring or receiving the same is not lawfully entitled—

Shall be fined under this title or imprisoned not more than five years, or both.

(June 25, 1948, ch. 645, 62 Stat. 801; Pub. L. 103–322, title XXXIII, §330016(1)(K), Sept. 13, 1994, 108 Stat. 2147.)

Historical and Revision Notes

Based on section 710a of title 46, U.S.C., 1940 ed., Shipping (June 25, 1936, ch. 816, §6, 49 Stat. 1936).

The phrase "the Bureau of Marine Inspection and Navigation," identifying the agency issuing the certificate, license or document, was omitted without change of substance. The functions of the Bureau of Marine Inspection and Navigation were transferred to the Bureau of Customs and the Coast Guard by Executive Order 9083 Feb. 28, 1942, title 50, App. U.S.C., 1940 ed., following §601. Such transfer is temporary under section 621 of title 50, App., U.S.C., 1940 ed. (First War Powers Act).

As revised the section is broad enough to embrace certificates, licenses and documents issued by the officers or employees of the Coast Guard and Customs Service, as the case may be.

Reference to persons causing, procuring, aiding or abetting was omitted as such persons are principals under section 2 of this title.

Words "upon conviction thereof" were omitted as unnecessary, since punishment cannot be imposed until a conviction is secured.

Changes were made in phraseology and arrangement.

Amendments

1994—Pub. L. 103–322 substituted "fined under this title" for "fined not more than $5,000" in last par.

[§2198. Repealed. Pub. L. 101–647, title XII, §1207(b), Nov. 29, 1990, 104

Section, act June 25, 1948, ch. 645, 62 Stat. 802, related to penalties for seducing a female passenger on an American vessel by employees of the vessel.

§2199. Stowaways on vessels or aircraft

Whoever, without the consent of the owner, charterer, master, or person in command of any vessel, or aircraft, with intent to obtain transportation, boards, enters or secretes himself aboard such vessel or aircraft and is thereon at the time of departure of said vessel or aircraft from a port, harbor, wharf, airport or other place within the jurisdiction of the United States; or

Whoever, with like intent, having boarded, entered or secreted himself aboard a vessel or aircraft at any place within or without the jurisdiction of the United States, remains aboard after the vessel or aircraft has left such place and is thereon at any place within the jurisdiction of the United States; or

Whoever, with intent to obtain a ride or transportation, boards or enters any aircraft owned or operated by the United States without the consent of the person in command or other duly authorized officer or agent—

(1) shall be fined under this title, imprisoned not more than 5 years, or both;

(2) if the person commits an act proscribed by this section, with the intent to commit serious bodily injury, and serious bodily injury occurs (as defined under section 1365, including any conduct that, if the conduct occurred in the special maritime and territorial jurisdiction of the United States, would violate section 2241 or 2242) to any person other than a participant as a result of a violation of this section, shall be fined under this title or imprisoned not more than 20 years, or both; and

(3) if an individual commits an act proscribed by this section, with the intent to cause death, and if the death of any person other than a participant occurs as a result of a violation of this section, shall be fined under this title, imprisoned for any number of years or for life, or both.

The word "aircraft" as used in this section includes any contrivance for navigation or flight in the air.

(June 25, 1948, ch. 645, 62 Stat. 802; Pub. L. 104–294, title VI, §601(a)(8), Oct. 11, 1996, 110 Stat. 3498; Pub. L. 109–177, title III, §308, Mar. 9, 2006, 120 Stat. 241.)

Historical and Revision Notes

Based on title 18, U.S.C., 1940 ed., §§469–474 (June 11, 1940, ch. 326, §§1–3, 54 Stat. 306; Mar. 4, 1944, ch. 82, §§1–4, 58 Stat. 111; Apr. 10, 1944, ch. 162, 58 Stat. 188).

Sections consolidated and rewritten with changes of phraseology and substance.

In section 469 of title 18, U.S.C., 1940 ed., the element of intent not to pay for transportation was omitted as unnecessary since the payment of transportation will invariably remove the stowaway from the operation of the section by purchasing the master's "consent".

In section 472 of title 18, U.S.C., 1940 ed., the enumerations of State, Territory, Possession, District of Columbia, and The Canal Zone, was omitted as adequately covered by "place within the jurisdiction of the United States."

The punishment provision is the same as in sections 470, 472, and 473 of title 18, U.S.C., 1940 ed., but the fine is $500 more than the maximum fine provided by said section 469. There seemed no point, however, in preserving a differential in favor of the stowaway as against the aider and abettor of $500. The court can be trusted to exercise a wise discretion within the slightly larger limits provided by the revised section.

The provision for punishment of aiders and abettors in section 470 of title 18, U.S.C., 1940 ed., was omitted as unnecessary since they are punishable as principals by section 2 of this title. Sections 471 and 474 of title 18, U.S.C., 1940 ed., were omitted as obviously unnecessary.

Amendments

2006—Pub. L. 109–177 added pars. (1) to (3) and struck out former fourth undesignated par.

which read as follows: "Shall be fined under this title or imprisoned not more than one year, or both."

1996—Pub. L. 104–294 substituted "fined under this title" for "fined not more than $1,000" in fourth undesignated par.

CHAPTER 109 - SEARCHES AND SEIZURES

Amendments

2006—Pub. L. 109–177, title III, §303(b), Mar. 9, 2006, 120 Stat. 234, added item 2237.

§2231. Assault or resistance

(a) Whoever forcibly assaults, resists, opposes, prevents, impedes, intimidates, or interferes with any person authorized to serve or execute search warrants or to make searches and seizures while engaged in the performance of his duties with regard thereto or on account of the performance of such duties, shall be fined under this title or imprisoned not more than three years, or both; and—

(b) Whoever, in committing any act in violation of this section, uses any deadly or dangerous weapon, shall be fined under this title or imprisoned not more than ten years, or both.

(June 25, 1948, ch. 645, 62 Stat. 802; Pub. L. 103–322, title XXXIII, §330016(1)(K), (L), Sept. 13, 1994, 108 Stat. 2147.)

Historical and Revision Notes

Based on title 18, U.S.C., 1940 ed., §§121, 253, 254, 628 (Mar. 4, 1909, ch. 321, §65, 35 Stat. 1100; June 15, 1917, ch. 30, title XI, §18, 40 Stat. 230; May 18, 1934, ch. 299, §§1, 2, 48 Stat. 780, 781; Feb. 8, 1936, ch. 40, 49 Stat. 1105; June 26, 1936, ch. 830, title I, §3, 49 Stat. 1940; Reorg. Plan No. II, §4(f), eff. July 1, 1939, 4 Fed. Reg. 2731, 53 Stat. 1433; June 13, 1940, ch. 359, 54 Stat. 391).

Section consolidates section 628 of title 18, U.S.C., 1940 ed., and the portion of section 121 of said title relating to resistance of persons authorized to make searches.

Punishment provided by section 121 of title 18, U.S.C., 1940 ed., was $2,000 fine and imprisonment for 1 year. Section 628 of said title was part of Espionage Act of June 15, 1917, ch. 30, title XIII, §1, 40 Stat. 231, prescribing fine of not more than $1,000 and imprisonment not exceeding 2 years for resisting service, execution of search warrant, or assaulting an officer.

Section 253 of title 18, U.S.C., 1940 ed., enumerated United States marshals, deputies, and assistants, Federal Bureau of Investigation agents, and numerous other officers, the killing of whom is denounced as a Federal offense.

Section 254 of title 18, U.S.C., 1940 ed., denounced the assaulting of such officers and prescribed punishment therefor without regard to nature of duties involved or performed.

In other words sections 253 and 254 of title 18, U.S.C., 1940 ed., were not limited to officers executing search warrants.

Officers enumerated in section 253 of title 18, U.S.C., 1940 ed., were substantially all those who serve or execute search warrants. Therefore, the language and punishment under section 254 of said title constitute basis of this revised section. No change in legislative intent is involved, as the amendments of sections 253 and 254 of said title are the latest enactments.

The provisions of section 121 of title 18, U.S.C., 1940 ed., relating to rescue of property from seizing officer or its destruction to prevent seizure, are incorporated in sections 2232 and 2233 of this title.

Minor changes were made in translation and phraseology.

Amendments

1994—Subsec. (a). Pub. L. 103–322, §330016(1)(K), substituted "fined under this title" for "fined not more than $5,000".

Subsec. (b). Pub. L. 103–322, §330016(1)(L), substituted "fined under this title" for "fined not more than $10,000".

§2232. Destruction or removal of property to prevent seizure

(a) Destruction or Removal of Property To Prevent Seizure.—Whoever, before, during, or after any search for or seizure of property by any person authorized to make such search or seizure, knowingly destroys, damages, wastes, disposes of, transfers, or otherwise takes any action, or knowingly attempts to destroy, damage, waste, dispose of, transfer, or otherwise take any action, for the purpose of preventing or impairing the Government's lawful authority to take such property into its custody or control or to continue holding such property under its lawful custody and control, shall be fined under this title or imprisoned not more than 5 years, or both.

(b) Impairment of In Rem Jurisdiction.—Whoever, knowing that property is subject to the in rem jurisdiction of a United States court for purposes of civil forfeiture under Federal law, knowingly and without authority from that court, destroys, damages, wastes, disposes of, transfers, or otherwise takes any action, or knowingly attempts to destroy, damage, waste, dispose of, transfer, or otherwise take any action, for the purpose of impairing or defeating the court's continuing in rem jurisdiction over the property, shall be fined under this title or imprisoned not more than 5 years, or both.

(c) Notice of Search or Execution of Seizure Warrant or Warrant of Arrest In Rem.—Whoever, having knowledge that any person authorized to make searches and seizures, or to execute a seizure warrant or warrant of arrest in rem, in order to prevent the authorized seizing or securing of any person or property, gives notice or attempts to give notice in advance of the search, seizure, or execution of a seizure warrant or warrant of arrest in rem, to any person shall be fined under this title or imprisoned not more than 5 years, or both.

(d) Notice of Certain Electronic Surveillance.—Whoever, having knowledge that a Federal investigative or law enforcement officer has been authorized or has applied for authorization under chapter 119 to intercept a wire, oral, or electronic communication, in order to obstruct, impede, or prevent such interception, gives notice or attempts to give notice of the possible interception to any person shall be fined under this title or imprisoned not more than five years, or both.

(e) Foreign Intelligence Surveillance.—Whoever, having knowledge that a Federal officer has been authorized or has applied for authorization to conduct electronic surveillance under the Foreign Intelligence Surveillance Act of 1978 (50 U.S.C. 1801, et seq.), in order to obstruct, impede, or prevent such activity, gives notice or attempts to give notice of the possible activity to any person shall be fined under this title or imprisoned not more than five years, or both.

(June 25, 1948, ch. 645, 62 Stat. 802; Pub. L. 98–473, title II, §1103, Oct. 12, 1984, 98 Stat. 2143; Pub. L. 99–508, title I, §109, Oct. 21, 1986, 100 Stat. 1858; Pub. L. 99–646, §33, Nov. 10, 1986, 100 Stat. 3598; Pub. L. 100–690, title VII, §7066, Nov. 18, 1988, 102 Stat. 4404; Pub. L. 103–322, title XXXIII, §330016(1)(L), Sept. 13, 1994, 108 Stat. 2147; Pub. L. 106–185, §12, Apr. 25, 2000, 114 Stat. 218.)

Historical and Revision Notes

Based on title 18, U.S.C., 1940 ed., §121 (Mar. 4, 1909, ch. 321, §65, 35 Stat. 1100).

Section was formed from the words following the first semicolon and ending with the second semicolon, in section 121 of title 18, U.S.C., 1940 ed.

The remaining provisions of section 121 of title 18, U.S.C., 1940 ed., relating to assaulting, resisting, or interfering with customs officers, revenue officers, or other persons, and to the rescue of seized property, constitute, along with provisions from other sections, sections 2231 and 2233 of this title.

Minor changes were made in phraseology.

References in Text

The Foreign Intelligence Surveillance Act of 1978, referred to in subsec. (e), is Pub. L. 95–511, Oct. 25, 1978, 92 Stat. 1783, as amended, which is classified principally to chapter 36 (§1801 et seq.) of Title 50, War and National Defense. For complete classification of this Act to the Code, see Short Title note set out under section 1801 of Title 50 and Tables.

Amendments

2000—Pub. L. 106–185 added subsecs. (a) to (c), redesignated first and second pars. of former subsec. (c) as subsecs. (d) and (e), respectively, inserted subsec. (e) heading, and struck out former subsecs. (a) and (b) which related to physical interference with search and notice of search, respectively.

1994—Subsecs. (a), (b). Pub. L. 103–322 substituted "fined under this title" for "fined not more than $10,000".

1988—Subsec. (c). Pub. L. 100–690 inserted "of 1978" after "Surveillance Act".

1986—Pub. L. 99–646 directed the designation of first and second pars. as subsecs. (a) and (b), respectively, which had been previously so designated by Pub. L. 99–508, and substituted "imprisoned not" for "imprisoned" in subsec. (a).

Pub. L. 99–508 designated first and second pars. as subsecs. (a) and (b), respectively, and inserted headings, and added subsec. (c).

1984—Pub. L. 98–473, §1103(a), substituted provisions raising the maximum fine from $2,000 to $10,000 and raising the maximum term of imprisonment from two years to five years.

Pub. L. 98–473, §1103(b), inserted paragraph relating to the penalties for warning the subject of a search.

Effective Date of 2000 Amendment

Amendment by Pub. L. 106–185 applicable to any forfeiture proceeding commenced on or after the date that is 120 days after Apr. 25, 2000, see section 21 of Pub. L. 106–185, set out as a note under section 1324 of Title 8, Aliens and Nationality.

Effective Date of 1986 Amendment

Amendment by Pub. L. 99–508 effective 90 days after Oct. 21, 1986, and, in case of conduct pursuant to court order or extension, applicable only with respect to court orders and extensions made after such date, with special rule for State authorizations of interceptions, see section 111 of Pub. L. 99–508, set out as a note under section 2510 of this title.

§2233. Rescue of seized property

Whoever forcibly rescues, dispossesses, or attempts to rescue or dispossess any property, articles, or objects after the same shall have been taken, detained, or seized by any officer or other person under the authority of any revenue law of the United States, or by any person authorized to make searches and seizures, shall be fined under this title or imprisoned not more than two years, or both.

(June 25, 1948, ch. 645, 62 Stat. 802; Pub. L. 103 322, title XXXIII, §330016(1)(I), Sept. 13, 1994, 108 Stat. 2147.)

Historical and Revision Notes

Based on title 18, U.S.C., 1940 ed., §§121, 128 (Mar. 4, 1909, ch. 321, §§65, 71, 35 Stat. 1100, 1101).

Section consolidates that portion of section 121 of title 18, U.S.C., 1940 ed., relating to rescue of seized property, with section 128 of title 18, U.S.C., 1940 ed.

The remaining provisions of section 121 of present title 18, U.S.C., 1940 ed., relating to assaulting, resisting, or interfering with customs officers, revenue officers, or other persons, and to the destruction or removal of property to prevent seizure, constitute sections 2231 and 2232 of this title, the former provisions being consolidated with certain provisions of other sections.

Said section 121 of present title 18, U.S.C., 1940 ed., provided for punishment by fine of not more than $2,000 or imprisonment of not more than 1 year, or both, of persons rescuing, attempting to rescue, or causing to be rescued, "any property" which has been seized by "any person" authorized to make searches and seizures.

Said section 128 of present title 18, U.S.C., 1940 ed., provided for punishment by fine of not more than $300 and imprisonment for not more than 1 year of persons dispossessing, rescuing, or attempting to dispossess or rescue, or aiding or assisting in dispossessing or rescuing, "any property taken or detained by any officer or other person under the authority of any revenue law of the United States."

This revised section adopts the maximum fine provisions of section 121 of title 18, U.S.C., 1940 ed., and extends the maximum term of imprisonment to 2 years. This was deemed advisable so that uniformity of punishment would be established and the provisions would be sufficiently broad to impose punishment commensurate with the gravity of the offense. (See section 3601(c)(2) of title 26, U.S.C., 1940 ed., Internal Revenue Code.)

Reference to persons causing, procuring, aiding or assisting was omitted as unnecessary in view of definition of "principal" in section 2 of this title.

Changes were made in phraseology.

Amendments

1994—Pub. L. 103–322 substituted "fined under this title" for "fined not more than $2,000".

§2234. Authority exceeded in executing warrant

Whoever, in executing a search warrant, willfully exceeds his authority or exercises it with unnecessary severity, shall be fined under this title or imprisoned not more than one year, or both.

(June 25, 1948, ch. 645, 62 Stat. 803; Pub. L. 104–294, title VI, §601(a)(8), Oct. 11, 1996, 110 Stat. 3498; Pub. L. 107–273, div. B, title III, §3002(a)(3), Nov. 2, 2002, 116 Stat. 1805.)

Historical and Revision Notes

Based on title 18, U.S.C., 1940 ed., §631 (June 15, 1917, ch. 30, title XI, §21, 40 Stat. 230).
Minor changes were made in phraseology.

Amendments

2002—Pub. L. 107–273 inserted ", or both" after "year".
1996—Pub. L. 104–294 substituted "fined under this title" for "fined not more than $1,000".

§2235. Search warrant procured maliciously

Whoever maliciously and without probable cause procures a search warrant to be issued and executed, shall be fined under this title or imprisoned not more than one year, or both.

(June 25, 1948, ch. 645, 62 Stat. 803; Pub. L. 104–294, title VI, §601(a)(8), Oct. 11, 1996, 110 Stat. 3498; Pub. L. 107–273, div. B, title III, §3002(a)(3), Nov. 2, 2002, 116 Stat. 1805.)

Historical and Revision Notes

Based on title 18, U.S.C., 1940 ed., §630 (June 15, 1917, ch. 30, title XI, §20, 40 Stat. 230). Minor changes were made in phraseology.

Amendments

2002—Pub. L. 107–273 inserted ", or both" after "year".

1996—Pub. L. 104–294 substituted "fined under this title" for "fined not more than $1,000".

§2236. Searches without warrant

Whoever, being an officer, agent, or employee of the United States or any department or agency thereof, engaged in the enforcement of any law of the United States, searches any private dwelling used and occupied as such dwelling without a warrant directing such search, or maliciously and without reasonable cause searches any other building or property without a search warrant, shall be fined under this title for a first offense; and, for a subsequent offense, shall be fined under this title or imprisoned not more than one year, or both.

This section shall not apply to any person—

(a) serving a warrant of arrest; or

(b) arresting or attempting to arrest a person committing or attempting to commit an offense in his presence, or who has committed or is suspected on reasonable grounds of having committed a felony; or

(c) making a search at the request or invitation or with the consent of the occupant of the premises.

(June 25, 1948, ch. 645, 62 Stat. 803; Pub. L. 104–294, title VI, §601(a)(8), Oct. 11, 1996, 110 Stat. 3498; Pub. L. 107–273, div. B, title IV, §4002(d)(1)(C)(iii), Nov. 2, 2002, 116 Stat. 1809.)

Historical and Revision Notes

Based on title 18, U.S.C., 1940 ed., §53a (Aug. 27, 1935, ch. 740, §201, 49 Stat. 877).

Words "or any department or agency thereof" were inserted to avoid ambiguity as to scope of section. (See definitive section 6 of this title.)

The exception in the case of an invitation or the consent of the occupant, was inserted to make the section complete and remove any doubt as to the application of this section to searches which have uniformly been upheld.

Reference to misdemeanor was omitted in view of definitive section 1 of this title. (See reviser's note under section 212 of this title.)

Words "upon conviction thereof shall be" were omitted as surplusage, since punishment cannot be imposed until conviction is secured.

Minor changes were made in phraseology.

Amendments

2002—Pub. L. 107–273 inserted "under this title" after "warrant, shall be fined" and struck out "not more than $1,000" after "for a first offense".

1996—Pub. L. 104–294 substituted "fined under this title" for "fined not more than $1,000".

§2237. Criminal sanctions for failure to heave to, obstruction of boarding, or providing false information

(a)(1) It shall be unlawful for the master, operator, or person in charge of a vessel of the United States, or a vessel subject to the jurisdiction of the United States, to knowingly fail to obey an order by an authorized Federal law enforcement officer to heave to that vessel.

(2) It shall be unlawful for any person on board a vessel of the United States, or a vessel subject to the jurisdiction of the United States, to—

(A) forcibly resist, oppose, prevent, impede, intimidate, or interfere with a boarding or other law enforcement action authorized by any Federal law or to resist a lawful arrest; or

(B) provide materially false information to a Federal law enforcement officer during a boarding of a vessel regarding the vessel's destination, origin, ownership, registration, nationality, cargo, or crew.

(b)(1) Except as otherwise provided in this subsection, whoever knowingly violates subsection (a) shall be fined under this title or imprisoned for not more than 5 years, or both.

(2)(A) If the offense is one under paragraph (1) or (2)(A) of subsection (a) and has an aggravating factor set forth in subparagraph (B) of this paragraph, the offender shall be fined under this title or imprisoned for any term of years or life, or both.

(B) The aggravating factor referred to in subparagraph (A) is that the offense—

(i) results in death; or

(ii) involves—

(I) an attempt to kill;

(II) kidnapping or an attempt to kidnap; or

(III) an offense under section 2241.

(3) If the offense is one under paragraph (1) or (2)(A) of subsection (a) and results in serious bodily injury (as defined in section 1365), the offender shall be fined under this title or imprisoned for not more than 15 years, or both.

(4) If the offense is one under paragraph (1) or (2)(A) of subsection (a), involves knowing transportation under inhumane conditions, and is committed in the course of a violation of section 274 of the Immigration and Nationality Act, or chapter 77 or section 113 (other than under subsection (a)(4) or (a)(5) of such section) or 117 of this title, the offender shall be fined under this title or imprisoned for not more than 15 years, or both.

(c) This section does not limit the authority of a customs officer under section 581 of the Tariff Act of 1930 (19 U.S.C. 1581), or any other provision of law enforced or administered by the Secretary of the Treasury or the Secretary of Homeland Security, or the authority of any Federal law enforcement officer under any law of the United States, to order a vessel to stop or heave to.

(d) A foreign nation may consent or waive objection to the enforcement of United States law by the United States under this section by radio, telephone, or similar oral or electronic means. Consent or waiver may be proven by certification of the Secretary of State or the designee of the Secretary of State.

(e) In this section—

(1) the term "Federal law enforcement officer" has the meaning given the term in section 115(c);

(2) the term "heave to" means to cause a vessel to slow, come to a stop, or adjust its course or speed to account for the weather conditions and sea state to facilitate a law enforcement boarding;

(3) the term "vessel subject to the jurisdiction of the United States" has the meaning given the term in section 70502 of title 46;

(4) the term "vessel of the United States" has the meaning given the term in section 70502 of title 46; and

(5) the term "transportation under inhumane conditions" means—

(A) transportation—

(i) of one or more persons in an engine compartment, storage compartment, or other confined space;

(ii) at an excessive speed; or

(iii) of a number of persons in excess of the rated capacity of the vessel; or

(B) intentional grounding of a vessel in which persons are being transported.

(Added Pub. L. 109–177, title III, §303(a), Mar. 9, 2006, 120 Stat. 233; amended Pub. L. 111–281, title IX, §917, Oct. 15, 2010, 124 Stat. 3021.)

References in Text

Section 274 of the Immigration and Nationality Act, referred to in subsec. (b)(4), is classified to section 1324 of Title 8, Aliens and Nationality.

Amendments

2010—Subsec. (b). Pub. L. 111–281, §917(a), amended subsec. (b) generally. Prior to amendment subsec. (b) read as follows: "Any person who intentionally violates this section shall be fined under this title or imprisoned for not more than 5 years, or both."

Subsec. (e)(3). Pub. L. 111–281, §917(b)(1), amended par. (3) generally. Prior to amendment, par. (3) read as follows: "the term 'vessel subject to the jurisdiction of the United States' has the meaning given the term in section 2 of the Maritime Drug Law Enforcement Act (46 U.S.C. App. 1903); and".

Subsec. (e)(4). Pub. L. 111–281, §917(b)(2), substituted "section 70502 of title 46; and" for "section 2 of the Maritime Drug Law Enforcement Act (46 U.S.C. App. 1903)."

Subsec. (e)(5). Pub. L. 111–281, §917(b)(3), added par. (5).

CHAPTER 109A - SEXUAL ABUSE

Codification
Pub. L. 99–646 and Pub. L. 99–654 added identical chapters 109A.

Amendments
1994—Pub. L. 103–322, title IV, §§40111(c), 40113(a)(2), title VI, §60010(b), Sept. 13, 1994, 108 Stat. 1903, 1907, 1973, redesignated item 2245 as 2246 and added items 2245, 2247, and 2248.

§2241. Aggravated sexual abuse
(a) By Force or Threat.—Whoever, in the special maritime and territorial jurisdiction of the United States or in a Federal prison, or in any prison, institution, or facility in which persons are held in custody by direction of or pursuant to a contract or agreement with the head of any Federal department or agency, knowingly causes another person to engage in a sexual act—

(1) by using force against that other person; or

(2) by threatening or placing that other person in fear that any person will be subjected to death, serious bodily injury, or kidnapping;

or attempts to do so, shall be fined under this title, imprisoned for any term of years or life, or both.

(b) By Other Means.—Whoever, in the special maritime and territorial jurisdiction of the United States or in a Federal prison, or in any prison, institution, or facility in which persons are held in custody by direction of or pursuant to a contract or agreement with the head of any Federal department or agency, knowingly—

(1) renders another person unconscious and thereby engages in a sexual act with that other person; or

(2) administers to another person by force or threat of force, or without the knowledge or permission of that person, a drug, intoxicant, or other similar substance and thereby—

(A) substantially impairs the ability of that other person to appraise or control conduct; and

(B) engages in a sexual act with that other person;

or attempts to do so, shall be fined under this title, imprisoned for any term of years or life, or both.

(c) With Children.—Whoever crosses a State line with intent to engage in a sexual act with a person who has not attained the age of 12 years, or in the special maritime and territorial jurisdiction of the United States or in a Federal prison, or in any prison, institution, or facility in which persons are held in custody by direction of or pursuant to a contract or agreement with the head of any Federal department or agency, knowingly engages in a sexual act with another person who has not attained the age of 12 years, or knowingly engages in a sexual act under the circumstances described in subsections (a) and (b) with another person who has attained the age of 12 years but has not attained the age of 16 years (and is at least 4 years younger than the person so engaging), or attempts to do so, shall be fined under this title and imprisoned for not less than 30 years or for life. If the defendant has previously been convicted of another Federal offense under this subsection, or of a State offense that would have been an offense under either such provision had the offense occurred in a Federal prison, unless the death penalty is imposed, the defendant shall be sentenced to life in prison.

(d) State of Mind Proof Requirement.—In a prosecution under subsection (c) of this section, the Government need not prove that the defendant knew that the other person engaging in the sexual act had not attained the age of 12 years.

(Added Pub. L. 99–646, §87(b), Nov. 10, 1986, 100 Stat. 3620, and Pub. L. 99–654, §2, Nov. 14, 1986, 100 Stat. 3660; amended Pub. L. 103–322, title XXXIII, §330021(1), Sept. 13, 1994, 108 Stat. 2150; Pub. L. 104–208, div. A, title I, §101(a) [title I, §121[7(b)]], Sept. 30, 1996, 110 Stat. 3009, 3009–26, 3009–31; Pub. L. 105–314, title III, §301(a), Oct. 30, 1998, 112 Stat. 2978; Pub. L. 109–162, title XI, §1177(a)(1), (2), Jan. 5, 2006, 119 Stat. 3125; Pub. L. 109–248, title II, §§206(a)(1), 207(2), July 27, 2006, 120 Stat. 613, 615; Pub. L. 110–161, div. E, title V, §554, Dec. 26, 2007, 121 Stat. 2082.)

Codification

Pub. L. 99–646 and Pub. L. 99–654 added identical sections 2241.

Amendments

2007—Subsecs. (a) to (c). Pub. L. 110–161 substituted "the head of any Federal department or agency" for "the Attorney General".

2006—Subsecs. (a), (b). Pub. L. 109–248, §207(2), inserted comma after "Attorney General" in introductory provisions.

Pub. L. 109–162, §1177(a)(1), inserted "or in any prison, institution, or facility in which persons are held in custody by direction of or pursuant to a contract or agreement with the Attorney General" after "in a Federal prison," in introductory provisions.

Subsec. (c). Pub. L. 109–248 inserted comma after "Attorney General" and substituted "and imprisoned for not less than 30 years or for life" for ", imprisoned for any term of years or life, or both" in first sentence.

Pub. L. 109–162, §1177(a)(2), inserted "or in any prison, institution, or facility in which persons are held in custody by direction of or pursuant to a contract or agreement with the Attorney General" after "in a Federal prison," in first sentence.

1998—Subsec. (c). Pub. L. 105–314 substituted "younger than the person so engaging" for "younger than that person".

1996—Subsec. (c). Pub. L. 104–208 reenacted heading without change and amended text generally. Prior to amendment, text read as follows: "Whoever, in the special maritime and territorial jurisdiction of the United States or in a Federal prison, knowingly engages in a sexual act with another person who has not attained the age of 12 years, or attempts to do so, shall be fined under this title, imprisoned for any term of years or life, or both."

1994—Subsec. (a)(2). Pub. L. 103–322 substituted "kidnapping" for "kidnaping".

Effective Date

Pub. L. 99–646, §87(e), Nov. 10, 1986, 100 Stat. 3624, and Pub. L. 99–654, §4, Nov. 14, 1986, 100 Stat. 3664, provided, respectively, that: "This section and the amendments made by this section [see Short Title note below] shall take effect 30 days after the date of the enactment of this Act [Nov. 10, 1986]." and "This Act and the amendments made by this Act [see Short Title note below] shall take effect 30 days after the date of the enactment of this Act [Nov. 14, 1986]."

Short Title of 1996 Amendment

Pub. L. 104–208, div. A, title I, §101(a) [title I, §121[7(a)]], Sept. 30, 1996, 110 Stat. 3009, 3009–31, provided that: "This section [probably means subsec. 7 of section 121 of Pub. L. 104–208, div. A, title I, §101(a), which amended sections 2241 and 2243 of this title] may be cited as the 'Amber Hagerman Child Protection Act of 1996'."

Short Title of 1986 Amendment

Pub. L. 99–646, §87(a), Nov. 10, 1986, 100 Stat. 3620, and Pub. L. 99–654, §1, Nov. 14, 1986, 100 Stat. 3660, provided, respectively, that: "This section [enacting this chapter, amending sections 113, 1111, 1153, and 3185 of this title, sections 300w–3, 300w–4, and 9511 of Title 42, The Public Health and Welfare, and section 1472 of former Title 49, Transportation, and repealing chapter 99 of this title] may be cited as the 'Sexual Abuse Act of 1986'." and "This Act [enacting this chapter, amending sections 113, 1111, 1153, and 3185 of this title, sections 300w–3, 300w–4, and 9511 of Title 42, and section 1472 of former Title 49, Transportation, and repealing chapter 99 of this title] may be cited as the 'Sexual Abuse Act of 1986'."

§2242. Sexual abuse

Whoever, in the special maritime and territorial jurisdiction of the United States or in a Federal prison, or in any prison, institution, or facility in which persons are held in custody by direction of or pursuant to a contract or agreement with the head of any Federal department or agency, knowingly—

(1) causes another person to engage in a sexual act by threatening or placing that other person in fear (other than by threatening or placing that other person in fear that any person will be subjected to death, serious bodily injury, or kidnapping); or

(2) engages in a sexual act with another person if that other person is—

(A) incapable of appraising the nature of the conduct; or

(B) physically incapable of declining participation in, or communicating unwillingness to engage in, that sexual act;

or attempts to do so, shall be fined under this title and imprisoned for any term of years or for life.

(Added Pub. L. 99–646, §87(b), Nov. 10, 1986, 100 Stat. 3621, and Pub. L. 99–654, §2, Nov. 14, 1986, 100 Stat. 3661; amended Pub. L. 103–322, title XXXIII, §330021(1), Sept. 13, 1994, 108 Stat. 2150; Pub. L. 109–162, title XI, §1177(a)(3), Jan. 5, 2006, 119 Stat. 3125; Pub. L. 109–248, title II, §§205, 207(2), July 27, 2006, 120 Stat. 613, 615; Pub. L. 110–161, div. E, title V, §554, Dec. 26, 2007, 121 Stat. 2082.)

Codification

Pub. L. 99–646 and Pub. L. 99–654 added identical sections 2242.

Amendments

2007—Pub. L. 110–161 substituted "the head of any Federal department or agency" for "the Attorney General" in introductory provisions.

2006—Pub. L. 109–248 inserted comma after "Attorney General" in introductory provisions and substituted "and imprisoned for any term of years or for life" for ", imprisoned not more than 20 years, or both" in concluding provisions.

Pub. L. 109–162 inserted "or in any prison, institution, or facility in which persons are held in custody by direction of or pursuant to a contract or agreement with the Attorney General" after "in a Federal prison," in introductory provisions.

1994—Par. (1). Pub. L. 103–322 substituted "kidnapping" for "kidnaping".

§2243. Sexual abuse of a minor or ward

(a) Of a Minor.—Whoever, in the special maritime and territorial jurisdiction of the United States or in a Federal prison, or in any prison, institution, or facility in which persons are held in custody by direction of or pursuant to a contract or agreement with the head of any Federal department or agency, knowingly engages in a sexual act with another person who—

(1) has attained the age of 12 years but has not attained the age of 16 years; and

(2) is at least four years younger than the person so engaging;

or attempts to do so, shall be fined under this title, imprisoned not more than 15 years, or both.

(b) Of a Ward.—Whoever, in the special maritime and territorial jurisdiction of the United States or in a Federal prison, or in any prison, institution, or facility in which persons are held in custody by direction of or pursuant to a contract or agreement with the head of any Federal department or agency, knowingly engages in a sexual act with another person who is—

(1) in official detention; and

(2) under the custodial, supervisory, or disciplinary authority of the person so engaging;

or attempts to do so, shall be fined under this title, imprisoned not more than 15 years, or both.

(c) Defenses.—(1) In a prosecution under subsection (a) of this section, it is a defense, which the defendant must establish by a preponderance of the evidence, that the defendant reasonably believed that the other person had attained the age of 16 years.

(2) In a prosecution under this section, it is a defense, which the defendant must establish by a preponderance of the evidence, that the persons engaging in the sexual act were at that time married to each other.

(d) State of Mind Proof Requirement.—In a prosecution under subsection (a) of this section, the Government need not prove that the defendant knew—

(1) the age of the other person engaging in the sexual act; or

(2) that the requisite age difference existed between the persons so engaging.

(Added Pub. L. 99–646, §87(b), Nov. 10, 1986, 100 Stat. 3621, and Pub. L. 99–654, §2, Nov. 14, 1986, 100 Stat. 3661; amended Pub. L. 101–647, title III, §322, Nov. 29, 1990, 104 Stat. 4818; Pub. L. 104–208, div. A, title I, §101(a) [title I, §121[7(c)]], Sept. 30, 1996, 110 Stat. 3009, 3009–26, 3009–31; Pub. L. 105–314, title III, §301(b), Oct. 30, 1998, 112 Stat. 2979; Pub. L. 109–162, title XI, §1177(a)(4), (b)(1), Jan. 5, 2006, 119 Stat. 3125; Pub. L. 109–248, title II, §207, July 27, 2006, 120 Stat. 615; Pub. L. 110–161, div. E, title V, §554, Dec. 26, 2007, 121 Stat. 2082.)

Codification

Pub. L. 99–646 and Pub. L. 99–654 added identical sections 2243.

Amendments

2007—Subsecs. (a), (b). Pub. L. 110–161 substituted "the head of any Federal department or agency" for "the Attorney General" in introductory provisions.

2006—Subsec. (a). Pub. L. 109–248, §207(2), inserted comma after "Attorney General" in introductory provisions.

Pub. L. 109–162, §1177(a)(4), inserted "or in any prison, institution, or facility in which persons are held in custody by direction of or pursuant to a contract or agreement with the Attorney General" after "in a Federal prison," in introductory provisions.

Subsec. (b). Pub. L. 109–248 inserted comma after "Attorney General" in introductory provisions and substituted "15 years" for "five years" in concluding provisions.

Pub. L. 109–162, §1177(a)(4), (b)(1), inserted "or in any prison, institution, or facility in which persons are held in custody by direction of or pursuant to a contract or agreement with the

Attorney General" after "in a Federal prison," in introductory provisions and substituted "five years" for "one year" in concluding provisions.

1998—Subsec. (a). Pub. L. 105–314 struck out "crosses a State line with intent to engage in a sexual act with a person who has not attained the age of 12 years, or" after "Whoever" in introductory provisions.

1996—Subsec. (a). Pub. L. 104–208 inserted "crosses a State line with intent to engage in a sexual act with a person who has not attained the age of 12 years, or" after "Whoever" in introductory provisions.

1990—Subsec. (a). Pub. L. 101–647 substituted "15 years" for "five years" in concluding provisions.

§2244. Abusive sexual contact

(a) Sexual Conduct in Circumstances Where Sexual Acts Are Punished by This Chapter.— Whoever, in the special maritime and territorial jurisdiction of the United States or in a Federal prison, or in any prison, institution, or facility in which persons are held in custody by direction of or pursuant to a contract or agreement with the head of any Federal department or agency, knowingly engages in or causes sexual contact with or by another person, if so to do would violate—

(1) subsection (a) or (b) of section 2241 of this title had the sexual contact been a sexual act, shall be fined under this title, imprisoned not more than ten years, or both;

(2) section 2242 of this title had the sexual contact been a sexual act, shall be fined under this title, imprisoned not more than three years, or both;

(3) subsection (a) of section 2243 of this title had the sexual contact been a sexual act, shall be fined under this title, imprisoned not more than two years, or both;

(4) subsection (b) of section 2243 of this title had the sexual contact been a sexual act, shall be fined under this title, imprisoned not more than two years, or both; or

(5) subsection (c) of section 2241 of this title had the sexual contact been a sexual act, shall be fined under this title and imprisoned for any term of years or for life.

(b) In Other Circumstances.—Whoever, in the special maritime and territorial jurisdiction of the United States or in a Federal prison, or in any prison, institution, or facility in which persons are held in custody by direction of or pursuant to a contract or agreement with the head of any Federal department or agency, knowingly engages in sexual contact with another person without that other person's permission shall be fined under this title, imprisoned not more than two years, or both.

(c) Offenses Involving Young Children.—If the sexual contact that violates this section (other than subsection (a)(5)) is with an individual who has not attained the age of 12 years, the maximum term of imprisonment that may be imposed for the offense shall be twice that otherwise provided in this section.

(Added Pub. L. 99–646, §87(b), Nov. 10, 1986, 100 Stat. 3622, and Pub. L. 99–654, §2, Nov. 14, 1986, 100 Stat. 3661; amended Pub. L. 100–690, title VII, §7058(a), Nov. 18, 1988, 102 Stat. 4403; Pub. L. 103–322, title XXXIII, §330016(1)(K), Sept. 13, 1994, 108 Stat. 2147; Pub. L. 105–314, title III, §302, Oct. 30, 1998, 112 Stat. 2979; Pub. L. 109–162, title XI, §1177(a)(5), (b)(2), Jan. 5, 2006, 119 Stat. 3125; Pub. L. 109–248, title II, §§206(a)(2), 207(2), July 27, 2006, 120 Stat. 613, 615; Pub. L. 110–161, div. E, title V, §554, Dec. 26, 2007, 121 Stat. 2082.)

Codification

Pub. L. 99–646 and Pub. L. 99–654 added identical sections 2244.

Amendments

2007—Subsecs. (a), (b). Pub. L. 110–161 substituted "the head of any Federal department or agency" for "the Attorney General".

2006—Subsec. (a). Pub. L. 109–248, §207(2), inserted comma after "Attorney General" in introductory provisions.

Pub. L. 109–162, §1177(a)(5), inserted "or in any prison, institution, or facility in which persons are held in custody by direction of or pursuant to a contract or agreement with the Attorney General" after "in a Federal prison," in introductory provisions.

Subsec. (a)(1). Pub. L. 109–248, §206(a)(2)(A)(i), inserted "subsection (a) or (b) of" before "section 2241 of this title".

Subsec. (a)(4). Pub. L. 109–162, §1177(b)(2), substituted "two years" for "six months".

Subsec. (a)(5). Pub. L. 109–248, §206(a)(2)(A)(ii)–(iv), added par. (5).

Subsec. (b). Pub. L. 109–248, §207(2), inserted comma after "Attorney General".

Pub. L. 109–162, §1177(a)(5), (b)(2), inserted "or in any prison, institution, or facility in which persons are held in custody by direction of or pursuant to a contract or agreement with the Attorney General" after "in a Federal prison," and substituted "two years" for "six months".

Subsec. (c). Pub. L. 109–248, §206(a)(2)(B), inserted "(other than subsection (a)(5))" after "violates this section".

1998—Subsec. (c). Pub. L. 105–314 added subsec. (c).

1994—Subsecs. (a)(4), (b). Pub. L. 103–322 substituted "fined under this title" for "fined not more than $5,000".

1988—Subsec. (a). Pub. L. 100–690 substituted "ten years" for "five years" in par. (1) and "two years" for "one year" in par. (3).

§2245. Offenses resulting in death

(a) 1 In General.—A person who, in the course of an offense under this chapter, or section 1591, 2251, 2251A, 2260, 2421, 2422, 2423, or 2425, murders an individual, shall be punished by death or imprisoned for any term of years or for life.

(Added Pub. L. 103–322, title VI, §60010(a)(2), Sept. 13, 1994, 108 Stat. 1972; amended Pub. L. 109–248, title II, §206(a)(3), July 27, 2006, 120 Stat. 613.)

Prior Provisions

A prior section 2245 was renumbered section 2246 of this title.

Amendments

2006—Pub. L. 109–248 amended section catchline and text generally. Prior to amendment, text read as follows: "A person who, in the course of an offense under this chapter, engages in conduct that results in the death of a person, shall be punished by death or imprisoned for any term of years or for life."

§2246. Definitions for chapter

As used in this chapter—

(1) the term "prison" means a correctional, detention, or penal facility;

(2) the term "sexual act" means—

(A) contact between the penis and the vulva or the penis and the anus, and for purposes of this subparagraph contact involving the penis occurs upon penetration, however slight;

(B) contact between the mouth and the penis, the mouth and the vulva, or the mouth and the anus;

(C) the penetration, however slight, of the anal or genital opening of another by a hand or finger or by any object, with an intent to abuse, humiliate, harass, degrade, or arouse or gratify the sexual desire of any person; or

(D) the intentional touching, not through the clothing, of the genitalia of another person who has not attained the age of 16 years with an intent to abuse, humiliate, harass, degrade, or arouse or gratify the sexual desire of any person;

(3) the term "sexual contact" means the intentional touching, either directly or through the clothing, of the genitalia, anus, groin, breast, inner thigh, or buttocks of any person with an intent to abuse, humiliate, harass, degrade, or arouse or gratify the sexual desire of any person;

(4) the term "serious bodily injury" means bodily injury that involves a substantial risk of death,

unconsciousness, extreme physical pain, protracted and obvious disfigurement, or protracted loss or impairment of the function of a bodily member, organ, or mental faculty;

(5) the term "official detention" means—

(A) detention by a Federal officer or employee, or under the direction of a Federal officer or employee, following arrest for an offense; following surrender in lieu of arrest for an offense; following a charge or conviction of an offense, or an allegation or finding of juvenile delinquency; following commitment as a material witness; following civil commitment in lieu of criminal proceedings or pending resumption of criminal proceedings that are being held in abeyance, or pending extradition, deportation, or exclusion; or

(B) custody by a Federal officer or employee, or under the direction of a Federal officer or employee, for purposes incident to any detention described in subparagraph (A) of this paragraph, including transportation, medical diagnosis or treatment, court appearance, work, and recreation; but does not include supervision or other control (other than custody during specified hours or days) after release on bail, probation, or parole, or after release following a finding of juvenile delinquency; and

(6) the term "State" means a State of the United States, the District of Columbia, and any commonwealth, possession, or territory of the United States.

(Added Pub. L. 99–646, §87(b), Nov. 10, 1986, 100 Stat. 3622, §2245, and Pub. L. 99–654, §2, Nov. 14, 1986, 100 Stat. 3662, §2245; renumbered §2246 and amended Pub. L. 103–322, title IV, §40502, title VI, §60010(a)(1), Sept. 13, 1994, 108 Stat. 1945, 1972; Pub. L. 105–314, title III, §301(c), Oct. 30, 1998, 112 Stat. 2979.)

Codification

Pub. L. 99–646 and Pub. L. 99–654 added identical sections.

Amendments

1998—Par. (6). Pub. L. 105–314 added par. (6).

1994—Pub. L. 103–322, §60010(a)(1), renumbered section 2245 of this title as this section.

Par. (2)(D). Pub. L. 103–322, §40502, added subpar. (D).

§2247. Repeat offenders

(a) Maximum Term of Imprisonment.—The maximum term of imprisonment for a violation of this chapter after a prior sex offense conviction shall be twice the term otherwise provided by this chapter, unless section 3559(e) applies.

(b) Prior Sex Offense Conviction Defined.—In this section, the term "prior sex offense conviction" has the meaning given that term in section 2426(b).

(Added Pub. L. 103–322, title IV, §40111(a), Sept. 13, 1994, 108 Stat. 1903; amended Pub. L. 105–314, title III, §303, Oct. 30, 1998, 112 Stat. 2979; Pub. L. 108–21, title I, §106(b), Apr. 30, 2003, 117 Stat. 655.)

Amendments

2003—Subsec. (a). Pub. L. 108–21 inserted ", unless section 3559(e) applies" before period at end.

1998—Pub. L. 105–314 reenacted section catchline without change and amended text generally. Prior to amendment, text read as follows: "Any person who violates a provision of this chapter, after one or more prior convictions for an offense punishable under this chapter, or after one or more prior convictions under the laws of any State relating to aggravated sexual abuse, sexual abuse, or abusive sexual contact have become final, is punishable by a term of imprisonment up to twice that otherwise authorized."

§2248. Mandatory restitution

(a) In General.—Notwithstanding section 3663 or 3663A, and in addition to any other civil or criminal penalty authorized by law, the court shall order restitution for any offense under this chapter.

(b) Scope and Nature of Order.—

(1) Directions.—The order of restitution under this section shall direct the defendant to pay to the victim (through the appropriate court mechanism) the full amount of the victim's losses as determined by the court pursuant to paragraph (2).

(2) Enforcement.—An order of restitution under this section shall be issued and enforced in accordance with section 3664 in the same manner as an order under section 3663A.

(3) Definition.—For purposes of this subsection, the term "full amount of the victim's losses" includes any costs incurred by the victim for—

(A) medical services relating to physical, psychiatric, or psychological care;

(B) physical and occupational therapy or rehabilitation;

(C) necessary transportation, temporary housing, and child care expenses;

(D) lost income;

(E) attorneys' fees, plus any costs incurred in obtaining a civil protection order; and

(F) any other losses suffered by the victim as a proximate result of the offense.

(4) Order mandatory.—(A) The issuance of a restitution order under this section is mandatory.

(B) A court may not decline to issue an order under this section because of—

(i) the economic circumstances of the defendant; or

(ii) the fact that a victim has, or is entitled to, receive compensation for his or her injuries from the proceeds of insurance or any other source.

(c) Definition.—For purposes of this section, the term "victim" means the individual harmed as a result of a commission of a crime under this chapter, including, in the case of a victim who is under 18 years of age, incompetent, incapacitated, or deceased, the legal guardian of the victim or representative of the victim's estate, another family member, or any other person appointed as suitable by the court, but in no event shall the defendant be named as such representative or guardian.

(Added Pub. L. 103–322, title IV, §40113(a)(1), Sept. 13, 1994, 108 Stat. 1904; amended Pub. L. 104–132, title II, §205(b), Apr. 24, 1996, 110 Stat. 1231.)

Amendments

1996—Subsec. (a). Pub. L. 104–132, §205(b)(1), inserted "or 3663A" after "3663".

Subsec. (b)(1). Pub. L. 104–132, §205(b)(2)(A), reenacted heading without change and amended text generally. Prior to amendment, text read as follows: "The order of restitution under this section shall direct that—

"(A) the defendant pay to the victim (through the appropriate court mechanism) the full amount of the victim's losses as determined by the court, pursuant to paragraph (3); and

"(B) the United States Attorney enforce the restitution order by all available and reasonable means."

Subsec. (b)(2). Pub. L. 104–132, §205(b)(2)(B), struck out "by victim" after "Enforcement" in heading and amended text generally. Prior to amendment, text read as follows: "An order of restitution also may be enforced by a victim named in the order to receive the restitution in the same manner as a judgment in a civil action."

Subsec. (b)(4)(C), (D). Pub. L. 104–132, §205(b)(2)(C), struck out subpars. (C) and (D), which related to court's consideration of economic circumstances of defendant in determining schedule of payment of restitution orders, and court's entry of nominal restitution awards where economic circumstances of defendant do not allow for payment of restitution, respectively.

Subsec. (b)(5) to (10). Pub. L. 104–132, §205(b)(2)(D), struck out pars. (5) to (10), which related, respectively, to more than 1 offender, more than 1 victim, payment schedule, setoff, effect on other sources of compensation, and condition of probation or supervised release.

Subsec. (c). Pub. L. 104–132, §205(b)(3), (4), redesignated subsec. (f) as (c) and struck out former subsec. (c) relating to proof of claim.

Subsecs. (d), (e). Pub. L. 104–132, §205(b)(3), struck out subsecs. (d) and (e) which read as follows:

"(d) Modification of Order.—A victim or the offender may petition the court at any time to modify a restitution order as appropriate in view of a change in the economic circumstances of the offender.

"(e) Reference to Magistrate or Special Master.—The court may refer any issue arising in connection with a proposed order of restitution to a magistrate or special master for proposed findings of fact and recommendations as to disposition, subject to a de novo determination of the issue by the court."

Subsec. (f). Pub. L. 104–132, §205(b)(4), redesignated subsec. (f) as (c).

Effective Date of 1996 Amendment

Pub. L. 104–132, title II, §211, Apr. 24, 1996, 110 Stat. 1241, provided that: "The amendments made by this subtitle [subtitle A (§§201–211) of title II of Pub. L. 104–132, see Short Title of 1996 Amendment note set out under section 3551 of this title] shall, to the extent constitutionally permissible, be effective for sentencing proceedings in cases in which the defendant is convicted on or after the date of enactment of this Act [Apr. 24, 1996]."

CHAPTER 109B - SEX OFFENDER AND CRIMES AGAINST CHILDREN REGISTRY

| 2250. | Failure to register. |

§2250. Failure to register

(a) In General.—Whoever—

(1) is required to register under the Sex Offender Registration and Notification Act;

(2)(A) is a sex offender as defined for the purposes of the Sex Offender Registration and Notification Act by reason of a conviction under Federal law (including the Uniform Code of Military Justice), the law of the District of Columbia, Indian tribal law, or the law of any territory or possession of the United States; or

(B) travels in interstate or foreign commerce, or enters or leaves, or resides in, Indian country; and

(3) knowingly fails to register or update a registration as required by the Sex Offender Registration and Notification Act;

shall be fined under this title or imprisoned not more than 10 years, or both.

(b) International Travel Reporting Violations.—Whoever—

(1) is required to register under the Sex Offender Registration and Notification Act (42 U.S.C. 16901 et seq.); 1

(2) knowingly fails to provide information required by the Sex Offender Registration and Notification Act relating to intended travel in foreign commerce; and

(3) engages or attempts to engage in the intended travel in foreign commerce;

shall be fined under this title, imprisoned not more than 10 years, or both.

(c) Affirmative Defense.—In a prosecution for a violation under subsection (a) or (b), it is an affirmative defense that—

(1) uncontrollable circumstances prevented the individual from complying;

(2) the individual did not contribute to the creation of such circumstances in reckless disregard of the requirement to comply; and

(3) the individual complied as soon as such circumstances ceased to exist.

(d) Crime of Violence.—

(1) In general.—An individual described in subsection (a) or (b) who commits a crime of violence under Federal law (including the Uniform Code of Military Justice), the law of the District of

Columbia, Indian tribal law, or the law of any territory or possession of the United States shall be imprisoned for not less than 5 years and not more than 30 years.

(2) Additional punishment.—The punishment provided in paragraph (1) shall be in addition and consecutive to the punishment provided for the violation described in subsection (a) or (b).

(Added Pub. L. 109–248, title I, §141(a)(1), July 27, 2006, 120 Stat. 602; amended Pub. L. 114–119, §6(b), Feb. 8, 2016, 130 Stat. 23.)

References in Text

The Sex Offender Registration and Notification Act, referred to in subsecs. (a)(1), (2)(A), (3) and (b)(1), (2), is title I of Pub. L. 109–248, July 27, 2006, 120 Stat. 590, which was classified principally to subchapter I (§16901 et seq.) of chapter 151 of Title 42, The Public Health and Welfare, prior to editorial reclassification as chapter 209 (§20901 et seq.) of Title 34, Crime Control and Law Enforcement. For complete classification of this Act to the Code, see Short Title of 2006 Act note set out under section 10101 of Title 34 and Tables.

The Uniform Code of Military Justice, referred to in subsecs. (a)(2)(A) and (d)(1), is classified generally to chapter 47 (§801 et seq.) of Title 10, Armed Forces.

Amendments

2016—Subsecs. (b) to (d). Pub. L. 114–119 added subsec. (b), redesignated former subsecs. (b) and (c) as (c) and (d), respectively, and in subsecs. (c) and (d), substituted "subsection (a) or (b)" for "subsection (a)" wherever appearing.

CHAPTER 110 - SEXUAL EXPLOITATION AND OTHER ABUSE OF CHILDREN

Amendments

2008—Pub. L. 110–401, title V, §501(b)(3), Oct. 13, 2008, 122 Stat. 4251, added items 2258A to 2258E.

2006—Pub. L. 109–248, title V, §503(b), title VII, §§702(b), 703(b), July 27, 2006, 120 Stat. 629, 648, 649, added items 2252C, 2257A, and 2260A.

2003—Pub. L. 108–21, title V, §521(b), Apr. 30, 2003, 117 Stat. 686, added item 2252B.

1996—Pub. L. 104–294, title VI, §601(i)(2), Oct. 11, 1996, 110 Stat. 3501, redesignated item 2258, relating to production of sexually explicit depictions of a minor, as 2260.

Pub. L. 104–208, div. A, title I, §101(a) [title I, §121[3(b)]], Sept. 30, 1996, 110 Stat. 3009, 3009–26, 3009–30, added item 2252A.

1994—Pub. L. 103–322, title IV, §40113(b)(2), title XVI, §160001(b)(1), Sept. 13, 1994, 108 Stat. 1910, 2037, added items 2258, relating to production of sexually explicit depictions of a minor, and 2259.

1990—Pub. L. 101–647, title II, §226(g)(2), Nov. 29, 1990, 104 Stat. 4808, inserted "AND OTHER ABUSE" after "EXPLOITATION" in chapter heading and added item 2258.

1988—Pub. L. 100–690, title VII, §§7512(c), 7513(b), Nov. 18, 1988, 102 Stat. 4487, 4488, added items 2251A and 2257.

1986—Pub. L. 99–500, §101(b), [title VII, §703(b)], Oct. 18, 1986, 100 Stat. 1783–39, 1783–75, and Pub. L. 99–591, §101(b) [title VII, §703(b)], Oct. 30, 1986, 100 Stat. 3341–39, 3341–75, added item 2255 and redesignated former item 2255 as 2256.

1984—Pub. L. 98–292, §7, May 21, 1984, 98 Stat. 206, added items 2253 and 2254 and redesignated former item 2253 as 2255.

§2251. Sexual exploitation of children

(a) Any person who employs, uses, persuades, induces, entices, or coerces any minor to engage in, or who has a minor assist any other person to engage in, or who transports any minor in or affecting interstate or foreign commerce, or in any Territory or Possession of the United States, with the intent that such minor engage in, any sexually explicit conduct for the purpose of producing any visual depiction of such conduct or for the purpose of transmitting a live visual depiction of such conduct, shall be punished as provided under subsection (e), if such person knows or has reason to know that such visual depiction will be transported or transmitted using any means or facility of interstate or foreign commerce or in or affecting interstate or foreign commerce or mailed, if that visual depiction was produced or transmitted using materials that have been mailed, shipped, or transported in or affecting interstate or foreign commerce by any means, including by computer, or if such visual depiction has actually been transported or transmitted using any means or facility of interstate or foreign commerce or in or affecting interstate or foreign commerce or mailed.

(b) Any parent, legal guardian, or person having custody or control of a minor who knowingly permits such minor to engage in, or to assist any other person to engage in, sexually explicit conduct for the purpose of producing any visual depiction of such conduct or for the purpose of transmitting a live visual depiction of such conduct shall be punished as provided under subsection (e) of this section, if such parent, legal guardian, or person knows or has reason to know that such visual depiction will be transported or transmitted using any means or facility of interstate or foreign commerce or in or affecting interstate or foreign commerce or mailed, if that visual depiction was produced or transmitted using materials that have been mailed, shipped, or transported in or affecting interstate or foreign commerce by any means, including by computer, or if such visual depiction has actually been transported or transmitted using any means or facility of interstate or foreign commerce or in or affecting interstate or foreign commerce or mailed.

(c)(1) Any person who, in a circumstance described in paragraph (2), employs, uses, persuades, induces, entices, or coerces any minor to engage in, or who has a minor assist any other person to engage in, any sexually explicit conduct outside of the United States, its territories or possessions, for the purpose of producing any visual depiction of such conduct, shall be punished as provided under subsection (e).

(2) The circumstance referred to in paragraph (1) is that—

(A) the person intends such visual depiction to be transported to the United States, its territories or possessions, by any means, including by using any means or facility of interstate or foreign commerce or mail; or

(B) the person transports such visual depiction to the United States, its territories or possessions, by any means, including by using any means or facility of interstate or foreign commerce or mail.

(d)(1) Any person who, in a circumstance described in paragraph (2), knowingly makes, prints, or publishes, or causes to be made, printed, or published, any notice or advertisement seeking or offering—

(A) to receive, exchange, buy, produce, display, distribute, or reproduce, any visual depiction, if the production of such visual depiction involves the use of a minor engaging in sexually explicit conduct and such visual depiction is of such conduct; or

(B) participation in any act of sexually explicit conduct by or with any minor for the purpose of producing a visual depiction of such conduct;

shall be punished as provided under subsection (e).

(2) The circumstance referred to in paragraph (1) is that—

(A) such person knows or has reason to know that such notice or advertisement will be transported using any means or facility of interstate or foreign commerce or in or affecting interstate or foreign commerce by any means including by computer or mailed; or

(B) such notice or advertisement is transported using any means or facility of interstate or foreign commerce or in or affecting interstate or foreign commerce by any means including by computer or mailed.

(e) Any individual who violates, or attempts or conspires to violate, this section shall be fined under this title and imprisoned not less than 15 years nor more than 30 years, but if such person has one prior conviction under this chapter, section 1591, chapter 71, chapter 109A, or chapter 117, or under section 920 of title 10 (article 120 of the Uniform Code of Military Justice), or under the laws of any State relating to aggravated sexual abuse, sexual abuse, abusive sexual contact involving a minor or ward, or sex trafficking of children, or the production, possession, receipt, mailing, sale, distribution, shipment, or transportation of child pornography, such person shall be fined under this title and imprisoned for not less than 25 years nor more than 50 years, but if such person has 2 or more prior convictions under this chapter, chapter 71, chapter 109A, or chapter 117, or under section 920 of title 10 (article 120 of the Uniform Code of Military Justice), or under the laws of any State relating to the sexual exploitation of children, such person shall be fined under this title and imprisoned not less than 35 years nor more than life. Any organization that violates, or attempts or conspires to violate, this section shall be fined under this title. Whoever, in the course of an offense under this section, engages in conduct that results in the death of a person, shall be punished by death or imprisoned for not less than 30 years or for life.

(Added Pub. L. 95–225, §2(a), Feb. 6, 1978, 92 Stat. 7; amended Pub. L. 98–292, §3, May 21, 1984, 98 Stat. 204; Pub. L. 99–500, §101(b) [title VII, §704(a)], Oct. 18, 1986, 100 Stat. 1783–39, 1783–75, and Pub. L. 99–591, §101(b) [title VII, §704(a)], Oct. 30, 1986, 100 Stat. 3341–39, 3341–75; Pub. L. 99–628, §§2, 3, Nov. 7, 1986, 100 Stat. 3510; Pub. L. 100–690, title VII, §7511(a), Nov. 18, 1988, 102 Stat. 4485; Pub. L. 101–647, title XXXV, §3563, Nov. 29, 1990, 104 Stat. 4928; Pub. L. 103–322, title VI, §60011, title XVI, §160001(b)(2), (c), (e), title XXXIII, §330016(1)(S)–(U), Sept. 13, 1994, 108 Stat. 1973, 2037, 2148; Pub. L. 104–208, div. A, title I, §101(a) [title I, §121[4]], Sept. 30, 1996, 110 Stat. 3009, 3009–26, 3009–30; Pub. L. 105–314, title II, §201, Oct. 30, 1998, 112 Stat. 2977; Pub. L. 108–21, title I, §103(a)(1)(A), (b)(1)(A), title V, §§506, 507, Apr. 30, 2003, 117 Stat. 652, 653, 683; Pub. L. 109–248, title II, §206(b)(1), July 27, 2006, 120 Stat. 614; Pub. L. 110–358, title I, §103(a)(1), (b), Oct. 8, 2008, 122 Stat. 4002, 4003; Pub. L. 110–401, title III, §301, Oct. 13, 2008, 122 Stat. 4242.)

Codification

Pub. L. 99–591 is a corrected version of Pub. L. 99–500.

Amendments

2008—Subsecs. (a), (b). Pub. L. 110–401 inserted "or for the purpose of transmitting a live visual depiction of such conduct" after "for the purpose of producing any visual depiction of such conduct" and "or transmitted" after "will be transported", after "was produced", and after "has actually been transported".

Pub. L. 110–358, §103(a)(1)(A), (B), (b), inserted "using any means or facility of interstate or foreign commerce or" after "be transported" and after "been transported" and substituted "in or affecting interstate" for "in interstate" wherever appearing.

Subsec. (c)(2). Pub. L. 110–358, §103(a)(1)(C), substituted "using any means or facility of interstate or foreign commerce" for "computer" in subpars. (A) and (B).

Subsec. (d)(2)(A). Pub. L. 110–358, §103(a)(1)(A), (b), inserted "using any means or facility of interstate or foreign commerce or" after "be transported" and substituted "in or affecting interstate" for "in interstate".

Subsec. (d)(2)(B). Pub. L. 110–358, §103(a)(1)(D), (b), inserted "using any means or facility of interstate or foreign commerce or" after "is transported" and substituted "in or affecting interstate" for "in interstate".

2006—Subsec. (e). Pub. L. 109–248 inserted "section 1591," after "one prior conviction under this chapter," and substituted "aggravated sexual abuse, sexual abuse, abusive sexual contact involving a minor or ward, or sex trafficking of children, or the production, possession, receipt, mailing, sale, distribution, shipment, or transportation of child pornography" for "the sexual exploitation of children" and "not less than 30 years or for life" for "any term of years or for life".

2003—Subsecs. (a), (b). Pub. L. 108–21, §506(1), substituted "subsection (e)" for "subsection (d)".

Subsec. (c). Pub. L. 108–21, §506(3), added subsec. (c). Former subsec. (c) redesignated (d).

Subsec. (c)(1). Pub. L. 108–21, §506(1), substituted "subsection (e)" for "subsection (d)" in concluding provisions.

Subsec. (d). Pub. L. 108–21, §506(2), redesignated subsec. (c) as (d). Former subsec. (d) redesignated (e).

Pub. L. 108–21, §103(a)(1)(A), (b)(1)(A), substituted "and imprisoned not less than 15" for "or imprisoned not less than 10", "30 years" for "20 years", "25 years" for "15 years", "more than 50 years" for "more than 30 years", and "35 years nor more than life" for "30 years nor more than life", and struck out "and both," before "but if such person has one".

Subsec. (e). Pub. L. 108–21, §507, inserted "chapter 71," before "chapter 109A," in two places and "or under section 920 of title 10 (article 120 of the Uniform Code of Military Justice)," before "or under the laws" in two places.

Pub. L. 108–21, §506(2), redesignated subsec. (d) as (e).

1998—Subsec. (a). Pub. L. 105–314, §201(a), inserted "if that visual depiction was produced using materials that have been mailed, shipped, or transported in interstate or foreign commerce by any means, including by computer," before "or if".

Subsec. (b). Pub. L. 105–314, §201(b), inserted ", if that visual depiction was produced using materials that have been mailed, shipped, or transported in interstate or foreign commerce by any means, including by computer," before "or if".

Subsec. (d). Pub. L. 105–314, §201(c), substituted ", chapter 109A, or chapter 117" for "or chapter 109A" in two places.

1996—Subsec. (d). Pub. L. 104–208 amended subsec. (d) generally. Prior to amendment, subsec. (d) read as follows: "Any individual who violates, or attempts or conspires to violate, this section shall be fined under this title, imprisoned not more than 10 years, or both, but, if such individual has a prior conviction under this chapter or chapter 109A, such individual shall be fined under this title, imprisoned not less than five years nor more than 15 years, or both. Any organization which violates, or attempts or conspires to violate, this section shall be fined under this title. Whoever, in the course of an offense under this section, engages in conduct that results in the death of a person, shall be punished by death or imprisoned for any term of years or for life."

1994—Pub. L. 103–322, §330016(1)(S)–(U), which directed the amendment of this section by substituting "under this title" for "not more than $100,000", "not more than $200,000", and "not more than $250,000", could not be executed because those phrases did not appear in text subsequent to amendment of subsec. (d) by Pub. L. 103–322, §160001(b)(2). See below.

Subsec. (d). Pub. L. 103–322, §160001(e), inserted ", or attempts or conspires to violate," after "violates" in two places.

Pub. L. 103–322, §160001(c), substituted "conviction under this chapter or chapter 109A" for "conviction under this section".

Pub. L. 103–322, §160001(b)(2)(C), substituted "fined under this title" for "fined not more than $250,000" in penultimate sentence.

Pub. L. 103–322, §160001(b)(2)(B), substituted "fined under this title," for "fined not more than $200,000, or" before "imprisoned not less than five years".

Pub. L. 103–322, §160001(b)(2)(A), substituted "fined under this title," for "fined not more than $100,000, or" before "imprisoned not more than 10 years".

Pub. L. 103–322, §60011, inserted at end "Whoever, in the course of an offense under this section, engages in conduct that results in the death of a person, shall be punished by death or imprisoned for any term of years or for life."

1990—Subsec. (a). Pub. L. 101–647 substituted "person to engage in," for "person to engage in,,".

1988—Subsec. (c)(2)(A), (B). Pub. L. 100–690 inserted "by any means including by computer" after "commerce".

1986—Subsec. (a). Pub. L. 99–628, §§2(1), (3), inserted ", or who transports any minor in interstate or foreign commerce, or in any Territory or Possession of the United States, with the intent that such minor engage in," after "assist any other person to engage in," and substituted "subsection (d)" for "subsection (c)".

Subsec. (b). Pub. L. 99–628, §2(2), substituted "subsection (d)" for "subsection (c)".

Subsecs. (c), (d). Pub. L. 99–628, §2(3), (4), added subsec. (c) and redesignated former subsec. (c) as (d).

Pub. L. 99–500 and Pub. L. 99–591 substituted "five years" for "two years" in subsec. (c).

1984—Subsecs. (a), (b). Pub. L. 98–292, §3(1), (2), substituted "visual depiction" for "visual or print medium" in three places and substituted "of" for "depicting" before "such conduct".

Subsec. (c). Pub. L. 98–292, §3(3)–(6), substituted "individual" for "person" in three places, "$100,000" for "$10,000", and "$200,000" for "$15,000", and inserted "Any organization which violates this section shall be fined not more than $250,000."

Short Title of 2006 Amendment

Pub. L. 109–248, title VII, §707(a), July 27, 2006, 120 Stat. 650, provided that: "This section [amending section 2255 of this title] may be cited as 'Masha's Law'."

Short Title of 1996 Amendment

Pub. L. 104–208, div. A, title I, §101(a) [title I, §121], Sept. 30, 1996, 110 Stat. 3009–26, provided in part that: "This section [enacting section 2252A of this title, amending this section, sections 2241, 2243, 2252, and 2256 of this title, and section 2000aa of Title 42, The Public Health and Welfare, and enacting provisions set out as notes under this section and section 2241 of this title] may be cited as the 'Child Pornography Prevention Act of 1996'."

Short Title of 1990 Amendment

Pub. L. 101–647, title III, §301(a), Nov. 29, 1990, 104 Stat. 4816, provided that: "This title [amending sections 1460, 2243, 2252, and 2257 of this title and enacting provisions set out as notes under section 2257 of this title and section 994 of Title 28, Judiciary and Judicial Procedure] may be cited as the 'Child Protection Restoration and Penalties Enhancement Act of 1990'."

Short Title of 1988 Amendment

Pub. L. 100–690, title VII, §7501, Nov. 18, 1988, 102 Stat. 4485, provided that: "This subtitle [subtitle N (§§7501–7526) of title VII of Pub. L. 100–690, enacting sections 1460, 1466 to 1469, 2251A, and 2257 of this title, amending this section, sections 1465, 1961, 2252 to 2254, 2256, and 2516 of this title, section 1305 of Title 19, Customs Duties, and section 223 of Title 47, Telecommunications, and enacting provisions set out as a note under section 2257 of this title] may be cited as the 'Child Protection and Obscenity Enforcement Act of 1988'."

Short Title of 1986 Amendments

Pub. L. 99–628, §1, Nov. 7, 1986, 100 Stat. 3510, provided that: "This Act [enacting sections 2421 to 2423 of this title, amending this section and sections 2255 and 2424 of this title, and repealing former sections 2421 to 2423 of this title] may be cited as the 'Child Sexual Abuse and Pornography Act of 1986'."

Pub. L. 99–500, §101(b) [title VII, §701], Oct. 18, 1986, 100 Stat. 1783–39, 1783–74, and Pub. L. 99–591, §101(b) [title VII, §701], Oct. 30, 1986, 100 Stat. 3341–39, 3341–74, provided that: "This title [enacting section 2255 of this title, amending this section and section 2252 of this title, redesignating former section 2255 of this title as 2256, and enacting provisions set out as notes under this section] may be cited as the 'Child Abuse Victims' Rights Act of 1986'."

Short Title of 1984 Amendment

Pub. L. 98–292, §1, May 21, 1984, 98 Stat. 204, provided: "That this Act [enacting sections 2253 and 2254 of this title, amending this section and sections 2252, 2255, and 2516 of this title, and enacting provisions set out as notes under this section and section 522 of Title 28, Judiciary and Judicial Procedure] may be cited as the 'Child Protection Act of 1984'."

Short Title

Pub. L. 95–225, §1, Feb. 6, 1978, 92 Stat. 7, provided: "That this Act [enacting this chapter and amending section 2423 of this title] may be cited as the 'Protection of Children Against Sexual Exploitation Act of 1977'."

Severability

Pub. L. 110–401, title V, §503, Oct. 13, 2008, 122 Stat. 4252, provided that: "If any provision of this title [enacting sections 2258A to 2258E of this title, amending section 2702 of this title, and repealing section 13032 of Title 42, The Public Health and Welfare] or amendment made by this title is held to be unconstitutional, the remainder of the provisions of this title or amendments made by this title—

"(1) shall remain in full force and effect; and

"(2) shall not be affected by the holding."

Pub. L. 104–208, div. A, title I, §101(a) [title I, §121[8]], Sept. 30, 1996, 110 Stat. 3009–31, provided that: "If any provision of this Act [probably means section 121 of Pub. L. 104–208, div. A, title I, §101(a), see Short Title of 1996 Amendment note above], including any provision or section of the definition of the term child pornography, an amendment made by this Act, or the application of such provision or amendment to any person or circumstance is held to be unconstitutional, the remainder of this Act, including any other provision or section of the definition of the term child pornography, the amendments made by this Act, and the application of such to any other person or circumstance shall not be affected thereby."

Pub. L. 95–225, §4, Feb. 6, 1978, 92 Stat. 9, provided that: "If any provision of this Act [see Short Title note set out above] or the application thereof to any person or circumstances is held invalid, the remainder of the Act and the application of the provision to other persons not similarly situated or to other circumstances shall not be affected thereby."

Congressional Findings

Pub. L. 110–358, title I, §102, Oct. 8, 2008, 122 Stat. 4001, provided that: "Congress finds the following:

"(1) Child pornography is estimated to be a multibillion dollar industry of global proportions, facilitated by the growth of the Internet.

"(2) Data has shown that 83 percent of child pornography possessors had images of children younger than 12 years old, 39 percent had images of children younger than 6 years old, and 19 percent had images of children younger than 3 years old.

"(3) Child pornography is a permanent record of a child's abuse and the distribution of child pornography images revictimizes the child each time the image is viewed.

"(4) Child pornography is readily available through virtually every Internet technology, including Web sites, email, instant messaging, Internet Relay Chat, newsgroups, bulletin boards, and peer-to-peer.

"(5) The technological ease, lack of expense, and anonymity in obtaining and distributing child pornography over the Internet has resulted in an explosion in the multijurisdictional distribution of child pornography.

"(6) The Internet is well recognized as a method of distributing goods and services across State lines.

"(7) The transmission of child pornography using the Internet constitutes transportation in interstate commerce."

Pub. L. 109–248, title V, §501, July 27, 2006, 120 Stat. 623, provided that: "Congress makes the following findings:

"(1) The effect of the intrastate production, transportation, distribution, receipt, advertising, and possession of child pornography on the interstate market in child pornography:

"(A) The illegal production, transportation, distribution, receipt, advertising and possession of child pornography, as defined in section 2256(8) of title 18, United States Code, as well as the transfer of custody of children for the production of child pornography, is harmful to the physiological, emotional, and mental health of the children depicted in child pornography and has a substantial and detrimental effect on society as a whole.

"(B) A substantial interstate market in child pornography exists, including not only a multimillion dollar industry, but also a nationwide network of individuals openly advertising their desire to exploit children and to traffic in child pornography. Many of these individuals distribute child pornography with the expectation of receiving other child pornography in return.

"(C) The interstate market in child pornography is carried on to a substantial extent through the mails and other instrumentalities of interstate and foreign commerce, such as the Internet. The advent of the Internet has greatly increased the ease of transporting, distributing, receiving, and advertising child pornography in interstate commerce. The advent of digital cameras and digital video cameras, as well as videotape cameras, has greatly increased the ease of producing child pornography. The advent of inexpensive computer equipment with the capacity to store large numbers of digital images of child pornography has greatly increased the ease of possessing child pornography. Taken together, these technological advances have had the unfortunate result of greatly increasing the interstate market in child pornography.

"(D) Intrastate incidents of production, transportation, distribution, receipt, advertising, and possession of child pornography, as well as the transfer of custody of children for the production of child pornography, have a substantial and direct effect upon interstate commerce because:

"(i) Some persons engaged in the production, transportation, distribution, receipt, advertising, and possession of child pornography conduct such activities entirely within the boundaries of one state. These persons are unlikely to be content with the amount of child pornography they produce, transport, distribute, receive, advertise, or possess. These persons are therefore likely to enter the interstate market in child pornography in search of additional child pornography, thereby stimulating demand in the interstate market in child pornography.

"(ii) When the persons described in subparagraph (D)(i) enter the interstate market in search of additional child pornography, they are likely to distribute the child pornography they already produce, transport, distribute, receive, advertise, or possess to persons who will distribute additional child pornography to them, thereby stimulating supply in the interstate market in child pornography.

"(iii) Much of the child pornography that supplies the interstate market in child pornography is produced entirely within the boundaries of one state, is not traceable, and enters the interstate market surreptitiously. This child pornography supports demand in the interstate market in child pornography and is essential to its existence.

"(E) Prohibiting the intrastate production, transportation, distribution, receipt, advertising, and possession of child pornography, as well as the intrastate transfer of custody of children for the production of child pornography, will cause some persons engaged in such intrastate activities to cease all such activities, thereby reducing both supply and demand in the interstate market for child pornography.

"(F) Federal control of the intrastate incidents of the production, transportation, distribution, receipt, advertising, and possession of child pornography, as well as the intrastate transfer of children for the production of child pornography, is essential to the effective control of the interstate market in child pornography.

"(2) The importance of protecting children from repeat exploitation in child pornography:

"(A) The vast majority of child pornography prosecutions today involve images contained on computer hard drives, computer disks, and related media.

"(B) Child pornography is not entitled to protection under the First Amendment and thus may be prohibited.

"(C) The government has a compelling State interest in protecting children from those who sexually exploit them, and this interest extends to stamping out the vice of child pornography at all levels in the distribution chain.

"(D) Every instance of viewing images of child pornography represents a renewed violation of the privacy of the victims and a repetition of their abuse.

"(E) Child pornography constitutes prima facie contraband, and as such should not be distributed to, or copied by, child pornography defendants or their attorneys.

"(F) It is imperative to prohibit the reproduction of child pornography in criminal cases so as to avoid repeated violation and abuse of victims, so long as the government makes reasonable accommodations for the inspection, viewing, and examination of such material for the purposes of mounting a criminal defense."

Pub. L. 108–21, title V, §501, Apr. 30, 2003, 117 Stat. 676, provided that: "Congress finds the following:

"(1) Obscenity and child pornography are not entitled to protection under the First Amendment under Miller v. California, 413 U.S. 15 (1973) (obscenity), or New York v. Ferber, 458 U.S. 747 (1982) (child pornography) and thus may be prohibited.

"(2) The Government has a compelling state interest in protecting children from those who sexually exploit them, including both child molesters and child pornographers. 'The prevention of sexual exploitation and abuse of children constitutes a government objective of surpassing importance,' New York v. Ferber, 458 U.S. 747, 757 (1982), and this interest extends to stamping out the vice of child pornography at all levels in the distribution chain. Osborne v. Ohio, 495 U.S. 103, 110 (1990).

"(3) The Government thus has a compelling interest in ensuring that the criminal prohibitions against child pornography remain enforceable and effective. 'The most expeditious if not the only practical method of law enforcement may be to dry up the market for this material by imposing severe criminal penalties on persons selling, advertising, or otherwise promoting the product.' Ferber, 458 U.S. at 760.

"(4) In 1982, when the Supreme Court decided Ferber, the technology did not exist to—

"(A) computer generate depictions of children that are indistinguishable from depictions of real children;

"(B) use parts of images of real children to create a composite image that is unidentifiable as a particular child and in a way that prevents even an expert from concluding that parts of images of real children were used; or

"(C) disguise pictures of real children being abused by making the image look computer-generated.

"(5) Evidence submitted to the Congress, including from the National Center for Missing and Exploited Children, demonstrates that technology already exists to disguise depictions of real children to make them unidentifiable and to make depictions of real children appear computer-generated. The technology will soon exist, if it does not already, to computer generate realistic images of children.

"(6) The vast majority of child pornography prosecutions today involve images contained on computer hard drives, computer disks, and/or related media.

"(7) There is no substantial evidence that any of the child pornography images being trafficked today were made other than by the abuse of real children. Nevertheless, technological advances since Ferber have led many criminal defendants to suggest that the images of child pornography they possess are not those of real children, insisting that the government prove beyond a reasonable doubt that the images are not computer-generated. Such challenges increased significantly after the decision in Ashcroft v. Free Speech Coalition, 535 U.S. 234 (2002).

"(8) Child pornography circulating on the Internet has, by definition, been digitally uploaded or scanned into computers and has been transferred over the Internet, often in different file formats, from trafficker to trafficker. An image seized from a collector of child pornography is rarely a first-generation product, and the retransmission of images can alter the image so as to make it difficult for even an expert conclusively to opine that a particular image depicts a real child. If the original image has been scanned from a paper version into a digital format, this task can be even harder since proper forensic assessment may depend on the quality of the image scanned and the tools used to scan it.

"(9) The impact of the Free Speech Coalition decision on the Government's ability to prosecute child pornography offenders is already evident. The Ninth Circuit has seen a significant adverse effect on prosecutions since the 1999 Ninth Circuit Court of Appeals decision in Free Speech Coalition. After that decision, prosecutions generally have been brought in the Ninth Circuit only in the most clear-cut cases in which the government can specifically identify the child in the depiction or otherwise identify the origin of the image. This is a fraction of meritorious child pornography cases. The National Center for Missing and Exploited Children testified that, in light of the Supreme Court's affirmation of the Ninth Circuit decision, prosecutors in various parts of the country have expressed concern about the continued viability of previously indicted cases as well as declined potentially meritorious prosecutions.

"(10) Since the Supreme Court's decision in Free Speech Coalition, defendants in child pornography cases have almost universally raised the contention that the images in question could be virtual, thereby requiring the government, in nearly every child pornography prosecution, to find proof that the child is real. Some of these defense efforts have already been successful. In addition, the number of prosecutions being brought has been significantly and adversely affected as the resources required to be dedicated to each child pornography case now are significantly higher than ever before.

"(11) Leading experts agree that, to the extent that the technology exists to computer generate realistic images of child pornography, the cost in terms of time, money, and expertise is—and for the foreseeable future will remain—prohibitively expensive. As a result, for the foreseeable future, it will be more cost-effective to produce child pornography using real children. It will not, however, be difficult or expensive to use readily available technology to disguise those depictions of real children to make them unidentifiable or to make them appear computer-generated.

"(12) Child pornography results from the abuse of real children by sex offenders; the production of child pornography is a byproduct of, and not the primary reason for, the sexual abuse of children. There is no evidence that the future development of easy and inexpensive means of computer generating realistic images of children would stop or even reduce the sexual abuse of real children or the practice of visually recording that abuse.

"(13) In the absence of congressional action, the difficulties in enforcing the child pornography laws will continue to grow increasingly worse. The mere prospect that the technology exists to create composite or computer-generated depictions that are indistinguishable from depictions of real children will allow defendants who possess images of real children to escape prosecution; for it threatens to create a reasonable doubt in every case of computer images even when a real child was abused. This threatens to render child pornography laws that protect real children unenforceable. Moreover, imposing an additional requirement that the Government prove beyond a reasonable doubt that the defendant knew that the image was in fact a real child—as some courts have done—threatens to result in the de facto legalization of the possession, receipt, and distribution of child pornography for all except the original producers of the material.

"(14) To avoid this grave threat to the Government's unquestioned compelling interest in effective enforcement of the child pornography laws that protect real children, a statute must be adopted that prohibits a narrowly-defined subcategory of images.

"(15) The Supreme Court's 1982 Ferber v. New York decision holding that child pornography was not protected drove child pornography off the shelves of adult bookstores. Congressional action is necessary now to ensure that open and notorious trafficking in such materials does not reappear, and even increase, on the Internet."

Pub. L. 104–208, div. A, title I, §101(a) [title I, §121[1]], Sept. 30, 1996, 110 Stat. 3009–26, provided that: "Congress finds that—

"(1) the use of children in the production of sexually explicit material, including photographs, films, videos, computer images, and other visual depictions, is a form of sexual abuse which can result in physical or psychological harm, or both, to the children involved;

"(2) where children are used in its production, child pornography permanently records the victim's abuse, and its continued existence causes the child victims of sexual abuse continuing harm by haunting those children in future years;

"(3) child pornography is often used as part of a method of seducing other children into sexual activity; a child who is reluctant to engage in sexual activity with an adult, or to pose for sexually explicit photographs, can sometimes be convinced by viewing depictions of other children 'having fun' participating in such activity;

"(4) child pornography is often used by pedophiles and child sexual abusers to stimulate and whet their own sexual appetites, and as a model for sexual acting out with children; such use of child pornography can desensitize the viewer to the pathology of sexual abuse or exploitation of children, so that it can become acceptable to and even preferred by the viewer;

"(5) new photographic and computer imagining [sic] technologies make it possible to produce by electronic, mechanical, or other means, visual depictions of what appear to be children engaging in sexually explicit conduct that are virtually indistinguishable to the unsuspecting viewer from unretouched photographic images of actual children engaging in sexually explicit conduct;

"(6) computers and computer imaging technology can be used to—

"(A) alter sexually explicit photographs, films, and videos in such a way as to make it virtually impossible for unsuspecting viewers to identify individuals, or to determine if the offending material was produced using children;

"(B) produce visual depictions of child sexual activity designed to satisfy the preferences of individual child molesters, pedophiles, and pornography collectors; and

"(C) alter innocent pictures of children to create visual depictions of those children engaging in sexual conduct;

"(7) the creation or distribution of child pornography which includes an image of a recognizable minor invades the child's privacy and reputational interests, since images that are created showing a child's face or other identifiable feature on a body engaging in sexually explicit conduct can haunt the minor for years to come;

"(8) the effect of visual depictions of child sexual activity on a child molester or pedophile using that material to stimulate or whet his own sexual appetites, or on a child where the material is being used as a means of seducing or breaking down the child's inhibitions to sexual abuse or exploitation, is the same whether the child pornography consists of photographic depictions of actual children or visual depictions produced wholly or in part by electronic, mechanical, or other means, including by computer, which are virtually indistinguishable to the unsuspecting viewer from photographic images of actual children;

"(9) the danger to children who are seduced and molested with the aid of child sex pictures is just as great when the child pornographer or child molester uses visual depictions of child sexual activity produced wholly or in part by electronic, mechanical, or other means, including by computer, as when the material consists of unretouched photographic images of actual children engaging in sexually explicit conduct;

"(10)(A) the existence of and traffic in child pornographic images creates the potential for many types of harm in the community and presents a clear and present danger to all children; and

"(B) it inflames the desires of child molesters, pedophiles, and child pornographers who prey on children, thereby increasing the creation and distribution of child pornography and the sexual abuse and exploitation of actual children who are victimized as a result of the existence and use of these materials;

"(11)(A) the sexualization and eroticization of minors through any form of child pornographic images has a deleterious effect on all children by encouraging a societal perception of children as sexual objects and leading to further sexual abuse and exploitation of them; and

"(B) this sexualization of minors creates an unwholesome environment which affects the psychological, mental and emotional development of children and undermines the efforts of parents and families to encourage the sound mental, moral and emotional development of children;

"(12) prohibiting the possession and viewing of child pornography will encourage the possessors of such material to rid themselves of or destroy the material, thereby helping to protect the victims of child pornography and to eliminate the market for the sexual exploitative use of children; and

"(13) the elimination of child pornography and the protection of children from sexual exploitation provide a compelling governmental interest for prohibiting the production, distribution, possession, sale, or viewing of visual depictions of children engaging in sexually explicit conduct, including both photographic images of actual children engaging in such conduct and depictions produced by computer or other means which are virtually indistinguishable to the unsuspecting viewer from photographic images of actual children engaging in such conduct."

Pub. L. 99–500, §101(b) [title VII, §702], Oct. 18, 1986, 100 Stat. 1783–39, 1783–74, and Pub. L. 99–591, §101(b) [title VII, §702], Oct. 30, 1986, 100 Stat. 3341–39, 3341–74 provided that: "The Congress finds that—

"(1) child exploitation has become a multi-million dollar industry, infiltrated and operated by elements of organized crime, and by a nationwide network of individuals openly advertising their desire to exploit children;

"(2) Congress has recognized the physiological, psychological, and emotional harm caused by the production, distribution, and display of child pornography by strengthening laws prescribing such activity;

"(3) the Federal Government lacks sufficient enforcement tools to combat concerted efforts to exploit children prescribed by Federal law, and exploitation victims lack effective remedies under Federal law; and

"(4) current rules of evidence, criminal procedure, and civil procedure and other courtroom and investigative procedures inhibit the participation of child victims as witnesses and damage their credibility when they do testify, impairing the prosecution of child exploitation offenses."

Pub. L. 98–292, §2, May 21, 1984, 98 Stat. 204, provided that: "The Congress finds that—

"(1) child pornography has developed into a highly organized, multi-million-dollar industry which operates on a nationwide scale;

"(2) thousands of children including large numbers of runaway and homeless youth are exploited in the production and distribution of pornographic materials; and

"(3) the use of children as subjects of pornographic materials is harmful to the physiological, emotional, and mental health of the individual child and to society."

Report by Attorney General

Pub. L. 99–500, §101(b) [title VII, §705], Oct. 18, 1986, 100 Stat. 1783–39, 1783–75, and Pub. L. 99–591, §101(b) [title VII, §705], Oct. 30, 1986, 100 Stat. 3341–39, 3341–75, required Attorney General, within one year after Oct. 18, 1986, to submit a report to Congress detailing possible changes in Federal Rules of Evidence, Federal Rules of Criminal Procedure, Federal Rules of Civil Procedure, and other Federal courtroom, prosecutorial, and investigative procedures which would facilitate the participation of child witnesses in cases involving child abuse and sexual exploitation.

Annual Report to Congress

Attorney General to report annually to Congress on prosecutions, convictions, and forfeitures under this chapter, see section 41301 of Title 34, Crime Control and Law Enforcement.

§2251A. Selling or buying of children

(a) Any parent, legal guardian, or other person having custody or control of a minor who sells or otherwise transfers custody or control of such minor, or offers to sell or otherwise transfer custody of such minor either—

(1) with knowledge that, as a consequence of the sale or transfer, the minor will be portrayed in a visual depiction engaging in, or assisting another person to engage in, sexually explicit conduct; or

(2) with intent to promote either—

(A) the engaging in of sexually explicit conduct by such minor for the purpose of producing any visual depiction of such conduct; or

(B) the rendering of assistance by the minor to any other person to engage in sexually explicit conduct for the purpose of producing any visual depiction of such conduct;

shall be punished by imprisonment for not less than 30 years or for life and by a fine under this title, if any of the circumstances described in subsection (c) of this section exist.

(b) Whoever purchases or otherwise obtains custody or control of a minor, or offers to purchase or otherwise obtain custody or control of a minor either—

(1) with knowledge that, as a consequence of the purchase or obtaining of custody, the minor will be portrayed in a visual depiction engaging in, or assisting another person to engage in, sexually explicit conduct; or

(2) with intent to promote either—

(A) the engaging in of sexually explicit conduct by such minor for the purpose of producing any visual depiction of such conduct; or

(B) the rendering of assistance by the minor to any other person to engage in sexually explicit conduct for the purpose of producing any visual depiction of such conduct;

shall be punished by imprisonment for not less than 30 years or for life and by a fine under this title, if any of the circumstances described in subsection (c) of this section exist.

(c) The circumstances referred to in subsections (a) and (b) are that—

(1) in the course of the conduct described in such subsections the minor or the actor traveled in or was transported in or affecting interstate or foreign commerce;

(2) any offer described in such subsections was communicated or transported using any means or facility of interstate or foreign commerce or in or affecting interstate or foreign commerce by any means including by computer or mail; or

(3) the conduct described in such subsections took place in any territory or possession of the United States.

(Added Pub. L. 100–690, title VII, §7512(a), Nov. 18, 1988, 102 Stat. 4486; amended Pub. L. 108–21, title I, §103(b)(1)(B), Apr. 30, 2003, 117 Stat. 653; Pub. L. 110–358, title I, §103(a)(2), (b), Oct. 8, 2008, 122 Stat. 4002, 4003.)

Amendments

2008—Subsec. (c). Pub. L. 110–358, §103(b), substituted "in or affecting interstate" for "in interstate" in pars. (1) and (2).

Subsec. (c)(2). Pub. L. 110–358, §103(a)(2), inserted "using any means or facility of interstate or foreign commerce or" after "or transported".

2003—Subsecs. (a), (b). Pub. L. 108–21 substituted "30 years" for "20 years" in concluding provisions.

§2252. Certain activities relating to material involving the sexual exploitation of minors

(a) Any person who—

(1) knowingly transports or ships using any means or facility of interstate or foreign commerce or in or affecting interstate or foreign commerce by any means including by computer or mails, any visual depiction, if—

(A) the producing of such visual depiction involves the use of a minor engaging in sexually explicit conduct; and

(B) such visual depiction is of such conduct;

(2) knowingly receives, or distributes, any visual depiction using any means or facility of interstate or foreign commerce or that has been mailed, or has been shipped or transported in or affecting interstate or foreign commerce, or which contains materials which have been mailed or so shipped or transported, by any means including by computer, or knowingly reproduces any visual depiction for distribution using any means or facility of interstate or foreign commerce or in or affecting interstate or foreign commerce or through the mails, if—

(A) the producing of such visual depiction involves the use of a minor engaging in sexually explicit conduct; and

(B) such visual depiction is of such conduct;

(3) either—

(A) in the special maritime and territorial jurisdiction of the United States, or on any land or building owned by, leased to, or otherwise used by or under the control of the Government of the United States, or in the Indian country as defined in section 1151 of this title, knowingly sells or possesses with intent to sell any visual depiction; or

(B) knowingly sells or possesses with intent to sell any visual depiction that has been mailed, shipped, or transported using any means or facility of interstate or foreign commerce, or has been shipped or transported in or affecting interstate or foreign commerce, or which was produced using materials which have been mailed or so shipped or transported using any means or facility of interstate or foreign commerce, including by computer, if—

(i) the producing of such visual depiction involves the use of a minor engaging in sexually explicit conduct; and

(ii) such visual depiction is of such conduct; or

(4) either—

(A) in the special maritime and territorial jurisdiction of the United States, or on any land or building owned by, leased to, or otherwise used by or under the control of the Government of the United States, or in the Indian country as defined in section 1151 of this title, knowingly possesses, or knowingly accesses with intent to view, 1 or more books, magazines, periodicals, films, video tapes, or other matter which contain any visual depiction; or

(B) knowingly possesses, or knowingly accesses with intent to view, 1 or more books, magazines, periodicals, films, video tapes, or other matter which contain any visual depiction that has been mailed, or has been shipped or transported using any means or facility of interstate or foreign commerce or in or affecting interstate or foreign commerce, or which was produced using materials which have been mailed or so shipped or transported, by any means including by computer, if—

(i) the producing of such visual depiction involves the use of a minor engaging in sexually explicit conduct; and

(ii) such visual depiction is of such conduct;

shall be punished as provided in subsection (b) of this section.

(b)(1) Whoever violates, or attempts or conspires to violate, paragraph (1), (2), or (3) of subsection (a) shall be fined under this title and imprisoned not less than 5 years and not more than 20 years, but if such person has a prior conviction under this chapter, section 1591, chapter 71, chapter 109A, or chapter 117, or under section 920 of title 10 (article 120 of the Uniform Code of Military Justice), or under the laws of any State relating to aggravated sexual abuse, sexual abuse, or abusive sexual conduct involving a minor or ward, or the production, possession, receipt, mailing, sale, distribution, shipment, or transportation of child pornography, or sex trafficking of children, such person shall be fined under this title and imprisoned for not less than 15 years nor more than 40 years.

(2) Whoever violates, or attempts or conspires to violate, paragraph (4) of subsection (a) shall be fined under this title or imprisoned not more than 10 years, or both, but if any visual depiction involved in the offense involved a prepubescent minor or a minor who had not attained 12 years of age, such person shall be fined under this title and imprisoned for not more than 20 years, or if such person has a prior conviction under this chapter, chapter 71, chapter 109A, or chapter 117, or under section 920 of title 10 (article 120 of the Uniform Code of Military Justice), or under the laws of any State relating to aggravated sexual abuse, sexual abuse, or abusive sexual conduct involving a minor or ward, or the production, possession, receipt, mailing, sale, distribution, shipment, or transportation of child pornography, such person shall be fined under this title and imprisoned for not less than 10 years nor more than 20 years.

(c) Affirmative Defense.—It shall be an affirmative defense to a charge of violating paragraph (4) of subsection (a) that the defendant—

(1) possessed less than three matters containing any visual depiction proscribed by that paragraph; and

(2) promptly and in good faith, and without retaining or allowing any person, other than a law enforcement agency, to access any visual depiction or copy thereof—

(A) took reasonable steps to destroy each such visual depiction; or

(B) reported the matter to a law enforcement agency and afforded that agency access to each such visual depiction.

(Added Pub. L. 95–225, §2(a), Feb. 6, 1978, 92 Stat. 7; amended Pub. L. 98–292, §4, May 21, 1984, 98 Stat. 204; Pub. L. 99–500, §101(b) [title VII, §704(b)], Oct. 18, 1986, 100 Stat. 1783–39, 1783–75, and Pub. L. 99–591, §101(b) [title VII, §704(b)], Oct. 30, 1986, 100 Stat. 3341–39, 3341–75; Pub. L. 100–690, title VII, §7511(b), Nov. 18, 1988, 102 Stat. 4485; Pub. L. 101–647, title III, §323(a), (b), Nov. 29, 1990, 104 Stat. 4818, 4819; Pub. L. 103–322, title XVI, §160001(d), (e), title XXXIII, §330010(8), Sept. 13, 1994, 108 Stat. 2037, 2143; Pub. L. 104–208, div. A, title I, §101(a) [title I, §121[5]], Sept. 30, 1996, 110 Stat. 3009, 3009–26, 3009–30; Pub. L. 105–314, title II, §§202(a), 203(a), Oct. 30, 1998, 112 Stat. 2977, 2978; Pub. L. 108–21, title I, §103(a)(1)(B), (C), (b)(1)(C), (D), title V, §507, Apr. 30, 2003, 117 Stat. 652, 653, 683; Pub. L. 109–248, title II, §206(b)(2), July 27, 2006, 120 Stat. 614; Pub. L. 110–358, title I, §103(a)(3), (b), (c), title II, §203(a), Oct. 8, 2008, 122 Stat. 4002, 4003; Pub. L. 112–206, §2(a), Dec. 7, 2012, 126 Stat. 1490.)

Codification

Pub. L. 99–591 is a corrected version of Pub. L. 99–500.

Amendments

2012—Subsec. (b)(2). Pub. L. 112–206 inserted "any visual depiction involved in the offense involved a prepubescent minor or a minor who had not attained 12 years of age, such person shall be fined under this title and imprisoned for not more than 20 years, or if" after "but if".

2008—Subsec. (a)(1). Pub. L. 110–358, §103(a)(3)(A), (b), inserted "using any means or facility of interstate or foreign commerce or" after "ships" and substituted "in or affecting interstate" for "in interstate".

Subsec. (a)(2). Pub. L. 110–358, §103(a)(3)(B), (b), inserted "using any means or facility of interstate or foreign commerce or" after "distributes, any visual depiction" and after "depiction for distribution" and substituted "in or affecting interstate" for "in interstate" in two places.

Subsec. (a)(3)(B). Pub. L. 110–358, §103(a)(3)(C), (b), (c), inserted ", shipped, or transported using any means or facility of interstate or foreign commerce" after "that has been mailed" and "using any means or facility of interstate or foreign commerce" after "so shipped or transported", substituted "in or affecting interstate" for "in interstate" and struck out "by any means," before "including".

Subsec. (a)(4)(A). Pub. L. 110–358, §203(a)(1), inserted ", or knowingly accesses with intent to view," after "possesses".

Subsec. (a)(4)(B). Pub. L. 110–358, §§103(a)(3)(D), (b), 203(a)(2), inserted ", or knowingly accesses with intent to view," after "possesses" and "using any means or facility of interstate or foreign commerce or" after "has been shipped or transported" and substituted "in or affecting interstate" for "in interstate".

2006—Subsec. (b)(1). Pub. L. 109–248 substituted "paragraph (1)" for "paragraphs (1)" and inserted "section 1591," after "this chapter," and ", or sex trafficking of children" after "pornography".

2003—Subsec. (b)(1). Pub. L. 108–21, §507, inserted "chapter 71," before "chapter 109A," and "or under section 920 of title 10 (article 120 of the Uniform Code of Military Justice)," before "or under the laws".

Pub. L. 108–21, §103(a)(1)(B), (C), substituted "and imprisoned not less than 5 years and" for "or imprisoned", "20 years" for "15 years", "40 years" for "30 years", and "15 years" for "5 years" and struck out "or both," before "but if such person has a prior".

Subsec. (b)(2). Pub. L. 108–21, §507, inserted "chapter 71," before "chapter 109A," and "or under section 920 of title 10 (article 120 of the Uniform Code of Military Justice)," before "or under the laws".

Pub. L. 108–21, §103(a)(1)(C), (D), substituted "more than 10 years" for "more than 5 years", "less than 10 years" for "less than 2 years", and "20 years" for "10 years".

1998—Subsec. (a)(4)(A), (B). Pub. L. 105–314, §203(a)(1), substituted "1 or more" for "3 or more".

Subsec. (b). Pub. L. 105–314, §202(a), substituted ", chapter 109A, or chapter 117" for "or chapter 109A" in pars. (1) and (2) and substituted "aggravated sexual abuse, sexual abuse, or abusive sexual conduct involving a minor or ward, or the production, possession, receipt, mailing, sale, distribution, shipment, or transportation of child pornography" for "the possession of child pornography" in par. (2).

Subsec. (c). Pub. L. 105–314, §203(a)(2), added subsec. (c).

1996—Subsec. (b). Pub. L. 104–208 added subsec. (b) and struck out former subsec. (b) which read as follows:

"(b)(1) Whoever violates, or attempts or conspires to violate, paragraph (1), (2), or (3) of subsection (a) shall be fined under this title or imprisoned not more than ten years, or both, but, if such person has a prior conviction under this chapter or chapter 109A, such person shall be fined under this title and imprisoned for not less than five years nor more than fifteen years.

"(2) Whoever violates, or attempts or conspires to violate, paragraph (4) of subsection (a) shall be fined under this title or imprisoned for not more than five years, or both."

1994—Subsec. (a)(3)(B). Pub. L. 103–322, §330010(8), substituted "materials" for "materails" in introductory provisions.

Subsec. (b)(1). Pub. L. 103–322, §160001(d), (e), inserted ", or attempts or conspires to violate," after "violates" and substituted "conviction under this chapter or chapter 109A" for "conviction under this section".

Subsec. (b)(2). Pub. L. 103–322, §160001(e), inserted ", or attempts or conspires to violate," after "violates".

1990—Subsec. (a). Pub. L. 101–647, §323(a), (b), struck out "or" at end of par. (1), substituted "that has been mailed, or has been shipped or transported in interstate or foreign commerce, or which contains materials which have been mailed or so shipped or transported, by any means including by computer," for "that has been transported or shipped in interstate or foreign commerce by any means including by computer or mailed" in par. (2), struck out at end "shall be punished as provided in subsection (b) of this section.", and added pars. (3) and (4) and concluding provisions.

Subsec. (b). Pub. L. 101–647, §323(a)(2), added subsec. (b) and struck out former subsec. (b) which read as follows: "Any individual who violates this section shall be fined not more than $100,000, or imprisoned not more than 10 years, or both, but, if such individual has a prior conviction under this section, such individual shall be fined not more than $200,000, or imprisoned not less than five years nor more than 15 years, or both. Any organization which violates this section shall be fined not more than $250,000."

1988—Subsec. (a)(1), (2). Pub. L. 100–690 inserted "by any means including by computer" after "commerce" in introductory provisions.

1986—Subsec. (b). Pub. L. 99–500 and Pub. L. 99–591 substituted "five years" for "two years".

1984—Subsec. (a)(1). Pub. L. 98–292, §4(1), (3), (4), substituted "any visual depiction" for "for the purpose of sale or distribution for sale, any obscene visual or print medium" in provisions preceding subpar. (A).

Subsec. (a)(1)(A). Pub. L. 98–292, §4(4), substituted "visual depiction" for "visual or print medium".

Subsec. (a)(1)(B). Pub. L. 98–292, §4(4), (5), substituted "visual depiction is of" for "visual or print medium depicts".

Subsec. (a)(2). Pub. L. 98–292, §4(2)–(4), (6), (7), substituted ", or distributes, any visual depiction" for "for the purpose of sale or distribution for sale, or knowingly sells or distributes for sale, any obscene visual or print medium" and inserted "or knowingly reproduces any visual depiction for distribution in interstate or foreign commerce or through the mails" in provisions preceding subpar. (A).

Subsec. (a)(2)(A). Pub. L. 98–292, §4(4), substituted "visual depiction" for "visual or print medium".

Subsec. (a)(2)(B). Pub. L. 98–292, §4(4), (5), substituted "visual depiction is of" for "visual or print medium depicts".

Subsec. (b). Pub. L. 98–292, §4(8)–(11), substituted "individual" for "person" in three places, "$100,000" for "$10,000", and "$200,000" for "$15,000", and inserted "Any organization which violates this section shall be fined not more than $250,000."

Confirmation of Intent of Congress in Enacting Sections 2252 and 2256 of This Title

Pub. L. 103–322, title XVI, §160003(a), Sept. 13, 1994, 108 Stat. 2038, provided that:

"(a) Declaration.—The Congress declares that in enacting sections 2252 and 2256 of title 18, United States Code, it was and is the intent of Congress that—

"(1) the scope of 'exhibition of the genitals or pubic area' in section 2256(2)(E), in the definition of 'sexually explicit conduct', is not limited to nude exhibitions or exhibitions in which the outlines of those areas were discernible through clothing; and

"(2) the requirements in section 2252(a)(1)(A), (2)(A), (3)(B)(i), and (4)(B)(i) that the production of a visual depiction involve the use of a minor engaging in 'sexually explicit conduct' of the kind described in section 2256(2)(E) are satisfied if a person photographs a minor in such a way as to exhibit the child in a lascivious manner."

§2252A. Certain activities relating to material constituting or containing child pornography

(a) Any person who—

(1) knowingly mails, or transports or ships using any means or facility of interstate or foreign commerce or in or affecting interstate or foreign commerce by any means, including by computer,

any child pornography;

(2) knowingly receives or distributes—

(A) any child pornography that has been mailed, or using any means or facility of interstate or foreign commerce shipped or transported in or affecting interstate or foreign commerce by any means, including by computer; or

(B) any material that contains child pornography that has been mailed, or using any means or facility of interstate or foreign commerce shipped or transported in or affecting interstate or foreign commerce by any means, including by computer;

(3) knowingly—

(A) reproduces any child pornography for distribution through the mails, or using any means or facility of interstate or foreign commerce or in or affecting interstate or foreign commerce by any means, including by computer; or

(B) advertises, promotes, presents, distributes, or solicits through the mails, or using any means or facility of interstate or foreign commerce or in or affecting interstate or foreign commerce by any means, including by computer, any material or purported material in a manner that reflects the belief, or that is intended to cause another to believe, that the material or purported material is, or contains—

(i) an obscene visual depiction of a minor engaging in sexually explicit conduct; or

(ii) a visual depiction of an actual minor engaging in sexually explicit conduct;

(4) either—

(A) in the special maritime and territorial jurisdiction of the United States, or on any land or building owned by, leased to, or otherwise used by or under the control of the United States Government, or in the Indian country (as defined in section 1151), knowingly sells or possesses with the intent to sell any child pornography; or

(B) knowingly sells or possesses with the intent to sell any child pornography that has been mailed, or shipped or transported using any means or facility of interstate or foreign commerce or in or affecting interstate or foreign commerce by any means, including by computer, or that was produced using materials that have been mailed, or shipped or transported in or affecting interstate or foreign commerce by any means, including by computer;

(5) either—

(A) in the special maritime and territorial jurisdiction of the United States, or on any land or building owned by, leased to, or otherwise used by or under the control of the United States Government, or in the Indian country (as defined in section 1151), knowingly possesses, or knowingly accesses with intent to view, any book, magazine, periodical, film, videotape, computer disk, or any other material that contains an image of child pornography; or

(B) knowingly possesses, or knowingly accesses with intent to view, any book, magazine, periodical, film, videotape, computer disk, or any other material that contains an image of child pornography that has been mailed, or shipped or transported using any means or facility of interstate or foreign commerce or in or affecting interstate or foreign commerce by any means, including by computer, or that was produced using materials that have been mailed, or shipped or transported in or affecting interstate or foreign commerce by any means, including by computer;

(6) knowingly distributes, offers, sends, or provides to a minor any visual depiction, including any photograph, film, video, picture, or computer generated image or picture, whether made or produced by electronic, mechanical, or other means, where such visual depiction is, or appears to be, of a minor engaging in sexually explicit conduct—

(A) that has been mailed, shipped, or transported using any means or facility of interstate or foreign commerce or in or affecting interstate or foreign commerce by any means, including by computer;

(B) that was produced using materials that have been mailed, shipped, or transported in or affecting interstate or foreign commerce by any means, including by computer; or

(C) which distribution, offer, sending, or provision is accomplished using the mails or any means or facility of interstate or foreign commerce,

for purposes of inducing or persuading a minor to participate in any activity that is illegal; or

(7) knowingly produces with intent to distribute, or distributes, by any means, including a computer, in or affecting interstate or foreign commerce, child pornography that is an adapted or modified depiction of an identifiable minor.1

shall be punished as provided in subsection (b).

(b)(1) Whoever violates, or attempts or conspires to violate, paragraph (1), (2), (3), (4), or (6) of subsection (a) shall be fined under this title and imprisoned not less than 5 years and not more than 20 years, but, if such person has a prior conviction under this chapter, section 1591, chapter 71, chapter 109A, or chapter 117, or under section 920 of title 10 (article 120 of the Uniform Code of Military Justice), or under the laws of any State relating to aggravated sexual abuse, sexual abuse, or abusive sexual conduct involving a minor or ward, or the production, possession, receipt, mailing, sale, distribution, shipment, or transportation of child pornography, or sex trafficking of children, such person shall be fined under this title and imprisoned for not less than 15 years nor more than 40 years.

(2) Whoever violates, or attempts or conspires to violate, subsection (a)(5) shall be fined under this title or imprisoned not more than 10 years, or both, but, if any image of child pornography involved in the offense involved a prepubescent minor or a minor who had not attained 12 years of age, such person shall be fined under this title and imprisoned for not more than 20 years, or if such person has a prior conviction under this chapter, chapter 71, chapter 109A, or chapter 117, or under section 920 of title 10 (article 120 of the Uniform Code of Military Justice), or under the laws of any State relating to aggravated sexual abuse, sexual abuse, or abusive sexual conduct involving a minor or ward, or the production, possession, receipt, mailing, sale, distribution, shipment, or transportation of child pornography, such person shall be fined under this title and imprisoned for not less than 10 years nor more than 20 years.

(3) Whoever violates, or attempts or conspires to violate, subsection (a)(7) shall be fined under this title or imprisoned not more than 15 years, or both.

(c) It shall be an affirmative defense to a charge of violating paragraph (1), (2), (3)(A), (4), or (5) of subsection (a) that—

(1)(A) the alleged child pornography was produced using an actual person or persons engaging in sexually explicit conduct; and

(B) each such person was an adult at the time the material was produced; or

(2) the alleged child pornography was not produced using any actual minor or minors.

No affirmative defense under subsection (c)(2) shall be available in any prosecution that involves child pornography as described in section 2256(8)(C). A defendant may not assert an affirmative defense to a charge of violating paragraph (1), (2), (3)(A), (4), or (5) of subsection (a) unless, within the time provided for filing pretrial motions or at such time prior to trial as the judge may direct, but in no event later than 14 days before the commencement of the trial, the defendant provides the court and the United States with notice of the intent to assert such defense and the substance of any expert or other specialized testimony or evidence upon which the defendant intends to rely. If the defendant fails to comply with this subsection, the court shall, absent a finding of extraordinary circumstances that prevented timely compliance, prohibit the defendant from asserting such defense to a charge of violating paragraph (1), (2), (3)(A), (4), or (5) of subsection (a) or presenting any evidence for which the defendant has failed to provide proper and timely notice.

(d) Affirmative Defense.—It shall be an affirmative defense to a charge of violating subsection (a)(5) that the defendant—

(1) possessed less than three images of child pornography; and

(2) promptly and in good faith, and without retaining or allowing any person, other than a law enforcement agency, to access any image or copy thereof—

(A) took reasonable steps to destroy each such image; or

(B) reported the matter to a law enforcement agency and afforded that agency access to each such image.

(e) Admissibility of Evidence.—On motion of the government, in any prosecution under this chapter or section 1466A, except for good cause shown, the name, address, social security number, or other nonphysical identifying information, other than the age or approximate age, of any minor who is depicted in any child pornography shall not be admissible and may be redacted from any otherwise admissible evidence, and the jury shall be instructed, upon request of the United States, that it can draw no inference from the absence of such evidence in deciding whether the child pornography depicts an actual minor.

(f) Civil Remedies.—

(1) In general.—Any person aggrieved by reason of the conduct prohibited under subsection (a) or (b) or section 1466A may commence a civil action for the relief set forth in paragraph (2).

(2) Relief.—In any action commenced in accordance with paragraph (1), the court may award appropriate relief, including—

(A) temporary, preliminary, or permanent injunctive relief;

(B) compensatory and punitive damages; and

(C) the costs of the civil action and reasonable fees for attorneys and expert witnesses.

(g) Child Exploitation Enterprises.—

(1) Whoever engages in a child exploitation enterprise shall be fined under this title and imprisoned for any term of years not less than 20 or for life.

(2) A person engages in a child exploitation enterprise for the purposes of this section if the person violates section 1591, section 1201 if the victim is a minor, or chapter 109A (involving a minor victim), 110 (except for sections 2257 and 2257A), or 117 (involving a minor victim), as a part of a series of felony violations constituting three or more separate incidents and involving more than one victim, and commits those offenses in concert with three or more other persons.

(Added Pub. L. 104–208, div. A, title I, §101(a) [title I, §121[3(a)]], Sept. 30, 1996, 110 Stat. 3009, 3009–26, 3009–28; amended Pub. L. 105–314, title II, §§202(b), 203(b), Oct. 30, 1998, 112 Stat. 2978; Pub. L. 107–273, div. B, title IV, §4003(a)(5), Nov. 2, 2002, 116 Stat. 1811; Pub. L. 108–21, title I, §103(a)(1)(D), (E), (b)(1)(E), (F), title V, §§502(d), 503, 505, 507, 510, Apr. 30, 2003, 117 Stat. 652, 653, 679, 680, 682–684; Pub. L. 109–248, title II, §206(b)(3), title VII, §701, July 27, 2006, 120 Stat. 614, 647; Pub. L. 110–358, title I, §103(a)(4), (b), (d), title II, §203(b), Oct. 8, 2008, 122 Stat. 4002, 4003; Pub. L. 110–401, title III, §304, Oct. 13, 2008, 122 Stat. 4242; Pub. L. 111–16, §3(5), May 7, 2009, 123 Stat. 1607; Pub. L. 112–206, §2(b), Dec. 7, 2012, 126 Stat. 1490.)

Amendments

2012—Subsec. (b)(2). Pub. L. 112–206 inserted "any image of child pornography involved in the offense involved a prepubescent minor or a minor who had not attained 12 years of age, such person shall be fined under this title and imprisoned for not more than 20 years, or if" after "but, if".

2009—Subsec. (c). Pub. L. 111–16 substituted "14 days" for "10 days" in concluding provisions.

2008—Subsec. (a)(1). Pub. L. 110–358, §103(a)(4)(A), (b), inserted "using any means or facility of interstate or foreign commerce or" after "ships" and substituted "in or affecting interstate" for "in interstate".

Subsec. (a)(2). Pub. L. 110–358, §103(a)(4)(B), (b), in pars. (A) and (B), inserted "using any means or facility of interstate or foreign commerce" after "mailed, or" and substituted "in or affecting interstate" for "in interstate".

Subsec. (a)(3). Pub. L. 110–358, §103(a)(4)(C), (b), in pars. (A) and (B), inserted "using any means or facility of interstate or foreign commerce or" after "mails, or" and substituted "in or affecting interstate" for "in interstate".

Subsec. (a)(4)(B). Pub. L. 110–358, §103(a)(4)(D), (b), inserted "using any means or facility of interstate or foreign commerce or" after "has been mailed, or shipped or transported" and substituted "in or affecting interstate" for "in interstate" in two places.

Subsec. (a)(5)(A). Pub. L. 110–358, §203(b)(1), inserted ", or knowingly accesses with intent to view," after "possesses".

Subsec. (a)(5)(B). Pub. L. 110–358, §§103(a)(4)(D), (b), 203(b)(2), inserted ", or knowingly accesses with intent to view," after "possesses" and "using any means or facility of interstate or foreign commerce or" after "has been mailed, or shipped or transported" and substituted "in or affecting interstate" for "in interstate" in two places.

Subsec. (a)(6)(A). Pub. L. 110–358, §103(a)(4)(E), (b), inserted "using any means or facility of interstate or foreign commerce or" after "has been mailed, shipped, or transported" and substituted "in or affecting interstate" for "in interstate".

Subsec. (a)(6)(B). Pub. L. 110–358, §103(b), substituted "in or affecting interstate" for "in interstate".

Subsec. (a)(6)(C). Pub. L. 110–358, §103(d), substituted "or any means or facility of interstate or foreign commerce," for "or by transmitting or causing to be transmitted any wire communication in interstate or foreign commerce, including by computer,".

Subsec. (a)(7). Pub. L. 110–401, §304(a), added par. (7).

Subsec. (b)(3). Pub. L. 110–401, §304(b), added par. (3).

2006—Subsec. (b)(1). Pub. L. 109–248, §206(b)(3), inserted "section 1591," after "this chapter," and ", or sex trafficking of children" after "pornography".

Subsec. (g). Pub. L. 109–248, §701, added subsec. (g).

2003—Subsec. (a)(3). Pub. L. 108–21, §503(1)(A), added par. (3) and struck out former par. (3) which read as follows: "knowingly reproduces any child pornography for distribution through the mails, or in interstate or foreign commerce by any means, including by computer;".

Subsec. (a)(6). Pub. L. 108–21, §503(1)(B)–(D), added par. (6).

Subsec. (b)(1). Pub. L. 108–21, §507, inserted "chapter 71," before "chapter 109A," and "or under section 920 of title 10 (article 120 of the Uniform Code of Military Justice)," before "or under the laws".

Pub. L. 108–21, §503(2), which directed the substitution of "paragraph (1), (2), (3), (4), or (6)" for "paragraphs (1), (2), (3), or (4)", was executed by making the substitution for "paragraph (1), (2), (3), or (4)", to reflect the probable intent of Congress.

Pub. L. 108–21, §103(a)(1)(D), (b)(1)(E), substituted "20 years" for "15 years", "and imprisoned not less than 5 years and" for "or imprisoned", "15 years" for "5 years", and "40 years" for "30 years" and struck out "or both," before "but, if such person".

Subsec. (b)(2). Pub. L. 108–21, §507, inserted "chapter 71," before "chapter 109A," and "or under section 920 of title 10 (article 120 of the Uniform Code of Military Justice)," before "or under the laws".

Pub. L. 108–21, §103(a)(1)(E), (F), substituted "more than 10 years" for "more than 5 years", "less than 10 years" for "less than 2 years", and "20 years" for "10 years".

Subsec. (c). Pub. L. 108–21, §502(d), amended subsec. (c) generally. Prior to amendment, subsec. (c) read as follows: "It shall be an affirmative defense to a charge of violating paragraph (1), (2), (3), or (4) of subsection (a) that—

"(1) the alleged child pornography was produced using an actual person or persons engaging in sexually explicit conduct;

"(2) each such person was an adult at the time the material was produced; and

"(3) the defendant did not advertise, promote, present, describe, or distribute the material in such a manner as to convey the impression that it is or contains a visual depiction of a minor engaging in sexually explicit conduct."

Subsec. (e). Pub. L. 108–21, §505, added subsec. (e).

Subsec. (f). Pub. L. 108–21, §510, added subsec. (f).

2002—Subsecs. (b)(1), (c). Pub. L. 107–273 substituted "paragraph" for "paragraphs".

1998—Subsec. (a)(5)(A), (B). Pub. L. 105–314, §203(b)(1), substituted "an image" for "3 or more images".

Subsec. (b). Pub. L. 105–314, §202(b), substituted ", chapter 109A, or chapter 117" for "or chapter 109A" in pars. (1) and (2) and substituted "aggravated sexual abuse, sexual abuse, or abusive sexual conduct involving a minor or ward, or the production, possession, receipt, mailing, sale, distribution, shipment, or transportation of child pornography" for "the possession of child pornography" in par. (2).

Subsec. (d). Pub. L. 105–314, §203(b)(2), added subsec. (d).

Effective Date of 2009 Amendment
Amendment by Pub. L. 111–16 effective Dec. 1, 2009, see section 7 of Pub. L. 111–16, set out as a note under section 109 of Title 11, Bankruptcy.

§2252B. Misleading domain names on the Internet
(a) Whoever knowingly uses a misleading domain name on the Internet with the intent to deceive a person into viewing material constituting obscenity shall be fined under this title or imprisoned not more than 2 years, or both.

(b) Whoever knowingly uses a misleading domain name on the Internet with the intent to deceive a minor into viewing material that is harmful to minors on the Internet shall be fined under this title or imprisoned not more than 10 years, or both.

(c) For the purposes of this section, a domain name that includes a word or words to indicate the sexual content of the site, such as "sex" or "porn", is not misleading.

(d) For the purposes of this section, the term "material that is harmful to minors" means any communication, consisting of nudity, sex, or excretion, that, taken as a whole and with reference to its context—

(1) predominantly appeals to a prurient interest of minors;

(2) is patently offensive to prevailing standards in the adult community as a whole with respect to what is suitable material for minors; and

(3) lacks serious literary, artistic, political, or scientific value for minors.

(e) For the purposes of subsection (d), the term "sex" means acts of masturbation, sexual intercourse, or physcial 1 contact with a person's genitals, or the condition of human male or female genitals when in a state of sexual stimulation or arousal.

(Added Pub. L. 108–21, title V, §521(a), Apr. 30, 2003, 117 Stat. 686; amended Pub. L. 109–248, title II, §206(b)(4), July 27, 2006, 120 Stat. 614.)

Amendments
2006—Subsec. (b). Pub. L. 109–248 substituted "10 years" for "4 years".

§2252C. Misleading words or digital images on the Internet
(a) In General.—Whoever knowingly embeds words or digital images into the source code of a website with the intent to deceive a person into viewing material constituting obscenity shall be fined under this title and imprisoned for not more than 10 years.

(b) Minors.—Whoever knowingly embeds words or digital images into the source code of a website with the intent to deceive a minor into viewing material harmful to minors on the Internet shall be fined under this title and imprisoned for not more than 20 years.

(c) Construction.—For the purposes of this section, a word or digital image that clearly indicates the sexual content of the site, such as "sex" or "porn", is not misleading.

(d) Definitions.—As used in this section—

(1) the terms "material that is harmful to minors" and "sex" have the meaning given such terms in section 2252B; and

(2) the term "source code" means the combination of text and other characters comprising the content, both viewable and nonviewable, of a web page, including any website publishing language, programming language, protocol or functional content, as well as any successor languages or protocols.

(Added Pub. L. 109–248, title VII, §703(a), July 27, 2006, 120 Stat. 648.)

§2253. Criminal forfeiture
(a) Property Subject to Criminal Forfeiture.—A person who is convicted of an offense under this chapter involving a visual depiction described in section 2251, 2251A, 2252, 2252A, or 2260 of

this chapter or who is convicted of an offense under section 2252B of this chapter,,1 or who is convicted of an offense under chapter 109A, shall forfeit to the United States such person's interest in—

(1) any visual depiction described in section 2251, 2251A, or 2252 2 2252A, 2252B, or 2260 of this chapter, or any book, magazine, periodical, film, videotape, or other matter which contains any such visual depiction, which was produced, transported, mailed, shipped or received in violation of this chapter;

(2) any property, real or personal, constituting or traceable to gross profits or other proceeds obtained from such offense; and

(3) any property, real or personal, used or intended to be used to commit or to promote the commission of such offense or any property traceable to such property.

(b) Section 413 of the Controlled Substances Act (21 U.S.C. 853) with the exception of subsections (a) and (d), applies to the criminal forfeiture of property pursuant to subsection (a). (Added Pub. L. 98–292, §6, May 21, 1984, 98 Stat. 205; amended Pub. L. 100–690, title VII, §7522(c), Nov. 18, 1988, 102 Stat. 4494; Pub. L. 101–647, title XXXV, §3564, Nov. 29, 1990, 104 Stat. 4928; Pub. L. 103–322, title XXXIII, §330011(m)(1), Sept. 13, 1994, 108 Stat. 2145; Pub. L. 105–314, title VI, §602, Oct. 30, 1998, 112 Stat. 2982; Pub. L. 109–248, title V, §505(b), (c), July 27, 2006, 120 Stat. 630.)

Prior Provisions

A prior section 2253 was redesignated section 2256 of this title.

Amendments

2006—Subsec. (a). Pub. L. 109–248, §505(b)(1), inserted "or who is convicted of an offense under section 2252B of this chapter," after "2260 of this chapter" and substituted "an offense under chapter 109A" for "an offense under section 2421, 2422, or 2423 of chapter 117" in introductory provisions.

Subsec. (a)(1). Pub. L. 109–248, §505(b)(2), inserted "2252A, 2252B, or 2260" after "2252".

Subsec. (a)(3). Pub. L. 109–248, §505(b)(3), inserted "or any property traceable to such property" before period at end.

Subsecs. (b) to (o). Pub. L. 109–248, §505(c), added subsec. (b) and struck out former subsecs. (b) to (o) which related, respectively, to third party transfers, protective orders, warrant of seizure, order of forfeiture, execution of order, disposition of property, authority of Attorney General, applicability of civil forfeiture provisions, bar on intervention, jurisdiction to enter orders, depositions, third party interests, construction of section, and substitute assets.

1998—Subsec. (a). Pub. L. 105–314 substituted "2252, 2252A, or 2260 of this chapter, or who is convicted of an offense under section 2421, 2422, or 2423 of chapter 117," for "or 2252 of this chapter".

1994—Subsec. (a). Pub. L. 103–322, §330011(m)(1), amended directory language of Pub. L. 101–647, §3564(1). See 1990 Amendment note below.

1990—Subsec. (a). Pub. L. 101–647, §3564(1), as amended by Pub. L. 103–322, §330011(m)(1), substituted "section 2251" for "sections 2251" in introductory provisions and in par. (1).

Subsec. (h)(4). Pub. L. 101–647, §3564(2), substituted "under section 616 of the Tariff Act of 1930" for "in accordance with the provisions of section 1616, title 19, United States Code".

1988—Pub. L. 100–690 amended section generally, substituting subsecs. (a) to (o) for former subsecs. (a) to (d).

Effective Date of 1994 Amendment

Pub. L. 103–322, title XXXIII, §330011(m), Sept. 13, 1994, 108 Stat. 2145, provided that the amendment made by that section is effective as of Nov. 29, 1990.

§2254. Civil forfeiture

Any property subject to forfeiture pursuant to section 2253 may be forfeited to the United States in a civil case in accordance with the procedures set forth in chapter 46.

(Added Pub. L. 98–292, §6, May 21, 1984, 98 Stat. 205; amended Pub. L. 99–500, §101(m) [title II, §201(a), (c)], Oct. 18, 1986, 100 Stat. 1783–308, 1783–314, and Pub. L. 99–591, §101(m) [title II, §201(a), (c)], Oct. 30, 1986, 100 Stat. 3341–308, 3341–314; Pub. L. 100–690, title VII, §7522(c), Nov. 18, 1988, 102 Stat. 4498; Pub. L. 101–647, title XX, §2003, title XXXV, §3565, Nov. 29, 1990, 104 Stat. 4855, 4928; Pub. L. 103–322, title XXXIII, §330011(m)(2), Sept. 13, 1994, 108 Stat. 2145; Pub. L. 105–314, title VI, §603, Oct. 30, 1998, 112 Stat. 2982; Pub. L. 106–185, §2(c)(4), Apr. 25, 2000, 114 Stat. 211; Pub. L. 107–273, div. B, title IV, §4003(a)(6), Nov. 2, 2002, 116 Stat. 1811; Pub. L. 109–248, title V, §505(d), July 27, 2006, 120 Stat. 630.)

Codification

Pub. L. 99–591 is a corrected version of Pub. L. 99–500.

Amendments

2006—Pub. L. 109–248 amended section generally. Prior to amendment, section related to civil forfeiture of certain types of property described in this chapter and laws applicable to civil forfeiture proceedings.

2002—Subsec. (a)(3). Pub. L. 107–273 struck out comma before period at end.

2000—Subsec. (a)(2), (3). Pub. L. 106–185 struck out before period at end ", except that no property shall be forfeited under this paragraph, to the extent of the interest of an owner, by reason of any act or omission established by that owner to have been committed or omitted without the knowledge or consent of that owner".

1998—Subsec. (a)(2). Pub. L. 105–314, §603(1), substituted "2252, 2252A, or 2260 of this chapter, or used or intended to be used to commit or to promote the commission of an offense under section 2421, 2422, or 2423 of chapter 117," for "or 2252 of this chapter".

Subsec. (a)(3). Pub. L. 105–314, §603(2), substituted "2252, 2252A, or 2260 of this chapter, or obtained from a violation of section 2421, 2422, or 2423 of chapter 117," for "or 2252 of this chapter".

1994—Subsec. (f). Pub. L. 103–322, §330011(m)(2), amended directory language of Pub. L. 101–647, §3565(3)(A). See 1990 Amendment note below.

1990—Subsec. (a)(1) to (3). Pub. L. 101–647, §3565(1), substituted "section 2251" for "sections 2251".

Subsec. (e). Pub. L. 101–647, §3565(2), inserted heading.

Subsec. (f). Pub. L. 101–647, §3565(3)(A), as amended by Pub. L. 103–322, §330011(m)(2), substituted "section" for "subchapter" after "forfeited under this" in two places in concluding provisions.

Subsec. (f)(1). Pub. L. 101–647, §3565(3)(B), substituted "under section 616 of the Tariff Act of 1930" for "pursuant to section 1616 of title 19".

Subsec. (f)(2). Pub. L. 101–647, §2003, inserted ", by public sale or any other commercially feasible means," after "sell".

1988—Pub. L. 100–690 amended section generally, substituting subsecs. (a) to (i) for former subsecs. (a) to (d).

1986—Pub. L. 99–500 and Pub. L. 99–591 amended section identically, inserting ", and any property, real or personal, tangible or intangible, which was used or intended to be used, in any manner or part, to facilitate a violation of this chapter" in subsec. (a)(1), substituting "Attorney General or the Postal Service" for "Attorney General" in subsec. (b), and adding subsecs. (c) and (d).

Effective Date of 2000 Amendment

Amendment by Pub. L. 106–185 applicable to any forfeiture proceeding commenced on or after the date that is 120 days after Apr. 25, 2000, see section 21 of Pub. L. 106–185, set out as a note under section 1324 of Title 8, Aliens and Nationality.

Effective Date of 1994 Amendment
Pub. L. 103–322, title XXXIII, §330011(m), Sept. 13, 1994, 108 Stat. 2145, provided that the amendment made by that section is effective as of Nov. 29, 1990.

§2255. Civil remedy for personal injuries
(a) In General.—Any person who, while a minor, was a victim of a violation of section 1589, 1590, 1591, 2241(c), 2242, 2243, 2251, 2251A, 2252, 2252A, 2260, 2421, 2422, or 2423 of this title and who suffers personal injury as a result of such violation, regardless of whether the injury occurred while such person was a minor, may sue in any appropriate United States District Court and shall recover the actual damages such person sustains or liquidated damages in the amount of $150,000, and the cost of the action, including reasonable attorney's fees and other litigation costs reasonably incurred. The court may also award punitive damages and such other preliminary and equitable relief as the court determines to be appropriate.
(b) Statute of Limitations.—Any action commenced under this section shall be barred unless the complaint is filed—
(1) not later than 10 years after the date on which the plaintiff reasonably discovers the later of—
(A) the violation that forms the basis for the claim; or
(B) the injury that forms the basis for the claim; or
(2) not later than 10 years after the date on which the victim reaches 18 years of age.
(c) Venue; Service of Process.—
(1) Venue.—Any action brought under subsection (a) may be brought in the district court of the United States that meets applicable requirements relating to venue under section 1391 of title 28.
(2) Service of process.—In an action brought under subsection (a), process may be served in any district in which the defendant—
(A) is an inhabitant; or
(B) may be found.
(Added Pub. L. 99–500, §101(b) [title VII, §703(a)], Oct. 18, 1986, 100 Stat. 1783–39, 1783–74, and Pub. L. 99–591, §101(b) [title VII, §703(a)], Oct. 30, 1986, 100 Stat. 3341–39, 3341–74; amended Pub. L. 105–314, title VI, §605, Oct. 30, 1998, 112 Stat. 2984; Pub. L. 109–248, title VII, §707(b), (c), July 27, 2006, 120 Stat. 650; Pub. L. 113–4, title XII, §1212(a), Mar. 7, 2013, 127 Stat. 143; Pub. L. 115–126, title I, §102, Feb. 14, 2018, 132 Stat. 319.)

Codification
Pub. L. 99–591 is a corrected version of Pub. L. 99–500.

Prior Provisions
A prior section 2255 was renumbered section 2256 of this title.

Amendments
2018—Subsec. (a). Pub. L. 115–126, §102(1), added subsec. (a) and struck out former subsec. (a) related to civil remedy for personal injuries in general.
Subsec. (b). Pub. L. 115–126, §102(2), substituted "filed—" for "filed within 10 years after the right of action first accrues or in the case of a person under a legal disability, not later than three years after the disability." and added pars. (1) and (2).
Subsec. (c). Pub. L. 115–126, §102(3), added subsec. (c).
2013—Subsec. (a). Pub. L. 113–4, §1212(a)(1), substituted "section 1589, 1590, 1591, 2241(c)" for "section 2241(c)".
Subsec. (b). Pub. L. 113–4, §1212(a)(2), substituted "10 years" for "six years".
2006—Subsec. (a). Pub. L. 109–248, §707(b), inserted heading, inserted ", regardless of whether the injury occurred while such person was a minor," after "such violation", and substituted "Any

person who, while a minor, was" for "Any minor who is", "such person" for "such minor", "Any person as described" for "Any minor as described", and "$150,000" for "$50,000".

Subsec. (b). Pub. L. 109–248, §707(c), inserted heading.

1998—Subsec. (a). Pub. L. 105–314 substituted "2241(c), 2242, 2243, 2251, 2251A, 2252, 2252A, 2260, 2421, 2422, or 2423" for "2251 or 2252".

§2256. Definitions for chapter

For the purposes of this chapter, the term—

(1) "minor" means any person under the age of eighteen years;

(2)(A) Except as provided in subparagraph (B), "sexually explicit conduct" means actual or simulated—

(i) sexual intercourse, including genital-genital, oral-genital, anal-genital, or oral-anal, whether between persons of the same or opposite sex;

(ii) bestiality;

(iii) masturbation;

(iv) sadistic or masochistic abuse; or

(v) lascivious exhibition of the genitals or pubic area of any person;

(B) For purposes of subsection 8(B) 1 of this section, "sexually explicit conduct" means—

(i) graphic sexual intercourse, including genital-genital, oral-genital, anal-genital, or oral-anal, whether between persons of the same or opposite sex, or lascivious simulated sexual intercourse where the genitals, breast, or pubic area of any person is exhibited;

(ii) graphic or lascivious simulated;

(I) bestiality;

(II) masturbation; or

(III) sadistic or masochistic abuse; or

(iii) graphic or simulated lascivious exhibition of the genitals or pubic area of any person;

(3) "producing" means producing, directing, manufacturing, issuing, publishing, or advertising;

(4) "organization" means a person other than an individual;

(5) "visual depiction" includes undeveloped film and videotape, data stored on computer disk or by electronic means which is capable of conversion into a visual image, and data which is capable of conversion into a visual image that has been transmitted by any means, whether or not stored in a permanent format;

(6) "computer" has the meaning given that term in section 1030 of this title;

(7) "custody or control" includes temporary supervision over or responsibility for a minor whether legally or illegally obtained;

(8) "child pornography" means any visual depiction, including any photograph, film, video, picture, or computer or computer-generated image or picture, whether made or produced by electronic, mechanical, or other means, of sexually explicit conduct, where—

(A) the production of such visual depiction involves the use of a minor engaging in sexually explicit conduct;

(B) such visual depiction is a digital image, computer image, or computer-generated image that is, or is indistinguishable from, that of a minor engaging in sexually explicit conduct; or

(C) such visual depiction has been created, adapted, or modified to appear that an identifiable minor is engaging in sexually explicit conduct.

(9) "identifiable minor"—

(A) means a person—

(i)(I) who was a minor at the time the visual depiction was created, adapted, or modified; or

(II) whose image as a minor was used in creating, adapting, or modifying the visual depiction; and

(ii) who is recognizable as an actual person by the person's face, likeness, or other distinguishing characteristic, such as a unique birthmark or other recognizable feature; and

(B) shall not be construed to require proof of the actual identity of the identifiable minor.

(10) "graphic", when used with respect to a depiction of sexually explicit conduct, means that a

viewer can observe any part of the genitals or pubic area of any depicted person or animal during any part of the time that the sexually explicit conduct is being depicted; and

(11) the term "indistinguishable" used with respect to a depiction, means virtually indistinguishable, in that the depiction is such that an ordinary person viewing the depiction would conclude that the depiction is of an actual minor engaged in sexually explicit conduct. This definition does not apply to depictions that are drawings, cartoons, sculptures, or paintings depicting minors or adults.

(Added Pub. L. 95–225, §2(a), Feb. 6, 1978, 92 Stat. 8, §2253; renumbered §2255 and amended Pub. L. 98–292, §5, May 21, 1984, 98 Stat. 205; renumbered §2256, Pub. L. 99–500, §101(b) [title VII, §703(a)], Oct. 18, 1986, 100 Stat. 1783–39, 1783–74, and Pub. L. 99–591, §101(b) [title VII, §703(a)], Oct. 30, 1986, 100 Stat. 3341–39, 3341–74; Pub. L. 99–628, §4, Nov. 7, 1986, 100 Stat. 3510; Pub. L. 100–690, title VII, §§7511(c), 7512(b), Nov. 18, 1988, 102 Stat. 4485, 4486; Pub. L. 104–208, div. A, title I, §101(a) [title I, §121[2]], Sept. 30, 1996, 110 Stat. 3009, 3009–26, 3009–27; Pub. L. 108–21, title V, §502(a)–(c), Apr. 30, 2003, 117 Stat. 678, 679; Pub. L. 110–401, title III, §302, Oct. 13, 2008, 122 Stat. 4242.)

Codification

Pub. L. 99–591 is a corrected version of Pub. L. 99–500.

Amendments

2008—Par. (5). Pub. L. 110–401 struck out "and" before "data stored" and inserted ", and data which is capable of conversion into a visual image that has been transmitted by any means, whether or not stored in a permanent format" before semicolon at end.

2003—Par. (2). Pub. L. 108–21, §502(b), amended par. (2) generally. Prior to amendment, par. (2) read as follows:

"(2) 'sexually explicit conduct' means actual or simulated—

"(A) sexual intercourse, including genital-genital, oral-genital, anal-genital, or oral-anal, whether between persons of the same or opposite sex;

"(B) bestiality;

"(C) masturbation;

"(D) sadistic or masochistic abuse; or

"(E) lascivious exhibition of the genitals or pubic area of any person;".

Par. (8)(B). Pub. L. 108–21, §502(a)(1), amended subpar. (B) generally. Prior to amendment, subpar. (B) read as follows: "such visual depiction is, or appears to be, of a minor engaging in sexually explicit conduct;".

Par. (8)(C). Pub. L. 108–21, §502(a)(2), substituted a period for "; or" at end.

Par. (8)(D). Pub. L. 108–21, §502(a)(3), struck out subpar. (D) which read as follows: "such visual depiction is advertised, promoted, presented, described, or distributed in such a manner that conveys the impression that the material is or contains a visual depiction of a minor engaging in sexually explicit conduct; and".

Pars. (10), (11). Pub. L. 108–21, §502(c), added pars. (10) and (11).

1996—Par. (5). Pub. L. 104–208, §101(a) [title I, §121[2(1)]], inserted ", and data stored on computer disk or by electronic means which is capable of conversion into a visual image" before semicolon at end.

Pars. (8), (9). Pub. L. 104–208, §101(a) [title I, §121[2(2)–(4)]], added pars. (8) and (9).

1988—Par. (6). Pub. L. 100–690, §7511(c), added par. (6).

Par. (7). Pub. L. 100–690, §7512(b), added par. (7).

1986—Pub. L. 99–500 and Pub. L. 99–591 renumbered section 2255 of this title as this section.

Par. (5). Pub. L. 99–628, which directed that par. (5) be added to section 2255 of this title, was executed by adding par. (5) to section 2256 of this title to reflect the probable intent of Congress and the renumbering of section 2255 as 2256 by Pub. L. 99–500 and Pub. L. 99–591.

1984—Pub. L. 98–292, §5(b), renumbered section 2253 of this title as this section.

Par. (1). Pub. L. 98–292, §5(a)(1), substituted "eighteen" for "sixteen".

Par. (2)(D). Pub. L. 98–292, §5(a)(2), (3), substituted "sadistic or masochistic" for "sado-masochistic" and struck out "(for the purpose of sexual stimulation)" after "abuse".

Par. (2)(E). Pub. L. 98–292, §5(a)(4), substituted "lascivious" for "lewd".

Par. (3). Pub. L. 98–292, §5(a)(5), struck out ", for pecuniary profit" after "advertising".

Par. (4). Pub. L. 98–292, §5(a)(6), substituted " 'organization' means a person other than an individual" for " 'visual or print medium' means any film, photograph, negative, slide, book, magazine, or other visual or print medium".

Confirmation of Intent of Congress in Enacting Sections 2252 and 2256 of This Title

For provisions declaring and confirming intent of Congress in enacting this section, see section 160003(a) of Pub. L. 103–322, set out as a note under section 2252 of this title.

§2257. Record keeping requirements

(a) Whoever produces any book, magazine, periodical, film, videotape, digital image, digitally- or computer-manipulated image of an actual human being, picture, or other matter which—

(1) contains one or more visual depictions made after November 1, 1990 of actual sexually explicit conduct; and

(2) is produced in whole or in part with materials which have been mailed or shipped in interstate or foreign commerce, or is shipped or transported or is intended for shipment or transportation in interstate or foreign commerce;

shall create and maintain individually identifiable records pertaining to every performer portrayed in such a visual depiction.

(b) Any person to whom subsection (a) applies shall, with respect to every performer portrayed in a visual depiction of actual sexually explicit conduct—

(1) ascertain, by examination of an identification document containing such information, the performer's name and date of birth, and require the performer to provide such other indicia of his or her identity as may be prescribed by regulations;

(2) ascertain any name, other than the performer's present and correct name, ever used by the performer including maiden name, alias, nickname, stage, or professional name; and

(3) record in the records required by subsection (a) the information required by paragraphs (1) and (2) of this subsection and such other identifying information as may be prescribed by regulation.

(c) Any person to whom subsection (a) applies shall maintain the records required by this section at his business premises, or at such other place as the Attorney General may by regulation prescribe and shall make such records available to the Attorney General for inspection at all reasonable times.

(d)(1) No information or evidence obtained from records required to be created or maintained by this section shall, except as provided in this section, directly or indirectly, be used as evidence against any person with respect to any violation of law.

(2) Paragraph (1) of this subsection shall not preclude the use of such information or evidence in a prosecution or other action for a violation of this chapter or chapter 71, or for a violation of any applicable provision of law with respect to the furnishing of false information.

(e)(1) Any person to whom subsection (a) applies shall cause to be affixed to every copy of any matter described in paragraph (1) of subsection (a) of this section, in such manner and in such form as the Attorney General shall by regulations prescribe, a statement describing where the records required by this section with respect to all performers depicted in that copy of the matter may be located. In this paragraph, the term "copy" includes every page of a website on which matter described in subsection (a) appears.

(2) If the person to whom subsection (a) of this section applies is an organization the statement required by this subsection shall include the name, title, and business address of the individual employed by such organization responsible for maintaining the records required by this section.

(f) It shall be unlawful—

(1) for any person to whom subsection (a) applies to fail to create or maintain the records as required by subsections (a) and (c) or by any regulation promulgated under this section;

(2) for any person to whom subsection (a) applies knowingly to make any false entry in or knowingly to fail to make an appropriate entry in, any record required by subsection (b) of this section or any regulation promulgated under this section;

(3) for any person to whom subsection (a) applies knowingly to fail to comply with the provisions of subsection (e) or any regulation promulgated pursuant to that subsection;

(4) for any person knowingly to sell or otherwise transfer, or offer for sale or transfer, any book, magazine, periodical, film, video, or other matter, produce in whole or in part with materials which have been mailed or shipped in interstate or foreign commerce or which is intended for shipment in interstate or foreign commerce, which—

(A) contains one or more visual depictions made after the effective date of this subsection of actual sexually explicit conduct; and

(B) is produced in whole or in part with materials which have been mailed or shipped in interstate or foreign commerce, or is shipped or transported or is intended for shipment or transportation in interstate or foreign commerce;

which does not have affixed thereto, in a manner prescribed as set forth in subsection (e)(1), a statement describing where the records required by this section may be located, but such person shall have no duty to determine the accuracy of the contents of the statement or the records required to be kept; and

(5) for any person to whom subsection (a) applies to refuse to permit the Attorney General or his or her designee to conduct an inspection under subsection (c).

(g) The Attorney General shall issue appropriate regulations to carry out this section.

(h) In this section—

(1) the term "actual sexually explicit conduct" means actual but not simulated conduct as defined in clauses (i) through (v) of section 2256(2)(A) of this title;

(2) the term "produces"—

(A) means—

(i) actually filming, videotaping, photographing, creating a picture, digital image, or digitally- or computer-manipulated image of an actual human being;

(ii) digitizing an image, of a visual depiction of sexually explicit conduct; or, assembling, manufacturing, publishing, duplicating, reproducing, or reissuing a book, magazine, periodical, film, videotape, digital image, or picture, or other matter intended for commercial distribution, that contains a visual depiction of sexually explicit conduct; or

(iii) inserting on a computer site or service a digital image of, or otherwise managing the sexually explicit content,1 of a computer site or service that contains a visual depiction of, sexually explicit conduct; and

(B) does not include activities that are limited to—

(i) photo or film processing, including digitization of previously existing visual depictions, as part of a commercial enterprise, with no other commercial interest in the sexually explicit material, printing, and video duplication;

(ii) distribution;

(iii) any activity, other than those activities identified in subparagraph (A), that does not involve the hiring, contracting for, managing, or otherwise arranging for the participation of the depicted performers;

(iv) the provision of a telecommunications service, or of an Internet access service or Internet information location tool (as those terms are defined in section 231 of the Communications Act of 1934 (47 U.S.C. 231)); or

(v) the transmission, storage, retrieval, hosting, formatting, or translation (or any combination thereof) of a communication, without selection or alteration of the content of the communication, except that deletion of a particular communication or material made by another person in a manner consistent with section 230(c) of the Communications Act of 1934 (47 U.S.C. 230(c)) shall not constitute such selection or alteration of the content of the communication; and

(3) the term "performer" includes any person portrayed in a visual depiction engaging in, or assisting another person to engage in, sexually explicit conduct.

(i) Whoever violates this section shall be imprisoned for not more than 5 years, and fined in accordance with the provisions of this title, or both. Whoever violates this section after having been convicted of a violation punishable under this section shall be imprisoned for any period of years not more than 10 years but not less than 2 years, and fined in accordance with the provisions of this title, or both.

(Added Pub. L. 100–690, title VII, §7513(a), Nov. 18, 1988, 102 Stat. 4487; amended Pub. L. 101–647, title III, §§301(b), 311, Nov. 29, 1990, 104 Stat. 4816; Pub. L. 103–322, title XXXIII, §330004(14), Sept. 13, 1994, 108 Stat. 2142; Pub. L. 108–21, title V, §511(a), Apr. 30, 2003, 117 Stat. 684; Pub. L. 109–248, title V, §502(a), July 27, 2006, 120 Stat. 625.)

References in Text

For effective date of this subsection, referred to in subsec. (f)(4)(A), see section 312 of Pub. L. 101–647, set out as an Effective Date of 1990 Amendment note below.

Amendments

2006—Subsec. (a). Pub. L. 109–248, §502(a)(1), inserted "digital image, digitally- or computer-manipulated image of an actual human being, picture," after "videotape,".

Subsec. (e)(1). Pub. L. 109–248, §502(a)(2), inserted at end "In this paragraph, the term 'copy' includes every page of a website on which matter described in subsection (a) appears."

Subsec. (f)(5). Pub. L. 109–248, §502(a)(3), added par. (5).

Subsec. (h). Pub. L. 109–248, §502(a)(4), added subsec. (h) and struck out former subsec. (h) which defined "actual sexually explicit conduct", "identification document", "produces", and "performer".

2003—Subsec. (d)(2). Pub. L. 108–21, §511(a)(1), substituted "of this chapter or chapter 71," for "of this section".

Subsec. (h)(3). Pub. L. 108–21, §511(a)(2), inserted ", computer generated image, digital image, or picture," after "video tape".

Subsec. (i). Pub. L. 108–21, §511(a)(3), substituted "not more than 5 years" for "not more than 2 years" and "10 years" for "5 years".

1994—Subsecs. (f), (g). Pub. L. 103–322 struck out subsecs. (f) and (g) as enacted by Pub. L. 100–690. Subsec. (f) authorized Attorney General to issue regulations to carry out this section and subsec. (g) defined "actual sexually explicit conduct", "identification document", "produces", and "performer".

1990—Subsec. (a)(1). Pub. L. 101–647, §301(b), substituted "November 1, 1990" for "February 6, 1978".

Subsec. (d). Pub. L. 101–647, §311, substituted pars. (1) and (2) for former pars. (1) and (2) which were substantially the same and struck out par. (3) which read as follows: "In a prosecution of any person to whom subsection (a) applies for an offense in violation of subsection 2251(a) of this title which has as an element the production of a visual depiction of a minor engaging in or assisting another person to engage in sexually explicit conduct and in which that element is sought to be established by showing that a performer within the meaning of this section is a minor—

"(A) proof that the person failed to comply with the provisions of subsection (a) or (b) of this section concerning the creation and maintenance of records, or a regulation issued pursuant thereto, shall raise a rebuttable presumption that such performer was a minor; and

"(B) proof that the person failed to comply with the provisions of subsection (e) of this section concerning the statement required by that subsection shall raise the rebuttable presumption that every performer in the matter was a minor."

Subsec. (e). Pub. L. 101–647, §311, substituted pars. (1) and (2) for former pars. (1) and (2) which were substantially the same and struck out par. (3) which read as follows: "In any prosecution of a person for an offense in violation of section 2252 of this title which has as an element the transporting, mailing, or distribution of a visual depiction involving the use of a minor engaging in sexually explicit conduct, and in which that element is sought to be established by a showing that a performer within the meaning of this section is a minor, proof that the matter in which the visual depiction is contained did not contain the statement required by this section shall raise a rebuttable presumption that such performer was a minor."

Subsec. (f). Pub. L. 101–647, §311, added subsec. (f) relating to unlawful acts and omissions.

Subsec. (g). Pub. L. 101–647, §311, added subsec. (g) relating to issuance of regulations.

Subsecs. (h), (i). Pub. L. 101–647, §311, added subsecs. (h) and (i).

Effective Date of 1990 Amendment

Pub. L. 101–647, title III, §312, Nov. 29, 1990, 104 Stat. 4817, provided that: "Subsections (d), (f), (g), (h), and (i) of section 2257 of title 18, United States Code, as added by this title shall take effect 90 days after the date of the enactment of this Act [Nov. 29, 1990] except—

"(1) the Attorney General shall prepare the initial set of regulations required or authorized by subsections (d), (f), (g), (h), and (i) of section 2257 within 60 days of the date of the enactment of this Act; and

"(2) subsection (e) of section 2257 and of any regulation issued pursuant thereto shall take effect 90 days after the date of the enactment of this Act."

Effective Date

Pub. L. 100–690, title VII, §7513(c), Nov. 18, 1988, 102 Stat. 4488, provided that: "Section 2257 of title 18, United States Code, as added by this section shall take effect 180 days after the date of the enactment of this Act [Nov. 18, 1988] except—

"(1) the Attorney General shall prepare the initial set of regulations required or authorized by section 2257 within 90 days of the date of the enactment of this Act; and

"(2) subsection (e) of section 2257 of such title and of any regulation issued pursuant thereto shall take effect 270 days after the date of the enactment of this Act."

Construction

Pub. L. 109–248, title V, §502(b), July 27, 2006, 120 Stat. 626, provided that: "The provisions of section 2257 [of title 18, United States Code] shall not apply to any depiction of actual sexually explicit conduct as described in clause (v) of section 2256(2)(A) of title 18, United States Code, produced in whole or in part, prior to the effective date of this section [July 27, 2006] unless that depiction also includes actual sexually explicit conduct as described in clauses (i) through (iv) of section 2256(2)(A) of title 18, United States Code."

Report

Pub. L. 108–21, title V, §511(b), Apr. 30, 2003, 117 Stat. 685, provided that, not later than 1 year after Apr. 30, 2003, the Attorney General was to submit to Congress a report detailing the number of times since January 1993 that the Department of Justice had inspected records pursuant to this section and section 75 of title 28 of the Code of Federal Regulations, and the number of violations prosecuted as a result of those inspections.

§2257A. Record keeping requirements for simulated sexual conduct

(a) Whoever produces any book, magazine, periodical, film, videotape, digital image, digitally- or computer-manipulated image of an actual human being, picture, or other matter that—

(1) contains 1 or more visual depictions of simulated sexually explicit conduct; and

(2) is produced in whole or in part with materials which have been mailed or shipped in interstate or foreign commerce, or is shipped or transported or is intended for shipment or transportation in interstate or foreign commerce;

shall create and maintain individually identifiable records pertaining to every performer portrayed in such a visual depiction.

(b) Any person to whom subsection (a) applies shall, with respect to every performer portrayed in a visual depiction of simulated sexually explicit conduct—

(1) ascertain, by examination of an identification document containing such information, the performer's name and date of birth, and require the performer to provide such other indicia of his or her identity as may be prescribed by regulations;

(2) ascertain any name, other than the performer's present and correct name, ever used by the performer including maiden name, alias, nickname, stage, or professional name; and

(3) record in the records required by subsection (a) the information required by paragraphs (1) and (2) and such other identifying information as may be prescribed by regulation.

(c) Any person to whom subsection (a) applies shall maintain the records required by this section at their business premises, or at such other place as the Attorney General may by regulation prescribe and shall make such records available to the Attorney General for inspection at all reasonable times.

(d)(1) No information or evidence obtained from records required to be created or maintained by this section shall, except as provided in this section, directly or indirectly, be used as evidence against any person with respect to any violation of law.

(2) Paragraph (1) shall not preclude the use of such information or evidence in a prosecution or other action for a violation of this chapter or chapter 71, or for a violation of any applicable provision of law with respect to the furnishing of false information.

(e)(1) Any person to whom subsection (a) applies shall cause to be affixed to every copy of any matter described in subsection (a)(1) in such manner and in such form as the Attorney General shall by regulations prescribe, a statement describing where the records required by this section with respect to all performers depicted in that copy of the matter may be located. In this paragraph, the term "copy" includes every page of a website on which matter described in subsection (a) appears.

(2) If the person to whom subsection (a) applies is an organization the statement required by this subsection shall include the name, title, and business address of the individual employed by such organization responsible for maintaining the records required by this section.

(f) It shall be unlawful—

(1) for any person to whom subsection (a) applies to fail to create or maintain the records as required by subsections (a) and (c) or by any regulation promulgated under this section;

(2) for any person to whom subsection (a) applies knowingly to make any false entry in or knowingly to fail to make an appropriate entry in, any record required by subsection (b) or any regulation promulgated under this section;

(3) for any person to whom subsection (a) applies knowingly to fail to comply with the provisions of subsection (e) or any regulation promulgated pursuant to that subsection; or

(4) for any person knowingly to sell or otherwise transfer, or offer for sale or transfer, any book, magazine, periodical, film, video, or other matter, produced in whole or in part with materials which have been mailed or shipped in interstate or foreign commerce or which is intended for shipment in interstate or foreign commerce, that—

(A) contains 1 or more visual depictions made after the date of enactment of this subsection of simulated sexually explicit conduct; and

(B) is produced in whole or in part with materials which have been mailed or shipped in interstate or foreign commerce, or is shipped or transported or is intended for shipment or transportation in interstate or foreign commerce;

which does not have affixed thereto, in a manner prescribed as set forth in subsection (e)(1), a statement describing where the records required by this section may be located, but such person shall have no duty to determine the accuracy of the contents of the statement or the records required to be kept.

(5) for any person to whom subsection (a) applies to refuse to permit the Attorney General or his or her designee to conduct an inspection under subsection (c).

(g) As used in this section, the terms "produces" and "performer" have the same meaning as in section 2257(h) of this title.

(h)(1) The provisions of this section and section 2257 shall not apply to matter, or any image therein, containing one or more visual depictions of simulated sexually explicit conduct, or actual sexually explicit conduct as described in clause (v) of section 2256(2)(A), if such matter—

(A)(i) is intended for commercial distribution;

(ii) is created as a part of a commercial enterprise by a person who certifies to the Attorney General that such person regularly and in the normal course of business collects and maintains individually identifiable information regarding all performers, including minor performers, employed by that person, pursuant to Federal and State tax, labor, and other laws, labor agreements, or otherwise pursuant to industry standards, where such information includes the name, address, and date of birth of the performer; and

(iii) is not produced, marketed or made available by the person described in clause (ii) to another in circumstances such than 1 an ordinary person would conclude that the matter contains a visual depiction that is child pornography as defined in section 2256(8); or

(B)(i) is subject to the authority and regulation of the Federal Communications Commission acting in its capacity to enforce section 1464 of this title, regarding the broadcast of obscene, indecent or profane programming; and

(ii) is created as a part of a commercial enterprise by a person who certifies to the Attorney General that such person regularly and in the normal course of business collects and maintains individually identifiable information regarding all performers, including minor performers, employed by that person, pursuant to Federal and State tax, labor, and other laws, labor agreements, or otherwise pursuant to industry standards, where such information includes the name, address, and date of birth of the performer.

(2) Nothing in subparagraphs (A) and (B) of paragraph (1) shall be construed to exempt any matter that contains any visual depiction that is child pornography, as defined in section 2256(8), or is actual sexually explicit conduct within the definitions in clauses (i) through (iv) of section 2256(2)(A).

(i)(1) Whoever violates this section shall be imprisoned for not more than 1 year, and 2 fined in accordance with the provisions of this title, or both.

(2) Whoever violates this section in an effort to conceal a substantive offense involving the causing, transporting, permitting or offering or seeking by notice or advertisement, a minor to engage in sexually explicit conduct for the purpose of producing a visual depiction of such conduct in violation of this title, or to conceal a substantive offense that involved trafficking in material involving the sexual exploitation of a minor, including receiving, transporting, advertising, or possessing material involving the sexual exploitation of a minor with intent to traffic, in violation of this title, shall be imprisoned for not more than 5 years and 2 fined in accordance with the provisions of this title, or both.

(3) Whoever violates paragraph (2) after having been previously convicted of a violation punishable under that paragraph shall be imprisoned for any period of years not more than 10 years but not less than 2 years, and 2 fined in accordance with the provisions of this title, or both. The 3 provisions of this section shall not become effective until 90 days after the final regulations implementing this section are published in the Federal Register. The provisions of this section shall not apply to any matter, or image therein, produced, in whole or in part, prior to the effective date of this section.

(k) On an annual basis, the Attorney General shall submit a report to Congress—

(1) concerning the enforcement of this section and section 2257 by the Department of Justice during the previous 12-month period; and

(2) including—

(A) the number of inspections undertaken pursuant to this section and section 2257;

(B) the number of open investigations pursuant to this section and section 2257;

(C) the number of cases in which a person has been charged with a violation of this section and section 2257; and

(D) for each case listed in response to subparagraph (C), the name of the lead defendant, the federal district in which the case was brought, the court tracking number, and a synopsis of the violation and its disposition, if any, including settlements, sentences, recoveries and penalties. (Added Pub. L. 109–248, title V, §503(a), July 27, 2006, 120 Stat. 626.)

References in Text
The date of enactment of this subsection, referred to in subsec. (f)(4)(A), means the date of enactment of Pub. L. 109–248, which was approved July 27, 2006.
Final regulations implementing this section, referred to in the undesignated subsec. preceding subsec. (k), were published in the Federal Register on Dec. 18, 2008, see 73 F.R. 77432.

§2258. Failure to report child abuse
A person who, while engaged in a professional capacity or activity described in subsection (b) of section 226 of the Victims of Child Abuse Act of 1990 on Federal land or in a federally operated (or contracted) facility, or a covered individual as described in subsection (a)(2) of such section 226 who, learns of facts that give reason to suspect that a child has suffered an incident of child abuse, as defined in subsection (c) of that section, and fails to make a timely report as required by subsection (a) of that section, shall be fined under this title or imprisoned not more than 1 year or both.
(Added Pub. L. 101–647, title II, §226(g)(1), Nov. 29, 1990, 104 Stat. 4808; amended Pub. L. 109–248, title II, §209, July 27, 2006, 120 Stat. 615; Pub. L. 115–126, title I, §101(b), Feb. 14, 2018, 132 Stat. 319.)

References in Text
Section 226 of the Victims of Child Abuse Act of 1990, referred to in text, is classified to section 20341 of Title 34, Crime Control and Law Enforcement.

Codification
Another section 2258 was renumbered section 2260 of this title.

Amendments
2018—Pub. L. 115–126 inserted "or a covered individual as described in subsection (a)(2) of such section 226 who," after "facility,".
2006—Pub. L. 109–248 substituted "fined under this title or imprisoned not more than 1 year or both" for "guilty of a Class B misdemeanor".

§2258A. Reporting requirements of electronic communication service providers and remote computing service providers
(a) Duty To Report.—
(1) In general.—Whoever, while engaged in providing an electronic communication service or a remote computing service to the public through a facility or means of interstate or foreign commerce, obtains actual knowledge of any facts or circumstances described in paragraph (2) shall, as soon as reasonably possible—
(A) provide to the CyberTipline of the National Center for Missing and Exploited Children, or any successor to the CyberTipline operated by such center, the mailing address, telephone number, facsimile number, electronic mail address of, and individual point of contact for, such electronic communication service provider or remote computing service provider; and
(B) make a report of such facts or circumstances to the CyberTipline, or any successor to the CyberTipline operated by such center.
(2) Facts or circumstances.—The facts or circumstances described in this paragraph are any facts or circumstances from which there is an apparent violation of—
(A) section 2251, 2251A, 2252, 2252A, 2252B, or 2260 that involves child pornography; or

(B) section 1466A.

(b) Contents of Report.—To the extent the information is within the custody or control of an electronic communication service provider or a remote computing service provider, the facts and circumstances included in each report under subsection (a)(1) may include the following information:

(1) Information about the involved individual.—Information relating to the identity of any individual who appears to have violated a Federal law described in subsection (a)(2), which may, to the extent reasonably practicable, include the electronic mail address, Internet Protocol address, uniform resource locator, or any other identifying information, including self-reported identifying information.

(2) Historical reference.—Information relating to when and how a customer or subscriber of an electronic communication service or a remote computing service uploaded, transmitted, or received apparent child pornography or when and how apparent child pornography was reported to, or discovered by the electronic communication service provider or remote computing service provider, including a date and time stamp and time zone.

(3) Geographic location information.—

(A) In general.—Information relating to the geographic location of the involved individual or website, which may include the Internet Protocol address or verified billing address, or, if not reasonably available, at least 1 form of geographic identifying information, including area code or zip code.

(B) Inclusion.—The information described in subparagraph (A) may also include any geographic information provided to the electronic communication service or remote computing service by the customer or subscriber.

(4) Images of apparent child pornography.—Any image of apparent child pornography relating to the incident such report is regarding.

(5) Complete communication.—The complete communication containing any image of apparent child pornography, including—

(A) any data or information regarding the transmission of the communication; and

(B) any images, data, or other digital files contained in, or attached to, the communication.

(c) Forwarding of Report to Law Enforcement.—

(1) In general.—The National Center for Missing and Exploited Children shall forward each report made under subsection (a)(1) to any appropriate law enforcement agency designated by the Attorney General under subsection (d)(2).

(2) State and local law enforcement.—The National Center for Missing and Exploited Children may forward any report made under subsection (a)(1) to an appropriate law enforcement official of a State or political subdivision of a State for the purpose of enforcing State criminal law.

(3) Foreign law enforcement.—

(A) In general.—The National Center for Missing and Exploited Children may forward any report made under subsection (a)(1) to any appropriate foreign law enforcement agency designated by the Attorney General under subsection (d)(3), subject to the conditions established by the Attorney General under subsection (d)(3).

(B) Transmittal to designated federal agencies.—If the National Center for Missing and Exploited Children forwards a report to a foreign law enforcement agency under subparagraph (A), the National Center for Missing and Exploited Children shall concurrently provide a copy of the report and the identity of the foreign law enforcement agency to—

(i) the Attorney General; or

(ii) the Federal law enforcement agency or agencies designated by the Attorney General under subsection (d)(2).

(d) Attorney General Responsibilities.—

(1) In general.—The Attorney General shall enforce this section.

(2) Designation of federal agencies.—The Attorney General shall designate promptly the Federal law enforcement agency or agencies to which a report shall be forwarded under subsection (c)(1).

(3) Designation of foreign agencies.—The Attorney General shall promptly—

(A) in consultation with the Secretary of State, designate the foreign law enforcement agencies to which a report may be forwarded under subsection (c)(3);

(B) establish the conditions under which such a report may be forwarded to such agencies; and

(C) develop a process for foreign law enforcement agencies to request assistance from Federal law enforcement agencies in obtaining evidence related to a report referred under subsection (c)(3).

(4) Reporting designated foreign agencies.—The Attorney General shall maintain and make available to the Department of State, the National Center for Missing and Exploited Children, electronic communication service providers, remote computing service providers, the Committee on the Judiciary of the Senate, and the Committee on the Judiciary of the House of Representatives a list of the foreign law enforcement agencies designated under paragraph (3).

(5) Sense of congress regarding designation of foreign agencies.—It is the sense of Congress that—

(A) combating the international manufacturing, possession, and trade in online child pornography requires cooperation with competent, qualified, and appropriately trained foreign law enforcement agencies; and

(B) the Attorney General, in cooperation with the Secretary of State, should make a substantial effort to expand the list of foreign agencies designated under paragraph (3).

(6) Notification to providers.—If an electronic communication service provider or remote computing service provider notifies the National Center for Missing and Exploited Children that the electronic communication service provider or remote computing service provider is making a report under this section as the result of a request by a foreign law enforcement agency, the National Center for Missing and Exploited Children shall—

(A) if the Center forwards the report to the requesting foreign law enforcement agency or another agency in the same country designated by the Attorney General under paragraph (3), notify the electronic communication service provider or remote computing service provider of—

(i) the identity of the foreign law enforcement agency to which the report was forwarded; and

(ii) the date on which the report was forwarded; or

(B) notify the electronic communication service provider or remote computing service provider if the Center declines to forward the report because the Center, in consultation with the Attorney General, determines that no law enforcement agency in the foreign country has been designated by the Attorney General under paragraph (3).

(e) Failure To Report.—An electronic communication service provider or remote computing service provider that knowingly and willfully fails to make a report required under subsection (a)(1) shall be fined—

(1) in the case of an initial knowing and willful failure to make a report, not more than $150,000; and

(2) in the case of any second or subsequent knowing and willful failure to make a report, not more than $300,000.

(f) Protection of Privacy.—Nothing in this section shall be construed to require an electronic communication service provider or a remote computing service provider to—

(1) monitor any user, subscriber, or customer of that provider;

(2) monitor the content of any communication of any person described in paragraph (1); or

(3) affirmatively seek facts or circumstances described in sections (a) and (b).

(g) Conditions of Disclosure Information Contained Within Report.—

(1) In general.—Except as provided in paragraph (2), a law enforcement agency that receives a report under subsection (c) shall not disclose any information contained in that report.

(2) Permitted disclosures by law enforcement.—

(A) In general.—A law enforcement agency may disclose information in a report received under subsection (c)—

(i) to an attorney for the government for use in the performance of the official duties of that attorney;

(ii) to such officers and employees of that law enforcement agency, as may be necessary in the performance of their investigative and recordkeeping functions;

(iii) to such other government personnel (including personnel of a State or subdivision of a State) as are determined to be necessary by an attorney for the government to assist the attorney in the performance of the official duties of the attorney in enforcing Federal criminal law;

(iv) if the report discloses a violation of State criminal law, to an appropriate official of a State or subdivision of a State for the purpose of enforcing such State law;

(v) to a defendant in a criminal case or the attorney for that defendant, subject to the terms and limitations under section 3509(m) or a similar State law, to the extent the information relates to a criminal charge pending against that defendant;

(vi) subject to subparagraph (B), to an electronic communication service provider or remote computing provider if necessary to facilitate response to legal process issued in connection to a criminal investigation, prosecution, or post-conviction remedy relating to that report; and

(vii) as ordered by a court upon a showing of good cause and pursuant to any protective orders or other conditions that the court may impose.

(B) Limitations.—

(i) Limitations on further disclosure.—The electronic communication service provider or remote computing service provider shall be prohibited from disclosing the contents of a report provided under subparagraph (A)(vi) to any person, except as necessary to respond to the legal process.

(ii) Effect.—Nothing in subparagraph (A)(vi) authorizes a law enforcement agency to provide child pornography images to an electronic communications service provider or a remote computing service.

(3) Permitted disclosures by the national center for missing and exploited children.—The National Center for Missing and Exploited Children may disclose information received in a report under subsection (a) only—

(A) to any Federal law enforcement agency designated by the Attorney General under subsection (d)(2);

(B) to any State, local, or tribal law enforcement agency involved in the investigation of child pornography, child exploitation, kidnapping, or enticement crimes;

(C) to any foreign law enforcement agency designated by the Attorney General under subsection (d)(3); and

(D) to an electronic communication service provider or remote computing service provider as described in section 2258C.

(h) Preservation.—

(1) In general.—For the purposes of this section, the notification to an electronic communication service provider or a remote computing service provider by the CyberTipline of receipt of a report under subsection (a)(1) shall be treated as a request to preserve, as if such request was made pursuant to section 2703(f).

(2) Preservation of report.—Pursuant to paragraph (1), an electronic communication service provider or a remote computing service shall preserve the contents of the report provided pursuant to subsection (b) for 90 days after such notification by the CyberTipline.

(3) Preservation of commingled images.—Pursuant to paragraph (1), an electronic communication service provider or a remote computing service shall preserve any images, data, or other digital files that are commingled or interspersed among the images of apparent child pornography within a particular communication or user-created folder or directory.

(4) Protection of preserved materials.—An electronic communications service or remote computing service preserving materials under this section shall maintain the materials in a secure location and take appropriate steps to limit access by agents or employees of the service to the materials to that access necessary to comply with the requirements of this subsection.

(5) Authorities and duties not affected.—Nothing in this section shall be construed as replacing, amending, or otherwise interfering with the authorities and duties under section 2703.

(Added Pub. L. 110–401, title V, §501(a), Oct. 13, 2008, 122 Stat. 4243.)

§2258B. Limited liability for electronic communication service providers,

remote computing service providers, or domain name registrar 1

(a) In General.—Except as provided in subsection (b), a civil claim or criminal charge against an electronic communication service provider, a remote computing service provider, or domain 2 name registrar, including any director, officer, employee, or agent of such electronic communication service provider, remote computing service provider, or domain name registrar arising from the performance of the reporting or preservation responsibilities of such electronic communication service provider, remote computing service provider, or domain name registrar under this section, section 2258A, or section 2258C may not be brought in any Federal or State court.

(b) Intentional, Reckless, or Other Misconduct.—Subsection (a) shall not apply to a claim if the electronic communication service provider, remote computing service provider, or domain name registrar, or a director, officer, employee, or agent of that electronic communication service provider, remote computing service provider, or domain name registrar—

(1) engaged in intentional misconduct; or

(2) acted, or failed to act—

(A) with actual malice;

(B) with reckless disregard to a substantial risk of causing physical injury without legal justification; or

(C) for a purpose unrelated to the performance of any responsibility or function under this section,3 sections 2258A, 2258C, 2702, or 2703.

(c) Minimizing Access.—An electronic communication service provider, a remote computing service provider, and domain 2 name registrar shall—

(1) minimize the number of employees that are provided access to any image provided under section 2258A or 2258C; and

(2) ensure that any such image is permanently destroyed, upon a request from a law enforcement agency to destroy the image.

(Added Pub. L. 110–401, title V, §501(a), Oct. 13, 2008, 122 Stat. 4248.)

§2258C. Use to combat child pornography of technical elements relating to images reported to the CyberTipline

(a) Elements.—

(1) In general.—The National Center for Missing and Exploited Children may provide elements relating to any apparent child pornography image of an identified child to an electronic communication service provider or a remote computing service provider for the sole and exclusive purpose of permitting that electronic communication service provider or remote computing service provider to stop the further transmission of images.

(2) Inclusions.—The elements authorized under paragraph (1) may include hash values or other unique identifiers associated with a specific image, Internet location of images, and other technological elements that can be used to identify and stop the transmission of child pornography.

(3) Exclusion.—The elements authorized under paragraph (1) may not include the actual images.

(b) Use by Electronic Communication Service Providers and Remote Computing Service Providers.—Any electronic communication service provider or remote computing service provider that receives elements relating to any apparent child pornography image of an identified child from the National Center for Missing and Exploited Children under this section may use such information only for the purposes described in this section, provided that such use shall not relieve that electronic communication service provider or remote computing service provider from its reporting obligations under section 2258A.

(c) Limitations.—Nothing in subsections 1 (a) or (b) requires electronic communication service providers or remote computing service providers receiving elements relating to any apparent child pornography image of an identified child from the National Center for Missing and Exploited Children to use the elements to stop the further transmission of the images.

(d) Provision of Elements to Law Enforcement.—The National Center for Missing and Exploited

Children shall make available to Federal, State, and local law enforcement involved in the investigation of child pornography crimes elements, including hash values, relating to any apparent child pornography image of an identified child reported to the National Center for Missing and Exploited Children.

(e) Use by Law Enforcement.—Any Federal, State, or local law enforcement agency that receives elements relating to any apparent child pornography image of an identified child from the National Center for Missing and Exploited Children under section 1 (d) may use such elements only in the performance of the official duties of that agency to investigate child pornography crimes.

(Added Pub. L. 110–401, title V, §501(a), Oct. 13, 2008, 122 Stat. 4249.)

§2258D. Limited liability for the National Center for Missing and Exploited Children

(a) In General.—Except as provided in subsections (b) and (c), a civil claim or criminal charge against the National Center for Missing and Exploited Children, including any director, officer, employee, or agent of such center, arising from the performance of the CyberTipline responsibilities or functions of such center, as described in this section, section 2258A or 2258C of this title, or section 404 of the Missing Children's Assistance Act (42 U.S.C. 5773),1 or from the effort of such center to identify child victims may not be brought in any Federal or State court.

(b) Intentional, Reckless, or Other Misconduct.—Subsection (a) shall not apply to a claim or charge if the National Center for Missing and Exploited Children, or a director, officer, employee, or agent of such center—

(1) engaged in intentional misconduct; or

(2) acted, or failed to act—

(A) with actual malice;

(B) with reckless disregard to a substantial risk of causing injury without legal justification; or

(C) for a purpose unrelated to the performance of any responsibility or function under this section, section 2258A or 2258C of this title, or section 404 of the Missing Children's Assistance Act (42 U.S.C. 5773).1

(c) Ordinary Business Activities.—Subsection (a) shall not apply to an act or omission relating to an ordinary business activity, including general administration or operations, the use of motor vehicles, or personnel management.

(d) Minimizing Access.—The National Center for Missing and Exploited Children shall—

(1) minimize the number of employees that are provided access to any image provided under section 2258A; and

(2) ensure that any such image is permanently destroyed upon notification from a law enforcement agency.

(Added Pub. L. 110–401, title V, §501(a), Oct. 13, 2008, 122 Stat. 4250.)

References in Text

Section 404 of the Missing Children's Assistance Act, referred to in subsecs. (a) and (b)(2)(C), is section 404 of title IV of Pub. L. 93–415, which was formerly classified to section 5773 of Title 42, The Public Health and Welfare, prior to editorial reclassification as section 11293 of Title 34, Crime Control and Law Enforcement.

§2258E. Definitions

In sections 2258A through 2258D—

(1) the terms "attorney for the government" and "State" have the meanings given those terms in rule 1 of the Federal Rules of Criminal Procedure;

(2) the term "electronic communication service" has the meaning given that term in section 2510;

(3) the term "electronic mail address" has the meaning given that term in section 3 of the CAN–SPAM Act of 2003 (15 U.S.C. 7702);

(4) the term "Internet" has the meaning given that term in section 1101 of the Internet Tax

Freedom Act (47 U.S.C. 151 note);

(5) the term "remote computing service" has the meaning given that term in section 2711; and

(6) the term "website" means any collection of material placed in a computer server-based file archive so that it is publicly accessible, over the Internet, using hypertext transfer protocol or any successor protocol.

(Added Pub. L. 110–401, title V, §501(a), Oct. 13, 2008, 122 Stat. 4250.)

References in Text

The Federal Rules of Criminal Procedure, referred to in par. (1), are set out in the Appendix to this title.

Section 1101 of the Internet Tax Freedom Act, referred to in par. (4), is section 1101 of title XI of div. C of Pub. L. 105–277, which is set out in a note under section 151 of Title 47, Telecommunications.

§2259. Mandatory restitution

(a) In General.—Notwithstanding section 3663 or 3663A, and in addition to any other civil or criminal penalty authorized by law, the court shall order restitution for any offense under this chapter.

(b) Scope and Nature of Order.—

(1) Directions.—The order of restitution under this section shall direct the defendant to pay the victim (through the appropriate court mechanism) the full amount of the victim's losses as determined by the court pursuant to paragraph (2).

(2) Enforcement.—An order of restitution under this section shall be issued and enforced in accordance with section 3664 in the same manner as an order under section 3663A.

(3) Definition.—For purposes of this subsection, the term "full amount of the victim's losses" includes any costs incurred by the victim for—

(Λ) medical services relating to physical, psychiatric, or psychological care;

(B) physical and occupational therapy or rehabilitation;

(C) necessary transportation, temporary housing, and child care expenses;

(D) lost income;

(E) attorneys' fees, as well as other costs incurred; and

(F) any other losses suffered by the victim as a proximate result of the offense.

(4) Order mandatory.—(A) The issuance of a restitution order under this section is mandatory.

(B) A court may not decline to issue an order under this section because of—

(i) the economic circumstances of the defendant; or

(ii) the fact that a victim has, or is entitled to, receive compensation for his or her injuries from the proceeds of insurance or any other source.

(c) Definition.—For purposes of this section, the term "victim" means the individual harmed as a result of a commission of a crime under this chapter, including, in the case of a victim who is under 18 years of age, incompetent, incapacitated, or deceased, the legal guardian of the victim or representative of the victim's estate, another family member, or any other person appointed as suitable by the court, but in no event shall the defendant be named as such representative or guardian.

(Added Pub. L. 103–322, title IV, §40113(b)(1), Sept. 13, 1994, 108 Stat. 1907; amended Pub. L. 104–132, title II, §205(c), Apr. 24, 1996, 110 Stat. 1231.)

Amendments

1996—Subsec. (a). Pub. L. 104–132, §205(c)(1), inserted "or 3663A" after "3663".

Subsec. (b)(1). Pub. L. 104–132, §205(c)(2)(A), reenacted heading without change and amended text generally. Prior to amendment, text read as follows: "The order of restitution under this section shall direct that—

"(A) the defendant pay to the victim (through the appropriate court mechanism) the full amount of the victim's losses as determined by the court, pursuant to paragraph (3); and

"(B) the United States Attorney enforce the restitution order by all available and reasonable means."

Subsec. (b)(2). Pub. L. 104–132, §205(c)(2)(B), struck out "by victim" after "Enforcement" in heading and amended text generally. Prior to amendment, text read as follows: "An order of restitution may also be enforced by a victim named in the order to receive the restitution in the same manner as a judgment in a civil action."

Subsec. (b)(4)(C), (D). Pub. L. 104–132, §205(c)(2)(C), struck out subpars. (C) and (D), which related to court's consideration of economic circumstances of defendant in determining schedule of payment of restitution orders, and court's entry of nominal restitution awards where economic circumstances of defendant do not allow for payment of restitution, respectively.

Subsec. (b)(5) to (10). Pub. L. 104–132, §205(c)(2)(D), struck out pars. (5) to (10), which related, respectively, to more than 1 offender, more than 1 victim, payment schedule, setoff, effect on other sources of compensation, and condition of probation or supervised release.

Subsec. (c). Pub. L. 104–132, §205(c)(3), (4), redesignated subsec. (f) as (c) and struck out former subsec. (c) relating to proof of claim.

Subsecs. (d), (e). Pub. L. 104–132, §205(c)(3), struck out subsecs. (d) and (e) which read as follows:

"(d) Modification of Order.—A victim or the offender may petition the court at any time to modify a restitution order as appropriate in view of a change in the economic circumstances of the offender.

"(e) Reference to Magistrate or Special Master.—The court may refer any issue arising in connection with a proposed order of restitution to a magistrate or special master for proposed findings of fact and recommendations as to disposition, subject to a de novo determination of the issue by the court."

Subsec. (f). Pub. L. 104–132, §205(c)(4), redesignated subsec. (f) as (c).

Effective Date of 1996 Amendment

Amendment by Pub. L. 104–132 effective, to extent constitutionally permissible, for sentencing proceedings in cases in which defendant is convicted on or after Apr. 24, 1996, see section 211 of Pub. L. 104–132, set out as a note under section 2248 of this title.

§2260. Production of sexually explicit depictions of a minor for importation into the United States

(a) Use of Minor.—A person who, outside the United States, employs, uses, persuades, induces, entices, or coerces any minor to engage in, or who has a minor assist any other person to engage in, or who transports any minor with the intent that the minor engage in any sexually explicit conduct for the purpose of producing any visual depiction of such conduct or for the purpose of transmitting a live visual depiction of such conduct, intending that the visual depiction will be imported or transmitted into the United States or into waters within 12 miles of the coast of the United States, shall be punished as provided in subsection (c).

(b) Use of Visual Depiction.—A person who, outside the United States, knowingly receives, transports, ships, distributes, sells, or possesses with intent to transport, ship, sell, or distribute any visual depiction of a minor engaging in sexually explicit conduct (if the production of the visual depiction involved the use of a minor engaging in sexually explicit conduct), intending that the visual depiction will be imported into the United States or into waters within a distance of 12 miles of the coast of the United States, shall be punished as provided in subsection (c).

(c) Penalties.—

(1) A person who violates subsection (a), or attempts or conspires to do so, shall be subject to the penalties provided in subsection (e) of section 2251 for a violation of that section, including the penalties provided for such a violation by a person with a prior conviction or convictions as described in that subsection.

(2) A person who violates subsection (b), or attempts or conspires to do so, shall be subject to the penalties provided in subsection (b)(1) of section 2252 for a violation of paragraph (1), (2), or (3) of subsection (a) of that section, including the penalties provided for such a violation by a person with a prior conviction or convictions as described in subsection (b)(1) of section 2252.
(Added Pub. L. 103–322, title XVI, §160001(a), Sept. 13, 1994, 108 Stat. 2036, §2258; renumbered §2260, Pub. L. 104–294, title VI, §601(i)(1), Oct. 11, 1996, 110 Stat. 3501; amended Pub. L. 109–248, title II, §206(b)(5), July 27, 2006, 120 Stat. 614; Pub. L. 110–401, title III, §303, Oct. 13, 2008, 122 Stat. 4242.)

Amendments

2008—Subsec. (a). Pub. L. 110–401 inserted "or for the purpose of transmitting a live visual depiction of such conduct" after "for the purpose of producing any visual depiction of such conduct" and "or transmitted" after "imported".
2006—Subsec. (c). Pub. L. 109–248 amended subsec. (c) generally. Prior to amendment, text read as follows: "A person who violates subsection (a) or (b), or conspires or attempts to do so—
"(1) shall be fined under this title, imprisoned not more than 10 years, or both; and
"(2) if the person has a prior conviction under this chapter or chapter 109A, shall be fined under this title, imprisoned not more than 20 years, or both."
1996—Pub. L. 104–294 renumbered section 2258, relating to production of sexually explicit depictions of minor, as this section.

§2260A. Penalties for registered sex offenders

Whoever, being required by Federal or other law to register as a sex offender, commits a felony offense involving a minor under section 1201, 1466A, 1470, 1591, 2241, 2242, 2243, 2244, 2245, 2251, 2251A, 2260, 2421, 2422, 2423, or 2425, shall be sentenced to a term of imprisonment of 10 years in addition to the imprisonment imposed for the offense under that provision. The sentence imposed under this section shall be consecutive to any sentence imposed for the offense under that provision.
(Added Pub. L. 109–248, title VII, §702(a), July 27, 2006, 120 Stat. 648.)

CHAPTER 110A - DOMESTIC VIOLENCE AND STALKING

Amendments

1996—Pub. L. 104–294, title VI, §604(a)(1), Oct. 11, 1996, 110 Stat. 3506, amended analysis by inserting "Sec." above section numbers.
Pub. L. 104–201, div. A, title X, §1069(b)(3), (c), Sept. 23, 1996, 110 Stat. 2656, inserted "AND STALKING" after "VIOLENCE" in chapter heading and added item 2261A.

§2261. Interstate domestic violence

(a) Offenses.—

(1) Travel or conduct of offender.—A person who travels in interstate or foreign commerce or enters or leaves Indian country or is present within the special maritime and territorial jurisdiction of the United States with the intent to kill, injure, harass, or intimidate a spouse, intimate partner, or dating partner, and who, in the course of or as a result of such travel or presence, commits or attempts to commit a crime of violence against that spouse, intimate partner, or dating partner, shall be punished as provided in subsection (b).

(2) Causing travel of victim.—A person who causes a spouse, intimate partner, or dating partner to travel in interstate or foreign commerce or to enter or leave Indian country by force, coercion, duress, or fraud, and who, in the course of, as a result of, or to facilitate such conduct or travel, commits or attempts to commit a crime of violence against that spouse, intimate partner, or dating partner, shall be punished as provided in subsection (b).

(b) Penalties.—A person who violates this section or section 2261A shall be fined under this title, imprisoned—

(1) for life or any term of years, if death of the victim results;

(2) for not more than 20 years if permanent disfigurement or life threatening bodily injury to the victim results;

(3) for not more than 10 years, if serious bodily injury to the victim results or if the offender uses a dangerous weapon during the offense;

(4) as provided for the applicable conduct under chapter 109A if the offense would constitute an offense under chapter 109A (without regard to whether the offense was committed in the special maritime and territorial jurisdiction of the United States or in a Federal prison); and

(5) for not more than 5 years, in any other case,

or both fined and imprisoned.

(6) Whoever commits the crime of stalking in violation of a temporary or permanent civil or criminal injunction, restraining order, no-contact order, or other order described in section 2266 of title 18, United States Code, shall be punished by imprisonment for not less than 1 year.

(Added Pub. L. 103–322, title IV, §40221(a), Sept. 13, 1994, 108 Stat. 1926; amended Pub. L. 104–201, div. A, title X, §1069(b)(1), (2), Sept. 23, 1996, 110 Stat. 2656; Pub. L. 106–386, div. B, title I, §1107(a), Oct. 28, 2000, 114 Stat. 1497; Pub. L. 109–162, title I, §§114(b), 116(a), 117(a), Jan. 5, 2006, 119 Stat. 2988, 2989; Pub. L. 113–4, title I, §107(a), Mar. 7, 2013, 127 Stat. 77.)

Amendments

2013—Subsec. (a)(1). Pub. L. 113–4 inserted "is present" after "Indian country or" and "or presence" after "as a result of such travel".

2006—Subsec. (a)(1). Pub. L. 109–162, §117(a), inserted "or within the special maritime and territorial jurisdiction of the United States" after "Indian country".

Pub. L. 109–162, §116(a)(1), which directed substitution of ", intimate partner, or dating partner" for "or intimate partner", was executed by making the substitution in two places to reflect the probable intent of Congress.

Subsec. (a)(2). Pub. L. 109–162, §116(a)(2), which directed substitution of ", intimate partner, or dating partner" for "or intimate partner", was executed by making the substitution in two places to reflect the probable intent of Congress.

Subsec. (b)(6). Pub. L. 109–162, §114(b), added par. (6).

2000—Subsec. (a). Pub. L. 106–386 added subsec. (a) and struck out heading and text of former subsec. (a). Text read as follows:

"(1) Crossing a state line.—A person who travels across a State line or enters or leaves Indian country with the intent to injure, harass, or intimidate that person's spouse or intimate partner, and who, in the course of or as a result of such travel, intentionally commits a crime of violence and thereby causes bodily injury to such spouse or intimate partner, shall be punished as provided in subsection (b).

"(2) Causing the crossing of a state line.—A person who causes a spouse or intimate partner to cross a State line or to enter or leave Indian country by force, coercion, duress, or fraud and, in the course or as a result of that conduct, intentionally commits a crime of violence and thereby causes bodily injury to the person's spouse or intimate partner, shall be punished as provided in subsection (b)."

1996—Subsec. (b). Pub. L. 104–201 inserted "or section 2261A" after "this section" in introductory provisions and substituted "victim" for "offender's spouse or intimate partner" in pars. (1) to (3).

Effective Date of 2013 Amendment

Pub. L. 113–4, §4, Mar. 7, 2013, 127 Stat. 64, provided that: "Except as otherwise specifically provided in this Act [see Tables for classification], the provisions of titles I, II, III, IV, VII, and sections 3, 602, 901, and 902 of this Act shall not take effect until the beginning of the fiscal year following the date of enactment of this Act [Mar. 7, 2013]."

§2261A. Stalking

Whoever—

(1) travels in interstate or foreign commerce or is present within the special maritime and territorial jurisdiction of the United States, or enters or leaves Indian country, with the intent to kill, injure, harass, intimidate, or place under surveillance with intent to kill, injure, harass, or intimidate another person, and in the course of, or as a result of, such travel or presence engages in conduct that—

(A) places that person in reasonable fear of the death of, or serious bodily injury to—

(i) that person;

(ii) an immediate family member (as defined in section 115) of that person; or

(iii) a spouse or intimate partner of that person; or

(B) causes, attempts to cause, or would be reasonably expected to cause substantial emotional distress to a person described in clause (i), (ii), or (iii) of subparagraph (A); or

(2) with the intent to kill, injure, harass, intimidate, or place under surveillance with intent to kill, injure, harass, or intimidate another person, uses the mail, any interactive computer service or electronic communication service or electronic communication system of interstate commerce, or any other facility of interstate or foreign commerce to engage in a course of conduct that—

(A) places that person in reasonable fear of the death of or serious bodily injury to a person described in clause (i), (ii), or (iii) of paragraph (1)(A); or

(B) causes, attempts to cause, or would be reasonably expected to cause substantial emotional distress to a person described in clause (i), (ii), or (iii) of paragraph (1)(A),

shall be punished as provided in section 2261(b) of this title.

(Added Pub. L. 104–201, div. A, title X, §1069(a), Sept. 23, 1996, 110 Stat. 2655; amended Pub. L. 106–386, div. B, title I, §1107(b)(1), Oct. 28, 2000, 114 Stat. 1498; Pub. L. 109–162, title I, §114(a), Jan. 5, 2006, 119 Stat. 2987; Pub. L. 113–4, title I, §107(b), Mar. 7, 2013, 127 Stat. 77.)

Amendments

2013—Pub. L. 113–4 amended section generally. Prior to amendment, section related to stalking.

2006—Pub. L. 109–162 amended section catchline and text generally, revising and restating former provisions relating to stalking so as to include surveillance with intent to kill, injure, harass, or intimidate which results in substantial emotional distress to a person within the purview of the offense proscribed.

2000—Pub. L. 106–386 reenacted section catchline without change and amended text generally. Prior to amendment, text read as follows: "Whoever travels across a State line or within the special maritime and territorial jurisdiction of the United States with the intent to injure or harass another person, and in the course of, or as a result of, such travel places that person in reasonable fear of the death of, or serious bodily injury (as defined in section 1365(g)(3) of this title) to, that person or a member of that person's immediate family (as defined in section 115 of this title) shall be punished as provided in section 2261 of this title."

Effective Date of 2013 Amendment

Amendment by Pub. L. 113–4 not effective until the beginning of the fiscal year following Mar. 7, 2013, see section 4 of Pub. L. 113–4, set out as a note under section 2261 of this title.

§2262. Interstate violation of protection order

(a) Offenses.—

(1) Travel or conduct of offender.—A person who travels in interstate or foreign commerce, or enters or leaves Indian country or is present within the special maritime and territorial jurisdiction of the United States, with the intent to engage in conduct that violates the portion of a protection order that prohibits or provides protection against violence, threats, or harassment against, contact or communication with, or physical proximity to, another person, or that would violate such a portion of a protection order in the jurisdiction in which the order was issued, and subsequently engages in such conduct, shall be punished as provided in subsection (b).

(2) Causing travel of victim.—A person who causes another person to travel in interstate or foreign commerce or to enter or leave Indian country by force, coercion, duress, or fraud, and in the course of, as a result of, or to facilitate such conduct or travel engages in conduct that violates the portion of a protection order that prohibits or provides protection against violence, threats, or harassment against, contact or communication with, or physical proximity to, another person, or that would violate such a portion of a protection order in the jurisdiction in which the order was issued, shall be punished as provided in subsection (b).

(b) Penalties.—A person who violates this section shall be fined under this title, imprisoned—

(1) for life or any term of years, if death of the victim results;

(2) for not more than 20 years if permanent disfigurement or life threatening bodily injury to the victim results;

(3) for not more than 10 years, if serious bodily injury to the victim results or if the offender uses a dangerous weapon during the offense;

(4) as provided for the applicable conduct under chapter 109A if the offense would constitute an offense under chapter 109A (without regard to whether the offense was committed in the special maritime and territorial jurisdiction of the United States or in a Federal prison); and

(5) for not more than 5 years, in any other case,

or both fined and imprisoned.

(Added Pub. L. 103–322, title IV, §40221(a), Sept. 13, 1994, 108 Stat. 1927; amended Pub. L. 104–201, div. A, title X, §1069(b)(2), Sept. 23, 1996, 110 Stat. 2656; Pub. L. 104–294, title VI, §605(d), Oct. 11, 1996, 110 Stat. 3509; Pub. L. 106–386, div. B, title I, §1107(c), Oct. 28, 2000, 114 Stat. 1498; Pub. L. 109–162, title I, §117(b), Jan. 5, 2006, 119 Stat. 2989; Pub. L. 113–4, title I, §107(c), Mar. 7, 2013, 127 Stat. 78.)

Amendments

2013—Subsec. (a)(1). Pub. L. 113–4, which directed amendment of subsec. (a)(2) by inserting "is present" after "Indian country or", was executed by making the insertion in subsec. (a)(1) to reflect the probable intent of Congress.

2006—Subsec. (a)(1). Pub. L. 109–162 inserted "or within the special maritime and territorial jurisdiction of the United States" after "Indian country".

2000—Subsec. (a). Pub. L. 106–386 added subsec. (a) and struck out heading and text of former subsec. (a). Text read as follows:

"(1) Crossing a state line.—A person who travels across a State line or enters or leaves Indian country with the intent to engage in conduct that—

"(A)(i) violates the portion of a protection order that involves protection against credible threats of violence, repeated harassment, or bodily injury to the person or persons for whom the protection order was issued; or

"(ii) would violate this subparagraph if the conduct occurred in the jurisdiction in which the order was issued; and

"(B) subsequently engages in such conduct,

shall be punished as provided in subsection (b).

"(2) Causing the crossing of a state line.—A person who causes a spouse or intimate partner to cross a State line or to enter or leave Indian country by force, coercion, duress, or fraud, and, in the course or as a result of that conduct, intentionally commits an act that injures the person's spouse or intimate partner in violation of a valid protection order issued by a State shall be punished as provided in subsection (b)."

1996—Subsec. (a)(1)(A)(ii). Pub. L. 104–294 substituted "violate this subparagraph" for "violate subparagraph (A)".

Subsec. (b)(1) to (3). Pub. L. 104–201 substituted "victim" for "offender's spouse or intimate partner".

Effective Date of 2013 Amendment

Amendment by Pub. L. 113–4 not effective until the beginning of the fiscal year following Mar. 7, 2013, see section 4 of Pub. L. 113–4, set out as a note under section 2261 of this title.

§2263. Pretrial release of defendant

In any proceeding pursuant to section 3142 for the purpose of determining whether a defendant charged under this chapter shall be released pending trial, or for the purpose of determining conditions of such release, the alleged victim shall be given an opportunity to be heard regarding the danger posed by the defendant.

(Added Pub. L. 103–322, title IV, §40221(a), Sept. 13, 1994, 108 Stat. 1928.)

§2264. Restitution

(a) In General.—Notwithstanding section 3663 or 3663A, and in addition to any other civil or criminal penalty authorized by law, the court shall order restitution for any offense under this chapter.

(b) Scope and Nature of Order.—

(1) Directions.—The order of restitution under this section shall direct the defendant to pay the victim (through the appropriate court mechanism) the full amount of the victim's losses as determined by the court pursuant to paragraph (2).

(2) Enforcement.—An order of restitution under this section shall be issued and enforced in accordance with section 3664 in the same manner as an order under section 3663A.

(3) Definition.—For purposes of this subsection, the term "full amount of the victim's losses" includes any costs incurred by the victim for—

(A) medical services relating to physical, psychiatric, or psychological care;

(B) physical and occupational therapy or rehabilitation;

(C) necessary transportation, temporary housing, and child care expenses;

(D) lost income;

(E) attorneys' fees, plus any costs incurred in obtaining a civil protection order; and

(F) any other losses suffered by the victim as a proximate result of the offense.

(4) Order mandatory.—(A) The issuance of a restitution order under this section is mandatory.

(B) A court may not decline to issue an order under this section because of—

(i) the economic circumstances of the defendant; or

(ii) the fact that a victim has, or is entitled to, receive compensation for his or her injuries from the proceeds of insurance or any other source.

(c) Victim Defined.—For purposes of this section, the term "victim" means the individual harmed as a result of a commission of a crime under this chapter, including, in the case of a victim who is under 18 years of age, incompetent, incapacitated, or deceased, the legal guardian of the victim or representative of the victim's estate, another family member, or any other person appointed as suitable by the court, but in no event shall the defendant be named as such representative or guardian.

(Added Pub. L. 103–322, title IV, §40221(a), Sept. 13, 1994, 108 Stat. 1928; amended Pub. L. 104–132, title II, §205(d), Apr. 24, 1996, 110 Stat. 1231.)

Amendments

1996—Subsec. (a). Pub. L. 104–132, §205(d)(1), inserted "or 3663A" after "3663".

Subsec. (b)(1). Pub. L. 104–132, §205(d)(2)(A), reenacted heading without change and amended text generally. Prior to amendment, text read as follows: "The order of restitution under this section shall direct that—

"(A) the defendant pay to the victim (through the appropriate court mechanism) the full amount of the victim's losses as determined by the court, pursuant to paragraph (3); and

"(B) the United States Attorney enforce the restitution order by all available and reasonable means."

Subsec. (b)(2). Pub. L. 104–132, §205(d)(2)(B), struck out "by victim" after "Enforcement" in heading and amended text generally. Prior to amendment, text read as follows: "An order of restitution also may be enforced by a victim named in the order to receive the restitution in the same manner as a judgment in a civil action."

Subsec. (b)(4)(C), (D). Pub. L. 104–132, §205(d)(2)(C), struck out subpars. (C) and (D), which related to court's consideration of economic circumstances of defendant in determining schedule of payment of restitution orders, and court's entry of nominal restitution awards where economic circumstances of defendant do not allow for payment of restitution, respectively.

Subsec. (b)(5) to (10). Pub. L. 104–132, §205(d)(2)(D), struck out pars. (5) to (10), which related, respectively, to more than 1 offender, more than 1 victim, payment schedule, setoff, effect on other sources of compensation, and condition of probation or supervised release.

Subsec. (c). Pub. L. 104–132, §205(d)(3), (4), added subsec. (c) and struck out former subsec. (c) which read as follows: "Affidavit.—Within 60 days after conviction and, in any event, not later than 10 days before sentencing, the United States Attorney (or such Attorney's delegate), after consulting with the victim, shall prepare and file an affidavit with the court listing the amounts subject to restitution under this section. The affidavit shall be signed by the United States Attorney (or the delegate) and the victim. Should the victim object to any of the information included in the affidavit, the United States Attorney (or the delegate) shall advise the victim that the victim may file a separate affidavit and assist the victim in the preparation of the affidavit."

Subsecs. (d) to (g). Pub. L. 104–132, §205(d)(3), struck out subsecs. (d) to (g), which related, respectively, to objection, additional documentation and testimony, final determination of losses, and restitution in addition to punishment.

Effective Date of 1996 Amendment

Amendment by Pub. L. 104–132 effective, to extent constitutionally permissible, for sentencing proceedings in cases in which defendant is convicted on or after Apr. 24, 1996, see section 211 of Pub. L. 104–132, set out as a note under section 2248 of this title.

§2265. Full faith and credit given to protection orders

(a) Full Faith and Credit.—Any protection order issued that is consistent with subsection (b) of this section by the court of one State, Indian tribe, or territory (the issuing State, Indian tribe, or territory) shall be accorded full faith and credit by the court of another State, Indian tribe, or territory (the enforcing State, Indian tribe, or territory) and enforced by the court and law enforcement personnel of the other State, Indian tribal government or Territory 1 as if it were the order of the enforcing State or tribe.

(b) Protection Order.—A protection order issued by a State, tribal, or territorial court is consistent with this subsection if—

(1) such court has jurisdiction over the parties and matter under the law of such State, Indian tribe, or territory; and

(2) reasonable notice and opportunity to be heard is given to the person against whom the order is sought sufficient to protect that person's right to due process. In the case of ex parte orders, notice and opportunity to be heard must be provided within the time required by State, tribal, or territorial law, and in any event within a reasonable time after the order is issued, sufficient to protect the respondent's due process rights.

(c) Cross or Counter Petition.—A protection order issued by a State, tribal, or territorial court against one who has petitioned, filed a complaint, or otherwise filed a written pleading for protection against abuse by a spouse or intimate partner is not entitled to full faith and credit if—

(1) no cross or counter petition, complaint, or other written pleading was filed seeking such a protection order; or

(2) a cross or counter petition has been filed and the court did not make specific findings that each party was entitled to such an order.

(d) Notification and Registration.—

(1) Notification.—A State, Indian tribe, or territory according full faith and credit to an order by a court of another State, Indian tribe, or territory shall not notify or require notification of the party against whom a protection order has been issued that the protection order has been registered or filed in that enforcing State, tribal, or territorial jurisdiction unless requested to do so by the party protected under such order.

(2) No prior registration or filing as prerequisite for enforcement.—Any protection order that is otherwise consistent with this section shall be accorded full faith and credit, notwithstanding failure to comply with any requirement that the order be registered or filed in the enforcing State, tribal, or territorial jurisdiction.

(3) Limits on internet publication of registration information.—A State, Indian tribe, or territory shall not make available publicly on the Internet any information regarding the registration, filing of a petition for, or issuance of a protection order, restraining order or injunction, restraining order, or injunction in either the issuing or enforcing State, tribal or territorial jurisdiction, if such publication would be likely to publicly reveal the identity or location of the party protected under such order. A State, Indian tribe, or territory may share court-generated and law enforcement-generated information contained in secure, governmental registries for protection order enforcement purposes.

(e) Tribal Court Jurisdiction.—For purposes of this section, a court of an Indian tribe shall have full civil jurisdiction to issue and enforce protection orders involving any person, including the authority to enforce any orders through civil contempt proceedings, to exclude violators from Indian land, and to use other appropriate mechanisms, in matters arising anywhere in the Indian country of the Indian tribe (as defined in section 1151) or otherwise within the authority of the Indian tribe.

(Added Pub. L. 103–322, title IV, §40221(a), Sept. 13, 1994, 108 Stat. 1930; amended Pub. L. 106–386, div. B, title I, §1101(b)(4), Oct. 28, 2000, 114 Stat. 1493; Pub. L. 109–162, title I, §106(a)–(c), Jan. 5, 2006, 119 Stat. 2981, 2982; Pub. L. 109–271, §2(n), Aug. 12, 2006, 120 Stat. 754; Pub. L. 113–4, title IX, §905, Mar. 7, 2013, 127 Stat. 124.)

Amendments

2013—Subsec. (e). Pub. L. 113–4 added subsec. (e) and struck out former subsec. (e). Prior to amendment, text read as follows: "For purposes of this section, a tribal court shall have full civil jurisdiction to enforce protection orders, including authority to enforce any orders through civil contempt proceedings, exclusion of violators from Indian lands, and other appropriate mechanisms, in matters arising within the authority of the tribe."

2006—Subsec. (a). Pub. L. 109–162, §106(a)(1), (b), substituted ", Indian tribe, or territory" for "or Indian tribe" wherever appearing and "and enforced by the court and law enforcement personnel of the other State, Indian tribal government or Territory as if it were" for "and enforced as if it were".

Subsec. (b). Pub. L. 109–162, §106(a)(2), substituted "State, tribal, or territorial" for "State or tribal" in introductory provisions.

Subsec. (b)(1). Pub. L. 109–162, §106(a)(1), substituted ", Indian tribe, or territory" for "or Indian tribe".

Subsec. (b)(2). Pub. L. 109–162, §106(a)(2), substituted "State, tribal, or territorial" for "State or tribal".

Subsec. (c). Pub. L. 109–162, §106(a)(2), substituted "State, tribal, or territorial" for "State or tribal" in introductory provisions.

Subsec. (d)(1). Pub. L. 109–162, §106(a), substituted ", Indian tribe, or territory" for "or Indian tribe" in two places and "State, tribal, or territorial" for "State or tribal".

Subsec. (d)(2). Pub. L. 109–162, §106(a)(2), substituted "State, tribal, or territorial" for "State or tribal".

Subsec. (d)(3). Pub. L. 109–271, which directed amendment of section 106(c) of Pub. L. 109–162 by substituting "the registration, filing of a petition for, or issuance of a protection order, restraining order or injunction" for "the registration or filing of a protection order", was executed by making the substitution in par. (3), which was added by section 106(c) of Pub. L. 109–162, to reflect the probable intent of Congress.

Pub. L. 109–162, §106(c), added par. (3).

2000—Subsecs. (d), (e). Pub. L. 106–386 added subsecs. (d) and (e).

Special Rule for the State of Alaska

Pub. L. 113–4, title IX, §910, Mar. 7, 2013, 127 Stat. 126, which provided that, in the State of Alaska, the amendments made by sections 904 and 905 of Pub. L. 113–4, which related to tribal jurisdiction over crimes of domestic violence and over issuance of protection orders, applied only to the Indian country of the Metlakatla Indian Community, Annette Island Reserve, was repealed by Pub. L. 113–275, Dec. 18, 2014, 128 Stat. 2988.

§2265A. Repeat offenders

(a) Maximum Term of Imprisonment.—The maximum term of imprisonment for a violation of this chapter after a prior domestic violence or stalking offense shall be twice the term otherwise provided under this chapter.

(b) Definition.—For purposes of this section—

(1) the term "prior domestic violence or stalking offense" means a conviction for an offense—

(A) under section 2261, 2261A, or 2262 of this chapter; or

(B) under State or tribal law for an offense consisting of conduct that would have been an offense under a section referred to in subparagraph (A) if the conduct had occurred within the special maritime and territorial jurisdiction of the United States, or in interstate or foreign commerce; and

(2) the term "State" means a State of the United States, the District of Columbia, or any commonwealth, territory, or possession of the United States.

(Added Pub. L. 109–162, title I, §115, Jan. 5, 2006, 119 Stat. 2988; amended Pub. L. 113–4, title IX, §906(c), Mar. 7, 2013, 127 Stat. 125.)

Amendments

2013—Subsec. (b)(1)(B). Pub. L. 113–4 inserted "or tribal" after "State".

§2266. Definitions

In this chapter:

(1) Bodily injury.—The term "bodily injury" means any act, except one done in self-defense, that results in physical injury or sexual abuse.

(2) Course of conduct.—The term "course of conduct" means a pattern of conduct composed of 2 or more acts, evidencing a continuity of purpose.

(3) Enter or leave indian country.—The term "enter or leave Indian country" includes leaving the jurisdiction of 1 tribal government and entering the jurisdiction of another tribal government.

(4) Indian country.—The term "Indian country" has the meaning stated in section 1151 of this title.

(5) Protection order.—The term "protection order" includes—

(A) any injunction, restraining order, or any other order issued by a civil or criminal court for the purpose of preventing violent or threatening acts or harassment against, sexual violence, or contact or communication with or physical proximity to, another person, including any temporary or final order issued by a civil or criminal court whether obtained by filing an independent action or as a pendente lite order in another proceeding so long as any civil or criminal order was issued in response to a complaint, petition, or motion filed by or on behalf of a person seeking protection; and

(B) any support, child custody or visitation provisions, orders, remedies or relief issued as part of a protection order, restraining order, or injunction pursuant to State, tribal, territorial, or local law authorizing the issuance of protection orders, restraining orders, or injunctions for the protection of victims of domestic violence, sexual assault, dating violence, or stalking.

(6) Serious bodily injury.—The term "serious bodily injury" has the meaning stated in section 2119(2).

(7) Spouse or intimate partner.—The term "spouse or intimate partner" includes—

(A) for purposes of—

(i) sections other than 2261A—

(I) a spouse or former spouse of the abuser, a person who shares a child in common with the abuser, and a person who cohabits or has cohabited as a spouse with the abuser; or

(II) a person who is or has been in a social relationship of a romantic or intimate nature with the abuser, as determined by the length of the relationship, the type of relationship, and the frequency of interaction between the persons involved in the relationship; and

(ii) section 2261A—

(I) a spouse or former spouse of the target of the stalking, a person who shares a child in common with the target of the stalking, and a person who cohabits or has cohabited as a spouse with the target of the stalking; or

(II) a person who is or has been in a social relationship of a romantic or intimate nature with the target of the stalking, as determined by the length of the relationship, the type of the relationship, and the frequency of interaction between the persons involved in the relationship.1

(B) any other person similarly situated to a spouse who is protected by the domestic or family violence laws of the State or tribal jurisdiction in which the injury occurred or where the victim resides.

(8) State.—The term "State" includes a State of the United States, the District of Columbia, and a commonwealth, territory, or possession of the United States.

(9) Travel in interstate or foreign commerce.—The term "travel in interstate or foreign commerce" does not include travel from 1 State to another by an individual who is a member of an Indian tribe and who remains at all times in the territory of the Indian tribe of which the individual is a member.

(10) Dating partner.—The term "dating partner" refers to a person who is or has been in a social relationship of a romantic or intimate nature with the abuser. The existence of such a relationship is based on a consideration of—

(A) the length of the relationship; and

(B) the type of relationship; and

(C) the frequency of interaction between the persons involved in the relationship.

(Added Pub. L. 103–322, title IV, §40221(a), Sept. 13, 1994, 108 Stat. 1931; amended Pub. L. 106–386, div. B, title I, §1107(d), Oct. 28, 2000, 114 Stat. 1499; Pub. L. 109–162, title I, §§106(d), 116(b), Jan. 5, 2006, 119 Stat. 2982, 2988; Pub. L. 109–271, §2(c), (i), Aug. 12, 2006, 120 Stat. 752.)

Amendments

2006—Par. (5). Pub. L. 109–162, §106(d)(1), added par. (5) and struck out heading and text of former par. (5). Text read as follows: "The term 'protection order' includes any injunction or other order issued for the purpose of preventing violent or threatening acts or harassment against, or contact or communication with or physical proximity to, another person, including any temporary or final order issued by a civil and criminal court (other than a support or child custody order issued pursuant to State divorce and child custody laws, except to the extent that such an order is entitled to full faith and credit under other Federal law) whether obtained by filing an independent action or as a pendente lite order in another proceeding so long as any civil order was issued in response to a complaint, petition, or motion filed by or on behalf of a person seeking protection."

Par. (7)(A). Pub. L. 109–162, §106(d)(2), which directed amendment of cls. (i) and (ii) by substituting "2261A—

"(I) a spouse or former spouse of the abuser, a person who shares a child in common with the abuser, and a person who cohabits or has cohabited as a spouse with the abuser; or

"(II) a person who is or has been in a social relationship of a romantic or intimate nature with the abuser, as determined by the length of the relationship, the type of relationship, and the frequency of interaction between the persons involved in the relationship"

for "2261A, a spouse or former spouse of the abuser, a person who shares a child in common with the abuser, and a person who cohabits or has cohabited as a spouse with the abuser", was executed only to cl. (i) to reflect the probable intent of Congress because the quoted language to be deleted does not appear in cl. (ii).

Par. (7)(A)(ii). Pub. L. 109–271, §2(c), added cl. (ii) and struck out former cl. (ii) which read as follows: "section 2261A, a spouse or former spouse of the target of the stalking, a person who shares a child in common with the target of the stalking, and a person who cohabits or has cohabited as a spouse with the target of the stalking; and".

Par. (10). Pub. L. 109–271, §2(i), substituted ". The existence of such a relationship is" for "and the existence of such a relationship" in introductory provisions.

Pub. L. 109–162, §116(b), added par. (10).

2000—Pub. L. 106–386 reenacted section catchline without change and amended text generally. Prior to amendment, text defined "bodily injury", "Indian country", "protection order", "spouse or intimate partner", "State", and "travel across State lines".

CHAPTER 111 - SHIPPING

Amendments

2015—Pub. L. 114–23, title VIII, §§802(b), 804(b), June 2, 2015, 129 Stat. 307, 308, added items 2280a and 2281a.

2008—Pub. L. 110–407, title I, §102(b), Oct. 13, 2008, 122 Stat. 4298, added item 2285.

2006—Pub. L. 109–177, title III, §§304(b)(2), 305(b), Mar. 9, 2006, 120 Stat. 235, 237, added items 2282B, 2283, and 2284.

Pub. L. 109–177, title III, §304(a)(2), Mar. 9, 2006, 120 Stat. 235, which directed amendment of table of sections for this chapter by adding item 2282A after item 2282, was executed by adding item 2282A after item 2281 to reflect the probable intent of Congress, because there is no item 2282.

1994—Pub. L. 103–322, title VI, §60019(b), Sept. 13, 1994, 108 Stat. 1979, added items 2280 and 2281.

1990—Pub. L. 101–647, title XXXV, §3566, Nov. 29, 1990, 104 Stat. 4928, substituted "vessels" for "vessel" in item 2271.

§2271. Conspiracy to destroy vessels

Whoever, on the high seas, or within the United States, willfully and corruptly conspires, combines, and confederates with any other person, such other person being either within or without the United States, to cast away or otherwise destroy any vessel, with intent to injure any person that may have underwritten or may thereafter underwrite any policy of insurance thereon or on goods on board thereof, or with intent to injure any person that has lent or advanced, or may lend or advance, any money on such vessel on bottomry or respondentia; or

Whoever, within the United States, builds, or fits out any vessel to be cast away or destroyed, with like intent—

Shall be fined under this title or imprisoned not more than ten years, or both.

(June 25, 1948, ch. 645, 62 Stat. 803; Pub. L. 103–322, title XXXIII, §330016(1)(L), Sept. 13, 1994, 108 Stat. 2147.)

Historical and Revision Notes

Based on title 18, U.S.C., 1940 ed., §487 (Mar. 4, 1909, ch. 321, §296, 35 Stat. 1146).

Mandatory punishment provision was rephrased in the alternative.

Reference to a person who "aids in building or fitting out any vessel" was omitted as unnecessary in view of section 2 making all aiders guilty as principal.

Changes in phraseology were made.

Amendments

1994—Pub. L. 103–322 substituted "fined under this title" for "fined not more than $10,000" in last par.

§2272. Destruction of vessel by owner

Whoever, upon the high seas or on any other waters within the admiralty and maritime jurisdiction of the United States, willfully and corruptly casts away or otherwise destroys any vessel of which he is owner, in whole or in part, with intent to injure any person that may underwrite any policy of insurance thereon, or any merchant that may have goods thereon, or any other owner of such vessel, shall be imprisoned for life or for any term of years.

(June 25, 1948, ch. 645, 62 Stat. 803.)

Historical and Revision Notes

Based on title 18, U.S.C., 1940 ed., §491 (Mar. 4, 1909, ch. 321, §300, 35 Stat. 1147).

§2273. Destruction of vessel by nonowner

Whoever, not being an owner, upon the high seas or on any other waters within the admiralty and maritime jurisdiction of the United States, willfully and corruptly casts away or otherwise destroys any vessel of the United States to which he belongs, or willfully attempts the destruction thereof, shall be imprisoned not more than ten years.
(June 25, 1948, ch. 645, 62 Stat. 804.)

Historical and Revision Notes

Based on title 18, U.S.C., 1940 ed., §492 (Mar. 4, 1909, ch. 321, §301, 35 Stat. 1147).
Words "with intent to destroy the same, sets fire to any such vessel, or otherwise" following "willfully" and preceding "attempts" were omitted as surplusage.

§2274. Destruction or misuse of vessel by person in charge

Whoever, being the owner, master or person in charge or command of any private vessel, foreign or domestic, or a member of the crew or other person, within the territorial waters of the United States, willfully causes or permits the destruction or injury of such vessel or knowingly permits said vessel to be used as a place of resort for any person conspiring with another or preparing to commit any offense against the United States, or any offense in violation of the treaties of the United States or of the obligations of the United States under the law of nations, or to defraud the United States; or knowingly permits such vessels to be used in violation of the rights and obligations of the United States under the law of nations, shall be fined under this title or imprisoned not more than ten years, or both.

In case such vessels are so used, with the knowledge of the owner or master or other person in charge or command thereof, the vessel, together with her tackle, apparel, furniture, and equipment, shall be subject to seizure and forfeiture to the United States in the same manner as merchandise is forfeited for violation of the customs revenue laws.
(June 25, 1948, ch. 645, 62 Stat. 804; Pub. L. 103–322, title XXXIII, §330016(1)(L), Sept. 13, 1994, 108 Stat. 2147.)

Historical and Revision Notes

Based on section 193 of title 50, U.S.C., 1940 ed., War and National Defense (June 15, 1917, ch. 30, title II, §3, 40 Stat. 220; Mar. 28, 1940, ch. 72, §3(b), 54 Stat. 79).
Mandatory punishment provision was rephrased in the alternative.
Minor changes were made in phraseology.

Amendments

1994—Pub. L. 103–322 substituted "fined under this title" for "fined not more than $10,000" in first par.

§2275. Firing or tampering with vessels

Whoever sets fire to any vessel of foreign registry, or any vessel of American registry entitled to engage in commerce with foreign nations, or to any vessel of the United States, or to the cargo of the same, or tampers with the motive power of instrumentalities of navigation of such vessel, or places bombs or explosives in or upon such vessel, or does any other act to or upon such vessel while within the jurisdiction of the United States, or, if such vessel is of American registry, while she is on the high sea, with intent to injure or endanger the safety of the vessel or of her cargo, or of persons on board, whether the injury or danger is so intended to take place within the jurisdiction of the United States, or after the vessel shall have departed therefrom and whoever attempts to do so shall be fined under this title or imprisoned not more than twenty years, or both.

(June 25, 1948, ch. 645, 62 Stat. 804; Pub. L. 103–322, title XXXIII, §330016(1)(L), Sept. 13, 1994, 108 Stat. 2147.)

Historical and Revision Notes

Based on title 18, U.S.C., 1940 ed., §502 (June 15, 1917, ch. 30, title III, §1, 40 Stat. 221).
Words "as defined in section 501 of this title," were omitted in view of section 9 of this title, defining vessel of the United States.
Last sentence of said section 502, defining "United States", was incorporated in section 5 of this title.
Provision prohibiting conspiracy was deleted as adequately covered by the general conspiracy statute, section 371 of this title.
Minor changes were made in phraseology.

Amendments

1994—Pub. L. 103–322 substituted "fined under this title" for "fined not more than $10,000".

§2276. Breaking and entering vessel

Whoever, upon the high seas or on any other waters within the admiralty and maritime jurisdiction of the United States, and out of the jurisdiction of any particular State, breaks or enters any vessel with intent to commit any felony, or maliciously cuts, spoils, or destroys any cordage, cable, buoys, buoy rope, head fast, or other fast, fixed to the anchor or moorings belonging to any vessel, shall be fined under this title or imprisoned not more than five years, or both.
(June 25, 1948, ch. 645, 62 Stat. 804; Pub. L. 103–322, title XXXIII, §330016(1)(H), Sept. 13, 1994, 108 Stat. 2147.)

Historical and Revision Notes

Based on title 18, U.S.C., 1940 ed., §490 (Mar. 4, 1909, ch. 321, §299, 35 Stat. 1147).
Mandatory punishment provision was rephrased in the alternative.

Amendments

1994—Pub. L. 103–322 substituted "fined under this title" for "fined not more than $1,000".

§2277. Explosives or dangerous weapons aboard vessels

(a) Whoever brings, carries, or possesses any dangerous weapon, instrument, or device, or any dynamite, nitroglycerin, or other explosive article or compound on board of any vessel documented under the laws of the United States, or any vessel purchased, requisitioned, chartered, or taken over by the United States pursuant to the provisions of Act June 6, 1941, ch. 174, 55 Stat. 242, as amended, without previously obtaining the permission of the owner or the master of such vessel; or

Whoever brings, carries, or possesses any such weapon or explosive on board of any vessel in the possession and under the control of the United States or which has been seized and forfeited by the United States or upon which a guard has been placed by the United States pursuant to the provisions of section 191 of Title 50, without previously obtaining the permission of the captain of the port in which such vessel is located, shall be fined under this title or imprisoned not more than one year, or both.

(b) This section shall not apply to the personnel of the Armed Forces of the United States or to officers or employees of the United States or of a State or of a political subdivision thereof, while acting in the performance of their duties, who are authorized by law or by rules or regulations to own or possess any such weapon or explosive.
(June 25, 1948, ch. 645, 62 Stat. 804; Pub. L. 103–322, title XXXIII, §330016(1)(H), Sept. 13, 1994, 108 Stat. 2147; Pub. L. 109–304, §17(d)(6), Oct. 6, 2006, 120 Stat. 1707.)

Historical and Revision Notes
Based on title 18, U.S.C., 1940 ed., §§503, 504 (Dec. 31, 1941, ch. 642, §§1, 2, 55 Stat. 876).
Section consolidates sections 503 and 504 of title 18, U.S.C., 1940 ed.
Words "This section" were substituted in subsection (b) for the words "The provisions of sections 503, 504 of this title".
Minor changes were made in phraseology.

References in Text
Act June 6, 1941, ch. 174, 55 Stat. 242, as amended, referred to in subsec. (a), expired July 1, 1953. For provisions covering the subject matter of that Act, see sections 196 to 198 of Title 50, War and National Defense.

Amendments
2006—Subsec. (a). Pub. L. 109–304 substituted "documented" for "registered, enrolled, or licensed".
1994—Subsec. (a). Pub. L. 103–322 substituted "fined under this title" for "fined not more than $1,000" in second par.

§2278. Explosives on vessels carrying steerage passengers
Whoever, being the master of a steamship or other vessel referred to in section 151 of Title 46, except as otherwise expressly provided by law, takes, carries, or has on board of any such vessel any nitroglycerin, dynamite, or any other explosive article or compound, or any vitriol or like acids, or gunpowder, except for the ship's use, or any article or number of articles, whether as a cargo or ballast, which, by reason of the nature or quantity or mode of storage thereof, shall, either singly or collectively, be likely to endanger the health or lives of the passengers or the safety of the vessel, shall be fined under this title or imprisoned not more than one year, or both.
(June 25, 1948, ch. 645, 62 Stat. 805; Pub. L. 103–322, title XXXIII, §330016(1)(H), Sept. 13, 1994, 108 Stat. 2147.)

Historical and Revision Notes
Based on section 171 of title 46, U.S.C., 1940 ed., Shipping (Aug. 2, 1882, ch. 374, §8, 22 Stat. 189).
Words "except as otherwise expressly provided by law" were inserted to remove obvious inconsistency between sections 831–835 of this title, section 170 of title 46, U.S.C., 1940 ed., Shipping, and this section.
Words "shall be deemed guilty of a misdemeanor and" were omitted because designation of the offense as a misdemeanor is unnecessary in view of definitive section 1 of this title.
Mandatory punishment provision was rephrased in the alternative.
Minor changes were made in phraseology.

References in Text
Section 151 of Title 46, referred to in text, which was based on section 1 of act Aug. 2, 1882, ch. 374, 22 Stat. 186, as amended, was repealed by Pub. L. 98–89, Aug. 26, 1983, §4(b), 97 Stat. 599.

Amendments
1994—Pub. L. 103–322 substituted "fined under this title" for "fined not more than $1,000".

§2279. Boarding vessels before arrival
Whoever, not being in the United States service, and not being duly authorized by law for the purpose, goes on board any vessel about to arrive at the place of her destination, before her actual

arrival, and before she has been completely moored, shall be fined under this title or imprisoned not more than six months, or both.

The master of such vessel may take any such person into custody, and deliver him up forthwith to any law enforcement officer, to be by him taken before any committing magistrate, to be dealt with according to law.

(June 25, 1948, ch. 645, 62 Stat. 805; Pub. L. 103–322, title XXXIII, §330016(1)(D), Sept. 13, 1994, 108 Stat. 2146.)

Historical and Revision Notes

Based on section 708 of title 46, U.S.C., 1940 ed., Shipping (R.S. §4606).

"Law enforcement officer" was substituted for "constable or police officer" and "committing magistrate" for "justice of the peace." The phraseology used in the statute was archaic. It originated when the government had few law enforcement officers and magistrates of its own. References to specific sections were made to read: "according to law" to achieve brevity. Mandatory punishment provision was rephrased in the alternative.

The words "without permission of the master" were deleted to remove an inconsistency with the provisions of section 163 of title 46, U.S.C., 1940 ed., and customs regulations. Customs regulations, 1943, section 4.1c, prohibit any person "with or without consent of the master" from boarding vessel, with specific enumerated exceptions. Said section 163 prescribes a "penalty of not more than $100 or imprisonment not to exceed six months, or both" for violating regulations. The revised section increases the fine from $100 to $200 for boarding the vessel "with the consent of the master."

Minor changes were made in phraseology.

Amendments

1994—Pub. L. 103–322 substituted "fined under this title" for "fined not more than $200" in first par.

§2280. Violence against maritime navigation

(a) Offenses.—

(1) In general.—A person who unlawfully and intentionally—

(A) seizes or exercises control over a ship by force or threat thereof or any other form of intimidation;

(B) performs an act of violence against a person on board a ship if that act is likely to endanger the safe navigation of that ship;

(C) destroys a ship or causes damage to a ship or to its cargo which is likely to endanger the safe navigation of that ship;

(D) places or causes to be placed on a ship, by any means whatsoever, a device or substance which is likely to destroy that ship, or cause damage to that ship or its cargo which endangers or is likely to endanger the safe navigation of that ship;

(E) destroys or seriously damages maritime navigational facilities or seriously interferes with their operation, if such act is likely to endanger the safe navigation of a ship;

(F) communicates information, knowing the information to be false and under circumstances in which such information may reasonably be believed, thereby endangering the safe navigation of a ship;

(G) injures or kills any person in connection with the commission or the attempted commission of any of the offenses set forth in subparagraphs (A) through (F); or

(H) attempts or conspires to do any act prohibited under subparagraphs (A) through (G), shall be fined under this title, imprisoned not more than 20 years, or both; and if the death of any person results from conduct prohibited by this paragraph, shall be punished by death or imprisoned for any term of years or for life.

(2) Threat to navigation.—A person who threatens to do any act prohibited under paragraph

(1)(B), (C) or (E), with apparent determination and will to carry the threat into execution, if the threatened act is likely to endanger the safe navigation of the ship in question, shall be fined under this title, imprisoned not more than 5 years, or both.

(b) Jurisdiction.—There is jurisdiction over the activity prohibited in subsection (a)—

(1) in the case of a covered ship, if—

(A) such activity is committed—

(i) against or on board a vessel of the United States or a vessel subject to the jurisdiction of the United States (as defined in section 70502 of title 46) at the time the prohibited activity is committed;

(ii) in the United States, including the territorial seas; or

(iii) by a national of the United States, by a United States corporation or legal entity, or by a stateless person whose habitual residence is in the United States;

(B) during the commission of such activity, a national of the United States is seized, threatened, injured or killed; or

(C) the offender is later found in the United States after such activity is committed;

(2) in the case of a ship navigating or scheduled to navigate solely within the territorial sea or internal waters of a country other than the United States, if the offender is later found in the United States after such activity is committed; and

(3) in the case of any vessel, if such activity is committed in an attempt to compel the United States to do or abstain from doing any act.

(c) Bar To Prosecution.—It is a bar to Federal prosecution under subsection (a) for conduct that occurred within the United States that the conduct involved was during or in relation to a labor dispute, and such conduct is prohibited as a felony under the law of the State in which it was committed. For purposes of this section, the term "labor dispute" has the meaning set forth in section 13(c) of the Norris-LaGuardia Act, as amended (29 U.S.C. 113(c)).

(d) Definitions.—As used in this section, section 2280a, section 2281, and section 2281a, the term—

(1) "applicable treaty" means—

(A) the Convention for the Suppression of Unlawful Seizure of Aircraft, done at The Hague on 16 December 1970;

(B) the Convention for the Suppression of Unlawful Acts against the Safety of Civil Aviation, done at Montreal on 23 September 1971;

(C) the Convention on the Prevention and Punishment of Crimes against Internationally Protected Persons, including Diplomatic Agents, adopted by the General Assembly of the United Nations on 14 December 1973;

(D) International Convention against the Taking of Hostages, adopted by the General Assembly of the United Nations on 17 December 1979;

(E) the Convention on the Physical Protection of Nuclear Material, done at Vienna on 26 October 1979;

(F) the Protocol for the Suppression of Unlawful Acts of Violence at Airports Serving International Civil Aviation, supplementary to the Convention for the Suppression of Unlawful Acts against the Safety of Civil Aviation, done at Montreal on 24 February 1988;

(G) the Protocol for the Suppression of Unlawful Acts against the Safety of Fixed Platforms Located on the Continental Shelf, done at Rome on 10 March 1988;

(H) International Convention for the Suppression of Terrorist Bombings, adopted by the General Assembly of the United Nations on 15 December 1997; and

(I) International Convention for the Suppression of the Financing of Terrorism, adopted by the General Assembly of the United Nations on 9 December 1999;

(2) "armed conflict" does not include internal disturbances and tensions, such as riots, isolated and sporadic acts of violence, and other acts of a similar nature;

(3) "biological weapon" means—

(A) microbial or other biological agents, or toxins whatever their origin or method of production, of types and in quantities that have no justification for prophylactic, protective, or other peaceful purposes; or

(B) weapons, equipment, or means of delivery designed to use such agents or toxins for hostile purposes or in armed conflict;

(4) "chemical weapon" means, together or separately—

(A) toxic chemicals and their precursors, except where intended for—

(i) industrial, agricultural, research, medical, pharmaceutical, or other peaceful purposes;

(ii) protective purposes, namely those purposes directly related to protection against toxic chemicals and to protection against chemical weapons;

(iii) military purposes not connected with the use of chemical weapons and not dependent on the use of the toxic properties of chemicals as a method of warfare; or

(iv) law enforcement including domestic riot control purposes,

as long as the types and quantities are consistent with such purposes;

(B) munitions and devices, specifically designed to cause death or other harm through the toxic properties of those toxic chemicals specified in subparagraph (A), which would be released as a result of the employment of such munitions and devices; and

(C) any equipment specifically designed for use directly in connection with the employment of munitions and devices specified in subparagraph (B);

(5) "covered ship" means a ship that is navigating or is scheduled to navigate into, through or from waters beyond the outer limit of the territorial sea of a single country or a lateral limit of that country's territorial sea with an adjacent country;

(6) "explosive material" has the meaning given the term in section 841(c) and includes explosive as defined in section 844(j) of this title;

(7) "infrastructure facility" has the meaning given the term in section 2332f(e)(5) of this title;

(8) "international organization" has the meaning given the term in section 831(f)(3) 1 of this title;

(9) "military forces of a state" means the armed forces of a state which are organized, trained, and equipped under its internal law for the primary purpose of national defense or security, and persons acting in support of those armed forces who are under their formal command, control, and responsibility;

(10) "national of the United States" has the meaning stated in section 101(a)(22) of the Immigration and Nationality Act (8 U.S.C. 1101(a)(22));

(11) "Non-Proliferation Treaty" means the Treaty on the Non-Proliferation of Nuclear Weapons, done at Washington, London, and Moscow on 1 July 1968;

(12) "Non-Proliferation Treaty State Party" means any State Party to the Non-Proliferation Treaty, to include Taiwan, which shall be considered to have the obligations under the Non-Proliferation Treaty of a party to that treaty other than a Nuclear Weapon State Party to the Non-Proliferation Treaty;

(13) "Nuclear Weapon State Party to the Non-Proliferation Treaty" means a State Party to the Non-Proliferation Treaty that is a nuclear-weapon State, as that term is defined in Article IX(3) of the Non-Proliferation Treaty;

(14) "place of public use" has the meaning given the term in section 2332f(e)(6) of this title;

(15) "precursor" has the meaning given the term in section 229F(6)(A) of this title;

(16) "public transport system" has the meaning given the term in section 2332f(e)(7) of this title;

(17) "serious injury or damage" means—

(A) serious bodily injury,

(B) extensive destruction of a place of public use, State or government facility, infrastructure facility, or public transportation system, resulting in major economic loss, or

(C) substantial damage to the environment, including air, soil, water, fauna, or flora;

(18) "ship" means a vessel of any type whatsoever not permanently attached to the sea-bed, including dynamically supported craft, submersibles, or any other floating craft, but does not include a warship, a ship owned or operated by a government when being used as a naval auxiliary or for customs or police purposes, or a ship which has been withdrawn from navigation or laid up;

(19) "source material" has the meaning given that term in the International Atomic Energy Agency Statute, done at New York on 26 October 1956;

(20) "special fissionable material" has the meaning given that term in the International Atomic Energy Agency Statute, done at New York on 26 October 1956;

(21) "territorial sea of the United States" means all waters extending seaward to 12 nautical miles from the baselines of the United States determined in accordance with international law;

(22) "toxic chemical" has the meaning given the term in section 229F(8)(A) of this title;

(23) "transport" means to initiate, arrange or exercise effective control, including decisionmaking authority, over the movement of a person or item; and

(24) "United States", when used in a geographical sense, includes the Commonwealth of Puerto Rico, the Commonwealth of the Northern Mariana Islands, and all territories and possessions of the United States.

(e) Exceptions.—This section shall not apply to—

(1) the activities of armed forces during an armed conflict, as those terms are understood under the law of war, which are governed by that law; or

(2) activities undertaken by military forces of a state in the exercise of their official duties.

(f) Delivery of Suspected Offender.—The master of a covered ship flying the flag of the United States who has reasonable grounds to believe that there is on board that ship any person who has committed an offense under section 2280 or section 2280a may deliver such person to the authorities of a country that is a party to the Convention for the Suppression of Unlawful Acts against the Safety of Maritime Navigation. Before delivering such person to the authorities of another country, the master shall notify in an appropriate manner the Attorney General of the United States of the alleged offense and await instructions from the Attorney General as to what action to take. When delivering the person to a country which is a state party to the Convention, the master shall, whenever practicable, and if possible before entering the territorial sea of such country, notify the authorities of such country of the master's intention to deliver such person and the reasons therefor. If the master delivers such person, the master shall furnish to the authorities of such country the evidence in the master's possession that pertains to the alleged offense.

(g)(1) Civil Forfeiture.—Any real or personal property used or intended to be used to commit or to facilitate the commission of a violation of this section, the gross proceeds of such violation, and any real or personal property traceable to such property or proceeds, shall be subject to forfeiture.

(2) Applicable Procedures.—Seizures and forfeitures under this section shall be governed by the provisions of chapter 46 of title 18, United States Code, relating to civil forfeitures, except that such duties as are imposed upon the Secretary of the Treasury under the customs laws described in section 981(d) shall be performed by such officers, agents, and other persons as may be designated for that purpose by the Secretary of Homeland Security, the Attorney General, or the Secretary of Defense.

(Added Pub. L. 103–322, title VI, §60019(a), Sept. 13, 1994, 108 Stat. 1975; amended Pub. L. 104–132, title VII, §§722, 723(a)(1), Apr. 24, 1996, 110 Stat. 1299, 1300; Pub. L. 114–23, title VIII, §801, June 2, 2015, 129 Stat. 300.)

References in Text

Section 831(f)(3) of this title, referred to in subsec. (d)(8), was redesignated section 831(g)(3) by Pub. L. 114–23, title VIII, §812(d), June 2, 2015, 129 Stat. 312.

Amendments

2015—Subsec. (b)(1)(A)(i). Pub. L. 114–23, §801(1)(A), substituted "a vessel of the United States or a vessel subject to the jurisdiction of the United States (as defined in section 70502 of title 46)" for "a ship flying the flag of the United States".

Subsec. (b)(1)(A)(ii). Pub. L. 114–23, §801(1)(B), inserted ", including the territorial seas" before semicolon.

Subsec. (b)(1)(A)(iii). Pub. L. 114–23, §801(1)(C), inserted ", by a United States corporation or legal entity," after "by a national of the United States".

Subsec. (c). Pub. L. 114–23, §801(2), substituted "section 13(c)" for "section 2(c)".

Subsecs. (d) to (g). Pub. L. 114–23, §801(3)–(5), added subsecs. (d) to (g) and struck out former subsecs. (d) and (e) which related to delivery of suspected offender and definitions, respectively.

1996—Subsec. (a)(1)(H). Pub. L. 104–132, §723(a)(1), inserted "or conspires" after "attempts".

Subsec. (b)(1)(A)(ii). Pub. L. 104–132, §722(1), struck out "and the activity is not prohibited as a crime by the State in which the activity takes place" after "the United States".

Subsec. (b)(1)(A)(iii). Pub. L. 104–132, §722(2), struck out "the activity takes place on a ship flying the flag of a foreign country or outside the United States," before "by a national of the United States".

Effective Date

Pub. L. 103–322, title VI, §60019(c), Sept. 13, 1994, 108 Stat. 1979, provided that: "This section [enacting this section and section 2281 of this title] and the amendments made by this section shall take effect on the later of—

"(1) the date of the enactment of this Act [Sept. 13, 1994]; or

"(2)(A) in the case of section 2280 of title 18, United States Code, the date the Convention for the Suppression of Unlawful Acts Against the Safety of Maritime Navigation has come into force and the United States has become a party to that Convention; and

"(B) in the case of section 2281 of title 18, United States Code, the date the Protocol for the Suppression of Unlawful Acts Against the Safety of Fixed Platforms Located on the Continental Shelf has come into force and the United States has become a party to that Protocol."

[Convention and Protocol came into force Mar. 1, 1992, and entered into force with respect to the United States Mar. 6, 1995, Treaty Doc. 101–1.]

Territorial Sea of United States

For extension of territorial sea of United States, see Proc. No. 5928, set out as a note under section 1331 of Title 43, Public Lands.

§2280a. Violence against maritime navigation and maritime transport involving weapons of mass destruction

(a) Offenses.—

(1) In general.—Subject to the exceptions in subsection (c), a person who unlawfully and intentionally—

(A) when the purpose of the act, by its nature or context, is to intimidate a population, or to compel a government or an international organization to do or to abstain from doing any act—

(i) uses against or on a ship or discharges from a ship any explosive or radioactive material, biological, chemical, or nuclear weapon or other nuclear explosive device in a manner that causes or is likely to cause death to any person or serious injury or damage;

(ii) discharges from a ship oil, liquefied natural gas, or another hazardous or noxious substance that is not covered by clause (i), in such quantity or concentration that causes or is likely to cause death to any person or serious injury or damage; or

(iii) uses a ship in a manner that causes death to any person or serious injury or damage;

(B) transports on board a ship—

(i) any explosive or radioactive material, knowing that it is intended to be used to cause, or in a threat to cause, death to any person or serious injury or damage for the purpose of intimidating a population, or compelling a government or an international organization to do or to abstain from doing any act;

(ii) any biological, chemical, or nuclear weapon or other nuclear explosive device, knowing it to be a biological, chemical, or nuclear weapon or other nuclear explosive device;

(iii) any source material, special fissionable material, or equipment or material especially designed or prepared for the processing, use, or production of special fissionable material, knowing that it is intended to be used in a nuclear explosive activity or in any other nuclear activity not under safeguards pursuant to an International Atomic Energy Agency comprehensive safeguards agreement, except where—

(I) such item is transported to or from the territory of, or otherwise under the control of, a Non-Proliferation Treaty State Party; and

(II) the resulting transfer or receipt (including internal to a country) is not contrary to the obligations under the Non-Proliferation Treaty of the Non-Proliferation Treaty State Party from which, to the territory of which, or otherwise under the control of which such item is transferred;

(iv) any equipment, materials, or software or related technology that significantly contributes to the design or manufacture of a nuclear weapon or other nuclear explosive device, with the intention that it will be used for such purpose, except where—

(I) the country to the territory of which or under the control of which such item is transferred is a Nuclear Weapon State Party to the Non-Proliferation Treaty; and

(II) the resulting transfer or receipt (including internal to a country) is not contrary to the obligations under the Non-Proliferation Treaty of a Non-Proliferation Treaty State Party from which, to the territory of which, or otherwise under the control of which such item is transferred;

(v) any equipment, materials, or software or related technology that significantly contributes to the delivery of a nuclear weapon or other nuclear explosive device, with the intention that it will be used for such purpose, except where—

(I) such item is transported to or from the territory of, or otherwise under the control of, a Non-Proliferation Treaty State Party; and

(II) such item is intended for the delivery system of a nuclear weapon or other nuclear explosive device of a Nuclear Weapon State Party to the Non-Proliferation Treaty; or

(vi) any equipment, materials, or software or related technology that significantly contributes to the design, manufacture, or delivery of a biological or chemical weapon, with the intention that it will be used for such purpose;

(C) transports another person on board a ship knowing that the person has committed an act that constitutes an offense under section 2280 or subparagraph (A), (B), (D), or (E) of this section 1 or an offense set forth in an applicable treaty, as specified in section 2280(d)(1), and intending to assist that person to evade criminal prosecution;

(D) injures or kills any person in connection with the commission or the attempted commission of any of the offenses set forth in subparagraphs (A) through (C), or subsection (a)(2), to the extent that the subsection (a)(2) offense pertains to subparagraph (A); or

(E) attempts to do any act prohibited under subparagraph (A), (B) or (D), or conspires to do any act prohibited by subparagraphs (A) through (E) or subsection (a)(2),

shall be fined under this title, imprisoned not more than 20 years, or both; and if the death of any person results from conduct prohibited by this paragraph, shall be imprisoned for any term of years or for life.

(2) Threats.—A person who threatens, with apparent determination and will to carry the threat into execution, to do any act prohibited under paragraph (1)(A) shall be fined under this title, imprisoned not more than 5 years, or both.

(b) Jurisdiction.—There is jurisdiction over the activity prohibited in subsection (a)—

(1) in the case of a covered ship, if—

(A) such activity is committed—

(i) against or on board a vessel of the United States or a vessel subject to the jurisdiction of the United States (as defined in section 70502 of title 46) at the time the prohibited activity is committed;

(ii) in the United States, including the territorial seas; or

(iii) by a national of the United States, by a United States corporation or legal entity, or by a stateless person whose habitual residence is in the United States;

(B) during the commission of such activity, a national of the United States is seized, threatened, injured, or killed; or

(C) the offender is later found in the United States after such activity is committed;

(2) in the case of a ship navigating or scheduled to navigate solely within the territorial sea or internal waters of a country other than the United States, if the offender is later found in the United

States after such activity is committed; or

(3) in the case of any vessel, if such activity is committed in an attempt to compel the United States to do or abstain from doing any act.

(c) Exceptions.—This section shall not apply to—

(1) the activities of armed forces during an armed conflict, as those terms are understood under the law of war, which are governed by that law; or

(2) activities undertaken by military forces of a state in the exercise of their official duties.

(d)(1) Civil Forfeiture.—Any real or personal property used or intended to be used to commit or to facilitate the commission of a violation of this section, the gross proceeds of such violation, and any real or personal property traceable to such property or proceeds, shall be subject to forfeiture.

(2) Applicable Procedures.—Seizures and forfeitures under this section shall be governed by the provisions of chapter 46 of title 18, United States Code, relating to civil forfeitures, except that such duties as are imposed upon the Secretary of the Treasury under the customs laws described in section 981(d) shall be performed by such officers, agents, and other persons as may be designated for that purpose by the Secretary of Homeland Security, the Attorney General, or the Secretary of Defense.

(Added Pub. L. 114–23, title VIII, §802(a), June 2, 2015, 129 Stat. 304.)

Definitions

For definitions of terms used in this section, see section 2280(d) of this title.

§2281. Violence against maritime fixed platforms

(a) Offenses.—

(1) In general.—A person who unlawfully and intentionally—

(A) seizes or exercises control over a fixed platform by force or threat thereof or any other form of intimidation;

(B) performs an act of violence against a person on board a fixed platform if that act is likely to endanger its safety;

(C) destroys a fixed platform or causes damage to it which is likely to endanger its safety;

(D) places or causes to be placed on a fixed platform, by any means whatsoever, a device or substance which is likely to destroy that fixed platform or likely to endanger its safety;

(E) injures or kills any person in connection with the commission or the attempted commission of any of the offenses set forth in subparagraphs (A) through (D); or

(F) attempts or conspires to do anything prohibited under subparagraphs (A) through (E),

shall be fined under this title, imprisoned not more than 20 years, or both; and if death results to any person from conduct prohibited by this paragraph, shall be punished by death or imprisoned for any term of years or for life.

(2) Threat to safety.—A person who threatens to do anything prohibited under paragraph (1)(B) or (C), with apparent determination and will to carry the threat into execution, if the threatened act is likely to endanger the safety of the fixed platform, shall be fined under this title, imprisoned not more than 5 years, or both.

(b) Jurisdiction.—There is jurisdiction over the activity prohibited in subsection (a) if—

(1) such activity is committed against or on board a fixed platform—

(A) that is located on the continental shelf of the United States;

(B) that is located on the continental shelf of another country, by a national of the United States or by a stateless person whose habitual residence is in the United States; or

(C) in an attempt to compel the United States to do or abstain from doing any act;

(2) during the commission of such activity against or on board a fixed platform located on a continental shelf, a national of the United States is seized, threatened, injured or killed; or

(3) such activity is committed against or on board a fixed platform located outside the United States and beyond the continental shelf of the United States and the offender is later found in the United States.

(c) Bar To Prosecution.—It is a bar to Federal prosecution under subsection (a) for conduct that occurred within the United States that the conduct involved was during or in relation to a labor dispute, and such conduct is prohibited as a felony under the law of the State in which it was committed. For purposes of this section, the term "labor dispute" has the meaning set forth in section 13(c) of the Norris-LaGuardia Act, as amended (29 U.S.C. 113(c)), and the term "State" means a State of the United States, the District of Columbia, and any commonwealth, territory, or possession of the United States.

(d) Definitions.—In this section—

"continental shelf" means the sea-bed and subsoil of the submarine areas that extend beyond a country's territorial sea to the limits provided by customary international law as reflected in Article 76 of the 1982 Convention on the Law of the Sea.

"fixed platform" means an artificial island, installation or structure permanently attached to the sea-bed for the purpose of exploration or exploitation of resources or for other economic purposes.

(e) Exceptions.—This section does not apply to—

(1) the activities of armed forces during an armed conflict, as those terms are understood under the law of war, which are governed by that law; or

(2) activities undertaken by military forces of a state in the exercise of their official duties.

(Added Pub. L. 103–322, title VI, §60019(a), Sept. 13, 1994, 108 Stat. 1977; amended Pub. L. 104–132, title VII, §723(a)(1), Apr. 24, 1996, 110 Stat. 1300; Pub. L. 104–294, title VI, §607(p), Oct. 11, 1996, 110 Stat. 3513; Pub. L. 114–23, title VIII, §803, June 2, 2015, 129 Stat. 307.)

Amendments

2015—Subsec. (c). Pub. L. 114–23, §803(1), substituted "section 13(c)" for "section 2(c)".

Subsec. (d). Pub. L. 114–23, §803(2), struck out definitions of "national of the United States", "territorial sea of the United States", and "United States".

Subsec. (e). Pub. L. 114–23, §803(3), added subsec. (e).

1996—Subsec. (a)(1)(F). Pub. L. 104–132 inserted "or conspires" after "attempts".

Subsec. (c). Pub. L. 104–294 inserted before period at end ", and the term 'State' means a State of the United States, the District of Columbia, and any commonwealth, territory, or possession of the United States".

Effective Date

Section effective Mar. 6, 1995, see section 60019(c)(1), (2)(B) of Pub. L. 103–322, set out as a note under section 2280 of this title.

Territorial Sea of United States

For extension of territorial sea of United States, see Proc. No. 5928, set out as a note under section 1331 of Title 43, Public Lands.

Definitions

For definitions of terms used in this section, see section 2280(d) of this title.

§2281a. Additional offenses against maritime fixed platforms

(a) Offenses.—

(1) In general.—A person who unlawfully and intentionally—

(A) when the purpose of the act, by its nature or context, is to intimidate a population, or to compel a government or an international organization to do or to abstain from doing any act—

(i) uses against or on a fixed platform or discharges from a fixed platform any explosive or radioactive material, biological, chemical, or nuclear weapon in a manner that causes or is likely to cause death or serious injury or damage; or

(ii) discharges from a fixed platform oil, liquefied natural gas, or another hazardous or noxious substance that is not covered by clause (i), in such quantity or concentration that causes or is likely to cause death or serious injury or damage;

(B) injures or kills any person in connection with the commission or the attempted commission of any of the offenses set forth in subparagraph (A); or

(C) attempts or conspires to do anything prohibited under subparagraph (A) or (B),

shall be fined under this title, imprisoned not more than 20 years, or both; and if death results to any person from conduct prohibited by this paragraph, shall be imprisoned for any term of years or for life.

(2) Threat to safety.—A person who threatens, with apparent determination and will to carry the threat into execution, to do any act prohibited under paragraph (1)(A), shall be fined under this title, imprisoned not more than 5 years, or both.

(b) Jurisdiction.—There is jurisdiction over the activity prohibited in subsection (a) if—

(1) such activity is committed against or on board a fixed platform—

(A) that is located on the continental shelf of the United States;

(B) that is located on the continental shelf of another country, by a national of the United States or by a stateless person whose habitual residence is in the United States; or

(C) in an attempt to compel the United States to do or abstain from doing any act;

(2) during the commission of such activity against or on board a fixed platform located on a continental shelf, a national of the United States is seized, threatened, injured, or killed; or

(3) such activity is committed against or on board a fixed platform located outside the United States and beyond the continental shelf of the United States and the offender is later found in the United States.

(c) Exceptions.—This section does not apply to—

(1) the activities of armed forces during an armed conflict, as those terms are understood under the law of war, which are governed by that law; or

(2) activities undertaken by military forces of a state in the exercise of their official duties.

(d) Definitions.—In this section—

(1) "continental shelf" means the sea-bed and subsoil of the submarine areas that extend beyond a country's territorial sea to the limits provided by customary international law as reflected in Article 76 of the 1982 Convention on the Law of the Sea; and

(2) "fixed platform" means an artificial island, installation, or structure permanently attached to the sea-bed for the purpose of exploration or exploitation of resources or for other economic purposes.

(Added Pub. L. 114–23, title VIII, §804(a), June 2, 2015, 129 Stat. 307.)

Definitions

For definitions of terms used in this section, see section 2280(d) of this title.

§2282A.1 Devices or dangerous substances in waters of the United States likely to destroy or damage ships or to interfere with maritime commerce

(a) A person who knowingly places, or causes to be placed, in navigable waters of the United States, by any means, a device or dangerous substance which is likely to destroy or cause damage to a vessel or its cargo, cause interference with the safe navigation of vessels, or interference with maritime commerce (such as by damaging or destroying marine terminals, facilities, or any other marine structure or entity used in maritime commerce) with the intent of causing such destruction or damage, interference with the safe navigation of vessels, or interference with maritime commerce shall be fined under this title or imprisoned for any term of years, or for life; or both.

(b) A person who causes the death of any person by engaging in conduct prohibited under subsection (a) may be punished by death.

(c) Nothing in this section shall be construed to apply to otherwise lawfully authorized and conducted activities of the United States Government.

(d) In this section:

(1) The term "dangerous substance" means any solid, liquid, or gaseous material that has the

capacity to cause damage to a vessel or its cargo, or cause interference with the safe navigation of a vessel.

(2) The term "device" means any object that, because of its physical, mechanical, structural, or chemical properties, has the capacity to cause damage to a vessel or its cargo, or cause interference with the safe navigation of a vessel.

(Added Pub. L. 109–177, title III, §304(a)(1), Mar. 9, 2006, 120 Stat. 234.)

§2282B. Violence against aids to maritime navigation

Whoever intentionally destroys, seriously damages, alters, moves, or tampers with any aid to maritime navigation maintained by the Saint Lawrence Seaway Development Corporation under the authority of section 4 of the Act of May 13, 1954 (33 U.S.C. 984), by the Coast Guard pursuant to section 81 of title 14, United States Code, or lawfully maintained under authority granted by the Coast Guard pursuant to section 83 of title 14, United States Code, if such act endangers or is likely to endanger the safe navigation of a ship, shall be fined under this title or imprisoned for not more than 20 years, or both.

(Added Pub. L. 109–177, title III, §304(b)(1), Mar. 9, 2006, 120 Stat. 235.)

§2283. Transportation of explosive, biological, chemical, or radioactive or nuclear materials

(a) In General.—Whoever knowingly transports aboard any vessel within the United States and on waters subject to the jurisdiction of the United States or any vessel outside the United States and on the high seas or having United States nationality an explosive or incendiary device, biological agent, chemical weapon, or radioactive or nuclear material, knowing that any such item is intended to be used to commit an offense listed under section 2332b(g)(5)(B), shall be fined under this title or imprisoned for any term of years or for life, or both.

(b) Causing Death.—Any person who causes the death of a person by engaging in conduct prohibited by subsection (a) may be punished by death.

(c) Definitions.—In this section:

(1) Biological agent.—The term "biological agent" means any biological agent, toxin, or vector (as those terms are defined in section 178).

(2) By-product material.—The term "by-product material" has the meaning given that term in section 11(e) of the Atomic Energy Act of 1954 (42 U.S.C. 2014(e)).

(3) Chemical weapon.—The term "chemical weapon" has the meaning given that term in section 229F(1).

(4) Explosive or incendiary device.—The term "explosive or incendiary device" has the meaning given the term in section 232(5) and includes explosive materials, as that term is defined in section 841(c) and explosive as defined in section 844(j).

(5) Nuclear material.—The term "nuclear material" has the meaning given that term in section 831(f)(1).1

(6) Radioactive material.—The term "radioactive material" means—

(A) source material and special nuclear material, but does not include natural or depleted uranium;

(B) nuclear by-product material;

(C) material made radioactive by bombardment in an accelerator; or

(D) all refined isotopes of radium.

(8) 2 Source material.—The term "source material" has the meaning given that term in section 11(z) of the Atomic Energy Act of 1954 (42 U.S.C. 2014(z)).

(9) Special nuclear material.—The term "special nuclear material" has the meaning given that term in section 11(aa) of the Atomic Energy Act of 1954 (42 U.S.C. 2014(aa)).

(Added Pub. L. 109–177, title III, §305(a), Mar. 9, 2006, 120 Stat. 236.)

References in Text

Section 831(f)(1), referred to in subsec. (c)(5), was redesignated section 831(g)(1) by Pub. L. 114–

23, title VIII, §812(d), June 2, 2015, 129 Stat. 312.

§2284. Transportation of terrorists

(a) In General.—Whoever knowingly and intentionally transports any terrorist aboard any vessel within the United States and on waters subject to the jurisdiction of the United States or any vessel outside the United States and on the high seas or having United States nationality, knowing that the transported person is a terrorist, shall be fined under this title or imprisoned for any term of years or for life, or both.

(b) Defined Term.—In this section, the term "terrorist" means any person who intends to commit, or is avoiding apprehension after having committed, an offense listed under section 2332b(g)(5)(B).

(Added Pub. L. 109–177, title III, §305(a), Mar. 9, 2006, 120 Stat. 237.)

§2285. Operation of submersible vessel or semi-submersible vessel without nationality

(a) Offense.—Whoever knowingly operates, or attempts or conspires to operate, by any means, or embarks in any submersible vessel or semi-submersible vessel that is without nationality and that is navigating or has navigated into, through, or from waters beyond the outer limit of the territorial sea of a single country or a lateral limit of that country's territorial sea with an adjacent country, with the intent to evade detection, shall be fined under this title, imprisoned not more than 15 years, or both.

(b) Evidence of Intent To Evade Detection.—For purposes of subsection (a), the presence of any of the indicia described in paragraph (1)(A), (E), (F), or (G), or in paragraph (4), (5), or (6), of section 70507(b) of title 46 may be considered, in the totality of the circumstances, to be prima facie evidence of intent to evade detection.

(c) Extraterritorial Jurisdiction.—There is extraterritorial Federal jurisdiction over an offense under this section, including an attempt or conspiracy to commit such an offense.

(d) Claim of Nationality or Registry.—A claim of nationality or registry under this section includes only—

(1) possession on board the vessel and production of documents evidencing the vessel's nationality as provided in article 5 of the 1958 Convention on the High Seas;

(2) flying its nation's ensign or flag; or

(3) a verbal claim of nationality or registry by the master or individual in charge of the vessel.

(e) Affirmative Defenses.—

(1) In general.—It is an affirmative defense to a prosecution for a violation of subsection (a), which the defendant has the burden to prove by a preponderance of the evidence, that the submersible vessel or semi-submersible vessel involved was, at the time of the offense—

(A) a vessel of the United States or lawfully registered in a foreign nation as claimed by the master or individual in charge of the vessel when requested to make a claim by an officer of the United States authorized to enforce applicable provisions of United States law;

(B) classed by and designed in accordance with the rules of a classification society;

(C) lawfully operated in government-regulated or licensed activity, including commerce, research, or exploration; or

(D) equipped with and using an operable automatic identification system, vessel monitoring system, or long range identification and tracking system.

(2) Production of documents.—The affirmative defenses provided by this subsection are proved conclusively by the production of—

(A) government documents evidencing the vessel's nationality at the time of the offense, as provided in article 5 of the 1958 Convention on the High Seas;

(B) a certificate of classification issued by the vessel's classification society upon completion of relevant classification surveys and valid at the time of the offense; or

(C) government documents evidencing licensure, regulation, or registration for commerce, research, or exploration.

(f) Federal Activities Excepted.—Nothing in this section applies to lawfully authorized activities carried out by or at the direction of the United States Government.

(g) Applicability of Other Provisions.—Sections 70504 and 70505 of title 46 apply to offenses under this section in the same manner as they apply to offenses under section 70503 of such title.

(h) Definitions.—In this section, the terms "submersible vessel", "semi-submersible vessel", "vessel of the United States", and "vessel without nationality" have the meaning given those terms in section 70502 of title 46.

(Added Pub. L. 110–407, title I, §102(a), Oct. 13, 2008, 122 Stat. 4296.)

Findings and Declarations

Pub. L. 110–407, title I, §101, Oct. 13, 2008, 122 Stat. 4296, provided that: "Congress finds and declares that operating or embarking in a submersible vessel or semi-submersible vessel without nationality and on an international voyage is a serious international problem, facilitates transnational crime, including drug trafficking, and terrorism, and presents a specific threat to the safety of maritime navigation and the security of the United States."

CHAPTER 111A - DESTRUCTION OF, OR INTERFERENCE WITH, VESSELS OR MARITIME FACILITIES

§2290. Jurisdiction and scope

(a) Jurisdiction.—There is jurisdiction, including extraterritorial jurisdiction, over an offense under this chapter if the prohibited activity takes place—

(1) within the United States and within waters subject to the jurisdiction of the United States; or

(2) outside United States and—

(A) an offender or a victim is a national of the United States (as that term is defined under section 101(a)(22) of the Immigration and Nationality Act (8 U.S.C. 1101(a)(22)); 1

(B) the activity involves a vessel in which a national of the United States was on board; or

(C) the activity involves a vessel of the United States (as that term is defined under section 2 2 of the Maritime Drug Law Enforcement Act (46 U.S.C. App. 1903).1

(b) Scope.—Nothing in this chapter shall apply to otherwise lawful activities carried out by or at the direction of the United States Government.

(Added Pub. L. 109–177, title III, §306(a), Mar. 9, 2006, 120 Stat. 237.)

References in Text

Section 2 of the Maritime Drug Law Enforcement Act, referred to in subsec. (a)(2)(C), probably means section 3 of the Maritime Drug Law Enforcement Act, Pub. L. 96–350, which was classified to section 1903 of former Title 46, Appendix, Shipping, and was repealed and restated in sections 70502 to 70506 of Title 46, Shipping, by Pub. L. 109–304, §§10(2), 19, Oct. 6, 2006, 120 Stat. 1683, 1710. Section 70502(b) of Title 46 defines "vessel of the United States".

§2291. Destruction of vessel or maritime facility

(a) Offense.—Whoever knowingly—

(1) sets fire to, damages, destroys, disables, or wrecks any vessel;

(2) places or causes to be placed a destructive device, as defined in section 921(a)(4), destructive substance, as defined in section 31(a)(3), or an explosive, as defined in section 844(j) in, upon, or near, or otherwise makes or causes to be made unworkable or unusable or hazardous to work or use, any vessel, or any part or other materials used or intended to be used in connection with the operation of a vessel;

(3) sets fire to, damages, destroys, or disables or places a destructive device or substance in, upon, or near, any maritime facility, including any aid to navigation, lock, canal, or vessel traffic service facility or equipment;

(4) interferes by force or violence with the operation of any maritime facility, including any aid to navigation, lock, canal, or vessel traffic service facility or equipment, if such action is likely to endanger the safety of any vessel in navigation;

(5) sets fire to, damages, destroys, or disables or places a destructive device or substance in, upon, or near, any appliance, structure, property, machine, or apparatus, or any facility or other material used, or intended to be used, in connection with the operation, maintenance, loading, unloading, or storage of any vessel or any passenger or cargo carried or intended to be carried on any vessel;

(6) performs an act of violence against or incapacitates any individual on any vessel, if such act of violence or incapacitation is likely to endanger the safety of the vessel or those on board;

(7) performs an act of violence against a person that causes or is likely to cause serious bodily injury, as defined in section 1365(h)(3), in, upon, or near, any appliance, structure, property, machine, or apparatus, or any facility or other material used, or intended to be used, in connection with the operation, maintenance, loading, unloading, or storage of any vessel or any passenger or cargo carried or intended to be carried on any vessel;

(8) communicates information, knowing the information to be false and under circumstances in which such information may reasonably be believed, thereby endangering the safety of any vessel in navigation; or

(9) attempts or conspires to do anything prohibited under paragraphs (1) through (8),

shall be fined under this title or imprisoned not more than 20 years, or both.

(b) Limitation.—Subsection (a) shall not apply to any person that is engaging in otherwise lawful activity, such as normal repair and salvage activities, and the transportation of hazardous materials regulated and allowed to be transported under chapter 51 of title 49.

(c) Penalty.—Whoever is fined or imprisoned under subsection (a) as a result of an act involving a vessel that, at the time of the violation, carried high-level radioactive waste (as that term is defined in section 2(12) of the Nuclear Waste Policy Act of 1982 (42 U.S.C. 10101(12)) 1 or spent nuclear fuel (as that term is defined in section 2(23) of the Nuclear Waste Policy Act of 1982 (42 U.S.C. 10101(23)),1 shall be fined under this title, imprisoned for a term up to life, or both.

(d) Penalty When Death Results.—Whoever is convicted of any crime prohibited by subsection (a) and intended to cause death by the prohibited conduct, if the conduct resulted in the death of any person, shall be subject also to the death penalty or to a term of imprisonment for a period up to life.

(e) Threats.—Whoever knowingly and intentionally imparts or conveys any threat to do an act which would violate this chapter, with an apparent determination and will to carry the threat into execution, shall be fined under this title or imprisoned not more than 5 years, or both, and is liable for all costs incurred as a result of such threat.

(Added Pub. L. 109–177, title III, §306(a), Mar. 9, 2006, 120 Stat. 237.)

§2292. Imparting or conveying false information

(a) In General.—Whoever imparts or conveys or causes to be imparted or conveyed false information, knowing the information to be false, concerning an attempt or alleged attempt being made or to be made, to do any act that would be a crime prohibited by this chapter or by chapter 111 of this title, shall be subject to a civil penalty of not more than $5,000, which shall be recoverable in a civil action brought in the name of the United States.

(b) Malicious Conduct.—Whoever knowingly, intentionally, maliciously, or with reckless disregard for the safety of human life, imparts or conveys or causes to be imparted or conveyed false information, knowing the information to be false, concerning an attempt or alleged attempt to do any act which would be a crime prohibited by this chapter or by chapter 111 of this title, shall be fined under this title or imprisoned not more than 5 years.

(c) Jurisdiction.—

(1) In general.—Except as provided under paragraph (2), section 2290(a) shall not apply to any offense under this section.

(2) Jurisdiction.—Jurisdiction over an offense under this section shall be determined in accordance with the provisions applicable to the crime prohibited by this chapter, or by chapter 111 of this title, to which the imparted or conveyed false information relates, as applicable.

(Added Pub. L. 109–177, title III, §306(a), Mar. 9, 2006, 120 Stat. 239.)

§2293. Bar to prosecution

(a) In General.—It is a bar to prosecution under this chapter if—

(1) the conduct in question occurred within the United States in relation to a labor dispute, and such conduct is prohibited as a felony under the law of the State in which it was committed; or

(2) such conduct is prohibited as a misdemeanor, and not as a felony, under the law of the State in which it was committed.

(b) Definitions.—In this section:

(1) Labor dispute.—The term "labor dispute" has the same meaning given that term in section 13(c) of the Act to amend the Judicial Code and to define and limit the jurisdiction of courts sitting in equity, and for other purposes (29 U.S.C. 113(c), commonly known as the Norris-LaGuardia Act).

(2) State.—The term "State" means a State of the United States, the District of Columbia, and any commonwealth, territory, or possession of the United States.

(Added Pub. L. 109–177, title III, §306(a), Mar. 9, 2006, 120 Stat. 239.)

CHAPTER 113 - STOLEN PROPERTY

Amendments

2008—Pub. L. 110–403, title II, §206(b), Oct. 13, 2008, 122 Stat. 4263, added item 2323.

2005—Pub. L. 109–9, title I, §102(b), Apr. 27, 2005, 119 Stat. 220, added item 2319B.

2004—Pub. L. 108–482, title I, §102(c), Dec. 23, 2004, 118 Stat. 3915, substituted "Trafficking in counterfeit labels, illicit labels, or counterfeit documentation or packaging" for "Trafficking in counterfeit labels for phonorecords, copies of computer programs or computer program documentation or packaging, and copies of motion pictures or other audio visual works, and trafficking in counterfeit computer program documentation or packaging" in item 2318.

1996—Pub. L. 104–153, §4(b)(2), July 2, 1996, 110 Stat. 1387, substituted "Trafficking in counterfeit labels for phonorecords, copies of computer programs or computer program documentation or packaging, and copies of motion pictures or other audio visual works, and trafficking in counterfeit computer program documentation or packaging" for "Trafficking in counterfeit labels for phonorecords and copies of motion pictures or other audiovisual works" in item 2318.

1994—Pub. L. 103–465, title V, §513(b), Dec. 8, 1994, 108 Stat. 4976, added item 2319A.

1992—Pub. L. 102–519, title I, §105(b), Oct. 25, 1992, 106 Stat. 3386, added item 2322.

1986—Pub. L. 99–646, §42(b), Nov. 10, 1986, 100 Stat. 3601, renumbered item 2320 relating to trafficking in certain motor vehicles or motor vehicle parts as item 2321.

1984—Pub. L. 98–547, title II, §204(b), Oct. 25, 1984, 98 Stat. 2770, added item 2320 relating to trafficking in certain motor vehicles or motor vehicle parts.

Pub. L. 98–473, title II, §§1115, 1502(b), Oct. 12, 1984, 98 Stat. 2149, 2179, substituted "livestock" for "cattle" in items 2316 and 2317 and added item 2320 relating to trafficking in counterfeit goods or services.

1982—Pub. L. 97–180, §4, May 24, 1982, 96 Stat. 92, substituted "Trafficking in counterfeit labels for phonorecords and copies of motion pictures or other audiovisual works" for "Transportation, sale, or receipt of phonograph records bearing forged or counterfeit labels" in item 2318 and added item 2319.

1962—Pub. L. 87–773, §2, Oct. 9, 1962, 76 Stat. 775, added item 2318.

1961—Pub. L. 87–371, §4, Oct. 4, 1961, 75 Stat. 802, inserted "fraudulent State tax stamps," in item 2314, and substituted "moneys, or fraudulent State tax stamps" for "or monies" in item 2315.

§2311. Definitions

As used in this chapter:

"Aircraft" means any contrivance now known or hereafter invented, used, or designed for navigation of or for flight in the air;

"Cattle" means one or more bulls, steers, oxen, cows, heifers, or calves, or the carcass or carcasses thereof;

"Livestock" means any domestic animals raised for home use, consumption, or profit, such as horses, pigs, llamas, goats, fowl, sheep, buffalo, and cattle, or the carcasses thereof;

"Money" means the legal tender of the United States or of any foreign country, or any counterfeit thereof;

"Motor vehicle" includes an automobile, automobile truck, automobile wagon, motorcycle, or any other self-propelled vehicle designed for running on land but not on rails;

"Securities" includes any note, stock certificate, bond, debenture, check, draft, warrant, traveler's check, letter of credit, warehouse receipt, negotiable bill of lading, evidence of indebtedness, certificate of interest or participation in any profit-sharing agreement, collateral-trust certificate, preorganization certificate or subscription, transferable share, investment contract, voting-trust certificate; valid or blank motor vehicle title; certificate of interest in property, tangible or intangible; instrument or document or writing evidencing ownership of goods, wares, and merchandise, or transferring or assigning any right, title, or interest in or to goods, wares, and merchandise; or, in general, any instrument commonly known as a "security", or any certificate of interest or participation in, temporary or interim certificate for, receipt for, warrant, or right to subscribe to or purchase any of the foregoing, or any forged, counterfeited, or spurious representation of any of the foregoing;

"Tax stamp" includes any tax stamp, tax token, tax meter imprint, or any other form of evidence of an obligation running to a State, or evidence of the discharge thereof;

"Value" means the face, par, or market value, whichever is the greatest, and the aggregate value of all goods, wares, and merchandise, securities, and money referred to in a single indictment shall constitute the value thereof.

"Vessel" means any watercraft or other contrivance used or designed for transportation or navigation on, under, or immediately above, water.

(June 25, 1948, ch. 645, 62 Stat. 805; Pub. L. 87–371, §1, Oct. 4, 1961, 75 Stat. 802; Pub. L. 98–547, title II, §202, Oct. 25, 1984, 98 Stat. 2770; Pub. L. 103–322, title XXXII, §320912, Sept. 13, 1994, 108 Stat. 2128; Pub. L. 104–294, title VI, §604(b)(20), Oct. 11, 1996, 110 Stat. 3507; Pub. L. 107–273, div. B, title IV, §4002(b)(8), Nov. 2, 2002, 116 Stat. 1808; Pub. L. 109–177, title III, §307(b)(1), Mar. 9, 2006, 120 Stat. 240.)

Historical and Revision Notes

Based on title 18, U.S.C., 1940 ed., §§408, 414(b), (c), 417, 419a(a) (Oct. 29, 1919, ch. 89, §2(a), 41 Stat. 324; May 22, 1934, ch. 333, §§2(b), (c), 5, 48 Stat. 794, 795; Aug. 3, 1939, ch. 413, §3, 53 Stat. 1178; Aug. 18, 1941, ch. 366, §2(a), 55 Stat. 631; Sept. 24, 1945, ch. 383, §1, 59 Stat. 536).

The definitive provisions in each of said sections were separated therefrom and consolidated into this one section defining terms used in this chapter.

The definitions of "interstate or foreign commerce", contained in said section 408 and in sections 414(a) and 419a(b) of title 18, U.S.C., 1940 ed., are incorporated in section 10 of this title.

Other provisions of section 408 of title 18, U.S.C., 1940 ed., are incorporated in sections 2312 and 2313 of this title.

In the definition of "motor vehicle", words "designed for running on land but not on rails" were substituted for "not designed for running on rails" so as to conform with the ruling in the case of McBoyle v. U.S. (1931, 51 S. Ct. 340, 283, U. S. 25, 75 L. Ed. 816), in which the Supreme Court held that "vehicle" is limited to vehicles running on land and that motor vehicle does not include an airplane.

In the paragraph defining "value" which came from said section 417 of title 18, U.S.C., 1940 ed., words "In the event that a defendant is charged in the same indictment with two or more violations of sections 413–419 of this title, then" were omitted and the same meaning was preserved by the substitution of the words "a single" for the word "such."

Minor changes were made in phraseology.

Amendments

2006—Pub. L. 109–177 inserted definition of "Vessel".

2002—Pub. L. 107–273 substituted semicolon for period at end of third par.

1996—Pub. L. 104–294 substituted "Livestock" for "livestock" in third par.

1994—Pub. L. 103–322 inserted definition of "livestock".

1984—Pub. L. 98–547 inserted "valid or blank motor vehicle title;" in definition of "Securities".

1961—Pub. L. 87–371 inserted definition of "Tax stamp".

Effective Date of 1996 Amendment

Amendment by Pub. L. 104–294 effective Sept. 13, 1994, see section 604(d) of Pub. L. 104–294, set out as a note under section 13 of this title.

Short Title of 2004 Amendment

Pub. L. 108–482, title I, §101, Dec. 23, 2004, 118 Stat. 3912, provided that: "This title [amending section 2318 of this title and enacting provisions set out as a note under section 2318 of this title] may be cited as the 'Anti-counterfeiting Amendments Act of 2004'."

Short Title of 1997 Amendment

Pub. L. 105–147, §1, Dec. 16, 1997, 111 Stat. 2678, provided that: "This Act [amending sections 2319 to 2320 of this title, sections 101, 506, and 507 of Title 17, Copyrights, and section 1498 of Title 28, Judiciary and Judicial Procedure, and enacting provisions set out as a note under section 994 of Title 28] may be cited as the 'No Electronic Theft (NET) Act'."

Short Title of 1996 Amendment

Pub. L. 104–153, §1, July 2, 1996, 110 Stat. 1386, provided that: "This Act [amending sections 1961, 2318, and 2320 of this title, sections 1116 and 1117 of Title 15, Commerce and Trade, section 603 of Title 17, Copyrights, sections 1431, 1484, and 1526 of Title 19, Customs Duties, and section 80302 of Title 49, Transportation, and enacting provisions set out as notes under this section and section 1431 of Title 19] may be cited as the 'Anticounterfeiting Consumer Protection Act of 1996'."

Short Title of 1992 Amendment

Pub. L. 102–519, §1, Oct. 25, 1992, 106 Stat. 3384, provided that: "This Act [enacting sections 2119 and 2322 of this title, sections 2026a to 2026c and 2041 to 2044 of Title 15, Commerce and Trade, sections 1646b and 1646c of Title 19, Customs Duties, and sections 3750a to 3750d of Title 42, The Public Health and Welfare, amending sections 553, 981, 982, 2312, and 2313 of this title, sections 2021 to 2023, 2025, 2027, and 2034 of Title 15, and enacting provisions set out as notes under section 2119 of this title, sections 2026a, 2026b, and 2041 of Title 15, and section 1646b of Title 19] may be cited as the 'Anti Car Theft Act of 1992'."

Short Title of 1984 Amendments

Pub. L. 98–547, §1(a), Oct. 25, 1984, 98 Stat. 2754, provided that: "This Act [enacting sections 511, 512, 553, and 2320 [now 2321] of this title, sections 2021 to 2034 of Title 15, Commerce and Trade, and section 1627 of Title 19, Customs Duties, amending this section, sections 1961 and 2313 of this title, and section 1901 of Title 15, and enacting provisions set out as a note under section 2021 of Title 15] may be cited as the 'Motor Vehicle Theft Law Enforcement Act of 1984'."

Pub. L. 98–473, title II, §1501, Oct. 12, 1984, 98 Stat. 2178, provided that: "This chapter [chapter XV (§§1501–1503) of title II of Pub. L. 98–473, enacting section 2320 of this title and amending sections 1116, 1117, and 1118 of Title 15, Commerce and Trade] may be cited as the 'Trademark Counterfeiting Act of 1984'."

Short Title of 1982 Amendment

Pub. L. 97–180, §1, May 24, 1982, 96 Stat. 91, provided: "That this Act [enacting section 2319 of this title and amending section 2318 of this title and section 506 of Title 17, Copyrights] may be cited as the 'Piracy and Counterfeiting Amendments Act of 1982'."

Counterfeiting of Trademarked and Copyrighted Merchandise; Congressional Statement of Findings

Pub. L. 104–153, §2, July 2, 1996, 110 Stat. 1386, provided that: "The counterfeiting of trademarked and copyrighted merchandise—

"(1) has been connected with organized crime;

"(2) deprives legitimate trademark and copyright owners of substantial revenues and consumer goodwill;

"(3) poses health and safety threats to United States consumers;

"(4) eliminates United States jobs; and

"(5) is a multibillion-dollar drain on the United States economy."

Congressional Declaration of Purpose of 1984 Amendment

Pub. L. 98–547, §2, Oct. 25, 1984, 98 Stat. 2754, provided that: "It is the purpose of this Act [see Short Title of 1984 Amendments note above]—

"(1) to provide for the identification of certain motor vehicles and their major replacement parts to impede motor vehicle theft;

"(2) to augment the Federal criminal penalties imposed upon persons trafficking in stolen motor vehicles;

"(3) to encourage decreases in premiums charged consumers for motor vehicle theft insurance; and

"(4) to reduce opportunities for exporting or importing stolen motor vehicles and off-highway mobile equipment."

§2312. Transportation of stolen vehicles

Whoever transports in interstate or foreign commerce a motor vehicle, vessel, or aircraft, knowing the same to have been stolen, shall be fined under this title or imprisoned not more than 10 years, or both.

(June 25, 1948, ch. 645, 62 Stat. 806; Pub. L. 102–519, title I, §103, Oct. 25, 1992, 106 Stat. 3385; Pub. L. 109–177, title III, §307(b)(2)(A), Mar. 9, 2006, 120 Stat. 240.)

Historical and Revision Notes

Based on title 18, U.S.C., 1940 ed., §408 (Oct. 29, 1919, ch. 89, §§1, 3, 5, 41 Stat. 324, 325; Sept. 24, 1945, ch. 383, §§2, 3, 59 Stat. 536).

The first sentence of said section 408, providing the short title "An Act to punish the transportation of stolen motor vehicles or aircraft in interstate or foreign commerce," and derived from section 1 of said act of October 29, 1919, as amended, was omitted as not appropriate in a revision.

Definitions of "aircraft," "motor vehicle," and "interstate or foreign commerce," which constituted the second sentence of said section 408 of title 18, U.S.C., 1940 ed., and were derived from section 2 of said act of October 29, 1919, as amended, are incorporated in sections 10 and 2311 of this title.

Provision relating to receiving or selling stolen aircraft or motor vehicles, which was derived from section 4 of the act of October 29, 1919, as amended, is incorporated in section 2313 of this title.

Venue provision, which was derived from section 5 of the act of October 29, 1919, was omitted as unnecessary, being covered by section 3237 of this title.

Reference to persons causing or procuring was omitted as unnecessary in view of definition of "principal" in section 2 of this title.

Minor changes were made in phraseology.

Amendments

2006—Pub. L. 109–177 substituted "motor vehicle, vessel, or aircraft" for "motor vehicle or aircraft".

1992—Pub. L. 102–519 substituted "fined under this title or imprisoned not more than 10 years" for "fined not more than $5,000 or imprisoned not more than five years".

§2313. Sale or receipt of stolen vehicles

(a) Whoever receives, possesses, conceals, stores, barters, sells, or disposes of any motor vehicle, vessel, or aircraft, which has crossed a State or United States boundary after being stolen, knowing the same to have been stolen, shall be fined under this title or imprisoned not more than 10 years, or both.

(b) For purposes of this section, the term "State" includes a State of the United States, the District of Columbia, and any commonwealth, territory, or possession of the United States.

(June 25, 1948, ch. 645, 62 Stat. 806; Pub. L. 98–547, title II, §203, Oct. 25, 1984, 98 Stat. 2770; Pub. L. 101–647, title XII, §1205(l), Nov. 29, 1990, 104 Stat. 4831; Pub. L. 102–519, title I, §103, Oct. 25, 1992, 106 Stat. 3385; Pub. L. 109–177, title III, §307(b)(2)(B), Mar. 9, 2006, 120 Stat.

240.)

Historical and Revision Notes

Based on title 18, U.S.C., 1940 ed., §408 (Oct. 29, 1919, ch. 89, §4, 41 Stat. 325; Sept. 24, 1945, ch. 383, §§2, 3, 59 Stat. 536).

Section constitutes the fourth sentence of said section 408 of title 18, U.S.C., 1940 ed.

Definitions of "aircraft," "motor vehicle," and "interstate or foreign commerce," which constituted the second sentence of said section 408, are incorporated in sections 10 and 2311 of this title.

The third sentence of said section 408, relating to transporting stolen aircraft or motor vehicles, is incorporated in section 2312 of this title.

The first sentence of said section 408, providing the short title, and the fifth sentence thereof, relating to venue, were omitted. (See reviser's note under section 2312 of this title.)

Minor changes were made in phraseology.

Amendments

2006—Subsec. (a). Pub. L. 109–177 substituted "motor vehicle, vessel, or aircraft" for "motor vehicle or aircraft".

1992—Subsec. (a). Pub. L. 102–519 substituted "fined under this title or imprisoned not more than 10 years" for "fined not more than $5,000 or imprisoned not more than five years".

1990—Pub. L. 101–647 designated existing provisions as subsec. (a) and added subsec. (b).

1984—Pub. L. 98–547 inserted "possesses," after "receives," and substituted "which has crossed a State or United States boundary after being stolen," for "moving as, or which is a part of, or which constitutes interstate or foreign commerce,".

§2314. Transportation of stolen goods, securities, moneys, fraudulent State tax stamps, or articles used in counterfeiting

Whoever transports, transmits, or transfers in interstate or foreign commerce any goods, wares, merchandise, securities or money, of the value of $5,000 or more, knowing the same to have been stolen, converted or taken by fraud; or

Whoever, having devised or intending to devise any scheme or artifice to defraud, or for obtaining money or property by means of false or fraudulent pretenses, representations, or promises, transports or causes to be transported, or induces any person or persons to travel in, or to be transported in interstate or foreign commerce in the execution or concealment of a scheme or artifice to defraud that person or those persons of money or property having a value of $5,000 or more; or

Whoever, with unlawful or fraudulent intent, transports in interstate or foreign commerce any falsely made, forged, altered, or counterfeited securities or tax stamps, knowing the same to have been falsely made, forged, altered, or counterfeited; or

Whoever, with unlawful or fraudulent intent, transports in interstate or foreign commerce any traveler's check bearing a forged countersignature; or

Whoever, with unlawful or fraudulent intent, transports in interstate or foreign commerce, any tool, implement, or thing used or fitted to be used in falsely making, forging, altering, or counterfeiting any security or tax stamps, or any part thereof; or

Whoever transports, transmits, or transfers in interstate or foreign commerce any veterans' memorial object, knowing the same to have been stolen, converted or taken by fraud—

Shall be fined under this title or imprisoned not more than ten years, or both. If the offense involves a pre-retail medical product (as defined in section 670) the punishment for the offense shall be the same as the punishment for an offense under section 670 unless the punishment under this section is greater. If the offense involves the transportation, transmission, or transfer in interstate or foreign commerce of veterans' memorial objects with a value, in the aggregate, of less than $1,000, the defendant shall be fined under this title or imprisoned not more than one year, or both.

This section shall not apply to any falsely made, forged, altered, counterfeited or spurious representation of an obligation or other security of the United States, or of an obligation, bond, certificate, security, treasury note, bill, promise to pay or bank note issued by any foreign government. This section also shall not apply to any falsely made, forged, altered, counterfeited, or spurious representation of any bank note or bill issued by a bank or corporation of any foreign country which is intended by the laws or usage of such country to circulate as money.

For purposes of this section the term "veterans' memorial object" means a grave marker, headstone, monument, or other object, intended to permanently honor a veteran or mark a veteran's grave, or any monument that signifies an event of national military historical significance.

(June 25, 1948, ch. 645, 62 Stat. 806; May 24, 1949, ch. 139, §45, 63 Stat. 96; July 9, 1956, ch. 519, 70 Stat. 507; Pub. L. 87–371, §2, Oct. 4, 1961, 75 Stat. 802; Pub. L. 90–535, Sept. 28, 1968, 82 Stat. 885; Pub. L. 100–690, title VII, §§7057, 7080, Nov. 18, 1988, 102 Stat. 4402, 4406; Pub. L. 101–647, title XII, §1208, Nov. 29, 1990, 104 Stat. 4832; Pub. L. 103–322, title XXXIII, §330016(1)(K), (L), Sept. 13, 1994, 108 Stat. 2147; Pub. L. 112–186, §4(d)(1), Oct. 5, 2012, 126 Stat. 1429; Pub. L. 112–239, div. A, title X, §1084(a), Jan. 2, 2013, 126 Stat. 1963.)

Historical and Revision Notes

1948 Act

Based on title 18, U.S.C., 1940 ed., §§413, 415, 418, 418a, 419 (May 22, 1934, ch. 333, §§1, 3, 6, 48 Stat. 794, 795; May 22, 1934, ch. 333, §7, as added Aug. 3, 1939, ch. 413, §5, 53 Stat. 1179; May 22, 1934, ch. 333, §7, renumbered §8 by Aug. 3, 1939, ch. 413, §6, 53 Stat. 1179; Aug. 3, 1939, ch. 413, §§1, 4, 5, 53 Stat. 1178, 1179).

Section consolidates sections 413, 415, 417, 418, 418a, and 419 of title 18, U.S.C., 1940 ed. Words "or with intent to steal or purloin, knowing the same to have been so stolen, converted, or taken" were omitted as surplusage, since property so "taken" is "stolen," and insertion of word "knowingly" after "Whoever" at beginning of section renders such omission possible.

Reference to persons causing or procuring was omitted as unnecessary in view of definition of "principal" in section 2 of this title.

Section 413 of title 18, U.S.C., 1940 ed., providing the short title "National Stolen Property Act," was omitted as not appropriate in a revision.

Section 414 of title 18, U.S.C., 1940 ed., containing definitions of "interstate or foreign commerce," "securities," and "money," is incorporated in sections 10 and 2311 of this title.

Section 417 of title 18, U.S.C., 1940 ed., relating to indictments and determination of "value" of goods, wares, merchandise, securities, and money referred to in indictments, is also incorporated in section 2311 of this title.

Section 418 of title 18, U.S.C., 1940 ed., relating to venue, was omitted as completely covered by section 3237 of this title.

Section 418a of title 18, U.S.C., 1940 ed., relating to conspiracy, was omitted as covered by section 371 of this title, the general conspiracy section.

Section 419 of title 18, U.S.C., 1940 ed., providing that nothing contained in the National Stolen Property Act should be construed to repeal, modify, or amend any part of the National Motor Vehicle Theft Act, was omitted as unnecessary, in view of this revision and reenactment of the provisions of the latter act (sections 10, 2311–2313 of this title).

Changes were made in phraseology and arrangement.

1949 Act

This amendment [see section 45] restates and clarifies the first paragraph of section 2314 of title 18, U.S.C., to conform to the original law upon which the section is based.

Amendments

2013—Pub. L. 112–239, §1084(a)(4), inserted par. at end defining "veterans' memorial object".

Pub. L. 112–239, §1084(a)(3), inserted at end of seventh par. "If the offense involves the transportation, transmission, or transfer in interstate or foreign commerce of veterans' memorial objects with a value, in the aggregate, of less than $1,000, the defendant shall be fined under this title or imprisoned not more than one year, or both."

Pub. L. 112–239, §1084(a)(1), (2), inserted sixth par. relating to veterans' memorial objects.

2012—Pub. L. 112–186 inserted at end of sixth par. "If the offense involves a pre-retail medical product (as defined in section 670) the punishment for the offense shall be the same as the punishment for an offense under section 670 unless the punishment under this section is greater."

1994—Pub. L. 103–322, §330016(1)(L), substituted "fined under this title" for "fined not more than $10,000" in sixth par.

Pub. L. 103–322, §330016(1)(K), which directed the amendment of this section by striking "not more than $5,000" and inserting "under this title", could not be executed because the phrase "not more than $5,000" did not appear in text.

1990—Pub. L. 101–647 inserted "or foreign" after "interstate" in second par.

1988—Pub. L. 100–690, §7057(a), substituted "transports, transmits, or transfers" for "transports" in first par.

Pub. L. 100–690, §7080, inserted "or persons" after "any person" and "or those persons" after "that person" in second par.

Pub. L. 100–690, §7057(b), struck out "or by a bank or corporation of any foreign country" after "foreign government" in last par. and inserted at end "This section also shall not apply to any falsely made, forged, altered, counterfeited, or spurious representation of any bank note or bill issued by a bank or corporation of any foreign country which is intended by the laws or usage of such country to circulate as money."

1968—Pub. L. 90–535 prohibited transportation with unlawful or fraudulent intent in interstate or foreign commerce of traveler's checks bearing forged countersignatures.

1961—Pub. L. 87–371 inserted "or tax stamps" after "securities" in third par. and after "security" in fourth par., and "fraudulent State tax stamps," in section catchline.

1956—Act July 9, 1956, inserted par. relating to interstate transportation of persons in schemes to defraud.

1949—Act May 24, 1949, substituted "knowing the same to have been stolen, converted or taken by fraud" for "theretofore stolen, converted, or taken by fraud" in first par.

§2315. Sale or receipt of stolen goods, securities, moneys, or fraudulent State tax stamps

Whoever receives, possesses, conceals, stores, barters, sells, or disposes of any goods, wares, or merchandise, securities, or money of the value of $5,000 or more, or pledges or accepts as security for a loan any goods, wares, or merchandise, or securities, of the value of $500 or more, which have crossed a State or United States boundary after being stolen, unlawfully converted, or taken, knowing the same to have been stolen, unlawfully converted, or taken; or

Whoever receives, possesses, conceals, stores, barters, sells, or disposes of any falsely made, forged, altered, or counterfeited securities or tax stamps, or pledges or accepts as security for a loan any falsely made, forged, altered, or counterfeited securities or tax stamps, moving as, or which are a part of, or which constitute interstate or foreign commerce, knowing the same to have been so falsely made, forged, altered, or counterfeited; or

Whoever receives in interstate or foreign commerce, or conceals, stores, barters, sells, or disposes of, any tool, implement, or thing used or intended to be used in falsely making, forging, altering, or counterfeiting any security or tax stamp, or any part thereof, moving as, or which is a part of, or which constitutes interstate or foreign commerce, knowing that the same is fitted to be used, or has been used, in falsely making, forging, altering, or counterfeiting any security or tax stamp, or any part thereof; or

'Whoever ¹ receives, possesses, conceals, stores, barters, sells, or disposes of any veterans' memorial object which has crossed a State or United States boundary after being stolen, unlawfully converted, or taken, knowing the same to have been stolen, unlawfully converted, or taken—' 1

Shall be fined under this title or imprisoned not more than ten years, or both. If the offense involves a pre-retail medical product (as defined in section 670) the punishment for the offense shall be the same as the punishment for an offense under section 670 unless the punishment under this section is greater. If the offense involves the receipt, possession, concealment, storage, barter, sale, or disposal of veterans' memorial objects with a value, in the aggregate, of less than $1,000, the defendant shall be fined under this title or imprisoned not more than one year, or both.

This section shall not apply to any falsely made, forged, altered, counterfeited, or spurious representation of an obligation or other security of the United States or of an obligation, bond, certificate, security, treasury note, bill, promise to pay, or bank note, issued by any foreign government. This section also shall not apply to any falsely made, forged, altered, counterfeited, or spurious representation of any bank note or bill issued by a bank or corporation of any foreign country which is intended by the laws or usage of such country to circulate as money.

For purposes of this section, the term "State" includes a State of the United States, the District of Columbia, and any commonwealth, territory, or possession of the United States. For purposes of this section the term "veterans' memorial object" means a grave marker, headstone, monument, or other object, intended to permanently honor a veteran or mark a veteran's grave, or any monument that signifies an event of national military historical significance.

(June 25, 1948, ch. 645, 62 Stat. 806; Pub. L. 87–371, §3, Oct. 4, 1961, 75 Stat. 802; Pub. L. 99–646, §76, Nov. 10, 1986, 100 Stat. 3618; Pub. L. 100–690, title VII, §§7048, 7057(b), Nov. 18, 1988, 102 Stat. 4401, 4402; Pub. L. 101–647, title XII, §1205(m), Nov. 29, 1990, 104 Stat. 4831; Pub. L. 103–322, title XXXIII, §330016(1)(L), Sept. 13, 1994, 108 Stat. 2147; Pub. L. 112–186, §4(d)(2), Oct. 5, 2012, 126 Stat. 1429; Pub. L. 112–239, div. A, title X, §1084(b), Jan. 2, 2013, 126 Stat. 1963.)

Historical and Revision Notes

Based on title 18, U.S.C., 1940 ed., §416 (May 22, 1934, ch. 333, §4, 48 Stat. 795; Aug. 3, 1939, ch. 413, §2, 53 Stat. 1178).

(See reviser's notes under sections 10, 2311 and 2314 of this title for explanation of consolidation or omission of other sections of title 18, U.S.C., 1940 ed., which were derived from the National Stolen Property Act.)

Minor changes were made in phraseology.

Amendments

2013—Pub. L. 112–239, §1084(b)(4), inserted at end "For purposes of this section the term 'veterans' memorial object' means a grave marker, headstone, monument, or other object, intended to permanently honor a veteran or mark a veteran's grave, or any monument that signifies an event of national military historical significance."

Pub. L. 112–239, §1084(b)(3), inserted at end of fifth par. "If the offense involves the receipt, possession, concealment, storage, barter, sale, or disposal of veterans' memorial objects with a value, in the aggregate, of less than $1,000, the defendant shall be fined under this title or imprisoned not more than one year, or both."

Pub. L. 112–239, §1084(b)(1), (2), inserted fourth par. relating to veterans' memorial objects.

2012—Pub. L. 112–186 inserted at end of fourth par. "If the offense involves a pre-retail medical product (as defined in section 670) the punishment for the offense shall be the same as the punishment for an offense under section 670 unless the punishment under this section is greater."

1994—Pub. L. 103–322 substituted "fined under this title" for "fined not more than $10,000" in fourth par.

1990—Pub. L. 101–647 inserted par. at end defining "State".

1988—Pub. L. 100–690, §7048, substituted "moving as, or which are a part of, or which constitute interstate or foreign commerce" for "which have crossed a State or United States boundary after being stolen, unlawfully converted, or taken" in second par.

Pub. L. 100–690, §7057(b), struck out "or by a bank or corporation of any foreign country" after "foreign government" in last par. and inserted at end "This section also shall not apply to any falsely made, forged, altered, counterfeited, or spurious representation of any bank note or bill issued by a bank or corporation of any foreign country which is intended by the laws or usage of such country to circulate as money."

1986—Pub. L. 99–646 substituted "receives, possesses, conceals" for "receives, conceals" and "which have crossed a State or United States boundary after being stolen, unlawfully converted, or taken" for "moving as, or which are part of, or which constitute interstate or foreign commerce" in first and second pars.

1961—Pub. L. 87–371 inserted "or tax stamps" after "securities", wherever appearing, in second par., and "or tax stamp" after "security", wherever appearing, in third par., and substituted "moneys, or fraudulent State tax stamps" for "or monies" in section catchline.

§2316. Transportation of livestock

Whoever transports in interstate or foreign commerce any livestock, knowing the same to have been stolen, shall be fined under this title or imprisoned not more than five years, or both.

(June 25, 1948, ch. 645, 62 Stat. 807; Pub. L. 98–473, title II, §1113, Oct. 12, 1984, 98 Stat. 2149; Pub. L. 103–322, title XXXIII, §330016(1)(K), Sept. 13, 1994, 108 Stat. 2147.)

Historical and Revision Notes

Based on title 18, U.S.C., 1940 ed., §§419b, 419d (Aug. 18, 1941, ch. 366, §§3, 5, 55 Stat. 631).

This section consolidates sections 419b and 419d of title 18, U.S.C., 1940 ed.

Definition of "cattle", contained in section 419a(a) of title 18, U.S.C., 1940 ed., is incorporated in section 2311 of this title.

Definition of "interstate or foreign commerce", constituting section 419a(b) of title 18, U.S.C., 1940 ed., is incorporated in section 10 of this title.

The venue provision of said section 419d of title 18, U.S.C., 1940 ed., was omitted as completely covered by section 3237 of this title.

Reference to persons causing or procuring was omitted as unnecessary in view of definition of "principal" in section 2 of this title.

Minor changes were made in phraseology.

Amendments

1994—Pub. L. 103–322 substituted "fined under this title" for "fined not more than $5,000".

1984—Pub. L. 98–473 substituted "livestock" for "cattle" in section catchline and text.

§2317. Sale or receipt of livestock

Whoever receives, conceals, stores, barters, buys, sells, or disposes of any livestock, moving in or constituting a part of interstate or foreign commerce, knowing the same to have been stolen, shall be fined under this title or imprisoned not more than five years, or both.

(June 25, 1948, ch. 645, 62 Stat. 807; Pub. L. 98–473, title II, §1114, Oct. 12, 1984, 98 Stat. 2149; Pub. L. 103–322, title XXXIII, §330016(1)(K), Sept. 13, 1994, 108 Stat. 2147.)

Historical and Revision Notes

Based on title 18, U.S.C., 1940 ed., §§419c, 419d (Aug. 18, 1941, ch. 366, §§4, 5, 55 Stat. 632).

Definitions of "cattle" and "interstate or foreign commerce", contained in section 419a of title 18, U.S.C., 1940 ed., are incorporated in sections 10 and 2311 of this title.

Venue provision of said section 419d of title 18, U.S.C., 1940 ed., was omitted as completely covered by section 3237 of this title.

Minor changes were made in phraseology.

Amendments

1994—Pub. L. 103–322 substituted "fined under this title" for "fined not more than $5,000".
1984—Pub. L. 98–473 substituted "livestock" for "cattle" in section catchline and text.

§2318. Trafficking in counterfeit labels, illicit labels, or counterfeit documentation or packaging

(a)(1) 1 Whoever, in any of the circumstances described in subsection (c), knowingly traffics in—

(A) a counterfeit label or illicit label affixed to, enclosing, or accompanying, or designed to be affixed to, enclose, or accompany—

(i) a phonorecord;

(ii) a copy of a computer program;

(iii) a copy of a motion picture or other audiovisual work;

(iv) a copy of a literary work;

(v) a copy of a pictorial, graphic, or sculptural work;

(vi) a work of visual art; or

(vii) documentation or packaging; or

(B) counterfeit documentation or packaging,

shall be fined under this title or imprisoned for not more than 5 years, or both.

(b) As used in this section—

(1) the term "counterfeit label" means an identifying label or container that appears to be genuine, but is not;

(2) the term "traffic" has the same meaning as in section 2320(f) of this title;

(3) the terms "copy", "phonorecord", "motion picture", "computer program", "audiovisual work", "literary work", "pictorial, graphic, or sculptural work", "sound recording", "work of visual art", and "copyright owner" have, respectively, the meanings given those terms in section 101 (relating to definitions) of title 17;

(4) the term "illicit label" means a genuine certificate, licensing document, registration card, or similar labeling component—

(A) that is used by the copyright owner to verify that a phonorecord, a copy of a computer program, a copy of a motion picture or other audiovisual work, a copy of a literary work, a copy of a pictorial, graphic, or sculptural work, a work of visual art, or documentation or packaging is not counterfeit or infringing of any copyright; and

(B) that is, without the authorization of the copyright owner—

(i) distributed or intended for distribution not in connection with the copy, phonorecord, or work of visual art to which such labeling component was intended to be affixed by the respective copyright owner; or

(ii) in connection with a genuine certificate or licensing document, knowingly falsified in order to designate a higher number of licensed users or copies than authorized by the copyright owner, unless that certificate or document is used by the copyright owner solely for the purpose of monitoring or tracking the copyright owner's distribution channel and not for the purpose of verifying that a copy or phonorecord is noninfringing;

(5) the term "documentation or packaging" means documentation or packaging, in physical form, for a phonorecord, copy of a computer program, copy of a motion picture or other audiovisual work, copy of a literary work, copy of a pictorial, graphic, or sculptural work, or work of visual art; and

(6) the term "counterfeit documentation or packaging" means documentation or packaging that appears to be genuine, but is not.

(c) The circumstances referred to in subsection (a) of this section are—

(1) the offense is committed within the special maritime and territorial jurisdiction of the United States; or within the special aircraft jurisdiction of the United States (as defined in section 46501 of title 49);

(2) the mail or a facility of interstate or foreign commerce is used or intended to be used in the commission of the offense;

(3) the counterfeit label or illicit label is affixed to, encloses, or accompanies, or is designed to be affixed to, enclose, or accompany—

(A) a phonorecord of a copyrighted sound recording or copyrighted musical work;

(B) a copy of a copyrighted computer program;

(C) a copy of a copyrighted motion picture or other audiovisual work;

(D) a copy of a literary work;

(E) a copy of a pictorial, graphic, or sculptural work;

(F) a work of visual art; or

(G) copyrighted documentation or packaging; or

(4) the counterfeited documentation or packaging is copyrighted.

(d) Forfeiture and Destruction of Property; Restitution.—Forfeiture, destruction, and restitution relating to this section shall be subject to section 2323, to the extent provided in that section, in addition to any other similar remedies provided by law.

(e) Civil Remedies.—

(1) In general.—Any copyright owner who is injured, or is threatened with injury, by a violation of subsection (a) may bring a civil action in an appropriate United States district court.

(2) Discretion of court.—In any action brought under paragraph (1), the court—

(A) may grant 1 or more temporary or permanent injunctions on such terms as the court determines to be reasonable to prevent or restrain a violation of subsection (a);

(B) at any time while the action is pending, may order the impounding, on such terms as the court determines to be reasonable, of any article that is in the custody or control of the alleged violator and that the court has reasonable cause to believe was involved in a violation of subsection (a); and

(C) may award to the injured party—

(i) reasonable attorney fees and costs; and

(ii)(I) actual damages and any additional profits of the violator, as provided in paragraph (3); or

(II) statutory damages, as provided in paragraph (4).

(3) Actual damages and profits.—

(A) In general.—The injured party is entitled to recover—

(i) the actual damages suffered by the injured party as a result of a violation of subsection (a), as provided in subparagraph (B) of this paragraph; and

(ii) any profits of the violator that are attributable to a violation of subsection (a) and are not taken into account in computing the actual damages.

(B) Calculation of damages.—The court shall calculate actual damages by multiplying—

(i) the value of the phonorecords, copies, or works of visual art which are, or are intended to be, affixed with, enclosed in, or accompanied by any counterfeit labels, illicit labels, or counterfeit documentation or packaging, by

(ii) the number of phonorecords, copies, or works of visual art which are, or are intended to be, affixed with, enclosed in, or accompanied by any counterfeit labels, illicit labels, or counterfeit documentation or packaging.

(C) Definition.—For purposes of this paragraph, the "value" of a phonorecord, copy, or work of visual art is—

(i) in the case of a copyrighted sound recording or copyrighted musical work, the retail value of an authorized phonorecord of that sound recording or musical work;

(ii) in the case of a copyrighted computer program, the retail value of an authorized copy of that computer program;

(iii) in the case of a copyrighted motion picture or other audiovisual work, the retail value of an authorized copy of that motion picture or audiovisual work;

(iv) in the case of a copyrighted literary work, the retail value of an authorized copy of that literary work;

(v) in the case of a pictorial, graphic, or sculptural work, the retail value of an authorized copy of that work; and

(vi) in the case of a work of visual art, the retail value of that work.

(4) Statutory damages.—The injured party may elect, at any time before final judgment is rendered, to recover, instead of actual damages and profits, an award of statutory damages for each violation of subsection (a) in a sum of not less than $2,500 or more than $25,000, as the court considers appropriate.

(5) Subsequent violation.—The court may increase an award of damages under this subsection by 3 times the amount that would otherwise be awarded, as the court considers appropriate, if the court finds that a person has subsequently violated subsection (a) within 3 years after a final judgment was entered against that person for a violation of that subsection.

(6) Limitation on actions.—A civil action may not be commenced under this subsection unless it is commenced within 3 years after the date on which the claimant discovers the violation of subsection (a).

(Added Pub. L. 87–773, §1, Oct. 9, 1962, 76 Stat. 775; amended Pub. L. 93–573, title I, §103, Dec. 31, 1974, 88 Stat. 1873; Pub. L. 94–553, title I, §111, Oct. 19, 1976, 90 Stat. 2600; Pub. L. 97–180, §2, May 24, 1982, 96 Stat. 91; Pub. L. 101–647, title XXXV, §3567, Nov. 29, 1990, 104 Stat. 4928; Pub. L. 103–272, §5(e)(10), July 5, 1994, 108 Stat. 1374; Pub. L. 103–322, title XXXIII, §330016(1)(U), Sept. 13, 1994, 108 Stat. 2148; Pub. L. 104–153, §4(a), (b)(1), July 2, 1996, 110 Stat. 1386, 1387; Pub. L. 108–482, title I, §102(a), (b), Dec. 23, 2004, 118 Stat. 3912, 3914; Pub. L. 109–181, §2(c)(2), Mar. 16, 2006, 120 Stat. 288; Pub. L. 110–403, title II, §202, Oct. 13, 2008, 122 Stat. 4260; Pub. L. 111–295, §6(i), Dec. 9, 2010, 124 Stat. 3182; Pub. L. 114–154, §3(1), May 16, 2016, 130 Stat. 387.)

Amendments

2016—Subsec. (b)(2). Pub. L. 114–154 substituted "section 2320(f)" for "section 2320(e)".

2010—Subsec. (e)(6). Pub. L. 111–295 substituted "under this subsection" for "under section".

2008—Subsec. (a). Pub. L. 110–403, §202(1), designated existing provisions as par. (1) and redesignated former pars. (1) and (2) as subpars. (A) and (B), respectively, of par. (1), and former subpars. (A) to (G) as cls. (i) to (vii), respectively, of subpar. (A).

Subsec. (d). Pub. L. 110–403, §202(2), amended subsec. (d) generally. Prior to amendment, subsec. (d) read as follows: "When any person is convicted of any violation of subsection (a), the court in its judgment of conviction shall in addition to the penalty therein prescribed, order the forfeiture and destruction or other disposition of all counterfeit labels or illicit labels and all articles to which counterfeit labels or illicit labels have been affixed or which were intended to have had such labels affixed, and of any equipment, device, or material used to manufacture, reproduce, or assemble the counterfeit labels or illicit labels."

Subsecs. (e), (f). Pub. L. 110–403, §202(3), redesignated subsec. (f) as (e) and struck out former subsec. (e) which read as follows: "Except to the extent they are inconsistent with the provisions of this title, all provisions of section 509, title 17, United States Code, are applicable to violations of subsection (a)."

2006—Subsec. (b)(2). Pub. L. 109–181 added par. (2) and struck out former par. (2) which read as follows: "the term 'traffic' means to transport, transfer or otherwise dispose of, to another, as consideration for anything of value or to make or obtain control of with intent to so transport, transfer or dispose of;".

2004—Pub. L. 108–482, §102(a)(1), substituted "Trafficking in counterfeit labels, illicit labels, or counterfeit documentation or packaging" for "Trafficking in counterfeit labels for phonorecords, copies of computer programs or computer program documentation or packaging, and copies of motion pictures or other audio visual works, and trafficking in counterfeit computer program documentation or packaging" in section catchline.

Subsec. (a). Pub. L. 108–482, §102(a)(2), added subsec. (a) and struck out former subsec. (a) which read as follows: "Whoever, in any of the circumstances described in subsection (c) of this section, knowingly traffics in a counterfeit label affixed or designed to be affixed to a phonorecord, or a copy of a computer program or documentation or packaging for a computer program, or a copy of a motion picture or other audiovisual work, and whoever, in any of the circumstances described in subsection (c) of this section, knowingly traffics in counterfeit documentation or packaging for a computer program, shall be fined under this title or imprisoned for not more than five years, or both."

Subsec. (b)(2). Pub. L. 108–482, §102(a)(3)(A), struck out "and" after the semicolon at end.

Subsec. (b)(3). Pub. L. 108–482, §102(a)(3)(B), substituted " 'audiovisual work', 'literary work', 'pictorial, graphic, or sculptural work', 'sound recording', 'work of visual art', and 'copyright owner' have" for "and 'audiovisual work' have" and a semicolon for the period at end.

Subsec. (b)(4) to (6). Pub. L. 108–482, §102(a)(3)(C), added pars. (4) to (6).

Subsec. (c)(3). Pub. L. 108–482, §102(a)(4)(A), added par. (3) and struck former par. (3) which read as follows: "the counterfeit label is affixed to or encloses, or is designed to be affixed to or enclose, a copy of a copyrighted computer program or copyrighted documentation or packaging for a computer program, a copyrighted motion picture or other audiovisual work, or a phonorecord of a copyrighted sound recording; or".

Subsec. (c)(4). Pub. L. 108–482, §102(a)(4)(B), struck out "for a computer program" after "packaging".

Subsec. (d). Pub. L. 108–482, §102(a)(5), inserted "or illicit labels" after "counterfeit labels" in two places and inserted ", and of any equipment, device, or material used to manufacture, reproduce, or assemble the counterfeit labels or illicit labels" before period at end.

Subsec. (f). Pub. L. 108–482, §102(b), added subsec. (f).

1996—Pub. L. 104–153, §4(b)(1), substituted "Trafficking in counterfeit labels for phonorecords, copies of computer programs or computer program documentation or packaging, and copies of motion pictures or other audio visual works, and trafficking in counterfeit computer program documentation or packaging" for "Trafficking in counterfeit labels for phonorecords and copies of motion pictures or other audiovisual works" in section catchline.

Subsec. (a). Pub. L. 104–153, §4(a)(1), substituted "a computer program or documentation or packaging for a computer program, or a copy of a motion picture or other audiovisual work, and whoever, in any of the circumstances described in subsection (c) of this section, knowingly traffics in counterfeit documentation or packaging for a computer program," for "a motion picture or other audiovisual work,".

Subsec. (b)(3). Pub. L. 104–153, §4(a)(2), inserted " 'computer program'," after " 'motion picture',".

Subsec. (c)(2). Pub. L. 104–153, §4(a)(3)(A), struck out "or" at end.

Subsec. (c)(3). Pub. L. 104–153, §4(a)(3)(B), inserted "a copy of a copyrighted computer program or copyrighted documentation or packaging for a computer program," after "enclose," and substituted "; or" for period at end.

Subsec. (c)(4). Pub. L. 104–153, §4(a)(3)(C), added par. (4).

1994—Subsec. (a). Pub. L. 103–322 substituted "fined under this title" for "fined not more than $250,000".

Subsec. (c)(1). Pub. L. 103–272 substituted "section 46501 of title 49" for "section 101 of the Federal Aviation Act of 1958".

1990—Pub. L. 101–647 struck out comma after "phonorecords" in section catchline.

1982—Pub. L. 97–180 substituted "Trafficking in counterfeit labels for phonorecords, and copies of motion pictures or other audiovisual works" for "Transportation, sale or receipt of phonograph records bearing forged or counterfeit labels" in section catchline.

Subsec. (a). Pub. L. 97–180 substituted provision that violators of this section shall be fined not more than $250,000 or imprisoned for not more than five years or both for provision that whoever knowingly and with fraudulent intent transported, caused to be transported, received, sold, or offered for sale in interstate or foreign commerce any phonograph record, disk, wire, tape, film, or other article on which sounds were recorded, to which or upon which was stamped, pasted, or affixed any forged or counterfeited label, knowing the label to have been falsely made, forged, or counterfeited would be fined not more than $10,000 or imprisoned for not more than one year, or both, for the first such offense and would be fined not more than $25,000 or imprisoned for not more than two years, or both, for any subsequent offense.

Subsecs. (b) to (e). Pub. L. 97–180 added subsecs. (b) and (c), redesignated former subsecs. (b) and (c) as (d) and (e), respectively, and in subsec. (d) as so redesignated struck out the comma after "judgment of conviction shall".

1976—Pub. L. 94–553 designated existing provisions as subsec. (a) and substituted "$10,000" for "$25,000" and "$25,000" for "$50,000", and added subsecs. (b) and (c).

1974—Pub. L. 93–573 substituted "not more than $25,000 or imprisoned for not more than one year, or both, for the first offense and shall be fined not more than $50,000 or imprisoned not more than 2 years, or both, for any subsequent offense" for "not more than $1,000 or imprisoned not more than one year or both".

Effective Date of 1976 Amendment

Amendment by Pub. L. 94–553 effective Jan. 1, 1978, see section 102 of Pub. L. 94–553, set out as a note preceding section 101 of Title 17, Copyrights.

Other Rights Not Affected by Anti-Counterfeiting Provisions

Pub. L. 108–482, title I, §103, Dec. 23, 2004, 118 Stat. 3915, provided that:

"(a) Chapters 5 and 12 of Title 17; Electronic Transmissions.—The amendments made by this title [amending this section]—

"(1) shall not enlarge, diminish, or otherwise affect any liability or limitations on liability under sections 512, 1201 or 1202 of title 17, United States Code; and

"(2) shall not be construed to apply—

"(A) in any case, to the electronic transmission of a genuine certificate, licensing document, registration card, similar labeling component, or documentation or packaging described in paragraph (4) or (5) of section 2318(b) of title 18, United States Code, as amended by this title; and

"(B) in the case of a civil action under section 2318(f) [now 2318(e)] of title 18, United States Code, to the electronic transmission of a counterfeit label or counterfeit documentation or packaging defined in paragraph (1) or (6) of section 2318(b) of title 18, United States Code.

"(b) Fair Use.—The amendments made by this title shall not affect the fair use, under section 107 of title 17, United States Code, of a genuine certificate, licensing document, registration card, similar labeling component, or documentation or packaging described in paragraph (4) or (5) of section 2318(b) of title 18, United States Code, as amended by this title."

§2319. Criminal infringement of a copyright

(a) Any person who violates section 506(a) (relating to criminal offenses) of title 17 shall be punished as provided in subsections (b), (c), and (d) and such penalties shall be in addition to any other provisions of title 17 or any other law.

(b) Any person who commits an offense under section 506(a)(1)(A) of title 17—

(1) shall be imprisoned not more than 5 years, or fined in the amount set forth in this title, or both, if the offense consists of the reproduction or distribution, including by electronic means, during any 180-day period, of at least 10 copies or phonorecords, of 1 or more copyrighted works, which have a total retail value of more than $2,500;

(2) shall be imprisoned not more than 10 years, or fined in the amount set forth in this title, or both, if the offense is a felony and is a second or subsequent offense under subsection (a); and

(3) shall be imprisoned not more than 1 year, or fined in the amount set forth in this title, or both, in any other case.

(c) Any person who commits an offense under section 506(a)(1)(B) of title 17—

(1) shall be imprisoned not more than 3 years, or fined in the amount set forth in this title, or both, if the offense consists of the reproduction or distribution of 10 or more copies or phonorecords of 1 or more copyrighted works, which have a total retail value of $2,500 or more;

(2) shall be imprisoned not more than 6 years, or fined in the amount set forth in this title, or both, if the offense is a felony and is a second or subsequent offense under subsection (a); and

(3) shall be imprisoned not more than 1 year, or fined in the amount set forth in this title, or both, if the offense consists of the reproduction or distribution of 1 or more copies or phonorecords of 1 or more copyrighted works, which have a total retail value of more than $1,000.

(d) Any person who commits an offense under section 506(a)(1)(C) of title 17—

(1) shall be imprisoned not more than 3 years, fined under this title, or both;

(2) shall be imprisoned not more than 5 years, fined under this title, or both, if the offense was committed for purposes of commercial advantage or private financial gain;

(3) shall be imprisoned not more than 6 years, fined under this title, or both, if the offense is a felony and is a second or subsequent offense under subsection (a); and

(4) shall be imprisoned not more than 10 years, fined under this title, or both, if the offense is a felony and is a second or subsequent offense under paragraph (2).

(e)(1) During preparation of the presentence report pursuant to Rule 32(c) of the Federal Rules of Criminal Procedure, victims of the offense shall be permitted to submit, and the probation officer shall receive, a victim impact statement that identifies the victim of the offense and the extent and scope of the injury and loss suffered by the victim, including the estimated economic impact of the offense on that victim.

(2) Persons permitted to submit victim impact statements shall include—

(A) producers and sellers of legitimate works affected by conduct involved in the offense;

(B) holders of intellectual property rights in such works; and

(C) the legal representatives of such producers, sellers, and holders.

(f) As used in this section—

(1) the terms "phonorecord" and "copies" have, respectively, the meanings set forth in section 101 (relating to definitions) of title 17;

(2) the terms "reproduction" and "distribution" refer to the exclusive rights of a copyright owner under clauses (1) and (3) respectively of section 106 (relating to exclusive rights in copyrighted works), as limited by sections 107 through 122, of title 17;

(3) the term "financial gain" has the meaning given the term in section 101 of title 17; and

(4) the term "work being prepared for commercial distribution" has the meaning given the term in section 506(a) of title 17.

(Added Pub. L. 97–180, §3, May 24, 1982, 96 Stat. 92; amended Pub. L. 102–561, Oct. 28, 1992, 106 Stat. 4233; Pub. L. 105–80, §12(b)(2), Nov. 13, 1997, 111 Stat. 1536; Pub. L. 105–147, §2(d), Dec. 16, 1997, 111 Stat. 2678; Pub. L. 107–273, div. C, title III, §13211(a), Nov. 2, 2002, 116 Stat. 1910; Pub. L. 109–9, title I, §103(b), Apr. 27, 2005, 119 Stat. 220; Pub. L. 110–403, title II, §208, Oct. 13, 2008, 122 Stat. 4263.)

References in Text

The Federal Rules of Criminal Procedure, referred to in subsec. (e)(1), are set out in the Appendix to this title.

Amendments

2008—Subsecs. (b)(2), (c)(2). Pub. L. 110–403, §208(1), (2), inserted "is a felony and" after "the offense" and substituted "subsection (a)" for "paragraph (1)".

Subsec. (d)(3). Pub. L. 110–403, §208(3), inserted "is a felony and" after "the offense" and "under subsection (a)" before the semicolon.

Subsec. (d)(4). Pub. L. 110–403, §208(4), inserted "is a felony and" after "the offense".

2005—Subsec. (a). Pub. L. 109–9, §103(b)(1), substituted "Any person who" for "Whoever" and ", (c), and (d)" for "and (c) of this section".

Subsec. (b). Pub. L. 109–9, §103(b)(2), substituted "section 506(a)(1)(A)" for "section 506(a)(1)" in introductory provisions.

Subsec. (c). Pub. L. 109–9, §103(b)(3), substituted "section 506(a)(1)(B) of title 17" for "section

506(a)(2) of title 17, United States Code" in introductory provisions.

Subsecs. (d), (e). Pub. L. 109–9, §103(b)(4), (5), added subsec. (d) and redesignated former subsec. (d) as (e). Former subsec. (e) redesignated (f).

Subsec. (f). Pub. L. 109–9, §103(b)(4), (6), redesignated subsec. (e) as (f) and added pars. (3) and (4).

2002—Subsec. (e)(2). Pub. L. 107–273 substituted "107 through 122" for "107 through 120".

1997—Subsec. (a). Pub. L. 105–147, §2(d)(1), substituted "subsections (b) and (c)" for "subsection (b)".

Subsec. (b). Pub. L. 105–147, §2(d)(2)(A), substituted "section 506(a)(1) of title 17" for "subsection (a) of this section" in introductory provisions.

Subsec. (b)(1). Pub. L. 105–147, §2(d)(2)(B), inserted "including by electronic means," after "if the offense consists of the reproduction or distribution," and substituted "which have a total retail value of more than $2,500" for "with a retail value of more than $2,500".

Pub. L. 105–80, substituted "at least 10 copies" for "at last 10 copies".

Subsecs. (c) to (e). Pub. L. 105–147, §2(d)(3), added subsecs. (c) and (d) and redesignated former subsec. (c) as (e).

1992—Subsec. (b). Pub. L. 102–561, §1, amended subsec. (b) generally. Prior to amendment, subsec. (b) read as follows: "Any person who commits an offense under subsection (a) of this section—

"(1) shall be fined not more than $250,000 or imprisoned for not more than five years, or both, if the offense—

"(A) involves the reproduction or distribution, during any one-hundred-and-eighty-day period, of at least one thousand phonorecords or copies infringing the copyright in one or more sound recordings;

"(B) involves the reproduction or distribution, during any one-hundred-and-eighty-day period, of at least sixty-five copies infringing the copyright in one or more motion pictures or other audiovisual works; or

"(C) is a second or subsequent offense under either of subsection (b)(1) or (b)(2) of this section, where a prior offense involved a sound recording, or a motion picture or other audiovisual work;

"(2) shall be fined not more than $250,000 or imprisoned for not more than two years, or both, if the offense—

"(A) involves the reproduction or distribution, during any one-hundred-and-eighty-day period, of more than one hundred but less than one thousand phonorecords or copies infringing the copyright in one or more sound recordings; or

"(B) involves the reproduction or distribution, during any one-hundred-and-eighty-day period, of more than seven but less than sixty-five copies infringing the copyright in one or more motion pictures or other audiovisual works; and

"(3) shall be fined not more than $25,000 or imprisoned for not more than one year, or both, in any other case."

Subsec. (c). Pub. L. 102–561, §2, substituted " 'phonorecord' " for " 'sound recording', 'motion picture', 'audiovisual work', 'phonorecord'," in par. (1) and "120" for "118" in par. (2).

§2319A. Unauthorized fixation of and trafficking in sound recordings and music videos of live musical performances

(a) Offense.—Whoever, without the consent of the performer or performers involved, knowingly and for purposes of commercial advantage or private financial gain—

(1) fixes the sounds or sounds and images of a live musical performance in a copy or phonorecord, or reproduces copies or phonorecords of such a performance from an unauthorized fixation;

(2) transmits or otherwise communicates to the public the sounds or sounds and images of a live musical performance; or

(3) distributes or offers to distribute, sells or offers to sell, rents or offers to rent, or traffics in any copy or phonorecord fixed as described in paragraph (1), regardless of whether the fixations

occurred in the United States;

shall be imprisoned for not more than 5 years or fined in the amount set forth in this title, or both, or if the offense is a second or subsequent offense, shall be imprisoned for not more than 10 years or fined in the amount set forth in this title, or both.

(b) Forfeiture and Destruction of Property; Restitution.—Forfeiture, destruction, and restitution relating to this section shall be subject to section 2323, to the extent provided in that section, in addition to any other similar remedies provided by law.

(c) Seizure and Forfeiture.—If copies or phonorecords of sounds or sounds and images of a live musical performance are fixed outside of the United States without the consent of the performer or performers involved, such copies or phonorecords are subject to seizure and forfeiture in the United States in the same manner as property imported in violation of the customs laws. The Secretary of Homeland Security shall issue regulations by which any performer may, upon payment of a specified fee, be entitled to notification by United States Customs and Border Protection of the importation of copies or phonorecords that appear to consist of unauthorized fixations of the sounds or sounds and images of a live musical performance.

(d) Victim Impact Statement.—(1) During preparation of the presentence report pursuant to Rule 32(c) of the Federal Rules of Criminal Procedure, victims of the offense shall be permitted to submit, and the probation officer shall receive, a victim impact statement that identifies the victim of the offense and the extent and scope of the injury and loss suffered by the victim, including the estimated economic impact of the offense on that victim.

(2) Persons permitted to submit victim impact statements shall include—

(A) producers and sellers of legitimate works affected by conduct involved in the offense;

(B) holders of intellectual property rights in such works; and

(C) the legal representatives of such producers, sellers, and holders.

(e) Definitions.—As used in this section—

(1) the terms "copy", "fixed", "musical work", "phonorecord", "reproduce", "sound recordings", and "transmit" mean those terms within the meaning of title 17; and

(2) the term "traffic" has the same meaning as in section 2320(e) 1 of this title.

(f) Applicability.—This section shall apply to any Act or Acts that occur on or after the date of the enactment of the Uruguay Round Agreements Act.

(Added Pub. L. 103–465, title V, §513(a), Dec. 8, 1994, 108 Stat. 4974; amended Pub. L. 105–147, §2(e), Dec. 16, 1997, 111 Stat. 2679; Pub. L. 109–181, §2(c)(1), Mar. 16, 2006, 120 Stat. 288; Pub. L. 110–403, title II, §203, Oct. 13, 2008, 122 Stat. 4261.)

References in Text

The Federal Rules of Criminal Procedure, referred to in subsec. (d)(1), are set out in the Appendix to this title.

Section 2320 of this title, referred to in subsec. (e)(2), was amended generally by Pub. L. 112–81, div. A, title VIII, §818(h), Dec. 31, 2011, 125 Stat. 1497, and, as so amended, provisions similar to those formerly appearing in subsec. (e) are now contained in subsec. (f).

The date of the enactment of the Uruguay Round Agreements Act, referred to in subsec. (f), is the date of enactment of Pub. L. 103–465, which was approved Dec. 8, 1994.

Amendments

2008—Subsec. (b). Pub. L. 110–403, §203(a), amended subsec. (b) generally. Prior to amendment, text read as follows: "When a person is convicted of a violation of subsection (a), the court shall order the forfeiture and destruction of any copies or phonorecords created in violation thereof, as well as any plates, molds, matrices, masters, tapes, and film negatives by means of which such copies or phonorecords may be made. The court may also, in its discretion, order the forfeiture and destruction of any other equipment by means of which such copies or phonorecords may be reproduced, taking into account the nature, scope, and proportionality of the use of the equipment in the offense."

Subsec. (c). Pub. L. 110–403, §203(b), substituted "The Secretary of Homeland Security shall issue regulations by which any performer may, upon payment of a specified fee, be entitled to notification by United States Customs and Border Protection of the importation of copies or phonorecords that appear to consist of unauthorized fixations of the sounds or sounds and images of a live musical performance." for "The Secretary of the Treasury shall, not later than 60 days after the date of the enactment of the Uruguay Round Agreements Act, issue regulations to carry out this subsection, including regulations by which any performer may, upon payment of a specified fee, be entitled to notification by the United States Customs Service of the importation of copies or phonorecords that appear to consist of unauthorized fixations of the sounds or sounds and images of a live musical performance."

2006—Subsec. (e)(2). Pub. L. 109–181 added par. (2) and struck out former par. (2) which read as follows: "the term 'traffic in' means transport, transfer, or otherwise dispose of, to another, as consideration for anything of value, or make or obtain control of with intent to transport, transfer, or dispose of."

1997—Subsecs. (d) to (f). Pub. L. 105–147 added subsec. (d) and redesignated former subsecs. (d) and (e) as (e) and (f), respectively.

Transfer of Functions

For transfer of functions, personnel, assets, and liabilities of the United States Customs Service of the Department of the Treasury, including functions of the Secretary of the Treasury relating thereto, to the Secretary of Homeland Security, and for treatment of related references, see sections 203(1), 551(d), 552(d), and 557 of Title 6, Domestic Security, and the Department of Homeland Security Reorganization Plan of November 25, 2002, as modified, set out as a note under section 542 of Title 6. For establishment of U.S. Customs and Border Protection in the Department of Homeland Security, treated as if included in Pub. L. 107–296 as of Nov. 25, 2002, see section 211 of Title 6, as amended generally by Pub. L. 114–125, and section 802(b) of Pub. L. 114–125, set out as a note under section 211 of Title 6.

§2319B. Unauthorized recording of Motion pictures in a Motion picture exhibition facility

(a) Offense.—Any person who, without the authorization of the copyright owner, knowingly uses or attempts to use an audiovisual recording device to transmit or make a copy of a motion picture or other audiovisual work protected under title 17, or any part thereof, from a performance of such work in a motion picture exhibition facility, shall—

(1) be imprisoned for not more than 3 years, fined under this title, or both; or

(2) if the offense is a second or subsequent offense, be imprisoned for no more than 6 years, fined under this title, or both.

The possession by a person of an audiovisual recording device in a motion picture exhibition facility may be considered as evidence in any proceeding to determine whether that person committed an offense under this subsection, but shall not, by itself, be sufficient to support a conviction of that person for such offense.

(b) Forfeiture and Destruction of Property; Restitution.—Forfeiture, destruction, and restitution relating to this section shall be subject to section 2323, to the extent provided in that section, in addition to any other similar remedies provided by law.

(c) Authorized Activities.—This section does not prevent any lawfully authorized investigative, protective, or intelligence activity by an officer, agent, or employee of the United States, a State, or a political subdivision of a State, or by a person acting under a contract with the United States, a State, or a political subdivision of a State.

(d) Immunity for Theaters.—With reasonable cause, the owner or lessee of a motion picture exhibition facility where a motion picture or other audiovisual work is being exhibited, the authorized agent or employee of such owner or lessee, the licensor of the motion picture or other audiovisual work being exhibited, or the agent or employee of such licensor—

(1) may detain, in a reasonable manner and for a reasonable time, any person suspected of a violation of this section with respect to that motion picture or audiovisual work for the purpose of questioning or summoning a law enforcement officer; and

(2) shall not be held liable in any civil or criminal action arising out of a detention under paragraph (1).

(e) Victim Impact Statement.—

(1) In general.—During the preparation of the presentence report under rule 32(c) of the Federal Rules of Criminal Procedure, victims of an offense under this section shall be permitted to submit to the probation officer a victim impact statement that identifies the victim of the offense and the extent and scope of the injury and loss suffered by the victim, including the estimated economic impact of the offense on that victim.

(2) Contents.—A victim impact statement submitted under this subsection shall include—

(A) producers and sellers of legitimate works affected by conduct involved in the offense;

(B) holders of intellectual property rights in the works described in subparagraph (A); and

(C) the legal representatives of such producers, sellers, and holders.

(f) State Law Not Preempted.—Nothing in this section may be construed to annul or limit any rights or remedies under the laws of any State.

(g) Definitions.—In this section, the following definitions shall apply:

(1) Title 17 definitions.—The terms "audiovisual work", "copy", "copyright owner", "motion picture", "motion picture exhibition facility", and "transmit" have, respectively, the meanings given those terms in section 101 of title 17.

(2) Audiovisual recording device.—The term "audiovisual recording device" means a digital or analog photographic or video camera, or any other technology or device capable of enabling the recording or transmission of a copyrighted motion picture or other audiovisual work, or any part thereof, regardless of whether audiovisual recording is the sole or primary purpose of the device.

(Added Pub. L. 109–9, title I, §102(a), Apr. 27, 2005, 119 Stat. 218; amended Pub. L. 110–403, title II, §204, Oct. 13, 2008, 122 Stat. 4261.)

References in Text

The Federal Rules of Criminal Procedure, referred to in subsec. (e)(1), are set out in the Appendix to this title.

Amendments

2008—Subsec. (b). Pub. L. 110–403 amended subsec. (b) generally. Prior to amendment, text read as follows: "When a person is convicted of a violation of subsection (a), the court in its judgment of conviction shall, in addition to any penalty provided, order the forfeiture and destruction or other disposition of all unauthorized copies of motion pictures or other audiovisual works protected under title 17, or parts thereof, and any audiovisual recording devices or other equipment used in connection with the offense."

§2320. Trafficking in counterfeit goods or services

(a) Offenses.—Whoever intentionally—

(1) traffics in goods or services and knowingly uses a counterfeit mark on or in connection with such goods or services,

(2) traffics in labels, patches, stickers, wrappers, badges, emblems, medallions, charms, boxes, containers, cans, cases, hangtags, documentation, or packaging of any type or nature, knowing that a counterfeit mark has been applied thereto, the use of which is likely to cause confusion, to cause mistake, or to deceive,

(3) traffics in goods or services knowing that such good or service is a counterfeit military good or service the use, malfunction, or failure of which is likely to cause serious bodily injury or death, the disclosure of classified information, impairment of combat operations, or other significant harm to a combat operation, a member of the Armed Forces, or to national security, or

(4) traffics in a drug and knowingly uses a counterfeit mark on or in connection with such drug, or attempts or conspires to violate any of paragraphs (1) through (4) shall be punished as provided in subsection (b).

(b) Penalties.—

(1) In general.—Whoever commits an offense under subsection (a)—

(A) if an individual, shall be fined not more than $2,000,000 or imprisoned not more than 10 years, or both, and, if a person other than an individual, shall be fined not more than $5,000,000; and

(B) for a second or subsequent offense under subsection (a), if an individual, shall be fined not more than $5,000,000 or imprisoned not more than 20 years, or both, and if other than an individual, shall be fined not more than $15,000,000.

(2) Serious bodily injury or death.—

(A) Serious bodily injury.—Whoever knowingly or recklessly causes or attempts to cause serious bodily injury from conduct in violation of subsection (a), if an individual, shall be fined not more than $5,000,000 or imprisoned for not more than 20 years, or both, and if other than an individual, shall be fined not more than $15,000,000.

(B) Death.—Whoever knowingly or recklessly causes or attempts to cause death from conduct in violation of subsection (a), if an individual, shall be fined not more than $5,000,000 or imprisoned for any term of years or for life, or both, and if other than an individual, shall be fined not more than $15,000,000.

(3) Counterfeit military goods or services and counterfeit drugs.—Whoever commits an offense under subsection (a) involving a counterfeit military good or service or drug that uses a counterfeit mark on or in connection with the drug—

(A) if an individual, shall be fined not more than $5,000,000, imprisoned not more than 20 years, or both, and if other than an individual, be fined not more than $15,000,000; and

(B) for a second or subsequent offense, if an individual, shall be fined not more than $15,000,000, imprisoned not more than 30 years, or both, and if other than an individual, shall be fined not more than $30,000,000.

(c) Forfeiture and Destruction of Property; Restitution.—Forfeiture, destruction, and restitution relating to this section shall be subject to section 2323, to the extent provided in that section, in addition to any other similar remedies provided by law.

(d) Defenses.—All defenses, affirmative defenses, and limitations on remedies that would be applicable in an action under the Lanham Act shall be applicable in a prosecution under this section. In a prosecution under this section, the defendant shall have the burden of proof, by a preponderance of the evidence, of any such affirmative defense.

(e) Presentence Report.—(1) During preparation of the presentence report pursuant to Rule 32(c) of the Federal Rules of Criminal Procedure, victims of the offense shall be permitted to submit, and the probation officer shall receive, a victim impact statement that identifies the victim of the offense and the extent and scope of the injury and loss suffered by the victim, including the estimated economic impact of the offense on that victim.

(2) Persons permitted to submit victim impact statements shall include—

(A) producers and sellers of legitimate goods or services affected by conduct involved in the offense;

(B) holders of intellectual property rights in such goods or services; and

(C) the legal representatives of such producers, sellers, and holders.

(f) Definitions.—For the purposes of this section—

(1) the term "counterfeit mark" means—

(A) a spurious mark—

(i) that is used in connection with trafficking in any goods, services, labels, patches, stickers, wrappers, badges, emblems, medallions, charms, boxes, containers, cans, cases, hangtags, documentation, or packaging of any type or nature;

(ii) that is identical with, or substantially indistinguishable from, a mark registered on the principal register in the United States Patent and Trademark Office and in use, whether or not the defendant knew such mark was so registered;

(iii) that is applied to or used in connection with the goods or services for which the mark is registered with the United States Patent and Trademark Office, or is applied to or consists of a label, patch, sticker, wrapper, badge, emblem, medallion, charm, box, container, can, case, hangtag, documentation, or packaging of any type or nature that is designed, marketed, or otherwise intended to be used on or in connection with the goods or services for which the mark is registered in the United States Patent and Trademark Office; and

(iv) the use of which is likely to cause confusion, to cause mistake, or to deceive; or

(B) a spurious designation that is identical with, or substantially indistinguishable from, a designation as to which the remedies of the Lanham Act are made available by reason of section 220506 of title 36;

but such term does not include any mark or designation used in connection with goods or services, or a mark or designation applied to labels, patches, stickers, wrappers, badges, emblems, medallions, charms, boxes, containers, cans, cases, hangtags, documentation, or packaging of any type or nature used in connection with such goods or services, of which the manufacturer or producer was, at the time of the manufacture or production in question, authorized to use the mark or designation for the type of goods or services so manufactured or produced, by the holder of the right to use such mark or designation;

(2) the term "financial gain" includes the receipt, or expected receipt, of anything of value;

(3) the term "Lanham Act" means the Act entitled "An Act to provide for the registration and protection of trademarks used in commerce, to carry out the provisions of certain international conventions, and for other purposes", approved July 5, 1946 (15 U.S.C. 1051 et seq.);

(4) the term "counterfeit military good or service" means a good or service that uses a counterfeit mark on or in connection with such good or service and that—

(A) is falsely identified or labeled as meeting military specifications, or

(B) is intended for use in a military or national security application;

(5) the term "traffic" means to transport, transfer, or otherwise dispose of, to another, for purposes of commercial advantage or private financial gain, or to make, import, export, obtain control of, or possess, with intent to so transport, transfer, or otherwise dispose of; and

(6) the term "drug" means a drug, as defined in section 201 of the Federal Food, Drug, and Cosmetic Act (21 U.S.C. 321).

(g) Limitation on Cause of Action.—Nothing in this section shall entitle the United States to bring a criminal cause of action under this section for the repackaging of genuine goods or services not intended to deceive or confuse.

(h) Report to Congress.—(1) Beginning with the first year after the date of enactment of this subsection, the Attorney General shall include in the report of the Attorney General to Congress on the business of the Department of Justice prepared pursuant to section 522 of title 28, an accounting, on a district by district basis, of the following with respect to all actions taken by the Department of Justice that involve trafficking in counterfeit labels for phonorecords, copies of computer programs or computer program documentation or packaging, copies of motion pictures or other audiovisual works (as defined in section 2318 of this title), criminal infringement of copyrights (as defined in section 2319 of this title), unauthorized fixation of and trafficking in sound recordings and music videos of live musical performances (as defined in section 2319A of this title), or trafficking in goods or services bearing counterfeit marks (as defined in section 2320 of this title):

(A) The number of open investigations.

(B) The number of cases referred by the United States Customs Service.

(C) The number of cases referred by other agencies or sources.

(D) The number and outcome, including settlements, sentences, recoveries, and penalties, of all prosecutions brought under sections 2318, 2319, 2319A, and 2320 of title 18.

(2)(A) The report under paragraph (1), with respect to criminal infringement of copyright, shall include the following:

(i) The number of infringement cases in these categories: audiovisual (videos and films); audio (sound recordings); literary works (books and musical compositions); computer programs; video games; and, others.

(ii) The number of online infringement cases.

(iii) The number and dollar amounts of fines assessed in specific categories of dollar amounts. These categories shall be: no fines ordered; fines under $500; fines from $500 to $1,000; fines from $1,000 to $5,000; fines from $5,000 to $10,000; and fines over $10,000.

(iv) The total amount of restitution ordered in all copyright infringement cases.

(B) In this paragraph, the term "online infringement cases" as used in paragraph (2) means those cases where the infringer—

(i) advertised or publicized the infringing work on the Internet; or

(ii) made the infringing work available on the Internet for download, reproduction, performance, or distribution by other persons.

(C) The information required under subparagraph (A) shall be submitted in the report required in fiscal year 2005 and thereafter.

(i) Transshipment and Exportation.—No goods or services, the trafficking in of which is prohibited by this section, shall be transshipped through or exported from the United States. Any such transshipment or exportation shall be deemed a violation of section 42 of an Act to provide for the registration of trademarks used in commerce, to carry out the provisions of certain international conventions, and for other purposes, approved July 5, 1946 (commonly referred to as the "Trademark Act of 1946" or the "Lanham Act").

(Added Pub. L. 98–473, title II, §1502(a), Oct. 12, 1984, 98 Stat. 2178; amended Pub. L. 103–322, title XXXII, §320104(a), title XXXIII, §330016(1)(U), Sept. 13, 1994, 108 Stat. 2110, 2148; Pub. L. 104–153, §5, July 2, 1996, 110 Stat. 1387; Pub. L. 105–147, §2(f), Dec. 16, 1997, 111 Stat. 2679; Pub. L. 105–225, §4(b), Aug. 12, 1998, 112 Stat. 1499; Pub. L. 105–354, §2(c)(1), Nov. 3, 1998, 112 Stat. 3244; Pub. L. 107–140, §1, Feb. 8, 2002, 116 Stat. 12; Pub. L. 107–273, div. A, title II, §205(e), Nov. 2, 2002, 116 Stat. 1778; Pub. L. 109–181, §§1(b), 2(b), Mar. 16, 2006, 120 Stat. 285, 288; Pub. L. 110–403, title II, §205, Oct. 13, 2008, 122 Stat. 4261; Pub. L. 112–81, div. A, title VIII, §818(h), Dec. 31, 2011, 125 Stat. 1497; Pub. L. 112–144, title VII, §717(a)(1)–(3), July 9, 2012, 126 Stat. 1076; Pub. L. 114–154, §3(2), May 16, 2016, 130 Stat. 387.)

References in Text

The Lanham Act, referred to in subsecs. (d), (f)(1)(B), (3), and (i), also known as the Trademark Act of 1946, is act July 5, 1946, ch. 540, 60 Stat. 427, which is classified generally to chapter 22 (§1051 et seq.) of Title 15, Commerce and Trade. For complete classification of this Act to the Code, see Short Title note set out under section 1051 of Title 15 and Tables.

The Federal Rules of Criminal Procedure, referred to in subsec. (e)(1), are set out in the Appendix to this title.

The date of enactment of this subsection, referred to in subsec. (h)(1), is the date of enactment of Pub. L. 112–81, which was approved Dec. 31, 2011.

Codification

Another section 2320 was renumbered section 2321 of this title.

Amendments

2016—Subsec. (a)(4). Pub. L. 114–154, §3(2)(A), added par. (4) and struck out former par. (4) which read as follows: "traffics in a counterfeit drug,".

Subsec. (b)(3). Pub. L. 114–154, §3(2)(B), substituted "drug that uses a counterfeit mark on or in connection with the drug" for "counterfeit drug" in introductory provisions.

Subsec. (f)(6). Pub. L. 114–154, §3(2)(C), added par. (6) and struck out former par. (6) which defined "counterfeit drug".

2012—Subsec. (a). Pub. L. 112–144, §717(a)(1), added par. (4) and substituted "through (4)" for "through (3)" in concluding provisions.

Subsec. (b)(3). Pub. L. 112–144, §717(a)(2), inserted "and counterfeit drugs" after "services" in heading and "or counterfeit drug" after "service" in introductory provisions.

Subsec. (f)(6). Pub. L. 112–144, §717(a)(3), added par. (6).

2011—Pub. L. 112–81 amended section generally, adding provisions relating to counterfeit military goods and services.

2008—Subsec. (a). Pub. L. 110–403, §205(a)(1), inserted subsec. heading, designated existing provisions as par. (1) and inserted par. heading, substituted "Whoever;" for "Whoever", realigned margin, and added par. (2).

Subsec. (b). Pub. L. 110–403, §205(b), amended subsec. (b) generally. Prior to amendment, subsec. (b) related to property subject to forfeiture, forfeiture procedures, and restitution.

Subsec. (h). Pub. L. 110–403, §205(a)(2), added subsec. (h).

2006—Subsec. (a). Pub. L. 109–181, §1(b)(1), inserted ", or intentionally traffics or attempts to traffic in labels, patches, stickers, wrappers, badges, emblems, medallions, charms, boxes, containers, cans, cases, hangtags, documentation, or packaging of any type or nature, knowing that a counterfeit mark has been applied thereto, the use of which is likely to cause confusion, to cause mistake, or to deceive," after "such goods or services".

Subsec. (b). Pub. L. 109–181, §1(b)(2), amended subsec. (b) generally. Prior to amendment, subsec. (b) read as follows: "Upon a determination by a preponderance of the evidence that any articles in the possession of a defendant in a prosecution under this section bear counterfeit marks, the United States may obtain an order for the destruction of such articles."

Subsec. (e)(1). Pub. L. 109–181, §1(b)(3)(B), amended concluding provisions generally. Prior to amendment, concluding provisions read as follows: "but such term does not include any mark or designation used in connection with goods or services of which the manufacturer or producer was, at the time of the manufacture or production in question authorized to use the mark or designation for the type of goods or services so manufactured or produced, by the holder of the right to use such mark or designation;".

Subsec. (e)(1)(A). Pub. L. 109–181, §1(b)(3)(A), added subpar. (A) and struck out former subpar. (A) which read as follows: "a spurious mark—

"(i) that is used in connection with trafficking in goods or services;

"(ii) that is identical with, or substantially indistinguishable from, a mark registered for those goods or services on the principal register in the United States Patent and Trademark Office and in use, whether or not the defendant knew such mark was so registered; and

"(iii) the use of which is likely to cause confusion, to cause mistake, or to deceive; or".

Subsec. (e)(2). Pub. L. 109–181, §2(b)(1), added par. (2) and struck out former par. (2) which read as follows: "the term 'traffic' means transport, transfer, or otherwise dispose of, to another, as consideration for anything of value, or make or obtain control of with intent so to transport, transfer, or dispose of; and".

Subsec. (e)(3), (4). Pub. L. 109–181, §2(b)(2), (3), added par. (3) and redesignated former par. (3) as (4).

Subsecs. (f), (g). Pub. L. 109–181, §1(b)(4), added subsec. (f) and redesignated former subsec. (f) as (g).

2002—Subsec. (e)(1)(B). Pub. L. 107–140 substituted "section 220506 of title 36" for "section 220706 of title 36".

Subsec. (f). Pub. L. 107–273, §205(e), designated existing provisions as par. (1), substituted "this title" for "title 18" wherever appearing, redesignated former pars. (1) to (4) as subpars. (A) to (D), respectively, of par. (1), and added par. (2).

1998—Subsec. (e)(1)(B). Pub. L. 105–225, §4(b)(1), as amended by Pub. L. 105–354, §2(c)(1), substituted "section 220706 of title 36" for "section 110 of the Olympic Charter Act".

Subsec. (e)(2). Pub. L. 105–225, §4(b)(2), as amended by Pub. L. 105–354, §2(c)(1), inserted "and" after semicolon at end.

Subsec. (e)(3). Pub. L. 105–225, §4(b)(3), as amended by Pub. L. 105–354, §2(c)(1), substituted a period for "; and" at end.

Subsec. (e)(4). Pub. L. 105–225, §4(b)(4), as amended by Pub. L. 105–354, §2(c)(1), struck out par. (4) which read as follows: "the term 'Olympic Charter Act' means the Act entitled 'An Act to incorporate the United States Olympic Association', approved September 21, 1950 (36 U.S.C. 371 et seq.)."

1997—Subsecs. (d) to (f). Pub. L. 105–147 added subsec. (d) and redesignated former subsecs. (d) and (e) as (e) and (f), respectively.

1996—Subsec. (e). Pub. L. 104–153 added subsec. (e).

1994—Pub. L. 103–322, §330016(1)(U), which directed the amendment of this section by striking "not more than $250,000" and inserting "under this title", could not be executed because the phrase "not more than $250,000" did not appear in text subsequent to amendment of subsec. (a) by Pub. L. 103–322, §320104(a). See below.

Subsec. (a). Pub. L. 103–322, §320104(a), in first sentence, substituted "$2,000,000 or imprisoned not more than 10 years" for "$250,000 or imprisoned not more than five years" and "$5,000,000" for "$1,000,000", and in second sentence, substituted "$5,000,000 or imprisoned not more than 20 years" for "$1,000,000 or imprisoned not more than fifteen years" and "$15,000,000" for "$5,000,000".

Effective Date of 1998 Amendment

Pub. L. 105–354, §2(c), Nov. 3, 1998, 112 Stat. 3244, provided that the amendment made by section 2(c) is effective Aug. 12, 1998.

Transfer of Functions

For transfer of functions, personnel, assets, and liabilities of the United States Customs Service of the Department of the Treasury, including functions of the Secretary of the Treasury relating thereto, to the Secretary of Homeland Security, and for treatment of related references, see sections 203(1), 551(d), 552(d), and 557 of Title 6, Domestic Security, and the Department of Homeland Security Reorganization Plan of November 25, 2002, as modified, set out as a note under section 542 of Title 6. For establishment of U.S. Customs and Border Protection in the Department of Homeland Security, treated as if included in Pub. L. 107–296 as of Nov. 25, 2002, see section 211 of Title 6, as amended generally by Pub. L. 114–125, and section 802(b) of Pub. L. 114–125, set out as a note under section 211 of Title 6.

Priority Given to Certain Investigations and Prosecutions

Pub. L. 112–144, title VII, §717(a)(4), July 9, 2012, 126 Stat. 1076, provided that: "The Attorney General shall give increased priority to efforts to investigate and prosecute offenses under section 2320 of title 18, United States Code, that involve counterfeit drugs."

Findings

Pub. L. 109–181, §1(a)(2), Mar. 16, 2006, 120 Stat. 285, provided that: "The Congress finds that—

"(A) the United States economy is losing millions of dollars in tax revenue and tens of thousands of jobs because of the manufacture, distribution, and sale of counterfeit goods;

"(B) the Bureau of Customs and Border Protection estimates that counterfeiting costs the United States $200 billion annually;

"(C) counterfeit automobile parts, including brake pads, cost the auto industry alone billions of dollars in lost sales each year;

"(D) counterfeit products have invaded numerous industries, including those producing auto parts, electrical appliances, medicines, tools, toys, office equipment, clothing, and many other products;

"(E) ties have been established between counterfeiting and terrorist organizations that use the sale of counterfeit goods to raise and launder money;

"(F) ongoing counterfeiting of manufactured goods poses a widespread threat to public health and safety; and

"(G) strong domestic criminal remedies against counterfeiting will permit the United States to seek stronger anticounterfeiting provisions in bilateral and international agreements with trading partners."

§2321. Trafficking in certain motor vehicles or motor vehicle parts

(a) Whoever buys, receives, possesses, or obtains control of, with intent to sell or otherwise dispose of, a motor vehicle or motor vehicle part, knowing that an identification number for such motor vehicle or part has been removed, obliterated, tampered with, or altered, shall be fined under this title or imprisoned not more than ten years, or both.

(b) Subsection (a) does not apply if the removal, obliteration, tampering, or alteration—

(1) is caused by collision or fire; or

(2) is not a violation of section 511 of this title.

(c) As used in this section, the terms "identification number" and "motor vehicle" have the meaning given those terms in section 511 of this title.

(Added Pub. L. 98–547, title II, §204(a), Oct. 25, 1984, 98 Stat. 2770, §2320; renumbered §2321, Pub. L. 99–646, §42(a), Nov. 10, 1986, 100 Stat. 3601; amended Pub. L. 103–322, title XXXIII, §330016(1)(N), Sept. 13, 1994, 108 Stat. 2148.)

Amendments

1994—Subsec. (a). Pub. L. 103–322 substituted "fined under this title" for "fined not more than $20,000".

§2322. Chop shops

(a) In General.—

(1) Unlawful action.—Any person who knowingly owns, operates, maintains, or controls a chop shop or conducts operations in a chop shop shall be punished by a fine under this title or by imprisonment for not more than 15 years, or both. If a conviction of a person under this paragraph is for a violation committed after the first conviction of such person under this paragraph, the maximum punishment shall be doubled with respect to any fine and imprisonment.

(2) Injunctions.—The Attorney General shall, as appropriate, in the case of any person who violates paragraph (1), commence a civil action for permanent or temporary injunction to restrain such violation.

(b) Definition.—For purposes of this section, the term "chop shop" means any building, lot, facility, or other structure or premise where one or more persons engage in receiving, concealing, destroying, disassembling, dismantling, reassembling, or storing any passenger motor vehicle or passenger motor vehicle part which has been unlawfully obtained in order to alter, counterfeit, deface, destroy, disguise, falsify, forge, obliterate, or remove the identity, including the vehicle identification number or derivative thereof, of such vehicle or vehicle part and to distribute, sell, or dispose of such vehicle or vehicle part in interstate or foreign commerce.

(Added Pub. L. 102–519, title I, §105(a), Oct. 25, 1992, 106 Stat. 3385.)

§2323. Forfeiture, destruction, and restitution

(a) Civil Forfeiture.—

(1) Property subject to forfeiture.—The following property is subject to forfeiture to the United States Government:

(A) Any article, the making or trafficking of which is, prohibited under section 506 of title 17, or section 2318, 2319, 2319A, 2319B, or 2320, or chapter 90, of this title.

(B) Any property used, or intended to be used, in any manner or part to commit or facilitate the commission of an offense referred to in subparagraph (A).

(C) Any property constituting or derived from any proceeds obtained directly or indirectly as a result of the commission of an offense referred to in subparagraph (A).

(2) Procedures.—The provisions of chapter 46 relating to civil forfeitures shall extend to any seizure or civil forfeiture under this section. For seizures made under this section, the court shall

enter an appropriate protective order with respect to discovery and use of any records or information that has been seized. The protective order shall provide for appropriate procedures to ensure that confidential, private, proprietary, or privileged information contained in such records is not improperly disclosed or used. At the conclusion of the forfeiture proceedings, unless otherwise requested by an agency of the United States, the court shall order that any property forfeited under paragraph (1) be destroyed, or otherwise disposed of according to law.

(b) Criminal Forfeiture.—

(1) Property subject to forfeiture.—The court, in imposing sentence on a person convicted of an offense under section 506 of title 17, or section 2318, 2319, 2319A, 2319B, or 2320, or chapter 90, of this title, shall order, in addition to any other sentence imposed, that the person forfeit to the United States Government any property subject to forfeiture under subsection (a) for that offense.

(2) Procedures.—

(A) In general.—The forfeiture of property under paragraph (1), including any seizure and disposition of the property and any related judicial or administrative proceeding, shall be governed by the procedures set forth in section 413 of the Comprehensive Drug Abuse Prevention and Control Act of 1970 (21 U.S.C. 853), other than subsection (d) of that section.

(B) Destruction.—At the conclusion of the forfeiture proceedings, the court, unless otherwise requested by an agency of the United States shall order that any—

(i) forfeited article or component of an article bearing or consisting of a counterfeit mark be destroyed or otherwise disposed of according to law; and

(ii) infringing items or other property described in subsection (a)(1)(A) and forfeited under paragraph (1) of this subsection be destroyed or otherwise disposed of according to law.

(c) Restitution.—When a person is convicted of an offense under section 506 of title 17 or section 2318, 2319, 2319A, 2319B, or 2320, or chapter 90, of this title, the court, pursuant to sections 3556, 3663A, and 3664 of this title, shall order the person to pay restitution to any victim of the offense as an offense against property referred to in section 3663A(c)(1)(A)(ii) of this title.

(Added Pub. L. 110–403, title II, §206(a), Oct. 13, 2008, 122 Stat. 4262.)

CHAPTER 113A - TELEMARKETING AND EMAIL MARKETING FRAUD

Prior Provisions

A prior chapter 113A of part I of this title, consisting of section 2331 et seq. and relating to terrorism, was renumbered chapter 113B of part I of this title by Pub. L. 103–322, title XXV, §250002(a)(1), Sept. 13, 1994, 108 Stat. 2082.

Amendments

2017—Pub. L. 115–70, title IV, §402(a)(1), (b)(2), Oct. 18, 2017, 131 Stat. 1213, 1214, inserted "AND EMAIL MARKETING" after "TELEMARKETING" in chapter heading and added item 2328.

§2325. Definition

In this chapter, the term "telemarketing or email marketing"—

(1) means a plan, program, promotion, or campaign that is conducted to induce—

(A) purchases of goods or services;

(B) participation in a contest or sweepstakes;

(C) a charitable contribution, donation, or gift of money or any other thing of value;

(D) investment for financial profit;

(E) participation in a business opportunity;

(F) commitment to a loan; or

(G) participation in a fraudulent medical study, research study, or pilot study,

by use of one or more interstate telephone calls, emails, text messages, or electronic instant messages initiated either by a person who is conducting the plan, program, promotion, or campaign or by a prospective purchaser or contest or sweepstakes participant or charitable contributor, donor, or investor; and

(2) does not include the solicitation through the posting, publication, or mailing of a catalog or brochure that—

(A) contains a written description or illustration of the goods, services, or other opportunities being offered;

(B) includes the business address of the solicitor;

(C) includes multiple pages of written material or illustration; and

(D) has been issued not less frequently than once a year,

if the person making the solicitation does not solicit customers by telephone, email, text message, or electronic instant message, but only receives interstate telephone calls, emails, text messages, or electronic instant messages initiated by customers in response to the written materials, whether in hard copy or digital format, and in response to those interstate telephone calls, emails, text messages, or electronic instant messages does not conduct further solicitation.

(Added Pub. L. 115–70, title IV, §402(a)(2), Oct. 18, 2017, 131 Stat. 1213.)

Prior Provisions

A prior section 2325, added Pub. L. 103–322, title XXV, §250002(a)(2), Sept. 13, 1994, 108 Stat. 2082; amended Pub. L. 107–56, title X, §1011(d), Oct. 26, 2001, 115 Stat. 396, related to definition of "telemarketing", prior to repeal by Pub. L. 115–70, title IV, §402(a)(2), Oct. 18, 2017, 131 Stat. 1213.

Short Title

Pub. L. 103–322, title XXV, §250001, Sept. 13, 1994, 108 Stat. 2081, provided that: "This Act [probably should be "title", meaning title XXV (§§250001–250008) of Pub. L. 103–322, which enacted this chapter, amended sections 1029, 1341, and 3059 of this title, and enacted provisions set out as notes under this section and section 994 of Title 28, Judiciary and Judicial Procedure] may be cited as the 'Senior Citizens Against Marketing Scams Act of 1994'."

Information Network

Pub. L. 103–322, title XXV, §250008, Sept. 13, 1994, 108 Stat. 2088, as amended by Pub. L. 104–294, title VI, §604(b)(29), Oct. 11, 1996, 110 Stat. 3508, provided that:

"(a) Hotline.—The Attorney General shall, subject to the availability of appropriations, establish a national toll-free hotline for the purpose of—

"(1) providing general information on telemarketing fraud to interested persons; and

"(2) gathering information related to possible violations of provisions of law amended by this title [see Short Title note above].

"(b) Action on Information Gathered.—The Attorney General shall work in cooperation with the Federal Trade Commission to ensure that information gathered through the hotline shall be acted on in an appropriate manner."

§2326. Enhanced penalties

A person who is convicted of an offense under section 1028, 1029, 1341, 1342, 1343, 1344, or 1347 or section 1128B of the Social Security Act (42 U.S.C. 1320a–7b), or a conspiracy to commit such an offense, in connection with the conduct of telemarketing or email marketing—

(1) shall be imprisoned for a term of up to 5 years in addition to any term of imprisonment imposed under any of those sections, respectively; and

(2) in the case of an offense under any of those sections that—

(A) victimized ten or more persons over the age of 55; or

(B) targeted persons over the age of 55,

shall be imprisoned for a term of up to 10 years in addition to any term of imprisonment imposed under any of those sections, respectively.

(Added Pub. L. 103–322, title XXV, §250002(a)(2), Sept. 13, 1994, 108 Stat. 2082; amended Pub. L. 105–184, §§3, 4, June 23, 1998, 112 Stat. 520; Pub. L. 115–70, title IV, §402(a)(3), Oct. 18, 2017, 131 Stat. 1214.)

Amendments

2017—Pub. L. 115–70 substituted "1344, or 1347 or section 1128B of the Social Security Act (42 U.S.C. 1320a–7b)" for "or 1344" and inserted "or email marketing" after "telemarketing" in introductory provisions.

1998—Pub. L. 105–184 inserted ", or a conspiracy to commit such an offense," after "or 1344" in introductory provisions and substituted "shall" for "may" in two places.

§2327. Mandatory restitution

(a) In General.—Notwithstanding section 3663 or 3663A, and in addition to any other civil or criminal penalty authorized by law, the court shall order restitution to all victims of any offense for which an enhanced penalty is provided under section 2326.

(b) Scope and Nature of Order.—

(1) Directions.—The order of restitution under this section shall direct the defendant to pay to the victim (through the appropriate court mechanism) the full amount of the victim's losses as determined by the court pursuant to paragraph (2).

(2) Enforcement.—An order of restitution under this section shall be issued and enforced in accordance with section 3664 in the same manner as an order under section 3663A.

(3) Definition.—For purposes of this subsection, the term "full amount of the victim's losses" means all losses suffered by the victim as a proximate result of the offense.

(4) Order mandatory.—(A) The issuance of a restitution order under this section is mandatory.

(B) A court may not decline to issue an order under this section because of—

(i) the economic circumstances of the defendant; or

(ii) the fact that a victim has, or is entitled to, receive compensation for his or her injuries from the proceeds of insurance or any other source.

(c) Victim Defined.—In this section, the term "victim" has the meaning given that term in section 3663A(a)(2).

(Added Pub. L. 103–322, title XXV, §250002(a)(2), Sept. 13, 1994, 108 Stat. 2082; amended Pub. L. 104–132, title II, §205(e), Apr. 24, 1996, 110 Stat. 1232; Pub. L. 104–294, title VI, §601(n), Oct. 11, 1996, 110 Stat. 3502; Pub. L. 105–184, §5, June 23, 1998, 112 Stat. 520.)

Amendments

1998—Subsec. (a). Pub. L. 105–184, §5(1), substituted "to all victims of any offense for which an enhanced penalty is provided under section 2326" for "for any offense under this chapter".

Subsec. (c). Pub. L. 105–184, §5(2), added subsec. (c) and struck out former subsec. (c) which read as follows:

"(c) Definition.—For purposes of this section, the term 'victim' includes the individual harmed as a result of a commission of a crime under this chapter, including, in the case of a victim who is incompetent, incapacitated, or deceased, the legal guardian of the victim or representative of the victim's estate, another family member, or any other person appointed as suitable by the court, but in no event shall the defendant be named as such representative or guardian."

1996—Subsec. (a). Pub. L. 104–132, §205(e)(1), inserted "or 3663A" after "3663".

Subsec. (b)(1). Pub. L. 104–132, §205(e)(2)(A), reenacted heading without change and amended text generally. Prior to amendment, text read as follows: "The order of restitution under this section shall direct that—

"(A) the defendant pay to the victim (through the appropriate court mechanism) the full amount of the victim's losses as determined by the court, pursuant to paragraph (3); and

"(B) the United States Attorney enforce the restitution order by all available and reasonable means."

Subsec. (b)(2). Pub. L. 104–132, §205(e)(2)(B), struck out "by victim" after "Enforcement" in heading and amended text generally. Prior to amendment, text read as follows: "An order of restitution may be enforced by a victim named in the order to receive the restitution as well as by the United States Attorney, in the same manner as a judgment in a civil action."

Subsec. (b)(4)(C), (D). Pub. L. 104–132, §205(e)(2)(C), struck out subpars. (C) and (D), which related to court's consideration of economic circumstances of defendant in determining schedule of payment of restitution orders, and court's entry of nominal restitution awards where economic circumstances of defendant do not allow for payment of restitution, respectively.

Subsec. (b)(5) to (10). Pub. L. 104–132, §205(e)(2)(D), struck out pars. (5) to (10), which related, respectively, to more than 1 offender, more than 1 victim, payment schedule, setoff, effect on other sources of compensation, and condition of probation or supervised release.

Subsec. (c). Pub. L. 104–294, which directed substitution of "designee" for "delegee" wherever appearing, could not be executed because of amendment by Pub. L. 104–132, §205(e)(3), (4). See below.

Pub. L. 104–132, §205(e)(3), (4), redesignated subsec. (f) as (c) and struck out former subsec. (c) relating to proof of claim.

Subsecs. (d), (e). Pub. L. 104–132, §205(e)(3), struck out subsecs. (d) and (e) which read as follows:

"(d) Modification of Order.—A victim or the offender may petition the court at any time to modify a restitution order as appropriate in view of a change in the economic circumstances of the offender.

"(e) Reference to Magistrate or Special Master.—The court may refer any issue arising in connection with a proposed order of restitution to a magistrate or special master for proposed findings of fact and recommendations as to disposition, subject to a de novo determination of the issue by the court."

Subsec. (f). Pub. L. 104–132, §205(e)(4), redesignated subsec. (f) as (c).

Effective Date of 1996 Amendment

Amendment by Pub. L. 104–132 effective, to extent constitutionally permissible, for sentencing proceedings in cases in which defendant is convicted on or after Apr. 24, 1996, see section 211 of Pub. L. 104–132, set out as a note under section 2248 of this title.

§2328. Mandatory forfeiture

(a) In General.—The court, in imposing sentence on a person who is convicted of any offense for which an enhanced penalty is provided under section 2326, shall order that the defendant forfeit to the United States—

(1) any property, real or personal, constituting or traceable to gross proceeds obtained from such offense; and

(2) any equipment, software, or other technology used or intended to be used to commit or to facilitate the commission of such offense.

(b) Procedures.—The procedures set forth in section 413 of the Controlled Substances Act (21 U.S.C. 853), other than subsection (d) of that section, and in Rule 32.2 of the Federal Rules of Criminal Procedure, shall apply to all stages of a criminal forfeiture proceeding under this section.

(Added Pub. L. 115–70, title IV, §402(a)(4), Oct. 18, 2017, 131 Stat. 1214.)

References in Text

The Federal Rules of Criminal Procedure, referred to in subsec. (b), are set out in the Appendix to this title.

CHAPTER 113B - TERRORISM

Codification

Pub. L. 101–519, §132, Nov. 5, 1990, 104 Stat. 2250, known as the "Antiterrorism Act of 1990", amended this chapter by adding sections 2331 and 2333 to 2338 and by amending former section 2331 and renumbering it as section 2332. Pub. L. 102–27, title IV, §402, Apr. 10, 1991, 105 Stat. 155, as amended by Pub. L. 102–136, §126, Oct. 25, 1991, 105 Stat. 643, repealed section 132 of Pub. L. 101–519, effective Nov. 5, 1990, and provided that effective Nov. 5, 1990, this chapter is amended to read as if section 132 of Pub. L. 101–519 had not been enacted.

Prior Provisions

Another chapter 113B, consisting of sections 2340 to 2340B, was renumbered chapter 113C.

Amendments

2015—Pub. L. 114–23, title VIII, §811(b), June 2, 2015, 129 Stat. 311, added item 2332i.

2004—Pub. L. 108–458, title VI, §6911(a), Dec. 17, 2004, 118 Stat. 3775, added items 2332g and 2332h.

2002—Pub. L. 107–197, title I, §102(b), title II, §202(b), June 25, 2002, 116 Stat. 724, 727, added items 2332f and 2339C.

2001—Pub. L. 107–56, title VIII, §803(b), Oct. 26, 2001, 115 Stat. 377, added item 2339.

1998—Pub. L. 105–277, div. I, title II, §201(c)(2), Oct. 21, 1998, 112 Stat. 2681–871, struck out item 2332c "Use of chemical weapons".

1996—Pub. L. 104–294, title VI, §605(q), Oct. 11, 1996, 110 Stat. 3510, redesignated item 2332d, relating to requests for military assistance to enforce prohibition in certain emergencies, as item 2332e, and moved the item to follow item 2332d, relating to financial transactions.

Pub. L. 104–294, title VI, §604(b)(5), Oct. 11, 1996, 110 Stat. 3506, amended directory language of Pub. L. 103–322, title XII, §120005(b), Sept. 13, 1994, 108 Stat. 2023. See 1994 Amendment note below.

Pub. L. 104–201, div. A, title XIV, §1416(c)(2)(B), Sept. 23, 1996, 110 Stat. 2723, which directed amendment of table of sections at beginning of the chapter 133B of this title, that relates to terrorism, by adding item 2332d relating to requests for military assistance to enforce prohibition in certain emergencies, after item 2332c, was executed by making the addition after item 2332c in the table of sections at the beginning of this chapter to reflect the probable intent of Congress. This title does not contain a chapter 133B.

Pub. L. 104–132, title III, §§303(b), 321(b), title V, §521(c), title VII, §702(b), Apr. 24, 1996, 110 Stat. 1253, 1254, 1287, 1294, added items 2332b to 2332d and 2339B.

1994—Pub. L. 103–322, title XII, §120005(b), Sept. 13, 1994, 108 Stat. 2023, as amended by Pub. L. 104–294, title VI, §604(b)(5), Oct. 11, 1996, 110 Stat. 3506, added item 2339A.

Pub. L. 103–322, title VI, §60023(b), title XXV, §250002(a)(1), (b)(2), Sept. 13, 1994, 108 Stat. 1981, 2082, 2085, renumbered chapter 113A as 113B, amended chapter heading generally, substituting "113B" for "113A", and added item 2332a.

1992—Pub. L. 102–572, title X, §1003(a)(5), Oct. 29, 1992, 106 Stat. 4524, substituted "TERRORISM" for "EXTRATERRITORIAL JURISDICTION OVER TERRORIST ACTS ABROAD AGAINST UNITED STATES NATIONALS" in chapter heading and amended chapter analysis generally, substituting "Definitions" for "Terrorist acts abroad against United States nationals" in item 2331 and adding items 2332 to 2338.

1988—Pub. L. 100–690, title VII, §7062, Nov. 18, 1988, 102 Stat. 4404, added item 2331.

§2331. Definitions

As used in this chapter—

(1) the term "international terrorism" means activities that—

(A) involve violent acts or acts dangerous to human life that are a violation of the criminal laws of the United States or of any State, or that would be a criminal violation if committed within the jurisdiction of the United States or of any State;

(B) appear to be intended—

(i) to intimidate or coerce a civilian population;

(ii) to influence the policy of a government by intimidation or coercion; or

(iii) to affect the conduct of a government by mass destruction, assassination, or kidnapping; and

(C) occur primarily outside the territorial jurisdiction of the United States, or transcend national boundaries in terms of the means by which they are accomplished, the persons they appear intended to intimidate or coerce, or the locale in which their perpetrators operate or seek asylum;

(2) the term "national of the United States" has the meaning given such term in section 101(a)(22) of the Immigration and Nationality Act;

(3) the term "person" means any individual or entity capable of holding a legal or beneficial interest in property;

(4) the term "act of war" means any act occurring in the course of—

(A) declared war;

(B) armed conflict, whether or not war has been declared, between two or more nations; or

(C) armed conflict between military forces of any origin; and

(5) the term "domestic terrorism" means activities that—

(A) involve acts dangerous to human life that are a violation of the criminal laws of the United States or of any State;

(B) appear to be intended—

(i) to intimidate or coerce a civilian population;

(ii) to influence the policy of a government by intimidation or coercion; or

(iii) to affect the conduct of a government by mass destruction, assassination, or kidnapping; and

(C) occur primarily within the territorial jurisdiction of the United States.

(Added Pub. L. 102–572, title X, §1003(a)(3), Oct. 29, 1992, 106 Stat. 4521; amended Pub. L. 107–56, title VIII, §802(a), Oct. 26, 2001, 115 Stat. 376.)

References in Text

Section 101(a)(22) of the Immigration and Nationality Act, referred to in par. (2), is classified to section 1101(a)(22) of Title 8, Aliens and Nationality.

Prior Provisions

A prior section 2331 was renumbered 2332 of this title.

Amendments

2001—Par. (1)(B)(iii). Pub. L. 107–56, §802(a)(1), substituted "by mass destruction, assassination, or kidnapping" for "by assassination or kidnapping".

Par. (5). Pub. L. 107–56, §802(a)(2)–(4), added par. (5).

Effective Date

Pub. L. 102–572, title X, §1003(c), Oct. 29, 1992, 106 Stat. 4524, provided that: "This section [enacting this section and sections 2333 to 2338 of this title, amending former section 2331 of this title, and renumbering former section 2331 of this title as 2332] and the amendments made by this section shall apply to any pending case or any cause of action arising on or after 4 years before the date of enactment of this Act [Oct. 29, 1992]."

Short Title of 2004 Amendment

Pub. L. 108–458, title VI, §6601, Dec. 17, 2004, 118 Stat. 3761, provided that: "This subtitle [subtitle G (§§6601–6604) of title VI of Pub. L. 108–458, enacting section 2339D of this title, amending sections 2332b and 2339A to 2339C of this title, and enacting provisions set out as a note under section 2332b of this title] may be cited as the 'Material Support to Terrorism Prohibition Enhancement Act of 2004'."

Short Title of 2002 Amendment

Pub. L. 107–197, title I, §101, June 25, 2002, 116 Stat. 721, provided that: "This title [enacting section 2332f of this title and provisions set out as notes under section 2332f of this title] may be cited as the 'Terrorist Bombings Convention Implementation Act of 2002'."

Pub. L. 107–197, title II, §201, June 25, 2002, 116 Stat. 724, provided that: "This title [enacting section 2339C of this title and provisions set out as notes under section 2339C of this title] may be cited as the 'Suppression of the Financing of Terrorism Convention Implementation Act of 2002'."

§2332. Criminal penalties

(a) Homicide.—Whoever kills a national of the United States, while such national is outside the United States, shall—

(1) if the killing is murder (as defined in section 1111(a)), be fined under this title, punished by death or imprisonment for any term of years or for life, or both;

(2) if the killing is a voluntary manslaughter as defined in section 1112(a) of this title, be fined under this title or imprisoned not more than ten years, or both; and

(3) if the killing is an involuntary manslaughter as defined in section 1112(a) of this title, be fined under this title or imprisoned not more than three years, or both.

(b) Attempt or Conspiracy With Respect to Homicide.—Whoever outside the United States attempts to kill, or engages in a conspiracy to kill, a national of the United States shall—

(1) in the case of an attempt to commit a killing that is a murder as defined in this chapter, be fined under this title or imprisoned not more than 20 years, or both; and

(2) in the case of a conspiracy by two or more persons to commit a killing that is a murder as defined in section 1111(a) of this title, if one or more of such persons do any overt act to effect the object of the conspiracy, be fined under this title or imprisoned for any term of years or for life, or both so fined and so imprisoned.

(c) Other Conduct.—Whoever outside the United States engages in physical violence—

(1) with intent to cause serious bodily injury to a national of the United States; or

(2) with the result that serious bodily injury is caused to a national of the United States;

shall be fined under this title or imprisoned not more than ten years, or both.

(d) Limitation on Prosecution.—No prosecution for any offense described in this section shall be undertaken by the United States except on written certification of the Attorney General or the highest ranking subordinate of the Attorney General with responsibility for criminal prosecutions that, in the judgment of the certifying official, such offense was intended to coerce, intimidate, or retaliate against a government or a civilian population.

(Added Pub. L. 99–399, title XII, §1202(a), Aug. 27, 1986, 100 Stat. 896, §2331; amended Pub. L. 101–519, §132(b), Nov. 5, 1990, 104 Stat. 2250; Pub. L. 102–27, title IV, §402, Apr. 10, 1991, 105 Stat. 155; Pub. L. 102–136, §126, Oct. 25, 1991, 105 Stat. 643; renumbered §2332 and amended Pub. L. 102–572, title X, §1003(a)(1), (2), Oct. 29, 1992, 106 Stat. 4521; Pub. L. 103–322, title VI, §60022, Sept. 13, 1994, 108 Stat. 1980; Pub. L. 104–132, title VII, §705(a)(6), Apr. 24, 1996, 110 Stat. 1295.)

Amendments

1996—Subsec. (c). Pub. L. 104–132 substituted "ten years" for "five years" in concluding provisions.

1994—Subsec. (a)(1). Pub. L. 103–322 amended par. (1) generally. Prior to amendment, par. (1) read as follows: "if the killing is a murder as defined in section 1111(a) of this title, be fined under this title or imprisoned for any term of years or for life, or both so fined and so imprisoned;".

1992—Pub. L. 102–572 renumbered section 2331 of this title as this section, substituted "Criminal penalties" for "Terrorist acts abroad against United States national" in section catchline, redesignated subsec. (e) as (d), and struck out former subsec. (d) which read as follows: "Definition.—As used in this section the term 'national of the United States' has the meaning given such term in section 101(a)(22) of the Immigration and Nationality Act (8 U.S.C. 1101(a)(22))."

1991—Pub. L. 102–27, §402, as amended by Pub. L. 102–136, §126, repealed Pub. L. 101–519, §132, and amended this section to read as if Pub. L. 101–519, §132, had not been enacted, effective as of Nov. 5, 1990, the date of enactment of Pub. L. 101–519. See Codification note preceding this section.

1990—Pub. L. 101–519, §132, which amended this section, was repealed by Pub. L. 102–27, §402, as amended. See 1991 Amendment note above.

Effective Date of 1992 Amendment

Amendment by Pub. L. 102–572 applicable to any pending case or any cause of action arising on or after 4 years before Oct. 29, 1992, see section 1003(c) of Pub. L. 102–572, set out as an Effective Date note under section 2331 of this title.

§2332a. Use of weapons of mass destruction

(a) Offense Against a National of the United States or Within the United States.—A person who, without lawful authority, uses, threatens, or attempts or conspires to use, a weapon of mass destruction—

(1) against a national of the United States while such national is outside of the United States;

(2) against any person or property within the United States, and

(A) the mail or any facility of interstate or foreign commerce is used in furtherance of the offense;

(B) such property is used in interstate or foreign commerce or in an activity that affects interstate or foreign commerce;

(C) any perpetrator travels in or causes another to travel in interstate or foreign commerce in furtherance of the offense; or

(D) the offense, or the results of the offense, affect interstate or foreign commerce, or, in the case of a threat, attempt, or conspiracy, would have affected interstate or foreign commerce;

(3) against any property that is owned, leased or used by the United States or by any department or agency of the United States, whether the property is within or outside of the United States; or

(4) against any property within the United States that is owned, leased, or used by a foreign government,

shall be imprisoned for any term of years or for life, and if death results, shall be punished by death or imprisoned for any term of years or for life.

(b) Offense by National of the United States Outside of the United States.—Any national of the United States who, without lawful authority, uses, or threatens, attempts, or conspires to use, a weapon of mass destruction outside of the United States shall be imprisoned for any term of years or for life, and if death results, shall be punished by death, or by imprisonment for any term of years or for life.

(c) Definitions.—For purposes of this section—

(1) the term "national of the United States" has the meaning given in section 101(a)(22) of the Immigration and Nationality Act (8 U.S.C. 1101(a)(22));

(2) the term "weapon of mass destruction" means—

(A) any destructive device as defined in section 921 of this title;

(B) any weapon that is designed or intended to cause death or serious bodily injury through the release, dissemination, or impact of toxic or poisonous chemicals, or their precursors;

(C) any weapon involving a biological agent, toxin, or vector (as those terms are defined in section 178 of this title); or

(D) any weapon that is designed to release radiation or radioactivity at a level dangerous to human life; and

(3) the term "property" includes all real and personal property.

(Added Pub. L. 103–322, title VI, §60023(a), Sept. 13, 1994, 108 Stat. 1980; amended Pub. L. 104–132, title V, §511(c), title VII, §725, Apr. 24, 1996, 110 Stat. 1284, 1300; Pub. L. 104–294, title VI, §605(m), Oct. 11, 1996, 110 Stat. 3510; Pub. L. 105–277, div. I, title II, §201(b)(1), Oct. 21, 1998, 112 Stat. 2681–871; Pub. L. 107–188, title II, §231(d), June 12, 2002, 116 Stat. 661; Pub. L. 108–458, title VI, §6802(a), (b), Dec. 17, 2004, 118 Stat. 3766, 3767.)

Amendments

2004—Pub. L. 108–458, §6802(b)(1), struck out "certain" before "weapons" in section catchline.

Subsec. (a). Pub. L. 108–458, §6802(b)(2), struck out "(other than a chemical weapon as that term is defined in section 229F)" after "mass destruction" in introductory provisions.

Subsec. (a)(2). Pub. L. 108–458, §6802(a)(1), amended par. (2) generally. Prior to amendment, par. (2) read as follows: "against any person within the United States, and the results of such use affect interstate or foreign commerce or, in the case of a threat, attempt, or conspiracy, would have affected interstate or foreign commerce; or".

Subsec. (a)(4). Pub. L. 108–458, §6802(a)(2), (3), added par. (4).

Subsec. (b). Pub. L. 108–458, §6802(b)(3), struck out "(other than a chemical weapon (as that term is defined in section 229F))" after "mass destruction".

Subsec. (c)(3). Pub. L. 108–458, §6802(a)(4)–(6), added par. (3).

2002—Subsec. (a). Pub. L. 107–188, §231(d)(1), substituted "section 229F)—" for "section 229F), including any biological agent, toxin, or vector (as those terms are defined in section 178)—" in introductory provisions.

Subsec. (c)(2)(C). Pub. L. 107–188, §231(d)(2), substituted "a biological agent, toxin, or vector (as those terms are defined in section 178 of this title)" for "a disease organism".

1998—Pub. L. 105–277, §201(b)(1)(A), inserted "certain" before "weapons" in section catchline.

Subsec. (a). Pub. L. 105–277, §201(b)(1)(B), inserted "(other than a chemical weapon as that term is defined in section 229F)" after "weapon of mass destruction" in introductory provisions.

Subsec. (b). Pub. L. 105–277, §201(b)(1)(C), inserted "(other than a chemical weapon (as that term is defined in section 229F))" after "weapon of mass destruction".

1996—Subsec. (a). Pub. L. 104–132, §§511(c), 725(1)(A), (B), in heading, inserted "Against a National of the United States or Within the United States" after "Offense", and in introductory provisions, substituted ", without lawful authority, uses, threatens, or attempts" for "uses, or attempts" and inserted ", including any biological agent, toxin, or vector (as those terms are defined in section 178)" after "mass destruction".

Subsec. (a)(2). Pub. L. 104–132, §725(1)(C), inserted before semicolon at end ", and the results of such use affect interstate or foreign commerce or, in the case of a threat, attempt, or conspiracy, would have affected interstate or foreign commerce".

Subsec. (b). Pub. L. 104–132, §725(4), added subsec. (b). Former subsec. (b) redesignated (c).

Subsec. (b)(2)(B). Pub. L. 104–132, §725(2), as amended by Pub. L. 104–294, §605(m), added subpar. (B) and struck out former subpar. (B) which read as follows: "poison gas;".

Subsec. (c). Pub. L. 104–132, §725(3), redesignated subsec. (b) as (c).

§2332b. Acts of terrorism transcending national boundaries

(a) Prohibited Acts.—

(1) Offenses.—Whoever, involving conduct transcending national boundaries and in a circumstance described in subsection (b)—

(A) kills, kidnaps, maims, commits an assault resulting in serious bodily injury, or assaults with a dangerous weapon any person within the United States; or

(B) creates a substantial risk of serious bodily injury to any other person by destroying or damaging any structure, conveyance, or other real or personal property within the United States or by attempting or conspiring to destroy or damage any structure, conveyance, or other real or personal property within the United States;

in violation of the laws of any State, or the United States, shall be punished as prescribed in subsection (c).

(2) Treatment of threats, attempts and conspiracies.—Whoever threatens to commit an offense under paragraph (1), or attempts or conspires to do so, shall be punished under subsection (c).

(b) Jurisdictional Bases.—

(1) Circumstances.—The circumstances referred to in subsection (a) are—

(A) the mail or any facility of interstate or foreign commerce is used in furtherance of the offense;

(B) the offense obstructs, delays, or affects interstate or foreign commerce, or would have so obstructed, delayed, or affected interstate or foreign commerce if the offense had been consummated;

(C) the victim, or intended victim, is the United States Government, a member of the uniformed services, or any official, officer, employee, or agent of the legislative, executive, or judicial branches, or of any department or agency, of the United States;

(D) the structure, conveyance, or other real or personal property is, in whole or in part, owned, possessed, or leased to the United States, or any department or agency of the United States;

(E) the offense is committed in the territorial sea (including the airspace above and the seabed and subsoil below, and artificial islands and fixed structures erected thereon) of the United States; or

(F) the offense is committed within the special maritime and territorial jurisdiction of the United States.

(2) Co-conspirators and accessories after the fact.—Jurisdiction shall exist over all principals and co-conspirators of an offense under this section, and accessories after the fact to any offense under this section, if at least one of the circumstances described in subparagraphs (A) through (F) of paragraph (1) is applicable to at least one offender.

(c) Penalties.—

(1) Penalties.—Whoever violates this section shall be punished—

(A) for a killing, or if death results to any person from any other conduct prohibited by this section, by death, or by imprisonment for any term of years or for life;

(B) for kidnapping, by imprisonment for any term of years or for life;

(C) for maiming, by imprisonment for not more than 35 years;

(D) for assault with a dangerous weapon or assault resulting in serious bodily injury, by imprisonment for not more than 30 years;

(E) for destroying or damaging any structure, conveyance, or other real or personal property, by imprisonment for not more than 25 years;

(F) for attempting or conspiring to commit an offense, for any term of years up to the maximum punishment that would have applied had the offense been completed; and

(G) for threatening to commit an offense under this section, by imprisonment for not more than 10 years.

(2) Consecutive sentence.—Notwithstanding any other provision of law, the court shall not place on probation any person convicted of a violation of this section; nor shall the term of imprisonment imposed under this section run concurrently with any other term of imprisonment.

(d) Proof Requirements.—The following shall apply to prosecutions under this section:

(1) Knowledge.—The prosecution is not required to prove knowledge by any defendant of a jurisdictional base alleged in the indictment.

(2) State law.—In a prosecution under this section that is based upon the adoption of State law, only the elements of the offense under State law, and not any provisions pertaining to criminal procedure or evidence, are adopted.

(e) Extraterritorial Jurisdiction.—There is extraterritorial Federal jurisdiction—

(1) over any offense under subsection (a), including any threat, attempt, or conspiracy to commit such offense; and

(2) over conduct which, under section 3, renders any person an accessory after the fact to an offense under subsection (a).

(f) Investigative Authority.—In addition to any other investigative authority with respect to violations of this title, the Attorney General shall have primary investigative responsibility for all Federal crimes of terrorism, and any violation of section 351(e), 844(e), 844(f)(1), 956(b), 1361, 1366(b), 1366(c), 1751(e), 2152, or 2156 of this title, and the Secretary of the Treasury shall assist the Attorney General at the request of the Attorney General. Nothing in this section shall be construed to interfere with the authority of the United States Secret Service under section 3056.

(g) Definitions.—As used in this section—

(1) the term "conduct transcending national boundaries" means conduct occurring outside of the United States in addition to the conduct occurring in the United States;

(2) the term "facility of interstate or foreign commerce" has the meaning given that term in section 1958(b)(2);

(3) the term "serious bodily injury" has the meaning given that term in section 1365(g)(3); 1

(4) the term "territorial sea of the United States" means all waters extending seaward to 12 nautical miles from the baselines of the United States, determined in accordance with international law; and

(5) the term "Federal crime of terrorism" means an offense that—

(A) is calculated to influence or affect the conduct of government by intimidation or coercion, or to retaliate against government conduct; and

(B) is a violation of—

(i) section 32 (relating to destruction of aircraft or aircraft facilities), 37 (relating to violence at international airports), 81 (relating to arson within special maritime and territorial jurisdiction), 175 or 175b (relating to biological weapons), 175c (relating to variola virus), 229 (relating to chemical weapons), subsection (a), (b), (c), or (d) of section 351 (relating to congressional, cabinet, and Supreme Court assassination and kidnaping), 831 (relating to nuclear materials), 832 (relating to participation in nuclear and weapons of mass destruction threats to the United States) 2

842(m) or (n) (relating to plastic explosives), 844(f)(2) or (3) (relating to arson and bombing of Government property risking or causing death), 844(i) (relating to arson and bombing of property used in interstate commerce), 930(c) (relating to killing or attempted killing during an attack on a Federal facility with a dangerous weapon), 956(a)(1) (relating to conspiracy to murder, kidnap, or maim persons abroad), 1030(a)(1) (relating to protection of computers), 1030(a)(5)(A) resulting in damage as defined in 1030(c)(4)(A)(i)(II) through (VI) (relating to protection of computers), 1114 (relating to killing or attempted killing of officers and employees of the United States), 1116 (relating to murder or manslaughter of foreign officials, official guests, or internationally protected persons), 1203 (relating to hostage taking), 1361 (relating to government property or contracts), 1362 (relating to destruction of communication lines, stations, or systems), 1363 (relating to injury to buildings or property within special maritime and territorial jurisdiction of the United States), 1366(a) (relating to destruction of an energy facility), 1751(a), (b), (c), or (d) (relating to Presidential and Presidential staff assassination and kidnaping), 1992 (relating to terrorist attacks and other acts of violence against railroad carriers and against mass transportation systems on land, on water, or through the air), 2155 (relating to destruction of national defense materials, premises, or utilities), 2156 (relating to national defense material, premises, or utilities), 2280 (relating to violence against maritime navigation), 2280a (relating to maritime safety), 2281 through 2281a (relating to violence against maritime fixed platforms), 2332 (relating to certain homicides and other violence against United States nationals occurring outside of the United States), 2332a (relating to use of weapons of mass destruction), 2332b (relating to acts of terrorism transcending national boundaries), 2332f (relating to bombing of public places and facilities), 2332g (relating to missile systems designed to destroy aircraft), 2332h (relating to radiological dispersal devices), 2332i (relating to acts of nuclear terrorism), 2339 (relating to harboring terrorists), 2339A (relating to providing material support to terrorists), 2339B (relating to providing material support to terrorist organizations), 2339C (relating to financing of terrorism), 2339D (relating to military-type training from a foreign terrorist organization), or 2340A (relating to torture) of this title;

(ii) sections 92 (relating to prohibitions governing atomic weapons) or 236 (relating to sabotage of nuclear facilities or fuel) of the Atomic Energy Act of 1954 (42 U.S.C. 2122 or 2284);

(iii) section 46502 (relating to aircraft piracy), the second sentence of section 46504 (relating to assault on a flight crew with a dangerous weapon), section 46505(b)(3) or (c) (relating to explosive or incendiary devices, or endangerment of human life by means of weapons, on aircraft), section 46506 if homicide or attempted homicide is involved (relating to application of certain criminal laws to acts on aircraft), or section 60123(b) (relating to destruction of interstate gas or hazardous liquid pipeline facility) of title 49; or

(iv) section 1010A of the Controlled Substances Import and Export Act (relating to narco-terrorism).

(Added Pub. L. 104–132, title VII, §702(a), Apr. 24, 1996, 110 Stat. 1291; amended Pub. L. 104–294, title VI, §601(s)(1), (3), Oct. 11, 1996, 110 Stat. 3502; Pub. L. 107–56, title VIII, §808, Oct. 26, 2001, 115 Stat. 378; Pub. L. 107–197, title III, §301(b), June 25, 2002, 116 Stat. 728; Pub. L. 108–458, title VI, §§6603(a)(1), 6803(c)(3), 6908, Dec. 17, 2004, 118 Stat. 3762, 3769, 3774; Pub. L. 109–177, title I, §§110(b)(3)(A), 112, Mar. 9, 2006, 120 Stat. 208, 209; Pub. L. 110–326, title II, §204(b), Sept. 26, 2008, 122 Stat. 3562; Pub. L. 114–23, title VIII, §§805, 811(d), June 2, 2015, 129 Stat. 309, 311.)

References in Text

Section 1365(g)(3), referred to in subsec. (g)(3), was redesignated section 1365(h)(3) by Pub. L. 107–307, §2(1), Dec. 2, 2002, 116 Stat. 2445.

Section 1010A of the Controlled Substances Import and Export Act, referred to in subsec. (g)(5)(B)(iv), is classified to section 960a of Title 21, Food and Drugs.

Amendments

2015—Subsec. (g)(5)(B)(i). Pub. L. 114–23 substituted "2280a (relating to maritime safety), 2281 through 2281a" for "2281" and inserted "2332i (relating to acts of nuclear terrorism)," before "2339 (relating to harboring terrorists)".

2008—Subsec. (g)(5)(B)(i). Pub. L. 110–326 substituted "1030(a)(5)(A) resulting in damage as defined in 1030(c)(4)(A)(i)(II) through (VI)" for "1030(a)(5)(A)(i) resulting in damage as defined in 1030(a)(5)(B)(ii) through (v)".

2006—Subsec. (g)(5)(B)(i). Pub. L. 109–177, §§110(b)(3)(A), 112(a)(1), (b), substituted "1992 (relating to terrorist attacks and other acts of violence against railroad carriers and against mass transportation systems on land, on water, or through the air)," for "1992 (relating to wrecking trains), 1993 (relating to terrorist attacks and other acts of violence against mass transportation systems)," and "terrorism), 2339D (relating to military-type training from a foreign terrorist organization), or 2340A" for "terrorism, or 2340A".

Subsec. (g)(5)(B)(iv). Pub. L. 109–177, §112(a)(2)–(4), added cl. (iv).

2004—Subsec. (g)(5)(B)(i). Pub. L. 108–458, §6908(1), inserted "175c (relating to variola virus)," after "175 or 175b (relating to biological weapons)," and "2332g (relating to missile systems designed to destroy aircraft), 2332h (relating to radiological dispersal devices)," before "2339 (relating to harboring terrorists)".

Pub. L. 108–458, §6803(c)(3), inserted "832 (relating to participation in nuclear and weapons of mass destruction threats to the United States)" after "831 (relating to nuclear materials),".

Pub. L. 108–458, §6603(a)(1), inserted "1361 (relating to government property or contracts)," after "1203 (relating to hostage taking)," and "2156 (relating to national defense material, premises, or utilities)," after "2155 (relating to destruction of national defense materials, premises, or utilities),".

Subsec. (g)(5)(B)(ii). Pub. L. 108–458, §6908(2), substituted "sections 92 (relating to prohibitions governing atomic weapons) or" for "section" and inserted "2122 or" before "2284".

2002—Subsec. (g)(5)(B)(i). Pub. L. 107–197 inserted "2332f (relating to bombing of public places and facilities)," after "2332b (relating to acts of terrorism transcending national boundaries)," and "2339C (relating to financing of terrorism," after "2339B (relating to providing material support to terrorist organizations),".

2001—Subsec. (f). Pub. L. 107–56, §808(1), inserted "and any violation of section 351(e), 844(e), 844(f)(1), 956(b), 1361, 1366(b), 1366(c), 1751(e), 2152, or 2156 of this title," before "and the Secretary".

Subsec. (g)(5)(B)(i) to (iii). Pub. L. 107–56, §808(2), added cls. (i) to (iii) and struck out former cls. (i) to (iii), inserting references to sections 175b, 229, 1030, 1993, and 2339 of this title and striking out references to 1361, 2152, 2156, 2332c of this title in cl. (i) and inserting references to sections 46504, 46505, and 46506 of title 49 in cl. (iii).

1996—Subsec. (b)(1)(A). Pub. L. 104–294, §601(s)(1), struck out "any of the offenders uses" before "the mail or any facility" and inserted "is used" after "foreign commerce".

Subsec. (g)(5)(B)(i). Pub. L. 104–294, §601(s)(3), inserted "930(c)," before "956 (relating to conspiracy to injure property of a foreign government)", "1992," before "2152 (relating to injury of fortifications, harbor defenses, or defensive sea areas)", and "2332c," before "2339A (relating to providing material support to terrorists)".

Termination Date of 2004 Amendment

Pub. L. 108–458, title VI, §6603(g), Dec. 17, 2004, 118 Stat. 3764, which provided that section 6603 of Pub. L. 108–458 (amending this section and sections 2339A and 2339B of this title) and the amendments made by section 6603 would cease to be effective on Dec. 31, 2006, with certain exceptions, was repealed by Pub. L. 109–177, title I, §104, Mar. 9, 2006, 120 Stat. 195.

Transfer of Functions

For transfer of the functions, personnel, assets, and obligations of the United States Secret Service, including the functions of the Secretary of the Treasury relating thereto, to the Secretary of

Homeland Security, and for treatment of related references, see sections 381, 551(d), 552(d), and 557 of Title 6, Domestic Security, and the Department of Homeland Security Reorganization Plan of November 25, 2002, as modified, set out as a note under section 542 of Title 6.

Territorial Sea of United States

For extension of territorial sea of United States, see Proc. No. 5928, set out as a note under section 1331 of Title 43, Public Lands.

Disclaimer

Pub. L. 114–23, title VIII, §811(c), June 2, 2015, 129 Stat. 311, provided that: "Nothing contained in this section [enacting section 2332i of this title and amending this section] is intended to affect the applicability of any other Federal or State law that might pertain to the underlying conduct."

[§2332c. Repealed. Pub. L. 105–277, div. I, title II, §201(c)(1), Oct. 21, 1998, 112 Stat. 2681–871]

Section, added Pub. L. 104–132, title V, §521(a), Apr. 24, 1996, 110 Stat. 1286, related to use of chemical weapons.

§2332d. Financial transactions

(a) Offense.—Except as provided in regulations issued by the Secretary of the Treasury, in consultation with the Secretary of State, whoever, being a United States person, knowing or having reasonable cause to know that a country is designated under section 6(j) of the Export Administration Act of 1979 (50 U.S.C. App. 2405) 1 as a country supporting international terrorism, engages in a financial transaction with the government of that country, shall be fined under this title, imprisoned for not more than 10 years, or both.

(b) Definitions.—As used in this section—

(1) the term "financial transaction" has the same meaning as in section 1956(c)(4); and

(2) the term "United States person" means any—

(A) United States citizen or national;

(B) permanent resident alien;

(C) juridical person organized under the laws of the United States; or

(D) any person in the United States.

(Added Pub. L. 104–132, title III, §321(a), Apr. 24, 1996, 110 Stat. 1254; amended Pub. L. 107–273, div. B, title IV, §4002(a)(5), Nov. 2, 2002, 116 Stat. 1806.)

References in Text

Section 6(j) of the Export Administration Act of 1979, referred to in subsec. (a), was classified to section 2405(j) of the former Appendix to Title 50, War and National Defense, prior to editorial reclassification and renumbering as section 4605(j) of Title 50.

Codification

Another section 2332d was renumbered section 2332e of this title.

Amendments

2002—Subsec. (a). Pub. L. 107–273 inserted "of 1979" after "Export Administration Act".

Effective Date

Pub. L. 104–132, title III, §321(c), Apr. 24, 1996, 110 Stat. 1254, provided that: "The amendments made by this section [enacting this section] shall become effective 120 days after the date of enactment of this Act [Apr. 24, 1996]."

§2332e. Requests for military assistance to enforce prohibition in certain emergencies

The Attorney General may request the Secretary of Defense to provide assistance under section 382 of title 10 1 in support of Department of Justice activities relating to the enforcement of section 2332a of this title during an emergency situation involving a weapon of mass destruction. The authority to make such a request may be exercised by another official of the Department of Justice in accordance with section 382(f)(2) of title 10.1

(Added Pub. L. 104–201, title XIV, §1416(c)(2)(A), Sept. 23, 1996, 110 Stat. 2723, §2332d; renumbered §2332e, Pub. L. 104–294, title VI, §605(q), Oct. 11, 1996, 110 Stat. 3510; amended Pub. L. 107–56, title I, §104, Oct. 26, 2001, 115 Stat. 277.)

References in Text

Section 382 of title 10, referred to in text, was renumbered section 282 of title 10, Armed Forces, by Pub. L. 114–328, div. A, title XII, §1241(a)(2), Dec. 23, 2016, 130 Stat. 2497.

Codification

Pub. L. 104–201, §1416(c)(2)(A), which directed amendment of the chapter 133B of this title that relates to terrorism by adding this section, was executed by adding this section to this chapter to reflect the probable intent of Congress. This title does not contain a chapter 133B.

Amendments

2001—Pub. L. 107–56 substituted "2332a of this title" for "2332c of this title" and struck out "chemical" before "weapon of".

1996—Pub. L. 104–294 renumbered section 2332d of this title, relating to requests for military assistance to enforce prohibition in certain emergencies, as this section.

§2332f. Bombings of places of public use, government facilities, public transportation systems and infrastructure facilities

(a) Offenses.—

(1) In general.—Whoever unlawfully delivers, places, discharges, or detonates an explosive or other lethal device in, into, or against a place of public use, a state or government facility, a public transportation system, or an infrastructure facility—

(A) with the intent to cause death or serious bodily injury, or

(B) with the intent to cause extensive destruction of such a place, facility, or system, where such destruction results in or is likely to result in major economic loss,

shall be punished as prescribed in subsection (c).

(2) Attempts and conspiracies.—Whoever attempts or conspires to commit an offense under paragraph (1) shall be punished as prescribed in subsection (c).

(b) Jurisdiction.—There is jurisdiction over the offenses in subsection (a) if—

(1) the offense takes place in the United States and—

(A) the offense is committed against another state or a government facility of such state, including its embassy or other diplomatic or consular premises of that state;

(B) the offense is committed in an attempt to compel another state or the United States to do or abstain from doing any act;

(C) at the time the offense is committed, it is committed—

(i) on board a vessel flying the flag of another state;

(ii) on board an aircraft which is registered under the laws of another state; or

(iii) on board an aircraft which is operated by the government of another state;

(D) a perpetrator is found outside the United States;

(E) a perpetrator is a national of another state or a stateless person; or

(F) a victim is a national of another state or a stateless person;

(2) the offense takes place outside the United States and—

(A) a perpetrator is a national of the United States or is a stateless person whose habitual residence is in the United States;

(B) a victim is a national of the United States;

(C) a perpetrator is found in the United States;

(D) the offense is committed in an attempt to compel the United States to do or abstain from doing any act;

(E) the offense is committed against a state or government facility of the United States, including an embassy or other diplomatic or consular premises of the United States;

(F) the offense is committed on board a vessel flying the flag of the United States or an aircraft which is registered under the laws of the United States at the time the offense is committed; or

(G) the offense is committed on board an aircraft which is operated by the United States.

(c) Penalties.—Whoever violates this section shall be punished as provided under section 2332a(a) of this title.

(d) Exemptions to Jurisdiction.—This section does not apply to—

(1) the activities of armed forces during an armed conflict, as those terms are understood under the law of war, which are governed by that law,

(2) activities undertaken by military forces of a state in the exercise of their official duties; or

(3) offenses committed within the United States, where the alleged offender and the victims are United States citizens and the alleged offender is found in the United States, or where jurisdiction is predicated solely on the nationality of the victims or the alleged offender and the offense has no substantial effect on interstate or foreign commerce.

(e) Definitions.—As used in this section, the term—

(1) "serious bodily injury" has the meaning given that term in section 1365(g)(3) of this title; 1

(2) "national of the United States" has the meaning given that term in section 101(a)(22) of the Immigration and Nationality Act (8 U.S.C. 1101(a)(22));

(3) "state or government facility" includes any permanent or temporary facility or conveyance that is used or occupied by representatives of a state, members of Government, the legislature or the judiciary or by officials or employees of a state or any other public authority or entity or by employees or officials of an intergovernmental organization in connection with their official duties;

(4) "intergovernmental organization" includes international organization (as defined in section 1116(b)(5) of this title);

(5) "infrastructure facility" means any publicly or privately owned facility providing or distributing services for the benefit of the public, such as water, sewage, energy, fuel, or communications;

(6) "place of public use" means those parts of any building, land, street, waterway, or other location that are accessible or open to members of the public, whether continuously, periodically, or occasionally, and encompasses any commercial, business, cultural, historical, educational, religious, governmental, entertainment, recreational, or similar place that is so accessible or open to the public;

(7) "public transportation system" means all facilities, conveyances, and instrumentalities, whether publicly or privately owned, that are used in or for publicly available services for the transportation of persons or cargo;

(8) "explosive" has the meaning given in section 844(j) of this title insofar that it is designed, or has the capability, to cause death, serious bodily injury, or substantial material damage;

(9) "other lethal device" means any weapon or device that is designed or has the capability to cause death, serious bodily injury, or substantial damage to property through the release, dissemination, or impact of toxic chemicals, biological agents, or toxins (as those terms are defined in section 178 of this title) or radiation or radioactive material;

(10) "military forces of a state" means the armed forces of a state which are organized, trained, and equipped under its internal law for the primary purpose of national defense or security, and persons acting in support of those armed forces who are under their formal command, control, and

responsibility;

(11) "armed conflict" does not include internal disturbances and tensions, such as riots, isolated and sporadic acts of violence, and other acts of a similar nature; and

(12) "state" has the same meaning as that term has under international law, and includes all political subdivisions thereof.

(Added Pub. L. 107–197, title I, §102(a), June 25, 2002, 116 Stat. 721.)

References in Text

Section 1365(g)(3), referred to in subsec. (e)(1), was redesignated section 1365(h)(3) by Pub. L. 107–307, §2(1), Dec. 2, 2002, 116 Stat. 2445.

Effective Date

Pub. L. 107–197, title I, §103, June 25, 2002, 116 Stat. 724, provided that: "Section 102 [enacting this section and provisions set out as a note below] shall take effect on the date that the International Convention for the Suppression of Terrorist Bombings enters into force for the United States [July 26, 2002]."

Disclaimer

Pub. L. 107–197, title I, §102(c), June 25, 2002, 116 Stat. 724, provided that: "Nothing contained in this section [enacting this section and provisions set out as a note above] is intended to affect the applicability of any other Federal or State law which might pertain to the underlying conduct."

§2332g. Missile systems designed to destroy aircraft

(a) Unlawful Conduct.—

(1) In general.—Except as provided in paragraph (3), it shall be unlawful for any person to knowingly produce, construct, otherwise acquire, transfer directly or indirectly, receive, possess, import, export, or use, or possess and threaten to use—

(A) an explosive or incendiary rocket or missile that is guided by any system designed to enable the rocket or missile to—

(i) seek or proceed toward energy radiated or reflected from an aircraft or toward an image locating an aircraft; or

(ii) otherwise direct or guide the rocket or missile to an aircraft;

(B) any device designed or intended to launch or guide a rocket or missile described in subparagraph (A); or

(C) any part or combination of parts designed or redesigned for use in assembling or fabricating a rocket, missile, or device described in subparagraph (A) or (B).

(2) Nonweapon.—Paragraph (1)(A) does not apply to any device that is neither designed nor redesigned for use as a weapon.

(3) Excluded conduct.—This subsection does not apply with respect to—

(A) conduct by or under the authority of the United States or any department or agency thereof or of a State or any department or agency thereof; or

(B) conduct pursuant to the terms of a contract with the United States or any department or agency thereof or with a State or any department or agency thereof.

(b) Jurisdiction.—Conduct prohibited by subsection (a) is within the jurisdiction of the United States if—

(1) the offense occurs in or affects interstate or foreign commerce;

(2) the offense occurs outside of the United States and is committed by a national of the United States;

(3) the offense is committed against a national of the United States while the national is outside the United States;

(4) the offense is committed against any property that is owned, leased, or used by the United States or by any department or agency of the United States, whether the property is within or

outside the United States; or

(5) an offender aids or abets any person over whom jurisdiction exists under this subsection in committing an offense under this section or conspires with any person over whom jurisdiction exists under this subsection to commit an offense under this section.

(c) Criminal Penalties.—

(1) In general.—Any person who violates, or attempts or conspires to violate, subsection (a) shall be fined not more than $2,000,000 and shall be sentenced to a term of imprisonment not less than 25 years or to imprisonment for life.

(2) Other circumstances.—Any person who, in the course of a violation of subsection (a), uses, attempts or conspires to use, or possesses and threatens to use, any item or items described in subsection (a), shall be fined not more than $2,000,000 and imprisoned for not less than 30 years or imprisoned for life.

(3) Special circumstances.—If the death of another results from a person's violation of subsection (a), the person shall be fined not more than $2,000,000 and punished by imprisonment for life.

(d) Definition.—As used in this section, the term "aircraft" has the definition set forth in section 40102(a)(6) of title 49, United States Code.

(Added Pub. L. 108–458, title VI, §6903, Dec. 17, 2004, 118 Stat. 3770.)

§2332h. Radiological dispersal devices

(a) Unlawful Conduct.—

(1) In general.—Except as provided in paragraph (2), it shall be unlawful for any person to knowingly produce, construct, otherwise acquire, transfer directly or indirectly, receive, possess, import, export, or use, or possess and threaten to use—

(A) any weapon that is designed or intended to release radiation or radioactivity at a level dangerous to human life; or

(B) any device or other object that is capable of and designed or intended to endanger human life through the release of radiation or radioactivity.

(2) Exception.—This subsection does not apply with respect to—

(A) conduct by or under the authority of the United States or any department or agency thereof; or

(B) conduct pursuant to the terms of a contract with the United States or any department or agency thereof.

(b) Jurisdiction.—Conduct prohibited by subsection (a) is within the jurisdiction of the United States if—

(1) the offense occurs in or affects interstate or foreign commerce;

(2) the offense occurs outside of the United States and is committed by a national of the United States;

(3) the offense is committed against a national of the United States while the national is outside the United States;

(4) the offense is committed against any property that is owned, leased, or used by the United States or by any department or agency of the United States, whether the property is within or outside the United States; or

(5) an offender aids or abets any person over whom jurisdiction exists under this subsection in committing an offense under this section or conspires with any person over whom jurisdiction exists under this subsection to commit an offense under this section.

(c) Criminal Penalties.—

(1) In general.—Any person who violates, or attempts or conspires to violate, subsection (a) shall be fined not more than $2,000,000 and shall be sentenced to a term of imprisonment not less than 25 years or to imprisonment for life.

(2) Other circumstances.—Any person who, in the course of a violation of subsection (a), uses, attempts or conspires to use, or possesses and threatens to use, any item or items described in subsection (a), shall be fined not more than $2,000,000 and imprisoned for not less than 30 years or imprisoned for life.

(3) Special circumstances.—If the death of another results from a person's violation of subsection (a), the person shall be fined not more than $2,000,000 and punished by imprisonment for life. (Added Pub. L. 108–458, title VI, §6905, Dec. 17, 2004, 118 Stat. 3772.)

§2332i. Acts of nuclear terrorism

(a) Offenses.—

(1) In general.—Whoever knowingly and unlawfully—

(A) possesses radioactive material or makes or possesses a device—

(i) with the intent to cause death or serious bodily injury; or

(ii) with the intent to cause substantial damage to property or the environment; or

(B) uses in any way radioactive material or a device, or uses or damages or interferes with the operation of a nuclear facility in a manner that causes the release of or increases the risk of the release of radioactive material, or causes radioactive contamination or exposure to radiation—

(i) with the intent to cause death or serious bodily injury or with the knowledge that such act is likely to cause death or serious bodily injury;

(ii) with the intent to cause substantial damage to property or the environment or with the knowledge that such act is likely to cause substantial damage to property or the environment; or

(iii) with the intent to compel a person, an international organization or a country to do or refrain from doing an act,

shall be punished as prescribed in subsection (c).

(2) Threats.—Whoever, under circumstances in which the threat may reasonably be believed, threatens to commit an offense under paragraph (1) shall be punished as prescribed in subsection (c). Whoever demands possession of or access to radioactive material, a device or a nuclear facility by threat or by use of force shall be punished as prescribed in subsection (c).

(3) Attempts and conspiracies.—Whoever attempts to commit an offense under paragraph (1) or conspires to commit an offense under paragraph (1) or (2) shall be punished as prescribed in subsection (c).

(b) Jurisdiction.—Conduct prohibited by subsection (a) is within the jurisdiction of the United States if—

(1) the prohibited conduct takes place in the United States or the special aircraft jurisdiction of the United States;

(2) the prohibited conduct takes place outside of the United States and—

(A) is committed by a national of the United States, a United States corporation or legal entity or a stateless person whose habitual residence is in the United States;

(B) is committed on board a vessel of the United States or a vessel subject to the jurisdiction of the United States (as defined in section 70502 of title 46) or on board an aircraft that is registered under United States law, at the time the offense is committed; or

(C) is committed in an attempt to compel the United States to do or abstain from doing any act, or constitutes a threat directed at the United States;

(3) the prohibited conduct takes place outside of the United States and a victim or an intended victim is a national of the United States or a United States corporation or legal entity, or the offense is committed against any state or government facility of the United States; or

(4) a perpetrator of the prohibited conduct is found in the United States.

(c) Penalties.—Whoever violates this section shall be fined not more than $2,000,000 and shall be imprisoned for any term of years or for life.

(d) Nonapplicability.—This section does not apply to—

(1) the activities of armed forces during an armed conflict, as those terms are understood under the law of war, which are governed by that law; or

(2) activities undertaken by military forces of a state in the exercise of their official duties.

(e) Definitions.—As used in this section, the term—

(1) "armed conflict" has the meaning given that term in section 2332f(e)(11) of this title;

(2) "device" means:

(A) any nuclear explosive device; or

(B) any radioactive material dispersal or radiation-emitting device that may, owing to its radiological properties, cause death, serious bodily injury or substantial damage to property or the environment;

(3) "international organization" has the meaning given that term in section 831(f)(3) 1 of this title;

(4) "military forces of a state" means the armed forces of a country that are organized, trained and equipped under its internal law for the primary purpose of national defense or security and persons acting in support of those armed forces who are under their formal command, control and responsibility;

(5) "national of the United States" has the meaning given that term in section 101(a)(22) of the Immigration and Nationality Act (8 U.S.C. 1101(a)(22));

(6) "nuclear facility" means:

(A) any nuclear reactor, including reactors on vessels, vehicles, aircraft or space objects for use as an energy source in order to propel such vessels, vehicles, aircraft or space objects or for any other purpose;

(B) any plant or conveyance being used for the production, storage, processing or transport of radioactive material; or

(C) a facility (including associated buildings and equipment) in which nuclear material is produced, processed, used, handled, stored or disposed of, if damage to or interference with such facility could lead to the release of significant amounts of radiation or radioactive material;

(7) "nuclear material" has the meaning given that term in section 831(f)(1) 1 of this title;

(8) "radioactive material" means nuclear material and other radioactive substances that contain nuclides that undergo spontaneous disintegration (a process accompanied by emission of one or more types of ionizing radiation, such as alpha-, beta-, neutron particles and gamma rays) and that may, owing to their radiological or fissile properties, cause death, serious bodily injury or substantial damage to property or to the environment;

(9) "serious bodily injury" has the meaning given that term in section 831(f)(4) 1 of this title;

(10) "state" has the same meaning as that term has under international law, and includes all political subdivisions thereof;

(11) "state or government facility" has the meaning given that term in section 2332f(e)(3) of this title;

(12) "United States corporation or legal entity" means any corporation or other entity organized under the laws of the United States or any State, Commonwealth, territory, possession or district of the United States;

(13) "vessel" has the meaning given that term in section 1502(19) of title 33; 1 and

(14) "vessel of the United States" has the meaning given that term in section 70502 of title 46.

(Added Pub. L. 114–23, title VIII, §811(a), June 2, 2015, 129 Stat. 309.)

References in Text

Section 831(f) of this title, referred to in subsec. (e)(3), (7), (9), was redesignated section 831(g) by Pub. L. 114–23, title VIII, §812(d), June 2, 2015, 129 Stat. 312.

Section 1502(19) of title 33, referred to in subsec. (e)(13), probably should be a reference to section 3(19) of the Deepwater Port Act of 1974, which is classified to section 1502(19) of Title 33, Navigation and Navigable Waters.

§2333. Civil remedies

(a) Action and Jurisdiction.—Any national of the United States injured in his or her person, property, or business by reason of an act of international terrorism, or his or her estate, survivors, or heirs, may sue therefor in any appropriate district court of the United States and shall recover threefold the damages he or she sustains and the cost of the suit, including attorney's fees.

(b) Estoppel Under United States Law.—A final judgment or decree rendered in favor of the United States in any criminal proceeding under section 1116, 1201, 1203, or 2332 of this title or section 46314, 46502, 46505, or 46506 of title 49 shall estop the defendant from denying the essential allegations of the criminal offense in any subsequent civil proceeding under this section.

(c) Estoppel Under Foreign Law.—A final judgment or decree rendered in favor of any foreign state in any criminal proceeding shall, to the extent that such judgment or decree may be accorded full faith and credit under the law of the United States, estop the defendant from denying the essential allegations of the criminal offense in any subsequent civil proceeding under this section.

(d) Liability.—

(1) Definition.—In this subsection, the term "person" has the meaning given the term in section 1 of title 1.

(2) Liability.—In an action under subsection (a) for an injury arising from an act of international terrorism committed, planned, or authorized by an organization that had been designated as a foreign terrorist organization under section 219 of the Immigration and Nationality Act (8 U.S.C. 1189), as of the date on which such act of international terrorism was committed, planned, or authorized, liability may be asserted as to any person who aids and abets, by knowingly providing substantial assistance, or who conspires with the person who committed such an act of international terrorism.

(Added Pub. L. 102–572, title X, §1003(a)(4), Oct. 29, 1992, 106 Stat. 4522; amended Pub. L. 103–429, §2(1), Oct. 31, 1994, 108 Stat. 4377; Pub. L. 114–222, §4(a), Sept. 28, 2016, 130 Stat. 854.)

Amendments

2016—Subsec. (d). Pub. L. 114–222 added subsec. (d).

1994—Subsec. (b). Pub. L. 103–429 substituted "section 46314, 46502, 46505, or 46506 of title 49" for "section 902(i), (k), (l), (n), or (r) of the Federal Aviation Act of 1958 (49 U.S.C. App. 1472(i), (k), (l), (n), or (r))".

Effective Date of 2016 Amendment

Pub. L. 114–222, §7, Sept. 28, 2016, 130 Stat. 855, provided that: "The amendments made by this Act [enacting section 1605B of Title 28, Judiciary and Judicial Procedure, and amending this section and section 1605 of Title 28] shall apply to any civil action—

"(1) pending on, or commenced on or after, the date of enactment of this Act [Sept. 28, 2016]; and

"(2) arising out of an injury to a person, property, or business on or after September 11, 2001."

Effective Date

Section applicable to any pending case or any cause of action arising on or after 4 years before Oct. 29, 1992, see section 1003(c) of Pub. L. 102–572, set out as a note under section 2331 of this title.

Severability

Pub. L. 114–222, §6, Sept. 28, 2016, 130 Stat. 855, provided that: "If any provision of this Act [enacting section 1605B of Title 28, Judiciary and Judicial Procedure, amending this section and section 1605 of Title 28, and enacting provisions set out as notes under this section, section 1 of this title, and section 1605B of Title 28] or any amendment made by this Act, or the application of a provision or amendment to any person or circumstance, is held to be invalid, the remainder of this Act and the amendments made by this Act, and the application of the provisions and amendments to any other person not similarly situated or to other circumstances, shall not be affected by the holding."

Findings and Purpose

Pub. L. 114–222, §2, Sept. 28, 2016, 130 Stat. 852, provided that:

"(a) Findings.—Congress finds the following:

"(1) International terrorism is a serious and deadly problem that threatens the vital interests of the

United States.

"(2) International terrorism affects the interstate and foreign commerce of the United States by harming international trade and market stability, and limiting international travel by United States citizens as well as foreign visitors to the United States.

"(3) Some foreign terrorist organizations, acting through affiliated groups or individuals, raise significant funds outside of the United States for conduct directed and targeted at the United States.

"(4) It is necessary to recognize the substantive causes of action for aiding and abetting and conspiracy liability under chapter 113B of title 18, United States Code.

"(5) The decision of the United States Court of Appeals for the District of Columbia in Halberstam v. Welch, 705 F.2d 472 (D.C. Cir. 1983), which has been widely recognized as the leading case regarding Federal civil aiding and abetting and conspiracy liability, including by the Supreme Court of the United States, provides the proper legal framework for how such liability should function in the context of chapter 113B of title 18, United States Code.

"(6) Persons, entities, or countries that knowingly or recklessly contribute material support or resources, directly or indirectly, to persons or organizations that pose a significant risk of committing acts of terrorism that threaten the security of nationals of the United States or the national security, foreign policy, or economy of the United States, necessarily direct their conduct at the United States, and should reasonably anticipate being brought to court in the United States to answer for such activities.

"(7) The United States has a vital interest in providing persons and entities injured as a result of terrorist attacks committed within the United States with full access to the court system in order to pursue civil claims against persons, entities, or countries that have knowingly or recklessly provided material support or resources, directly or indirectly, to the persons or organizations responsible for their injuries.

"(b) Purpose.—The purpose of this Act [enacting section 1605B of Title 28, Judiciary and Judicial Procedure, amending this section and section 1605 of Title 28, and enacting provisions set out as notes under this section, section 1 of this title, and section 1605B of Title 28] is to provide civil litigants with the broadest possible basis, consistent with the Constitution of the United States, to seek relief against persons, entities, and foreign countries, wherever acting and wherever they may be found, that have provided material support, directly or indirectly, to foreign organizations or persons that engage in terrorist activities against the United States."

Effect on Foreign Sovereign Immunities Act

Pub. L. 114–222, §4(b), Sept. 28, 2016, 130 Stat. 854, provided that: "Nothing in the amendment made by this section [amending this section] affects immunity of a foreign state, as that term is defined in section 1603 of title 28, United States Code, from jurisdiction under other law."

Special Rule Relating to Certain Acts of International Terrorism

Pub. L. 112–239, div. A, title XII, §1251(c), Jan. 2, 2013, 126 Stat. 2017, provided that: "Notwithstanding section 2335 of title 18, United States Code, as amended by subsection (a), a civil action under section 2333 of such title resulting from an act of international terrorism that occurred on or after September 11, 2001, and before the date that is 4 years before the date of the enactment of this Act [Jan. 2, 2013], may be maintained if the civil action is commenced during the 6-year period beginning on such date of enactment."

§2334. Jurisdiction and venue

(a) General Venue.—Any civil action under section 2333 of this title against any person may be instituted in the district court of the United States for any district where any plaintiff resides or where any defendant resides or is served, or has an agent. Process in such a civil action may be served in any district where the defendant resides, is found, or has an agent.

(b) Special Maritime or Territorial Jurisdiction.—If the actions giving rise to the claim occurred within the special maritime and territorial jurisdiction of the United States, as defined in section 7 of this title, then any civil action under section 2333 of this title against any person may be instituted in the district court of the United States for any district in which any plaintiff resides or the defendant resides, is served, or has an agent.

(c) Service on Witnesses.—A witness in a civil action brought under section 2333 of this title may be served in any other district where the defendant resides, is found, or has an agent.

(d) Convenience of the Forum.—The district court shall not dismiss any action brought under section 2333 of this title on the grounds of the inconvenience or inappropriateness of the forum chosen, unless—

(1) the action may be maintained in a foreign court that has jurisdiction over the subject matter and over all the defendants;

(2) that foreign court is significantly more convenient and appropriate; and

(3) that foreign court offers a remedy which is substantially the same as the one available in the courts of the United States.

(Added Pub. L. 102–572, title X, §1003(a)(4), Oct. 29, 1992, 106 Stat. 4522.)

Effective Date

Section applicable to any pending case or any cause of action arising on or after 4 years before Oct. 29, 1992, see section 1003(c) of Pub. L. 102–572, set out as a note under section 2331 of this title.

§2335. Limitation of actions

(a) In General.—Subject to subsection (b), a suit for recovery of damages under section 2333 of this title shall not be maintained unless commenced within 10 years after the date the cause of action accrued.

(b) Calculation of Period.—The time of the absence of the defendant from the United States or from any jurisdiction in which the same or a similar action arising from the same facts may be maintained by the plaintiff, or of any concealment of the defendant's whereabouts, shall not be included in the 10-year period set forth in subsection (a).

(Added Pub. L. 102–572, title X, §1003(a)(4), Oct. 29, 1992, 106 Stat. 4523; amended Pub. L. 112–239, div. A, title XII, §1251(a), Jan. 2, 2013, 126 Stat. 2017.)

Amendments

2013—Subsec. (a). Pub. L. 112–239, §1251(a)(1), substituted "10 years" for "4 years".
Subsec. (b). Pub. L. 112–239, §1251(a)(2), substituted "10-year period" for "4-year period".

Effective Date of 2013 Amendment

Pub. L. 112–239, div. A, title XII, §1251(b), Jan. 2, 2013, 126 Stat. 2017, provided that: "The amendments made by this section [amending this section] shall apply to any civil action arising under section 2333 of title 18, United States Code, that is pending on, or commenced on or after, the date of the enactment of this Act [Jan. 2, 2013]."

Effective Date

Section applicable to any pending case or any cause of action arising on or after 4 years before Oct. 29, 1992, see section 1003(c) of Pub. L. 102–572, set out as a note under section 2331 of this title.

§2336. Other limitations

(a) Acts of War.—No action shall be maintained under section 2333 of this title for injury or loss by reason of an act of war.

(b) Limitation on Discovery.—If a party to an action under section 2333 seeks to discover the investigative files of the Department of Justice, the Assistant Attorney General, Deputy Attorney General, or Attorney General may object on the ground that compliance will interfere with a criminal investigation or prosecution of the incident, or a national security operation related to the incident, which is the subject of the civil litigation. The court shall evaluate any such objections in camera and shall stay the discovery if the court finds that granting the discovery request will substantially interfere with a criminal investigation or prosecution of the incident or a national security operation related to the incident. The court shall consider the likelihood of criminal prosecution by the Government and other factors it deems to be appropriate. A stay of discovery under this subsection shall constitute a bar to the granting of a motion to dismiss under rules 12(b)(6) and 56 of the Federal Rules of Civil Procedure. If the court grants a stay of discovery under this subsection, it may stay the action in the interests of justice.

(c) Stay of Action for Civil Remedies.—(1) The Attorney General may intervene in any civil action brought under section 2333 for the purpose of seeking a stay of the civil action. A stay shall be granted if the court finds that the continuation of the civil action will substantially interfere with a criminal prosecution which involves the same subject matter and in which an indictment has been returned, or interfere with national security operations related to the terrorist incident that is the subject of the civil action. A stay may be granted for up to 6 months. The Attorney General may petition the court for an extension of the stay for additional 6-month periods until the criminal prosecution is completed or dismissed.

(2) In a proceeding under this subsection, the Attorney General may request that any order issued by the court for release to the parties and the public omit any reference to the basis on which the stay was sought.

(Added Pub. L. 102–572, title X, §1003(a)(4), Oct. 29, 1992, 106 Stat. 4523.)

References in Text

The Federal Rules of Civil Procedure, referred to in subsec. (b), are set out in the Appendix to Title 28, Judiciary and Judicial Procedure.

Effective Date

Section applicable to any pending case or any cause of action arising on or after 4 years before Oct. 29, 1992, see section 1003(c) of Pub. L. 102–572, set out as a note under section 2331 of this title.

§2337. Suits against Government officials

No action shall be maintained under section 2333 of this title against—

(1) the United States, an agency of the United States, or an officer or employee of the United States or any agency thereof acting within his or her official capacity or under color of legal authority; or

(2) a foreign state, an agency of a foreign state, or an officer or employee of a foreign state or an agency thereof acting within his or her official capacity or under color of legal authority.

(Added Pub. L. 102–572, title X, §1003(a)(4), Oct. 29, 1992, 106 Stat. 4523.)

Effective Date

Section applicable to any pending case or any cause of action arising on or after 4 years before Oct. 29, 1992, see section 1003(c) of Pub. L. 102–572, set out as a note under section 2331 of this title.

§2338. Exclusive Federal jurisdiction

The district courts of the United States shall have exclusive jurisdiction over an action brought under this chapter.

(Added Pub. L. 102–572, title X, §1003(a)(4), Oct. 29, 1992, 106 Stat. 4524.)

Effective Date

Section applicable to any pending case or any cause of action arising on or after 4 years before Oct. 29, 1992, see section 1003(c) of Pub. L. 102–572, set out as a note under section 2331 of this title.

§2339. Harboring or concealing terrorists

(a) Whoever harbors or conceals any person who he knows, or has reasonable grounds to believe, has committed, or is about to commit, an offense under section 32 (relating to destruction of aircraft or aircraft facilities), section 175 (relating to biological weapons), section 229 (relating to chemical weapons), section 831 (relating to nuclear materials), paragraph (2) or (3) of section 844(f) (relating to arson and bombing of government property risking or causing injury or death), section 1366(a) (relating to the destruction of an energy facility), section 2280 (relating to violence against maritime navigation), section 2332a (relating to weapons of mass destruction), or section 2332b (relating to acts of terrorism transcending national boundaries) of this title, section 236(a) (relating to sabotage of nuclear facilities or fuel) of the Atomic Energy Act of 1954 (42 U.S.C. 2284(a)), or section 46502 (relating to aircraft piracy) of title 49, shall be fined under this title or imprisoned not more than ten years, or both.

(b) A violation of this section may be prosecuted in any Federal judicial district in which the underlying offense was committed, or in any other Federal judicial district as provided by law. (Added Pub. L. 107–56, title VIII, §803(a), Oct. 26, 2001, 115 Stat. 376; amended Pub. L. 107–273, div. B, title IV, §4005(d)(2), Nov. 2, 2002, 116 Stat. 1813.)

Amendments

2002—Pub. L. 107–273 made technical correction to directory language of Pub. L. 107–56, §803(a), which enacted this section.

Effective Date of 2002 Amendment

Pub. L. 107–273, div. B, title IV, §4005(d)(2), Nov. 2, 2002, 116 Stat. 1813, provided that the amendment made by section 4005(d)(2) is effective Oct. 26, 2001.

§2339A. Providing material support to terrorists

(a) Offense.—Whoever provides material support or resources or conceals or disguises the nature, location, source, or ownership of material support or resources, knowing or intending that they are to be used in preparation for, or in carrying out, a violation of section 32, 37, 81, 175, 229, 351, 831, 842(m) or (n), 844(f) or (i), 930(c), 956, 1091, 1114, 1116, 1203, 1361, 1362, 1363, 1366, 1751, 1992, 2155, 2156, 2280, 2281, 2332, 2332a, 2332b, 2332f, 2340A, or 2442 of this title, section 236 of the Atomic Energy Act of 1954 (42 U.S.C. 2284), section 46502 or 60123(b) of title 49, or any offense listed in section 2332b(g)(5)(B) (except for sections 2339A and 2339B) or in preparation for, or in carrying out, the concealment of an escape from the commission of any such violation, or attempts or conspires to do such an act, shall be fined under this title, imprisoned not more than 15 years, or both, and, if the death of any person results, shall be imprisoned for any term of years or for life. A violation of this section may be prosecuted in any Federal judicial district in which the underlying offense was committed, or in any other Federal judicial district as provided by law.

(b) Definitions.—As used in this section—

(1) the term "material support or resources" means any property, tangible or intangible, or service, including currency or monetary instruments or financial securities, financial services, lodging, training, expert advice or assistance, safehouses, false documentation or identification, communications equipment, facilities, weapons, lethal substances, explosives, personnel (1 or more individuals who may be or include oneself), and transportation, except medicine or religious materials;

(2) the term "training" means instruction or teaching designed to impart a specific skill, as opposed

to general knowledge; and

(3) the term "expert advice or assistance" means advice or assistance derived from scientific, technical or other specialized knowledge.

(Added Pub. L. 103–322, title XII, §120005(a), Sept. 13, 1994, 108 Stat. 2022; amended Pub. L. 104–132, title III, §323, Apr. 24, 1996, 110 Stat. 1255; Pub. L. 104–294, title VI, §§601(b)(2), (s)(2), (3), 604(b)(5), Oct. 11, 1996, 110 Stat. 3498, 3502, 3506; Pub. L. 107–56, title VIII, §§805(a), 810(c), 811(f), Oct. 26, 2001, 115 Stat. 377, 380, 381; Pub. L. 107–197, title III, §301(c), June 25, 2002, 116 Stat. 728; Pub. L. 107–273, div. B, title IV, §4002(a)(7), (c)(1), (e)(11), Nov. 2, 2002, 116 Stat. 1807, 1808, 1811; Pub. L. 108–458, title VI, §6603(a)(2), (b), Dec. 17, 2004, 118 Stat. 3762; Pub. L. 109–177, title I, §110(b)(3)(B), Mar. 9, 2006, 120 Stat. 208; Pub. L. 111–122, §3(d), Dec. 22, 2009, 123 Stat. 3481.)

Amendments

2009—Subsec. (a). Pub. L. 111–122 inserted ", 1091" after "956" and substituted ", 2340A, or 2442" for ", or 2340A".

2006—Subsec. (a). Pub. L. 109–177 struck out "1993," after "1992,".

2004—Subsec. (a). Pub. L. 108–458, §6603(a)(2)(B), which directed amendment of this section by inserting "or any offense listed in section 2332b(g)(5)(B) (except for sections 2339A and 2339B)" after "section 60123(b) of title 49,", was executed by making the insertion in subsec. (a) after "section 46502 or 60123(b) of title 49," to reflect the probable intent of Congress.

Pub. L. 108–458, §6603(a)(2)(A), struck out "or" before "section 46502".

Subsec. (b). Pub. L. 108–458, §6603(b), reenacted heading without change and amended text generally. Prior to amendment, text read as follows: "In this section, the term 'material support or resources' means currency or monetary instruments or financial securities, financial services, lodging, training, expert advice or assistance, safehouses, false documentation or identification, communications equipment, facilities, weapons, lethal substances, explosives, personnel, transportation, and other physical assets, except medicine or religious materials."

2002—Subsec. (a). Pub. L. 107–273, §4002(a)(7), (e)(11), struck out "2332c," after "2332b," and substituted "of an escape" for "or an escape".

Pub. L. 107–197 inserted "2332f," before "or 2340A".

Subsec. (b). Pub. L. 107–273, §4002(c)(1), repealed amendment by Pub. L. 104–294, §601(b)(2). See 1996 Amendment note below.

2001—Subsec. (a). Pub. L. 107–56, §811(f), inserted "or attempts or conspires to do such an act," before "shall be fined".

Pub. L. 107–56, §810(c)(1), substituted "15 years" for "10 years".

Pub. L. 107–56, §810(c)(2), which directed substitution of ", and, if the death of any person results, shall be imprisoned for any term of years or for life." for period, was executed by making the substitution for the period at end of the first sentence to reflect the probable intent of Congress and the intervening amendment by section 805(a)(1)(F) of Pub. L. 107–56. See below.

Pub. L. 107–56, §805(a)(1)(F), inserted at end "A violation of this section may be prosecuted in any Federal judicial district in which the underlying offense was committed, or in any other Federal judicial district as provided by law."

Pub. L. 107–56, §§805(a)(1)(A)–(E), struck out ", within the United States," after "Whoever", and inserted "229," after "175,", "1993," after "1992,", ", section 236 of the Atomic Energy Act of 1954 (42 U.S.C. 2284)," after "2340A of this title", and "or 60123(b)" after "section 46502".

Subsec. (b). Pub. L. 107–56, §805(a)(2), substituted "or monetary instruments or financial securities" for "or other financial securities" and inserted "expert advice or assistance," after "training,".

1996—Pub. L. 104–294, §604(b)(5), amended directory language of Pub. L. 103–322, §120005(a), which enacted this section.

Pub. L. 104–132 amended section generally, reenacting section catchline without change and redesignating provisions which detailed what constitutes offense, formerly contained in subsec.

(b), as subsec. (a), inserting references to sections 37, 81, 175, 831, 842, 956, 1362, 1366, 2155, 2156, 2332, 2332a, 2332b, and 2340A of this title, striking out references to sections 36, 2331, and 2339 of this title, redesignating provisions which define "material support or resource", formerly contained in subsec. (a), as subsec. (b), substituting provisions excepting medicine or religious materials from definition for provisions excepting humanitarian assistance to persons not directly involved in violations, and struck out subsec. (c) which authorized investigations into possible violations, except activities involving First Amendment rights.

Subsec. (a). Pub. L. 104–294, §601(s)(2), (3), inserted "930(c)," before "956,", "1992," before "2155,", "2332c," before "or 2340A of this title", and "or an escape" after "concealment".

Subsec. (b). Pub. L. 104–294, §601(b)(2), which directed substitution of "2332" for "2331", "2332a" for "2339", "37" for "36", and "or an escape" for "of an escape" and which could not be executed after the general amendment by Pub. L. 104–132, was repealed by Pub. L. 107–273, §4002(c)(1). See above.

Effective Date of 2002 Amendment
Pub. L. 107–273, div. B, title IV, §4002(c)(1), Nov. 2, 2002, 116 Stat. 1808, provided that the amendment made by section 4002(c)(1) is effective Oct. 11, 1996.

Effective Date of 1996 Amendment
Amendment by section 604(b)(5) of Pub. L. 104–294 effective Sept. 13, 1994, see section 604(d) of Pub. L. 104–294, set out as a note under section 13 of this title.

§2339B. Providing material support or resources to designated foreign terrorist organizations
(a) Prohibited Activities.—

(1) Unlawful conduct.—Whoever knowingly provides material support or resources to a foreign terrorist organization, or attempts or conspires to do so, shall be fined under this title or imprisoned not more than 20 years, or both, and, if the death of any person results, shall be imprisoned for any term of years or for life. To violate this paragraph, a person must have knowledge that the organization is a designated terrorist organization (as defined in subsection (g)(6)), that the organization has engaged or engages in terrorist activity (as defined in section 212(a)(3)(B) of the Immigration and Nationality Act), or that the organization has engaged or engages in terrorism (as defined in section 140(d)(2) of the Foreign Relations Authorization Act, Fiscal Years 1988 and 1989).

(2) Financial institutions.—Except as authorized by the Secretary, any financial institution that becomes aware that it has possession of, or control over, any funds in which a foreign terrorist organization, or its agent, has an interest, shall—

(A) retain possession of, or maintain control over, such funds; and

(B) report to the Secretary the existence of such funds in accordance with regulations issued by the Secretary.

(b) Civil Penalty.—Any financial institution that knowingly fails to comply with subsection (a)(2) shall be subject to a civil penalty in an amount that is the greater of—

(A) $50,000 per violation; or

(B) twice the amount of which the financial institution was required under subsection (a)(2) to retain possession or control.

(c) Injunction.—Whenever it appears to the Secretary or the Attorney General that any person is engaged in, or is about to engage in, any act that constitutes, or would constitute, a violation of this section, the Attorney General may initiate civil action in a district court of the United States to enjoin such violation.

(d) Extraterritorial Jurisdiction.—

(1) In general.—There is jurisdiction over an offense under subsection (a) if—

(A) an offender is a national of the United States (as defined in section 101(a)(22) of the

Immigration and Nationality Act (8 U.S.C. 1101(a)(22))) or an alien lawfully admitted for permanent residence in the United States (as defined in section 101(a)(20) of the Immigration and Nationality Act (8 U.S.C. 1101(a)(20)));

(B) an offender is a stateless person whose habitual residence is in the United States;

(C) after the conduct required for the offense occurs an offender is brought into or found in the United States, even if the conduct required for the offense occurs outside the United States;

(D) the offense occurs in whole or in part within the United States;

(E) the offense occurs in or affects interstate or foreign commerce; or

(F) an offender aids or abets any person over whom jurisdiction exists under this paragraph in committing an offense under subsection (a) or conspires with any person over whom jurisdiction exists under this paragraph to commit an offense under subsection (a).

(2) Extraterritorial jurisdiction.—There is extraterritorial Federal jurisdiction over an offense under this section.

(e) Investigations.—

(1) In general.—The Attorney General shall conduct any investigation of a possible violation of this section, or of any license, order, or regulation issued pursuant to this section.

(2) Coordination with the department of the treasury.—The Attorney General shall work in coordination with the Secretary in investigations relating to—

(A) the compliance or noncompliance by a financial institution with the requirements of subsection (a)(2); and

(B) civil penalty proceedings authorized under subsection (b).

(3) Referral.—Any evidence of a criminal violation of this section arising in the course of an investigation by the Secretary or any other Federal agency shall be referred immediately to the Attorney General for further investigation. The Attorney General shall timely notify the Secretary of any action taken on referrals from the Secretary, and may refer investigations to the Secretary for remedial licensing or civil penalty action.

(f) Classified Information in Civil Proceedings Brought by the United States.—

(1) Discovery of classified information by defendants.—

(A) Request by united states.—In any civil proceeding under this section, upon request made ex parte and in writing by the United States, a court, upon a sufficient showing, may authorize the United States to—

(i) redact specified items of classified information from documents to be introduced into evidence or made available to the defendant through discovery under the Federal Rules of Civil Procedure;

(ii) substitute a summary of the information for such classified documents; or

(iii) substitute a statement admitting relevant facts that the classified information would tend to prove.

(B) Order granting request.—If the court enters an order granting a request under this paragraph, the entire text of the documents to which the request relates shall be sealed and preserved in the records of the court to be made available to the appellate court in the event of an appeal.

(C) Denial of request.—If the court enters an order denying a request of the United States under this paragraph, the United States may take an immediate, interlocutory appeal in accordance with paragraph (5). For purposes of such an appeal, the entire text of the documents to which the request relates, together with any transcripts of arguments made ex parte to the court in connection therewith, shall be maintained under seal and delivered to the appellate court.

(2) Introduction of classified information; precautions by court.—

(A) Exhibits.—To prevent unnecessary or inadvertent disclosure of classified information in a civil proceeding brought by the United States under this section, the United States may petition the court ex parte to admit, in lieu of classified writings, recordings, or photographs, one or more of the following:

(i) Copies of items from which classified information has been redacted.

(ii) Stipulations admitting relevant facts that specific classified information would tend to prove.

(iii) A declassified summary of the specific classified information.

(B) Determination by court.—The court shall grant a request under this paragraph if the court finds that the redacted item, stipulation, or summary is sufficient to allow the defendant to prepare a defense.

(3) Taking of trial testimony.—

(A) Objection.—During the examination of a witness in any civil proceeding brought by the United States under this subsection, the United States may object to any question or line of inquiry that may require the witness to disclose classified information not previously found to be admissible.

(B) Action by court.—In determining whether a response is admissible, the court shall take precautions to guard against the compromise of any classified information, including—

(i) permitting the United States to provide the court, ex parte, with a proffer of the witness's response to the question or line of inquiry; and

(ii) requiring the defendant to provide the court with a proffer of the nature of the information that the defendant seeks to elicit.

(C) Obligation of defendant.—In any civil proceeding under this section, it shall be the defendant's obligation to establish the relevance and materiality of any classified information sought to be introduced.

(4) Appeal.—If the court enters an order denying a request of the United States under this subsection, the United States may take an immediate interlocutory appeal in accordance with paragraph (5).

(5) Interlocutory appeal.—

(A) Subject of appeal.—An interlocutory appeal by the United States shall lie to a court of appeals from a decision or order of a district court—

(i) authorizing the disclosure of classified information;

(ii) imposing sanctions for nondisclosure of classified information; or

(iii) refusing a protective order sought by the United States to prevent the disclosure of classified information.

(B) Expedited consideration.—

(i) In general.—An appeal taken pursuant to this paragraph, either before or during trial, shall be expedited by the court of appeals.

(ii) Appeals prior to trial.—If an appeal is of an order made prior to trial, an appeal shall be taken not later than 14 days after the decision or order appealed from, and the trial shall not commence until the appeal is resolved.

(iii) Appeals during trial.—If an appeal is taken during trial, the trial court shall adjourn the trial until the appeal is resolved, and the court of appeals—

(I) shall hear argument on such appeal not later than 4 days after the adjournment of the trial, excluding intermediate weekends and holidays;

(II) may dispense with written briefs other than the supporting materials previously submitted to the trial court;

(III) shall render its decision not later than 4 days after argument on appeal, excluding intermediate weekends and holidays; and

(IV) may dispense with the issuance of a written opinion in rendering its decision.

(C) Effect of ruling.—An interlocutory appeal and decision shall not affect the right of the defendant, in a subsequent appeal from a final judgment, to claim as error reversal by the trial court on remand of a ruling appealed from during trial.

(6) Construction.—Nothing in this subsection shall prevent the United States from seeking protective orders or asserting privileges ordinarily available to the United States to protect against the disclosure of classified information, including the invocation of the military and State secrets privilege.

(g) Definitions.—As used in this section—

(1) the term "classified information" has the meaning given that term in section 1(a) of the Classified Information Procedures Act (18 U.S.C. App.);

(2) the term "financial institution" has the same meaning as in section 5312(a)(2) of title 31, United States Code;

(3) the term "funds" includes coin or currency of the United States or any other country, traveler's checks, personal checks, bank checks, money orders, stocks, bonds, debentures, drafts, letters of credit, any other negotiable instrument, and any electronic representation of any of the foregoing;

(4) the term "material support or resources" has the same meaning given that term in section 2339A (including the definitions of "training" and "expert advice or assistance" in that section);

(5) the term "Secretary" means the Secretary of the Treasury; and

(6) the term "terrorist organization" means an organization designated as a terrorist organization under section 219 of the Immigration and Nationality Act.

(h) Provision of Personnel.—No person may be prosecuted under this section in connection with the term "personnel" unless that person has knowingly provided, attempted to provide, or conspired to provide a foreign terrorist organization with 1 or more individuals (who may be or include himself) to work under that terrorist organization's direction or control or to organize, manage, supervise, or otherwise direct the operation of that organization. Individuals who act entirely independently of the foreign terrorist organization to advance its goals or objectives shall not be considered to be working under the foreign terrorist organization's direction and control.

(i) Rule of Construction.—Nothing in this section shall be construed or applied so as to abridge the exercise of rights guaranteed under the First Amendment to the Constitution of the United States.

(j) Exception.—No person may be prosecuted under this section in connection with the term "personnel", "training", or "expert advice or assistance" if the provision of that material support or resources to a foreign terrorist organization was approved by the Secretary of State with the concurrence of the Attorney General. The Secretary of State may not approve the provision of any material support that may be used to carry out terrorist activity (as defined in section 212(a)(3)(B)(iii) of the Immigration and Nationality Act).

(Added Pub. L. 104–132, title III, §303(a), Apr. 24, 1996, 110 Stat. 1250; amended Pub. L. 107–56, title VIII, §810(d), Oct. 26, 2001, 115 Stat. 380; Pub. L. 108–458, title VI, §6603(c)–(f), Dec. 17, 2004, 118 Stat. 3762, 3763; Pub. L. 111–16, §3(6)–(8), May 7, 2009, 123 Stat. 1608; Pub. L. 114–23, title VII, §704, June 2, 2015, 129 Stat. 300.)

References in Text

Section 212(a)(3)(B) of the Immigration and Nationality Act, referred to in subsecs. (a)(1) and (j), is classified to section 1182(a)(3)(B) of Title 8, Aliens and Nationality.

Section 140(d)(2) of the Foreign Relations Authorization Act, Fiscal Years 1988 and 1989, referred to in subsec. (a)(1), is classified to section 2656f(d)(2) of Title 22, Foreign Relations and Intercourse.

The Federal Rules of Civil Procedure, referred to in subsec. (f)(1)(A)(i), are set out in the Appendix to Title 28, Judiciary and Judicial Procedure.

Section 1(a) of the Classified Information Procedures Act, referred to in subsec. (g)(1), is section 1(a) of Pub. L. 95–456, which is set out in the Appendix to this title.

Section 219 of the Immigration and Nationality Act, referred to in subsec. (g)(6), is classified to section 1189 of Title 8, Aliens and Nationality.

Amendments

2015—Subsec. (a)(1). Pub. L. 114–23 substituted "20 years" for "15 years".

2009—Subsec. (f)(5)(B)(ii). Pub. L. 111–16, §3(6), substituted "14 days" for "10 days".

Subsec. (f)(5)(B)(iii)(I). Pub. L. 111–16, §3(7), inserted ", excluding intermediate weekends and holidays" after "trial".

Subsec. (f)(5)(B)(iii)(III). Pub. L. 111–16, §3(8), inserted ", excluding intermediate weekends and holidays" after "appeal".

2004—Subsec. (a)(1). Pub. L. 108–458, §6603(c), struck out ", within the United States or subject to the jurisdiction of the United States," after "Whoever" and inserted at end "To violate this paragraph, a person must have knowledge that the organization is a designated terrorist organization (as defined in subsection (g)(6)), that the organization has engaged or engages in terrorist activity (as defined in section 212(a)(3)(B) of the Immigration and Nationality Act), or that the organization has engaged or engages in terrorism (as defined in section 140(d)(2) of the Foreign Relations Authorization Act, Fiscal Years 1988 and 1989)."

Subsec. (d). Pub. L. 108–458, §6603(d), designated existing provisions as par. (2), inserted par. (2) heading, and added par. (1).

Subsec. (g)(4). Pub. L. 108–458, §6603(e), amended par. (4) generally. Prior to amendment, par. (4) read as follows: "the term 'material support or resources' has the same meaning as in section 2339A;".

Subsecs. (h) to (j). Pub. L. 108–458, §6603(f), added subsecs. (h) to (j).

2001—Subsec. (a)(1). Pub. L. 107–56 substituted "15 years, or both, and, if the death of any person results, shall be imprisoned for any term of years or for life" for "10 years, or both".

Effective Date of 2009 Amendment

Amendment by Pub. L. 111–16 effective Dec. 1, 2009, see section 7 of Pub. L. 111–16, set out as a note under section 109 of Title 11, Bankruptcy.

Findings and Purpose

Pub. L. 104–132, title III, §301, Apr. 24, 1996, 110 Stat. 1247, provided that:

"(a) Findings.—The Congress finds that—

"(1) international terrorism is a serious and deadly problem that threatens the vital interests of the United States;

"(2) the Constitution confers upon Congress the power to punish crimes against the law of nations and to carry out the treaty obligations of the United States, and therefore Congress may by law impose penalties relating to the provision of material support to foreign organizations engaged in terrorist activity;

"(3) the power of the United States over immigration and naturalization permits the exclusion from the United States of persons belonging to international terrorist organizations;

"(4) international terrorism affects the interstate and foreign commerce of the United States by harming international trade and market stability, and limiting international travel by United States citizens as well as foreign visitors to the United States;

"(5) international cooperation is required for an effective response to terrorism, as demonstrated by the numerous multilateral conventions in force providing universal prosecutive jurisdiction over persons involved in a variety of terrorist acts, including hostage taking, murder of an internationally protected person, and aircraft piracy and sabotage;

"(6) some foreign terrorist organizations, acting through affiliated groups or individuals, raise significant funds within the United States, or use the United States as a conduit for the receipt of funds raised in other nations; and

"(7) foreign organizations that engage in terrorist activity are so tainted by their criminal conduct that any contribution to such an organization facilitates that conduct.

"(b) Purpose.—The purpose of this subtitle [subtitle A (§§301–303) of title III of Pub. L. 104–132, enacting this section and section 1189 of Title 8, Aliens and Nationality] is to provide the Federal Government the fullest possible basis, consistent with the Constitution, to prevent persons within the United States, or subject to the jurisdiction of the United States, from providing material support or resources to foreign organizations that engage in terrorist activities."

§2339C. Prohibitions against the financing of terrorism

(a) Offenses.—

(1) In general.—Whoever, in a circumstance described in subsection (b), by any means, directly or indirectly, unlawfully and willfully provides or collects funds with the intention that such funds be used, or with the knowledge that such funds are to be used, in full or in part, in order to carry out—

(A) an act which constitutes an offense within the scope of a treaty specified in subsection (e)(7), as implemented by the United States, or

(B) any other act intended to cause death or serious bodily injury to a civilian, or to any other person not taking an active part in the hostilities in a situation of armed conflict, when the purpose of such act, by its nature or context, is to intimidate a population, or to compel a government or an international organization to do or to abstain from doing any act,

shall be punished as prescribed in subsection (d)(1).

(2) Attempts and conspiracies.—Whoever attempts or conspires to commit an offense under paragraph (1) shall be punished as prescribed in subsection (d)(1).

(3) Relationship to predicate act.—For an act to constitute an offense set forth in this subsection, it shall not be necessary that the funds were actually used to carry out a predicate act.

(b) Jurisdiction.—There is jurisdiction over the offenses in subsection (a) in the following circumstances—

(1) the offense takes place in the United States and—

(A) a perpetrator was a national of another state or a stateless person;

(B) on board a vessel flying the flag of another state or an aircraft which is registered under the laws of another state at the time the offense is committed;

(C) on board an aircraft which is operated by the government of another state;

(D) a perpetrator is found outside the United States;

(E) was directed toward or resulted in the carrying out of a predicate act against—

(i) a national of another state; or

(ii) another state or a government facility of such state, including its embassy or other diplomatic or consular premises of that state;

(F) was directed toward or resulted in the carrying out of a predicate act committed in an attempt to compel another state or international organization to do or abstain from doing any act; or

(G) was directed toward or resulted in the carrying out of a predicate act—

(i) outside the United States; or

(ii) within the United States, and either the offense or the predicate act was conducted in, or the results thereof affected, interstate or foreign commerce;

(2) the offense takes place outside the United States and—

(A) a perpetrator is a national of the United States or is a stateless person whose habitual residence is in the United States;

(B) a perpetrator is found in the United States; or

(C) was directed toward or resulted in the carrying out of a predicate act against—

(i) any property that is owned, leased, or used by the United States or by any department or agency of the United States, including an embassy or other diplomatic or consular premises of the United States;

(ii) any person or property within the United States;

(iii) any national of the United States or the property of such national; or

(iv) any property of any legal entity organized under the laws of the United States, including any of its States, districts, commonwealths, territories, or possessions;

(3) the offense is committed on board a vessel flying the flag of the United States or an aircraft which is registered under the laws of the United States at the time the offense is committed;

(4) the offense is committed on board an aircraft which is operated by the United States; or

(5) the offense was directed toward or resulted in the carrying out of a predicate act committed in an attempt to compel the United States to do or abstain from doing any act.

(c) Concealment.—Whoever—

(1)(A) is in the United States; or

(B) is outside the United States and is a national of the United States or a legal entity organized under the laws of the United States (including any of its States, districts, commonwealths, territories, or possessions); and

(2) knowingly conceals or disguises the nature, location, source, ownership, or control of any material support or resources, or any funds or proceeds of such funds—

(A) knowing or intending that the support or resources are to be provided, or knowing that the support or resources were provided, in violation of section 2339B of this title; or

(B) knowing or intending that any such funds are to be provided or collected, or knowing that the funds were provided or collected, in violation of subsection (a),

shall be punished as prescribed in subsection (d)(2).

(d) Penalties.—

(1) Subsection (a).—Whoever violates subsection (a) shall be fined under this title, imprisoned for not more than 20 years, or both.

(2) Subsection (c).—Whoever violates subsection (c) shall be fined under this title, imprisoned for not more than 10 years, or both.

(e) Definitions.—In this section—

(1) the term "funds" means assets of every kind, whether tangible or intangible, movable or immovable, however acquired, and legal documents or instruments in any form, including electronic or digital, evidencing title to, or interest in, such assets, including coin, currency, bank credits, travelers checks, bank checks, money orders, shares, securities, bonds, drafts, and letters of credit;

(2) the term "government facility" means any permanent or temporary facility or conveyance that is used or occupied by representatives of a state, members of a government, the legislature, or the judiciary, or by officials or employees of a state or any other public authority or entity or by employees or officials of an intergovernmental organization in connection with their official duties;

(3) the term "proceeds" means any funds derived from or obtained, directly or indirectly, through the commission of an offense set forth in subsection (a);

(4) the term "provides" includes giving, donating, and transmitting;

(5) the term "collects" includes raising and receiving;

(6) the term "predicate act" means any act referred to in subparagraph (A) or (B) of subsection (a)(1);

(7) the term "treaty" means—

(A) the Convention for the Suppression of Unlawful Seizure of Aircraft, done at The Hague on December 16, 1970;

(B) the Convention for the Suppression of Unlawful Acts against the Safety of Civil Aviation, done at Montreal on September 23, 1971;

(C) the Convention on the Prevention and Punishment of Crimes against Internationally Protected Persons, including Diplomatic Agents, adopted by the General Assembly of the United Nations on December 14, 1973;

(D) the International Convention against the Taking of Hostages, adopted by the General Assembly of the United Nations on December 17, 1979;

(E) the Convention on the Physical Protection of Nuclear Material, adopted at Vienna on March 3, 1980;

(F) the Protocol for the Suppression of Unlawful Acts of Violence at Airports Serving International Civil Aviation, supplementary to the Convention for the Suppression of Unlawful Acts against the Safety of Civil Aviation, done at Montreal on February 24, 1988;

(G) the Convention for the Suppression of Unlawful Acts against the Safety of Maritime Navigation, done at Rome on March 10, 1988;

(H) the Protocol for the Suppression of Unlawful Acts against the Safety of Fixed Platforms located on the Continental Shelf, done at Rome on March 10, 1988; or

(I) the International Convention for the Suppression of Terrorist Bombings, adopted by the General Assembly of the United Nations on December 15, 1997;

(8) the term "intergovernmental organization" includes international organizations;

(9) the term "international organization" has the same meaning as in section 1116(b)(5) of this title;

(10) the term "armed conflict" does not include internal disturbances and tensions, such as riots, isolated and sporadic acts of violence, and other acts of a similar nature;

(11) the term "serious bodily injury" has the same meaning as in section 1365(g)(3) of this title; 1

(12) the term "national of the United States" has the meaning given that term in section 101(a)(22) of the Immigration and Nationality Act (8 U.S.C. 1101(a)(22));

(13) the term "material support or resources" has the same meaning given that term in section 2339B(g)(4) of this title; and

(14) the term "state" has the same meaning as that term has under international law, and includes all political subdivisions thereof.

(f) Civil Penalty.—In addition to any other criminal, civil, or administrative liability or penalty, any legal entity located within the United States or organized under the laws of the United States, including any of the laws of its States, districts, commonwealths, territories, or possessions, shall be liable to the United States for the sum of at least $10,000, if a person responsible for the management or control of that legal entity has, in that capacity, committed an offense set forth in subsection (a).

(Added Pub. L. 107–197, title II, §202(a), June 25, 2002, 116 Stat. 724; amended Pub. L. 107–273, div. B, title IV, §4006, Nov. 2, 2002, 116 Stat. 1813; Pub. L. 108–458, title VI, §6604, Dec. 17, 2004, 118 Stat. 3764; Pub. L. 109–177, title IV, §408, Mar. 9, 2006, 120 Stat. 245.)

References in Text

Section 1365(g)(3), referred to in subsec. (e)(11), was redesignated section 1365(h)(3) by Pub. L. 107–307, §2(1), Dec. 2, 2002, 116 Stat. 2445.

Amendments

2006—Pub. L. 109–177 amended directory language of Pub. L. 108–458, §6604. See 2004 Amendment notes below.

2004—Subsec. (c)(2). Pub. L. 108–458, §6604(a)(1), as amended by Pub. L. 109–177, §408(1), substituted "or resources, or any funds or proceeds of such funds" for ", resources, or funds" in introductory provisions.

Subsec. (c)(2)(A). Pub. L. 108–458, §6604(a)(2), as amended by Pub. L. 109–177, §408(1), substituted "are to be provided, or knowing that the support or resources were provided," for "were provided".

Subsec. (c)(2)(B). Pub. L. 108–458, §6604(a)(3), as amended by Pub. L. 109–177, §408(1), struck out "or any proceeds of such funds" after "any such funds" and substituted "are to be provided or collected, or knowing that the funds were provided or collected," for "were provided or collected".

Subsec. (e)(13), (14). Pub. L. 108–458, §6604(b), as amended by Pub. L. 109–177, §408(2), added par. (13) and redesignated former par. (13) as (14).

2002—Subsec. (a)(1). Pub. L. 107–273 substituted "described in subsection (b)" for "described in subsection (c)".

Effective Date of 2006 Amendment

Pub. L. 109–177, title IV, §408, Mar. 9, 2006, 120 Stat. 245, provided that the amendment by Pub. L. 109–177 to section 6604 of Pub. L. 108–458 (amending this section) is effective on the date of enactment of Pub. L. 108–458 (Dec. 17, 2004).

Effective Date

Pub. L. 107–197, title II, §203, June 25, 2002, 116 Stat. 727, provided that: "Except for paragraphs (1)(D) and (2)(B) of section 2339C(b) of title 18, United States Code, which shall become effective on the date that the International Convention for the Suppression of the Financing of Terrorism enters into force for the United States [July 26, 2002], and for the provisions of section 2339C(e)(7)(I) of title 18, United States Code, which shall become effective on the date that the International Convention for the Suppression of Terrorist Bombing enters into force for the United States [July 26, 2002], section 202 [enacting this section and provisions set out as a note below] shall take effect on the date of enactment of this Act [June 25, 2002]."

Disclaimer

Pub. L. 107–197, title II, §202(c), June 25, 2002, 116 Stat. 727, provided that: "Nothing contained in this section [enacting this section] is intended to affect the scope or applicability of any other Federal or State law."

§2339D. Receiving military-type training from a foreign terrorist organization

(a) Offense.—Whoever knowingly receives military-type training from or on behalf of any organization designated at the time of the training by the Secretary of State under section 219(a)(1) of the Immigration and Nationality Act as a foreign terrorist organization shall be fined under this title or imprisoned for ten years, or both. To violate this subsection, a person must have knowledge that the organization is a designated terrorist organization (as defined in subsection (c)(4)), that the organization has engaged or engages in terrorist activity (as defined in section 212 of the Immigration and Nationality Act), or that the organization has engaged or engages in terrorism (as defined in section 140(d)(2) of the Foreign Relations Authorization Act, Fiscal Years 1988 and 1989).

(b) Extraterritorial Jurisdiction.—There is extraterritorial Federal jurisdiction over an offense under this section. There is jurisdiction over an offense under subsection (a) if—

(1) an offender is a national of the United States (as defined in 1 101(a)(22) of the Immigration and Nationality Act) or an alien lawfully admitted for permanent residence in the United States (as defined in section 101(a)(20) of the Immigration and Nationality Act);

(2) an offender is a stateless person whose habitual residence is in the United States;

(3) after the conduct required for the offense occurs an offender is brought into or found in the United States, even if the conduct required for the offense occurs outside the United States;

(4) the offense occurs in whole or in part within the United States;

(5) the offense occurs in or affects interstate or foreign commerce; or

(6) an offender aids or abets any person over whom jurisdiction exists under this paragraph in committing an offense under subsection (a) or conspires with any person over whom jurisdiction exists under this paragraph to commit an offense under subsection (a).

(c) Definitions.—As used in this section—

(1) the term "military-type training" includes training in means or methods that can cause death or serious bodily injury, destroy or damage property, or disrupt services to critical infrastructure, or training on the use, storage, production, or assembly of any explosive, firearm or other weapon, including any weapon of mass destruction (as defined in section 2232a(c)(2) 2);

(2) the term "serious bodily injury" has the meaning given that term in section 1365(h)(3);

(3) the term "critical infrastructure" means systems and assets vital to national defense, national security, economic security, public health or safety including both regional and national infrastructure. Critical infrastructure may be publicly or privately owned; examples of critical infrastructure include gas and oil production, storage, or delivery systems, water supply systems, telecommunications networks, electrical power generation or delivery systems, financing and banking systems, emergency services (including medical, police, fire, and rescue services), and transportation systems and services (including highways, mass transit, airlines, and airports); and

(4) the term "foreign terrorist organization" means an organization designated as a terrorist organization under section 219(a)(1) of the Immigration and Nationality Act.

(Added Pub. L. 108–458, title VI, §6602, Dec. 17, 2004, 118 Stat. 3761.)

References in Text

Sections 101, 212, and 219 of the Immigration and Nationality Act, referred to in subsecs. (a), (b)(1), and (c)(4), are classified to sections 1101, 1182, and 1189, respectively, of Title 8, Aliens and Nationality.

Section 140(d)(2) of the Foreign Relations Authorization Act, Fiscal Years 1988 and 1989, referred to in subsec. (a), is classified to section 2656f(d)(2) of Title 22, Foreign Relations and Intercourse.

CHAPTER 113C - TORTURE

Amendments

2002—Pub. L. 107–273, div. B, title IV, §4002(c)(1), Nov. 2, 2002, 116 Stat. 1808, repealed Pub. L. 104–294, title VI, §601(j)(1), Oct. 11, 1996, 110 Stat. 3501. See 1996 Amendment note below. 1996—Pub. L. 104–132, title III, §303(c)(1), Apr. 24, 1996, 110 Stat. 1253, redesignated chapter 113B as 113C. Pub. L. 104–294, title VI, §601(j)(1), Oct. 11, 1996, 110 Stat. 3501, which made identical amendment, was repealed by Pub. L. 107–273, div. B, title IV, §4002(c)(1), Nov. 2, 2002, 116 Stat. 1808, effective Oct. 11, 1996.

§2340. Definitions

As used in this chapter—

(1) "torture" means an act committed by a person acting under the color of law specifically intended to inflict severe physical or mental pain or suffering (other than pain or suffering incidental to lawful sanctions) upon another person within his custody or physical control;

(2) "severe mental pain or suffering" means the prolonged mental harm caused by or resulting from—

(A) the intentional infliction or threatened infliction of severe physical pain or suffering;

(B) the administration or application, or threatened administration or application, of mind-altering substances or other procedures calculated to disrupt profoundly the senses or the personality;

(C) the threat of imminent death; or

(D) the threat that another person will imminently be subjected to death, severe physical pain or suffering, or the administration or application of mind-altering substances or other procedures calculated to disrupt profoundly the senses or personality; and

(3) "United States" means the several States of the United States, the District of Columbia, and the commonwealths, territories, and possessions of the United States.

(Added Pub. L. 103–236, title V, §506(a), Apr. 30, 1994, 108 Stat. 463; amended Pub. L. 103–415, §1(k), Oct. 25, 1994, 108 Stat. 4301; Pub. L. 103–429, §2(2), Oct. 31, 1994, 108 Stat. 4377; Pub. L. 108–375, div. A, title X, §1089, Oct. 28, 2004, 118 Stat. 2067.)

Amendments

2004—Par. (3). Pub. L. 108–375 amended par. (3) generally. Prior to amendment, par. (3) read as follows: " 'United States' includes all areas under the jurisdiction of the United States including any of the places described in sections 5 and 7 of this title and section 46501(2) of title 49." 1994—Par. (1). Pub. L. 103–415 substituted "within his custody" for "with custody". Par. (3). Pub. L. 103–429 substituted "section 46501(2) of title 49" for "section 101(38) of the Federal Aviation Act of 1958 (49 U.S.C. App. 1301(38))".

Effective Date

Pub. L. 103–236, title V, §506(c), Apr. 30, 1994, 108 Stat. 464, provided that: "The amendments made by this section [enacting this chapter] shall take effect on the later of—

"(1) the date of enactment of this Act [Apr. 30, 1994]; or

"(2) the date on which the United States has become a party to the Convention Against Torture and Other Cruel, Inhuman or Degrading Treatment or Punishment." [Convention entered into Force with respect to United States Nov. 20, 1994, Treaty Doc. 100–20.]

§2340A. Torture

(a) Offense.—Whoever outside the United States commits or attempts to commit torture shall be fined under this title or imprisoned not more than 20 years, or both, and if death results to any person from conduct prohibited by this subsection, shall be punished by death or imprisoned for any term of years or for life.

(b) Jurisdiction.—There is jurisdiction over the activity prohibited in subsection (a) if—

(1) the alleged offender is a national of the United States; or

(2) the alleged offender is present in the United States, irrespective of the nationality of the victim or alleged offender.

(c) Conspiracy.—A person who conspires to commit an offense under this section shall be subject to the same penalties (other than the penalty of death) as the penalties prescribed for the offense, the commission of which was the object of the conspiracy.

(Added Pub. L. 103–236, title V, §506(a), Apr. 30, 1994, 108 Stat. 463; amended Pub. L. 103–322, title VI, §60020, Sept. 13, 1994, 108 Stat. 1979; Pub. L. 107–56, title VIII, §811(g), Oct. 26, 2001, 115 Stat. 381.)

Amendments

2001—Subsec. (c). Pub. L. 107–56 added subsec. (c).

1994—Subsec. (a). Pub. L. 103–322 inserted "punished by death or" before "imprisoned for any term of years or for life".

Effective Date

Section effective on the later of Apr. 30, 1994, or the date on which the United States has become a party to the Convention Against Torture and Other Cruel, Inhuman or Degrading Treatment or Punishment (Nov. 20, 1994), see section 506(c) of Pub. L. 103–236, set out as a note under section 2340 of this title.

§2340B. Exclusive remedies

Nothing in this chapter shall be construed as precluding the application of State or local laws on the same subject, nor shall anything in this chapter be construed as creating any substantive or procedural right enforceable by law by any party in any civil proceeding.

(Added Pub. L. 103–236, title V, §506(a), Apr. 30, 1994, 108 Stat. 464.)

Effective Date

Section effective on the later of Apr. 30, 1994, or the date on which the United States has become a party to the Convention Against Torture and Other Cruel, Inhuman or Degrading Treatment or Punishment (Nov. 20, 1994), see section 506(c) of Pub. L. 103–236, set out as a note under section 2340 of this title.

CHAPTER 114 - TRAFFICKING IN CONTRABAND CIGARETTES AND SMOKELESS TOBACCO

Amendments

2006—Pub. L. 109–177, title I, §121(g)(3), (4)(A), Mar. 9, 2006, 120 Stat. 224, substituted "TRAFFICKING IN CONTRABAND CIGARETTES AND SMOKELESS TOBACCO" for "TRAFFICKING IN CONTRABAND CIGARETTES" in chapter heading, added items 2343 and 2345, and struck out former items 2343 "Recordkeeping and inspection" and 2345 "Effect on State law".

§2341. Definitions

As used in this chapter—

(1) the term "cigarette" means—

(A) any roll of tobacco wrapped in paper or in any substance not containing tobacco; and

(B) any roll of tobacco wrapped in any substance containing tobacco which, because of its appearance, the type of tobacco used in the filler, or its packaging and labeling, is likely to be offered to, or purchased by, consumers as a cigarette described in subparagraph (A);

(2) the term "contraband cigarettes" means a quantity in excess of 10,000 cigarettes, which bear no evidence of the payment of applicable State or local cigarette taxes in the State or locality where such cigarettes are found, if the State or local government requires a stamp, impression, or other indication to be placed on packages or other containers of cigarettes to evidence payment of cigarette taxes, and which are in the possession of any person other than—

(A) a person holding a permit issued pursuant to chapter 52 of the Internal Revenue Code of 1986 as a manufacturer of tobacco products or as an export warehouse proprietor, or a person operating a customs bonded warehouse pursuant to section 311 or 555 of the Tariff Act of 1930 (19 U.S.C. 1311 or 1555) or an agent of such person;

(B) a common or contract carrier transporting the cigarettes involved under a proper bill of lading or freight bill which states the quantity, source, and destination of such cigarettes;

(C) a person—

(i) who is licensed or otherwise authorized by the State where the cigarettes are found to account for and pay cigarette taxes imposed by such State; and

(ii) who has complied with the accounting and payment requirements relating to such license or authorization with respect to the cigarettes involved; or

(D) an officer, employee, or other agent of the United States or a State, or any department, agency, or instrumentality of the United States or a State (including any political subdivision of a State) having possession of such cigarettes in connection with the performance of official duties;

(3) the term "common or contract carrier" means a carrier holding a certificate of convenience and necessity, a permit for contract carrier by motor vehicle, or other valid operating authority under subtitle IV of title 49, or under equivalent operating authority from a regulatory agency of the United States or of any State;

(4) the term "State" means a State of the United States, the District of Columbia, the Commonwealth of Puerto Rico, or the Virgin Islands;

(5) the term "Attorney General" means the Attorney General of the United States;

(6) the term "smokeless tobacco" means any finely cut, ground, powdered, or leaf tobacco that is intended to be placed in the oral or nasal cavity or otherwise consumed without being combusted;

(7) the term "contraband smokeless tobacco" means a quantity in excess of 500 single-unit consumer-sized cans or packages of smokeless tobacco, or their equivalent, that are in the possession of any person other than—

(A) a person holding a permit issued pursuant to chapter 52 of the Internal Revenue Code of 1986 as manufacturer 1 of tobacco products or as an export warehouse proprietor, a person operating a customs bonded warehouse pursuant to section 311 or 555 of the Tariff Act of 1930 (19 U.S.C. 1311, 1555), or an agent of such person;

(B) a common carrier transporting such smokeless tobacco under a proper bill of lading or freight bill which states the quantity, source, and designation of such smokeless tobacco;

(C) a person who—

(i) is licensed or otherwise authorized by the State where such smokeless tobacco is found to engage in the business of selling or distributing tobacco products; and

(ii) has complied with the accounting, tax, and payment requirements relating to such license or authorization with respect to such smokeless tobacco; or

(D) an officer, employee, or agent of the United States or a State, or any department, agency, or instrumentality of the United States or a State (including any political subdivision of a State), having possession of such smokeless tobacco in connection with the performance of official duties; 2

(Added Pub. L. 95–575, §1, Nov. 2, 1978, 92 Stat. 2463; amended Pub. L. 97–449, §5(c), Jan. 12, 1983, 96 Stat. 2442; Pub. L. 99–514, §2, Oct. 22, 1986, 100 Stat. 2095; Pub. L. 107–296, title XI, §1112(i)(1), Nov. 25, 2002, 116 Stat. 2277; Pub. L. 109–177, title I, §121(a)(1), (b)(1), (6), Mar. 9, 2006, 120 Stat. 221, 222.)

References in Text

Chapter 52 of the Internal Revenue Code of 1986, referred to in pars. (2)(A) and (7)(A), is classified generally to chapter 52 (§5701 et seq.) of Title 26, Internal Revenue Code.

Amendments

2006—Par. (2). Pub. L. 109–177, §121(b)(6), which directed amendment of par. (2) by substituting "State or local cigarette taxes in the State or locality where such cigarettes are found, if the State or local government" for "State cigarette taxes in the State where such cigarettes are found, if the State" in introductory provisions, was executed by making the substitution for "State cigarette taxes in the State where such cigarettes are found, if such State", to reflect the probable intent of Congress.

Pub. L. 109–177, §121(a)(1), substituted "10,000 cigarettes" for "60,000 cigarettes" in introductory provisions.

Pars. (6), (7). Pub. L. 109–177, §121(b)(1), added pars. (6) and (7).

2002—Par. (5). Pub. L. 107–296 added par. (5) and struck out former par. (5) which read as follows: "the term 'Secretary' means the Secretary of the Treasury."

1986—Par. (2)(A). Pub. L. 99–514 substituted "Internal Revenue Code of 1986" for "Internal Revenue Code of 1954".

1983—Par. (3). Pub. L. 97–449 substituted "subtitle IV of title 49" for "the Interstate Commerce Act".

Effective Date of 2002 Amendment

Amendment by Pub. L. 107–296 effective 60 days after Nov. 25, 2002, see section 4 of Pub. L. 107–296, set out as an Effective Date note under section 101 of Title 6, Domestic Security.

Effective Date

Pub. L. 95–575, §4, Nov. 2, 1978, 92 Stat. 2466, provided:

"(a) Except as provided in subsection (b), this Act [enacting this chapter, amending section 1961 of this title and sections 781 and 787 of former Title 49, Transportation, and enacting provisions set out as a note under this section] shall take effect on the date of its enactment [Nov. 2, 1978].

"(b) Sections 2342(b) and 2343 of title 18, United States Code as enacted by the first section of this Act, shall take effect on the first day of the first month beginning more than 120 days after the date of the enactment of this Act [Nov. 2, 1978]."

Authorization of Appropriations

Pub. L. 95–575, §5, Nov. 2, 1978, 92 Stat. 2466, provided that: "There are hereby authorized to be appropriated such sums as may be necessary to carry out the provisions of chapter 114 of title 18, United States Code, added by the first section of this Act."

§2342. Unlawful acts

(a) It shall be unlawful for any person knowingly to ship, transport, receive, possess, sell, distribute, or purchase contraband cigarettes or contraband smokeless tobacco.

(b) It shall be unlawful for any person knowingly to make any false statement or representation with respect to the information required by this chapter to be kept in the records of any person who ships, sells, or distributes any quantity of cigarettes in excess of 10,000 in a single transaction. (Added Pub. L. 95–575, §1, Nov. 2, 1978, 92 Stat. 2464; amended Pub. L. 109–177, title I, §121(a)(2), (b)(2), Mar. 9, 2006, 120 Stat. 221, 222.)

Amendments

2006—Subsec. (a). Pub. L. 109–177, §121(b)(2), inserted "or contraband smokeless tobacco" after "contraband cigarettes".
Subsec. (b). Pub. L. 109–177, §121(a)(2), substituted "10,000" for "60,000".

Effective Date

Subsec. (a) of this section effective Nov. 2, 1978, and subsec. (b) of this section effective on first day of first month beginning more than 120 days after Nov. 2, 1978, see section 4 of Pub. L. 95–575, set out as a note under section 2341 of this title.

§2343. Recordkeeping, reporting, and inspection

(a) Any person who ships, sells, or distributes any quantity of cigarettes in excess of 10,000, or any quantity of smokeless tobacco in excess of 500 single-unit consumer-sized cans or packages, in a single transaction shall maintain such information about the shipment, receipt, sale, and distribution of cigarettes as the Attorney General may prescribe by rule or regulation. The Attorney General may require such person to keep such information as the Attorney General considers appropriate for purposes of enforcement of this chapter, including—

(1) the name, address, destination (including street address), vehicle license number, driver's license number, signature of the person receiving such cigarettes, and the name of the purchaser;

(2) a declaration of the specific purpose of the receipt (personal use, resale, or delivery to another); and

(3) a declaration of the name and address of the recipient's principal in all cases when the recipient is acting as an agent.

Such information shall be contained on business records kept in the normal course of business.

(b) Any person, except for a tribal government, who engages in a delivery sale, and who ships, sells, or distributes any quantity in excess of 10,000 cigarettes, or any quantity in excess of 500 single-unit consumer-sized cans or packages of smokeless tobacco, or their equivalent, within a single month, shall submit to the Attorney General, pursuant to rules or regulations prescribed by the Attorney General, a report that sets forth the following:

(1) The person's beginning and ending inventory of cigarettes and cans or packages of smokeless tobacco (in total) for such month.

(2) The total quantity of cigarettes and cans or packages of smokeless tobacco that the person received within such month from each other person (itemized by name and address).

(3) The total quantity of cigarettes and cans or packages of smokeless tobacco that the person distributed within such month to each person (itemized by name and address) other than a retail purchaser.

(c)(1) Any officer of the Bureau of Alcohol, Tobacco, Firearms, and Explosives may, during normal business hours, enter the premises of any person described in subsection (a) or (b) for the purposes of inspecting—

(A) any records or information required to be maintained by the person under this chapter; or

(B) any cigarettes or smokeless tobacco kept or stored by the person at the premises.

(2) The district courts of the United States shall have the authority in a civil action under this subsection to compel inspections authorized by paragraph (1).

(3) Whoever denies access to an officer under paragraph (1), or who fails to comply with an order issued under paragraph (2), shall be subject to a civil penalty in an amount not to exceed $10,000.

(d) Any report required to be submitted under this chapter to the Attorney General shall also be submitted to the Secretary of the Treasury and to the attorneys general and the tax administrators of the States from where the shipments, deliveries, or distributions both originated and concluded.

(e) In this section, the term "delivery sale" means any sale of cigarettes or smokeless tobacco in interstate commerce to a consumer if—

(1) the consumer submits the order for such sale by means of a telephone or other method of voice transmission, the mails, or the Internet or other online service, or by any other means where the consumer is not in the same physical location as the seller when the purchase or offer of sale is made; or

(2) the cigarettes or smokeless tobacco are delivered by use of the mails, common carrier, private delivery service, or any other means where the consumer is not in the same physical location as the seller when the consumer obtains physical possession of the cigarettes or smokeless tobacco.

(f) In this section, the term "interstate commerce" means commerce between a State and any place outside the State, or commerce between points in the same State but through any place outside the State.

(Added Pub. L. 95–575, §1, Nov. 2, 1978, 92 Stat. 2464; amended Pub. L. 107–296, title XI, §1112(i)(2), Nov. 25, 2002, 116 Stat. 2277; Pub. L. 109–177, title I, §121(a)(3), (b)(3), (c), (g)(1), Mar. 9, 2006, 120 Stat. 221, 222, 224; Pub. L. 111–154, §4, Mar. 31, 2010, 124 Stat. 1109.)

Amendments

2010—Subsec. (c). Pub. L. 111–154 amended subsec. (c) generally. Prior to amendment, subsec. (c) read as follows: "Upon the consent of any person who ships, sells, or distributes any quantity of cigarettes in excess of 10,000 in a single transaction, or pursuant to a duly issued search warrant, the Attorney General may enter the premises (including places of storage) of such person for the purpose of inspecting any records or information required to be maintained by such person under this chapter, and any cigarettes kept or stored by such person at such premises."

2006—Pub. L. 109–177, §121(g)(1), substituted "Recordkeeping, reporting, and inspection" for "Recordkeeping and inspection" in section catchline.

Subsec. (a). Pub. L. 109–177, §121(a)(3)(A), (b)(3), (c)(1), in introductory provisions, substituted "10,000, or any quantity of smokeless tobacco in excess of 500 single-unit consumer-sized cans or packages," for "60,000" and "such information as the Attorney General considers appropriate for purposes of enforcement of this chapter, including—" for "only—" and, in concluding provisions, struck out "Nothing contained herein shall authorize the Attorney General to require reporting under this section." at end.

Subsec. (b). Pub. L. 109–177, §121(c)(3), added subsec. (b). Former subsec. (b) redesignated (c).

Pub. L. 109–177, §121(a)(3)(B), substituted "10,000" for "60,000".

Subsec. (c). Pub. L. 109–177, §121(c)(2), redesignated subsec. (b) as (c).

Subsecs. (d) to (f). Pub. L. 109–177, §121(c)(4), added subsecs. (d) to (f).

2002—Pub. L. 107–296 substituted "Attorney General" for "Secretary" wherever appearing.

Effective Date of 2002 Amendment

Amendment by Pub. L. 107–296 effective 60 days after Nov. 25, 2002, see section 4 of Pub. L. 107–296, set out as an Effective Date note under section 101 of Title 6, Domestic Security.

Effective Date

Section effective on first day of first month beginning more than 120 days after Nov. 2, 1978, see section 4 of Pub. L. 95–575, set out as a note under section 2341 of this title.

§2344. Penalties

(a) Whoever knowingly violates section 2342(a) of this title shall be fined under this title or imprisoned not more than five years, or both.

(b) Whoever knowingly violates any rule or regulation promulgated under section 2343(a) or 2346 of this title or violates section 2342(b) of this title shall be fined under this title or imprisoned not more than three years, or both.

(c) Any contraband cigarettes or contraband smokeless tobacco involved in any violation of the provisions of this chapter shall be subject to seizure and forfeiture. The provisions of chapter 46 of title 18 relating to civil forfeitures shall extend to any seizure or civil forfeiture under this section. Any cigarettes or smokeless tobacco so seized and forfeited shall be either—

(1) destroyed and not resold; or

(2) used for undercover investigative operations for the detection and prosecution of crimes, and then destroyed and not resold.

(Added Pub. L. 95–575, §1, Nov. 2, 1978, 92 Stat. 2464; amended Pub. L. 99–514, §2, Oct. 22, 1986, 100 Stat. 2095; Pub. L. 103–322, title XXXIII, §330016(1)(K), (S), Sept. 13, 1994, 108 Stat. 2147, 2148; Pub. L. 109–177, title I, §121(b)(4), (d), Mar. 9, 2006, 120 Stat. 222, 223.)

Amendments

2006—Subsec. (c). Pub. L. 109–177 inserted "or contraband smokeless tobacco" after "contraband cigarettes", substituted "seizure and forfeiture. The provisions of chapter 46 of title 18 relating to civil forfeitures shall extend to any seizure or civil forfeiture under this section. Any cigarettes or smokeless tobacco so seized and forfeited shall be either—" for "seizure and forfeiture, and all provisions of the Internal Revenue Code of 1986 relating to the seizure, forfeiture, and disposition of firearms, as defined in section 5845(a) of such Code, shall, so far as applicable, extend to seizures and forfeitures under the provisions of this chapter.", and added pars. (1) and (2).

1994   Subsec. (a). Pub. L. 103–322, §330016(1)(S), substituted "fined under this title" for "fined not more than $100,000".

Subsec. (b). Pub. L. 103–322, §330016(1)(K), substituted "fined under this title" for "fined not more than $5,000".

1986—Subsec. (c). Pub. L. 99–514 substituted "Internal Revenue Code of 1986" for "Internal Revenue Code of 1954".

§2345. Effect on State and local law

(a) Nothing in this chapter shall be construed to affect the concurrent jurisdiction of a State or local government to enact and enforce its own cigarette tax laws, to provide for the confiscation of cigarettes or smokeless tobacco and other property seized for violation of such laws, and to provide for penalties for the violation of such laws.

(b) Nothing in this chapter shall be construed to inhibit or otherwise affect any coordinated law enforcement effort by a number of State or local governments, through interstate compact or otherwise, to provide for the administration of State or local cigarette tax laws, to provide for the confiscation of cigarettes or smokeless tobacco and other property seized in violation of such laws, and to establish cooperative programs for the administration of such laws.

(Added Pub. L. 95–575, §1, Nov. 2, 1978, 92 Stat. 2465; amended Pub. L. 109–177, title I, §121(b)(5), (e), (g)(2), Mar. 9, 2006, 120 Stat. 222–224.)

Amendments

2006—Pub. L. 109–177, §121(g)(2), substituted "Effect on State and local law" for "Effect on State law" in section catchline.

Subsec. (a). Pub. L. 109–177, §121(b)(5), (e)(1), substituted "a State or local government to enact and enforce its own" for "a State to enact and enforce" and inserted "or smokeless tobacco" after "cigarettes".

Subsec. (b). Pub. L. 109–177, §121(b)(5), (e)(2), substituted "of State or local governments, through interstate compact or otherwise, to provide for the administration of State or local" for "of States, through interstate compact or otherwise, to provide for the administration of State" and inserted "or smokeless tobacco" after "cigarettes".

§2346. Enforcement and regulations

(a) The Attorney General, subject to the provisions of section 2343(a) of this title, shall enforce the provisions of this chapter and may prescribe such rules and regulations as he deems reasonably necessary to carry out the provisions of this chapter.

(b)(1) A State, through its attorney general, a local government, through its chief law enforcement officer (or a designee thereof), or any person who holds a permit under chapter 52 of the Internal Revenue Code of 1986, may bring an action in the United States district courts to prevent and restrain violations of this chapter by any person (or by any person controlling such person), except that any person who holds a permit under chapter 52 of the Internal Revenue Code of 1986 may not bring such an action against a State or local government. No civil action may be commenced under this paragraph against an Indian tribe or an Indian in Indian country (as defined in section 1151).

(2) A State, through its attorney general, or a local government, through its chief law enforcement officer (or a designee thereof), may in a civil action under paragraph (1) also obtain any other appropriate relief for violations of this chapter from any person (or by any person controlling such person), including civil penalties, money damages, and injunctive or other equitable relief. Nothing in this chapter shall be deemed to abrogate or constitute a waiver of any sovereign immunity of a State or local government, or an Indian tribe against any unconsented lawsuit under this chapter, or otherwise to restrict, expand, or modify any sovereign immunity of a State or local government, or an Indian tribe.

(3) The remedies under paragraphs (1) and (2) are in addition to any other remedies under Federal, State, local, or other law.

(4) Nothing in this chapter shall be construed to expand, restrict, or otherwise modify any right of an authorized State official to proceed in State court, or take other enforcement actions, on the basis of an alleged violation of State or other law.

(5) Nothing in this chapter shall be construed to expand, restrict, or otherwise modify any right of an authorized local government official to proceed in State court, or take other enforcement actions, on the basis of an alleged violation of local or other law.

(Added Pub. L. 95–575, §1, Nov. 2, 1978, 92 Stat. 2465; amended Pub. L. 107–296, title XI, §1112(i)(2), Nov. 25, 2002, 116 Stat. 2277; Pub. L. 109–177, title I, §121(f), Mar. 9, 2006, 120 Stat. 223.)

References in Text

Chapter 52 of the Internal Revenue Code of 1986, referred to in subsec. (b)(1), is classified generally to chapter 52 (§5701 et seq.) of Title 26, Internal Revenue Code.

Amendments

2006—Pub. L. 109–177 designated existing provisions as subsec. (a) and added subsec. (b).
2002—Pub. L. 107–296 substituted "Attorney General" for "Secretary".

Effective Date of 2002 Amendment

Amendment by Pub. L. 107–296 effective 60 days after Nov. 25, 2002, see section 4 of Pub. L. 107–296, set out as an Effective Date note under section 101 of Title 6, Domestic Security.

CHAPTER 115 - TREASON, SEDITION, AND SUBVERSIVE ACTIVITIES

Amendments

1994—Pub. L. 103–322, title XXXIII, §330004(13), Sept. 13, 1994, 108 Stat. 2142, struck out item 2391 "Temporary extension of section 2388".
1953—Act June 30, 1953, ch. 175, §5, 67 Stat. 134, added item 2391.

§2381. Treason

Whoever, owing allegiance to the United States, levies war against them or adheres to their enemies, giving them aid and comfort within the United States or elsewhere, is guilty of treason and shall suffer death, or shall be imprisoned not less than five years and fined under this title but not less than $10,000; and shall be incapable of holding any office under the United States. (June 25, 1948, ch. 645, 62 Stat. 807; Pub. L. 103–322, title XXXIII, §330016(2)(J), Sept. 13, 1994, 108 Stat. 2148.)

Historical and Revision Notes

Based on title 18, U.S.C., 1940 ed., §§1, 2 (Mar. 4, 1909, ch. 321, §§1, 2, 35 Stat. 1088).
Section consolidates sections 1 and 2 of title 18, U.S.C., 1940 ed.
The language referring to collection of the fine was omitted as obsolete and repugnant to the more humane policy of modern law which does not impose criminal consequences on the innocent.
The words "every person so convicted of treason" were omitted as redundant.
Minor change was made in phraseology.

Amendments

1994—Pub. L. 103–322 inserted "under this title but" before "not less than $10,000".

§2382. Misprision of treason

Whoever, owing allegiance to the United States and having knowledge of the commission of any treason against them, conceals and does not, as soon as may be, disclose and make known the same to the President or to some judge of the United States, or to the governor or to some judge or justice of a particular State, is guilty of misprision of treason and shall be fined under this title or imprisoned not more than seven years, or both. (June 25, 1948, ch. 645, 62 Stat. 807; Pub. L. 103–322, title XXXIII, §330016(1)(H), Sept. 13, 1994, 108 Stat. 2147.)

Historical and Revision Notes

Based on title 18, U.S.C., 1940 ed., §3 (Mar. 4, 1909, ch. 321, §3, 35 Stat. 1088).

Mandatory punishment provision was rephrased in the alternative.

Amendments
1994—Pub. L. 103–322 substituted "fined under this title" for "fined not more than $1,000".

§2383. Rebellion or insurrection
Whoever incites, sets on foot, assists, or engages in any rebellion or insurrection against the authority of the United States or the laws thereof, or gives aid or comfort thereto, shall be fined under this title or imprisoned not more than ten years, or both; and shall be incapable of holding any office under the United States.
(June 25, 1948, ch. 645, 62 Stat. 808; Pub. L. 103–322, title XXXIII, §330016(1)(L), Sept. 13, 1994, 108 Stat. 2147.)

Historical and Revision Notes
Based on title 18, U.S.C., 1940 ed., §4 (Mar. 4, 1909, ch. 321, §4, 35 Stat. 1088).
Word "moreover" was deleted as surplusage and minor changes were made in phraseology.

Amendments
1994—Pub. L. 103–322 substituted "fined under this title" for "fined not more than $10,000".

§2384. Seditious conspiracy
If two or more persons in any State or Territory, or in any place subject to the jurisdiction of the United States, conspire to overthrow, put down, or to destroy by force the Government of the United States, or to levy war against them, or to oppose by force the authority thereof, or by force to prevent, hinder, or delay the execution of any law of the United States, or by force to seize, take, or possess any property of the United States contrary to the authority thereof, they shall each be fined under this title or imprisoned not more than twenty years, or both.
(June 25, 1948, ch. 645, 62 Stat. 808; July 24, 1956, ch. 678, §1, 70 Stat. 623; Pub. L. 103–322, title XXXIII, §330016(1)(N), Sept. 13, 1994, 108 Stat. 2148.)

Historical and Revision Notes
Based on title 18, U.S.C., 1940 ed., §6 (Mar. 4, 1909, ch. 321, §6, 35 Stat. 1089).

Amendments
1994—Pub. L. 103–322 substituted "fined under this title" for "fined not more than $20,000".
1956—Act July 24, 1956, substituted "$20,000" for "$5,000", and "twenty years" for "six years".

Effective Date of 1956 Amendment
Act July 24, 1956, ch. 678, §3, 70 Stat. 624, provided that: "The foregoing amendments [amending this section and section 2385 of this title] shall apply only with respect to offenses committed on and after the date of the enactment of this Act [July 24, 1956]."

§2385. Advocating overthrow of Government
Whoever knowingly or willfully advocates, abets, advises, or teaches the duty, necessity, desirability, or propriety of overthrowing or destroying the government of the United States or the government of any State, Territory, District or Possession thereof, or the government of any political subdivision therein, by force or violence, or by the assassination of any officer of any such government; or
Whoever, with intent to cause the overthrow or destruction of any such government, prints, publishes, edits, issues, circulates, sells, distributes, or publicly displays any written or printed matter advocating, advising, or teaching the duty, necessity, desirability, or propriety of

overthrowing or destroying any government in the United States by force or violence, or attempts to do so; or

Whoever organizes or helps or attempts to organize any society, group, or assembly of persons who teach, advocate, or encourage the overthrow or destruction of any such government by force or violence; or becomes or is a member of, or affiliates with, any such society, group, or assembly of persons, knowing the purposes thereof—

Shall be fined under this title or imprisoned not more than twenty years, or both, and shall be ineligible for employment by the United States or any department or agency thereof, for the five years next following his conviction.

If two or more persons conspire to commit any offense named in this section, each shall be fined under this title or imprisoned not more than twenty years, or both, and shall be ineligible for employment by the United States or any department or agency thereof, for the five years next following his conviction.

As used in this section, the terms "organizes" and "organize", with respect to any society, group, or assembly of persons, include the recruiting of new members, the forming of new units, and the regrouping or expansion of existing clubs, classes, and other units of such society, group, or assembly of persons.

(June 25, 1948, ch. 645, 62 Stat. 808; July 24, 1956, ch. 678, §2, 70 Stat. 623; Pub. L. 87–486, June 19, 1962, 76 Stat. 103; Pub. L. 103–322, title XXXIII, §330016(1)(N), Sept. 13, 1994, 108 Stat. 2148.)

Historical and Revision Notes

Based on title 18, U.S.C., 1940 ed., §§10, 11, 13 (June 28, 1940, ch. 439, title I, §§2, 3, 5, 54 Stat. 670, 671).

Section consolidates sections 10, 11, and 13 of title 18, U.S.C., 1940 ed. Section 13 of title 18, U.S.C., 1940 ed., which contained the punishment provisions applicable to sections 10 and 11 of title 18, U.S.C., 1940 ed., was combined with section 11 of title 18, U.S.C., 1940 ed., and added to this section.

In first paragraph, words "the Government of the United States or the government of any State, Territory, District or possession thereof, or the government of any political subdivision therein" were substituted for "any government in the United States".

In second and third paragraphs, word "such" was inserted after "any" and before "government", and words "in the United States" which followed "government" were omitted.

In view of these changes, the provisions of subsection (b) of section 10 of title 18, U.S.C., 1940 ed., which defined the term "government in the United States" were omitted as unnecessary.

Reference to conspiracy to commit any of the prohibited acts was omitted as covered by the general conspiracy provision, incorporated in section 371 of this title. (See reviser's note under that section.)

Words "upon conviction thereof" which preceded "be fined" were omitted as surplusage, as punishment cannot be imposed until a conviction is secured.

The phraseology was considerably changed to effect consolidation but without any change of substance.

Amendments

1994—Pub. L. 103–322 substituted "fined under this title" for "fined not more than $20,000" in fourth and fifth pars.

1962—Pub. L. 87–486 defined the terms "organizes" and "organize".

1956—Act July 24, 1956, substituted "$20,000" for "$10,000", and "twenty years" for "ten years" in the paragraph prescribing penalties applicable to advocating overthrow of government and inserted provisions relating to conspiracy to commit any offense named in this section.

Effective Date of 1956 Amendment

Amendment by act July 24, 1956, as applicable only with respect to offenses committed on and after July 24, 1956, see section 3 of act July 24, 1956, set out as a note under section 2384 of this title.

§2386. Registration of certain organizations

(A) For the purposes of this section:

"Attorney General" means the Attorney General of the United States;

"Organization" means any group, club, league, society, committee, association, political party, or combination of individuals, whether incorporated or otherwise, but such term shall not include any corporation, association, community chest, fund, or foundation, organized and operated exclusively for religious, charitable, scientific, literary, or educational purposes;

"Political activity" means any activity the purpose or aim of which, or one of the purposes or aims of which, is the control by force or overthrow of the Government of the United States or a political subdivision thereof, or any State or political subdivision thereof;

An organization is engaged in "civilian military activity" if:

(1) it gives instruction to, or prescribes instruction for, its members in the use of firearms or other weapons or any substitute therefor, or military or naval science; or

(2) it receives from any other organization or from any individual instruction in military or naval science; or

(3) it engages in any military or naval maneuvers or activities; or

(4) it engages, either with or without arms, in drills or parades of a military or naval character; or

(5) it engages in any other form of organized activity which in the opinion of the Attorney General constitutes preparation for military action;

An organization is "subject to foreign control" if:

(a) it solicits or accepts financial contributions, loans, or support of any kind, directly or indirectly, from, or is affiliated directly or indirectly with, a foreign government or a political subdivision thereof, or an agent, agency, or instrumentality of a foreign government or political subdivision thereof, or a political party in a foreign country, or an international political organization; or

(b) its policies, or any of them, are determined by or at the suggestion of, or in collaboration with, a foreign government or political subdivision thereof, or an agent, agency, or instrumentality of a foreign government or a political subdivision thereof, or a political party in a foreign country, or an international political organization.

(B)(1) The following organizations shall be required to register with the Attorney General:

Every organization subject to foreign control which engages in political activity;

Every organization which engages both in civilian military activity and in political activity;

Every organization subject to foreign control which engages in civilian military activity; and

Every organization, the purpose or aim of which, or one of the purposes or aims of which, is the establishment, control, conduct, seizure, or overthrow of a government or subdivision thereof by the use of force, violence, military measures, or threats of any one or more of the foregoing.

Every such organization shall register by filing with the Attorney General, on such forms and in such detail as the Attorney General may by rules and regulations prescribe, a registration statement containing the information and documents prescribed in subsection (B)(3) and shall within thirty days after the expiration of each period of six months succeeding the filing of such registration statement, file with the Attorney General, on such forms and in such detail as the Attorney General may by rules and regulations prescribe, a supplemental statement containing such information and documents as may be necessary to make the information and documents previously filed under this section accurate and current with respect to such preceding six months' period. Every statement required to be filed by this section shall be subscribed, under oath, by all of the officers of the organization.

(2) This section shall not require registration or the filing of any statement with the Attorney General by:

(a) The armed forces of the United States; or

(b) The organized militia or National Guard of any State, Territory, District, or possession of the United States; or

(c) Any law-enforcement agency of the United States or of any Territory, District or possession thereof, or of any State or political subdivision of a State, or of any agency or instrumentality of one or more States; or

(d) Any duly established diplomatic mission or consular office of a foreign government which is so recognized by the Department of State; or

(e) Any nationally recognized organization of persons who are veterans of the armed forces of the United States, or affiliates of such organizations.

(3) Every registration statement required to be filed by any organization shall contain the following information and documents:

(a) The name and post-office address of the organization in the United States, and the names and addresses of all branches, chapters, and affiliates of such organization;

(b) The name, address, and nationality of each officer, and of each person who performs the functions of an officer, of the organization, and of each branch, chapter, and affiliate of the organization;

(c) The qualifications for membership in the organization;

(d) The existing and proposed aims and purposes of the organization, and all the means by which these aims or purposes are being attained or are to be attained;

(e) The address or addresses of meeting places of the organization, and of each branch, chapter, or affiliate of the organization, and the times of meetings;

(f) The name and address of each person who has contributed any money, dues, property, or other thing of value to the organization or to any branch, chapter, or affiliate of the organization;

(g) A detailed statement of the assets of the organization, and of each branch, chapter, and affiliate of the organization, the manner in which such assets were acquired, and a detailed statement of the liabilities and income of the organization and of each branch, chapter, and affiliate of the organization;

(h) A detailed description of the activities of the organization, and of each chapter, branch, and affiliate of the organization;

(i) A description of the uniforms, badges, insignia, or other means of identification prescribed by the organization, and worn or carried by its officers or members, or any of such officers or members;

(j) A copy of each book, pamphlet, leaflet, or other publication or item of written, printed, or graphic matter issued or distributed directly or indirectly by the organization, or by any chapter, branch, or affiliate of the organization, or by any of the members of the organization under its authority or within its knowledge, together with the name of its author or authors and the name and address of the publisher;

(k) A description of all firearms or other weapons owned by the organization, or by any chapter, branch, or affiliate of the organization, identified by the manufacturer's number thereon;

(l) In case the organization is subject to foreign control, the manner in which it is so subject;

(m) A copy of the charter, articles of association, constitution, bylaws, rules, regulations, agreements, resolutions, and all other instruments relating to the organization, powers, and purposes of the organization and to the powers of the officers of the organization and of each chapter, branch, and affiliate of the organization; and

(n) Such other information and documents pertinent to the purposes of this section as the Attorney General may from time to time require.

All statements filed under this section shall be public records and open to public examination and inspection at all reasonable hours under such rules and regulations as the Attorney General may prescribe.

(C) The Attorney General is authorized at any time to make, amend, and rescind such rules and regulations as may be necessary to carry out this section, including rules and regulations governing the statements required to be filed.

(D) Whoever violates any of the provisions of this section shall be fined under this title or imprisoned not more than five years, or both.

Whoever in a statement filed pursuant to this section willfully makes any false statement or willfully omits to state any fact which is required to be stated, or which is necessary to make the statements made not misleading, shall be fined under this title or imprisoned not more than five years, or both.

(June 25, 1948, ch. 645, 62 Stat. 808; Pub. L. 103–322, title XXXIII, §330016(1)(I), (L), Sept. 13, 1994, 108 Stat. 2147.)

Historical and Revision Notes

Based on title 18, U.S.C., 1940 ed., §§14–17 (Oct. 17, 1940, ch. 897, §§1–4, 54 Stat. 1201–1204). Section consolidates sections 14–17 of title 18, U.S.C., 1940 ed., as subsections (a), (b), (c), and (d), respectively, of this section, with necessary changes of phraseology and translation of section references.

Words "upon conviction" which preceded "be subject" were omitted as surplusage, as punishment cannot otherwise be imposed.

Amendments

1994—Pub. L. 103–322 substituted "fined under this title" for "fined not more than $10,000" in penultimate par. and for "fined not more than $2,000" in last par.

§2387. Activities affecting armed forces generally

(a) Whoever, with intent to interfere with, impair, or influence the loyalty, morale, or discipline of the military or naval forces of the United States:

(1) advises, counsels, urges, or in any manner causes or attempts to cause insubordination, disloyalty, mutiny, or refusal of duty by any member of the military or naval forces of the United States; or

(2) distributes or attempts to distribute any written or printed matter which advises, counsels, or urges insubordination, disloyalty, mutiny, or refusal of duty by any member of the military or naval forces of the United States—

Shall be fined under this title or imprisoned not more than ten years, or both, and shall be ineligible for employment by the United States or any department or agency thereof, for the five years next following his conviction.

(b) For the purposes of this section, the term "military or naval forces of the United States" includes the Army of the United States, the Navy, Air Force, Marine Corps, Coast Guard, Navy Reserve, Marine Corps Reserve, and Coast Guard Reserve of the United States; and, when any merchant vessel is commissioned in the Navy or is in the service of the Army or the Navy, includes the master, officers, and crew of such vessel.

(June 25, 1948, ch. 645, 62 Stat. 811; May 24, 1949, ch. 139, §46, 63 Stat. 96; Pub. L. 103–322, title XXXIII, §330016(1)(L), Sept. 13, 1994, 108 Stat. 2147; Pub. L. 109–163, div. A, title V, §515(f)(2), Jan. 6, 2006, 119 Stat. 3236.)

Historical and Revision Notes

1948 Act

Based on title 18, U.S.C., 1940 ed., §§9, 11, 13 (June 28, 1940, ch. 439, title I, §§1, 3, 5, 54 Stat. 670, 671).

Section consolidates sections 9, 11, and 13 of title 18, U.S.C., 1940 ed., with only such changes of phraseology as were necessary to effect consolidation.

The revised section extends the provisions so as to include the Coast Guard Reserve in its coverage.

Words "upon conviction thereof" were omitted as unnecessary, as punishment cannot be imposed until conviction is secured.

Reference to conspiracy to commit any of the prohibited acts was omitted as covered by the general law incorporated in section 371 of this title. (See reviser's note under that section.) Minor changes were made in arrangement and phraseology.

1949 Act

This section [section 46] inserts the words, "Air Force," in subsection (b) of section 2387 of title 18, U.S.C., in view of the establishment in 1947 of this separate branch of the armed services.

Amendments

2006—Subsec. (b). Pub. L. 109–163 substituted "Navy Reserve" for "Naval Reserve".

1994—Subsec. (a). Pub. L. 103–322 substituted "fined under this title" for "fined not more than $10,000" in last par.

1949—Subsec. (b). Act May 24, 1949, made section applicable to the Air Force.

Transfer of Functions

For transfer of authorities, functions, personnel, and assets of the Coast Guard, including the authorities and functions of the Secretary of Transportation relating thereto, to the Department of Homeland Security, and for treatment of related references, see sections 468(b), 551(d), 552(d), and 557 of Title 6, Domestic Security, and the Department of Homeland Security Reorganization Plan of November 25, 2002, as modified, set out as a note under section 542 of Title 6.

Coast Guard transferred to Department of Transportation and functions, powers, and duties, relating to Coast Guard, of Secretary of the Treasury and of other offices and officers of Department of the Treasury transferred to Secretary of Transportation by Pub. L. 89–670, Oct. 15, 1966, 80 Stat. 931, which created Department of Transportation. See section 108 of Title 49, Transportation.

Functions of all officers of Department of the Treasury and functions of all agencies and employees of such Department transferred, with certain exceptions, to Secretary of the Treasury, with power vested in him to authorize their performance or performance of any of his functions, by any of such officers, agencies, and employees, by Reorg. Plan No. 26, of 1950, §§1, 2, eff. July 31, 1950, 15 F.R. 4935, 64 Stat. 1280, set out in the Appendix to Title 5, Government Organization and Employees. Such plan excepted from transfer functions of Coast Guard and Commandant thereof when Coast Guard is operating as a part of the Navy under section 1 and 3 of Title 14, Coast Guard.

§2388. Activities affecting armed forces during war

(a) Whoever, when the United States is at war, willfully makes or conveys false reports or false statements with intent to interfere with the operation or success of the military or naval forces of the United States or to promote the success of its enemies; or

Whoever, when the United States is at war, willfully causes or attempts to cause insubordination, disloyalty, mutiny, or refusal of duty, in the military or naval forces of the United States, or willfully obstructs the recruiting or enlistment service of the United States, to the injury of the service or the United States, or attempts to do so—

Shall be fined under this title or imprisoned not more than twenty years, or both.

(b) If two or more persons conspire to violate subsection (a) of this section and one or more such persons do any act to effect the object of the conspiracy, each of the parties to such conspiracy shall be punished as provided in said subsection (a).

(c) Whoever harbors or conceals any person who he knows, or has reasonable grounds to believe or suspect, has committed, or is about to commit, an offense under this section, shall be fined under this title or imprisoned not more than ten years, or both.

(d) This section shall apply within the admiralty and maritime jurisdiction of the United States, and on the high seas, as well as within the United States.

(June 25, 1948, ch. 645, 62 Stat. 811; Pub. L. 103–322, title XXXIII, §330016(1)(L), Sept. 13,

1994, 108 Stat. 2147.)

Historical and Revision Notes

Based on sections 33, 34, 35, 37 of title 50, U.S.C., 1940 ed., War and National Defense (June 15, 1917, ch. 30, title I, §§3, 4, 5, 8, 40 Stat. 219; Mar. 3, 1921, ch. 136, 41 Stat. 1359; Mar. 28, 1940, ch. 72, §2, 54 Stat. 79).

Sections 33, 34, 35, and 37 of title 50, U.S.C., 1940 ed., War and National Defense, were consolidated. Sections 34, 35, and 37 of title 50, U.S.C., 1940 ed., War and National Defense, are also incorporated in sections 791, 792, and 794 of this title, to which they relate.

Minor changes were made in phraseology.

Amendments

1994—Pub. L. 103–322 substituted "fined under this title" for "fined not more than $10,000" in last par. of subsec. (a) and in subsec. (c).

Repeals

Section 7 of act June 30, 1953, ch. 175, 67 Stat. 134, repealed Joint Res. July 3, 1952, ch. 570, §1(a)(29), 66 Stat. 333; Joint Res. Mar. 31, 1953, ch. 13, §1, 67 Stat. 18, which had provided that this section should continue in force until six months after the termination of the National emergency proclaimed by 1950 Proc. No. 2914, which is set out as a note preceding section 1 of Title 50, War and National Defense.

Repeal of Extensions of War-time Provisions

Section 6 of Joint Res. July 3, 1952, repealed Joint Res. Apr. 14, 1952, ch. 204, 66 Stat. 54, as amended by Joint Res. May 28, 1952, ch. 339, 66 Stat. 96. Intermediate extensions by Joint Res. June 14, 1952, ch. 437, 66 Stat. 137, and Joint Res. June 30, 1952, ch. 526, 66 Stat. 296, which continued provisions until July 3, 1952, expired by their own terms.

§2389. Recruiting for service against United States

Whoever recruits soldiers or sailors within the United States, or in any place subject to the jurisdiction thereof, to engage in armed hostility against the same; or

Whoever opens within the United States, or in any place subject to the jurisdiction thereof, a recruiting station for the enlistment of such soldiers or sailors to serve in any manner in armed hostility against the United States—

Shall be fined under this title or imprisoned not more than five years, or both.

(June 25, 1948, ch. 645, 62 Stat. 811; Pub. L. 103–322, title XXXIII, §330016(1)(H), Sept. 13, 1994, 108 Stat. 2147.)

Historical and Revision Notes

Based on title 18, U.S.C., 1940 ed., §7 (Mar. 4, 1909, ch. 321, §7, 35 Stat. 1089).

Mandatory punishment provision was rephrased in the alternative.

Minor changes were made in phraseology.

Amendments

1994—Pub. L. 103–322 substituted "fined under this title" for "fined not more than $1,000" in last par.

§2390. Enlistment to serve against United States

Whoever enlists or is engaged within the United States or in any place subject to the jurisdiction thereof, with intent to serve in armed hostility against the United States, shall be fined under this title 1 or imprisoned not more than three years, or both.

(June 25, 1948, ch. 645, 62 Stat. 812; Pub. L. 103–322, title XXXIII, §330016(1)(B), Sept. 13, 1994, 108 Stat. 2146.)

Historical and Revision Notes
Based on title 18, U.S.C., 1940 ed., §8 (Mar. 4, 1909, ch. 321, §8, 35 Stat. 1089).
Mandatory punishment provision was rephrased in the alternative.
Minor changes were made in phraseology.

Amendments
1994—Pub. L. 103–322, which directed the amendment of this section by striking "fined not more than $100" and inserting "fined under this title", was executed by substituting "fined under this title" for "fined $100", to reflect the probable intent of Congress.

[§2391. Repealed. Pub. L. 103–322, title XXXIII, §330004(13), Sept. 13, 1994, 108 Stat. 2142]
Section, added June 30, 1953, ch. 175, §6, 67 Stat. 134, related to temporary extension of section 2388 of this title.

CHAPTER 117 - TRANSPORTATION FOR ILLEGAL SEXUAL ACTIVITY AND RELATED CRIMES

2421.	Transportation generally.
2421A.	Promotion or facilitation of prostitution and reckless disregard of sex trafficking.
2422.	Coercion and enticement.
2423.	Transportation of minors.
2424.	Filing factual statement about alien individual.
2425.	Use of interstate facilities to transmit information about a minor.
2426.	Repeat offenders.
2427.	Inclusion of offenses relating to child pornography in definition of sexual activity for which any person can be charged with a criminal offense.
2428.	Forfeitures.

Amendments
2018—Pub. L. 115–164, §3(b), Apr. 11, 2018, 132 Stat. 1254, added item 2421A.
2006—Pub. L. 109–164, title I, §103(d)(2), Jan. 10, 2006, 119 Stat. 3563, added item 2428.
1998—Pub. L. 105–314, title I, §§101(b), 104(b), 105(b), Oct. 30, 1998, 112 Stat. 2975–2977, added items 2425, 2426, and 2427.
1988—Pub. L. 100–690, title VII, §7071, Nov. 18, 1988, 102 Stat. 4405, substituted "individual" for "female" in item 2424.
1986—Pub. L. 99–628, §5(a)(1), (b)(2), Nov. 7, 1986, 100 Stat. 3511, substituted "TRANSPORTATION FOR ILLEGAL SEXUAL ACTIVITY AND RELATED CRIMES" for "WHITE SLAVE TRAFFIC" as chapter heading and substituted "and enticement" for "or enticement of female" in item 2422.
1978—Pub. L. 95–225, §3(b), Feb. 6, 1978, 92 Stat. 9, substituted "Transportation of minors" for "Coercion or enticement of minor female" in item 2423.

§2421. Transportation generally
(a) In General.—Whoever knowingly transports any individual in interstate or foreign commerce, or in any Territory or Possession of the United States, with intent that such individual engage in

prostitution, or in any sexual activity for which any person can be charged with a criminal offense, or attempts to do so, shall be fined under this title or imprisoned not more than 10 years, or both.

(b) Requests To Prosecute Violations by State Attorneys General.—

(1) In general.—The Attorney General shall grant a request by a State attorney general that a State or local attorney be cross designated to prosecute a violation of this section unless the Attorney General determines that granting the request would undermine the administration of justice.

(2) Reason for denial.—If the Attorney General denies a request under paragraph (1), the Attorney General shall submit to the State attorney general a detailed reason for the denial not later than 60 days after the date on which a request is received.

(Added Pub. L. 114–22, title III, §303, May 29, 2015, 129 Stat. 255.)

Prior Provisions

A prior section 2421, act June 25, 1948, ch. 645, 62 Stat. 812; May 24, 1949, ch. 139, §47, 63 Stat. 96; Pub. L. 99–628, §5(b)(1), Nov. 7, 1986, 100 Stat. 3511; Pub. L. 105–314, title I, §106, Oct. 30, 1998, 112 Stat. 2977, related to transportation of individuals generally, prior to repeal by Pub. L. 114–22, title III, §303, May 29, 2015, 129 Stat. 255.

§2421A. Promotion or facilitation of prostitution and reckless disregard of sex trafficking

(a) In General.—Whoever, using a facility or means of interstate or foreign commerce or in or affecting interstate or foreign commerce, owns, manages, or operates an interactive computer service (as such term is defined in defined in 1 section 230(f) the Communications Act of 1934 (47 U.S.C. 230(f))), or conspires or attempts to do so, with the intent to promote or facilitate the prostitution of another person shall be fined under this title, imprisoned for not more than 10 years, or both.

(b) Aggravated Violation.—Whoever, using a facility or means of interstate or foreign commerce or in or affecting interstate or foreign commerce, owns, manages, or operates an interactive computer service (as such term is defined in defined in 1 section 230(f) the Communications Act of 1934 (47 U.S.C. 230(f))), or conspires or attempts to do so, with the intent to promote or facilitate the prostitution of another person and—

(1) promotes or facilitates the prostitution of 5 or more persons; or

(2) acts in reckless disregard of the fact that such conduct contributed to sex trafficking, in violation of 2 1591(a),

shall be fined under this title, imprisoned for not more than 25 years, or both.

(c) Civil Recovery.—Any person injured by reason of a violation of section 2421A(b) may recover damages and reasonable attorneys' fees in an action before any appropriate United States district court.

(d) Mandatory Restitution.—Notwithstanding sections 3 3663 or 3663A and in addition to any other civil or criminal penalties authorized by law, the court shall order restitution for any violation of subsection (b)(2). The scope and nature of such restitution shall be consistent with section 2327(b).

(e) Affirmative Defense.—It shall be an affirmative defense to a charge of violating subsection (a), or subsection (b)(1) where the defendant proves, by a preponderance of the evidence, that the promotion or facilitation of prostitution is legal in the jurisdiction where the promotion or facilitation was targeted.

(Added Pub. L. 115–164, §3(a), Apr. 11, 2018, 132 Stat. 1253.)

§2422. Coercion and enticement

(a) Whoever knowingly persuades, induces, entices, or coerces any individual to travel in interstate or foreign commerce, or in any Territory or Possession of the United States, to engage in prostitution, or in any sexual activity for which any person can be charged with a criminal offense, or attempts to do so, shall be fined under this title or imprisoned not more than 20 years, or both.

(b) Whoever, using the mail or any facility or means of interstate or foreign commerce, or within the special maritime and territorial jurisdiction of the United States knowingly persuades, induces, entices, or coerces any individual who has not attained the age of 18 years, to engage in prostitution or any sexual activity for which any person can be charged with a criminal offense, or attempts to do so, shall be fined under this title and imprisoned not less than 10 years or for life. (June 25, 1948, ch. 645, 62 Stat. 812; Pub. L. 99–628, §5(b)(1), Nov. 7, 1986, 100 Stat. 3511; Pub. L. 100–690, title VII, §7070, Nov. 18, 1988, 102 Stat. 4405; Pub. L. 104–104, title V, §508, Feb. 8, 1996, 110 Stat. 137; Pub. L. 105–314, title I, §102, Oct. 30, 1998, 112 Stat. 2975; Pub. L. 108–21, title I, §103(a)(2)(A), (B), (b)(2)(A), Apr. 30, 2003, 117 Stat. 652, 653; Pub. L. 109–248, title II, §203, July 27, 2006, 120 Stat. 613.)

Historical and Revision Notes

Based on title 18, U.S.C., 1940 ed., §399 (June 25, 1910, ch. 395, §3, 36 Stat. 825).

Words "deemed guilty of a felony" were deleted as unnecessary in view of definition of felony in section 1 of this title. (See reviser's note under section 550 of this title.)

Words "and on conviction thereof shall be" were deleted as surplusage since punishment cannot be imposed until a conviction is secured.

The references to persons causing, procuring, aiding or assisting were omitted as unnecessary as such persons are made principals by section 2 of this title.

Words "Possession of the United States" were inserted twice. (See reviser's note under section 2421 of this title.)

Minor changes were made in phraseology.

Amendments

2006—Subsec. (b). Pub. L. 109–248 substituted "not less than 10 years or for life" for "not less than 5 years and not more than 30 years".

2003—Subsec. (a). Pub. L. 108–21, §103(a)(2)(A), substituted "20 years" for "10 years".

Subsec. (b). Pub. L. 108–21, §103(a)(2)(B), (b)(2)(A), substituted "and imprisoned not less than 5 years and" for ", imprisoned" and "30 years" for "15 years, or both".

1998—Subsec. (a). Pub. L. 105–314, §102(1), inserted "or attempts to do so," before "shall be fined" and substituted "10 years" for "five years".

Subsec. (b). Pub. L. 105–314, §102(2), added subsec. (b) and struck out former subsec. (b) which read as follows: "Whoever, using any facility or means of interstate or foreign commerce, including the mail, or within the special maritime and territorial jurisdiction of the United States, knowingly persuades, induces, entices, or coerces any individual who has not attained the age of 18 years to engage in prostitution or any sexual act for which any person may be criminally prosecuted, or attempts to do so, shall be fined under this title or imprisoned not more than 10 years, or both."

1996—Pub. L. 104–104 designated existing provisions as subsec. (a) and added subsec. (b).

1988—Pub. L. 100–690 substituted "or" for "of" before "foreign commerce".

1986—Pub. L. 99–628 substituted "and enticement" for "or enticement of female" in section catchline and amended text generally. Prior to amendment, text read as follows: "Whoever knowingly persuades, induces, entices, or coerces any woman or girl to go from one place to another in interstate or foreign commerce, or in the District of Columbia or in any Territory or Possession of the United States, for the purpose of prostitution or debauchery, or for any other immoral purpose, or with the intent and purpose on the part of such person that such woman or girl shall engage in the practice of prostitution or debauchery, or any other immoral practice, whether with or without her consent, and thereby knowingly causes such woman or girl to go and to be carried or transported as a passenger upon the line or route of any common carrier or carriers in interstate or foreign commerce, or in the District of Columbia or in any Territory or Possession of the United States, shall be fined not more than $5,000 or imprisoned not more than five years, or both."

§2423. Transportation of minors

(a) Transportation With Intent To Engage in Criminal Sexual Activity.—A person who knowingly transports an individual who has not attained the age of 18 years in interstate or foreign commerce, or in any commonwealth, territory or possession of the United States, with intent that the individual engage in prostitution, or in any sexual activity for which any person can be charged with a criminal offense, shall be fined under this title and imprisoned not less than 10 years or for life.

(b) Travel With Intent To Engage in Illicit Sexual Conduct.—A person who travels in interstate commerce or travels into the United States, or a United States citizen or an alien admitted for permanent residence in the United States who travels in foreign commerce, for the purpose of engaging in any illicit sexual conduct with another person shall be fined under this title or imprisoned not more than 30 years, or both.

(c) Engaging in Illicit Sexual Conduct in Foreign Places.—Any United States citizen or alien admitted for permanent residence who travels in foreign commerce or resides, either temporarily or permanently, in a foreign country, and engages in any illicit sexual conduct with another person shall be fined under this title or imprisoned not more than 30 years, or both.

(d) Ancillary Offenses.—Whoever, for the purpose of commercial advantage or private financial gain, arranges, induces, procures, or facilitates the travel of a person knowing that such a person is traveling in interstate commerce or foreign commerce for the purpose of engaging in illicit sexual conduct shall be fined under this title, imprisoned not more than 30 years, or both.

(e) Attempt and Conspiracy.—Whoever attempts or conspires to violate subsection (a), (b), (c), or (d) shall be punishable in the same manner as a completed violation of that subsection.

(f) Definition.—As used in this section, the term "illicit sexual conduct" means—

(1) a sexual act (as defined in section 2246) with a person under 18 years of age that would be in violation of chapter 109A if the sexual act occurred in the special maritime and territorial jurisdiction of the United States;

(2) any commercial sex act (as defined in section 1591) with a person under 18 years of age; or

(3) production of child pornography (as defined in section 2256(8)).

(g) Defense.—In a prosecution under this section based on illicit sexual conduct as defined in subsection (f)(2), it is a defense, which the defendant must establish by clear and convincing evidence, that the defendant reasonably believed that the person with whom the defendant engaged in the commercial sex act had attained the age of 18 years.

(June 25, 1948, ch. 645, 62 Stat. 812; Pub. L. 95–225, §3(a), Feb. 6, 1978, 92 Stat. 8; Pub. L. 99–628, §5(b)(1), Nov. 7, 1986, 100 Stat. 3511; Pub. L. 103–322, title XVI, §160001(g), Sept. 13, 1994, 108 Stat. 2037; Pub. L. 104–71, §5, Dec. 23, 1995, 109 Stat. 774; Pub. L. 104–294, title VI, §§601(b)(4), 604(b)(33), Oct. 11, 1996, 110 Stat. 3499, 3508; Pub. L. 105–314, title I, §103, Oct. 30, 1998, 112 Stat. 2976; Pub. L. 107–273, div. B, title IV, §4002(c)(1), Nov. 2, 2002, 116 Stat. 1808; Pub. L. 108–21, title I, §§103(a)(2)(C), (b)(2)(B), 105, Apr. 30, 2003, 117 Stat. 652, 653; Pub. L. 109–248, title II, §204, July 27, 2006, 120 Stat. 613; Pub. L. 113–4, title XII, §1211(b), Mar. 7, 2013, 127 Stat. 142; Pub. L. 114–22, title I, §111, May 29, 2015, 129 Stat. 240.)

Historical and Revision Notes

Based on title 18, U.S.C., 1940 ed., §400 (June 25, 1910, ch. 395, §4, 36 Stat. 826).

Words "deemed guilty of a felony" were deleted as unnecessary in view of definition of felony in section 1 of this title. (See reviser's note under section 550 of this title.)

Words "and on conviction thereof shall be" were deleted as surplusage since punishment cannot be imposed until a conviction is secured.

Words "Possession of the United States" were inserted twice. (See reviser's note under section 2421 of this title.)

Minor changes were made in phraseology.

Amendments

2015—Subsec. (f). Pub. L. 114–22, §111(a), inserted a dash after "means", designated existing provisions containing designations (1) and (2) as pars. (1) and (2), and added par. (3).

Subsec. (g). Pub. L. 114–22, §111(b), substituted "clear and convincing evidence" for "a preponderance of the evidence".

2013—Subsec. (c). Pub. L. 113–4 inserted "or resides, either temporarily or permanently, in a foreign country" after "commerce".

2006—Subsec. (a). Pub. L. 109–248 substituted "10 years or for life" for "5 years and not more than 30 years".

2003—Subsec. (a). Pub. L. 108–21, §105(b), struck out "or attempts to do so," before "shall be fined".

Pub. L. 108–21, §103(a)(2)(C), (b)(2)(B), substituted "and imprisoned not less than 5 years and" for ", imprisoned" and "30 years" for "15 years, or both".

Subsec. (b) to (g). Pub. L. 108–21, §105(a), added subsecs. (b) to (g) and struck out former subsec. (b) which read as follows:

"(b) Travel With Intent To Engage in Sexual Act With a Juvenile.—A person who travels in interstate commerce, or conspires to do so, or a United States citizen or an alien admitted for permanent residence in the United States who travels in foreign commerce, or conspires to do so, for the purpose of engaging in any sexual act (as defined in section 2246) with a person under 18 years of age that would be in violation of chapter 109A if the sexual act occurred in the special maritime and territorial jurisdiction of the United States shall be fined under this title, imprisoned not more than 15 years, or both."

2002—Subsec. (b). Pub. L. 107–273 repealed Pub. L. 104–294, §601(b)(4). See 1996 Amendment note below.

1998—Subsec. (a). Pub. L. 105–314, §103(1), added subsec. (a) and struck out former subsec. (a) which read as follows:

"(a) Transportation With Intent To Engage in Criminal Sexual Activity.—A person who knowingly transports any individual under the age of 18 years in interstate or foreign commerce, or in any Territory or Possession of the United States, with intent that such individual engage in prostitution, or in any sexual activity for which any person can be charged with a criminal offense, shall be fined under this title or imprisoned not more than ten years, or both."

Subsec. (b). Pub. L. 105–314, §103(2), substituted "15 years" for "10 years".

1996—Pub. L. 104–294, §604(b)(33), amended directory language of Pub. L. 103–322, §160001(g). See 1994 Amendment note below.

Subsec. (b). Pub. L. 104–294, §601(b)(4), which made amendment identical to that made by Pub. L. 104–71, was repealed by Pub. L. 107–273. See 1995 Amendment note below.

1995—Subsec. (b). Pub. L. 104–71 substituted "2246" for "2245".

1994—Pub. L. 103–322, as amended by Pub. L. 104–294, §604(b)(33), added subsec. (b) and substituted "(a) Transportation With Intent To Engage in Criminal Sexual Activity.—A person who" for "Whoever".

1986—Pub. L. 99–628 amended section generally, revising and restating as one paragraph provisions formerly contained in subsec. (a) and striking out subsec. (b) which provided definitions.

1978—Pub. L. 95–225 substituted "Transportation of minors" for "Coercion or enticement of minor female" in section catchline, designated existing provision as subsec. (a), substituted provisions relating to conduct prohibiting the transportation of minors for provisions relating to conduct prohibiting the coercion or enticement of a minor female, and added subsec. (b).

Effective Date of 2002 Amendment

Pub. L. 107–273, div. B, title IV, §4002(c)(1), Nov. 2, 2002, 116 Stat. 1808, provided that the amendment made by section 4002(c)(1) is effective Oct. 11, 1996.

Effective Date of 1996 Amendment

Amendment by section 604(b)(33) of Pub. L. 104–294 effective Sept. 13, 1994, see section 604(d) of Pub. L. 104–294, set out as a note under section 13 of this title.

§2424. Filing factual statement about alien individual

(a) Whoever keeps, maintains, controls, supports, or harbors in any house or place for the purpose of prostitution, or for any other immoral purpose, any individual, knowing or in reckless disregard of the fact that the individual is an alien, shall file with the Commissioner of Immigration and Naturalization a statement in writing setting forth the name of such individual, the place at which that individual is kept, and all facts as to the date of that individual's entry into the United States, the port through which that individual entered, that individual's age, nationality, and parentage, and concerning that individual's procuration to come to this country within the knowledge of such person; and

Whoever fails within five business days after commencing to keep, maintain, control, support, or harbor in any house or place for the purpose of prostitution, or for any other immoral purpose, any alien individual to file such statement concerning such alien individual with the Commissioner of Immigration and Naturalization; or

Whoever knowingly and willfully states falsely or fails to disclose in such statement any fact within that person's knowledge or belief with reference to the age, nationality, or parentage of any such alien individual, or concerning that individual's procuration to come to this country—

Shall be fined under this title or imprisoned not more than 10 years, or both.

(b) In any prosecution brought under this section, if it appears that any such statement required is not on file in the office of the Commissioner of Immigration and Naturalization, the person whose duty it is to file such statement shall be presumed to have failed to file said statement, unless such person or persons shall prove otherwise. No person shall be excused from furnishing the statement, as required by this section, on the ground or for the reason that the statement so required by that person, or the information therein contained, might tend to criminate that person or subject that person to a penalty or forfeiture, but no information contained in the statement or any evidence which is directly or indirectly derived from such information may be used against any person making such statement in any criminal case, except a prosecution for perjury, giving a false statement or otherwise failing to comply with this section.

(June 25, 1948, ch. 645, 62 Stat. 813; Pub. L. 91–452, title II, §226, Oct. 15, 1970, 84 Stat. 930; Pub. L. 99–628, §5(c), Nov. 7, 1986, 100 Stat. 3511; Pub. L. 103–322, title XXXIII, §330016(1)(I), Sept. 13, 1994, 108 Stat. 2147; Pub. L. 104–208, div. C, title III, §325, Sept. 30, 1996, 110 Stat. 3009–629.)

Historical and Revision Notes

Based on title 18, U.S.C., 1940 ed., §402(2), (3) (June 25, 1910, ch. 395, §6, 36 Stat. 826).

First paragraph of section 402 of title 18, U.S.C., 1940 ed., was omitted from this section and recommended for transfer to Title 8, Aliens and Nationality.

Words "shall be deemed guilty of a misdemeanor" were omitted as unnecessary in view of the definition of a misdemeanor in section 1 of this title. (See reviser's note under section 212 of this title.)

Minor changes were made in phraseology.

Amendments

1996—Subsec. (a). Pub. L. 104–208, §325(1), in first par. substituted "individual, knowing or in reckless disregard of the fact that the individual is an alien" for "alien individual within three years after that individual has entered the United States from any country, party to the arrangement adopted July 25, 1902, for the suppression of the white-slave traffic" and struck out "alien" after "the name of such".

Pub. L. 104–208, §325(2), in second par. substituted "five business" for "thirty" and struck out "within three years after that individual has entered the United States from any country, party to the said arrangement for the suppression of the white-slave traffic," after "any alien individual". Pub. L. 104–208, §325(3), substituted "10" for "two" in last par.

1994—Subsec. (a). Pub. L. 103–322 substituted "fined under this title" for "fined not more than $2,000" in last par.

1986—Pub. L. 99–628, §5(c)(1), substituted "individual" for "female" in section catchline.

Subsec. (a). Pub. L. 99–628, §5(c)(2)–(4), (6), substituted "individual" for "woman or girl", "that individual" for "she", "that individual's" for "her", and "that person's" for "his" wherever appearing.

Subsec. (b). Pub. L. 99–628, §5(c)(5), substituted "that person" for "him" wherever appearing.

1970—Subsec. (b). Pub. L. 91–452 substituted provisions that no information contained in the statement or any evidence directly or indirectly derived from such information be used against any person making such statement in any criminal case, except a prosecution for perjury, giving a false statement, or otherwise failing to comply with this section, for provisions that no person be prosecuted or subjected to any penalty or forfeiture under any law of the United States for or on account of any transaction, etc., truthfully reported in his statement.

Effective Date of 1970 Amendment

Amendment by Pub. L. 91–452 effective on sixtieth day following Oct. 15, 1970, and not to affect any immunity to which any individual is entitled under this section by reason of any testimony given before sixtieth day following Oct. 15, 1970, see section 260 of Pub. L. 91–452, set out as an Effective Date; Savings Provision note under section 6001 of this title.

Abolition of Immigration and Naturalization Service and Transfer of Functions

For abolition of Immigration and Naturalization Service, transfer of functions, and treatment of related references, see note set out under section 1551 of Title 8, Aliens and Nationality.

§2425. Use of interstate facilities to transmit information about a minor

Whoever, using the mail or any facility or means of interstate or foreign commerce, or within the special maritime and territorial jurisdiction of the United States, knowingly initiates the transmission of the name, address, telephone number, social security number, or electronic mail address of another individual, knowing that such other individual has not attained the age of 16 years, with the intent to entice, encourage, offer, or solicit any person to engage in any sexual activity for which any person can be charged with a criminal offense, or attempts to do so, shall be fined under this title, imprisoned not more than 5 years, or both.

(Added Pub. L. 105–314, title I, §101(a), Oct. 30, 1998, 112 Stat. 2975.)

§2426. Repeat offenders

(a) Maximum Term of Imprisonment.—The maximum term of imprisonment for a violation of this chapter after a prior sex offense conviction shall be twice the term of imprisonment otherwise provided by this chapter, unless section 3559(e) applies.

(b) Definitions.—In this section—

(1) the term "prior sex offense conviction" means a conviction for an offense—

(A) under this chapter, chapter 109A, chapter 110, or section 1591; or

(B) under State law for an offense consisting of conduct that would have been an offense under a chapter referred to in paragraph (1) if the conduct had occurred within the special maritime and territorial jurisdiction of the United States; and

(2) the term "State" means a State of the United States, the District of Columbia, and any commonwealth, territory, or possession of the United States.

(Added Pub. L. 105–314, title I, §104(a), Oct. 30, 1998, 112 Stat. 2976; amended Pub. L. 108–21, title I, §106(b), Apr. 30, 2003, 117 Stat. 655; Pub. L. 110–457, title II, §224(c), Dec. 23, 2008, 122

Stat. 5072.)

Amendments

2008—Subsec. (b)(1)(A). Pub. L. 110–457 substituted "chapter 110, or section 1591" for "or chapter 110".

2003—Subsec. (a). Pub. L. 108–21 inserted ", unless section 3559(e) applies" before period at end.

§2427. Inclusion of offenses relating to child pornography in definition of sexual activity for which any person can be charged with a criminal offense

In this chapter, the term "sexual activity for which any person can be charged with a criminal offense" includes the production of child pornography, as defined in section 2256(8).

(Added Pub. L. 105–314, title I, §105(a), Oct. 30, 1998, 112 Stat. 2977.)

§2428. Forfeitures

(a) In General.—The court, in imposing sentence on any person convicted of a violation of this chapter, shall order, in addition to any other sentence imposed and irrespective of any provision of State law, that such person shall forfeit to the United States—

(1) such person's interest in any property, real or personal, that was used or intended to be used to commit or to facilitate the commission of such violation; and

(2) any property, real or personal, constituting or derived from any proceeds that such person obtained, directly or indirectly, as a result of such violation.

(b) Property Subject to Forfeiture.—

(1) In general.—The following shall be subject to forfeiture to the United States and no property right shall exist in them:

(A) Any property, real or personal, used or intended to be used to commit or to facilitate the commission of any violation of this chapter.

(B) Any property, real or personal, that constitutes or is derived from proceeds traceable to any violation of this chapter.

(2) Applicability of chapter 46.—The provisions of chapter 46 of this title relating to civil forfeitures shall apply to any seizure or civil forfeiture under this subsection.

(Added Pub. L. 109–164, title I, §103(d)(1), Jan. 10, 2006, 119 Stat. 3563.)

CHAPTER 118 - WAR CRIMES

Amendments

2008—Pub. L. 110–340, §2(a)(3)(A), Oct. 3, 2008, 122 Stat. 3736, added item 2442.

1996—Pub. L. 104–294, title VI, §605(p)(2), Oct. 11, 1996, 110 Stat. 3510, redesignated item 2401 as 2441.

§2441. War crimes

(a) Offense.—Whoever, whether inside or outside the United States, commits a war crime, in any of the circumstances described in subsection (b), shall be fined under this title or imprisoned for life or any term of years, or both, and if death results to the victim, shall also be subject to the penalty of death.

(b) Circumstances.—The circumstances referred to in subsection (a) are that the person committing such war crime or the victim of such war crime is a member of the Armed Forces of the United States or a national of the United States (as defined in section 101 of the Immigration and Nationality Act).

(c) Definition.—As used in this section the term "war crime" means any conduct—

(1) defined as a grave breach in any of the international conventions signed at Geneva 12 August 1949, or any protocol to such convention to which the United States is a party;

(2) prohibited by Article 23, 25, 27, or 28 of the Annex to the Hague Convention IV, Respecting the Laws and Customs of War on Land, signed 18 October 1907;

(3) which constitutes a grave breach of common Article 3 (as defined in subsection (d)) when committed in the context of and in association with an armed conflict not of an international character; or

(4) of a person who, in relation to an armed conflict and contrary to the provisions of the Protocol on Prohibitions or Restrictions on the Use of Mines, Booby-Traps and Other Devices as amended at Geneva on 3 May 1996 (Protocol II as amended on 3 May 1996), when the United States is a party to such Protocol, willfully kills or causes serious injury to civilians.

(d) Common Article 3 Violations.—

(1) Prohibited conduct.—In subsection (c)(3), the term "grave breach of common Article 3" means any conduct (such conduct constituting a grave breach of common Article 3 of the international conventions done at Geneva August 12, 1949), as follows:

(A) Torture.—The act of a person who commits, or conspires or attempts to commit, an act specifically intended to inflict severe physical or mental pain or suffering (other than pain or suffering incidental to lawful sanctions) upon another person within his custody or physical control for the purpose of obtaining information or a confession, punishment, intimidation, coercion, or any reason based on discrimination of any kind.

(B) Cruel or inhuman treatment.—The act of a person who commits, or conspires or attempts to commit, an act intended to inflict severe or serious physical or mental pain or suffering (other than pain or suffering incidental to lawful sanctions), including serious physical abuse, upon another within his custody or control.

(C) Performing biological experiments.—The act of a person who subjects, or conspires or attempts to subject, one or more persons within his custody or physical control to biological experiments without a legitimate medical or dental purpose and in so doing endangers the body or health of such person or persons.

(D) Murder.—The act of a person who intentionally kills, or conspires or attempts to kill, or kills whether intentionally or unintentionally in the course of committing any other offense under this subsection, one or more persons taking no active part in the hostilities, including those placed out of combat by sickness, wounds, detention, or any other cause.

(E) Mutilation or maiming.—The act of a person who intentionally injures, or conspires or attempts to injure, or injures whether intentionally or unintentionally in the course of committing any other offense under this subsection, one or more persons taking no active part in the hostilities, including those placed out of combat by sickness, wounds, detention, or any other cause, by disfiguring the person or persons by any mutilation thereof or by permanently disabling any member, limb, or organ of his body, without any legitimate medical or dental purpose.

(F) Intentionally causing serious bodily injury.—The act of a person who intentionally causes, or conspires or attempts to cause, serious bodily injury to one or more persons, including lawful combatants, in violation of the law of war.

(G) Rape.—The act of a person who forcibly or with coercion or threat of force wrongfully invades, or conspires or attempts to invade, the body of a person by penetrating, however slightly, the anal or genital opening of the victim with any part of the body of the accused, or with any foreign object.

(H) Sexual assault or abuse.—The act of a person who forcibly or with coercion or threat of force engages, or conspires or attempts to engage, in sexual contact with one or more persons, or causes, or conspires or attempts to cause, one or more persons to engage in sexual contact.

(I) Taking hostages.—The act of a person who, having knowingly seized or detained one or more persons, threatens to kill, injure, or continue to detain such person or persons with the intent of compelling any nation, person other than the hostage, or group of persons to act or refrain from acting as an explicit or implicit condition for the safety or release of such person or persons.

(2) Definitions.—In the case of an offense under subsection (a) by reason of subsection (c)(3)—

(A) the term "severe mental pain or suffering" shall be applied for purposes of paragraphs (1)(A) and (1)(B) in accordance with the meaning given that term in section 2340(2) of this title;

(B) the term "serious bodily injury" shall be applied for purposes of paragraph (1)(F) in accordance with the meaning given that term in section 113(b)(2) of this title;

(C) the term "sexual contact" shall be applied for purposes of paragraph (1)(G) in accordance with the meaning given that term in section 2246(3) of this title;

(D) the term "serious physical pain or suffering" shall be applied for purposes of paragraph (1)(B) as meaning bodily injury that involves—

(i) a substantial risk of death;

(ii) extreme physical pain;

(iii) a burn or physical disfigurement of a serious nature (other than cuts, abrasions, or bruises); or

(iv) significant loss or impairment of the function of a bodily member, organ, or mental faculty; and

(E) the term "serious mental pain or suffering" shall be applied for purposes of paragraph (1)(B) in accordance with the meaning given the term "severe mental pain or suffering" (as defined in section 2340(2) of this title), except that—

(i) the term "serious" shall replace the term "severe" where it appears; and

(ii) as to conduct occurring after the date of the enactment of the Military Commissions Act of 2006, the term "serious and non-transitory mental harm (which need not be prolonged)" shall replace the term "prolonged mental harm" where it appears.

(3) Inapplicability of certain provisions with respect to collateral damage or incident of lawful attack.—The intent specified for the conduct stated in subparagraphs (D), (E), and (F) or paragraph (1) precludes the applicability of those subparagraphs to an offense under subsection (a) by reasons of subsection (c)(3) with respect to—

(A) collateral damage; or

(B) death, damage, or injury incident to a lawful attack.

(4) Inapplicability of taking hostages to prisoner exchange.—Paragraph (1)(I) does not apply to an offense under subsection (a) by reason of subsection (c)(3) in the case of a prisoner exchange during wartime.

(5) Definition of grave breaches.—The definitions in this subsection are intended only to define the grave breaches of common Article 3 and not the full scope of United States obligations under that Article.

(Added Pub. L. 104–192, §2(a), Aug. 21, 1996, 110 Stat. 2104, §2401; renumbered §2441, Pub. L. 104–294, title VI, §605(p)(1), Oct. 11, 1996, 110 Stat. 3510; amended Pub. L. 105–118, title V, §583, Nov. 26, 1997, 111 Stat. 2436; Pub. L. 107–273, div. B, title IV, §4002(e)(7), Nov. 2, 2002, 116 Stat. 1810; Pub. L. 109–366, §6(b)(1), Oct. 17, 2006, 120 Stat. 2633.)

References in Text

Section 101 of the Immigration and Nationality Act, referred to in subsec. (b), is classified to section 1101 of Title 8, Aliens and Nationality.

The date of the enactment of the Military Commissions Act of 2006, referred to in subsec. (d)(2)(E)(ii), is the date of enactment of Pub. L. 109–366, which was approved Oct. 17, 2006.

Amendments

2006—Subsec. (c)(3). Pub. L. 109–366, §6(b)(1)(A), added par. (3) and struck out former par. (3) which read as follows: "which constitutes a violation of common Article 3 of the international conventions signed at Geneva, 12 August 1949, or any protocol to such convention to which the United States is a party and which deals with non-international armed conflict; or".

Subsec. (d). Pub. L. 109–366, §6(b)(1)(B), added subsec. (d).

2002—Subsecs. (a) to (c). Pub. L. 107–273 made technical correction to directory language of Pub. L. 105–118, §583. See 1997 Amendment notes below.

1997—Subsec. (a). Pub. L. 105–118, §583(1), as amended by Pub. L. 107–273, substituted "war crime" for "grave breach of the Geneva Conventions".

Subsec. (b). Pub. L. 105–118, §583(2), as amended by Pub. L. 107–273, substituted "war crime" for "breach" in two places.

Subsec. (c). Pub. L. 105–118, §583(3), as amended by Pub. L. 107–273, amended subsec. (c) generally. Prior to amendment, subsec. (c) read as follows:

"(c) Definitions.—As used in this section, the term 'grave breach of the Geneva Conventions' means conduct defined as a grave breach in any of the international conventions relating to the laws of warfare signed at Geneva 12 August 1949 or any protocol to any such convention, to which the United States is a party."

1996—Pub. L. 104–294 renumbered section 2401 of this title as this section.

Effective Date of 2006 Amendment

Pub. L. 109–366, §6(b)(2), Oct. 17, 2006, 120 Stat. 2635, provided that: "The amendments made by this subsection [amending this section], except as specified in subsection (d)(2)(E) of section 2441 of title 18, United States Code, shall take effect as of November 26, 1997, as if enacted immediately after the amendments made by section 583 of Public Law 105–118 [amending this section] (as amended by section 4002(e)(7) of Public Law 107–273)."

Effective Date of 2002 Amendment

Pub. L. 107–273, div. B, title IV, §4002(e)(7), Nov. 2, 2002, 116 Stat. 1810, provided that the amendment made by section 4002(e)(7) is effective Nov. 26, 1997.

Short Title

Pub. L. 104–192, §1, Aug. 21, 1996, 110 Stat. 2104, provided that: "This Act [enacting this chapter] may be cited as the 'War Crimes Act of 1996'."

Implementation of Treaty Obligations

Pub. L. 109–366, §6(a), Oct. 17, 2006, 120 Stat. 2632, provided that:

"(1) In general.—The acts enumerated in subsection (d) of section 2441 of title 18, United States Code, as added by subsection (b) of this section, and in subsection (c) of this section [enacting section 2000dd–0 of Title 42, The Public Health and Welfare], constitute violations of common Article 3 of the Geneva Conventions prohibited by United States law.

"(2) Prohibition on grave breaches.—The provisions of section 2441 of title 18, United States Code, as amended by this section, fully satisfy the obligation under Article 129 of the Third Geneva Convention for the United States to provide effective penal sanctions for grave breaches which are encompassed in common Article 3 in the context of an armed conflict not of an international character. No foreign or international source of law shall supply a basis for a rule of decision in the courts of the United States in interpreting the prohibitions enumerated in subsection (d) of such section 2441.

"(3) Interpretation by the president.—

"(A) As provided by the Constitution and by this section, the President has the authority for the United States to interpret the meaning and application of the Geneva Conventions and to promulgate higher standards and administrative regulations for violations of treaty obligations which are not grave breaches of the Geneva Conventions.

"(B) The President shall issue interpretations described by subparagraph (A) by Executive Order published in the Federal Register.

"(C) Any Executive Order published under this paragraph shall be authoritative (except as to grave breaches of common Article 3) as a matter of United States law, in the same manner as other administrative regulations.

"(D) Nothing in this section shall be construed to affect the constitutional functions and responsibilities of Congress and the judicial branch of the United States.

"(4) Definitions.—In this subsection:

"(A) Geneva conventions.—The term 'Geneva Conventions' means—

"(i) the Convention for the Amelioration of the Condition of the Wounded and Sick in Armed Forces in the Field, done at Geneva August 12, 1949 (6 UST 3217);

"(ii) the Convention for the Amelioration of the Condition of the Wounded, Sick, and Shipwrecked Members of the Armed Forces at Sea, done at Geneva August 12, 1949 (6 UST 3217);

"(iii) the Convention Relative to the Treatment of Prisoners of War, done at Geneva August 12, 1949 (6 UST 3316); and

"(iv) the Convention Relative to the Protection of Civilian Persons in Time of War, done at Geneva August 12, 1949 (6 UST 3516).

"(B) Third geneva convention.—The term 'Third Geneva Convention' means the international convention referred to in subparagraph (A)(iii)."

Executive Order No. 13440

Ex. Ord. No. 13440, July 20, 2007, 72 F.R. 40707, which interpreted the Geneva Conventions Common Article 3 as applied to a program of detention and interrogation operated by the Central Intelligence Agency, was revoked by Ex. Ord. No. 13491, §1, Jan. 22, 2009, 74 F.R. 4893, set out as a note under section 2000dd of Title 42, The Public Health and Welfare.

§2442. Recruitment or use of child soldiers

(a) Offense.—Whoever knowingly—

(1) recruits, enlists, or conscripts a person to serve while such person is under 15 years of age in an armed force or group; or

(2) uses a person under 15 years of age to participate actively in hostilities;

knowing such person is under 15 years of age, shall be punished as provided in subsection (b).

(b) Penalty.—Whoever violates, or attempts or conspires to violate, subsection (a) shall be fined under this title or imprisoned not more than 20 years, or both and, if death of any person results, shall be fined under this title and imprisoned for any term of years or for life.

(c) Jurisdiction.—There is jurisdiction over an offense described in subsection (a), and any attempt or conspiracy to commit such offense, if—

(1) the alleged offender is a national of the United States (as defined in section 101(a)(22) of the Immigration and Nationality Act (8 U.S.C. 1101(a)(22))) or an alien lawfully admitted for permanent residence in the United States (as defined in section 101(a)(20) of such Act (8 U.S.C. 1101(a)(20)); 1

(2) the alleged offender is a stateless person whose habitual residence is in the United States;

(3) the alleged offender is present in the United States, irrespective of the nationality of the alleged offender; or

(4) the offense occurs in whole or in part within the United States.

(d) Definitions.—In this section:

(1) Participate actively in hostilities.—The term "participate actively in hostilities" means taking part in—

(A) combat or military activities related to combat, including sabotage and serving as a decoy, a courier, or at a military checkpoint; or

(B) direct support functions related to combat, including transporting supplies or providing other services.

(2) Armed force or group.—The term "armed force or group" means any army, militia, or other military organization, whether or not it is state-sponsored, excluding any group assembled solely for nonviolent political association.

(Added Pub. L. 110–340, §2(a)(1), Oct. 3, 2008, 122 Stat. 3735.)

CHAPTER 119 - WIRE AND ELECTRONIC COMMUNICATIONS INTERCEPTION AND INTERCEPTION OF ORAL COMMUNICATIONS

Amendments

1994—Pub. L. 103–414, title II, §201(b)(3), Oct. 25, 1994, 108 Stat. 4290, added item 2522.

1988—Pub. L. 100–690, title VII, §7035, Nov. 18, 1988, 102 Stat. 4398, substituted "wire, oral, or electronic" for "wire or oral" in items 2511, 2512, 2513, 2516, 2517, 2518, and 2519.

1986—Pub. L. 99–508, title I, §§101(c)(2), 110(b), Oct. 21, 1986, 100 Stat. 1851, 1859, inserted "AND ELECTRONIC COMMUNICATIONS" in chapter heading and added item 2521.

1970—Pub. L. 91–452, title II, §227(b), Oct. 15, 1970, 84 Stat. 930, struck out item 2514 "Immunity of witnesses", which section was repealed four years following the sixtieth day after Oct. 15, 1970.

1968—Pub. L. 90–351, title III, §802, June 19, 1968, 82 Stat. 212, added chapter 119 and items 2510 to 2520.

§2510. Definitions

As used in this chapter—

(1) "wire communication" means any aural transfer made in whole or in part through the use of facilities for the transmission of communications by the aid of wire, cable, or other like connection between the point of origin and the point of reception (including the use of such connection in a switching station) furnished or operated by any person engaged in providing or operating such facilities for the transmission of interstate or foreign communications or communications affecting interstate or foreign commerce;

(2) "oral communication" means any oral communication uttered by a person exhibiting an expectation that such communication is not subject to interception under circumstances justifying such expectation, but such term does not include any electronic communication;

(3) "State" means any State of the United States, the District of Columbia, the Commonwealth of Puerto Rico, and any territory or possession of the United States;

(4) "intercept" means the aural or other acquisition of the contents of any wire, electronic, or oral communication through the use of any electronic, mechanical, or other device.1

(5) "electronic, mechanical, or other device" means any device or apparatus which can be used to

intercept a wire, oral, or electronic communication other than—

(a) any telephone or telegraph instrument, equipment or facility, or any component thereof, (i) furnished to the subscriber or user by a provider of wire or electronic communication service in the ordinary course of its business and being used by the subscriber or user in the ordinary course of its business or furnished by such subscriber or user for connection to the facilities of such service and used in the ordinary course of its business; or (ii) being used by a provider of wire or electronic communication service in the ordinary course of its business, or by an investigative or law enforcement officer in the ordinary course of his duties;

(b) a hearing aid or similar device being used to correct subnormal hearing to not better than normal;

(6) "person" means any employee, or agent of the United States or any State or political subdivision thereof, and any individual, partnership, association, joint stock company, trust, or corporation;

(7) "Investigative or law enforcement officer" means any officer of the United States or of a State or political subdivision thereof, who is empowered by law to conduct investigations of or to make arrests for offenses enumerated in this chapter, and any attorney authorized by law to prosecute or participate in the prosecution of such offenses;

(8) "contents", when used with respect to any wire, oral, or electronic communication, includes any information concerning the substance, purport, or meaning of that communication;

(9) "Judge of competent jurisdiction" means—

(a) a judge of a United States district court or a United States court of appeals; and

(b) a judge of any court of general criminal jurisdiction of a State who is authorized by a statute of that State to enter orders authorizing interceptions of wire, oral, or electronic communications;

(10) "communication common carrier" has the meaning given that term in section 3 of the Communications Act of 1934;

(11) "aggrieved person" means a person who was a party to any intercepted wire, oral, or electronic communication or a person against whom the interception was directed;

(12) "electronic communication" means any transfer of signs, signals, writing, images, sounds, data, or intelligence of any nature transmitted in whole or in part by a wire, radio, electromagnetic, photoelectronic or photooptical system that affects interstate or foreign commerce, but does not include—

(A) any wire or oral communication;

(B) any communication made through a tone-only paging device;

(C) any communication from a tracking device (as defined in section 3117 of this title); or

(D) electronic funds transfer information stored by a financial institution in a communications system used for the electronic storage and transfer of funds;

(13) "user" means any person or entity who—

(A) uses an electronic communication service; and

(B) is duly authorized by the provider of such service to engage in such use;

(14) "electronic communications system" means any wire, radio, electromagnetic, photooptical or photoelectronic facilities for the transmission of wire or electronic communications, and any computer facilities or related electronic equipment for the electronic storage of such communications;

(15) "electronic communication service" means any service which provides to users thereof the ability to send or receive wire or electronic communications;

(16) "readily accessible to the general public" means, with respect to a radio communication, that such communication is not—

(A) scrambled or encrypted;

(B) transmitted using modulation techniques whose essential parameters have been withheld from the public with the intention of preserving the privacy of such communication;

(C) carried on a subcarrier or other signal subsidiary to a radio transmission;

(D) transmitted over a communication system provided by a common carrier, unless the communication is a tone only paging system communication; or

(E) transmitted on frequencies allocated under part 25, subpart D, E, or F of part 74, or part 94 of the Rules of the Federal Communications Commission, unless, in the case of a communication transmitted on a frequency allocated under part 74 that is not exclusively allocated to broadcast auxiliary services, the communication is a two-way voice communication by radio;

(17) "electronic storage" means—

(A) any temporary, intermediate storage of a wire or electronic communication incidental to the electronic transmission thereof; and

(B) any storage of such communication by an electronic communication service for purposes of backup protection of such communication;

(18) "aural transfer" means a transfer containing the human voice at any point between and including the point of origin and the point of reception;

(19) "foreign intelligence information", for purposes of section 2517(6) of this title, means—

(A) information, whether or not concerning a United States person, that relates to the ability of the United States to protect against—

(i) actual or potential attack or other grave hostile acts of a foreign power or an agent of a foreign power;

(ii) sabotage or international terrorism by a foreign power or an agent of a foreign power; or

(iii) clandestine intelligence activities by an intelligence service or network of a foreign power or by an agent of a foreign power; or

(B) information, whether or not concerning a United States person, with respect to a foreign power or foreign territory that relates to—

(i) the national defense or the security of the United States; or

(ii) the conduct of the foreign affairs of the United States;

(20) "protected computer" has the meaning set forth in section 1030; and

(21) "computer trespasser"—

(A) means a person who accesses a protected computer without authorization and thus has no reasonable expectation of privacy in any communication transmitted to, through, or from the protected computer; and

(B) does not include a person known by the owner or operator of the protected computer to have an existing contractual relationship with the owner or operator of the protected computer for access to all or part of the protected computer.

(Added Pub. L. 90–351, title III, §802, June 19, 1968, 82 Stat. 212; amended Pub. L. 99–508, title I, §101(a), (c)(1)(A), (4), Oct. 21, 1986, 100 Stat. 1848, 1851; Pub. L. 103–414, title II, §§202(a), 203, Oct. 25, 1994, 108 Stat. 4290, 4291; Pub. L. 104–132, title VII, §731, Apr. 24, 1996, 110 Stat. 1303; Pub. L. 107–56, title II, §§203(b)(2), 209(1), 217(1), Oct. 26, 2001, 115 Stat. 280, 283, 290; Pub. L. 107–108, title III, §314(b), Dec. 28, 2001, 115 Stat. 1402; Pub. L. 107–273, div. B, title IV, §4002(e)(10), Nov. 2, 2002, 116 Stat. 1810.)

References in Text

Section 3 of the Communications Act of 1934, referred to in par. (10), is classified to section 153 of Title 47, Telecommunications.

Amendments

2002—Par. (10). Pub. L. 107–273 substituted "has the meaning given that term in section 3 of the Communications Act of 1934;" for "shall have the same meaning which is given the term 'common carrier' by section 153(h) of title 47 of the United States Code;".

2001—Par. (1). Pub. L. 107–56, §209(1)(A), struck out "and such term includes any electronic storage of such communication" before semicolon at end.

Par. (14). Pub. L. 107–56, §209(1)(B), inserted "wire or" after "transmission of".

Par. (19). Pub. L. 107–108 inserted ", for purposes of section 2517(6) of this title," before "means" in introductory provisions.

Pub. L. 107–56, §203(b)(2), added par. (19).

Pars. (20), (21). Pub. L. 107–56, §217(1), added pars. (20) and (21).

1996—Par. (12)(D). Pub. L. 104–132, §731(1), added subpar. (D).

Par. (16)(F). Pub. L. 104–132, §731(2), struck out subpar. (F) which read as follows: "an electronic communication;".

1994—Par. (1). Pub. L. 103–414, §202(a)(1), struck out before semicolon at end ", but such term does not include the radio portion of a cordless telephone communication that is transmitted between the cordless telephone handset and the base unit".

Par. (12). Pub. L. 103–414, §202(a)(2), redesignated subpars. (B) to (D) as (A) to (C), respectively, and struck out former subpar. (A) which read as follows: "the radio portion of a cordless telephone communication that is transmitted between the cordless telephone handset and the base unit;".

Par. (16)(F). Pub. L. 103–414, §203, added subpar. (F).

1986—Par. (1). Pub. L. 99–508, §101(a)(1), substituted "any aural transfer" for "any communication", inserted "(including the use of such connection in a switching station)" after "reception", struck out "as a common carrier" after "person engaged", and inserted "or communications affecting interstate or foreign commerce and such term includes any electronic storage of such communication, but such term does not include the radio portion of a cordless telephone communication that is transmitted between the cordless telephone handset and the base unit" before the semicolon at end.

Par. (2). Pub. L. 99–508, §101(a)(2), inserted ", but such term does not include any electronic communication" before the semicolon at end.

Par. (4). Pub. L. 99–508, §101(a)(3), inserted "or other" after "aural" and ", electronic," after "wire".

Par. (5). Pub. L. 99–508, §101(a)(4), (c)(1)(A), (4), substituted "wire, oral, or electronic" for "wire or oral" in introductory provisions, substituted "provider of wire or electronic communication service" for "communications common carrier" in subpars. (a)(i) and (ii), and inserted "or furnished by such subscriber or user for connection to the facilities of such service and used in the ordinary course of its business" before the semicolon in subpar. (a)(i).

Par. (8). Pub. L. 99–508, §101(a)(5), (c)(1)(A), substituted "wire, oral, or electronic" for "wire or oral" and struck out "identity of the parties to such communication or the existence," after "concerning the".

Pars. (9)(b), (11). Pub. L. 99–508, §101(c)(1)(A), substituted "wire, oral, or electronic" for "wire or oral".

Pars. (12) to (18). Pub. L. 99–508, §101(a)(6), added pars. (12) to (18).

Termination Date of 2001 Amendment

Pub. L. 107–56, title II, §224, Oct. 26, 2001, 115 Stat. 295, as amended by Pub. L. 109–160, §1, Dec. 30, 2005, 119 Stat. 2957; Pub. L. 109–170, §1, Feb. 3, 2006, 120 Stat. 3, which provided that title II of Pub. L. 107–56 and the amendments made by that title would cease to have effect on Mar. 10, 2006, with certain exceptions, was repealed by Pub. L. 109–177, title I, §102(a), Mar. 9, 2006, 120 Stat. 194.

Effective Date of 1986 Amendment

Pub. L. 99–508, title I, §111, Oct. 21, 1986, 100 Stat. 1859, provided that:

"(a) In General.—Except as provided in subsection (b) or (c), this title and the amendments made by this title [enacting sections 2521 and 3117 of this title, amending this section and sections 2232, 2511 to 2513, and 2516 to 2520 of this title, and enacting provisions set out as notes under this section] shall take effect 90 days after the date of the enactment of this Act [Oct. 21, 1986] and shall, in the case of conduct pursuant to a court order or extension, apply only with respect to court orders or extensions made after this title takes effect.

"(b) Special Rule for State Authorizations of Interceptions.—Any interception pursuant to section 2516(2) of title 18 of the United States Code which would be valid and lawful without regard to the amendments made by this title shall be valid and lawful notwithstanding such amendments if such interception occurs during the period beginning on the date such amendments take effect and ending on the earlier of—

"(1) the day before the date of the taking effect of State law conforming the applicable State statute with chapter 119 of title 18, United States Code, as so amended; or

"(2) the date two years after the date of the enactment of this Act [Oct. 21, 1986].

"(c) Effective Date for Certain Approvals by Justice Department Officials.—Section 104 of this Act [amending section 2516 of this title] shall take effect on the date of enactment of this Act [Oct. 21, 1986]."

Short Title of 1997 Amendment

Pub. L. 105–112, §1, Nov. 21, 1997, 111 Stat. 2273, provided that: "This Act [amending section 2512 of this title] may be cited as the 'Law Enforcement Technology Advertisement Clarification Act of 1997'."

Short Title of 1986 Amendment

Pub. L. 99–508, §1, Oct. 21, 1986, 100 Stat. 1848, provided that: "This Act [enacting sections 1367, 2521, 2701 to 2710, 3117, and 3121 to 3126 of this title, amending sections 2232, 2511 to 2513, and 2516 to 2520 of this title, and enacting provisions set out as notes under this section and sections 2701 and 3121 of this title] may be cited as the 'Electronic Communications Privacy Act of 1986'."

Intelligence Activities

Pub. L. 99–508, title I, §107, Oct. 21, 1986, 100 Stat. 1858, provided that:

"(a) In General.—Nothing in this Act or the amendments made by this Act [see Short Title of 1986 Amendment note above] constitutes authority for the conduct of any intelligence activity.

"(b) Certain Activities Under Procedures Approved by the Attorney General.—Nothing in chapter 119 or chapter 121 of title 18, United States Code, shall affect the conduct, by officers or employees of the United States Government in accordance with other applicable Federal law, under procedures approved by the Attorney General of activities intended to—

"(1) intercept encrypted or other official communications of United States executive branch entities or United States Government contractors for communications security purposes;

"(2) intercept radio communications transmitted between or among foreign powers or agents of a foreign power as defined by the Foreign Intelligence Surveillance Act of 1978 [50 U.S.C. 1801 et seq.]; or

"(3) access an electronic communication system used exclusively by a foreign power or agent of a foreign power as defined by the Foreign Intelligence Surveillance Act of 1978."

Congressional Findings

Pub. L. 90–351, title III, §801, June 19, 1968, 82 Stat. 211, provided that: "On the basis of its own investigations and of published studies, the Congress makes the following findings:

"(a) Wire communications are normally conducted through the use of facilities which form part of an interstate network. The same facilities are used for interstate and intrastate communications. There has been extensive wiretapping carried on without legal sanctions, and without the consent of any of the parties to the conversation. Electronic, mechanical, and other intercepting devices are being used to overhear oral conversations made in private, without the consent of any of the parties to such communications. The contents of these communications and evidence derived therefrom are being used by public and private parties as evidence in court and administrative proceedings, and by persons whose activities affect interstate commerce. The possession, manufacture, distribution, advertising, and use of these devices are facilitated by interstate commerce.

"(b) In order to protect effectively the privacy of wire and oral communications, to protect the integrity of court and administrative proceedings, and to prevent the obstruction of interstate commerce, it is necessary for Congress to define on a uniform basis the circumstances and conditions under which the interception of wire and oral communications may be authorized, to prohibit any unauthorized interception of such communications, and the use of the contents thereof in evidence in courts and administrative proceedings.

"(c) Organized criminals make extensive use of wire and oral communications in their criminal activities. The interception of such communications to obtain evidence of the commission of crimes or to prevent their commission is an indispensable aid to law enforcement and the administration of justice.

"(d) To safeguard the privacy of innocent persons, the interception of wire or oral communications where none of the parties to the communication has consented to the interception should be allowed only when authorized by a court of competent jurisdiction and should remain under the control and supervision of the authorizing court. Interception of wire and oral communications should further be limited to certain major types of offenses and specific categories of crime with assurances that the interception is justified and that the information obtained thereby will not be misused."

National Commission for the Review of Federal and State Laws Relating to Wiretapping and Electronic Surveillance

Pub. L. 90–351, title III, §804, June 19, 1968, 82 Stat. 223, as amended by Pub. L. 91–452, title XII, §1212, Oct. 15, 1970, 84 Stat. 961; Pub. L. 91–644, title VI, §20, Jan. 2, 1971, 84 Stat. 1892; Pub. L. 93–609, §§1–4, Jan. 2, 1975, 88 Stat. 1972, 1973; Pub. L. 94–176, Dec. 23, 1975, 89 Stat. 1031, established a National Commission for the Review of Federal and State Laws Relating to Wiretapping and Electronic Surveillance, provided for its membership, Chairman, powers and functions, compensation and allowances, required the Commission to study and review the operation of the provisions of this chapter to determine their effectiveness and to submit interim reports and a final report to the President and to the Congress of its findings and recommendations on or before Apr. 30, 1976, and also provided for its termination sixty days after submission of the final report.

§2511. Interception and disclosure of wire, oral, or electronic communications prohibited

(1) Except as otherwise specifically provided in this chapter any person who—

(a) intentionally intercepts, endeavors to intercept, or procures any other person to intercept or endeavor to intercept, any wire, oral, or electronic communication;

(b) intentionally uses, endeavors to use, or procures any other person to use or endeavor to use any electronic, mechanical, or other device to intercept any oral communication when—

(i) such device is affixed to, or otherwise transmits a signal through, a wire, cable, or other like connection used in wire communication; or

(ii) such device transmits communications by radio, or interferes with the transmission of such communication; or

(iii) such person knows, or has reason to know, that such device or any component thereof has been sent through the mail or transported in interstate or foreign commerce; or

(iv) such use or endeavor to use (A) takes place on the premises of any business or other commercial establishment the operations of which affect interstate or foreign commerce; or (B) obtains or is for the purpose of obtaining information relating to the operations of any business or other commercial establishment the operations of which affect interstate or foreign commerce; or

(v) such person acts in the District of Columbia, the Commonwealth of Puerto Rico, or any territory or possession of the United States;

(c) intentionally discloses, or endeavors to disclose, to any other person the contents of any wire, oral, or electronic communication, knowing or having reason to know that the information was obtained through the interception of a wire, oral, or electronic communication in violation of this subsection;

(d) intentionally uses, or endeavors to use, the contents of any wire, oral, or electronic communication, knowing or having reason to know that the information was obtained through the interception of a wire, oral, or electronic communication in violation of this subsection; or

(e)(i) intentionally discloses, or endeavors to disclose, to any other person the contents of any wire, oral, or electronic communication, intercepted by means authorized by sections 2511(2)(a)(ii), 2511(2)(b)–(c), 2511(2)(e), 2516, and 2518 of this chapter, (ii) knowing or having reason to know that the information was obtained through the interception of such a communication in connection with a criminal investigation, (iii) having obtained or received the information in connection with a criminal investigation, and (iv) with intent to improperly obstruct, impede, or interfere with a duly authorized criminal investigation,

shall be punished as provided in subsection (4) or shall be subject to suit as provided in subsection (5).

(2)(a)(i) It shall not be unlawful under this chapter for an operator of a switchboard, or an officer, employee, or agent of a provider of wire or electronic communication service, whose facilities are used in the transmission of a wire or electronic communication, to intercept, disclose, or use that communication in the normal course of his employment while engaged in any activity which is a necessary incident to the rendition of his service or to the protection of the rights or property of the provider of that service, except that a provider of wire communication service to the public shall not utilize service observing or random monitoring except for mechanical or service quality control checks.

(ii) Notwithstanding any other law, providers of wire or electronic communication service, their officers, employees, and agents, landlords, custodians, or other persons, are authorized to provide information, facilities, or technical assistance to persons authorized by law to intercept wire, oral, or electronic communications or to conduct electronic surveillance, as defined in section 101 of the Foreign Intelligence Surveillance Act of 1978, if such provider, its officers, employees, or agents, landlord, custodian, or other specified person, has been provided with—

(A) a court order directing such assistance or a court order pursuant to section 704 of the Foreign Intelligence Surveillance Act of 1978 signed by the authorizing judge, or

(B) a certification in writing by a person specified in section 2518(7) of this title or the Attorney General of the United States that no warrant or court order is required by law, that all statutory requirements have been met, and that the specified assistance is required,

setting forth the period of time during which the provision of the information, facilities, or technical assistance is authorized and specifying the information, facilities, or technical assistance required. No provider of wire or electronic communication service, officer, employee, or agent thereof, or landlord, custodian, or other specified person shall disclose the existence of any interception or surveillance or the device used to accomplish the interception or surveillance with respect to which the person has been furnished a court order or certification under this chapter, except as may otherwise be required by legal process and then only after prior notification to the Attorney General or to the principal prosecuting attorney of a State or any political subdivision of a State, as may be appropriate. Any such disclosure, shall render such person liable for the civil damages provided for in section 2520. No cause of action shall lie in any court against any provider of wire or electronic communication service, its officers, employees, or agents, landlord, custodian, or other specified person for providing information, facilities, or assistance in accordance with the terms of a court order, statutory authorization, or certification under this chapter.

(iii) If a certification under subparagraph (ii)(B) for assistance to obtain foreign intelligence information is based on statutory authority, the certification shall identify the specific statutory provision and shall certify that the statutory requirements have been met.

(b) It shall not be unlawful under this chapter for an officer, employee, or agent of the Federal Communications Commission, in the normal course of his employment and in discharge of the monitoring responsibilities exercised by the Commission in the enforcement of chapter 5 of title 47 of the United States Code, to intercept a wire or electronic communication, or oral communication transmitted by radio, or to disclose or use the information thereby obtained.

(c) It shall not be unlawful under this chapter for a person acting under color of law to intercept a wire, oral, or electronic communication, where such person is a party to the communication or one of the parties to the communication has given prior consent to such interception.

(d) It shall not be unlawful under this chapter for a person not acting under color of law to intercept a wire, oral, or electronic communication where such person is a party to the communication or where one of the parties to the communication has given prior consent to such interception unless such communication is intercepted for the purpose of committing any criminal or tortious act in violation of the Constitution or laws of the United States or of any State.

(e) Notwithstanding any other provision of this title or section 705 or 706 of the Communications Act of 1934, it shall not be unlawful for an officer, employee, or agent of the United States in the normal course of his official duty to conduct electronic surveillance, as defined in section 101 of the Foreign Intelligence Surveillance Act of 1978, as authorized by that Act.

(f) Nothing contained in this chapter or chapter 121 or 206 of this title, or section 705 of the Communications Act of 1934, shall be deemed to affect the acquisition by the United States Government of foreign intelligence information from international or foreign communications, or foreign intelligence activities conducted in accordance with otherwise applicable Federal law involving a foreign electronic communications system, utilizing a means other than electronic surveillance as defined in section 101 of the Foreign Intelligence Surveillance Act of 1978, and procedures in this chapter or chapter 121 and the Foreign Intelligence Surveillance Act of 1978 shall be the exclusive means by which electronic surveillance, as defined in section 101 of such Act, and the interception of domestic wire, oral, and electronic communications may be conducted.

(g) It shall not be unlawful under this chapter or chapter 121 of this title for any person—

(i) to intercept or access an electronic communication made through an electronic communication system that is configured so that such electronic communication is readily accessible to the general public;

(ii) to intercept any radio communication which is transmitted—

(I) by any station for the use of the general public, or that relates to ships, aircraft, vehicles, or persons in distress;

(II) by any governmental, law enforcement, civil defense, private land mobile, or public safety communications system, including police and fire, readily accessible to the general public;

(III) by a station operating on an authorized frequency within the bands allocated to the amateur, citizens band, or general mobile radio services; or

(IV) by any marine or aeronautical communications system;

(iii) to engage in any conduct which—

(I) is prohibited by section 633 of the Communications Act of 1934; or

(II) is excepted from the application of section 705(a) of the Communications Act of 1934 by section 705(b) of that Act;

(iv) to intercept any wire or electronic communication the transmission of which is causing harmful interference to any lawfully operating station or consumer electronic equipment, to the extent necessary to identify the source of such interference; or

(v) for other users of the same frequency to intercept any radio communication made through a system that utilizes frequencies monitored by individuals engaged in the provision or the use of such system, if such communication is not scrambled or encrypted.

(h) It shall not be unlawful under this chapter—

(i) to use a pen register or a trap and trace device (as those terms are defined for the purposes of chapter 206 (relating to pen registers and trap and trace devices) of this title); or

(ii) for a provider of electronic communication service to record the fact that a wire or electronic communication was initiated or completed in order to protect such provider, another provider furnishing service toward the completion of the wire or electronic communication, or a user of that service, from fraudulent, unlawful or abusive use of such service.

(i) It shall not be unlawful under this chapter for a person acting under color of law to intercept the wire or electronic communications of a computer trespasser transmitted to, through, or from the protected computer, if—

(I) the owner or operator of the protected computer authorizes the interception of the computer trespasser's communications on the protected computer;

(II) the person acting under color of law is lawfully engaged in an investigation;

(III) the person acting under color of law has reasonable grounds to believe that the contents of the computer trespasser's communications will be relevant to the investigation; and

(IV) such interception does not acquire communications other than those transmitted to or from the computer trespasser.

(3)(a) Except as provided in paragraph (b) of this subsection, a person or entity providing an electronic communication service to the public shall not intentionally divulge the contents of any communication (other than one to such person or entity, or an agent thereof) while in transmission on that service to any person or entity other than an addressee or intended recipient of such communication or an agent of such addressee or intended recipient.

(b) A person or entity providing electronic communication service to the public may divulge the contents of any such communication—

(i) as otherwise authorized in section 2511(2)(a) or 2517 of this title;

(ii) with the lawful consent of the originator or any addressee or intended recipient of such communication;

(iii) to a person employed or authorized, or whose facilities are used, to forward such communication to its destination; or

(iv) which were inadvertently obtained by the service provider and which appear to pertain to the commission of a crime, if such divulgence is made to a law enforcement agency.

(4)(a) Except as provided in paragraph (b) of this subsection or in subsection (5), whoever violates subsection (1) of this section shall be fined under this title or imprisoned not more than five years, or both.

(b) Conduct otherwise an offense under this subsection that consists of or relates to the interception of a satellite transmission that is not encrypted or scrambled and that is transmitted—

(i) to a broadcasting station for purposes of retransmission to the general public; or

(ii) as an audio subcarrier intended for redistribution to facilities open to the public, but not including data transmissions or telephone calls,

is not an offense under this subsection unless the conduct is for the purposes of direct or indirect commercial advantage or private financial gain.

(5)(a)(i) If the communication is—

(A) a private satellite video communication that is not scrambled or encrypted and the conduct in violation of this chapter is the private viewing of that communication and is not for a tortious or illegal purpose or for purposes of direct or indirect commercial advantage or private commercial gain; or

(B) a radio communication that is transmitted on frequencies allocated under subpart D of part 74 of the rules of the Federal Communications Commission that is not scrambled or encrypted and the conduct in violation of this chapter is not for a tortious or illegal purpose or for purposes of direct or indirect commercial advantage or private commercial gain,

then the person who engages in such conduct shall be subject to suit by the Federal Government in a court of competent jurisdiction.

(ii) In an action under this subsection—

(A) if the violation of this chapter is a first offense for the person under paragraph (a) of subsection (4) and such person has not been found liable in a civil action under section 2520 of this title, the Federal Government shall be entitled to appropriate injunctive relief; and

(B) if the violation of this chapter is a second or subsequent offense under paragraph (a) of subsection (4) or such person has been found liable in any prior civil action under section 2520, the person shall be subject to a mandatory $500 civil fine.

(b) The court may use any means within its authority to enforce an injunction issued under paragraph (ii)(A), and shall impose a civil fine of not less than $500 for each violation of such an injunction.

(Added Pub. L. 90–351, title III, §802, June 19, 1968, 82 Stat. 213; amended Pub. L. 91–358, title II, §211(a), July 29, 1970, 84 Stat. 654; Pub. L. 95–511, title II, §201(a)–(c), Oct. 25, 1978, 92 Stat. 1796, 1797; Pub. L. 98–549, §6(b)(2), Oct. 30, 1984, 98 Stat. 2804; Pub. L. 99–508, title I, §§101(b), (c)(1), (5), (6), (d), (f)[(1)], 102, Oct. 21, 1986, 100 Stat. 1849, 1851–1853; Pub. L. 103–322, title XXXII, §320901, title XXXIII, §330016(1)(G), Sept. 13, 1994, 108 Stat. 2123, 2147; Pub. L. 103–414, title II, §§202(b), 204, 205, Oct. 25, 1994, 108 Stat. 4290, 4291; Pub. L. 104–294, title VI, §604(b)(42), Oct. 11, 1996, 110 Stat. 3509; Pub. L. 107–56, title II, §§204, 217(2), Oct. 26, 2001, 115 Stat. 281, 291; Pub. L. 107–296, title II, §225(h)(2), (j)(1), Nov. 25, 2002, 116 Stat. 2158; Pub. L. 110–261, title I, §§101(c)(1), 102(c)(1), title IV, §403(b)(2)(C), July 10, 2008, 122 Stat. 2459, 2474.)

Amendment of Paragraph (2)(a)(ii)(A)

Pub. L. 110–261, title IV, §403(b)(2), July 10, 2008, 122 Stat. 2474, as amended by Pub. L. 112–238, §2(a)(2), Dec. 30, 2012, 126 Stat. 1631; Pub. L. 115–118, title II, §201(a)(2), Jan. 19, 2018, 132 Stat. 19, provided that, except as provided in section 404 of Pub. L. 110–261, set out as a note under section 1801 of Title 50, War and National Defense, effective Dec. 31, 2023, paragraph (2)(a)(ii)(A) of this section is amended by striking "or a court order pursuant to section 704 of the Foreign Intelligence Surveillance Act of 1978".

References in Text

The Foreign Intelligence Surveillance Act of 1978, referred to in par. (2)(e), (f), is Pub. L. 95–511, Oct. 25, 1978, 92 Stat. 1783, which is classified principally to chapter 36 (§1801 et seq.) of Title 50, War and National Defense. Sections 101 and 704 of the Foreign Intelligence Surveillance Act of 1978, referred to in par. (2)(a)(ii), (e), and (f), are classified to sections 1801 and 1881c of Title 50, respectively. For complete classification of this Act to the Code, see Short Title note set out under section 1801 of Title 50 and Tables.

Sections 633, 705, and 706 of the Communications Act of 1934, referred to in par. (2)(e), (f), (g)(iii), are classified to sections 553, 605, and 606 of Title 47, Telecommunications, respectively.

Constitutionality

For information regarding constitutionality of certain provisions of this section, as amended by section 101(c)(1)(A) of Pub. L. 99–508, see Congressional Research Service, The Constitution of the United States of America: Analysis and Interpretation, Appendix 1, Acts of Congress Held Unconstitutional in Whole or in Part by the Supreme Court of the United States.

Amendments

2008—Par. (2)(a)(ii)(A). Pub. L. 110–261, §101(c)(1), inserted "or a court order pursuant to section 704 of the Foreign Intelligence Surveillance Act of 1978" after "assistance".

Par. (2)(a)(iii). Pub. L. 110–261, §102(c)(1), added cl. (iii).

2002—Par. (2)(a)(ii). Pub. L. 107–296, §225(h)(2), inserted ", statutory authorization," after "terms of a court order" in concluding provisions.

Par. (4)(b), (c). Pub. L. 107–296, §225(j)(1), redesignated subpar. (c) as (b) and struck out former subpar. (b) which read as follows: "If the offense is a first offense under paragraph (a) of this subsection and is not for a tortious or illegal purpose or for purposes of direct or indirect commercial advantage or private commercial gain, and the wire or electronic communication with respect to which the offense under paragraph (a) is a radio communication that is not scrambled, encrypted, or transmitted using modulation techniques the essential parameters of which have been withheld from the public with the intention of preserving the privacy of such communication, then—

"(i) if the communication is not the radio portion of a cellular telephone communication, a cordless telephone communication that is transmitted between the cordless telephone handset and the base unit, a public land mobile radio service communication or a paging service communication, and the conduct is not that described in subsection (5), the offender shall be fined under this title or imprisoned not more than one year, or both; and

"(ii) if the communication is the radio portion of a cellular telephone communication, a cordless telephone communication that is transmitted between the cordless telephone handset and the base unit, a public land mobile radio service communication or a paging service communication, the offender shall be fined under this title."

2001—Par. (2)(f). Pub. L. 107–56, §204, substituted "this chapter or chapter 121 or 206 of this title, or section 705 of the Communications Act of 1934" for "this chapter or chapter 121, or section 705 of the Communications Act of 1934" and "wire, oral, and electronic communications" for "wire and oral communications".

Par. (2)(i). Pub. L. 107–56, §217(2), added subpar. (i).

1996—Par. (1)(e)(i). Pub. L. 104–294 substituted "sections 2511(2)(a)(ii), 2511(2)(b)–(c), 2511(2)(e), 2516, and 2518 of this chapter" for "sections 2511(2)(A)(ii), 2511(b)–(c), 2511(e), 2516, and 2518 of this subchapter".

1994—Par. (1)(e). Pub. L. 103–322, §320901, added par. (1)(e).

Par. (2)(a)(i). Pub. L. 103–414, §205, inserted "or electronic" after "transmission of a wire".

Par. (4)(b). Pub. L. 103–414, §204, in introductory provisions substituted ", encrypted, or transmitted using modulation techniques the essential parameters of which have been withheld from the public with the intention of preserving the privacy of such communication, then" for "or encrypted, then".

Par. (4)(b)(i). Pub. L. 103–414, §202(b)(1), inserted "a cordless telephone communication that is transmitted between the cordless telephone handset and the base unit," after "cellular telephone communication,".

Par. (4)(b)(ii). Pub. L. 103–414, §202(b)(2), inserted "a cordless telephone communication that is transmitted between the cordless telephone handset and the base unit," after "cellular telephone communication,".

Pub. L. 103–322, §330016(1)(G), substituted "fined under this title" for "fined not more than $500".

1986—Pub. L. 99–508, §101(c)(1)(A), substituted "wire, oral, or electronic" for "wire or oral" in section catchline.

Par. (1). Pub. L. 99–508, §101(c)(1)(A), (d)(1), (f)[(1)], substituted "intentionally" for "willfully" in subpars. (a) to (d) and "wire, oral, or electronic' for "wire or oral" wherever appearing in subpars. (a), (c), and (d), and in concluding provisions substituted "shall be punished as provided in subsection (4) or shall be subject to suit as provided in subsection (5)" for "shall be fined not more than $10,000 or imprisoned not more than five years, or both".

Par. (2)(a)(i). Pub. L. 99–508, §101(c)(5), substituted "a provider of wire or electronic communication service" for "any communication common carrier" and "of the provider of that service, except that a provider of wire communication service to the public" for "of the carrier of such communication: Provided, That said communication common carriers".

Par. (2)(a)(ii). Pub. L. 99–508, §101(b)(1), (c)(1)(A), (6), substituted "providers of wire or electronic communication service" for "communication common carriers", "wire, oral, or electronic" for "wire or oral", "if such provider" for "if the common carrier", "provider of wire or electronic communication service" for "communication common carrier" wherever appearing, "such disclosure" for "violation of this subparagraph by a communication common carrier or an officer, employee, or agent thereof", "render such person liable" for "render the carrier liable", and "a court order or certification under this chapter" for "an order or certification under this subparagraph" in two places.

Par. (2)(b). Pub. L. 99–508, §101(c)(1)(B), inserted "or electronic" after "wire".

Par. (2)(c). Pub. L. 99–508, §101(c)(1)(A), substituted "wire, oral, or electronic" for "wire or oral".

Par. (2)(d). Pub. L. 99–508, §101(b)(2), (c)(1)(A), substituted "wire, oral, or electronic" for "wire or oral" and struck out "or for the purpose of committing any other injurious act" after "of any State".

Par. (2)(f). Pub. L. 99–508, §101(b)(3), inserted "or chapter 121" in two places and substituted "foreign communications, or foreign intelligence activities conducted in accordance with otherwise applicable Federal law involving a foreign electronic communications system, utilizing a means" for "foreign communications by a means".

Par. (2)(g), (h). Pub. L. 99–508, §101(b)(4), added subpars. (g) and (h).

Par. (3). Pub. L. 99–508, §102, added par. (3).

Pars. (4), (5). Pub. L. 99–508, §101(d)(2), added pars. (4) and (5).

1984—Par. (2)(e). Pub. L. 98–549, §6(b)(2)(A), substituted "section 705 or 706" for "section 605 or 606".

Par. (2)(f). Pub. L. 98–549, §6(b)(2)(B), substituted "section 705" for "section 605".

1978—Par. (2)(a)(ii). Pub. L. 95–511, §201(a), substituted provisions authorizing communication common carriers etc., to provide information to designated persons, prohibiting disclosure of intercepted information, and rendering violators civilly liable for provision exempting communication common carriers from criminality for giving information to designated officers.

Par. (2)(e), (f). Pub. L. 95–511, §201(b), added par. (2)(e) and (f).

Par. (3). Pub. L. 95–511, §201(c), struck out par. (3) which provided that nothing in this chapter or section 605 of title 47 limited the President's constitutional power to gather necessary intelligence to protect the national security and stated the conditions necessary for the reception into evidence and disclosure of communications intercepted by the President.

1970—Par. (2)(a). Pub. L. 91–358 designated existing provisions as cl. (i) and added cl. (ii).

Effective Date of 2008 Amendment

Amendments by sections 101(c)(1) and 102(c)(1) of Pub. L. 110–261 effective July 10, 2008, except as otherwise provided in section 404 of Pub. L. 110–261, set out as a Transition Procedures note under section 1801 of Title 50, War and National Defense, see section 402 of Pub. L. 110–261, set out as a note under section 1801 of Title 50.

Pub. L. 110–261, title IV, §403(b)(2), July 10, 2008, 122 Stat. 2474, as amended by Pub. L. 112–238, §2(a)(2), Dec. 30, 2012, 126 Stat. 1631; Pub. L. 115–118, title II, §201(a)(2), Jan. 19, 2018, 132 Stat. 19, provided that, except as provided in section 404 of Pub. L. 110–261, set out as a Transition Procedures note under section 1801 of Title 50, War and National Defense, the amendments made by section 403(b)(2) are effective Dec. 31, 2023.

Effective Date of 2002 Amendment

Amendment by Pub. L. 107–296 effective 60 days after Nov. 25, 2002, see section 4 of Pub. L. 107–296, set out as an Effective Date note under section 101 of Title 6, Domestic Security.

Effective Date of 1996 Amendment

Amendment by Pub. L. 104–294 effective Sept. 13, 1994, see section 604(d) of Pub. L. 104–294, set out as a note under section 13 of this title.

Effective Date of 1986 Amendment

Amendment by Pub. L. 99–508 effective 90 days after Oct. 21, 1986, and, in case of conduct pursuant to court order or extension, applicable only with respect to court orders and extensions made after such date, with special rule for State authorizations of interceptions, see section 111 of Pub. L. 99–508, set out as a note under section 2510 of this title.

Effective Date of 1984 Amendment

Amendment by Pub. L. 98–549 effective 60 days after Oct. 30, 1984, see section 9(a) of Pub. L. 98–549, set out as an Effective Date note under section 521 of Title 47, Telecommunications.

Effective Date of 1978 Amendment

Amendment by Pub. L. 95–511 effective Oct. 25, 1978, except as specifically provided, see section 401 of Pub. L. 95–511, formerly set out as an Effective Date note under section 1801 of Title 50, War and National Defense.

Effective Date of 1970 Amendment
Amendment by Pub. L. 91–358 effective on first day of seventh calendar month which begins after July 29, 1970, see section 901(a) of Pub. L. 91–358.

§2512. Manufacture, distribution, possession, and advertising of wire, oral, or electronic communication intercepting devices prohibited

(1) Except as otherwise specifically provided in this chapter, any person who intentionally—

(a) sends through the mail, or sends or carries in interstate or foreign commerce, any electronic, mechanical, or other device, knowing or having reason to know that the design of such device renders it primarily useful for the purpose of the surreptitious interception of wire, oral, or electronic communications;

(b) manufactures, assembles, possesses, or sells any electronic, mechanical, or other device, knowing or having reason to know that the design of such device renders it primarily useful for the purpose of the surreptitious interception of wire, oral, or electronic communications, and that such device or any component thereof has been or will be sent through the mail or transported in interstate or foreign commerce; or

(c) places in any newspaper, magazine, handbill, or other publication or disseminates by electronic means any advertisement of—

(i) any electronic, mechanical, or other device knowing or having reason to know that the design of such device renders it primarily useful for the purpose of the surreptitious interception of wire, oral, or electronic communications; or

(ii) any other electronic, mechanical, or other device, where such advertisement promotes the use of such device for the purpose of the surreptitious interception of wire, oral, or electronic communications,

knowing the content of the advertisement and knowing or having reason to know that such advertisement will be sent through the mail or transported in interstate or foreign commerce, shall be fined under this title or imprisoned not more than five years, or both.

(2) It shall not be unlawful under this section for—

(a) a provider of wire or electronic communication service or an officer, agent, or employee of, or a person under contract with, such a provider, in the normal course of the business of providing that wire or electronic communication service, or

(b) an officer, agent, or employee of, or a person under contract with, the United States, a State, or a political subdivision thereof, in the normal course of the activities of the United States, a State, or a political subdivision thereof,

to send through the mail, send or carry in interstate or foreign commerce, or manufacture, assemble, possess, or sell any electronic, mechanical, or other device knowing or having reason to know that the design of such device renders it primarily useful for the purpose of the surreptitious interception of wire, oral, or electronic communications.

(3) It shall not be unlawful under this section to advertise for sale a device described in subsection (1) of this section if the advertisement is mailed, sent, or carried in interstate or foreign commerce solely to a domestic provider of wire or electronic communication service or to an agency of the United States, a State, or a political subdivision thereof which is duly authorized to use such device.

(Added Pub. L. 90–351, title III, §802, June 19, 1968, 82 Stat. 214; amended Pub. L. 99–508, title I, §101(c)(1)(A), (7), (f)(2), Oct. 21, 1986, 100 Stat. 1851, 1853; Pub. L. 103–322, title XXXIII, §§330016(1)(L), 330022, Sept. 13, 1994, 108 Stat. 2147, 2150; Pub. L. 104–294, title VI, §604(b)(45), Oct. 11, 1996, 110 Stat. 3509; Pub. L. 105–112, §2, Nov. 21, 1997, 111 Stat. 2273; Pub. L. 107–296, title II, §225(f), Nov. 25, 2002, 116 Stat. 2158.)

Amendments

2002—Par. (1)(c). Pub. L. 107–296, in introductory provisions, inserted "or disseminates by electronic means" after "or other publication" and, in concluding provisions, inserted "knowing the content of the advertisement and" before "knowing or having reason to know".

1997—Par. (3). Pub. L. 105–112 added par. (3).

1996—Par. (2). Pub. L. 104–294 amended directory language of Pub. L. 103–322, §330022. See 1994 Amendment note below.

1994—Par. (1). Pub. L. 103–322, §330016(1)(L), substituted "fined under this title" for "fined not more than $10,000" in concluding provisions.

Par. (2). Pub. L. 103–322, §330022, as amended by Pub. L. 104–294, realigned margins of concluding provisions.

1986—Pub. L. 99–508, §101(c)(1)(A), substituted "wire, oral, or electronic" for "wire or oral" in section catchline.

Par. (1). Pub. L. 99–508, §101(c)(1)(A), (f)(2), substituted "intentionally" for "willfully" in introductory provision and "wire, oral, or electronic" for "wire or oral" in subpars. (a), (b), and (c)(i), (ii).

Par. (2)(a). Pub. L. 99–508, §101(c)(7), substituted "a provider of wire or electronic communication service or" for "a communications common carrier or", "such a provider, in" for "a communications common carrier, in", and "business of providing that wire or electronic communication service" for "communications common carrier's business".

Par. (2)(b). Pub. L. 99–508, §101(c)(1)(A), substituted "wire, oral, or electronic" for "wire or oral".

Effective Date of 2002 Amendment

Amendment by Pub. L. 107–296 effective 60 days after Nov. 25, 2002, see section 4 of Pub. L. 107–296, set out as an Effective Date note under section 101 of Title 6, Domestic Security.

Effective Date of 1996 Amendment

Amendment by Pub. L. 104–294 effective Sept. 13, 1994, see section 604(d) of Pub. L. 104–294, set out as a note under section 13 of this title.

Effective Date of 1986 Amendment

Amendment by Pub. L. 99–508 effective 90 days after Oct. 21, 1986, and, in case of conduct pursuant to court order or extension, applicable only with respect to court orders and extensions made after such date, with special rule for State authorizations of interceptions, see section 111 of Pub. L. 99–508, set out as a note under section 2510 of this title.

§2513. Confiscation of wire, oral, or electronic communication intercepting devices

Any electronic, mechanical, or other device used, sent, carried, manufactured, assembled, possessed, sold, or advertised in violation of section 2511 or section 2512 of this chapter may be seized and forfeited to the United States. All provisions of law relating to (1) the seizure, summary and judicial forfeiture, and condemnation of vessels, vehicles, merchandise, and baggage for violations of the customs laws contained in title 19 of the United States Code, (2) the disposition of such vessels, vehicles, merchandise, and baggage or the proceeds from the sale thereof, (3) the remission or mitigation of such forfeiture, (4) the compromise of claims, and (5) the award of compensation to informers in respect of such forfeitures, shall apply to seizures and forfeitures incurred, or alleged to have been incurred, under the provisions of this section, insofar as applicable and not inconsistent with the provisions of this section; except that such duties as are imposed upon the collector of customs or any other person with respect to the seizure and forfeiture of vessels, vehicles, merchandise, and baggage under the provisions of the customs laws contained in title 19 of the United States Code shall be performed with respect to seizure and forfeiture of electronic, mechanical, or other intercepting devices under this section by such officers, agents, or other persons as may be authorized or designated for that purpose by the Attorney General.

(Added Pub. L. 90–351, title III, §802, June 19, 1968, 82 Stat. 215; amended Pub. L. 99–508, title I, §101(c)(1)(A), Oct. 21, 1986, 100 Stat. 1851.)

Amendments

1986—Pub. L. 99–508 substituted "wire, oral, or electronic" for "wire or oral" in section catchline.

Effective Date of 1986 Amendment

Amendment by Pub. L. 99–508 effective 90 days after Oct. 21, 1986, and, in case of conduct pursuant to court order or extension, applicable only with respect to court orders and extensions made after such date, with special rule for State authorizations of interceptions, see section 111 of Pub. L. 99–508, set out as a note under section 2510 of this title.

[§2514. Repealed. Pub. L. 91–452, title II, §227(a), Oct. 15, 1970, 84 Stat. 930]

Section, Pub. L. 90–351, title II, §802, June 19, 1968, 82 Stat. 216, provided for immunity of witnesses giving testimony or producing evidence under compulsion in Federal grand jury or court proceedings. Subject matter is covered in sections 6002 and 6003 of this title.

Effective Date of Repeal

Sections 227(a) and 260 of Pub. L. 91–452 provided for repeal of this section effective four years following sixtieth day after date of enactment of Pub. L. 91–452, which was approved Oct. 15, 1970, such repeal not affecting any immunity to which any individual was entitled under this section by reason of any testimony or other information given before such date. See section 260 of Pub. L. 91–452, set out as an Effective Date; Savings Provision note under section 6001 of this title.

§2515. Prohibition of use as evidence of intercepted wire or oral communications

Whenever any wire or oral communication has been intercepted, no part of the contents of such communication and no evidence derived therefrom may be received in evidence in any trial, hearing, or other proceeding in or before any court, grand jury, department, officer, agency, regulatory body, legislative committee, or other authority of the United States, a State, or a political subdivision thereof if the disclosure of that information would be in violation of this chapter.

(Added Pub. L. 90–351, title III, §802, June 19, 1968, 82 Stat. 216.)

§2516. Authorization for interception of wire, oral, or electronic communications

(1) The Attorney General, Deputy Attorney General, Associate Attorney General,1 or any Assistant Attorney General, any acting Assistant Attorney General, or any Deputy Assistant Attorney General or acting Deputy Assistant Attorney General in the Criminal Division or National Security Division specially designated by the Attorney General, may authorize an application to a Federal judge of competent jurisdiction for, and such judge may grant in conformity with section 2518 of this chapter an order authorizing or approving the interception of wire or oral communications by the Federal Bureau of Investigation, or a Federal agency having responsibility for the investigation of the offense as to which the application is made, when such interception may provide or has provided evidence of—

(a) any offense punishable by death or by imprisonment for more than one year under sections 2122 and 2274 through 2277 of title 42 of the United States Code (relating to the enforcement of the Atomic Energy Act of 1954), section 2284 of title 42 of the United States Code (relating to sabotage of nuclear facilities or fuel), or under the following chapters of this title: chapter 10 (relating to biological weapons), chapter 37 (relating to espionage), chapter 55 (relating to kidnapping), chapter 90 (relating to protection of trade secrets), chapter 105 (relating to sabotage), chapter 115 (relating to treason), chapter 102 (relating to riots), chapter 65 (relating to malicious mischief), chapter 111 (relating to destruction of vessels), or chapter 81 (relating to piracy);

(b) a violation of section 186 or section 501(c) of title 29, United States Code (dealing with restrictions on payments and loans to labor organizations), or any offense which involves murder, kidnapping, robbery, or extortion, and which is punishable under this title;

(c) any offense which is punishable under the following sections of this title: section 37 (relating to violence at international airports), section 43 (relating to animal enterprise terrorism), section 81 (arson within special maritime and territorial jurisdiction), section 201 (bribery of public officials and witnesses), section 215 (relating to bribery of bank officials), section 224 (bribery in sporting contests), subsection (d), (e), (f), (g), (h), or (i) of section 844 (unlawful use of explosives), section 1032 (relating to concealment of assets), section 1084 (transmission of wagering information), section 751 (relating to escape), section 832 (relating to nuclear and weapons of mass destruction threats), section 842 (relating to explosive materials), section 930 (relating to possession of weapons in Federal facilities), section 1014 (relating to loans and credit applications generally; renewals and discounts), section 1114 (relating to officers and employees of the United States), section 1116 (relating to protection of foreign officials), sections 1503, 1512, and 1513 (influencing or injuring an officer, juror, or witness generally), section 1510 (obstruction of criminal investigations), section 1511 (obstruction of State or local law enforcement), section 1581 (peonage), section 1584 (involuntary servitude), section 1589 (forced labor), section 1590 (trafficking with respect to peonage, slavery, involuntary servitude, or forced labor), section 1591 (sex trafficking of children by force, fraud, or coercion), section 1592 (unlawful conduct with respect to documents in furtherance of trafficking, peonage, slavery, involuntary servitude, or forced labor), section 1751 (Presidential and Presidential staff assassination, kidnapping, and assault), section 1951 (interference with commerce by threats or violence), section 1952 (interstate and foreign travel or transportation in aid of racketeering enterprises), section 1958 (relating to use of interstate commerce facilities in the commission of murder for hire), section 1959 (relating to violent crimes in aid of racketeering activity), section 1954 (offer, acceptance, or solicitation to influence operations of employee benefit plan), section 1955 (prohibition of business enterprises of gambling), section 1956 (laundering of monetary instruments), section 1957 (relating to engaging in monetary transactions in property derived from specified unlawful activity), section 659 (theft from interstate shipment), section 664 (embezzlement from pension and welfare funds), section 1343 (fraud by wire, radio, or television), section 1344 (relating to bank fraud), section 1992 (relating to terrorist attacks against mass transportation), sections 2251 and 2252 (sexual exploitation of children), section 2251A (selling or buying of children), section 2252A (relating to material constituting or containing child pornography), section 1466A (relating to child obscenity), section 2260 (production of sexually explicit depictions of a minor for importation into the United States), sections 2421, 2422, 2423, and 2425 (relating to transportation for illegal sexual activity and related crimes), sections 2312, 2313, 2314, and 2315 (interstate transportation of stolen property), section 2321 (relating to trafficking in certain motor vehicles or motor vehicle parts), section 2340A (relating to torture), section 1203 (relating to hostage taking), section 1029 (relating to fraud and related activity in connection with access devices), section 3146 (relating to penalty for failure to appear), section 3521(b)(3) (relating to witness relocation and assistance), section 32 (relating to destruction of aircraft or aircraft facilities), section 38 (relating to aircraft parts fraud), section 1963 (violations with respect to racketeer influenced and corrupt organizations), section 115 (relating to threatening or retaliating against a Federal official), section 1341 (relating to mail fraud), a felony violation of section 1030 (relating to computer fraud and abuse), section 351 (violations with respect to congressional, Cabinet, or Supreme Court assassinations, kidnapping, and assault), section 831 (relating to prohibited transactions involving nuclear materials), section 33 (relating to destruction of motor vehicles or motor vehicle facilities), section 175 (relating to biological weapons), section 175c (relating to variola virus), section 956 (conspiracy to harm persons or property overseas), a felony violation of section 1028 (relating to production of false identification documentation), section 1425 (relating to the procurement of citizenship or nationalization unlawfully), section 1426 (relating to the reproduction of naturalization or citizenship papers), section 1427 (relating to the sale of naturalization or citizenship papers), section 1541 (relating to passport issuance without authority), section 1542 (relating to false statements in passport applications), section 1543 (relating to forgery or false use of passports), section 1544 (relating to misuse of passports), section 1546 (relating to fraud and misuse of visas, permits, and other documents), or section 555 (relating to construction or use of international border tunnels);

(d) any offense involving counterfeiting punishable under section 471, 472, or 473 of this title;

(e) any offense involving fraud connected with a case under title 11 or the manufacture, importation, receiving, concealment, buying, selling, or otherwise dealing in narcotic drugs, marihuana, or other dangerous drugs, punishable under any law of the United States;

(f) any offense including extortionate credit transactions under sections 892, 893, or 894 of this title;

(g) a violation of section 5322 of title 31, United States Code (dealing with the reporting of currency transactions), or section 5324 of title 31, United States Code (relating to structuring transactions to evade reporting requirement prohibited);

(h) any felony violation of sections 2511 and 2512 (relating to interception and disclosure of certain communications and to certain intercepting devices) of this title;

(i) any felony violation of chapter 71 (relating to obscenity) of this title;

(j) any violation of section 60123(b) (relating to destruction of a natural gas pipeline), section 46502 (relating to aircraft piracy), the second sentence of section 46504 (relating to assault on a flight crew with dangerous weapon), or section 46505(b)(3) or (c) (relating to explosive or incendiary devices, or endangerment of human life, by means of weapons on aircraft) of title 49;

(k) any criminal violation of section 2778 of title 22 (relating to the Arms Export Control Act);

(l) the location of any fugitive from justice from an offense described in this section;

(m) a violation of section 274, 277, or 278 of the Immigration and Nationality Act (8 U.S.C. 1324, 1327, or 1328) (relating to the smuggling of aliens);

(n) any felony violation of sections 922 and 924 of title 18, United States Code (relating to firearms);

(o) any violation of section 5861 of the Internal Revenue Code of 1986 (relating to firearms);

(p) a felony violation of section 1028 (relating to production of false identification documents), section 1542 (relating to false statements in passport applications), section 1546 (relating to fraud and misuse of visas, permits, and other documents), section 1028A (relating to aggravated identity theft) of this title or a violation of section 274, 277, or 278 of the Immigration and Nationality Act (relating to the smuggling of aliens); or 2

(q) any criminal violation of section 229 (relating to chemical weapons) or section 2332, 2332a, 2332b, 2332d, 2332f, 2332g, 2332h 3 2339, 2339A, 2339B, 2339C, or 2339D of this title (relating to terrorism);

(r) any criminal violation of section 1 (relating to illegal restraints of trade or commerce), 2 (relating to illegal monopolizing of trade or commerce), or 3 (relating to illegal restraints of trade or commerce in territories or the District of Columbia) of the Sherman Act (15 U.S.C. 1, 2, 3);

(s) any violation of section 670 (relating to theft of medical products); or

(t) any conspiracy to commit any offense described in any subparagraph of this paragraph.

(2) The principal prosecuting attorney of any State, or the principal prosecuting attorney of any political subdivision thereof, if such attorney is authorized by a statute of that State to make application to a State court judge of competent jurisdiction for an order authorizing or approving the interception of wire, oral, or electronic communications, may apply to such judge for, and such judge may grant in conformity with section 2518 of this chapter and with the applicable State

statute an order authorizing, or approving the interception of wire, oral, or electronic communications by investigative or law enforcement officers having responsibility for the investigation of the offense as to which the application is made, when such interception may provide or has provided evidence of the commission of the offense of murder, kidnapping 3 human trafficking, child sexual exploitation, child pornography production,,4 gambling, robbery, bribery, extortion, or dealing in narcotic drugs, marihuana or other dangerous drugs, or other crime dangerous to life, limb, or property, and punishable by imprisonment for more than one year, designated in any applicable State statute authorizing such interception, or any conspiracy to commit any of the foregoing offenses.

(3) Any attorney for the Government (as such term is defined for the purposes of the Federal Rules of Criminal Procedure) may authorize an application to a Federal judge of competent jurisdiction for, and such judge may grant, in conformity with section 2518 of this title, an order authorizing or approving the interception of electronic communications by an investigative or law enforcement officer having responsibility for the investigation of the offense as to which the application is made, when such interception may provide or has provided evidence of any Federal felony.

(Added Pub. L. 90–351, title III, §802, June 19, 1968, 82 Stat. 216; amended Pub. L. 91–452, title VIII, §810, title IX, §902(a), title XI, §1103, Oct. 15, 1970, 84 Stat. 940, 947, 959; Pub. L. 91–644, title IV, §16, Jan. 2, 1971, 84 Stat. 1891; Pub. L. 95–598, title III, §314(h), Nov. 6, 1978, 92 Stat. 2677; Pub. L. 97–285, §§2(e), 4(e), Oct. 6, 1982, 96 Stat. 1220, 1221; Pub. L. 98–292, §8, May 21, 1984, 98 Stat. 206; Pub. L. 98–473, title II, §1203(c), Oct. 12, 1984, 98 Stat. 2152; Pub. L. 99–508, title I, §§101(c)(1)(A), 104, 105, Oct. 21, 1986, 100 Stat. 1851, 1855; Pub. L. 99–570, title I, §1365(c), Oct. 27, 1986, 100 Stat. 3207–35; Pub. L. 100–690, title VI, §6461, title VII, §§7036, 7053(d), 7525, Nov. 18, 1988, 102 Stat. 4374, 4399, 4402, 4502; Pub. L. 101–298, §3(b), May 22, 1990, 104 Stat. 203; Pub. L. 101–647, title XXV, §2531, title XXXV, §3568, Nov. 29, 1990, 104 Stat. 4879, 4928; Pub. L. 103–272, §5(e)(11), July 5, 1994, 108 Stat. 1374; Pub. L. 103–322, title XXXIII, §§330011(c)(1), (q)(1), (r), 330021(1), Sept. 13, 1994, 108 Stat. 2144, 2145, 2150; Pub. L. 103–414, title II, §208, Oct. 25, 1994, 108 Stat. 4292; Pub. L. 103–429, §7(a)(4)(A), Oct. 31, 1994, 108 Stat. 4389; Pub. L. 104–132, title IV, §434, Apr. 24, 1996, 110 Stat. 1274; Pub. L. 104–208, div. C, title II, §201, Sept. 30, 1996, 110 Stat. 3009–564; Pub. L. 104–287, §6(a)(2), Oct. 11, 1996, 110 Stat. 3398; Pub. L. 104–294, title I, §102, title VI, §601(d), Oct. 11, 1996, 110 Stat. 3491, 3499; Pub. L. 105–318, §6(b), Oct. 30, 1998, 112 Stat. 3011; Pub. L. 106–181, title V, §506(c)(2)(B), Apr. 5, 2000, 114 Stat. 139; Pub. L. 107–56, title II, §§201, 202, Oct. 26, 2001, 115 Stat. 278; Pub. L. 107–197, title III, §301(a), June 25, 2002, 116 Stat. 728; Pub. L. 107–273, div. B, title IV, §§4002(c)(1), 4005(a)(1), Nov. 2, 2002, 116 Stat. 1808, 1812; Pub. L. 108–21, title II, §201, Apr. 30, 2003, 117 Stat. 659; Pub. L. 108–458, title VI, §6907, Dec. 17, 2004, 118 Stat. 3774; Pub. L. 109–162, title XI, §1171(b), Jan. 5, 2006, 119 Stat. 3123; Pub. L. 109–177, title I, §§110(b)(3)(C), 113, title V, §506(a)(6), Mar. 9, 2006, 120 Stat. 208, 209, 248; Pub. L. 112–127, §4, June 5, 2012, 126 Stat. 371; Pub. L. 112–186, §5, Oct. 5, 2012, 126 Stat. 1429; Pub. L. 114–22, title I, §106, May 29, 2015, 129 Stat. 238.)

References in Text

The Atomic Energy Act of 1954, referred to in par. (1)(a), is act Aug. 1, 1946, ch. 724, as added by act Aug. 30, 1954, ch. 1073, §1, 68 Stat. 919, which is classified principally to chapter 23 (§2011 et seq.) of Title 42, The Public Health and Welfare. For complete classification of this Act to the Code, see Short Title note set out under section 2011 of Title 42 and Tables.

The Arms Export Control Act, referred to in par. (1)(k), is Pub. L. 90–269, Oct. 22, 1968, 82 Stat. 1320, as amended, which is classified principally to chapter 39 (§2751 et seq.) of Title 22, Foreign Relations and Intercourse. For complete classification of this Act to the Code, see Short Title note set out under section 2751 of Title 22 and Tables.

Section 5861 of the Internal Revenue Code of 1986, referred to in par. (1)(o), is classified to section 5861 of Title 26, Internal Revenue Code.

The Federal Rules of Criminal Procedure, referred to in par. (3), are set out in the Appendix to this title.

Amendments

2015—Par. (1)(a). Pub. L. 114–22, §106(1)(A), inserted a comma after "weapons)".

Par. (1)(c). Pub. L. 114–22, §106(1)(B)(v), (vi), struck out "or" after "misuse of passports)," and inserted "or" before "section 555".

Pub. L. 114–22, §106(1)(B)(iii), (iv), inserted a comma after "virus)" and substituted "overseas), a felony" for "overseas),, section a felony".

Pub. L. 114–22, §106(1)(B)(i), (ii), inserted "section 1581 (peonage), section 1584 (involuntary servitude), section 1589 (forced labor), section 1590 (trafficking with respect to peonage, slavery, involuntary servitude, or forced labor)," before "section 1591" and "section 1592 (unlawful conduct with respect to documents in furtherance of trafficking, peonage, slavery, involuntary servitude, or forced labor)," before "section 1751".

Par. (1)(j). Pub. L. 114–22, §106(1)(C), substituted "pipeline)," for "pipeline,)".

Par. (1)(p). Pub. L. 114–22, §106(1)(D), substituted "documents), section 1028A (relating to aggravated identity theft)" for "documents, section 1028A (relating to aggravated identity theft))".

Par. (2). Pub. L. 114–22, §106(2), inserted "human trafficking, child sexual exploitation, child pornography production," after "kidnapping".

2012—Par. (1)(c). Pub. L. 112–127 inserted ", section 555 (relating to construction or use of international border tunnels)" before semicolon at end.

Par. (1)(s), (t). Pub. L. 112–186 added subpar. (s) and redesignated former subpar. (s) as (t).

2006—Par. (1). Pub. L. 109–177, §506(a)(6), inserted "or National Security Division" after "the Criminal Division" in introductory provisions.

Par. (1)(a). Pub. L. 109–177, §113(a), inserted "chapter 10 (relating to biological weapons)" after "under the following chapters of this title:".

Par. (1)(c). Pub. L. 109–177, §§110(b)(3)(C), 113(b), struck out "1992 (relating to wrecking trains)," before "a felony violation of section 1028" and inserted "section 37 (relating to violence at international airports), section 43 (relating to animal enterprise terrorism), section 81 (arson within special maritime and territorial jurisdiction)," after "the following sections of this title:", "section 832 (relating to nuclear and weapons of mass destruction threats), section 842 (relating to explosive materials), section 930 (relating to possession of weapons in Federal facilities)," after "section 751 (relating to escape),", "section 1114 (relating to officers and employees of the United States), section 1116 (relating to protection of foreign officials)," after "section 1014 (relating to loans and credit applications generally; renewals and discounts),", "section 1992 (relating to terrorist attacks against mass transportation)," after "section 1344 (relating to bank fraud),", "section 2340A (relating to torture)," after "section 2321 (relating to trafficking in certain motor vehicles or motor vehicle parts),", and "section 956 (conspiracy to harm persons or property overseas)," after "section 175c (relating to variola virus)".

Par. (1)(g). Pub. L. 109–177, §113(c), inserted ", or section 5324 of title 31, United States Code (relating to structuring transactions to evade reporting requirement prohibited)" before semicolon at end.

Par. (1)(j). Pub. L. 109–177, §113(d)(2), inserted ", the second sentence of section 46504 (relating to assault on a flight crew with dangerous weapon), or section 46505(b)(3) or (c) (relating to explosive or incendiary devices, or endangerment of human life, by means of weapons on aircraft)" before "of title 49".

Pub. L. 109–177, §113(d)(1), which directed amendment of par. (1)(j) by inserting a comma after "section 60123(b) (relating to the destruction of a natural gas pipeline", was executed by making the insertion after "section 60123(b) (relating to destruction of a natural gas pipeline", to reflect the probable intent of Congress.

Pub. L. 109–177, §113(d)(1), struck out "or" before "section 46502 (relating to aircraft piracy)".

Par. (1)(p). Pub. L. 109–177, §113(e), inserted ", section 1028A (relating to aggravated identity theft)" after "other documents".

Par. (1)(q). Pub. L. 109–177, §113(f), inserted "2339" after "2332h" and substituted "2339C, or 2339D" for "or 2339C".

Pub. L. 109–162 struck out semicolon after "(relating to chemical weapons)" and substituted "section 2332" for "sections 2332".

Par. (1)(r), (s). Pub. L. 109–177, §113(g), added subpar. (r) and redesignated former subpar. (r) as (s).

2004—Par. (1)(a). Pub. L. 108–458, §6907(1), inserted "2122 and" after "sections".

Par. (1)(c). Pub. L. 108–458, §6907(2), inserted "section 175c (relating to variola virus)," after "section 175 (relating to biological weapons),".

Par. (1)(q). Pub. L. 108–458, §6907(3), inserted "2332g, 2332h," after "2332f,".

2003—Par. (1)(a). Pub. L. 108–21, §201(1), inserted "chapter 55 (relating to kidnapping)," after "chapter 37 (relating to espionage),".

Par. (1)(c). Pub. L. 108–21, §201(2), inserted "section 1591 (sex trafficking of children by force, fraud, or coercion)," after "section 1511 (obstruction of State or local law enforcement)," and "section 2251A (selling or buying of children), section 2252A (relating to material constituting or containing child pornography), section 1466A (relating to child obscenity), section 2260 (production of sexually explicit depictions of a minor for importation into the United States), sections 2421, 2422, 2423, and 2425 (relating to transportation for illegal sexual activity and related crimes)," after "sections 2251 and 2252 (sexual exploitation of children),".

2002—Par. (1)(n). Pub. L. 107–273, §4002(c)(1), repealed Pub. L. 104–294, §601(d)(2). See 1996 Amendment note below.

Par. (1)(q). Pub. L. 107–273, §4005(a)(1), realigned margins.

Pub. L. 107–197 inserted "2332f," after "2332d," and substituted "2339B, or 2339C" for "or 2339B".

2001—Par. (1)(c). Pub. L. 107–56, §202, substituted "section 1341 (relating to mail fraud), a felony violation of section 1030 (relating to computer fraud and abuse)," for "and section 1341 (relating to mail fraud),".

Par. (1)(p). Pub. L. 107–56, §201(1), redesignated subpar. (p), relating to conspiracy, as (r).

Par. (1)(q). Pub. L. 107–56, §201(2), added subpar. (q).

Par. (1)(r). Pub. L. 107–56, §201(1), redesignated subpar. (p), relating to conspiracy, as (r).

2000—Par. (1)(c). Pub. L. 106–181 inserted "section 38 (relating to aircraft parts fraud)," after "section 32 (relating to destruction of aircraft or aircraft facilities),".

1998—Par. (1)(a). Pub. L. 105–318 inserted "chapter 90 (relating to protection of trade secrets)," after "chapter 37 (relating to espionage),".

1996—Par. (1)(c). Pub. L. 104–294, §102, which directed amendment of par. 1(c) by inserting "chapter 90 (relating to protection of trade secrets)," after "chapter 37 (relating to espionage),", could not be executed because phrase "chapter 37 (relating to espionage)," did not appear.

Pub. L. 104–208, §201(1), substituted "section 1992 (relating to wrecking trains), a felony violation of section 1028 (relating to production of false identification documentation), section 1425 (relating to the procurement of citizenship or nationalization unlawfully), section 1426 (relating to the reproduction of naturalization or citizenship papers), section 1427 (relating to the sale of naturalization or citizenship papers), section 1541 (relating to passport issuance without authority), section 1542 (relating to false statements in passport applications), section 1543 (relating to forgery or false use of passports), section 1544 (relating to misuse of passports), or section 1546 (relating to fraud and misuse of visas, permits, and other documents)" for "or section 1992 (relating to wrecking trains)" before semicolon at end.

Par. (1)(j). Pub. L. 104–287, §6(a)(2), amended directory language of Pub. L. 103–272, §5(e)(11) as amended by Pub. L. 103–429, §7(a)(4)(A). See 1994 Amendment note below.

Par. (1)(l). Pub. L. 104–208, §201(2), and Pub. L. 104–294, §601(d)(1), amended subpar. (l) identically, striking out "or" after semicolon at end.

Par. (1)(m). Pub. L. 104–208, §201(3), (4), added subpar. (m). Former subpar. (m) redesignated (n).

Par. (1)(n). Pub. L. 104–294, §601(d)(2), which could not be executed because of prior amendments by Pub. L. 104–132, §434(1) and Pub. L. 104–208, §201(3), was repealed by Pub. L. 107–273, §4002(c)(1). See below.

Pub. L. 104–208, §201(3), redesignated subpar. (m) as (n). Former subpar. (n) redesignated (o). Pub. L. 104–132, §434(1), struck out "and" at end.

Par. (1)(o). Pub. L. 104–208, §201(3), redesignated subpar. (n) as (o). Former subpar. (o) redesignated (p).

Pub. L. 104–132 added subpar. (o) and redesignated former subpar. (o) as (p).

Par. (1)(p). Pub. L. 104–208, §201(3), redesignated subpar. (o), relating to felony violation of section 1028, etc., as (p).

Pub. L. 104–132, §434(2), redesignated subpar. (o), relating to conspiracy, as (p).

1994—Par. (1). Pub. L. 103–414 in introductory provisions inserted "or acting Deputy Assistant Attorney General" after "Deputy Assistant Attorney General".

Par. (1)(c). Pub. L. 103–322, §330021(1), substituted "kidnapping" for "kidnaping" in two places. Pub. L. 103–322, §330011(c)(1), amended directory language of Pub. L. 101–298, §3(b). See 1990 Amendment note below.

Par. (1)(j). Pub. L. 103–322, §330011(r), amended directory language of Pub. L. 101–647, §2531(3). See 1990 Amendment note below.

Pub. L. 103–322, §330011(q)(1), repealed Pub. L. 101–647, §3568. See 1990 Amendment note below.

Pub. L. 103–272, §5(e)(11), as amended by Pub. L. 103–429, §7(a)(4)(A); Pub. L. 104–287, §6(a)(2), substituted "section 60123(b) (relating to destruction of a natural gas pipeline) or section 46502 (relating to aircraft piracy) of title 49;" for "section 11(c)(2) of the Natural Gas Pipeline Safety Act of 1968 (relating to destruction of a natural gas pipeline) or subsection (i) or (n) of section 902 of the Federal Aviation Act of 1958 (relating to aircraft piracy);".

1990—Par. (1)(c). Pub. L. 101–647, §2531(1), inserted "section 215 (relating to bribery of bank officials)," before "section 224", "section 1032 (relating to concealment of assets)," before section 1084, "section 1014 (relating to loans and credit applications generally; renewals and discounts)," before "sections 1503," and "section 1344 (relating to bank fraud)," before "sections 2251 and 2252" and struck out "the section in chapter 65 relating to destruction of an energy facility," after "retaliating against a Federal official),".

Pub. L. 101–298, §3(b), as amended by Pub. L. 103–322, §330011(c)(1), inserted "section 175 (relating to biological weapons)," after "section 33 (relating to destruction of motor vehicles or motor vehicle facilities),".

Par. (1)(j). Pub. L. 101–647, §3568, which directed amendment of subsec. (j) by substituting "any violation of section 11(c)(2) of the Natural Gas Pipeline Safety Act of 1968 (relating to destruction of a natural gas pipeline) or section 902(i) or (n) of the Federal Aviation Act of 1958 (relating to aircraft piracy)" for "any violation of section 1679a(c)(2) (relating to destruction of a natural gas pipeline) or subsection (i) or (n) of section 1472 (relating to aircraft piracy) of title 49, of the United States Code", and which was probably intended as an amendment to par. (1)(j), was repealed by Pub. L. 103–322, §330011(q)(1).

Pub. L. 101–647, §2531(3), as amended by Pub. L. 103–322, §330011(r), substituted "any violation of section 11(c)(2) of the Natural Gas Pipeline Safety Act of 1968 (relating to destruction of a natural gas pipeline) or subsection (i) or (n) of section 902 of the Federal Aviation Act of 1958 (relating to aircraft piracy)" for "any violation of section 1679a(c)(2) (relating to destruction of a natural gas pipeline) or subsection (i) or (n) of section 1472 (relating to aircraft piracy) of title 49, of the United States Code".

Par. (1)(m). Pub. L. 101–647, §2531(2)(A), struck out subpar. (m) relating to conspiracy which read as follows: "any conspiracy to commit any of the foregoing offenses."

Par. (1)(o). Pub. L. 101–647, §2531(2)(B)–(D), added subpar. (o).

1988—Par. (1). Pub. L. 100–690, §7036(a)(1), inserted "or" after "Associate Attorney General," in introductory provisions.

Par. (1)(a). Pub. L. 100–690, §7036(c)(1), which directed the amendment of subpar. (a) by substituting "(relating to riots)," for "(relating to riots);" was executed by substituting "(relating to riots)," for "(relating to riots)" as the probable intent of Congress.

Par. (1)(c). Pub. L. 100–690, §7053(d), which directed the amendment of section 2516(c) by substituting "1958" for "1952A" and "1959" for "1952B" was executed by making the substitutions in par. (1)(c) as the probable intent of Congress.

Pub. L. 100–690, §7036(b), struck out "section 2252 or 2253 (sexual exploitation of children)," after "wire, radio, or television)," and substituted "section 2321" for "the second section 2320".

Pub. L. 100–690, §7036(a)(2), which directed the amendment of par. (1) by striking the comma that follows a comma was executed to subpar. (c) by striking out the second comma after "to mail fraud)".

Par. (1)(i). Pub. L. 100–690, §7525, added subpar. (i) and redesignated former subpar. (i) as (j).

Par. (1)(j). Pub. L. 100–690, §7525, redesignated former subpar. (i) as (j). Former subpar. (j) redesignated (k).

Pub. L. 100–690, §7036(c)(2), which directed amendment of subpar. (j) by striking "or;" was executed by striking "or" after "Export Control Act);" to reflect the probable intent of Congress.

Par. (1)(k). Pub. L. 100–690, §7525, redesignated former subpar. (j) as (k). Former subpar. (k) redesignated (l).

Pub. L. 100–690, §7036(c)(3), struck out "or" at end.

Par. (1)(l). Pub. L. 100–690, §7525, redesignated former subpar. (k) as (l). Former subpar. (l) redesignated (m).

Par. (1)(m). Pub. L. 100–690, §7525, redesignated former subpar. (l) relating to conspiracy as (m).

Pub. L. 100–690, §6461, added subpar. (m) relating to sections 922 and 924.

Par. (1)(n). Pub. L. 100–690, §6461, added subpar. (n).

1986—Pub. L. 99–508, §101(c)(1)(A), substituted "wire, oral, or electronic" for "wire or oral" in section catchline.

Par. (1). Pub. L. 99–508, §104, substituted "any Assistant Attorney General, any acting Assistant Attorney General, or any Deputy Assistant Attorney General in the Criminal Division" for "or any Assistant Attorney General" in introductory provisions.

Par. (1)(a). Pub. L. 99–508, §105(a)(5), inserted "section 2284 of title 42 of the United States Code (relating to sabotage of nuclear facilities or fuel)," struck out "or" after "(relating to treason)," and inserted "chapter 65 (relating to malicious mischief), chapter 111 (relating to destruction of vessels), or chapter 81 (relating to piracy)".

Par. (1)(c). Pub. L. 99–570, which directed the amendment of subpar. (c) by inserting "section 1956 (laundering of monetary instruments), section 1957 (relating to engaging in monetary transactions in property derived from specified unlawful activity)," after "section 1955 (prohibition of relating to business enterprises of gambling)," was executed by inserting this phrase after "section 1955 (prohibition of business enterprises of gambling)," as the probable intent of Congress.

Pub. L. 99–508, §105(a)(1), inserted "section 751 (relating to escape)," "the second section 2320 (relating to trafficking in certain motor vehicles or motor vehicle parts), section 1203 (relating to hostage taking), section 1029 (relating to fraud and related activity in connection with access devices), section 3146 (relating to penalty for failure to appear), section 3521(b)(3) (relating to witness relocation and assistance), section 32 (relating to destruction of aircraft or aircraft facilities)," and "section 1952A (relating to use of interstate commerce facilities in the commission of murder for hire), section 1952B (relating to violent crimes in aid of racketeering activity)," substituted "2312, 2313, 2314," for "2314", inserted ", section 115 (relating to threatening or retaliating against a Federal official), the section in chapter 65 relating to destruction of an energy facility, and section 1341 (relating to mail fraud)," substituted ", section 351" for "or section 351", and inserted ", section 831 (relating to prohibited transactions involving nuclear materials), section 33 (relating to destruction of motor vehicles or motor vehicle facilities), or section 1992 (relating to wrecking trains)".

Par. (1)(h) to (l). Pub. L. 99–508, §105(a)(2)–(4), added subpars. (h) to (k) and redesignated former subpar. (h) as (l).

Par. (2). Pub. L. 99–508, §101(c)(1)(A), substituted "wire, oral, or electronic" for "wire or oral" in two places.

Par. (3). Pub. L. 99–508, §105(b), added par. (3).

1984—Par. (1). Pub. L. 98–473, §1203(c)(4), which directed the amendment of the first par. of par. (1) by inserting "Deputy Attorney General, Associate Attorney General," after "Attorney General." was executed by making the insertion after the first reference to "Attorney General," to reflect the probable intent of Congress.

Par. (1)(c). Pub. L. 98–473, §1203(c)(2), inserted references to sections 1512 and 1513 after "1503".

Pub. L. 98–473, §1203(c)(1), inserted "section 1343 (fraud by wire, radio, or television), section 2252 or 2253 (sexual exploitation of children)," after "section 664 (embezzlement from pension and welfare funds),".

Pub. L. 98–292 inserted "sections 2251 and 2252 (sexual exploitation of children)," after "section 664 (embezzlement from pension and welfare funds),".

Par. (1)(g), (h). Pub. L. 98–473, §1203(c)(3), added par. (g) and redesignated former par. (g) as (h).

1982—Par. (1)(c). Pub. L. 97–285 substituted "(Presidential and Presidential staff assassination, kidnaping, and assault)" for "(Presidential assassinations, kidnapping, and assault)" after "section 1751" and substituted "(violations with respect to congressional, Cabinet, or Supreme Court assassinations, kidnaping, and assault)" for "(violations with respect to congressional assassination, kidnapping, and assault)" after "section 351".

1978—Par. (1)(e). Pub. L. 95–598 substituted "fraud connected with a case under title 11" for "bankruptcy fraud".

1971—Par. (1)(c). Pub. L. 91–644 inserted reference to section 351 offense (violations with respect to congressional assassination, kidnaping, and assault).

1970—Par. (1)(c). Pub. L. 91–452 inserted reference to sections 844(d), (e), (f), (g), (h), or (i), 1511, 1955, and 1963 of this title.

Effective Date of 2002 Amendment

Pub. L. 107–273, div. B, title IV, §4002(c)(1), Nov. 2, 2002, 116 Stat. 1808, provided that the amendment made by section 4002(c)(1) is effective Oct. 11, 1996.

Effective Date of 2000 Amendment

Amendment by Pub. L. 106–181 applicable only to fiscal years beginning after Sept. 30, 1999, see section 3 of Pub. L. 106–181, set out as a note under section 106 of Title 49, Transportation.

Effective Date of 1996 Amendment

Pub. L. 104–287, §6(a), Oct. 11, 1996, 110 Stat. 3398, provided that the amendment made by that section is effective July 5, 1994.

Effective Date of 1994 Amendments

Pub. L. 103–429, §7(a), Oct. 31, 1994, 108 Stat. 4388, provided that the amendment made by section 7(a)(4)(A) of Pub. L. 103–429 is effective July 5, 1994.

Pub. L. 103–322, title XXXIII, §330011(c)(1), Sept. 13, 1994, 108 Stat. 2144, provided that the amendment made by that section is effective as of the date on which section 3(b) of Pub. L. 101–298 took effect.

Pub. L. 103–322, title XXXIII, §330011(q)(1), Sept. 13, 1994, 108 Stat. 2145, provided that the amendment made by that section is effective as of the date on which section 3568 of Pub. L. 101–647 took effect.

Pub. L. 103–322, title XXXIII, §330011(r), Sept. 13, 1994, 108 Stat. 2145, provided that the amendment made by that section is effective as of the date on which section 2531(3) of Pub. L. 101–647 took effect.

Effective Date of 1986 Amendment

Amendment by sections 101(c)(1)(A) and 105 of Pub. L. 99–508 effective 90 days after Oct. 21, 1986, and, in case of conduct pursuant to court order or extension, applicable only with respect to court orders and extensions made after such date, with special rule for State authorizations of interceptions pursuant to section 2516(2) of this title, and amendment by section 104 of Pub. L. 99–508 effective Oct. 21, 1986, see section 111 of Pub. L. 99–508, set out as a note under section 2510 of this title.

Effective Date of 1978 Amendment

Amendment by Pub. L. 95–598 effective Oct. 1, 1979, see section 402(a) of Pub. L. 95–598, set out as an Effective Date note preceding section 101 of Title 11, Bankruptcy.

Savings Provision

Amendment by section 314 of Pub. L. 95–598 not to affect the application of chapter 9 (§151 et seq.), chapter 96 (§1961 et seq.), or section 2516, 3057, or 3284 of this title to any act of any person (1) committed before Oct. 1, 1979, or (2) committed after Oct. 1, 1979, in connection with a case commenced before such date, see section 403(d) of Pub. L. 95–598, set out as a note preceding section 101 of Title 11, Bankruptcy.

§2517. Authorization for disclosure and use of intercepted wire, oral, or electronic communications

(1) Any investigative or law enforcement officer who, by any means authorized by this chapter, has obtained knowledge of the contents of any wire, oral, or electronic communication, or evidence derived therefrom, may disclose such contents to another investigative or law enforcement officer to the extent that such disclosure is appropriate to the proper performance of the official duties of the officer making or receiving the disclosure.

(2) Any investigative or law enforcement officer who, by any means authorized by this chapter, has obtained knowledge of the contents of any wire, oral, or electronic communication or evidence derived therefrom may use such contents to the extent such use is appropriate to the proper performance of his official duties.

(3) Any person who has received, by any means authorized by this chapter, any information concerning a wire, oral, or electronic communication, or evidence derived therefrom intercepted in accordance with the provisions of this chapter may disclose the contents of that communication or such derivative evidence while giving testimony under oath or affirmation in any proceeding held under the authority of the United States or of any State or political subdivision thereof.

(4) No otherwise privileged wire, oral, or electronic communication intercepted in accordance with, or in violation of, the provisions of this chapter shall lose its privileged character.

(5) When an investigative or law enforcement officer, while engaged in intercepting wire, oral, or electronic communications in the manner authorized herein, intercepts wire, oral, or electronic communications relating to offenses other than those specified in the order of authorization or approval, the contents thereof, and evidence derived therefrom, may be disclosed or used as provided in subsections (1) and (2) of this section. Such contents and any evidence derived therefrom may be used under subsection (3) of this section when authorized or approved by a judge of competent jurisdiction where such judge finds on subsequent application that the contents were otherwise intercepted in accordance with the provisions of this chapter. Such application shall be made as soon as practicable.

(6) Any investigative or law enforcement officer, or attorney for the Government, who by any means authorized by this chapter, has obtained knowledge of the contents of any wire, oral, or electronic communication, or evidence derived therefrom, may disclose such contents to any other Federal law enforcement, intelligence, protective, immigration, national defense, or national security official to the extent that such contents include foreign intelligence or counterintelligence (as defined in section 3 of the National Security Act of 1947 (50 U.S.C. 401a)),1 or foreign

intelligence information (as defined in subsection (19) of section 2510 of this title), to assist the official who is to receive that information in the performance of his official duties. Any Federal official who receives information pursuant to this provision may use that information only as necessary in the conduct of that person's official duties subject to any limitations on the unauthorized disclosure of such information.

(7) Any investigative or law enforcement officer, or other Federal official in carrying out official duties as such Federal official, who by any means authorized by this chapter, has obtained knowledge of the contents of any wire, oral, or electronic communication, or evidence derived therefrom, may disclose such contents or derivative evidence to a foreign investigative or law enforcement officer to the extent that such disclosure is appropriate to the proper performance of the official duties of the officer making or receiving the disclosure, and foreign investigative or law enforcement officers may use or disclose such contents or derivative evidence to the extent such use or disclosure is appropriate to the proper performance of their official duties.

(8) Any investigative or law enforcement officer, or other Federal official in carrying out official duties as such Federal official, who by any means authorized by this chapter, has obtained knowledge of the contents of any wire, oral, or electronic communication, or evidence derived therefrom, may disclose such contents or derivative evidence to any appropriate Federal, State, local, or foreign government official to the extent that such contents or derivative evidence reveals a threat of actual or potential attack or other grave hostile acts of a foreign power or an agent of a foreign power, domestic or international sabotage, domestic or international terrorism, or clandestine intelligence gathering activities by an intelligence service or network of a foreign power or by an agent of a foreign power, within the United States or elsewhere, for the purpose of preventing or responding to such a threat. Any official who receives information pursuant to this provision may use that information only as necessary in the conduct of that person's official duties subject to any limitations on the unauthorized disclosure of such information, and any State, local, or foreign official who receives information pursuant to this provision may use that information only consistent with such guidelines as the Attorney General and Director of Central Intelligence shall jointly issue.

(Added Pub. L. 90–351, title III, §802, June 19, 1968, 82 Stat. 217; amended Pub. L. 91–452, title IX, §902(b), Oct. 15, 1970, 84 Stat. 947; Pub. L. 99–508, title I, §101(c)(1)(A), Oct. 21, 1986, 100 Stat. 1851; Pub. L. 107–56, title II, §203(b)(1), Oct. 26, 2001, 115 Stat. 280; Pub. L. 107–296, title VIII, §896, Nov. 25, 2002, 116 Stat. 2257.)

References in Text

The National Security Act of 1947, referred to in par. (6), is act July 26, 1947, ch. 343, 61 Stat. 495, which was formerly classified principally to chapter 15 (§401 et seq.) of Title 50, War and National Defense, prior to editorial reclassification in chapter 44 (§3001 et seq.) of Title 50. Section 3 of the Act is now classified to section 3003 of Title 50. For complete classification of this Act to the Code, see Tables.

Amendments

2002—Pars. (7), (8). Pub. L. 107–296 added pars. (7) and (8).

2001—Par. (6). Pub. L. 107–56 added par. (6).

1986—Pub. L. 99–508 substituted "wire, oral, or electronic" for "wire or oral" in section catchline and wherever appearing in text.

1970—Par. (3). Pub. L. 91–452 substituted "proceeding held under the authority of the United States or of any State or political subdivision thereof" for "criminal proceeding in any court of the United States or of any State or in any Federal or State grand jury proceeding".

Change of Name

Reference to the Director of Central Intelligence or the Director of the Central Intelligence Agency in the Director's capacity as the head of the intelligence community deemed to be a reference to the Director of National Intelligence. Reference to the Director of Central Intelligence or the Director of the Central Intelligence Agency in the Director's capacity as the head of the Central Intelligence Agency deemed to be a reference to the Director of the Central Intelligence Agency. See section 1081(a), (b) of Pub. L. 108–458, set out as a note under section 3001 of Title 50, War and National Defense.

Effective Date of 2002 Amendment

Amendment by Pub. L. 107–296 effective 60 days after Nov. 25, 2002, see section 4 of Pub. L. 107–296, set out as an Effective Date note under section 101 of Title 6, Domestic Security.

Effective Date of 1986 Amendment

Amendment by Pub. L. 99–508 effective 90 days after Oct. 21, 1986, and, in case of conduct pursuant to court order or extension, applicable only with respect to court orders and extensions made after such date, with special rule for State authorizations of interceptions, see section 111 of Pub. L. 99–508, set out as a note under section 2510 of this title.

Procedures for Disclosure of Information

Pub. L. 107–56, title II, §203(c), Oct. 26, 2001, 115 Stat. 280, as amended by Pub. L. 107–296, title VIII, §897(b), Nov. 25, 2002, 116 Stat. 2258; Pub. L. 108–458, title VI, §6501(b), Dec. 17, 2004, 118 Stat. 3760, provided that: "The Attorney General shall establish procedures for the disclosure of information pursuant to paragraphs (6) and (8) of section 2517 of title 18, United States Code, and Rule 6(e)(3)(D) of the Federal Rules of Criminal Procedure [18 U.S.C. App.] that identifies a United States person, as defined in section 101 of the Foreign Intelligence Surveillance Act of 1978 (50 U.S.C. 1801)) [sic]."

§2518. Procedure for interception of wire, oral, or electronic communications

(1) Each application for an order authorizing or approving the interception of a wire, oral, or electronic communication under this chapter shall be made in writing upon oath or affirmation to a judge of competent jurisdiction and shall state the applicant's authority to make such application. Each application shall include the following information:

(a) the identity of the investigative or law enforcement officer making the application, and the officer authorizing the application;

(b) a full and complete statement of the facts and circumstances relied upon by the applicant, to justify his belief that an order should be issued, including (i) details as to the particular offense that has been, is being, or is about to be committed, (ii) except as provided in subsection (11), a particular description of the nature and location of the facilities from which or the place where the communication is to be intercepted, (iii) a particular description of the type of communications sought to be intercepted, (iv) the identity of the person, if known, committing the offense and whose communications are to be intercepted;

(c) a full and complete statement as to whether or not other investigative procedures have been tried and failed or why they reasonably appear to be unlikely to succeed if tried or to be too dangerous;

(d) a statement of the period of time for which the interception is required to be maintained. If the nature of the investigation is such that the authorization for interception should not automatically terminate when the described type of communication has been first obtained, a particular description of facts establishing probable cause to believe that additional communications of the same type will occur thereafter;

(e) a full and complete statement of the facts concerning all previous applications known to the individual authorizing and making the application, made to any judge for authorization to intercept, or for approval of interceptions of, wire, oral, or electronic communications involving any of the same persons, facilities or places specified in the application, and the action taken by the judge on each such application; and

(f) where the application is for the extension of an order, a statement setting forth the results thus far obtained from the interception, or a reasonable explanation of the failure to obtain such results.

(2) The judge may require the applicant to furnish additional testimony or documentary evidence in support of the application.

(3) Upon such application the judge may enter an ex parte order, as requested or as modified, authorizing or approving interception of wire, oral, or electronic communications within the territorial jurisdiction of the court in which the judge is sitting (and outside that jurisdiction but within the United States in the case of a mobile interception device authorized by a Federal court within such jurisdiction), if the judge determines on the basis of the facts submitted by the applicant that—

(a) there is probable cause for belief that an individual is committing, has committed, or is about to commit a particular offense enumerated in section 2516 of this chapter;

(b) there is probable cause for belief that particular communications concerning that offense will be obtained through such interception;

(c) normal investigative procedures have been tried and have failed or reasonably appear to be unlikely to succeed if tried or to be too dangerous;

(d) except as provided in subsection (11), there is probable cause for belief that the facilities from which, or the place where, the wire, oral, or electronic communications are to be intercepted are being used, or are about to be used, in connection with the commission of such offense, or are leased to, listed in the name of, or commonly used by such person.

(4) Each order authorizing or approving the interception of any wire, oral, or electronic communication under this chapter shall specify—

(a) the identity of the person, if known, whose communications are to be intercepted;

(b) the nature and location of the communications facilities as to which, or the place where, authority to intercept is granted;

(c) a particular description of the type of communication sought to be intercepted, and a statement of the particular offense to which it relates;

(d) the identity of the agency authorized to intercept the communications, and of the person authorizing the application; and

(e) the period of time during which such interception is authorized, including a statement as to whether or not the interception shall automatically terminate when the described communication has been first obtained.

An order authorizing the interception of a wire, oral, or electronic communication under this chapter shall, upon request of the applicant, direct that a provider of wire or electronic communication service, landlord, custodian or other person shall furnish the applicant forthwith all information, facilities, and technical assistance necessary to accomplish the interception unobtrusively and with a minimum of interference with the services that such service provider, landlord, custodian, or person is according the person whose communications are to be intercepted. Any provider of wire or electronic communication service, landlord, custodian or other person furnishing such facilities or technical assistance shall be compensated therefor by the applicant for reasonable expenses incurred in providing such facilities or assistance. Pursuant to section 2522 of this chapter, an order may also be issued to enforce the assistance capability and capacity requirements under the Communications Assistance for Law Enforcement Act.

(5) No order entered under this section may authorize or approve the interception of any wire, oral, or electronic communication for any period longer than is necessary to achieve the objective of the authorization, nor in any event longer than thirty days. Such thirty-day period begins on the earlier of the day on which the investigative or law enforcement officer first begins to conduct an interception under the order or ten days after the order is entered. Extensions of an order may be granted, but only upon application for an extension made in accordance with subsection (1) of this section and the court making the findings required by subsection (3) of this section. The period of extension shall be no longer than the authorizing judge deems necessary to achieve the purposes for which it was granted and in no event for longer than thirty days. Every order and extension thereof shall contain a provision that the authorization to intercept shall be executed as soon as

practicable, shall be conducted in such a way as to minimize the interception of communications not otherwise subject to interception under this chapter, and must terminate upon attainment of the authorized objective, or in any event in thirty days. In the event the intercepted communication is in a code or foreign language, and an expert in that foreign language or code is not reasonably available during the interception period, minimization may be accomplished as soon as practicable after such interception. An interception under this chapter may be conducted in whole or in part by Government personnel, or by an individual operating under a contract with the Government, acting under the supervision of an investigative or law enforcement officer authorized to conduct the interception.

(6) Whenever an order authorizing interception is entered pursuant to this chapter, the order may require reports to be made to the judge who issued the order showing what progress has been made toward achievement of the authorized objective and the need for continued interception. Such reports shall be made at such intervals as the judge may require.

(7) Notwithstanding any other provision of this chapter, any investigative or law enforcement officer, specially designated by the Attorney General, the Deputy Attorney General, the Associate Attorney General, or by the principal prosecuting attorney of any State or subdivision thereof acting pursuant to a statute of that State, who reasonably determines that—

(a) an emergency situation exists that involves—

(i) immediate danger of death or serious physical injury to any person,

(ii) conspiratorial activities threatening the national security interest, or

(iii) conspiratorial activities characteristic of organized crime,

that requires a wire, oral, or electronic communication to be intercepted before an order authorizing such interception can, with due diligence, be obtained, and

(b) there are grounds upon which an order could be entered under this chapter to authorize such interception,

may intercept such wire, oral, or electronic communication if an application for an order approving the interception is made in accordance with this section within forty-eight hours after the interception has occurred, or begins to occur. In the absence of an order, such interception shall immediately terminate when the communication sought is obtained or when the application for the order is denied, whichever is earlier. In the event such application for approval is denied, or in any other case where the interception is terminated without an order having been issued, the contents of any wire, oral, or electronic communication intercepted shall be treated as having been obtained in violation of this chapter, and an inventory shall be served as provided for in subsection (d) of this section on the person named in the application.

(8)(a) The contents of any wire, oral, or electronic communication intercepted by any means authorized by this chapter shall, if possible, be recorded on tape or wire or other comparable device. The recording of the contents of any wire, oral, or electronic communication under this subsection shall be done in such a way as will protect the recording from editing or other alterations. Immediately upon the expiration of the period of the order, or extensions thereof, such recordings shall be made available to the judge issuing such order and sealed under his directions. Custody of the recordings shall be wherever the judge orders. They shall not be destroyed except upon an order of the issuing or denying judge and in any event shall be kept for ten years. Duplicate recordings may be made for use or disclosure pursuant to the provisions of subsections (1) and (2) of section 2517 of this chapter for investigations. The presence of the seal provided for by this subsection, or a satisfactory explanation for the absence thereof, shall be a prerequisite for the use or disclosure of the contents of any wire, oral, or electronic communication or evidence derived therefrom under subsection (3) of section 2517.

(b) Applications made and orders granted under this chapter shall be sealed by the judge. Custody of the applications and orders shall be wherever the judge directs. Such applications and orders shall be disclosed only upon a showing of good cause before a judge of competent jurisdiction and shall not be destroyed except on order of the issuing or denying judge, and in any event shall be kept for ten years.

(c) Any violation of the provisions of this subsection may be punished as contempt of the issuing or denying judge.

(d) Within a reasonable time but not later than ninety days after the filing of an application for an order of approval under section 2518(7)(b) which is denied or the termination of the period of an order or extensions thereof, the issuing or denying judge shall cause to be served, on the persons named in the order or the application, and such other parties to intercepted communications as the judge may determine in his discretion that is in the interest of justice, an inventory which shall include notice of—

(1) the fact of the entry of the order or the application;

(2) the date of the entry and the period of authorized, approved or disapproved interception, or the denial of the application; and

(3) the fact that during the period wire, oral, or electronic communications were or were not intercepted.

The judge, upon the filing of a motion, may in his discretion make available to such person or his counsel for inspection such portions of the intercepted communications, applications and orders as the judge determines to be in the interest of justice. On an ex parte showing of good cause to a judge of competent jurisdiction the serving of the inventory required by this subsection may be postponed.

(9) The contents of any wire, oral, or electronic communication intercepted pursuant to this chapter or evidence derived therefrom shall not be received in evidence or otherwise disclosed in any trial, hearing, or other proceeding in a Federal or State court unless each party, not less than ten days before the trial, hearing, or proceeding, has been furnished with a copy of the court order, and accompanying application, under which the interception was authorized or approved. This ten-day period may be waived by the judge if he finds that it was not possible to furnish the party with the above information ten days before the trial, hearing, or proceeding and that the party will not be prejudiced by the delay in receiving such information.

(10)(a) Any aggrieved person in any trial, hearing, or proceeding in or before any court, department, officer, agency, regulatory body, or other authority of the United States, a State, or a political subdivision thereof, may move to suppress the contents of any wire or oral communication intercepted pursuant to this chapter, or evidence derived therefrom, on the grounds that—

(i) the communication was unlawfully intercepted;

(ii) the order of authorization or approval under which it was intercepted is insufficient on its face; or

(iii) the interception was not made in conformity with the order of authorization or approval.

Such motion shall be made before the trial, hearing, or proceeding unless there was no opportunity to make such motion or the person was not aware of the grounds of the motion. If the motion is granted, the contents of the intercepted wire or oral communication, or evidence derived therefrom, shall be treated as having been obtained in violation of this chapter. The judge, upon the filing of such motion by the aggrieved person, may in his discretion make available to the aggrieved person or his counsel for inspection such portions of the intercepted communication or evidence derived therefrom as the judge determines to be in the interests of justice.

(b) In addition to any other right to appeal, the United States shall have the right to appeal from an order granting a motion to suppress made under paragraph (a) of this subsection, or the denial of an application for an order of approval, if the United States attorney shall certify to the judge or other official granting such motion or denying such application that the appeal is not taken for purposes of delay. Such appeal shall be taken within thirty days after the date the order was entered and shall be diligently prosecuted.

(c) The remedies and sanctions described in this chapter with respect to the interception of electronic communications are the only judicial remedies and sanctions for nonconstitutional violations of this chapter involving such communications.

(11) The requirements of subsections (1)(b)(ii) and (3)(d) of this section relating to the specification of the facilities from which, or the place where, the communication is to be intercepted do not apply if—

(a) in the case of an application with respect to the interception of an oral communication—

(i) the application is by a Federal investigative or law enforcement officer and is approved by the Attorney General, the Deputy Attorney General, the Associate Attorney General, an Assistant Attorney General, or an acting Assistant Attorney General;

(ii) the application contains a full and complete statement as to why such specification is not practical and identifies the person committing the offense and whose communications are to be intercepted; and

(iii) the judge finds that such specification is not practical; and

(b) in the case of an application with respect to a wire or electronic communication—

(i) the application is by a Federal investigative or law enforcement officer and is approved by the Attorney General, the Deputy Attorney General, the Associate Attorney General, an Assistant Attorney General, or an acting Assistant Attorney General;

(ii) the application identifies the person believed to be committing the offense and whose communications are to be intercepted and the applicant makes a showing that there is probable cause to believe that the person's actions could have the effect of thwarting interception from a specified facility;

(iii) the judge finds that such showing has been adequately made; and

(iv) the order authorizing or approving the interception is limited to interception only for such time as it is reasonable to presume that the person identified in the application is or was reasonably proximate to the instrument through which such communication will be or was transmitted.

(12) An interception of a communication under an order with respect to which the requirements of subsections (1)(b)(ii) and (3)(d) of this section do not apply by reason of subsection (11)(a) shall not begin until the place where the communication is to be intercepted is ascertained by the person implementing the interception order. A provider of wire or electronic communications service that has received an order as provided for in subsection (11)(b) may move the court to modify or quash the order on the ground that its assistance with respect to the interception cannot be performed in a timely or reasonable fashion. The court, upon notice to the government, shall decide such a motion expeditiously.

(Added Pub. L. 90–351, title III, §802, June 19, 1968, 82 Stat. 218; amended Pub. L. 91–358, title II, §211(b), July 29, 1970, 84 Stat. 654; Pub. L. 95–511, title II, §201(d)–(g), Oct. 25, 1978, 92 Stat. 1797, 1798; Pub. L. 98–473, title II, §1203(a), (b), Oct. 12, 1984, 98 Stat. 2152; Pub. L. 99–508, title I, §§101(c)(1)(A), (8), (e), 106(a)–(d)(3), Oct. 21, 1986, 100 Stat. 1851–1853, 1856, 1857; Pub. L. 103–414, title II, §201(b)(1), Oct. 25, 1994, 108 Stat. 4290; Pub. L. 105–272, title VI, §604, Oct. 20, 1998, 112 Stat. 2413.)

References in Text

The Communications Assistance for Law Enforcement Act, referred to in par. (4), is title I of Pub. L. 103–414, Oct. 25, 1994, 108 Stat. 4279, which is classified generally to subchapter I (§1001 et seq.) of chapter 9 of Title 47, Telecommunications. For complete classification of this Act to the Code, see Short Title note set out under section 1001 of Title 47 and Tables.

Amendments

1998—Par. (11)(b)(ii). Pub. L. 105–272, §604(a)(1), substituted "that there is probable cause to believe that the person's actions could have the effect of thwarting interception from a specified facility;" for "of a purpose, on the part of that person, to thwart interception by changing facilities; and".

Par. (11)(b)(iii). Pub. L. 105–272, §604(a)(2), substituted "such showing has been adequately made; and" for "such purpose has been adequately shown."

Par. (11)(b)(iv). Pub. L. 105–272, §604(a)(3), added cl. (iv).

Par. (12). Pub. L. 105–272, §604(b), substituted "by reason of subsection (11)(a)" for "by reason of subsection (11)", struck out "the facilities from which, or" after "shall not begin until", and struck out comma after "the place where".

1994—Par. (4). Pub. L. 103–414 inserted at end of concluding provisions "Pursuant to section 2522 of this chapter, an order may also be issued to enforce the assistance capability and capacity requirements under the Communications Assistance for Law Enforcement Act."

1986—Pub. L. 99–508, §101(c)(1)(A), substituted "wire, oral, or electronic" for "wire or oral" in section catchline.

Par. (1). Pub. L. 99–508, §101(c)(1)(A), substituted "wire, oral, or electronic" for "wire or oral" in introductory provisions.

Par. (1)(b)(ii). Pub. L. 99–508, §106(d)(1), inserted "except as provided in subsection (11),".

Par. (1)(e). Pub. L. 99–508, §101(c)(1)(A), substituted "wire, oral, or electronic" for "wire or oral".

Par. (3). Pub. L. 99–508, §§101(c)(1)(A), 106(a), in introductory provisions, substituted "wire, oral, or electronic" for "wire or oral" and inserted "(and outside that jurisdiction but within the United States in the case of a mobile interception device authorized by a Federal court within such jurisdiction)".

Par. (3)(d). Pub. L. 99–508, §§101(c)(1)(A), 106(d)(2), inserted "except as provided in subsection (11)," and substituted "wire, oral, or electronic" for "wire or oral".

Par. (4). Pub. L. 99–508, §§101(c)(1)(A), (8), 106(b), substituted "wire, oral, or electronic" for "wire or oral" wherever appearing and, in closing provisions, substituted "provider of wire or electronic communication service" for "communication common carrier" wherever appearing, "such service provider" for "such carrier", and "for reasonable expenses incurred in providing such facilities or assistance" for "at the prevailing rates".

Par. (5). Pub. L. 99–508, §§101(c)(1)(A), 106(c), substituted "wire, oral, or electronic" for "wire or oral" and inserted provisions which related to beginning of thirty-day period, minimization where intercepted communication is in code or foreign language and expert in that code or foreign language is not immediately available, and conduct of interception by Government personnel or by individual operating under Government contract, acting under supervision of investigative or law enforcement officer authorized to conduct interception.

Pars. (7), (8)(a), (d)(3), (9). Pub. L. 99–508, §101(c)(1)(A), substituted "wire, oral, or electronic" for "wire or oral" wherever appearing.

Par. (10)(c). Pub. L. 99–508, §101(e), added subpar. (c).

Pars. (11), (12). Pub. L. 99–508, §106(d)(3), added pars. (11) and (12).

1984—Par. (7). Pub. L. 98–473, §1203(a), inserted ", the Deputy Attorney General, the Associate Attorney General," after "Attorney General" in provisions preceding subpar. (a).

Par. (7)(a). Pub. L. 98–473, §1203(b), amended subpar. (a) generally, adding cl. (i) and designated existing provisions as cls. (ii) and (iii).

1978—Par. (1). Pub. L. 95–511, §201(d), inserted "under this chapter" after "communication".

Par. (4). Pub. L. 95–511, §201(e), inserted "under this chapter" after "wire or oral communication" wherever appearing.

Par. (9). Pub. L. 95–511, §201(e), substituted "any wire or oral communication intercepted pursuant to this chapter" for "any intercepted wire or oral communication".

Par. (10). Pub. L. 95–511, §201(g), substituted "any wire or oral communication intercepted pursuant to this chapter," for "any intercepted wire or oral communication,".

1970—Par. (4). Pub. L. 91–358 inserted the provision that, upon the request of the applicant, an order authorizing the interception of a wire or oral communication direct that a communication common carrier, landlord, custodian, or other person furnish the applicant with all information, facilities, and technical assistance necessary to accomplish the interception unobtrusively and with a minimum of interference with the services provided.

Effective Date of 1986 Amendment

Amendment by Pub. L. 99–508 effective 90 days after Oct. 21, 1986, and, in case of conduct pursuant to court order or extension, applicable only with respect to court orders and extensions made after such date, with special rule for State authorizations of interceptions, see section 111 of Pub. L. 99–508, set out as a note under section 2510 of this title.

Effective Date of 1978 Amendment

Amendment by Pub. L. 95–511 effective Oct. 25, 1978, except as specifically provided, see section 401 of Pub. L. 95–511, formerly set out as an Effective Date note under section 1801 of Title 50, War and National Defense.

Effective Date of 1970 Amendment

Amendment by Pub. L. 91–358 effective on first day of seventh calendar month which begins after July 29, 1970, see section 901(a) of Pub. L. 91–358.

§2519. Reports concerning intercepted wire, oral, or electronic communications

(1) In January of each year, any judge who has issued an order (or an extension thereof) under section 2518 that expired during the preceding year, or who has denied approval of an interception during that year, shall report to the Administrative Office of the United States Courts—

(a) the fact that an order or extension was applied for;

(b) the kind of order or extension applied for (including whether or not the order was an order with respect to which the requirements of sections 2518(1)(b)(ii) and 2518(3)(d) of this title did not apply by reason of section 2518(11) of this title);

(c) the fact that the order or extension was granted as applied for, was modified, or was denied;

(d) the period of interceptions authorized by the order, and the number and duration of any extensions of the order;

(e) the offense specified in the order or application, or extension of an order;

(f) the identity of the applying investigative or law enforcement officer and agency making the application and the person authorizing the application; and

(g) the nature of the facilities from which or the place where communications were to be intercepted.

(2) In March of each year the Attorney General, an Assistant Attorney General specially designated by the Attorney General, or the principal prosecuting attorney of a State, or the principal prosecuting attorney for any political subdivision of a State, shall report to the Administrative Office of the United States Courts—

(a) the information required by paragraphs (a) through (g) of subsection (1) of this section with respect to each application for an order or extension made during the preceding calendar year;

(b) a general description of the interceptions made under such order or extension, including (i) the approximate nature and frequency of incriminating communications intercepted, (ii) the approximate nature and frequency of other communications intercepted, (iii) the approximate number of persons whose communications were intercepted, (iv) the number of orders in which encryption was encountered and whether such encryption prevented law enforcement from obtaining the plain text of communications intercepted pursuant to such order, and (v) the approximate nature, amount, and cost of the manpower and other resources used in the interceptions;

(c) the number of arrests resulting from interceptions made under such order or extension, and the offenses for which arrests were made;

(d) the number of trials resulting from such interceptions;

(e) the number of motions to suppress made with respect to such interceptions, and the number granted or denied;

(f) the number of convictions resulting from such interceptions and the offenses for which the convictions were obtained and a general assessment of the importance of the interceptions; and

(g) the information required by paragraphs (b) through (f) of this subsection with respect to orders or extensions obtained in a preceding calendar year.

(3) In June of each year the Director of the Administrative Office of the United States Courts shall transmit to the Congress a full and complete report concerning the number of applications for

orders authorizing or approving the interception of wire, oral, or electronic communications pursuant to this chapter and the number of orders and extensions granted or denied pursuant to this chapter during the preceding calendar year. Such report shall include a summary and analysis of the data required to be filed with the Administrative Office by subsections (1) and (2) of this section. The Director of the Administrative Office of the United States Courts is authorized to issue binding regulations dealing with the content and form of the reports required to be filed by subsections (1) and (2) of this section.

(Added Pub. L. 90–351, title III, §802, June 19, 1968, 82 Stat. 222; amended Pub. L. 95–511, title II, §201(h), Oct. 25, 1978, 92 Stat. 1798; Pub. L. 99–508, title I, §§101(c)(1)(A), 106(d)(4), Oct. 21, 1986, 100 Stat. 1851, 1857; Pub. L. 106–197, §2(a), May 2, 2000, 114 Stat. 247; Pub. L. 111–174, §6, May 27, 2010, 124 Stat. 1217.)

Amendments

2010—Par. (1). Pub. L. 111–174, §6(1), substituted "In January of each year, any judge who has issued an order (or an extension thereof) under section 2518 that expired during the preceding year, or who has denied approval of an interception during that year," for "Within thirty days after the expiration of an order (or each extension thereof) entered under section 2518, or the denial of an order approving an interception, the issuing or denying judge" in introductory provisions.

Par. (2). Pub. L. 111–174, §6(2), substituted "In March of each year" for "In January of each year" in introductory provisions.

Par. (3). Pub. L. 111–174, §6(3), substituted "In June of each year" for "In April of each year".

2000—Par. (2)(b)(iv), (v). Pub. L. 106–197 added cl. (iv) and redesignated former cl. (iv) as (v).

1986—Pub. L. 99–508, §101(c)(1)(A), substituted "wire, oral, or electronic" for "wire or oral" in section catchline.

Par. (1)(b). Pub. L. 99–508, §106(d)(4), inserted "(including whether or not the order was an order with respect to which the requirements of sections 2518(1)(b)(ii) and 2518(3)(d) of this title did not apply by reason of section 2518(11) of this title)".

Par. (3). Pub. L. 99–508, §101(c)(1)(A), substituted "wire, oral, or electronic" for "wire or oral".

1978—Par. (3). Pub. L. 95–511 inserted "pursuant to this chapter" after "wire or oral communications" and "granted or denied".

Effective Date of 1986 Amendment

Amendment by Pub. L. 99–508 effective 90 days after Oct. 21, 1986, and, in case of conduct pursuant to court order or extension, applicable only with respect to court orders and extensions made after such date, with special rule for State authorizations of interceptions, see section 111 of Pub. L. 99–508, set out as a note under section 2510 of this title.

Effective Date of 1978 Amendment

Amendment by Pub. L. 95–511 effective Oct. 25, 1978, except as specifically provided, see section 401 of Pub. L. 95–511, formerly set out as an Effective Date note under section 1801 of Title 50, War and National Defense.

Report on Use of DCS 1000 (Carnivore) To Implement Orders Under Section 2518

Pub. L. 107–273, div. A, title III, §305(b), Nov. 2, 2002, 116 Stat. 1782, provided that: "At the same time that the Attorney General, or Assistant Attorney General specially designated by the Attorney General, submits to the Administrative Office of the United States Courts the annual report required by section 2519(2) of title 18, United States Code, that is respectively next due after the end of each of the fiscal years 2002 and 2003, the Attorney General shall also submit to the Chairmen and ranking minority members of the Committees on the Judiciary of the Senate and of the House of Representatives a report, covering the same respective time period, that contains the following information with respect to those orders described in that annual report that were applied for by law enforcement agencies of the Department of Justice and whose implementation involved the use of the DCS 1000 program (or any subsequent version of such program)—

"(1) the kind of order or extension applied for (including whether or not the order was an order with respect to which the requirements of sections 2518(1)(b)(ii) and 2518(3)(d) of title 18, United States Code, did not apply by reason of section 2518 (11) of title 18);

"(2) the period of interceptions authorized by the order, and the number and duration of any extensions of the order;

"(3) the offense specified in the order or application, or extension of an order;

"(4) the identity of the applying investigative or law enforcement officer and agency making the application and the person authorizing the application;

"(5) the nature of the facilities from which or place where communications were to be intercepted;

"(6) a general description of the interceptions made under such order or extension, including—

"(A) the approximate nature and frequency of incriminating communications intercepted;

"(B) the approximate nature and frequency of other communications intercepted;

"(C) the approximate number of persons whose communications were intercepted;

"(D) the number of orders in which encryption was encountered and whether such encryption prevented law enforcement from obtaining the plain text of communications intercepted pursuant to such order; and

"(E) the approximate nature, amount, and cost of the manpower and other resources used in the interceptions;

"(7) the number of arrests resulting from interceptions made under such order or extension, and the offenses for which arrests were made;

"(8) the number of trials resulting from such interceptions;

"(9) the number of motions to suppress made with respect to such interceptions, and the number granted or denied;

"(10) the number of convictions resulting from such interceptions and the offenses for which the convictions were obtained and a general assessment of the importance of the interceptions; and

"(11) the specific persons authorizing the use of the DCS 1000 program (or any subsequent version of such program) in the implementation of such order."

Encryption Reporting Requirements

Pub. L. 106–197, §2(b), May 2, 2000, 114 Stat. 247, provided that: "The encryption reporting requirement in subsection (a) [amending this section] shall be effective for the report transmitted by the Director of the Administrative Office of the Courts for calendar year 2000 and in subsequent reports."

§2520. Recovery of civil damages authorized

(a) In General.—Except as provided in section 2511(2)(a)(ii), any person whose wire, oral, or electronic communication is intercepted, disclosed, or intentionally used in violation of this chapter may in a civil action recover from the person or entity, other than the United States, which engaged in that violation such relief as may be appropriate.

(b) Relief.—In an action under this section, appropriate relief includes—

(1) such preliminary and other equitable or declaratory relief as may be appropriate;

(2) damages under subsection (c) and punitive damages in appropriate cases; and

(3) a reasonable attorney's fee and other litigation costs reasonably incurred.

(c) Computation of Damages.—(1) In an action under this section, if the conduct in violation of this chapter is the private viewing of a private satellite video communication that is not scrambled or encrypted or if the communication is a radio communication that is transmitted on frequencies allocated under subpart D of part 74 of the rules of the Federal Communications Commission that is not scrambled or encrypted and the conduct is not for a tortious or illegal purpose or for purposes of direct or indirect commercial advantage or private commercial gain, then the court shall assess damages as follows:

(A) If the person who engaged in that conduct has not previously been enjoined under section 2511(5) and has not been found liable in a prior civil action under this section, the court shall assess the greater of the sum of actual damages suffered by the plaintiff, or statutory damages of not less than $50 and not more than $500.

(B) If, on one prior occasion, the person who engaged in that conduct has been enjoined under section 2511(5) or has been found liable in a civil action under this section, the court shall assess the greater of the sum of actual damages suffered by the plaintiff, or statutory damages of not less than $100 and not more than $1000.

(2) In any other action under this section, the court may assess as damages whichever is the greater of—

(A) the sum of the actual damages suffered by the plaintiff and any profits made by the violator as a result of the violation; or

(B) statutory damages of whichever is the greater of $100 a day for each day of violation or $10,000.

(d) Defense.—A good faith reliance on—

(1) a court warrant or order, a grand jury subpoena, a legislative authorization, or a statutory authorization;

(2) a request of an investigative or law enforcement officer under section 2518(7) of this title; or

(3) a good faith determination that section 2511(3) or 2511(2)(i) of this title permitted the conduct complained of;

is a complete defense against any civil or criminal action brought under this chapter or any other law.

(e) Limitation.—A civil action under this section may not be commenced later than two years after the date upon which the claimant first has a reasonable opportunity to discover the violation.

(f) Administrative Discipline.—If a court or appropriate department or agency determines that the United States or any of its departments or agencies has violated any provision of this chapter, and the court or appropriate department or agency finds that the circumstances surrounding the violation raise serious questions about whether or not an officer or employee of the United States acted willfully or intentionally with respect to the violation, the department or agency shall, upon receipt of a true and correct copy of the decision and findings of the court or appropriate department or agency promptly initiate a proceeding to determine whether disciplinary action against the officer or employee is warranted. If the head of the department or agency involved determines that disciplinary action is not warranted, he or she shall notify the Inspector General with jurisdiction over the department or agency concerned and shall provide the Inspector General with the reasons for such determination.

(g) Improper Disclosure Is Violation.—Any willful disclosure or use by an investigative or law enforcement officer or governmental entity of information beyond the extent permitted by section 2517 is a violation of this chapter for purposes of section 2520(a).

(Added Pub. L. 90–351, title III, §802, June 19, 1968, 82 Stat. 223; amended Pub. L. 91–358, title II, §211(c), July 29, 1970, 84 Stat. 654; Pub. L. 99–508, title I, §103, Oct. 21, 1986, 100 Stat. 1853; Pub. L. 107–56, title II, §223(a), Oct. 26, 2001, 115 Stat. 293; Pub. L. 107–296, title II, §225(e), Nov. 25, 2002, 116 Stat. 2157.)

Amendments

2002—Subsec. (d)(3). Pub. L. 107–296 inserted "or 2511(2)(i)" after "2511(3)".

2001—Subsec. (a). Pub. L. 107–56, §223(a)(1), inserted ", other than the United States," after "person or entity".

Subsecs. (f), (g). Pub. L. 107–56, §223(a)(2), (3), added subsecs. (f) and (g).

1986—Pub. L. 99–508 amended section generally. Prior to amendment, section read as follows: "Any person whose wire or oral communication is intercepted, disclosed, or used in violation of this chapter shall (1) have a civil cause of action against any person who intercepts, discloses, or uses, or procures any other person to intercept, disclose, or use such communications, and (2) be entitled to recover from any such person—

"(a) actual damages but not less than liquidated damages computed at the rate of $100 a day for each day of violation or $1,000, whichever is higher;

"(b) punitive damages; and

"(c) a reasonable attorney's fee and other litigation costs reasonably incurred.

A good faith reliance on a court order or legislative authorization shall constitute a complete defense to any civil or criminal action brought under this chapter or under any other law."

1970—Pub. L. 91–358 substituted provisions that a good faith reliance on a court order or legislative authorization constitute a complete defense to any civil or criminal action brought under this chapter or under any other law, for provisions that a good faith reliance on a court order or on the provisions of section 2518(7) of this chapter constitute a complete defense to any civil or criminal action brought under this chapter.

Effective Date of 2002 Amendment

Amendment by Pub. L. 107–296 effective 60 days after Nov. 25, 2002, see section 4 of Pub. L. 107–296, set out as an Effective Date note under section 101 of Title 6, Domestic Security.

Effective Date of 1986 Amendment

Amendment by Pub. L. 99–508 effective 90 days after Oct. 21, 1986, and, in case of conduct pursuant to court order or extension, applicable only with respect to court orders and extensions made after such date, with special rule for State authorizations of interceptions, see section 111 of Pub. L. 99–508, set out as a note under section 2510 of this title.

Effective Date of 1970 Amendment

Amendment by Pub. L. 91–358 effective on first day of seventh calendar month which begins after July 29, 1970, see section 901(a) of Pub. L. 91–358.

§2521. Injunction against illegal interception

Whenever it shall appear that any person is engaged or is about to engage in any act which constitutes or will constitute a felony violation of this chapter, the Attorney General may initiate a civil action in a district court of the United States to enjoin such violation. The court shall proceed as soon as practicable to the hearing and determination of such an action, and may, at any time before final determination, enter such a restraining order or prohibition, or take such other action, as is warranted to prevent a continuing and substantial injury to the United States or to any person or class of persons for whose protection the action is brought. A proceeding under this section is governed by the Federal Rules of Civil Procedure, except that, if an indictment has been returned against the respondent, discovery is governed by the Federal Rules of Criminal Procedure.

(Added Pub. L. 99–508, title I, §110(a), Oct. 21, 1986, 100 Stat. 1859.)

References in Text

The Federal Rules of Civil Procedure, referred to in text, are set out in the Appendix to Title 28, Judiciary and Judicial Procedure.

The Federal Rules of Criminal Procedure, referred to in text, are set out in the Appendix to this title.

Effective Date

Section effective 90 days after Oct. 21, 1986, and, in case of conduct pursuant to court order or extension, applicable only with respect to court orders and extensions made after such date, with special rule for State authorizations of interceptions, see section 111 of Pub. L. 99–508, set out as an Effective Date of 1986 Amendment note under section 2510 of this title.

§2522. Enforcement of the Communications Assistance for Law Enforcement Act

(a) Enforcement by Court Issuing Surveillance Order.—If a court authorizing an interception under this chapter, a State statute, or the Foreign Intelligence Surveillance Act of 1978 (50 U.S.C. 1801 et seq.) or authorizing use of a pen register or a trap and trace device under chapter 206 or a State statute finds that a telecommunications carrier has failed to comply with the requirements of the Communications Assistance for Law Enforcement Act, the court may, in accordance with section 108 of such Act, direct that the carrier comply forthwith and may direct that a provider of support services to the carrier or the manufacturer of the carrier's transmission or switching equipment furnish forthwith modifications necessary for the carrier to comply.

(b) Enforcement Upon Application by Attorney General.—The Attorney General may, in a civil action in the appropriate United States district court, obtain an order, in accordance with section 108 of the Communications Assistance for Law Enforcement Act, directing that a telecommunications carrier, a manufacturer of telecommunications transmission or switching equipment, or a provider of telecommunications support services comply with such Act.

(c) Civil Penalty.—

(1) In general.—A court issuing an order under this section against a telecommunications carrier, a manufacturer of telecommunications transmission or switching equipment, or a provider of telecommunications support services may impose a civil penalty of up to $10,000 per day for each day in violation after the issuance of the order or after such future date as the court may specify.

(2) Considerations.—In determining whether to impose a civil penalty and in determining its amount, the court shall take into account—

(A) the nature, circumstances, and extent of the violation;

(B) the violator's ability to pay, the violator's good faith efforts to comply in a timely manner, any effect on the violator's ability to continue to do business, the degree of culpability, and the length of any delay in undertaking efforts to comply; and

(C) such other matters as justice may require.

(d) Definitions.—As used in this section, the terms defined in section 102 of the Communications Assistance for Law Enforcement Act have the meanings provided, respectively, in such section.

(Added Pub. L. 103–414, title II, §201(a), Oct. 25, 1994, 108 Stat. 4289.)

References in Text

The Foreign Intelligence Surveillance Act of 1978, referred to in subsec. (a), is Pub. L. 95–511, Oct. 25, 1978, 92 Stat. 1783, as amended, which is classified principally to chapter 36 (§1801 et seq.) of Title 50, War and National Defense. For complete classification of this Act to the Code, see Short Title note set out under section 1801 of Title 50 and Tables.

The Communications Assistance for Law Enforcement Act, referred to in subsecs. (a) and (b), is title I of Pub. L. 103–414, Oct. 25, 1994, 108 Stat. 4279, which is classified generally to subchapter I (§1001 et seq.) of chapter 9 of Title 47, Telecommunications. Sections 102 and 108 of the Act are classified to sections 1001 and 1007, respectively, of Title 47. For complete classification of this Act to the Code, see Short Title note set out under section 1001 of Title 47 and Tables.

CHAPTER 121 - STORED WIRE AND ELECTRONIC COMMUNICATIONS AND TRANSACTIONAL RECORDS ACCESS

Amendments

2002—Pub. L. 107–273, div. B, title IV, §4005(b), Nov. 2, 2002, 116 Stat. 1812, made technical correction to directory language of Pub. L. 107–56, title II, §223(c)(2), Oct. 26, 2001, 115 Stat. 295, effective Oct. 26, 2001. See 2001 Amendment note below.

2001—Pub. L. 107–56, title II, §§223(c)(2), 224, Oct. 26, 2001, 115 Stat. 295, as amended by Pub. L. 107–273, div. B, title IV, §4005(b), Nov. 2, 2002, 116 Stat. 1812, temporarily added item 2712.

Pub. L. 107–56, title II, §§212(a)(2), (b)(2), 224, Oct. 26, 2001, 115 Stat. 285, 295, temporarily substituted "Voluntary disclosure of customer communications or records" for "Disclosure of contents" in item 2702 and "Required disclosure of customer communications or records" for "Requirements for governmental access" in item 2703.

1988—Pub. L. 100–690, title VII, §7067, Nov. 18, 1988, 102 Stat. 4405, which directed amendment of item 2710 by inserting "for chapter" after "Definitions" was executed by making the insertion in item 2711 to reflect the probable intent of Congress and the intervening redesignation of item 2710 as 2711 by Pub. L. 100–618, see below.

Pub. L. 100–618, §2(b), Nov. 5, 1988, 102 Stat. 3197, added item 2710 and redesignated former item 2710 as 2711.

§2701. Unlawful access to stored communications

(a) Offense.—Except as provided in subsection (c) of this section whoever—

(1) intentionally accesses without authorization a facility through which an electronic communication service is provided; or

(2) intentionally exceeds an authorization to access that facility;

and thereby obtains, alters, or prevents authorized access to a wire or electronic communication while it is in electronic storage in such system shall be punished as provided in subsection (b) of this section.

(b) Punishment.—The punishment for an offense under subsection (a) of this section is—

(1) if the offense is committed for purposes of commercial advantage, malicious destruction or damage, or private commercial gain, or in furtherance of any criminal or tortious act in violation of the Constitution or laws of the United States or any State—

(A) a fine under this title or imprisonment for not more than 5 years, or both, in the case of a first offense under this subparagraph; and

(B) a fine under this title or imprisonment for not more than 10 years, or both, for any subsequent offense under this subparagraph; and

(2) in any other case—

(A) a fine under this title or imprisonment for not more than 1 year or both, in the case of a first offense under this paragraph; and

(B) a fine under this title or imprisonment for not more than 5 years, or both, in the case of an offense under this subparagraph that occurs after a conviction of another offense under this section.

(c) Exceptions.—Subsection (a) of this section does not apply with respect to conduct authorized—

(1) by the person or entity providing a wire or electronic communications service;

(2) by a user of that service with respect to a communication of or intended for that user; or

(3) in section 2703, 2704 or 2518 of this title.

(Added Pub. L. 99–508, title II, §201[(a)], Oct. 21, 1986, 100 Stat. 1860; amended Pub. L. 103–322, title XXXIII, §330016(1)(K), (U), Sept. 13, 1994, 108 Stat. 2147, 2148; Pub. L. 104–294, title VI, §601(a)(3), Oct. 11, 1996, 110 Stat. 3498; Pub. L. 107–296, title II, §225(j)(2), Nov. 25, 2002, 116 Stat. 2158.)

Amendments

2002—Subsec. (b)(1). Pub. L. 107–296, §225(j)(2)(A), in introductory provisions, inserted ", or in furtherance of any criminal or tortious act in violation of the Constitution or laws of the United States or any State" after "commercial gain".

Subsec. (b)(1)(A). Pub. L. 107–296, §225(j)(2)(B), substituted "5 years" for "one year".

Subsec. (b)(1)(B). Pub. L. 107–296, §225(j)(2)(C), substituted "10 years" for "two years".

Subsec. (b)(2). Pub. L. 107–296, §225(j)(2)(D), added par. (2) and struck out former par. (2) which read as follows: "a fine under this title or imprisonment for not more than six months, or both, in any other case."

1996—Subsec. (b)(1)(A), (2). Pub. L. 104–294 substituted "fine under this title" for "fine of under this title".

1994—Subsec. (b)(1)(A). Pub. L. 103–322, §330016(1)(U), substituted "under this title" for "not more than $250,000".

Subsec. (b)(2). Pub. L. 103–322, §330016(1)(K), substituted "under this title" for "not more than $5,000".

Effective Date of 2002 Amendment

Amendment by Pub. L. 107–296 effective 60 days after Nov. 25, 2002, see section 4 of Pub. L. 107–296, set out as an Effective Date note under section 101 of Title 6, Domestic Security.

Effective Date

Pub. L. 99–508, title II, §202, Oct. 21, 1986, 100 Stat. 1868, provided that: "This title and the amendments made by this title [enacting this chapter] shall take effect ninety days after the date of the enactment of this Act [Oct. 21, 1986] and shall, in the case of conduct pursuant to a court order or extension, apply only with respect to court orders or extensions made after this title takes effect."

Short Title of 1988 Amendment

Pub. L. 100–618, §1, Nov. 5, 1988, 102 Stat. 3195, provided that: "This Act [enacting section 2710 of this title and renumbering former section 2710 as 2711 of this title] may be cited as the 'Video Privacy Protection Act of 1988'."

§2702. Voluntary disclosure of customer communications or records

(a) Prohibitions.—Except as provided in subsection (b) or (c)—

(1) a person or entity providing an electronic communication service to the public shall not knowingly divulge to any person or entity the contents of a communication while in electronic storage by that service; and

(2) a person or entity providing remote computing service to the public shall not knowingly divulge to any person or entity the contents of any communication which is carried or maintained on that service—

(A) on behalf of, and received by means of electronic transmission from (or created by means of computer processing of communications received by means of electronic transmission from), a subscriber or customer of such service;

(B) solely for the purpose of providing storage or computer processing services to such subscriber or customer, if the provider is not authorized to access the contents of any such communications for purposes of providing any services other than storage or computer processing; and

(3) a provider of remote computing service or electronic communication service to the public shall not knowingly divulge a record or other information pertaining to a subscriber to or customer of such service (not including the contents of communications covered by paragraph (1) or (2)) to any governmental entity.

(b) Exceptions for disclosure of communications.—A provider described in subsection (a) may divulge the contents of a communication—

(1) to an addressee or intended recipient of such communication or an agent of such addressee or intended recipient;

(2) as otherwise authorized in section 2517, 2511(2)(a), or 2703 of this title;

(3) with the lawful consent of the originator or an addressee or intended recipient of such communication, or the subscriber in the case of remote computing service;

(4) to a person employed or authorized or whose facilities are used to forward such communication to its destination;

(5) as may be necessarily incident to the rendition of the service or to the protection of the rights or property of the provider of that service;

(6) to the National Center for Missing and Exploited Children, in connection with a report submitted thereto under section 2258A;

(7) to a law enforcement agency—

(A) if the contents—

(i) were inadvertently obtained by the service provider; and

(ii) appear to pertain to the commission of a crime; or

[(B) Repealed. Pub. L. 108–21, title V, §508(b)(1)(A), Apr. 30, 2003, 117 Stat. 684]

(8) to a governmental entity, if the provider, in good faith, believes that an emergency involving danger of death or serious physical injury to any person requires disclosure without delay of communications relating to the emergency.

(c) Exceptions for Disclosure of Customer Records.—A provider described in subsection (a) may divulge a record or other information pertaining to a subscriber to or customer of such service (not including the contents of communications covered by subsection (a)(1) or (a)(2))—

(1) as otherwise authorized in section 2703;

(2) with the lawful consent of the customer or subscriber;

(3) as may be necessarily incident to the rendition of the service or to the protection of the rights or property of the provider of that service;

(4) to a governmental entity, if the provider, in good faith, believes that an emergency involving danger of death or serious physical injury to any person requires disclosure without delay of information relating to the emergency;

(5) to the National Center for Missing and Exploited Children, in connection with a report submitted thereto under section 2258A; or

(6) to any person other than a governmental entity.

(d) Reporting of Emergency Disclosures.—On an annual basis, the Attorney General shall submit to the Committee on the Judiciary of the House of Representatives and the Committee on the Judiciary of the Senate a report containing—

(1) the number of accounts from which the Department of Justice has received voluntary disclosures under subsection (b)(8);

(2) a summary of the basis for disclosure in those instances where—

(A) voluntary disclosures under subsection (b)(8) were made to the Department of Justice; and

(B) the investigation pertaining to those disclosures was closed without the filing of criminal charges; and

(3) the number of accounts from which the Department of Justice has received voluntary disclosures under subsection (c)(4).

(Added Pub. L. 99–508, title II, §201[(a)], Oct. 21, 1986, 100 Stat. 1860; amended Pub. L. 100–

690, title VII, §7037, Nov. 18, 1988, 102 Stat. 4399; Pub. L. 105–314, title VI, §604(b), Oct. 30, 1998, 112 Stat. 2984; Pub. L. 107–56, title II, §212(a)(1), Oct. 26, 2001, 115 Stat. 284; Pub. L. 107–296, title II, §225(d)(1), Nov. 25, 2002, 116 Stat. 2157; Pub. L. 108–21, title V, §508(b), Apr. 30, 2003, 117 Stat. 684; Pub. L. 109–177, title I, §107(a), (b)(1), (c), Mar. 9, 2006, 120 Stat. 202, 203; Pub. L. 110–401, title V, §501(b)(2), Oct. 13, 2008, 122 Stat. 4251; Pub. L. 114–23, title VI, §602(d), June 2, 2015, 129 Stat. 295.)

Amendments

2015—Subsec. (d)(3). Pub. L. 114–23 added par. (3).

2008—Subsecs. (b)(6), (c)(5). Pub. L. 110–401 substituted "section 2258A" for "section 227 of the Victims of Child Abuse Act of 1990 (42 U.S.C. 13032)".

2006—Subsec. (a). Pub. L. 109–177, §107(c), inserted "or (c)" after "Except as provided in subsection (b)".

Subsec. (b)(8). Pub. L. 109–177, §107(b)(1)(A), struck out "Federal, State, or local" before "governmental entity".

Subsec. (c)(4). Pub. L. 109–177, §107(b)(1)(B), added par. (4) and struck out former par. (4) which read as follows: "to a governmental entity, if the provider reasonably believes that an emergency involving immediate danger of death or serious physical injury to any person justifies disclosure of the information;".

Subsec. (d). Pub. L. 109–177, §107(a), added subsec. (d).

2003—Subsec. (b)(5). Pub. L. 108–21, §508(b)(1)(C), which directed amendment of par. (5) by striking "or" at the end, could not be executed because "or" did not appear at the end. See 2002 Amendment note below.

Subsec. (b)(6). Pub. L. 108–21, §508(b)(1)(D), added par. (6). Former par. (6) redesignated (7).

Subsec. (b)(6)(B). Pub. L. 108–21, §508(b)(1)(A), struck out subpar. (B) which read as follows: "if required by section 227 of the Crime Control Act of 1990; or".

Subsec. (b)(7), (8). Pub. L. 108–21, §508(b)(1)(B), redesignated pars. (6) and (7) as (7) and (8), respectively.

Subsec. (c)(5), (6). Pub. L. 108–21, §508(b)(2), added par. (5) and redesignated former par. (5) as (6).

2002—Subsec. (b)(5). Pub. L. 107–296, §225(d)(1)(A), struck out "or" at end.

Subsec. (b)(6)(A). Pub. L. 107–296, §225(d)(1)(B), inserted "or" at end.

Subsec. (b)(6)(C). Pub. L. 107–296, §225(d)(1)(C), struck out subpar. (C) which read as follows: "if the provider reasonably believes that an emergency involving immediate danger of death or serious physical injury to any person requires disclosure of the information without delay."

Subsec. (b)(7). Pub. L. 107–296, §225(d)(1)(D), added par. (7).

2001—Pub. L. 107–56, §212(a)(1)(A), substituted "Voluntary disclosure of customer communications or records" for "Disclosure of contents" in section catchline.

Subsec. (a)(3). Pub. L. 107–56, §212(a)(1)(B), added par. (3).

Subsec. (b). Pub. L. 107–56, §212(a)(1)(C), substituted "Exceptions for disclosure of communications" for "Exceptions" in heading and "A provider described in subsection (a)" for "A person or entity" in introductory provisions.

Subsec. (b)(6)(C). Pub. L. 107–56, §212(a)(1)(D), added subpar. (C).

Subsec. (c). Pub. L. 107–56, §212(a)(1)(E), added subsec. (c).

1998—Subsec. (b)(6). Pub. L. 105–314 amended par. (6) generally. Prior to amendment, par. (6) read as follows: "to a law enforcement agency, if such contents—

"(A) were inadvertently obtained by the service provider; and

"(B) appear to pertain to the commission of a crime."

1988—Subsec. (b)(2). Pub. L. 100–690 substituted "2517" for "2516".

Effective Date of 2002 Amendment

Amendment by Pub. L. 107–296 effective 60 days after Nov. 25, 2002, see section 4 of Pub. L.

107–296, set out as an Effective Date note under section 101 of Title 6, Domestic Security.

Effective Date

Section effective 90 days after Oct. 21, 1986, and, in the case of conduct pursuant to a court order or extension, applicable only with respect to court orders or extensions made after such effective date, see section 202 of Pub. L. 99–508, set out as a note under section 2701 of this title.

§2703. Required disclosure of customer communications or records

(a) Contents of Wire or Electronic Communications in Electronic Storage.—A governmental entity may require the disclosure by a provider of electronic communication service of the contents of a wire or electronic communication, that is in electronic storage in an electronic communications system for one hundred and eighty days or less, only pursuant to a warrant issued using the procedures described in the Federal Rules of Criminal Procedure (or, in the case of a State court, issued using State warrant procedures) by a court of competent jurisdiction. A governmental entity may require the disclosure by a provider of electronic communications services of the contents of a wire or electronic communication that has been in electronic storage in an electronic communications system for more than one hundred and eighty days by the means available under subsection (b) of this section.

(b) Contents of Wire or Electronic Communications in a Remote Computing Service.—(1) A governmental entity may require a provider of remote computing service to disclose the contents of any wire or electronic communication to which this paragraph is made applicable by paragraph (2) of this subsection—

(A) without required notice to the subscriber or customer, if the governmental entity obtains a warrant issued using the procedures described in the Federal Rules of Criminal Procedure (or, in the case of a State court, issued using State warrant procedures) by a court of competent jurisdiction; or

(B) with prior notice from the governmental entity to the subscriber or customer if the governmental entity—

(i) uses an administrative subpoena authorized by a Federal or State statute or a Federal or State grand jury or trial subpoena; or

(ii) obtains a court order for such disclosure under subsection (d) of this section;

except that delayed notice may be given pursuant to section 2705 of this title.

(2) Paragraph (1) is applicable with respect to any wire or electronic communication that is held or maintained on that service—

(A) on behalf of, and received by means of electronic transmission from (or created by means of computer processing of communications received by means of electronic transmission from), a subscriber or customer of such remote computing service; and

(B) solely for the purpose of providing storage or computer processing services to such subscriber or customer, if the provider is not authorized to access the contents of any such communications for purposes of providing any services other than storage or computer processing.

(c) Records Concerning Electronic Communication Service or Remote Computing Service.—(1) A governmental entity may require a provider of electronic communication service or remote computing service to disclose a record or other information pertaining to a subscriber to or customer of such service (not including the contents of communications) only when the governmental entity—

(A) obtains a warrant issued using the procedures described in the Federal Rules of Criminal Procedure (or, in the case of a State court, issued using State warrant procedures) by a court of competent jurisdiction;

(B) obtains a court order for such disclosure under subsection (d) of this section;

(C) has the consent of the subscriber or customer to such disclosure;

(D) submits a formal written request relevant to a law enforcement investigation concerning telemarketing fraud for the name, address, and place of business of a subscriber or customer of such provider, which subscriber or customer is engaged in telemarketing (as such term is defined in section 2325 of this title); or

(E) seeks information under paragraph (2).

(2) A provider of electronic communication service or remote computing service shall disclose to a governmental entity the—

(A) name;

(B) address;

(C) local and long distance telephone connection records, or records of session times and durations;

(D) length of service (including start date) and types of service utilized;

(E) telephone or instrument number or other subscriber number or identity, including any temporarily assigned network address; and

(F) means and source of payment for such service (including any credit card or bank account number),

of a subscriber to or customer of such service when the governmental entity uses an administrative subpoena authorized by a Federal or State statute or a Federal or State grand jury or trial subpoena or any means available under paragraph (1).

(3) A governmental entity receiving records or information under this subsection is not required to provide notice to a subscriber or customer.

(d) Requirements for Court Order.—A court order for disclosure under subsection (b) or (c) may be issued by any court that is a court of competent jurisdiction and shall issue only if the governmental entity offers specific and articulable facts showing that there are reasonable grounds to believe that the contents of a wire or electronic communication, or the records or other information sought, are relevant and material to an ongoing criminal investigation. In the case of a State governmental authority, such a court order shall not issue if prohibited by the law of such State. A court issuing an order pursuant to this section, on a motion made promptly by the service provider, may quash or modify such order, if the information or records requested are unusually voluminous in nature or compliance with such order otherwise would cause an undue burden on such provider.

(e) No Cause of Action Against a Provider Disclosing Information Under This Chapter.—No cause of action shall lie in any court against any provider of wire or electronic communication service, its officers, employees, agents, or other specified persons for providing information, facilities, or assistance in accordance with the terms of a court order, warrant, subpoena, statutory authorization, or certification under this chapter.

(f) Requirement To Preserve Evidence.—

(1) In general.—A provider of wire or electronic communication services or a remote computing service, upon the request of a governmental entity, shall take all necessary steps to preserve records and other evidence in its possession pending the issuance of a court order or other process.

(2) Period of retention.—Records referred to in paragraph (1) shall be retained for a period of 90 days, which shall be extended for an additional 90-day period upon a renewed request by the governmental entity.

(g) Presence of Officer Not Required.—Notwithstanding section 3105 of this title, the presence of an officer shall not be required for service or execution of a search warrant issued in accordance with this chapter requiring disclosure by a provider of electronic communications service or remote computing service of the contents of communications or records or other information pertaining to a subscriber to or customer of such service.

(Added Pub. L. 99–508, title II, §201[(a)], Oct. 21, 1986, 100 Stat. 1861; amended Pub. L. 100–690, title VII, §§7038, 7039, Nov. 18, 1988, 102 Stat. 4399; Pub. L. 103–322, title XXXIII, §330003(b), Sept. 13, 1994, 108 Stat. 2140; Pub. L. 103–414, title II, §207(a), Oct. 25, 1994, 108 Stat. 4292; Pub. L. 104–132, title VIII, §804, Apr. 24, 1996, 110 Stat. 1305; Pub. L. 104–293, title VI, §601(b), Oct. 11, 1996, 110 Stat. 3469; Pub. L. 104–294, title VI, §605(f), Oct. 11, 1996, 110 Stat. 3510; Pub. L. 105–184, §8, June 23, 1998, 112 Stat. 522; Pub. L. 107–56, title II, §§209(2), 210, 212(b)(1), 220(a)(1), (b), Oct. 26, 2001, 115 Stat. 283, 285, 291, 292; Pub. L. 107–273, div.

B, title IV, §4005(a)(2), div. C, title I, §11010, Nov. 2, 2002, 116 Stat. 1812, 1822; Pub. L. 107–296, title II, §225(h)(1), Nov. 25, 2002, 116 Stat. 2158; Pub. L. 109–162, title XI, §1171(a)(1), Jan. 5, 2006, 119 Stat. 3123; Pub. L. 111–79, §2(1), Oct. 19, 2009, 123 Stat. 2086; Pub. L. 114–328, div. E, title LVII, §5228(b)(1), Dec. 23, 2016, 130 Stat. 2912.)

Amendment of Subsections (a), (b)(1)(A), and (c)(1)(A)

Pub. L. 114–328, div. E, title LVII, §5228(b)(1), title LXIII, §5542, Dec. 23, 2016, 130 Stat. 2912, 2967, provided that, effective on the date designated by the President, not later than the first day of the first calendar month beginning two years after Dec. 23, 2016, with implementing regulations prescribed by the President not later than one year after Dec. 23, 2016, and with provisions relating to applicability to various situations, this section is amended—
(1) in the first sentence of subsection (a);
(2) in subsection (b)(1)(A); and
(3) in subsection (c)(1)(A);
by inserting after "warrant procedures" the following: "and, in the case of a court-martial or other proceeding under chapter 47 of title 10 (the Uniform Code of Military Justice), issued under section 846 of that title, in accordance with regulations prescribed by the President". See 2016 Amendment note below.

References in Text

The Federal Rules of Criminal Procedure, referred to in subsecs. (a), (b)(1)(A), and (c)(1)(B)(i), are set out in the Appendix to this title.

Amendments

2016—Subsecs. (a), (b)(1)(A), (c)(1)(A). Pub. L. 114–328 inserted "and, in the case of a court-martial or other proceeding under chapter 47 of title 10 (the Uniform Code of Military Justice), issued under section 846 of that title, in accordance with regulations prescribed by the President" after "warrant procedures".
2009—Subsecs. (a), (b)(1)(A), (c)(1)(A). Pub. L. 111–79, which directed substitution of "(or, in the case of a State court, issued using State warrant procedures) by a court of competent jurisdiction" for "by a court with jurisdiction over the offense under investigation or an equivalent State warrant", was executed by making the substitution for "by a court with jurisdiction over the offense under investigation or equivalent State warrant" to reflect the probable intent of Congress.
2006—Subsec. (c)(1)(C). Pub. L. 109–162 struck out "or" at end.
2002—Subsec. (c)(1)(E). Pub. L. 107–273, §4005(a)(2), realigned margins.
Subsec. (e). Pub. L. 107–296 inserted ", statutory authorization" after "subpoena".
Subsec. (g). Pub. L. 107–273, §11010, added subsec. (g).
2001—Pub. L. 107–56, §212(b)(1)(A), substituted "Required disclosure of customer communications or records" for "Requirements for governmental access" in section catchline.
Subsec. (a). Pub. L. 107–56, §§209(2)(A), (B), 220(a)(1), substituted "Contents of Wire or Electronic" for "Contents of Electronic" in heading and "contents of a wire or electronic" for "contents of an electronic" in two places and "using the procedures described in the Federal Rules of Criminal Procedure by a court with jurisdiction over the offense under investigation" for "under the Federal Rules of Criminal Procedure" in text.
Subsec. (b). Pub. L. 107–56, §209(2)(A), substituted "Contents of Wire or Electronic" for "Contents of Electronic" in heading.
Subsec. (b)(1). Pub. L. 107–56, §§209(2)(C), 220(a)(1), substituted "any wire or electronic communication" for "any electronic communication" in introductory provisions and "using the procedures described in the Federal Rules of Criminal Procedure by a court with jurisdiction over the offense under investigation" for "under the Federal Rules of Criminal Procedure" in subpar. (A).
Subsec. (b)(2). Pub. L. 107–56, §209(2)(C), substituted "any wire or electronic communication"

for "any electronic communication" in introductory provisions.

Subsec. (c)(1). Pub. L. 107–56, §§212(b)(1)(C), 220(a)(1), designated subpar. (A) and introductory provisions of subpar. (B) as par. (1), substituted "A governmental entity may require a provider of electronic communication service or remote computing service to" for "(A) Except as provided in subparagraph (B), a provider of electronic communication service or remote computing service may" and a closing parenthesis for provisions which began with "covered by subsection (a) or (b) of this section) to any person other than a governmental entity." in former subpar. (A) and ended with "(B) A provider of electronic communication service or remote computing service shall disclose a record or other information pertaining to a subscriber to or customer of such service (not including the contents of communications covered by subsection (a) or (b) of this section) to a governmental entity", redesignated clauses (i) to (iv) of former subpar. (B) as subpars. (A) to (D), respectively, substituted "using the procedures described in the Federal Rules of Criminal Procedure by a court with jurisdiction over the offense under investigation" for "under the Federal Rules of Criminal Procedure" in subpar. (A) and "; or" for period at end of subpar. (D), added subpar. (E), and redesignated former subpar. (C) as par. (2).

Subsec. (c)(2). Pub. L. 107–56, §210, amended par. (2), as redesignated by section 212 of Pub. L. 107–56, by substituting "entity the—" for "entity the name, address, local and long distance telephone toll billing records, telephone number or other subscriber number or identity, and length of service of a subscriber" in introductory provisions, inserting subpars. (A) to (F), striking out "and the types of services the subscriber or customer utilized," before "when the governmental entity uses an administrative subpoena", inserting "of a subscriber" at beginning of concluding provisions and designating "to or customer of such service when the governmental entity uses an administrative subpoena authorized by a Federal or State statute or a Federal or State grand jury or trial subpoena or any means available under paragraph (1)." as remainder of concluding provisions.

Pub. L. 107–56, §212(b)(1)(C)(iii), (D), redesignated subpar. (C) of par. (1) as par. (2) and temporarily substituted "paragraph (1)" for "subparagraph (B)".

Pub. L. 107–56, §212(b)(1)(B), redesignated par. (2) as (3).

Subsec. (c)(3). Pub. L. 107–56, §212(b)(1)(B), redesignated par. (2) as (3).

Subsec. (d). Pub. L. 107–56, §220(b), struck out "described in section 3127(2)(A)" after "court of competent jurisdiction".

1998—Subsec. (c)(1)(B)(iv). Pub. L. 105–184 added cl. (iv).

1996—Subsec. (c)(1)(C). Pub. L. 104–293 inserted "local and long distance" after "address,".

Subsec. (d). Pub. L. 104–294 substituted "in section 3127(2)(A)" for "in section 3126(2)(A)".

Subsec. (f). Pub. L. 104–132 added subsec. (f).

1994—Subsec. (c)(1)(B). Pub. L. 103–414, §207(a)(1)(A), redesignated cls. (ii) to (iv) as (i) to (iii), respectively, and struck out former cl. (i) which read as follows: "uses an administrative subpoena authorized by a Federal or State statute, or a Federal or State grand jury or trial subpoena;".

Subsec. (c)(1)(C). Pub. L. 103–414, §207(a)(1)(B), added subpar. (C).

Subsec. (d). Pub. L. 103–414, §207(a)(2), amended first sentence generally. Prior to amendment, first sentence read as follows: "A court order for disclosure under subsection (b) or (c) of this section may be issued by any court that is a court of competent jurisdiction set forth in section 3127(2)(A) of this title and shall issue only if the governmental entity shows that there is reason to believe the contents of a wire or electronic communication, or the records or other information sought, are relevant to a legitimate law enforcement inquiry."

Pub. L. 103–322 substituted "section 3127(2)(A)" for "section 3126(2)(A)".

1988—Subsecs. (b)(1)(B)(i), (c)(1)(B)(i). Pub. L. 100–690, §7038, inserted "or trial" after "grand jury".

Subsec. (d). Pub. L. 100–690, §7039, inserted "may be issued by any court that is a court of competent jurisdiction set forth in section 3126(2)(A) of this title and" before "shall issue".

Effective Date of 2016 Amendment

Amendment by Pub. L. 114–328 effective on the date designated by the President, not later than the first day of the first calendar month beginning two years after Dec. 23, 2016, with implementing regulations prescribed by the President not later than one year after Dec. 23, 2016, and with provisions relating to applicability to various situations, see section 5542 of Pub. L. 114–328, set out as a note under section 801 of Title 10, Armed Forces.

Effective Date of 2002 Amendment

Amendment by Pub. L. 107–296 effective 60 days after Nov. 25, 2002, see section 4 of Pub. L. 107–296, set out as an Effective Date note under section 101 of Title 6, Domestic Security.

Effective Date

Section effective 90 days after Oct. 21, 1986, and, in the case of conduct pursuant to a court order or extension, applicable only with respect to court orders or extensions made after such effective date, see section 202 of Pub. L. 99–508, set out as a note under section 2701 of this title.

§2704. Backup preservation

(a) Backup Preservation.—(1) A governmental entity acting under section 2703(b)(2) may include in its subpoena or court order a requirement that the service provider to whom the request is directed create a backup copy of the contents of the electronic communications sought in order to preserve those communications. Without notifying the subscriber or customer of such subpoena or court order, such service provider shall create such backup copy as soon as practicable consistent with its regular business practices and shall confirm to the governmental entity that such backup copy has been made. Such backup copy shall be created within two business days after receipt by the service provider of the subpoena or court order.

(2) Notice to the subscriber or customer shall be made by the governmental entity within three days after receipt of such confirmation, unless such notice is delayed pursuant to section 2705(a).

(3) The service provider shall not destroy such backup copy until the later of—

(A) the delivery of the information; or

(B) the resolution of any proceedings (including appeals of any proceeding) concerning the government's subpoena or court order.

(4) The service provider shall release such backup copy to the requesting governmental entity no sooner than fourteen days after the governmental entity's notice to the subscriber or customer if such service provider—

(A) has not received notice from the subscriber or customer that the subscriber or customer has challenged the governmental entity's request; and

(B) has not initiated proceedings to challenge the request of the governmental entity.

(5) A governmental entity may seek to require the creation of a backup copy under subsection (a)(1) of this section if in its sole discretion such entity determines that there is reason to believe that notification under section 2703 of this title of the existence of the subpoena or court order may result in destruction of or tampering with evidence. This determination is not subject to challenge by the subscriber or customer or service provider.

(b) Customer Challenges.—(1) Within fourteen days after notice by the governmental entity to the subscriber or customer under subsection (a)(2) of this section, such subscriber or customer may file a motion to quash such subpoena or vacate such court order, with copies served upon the governmental entity and with written notice of such challenge to the service provider. A motion to vacate a court order shall be filed in the court which issued such order. A motion to quash a subpoena shall be filed in the appropriate United States district court or State court. Such motion or application shall contain an affidavit or sworn statement—

(A) stating that the applicant is a customer or subscriber to the service from which the contents of electronic communications maintained for him have been sought; and

(B) stating the applicant's reasons for believing that the records sought are not relevant to a legitimate law enforcement inquiry or that there has not been substantial compliance with the provisions of this chapter in some other respect.

(2) Service shall be made under this section upon a governmental entity by delivering or mailing by registered or certified mail a copy of the papers to the person, office, or department specified in the notice which the customer has received pursuant to this chapter. For the purposes of this section, the term "delivery" has the meaning given that term in the Federal Rules of Civil Procedure.

(3) If the court finds that the customer has complied with paragraphs (1) and (2) of this subsection, the court shall order the governmental entity to file a sworn response, which may be filed in camera if the governmental entity includes in its response the reasons which make in camera review appropriate. If the court is unable to determine the motion or application on the basis of the parties' initial allegations and response, the court may conduct such additional proceedings as it deems appropriate. All such proceedings shall be completed and the motion or application decided as soon as practicable after the filing of the governmental entity's response.

(4) If the court finds that the applicant is not the subscriber or customer for whom the communications sought by the governmental entity are maintained, or that there is a reason to believe that the law enforcement inquiry is legitimate and that the communications sought are relevant to that inquiry, it shall deny the motion or application and order such process enforced. If the court finds that the applicant is the subscriber or customer for whom the communications sought by the governmental entity are maintained, and that there is not a reason to believe that the communications sought are relevant to a legitimate law enforcement inquiry, or that there has not been substantial compliance with the provisions of this chapter, it shall order the process quashed.

(5) A court order denying a motion or application under this section shall not be deemed a final order and no interlocutory appeal may be taken therefrom by the customer.

(Added Pub. L. 99–508, title II, §201[(a)], Oct. 21, 1986, 100 Stat. 1863.)

References in Text

The Federal Rules of Civil Procedure, referred to in subsec. (b)(2), are set out in the Appendix to Title 28, Judiciary and Judicial Procedure.

Effective Date

Section effective 90 days after Oct. 21, 1986, and, in the case of conduct pursuant to a court order or extension, applicable only with respect to court orders or extensions made after such effective date, see section 202 of Pub. L. 99–508, set out as a note under section 2701 of this title.

§2705. Delayed notice

(a) Delay of Notification.—(1) A governmental entity acting under section 2703(b) of this title may—

(A) where a court order is sought, include in the application a request, which the court shall grant, for an order delaying the notification required under section 2703(b) of this title for a period not to exceed ninety days, if the court determines that there is reason to believe that notification of the existence of the court order may have an adverse result described in paragraph (2) of this subsection; or

(B) where an administrative subpoena authorized by a Federal or State statute or a Federal or State grand jury subpoena is obtained, delay the notification required under section 2703(b) of this title for a period not to exceed ninety days upon the execution of a written certification of a supervisory official that there is reason to believe that notification of the existence of the subpoena may have an adverse result described in paragraph (2) of this subsection.

(2) An adverse result for the purposes of paragraph (1) of this subsection is—

(A) endangering the life or physical safety of an individual;

(B) flight from prosecution;

(C) destruction of or tampering with evidence;

(D) intimidation of potential witnesses; or

(E) otherwise seriously jeopardizing an investigation or unduly delaying a trial.

(3) The governmental entity shall maintain a true copy of certification under paragraph (1)(B).

(4) Extensions of the delay of notification provided in section 2703 of up to ninety days each may be granted by the court upon application, or by certification by a governmental entity, but only in accordance with subsection (b) of this section.

(5) Upon expiration of the period of delay of notification under paragraph (1) or (4) of this subsection, the governmental entity shall serve upon, or deliver by registered or first-class mail to, the customer or subscriber a copy of the process or request together with notice that—

(A) states with reasonable specificity the nature of the law enforcement inquiry; and

(B) informs such customer or subscriber—

(i) that information maintained for such customer or subscriber by the service provider named in such process or request was supplied to or requested by that governmental authority and the date on which the supplying or request took place;

(ii) that notification of such customer or subscriber was delayed;

(iii) what governmental entity or court made the certification or determination pursuant to which that delay was made; and

(iv) which provision of this chapter allowed such delay.

(6) As used in this subsection, the term "supervisory official" means the investigative agent in charge or assistant investigative agent in charge or an equivalent of an investigating agency's headquarters or regional office, or the chief prosecuting attorney or the first assistant prosecuting attorney or an equivalent of a prosecuting attorney's headquarters or regional office.

(b) Preclusion of Notice to Subject of Governmental Access.—A governmental entity acting under section 2703, when it is not required to notify the subscriber or customer under section 2703(b)(1), or to the extent that it may delay such notice pursuant to subsection (a) of this section, may apply to a court for an order commanding a provider of electronic communications service or remote computing service to whom a warrant, subpoena, or court order is directed, for such period as the court deems appropriate, not to notify any other person of the existence of the warrant, subpoena, or court order. The court shall enter such an order if it determines that there is reason to believe that notification of the existence of the warrant, subpoena, or court order will result in—

(1) endangering the life or physical safety of an individual;

(2) flight from prosecution;

(3) destruction of or tampering with evidence;

(4) intimidation of potential witnesses; or

(5) otherwise seriously jeopardizing an investigation or unduly delaying a trial.

(Added Pub. L. 99–508, title II, §201[(a)], Oct. 21, 1986, 100 Stat. 1864.)

Effective Date

Section effective 90 days after Oct. 21, 1986, and, in the case of conduct pursuant to a court order or extension, applicable only with respect to court orders or extensions made after such effective date, see section 202 of Pub. L. 99–508, set out as a note under section 2701 of this title.

§2706. Cost reimbursement

(a) Payment.—Except as otherwise provided in subsection (c), a governmental entity obtaining the contents of communications, records, or other information under section 2702, 2703, or 2704 of this title shall pay to the person or entity assembling or providing such information a fee for reimbursement for such costs as are reasonably necessary and which have been directly incurred in searching for, assembling, reproducing, or otherwise providing such information. Such reimbursable costs shall include any costs due to necessary disruption of normal operations of any electronic communication service or remote computing service in which such information may be stored.

(b) Amount.—The amount of the fee provided by subsection (a) shall be as mutually agreed by the governmental entity and the person or entity providing the information, or, in the absence of agreement, shall be as determined by the court which issued the order for production of such information (or the court before which a criminal prosecution relating to such information would be brought, if no court order was issued for production of the information).

(c) Exception.—The requirement of subsection (a) of this section does not apply with respect to records or other information maintained by a communications common carrier that relate to telephone toll records and telephone listings obtained under section 2703 of this title. The court may, however, order a payment as described in subsection (a) if the court determines the information required is unusually voluminous in nature or otherwise caused an undue burden on the provider.

(Added Pub. L. 99–508, title II, §201[(a)], Oct. 21, 1986, 100 Stat. 1866; amended Pub. L. 100–690, title VII, §7061, Nov. 18, 1988, 102 Stat. 4404.)

Amendments

1988—Subsec. (c). Pub. L. 100–690 inserted heading.

Effective Date

Section effective 90 days after Oct. 21, 1986, and, in the case of conduct pursuant to a court order or extension, applicable only with respect to court orders or extensions made after such effective date, see section 202 of Pub. L. 99–508, set out as a note under section 2701 of this title.

§2707. Civil action

(a) Cause of Action.—Except as provided in section 2703(e), any provider of electronic communication service, subscriber, or other person aggrieved by any violation of this chapter in which the conduct constituting the violation is engaged in with a knowing or intentional state of mind may, in a civil action, recover from the person or entity, other than the United States, which engaged in that violation such relief as may be appropriate.

(b) Relief.—In a civil action under this section, appropriate relief includes—

(1) such preliminary and other equitable or declaratory relief as may be appropriate;

(2) damages under subsection (c); and

(3) a reasonable attorney's fee and other litigation costs reasonably incurred.

(c) Damages.—The court may assess as damages in a civil action under this section the sum of the actual damages suffered by the plaintiff and any profits made by the violator as a result of the violation, but in no case shall a person entitled to recover receive less than the sum of $1,000. If the violation is willful or intentional, the court may assess punitive damages. In the case of a successful action to enforce liability under this section, the court may assess the costs of the action, together with reasonable attorney fees determined by the court.

(d) Administrative Discipline.—If a court or appropriate department or agency determines that the United States or any of its departments or agencies has violated any provision of this chapter, and the court or appropriate department or agency finds that the circumstances surrounding the violation raise serious questions about whether or not an officer or employee of the United States acted willfully or intentionally with respect to the violation, the department or agency shall, upon receipt of a true and correct copy of the decision and findings of the court or appropriate department or agency promptly initiate a proceeding to determine whether disciplinary action against the officer or employee is warranted. If the head of the department or agency involved determines that disciplinary action is not warranted, he or she shall notify the Inspector General with jurisdiction over the department or agency concerned and shall provide the Inspector General with the reasons for such determination.

(e) Defense.—A good faith reliance on—

(1) a court warrant or order, a grand jury subpoena, a legislative authorization, or a statutory authorization (including a request of a governmental entity under section 2703(f) of this title);

(2) a request of an investigative or law enforcement officer under section 2518(7) of this title; or

(3) a good faith determination that section 2511(3) of this title permitted the conduct complained of;

is a complete defense to any civil or criminal action brought under this chapter or any other law.

(f) Limitation.—A civil action under this section may not be commenced later than two years after the date upon which the claimant first discovered or had a reasonable opportunity to discover the violation.

(g) Improper Disclosure.—Any willful disclosure of a "record", as that term is defined in section 552a(a) of title 5, United States Code, obtained by an investigative or law enforcement officer, or a governmental entity, pursuant to section 2703 of this title, or from a device installed pursuant to section 3123 or 3125 of this title, that is not a disclosure made in the proper performance of the official functions of the officer or governmental entity making the disclosure, is a violation of this chapter. This provision shall not apply to information previously lawfully disclosed (prior to the commencement of any civil or administrative proceeding under this chapter) to the public by a Federal, State, or local governmental entity or by the plaintiff in a civil action under this chapter.

(Added Pub. L. 99–508, title II, §201[(a)], Oct. 21, 1986, 100 Stat. 1866; amended Pub. L. 104–293, title VI, §601(c), Oct. 11, 1996, 110 Stat. 3469; Pub. L. 107–56, title II, §§223(b), title VIII, §815, Oct. 26, 2001, 115 Stat. 293, 384; Pub. L. 107–273, div. B, title IV, §4005(f)(2), Nov. 2, 2002, 116 Stat. 1813.)

Amendments

2002—Subsec. (e)(1). Pub. L. 107–273 made technical correction to directory language of Pub. L. 107–56, §815. See 2001 Amendment note below.

2001—Subsec. (a). Pub. L. 107–56, §223(b)(1), inserted ", other than the United States," after "person or entity".

Subsec. (d). Pub. L. 107–56, §223(b)(2), added subsec. (d) and struck out heading and text of former subsec. (d). Text read as follows: "If a court determines that any agency or department of the United States has violated this chapter and the court finds that the circumstances surrounding the violation raise the question whether or not an officer or employee of the agency or department acted willfully or intentionally with respect to the violation, the agency or department concerned shall promptly initiate a proceeding to determine whether or not disciplinary action is warranted against the officer or employee."

Subsec. (e)(1). Pub. L. 107–56, §815, as amended by Pub. L. 107–273, inserted "(including a request of a governmental entity under section 2703(f) of this title)" after "or a statutory authorization".

Subsec. (g). Pub. L. 107–56, §223(b)(3), added subsec. (g).

1996—Subsec. (a). Pub. L. 104–293, §601(c)(1), substituted "other person" for "customer".

Subsec. (c). Pub. L. 104–293, §601(c)(2), inserted at end "If the violation is willful or intentional, the court may assess punitive damages. In the case of a successful action to enforce liability under this section, the court may assess the costs of the action, together with reasonable attorney fees determined by the court."

Subsecs. (d) to (f). Pub. L. 104–293, §601(c)(3), (4), added subsec. (d) and redesignated former subsecs. (d) and (e) as (e) and (f), respectively.

Effective Date of 2002 Amendment

Pub. L. 107–273, div. B, title IV, §4005(f)(2), Nov. 2, 2002, 116 Stat. 1813, provided that the amendment made by section 4005(f)(2) is effective Oct. 26, 2001.

Effective Date

Section effective 90 days after Oct. 21, 1986, and, in the case of conduct pursuant to a court order or extension, applicable only with respect to court orders or extensions made after such effective date, see section 202 of Pub. L. 99–508, set out as a note under section 2701 of this title.

§2708. Exclusivity of remedies

The remedies and sanctions described in this chapter are the only judicial remedies and sanctions for nonconstitutional violations of this chapter.

(Added Pub. L. 99–508, title II, §201[(a)], Oct. 21, 1986, 100 Stat. 1867.)

Effective Date

Section effective 90 days after Oct. 21, 1986, and, in the case of conduct pursuant to a court order or extension, applicable only with respect to court orders or extensions made after such effective date, see section 202 of Pub. L. 99–508, set out as a note under section 2701 of this title.

§2709. Counterintelligence access to telephone toll and transactional records

(a) Duty to Provide.—A wire or electronic communication service provider shall comply with a request for subscriber information and toll billing records information, or electronic communication transactional records in its custody or possession made by the Director of the Federal Bureau of Investigation under subsection (b) of this section.

(b) Required Certification.—The Director of the Federal Bureau of Investigation, or his designee in a position not lower than Deputy Assistant Director at Bureau headquarters or a Special Agent in Charge in a Bureau field office designated by the Director, may, using a term that specifically identifies a person, entity, telephone number, or account as the basis for a request—

(1) request the name, address, length of service, and local and long distance toll billing records of a person or entity if the Director (or his designee) certifies in writing to the wire or electronic communication service provider to which the request is made that the name, address, length of service, and toll billing records sought are relevant to an authorized investigation to protect against international terrorism or clandestine intelligence activities, provided that such an investigation of a United States person is not conducted solely on the basis of activities protected by the first amendment to the Constitution of the United States; and

(2) request the name, address, and length of service of a person or entity if the Director (or his designee) certifies in writing to the wire or electronic communication service provider to which the request is made that the information sought is relevant to an authorized investigation to protect against international terrorism or clandestine intelligence activities, provided that such an investigation of a United States person is not conducted solely upon the basis of activities protected by the first amendment to the Constitution of the United States.

(c) Prohibition of Certain Disclosure.—

(1) Prohibition.—

(A) In general.—If a certification is issued under subparagraph (B) and notice of the right to judicial review under subsection (d) is provided, no wire or electronic communication service provider that receives a request under subsection (b), or officer, employee, or agent thereof, shall disclose to any person that the Federal Bureau of Investigation has sought or obtained access to information or records under this section.

(B) Certification.—The requirements of subparagraph (A) shall apply if the Director of the Federal Bureau of Investigation, or a designee of the Director whose rank shall be no lower than Deputy Assistant Director at Bureau headquarters or a Special Agent in Charge of a Bureau field office, certifies that the absence of a prohibition of disclosure under this subsection may result in—

(i) a danger to the national security of the United States;

(ii) interference with a criminal, counterterrorism, or counterintelligence investigation;

(iii) interference with diplomatic relations; or

(iv) danger to the life or physical safety of any person.

(2) Exception.—

(A) In general.—A wire or electronic communication service provider that receives a request under subsection (b), or officer, employee, or agent thereof, may disclose information otherwise subject to any applicable nondisclosure requirement to—

(i) those persons to whom disclosure is necessary in order to comply with the request;

(ii) an attorney in order to obtain legal advice or assistance regarding the request; or

(iii) other persons as permitted by the Director of the Federal Bureau of Investigation or the designee of the Director.

(B) Application.—A person to whom disclosure is made under subparagraph (A) shall be subject to the nondisclosure requirements applicable to a person to whom a request is issued under subsection (b) in the same manner as the person to whom the request is issued.

(C) Notice.—Any recipient that discloses to a person described in subparagraph (A) information otherwise subject to a nondisclosure requirement shall notify the person of the applicable nondisclosure requirement.

(D) Identification of disclosure recipients.—At the request of the Director of the Federal Bureau of Investigation or the designee of the Director, any person making or intending to make a disclosure under clause (i) or (iii) of subparagraph (A) shall identify to the Director or such designee the person to whom such disclosure will be made or to whom such disclosure was made prior to the request.

(d) Judicial Review.—

(1) In general.—A request under subsection (b) or a nondisclosure requirement imposed in connection with such request under subsection (c) shall be subject to judicial review under section 3511.

(2) Notice.—A request under subsection (b) shall include notice of the availability of judicial review described in paragraph (1).

(e) Dissemination by Bureau.—The Federal Bureau of Investigation may disseminate information and records obtained under this section only as provided in guidelines approved by the Attorney General for foreign intelligence collection and foreign counterintelligence investigations conducted by the Federal Bureau of Investigation, and, with respect to dissemination to an agency of the United States, only if such information is clearly relevant to the authorized responsibilities of such agency.

(f) Requirement That Certain Congressional Bodies Be Informed.—On a semiannual basis the Director of the Federal Bureau of Investigation shall fully inform the Permanent Select Committee on Intelligence of the House of Representatives and the Select Committee on Intelligence of the Senate, and the Committee on the Judiciary of the House of Representatives and the Committee on the Judiciary of the Senate, concerning all requests made under subsection (b) of this section.

(g) Libraries.—A library (as that term is defined in section 213(1) of the Library Services and Technology Act (20 U.S.C. 9122(1)), the services of which include access to the Internet, books, journals, magazines, newspapers, or other similar forms of communication in print or digitally by patrons for their use, review, examination, or circulation, is not a wire or electronic communication service provider for purposes of this section, unless the library is providing the services defined in section 2510(15) ("electronic communication service") of this title.

(Added Pub. L. 99–508, title II, §201[(a)], Oct. 21, 1986, 100 Stat. 1867; amended Pub. L. 103–142, Nov. 17, 1993, 107 Stat. 1491; Pub. L. 104–293, title VI, §601(a), Oct. 11, 1996, 110 Stat. 3469; Pub. L. 107–56, title V, §505(a), Oct. 26, 2001, 115 Stat. 365; Pub. L. 109–177, title I, §116(a), Mar. 9, 2006, 120 Stat. 213; Pub. L. 109–178, §§4(b), 5, Mar. 9, 2006, 120 Stat. 280, 281; Pub. L. 114–23, title V, §§501(a), 502(a), 503(a), June 2, 2015, 129 Stat. 282, 283, 289.)

Amendments

2015—Subsec. (b). Pub. L. 114–23, §501(a), substituted "may, using a term that specifically identifies a person, entity, telephone number, or account as the basis for a request" for "may" in introductory provisions.

Subsec. (c). Pub. L. 114–23, §502(a), added subsec. (c) and struck out former subsec. (c) which related to prohibition of certain disclosure.

Subsecs. (d) to (g). Pub. L. 114–23, §503(a), added subsec. (d) and redesignated former subsecs. (d) to (f) as (e) to (g), respectively.

2006—Subsec. (c). Pub. L. 109–177 reenacted heading without change and amended text generally. Prior to amendment, text read as follows: "No wire or electronic communication service provider, or officer, employee, or agent thereof, shall disclose to any person that the Federal Bureau of Investigation has sought or obtained access to information or records under this section."

Subsec. (c)(4). Pub. L. 109–178, §4(b), amended par. (4) generally. Prior to amendment, par. (4) read as follows: "At the request of the Director of the Federal Bureau of Investigation or the designee of the Director, any person making or intending to make a disclosure under this section shall identify to the Director or such designee the person to whom such disclosure will be made or to whom such disclosure was made prior to the request, but in no circumstance shall a person be required to inform the Director or such designee that the person intends to consult an attorney to obtain legal advice or legal assistance."

Subsec. (f). Pub. L. 109–178, §5, added subsec. (f).

2001—Subsec. (b). Pub. L. 107–56, §505(a)(1), inserted "at Bureau headquarters or a Special Agent in Charge in a Bureau field office designated by the Director" after "Deputy Assistant Director" in introductory provisions.

Subsec. (b)(1). Pub. L. 107–56, §505(a)(2), struck out "in a position not lower than Deputy Assistant Director" after "(or his designee" and substituted "made that the name, address, length of service, and toll billing records sought are relevant to an authorized investigation to protect against international terrorism or clandestine intelligence activities, provided that such an investigation of a United States person is not conducted solely on the basis of activities protected by the first amendment to the Constitution of the United States; and" for "made that—

"(A) the name, address, length of service, and toll billing records sought are relevant to an authorized foreign counterintelligence investigation; and

"(B) there are specific and articulable facts giving reason to believe that the person or entity to whom the information sought pertains is a foreign power or an agent of a foreign power as defined in section 101 of the Foreign Intelligence Surveillance Act of 1978 (50 U.S.C. 1801); and".

Subsec. (b)(2). Pub. L. 107–56, §505(a)(3), struck out "in a position not lower than Deputy Assistant Director" after "(or his designee" and substituted "made that the information sought is relevant to an authorized investigation to protect against international terrorism or clandestine intelligence activities, provided that such an investigation of a United States person is not conducted solely upon the basis of activities protected by the first amendment to the Constitution of the United States." for "made that—

"(A) the information sought is relevant to an authorized foreign counterintelligence investigation; and

"(B) there are specific and articulable facts giving reason to believe that communication facilities registered in the name of the person or entity have been used, through the services of such provider, in communication with—

"(i) an individual who is engaging or has engaged in international terrorism as defined in section 101(c) of the Foreign Intelligence Surveillance Act or clandestine intelligence activities that involve or may involve a violation of the criminal statutes of the United States; or

"(ii) a foreign power or an agent of a foreign power under circumstances giving reason to believe that the communication concerned international terrorism as defined in section 101(c) of the Foreign Intelligence Surveillance Act or clandestine intelligence activities that involve or may involve a violation of the criminal statutes of the United States."

1996—Subsec. (b)(1). Pub. L. 104–293 inserted "local and long distance" before "toll billing records".

1993—Subsec. (b). Pub. L. 103–142, §1, amended subsec. (b) generally. Prior to amendment, subsec. (b) read as follows: "Required Certification.—The Director of the Federal Bureau of Investigation (or an individual within the Federal Bureau of Investigation designated for this purpose by the Director) may request any such information and records if the Director (or the Director's designee) certifies in writing to the wire or electronic communication service provider to which the request is made that—

"(1) the information sought is relevant to an authorized foreign counterintelligence investigation;

and

"(2) there are specific and articulable facts giving reason to believe that the person or entity to whom the information sought pertains is a foreign power or an agent of a foreign power as defined in section 101 of the Foreign Intelligence Surveillance Act of 1978 (50 U.S.C. 1801)."

Subsec. (e). Pub. L. 103–142, §2, inserted ", and the Committee on the Judiciary of the House of Representatives and the Committee on the Judiciary of the Senate," after "Senate".

Effective Date

Section effective 90 days after Oct. 21, 1986, and, in the case of conduct pursuant to a court order or extension, applicable only with respect to court orders or extensions made after such effective date, see section 202 of Pub. L. 99–508, set out as a note under section 2701 of this title.

§2710. Wrongful disclosure of video tape rental or sale records

(a) Definitions.—For purposes of this section—

(1) the term "consumer" means any renter, purchaser, or subscriber of goods or services from a video tape service provider;

(2) the term "ordinary course of business" means only debt collection activities, order fulfillment, request processing, and the transfer of ownership;

(3) the term "personally identifiable information" includes information which identifies a person as having requested or obtained specific video materials or services from a video tape service provider; and

(4) the term "video tape service provider" means any person, engaged in the business, in or affecting interstate or foreign commerce, of rental, sale, or delivery of prerecorded video cassette tapes or similar audio visual materials, or any person or other entity to whom a disclosure is made under subparagraph (D) or (E) of subsection (b)(2), but only with respect to the information contained in the disclosure.

(b) Video Tape Rental and Sale Records.—(1) A video tape service provider who knowingly discloses, to any person, personally identifiable information concerning any consumer of such provider shall be liable to the aggrieved person for the relief provided in subsection (d).

(2) A video tape service provider may disclose personally identifiable information concerning any consumer—

(A) to the consumer;

(B) to any person with the informed, written consent (including through an electronic means using the Internet) of the consumer that—

(i) is in a form distinct and separate from any form setting forth other legal or financial obligations of the consumer;

(ii) at the election of the consumer—

(I) is given at the time the disclosure is sought; or

(II) is given in advance for a set period of time, not to exceed 2 years or until consent is withdrawn by the consumer, whichever is sooner; and

(iii) the video tape service provider has provided an opportunity, in a clear and conspicuous manner, for the consumer to withdraw on a case-by-case basis or to withdraw from ongoing disclosures, at the consumer's election;

(C) to a law enforcement agency pursuant to a warrant issued under the Federal Rules of Criminal Procedure, an equivalent State warrant, a grand jury subpoena, or a court order;

(D) to any person if the disclosure is solely of the names and addresses of consumers and if—

(i) the video tape service provider has provided the consumer with the opportunity, in a clear and conspicuous manner, to prohibit such disclosure; and

(ii) the disclosure does not identify the title, description, or subject matter of any video tapes or other audio visual material; however, the subject matter of such materials may be disclosed if the disclosure is for the exclusive use of marketing goods and services directly to the consumer;

(E) to any person if the disclosure is incident to the ordinary course of business of the video tape service provider; or

(F) pursuant to a court order, in a civil proceeding upon a showing of compelling need for the information that cannot be accommodated by any other means, if—

(i) the consumer is given reasonable notice, by the person seeking the disclosure, of the court proceeding relevant to the issuance of the court order; and

(ii) the consumer is afforded the opportunity to appear and contest the claim of the person seeking the disclosure.

If an order is granted pursuant to subparagraph (C) or (F), the court shall impose appropriate safeguards against unauthorized disclosure.

(3) Court orders authorizing disclosure under subparagraph (C) shall issue only with prior notice to the consumer and only if the law enforcement agency shows that there is probable cause to believe that the records or other information sought are relevant to a legitimate law enforcement inquiry. In the case of a State government authority, such a court order shall not issue if prohibited by the law of such State. A court issuing an order pursuant to this section, on a motion made promptly by the video tape service provider, may quash or modify such order if the information or records requested are unreasonably voluminous in nature or if compliance with such order otherwise would cause an unreasonable burden on such provider.

(c) Civil Action.—(1) Any person aggrieved by any act of a person in violation of this section may bring a civil action in a United States district court.

(2) The court may award—

(A) actual damages but not less than liquidated damages in an amount of $2,500;

(B) punitive damages;

(C) reasonable attorneys' fees and other litigation costs reasonably incurred; and

(D) such other preliminary and equitable relief as the court determines to be appropriate.

(3) No action may be brought under this subsection unless such action is begun within 2 years from the date of the act complained of or the date of discovery.

(4) No liability shall result from lawful disclosure permitted by this section.

(d) Personally Identifiable Information.—Personally identifiable information obtained in any manner other than as provided in this section shall not be received in evidence in any trial, hearing, arbitration, or other proceeding in or before any court, grand jury, department, officer, agency, regulatory body, legislative committee, or other authority of the United States, a State, or a political subdivision of a State.

(e) Destruction of Old Records.—A person subject to this section shall destroy personally identifiable information as soon as practicable, but no later than one year from the date the information is no longer necessary for the purpose for which it was collected and there are no pending requests or orders for access to such information under subsection (b)(2) or (c)(2) or pursuant to a court order.

(f) Preemption.—The provisions of this section preempt only the provisions of State or local law that require disclosure prohibited by this section.

(Added Pub. L. 100–618, §2(a)(2), Nov. 5, 1988, 102 Stat. 3195; amended Pub. L. 112–258, §2, Jan. 10, 2013, 126 Stat. 2414.)

References in Text

The Federal Rules of Criminal Procedure, referred to in subsec. (b)(2)(C), are set out in the Appendix to this title.

Prior Provisions

A prior section 2710 was renumbered section 2711 of this title.

Amendments

2013—Subsec. (b)(2)(B). Pub. L. 112–258 added subpar. (B) and struck out former subpar. (B) which read as follows: "to any person with the informed, written consent of the consumer given at the time the disclosure is sought;".

§2711. Definitions for chapter

As used in this chapter—

(1) the terms defined in section 2510 of this title have, respectively, the definitions given such terms in that section;

(2) the term "remote computing service" means the provision to the public of computer storage or processing services by means of an electronic communications system;

(3) the term "court of competent jurisdiction" includes—

(A) any district court of the United States (including a magistrate judge of such a court) or any United States court of appeals that—

(i) has jurisdiction over the offense being investigated;

(ii) is in or for a district in which the provider of a wire or electronic communication service is located or in which the wire or electronic communications, records, or other information are stored; or

(iii) is acting on a request for foreign assistance pursuant to section 3512 of this title; or

(B) a court of general criminal jurisdiction of a State authorized by the law of that State to issue search warrants; and

(4) the term "governmental entity" means a department or agency of the United States or any State or political subdivision thereof.

(Added Pub. L. 99–508, title II, §201[(a)], Oct. 21, 1986, 100 Stat. 1868, §2710; renumbered §2711, Pub. L. 100–618, §2(a)(1), Nov. 5, 1988, 102 Stat. 3195; amended Pub. L. 107–56, title II, §220(a)(2), Oct. 26, 2001, 115 Stat. 292; Pub. L. 109–177, title I, §107(b)(2), Mar. 9, 2006, 120 Stat. 202; Pub. L. 111–79, §2(2), Oct. 19, 2009, 123 Stat. 2086; Pub. L. 114–328, div. E, title LVII, §5228(b)(2), Dec. 23, 2016, 130 Stat. 2913.)

Amendment of Paragraph (3)

Pub. L. 114–328, Dec. 23, 2016, div. E, title LVII, §5228(b)(2), title LXIII, §5542, Dec. 23, 2016, 130 Stat. 2913, 2967, provided that, effective on the date designated by the President, not later than the first day of the first calendar month beginning two years after Dec. 23, 2016, with implementing regulations prescribed by the President not later than one year after Dec. 23, 2016, and with provisions relating to applicability to various situations, paragraph (3) of this section is amended—

(1) in subparagraph (A), by striking "or" at the end;

(2) in subparagraph (B), by striking "and" at the end and inserting "or"; and

(3) by adding at the end the following new subparagraph:

"(C) a court-martial or other proceeding under chapter 47 of title 10 (the Uniform Code of Military Justice) to which a military judge has been detailed; and".

See 2016 Amendment note below.

Amendments

2016—Par. (3)(C). Pub. L. 114–328 added subpar. (C).

2009—Par. (3). Pub. L. 111–79 substituted "includes—" and subpars. (A) and (B) for "has the meaning assigned by section 3127, and includes any Federal court within that definition, without geographic limitation; and".

2006—Par. (4). Pub. L. 109–177 added par. (4).

2001—Par. (3). Pub. L. 107–56 added par. (3).

1988—Pub. L. 100–618 renumbered section 2710 of this title as this section.

Effective Date of 2016 Amendment

Amendment by Pub. L. 114–328 effective on the date designated by the President, not later than the first day of the first calendar month beginning two years after Dec. 23, 2016, with implementing regulations prescribed by the President not later than one year after Dec. 23, 2016, and with provisions relating to applicability to various situations, see section 5542 of Pub. L. 114–328, set out as a note under section 801 of Title 10, Armed Forces.

Effective Date

Section effective 90 days after Oct. 21, 1986, and, in the case of conduct pursuant to a court order or extension, applicable only with respect to court orders or extensions made after such effective date, see section 202 of Pub. L. 99–508, set out as a note under section 2701 of this title.

§2712. Civil actions against the United States

(a) In General.—Any person who is aggrieved by any willful violation of this chapter or of chapter 119 of this title or of sections 106(a), 305(a), or 405(a) of the Foreign Intelligence Surveillance Act of 1978 (50 U.S.C. 1801 et seq.) may commence an action in United States District Court against the United States to recover money damages. In any such action, if a person who is aggrieved successfully establishes such a violation of this chapter or of chapter 119 of this title or of the above specific provisions of title 50, the Court may assess as damages—

(1) actual damages, but not less than $10,000, whichever amount is greater; and

(2) litigation costs, reasonably incurred.

(b) Procedures.—(1) Any action against the United States under this section may be commenced only after a claim is presented to the appropriate department or agency under the procedures of the Federal Tort Claims Act, as set forth in title 28, United States Code.

(2) Any action against the United States under this section shall be forever barred unless it is presented in writing to the appropriate Federal agency within 2 years after such claim accrues or unless action is begun within 6 months after the date of mailing, by certified or registered mail, of notice of final denial of the claim by the agency to which it was presented. The claim shall accrue on the date upon which the claimant first has a reasonable opportunity to discover the violation.

(3) Any action under this section shall be tried to the court without a jury.

(4) Notwithstanding any other provision of law, the procedures set forth in section 106(f), 305(g), or 405(f) of the Foreign Intelligence Surveillance Act of 1978 (50 U.S.C. 1801 et seq.) shall be the exclusive means by which materials governed by those sections may be reviewed.

(5) An amount equal to any award against the United States under this section shall be reimbursed by the department or agency concerned to the fund described in section 1304 of title 31, United States Code, out of any appropriation, fund, or other account (excluding any part of such appropriation, fund, or account that is available for the enforcement of any Federal law) that is available for the operating expenses of the department or agency concerned.

(c) Administrative Discipline.—If a court or appropriate department or agency determines that the United States or any of its departments or agencies has violated any provision of this chapter, and the court or appropriate department or agency finds that the circumstances surrounding the violation raise serious questions about whether or not an officer or employee of the United States acted willfully or intentionally with respect to the violation, the department or agency shall, upon receipt of a true and correct copy of the decision and findings of the court or appropriate department or agency promptly initiate a proceeding to determine whether disciplinary action against the officer or employee is warranted. If the head of the department or agency involved determines that disciplinary action is not warranted, he or she shall notify the Inspector General with jurisdiction over the department or agency concerned and shall provide the Inspector General with the reasons for such determination.

(d) Exclusive Remedy.—Any action against the United States under this subsection shall be the exclusive remedy against the United States for any claims within the purview of this section.

(e) Stay of Proceedings.—(1) Upon the motion of the United States, the court shall stay any action commenced under this section if the court determines that civil discovery will adversely affect the ability of the Government to conduct a related investigation or the prosecution of a related criminal case. Such a stay shall toll the limitations periods of paragraph (2) of subsection (b).

(2) In this subsection, the terms "related criminal case" and "related investigation" mean an actual prosecution or investigation in progress at the time at which the request for the stay or any subsequent motion to lift the stay is made. In determining whether an investigation or a criminal case is related to an action commenced under this section, the court shall consider the degree of similarity between the parties, witnesses, facts, and circumstances involved in the 2 proceedings, without requiring that any one or more factors be identical.

(3) In requesting a stay under paragraph (1), the Government may, in appropriate cases, submit evidence ex parte in order to avoid disclosing any matter that may adversely affect a related investigation or a related criminal case. If the Government makes such an ex parte submission, the plaintiff shall be given an opportunity to make a submission to the court, not ex parte, and the court may, in its discretion, request further information from either party.

(Added Pub. L. 107–56, title II, §223(c)(1), Oct. 26, 2001, 115 Stat. 294.)

References in Text

Sections 106, 305, and 405 of the Foreign Intelligence Surveillance Act of 1978, referred to in subsecs. (a) and (b)(4), are classified to sections 1806, 1825, and 1845, respectively, of Title 50, War and National Defense.

The Federal Tort Claims Act, referred to in subsec. (b)(1), is title IV of act Aug. 2, 1946, ch. 753, 60 Stat. 842, which was classified principally to chapter 20 (§§921, 922, 931–934, 941–946) of former Title 28, Judicial Code and Judiciary. Title IV of act Aug. 2, 1946, was substantially repealed and reenacted as sections 1346(b) and 2671 et seq. of Title 28, Judiciary and Judicial Procedure, by act June 25, 1948, ch. 646, 62 Stat. 992, the first section of which enacted Title 28. The Federal Tort Claims Act is also commonly used to refer to chapter 171 of Title 28, Judiciary and Judicial Procedure. For complete classification of title IV to the Code, see Tables. For distribution of former sections of Title 28 into the revised Title 28, see Table at the beginning of Title 28.

CHAPTER 123 - PROHIBITION ON RELEASE AND USE OF CERTAIN PERSONAL INFORMATION FROM STATE MOTOR VEHICLE RECORDS

Amendments

1996—Pub. L. 104–294, title VI, §604(a)(3), Oct. 11, 1996, 110 Stat. 3506, added analysis.

§2721. Prohibition on release and use of certain personal information from State motor vehicle records

(a) In General.—A State department of motor vehicles, and any officer, employee, or contractor thereof, shall not knowingly disclose or otherwise make available to any person or entity:

(1) personal information, as defined in 18 U.S.C. 2725(3), about any individual obtained by the department in connection with a motor vehicle record, except as provided in subsection (b) of this section; or

(2) highly restricted personal information, as defined in 18 U.S.C. 2725(4), about any individual

254

obtained by the department in connection with a motor vehicle record, without the express consent of the person to whom such information applies, except uses permitted in subsections (b)(1), (b)(4), (b)(6), and (b)(9): Provided, That subsection (a)(2) shall not in any way affect the use of organ donation information on an individual's driver's license or affect the administration of organ donation initiatives in the States.

(b) Permissible Uses.—Personal information referred to in subsection (a) shall be disclosed for use in connection with matters of motor vehicle or driver safety and theft, motor vehicle emissions, motor vehicle product alterations, recalls, or advisories, performance monitoring of motor vehicles and dealers by motor vehicle manufacturers, and removal of non-owner records from the original owner records of motor vehicle manufacturers to carry out the purposes of titles I and IV of the Anti Car Theft Act of 1992, the Automobile Information Disclosure Act (15 U.S.C. 1231 et seq.), the Clean Air Act (42 U.S.C. 7401 et seq.), and chapters 301, 305, and 321–331 of title 49, and, subject to subsection (a)(2), may be disclosed as follows:

(1) For use by any government agency, including any court or law enforcement agency, in carrying out its functions, or any private person or entity acting on behalf of a Federal, State, or local agency in carrying out its functions.

(2) For use in connection with matters of motor vehicle or driver safety and theft; motor vehicle emissions; motor vehicle product alterations, recalls, or advisories; performance monitoring of motor vehicles, motor vehicle parts and dealers; motor vehicle market research activities, including survey research; and removal of non-owner records from the original owner records of motor vehicle manufacturers.

(3) For use in the normal course of business by a legitimate business or its agents, employees, or contractors, but only—

(A) to verify the accuracy of personal information submitted by the individual to the business or its agents, employees, or contractors; and

(B) if such information as so submitted is not correct or is no longer correct, to obtain the correct information, but only for the purposes of preventing fraud by, pursuing legal remedies against, or recovering on a debt or security interest against, the individual.

(4) For use in connection with any civil, criminal, administrative, or arbitral proceeding in any Federal, State, or local court or agency or before any self-regulatory body, including the service of process, investigation in anticipation of litigation, and the execution or enforcement of judgments and orders, or pursuant to an order of a Federal, State, or local court.

(5) For use in research activities, and for use in producing statistical reports, so long as the personal information is not published, redisclosed, or used to contact individuals.

(6) For use by any insurer or insurance support organization, or by a self-insured entity, or its agents, employees, or contractors, in connection with claims investigation activities, antifraud activities, rating or underwriting.

(7) For use in providing notice to the owners of towed or impounded vehicles.

(8) For use by any licensed private investigative agency or licensed security service for any purpose permitted under this subsection.

(9) For use by an employer or its agent or insurer to obtain or verify information relating to a holder of a commercial driver's license that is required under chapter 313 of title 49.

(10) For use in connection with the operation of private toll transportation facilities.

(11) For any other use in response to requests for individual motor vehicle records if the State has obtained the express consent of the person to whom such personal information pertains.

(12) For bulk distribution for surveys, marketing or solicitations if the State has obtained the express consent of the person to whom such personal information pertains.

(13) For use by any requester, if the requester demonstrates it has obtained the written consent of the individual to whom the information pertains.

(14) For any other use specifically authorized under the law of the State that holds the record, if such use is related to the operation of a motor vehicle or public safety.

(c) Resale or Redisclosure.—An authorized recipient of personal information (except a recipient under subsection (b)(11) or (12)) may resell or redisclose the information only for a use permitted under subsection (b) (but not for uses under subsection (b)(11) or (12)). An authorized recipient under subsection (b)(11) may resell or redisclose personal information for any purpose. An authorized recipient under subsection (b)(12) may resell or redisclose personal information pursuant to subsection (b)(12). Any authorized recipient (except a recipient under subsection (b)(11)) that resells or rediscloses personal information covered by this chapter must keep for a period of 5 years records identifying each person or entity that receives information and the permitted purpose for which the information will be used and must make such records available to the motor vehicle department upon request.

(d) Waiver Procedures.—A State motor vehicle department may establish and carry out procedures under which the department or its agents, upon receiving a request for personal information that does not fall within one of the exceptions in subsection (b), may mail a copy of the request to the individual about whom the information was requested, informing such individual of the request, together with a statement to the effect that the information will not be released unless the individual waives such individual's right to privacy under this section.

(e) Prohibition on Conditions.—No State may condition or burden in any way the issuance of an individual's motor vehicle record as defined in 18 U.S.C. 2725(1) to obtain express consent. Nothing in this paragraph shall be construed to prohibit a State from charging an administrative fee for issuance of a motor vehicle record.

(Added Pub. L. 103–322, title XXX, §300002(a), Sept. 13, 1994, 108 Stat. 2099; amended Pub. L. 104–287, §1, Oct. 11, 1996, 110 Stat. 3388; Pub. L. 104–294, title VI, §604(b)(46), Oct. 11, 1996, 110 Stat. 3509; Pub. L. 106–69, title III, §350(c), (d), Oct. 9, 1999, 113 Stat. 1025; Pub. L. 106–346, §101(a) [title III, §309(c)–(e)], Oct. 23, 2000, 114 Stat. 1356, 1356A–24.)

References in Text

The Anti Car Theft Act of 1992, referred to in subsec. (b), is Pub. L. 102–519, Oct. 25, 1992, 106 Stat. 3384. For complete classification of titles I and IV of the Act to the Code, see Tables.

The Automobile Information Disclosure Act, referred to in subsec. (b), is Pub. L. 85–506, July 7, 1958, 72 Stat. 325, as amended, which is classified generally to chapter 28 (§1231 et seq.) of Title 15, Commerce and Trade. For complete classification of this Act to the Code, see Short Title note set out under section 1231 of Title 15 and Tables.

The Clean Air Act, referred to in subsec. (b), is act July 14, 1955, ch. 360, 69 Stat. 322, as amended, which is classified generally to chapter 85 (§7401 et seq.) of Title 42, The Public Health and Welfare. For complete classification of this Act to the Code, see Short Title note set out under section 7401 of Title 42 and Tables.

Amendments

2000—Subsec. (a). Pub. L. 106–346, §101(a) [title III, §309(c)], reenacted heading without change and amended text generally. Prior to amendment, text read as follows: "Except as provided in subsection (b), a State department of motor vehicles, and any officer, employee, or contractor, thereof, shall not knowingly disclose or otherwise make available to any person or entity personal information about any individual obtained by the department in connection with a motor vehicle record."

Subsec. (b). Pub. L. 106–346, §101(a) [title III, §309(d)], inserted ", subject to subsection (a)(2)," before "may be disclosed" in introductory provisions.

Subsec. (e). Pub. L. 106–346, §101(a) [title III, §309(e)], added subsec. (e).

1999—Subsec. (b)(11). Pub. L. 106–69, §350(c), substituted "if the State has obtained the express consent of the person to whom such personal information pertains" for "if the motor vehicle department has provided in a clear and conspicuous manner on forms for issuance or renewal of operator's permits, titles, registrations, or identification cards, notice that personal information collected by the department may be disclosed to any business or person, and has provided in a clear and conspicuous manner on such forms an opportunity to prohibit such disclosures".

Subsec. (b)(12). Pub. L. 106–69, §350(d), substituted "if the State has obtained the express consent of the person to whom such personal information pertains" for "if the motor vehicle department has implemented methods and procedures to ensure that—

"(A) individuals are provided an opportunity, in a clear and conspicuous manner, to prohibit such uses; and

"(B) the information will be used, rented, or sold solely for bulk distribution for surveys, marketing, and solicitations, and that surveys, marketing, and solicitations will not be directed at those individuals who have requested in a timely fashion that they not be directed at them".

1996—Subsec. (b). Pub. L. 104–287, §1(1), in introductory provisions, substituted "titles I and IV of the Anti Car Theft Act of 1992, the Automobile Information Disclosure Act (15 U.S.C. 1231 et seq.), the Clean Air Act (42 U.S.C. 7401 et seq.), and chapters 301, 305, and 321–331 of title 49" for "the Automobile Information Disclosure Act, the Motor Vehicle Information and Cost Saving Act, the National Traffic and Motor Vehicle Safety Act of 1966, the Anti-Car Theft Act of 1992, and the Clean Air Act".

Subsec. (b)(9). Pub. L. 104–287, §1(2), substituted "chapter 313 of title 49" for "the Commercial Motor Vehicle Safety Act of 1986 (49 U.S.C. App. 2710 et seq.)".

Subsec. (c). Pub. L. 104–294 substituted "covered by this chapter" for "covered by this title".

Effective Date of 1999 Amendment

Pub. L. 106–69, title III, §350(g)(2), Oct. 9, 1999, 113 Stat. 1025, provided that: "Subsections (b), (c), and (d) [amending this section] shall be effective on June 1, 2000, excluding the States of Arkansas, Montana, Nevada, North Dakota, Oregon, and Texas that shall be in compliance with subsections (b), (c), and (d) within 90 days of the next convening of the State legislature and excluding the States of Wisconsin, South Carolina, and Oklahoma that shall be in compliance within 90 days following the day of issuance of a final decision on Reno vs. Condon by the United States Supreme Court if the State legislature is in session, or within 90 days of the next convening of the State legislature following the issuance of such final decision if the State legislature is not in session."

Effective Date of 1996 Amendment

Amendment by Pub. L. 104–294 effective Sept. 13, 1994, see section 604(d) of Pub. L. 104–294, set out as a note under section 13 of this title.

Effective Date

Pub. L. 103–322, title XXX, §300003, Sept. 13, 1994, 108 Stat. 2102, provided that: "The amendments made by section 300002 [enacting this chapter] shall become effective on the date that is 3 years after the date of enactment of this Act [Sept. 13, 1994]. After the effective date, if a State has implemented a procedure under section 2721(b)(11) and (12) of title 18, United States Code, as added by section 2902 [probably should be section "300002(a)"], for prohibiting disclosures or uses of personal information, and the procedure otherwise meets the requirements of subsection (b)(11) and (12), the State shall be in compliance with subsection (b)(11) and (12) even if the procedure is not available to individuals until they renew their license, title, registration or identification card, so long as the State provides some other procedure for individuals to contact the State on their own initiative to prohibit such uses or disclosures. Prior to the effective date, personal information covered by the amendment made by section 300002 may be released consistent with State law or practice."

Short Title

Pub. L. 103–322, title XXX, §300001, Sept. 13, 1994, 108 Stat. 2099, provided that: "This title [enacting this chapter] may be cited as the 'Driver's Privacy Protection Act of 1994'."

Relationship to Other Law

The Consumer Credit Reporting Reform Act of 1996 [see Short Title note set out under section

1601 of Title 15, Commerce and Trade] not to be considered to supersede or otherwise affect this section with respect to motor vehicle records for surveys, marketing, or solicitations, see section 2421 of Pub. L. 104–208, set out as a note under section 1681a of Title 15.

§2722. Additional unlawful acts
(a) Procurement for Unlawful Purpose.—It shall be unlawful for any person knowingly to obtain or disclose personal information, from a motor vehicle record, for any use not permitted under section 2721(b) of this title.
(b) False Representation.—It shall be unlawful for any person to make false representation to obtain any personal information from an individual's motor vehicle record.
(Added Pub. L. 103–322, title XXX, §300002(a), Sept. 13, 1994, 108 Stat. 2101.)

Effective Date
Section effective on the date that is 3 years after Sept. 13, 1994, with provisions relating to release of personal information before the effective date and compliance after such date, see section 300003 of Pub. L. 103–322, set out as a note under section 2721 of this title.

§2723. Penalties
(a) Criminal Fine.—A person who knowingly violates this chapter shall be fined under this title.
(b) Violations by State Department of Motor Vehicles.—Any State department of motor vehicles that has a policy or practice of substantial noncompliance with this chapter shall be subject to a civil penalty imposed by the Attorney General of not more than $5,000 a day for each day of substantial noncompliance.
(Added Pub. L. 103–322, title XXX, §300002(a), Sept. 13, 1994, 108 Stat. 2101.)

Effective Date
Section effective on the date that is 3 years after Sept. 13, 1994, with provisions relating to release of personal information before the effective date and compliance after such date, see section 300003 of Pub. L. 103–322, set out as a note under section 2721 of this title.

§2724. Civil action
(a) Cause of Action.—A person who knowingly obtains, discloses or uses personal information, from a motor vehicle record, for a purpose not permitted under this chapter shall be liable to the individual to whom the information pertains, who may bring a civil action in a United States district court.
(b) Remedies.—The court may award—
(1) actual damages, but not less than liquidated damages in the amount of $2,500;
(2) punitive damages upon proof of willful or reckless disregard of the law;
(3) reasonable attorneys' fees and other litigation costs reasonably incurred; and
(4) such other preliminary and equitable relief as the court determines to be appropriate.
(Added Pub. L. 103–322, title XXX, §300002(a), Sept. 13, 1994, 108 Stat. 2101.)

Effective Date
Section effective on the date that is 3 years after Sept. 13, 1994, with provisions relating to release of personal information before the effective date and compliance after such date, see section 300003 of Pub. L. 103–322, set out as a note under section 2721 of this title.

§2725. Definitions
In this chapter—
(1) "motor vehicle record" means any record that pertains to a motor vehicle operator's permit, motor vehicle title, motor vehicle registration, or identification card issued by a department of

motor vehicles;

(2) "person" means an individual, organization or entity, but does not include a State or agency thereof;

(3) "personal information" means information that identifies an individual, including an individual's photograph, social security number, driver identification number, name, address (but not the 5-digit zip code), telephone number, and medical or disability information, but does not include information on vehicular accidents, driving violations, and driver's status.1

(4) "highly restricted personal information" means an individual's photograph or image, social security number, medical or disability information; and

(5) "express consent" means consent in writing, including consent conveyed electronically that bears an electronic signature as defined in section 106(5) of Public Law 106–229.

(Added Pub. L. 103–322, title XXX, §300002(a), Sept. 13, 1994, 108 Stat. 2102; amended Pub. L. 106–346, §101(a) [title III, §309(b)], Oct. 23, 2000, 114 Stat. 1356, 1356A–24.)

References in Text

Section 106(5) of Public Law 106–229, referred to in par. (5), is classified to section 7006(5) of Title 15, Commerce and Trade.

Amendments

2000—Pars. (4), (5). Pub. L. 106–346 added pars. (4) and (5).

Effective Date

Section effective on the date that is 3 years after Sept. 13, 1994, with provisions relating to release of personal information before the effective date and compliance after such date, see section 300003 of Pub. L. 103–322, set out as a note under section 2721 of this title.

Amendments

2016—Pub. L. 114–316, §2(b)(1), Dec. 16, 2016, 130 Stat. 1593, struck out "trafficking in persons" before "offenses" in item for chapter 212A.

Pub. L. 114–236, §2(b), Oct. 7, 2016, 130 Stat. 967, added item for chapter 238.

2006—Pub. L. 109–164, title I, §103(a)(2), Jan. 10, 2006, 119 Stat. 3563, added item for chapter 212A.

2004—Pub. L. 108–405, title I, §102(b), title IV, §411(a)(2), Oct. 30, 2004, 118 Stat. 2264, 2284, added items for chapters 228A and 237.

2000—Pub. L. 106–523, §2(b), Nov. 22, 2000, 114 Stat. 2492, added item for chapter 212.

1994—Pub. L. 103–359, title VIII, §803(c)(1), Oct. 14, 1994, 108 Stat. 3439, substituted "terrorist acts and espionage" for "terrorists acts" in item for chapter 204.

Pub. L. 103–322, title VI, §60002(b), Sept. 13, 1994, 108 Stat. 1968, added item for chapter 228.

1988—Pub. L. 100–702, title IV, §404(a)(1), Nov. 19, 1988, 102 Stat. 4651, struck out item 237 "Rules of criminal procedure".

1986—Pub. L. 99–646, §41(d), Nov. 10, 1986, 100 Stat. 3600, struck out item for chapter 232 "Special forfeiture of collateral profits of crime" and added item for chapter 232A.

Pub. L. 99–508, title III, §301(b), Oct. 21, 1986, 100 Stat. 1872, added item for chapter 206.

1984—Pub. L. 98–533, title I, §101(b), Oct. 19, 1984, 98 Stat. 2708, added item for chapter 204.

Pub. L. 98–473, title II, §§203(d), 212(b), 1209(a), 1406(b), Oct. 12, 1984, 98 Stat. 1985, 2011, 2163, 2176, inserted "and detention pending judicial proceedings" in item for chapter 207, added items for chapters 224, 227, 229, 231, and 232, and struck out items for former chapters 227 "Sentence, judgment, and execution", 229 "Fines, penalties and forfeitures" and 231 "Probation".

1975—Pub. L. 93–619, title I, §102, Jan. 3, 1975, 88 Stat. 2086, added item for chapter 208.

1970—Pub. L. 91–452, title I, §101(b), Oct. 15, 1970, 84 Stat. 926, added item for chapter 216.

1968—Pub. L. 90–578, title III, §301(c), Oct. 17, 1968, 82 Stat. 1115, substituted "Trial by United States magistrates" for "Trial by commissioners" in item for chapter 219.

1966—Pub. L. 89–465, §5(e)(2), June 22, 1966, 80 Stat. 217, substituted "Release" for "Bail" in item for chapter 207.

Change of Name
"United States magistrate judges" substituted for "United States magistrates" in item for chapter 219 pursuant to section 321 of Pub. L. 101–650, set out as a note under section 631 of Title 28, Judiciary and Judicial Procedure.

CHAPTER 201 - GENERAL PROVISIONS

Amendments
2015—Pub. L. 114–22, title I, §101(b), May 29, 2015, 129 Stat. 230, added item 3014.
1984—Pub. L. 98–473, title II, §§218(c), 1405(b), Oct. 12, 1984, 98 Stat. 2027, 2175, added item 3013 and substituted "Repealed" for "Orders respecting persons in custody" in item 3012.
1964—Pub. L. 88–455, §4, Aug. 20, 1964, 78 Stat. 554, added item 3006A.

Law Enforcement Assistance Act of 1965
Note regarding Pub. L. 89–197, §§1–11, Sept. 22, 1965, 79 Stat. 828, which was amended and subsequently repealed, has been editorially reclassified in a note preceding section 10101 of Title 34, Crime Control and Law Enforcement.

Coordination of Federal Law Enforcement and Crime Prevention Programs
Designation of Attorney General to coordinate Federal law enforcement and crime prevention programs, see Ex. Ord. No. 11396, Feb. 7, 1968, 33 F.R. 2689, set out as a note preceding section 10101 of Title 34, Crime Control and Law Enforcement.

§3001. Procedure governed by rules; scope, purpose and effect; definition of terms; local rules; forms—(Rule)

See Federal Rules of Criminal Procedure
Scope, rule 1.
Purpose and construction, rule 2.
Proceedings to which rules apply, rules 54 and 59.

Definition, rule 54(c).
Rules of District Courts and Circuit Courts of Appeal, rule 57.
Forms, rule 58.
Effective date, rule 59.
Citation of rule, rule 60.
(June 25, 1948, ch. 645, 62 Stat. 814.)

§3002. Courts always open—(Rule)

See Federal Rules of Criminal Procedure
Business hours, rule 56.
(June 25, 1948, ch. 645, 62 Stat. 814.)

§3003. Calendars—(Rule)

See Federal Rules of Criminal Procedure
Preference to criminal cases, rule 50.
(June 25, 1948, ch. 645, 62 Stat. 814.)

§3004. Decorum in court room—(Rule)

See Federal Rules of Criminal Procedure
Photographing or radio broadcasting prohibited, rule 53.
(June 25, 1948, ch. 645, 62 Stat. 814.)

§3005. Counsel and witnesses in capital cases
Whoever is indicted for treason or other capital crime shall be allowed to make his full defense by counsel; and the court before which the defendant is to be tried, or a judge thereof, shall promptly, upon the defendant's request, assign 2 such counsel, of whom at least 1 shall be learned in the law applicable to capital cases, and who shall have free access to the accused at all reasonable hours. In assigning counsel under this section, the court shall consider the recommendation of the Federal Public Defender organization, or, if no such organization exists in the district, of the Administrative Office of the United States Courts. The defendant shall be allowed, in his defense to make any proof that he can produce by lawful witnesses, and shall have the like process of the court to compel his witnesses to appear at his trial, as is usually granted to compel witnesses to appear on behalf of the prosecution.
(June 25, 1948, ch. 645, 62 Stat. 814; Pub. L. 103–322, title VI, §60026, Sept. 13, 1994, 108 Stat. 1982.)

Historical and Revision Notes
Based on title 18, U.S.C., 1940 ed., §563 (R.S. §1034).
Changes were made in phraseology.

Amendments
1994—Pub. L. 103–322 substituted "; and the court before which the defendant is to be tried, or a judge thereof, shall promptly, upon the defendant's request, assign 2 such counsel, of whom at least 1 shall be learned in the law applicable to capital cases, and who shall have free access to the accused at all reasonable hours. In assigning counsel under this section, the court shall consider the recommendation of the Federal Public Defender organization, or, if no such organization exists in the district, of the Administrative Office of the United States Courts. The defendant shall" for "learned in the law; and the court before which he is tried, or some judge thereof, shall

immediately, upon his request, assign to him such counsel, not exceeding two, as he may desire, who shall have free access to him at all reasonable hours. He shall".

§3006. Assignment of counsel—(Rule)

See Federal Rules of Criminal Procedure
Appointment by court, rule 44.
Accused to be informed of right to counsel, rules 5 and 44.
(June 25, 1948, ch. 645, 62 Stat. 814.)

§3006A. Adequate representation of defendants
(a) Choice of Plan.—Each United States district court, with the approval of the judicial council of the circuit, shall place in operation throughout the district a plan for furnishing representation for any person financially unable to obtain adequate representation in accordance with this section. Representation under each plan shall include counsel and investigative, expert, and other services necessary for adequate representation. Each plan shall provide the following:
(1) Representation shall be provided for any financially eligible person who—
(A) is charged with a felony or a Class A misdemeanor;
(B) is a juvenile alleged to have committed an act of juvenile delinquency as defined in section 5031 of this title;
(C) is charged with a violation of probation;
(D) is under arrest, when such representation is required by law;
(E) is charged with a violation of supervised release or faces modification, reduction, or enlargement of a condition, or extension or revocation of a term of supervised release;
(F) is subject to a mental condition hearing under chapter 313 of this title;
(G) is in custody as a material witness;
(H) is entitled to appointment of counsel under the sixth amendment to the Constitution;
(I) faces loss of liberty in a case, and Federal law requires the appointment of counsel; or
(J) is entitled to the appointment of counsel under section 4109 of this title.
(2) Whenever the United States magistrate judge or the court determines that the interests of justice so require, representation may be provided for any financially eligible person who—
(A) is charged with a Class B or C misdemeanor, or an infraction for which a sentence to confinement is authorized; or
(B) is seeking relief under section 2241, 2254, or 2255 of title 28.
(3) Private attorneys shall be appointed in a substantial proportion of the cases. Each plan may include, in addition to the provisions for private attorneys, either of the following or both:
(A) Attorneys furnished by a bar association or a legal aid agency,
(B) Attorneys furnished by a defender organization established in accordance with the provisions of subsection (g).
Prior to approving the plan for a district, the judicial council of the circuit shall supplement the plan with provisions for representation on appeal. The district court may modify the plan at any time with the approval of the judicial council of the circuit. It shall modify the plan when directed by the judicial council of the circuit. The district court shall notify the Administrative Office of the United States Courts of any modification of its plan.
(b) Appointment of Counsel.—Counsel furnishing representation under the plan shall be selected from a panel of attorneys designated or approved by the court, or from a bar association, legal aid agency, or defender organization furnishing representation pursuant to the plan. In every case in which a person entitled to representation under a plan approved under subsection (a) appears without counsel, the United States magistrate judge or the court shall advise the person that he has the right to be represented by counsel and that counsel will be appointed to represent him if he is financially unable to obtain counsel. Unless the person waives representation by counsel, the United States magistrate judge or the court, if satisfied after appropriate inquiry that the person is

financially unable to obtain counsel, shall appoint counsel to represent him. Such appointment may be made retroactive to include any representation furnished pursuant to the plan prior to appointment. The United States magistrate judge or the court shall appoint separate counsel for persons having interests that cannot properly be represented by the same counsel, or when other good cause is shown.

(c) Duration and Substitution of Appointments.—A person for whom counsel is appointed shall be represented at every stage of the proceedings from his initial appearance before the United States magistrate judge or the court through appeal, including ancillary matters appropriate to the proceedings. If at any time after the appointment of counsel the United States magistrate judge or the court finds that the person is financially able to obtain counsel or to make partial payment for the representation, it may terminate the appointment of counsel or authorize payment as provided in subsection (f), as the interests of justice may dictate. If at any stage of the proceedings, including an appeal, the United States magistrate judge or the court finds that the person is financially unable to pay counsel whom he had retained, it may appoint counsel as provided in subsection (b) and authorize payment as provided in subsection (d), as the interests of justice may dictate. The United States magistrate judge or the court may, in the interests of justice, substitute one appointed counsel for another at any stage of the proceedings.

(d) Payment for Representation.—

(1) Hourly Rate.—Any attorney appointed pursuant to this section or a bar association or legal aid agency or community defender organization which has provided the appointed attorney shall, at the conclusion of the representation or any segment thereof, be compensated at a rate not exceeding $60 per hour for time expended in court or before a United States magistrate judge and $40 per hour for time reasonably expended out of court, unless the Judicial Conference determines that a higher rate of not in excess of $75 per hour is justified for a circuit or for particular districts within a circuit, for time expended in court or before a United States magistrate judge and for time expended out of court. The Judicial Conference shall develop guidelines for determining the maximum hourly rates for each circuit in accordance with the preceding sentence, with variations by district, where appropriate, taking into account such factors as the minimum range of the prevailing hourly rates for qualified attorneys in the district in which the representation is provided and the recommendations of the judicial councils of the circuits. Not less than 3 years after the effective date of the Criminal Justice Act Revision of 1986, the Judicial Conference is authorized to raise the maximum hourly rates specified in this paragraph up to the aggregate of the overall average percentages of the adjustments in the rates of pay under the General Schedule made pursuant to section 5305 1 of title 5 on or after such effective date. After the rates are raised under the preceding sentence, such maximum hourly rates may be raised at intervals of not less than 1 year each, up to the aggregate of the overall average percentages of such adjustments made since the last raise was made under this paragraph. Attorneys may be reimbursed for expenses reasonably incurred, including the costs of transcripts authorized by the United States magistrate 2 or the court, and the costs of defending actions alleging malpractice of counsel in furnishing representational services under this section. No reimbursement for expenses in defending against malpractice claims shall be made if a judgment of malpractice is rendered against the counsel furnishing representational services under this section. The United States magistrate 2 or the court shall make determinations relating to reimbursement of expenses under this paragraph.

(2) Maximum Amounts.—For representation of a defendant before the United States magistrate judge or the district court, or both, the compensation to be paid to an attorney or to a bar association or legal aid agency or community defender organization shall not exceed $7,000 for each attorney in a case in which one or more felonies are charged, and $2,000 for each attorney in a case in which only misdemeanors are charged. For representation of a defendant in an appellate court, the compensation to be paid to an attorney or to a bar association or legal aid agency or community defender organization shall not exceed $5,000 for each attorney in each court. For representation of a petitioner in a non-capital habeas corpus proceeding, the compensation for each attorney shall not exceed the amount applicable to a felony in this paragraph for representation of a defendant before a judicial officer of the district court. For representation of such petitioner in an

appellate court, the compensation for each attorney shall not exceed the amount applicable for representation of a defendant in an appellate court. For representation of an offender before the United States Parole Commission in a proceeding under section 4106A of this title, the compensation shall not exceed $1,500 for each attorney in each proceeding; for representation of an offender in an appeal from a determination of such Commission under such section, the compensation shall not exceed $5,000 for each attorney in each court. For any other representation required or authorized by this section, the compensation shall not exceed $1,500 for each attorney in each proceeding. The compensation maximum amounts provided in this paragraph shall increase simultaneously by the same percentage, rounded to the nearest multiple of $100, as the aggregate percentage increases in the maximum hourly compensation rate paid pursuant to paragraph (1) for time expended since the case maximum amounts were last adjusted.

(3) Waiving Maximum Amounts.—Payment in excess of any maximum amount provided in paragraph (2) of this subsection may be made for extended or complex representation whenever the court in which the representation was rendered, or the United States magistrate judge if the representation was furnished exclusively before him, certifies that the amount of the excess payment is necessary to provide fair compensation and the payment is approved by the chief judge of the circuit. The chief judge of the circuit may delegate such approval authority to an active or senior circuit judge.

(4) Disclosure of fees.—

(A) In general.—Subject to subparagraphs (B) through (E), the amounts paid under this subsection for services in any case shall be made available to the public by the court upon the court's approval of the payment.

(B) Pre-trial or trial in progress.—If a trial is in pre-trial status or still in progress and after considering the defendant's interests as set forth in subparagraph (D), the court shall—

(i) redact any detailed information on the payment voucher provided by defense counsel to justify the expenses to the court; and

(ii) make public only the amounts approved for payment to defense counsel by dividing those amounts into the following categories:

(I) Arraignment and or plea.

(II) Bail and detention hearings.

(III) Motions.

(IV) Hearings.

(V) Interviews and conferences.

(VI) Obtaining and reviewing records.

(VII) Legal research and brief writing.

(VIII) Travel time.

(IX) Investigative work.

(X) Experts.

(XI) Trial and appeals.

(XII) Other.

(C) Trial completed.—

(i) In general.—If a request for payment is not submitted until after the completion of the trial and subject to consideration of the defendant's interests as set forth in subparagraph (D), the court shall make available to the public an unredacted copy of the expense voucher.

(ii) Protection of the rights of the defendant.—If the court determines that defendant's interests as set forth in subparagraph (D) require a limited disclosure, the court shall disclose amounts as provided in subparagraph (B).

(D) Considerations.—The interests referred to in subparagraphs (B) and (C) are—

(i) to protect any person's 5th amendment right against self-incrimination;

(ii) to protect the defendant's 6th amendment rights to effective assistance of counsel;

(iii) the defendant's attorney-client privilege;

(iv) the work product privilege of the defendant's counsel;

(v) the safety of any person; and

(vi) any other interest that justice may require, except that the amount of the fees shall not be considered a reason justifying any limited disclosure under section 3006A(d)(4) of title 18, United States Code.

(E) Notice.—The court shall provide reasonable notice of disclosure to the counsel of the defendant prior to the approval of the payments in order to allow the counsel to request redaction based on the considerations set forth in subparagraph (D). Upon completion of the trial, the court shall release unredacted copies of the vouchers provided by defense counsel to justify the expenses to the court. If there is an appeal, the court shall not release unredacted copies of the vouchers provided by defense counsel to justify the expenses to the court until such time as the appeals process is completed, unless the court determines that none of the defendant's interests set forth in subparagraph (D) will be compromised.

(F) Effective date.—The amendment made by paragraph (4) shall become effective 60 days after enactment of this Act, will apply only to cases filed on or after the effective date, and shall be in effect for no longer than 24 months after the effective date.

(5) Filing Claims.—A separate claim for compensation and reimbursement shall be made to the district court for representation before the United States magistrate judge and the court, and to each appellate court before which the attorney provided representation to the person involved. Each claim shall be supported by a sworn written statement specifying the time expended, services rendered, and expenses incurred while the case was pending before the United States magistrate judge and the court, and the compensation and reimbursement applied for or received in the same case from any other source. The court shall fix the compensation and reimbursement to be paid to the attorney or to the bar association or legal aid agency or community defender organization which provided the appointed attorney. In cases where representation is furnished exclusively before a United States magistrate judge, the claim shall be submitted to him and he shall fix the compensation and reimbursement to be paid. In cases where representation is furnished other than before the United States magistrate judge, the district court, or an appellate court, claims shall be submitted to the district court which shall fix the compensation and reimbursement to be paid.

(6) New Trials.—For purposes of compensation and other payments authorized by this section, an order by a court granting a new trial shall be deemed to initiate a new case.

(7) Proceedings Before Appellate Courts.—If a person for whom counsel is appointed under this section appeals to an appellate court or petitions for a writ of certiorari, he may do so without prepayment of fees and costs or security therefor and without filing the affidavit required by section 1915(a) of title 28.

(e) Services Other Than Counsel.—

(1) Upon Request.—Counsel for a person who is financially unable to obtain investigative, expert, or other services necessary for adequate representation may request them in an ex parte application. Upon finding, after appropriate inquiry in an ex parte proceeding, that the services are necessary and that the person is financially unable to obtain them, the court, or the United States magistrate judge if the services are required in connection with a matter over which he has jurisdiction, shall authorize counsel to obtain the services.

(2) Without Prior Request.—(A) Counsel appointed under this section may obtain, subject to later review, investigative, expert, and other services without prior authorization if necessary for adequate representation. Except as provided in subparagraph (B) of this paragraph, the total cost of services obtained without prior authorization may not exceed $800 and expenses reasonably incurred.

(B) The court, or the United States magistrate judge (if the services were rendered in a case disposed of entirely before the United States magistrate judge), may, in the interest of justice, and upon the finding that timely procurement of necessary services could not await prior authorization, approve payment for such services after they have been obtained, even if the cost of such services exceeds $800.

(3) Maximum Amounts.—Compensation to be paid to a person for services rendered by him to a person under this subsection, or to be paid to an organization for services rendered by an employee thereof, shall not exceed $2,400, exclusive of reimbursement for expenses reasonably incurred,

unless payment in excess of that limit is certified by the court, or by the United States magistrate judge if the services were rendered in connection with a case disposed of entirely before him, as necessary to provide fair compensation for services of an unusual character or duration, and the amount of the excess payment is approved by the chief judge of the circuit. The chief judge of the circuit may delegate such approval authority to an active or senior circuit judge.

(4) Disclosure of fees.—The amounts paid under this subsection for services in any case shall be made available to the public.

(5) The dollar amounts provided in paragraphs (2) and (3) shall be adjusted simultaneously by an amount, rounded to the nearest multiple of $100, equal to the percentage of the cumulative adjustments taking effect under section 5303 of title 5 in the rates of pay under the General Schedule since the date the dollar amounts provided in paragraphs (2) and (3), respectively, were last enacted or adjusted by statute.

(f) Receipt of Other Payments.—Whenever the United States magistrate judge or the court finds that funds are available for payment from or on behalf of a person furnished representation, it may authorize or direct that such funds be paid to the appointed attorney, to the bar association or legal aid agency or community defender organization which provided the appointed attorney, to any person or organization authorized pursuant to subsection (e) to render investigative, expert, or other services, or to the court for deposit in the Treasury as a reimbursement to the appropriation, current at the time of payment, to carry out the provisions of this section. Except as so authorized or directed, no such person or organization may request or accept any payment or promise of payment for representing a defendant.

(g) Defender Organization.—

(1) Qualifications.—A district or a part of a district in which at least two hundred persons annually require the appointment of counsel may establish a defender organization as provided for either under subparagraphs (A) or (B) of paragraph (2) of this subsection or both. Two adjacent districts or parts of districts may aggregate the number of persons required to be represented to establish eligibility for a defender organization to serve both areas. In the event that adjacent districts or parts of districts are located in different circuits, the plan for furnishing representation shall be approved by the judicial council of each circuit.

(2) Types of Defender Organizations.—

(A) Federal Public Defender Organization.—A Federal Public Defender Organization shall consist of one or more full-time salaried attorneys. An organization for a district or part of a district or two adjacent districts or parts of districts shall be supervised by a Federal Public Defender appointed by the court of appeals of the circuit, without regard to the provisions of title 5 governing appointments in the competitive service, after considering recommendations from the district court or courts to be served. Nothing contained herein shall be deemed to authorize more than one Federal Public Defender within a single judicial district. The Federal Public Defender shall be appointed for a term of four years, unless sooner removed by the court of appeals of the circuit for incompetency, misconduct in office, or neglect of duty. Upon the expiration of his term, a Federal Public Defender may, by a majority vote of the judges of the court of appeals, continue to perform the duties of his office until his successor is appointed, or until one year after the expiration of such Defender's term, whichever is earlier. The compensation of the Federal Public Defender shall be fixed by the court of appeals of the circuit at a rate not to exceed the compensation received by the United States attorney for the district where representation is furnished or, if two districts or parts of districts are involved, the compensation of the higher paid United States attorney of the districts. The Federal Public Defender may appoint, without regard to the provisions of title 5 governing appointments in the competitive service, full-time attorneys in such number as may be approved by the court of appeals of the circuit and other personnel in such number as may be approved by the Director of the Administrative Office of the United States Courts. Compensation paid to such attorneys and other personnel of the organization shall be fixed by the Federal Public Defender at a rate not to exceed that paid to attorneys and other personnel of similar qualifications and experience in the Office of the United States attorney in the district where representation is furnished or, if two districts or parts of districts are involved, the higher compensation paid to persons of similar qualifications and experience in the districts. Neither the Federal Public Defender nor any attorney so appointed by him may engage in the private practice of law. Each organization shall submit to the Director of the Administrative Office of the United States Courts, at the time and in the form prescribed by him, reports of its activities and financial position and its proposed budget. The Director of the Administrative Office shall submit, in accordance with section 605 of title 28, a budget for each organization for each fiscal year and shall out of the appropriations therefor make payments to and on behalf of each organization. Payments under this subparagraph to an organization shall be in lieu of payments under subsection (d) or (e).

(B) Community Defender Organization.—A Community Defender Organization shall be a non-profit defense counsel service established and administered by any group authorized by the plan to provide representation. The organization shall be eligible to furnish attorneys and receive payments under this section if its bylaws are set forth in the plan of the district or districts in which it will serve. Each organization shall submit to the Judicial Conference of the United States an annual report setting forth its activities and financial position and the anticipated caseload and expenses for the next fiscal year. Upon application an organization may, to the extent approved by the Judicial Conference of the United States:

(i) receive an initial grant for expenses necessary to establish the organization; and

(ii) in lieu of payments under subsection (d) or (e), receive periodic sustaining grants to provide representation and other expenses pursuant to this section.

(3) Malpractice and Negligence Suits.—The Director of the Administrative Office of the United States Courts shall, to the extent the Director considers appropriate, provide representation for and hold harmless, or provide liability insurance for, any person who is an officer or employee of a Federal Public Defender Organization established under this subsection, or a Community Defender Organization established under this subsection which is receiving periodic sustaining grants, for money damages for injury, loss of liberty, loss of property, or personal injury or death arising from malpractice or negligence of any such officer or employee in furnishing representational services under this section while acting within the scope of that person's office or employment.

(h) Rules and Reports.—Each district court and court of appeals of a circuit shall submit a report on the appointment of counsel within its jurisdiction to the Administrative Office of the United States Courts in such form and at such times as the Judicial Conference of the United States may specify. The Judicial Conference of the United States may, from time to time, issue rules and regulations governing the operation of plans formulated under this section.

(i) Appropriations.—There are authorized to be appropriated to the United States courts, out of any money in the Treasury not otherwise appropriated, sums necessary to carry out the provisions of this section, including funds for the continuing education and training of persons providing representational services under this section. When so specified in appropriation acts, such appropriations shall remain available until expended. Payments from such appropriations shall be made under the supervision of the Director of the Administrative Office of the United States Courts.

(j) Districts Included.—As used in this section, the term "district court" means each district court of the United States created by chapter 5 of title 28, the District Court of the Virgin Islands, the District Court for the Northern Mariana Islands, and the District Court of Guam.

(k) Applicability in the District of Columbia.—The provisions of this section shall apply in the United States District Court for the District of Columbia and the United States Court of Appeals for the District of Columbia Circuit. The provisions of this section shall not apply to the Superior Court of the District of Columbia and the District of Columbia Court of Appeals.

(Added Pub. L. 88–455, §2, Aug. 20, 1964, 78 Stat. 552; amended Pub. L. 90–578, title III, §301(a)(1), Oct. 17, 1968, 82 Stat. 1115; Pub. L. 91–447, §1, Oct. 14, 1970, 84 Stat. 916; Pub. L. 93–412, §3, Sept. 3, 1974, 88 Stat. 1093; Pub. L. 97–164, title II, §206(a), (b), Apr. 2, 1982, 96 Stat. 53; Pub. L. 98–473, title II, §§223(e), 405, 1901, Oct. 12, 1984, 98 Stat. 2028, 2067, 2185; Pub. L. 99–651, title I, §§102, 103, Nov. 14, 1986, 100 Stat. 3642, 3645; Pub. L. 100–182, §19, Dec. 7, 1987, 101 Stat. 1270; Pub. L. 100–690, title VII, §7101(f), Nov. 18, 1988, 102 Stat. 4416;

Pub. L. 101–650, title III, §321, Dec. 1, 1990, 104 Stat. 5117; Pub. L. 104–132, title IX, §903(a), Apr. 24, 1996, 110 Stat. 1318; Pub. L. 105–119, title III, §308, Nov. 26, 1997, 111 Stat. 2493; Pub. L. 106–113, div. B, §1000(a)(1) [title III, §308(a)], Nov. 29, 1999, 113 Stat. 1535, 1501A–37; Pub. L. 106–518, title II, §§210, 211, Nov. 13, 2000, 114 Stat. 2415; Pub. L. 108–447, div. B, title III, §304, Dec. 8, 2004, 118 Stat. 2894; Pub. L. 110–406, §§11–12(b), Oct. 13, 2008, 122 Stat. 4293, 4294; Pub. L. 111–174, §7, May 27, 2010, 124 Stat. 1217.)

References in Text

The effective date of the Criminal Justice Act Revision of 1986, referred to in subsec. (d)(1), is, with qualifications, 120 days after Nov. 14, 1986. See section 105 of Pub. L. 99–651, set out below as an Effective Date of 1986 Amendment note.

Section 5305 of title 5, referred to in subsec. (d)(1), was amended generally by Pub. L. 101–509, title V, §529 [title I, §101(a)(1)], Nov. 5, 1990, 104 Stat. 1427, 1436, and, as so amended, does not relate to adjustments in the rate of pay under the General Schedule. See section 5303 of Title 5, Government Organization and Employees.

The amendment made by paragraph (4), referred to in subsec. (d)(4)(F), probably means the amendment by section 308 of Pub. L. 105–119, which struck out former par. (4) of subsec. (d) and inserted the new par. (4).

Enactment of this Act, referred to in subsec. (d)(4)(F), probably means the date of enactment of Pub. L. 105–119, which enacted subsec. (d)(4) of this section and was approved Nov. 26, 1997.

Amendments

2010—Subsec. (e)(2). Pub. L. 111–174, §7(1)(A), substituted "$800" for "$500" in subpars. (A) and (B).

Subsec. (e)(3). Pub. L. 111–174, §7(1)(B), substituted "$2,400" for "$1,600" in first sentence.

Subsec. (e)(5). Pub. L. 111–174, §7(2), added par. (5).

2008—Subsec. (d)(2). Pub. L. 110–406, §11, inserted at end "The compensation maximum amounts provided in this paragraph shall increase simultaneously by the same percentage, rounded to the nearest multiple of $100, as the aggregate percentage increases in the maximum hourly compensation rate paid pursuant to paragraph (1) for time expended since the case maximum amounts were last adjusted."

Subsecs. (d)(3), (e)(3). Pub. L. 110–406, §12(a), (b), inserted "or senior" after "active" in second sentence.

2004—Subsec. (d)(2). Pub. L. 108–447, §304(a), substituted "$7,000" for "$5,200" and "$2,000" for "$1,500" in first sentence, "$5,000" for "$3,700" in second sentence, "$1,500" for "$1,200" and "$5,000" for "$3,900" in fifth sentence, and "$1,500" for "$1,200" in last sentence.

Subsec. (e)(2). Pub. L. 108–447, §304(b)(1), substituted "$500" for "$300" in subpars. (A) and (B).

Subsec. (e)(3). Pub. L. 108–447, §304(b)(2), substituted "$1,600" for "$1,000" in first sentence.

2000—Subsec. (d)(1). Pub. L. 106–518, §211, substituted "Attorneys may be reimbursed for expenses reasonably incurred, including the costs of transcripts authorized by the United States magistrate or the court, and the costs of defending actions alleging malpractice of counsel in furnishing representational services under this section. No reimbursement for expenses in defending against malpractice claims shall be made if a judgment of malpractice is rendered against the counsel furnishing representational services under this section. The United States magistrate or the court shall make determinations relating to reimbursement of expenses under this paragraph." for "Attorneys shall be reimbursed for expenses reasonably incurred, including the costs of transcripts authorized by the United States magistrate or the court."

Subsec. (d)(2). Pub. L. 106–518, §210(4), (5), inserted after second sentence "For representation of a petitioner in a non-capital habeas corpus proceeding, the compensation for each attorney shall not exceed the amount applicable to a felony in this paragraph for representation of a defendant before a judicial officer of the district court. For representation of such petitioner in an appellate court, the compensation for each attorney shall not exceed the amount applicable for representation of a defendant in an appellate court." and substituted "$1,200" for "$750" in last sentence.

Pub. L. 106–518, §210(1)–(3), in first sentence, substituted "$5,200" for "$3,500" and "$1,500" for "$1,000", in second sentence, substituted "$3,700" for "$2,500", and in third sentence, substituted "$1,200" for "$750" and "$3,900" for "$2,500".

1999—Subsec. (d)(4)(D)(vi). Pub. L. 106–113 inserted ", except that the amount of the fees shall not be considered a reason justifying any limited disclosure under section 3006A(d)(4) of title 18, United States Code" after "require".

1997—Subsec. (d)(4). Pub. L. 105–119 reenacted par. heading without change and amended text generally. Prior to amendment, text read as follows: "The amounts paid under this subsection, for representation in any case, shall be made available to the public."

1996—Subsec. (d)(4) to (7). Pub. L. 104–132, §903(a)(1), added par. (4) and redesignated former pars. (4) to (6) as (5) to (7), respectively.

Subsec. (e)(4). Pub. L. 104–132, §903(a)(2), added par. (4).

1988—Subsec. (a)(1)(J). Pub. L. 100–690, §7101(f)(1), added subpar. (J).

Subsec. (d)(2). Pub. L. 100–690, §7101(f)(2), inserted provisions at end to representation of offender before United States Parole Commission, and in appeal from determination of such Commission.

1987—Subsec. (a)(1)(E) to (I). Pub. L. 100–182 added subpar. (E) and redesignated former subpars. (E) to (H) as (F) to (I), respectively.

1986—Subsec. (a). Pub. L. 99–651, §103, made technical amendments to Pub. L. 98–473, §223(e), see 1984 Amendment note below.

Pub. L. 99–651, §102(a)(1), substituted "in accordance with this section. Representation under each plan shall include counsel and investigative, expert, and other services necessary for adequate representation. Each plan shall provide the following:" and pars. (1) to (3) for prior provisions which read as follows: "(1) who is charged with a felony or misdemeanor (other than a petty offense as defined in section 1 of this title) or with juvenile delinquency by the commission of an act which, if committed by an adult, would be such a felony or misdemeanor or with a violation of probation, (2) who is under arrest, when such representation is required by law, (3) who is subject to revocation of parole, in custody as a material witness, or seeking collateral relief, as provided in subsection (g), (4) whose mental condition is the subject of a hearing pursuant to chapter 313 of this title, or (5) for whom the Sixth Amendment to the Constitution requires the appointment of counsel or for whom, in a case in which he faces loss of liberty, any Federal law requires the appointment of counsel. Representation under each plan shall include counsel and investigative, expert, and other services necessary for an adequate defense. Each plan shall include a provision for private attorneys. The plan may include, in addition to a provision for private attorneys in a substantial proportion of cases, either of the following or both:

"(1) attorneys furnished by a bar association or a legal aid agency; or

"(2) attorneys furnished by a defender organization established in accordance with the provisions of subsection (h)."

Subsec. (b). Pub. L. 99–651, §102(a)(2), substituted "In every case in which a person entitled to representation under a plan approved under subsection (a)" for "In every criminal case in which the defendant is charged with a felony or a misdemeanor (other than a petty offense as defined in section 1 of this title) or with juvenile delinquency by the commission of an act which, if committed by an adult, would be such a felony or misdemeanor or with a violation of probation and" and substituted "person" for "defendant" and "persons" for "defendants" wherever appearing.

Subsec. (d)(1). Pub. L. 99–651, §102(a)(3)(A), substituted "court, unless the Judicial Conference determines that a higher rate of not in excess of $75 per hour is justified for a circuit or for particular districts within a circuit, for time expended in court or before a United States magistrate and for time expended out of court. The Judicial Conference shall develop guidelines for determining the maximum hourly rates for each circuit in accordance with the preceding sentence, with variations by district, where appropriate, taking into account such factors as the minimum range of the prevailing hourly rates for qualified attorneys in the district in which the representation is provided and the recommendations of the judicial councils of the circuits. Not less than 3 years after the effective date of the Criminal Justice Act Revision of 1986, the Judicial Conference is authorized to raise the maximum hourly rates specified in this paragraph up to the aggregate of the overall average percentages of the adjustments in the rates of pay under the General Schedule made pursuant to section 5305 of title 5 on or after such effective date. After the rates are raised under the preceding sentence, such maximum hourly rates may be raised at intervals of not less than 1 year each, up to the aggregate of the overall average percentages of such adjustments made since the last raise was made under this paragraph. Attorneys" for "court. Such attorney".

Subsec. (d)(2). Pub. L. 99–651, §102(a)(3)(B), substituted "$3,500" for "$2,000", "$1,000" for "$800", "$2,500" for "$2,000", and substituted provision that for any other representation required or authorized by this section, the compensation shall not exceed $750 for each attorney in each proceeding, for provision that for representation in connection with a post-trial motion made after the entry of judgment or in a probation revocation proceeding or for representation provided under subsection (g) the compensation could not exceed $500 for each attorney in each proceeding in each court.

Subsec. (d)(3). Pub. L. 99–651, §102(a)(3)(C), inserted provision that the chief judge of the circuit may delegate such approval authority to an active circuit judge.

Subsec. (d)(4). Pub. L. 99–651, §102(a)(3)(D), substituted "provided representation to the person involved" for "represented the defendant".

Subsec. (e)(1). Pub. L. 99–651, §102(a)(4)(A), substituted "adequate representation" for "an adequate defense".

Subsec. (e)(2). Pub. L. 99–651, §102(a)(4)(B), designated existing provisions as subpar. (A), and substituted reference to adequate representation for reference to an adequate defense, inserted exception relating to subpar. (B), increased the authorized amount for services from $150 to $300, and added subpar. (B).

Subsec. (e)(3). Pub. L. 99–651, §102(a)(4)(C), substituted "$1,000" for "$300" and inserted provision that the chief judge of the circuit may delegate such approval authority to an active circuit judge.

Subsec. (g). Pub. L. 99–651, §102(b)(1), redesignated subsec. (h) as (g), and struck out former subsec. (g) which provided for discretionary appointments by the court or magistrate.

Subsec. (g)(2)(A), formerly (h)(2)(A). Pub. L. 99–651, §102(a)(5)(A), substituted "in accordance with section 605 of title 28" for "similarly as under title 28, United States Code, section 605, and subject to the conditions of that section", and after fourth sentence inserted provision authorizing the continuation in office, upon a majority vote of the judges of the court of appeals, of a Federal Public Defender whose term has expired until appointment of a successor or until one year after the expiration of such Defender's term, whichever is earlier.

Subsec. (g)(2)(B), formerly (h)(2)(B). Pub. L. 99–651, §102(a)(5)(B), substituted "for the next fiscal year" for "for the coming year" in introductory provisions.

Subsec. (g)(3), formerly (h)(3). Pub. L. 99–651, §102(a)(5)(C), added par. (3).

Subsec. (h). Pub. L. 99–651, §102(b)(1), redesignated subsec. (i) as (h). Former subsec. (h) redesignated (g).

Subsec. (i). Pub. L. 99–651, §102(a)(6), (b)(1), redesignated subsec. (j) as (i) and inserted provision for funding continuing education and training of persons providing representational services under this section. Former subsec. (i) redesignated (h).

Subsec. (j). Pub. L. 99–651, §102(b), redesignated subsec. (k) as (j), and amended subsec. (j) generally to include the District Court for the Northern Mariana Islands. Former subsec. (j) redesignated (i).

Subsecs. (k), (l). Pub. L. 99–651, §102(a)(7), (b)(1), redesignated subsec. (l) as (k) and substituted "this section shall apply" for "this Act, other than subsection (h) of section 1, shall apply" and "this section shall not apply" for "this Act shall not apply". Former subsec. (k) redesignated (j).

1984—Subsec. (a). Pub. L. 98–473, §405(a), added cl. (4) and redesignated former cl. (4) as (5).

Subsec. (a)(1)(A). Pub. L. 98–473, §223(e)(1), as amended by Pub. L. 99–651, §103, substituted "Class A misdemeanor" for "misdemeanor (other than a petty offense as defined in section 1 of this title)".

Subsec. (a)(1)(E) to (I). Pub. L. 98–473, §223(e)(2), as amended by Pub. L. 99–651, §103, redesignated subpars. (F) to (I) as (E) to (H), respectively, and struck out former subpar. (E) which required that representation be provided for any financially eligible person who was entitled to appointment of counsel in parole proceedings under chapter 311 of this title.

Subsec. (a)(2)(A). Pub. L. 98–473, §223(e)(3), as amended by Pub. L. 99–651, §103, substituted "Class B or C misdemeanor, or an infraction" for "petty offense".

Subsec. (d)(1). Pub. L. 98–473, §1901(1)–(3), substituted "$60" for "$30" and "$40" for "$20", and struck out ", or such other hourly rate, fixed by the Judicial Council of the Circuit, not to exceed the minimum hourly scale established by a bar association for similar services rendered in the district" at end of first sentence.

Subsec. (d)(2). Pub. L. 98–473, §1901(4)–(6), substituted "$2,000" for "$1,000" in two places, "$800" for "$400", and "$500" for "$250".

Subsec. (g). Pub. L. 98–473, §405(b), struck out reference to section 4245 of title 18.

1982—Subsec. (h)(2)(A). Pub. L. 97–164, §206(a), substituted "court of appeals" for "judicial council" wherever appearing and "court of appeals of the circuit" for "Judicial Council of the Circuit".

Subsec. (i). Pub. L. 97–164, §206(b), substituted "court of appeals" for "judicial council".

1974—Subsec. (l). Pub. L. 93–412 substituted "shall apply in the United States District Court for the District of Columbia and the United States Court of Appeals for the District of Columbia Circuit. The provisions of this Act shall not apply to the Superior Court of the District of Columbia and the District of Columbia Court of Appeals", for "shall be applicable in the District of Columbia", and struck out provisions that the plan of the District of Columbia shall be approved jointly by the Judicial Council of the District of Columbia Circuit and the District of Columbia Court of Appeals.

1970—Subsec. (a). Pub. L. 91–447, §1(a), expanded coverage of district court plan for furnishing representation to financially disabled persons to include defendants charged with violation of probation, any person under arrest when such representation is required by law, any person who is subject to revocation of parole, in custody as a material witness, or seeking collateral relief as provided in subsec. (g) of this section, and any person for whom the Sixth Amendment to the Constitution requires appointment of counsel or for whom, in a case in which he faces loss of liberty, any Federal law requires the appointment of counsel, and required each plan to include a provision for participation by private attorneys in a substantial proportion of cases, as well as permitting attorneys to be furnished by bar, legal aid, or defender organizations in accordance with subsec. (h) of this section.

Subsec. (b). Pub. L. 91–447, §1(a), provided for appointment of counsel from a bar association, legal aid agency, or defender organization as well as from a panel of attorneys approved by the court, expanded advice to defendant of right to appointment of counsel where defendant is charged with juvenile delinquency by the commission of an act which, if committed by an adult, would be a felony or misdemeanor or with violation of probation, and provided for appointment of counsel to be retroactive so as to include any representation furnished pursuant to the plan prior to appointment.

Subsec. (c). Pub. L. 91–447, §1(a), expanded the scope of representation by appointed counsel to include ancillary matters appropriate to the proceedings.

Subsec. (d). Pub. L. 91–447, §1(a), raised the rate of compensation not to exceed $30 per hour for time expended in court and $20 per hour for time reasonably expended out of court, increased the limit to $1,000 for each attorney in a case involving one or more alleged felonies and $400 for each attorney in a case in which one or more misdemeanors are charged, established a $1,000 maximum for each attorney in each court for cases on appeal and provided a $250 maximum for each attorney for representation in connection with a post-trial motion, probation revocation proceedings and matters covered by subsec. (g) such as parole revocation and collateral relief proceedings, provided for waiver of maximum amounts and payment in excess of those amounts for extended or complex representation upon approval of the chief judge of the circuit, provided for separate claims of compensation to be submitted to the appropriate court, thus a U.S. magistrate fixes compensation in cases before him, appellate court fixes compensation in cases before it and in all other instances claims are to be made to the district court, provided a court order granting a new trial is deemed to initiate a new case for the purpose of compensation, and facilitate appellate proceedings by allowing a defendant for whom counsel is appointed to appeal or petition for a writ of certiorari without prepayment of fees and cost of security therefore and without filing the affidavit required by section 1915(a).

Subsec. (e). Pub. L. 91–447, §1(a), limited to $150, plus reasonable expenses, subject to later review and approval by the court, the cost of investigative, expert, or other services necessary for an adequate defense where these services are obtained without prior authorization because circumstances prevented counsel from securing prior court authorization, maintained existing limit on payment for authorized services at a $300 maximum but permitted waiver of that maximum if the court certifies that payment in excess of that limit is necessary to provide fair compensation, and provided that the amount of any excess payment must be approved by the chief judge of the circuit.

Subsec. (f). Pub. L. 91–447, §1(a), substantially reenacted subsec. (f).

Subsecs. (g) to (k). Pub. L. 91–447, §1(b), added subsecs. (g) and (h) and redesignated existing subsecs. (g) to (i) as (i) to (k), respectively.

Subsec. (l). Pub. L. 91–447, §1(c), added subsec. (l).

1968—Subsecs. (b) to (d). Pub. L. 90–578 substituted "United States magistrate" for "United States commissioner" wherever appearing.

Change of Name

"United States magistrate judge" substituted for "United States magistrate" wherever appearing in text pursuant to section 321 of Pub. L. 101–650, set out as a note under section 631 of Title 28, Judiciary and Judicial Procedure.

Effective Date of 1999 Amendment

Pub. L. 106–113, div. B, §1000(a)(1) [title III, §308(b)], Nov. 29, 1999, 113 Stat. 1535, 1501A–37, provided that: "This section [amending this section] shall apply to all disclosures made under section 3006A(d) of title 18, United States Code, related to any criminal trial or appeal involving a sentence of death where the underlying alleged criminal conduct took place on or after April 19, 1995."

Effective Date of 1996 Amendment

Pub. L. 104–132, title IX, §903(c), Apr. 24, 1996, 100 Stat. 1318, provided that: "The amendments made by this section [amending this section and section 848 of Title 21, Food and Drugs] apply to—

"(1) cases commenced on or after the date of the enactment of this Act [Apr. 24, 1996]; and

"(2) appellate proceedings, in which an appeal is perfected, on or after the date of the enactment of this Act."

Effective Date of 1987 Amendment

Pub. L. 100–182, §26, Dec. 7, 1987, 101 Stat. 1272, provided that: "The amendments made by this Act [amending this section, sections 3553, 3561, 3563, 3564, 3583, 3663, 3672, 3742, and 4106 of this title, section 994 of Title 28, Judiciary and Judicial Procedure, and sections 504 and 1111 of Title 29, Labor, enacting provisions set out as notes under sections 3551 and 3553 of this title, rule 35 of the Federal Rules of Criminal Procedure, set out in the Appendix to this title, and section 994 of Title 28, and amending provisions set out as a note under section 3551 of this title] shall apply with respect to offenses committed after the enactment of this Act [Dec. 7, 1987]."

Effective Date of 1986 Amendment

Pub. L. 99–651, title I, §105, Nov. 14, 1986, 100 Stat. 3646, provided that: "This title and the amendments made by this title [amending this section and section 1825 of Title 28, Judiciary and Judicial Procedure, and enacting provisions set out as a note under this section] shall take effect one hundred and twenty days after the date of enactment of this Act [Nov. 14, 1986]. The maximum hourly rates provided in section 3006A(d)(1) of title 18, United States Code, as amended by section 102(a)(3)(A) of this Act, shall apply only to services performed on or after the effective date of this title. The maximum allowed for compensation for a case, as provided in section 3006A(d)(2) of title 18, United States Code, as amended by section 102(a)(3)(B) of this Act, shall apply only to compensation claims in which some portion of the claim is for services performed on or after the effective date of this title. The maximum compensation allowed pursuant to section 3006A(e) of title 18, United States Code, as amended by subparagraphs (B) and (C) of section 102(a)(4) of this Act, shall apply only to services obtained on or after the effective date of this title."

Effective Date of 1984 Amendment

Amendment by section 223(e) of Pub. L. 98–473 effective Nov. 1, 1987, and applicable only to offenses committed after the taking effect of such amendment, see section 235(a)(1) of Pub. L. 98–473, set out as an Effective Date note under section 3551 of this title.

Effective Date of 1982 Amendment

Amendment by Pub. L. 97–164 effective Oct. 1, 1982, see section 402 of Pub. L. 97–164, set out as a note under section 171 of Title 28, Judiciary and Judicial Procedure.

Effective Date of 1974 Amendment

Pub. L. 93–412, §4, Sept. 3, 1974, 88 Stat. 1093, provided in part that the amendment of subsec. (l) of this section by Pub. L. 93–412 shall take effect on Sept. 3, 1974.

Effective Date of 1970 Amendment

Pub. L. 91–447, §3, Oct. 14, 1970, 84 Stat. 920, provided that: "The amendments made by section 1 of this Act [amending this section] shall become effective one hundred and twenty days after the date of enactment [Oct. 14, 1970]."

Effective Date of 1968 Amendment

Amendment by Pub. L. 90–578 effective Oct. 17, 1968, except when a later effective date is applicable, which is the earlier of date when implementation of amendment by appointment of magistrates [now United States magistrate judges] and assumption of office takes place or third anniversary of enactment of Pub. L. 90–578 on Oct. 17, 1968, see section 403 of Pub. L. 90–578, set out as a note under section 631 of Title 28, Judiciary and Judicial Procedure.

Short Title of 1986 Amendment

Pub. L. 99–651, title I, §101, Nov. 14, 1986, 100 Stat. 3642, provided that: "This title [amending this section and section 1825 of Title 28, Judiciary and Judicial Procedure, and enacting provisions set out as a note under this section] may be referred to as the 'Criminal Justice Act Revision of 1986'."

Short Title of 1984 Amendment

Pub. L. 98–473, title II, Oct. 12, 1984, 98 Stat. 2185, provided in part that: "This chapter [chapter XIX (§1901) of title II of Pub. L. 98–473, amending this section] may be cited as the 'Criminal Justice Act Revision of 1984'."

Short Title

Pub. L. 88–455, §1, Aug. 20, 1964, 78 Stat. 552, provided: "That this Act [enacting this section and provisions set out as a note under this section] may be cited as the 'Criminal Justice Act of 1964.' "

Savings Provision

Pub. L. 97–164, title II, §206(c), Apr. 2, 1982, 96 Stat. 53, provided that: "The amendments made by subsection (a) of this section [amending subsec. (h)(2)(A) of this section] shall not affect the term of existing appointments."

Award of Attorney's Fees and Litigation Expenses to Defense

Pub. L. 105–119, title VI, §617, Nov. 26, 1997, 111 Stat. 2519, provided that: "During fiscal year 1998 and in any fiscal year thereafter, the court, in any criminal case (other than a case in which the defendant is represented by assigned counsel paid for by the public) pending on or after the date of the enactment of this Act [Nov. 26, 1997], may award to a prevailing party, other than the United States, a reasonable attorney's fee and other litigation expenses, where the court finds that the position of the United States was vexatious, frivolous, or in bad faith, unless the court finds that special circumstances make such an award unjust. Such awards shall be granted pursuant to the procedures and limitations (but not the burden of proof) provided for an award under section 2412 of title 28, United States Code. To determine whether or not to award fees and costs under this section, the court, for good cause shown, may receive evidence ex parte and in camera (which shall include the submission of classified evidence or evidence that reveals or might reveal the identity of an informant or undercover agent or matters occurring before a grand jury) and evidence or testimony so received shall be kept under seal. Fees and other expenses awarded under this provision to a party shall be paid by the agency over which the party prevails from any funds made available to the agency by appropriation. No new appropriations shall be made as a result of this provision."

Government Rates of Travel for Criminal Justice Act Attorneys and Experts

Pub. L. 102–572, title VII, §702, Oct. 29, 1992, 106 Stat. 4515, provided that: "The Administrator of General Services, in entering into contracts providing for special rates to be charged by Federal Government sources of supply, including common carriers and hotels (or other commercial providers of lodging) for official travel and accommodation of Federal Government employees, shall provide for charging the same rates for attorneys, experts, and other persons traveling primarily in connection with carrying out responsibilities under section 3006A of title 18, United States Code, including community defender organizations established under subsection (g) of that section."

Study of Federal Defender Program

Pub. L. 101–650, title III, §318, Dec. 1, 1990, 104 Stat. 5116, as amended by Pub. L. 102–198, §9, Dec. 9, 1991, 105 Stat. 1626, directed Judicial Conference of the United States to conduct a study of effectiveness of Federal defender program and to transmit a report on results of study to Committees on the Judiciary of Senate and House of Representatives no later than Mar. 31, 1993, with report to include recommendations for legislation, a proposed formula for compensation of Federal defender program counsel, and suggestions for procedural and operational changes by courts.

Funds for Payment of Compensation and Reimbursement

Pub. L. 101–45, title II, §102, June 30, 1989, 103 Stat. 122, provided in part: "That compensation and reimbursement of attorneys and others as authorized under section 3006A of title 18, United

States Code, and section 1875(d) of title 28, United States Code, may hereinafter be paid from funds appropriated for 'Defender Services' in the year in which payment is required."

Certification by Attorney General to Administrative Office of United States Courts of Payment of Obligated Expenses

Pub. L. 95–144, §5(c), Oct. 28, 1977, 91 Stat. 1222, provided that: "The Attorney General shall certify to the Administrative Office of the United States Courts those expenses which it is obligated to pay on behalf of an indigent offender under section 3006A of title 18, United States Code, and similar statutes."

Power and Function of a United States Commissioner

Pub. L. 91–447, §2, Oct. 14, 1970, 84 Stat. 920, provided that a United States commissioner for a district could exercise any power, function, or duty authorized to be performed by a United States magistrate under the amendments made by section 1 of Pub. L. 91–447, which amended this section, if such commissioner had authority to perform such power, function, or duty prior to the enactment of such amendments.

Submission of Plans

Pub. L. 88–455, §3, Aug. 20, 1964, 78 Stat. 554, directed each district court to submit a plan in accord with section 3006A of this title and the rules of the Judicial Conference of the United States to the judicial council of the circuit within 6 months from Aug. 20, 1964, further directed each judicial council to approve and send to the Administrative Office of the United States courts a plan for each district in its circuit within 9 months from Aug. 20, 1964, and also directed each district court and court of appeals to place its approved plan in operation within 1 year from Aug. 20, 1964.

§3007. Motions—(Rule)

See Federal Rules of Criminal Procedure

Motions substituted for pleas in abatement and special pleas in bar, rule 12.
Form and contents, rule 47.
(June 25, 1948, ch. 645, 62 Stat. 814.)

§3008. Service and filing of papers—(Rule)

See Federal Rules of Criminal Procedure

Requirement and manner of service; notice of orders; filing papers, rule 49.
(June 25, 1948, ch. 645, 62 Stat. 815.)

§3009. Records—(Rule)

See Federal Rules of Criminal Procedure

Keeping of records by district court clerks and magistrate judges, rule 55.
(June 25, 1948, ch. 645, 62 Stat. 815; Pub. L. 90–578, title III, §301(a)(4), Oct. 17, 1968, 82 Stat. 1115; Pub. L. 101–650, title III, §321, Dec. 1, 1990, 104 Stat. 5117.)

Amendments

1968—Pub. L. 90–578 substituted "magistrates" for "commissioners".

Change of Name

Words "magistrate judges" substituted for "magistrates" in text pursuant to section 321 of Pub. L. 101–650, set out as a note under section 631 of Title 28, Judiciary and Judicial Procedure.

§3010. Exceptions unnecessary—(Rule)

See Federal Rules of Criminal Procedure
Objections substituted for exceptions, rule 51.
(June 25, 1948, ch. 645, 62 Stat. 815.)

§3011. Computation of time—(Rule)

See Federal Rules of Criminal Procedure
Computation: enlargement; expiration of term; motions and affidavits; service by mail, rule 45.
(June 25, 1948, ch. 645, 62 Stat. 815.)

[§3012. Repealed. Pub. L. 98–473, title II, §218(a)(2), Oct. 12, 1984, 98 Stat. 2027]

Section, act June 25, 1948, ch. 645, 62 Stat. 815, related to orders respecting prisoners or persons in custody.

Effective Date of Repeal
Repeal of section effective Nov. 1, 1987, and applicable only to offenses committed after the taking effect of such repeal, see section 235(a)(1) of Pub. L. 98–473, set out as an Effective Date note under section 3551 of this title.

§3013. Special assessment on convicted persons
(a) The court shall assess on any person convicted of an offense against the United States—
(1) in the case of an infraction or a misdemeanor—
(A) if the defendant is an individual—
(i) the amount of $5 in the case of an infraction or a class C misdemeanor;
(ii) the amount of $10 in the case of a class B misdemeanor; and
(iii) the amount of $25 in the case of a class A misdemeanor; and
(B) if the defendant is a person other than an individual—
(i) the amount of $25 in the case of an infraction or a class C misdemeanor;
(ii) the amount of $50 in the case of a class B misdemeanor; and
(iii) the amount of $125 in the case of a class A misdemeanor;
(2) in the case of a felony—
(A) the amount of $100 if the defendant is an individual; and
(B) the amount of $400 if the defendant is a person other than an individual.
(b) Such amount so assessed shall be collected in the manner that fines are collected in criminal cases.
(c) The obligation to pay an assessment ceases five years after the date of the judgment. This subsection shall apply to all assessments irrespective of the date of imposition.
(d) For the purposes of this section, an offense under section 13 of this title is an offense against the United States.
(Added Pub. L. 98–473, title II, §1405(a), Oct. 12, 1984, 98 Stat. 2174; amended Pub. L. 100–185, §3, Dec. 11, 1987, 101 Stat. 1279; Pub. L. 100–690, title VII, §§7082(b), 7085, Nov. 18, 1988, 102 Stat. 4407, 4408; Pub. L. 101–647, title XXXV, §3569, Nov. 29, 1990, 104 Stat. 4928; Pub. L. 104–132, title II, §210, Apr. 24, 1996, 110 Stat. 1240; Pub. L. 104–294, title VI, §601(r)(4), Oct. 11, 1996, 110 Stat. 3502.)

Amendments

1996—Subsec. (a)(2). Pub. L. 104–294 struck out "not less than" before "$100" in subpar. (A) and before "$400" in subpar. (B).

Pub. L. 104–132 substituted "not less than $100" for "$50" in subpar. (A) and "not less than $400" for "$200" in subpar. (B).

1990—Subsec. (a)(1)(B). Pub. L. 101–647 substituted "an infraction" for "a infraction" in cl. (i) and a semicolon for a period at end of cl. (iii).

1988—Subsec. (a)(1). Pub. L. 100–690, §7085, amended par. (1) generally. Prior to amendment, par. (1) read as follows: "in the case of a misdemeanor—

"(A) the amount of $25 if the defendant is an individual; and

"(B) the amount of $100 if the defendant is a person other than an individual; and".

Subsec. (c). Pub. L. 100–690, §7082(b), inserted at end "This subsection shall apply to all assessments irrespective of the date of imposition."

1987—Subsecs. (c), (d). Pub. L. 100–185 added subsecs. (c) and (d).

Effective Date of 1996 Amendment

Amendment by Pub. L. 104–132 effective, to extent constitutionally permissible, for sentencing proceedings in cases in which defendant is convicted on or after Apr. 24, 1996, see section 211 of Pub. L. 104–132, set out as a note under section 2248 of this title.

Effective Date

Section effective 30 days after Oct. 12, 1984, see section 1409(a) of Pub. L. 98–473, set out as a note under section 20101 of Title 34, Crime Control and Law Enforcement.

§3014. Additional special assessment

(a) In General.—Beginning on the date of enactment of the Justice for Victims of Trafficking Act of 2015 and ending on September 30, 2019, in addition to the assessment imposed under section 3013, the court shall assess an amount of $5,000 on any non-indigent person or entity convicted of an offense under—

(1) chapter 77 (relating to peonage, slavery, and trafficking in persons);

(2) chapter 109A (relating to sexual abuse);

(3) chapter 110 (relating to sexual exploitation and other abuse of children);

(4) chapter 117 (relating to transportation for illegal sexual activity and related crimes); or

(5) section 274 of the Immigration and Nationality Act (8 U.S.C. 1324) (relating to human smuggling), unless the person induced, assisted, abetted, or aided only an individual who at the time of such action was the alien's spouse, parent, son, or daughter (and no other individual) to enter the United States in violation of law.

(b) Satisfaction of Other Court-Ordered Obligations.—An assessment under subsection (a) shall not be payable until the person subject to the assessment has satisfied all outstanding court-ordered fines, orders of restitution, and any other obligation related to victim-compensation arising from the criminal convictions on which the special assessment is based.

(c) Establishment of Domestic Trafficking Victims' Fund.—There is established in the Treasury of the United States a fund, to be known as the "Domestic Trafficking Victims' Fund" (referred to in this section as the "Fund"), to be administered by the Attorney General, in consultation with the Secretary of Homeland Security and the Secretary of Health and Human Services.

(d) Transfers.—In a manner consistent with section 3302(b) of title 31, there shall be transferred to the Fund from the General Fund of the Treasury an amount equal to the amount of the assessments collected under this section, which shall remain available until expended.

(e) Use of Funds.—

(1) In general.—From amounts in the Fund, in addition to any other amounts available, and without further appropriation, the Attorney General, in coordination with the Secretary of Health and Human Services shall, for each of fiscal years 2016 through 2019, use amounts available in

the Fund to award grants or enhance victims' programming under—

(A) section 204 of the Trafficking Victims Protection Reauthorization Act of 2005 (42 U.S.C. 14044c); 1

(B) subsections (b)(2) and (f) of section 107 of the Trafficking Victims Protection Act of 2000 (22 U.S.C. 7105);

(C) section 214(b) of the Victims of Child Abuse Act of 1990 (42 U.S.C. 13002(b)); 1 and

(D) section 106 of the PROTECT Our Children Act of 2008 (42 U.S.C. 17616).1

(2) Limitation.—Except as provided in subsection (h)(2), none of the amounts in the Fund may be used to provide health care or medical items or services.

(f) Collection Method.—The amount assessed under subsection (a) shall, subject to subsection (b), be collected in the manner that fines are collected in criminal cases.

(g) Duration of Obligation.—Subject to section 3613(b), the obligation to pay an assessment imposed on or after the date of enactment of the Justice for Victims of Trafficking Act of 2015 shall not cease until the assessment is paid in full.

(h) Health or Medical Services.—

(1) Transfer of funds.—From amounts appropriated under subparagraphs (E) and (F) of section 10503(b)(1) of the Patient Protection and Affordable Care Act (42 U.S.C. 254b–2(b)(1)), there shall be transferred to the Fund an amount equal to the amount transferred under subsection (d) for each fiscal year, except that the amount transferred under this paragraph shall not be less than $5,000,000 or more than $30,000,000 in each such fiscal year, and such amounts shall remain available until expended.

(2) Use of funds.—The Attorney General, in coordination with the Secretary of Health and Human Services, shall use amounts transferred to the Fund under paragraph (1) to award grants that may be used for the provision of health care or medical items or services to victims of trafficking under—

(A) sections 202, 203, and 204 of the Trafficking Victims Protection Reauthorization Act of 2005 (42 U.S.C. 14044a, 14044b, and 14044c); 1

(B) subsections (b)(2) and (f) of section 107 of the Trafficking Victims Protection Act of 2000 (22 U.S.C. 7105); and

(C) section 214(b) of the Victims of Child Abuse Act of 1990 (42 U.S.C. 13002(b)).1

(3) Grants.—Of the amounts in the Fund used under paragraph (1), not less than $2,000,000, if such amounts are available in the Fund during the relevant fiscal year, shall be used for grants to provide services for child pornography victims under section 214(b) of the Victims of Child Abuse Act of 1990 (42 U.S.C. 13002(b)).1

(4) Application of provision.—The application of the provisions of section 221(c) of the Medicare Access and CHIP Reauthorization Act of 2015 and section 50901(e) of the Advancing Chronic Care, Extenders, and Social Services Act shall continue to apply to the amounts transferred pursuant to paragraph (1).

(Added and amended Pub. L. 114–22, title I, §101(a), title IX, §905, May 29, 2015, 129 Stat. 228, 266; Pub. L. 115–96, div. C, title I, §3101(e), Dec. 22, 2017, 131 Stat. 2049; Pub. L. 115–123, div. E, title IX, §50901(f), Feb. 9, 2018, 132 Stat. 289.)

References in Text

The date of enactment of the Justice for Victims of Trafficking Act of 2015, referred to in subsecs. (a) and (g), is the date of enactment of Pub. L. 114–22, which was approved May 29, 2015.

Sections 202, 203, and 204 of the Trafficking Victims Protection Reauthorization Act of 2005, referred to in subsecs. (e)(1)(A) and (h)(2)(A), are sections 202, 203, and 204 of Pub. L. 109–164, which were classified to sections 14044a, 14044b, and 14044c, respectively, of Title 42, The Public Health and Welfare, prior to editorial reclassification as sections 20702, 20703, and 20705, respectively, of Title 34, Crime Control and Law Enforcement.

Section 214(b) of the Victims of Child Abuse Act of 1990, referred to in subsecs. (e)(1)(C) and (h)(2)(C), (3), is section 214(b) of title II of Pub. L. 101–647, which was classified to section

13002(b) of Title 42, The Public Health and Welfare, prior to editorial reclassification as section 20304(b) of Title 34, Crime Control and Law Enforcement.

Section 106 of the PROTECT Our Children Act of 2008, referred to in subsec. (e)(1)(D), is section 106 of Pub. L. 110–401, which was classified to section 17616 of Title 42, The Public Health and Welfare, prior to editorial reclassification as section 21116 of Title 34, Crime Control and Law Enforcement.

Section 221 of the Medicare Access and CHIP Reauthorization Act of 2015, referred to in subsec. (h)(1), (4), is section 221 of Pub. L. 114–10, title II, Apr. 16, 2015, 129 Stat. 154. Section 221(a)(1) of the Act amended section 254b–2(b)(1)(E) of Title 42, The Public Health and Welfare. Section 221(c) of the Act provided for a condition on certain appropriations and is not classified to the Code.

Section 50901(e) of the Advancing Chronic Care, Extenders, and Social Services Act, referred to in subsec. (h)(4), is section 50901(e) of Pub. L. 115–123, div. E, title IX, Feb. 9, 2018, 132 Stat. 289. Section 50901(e) of the Act related to application of amounts appropriated pursuant to that section and is not classified to the Code.

Amendments

2018—Subsec. (h)(4). Pub. L. 115–123 substituted "and section 50901(e) of the Advancing Chronic Care, Extenders, and Social Services Act" for "and section 3101(d) of the CHIP and Public Health Funding Extension Act".

2017—Subsec. (h)(1). Pub. L. 115–96, §3101(e)(1), substituted "subparagraphs (E) and (F) of section 10503(b)(1) of the Patient Protection and Affordable Care Act (42 U.S.C. 254b–2(b)(1))" for "section 10503(b)(1)(E) of the Patient Protection and Affordable Care Act (42 U.S.C. 254b–2(b)(1)(E)), as amended by section 221 of the Medicare Access and CHIP Reauthorization Act of 2015".

Subsec. (h)(4). Pub. L. 115–96, §3101(e)(2), inserted "and section 3101(d) of the CHIP and Public Health Funding Extension Act" after "section 221(c) of the Medicare Access and CHIP Reauthorization Act of 2015".

2015—Subsec. (e)(1)(D). Pub. L. 114–22, §905, added subpar. (D).

CHAPTER 203 - ARREST AND COMMITMENT

Amendments

2006—Pub. L. 109–177, title VI, §605(b), Mar. 9, 2006, 120 Stat. 255, added item 3056A.

Pub. L. 109–162, title XI, §1172(a), Jan. 5, 2006, 119 Stat. 3123, added item 3051.

2005—Pub. L. 109–59, title IV, §4143(c)(2), Aug. 10, 2005, 119 Stat. 1748, added item 3064.

1996—Pub. L. 104–294, title VI, §605(n), Oct. 11, 1996, 110 Stat. 3510, added item 3059B.

1994—Pub. L. 103–322, title XXXIII, §330010(18), Sept. 13, 1994, 108 Stat. 2144, inserted a period at end of item 3059A.

1990—Pub. L. 101–647, title XXXV, §3570, Nov. 29, 1990, 104 Stat. 4928, struck out item 3054 "Officer's powers involving animals and birds".

Pub. L. 101–647, title XXV, §2587(b), Nov. 29, 1990, 104 Stat. 4905, as amended, effective as of date section 2587(b) of Pub. L. 101–647 took effect, by Pub. L. 103–322, title XXXIII, §330011(a), Sept. 13, 1994, 108 Stat. 2144, added item 3059A.

1988—Pub. L. 100–690, title VI, §6251(b), Nov. 18, 1988, 102 Stat. 4362, substituted "Investigative powers of Postal Service personnel" for "Powers of postal personnel" in item 3061.

Pub. L. 100–582, §4(b), Nov. 1, 1988, 102 Stat. 2959, added item 3063.

1984—Pub. L. 98–587, §1(b), Oct. 30, 1984, 98 Stat. 3111, substituted "Powers, authorities, and duties of United States Secret Service" for "Secret Service powers" in item 3056.

Pub. L. 98–473, title II, §204(e), Oct. 12, 1984, 98 Stat. 1986, substituted "Repealed" for "Security of the peace and good behavior" in item 3043 and added item 3062.

1970—Pub. L. 91–375, §6(j)(38)(B), Aug. 12, 1970, 84 Stat. 782, substituted "postal personnel" for "postal inspectors" in item 3061.

1968—Pub. L. 90–578, title III, §303(b), Oct. 17, 1968, 82 Stat. 1118, struck out reference to "Rule" in item 3060.

Pub. L. 90–560, §5(b), Oct. 12, 1968, 82 Stat. 998, added item 3061.

1951—Act Oct. 31, 1951, ch. 655, §56(f), 65 Stat. 729, struck out item 3051 "Extradition agent's powers".

§3041. Power of courts and magistrates

For any offense against the United States, the offender may, by any justice or judge of the United States, or by any United States magistrate judge, or by any chancellor, judge of a supreme or superior court, chief or first judge of the common pleas, mayor of a city, justice of the peace, or other magistrate, of any state where the offender may be found, and at the expense of the United States, be arrested and imprisoned or released as provided in chapter 207 of this title, as the case may be, for trial before such court of the United States as by law has cognizance of the offense. Copies of the process shall be returned as speedily as may be into the office of the clerk of such court, together with the recognizances of the witnesses for their appearances to testify in the case. A United States judge or magistrate judge shall proceed under this section according to rules promulgated by the Supreme Court of the United States. Any state judge or magistrate acting hereunder may proceed according to the usual mode of procedure of his state but his acts and orders shall have no effect beyond determining, pursuant to the provisions of section 3142 of this title, whether to detain or conditionally release the prisoner prior to trial or to discharge him from arrest.

(June 25, 1948, ch. 645, 62 Stat. 815; Pub. L. 89–465, §5(a), June 22, 1966, 80 Stat. 217; Pub. L.

90–578, title III, §301(a)(1), (3), Oct. 17, 1968, 82 Stat. 1115; Pub. L. 98–473, title II, §204(a), Oct. 12, 1984, 98 Stat. 1985; Pub. L. 101–650, title III, §321, Dec. 1, 1990, 104 Stat. 5117.)

Historical and Revision Notes

Based on title 18, U.S.C., 1940 ed., §591 (R.S. §1014; May 28, 1896, ch. 252, §19, 29 Stat. 184; Mar. 2, 1901, ch. 814, 31 Stat. 956).

This section was completely rewritten to omit all provisions superseded by Federal Rules of Criminal Procedure, rules 3, 4, 5, 40 and 54(a) which prescribed the procedure for preliminary proceedings and examinations before United States judges and commissioners and for removal proceedings but not for preliminary examinations before State magistrates.

Amendments

1984—Pub. L. 98–473 substituted "determining, pursuant to the provisions of section 3142 of this title, whether to detain or conditionally release the prisoner prior to trial" for "determining to hold the prisoner for trial".

1968—Pub. L. 90–578 substituted "United States magistrate" and "magistrate" for "United States commissioner" and "commissioner", respectively.

1966—Pub. L. 89–465 substituted "or released as provided in chapter 207 of this title" for "or bailed".

Change of Name

"United States magistrate judge" substituted for "United States magistrate" in text pursuant to section 321 of Pub. L. 101–650, set out as a note under section 631 of Title 28, Judiciary and Judicial Procedure.

Effective Date of 1968 Amendment

Amendment by Pub. L. 90–578 effective Oct. 17, 1968, except when a later effective date is applicable, which is the earlier of date when implementation of amendment by appointment of magistrates [now United States magistrate judges] and assumption of office takes place or third anniversary of enactment of Pub. L. 90–578 on Oct. 17, 1968, see section 403 of Pub. L. 90–578, set out as a note under section 631 of Title 28, Judiciary and Judicial Procedure.

Effective Date of 1966 Amendment

Amendment by Pub. L. 89–465 effective ninety days after June 22, 1966, see section 6 of Pub. L. 89–465, set out as an Effective Date note under section 3146 of this title.

§3042. Extraterritorial jurisdiction

Section 3041 of this title shall apply in any country where the United States exercises extraterritorial jurisdiction for the arrest and removal therefrom to the United States of any citizen or national of the United States who is a fugitive from justice charged with or convicted of the commission of any offense against the United States, and shall also apply throughout the United States for the arrest and removal therefrom to the jurisdiction of any officer or representative of the United States vested with judicial authority in any country in which the United States exercises extraterritorial jurisdiction, of any citizen or national of the United States who is a fugitive from justice charged with or convicted of the commission of any offense against the United States in any country where it exercises extraterritorial jurisdiction.

Such fugitive first mentioned may, by any officer or representative of the United States vested with judicial authority in any country in which the United States exercises extraterritorial jurisdiction and agreeably to the usual mode of process against offenders subject to such jurisdiction, be arrested and detained or conditionally released pursuant to section 3142 of this title, as the case may be, pending the issuance of a warrant for his removal, which warrant the principal officer or representative of the United States vested with judicial authority in the country where the fugitive shall be found shall seasonably issue, and the United States marshal or corresponding officer shall execute.

Such marshal or other officer, or the deputies of such marshal or officer, when engaged in executing such warrant without the jurisdiction of the court to which they are attached, shall have all the powers of a marshal of the United States so far as such powers are requisite for the prisoner's safekeeping and the execution of the warrant.

(June 25, 1948, ch. 645, 62 Stat. 815; Pub. L. 98–473, title II, §204(b), Oct. 12, 1984, 98 Stat. 1985.)

Historical and Revision Notes

Based on title 18, U.S.C., 1940 ed., §662b (Mar. 22, 1934, ch. 73, §1, 48 Stat. 454).

Words "crime or" before "offense" were omitted as unnecessary.

Words "and the Philippine Islands" were deleted in two places as obsolete in view of the independence of the Commonwealth of the Philippines effective July 4, 1946.

Words "its Territories, Districts, or possessions, including the Panama Canal Zone or any other territory governed, occupied, or controlled by it" were omitted as covered by section 5 of this title defining the term "United States".

Minor changes were made in phraseology.

Amendments

1984—Pub. L. 98–473 substituted "detained or conditionally released pursuant to section 3142 of this title" for "imprisoned or admitted to bail".

[§3043. Repealed. Pub. L. 98–473, title II, §204(c), Oct. 12, 1984, 98 Stat. 1986]

Section, acts June 25, 1948, ch. 645, 62 Stat. 816; Oct. 17, 1968, Pub. L. 90–578, title III, §301(a)(2), 82 Stat. 1115, related to authority of justices, judges, and magistrates to hold to security of the peace and for good behavior. See section 3142 of this title.

§3044. Complaint—(Rule)

See Federal Rules of Criminal Procedure

Contents of complaint; oath, Rule 3.

(June 25, 1948, ch. 645, 62 Stat. 816.)

§3045. Internal revenue violations

Warrants of arrest for violations of internal revenue laws may be issued by United States magistrate judges upon the complaint of a United States attorney, assistant United States attorney, collector, or deputy collector of internal revenue or revenue agent, or private citizen; but no such warrant of arrest shall be issued upon the complaint of a private citizen unless first approved in writing by a United States attorney.

(June 25, 1948, ch. 645, 62 Stat. 816; Pub. L. 90–578, title III, §301(a)(2), Oct. 17, 1968, 82 Stat. 1115; Pub. L. 101–650, title III, §321, Dec. 1, 1990, 104 Stat. 5117.)

Historical and Revision Notes

Based on title 18, U.S.C., 1940 ed., §594 (May 28, 1896, ch. 252, §19, 29 Stat. 184; Mar. 2, 1901, ch. 814, 31 Stat. 956).

Minor changes were made in phraseology.

Amendments

1968—Pub. L. 90–578 substituted "United States magistrates" for "United States commissioners".

Change of Name
"United States magistrate judges" substituted for "United States magistrates" in text pursuant to section 321 of Pub. L. 101–650, set out as a note under section 631 of Title 28, Judiciary and Judicial Procedure.

Effective Date of 1968 Amendment
Amendment by Pub. L. 90–578 effective Oct. 17, 1968, except when a later effective date is applicable, which is the earlier of date when implementation of amendment by appointment of magistrates [now United States magistrate judges] and assumption of office takes place or third anniversary of enactment of Pub. L. 90–578 on Oct. 17, 1968, see section 403 of Pub. L. 90–578, set out as a note under section 631 of Title 28, Judiciary and Judicial Procedure.

Abolition of Offices of Collector and Deputy Collector of Internal Revenue
Offices of Collector and Deputy Collector of Internal Revenue abolished by Reorg. Plan No. 1 of 1952, §1, eff. Mar. 14, 1952, 17 F.R. 2243, 66 Stat. 823, set out in the Appendix to Title 5, Government Organization and Employees, and the offices of "district commissioner of internal revenue", and so many other offices, with titles to be determined by Secretary of the Treasury, were established by section 2(a) of the Plan.

§3046. Warrant or summons—(Rule)

See Federal Rules of Criminal Procedure
Issuance upon complaint, Rule 4.
Issuance upon indictment, Rule 9.
Summons on request of government; form; contents; service; return, Rules 4, 9.
(June 25, 1948, ch. 645, 62 Stat. 816.)

§3047. Multiple warrants unnecessary
When two or more charges are made, or two or more indictments are found against any person, only one writ or warrant shall be necessary to commit him for trial. It shall be sufficient to state in the writ the name or general character of the offenses, or to refer to them only in general terms.
(June 25, 1948, ch. 645, 62 Stat. 816.)

Historical and Revision Notes
Based on title 18, U.S.C., 1940 ed., §602 (R.S. §1027).
Minor changes were made in phraseology.

§3048. Commitment to another district; removal—(Rule)

See Federal Rules of Criminal Procedure
Arrest in nearby or distant districts; informative statement by judge or magistrate judge; hearing and removal; warrant; Rule 40.
(June 25, 1948, ch. 645, 62 Stat. 817; Pub. L. 90–578, title III, §301(a)(3), Oct. 17, 1968, 82 Stat. 1115; Pub. L. 101–650, title III, §321, Dec. 1, 1990, 104 Stat. 5117.)

Amendments
1968—Pub. L. 90–578 substituted "magistrate" for "commissioner".

Change of Name

Words "magistrate judge" substituted for "magistrate" in text pursuant to section 321 of Pub. L. 101–650, set out as a note under section 631 of Title 28, Judiciary and Judicial Procedure.

§3049. Warrant for removal

Only one writ or warrant is necessary to remove a prisoner from one district to another. One copy thereof may be delivered to the sheriff or jailer from whose custody the prisoner is taken, and another to the sheriff or jailer to whose custody he is committed, and the original writ, with the marshal's return thereon, shall be returned to the clerk of the district to which he is removed. (June 25, 1948, ch. 645, 62 Stat. 817.)

Historical and Revision Notes

Based on title 18, U.S.C., 1940 ed., §604 (R.S. §1029).

§3050. Bureau of Prisons employees' powers

An officer or employee of the Bureau of Prisons may—

(1) make arrests on or off of Bureau of Prisons property without warrant for violations of the following provisions regardless of where the violation may occur: sections 111 (assaulting officers), 751 (escape), and 752 (assisting escape) of title 18, United States Code, and section 1826(c) (escape) of title 28, United States Code;

(2) make arrests on Bureau of Prisons premises or reservation land of a penal, detention, or correctional facility without warrant for violations occurring thereon of the following provisions: sections 661 (theft), 1361 (depredation of property), 1363 (destruction of property), 1791 (contraband), 1792 (mutiny and riot), and 1793 (trespass) of title 18, United States Code; and

(3) arrest without warrant for any other offense described in title 18 or 21 of the United States Code, if committed on the premises or reservation of a penal or correctional facility of the Bureau of Prisons if necessary to safeguard security, good order, or government property;

if such officer or employee has reasonable grounds to believe that the arrested person is guilty of such offense, and if there is likelihood of such person's escaping before an arrest warrant can be obtained. If the arrested person is a fugitive from custody, such prisoner shall be returned to custody. Officers and employees of the said Bureau of Prisons may carry firearms under such rules and regulations as the Attorney General may prescribe.
(June 25, 1948, ch. 645, 62 Stat. 817; Pub. L. 99–646, §65, Nov. 10, 1986, 100 Stat. 3615.)

Historical and Revision Notes

Based on title 18, U.S.C., 1940 ed., §753k (June 29, 1940, ch. 449, §5, 54 Stat. 693).
Section was broadened to include authority to make arrests for mutiny, riot or traffic in dangerous instrumentalities, by reference to section 1792 of this title.
Minor changes were made in phraseology and provision for taking arrested person before magistrate was omitted as covered by rule 5(a) of the Federal Rules of Criminal Procedure.

Amendments

1986—Pub. L. 99–646 amended first sentence generally and substituted "such prisoner" for "he" in second sentence. Prior to amendment, first sentence read as follows: "An officer or employee of the Bureau of Prisons of the Department of Justice may make arrests without warrant for violations of any of the provisions of sections 751, 752, 1791, or 1792 of this title, if he has reasonable grounds to believe that the arrested person is guilty of such offense, and if there is likelihood of his escaping before a warrant can be obtained for his arrest."

Transfer of Functions

Functions of all other officers of Department of Justice and functions of all agencies and employees of such Department, with a few exceptions, transferred to Attorney General, with power vested in him to authorize their performance or performance of any of his functions by any of such officers, agencies, and employees, by Reorg. Plan No. 2 of 1950, §§1, 2, eff. May 24, 1950, 15 F.R. 3173, 64 Stat. 1261, set out in the Appendix to Title 5, Government Organization and Employees.

§3051. Powers of Special Agents 1 of Bureau of Alcohol, Tobacco, Firearms, and Explosives

(a) Special agents of the Bureau of Alcohol, Tobacco, Firearms, and Explosives, as well as any other investigator or officer charged by the Attorney General with the duty of enforcing any of the criminal, seizure, or forfeiture provisions of the laws of the United States, may carry firearms, serve warrants and subpoenas issued under the authority of the United States and make arrests without warrant for any offense against the United States committed in their presence, or for any felony cognizable under the laws of the United States if they have reasonable grounds to believe that the person to be arrested has committed or is committing such felony.

(b) Any special agent of the Bureau of Alcohol, Tobacco, Firearms, and Explosives may, in respect to the performance of his or her duties, make seizures of property subject to forfeiture to the United States.

(c)(1) Except as provided in paragraphs (2) and (3), and except to the extent that such provisions conflict with the provisions of section 983 of title 18, United States Code, insofar as section 983 applies, the provisions of the Customs laws relating to—

(A) the seizure, summary and judicial forfeiture, and condemnation of property;

(B) the disposition of such property;

(C) the remission or mitigation of such forfeiture; and

(D) the compromise of claims,

shall apply to seizures and forfeitures incurred, or alleged to have been incurred, under any applicable provision of law enforced or administered by the Bureau of Alcohol, Tobacco, Firearms, and Explosives.

(2) For purposes of paragraph (1), duties that are imposed upon a customs officer or any other person with respect to the seizure and forfeiture of property under the customs laws of the United States shall be performed with respect to seizures and forfeitures of property under this section by such officers, agents, or any other person as may be authorized or designated for that purpose by the Attorney General.

(3) Notwithstanding any other provision of law, the disposition of firearms forfeited by reason of a violation of any law of the United States shall be governed by the provisions of section 5872(b) of the Internal Revenue Code of 1986.

(Added Pub. L. 107–296, title XI, §1113, Nov. 25, 2002, 116 Stat. 2279.)

References in Text

Section 5872(b) of the Internal Revenue Code of 1986, referred to in subsec. (c)(3), is classified to section 5872(b) of Title 26, Internal Revenue Code.

Prior Provisions

A prior section 3051, act June 25, 1948, ch. 645, §1, 62 Stat. 817, related to powers of extradition agents, prior to repeal by act Oct. 31, 1951, ch. 655, §56(f), 65 Stat. 729. Substantially identical provisions are contained in section 3193 of this title.

Effective Date

Section effective 60 days after Nov. 25, 2002, see section 4 of Pub. L. 107–296, set out as a note under section 101 of Title 6, Domestic Security.

§3052. Powers of Federal Bureau of Investigation

The Director, Associate Director, Assistant to the Director, Assistant Directors, inspectors, and agents of the Federal Bureau of Investigation of the Department of Justice may carry firearms, serve warrants and subpoenas issued under the authority of the United States and make arrests without warrant for any offense against the United States committed in their presence, or for any felony cognizable under the laws of the United States if they have reasonable grounds to believe that the person to be arrested has committed or is committing such felony.

(June 25, 1948, ch. 645, 62 Stat. 817; Jan. 10, 1951, ch. 1221, §1, 64 Stat. 1239.)

Historical and Revision Notes

Based on section 300a of title 5, U.S.C., 1940 ed., Executive Departments and Government Officers and Employees (June 18, 1934, ch. 595, 48 Stat. 1008; Mar. 22, 1935, ch. 39, title II, 49 Stat. 77).

Language relating to seizures under warrant is in section 3107 of this title.

Minor changes were made in phraseology particularly with respect to omission of provision covered by rule 5(a) of Federal Rules of Criminal Procedure.

Amendments

1951—Act Jan. 10, 1951, allowed F. B. I. personnel to make arrests without a warrant for any offense against the United States committed in their presence.

Transfer of Functions

Functions of all other officers of Department of Justice and functions of all agencies and employees of such Department, with a few exceptions, transferred to Attorney General, with power vested in him to authorize their performance or performance of any of his functions by any of such officers, agencies, and employees, by Reorg. Plan No. 2 of 1950, §§1, 2, eff. May 24, 1950, 15 F.R. 3173, 64 Stat. 1261, set out in the Appendix to Title 5, Government Organization and Employees.

§3053. Powers of marshals and deputies

United States marshals and their deputies may carry firearms and may make arrests without warrant for any offense against the United States committed in their presence, or for any felony cognizable under the laws of the United States if they have reasonable grounds to believe that the person to be arrested has committed or is committing such felony.

(June 25, 1948, ch. 645, 62 Stat. 817.)

Historical and Revision Notes

Based on section 504a of title 28, U.S.C., 1940 ed., Judicial Code and Judiciary (June 15, 1935, ch. 259, §2, 49 Stat. 378).

Minor changes were made in phraseology.

Transfer of Functions

Functions of all other officers of Department of Justice and functions of all agencies and employees of such Department, with a few exceptions, transferred to Attorney General, with power vested in him to authorize their performance or performance of any of his functions by any of such officers, agencies, and employees, by Reorg. Plan No. 2 of 1950, §§1, 2, eff. May 24, 1950, 15 F.R. 3173, 64 Stat. 1261, set out in the Appendix to Title 5, Government Organization and Employees.

[§3054. Repealed. Pub. L. 97–79, §9(b)(3), Nov. 16, 1981, 95 Stat. 1079]

Section, acts June 25, 1948, ch. 645, 62 Stat. 817; Dec. 5, 1969, Pub. L. 91–135, §7(b), 83 Stat.

281, provided for an officer's power to act in enforcing sections 42, 43, and 44 of this title relating to animals and birds. See section 3375 of Title 16, Conservation.

§3055. Officers' powers to suppress Indian liquor traffic

The chief special officer for the suppression of the liquor traffic among Indians and duly authorized officers working under his supervision whose appointments are made or affirmed by the Commissioner of Indian Affairs or the Secretary of the Interior may execute all warrants of arrest and other lawful precepts issued under the authority of the United States and in the execution of his duty he may command all necessary assistance.
(June 25, 1948, ch. 645, 62 Stat. 817.)

Historical and Revision Notes

Based on section 250 of title 25, U.S.C., 1940 ed., Indians (Aug. 24, 1912, ch. 388, §1, 37 Stat. 519).

The only change was to delete the words at the beginning of the section, "The powers conferred by section 504 of title 28 upon marshals and their deputies are conferred upon." and the addition, at the end of the section, of the phrase expressing such powers beginning with the words "may execute all warrants".

§3056. Powers, authorities, and duties of United States Secret Service

(a) Under the direction of the Secretary of Homeland Security, the United States Secret Service is authorized to protect the following persons:

(1) The President, the Vice President (or other officer next in the order of succession to the Office of President), the President-elect, and the Vice President-elect.

(2) The immediate families of those individuals listed in paragraph (1).

(3) Former Presidents and their spouses for their lifetimes, except that protection of a spouse shall terminate in the event of remarriage.

(4) Children of a former President who are under 16 years of age.

(5) Visiting heads of foreign states or foreign governments.

(6) Other distinguished foreign visitors to the United States and official representatives of the United States performing special missions abroad when the President directs that such protection be provided.

(7) Major Presidential and Vice Presidential candidates and, within 120 days of the general Presidential election, the spouses of such candidates. As used in this paragraph, the term "major Presidential and Vice Presidential candidates" means those individuals identified as such by the Secretary of Homeland Security after consultation with an advisory committee consisting of the Speaker of the House of Representatives, the minority leader of the House of Representatives, the majority and minority leaders of the Senate, and one additional member selected by the other members of the committee. The Committee shall not be subject to the Federal Advisory Committee Act (5 U.S.C. App. 2).

(8) Former Vice Presidents, their spouses, and their children who are under 16 years of age, for a period of not more than six months after the date the former Vice President leaves office. The Secretary of Homeland Security shall have the authority to direct the Secret Service to provide temporary protection for any of these individuals at any time thereafter if the Secretary of Homeland Security or designee determines that information or conditions warrant such protection. The protection authorized in paragraphs (2) through (8) may be declined.

(b) Under the direction of the Secretary of Homeland Security, the Secret Service is authorized to detect and arrest any person who violates—

(1) section 508, 509, 510, 871, or 879 of this title or, with respect to the Federal Deposit Insurance Corporation, Federal land banks, and Federal land bank associations, section 213, 216,1 433, 493, 657, 709, 1006, 1007, 1011, 1013, 1014, 1907, or 1909 of this title;

(2) any of the laws of the United States relating to coins, obligations, and securities of the United

States and of foreign governments; or

(3) any of the laws of the United States relating to electronic fund transfer frauds, access device frauds, false identification documents or devices, and any fraud or other criminal or unlawful activity in or against any federally insured financial institution; except that the authority conferred by this paragraph shall be exercised subject to the agreement of the Attorney General and the Secretary of Homeland Security and shall not affect the authority of any other Federal law enforcement agency with respect to those laws.

(c)(1) Under the direction of the Secretary of Homeland Security, officers and agents of the Secret Service are authorized to—

(A) execute warrants issued under the laws of the United States;

(B) carry firearms;

(C) make arrests without warrant for any offense against the United States committed in their presence, or for any felony cognizable under the laws of the United States if they have reasonable grounds to believe that the person to be arrested has committed or is committing such felony;

(D) offer and pay rewards for services and information leading to the apprehension of persons involved in the violation or potential violation of those provisions of law which the Secret Service is authorized to enforce;

(E) pay expenses for unforeseen emergencies of a confidential nature under the direction of the Secretary of Homeland Security and accounted for solely on the Secretary's certificate; and

(F) perform such other functions and duties as are authorized by law.

(2) Funds expended from appropriations available to the Secret Service for the purchase of counterfeits and subsequently recovered shall be reimbursed to the appropriations available to the Secret Service at the time of the reimbursement.

(d) Whoever knowingly and willfully obstructs, resists, or interferes with a Federal law enforcement agent engaged in the performance of the protective functions authorized by this section or by section 1752 of this title shall be fined not more than $1,000 or imprisoned not more than one year, or both.

(e)(1) When directed by the President, the United States Secret Service is authorized to participate, under the direction of the Secretary of Homeland Security, in the planning, coordination, and implementation of security operations at special events of national significance, as determined by the President.

(2) At the end of each fiscal year, the President through such agency or office as the President may designate, shall report to the Congress—

(A) what events, if any, were designated special events of national significance for security purposes under paragraph (1); and

(B) the criteria and information used in making each designation.

(f) Under the direction of the Secretary of Homeland Security, the Secret Service is authorized, at the request of any State or local law enforcement agency, or at the request of the National Center for Missing and Exploited Children, to provide forensic and investigative assistance in support of any investigation involving missing or exploited children.

(g) The United States Secret Service shall be maintained as a distinct entity within the Department of Homeland Security and shall not be merged with any other Department function. No personnel and operational elements of the United States Secret Service shall report to an individual other than the Director of the United States Secret Service, who shall report directly to the Secretary of Homeland Security without being required to report through any other official of the Department.

(June 25, 1948, ch. 645, 62 Stat. 818; July 16, 1951, ch. 226, §4, 65 Stat. 122; Aug. 31, 1954, ch. 1143, §2, 68 Stat. 999; Pub. L. 86–168, title I, §104(h), Aug. 18, 1959, 73 Stat. 387; Pub. L. 87–791, Oct. 10, 1962, 76 Stat. 809; Pub. L. 87–829, §3, Oct. 15, 1962, 76 Stat. 956; Pub. L. 89–186, Sept. 15, 1965, 79 Stat. 791; Pub. L. 89–218, Sept. 29, 1965, 79 Stat. 890; Pub. L. 90–608, ch. XI, §1101, Oct. 21, 1968, 82 Stat. 1198; Pub. L. 91–644, title V, §19, Jan. 2, 1971, 84 Stat. 1892; Pub. L. 91–651, §4, Jan. 5, 1971, 84 Stat. 1941; Pub. L. 93–346, §8, July 12, 1974, as added Pub. L. 93–552, title VI, §609(a), Dec. 27, 1974, 88 Stat. 1765; Pub. L. 94–408, §2, Sept. 11, 1976, 90 Stat. 1239; Pub. L. 97–297, §3, Oct. 12, 1982, 96 Stat. 1318; Pub. L. 97–308, §2, Oct. 14, 1982,

96 Stat. 1452; Pub. L. 98–151, §115(b), Nov. 14, 1983, 97 Stat. 977; Pub. L. 98–587, §1(a), Oct. 30, 1984, 98 Stat. 3110; Pub. L. 103–329, title V, §530, Sept. 30, 1994, 108 Stat. 2412; Pub. L. 104–294, title VI, §605(i), Oct. 11, 1996, 110 Stat. 3510; Pub. L. 106–544, §3, Dec. 19, 2000, 114 Stat. 2716; Pub. L. 107–56, title V, §506(b), Oct. 26, 2001, 115 Stat. 367; Pub. L. 107–296, title XVII, §1703(a)(1), Nov. 25, 2002, 116 Stat. 2313; Pub. L. 108–21, title III, §322, Apr. 30, 2003, 117 Stat. 665; Pub. L. 109–177, title VI, §§604, 607, 608(a), Mar. 9, 2006, 120 Stat. 253, 256; Pub. L. 110–326, title I, §102, Sept. 26, 2008, 122 Stat. 3560; Pub. L. 112–257, §2, Jan. 10, 2013, 126 Stat. 2413.)

Historical and Revision Notes

Based on title 18, U.S.C., 1940 ed., §148, and on sections 264(x) and 986 of title 12, U.S.C., 1940 ed., Banks and Banking (Dec. 23, 1913, ch. 6, §12B, subsection (x), as added June 16, 1933, ch. 89, §8, 48 Stat. 178; July 17, 1916, ch. 245, §31, sixth paragraph, 39 Stat. 382 (384); Dec. 11, 1926, ch. 2, §3, 44 Stat. 918; Aug. 23, 1935, ch. 614, §101, 49 Stat. 684, 703).

Section consolidates said section 148 of title 18, U.S.C., 1940 ed., and said sections 264(x) and 986 of title 12, U.S.C., 1940 ed., Banks and Banking.

Said section 148 of title 12, U.S.C., 1940 ed., Banks and Banking, was concerned with offenses relating to counterfeiting and passing, etc., of transportation requests and to the unlawful possession or making of plates, stones, etc., used in making such requests, which were defined in sections 146 and 147 of said title 18, now sections 508 and 509 of this title.

Said sections 264(x) and 986 of title 12, U.S.C., 1940 ed., Banks and Banking, were concerned with various offenses as defined in sections 981–985, 987 of said title 12, relating to Federal land banks, joint-stock land banks and national farm loan associations, and as defined in section 264 of said title 12 relating to the Federal Deposit Insurance Corporation. All of the provisions of said sections 981–985, 987 of said title 12, and the criminal provisions of said section 264 of said title 12, were transferred to this title where they were, in some instances, consolidated with similar provisions from other sections. Such provisions are now incorporated in sections 218, 221, 433, 493, 657, 709, 1006, 1007, 1011, 1013, 1014, 1907, and 1909 of this title. In most instances, these sections, as the result of the consolidations, relate to other organizations as well as those mentioned above, but, by enumerating the Federal Deposit Insurance Corporation, Federal land banks, joint-stock land banks, and national farm loan associations in this section, the powers of the Secret Service are not broadened beyond what they were in said sections 264(x) and 986 of said title 12.

In this section, the wording of said section 148 of title 18, U.S.C., 1940 ed., and section 986 of title 12, U.S.C., 1940 ed., Banks and Banking reading "The Secretary of the Treasury is hereby authorized to direct and use the Secret Service Division of the Treasury Department" was adopted, rather than the wording of said section 264(x) of said title 12, which read "The Secret Service Division of the Treasury Department is authorized."

Words "of the United States marshal having jurisdiction", following "custody" in all three of said sections, were omitted as surplusage.

Changes were made in phraseology.

References in Text

The Federal Advisory Committee Act, referred to in subsec. (a)(7), is Pub. L. 92–463, Oct. 6, 1972, 86 Stat. 770, as amended, which is set out in the Appendix to Title 5, Government Organization and Employees.

Section 216 of this title, referred to in subsec. (b)(1), was repealed by Pub. L. 98–473, title II, §1107(b), Oct. 12, 1984, 98 Stat. 2146.

Amendments

2013—Subsec. (a)(3). Pub. L. 112–257, §2(a), struck out provisions limiting protection for certain former Presidents and their spouses to ten years from the date a former President leaves office, with certain exceptions, and authorizing the provision of temporary protection if determined to be warranted by the Secretary of Homeland Security.

Subsec. (a)(4). Pub. L. 112–257, §2(b), struck out "for a period not to exceed ten years or upon the child becoming 16 years of age, whichever comes first" after "16 years of age".

2008—Subsec. (a). Pub. L. 110–326, §102(2), substituted "(8)" for "(7)" in concluding provisions.

Subsec. (a)(8). Pub. L. 110–326, §102(1), added par. (8).

2006—Subsec. (a)(7). Pub. L. 109–177, §608(a), which directed amendment of subsec. (a)(7) by inserting "The Committee shall not be subject to the Federal Advisory Committee Act (5 U.S.C. App. 2)." after "other members of the Committee.", was executed by making the insertion after "other members of the committee.", to reflect the probable intent of Congress.

Subsec. (f). Pub. L. 109–177, §604, substituted "the Secret Service is" for "officers and agents of the Secret Service are".

Subsec. (g). Pub. L. 109–177, §607, added subsec. (g).

2003—Subsec. (f). Pub. L. 108–21 added subsec. (f).

2002—Subsecs. (a) to (c)(1), (e)(1). Pub. L. 107–296 substituted "of Homeland Security" for "of the Treasury" wherever appearing.

2001—Subsec. (b)(3). Pub. L. 107–56 substituted "access device frauds, false identification documents or devices, and any fraud or other criminal or unlawful activity in or against any federally insured financial institution" for "credit and debit card frauds, and false identification documents or devices".

2000—Subsec. (e). Pub. L. 106–544 added subsec. (e).

1996—Subsec. (a)(3). Pub. L. 104–294 redesignated subpars. (1) and (2) as (A) and (B), respectively, and realigned margins.

1994—Subsec. (a)(3). Pub. L. 103–329, §530(a), inserted before period at end "unless the former President did not serve as President prior to January 1, 1997, in which case, former Presidents and their spouses for a period of not more than ten years from the date a former President leaves office, except that—

"(1) protection of a spouse shall terminate in the event of remarriage or the divorce from, or death of a former President; and

"(2) should the death of a President occur while in office or within one year after leaving office, the spouse shall receive protection for one year from the time of such death:

Provided, That the Secretary of the Treasury shall have the authority to direct the Secret Service to provide temporary protection for any of these individuals at any time if the Secretary of the Treasury or designee determines that information or conditions warrant such protection".

Subsec. (a)(4). Pub. L. 103–329, §530(b), inserted before period at end "for a period not to exceed ten years or upon the child becoming 16 years of age, whichever comes first".

1984—Pub. L. 98–587 amended section generally, providing authority for the Secret Service to conduct criminal investigations of, make arrests in, and present for prosecutorial consideration, cases relating to electronic fund transfer frauds, and providing the Secret Service with authority to conduct investigations and make arrests relating to credit and debit card frauds, and false identification documents and devices, to be exercised subject to the agreement of the Attorney General and the Secretary of the Treasury.

1983—Subsec. (a). Pub. L. 98–151 inserted reference to section 510 of this section in fifth clause.

1982—Subsec. (a). Pub. L. 97–297, §3(1), substituted "871, and 879 of this title" for "and 871 of this title".

Pub. L. 97–297, §3(2), substituted "and Federal land bank associations are concerned, of sections 213, 216" for ", joint-stock land banks and Federal land bank associations are concerned, of sections 218, 221".

Subsec. (b). Pub. L. 97–308 increased the limitation on fines to $1,000 from $300.

1976—Subsec. (a). Pub. L. 94–408 substituted ", and the members of their immediate families unless the members decline such protection;" for "; protect the members of the immediate family of the Vice-President, unless such protection is declined;".

Subsec. (b). Pub. L. 94–408 inserted reference to other Federal law enforcement agents.

1974—Subsec. (a). Pub. L. 93–552 inserted provisions relating to the protection of the immediate family of the Vice President unless declined, and the payment of expenses for unforeseen emergencies of a confidential nature under the direction of the Secretary of the Treasury and accounted for solely on his certificate.

1971—Pub. L. 91–651 authorized the Secret Service to protect the person of a visiting head of a foreign state or foreign government and, at the direction of the President, other distinguished foreign visitors to the United States and official representatives of the United States performing special missions abroad, and substituted "Director, Deputy Director, Assistant Directors, Assistants to the Director" for "Chief, Deputy Chief, Assistant Chief".

Pub. L. 91–644 designated existing provisions as subsec. (a) and added subsec. (b).

1968—Pub. L. 90–608 substituted the death or remarriage of a former President's widow and the attainment by his minor children of age 16 for the passage of a period of four years after he leaves or dies in office as the events terminating Secret Service protection for the widow and minor children, respectively, of a former President.

1965—Pub. L. 89–218 authorized the Chief, Deputy Chief, Assistant Chief, inspectors, and agents of the Secret Service to make arrests without warrant for offenses committed against the United States in their presence or for any felony cognizable under the laws of the United States if they have reasonable grounds to believe that the person to be arrested has committed or is committing the felony and substituted "508, 509, and 871" for "508 and 509".

Pub. L. 89–186 substituted provision for the protection of the person of a former President and his wife during his lifetime and the person of a widow and minor children of a former President for a period of four years after he leaves or dies in office, unless the protection is declined, for provision calling for the protection of a former President, at his request, for a reasonable period after he leaves office.

1962—Pub. L. 87–829 authorized the protection of the Vice President, without requiring his request therefor, and any officer next in the order of succession to the office of President, the Vice-President-elect, and of a former president, at his request, for a reasonable period after he leaves office.

Pub. L. 87–791 required moneys expended from Secret Service appropriations for the purchase of counterfeits and subsequently recovered to be reimbursed to the appropriation current at the time of deposit.

1959—Pub. L. 86–168 substituted "Federal land bank associations" for "national farm loan associations".

1954—Act Aug. 31, 1954, struck out "detect, and arrest any person violating any laws of the United States directly concerning official matters administered by and under the direct control of the Treasury Department".

1951—Act July 16, 1951, provided basic authority for the Secret Service to perform certain functions and activities heretofore carried out by virtue of authority contained in appropriation acts.

Effective Date of 2008 Amendment

Pub. L. 110–326, title I, §103, Sept. 26, 2008, 122 Stat. 3560, provided that: "The amendments made by this Act [probably should be "title", meaning title I of Pub. L. 110–326, which amended this section and enacted provisions set out as a note under section 1 of this title] shall apply with respect to any Vice President holding office on or after the date of enactment of the Act [Sept. 26, 2008]."

Effective Date of 2002 Amendment

Pub. L. 107–296, title XVII, §1703(b), Nov. 25, 2002, 116 Stat. 2314, provided that: "The amendments made by this section [amending this section and former sections 202 and 208 of Title 3, The President] shall take effect on the date of transfer of the United States Secret Service to the Department [of Homeland Security]."

Effective Date of 1974 Amendment

Pub. L. 93–552, title VI, §609(b), Dec. 27, 1974, 88 Stat. 1765, provided that: "Except as otherwise provided therein, the amendment made by subsection (a) of this section [amending this section, former section 202 of Title 3, The President, and provisions set out as a note under section 111 of Title 3] shall become effective July 12, 1974."

Effective Date of 1959 Amendment

Amendment by Pub. L. 86–168 effective Dec. 31, 1959, see section 104(k) of Pub. L. 86–168.

Transfer of Functions

For transfer of the functions, personnel, assets, and obligations of the United States Secret Service, including the functions of the Secretary of the Treasury relating thereto, to the Secretary of Homeland Security, and for treatment of related references, see sections 381, 551(d), 552(d), and 557 of Title 6, Domestic Security, and the Department of Homeland Security Reorganization Plan of November 25, 2002, as modified, set out as a note under section 542 of Title 6.

Use of Funds for United States Secret Service Protection

Pub. L. 109–295, title V, §517(b), Oct. 4, 2006, 120 Stat. 1380, as amended by Pub. L. 110–161, div. E, title V, §517, Dec. 26, 2007, 121 Stat. 2073, provided that: "For fiscal year 2008, and each fiscal year thereafter, the Director of the United States Secret Service may enter into an agreement to perform protection of a Federal official other than a person granted protection under section 3056(a) of title 18, United States Code, on a fully reimbursable basis."

Funds for Training

Pub. L. 108–90, title II, Oct. 1, 2003, 117 Stat. 1145, provided in part: "That in fiscal year 2004 and thereafter, subject to the reimbursement of actual costs to this account, funds appropriated in this account shall be available, at the discretion of the Director, for the following: training United States Postal Service law enforcement personnel and Postal police officers, training Federal law enforcement officers, training State and local government law enforcement officers on a space-available basis, and training private sector security officials on a space-available basis".

Expansion of National Electronic Crime Task Force Initiative

Pub. L. 107–56, title I, §105, Oct. 26, 2001, 115 Stat. 277, as amended by Pub. L. 109–177, title VI, §608(b), Mar. 9, 2006, 120 Stat. 256, provided that: "The Director of the United States Secret Service shall take appropriate actions to develop a national network of electronic crime task forces, based on the New York Electronic Crimes Task Force model, throughout the United States, for the purpose of preventing, detecting, and investigating various forms of electronic crimes, including potential terrorist attacks against critical infrastructure and financial payment systems. The electronic crimes task forces shall not be subject to the Federal Advisory Committee Act (5 U.S.C. App. 2) [5 U.S.C. App.]."

National Threat Assessment Center

Pub. L. 106–544, §4, Dec. 19, 2000, 114 Stat. 2716, provided that:

"(a) Establishment.—The United States Secret Service (hereafter in this section referred to as the 'Service'), at the direction of the Secretary of the Treasury, may establish the National Threat Assessment Center (hereafter in this section referred to as the 'Center') as a unit within the Service.

"(b) Functions.—The Service may provide the following to Federal, State, and local law enforcement agencies through the Center:

"(1) Training in the area of threat assessment.

"(2) Consultation on complex threat assessment cases or plans.

"(3) Research on threat assessment and the prevention of targeted violence.

"(4) Facilitation of information sharing among all such agencies with protective or public safety responsibilities.

"(5) Programs to promote the standardization of Federal, State, and local threat assessments and investigations involving threats.

"(6) Any other activities the Secretary determines are necessary to implement a comprehensive threat assessment capability.

"(c) Report.—Not later than 1 year after the date of the enactment of this Act [Dec. 19, 2000], the Service shall submit a report to the Committees on the Judiciary of the Senate and the House of Representatives detailing the manner in which the Center will operate."

Telecommunications Support to United States Secret Service by White House Communications Agency

Pub. L. 104–208, div. A, title I, §101(b) [title VIII, §8100], Sept. 30, 1996, 110 Stat. 3009–71, 3009–108, as amended by Pub. L. 106–92, §2, Nov. 9, 1999, 113 Stat. 1309, provided that: "Beginning in fiscal year 1997 and thereafter, and notwithstanding any other provision of law, fixed and mobile telecommunications support shall be provided by the White House Communications Agency (WHCA) to the United States Secret Service (USSS), without reimbursement, in connection with the Secret Service's duties directly related to the protection of the President or the Vice President or other officer immediately next in order of succession to the office of the President at the White House Security Complex in the Washington, D.C. Metropolitan Area and Camp David, Maryland. For these purposes, the White House Security Complex includes the White House, the White House grounds, the Dwight D. Eisenhower Executive Office Building, the New Executive Office Building, the Blair House, the Treasury Building, and the Vice President's Residence at the Naval Observatory."

Off-Set of Costs of Protecting Former Presidents and Spouses

Pub. L. 104–208, div. A, title I, §101(f) [title V, §509], Sept. 30, 1996, 110 Stat. 3009–314, 3009–345, provided that: "The United States Secret Service may, during the fiscal year ending September 30, 1997, and hereafter, accept donations of money to off-set costs incurred while protecting former Presidents and spouses of former Presidents when the former President or spouse travels for the purpose of making an appearance or speech for a payment of money or any thing of value."

Similar provisions were contained in the following prior appropriations acts:

Pub. L. 104–52, title V, §509, Nov. 19, 1995, 109 Stat. 492.

Pub. L. 103–329, title V, §514, Sept. 30, 1994, 108 Stat. 2410.

Pub. L. 103–123, title V, §515, Oct. 28, 1993, 107 Stat. 1253.

Pub. L. 102–393, title V, §519, Oct. 6, 1992, 106 Stat. 1759.

Pub. L. 102–141, title V, §522, Oct. 28, 1991, 105 Stat. 865.

Pub. L. 101–509, title V, §525, Nov. 5, 1990, 104 Stat. 1426.

Former Vice President or Spouse; Protection

Pub. L. 103–1, Jan. 15, 1993, 107 Stat. 3, provided: "That—

"(1) the United States Secret Service, in addition to other duties now provided by law, is authorized to furnish protection to—

"(A) the person occupying the Office of Vice President of the United States immediately preceding January 20, 1993, or

"(B) his spouse,

if the President determines that such person may thereafter be in significant danger; and

"(2) protection of any such person, pursuant to the authority provided in paragraph (1), shall continue only for such period as the President determines, except that such protection shall not continue beyond July 20, 1993, unless otherwise permitted by law."

Pub. L. 96–503, Dec. 5, 1980, 94 Stat. 2740, provided: "That the United States Secret Service, in addition to other duties now provided by law, is authorized to furnish protection to (a) the person occupying the Office of Vice President of the United States immediately preceding January 20, 1981, or (b) his spouse, if the President determines that such person may thereafter be in significant danger: Provided, however, That protection of any such person shall continue only for such period as the President determines and shall not continue beyond July 20, 1981, unless otherwise permitted by law."

Secret Service Protection of Former Federal Officials

Pub. L. 95–1, Jan. 19, 1977, 91 Stat. 3, provided: "That the United States Secret Service, in addition to other duties now provided by law, is authorized to furnish protection to a person who (a) as a Federal Government official has been receiving protection by the United States Secret Service for a period immediately preceding January 20, 1977, or (b) as a member of such official's immediate family has been receiving protection by either the United States Secret Service or other security personnel of the official's department immediately preceding January 20, 1977, if the President determines that such person may thereafter be in significant danger: Provided, however, That protection of any such person shall continue only for such period as the President determines and shall not continue beyond July 20, 1977, unless otherwise permitted by law."

Presidential Protection Assistance Act of 1976

Pub. L. 94–524, Oct. 17, 1976, 90 Stat. 2475, as amended by Pub. L. 99–190, §143, Dec. 19, 1985, 99 Stat. 1324; Pub. L. 101–136, title V, §527, Nov. 3, 1989, 103 Stat. 815; Pub. L. 101–509, title V, §531(a), Nov. 5, 1990, 104 Stat. 1469; Pub. L. 102–141, title V, §533, Oct. 28, 1991, 105 Stat. 867; Pub. L. 104–52, title V, §529, Nov. 19, 1995, 109 Stat. 496; Pub. L. 104–316, title I, §109(a), Oct. 19, 1996, 110 Stat. 3832, provided: "That this Act may be cited as the 'Presidential Protection Assistance Act of 1976'.

"Sec. 2. As used in this Act the term—

"(1) 'Secret Service' means the United States Secret Service, the Department of the Treasury;

"(2) 'Director' means the Director of the Secret Service;

"(3) 'protectee' means any person eligible to receive the protection authorized by section 3056 of title 18, United States Code, or Public Law 90–331 (82 Stat. 170) [set out as a note above];

"(4) 'Executive departments' has the same meaning as provided in section 101 of title 5, United States Code;

"(5) 'Executive agencies' has the same meaning as provided in section 105 of title 5, United States Code;

"(6) 'Coast Guard' means the United States Coast Guard, Department of Transportation or such other Executive department or Executive agency to which the United States Coast Guard may subsequently be transferred;

"(7) 'duties' means all responsibilities of an Executive department or Executive agency relating to the protection of any protectee; and

"(8) 'non-Governmental property' means any property owned, leased, occupied, or otherwise utilized by a protectee which is not owned or controlled by the Government of the United States of America.

"Sec. 3. (a) Each protectee may designate one non-governmental property to be fully secured by the Secret Service on a permanent basis.

"(b) A protectee may thereafter designate a different non-Governmental property in lieu of the non-Governmental property previously designated under subsection (a) (hereinafter in this Act referred to as the 'previously designated property') as the one non-Governmental property to be fully secured by the Secret Service on a permanent basis under subsection (a). Thereafter, any expenditures by the Secret Service to maintain a permanent guard detail or for permanent facilities, equipment, and services to secure the non-Governmental property previously designated under subsection (a) shall be subject to the limitations imposed under section 4.

"(c) For the purposes of this section, where two or more protectees share the same domicile, such protectees shall be deemed a single protectee.

"Sec. 4. Expenditures by the Secret Service for maintaining a permanent guard detail and for permanent facilities, equipment, and services to secure any non-Governmental property in addition to the one non-Governmental property designated by each protectee under subsection 3(a) or 3(b) may not exceed a cumulative total of $200,000 at each such additional non-Governmental property, unless expenditures in excess of that amount are specifically approved by resolutions adopted by the Committees on Appropriations of the House and Senate, respectively.

"Sec. 5. (a) All improvements and other items acquired by the Federal Government and used for the purpose of securing any non-Governmental property in the performance of the duties of the Secret Service shall be the property of the United States.

"(b) Upon termination of Secret Service protection at any non-Governmental property all such improvements and other items shall be removed from the non-Governmental property unless the Director determines that it would not be economically feasible to do so; except that such improvements and other items shall be removed and the non-Governmental property shall be restored to its original state if the owner of such property at the time of termination requests the removal of such improvements or other items. If any such improvements or other items are not removed, the owner of the non-Governmental property at the time of termination shall compensate the United States for the original cost of such improvements or other items or for the amount by which they have increased the fair market value of the property, as determined by the Director, as of the date of termination, whichever is less.

"(c) In the event that any non-Governmental property becomes a previously designated property and Secret Service protection at that property has not been terminated, all such improvements and other items which the Director determines are not necessary to secure the previously designated property within the limitations imposed under section 4 shall be removed or compensated for in accordance with the procedures set forth under Subsection (b) of this section.

"Sec. 6. Executive departments and Executive agencies shall assist the Secret Service in the performance of its duties by providing services, equipment, and facilities on a temporary and reimbursable basis when requested by the Director and on a permanent and reimbursable basis upon advance written request of the Director; except that the Department of Defense and the Coast Guard shall provide such assistance on a temporary basis without reimbursement when assisting the Secret Service in its duties directly related to the protection of the President or the Vice President or other officer immediately next in order of succession to the office of the President.

"Sec. 7. No services, equipment, or facilities may be ordered, purchased, leased, or otherwise procured for the purposes of carrying out the duties of the Secret Service by persons other than officers or employees of the Federal Government duly authorized by the Director to make such orders, purchases, leases, or procurements.

"Sec. 8. No funds may be expended or obligated for the purpose of carrying out the purposes of section 3056 of title 18, United States Code, and section 1 of Public Law 90–331 [set out as a note above] other than funds specifically appropriated to the Secret Service for those purposes with the exception of—

"(1) expenditures made by the Department of Defense or the Coast Guard from funds appropriated to the Department of Defense or the Coast Guard in providing assistance on a temporary basis to the Secret Service in the performance of its duties directly related to the protection of the President or the Vice President or other officer next in order of succession to the office of the President; and

"(2) expenditures made by Executive departments and agencies, in providing assistance at the request of the Secret Service in the performance of its duties, and which will be reimbursed by the Secret Service under section 6 of this Act.

"Sec. 9. The Director, the Secretary of Defense, and the Commandant of the Coast Guard shall each transmit a detailed semi-annual report of expenditures made pursuant to this Act during the six-month period immediately preceding such report by the Secret Service, the Department of Defense, and the Coast Guard, respectively, to the Committees on Appropriations, Committees on the Judiciary, and Committees on Government Operations [now Committee on Oversight and

Government Reform of the House of Representatives and Committee on Homeland Security and Governmental Affairs of the Senate] of the House of Representatives and the Senate, respectively, on March 31 and September 30, of each year.

"Sec. 10. Expenditures made pursuant to this Act shall be subject to audit by the Comptroller General and his authorized representatives, who shall have access to all records relating to such expenditures. The Comptroller General shall transmit a report of the results of any such audit to the Committees on Appropriations, Committees on the Judiciary, and Committees on Government Operations [now Committee on Oversight and Government Reform of the House of Representatives and Committee on Homeland Security and Governmental Affairs of the Senate] of the House of Representatives and the Senate, respectively.

"Sec. 11. Section 2 of Public Law 90–331 (82 Stat. 170) [formerly set out as a note below] is repealed.

"Sec. 12. In carrying out the protection of the President of the United States, pursuant to section 3056(a) of title 18, at the one non-governmental property designated by the President of the United States to be fully secured by the United States Secret Service on a permanent basis, as provided in section 3.(a) of Public Law 94–524 [section 3(a) of this note], or at an airport facility used for travel en route to or from such property[,] the Secretary of the Treasury may utilize, with their consent, the law enforcement services, personnel, equipment, and facilities of the affected State and local governments. Further, the Secretary of the Treasury is authorized to reimburse such State and local governments for the utilization of such services, personnel, equipment, and facilities. All claims for such reimbursement by the affected governments will be submitted to the Secretary of the Treasury on a quarterly basis. Expenditures for this reimbursement are authorized not to exceed $300,000 at the one nongovernmental property, and $70,000 at the airport facility, in any one fiscal year: Provided, That the designated site is located in a municipality or political subdivision of any State where the permanent resident population is 7,000 or less and where the absence of such Federal assistance would place an undue economic burden on the affected State and local governments: Provided further, That the airport facility is wholly or partially located in a municipality or political subdivison [sic] of any State where the permanent resident population is 7,000 or less, the airport is located within 25 nautical miles of the designated nongovernmental property, and where the absence of such Federal assistance would place an undue economic burden on the affected State and local governments."

[For transfer of authorities, functions, personnel, and assets of the Coast Guard, including the authorities and functions of the Secretary of Transportation relating thereto, to the Department of Homeland Security, and for treatment of related references, see sections 468(b), 551(d), 552(d), and 557 of Title 6, Domestic Security, and the Department of Homeland Security Reorganization Plan of November 25, 2002, as modified, set out as a note under section 542 of Title 6.]

Major Presidential or Vice Presidential Candidates and Spouses; Personal Protection

Pub. L. 90–331, June 6, 1968, 82 Stat. 170, as amended by Pub. L. 94–408, §1, Sept. 11, 1976, 90 Stat. 1239; Pub. L. 94–524, §11, Oct. 17, 1976, 90 Stat. 2477; Pub. L. 96–329, Aug. 11, 1980, 94 Stat. 1029, which had provided for personal protection of major presidential or vice presidential candidates and had authorized protection of spouses commencing not more than 120 days before the general Presidential election, and appropriated for fiscal year ending June 30, 1968, $400,000 for execution of such provisions, was repealed by Pub. L. 98–587, §2, Oct. 30, 1984, 98 Stat. 3111. See subsec. (a)(7) of this section.

Extension of Protection of President's Widow and Children

Pub. L. 90–145, Nov. 17, 1967, 81 Stat. 466, extended until Mar. 1, 1969, the authority vested in the United States Secret Service by section 3056 of this title, as it existed prior to the amendment in 1968 by Pub. L. 90–608, to protect the widow and minor children of a former President who were receiving such protection on Nov. 17, 1967.

Applicability of Reorg. Plan No. 26 of 1950

Pub. L. 91–651, §5, Jan. 5, 1971, 84 Stat. 1941, provided that: "Section 3056 of title 18, United States Code, as amended by section 4 of this Act, shall be subject to Reorganization Plan Numbered 26 of 1950 (64 Stat. 1280) [set out in the Appendix to Title 5, Government Organization and Employees]."

§3056A. Powers, authorities, and duties of United States Secret Service Uniformed Division

(a) There is hereby created and established a permanent police force, to be known as the "United States Secret Service Uniformed Division". Subject to the supervision of the Secretary of Homeland Security, the United States Secret Service Uniformed Division shall perform such duties as the Director, United States Secret Service, may prescribe in connection with the protection of the following:

(1) The White House in the District of Columbia.

(2) Any building in which Presidential offices are located.

(3) The Treasury Building and grounds.

(4) The President, the Vice President (or other officer next in the order of succession to the Office of President), the President-elect, the Vice President-elect, and their immediate families.

(5) Foreign diplomatic missions located in the metropolitan area of the District of Columbia.

(6) The temporary official residence of the Vice President and grounds in the District of Columbia.

(7) Foreign diplomatic missions located in metropolitan areas (other than the District of Columbia) in the United States where there are located twenty or more such missions headed by full-time officers, except that such protection shall be provided only—

(A) on the basis of extraordinary protective need;

(B) upon request of an affected metropolitan area; and

(C) when the extraordinary protective need arises at or in association with a visit to—

(i) a permanent mission to, or an observer mission invited to participate in the work of, an international organization of which the United States is a member; or

(ii) an international organization of which the United States is a member;

except that such protection may also be provided for motorcades and at other places associated with any such visit and may be extended at places of temporary domicile in connection with any such visit.

(8) Foreign consular and diplomatic missions located in such areas in the United States, its territories and possessions, as the President, on a case-by-case basis, may direct.

(9) Visits of foreign government officials to metropolitan areas (other than the District of Columbia) where there are located twenty or more consular or diplomatic missions staffed by accredited personnel, including protection for motorcades and at other places associated with such visits when such officials are in the United States to conduct official business with the United States Government.

(10) Former Presidents and their spouses, as provided in section 3056(a)(3) of title 18.

(11) An event designated under section 3056(e) of title 18 as a special event of national significance.

(12) Major Presidential and Vice Presidential candidates and, within 120 days of the general Presidential election, the spouses of such candidates, as provided in section 3056(a)(7) of title 18.

(13) Visiting heads of foreign states or foreign governments.

(b)(1) Under the direction of the Director of the Secret Service, members of the United States Secret Service Uniformed Division are authorized to—

(A) carry firearms;

(B) make arrests without warrant for any offense against the United States committed in their presence, or for any felony cognizable under the laws of the United States if they have reasonable grounds to believe that the person to be arrested has committed or is committing such felony; and

(C) perform such other functions and duties as are authorized by law.

(2) Members of the United States Secret Service Uniformed Division shall possess privileges and powers similar to those of the members of the Metropolitan Police of the District of Columbia.

(c) Members of the United States Secret Service Uniformed Division shall be furnished with uniforms and other necessary equipment.

(d) In carrying out the functions pursuant to paragraphs (7) and (9) of subsection (a), the Secretary of Homeland Security may utilize, with their consent, on a reimbursable basis, the services, personnel, equipment, and facilities of State and local governments, and is authorized to reimburse such State and local governments for the utilization of such services, personnel, equipment, and facilities. The Secretary of Homeland Security may carry out the functions pursuant to paragraphs (7) and (9) of subsection (a) by contract. The authority of this subsection may be transferred by the President to the Secretary of State. In carrying out any duty under paragraphs (7) and (9) of subsection (a), the Secretary of State is authorized to utilize any authority available to the Secretary under title II of the State Department Basic Authorities Act of 1956.

(Added Pub. L. 109–177, title VI, §605(a), Mar. 9, 2006, 120 Stat. 253.)

References in Text

Title II of the State Department Basic Authorities Act of 1956, referred to in subsec. (d), is title II of act Aug. 1, 1956, ch. 841, as added Aug. 24, 1982, Pub. L. 97–241, title II, §202(b), 96 Stat. 283, known as the Foreign Missions Act, which is classified principally to chapter 53 (§4301 et seq.) of Title 22, Foreign Relations and Intercourse. For complete classification of title II to the Code, see Short Title note set out under section 4301 of Title 22 and Tables.

Change of Name

Pub. L. 95–179, Nov. 15, 1977, 91 Stat. 1371, provided in part that: "Any reference in any other law or in any regulation, document, record, or other paper of the United States to the Executive Protective Service shall be held to be a reference to the United States Secret Service Uniformed Division."

Pub. L. 91–297, title II, §202, June 30, 1970, 84 Stat. 358, provided that: "All laws of the United States in force on the date of enactment of this title [June 30, 1970] in which reference is made to the White House Police force are amended by substituting 'Executive Protective Service' for each such reference."

Savings Provisions

Pub. L. 109–177, title VI, §606, Mar. 9, 2006, 120 Stat. 256, provided that:

"(a) This title [see Tables for classification] does not affect the retirement benefits of current employees or annuitants that existed on the day before the effective date of this Act [probably means Mar. 9, 2006, the date of enactment of Pub. L. 109–177].

"(b) This title does not affect any Executive order transferring to the Secretary of State the authority of section 208 of title 3 (now section 3056A(d) of title 18) in effect on the day before the effective date of this Act."

Conversion to New Salary Schedule

Pub. L. 106–554, §1(a)(4) [div. B, title IX, §905], Dec. 21, 2000, 114 Stat. 2763, 2763A–306, as amended by Pub. L. 111–282, §4(b)(4), Oct. 15, 2010, 124 Stat. 3043, provided that:

"(a) In General.—

"(1) Determination of rates of basic pay.—Effective on the first day of the 1st pay period beginning 6 months after the date of enactment of this Act [Dec. 21, 2000], the Secretary of the Interior shall fix the rates of basic pay for officers and members of the United States Park Police, in accordance with this subsection.

"(2) Placement on revised salary schedule.—

"(A) In general.—Each officer and member shall be placed in and receive basic compensation at the corresponding scheduled service step of the salary schedule under section 501(c) of the District of Columbia Police and Firemen's Salary Act of 1958 [Pub. L. 85–584, title V, Aug. 1, 1958, 72 Stat. 485] (as amended by section 902(a)) in accordance with the member's total years of creditable service, receiving credit for all service step adjustments. If the scheduled rate of pay for the step to which the officer or member would be assigned in accordance with this paragraph is lower than the officer's or member's salary immediately prior to the enactment of this paragraph, the officer or member will be placed in and receive compensation at the next higher service step.

"(B) Credit for increases during transition.—Each member whose position is to be converted to the salary schedule under section 501(b) of the District of Columbia Police and Firemen's Salary Act of 1958 (as amended by subsection (a)) and who, prior to the effective date of this section [set out below] has earned, but has not been credited with, an increase in his or her rate of pay shall be afforded that increase before such member is placed in the corresponding service step in the salary schedule under section 501(b).

"(C) Creditable service described.—For purposes of this paragraph, an officer's or member's creditable service is any police service in pay status with the United States Secret Service Uniformed Division, United States Park Police, or Metropolitan Police Department.

"(b) Hold Harmless for Current Total Compensation.—Notwithstanding any other provision of law, if the total rate of compensation for an officer or employee for any pay period occurring after conversion to the salary schedule pursuant to subsection (a) (determined by taking into account any locality-based comparability adjustments, longevity pay, and other adjustments paid in addition to the rate of basic compensation) is less than the officer's or employee's total rate of compensation (as so determined) on the date of enactment [Dec. 21, 2000], the rate of compensation for the officer or employee for the pay period shall be equal to—

"(1) the rate of compensation on the date of enactment (as so determined); increased by

"(2) a percentage equal to 50 percent of sum of the percentage adjustments made in the rate of basic compensation under section 501(c) of the District of Columbia Police and Firemen's Salary Act of 1958 (as amended by subsection (a)) for pay periods occurring after the date of enactment and prior to the pay period involved.

"(c) Conversion Not Treated as Transfer or Promotion.—The conversion of positions and individuals to appropriate classes of the salary schedule under section 501(c) of the District of Columbia Police and Firemen's Salary Act of 1958 (as amended by section 902(a)) and the initial adjustments of rates of basic pay of those positions and individuals in accordance with subsection (a) shall not be considered to be transfers or promotions within the meaning of section 304 of the District of Columbia Police and Firemen's Salary Act of 1958 [Pub. L. 85–584, title III, Aug. 1, 1958, 72 Stat. 484] (sec. 4–413, D.C. Code).

"(d) Transfer of Credit for Satisfactory Service.—Each individual whose position is converted to the salary schedule under section 501(c) of the District of Columbia Police and Firemen's Salary Act of 1958 (as amended by section 902(a)) in accordance with subsection (a) shall be granted credit for purposes of such individual's first service step adjustment under the salary schedule in such section 501(c) for all satisfactory service performed by the individual since the individual's last increase in basic pay prior to the adjustment under that section.

"(e) Adjustment To Take Into Account General Schedule Adjustments During Transition.—The rates provided under the salary schedule under section 501(c) of the District of Columbia Police and Firemen's Salary Act of 1958 (as amended by section 902(a)) shall be increased by the percentage of any annual adjustment applicable to the General Schedule authorized under section 5303 of title 5, United States Code, which takes effect during the period which begins on the date of the enactment of this Act [Dec. 21, 2000] and ends on the first day of the first pay period beginning 6 months after the date of enactment of this Act.

"(f) Conversion Not Treated as Salary Increase for Purposes of Certain Pensions and Allowances.—The conversion of positions and individuals to appropriate classes of the salary schedule under section 501(c) of the District of Columbia Police and Firemen's Salary Act of 1958 (as amended by section 2[902](a)) and the initial adjustments of rates of basic pay of those positions and individuals in accordance with subsection (a) shall not be treated as an increase in salary for purposes of section 3 of the Act entitled 'An Act to provide increased pensions for widows and children of deceased members of the Police Department and the Fire Department of the District of Columbia', approved August 4, 1949 [ch. 394, 63 Stat. 566] (sec. 4–604, D.C. Code), or section 301 of the District of Columbia Police and Firemen's Salary Act of 1953 [June 20, 1953, ch. 146, title III, 67 Stat. 75] (sec. 4–605, D.C. Code)."

[Pub. L. 111–282, §4(b)(4), Oct. 15, 2010, 124 Stat. 3043, which directed amendment of section 1(a)(4) [div. B, title IX, §905(a)(1)] of Pub. L. 106–554, set out above, by striking out "the Secretary of Treasury" and all that followed through "United States Secret Service Uniformed Division, and", was executed by striking out "the Secretary of the Treasury shall fix the rates of basic pay for officers and members of the United States Secret Service Uniformed Division, and" to reflect the probable intent of Congress.

[Pub. L. 106–554, §1(a)(4) [div. B, title IX, §909], Dec. 21, 2000, 114 Stat. 2763, 2763A–310, provided that: "Except as provided in section 908(c) [114 Stat. 2763A–310], this title [enacting provisions set out as notes above and under sections 5301, 5304, and 5305 of Title 5, Government Organization and Employees, and amending provisions set out as a note under section 5305 of Title 5] and the amendments made by this title shall become effective on the first day of the first pay period beginning 6 months after the date of enactment [Dec. 21, 2000]."]

Secret Service Uniformed Division Compensation

Pub. L. 105–61, title I, §118, Oct. 10, 1997, 111 Stat. 1285, as amended by Pub. L. 111–282, §4(b)(3), Oct. 15, 2010, 124 Stat. 3043, provided that:

"(a) New Rates of Basic Pay.—[Amended Pub. L. 85–584, title V, §501, Aug. 1, 1958, 72 Stat. 485.]

"(b) [Repealed. Pub. L. 111–282, §4(b)(3), Oct. 15, 2010, 124 Stat. 3043.]

"(c) Limitation on Pay Period Earnings.—[Amended act Aug. 15, 1950, ch. 715, 64 Stat. 477.]

"(d) Savings Provision.—On the effective date of this section, any existing special salary rates authorized for members of the United States Secret Service Uniformed Division under section 5305 of title 5, United States Code (or any previous similar provision of law) and any special rates of pay or special pay adjustments under section 403, 404, or 405 of the Federal Law Enforcement Pay Reform Act of 1990 [Pub. L. 101–509, §529 [title IV, §§403–405], 5 U.S.C. 5305 note] applicable to members of the United States Secret Service Uniformed Division shall be rendered inapplicable.

"(e) Conforming Amendment.—[Amended Pub. L. 101–509, §529 [title IV, §405], set out as a note under section 5305 of Title 5, Government Organization and Employees.]

"(f) Effective Date.—The provisions of this section shall become effective on the first day of the first pay period beginning after the date of enactment of this Act [Oct. 10, 1997]."

Ex. Ord. No. 12478. Transfer of Authority to the Secretary of State To Make Reimbursements for Protection of Foreign Missions to International Organizations

Ex. Ord. No. 12478, May 23, 1984, 49 F.R. 22053, provided:

By authority vested in me as President by the Constitution and statutes of the United States of America, and in accordance with the provisions of the Act of December 31, 1975, Public Law 94–196 (89 Stat. 1109), codified as [former] sections 202(7) and 208(a) of Title 3, United States Code, as amended, it is hereby ordered as follows:

Section 1. There is transferred to the Secretary of State authority to determine the need for and to approve terms and conditions of the provision of reimbursable extraordinary protective activities for foreign diplomatic missions pursuant to [former] section 202(7), and the authority to make reimbursements to State and local governments for services, personnel, equipment, and facilities pursuant to [former] section 208(a) of Title 3, United States Code;

Sec. 2. There are transferred to the Secretary of State such unexpended moneys as may have been appropriated to the Department of the Treasury for the purpose of permitting reimbursements to be made under the provisions of [former] section 208(a) of Title 3, United States Code;

Sec. 3. The authority transferred pursuant to this Order shall be exercised in coordination with protective security programs administered by the Secretary of State under the Foreign Missions Act of 1982 [22 U.S.C. 4301 et seq.]; authority available under that Act may also be applied to any foreign mission to which [former] section 202(7) applies; and

Sec. 4. This Order shall be effective on October 1, 1984.

Ronald Reagan.

§3057. Bankruptcy investigations

(a) Any judge, receiver, or trustee having reasonable grounds for believing that any violation under chapter 9 of this title or other laws of the United States relating to insolvent debtors, receiverships or reorganization plans has been committed, or that an investigation should be had in connection therewith, shall report to the appropriate United States attorney all the facts and circumstances of the case, the names of the witnesses and the offense or offenses believed to have been committed. Where one of such officers has made such report, the others need not do so.

(b) The United States attorney thereupon shall inquire into the facts and report thereon to the judge, and if it appears probable that any such offense has been committed, shall without delay, present the matter to the grand jury, unless upon inquiry and examination he decides that the ends of public justice do not require investigation or prosecution, in which case he shall report the facts to the Attorney General for his direction.

(June 25, 1948, ch. 645, 62 Stat. 818; May 24, 1949, ch. 139, §48, 63 Stat. 96; Pub. L. 95–598, title III, §314(i), Nov. 6, 1978, 92 Stat. 2677.)

Historical and Revision Notes

1948 Act

Based on section 52(e)(1), (2) of title 11, U.S.C., 1940 ed., Bankruptcy (July 1, 1898, ch. 541, §29e(1), (2), as added by May 27, 1926, ch. 406, §11, 44 Stat. 665, 666; June 22, 1938, ch. 575, §1, 52 Stat. 840, 856).

Remaining provisions of section 52 of title 11, U.S.C., 1940 ed., Bankruptcy, constitute sections 151–154, and 3284 of this title.

The words "or laws relating to insolvent debtors, receiverships, or reorganization plans" were inserted to avoid reference to "Title 11".

Minor changes were made in phraseology.

1949 Act

This section [section 48] clarifies the meaning of section 3057 of title 18, U.S.C., by expressly limiting to laws "of the United States", violations of laws which are to be reported to the United States attorney.

Amendments

1978—Subsec. (a). Pub. L. 95–598, §314(i), substituted "judge" for "referee" and "violation under chapter 9 of this title" for "violations of the bankruptcy laws".

Subsec. (b). Pub. L. 95–598, §314(i)(1), substituted "judge" for "referee".

1949—Subsec. (a). Act May 24, 1949, substituted "or other laws of the United States" for "or laws".

Effective Date of 1978 Amendment

Amendment by Pub. L. 95–598 effective Oct. 1, 1979, see section 402(a) of Pub. L. 95–598, set out as an Effective Date note preceding section 101 of Title 11, Bankruptcy.

Savings Provision

Amendment by Pub. L. 95–598 not to affect the application of chapter 9 (§151 et seq.), chapter 96 (§1961 et seq.), or section 2516, 3057, or 3284 of this title to any act of any person (1) committed before Oct. 1, 1979, or (2) committed after Oct. 1, 1979, in connection with a case commenced before such date, see section 403(d) of Pub. L. 95–598, set out as a note preceding section 101 of Title 11, Bankruptcy.

Transfer of Functions

Functions of all other officers of Department of Justice and functions of all agencies and employees of such Department, with a few exceptions, transferred to Attorney General, with power vested in him to authorize their performance or performance of any of his functions by any of such officers, agencies, and employees, by Reorg. Plan No. 2 of 1950, §§1, 2, eff. May 24, 1950, 15 F.R. 3173, 64 Stat. 1261, set out in the Appendix to Title 5, Government Organization and Employees.

§3058. Interned belligerent nationals

Whoever, belonging to the armed land or naval forces of a belligerent nation or belligerent faction and being interned in the United States, in accordance with the law of nations, leaves or attempts to leave said jurisdiction, or leaves or attempts to leave the limits of internment without permission from the proper official of the United States in charge, or willfully overstays a leave of absence granted by such official, shall be subject to arrest by any marshal or deputy marshal of the United States, or by the military or naval authorities thereof, and shall be returned to the place of internment and there confined and safely kept for such period of time as the official of the United States in charge shall direct.

(June 25, 1948, ch. 645, 62 Stat. 818; Pub. L. 101–647, title XXXV, §3571, Nov. 29, 1990, 104 Stat. 4928.)

Historical and Revision Notes

Based on title 18, U.S.C., 1940 ed., §37 (June 15, 1917, ch. 30, title V, §7, 40 Stat. 223).
Said section 37 was incorporated in this section and section 756 of this title.
Minor verbal changes were made.

Amendments

1990—Pub. L. 101–647 substituted "belligerent" for "beligerent" before "nation".

[§§3059 to 3059B. Repealed. Pub. L. 107–273, div. A, title III, §301(c)(2), Nov. 2, 2002, 116 Stat. 1781]

Section 3059, act June 25, 1948, ch. 645, 62 Stat. 818; Pub. L. 97–258, §2(d)(2), Sept. 13, 1982, 96 Stat. 1058; Pub. L. 103–322, title XXV, §250004, Sept. 13, 1994, 108 Stat. 2086, related to rewards and appropriations therefor.

Section 3059A, added Pub. L. 101–647, title XXV, §2587(a), Nov. 29, 1990, 104 Stat. 4904; amended Pub. L. 103–322, title XXXII, §320607, title XXXIII, §330010(10), (17), Sept. 13, 1994, 108 Stat. 2120, 2143, 2144; Pub. L. 104–294, title VI, §§601(f)(4), 604(b)(24), Oct. 11, 1996, 110 Stat. 3499, 3508, related to special rewards for information relating to certain financial institution offenses.

Section 3059B, added Pub. L. 104–132, title VIII, §815(e)(1), Apr. 24, 1996, 110 Stat. 1315, set forth general reward authority.

§3060. Preliminary examination

(a) Except as otherwise provided by this section, a preliminary examination shall be held within the time set by the judge or magistrate judge pursuant to subsection (b) of this section, to determine whether there is probable cause to believe that an offense has been committed and that the arrested person has committed it.

(b) The date for the preliminary examination shall be fixed by the judge or magistrate judge at the initial appearance of the arrested person. Except as provided by subsection (c) of this section, or unless the arrested person waives the preliminary examination, such examination shall be held within a reasonable time following initial appearance, but in any event not later than—

(1) the fourteenth day following the date of the initial appearance of the arrested person before such officer if the arrested person is held in custody without any provision for release, or is held in custody for failure to meet the conditions of release imposed, or is released from custody only during specified hours of the day; or

(2) the twentieth day following the date of the initial appearance if the arrested person is released from custody under any condition other than a condition described in paragraph (1) of this subsection.

(c) With the consent of the arrested person, the date fixed by the judge or magistrate judge for the preliminary examination may be a date later than that prescribed by subsection (b), or may be continued one or more times to a date subsequent to the date initially fixed therefor. In the absence of such consent of the accused, the judge or magistrate judge may extend the time limits only on a showing that extraordinary circumstances exist and justice requires the delay.

(d) Except as provided by subsection (e) of this section, an arrested person who has not been accorded the preliminary examination required by subsection (a) within the period of time fixed by the judge or magistrate judge in compliance with subsections (b) and (c), shall be discharged from custody or from the requirement of bail or any other condition of release, without prejudice, however, to the institution of further criminal proceedings against him upon the charge upon which he was arrested.

(e) No preliminary examination in compliance with subsection (a) of this section shall be required to be accorded an arrested person, nor shall such arrested person be discharged from custody or from the requirement of bail or any other condition of release pursuant to subsection (d), if at any time subsequent to the initial appearance of such person before a judge or magistrate judge and prior to the date fixed for the preliminary examination pursuant to subsections (b) and (c) an indictment is returned or, in appropriate cases, an information is filed against such person in a court of the United States.

(f) Proceedings before United States magistrate judges under this section shall be taken down by a court reporter or recorded by suitable sound recording equipment. A copy of the record of such proceeding shall be made available at the expense of the United States to a person who makes affidavit that he is unable to pay or give security therefor, and the expense of such copy shall be paid by the Director of the Administrative Office of the United States Courts.

(June 25, 1948, ch. 645, 62 Stat. 819; Pub. L. 90–578, title III, §303(a), Oct. 17, 1968, 82 Stat. 1117; Pub. L. 101–650, title III, §321, Dec. 1, 1990, 104 Stat. 5117; Pub. L. 109–162, title XI, §1179, Jan. 5, 2006, 119 Stat. 3126; Pub. L. 111–16, §3(9), May 7, 2009, 123 Stat. 1608.)

Amendments

2009—Subsec. (b)(1). Pub. L. 111–16 substituted "fourteenth day" for "tenth day".

2006—Subsec. (c). Pub. L. 109–162 substituted "In the absence of such consent of the accused, the judge or magistrate judge may extend the time limits only on a showing that extraordinary circumstances exist and justice requires the delay." for "In the absence of such consent of the accused, the date fixed for the preliminary hearing may be a date later than that prescribed by subsection (b), or may be continued to a date subsequent to the date initially fixed therefor, only upon the order of a judge of the appropriate United States district court after a finding that extraordinary circumstances exist, and that the delay of the preliminary hearing is indispensable to the interests of justice."

1968—Pub. L. 90–578 substituted provisions of subsecs. (a) to (f) of this section detailing preliminary examination content for prior provisions which directed attention to the rule in section catchline, and directed one to see Federal Rules of Criminal Procedure, including "Proceedings before commissioner, appearance, advice as to right to counsel, hearing, Rule 5.".

Change of Name
Words "magistrate judge" and "United States magistrate judges" substituted for "magistrate" and "United States magistrates", respectively, wherever appearing in text pursuant to section 321 of Pub. L. 101–650, set out as a note under section 631 of Title 28, Judiciary and Judicial Procedure.

Effective Date of 2009 Amendment
Amendment by Pub. L. 111–16 effective Dec. 1, 2009, see section 7 of Pub. L. 111–16, set out as a note under section 109 of Title 11, Bankruptcy.

Effective Date of 1968 Amendment
Amendment by Pub. L. 90–578 effective Oct. 17, 1968, except when a later effective date is applicable, which is the earlier of date when implementation of amendment by appointment of magistrates [now United States magistrate judges] and assumption of office takes place or third anniversary of enactment of Pub. L. 90–578 on Oct. 17, 1968, see section 403 of Pub. L. 90–578, set out as a note under section 631 of Title 28, Judiciary and Judicial Procedure.

§3061. Investigative powers of Postal Service personnel
(a) Subject to subsection (b) of this section, Postal Inspectors and other agents of the United States Postal Service designated by the Board of Governors to investigate criminal matters related to the Postal Service and the mails may—
(1) serve warrants and subpoenas issued under the authority of the United States;
(2) make arrests without warrant for offenses against the United States committed in their presence;
(3) make arrests without warrant for felonies cognizable under the laws of the United States if they have reasonable grounds to believe that the person to be arrested has committed or is committing such a felony;
(4) carry firearms; and
(5) make seizures of property as provided by law.
(b) The powers granted by subsection (a) of this section shall be exercised only—
(1) in the enforcement of laws regarding property in the custody of the Postal Service, property of the Postal Service, the use of the mails, and other postal offenses; and
(2) to the extent authorized by the Attorney General pursuant to agreement between the Attorney General and the Postal Service, in the enforcement of other laws of the United States, if the Attorney General determines that violations of such laws have a detrimental effect upon the operations of the Postal Service.
(c)(1) The Postal Service may employ police officers for duty in connection with the protection of property owned or occupied by the Postal Service or under the charge and control of the Postal Service, and persons on that property, including duty in areas outside the property to the extent necessary to protect the property and persons on the property.
(2) With respect to such property, such officers shall have the power to—
(A) enforce Federal laws and regulations for the protection of persons and property;
(B) carry firearms; and
(C) make arrests without a warrant for any offense against the Unites 1 States committed in the presence of the officer or for any felony cognizable under the laws of the United States if the officer has reasonable grounds to believe that the person to be arrested has committed or is committing a felony.
(3) With respect to such property, such officers may have, to such extent as the Postal Service may by regulations prescribe, the power to—
(A) serve warrants and subpoenas issued under the authority of the United States; and

(B) conduct investigations, on and off the property in question, of offenses that may have been committed against property owned or occupied by the Postal Service or persons on the property.

(4)(A) As to such property, the Postmaster General may prescribe regulations necessary for the protection and administration of property owned or occupied by the Postal Service and persons on the property. The regulations may include reasonable penalties, within the limits prescribed in subparagraph (B), for violations of the regulations. The regulations shall be posted and remain posted in a conspicuous place on the property.

(B) A person violating a regulation prescribed under this subsection shall be fined under this title, imprisoned for not more than 30 days, or both.

(Added Pub. L. 90–560, §5(a), Oct. 12, 1968, 82 Stat. 998; amended Pub. L. 91–375, §6(j)(38)(A), Aug. 12, 1970, 84 Stat. 781; Pub. L. 100–690, title VI, §6251(a), Nov. 18, 1988, 102 Stat. 4362; Pub. L. 109–435, title X, §1001, Dec. 20, 2006, 120 Stat. 3254.)

Amendments

2006—Subsec. (c). Pub. L. 109–435 added subsec. (c).

1988—Pub. L. 100–690 substituted "Investigative powers of Postal Service personnel" for "Powers of postal personnel" in section catchline, and amended text generally. Prior to amendment, text read as follows:

"(a) Subject to subsection (b) of this section, officers and employees of the Postal Service performing duties related to the inspection of postal matters may, to the extent authorized by the Board of Governors—

"(1) serve warrants and subpenas issued under the authority of the United States;

"(2) make arrests without warrant for offenses against the United States committed in their presence; and

"(3) make arrests without warrant for felonies cognizable under the laws of the United States if they have reasonable grounds to believe that the person to be arrested has committed or is committing such a felony.

"(b) The powers granted by subsection (a) of this section shall be exercised only in the enforcement of laws regarding property of the United States in the custody of the Postal Service, including property of the Postal Service, the use of the mails, and other postal offenses."

1970—Pub. L. 91–375, §6(j)(38)(A)(i), substituted "postal personnel" for "postal inspectors" in section catchline.

Subsec. (a). Pub. L. 91–375, §6(j)(38)(A)(ii), substituted "officers and employees of the Postal Service performing duties related to the inspection of postal matters may, to the extent authorized by the Board of Governors—" for "postal inspectors may, to the extent authorized by the Postmaster General—".

Subsec. (b). Pub. L. 91–375, §6(j)(38)(A)(iii), substituted "Postal Service, including property of the Postal Service," for "postal service".

Effective Date of 1970 Amendment

Amendment by Pub. L. 91–375 effective within 1 year after Aug. 12, 1970, on date established therefor by the Board of Governors of the United States Postal Service and published by it in the Federal Register, see section 15(a) of Pub. L. 91–375, set out as an Effective Date note preceding section 101 of Title 39, Postal Service.

§3062. General arrest authority for violation of release conditions

A law enforcement officer, who is authorized to arrest for an offense committed in his presence, may arrest a person who is released pursuant to chapter 207 if the officer has reasonable grounds to believe that the person is violating, in his presence, a condition imposed on the person pursuant to section 3142(c)(1)(B)(iv), (v), (viii), (ix), or (xiii), or, if the violation involves a failure to remain in a specified institution as required, a condition imposed pursuant to section 3142(c)(1)(B)(x).

(Added Pub. L. 98–473, title II, §204(d), Oct. 12, 1984, 98 Stat. 1986; amended Pub. L. 100–690, title VII, §7052, Nov. 18, 1988, 102 Stat. 4401.)

Amendments

1988—Pub. L. 100–690 substituted "section 3142(c)(1)(B)(iv), (v), (viii), (ix), or (xiii)" for "section 3142(c)(2)(D), (c)(2)(E), (c)(2)(H), (c)(2)(I), or (c)(2)(M)" and "section 3142(c)(1)(B)(x)" for "section 3142(c)(2)(J)".

§3063. Powers of Environmental Protection Agency

(a) Upon designation by the Administrator of the Environmental Protection Agency, any law enforcement officer of the Environmental Protection Agency with responsibility for the investigation of criminal violations of a law administered by the Environmental Protection Agency, may—

(1) carry firearms;

(2) execute and serve any warrant or other processes issued under the authority of the United States; and

(3) make arrests without warrant for—

(A) any offense against the United States committed in such officer's presence; or

(B) any felony offense against the United States if such officer has probable cause to believe that the person to be arrested has committed or is committing that felony offense.

(b) The powers granted under subsection (a) of this section shall be exercised in accordance with guidelines approved by the Attorney General.

(Added Pub. L. 100–582, §4(a), Nov. 1, 1988, 102 Stat. 2958.)

§3064. Powers of Federal Motor Carrier Safety Administration

Authorized employees of the Federal Motor Carrier Safety Administration may direct a driver of a commercial motor vehicle (as defined in section 31132 of title 49) to stop for inspection of the vehicle, driver, cargo, and required records at or in the vicinity of an inspection site.

(Added Pub. L. 109–59, title IV, §4143(b), Aug. 10, 2005, 119 Stat. 1748.)

CHAPTER 204 - REWARDS FOR INFORMATION CONCERNING TERRORIST ACTS AND ESPIONAGE

Amendments

1994—Pub. L. 103–359, title VIII, §803(c)(2), Oct. 14, 1994, 108 Stat. 3439, inserted "AND ESPIONAGE" after "TERRORIST ACTS" in chapter heading.

§3071. Information for which rewards authorized

(a) With respect to acts of terrorism primarily within the territorial jurisdiction of the United States, the Attorney General may reward any individual who furnishes information—

(1) leading to the arrest or conviction, in any country, of any individual or individuals for the

commission of an act of terrorism against a United States person or United States property; or
(2) leading to the arrest or conviction, in any country, of any individual or individuals for conspiring or attempting to commit an act of terrorism against a United States person or property; or
(3) leading to the prevention, frustration, or favorable resolution of an act of terrorism against a United States person or property.
(b) With respect to acts of espionage involving or directed at the United States, the Attorney General may reward any individual who furnishes information—
(1) leading to the arrest or conviction, in any country, of any individual or individuals for commission of an act of espionage against the United States;
(2) leading to the arrest or conviction, in any country, of any individual or individuals for conspiring or attempting to commit an act of espionage against the United States; or
(3) leading to the prevention or frustration of an act of espionage against the United States.
(Added Pub. L. 98–533, title I, §101(a), Oct. 19, 1984, 98 Stat. 2706; amended Pub. L. 103–359, title VIII, §803(a), Oct. 14, 1994, 108 Stat. 3438.)

Amendments
1994—Pub. L. 103–359 designated existing provisions as subsec. (a) and added subsec. (b).

Short Title
Pub. L. 98–533, §1, Oct. 19, 1984, 98 Stat. 2706, provided that: "This Act [enacting this chapter and section 2708 of Title 22, Foreign Relations and Intercourse, amending sections 2669, 2678 and 2704 of Title 22, enacting provisions set out as a note under section 5928 of Title 5, Government Organization and Employees and amending provisions set out as a note under section 2651 of Title 22] may be cited as the '1984 Act to Combat International Terrorism'."

Attorney General's Authority To Pay Rewards To Combat Terrorism
Pub. L. 107–56, title V, §501, Oct. 26, 2001, 115 Stat. 363, which provided that funds available to Attorney General could be used for payment of rewards to combat terrorism and defend Nation against terrorist acts, in accordance with procedures and regulations established or issued by Attorney General, and set forth conditions in making such rewards, was repealed by Pub. L. 107–273, div. A, title III, §301(c)(1), Nov. 2, 2002, 116 Stat. 1781.

§3072. Determination of entitlement; maximum amount; Presidential approval; conclusiveness
The Attorney General shall determine whether an individual furnishing information described in section 3071 is entitled to a reward and the amount to be paid.
(Added Pub. L. 98–533, title I, §101(a), Oct. 19, 1984, 98 Stat. 2707; amended Pub. L. 107–273, div. A, title III, §301(c)(2), Nov. 2, 2002, 116 Stat. 1781.)

Amendments
2002—Pub. L. 107–273, which directed amendment of section 3072 of chapter 203, was executed to this section, which is in chapter 204, by striking out at end "A reward under this section may be in an amount not to exceed $500,000. A reward of $100,000 or more may not be made without the approval of the President or the Attorney General personally. A determination made by the Attorney General or the President under this chapter shall be final and conclusive, and no court shall have power or jurisdiction to review it."

§3073. Protection of identity
Any reward granted under this chapter shall be certified for payment by the Attorney General. If it is determined that the identity of the recipient of a reward or of the members of the recipient's

immediate family must be protected, the Attorney General may take such measures in connection with the payment of the reward as deemed necessary to effect such protection.

(Added Pub. L. 98–533, title I, §101(a), Oct. 19, 1984, 98 Stat. 2707.)

§3074. Exception of governmental officials

No officer or employee of any governmental entity who, while in the performance of his or her official duties, furnishes the information described in section 3071 shall be eligible for any monetary reward under this chapter.

(Added Pub. L. 98–533, title I, §101(a), Oct. 19, 1984, 98 Stat. 2707.)

[§3075. Repealed. Pub. L. 107–273, div. A, title III, §301(c)(2), Nov. 2, 2002, 116 Stat. 1781]

Section, added Pub. L. 98–533, title I, §101(a), Oct. 19, 1984, 98 Stat. 2707, authorized appropriations for the purpose of this chapter.

Pub. L. 107–273, which directed the repeal of section 3075 of chapter 203, was executed to this section which is in chapter 204.

§3076. Eligibility for witness security program

Any individual (and the immediate family of such individual) who furnishes information which would justify a reward by the Attorney General under this chapter or by the Secretary of State under section 36 of the State Department Basic Authorities Act of 1956 may, in the discretion of the Attorney General, participate in the Attorney General's witness security program authorized under chapter 224 of this title.

(Added Pub. L. 98–533, title I, §101(a), Oct. 19, 1984, 98 Stat. 2707; amended Pub. L. 99–646, §45, Nov. 10, 1986, 100 Stat. 3601.)

References in Text

Section 36 of the State Department Basic Authorities Act of 1956, referred to in text, is classified to section 2708 of Title 22, Foreign Relations and Intercourse.

Amendments

1986—Pub. L. 99–646 substituted "chapter 224 of this title" for "title V of the Organized Crime Control Act of 1970".

§3077. Definitions

As used in this chapter, the term—

(1) "act of terrorism" means an act of domestic or international terrorism as defined in section 2331;

(2) "United States person" means—

(A) a national of the United States as defined in section 101(a)(22) of the Immigration and Nationality Act (8 U.S.C. 1101(a)(22));

(B) an alien lawfully admitted for permanent residence in the United States as defined in section 101(a)(20) of the Immigration and Nationality Act (8 U.S.C. 1101(a)(20));

(C) any person within the United States;

(D) any employee or contractor of the United States Government, regardless of nationality, who is the victim or intended victim of an act of terrorism by virtue of that employment;

(E) a sole proprietorship, partnership, company, or association composed principally of nationals or permanent resident aliens of the United States; and

(F) a corporation organized under the laws of the United States, any State, the District of Columbia, or any territory or possession of the United States, and a foreign subsidiary of such corporation;

(3) "United States property" means any real or personal property which is within the United States or, if outside the United States, the actual or beneficial ownership of which rests in a United States person or any Federal or State governmental entity of the United States;

(4) "United States", when used in a geographical sense, includes Puerto Rico and all territories and possessions of the United States;

(5) "State" includes any State of the United States, the District of Columbia, the Commonwealth of Puerto Rico, and any other possession or territory of the United States;

(6) "government entity" includes the Government of the United States, any State or political subdivision thereof, any foreign country, and any state, provincial, municipal, or other political subdivision of a foreign country;

(7) "Attorney General" means the Attorney General of the United States or that official designated by the Attorney General to perform the Attorney General's responsibilities under this chapter; and

(8) "act of espionage" means an activity that is a violation of—

(A) section 793, 794, or 798 of this title; or

(B) section 4 of the Subversive Activities Control Act of 1950.

(Added Pub. L. 98–533, title I, §101(a), Oct. 19, 1984, 98 Stat. 2707; amended Pub. L. 100–690, title VII, §7051, Nov. 18, 1988, 102 Stat. 4401; Pub. L. 101–647, title XXXV, §3572, Nov. 29, 1990, 104 Stat. 4929; Pub. L. 103–322, title XXXIII, §330021(1), Sept. 13, 1994, 108 Stat. 2150; Pub. L. 103–359, title VIII, §803(b), Oct. 14, 1994, 108 Stat. 3439; Pub. L. 104–294, title VI, §605(g), Oct. 11, 1996, 110 Stat. 3510; Pub. L. 107–56, title VIII, §802(b), Oct. 26, 2001, 115 Stat. 376.)

References in Text

Section 4 of the Subversive Activities Control Act of 1950, referred to in par. (8)(B), is classified to section 783 of Title 50, War and National Defense.

Amendments

2001—Par. (1). Pub. L. 107–56 amended par. (1) generally. Prior to amendment, par. (1) read as follows: " 'act of terrorism' means an activity that—

"(A) involves a violent act or an act dangerous to human life that is a violation of the criminal laws of the United States or of any State, or that would be a criminal violation if committed within the jurisdiction of the United States or of any State; and

"(B) appears to be intended—

"(i) to intimidate or coerce a civilian population;

"(ii) to influence the policy of a government by intimidation or coercion; or

"(iii) to affect the conduct of a government by assassination or kidnapping;".

1996—Par. (8)(A). Pub. L. 104–294 substituted "this title" for "title 18, United States Code".

1994—Par. (1)(B)(iii). Pub. L. 103–322 substituted "kidnapping" for "kidnaping".

Par. (8). Pub. L. 103–359 added par. (8).

1990—Pub. L. 101–647 substituted a semicolon for a period at end of pars. (1) to (3), moved the comma from before the close quotation mark to after that mark in par. (4), substituted a semicolon for a period at end of par. (5), and substituted "; and" for period at end of par. (6).

1988—Par. (4). Pub. L. 100–690 amended par. (4) generally. Prior to amendment, par. (4) read as follows: " 'United States'—

"(A) when used in a geographical sense, includes Puerto Rico and all territories and possessions of the United States; and

"(B) when used in the context of section 3073 shall have the meaning given to it in the Immigration and Nationality Act (8 U.S.C. 1101 et seq.)."

CHAPTER 205 - SEARCHES AND SEIZURES

Codification

Pub. L. 90–351 enacted section 3103a of this title as part of chapter 204, and Pub. L. 90–462, §3, Aug. 8, 1968, 82 Stat. 638, corrected the chapter designation from 204 to 205.

Amendments

1990—Pub. L. 101–647, title XXXV, §3573(d), Nov. 29, 1990, 104 Stat. 4929, struck out item 3112 "Search warrants for seizure of animals, birds, or eggs" and renumbered item 3117, "Implied consent for certain tests", as 3118.

1988—Pub. L. 100–690, title VI, §6477(b)(2), Nov. 18, 1988, 102 Stat. 4381, added item 3117 "Implied consent for certain tests".

1986—Pub. L. 99–508, title I, §108(b), Oct. 21, 1986, 100 Stat. 1858, added item 3117 "Mobile tracking devices".

1968—Pub. L. 90–351, title IX, §1401(b), June 19, 1968, 82 Stat. 238, added item 3103a.

Change of Name

Words "magistrate judge" substituted for "magistrate" in item 3116 pursuant to section 321 of Pub. L. 101–650, set out as a note under section 631 of Title 28, Judiciary and Judicial Procedure.

§3101. Effect of rules of court—(Rule)

See Federal Rules of Criminal Procedure

Rules generally applicable throughout United States, Rule 54.
Acts of Congress superseded, Rule 41(g).
(June 25, 1948, ch. 645, 62 Stat. 819.)

References in Text

Rule 41(g), referred to in text, was relettered 41(h) by 1972 amendment eff. Oct. 1, 1972.

§3102. Authority to issue search warrant—(Rule)

See Federal Rules of Criminal Procedure

Federal, State or Territorial Judges, or U.S. magistrate judges authorized to issue search warrants, Rule 41(a).

(June 25, 1948, ch. 645, 62 Stat. 819; Pub. L. 90–578, title III, §301(a)(4), Oct. 17, 1968, 82 Stat. 1115; Pub. L. 101–650, title III, §321, Dec. 1, 1990, 104 Stat. 5117.)

Amendments

1968—Pub. L. 90–578 substituted "magistrates" for "Commissioners".

Change of Name

"U.S. magistrate judges" substituted for "U.S. magistrates" in text pursuant to section 321 of Pub. L. 101–650, set out as a note under section 631 of Title 28, Judiciary and Judicial Procedure.

Effective Date of 1968 Amendment

Amendment by Pub. L. 90–578 effective Oct. 17, 1968, except when a later effective date is applicable, which is the earlier of date when implementation of amendment by appointment of magistrates [now United States magistrate judges] and assumption of office takes place or third anniversary of enactment of Pub. L. 90–578 on Oct. 17, 1968, see section 403 of Pub. L. 90–578, set out as a note under section 631 of Title 28, Judiciary and Judicial Procedure.

§3103. Grounds for issuing search warrant—(Rule)

See Federal Rules of Criminal Procedure

Grounds prescribed for issuance of search warrant, Rule 41(b).

(June 25, 1948, ch. 645, 62 Stat. 819.)

§3103a. Additional grounds for issuing warrant

(a) In General.—In addition to the grounds for issuing a warrant in section 3103 of this title, a warrant may be issued to search for and seize any property that constitutes evidence of a criminal offense in violation of the laws of the United States.

(b) Delay.—With respect to the issuance of any warrant or court order under this section, or any other rule of law, to search for and seize any property or material that constitutes evidence of a criminal offense in violation of the laws of the United States, any notice required, or that may be required, to be given may be delayed if—

(1) the court finds reasonable cause to believe that providing immediate notification of the execution of the warrant may have an adverse result (as defined in section 2705, except if the adverse results consist only of unduly delaying a trial) 1 ;

(2) the warrant prohibits the seizure of any tangible property, any wire or electronic communication (as defined in section 2510), or, except as expressly provided in chapter 121, any stored wire or electronic information, except where the court finds reasonable necessity for the seizure; and

(3) the warrant provides for the giving of such notice within a reasonable period not to exceed 30 days after the date of its execution, or on a later date certain if the facts of the case justify a longer period of delay.

(c) Extensions of Delay.—Any period of delay authorized by this section may be extended by the court for good cause shown, subject to the condition that extensions should only be granted upon an updated showing of the need for further delay and that each additional delay should be limited to periods of 90 days or less, unless the facts of the case justify a longer period of delay.

(d) Reports.—

(1) Report by judge.—Not later than 30 days after the expiration of a warrant authorizing delayed notice (including any extension thereof) entered under this section, or the denial of such warrant (or request for extension), the issuing or denying judge shall report to the Administrative Office of

the United States Courts—

(A) the fact that a warrant was applied for;

(B) the fact that the warrant or any extension thereof was granted as applied for, was modified, or was denied;

(C) the period of delay in the giving of notice authorized by the warrant, and the number and duration of any extensions; and

(D) the offense specified in the warrant or application.

(2) Report by administrative office of the united states courts.—Beginning with the fiscal year ending September 30, 2007, the Director of the Administrative Office of the United States Courts shall transmit to Congress annually a full and complete report summarizing the data required to be filed with the Administrative Office by paragraph (1), including the number of applications for warrants and extensions of warrants authorizing delayed notice, and the number of such warrants and extensions granted or denied during the preceding fiscal year.

(3) Regulations.—The Director of the Administrative Office of the United States Courts, in consultation with the Attorney General, is authorized to issue binding regulations dealing with the content and form of the reports required to be filed under paragraph (1).

(Added Pub. L. 90–351, title IX, §1401(a), June 19, 1968, 82 Stat. 238; amended Pub. L. 107–56, title II, §213, Oct. 26, 2001, 115 Stat. 285; Pub. L. 109–177, title I, §114, Mar. 9, 2006, 120 Stat. 210.)

Codification

Pub. L. 90–351 enacted section 3103a of this title as part of chapter 204, and Pub. L. 90–462, §3, Aug. 8, 1968, 82 Stat. 638, corrected the chapter designation from 204 to 205.

Amendments

2006—Subsec. (b)(1). Pub. L. 109–177, §114(b), inserted ", except if the adverse results consist only of unduly delaying a trial" after "2705".

Subsec. (b)(3). Pub. L. 109–177, §114(a)(1), added par. (3) and struck out former par. (3) which read as follows: "the warrant provides for the giving of such notice within a reasonable period of its execution, which period may thereafter be extended by the court for good cause shown."

Subsecs. (c), (d). Pub. L. 109–177, §114(a)(2), (c), added subsecs. (c) and (d).

2001—Pub. L. 107–56 designated existing provisions as subsec. (a), inserted heading, and added subsec. (b).

§3104. Issuance of search warrant; contents—(Rule)

See Federal Rules of Criminal Procedure

Issuance of search warrant on affidavit; contents to identify persons or place; command to search forthwith, Rule 41(c).

(June 25, 1948, ch. 645, 62 Stat. 819.)

§3105. Persons authorized to serve search warrant

A search warrant may in all cases be served by any of the officers mentioned in its direction or by an officer authorized by law to serve such warrant, but by no other person, except in aid of the officer on his requiring it, he being present and acting in its execution.

(June 25, 1948, ch. 645, 62 Stat. 819.)

Historical and Revision Notes

Based on title 18, U.S.C., 1940 ed., §617 (June 15, 1917, ch. 30, title XI, §7, 40 Stat. 229). Minor change was made in phraseology.

§3106. Officer authorized to serve search warrant—(Rule)

See Federal Rules of Criminal Procedure

Officer to whom search warrant shall be directed, Rule 41(c).

(June 25, 1948, ch. 645, 62 Stat. 819.)

§3107. Service of warrants and seizures by Federal Bureau of Investigation

The Director, Associate Director, Assistant to the Director, Assistant Directors, agents, and inspectors of the Federal Bureau of Investigation of the Department of Justice are empowered to make seizures under warrant for violation of the laws of the United States.

(June 25, 1948, ch. 645, 62 Stat. 819; Jan. 10, 1951, ch. 1221, §2, 64 Stat. 1239.)

Historical and Revision Notes

Based on section 300a of title 5, U.S.C., 1940 ed., Executive Departments and Government Officers and Employees (June 18, 1934, ch. 595, 48 Stat. 1008; Mar. 22, 1935, ch. 39, title II, 49 Stat. 77).

Section 300a of title 5, U.S.C., 1940 ed., Executive Departments and Government Officers and Employees, was used as the basis for this section and section 3052 of this title.

Amendments

1951—Act Jan. 10, 1951, included within its provisions the Associate Director and the Assistant to the Director.

Transfer of Functions

Functions of all other officers of Department of Justice and functions of all agencies and employees of such Department, with a few exceptions, transferred to Attorney General, with power vested in him to authorize their performance or performance of any of his functions by any of such officers, agencies, and employees, by Reorg. Plan No. 2 of 1950, §§1, 2, eff. May 24, 1950, 15 F.R. 3173, 64 Stat. 1261, set out in the Appendix to Title 5, Government Organization and Employees.

§3108. Execution, service, and return—(Rule)

See Federal Rules of Criminal Procedure

Method and time for execution, service and return of search warrant, Rule 41(c), (d).

(June 25, 1948, ch. 645, 62 Stat. 819.)

§3109. Breaking doors or windows for entry or exit

The officer may break open any outer or inner door or window of a house, or any part of a house, or anything therein, to execute a search warrant, if, after notice of his authority and purpose, he is refused admittance or when necessary to liberate himself or a person aiding him in the execution of the warrant.

(June 25, 1948, ch. 645, 62 Stat. 820.)

Historical and Revision Notes

Based on title 18, U.S.C., 1940 ed., §§618, 619 (June 15, 1917, ch. 30, title XI, §§8, 9, 40 Stat. 229).

Said sections 618 and 619 were consolidated with minor changes in phraseology but without change of substance.

§3110. Property defined—(Rule)

See Federal Rules of Criminal Procedure

Term "property" as used in Rule 41 includes documents, books, papers and any other tangible objects, Rule 41(g).
(June 25, 1948, ch. 645, 62 Stat. 820.)

References in Text

Rule 41(g), referred to in text, was redesignated 41(h) by 1972 amendment eff. Oct. 1, 1972.

§3111. Property seizable on search warrant—(Rule)

See Federal Rules of Criminal Procedure

Specified property seizable on search warrant, Rule 41(b).
(June 25, 1948, ch. 645, 62 Stat. 820.)

[§3112. Repealed. Pub. L. 97–79, §9(b)(3), Nov. 16, 1981, 95 Stat. 1079]

Section, acts June 25, 1948, ch. 645, 62 Stat. 820; Dec. 5, 1969, Pub. L. 91–135, §7(c), 83 Stat. 281; Nov. 8, 1978, Pub. L. 95–616, §3(j)(1), 92 Stat. 3112, provided for issuance of search warrants for seizure of animals, birds, and eggs. See section 3375 of Title 16, Conservation.

§3113. Liquor violations in Indian country

If any superintendent of Indian affairs, or commanding officer of a military post, or special agent of the Office of Indian Affairs for the suppression of liquor traffic among Indians and in the Indian country and any authorized deputies under his supervision has probable cause to believe that any person is about to introduce or has introduced any spirituous liquor, beer, wine or other intoxicating liquors named in sections 1154 and 1156 of this title into the Indian country in violation of law, he may cause the places, conveyances, and packages of such person to be searched. If any such intoxicating liquor is found therein, the same, together with such conveyances and packages of such person, shall be seized and delivered to the proper officer, and shall be proceeded against by libel in the proper court, and forfeited, one-half to the informer and one-half to the use of the United States. If such person be a trader, his license shall be revoked and his bond put in suit.

Any person in the service of the United States authorized by this section to make searches and seizures, or any Indian may take and destroy any ardent spirits or wine found in the Indian country, except such as are kept or used for scientific, sacramental, medicinal, or mechanical purposes or such as may be introduced therein by the Department of the Army.
(June 25, 1948, ch. 645, 62 Stat. 820; Oct. 31, 1951, ch. 655, §30, 65 Stat. 721; Pub. L. 103–322, title XXXIII, §330004(15), Sept. 13, 1994, 108 Stat. 2142.)

Historical and Revision Notes

Based on sections 246, 248, 252 of title 25, U.S.C., 1940 ed., Indians (R.S. §2140; Mar. 1, 1907, ch. 2285, 34 Stat. 1017; May 18, 1916, ch. 125, §1, 39 Stat. 124).

Said sections 246, 248, and 252 were consolidated. References to Indian agent and subagent were deleted since those positions no longer exist. See section 64 of title 25, U.S.C., 1940 ed., Indians, and notes thereunder.

Words "except such as are kept or used for scientific, sacramental, medicinal or mechanical purposes" were inserted. See reviser's note under section 1154 of this title.

Words "conveyances and packages" were substituted for the enumeration, "boats, teams, wagons and sleds * * * and goods, packages and peltries."

Minor changes were made in phraseology.

Amendments

1994—Pub. L. 103–322 struck out last par. which read as follows: "In all cases arising under this section and sections 1154 and 1156 of this title, Indians shall be competent witnesses."
1951—Act Oct. 31, 1951, substituted "Department of the Army" for "War Department" in second par.

§3114. Return of seized property and suppression of evidence; motion—(Rule)

See Federal Rules of Criminal Procedure

Return of property and suppression of evidence upon motion, Rule 41(e).
(June 25, 1948, ch. 645, 62 Stat. 820.)

§3115. Inventory upon execution and return of search warrant—(Rule)

See Federal Rules of Criminal Procedure

Inventory of property seized under search warrant and copies to persons affected, Rule 41(d).
(June 25, 1948, ch. 645, 62 Stat. 820.)

§3116. Records of examining magistrate judge; return to clerk of court—(Rule)

See Federal Rules of Criminal Procedure

Magistrate judges and clerks of court to keep records as prescribed by Director of the Administrative Office of the United States Courts, Rule 55.
Return or filing of records with clerk, Rule 41(f).
(June 25, 1948, ch. 645, 62 Stat. 821; Pub. L. 90–578, title III, §301(a)(4), Oct. 17, 1968, 82 Stat. 1115; Pub. L. 101–650, title III, §321, Dec. 1, 1990, 104 Stat. 5117.)

Historical and Revision Notes

Section 627 of title 18, U.S.C., 1940 ed., relating to the filing of search warrants and companion papers, was omitted as unnecessary in view of Rule 41(f) of the Federal Rules of Criminal Procedure.

References in Text

Rule 41(f), referred to in text, was redesignated 41(g) by 1972 amendment eff. Oct. 1, 1972.

Amendments

1968—Pub. L. 90–578 substituted "Magistrates" for "Commissioners".

Change of Name

Words "magistrate judge" substituted for "magistrate" in section catchline and "Magistrate judges" substituted for "Magistrates" in text pursuant to section 321 of Pub. L. 101–650, set out as a note under section 631 of Title 28, Judiciary and Judicial Procedure.

Effective Date of 1968 Amendment

Amendment by Pub. L. 90–578 effective Oct. 17, 1968, except when a later effective date is applicable, which is the earlier of date when implementation of amendment by appointment of magistrates [now United States magistrate judges] and assumption of office takes place or third anniversary of enactment of Pub. L. 90–578 on Oct. 17, 1968, see section 403 of Pub. L. 90–578, set out as a note under section 631 of Title 28, Judiciary and Judicial Procedure.

§3117. Mobile tracking devices

(a) In General.—If a court is empowered to issue a warrant or other order for the installation of a mobile tracking device, such order may authorize the use of that device within the jurisdiction of the court, and outside that jurisdiction if the device is installed in that jurisdiction.

(b) Definition.—As used in this section, the term "tracking device" means an electronic or mechanical device which permits the tracking of the movement of a person or object.

(Added Pub. L. 99–508, title I, §108(a), Oct. 21, 1986, 100 Stat. 1858.)

Codification

Another section 3117 was renumbered section 3118 of this title.

Effective Date

Section effective 90 days after Oct. 21, 1986, and, in case of conduct pursuant to court order or extension, applicable only with respect to court orders and extensions made after such date, with special rule for State authorizations of interceptions, see section 111 of Pub. L. 99–508, set out as an Effective Date of 1986 Amendment note under section 2510 of this title.

§3118. Implied consent for certain tests

(a) Consent.—Whoever operates a motor vehicle in the special maritime and territorial jurisdiction of the United States consents thereby to a chemical test or tests of such person's blood, breath, or urine, if arrested for any offense arising from such person's driving while under the influence of a drug or alcohol in such jurisdiction. The test or tests shall be administered upon the request of a police officer having reasonable grounds to believe the person arrested to have been driving a motor vehicle upon the special maritime and territorial jurisdiction of the United States while under the influence of drugs or alcohol in violation of the laws of a State, territory, possession, or district.

(b) Effect of Refusal.—Whoever, having consented to a test or tests by reason of subsection (a), refuses to submit to such a test or tests, after having first been advised of the consequences of such a refusal, shall be denied the privilege of operating a motor vehicle upon the special maritime and territorial jurisdiction of the United States during the period of a year commencing on the date of arrest upon which such test or tests was refused, and such refusal may be admitted into evidence in any case arising from such person's driving while under the influence of a drug or alcohol in such jurisdiction. Any person who operates a motor vehicle in the special maritime and territorial jurisdiction of the United States after having been denied such privilege under this subsection shall be treated for the purposes of any civil or criminal proceedings arising out of such operation as operating such vehicle without a license to do so.

(Added Pub. L. 100–690, title VI, §6477(b)(1), Nov. 18, 1988, 102 Stat. 4381, §3117; renumbered §3118, Pub. L. 101–647, title XXXV, §3574, Nov. 29, 1990, 104 Stat. 4929.)

Amendments

1990—Pub. L. 101–647 renumbered second section 3117 of this title as this section.

CHAPTER 206 - PEN REGISTERS AND TRAP AND TRACE DEVICES

| 3121. | General prohibition on pen register and trap and trace device use; exception. |

Amendments

1988—Pub. L. 100–690, title VII, §§7068, 7092(c), Nov. 18, 1988, 102 Stat. 4405, 4411, substituted "trap and trace" for "trap or trace" in item 3123, added item 3125, and redesignated former items 3125 and 3126 as 3126 and 3127, respectively.

§3121. General prohibition on pen register and trap and trace device use; exception

(a) In General.—Except as provided in this section, no person may install or use a pen register or a trap and trace device without first obtaining a court order under section 3123 of this title or under the Foreign Intelligence Surveillance Act of 1978 (50 U.S.C. 1801 et seq.).

(b) Exception.—The prohibition of subsection (a) does not apply with respect to the use of a pen register or a trap and trace device by a provider of electronic or wire communication service—

(1) relating to the operation, maintenance, and testing of a wire or electronic communication service or to the protection of the rights or property of such provider, or to the protection of users of that service from abuse of service or unlawful use of service; or

(2) to record the fact that a wire or electronic communication was initiated or completed in order to protect such provider, another provider furnishing service toward the completion of the wire communication, or a user of that service, from fraudulent, unlawful or abusive use of service; or

(3) where the consent of the user of that service has been obtained.

(c) Limitation.—A government agency authorized to install and use a pen register or trap and trace device under this chapter or under State law shall use technology reasonably available to it that restricts the recording or decoding of electronic or other impulses to the dialing, routing, addressing, and signaling information utilized in the processing and transmitting of wire or electronic communications so as not to include the contents of any wire or electronic communications.

(d) Penalty.—Whoever knowingly violates subsection (a) shall be fined under this title or imprisoned not more than one year, or both.

(Added Pub. L. 99–508, title III, §301(a), Oct. 21, 1986, 100 Stat. 1868; amended Pub. L. 103–414, title II, §207(b), Oct. 25, 1994, 108 Stat. 4292; Pub. L. 107–56, title II, §216(a), Oct. 26, 2001, 115 Stat. 288.)

References in Text

The Foreign Intelligence Surveillance Act of 1978, referred to in subsec. (a), is Pub. L. 95–511, Oct. 25, 1978, 92 Stat. 1783, as amended, which is classified principally to chapter 36 (§1801 et seq.) of Title 50, War and National Defense. For complete classification of this Act to the Code, see Short Title note set out under section 1801 of Title 50 and Tables.

Amendments

2001—Subsec. (c). Pub. L. 107–56 inserted "or trap and trace device" after "pen register" and ", routing, addressing," after "dialing" and substituted "the processing and transmitting of wire or electronic communications so as not to include the contents of any wire or electronic communications" for "call processing".

1994—Subsecs. (c), (d). Pub. L. 103–414 added subsec. (c) and redesignated former subsec. (c) as (d).

Effective Date

Pub. L. 99–508, title III, §302, Oct. 21, 1986, 100 Stat. 1872, provided that:

"(a) In General.—Except as provided in subsection (b), this title and the amendments made by this title [enacting this chapter and section 1367 of this title] shall take effect ninety days after the date of the enactment of this Act [Oct. 21, 1986] and shall, in the case of conduct pursuant to a court order or extension, apply only with respect to court orders or extensions made after this title takes effect.

"(b) Special Rule for State Authorizations of Interceptions.—Any pen register or trap and trace device order or installation which would be valid and lawful without regard to the amendments made by this title shall be valid and lawful notwithstanding such amendments if such order or installation occurs during the period beginning on the date such amendments take effect and ending on the earlier of—

"(1) the day before the date of the taking effect of changes in State law required in order to make orders or installations under Federal law as amended by this title; or

"(2) the date two years after the date of the enactment of this Act [Oct. 21, 1986]."

§3122. Application for an order for a pen register or a trap and trace device

(a) Application.—(1) An attorney for the Government may make application for an order or an extension of an order under section 3123 of this title authorizing or approving the installation and use of a pen register or a trap and trace device under this chapter, in writing under oath or equivalent affirmation, to a court of competent jurisdiction.

(2) Unless prohibited by State law, a State investigative or law enforcement officer may make application for an order or an extension of an order under section 3123 of this title authorizing or approving the installation and use of a pen register or a trap and trace device under this chapter, in writing under oath or equivalent affirmation, to a court of competent jurisdiction of such State.

(b) Contents of Application.—An application under subsection (a) of this section shall include—

(1) the identity of the attorney for the Government or the State law enforcement or investigative officer making the application and the identity of the law enforcement agency conducting the investigation; and

(2) a certification by the applicant that the information likely to be obtained is relevant to an ongoing criminal investigation being conducted by that agency.

(Added Pub. L. 99–508, title III, §301(a), Oct. 21, 1986, 100 Stat. 1869.)

Effective Date

Section effective 90 days after Oct. 21, 1986, and, in case of conduct pursuant to court order or extension, applicable only with respect to court orders and extensions made after such date, with special rule for State authorizations of interceptions, see section 302 of Pub. L. 99–508, set out as a note under section 3121 of this title.

§3123. Issuance of an order for a pen register or a trap and trace device

(a) In General.—

(1) Attorney for the government.—Upon an application made under section 3122(a)(1), the court shall enter an ex parte order authorizing the installation and use of a pen register or trap and trace device anywhere within the United States, if the court finds that the attorney for the Government has certified to the court that the information likely to be obtained by such installation and use is relevant to an ongoing criminal investigation. The order, upon service of that order, shall apply to any person or entity providing wire or electronic communication service in the United States whose assistance may facilitate the execution of the order. Whenever such an order is served on any person or entity not specifically named in the order, upon request of such person or entity, the attorney for the Government or law enforcement or investigative officer that is serving the order shall provide written or electronic certification that the order applies to the person or entity being served.

(2) State investigative or law enforcement officer.—Upon an application made under section 3122(a)(2), the court shall enter an ex parte order authorizing the installation and use of a pen register or trap and trace device within the jurisdiction of the court, if the court finds that the State law enforcement or investigative officer has certified to the court that the information likely to be obtained by such installation and use is relevant to an ongoing criminal investigation.

(3)(A) Where the law enforcement agency implementing an ex parte order under this subsection seeks to do so by installing and using its own pen register or trap and trace device on a packet-switched data network of a provider of electronic communication service to the public, the agency shall ensure that a record will be maintained which will identify—

(i) any officer or officers who installed the device and any officer or officers who accessed the device to obtain information from the network;

(ii) the date and time the device was installed, the date and time the device was uninstalled, and the date, time, and duration of each time the device is accessed to obtain information;

(iii) the configuration of the device at the time of its installation and any subsequent modification thereof; and

(iv) any information which has been collected by the device.

To the extent that the pen register or trap and trace device can be set automatically to record this information electronically, the record shall be maintained electronically throughout the installation and use of such device.

(B) The record maintained under subparagraph (A) shall be provided ex parte and under seal to the court which entered the ex parte order authorizing the installation and use of the device within 30 days after termination of the order (including any extensions thereof).

(b) Contents of Order.—An order issued under this section—

(1) shall specify—

(A) the identity, if known, of the person to whom is leased or in whose name is listed the telephone line or other facility to which the pen register or trap and trace device is to be attached or applied;

(B) the identity, if known, of the person who is the subject of the criminal investigation;

(C) the attributes of the communications to which the order applies, including the number or other identifier and, if known, the location of the telephone line or other facility to which the pen register or trap and trace device is to be attached or applied, and, in the case of an order authorizing installation and use of a trap and trace device under subsection (a)(2), the geographic limits of the order; and

(D) a statement of the offense to which the information likely to be obtained by the pen register or trap and trace device relates; and

(2) shall direct, upon the request of the applicant, the furnishing of information, facilities, and technical assistance necessary to accomplish the installation of the pen register or trap and trace device under section 3124 of this title.

(c) Time Period and Extensions.—(1) An order issued under this section shall authorize the installation and use of a pen register or a trap and trace device for a period not to exceed sixty days.

(2) Extensions of such an order may be granted, but only upon an application for an order under section 3122 of this title and upon the judicial finding required by subsection (a) of this section. The period of extension shall be for a period not to exceed sixty days.

(d) Nondisclosure of Existence of Pen Register or a Trap and Trace Device.—An order authorizing or approving the installation and use of a pen register or a trap and trace device shall direct that—

(1) the order be sealed until otherwise ordered by the court; and

(2) the person owning or leasing the line or other facility to which the pen register or a trap and trace device is attached or applied, or who is obligated by the order to provide assistance to the applicant, not disclose the existence of the pen register or trap and trace device or the existence of the investigation to the listed subscriber, or to any other person, unless or until otherwise ordered by the court.

(Added Pub. L. 99–508, title III, §301(a), Oct. 21, 1986, 100 Stat. 1869; amended Pub. L. 107–56, title II, §216(b), Oct. 26, 2001, 115 Stat. 288.)

Amendments

2001—Subsec. (a). Pub. L. 107–56, §216(b)(1), reenacted heading without change and amended text generally. Prior to amendment, text read as follows: "Upon an application made under section 3122 of this title, the court shall enter an ex parte order authorizing the installation and use of a pen register or a trap and trace device within the jurisdiction of the court if the court finds that the attorney for the Government or the State law enforcement or investigative officer has certified to the court that the information likely to be obtained by such installation and use is relevant to an ongoing criminal investigation."

Subsec. (b)(1)(A). Pub. L. 107–56, §216(b)(2)(A), inserted "or other facility" after "telephone line" and "or applied" before semicolon at end.

Subsec. (b)(1)(C). Pub. L. 107–56, §216(b)(2)(B), added subpar. (C) and struck out former subpar (C) which read as follows: "the number and, if known, physical location of the telephone line to which the pen register or trap and trace device is to be attached and, in the case of a trap and trace device, the geographic limits of the trap and trace order; and".

Subsec. (d)(2). Pub. L. 107–56, §216(b)(3), inserted "or other facility" after "leasing the line" and substituted "or applied, or who is obligated by the order" for ", or who has been ordered by the court".

Effective Date

Section effective 90 days after Oct. 21, 1986, and, in case of conduct pursuant to court order or extension, applicable only with respect to court orders and extensions made after such date, with special rule for State authorizations of interceptions, see section 302 of Pub. L. 99–508, set out as a note under section 3121 of this title.

§3124. Assistance in installation and use of a pen register or a trap and trace device

(a) Pen Registers.—Upon the request of an attorney for the Government or an officer of a law enforcement agency authorized to install and use a pen register under this chapter, a provider of wire or electronic communication service, landlord, custodian, or other person shall furnish such investigative or law enforcement officer forthwith all information, facilities, and technical assistance necessary to accomplish the installation of the pen register unobtrusively and with a minimum of interference with the services that the person so ordered by the court accords the party with respect to whom the installation and use is to take place, if such assistance is directed by a court order as provided in section 3123(b)(2) of this title.

(b) Trap and Trace Device.—Upon the request of an attorney for the Government or an officer of a law enforcement agency authorized to receive the results of a trap and trace device under this chapter, a provider of a wire or electronic communication service, landlord, custodian, or other person shall install such device forthwith on the appropriate line or other facility and shall furnish such investigative or law enforcement officer all additional information, facilities and technical assistance including installation and operation of the device unobtrusively and with a minimum of interference with the services that the person so ordered by the court accords the party with respect to whom the installation and use is to take place, if such installation and assistance is directed by a court order as provided in section 3123(b)(2) of this title. Unless otherwise ordered by the court, the results of the trap and trace device shall be furnished, pursuant to section 3123(b) or section 3125 of this title, to the officer of a law enforcement agency, designated in the court order, at reasonable intervals during regular business hours for the duration of the order.

(c) Compensation.—A provider of a wire or electronic communication service, landlord, custodian, or other person who furnishes facilities or technical assistance pursuant to this section shall be reasonably compensated for such reasonable expenses incurred in providing such facilities and assistance.

(d) No Cause of Action Against a Provider Disclosing Information Under This Chapter.—No cause of action shall lie in any court against any provider of a wire or electronic communication service, its officers, employees, agents, or other specified persons for providing information, facilities, or assistance in accordance with a court order under this chapter or request pursuant to section 3125 of this title.

(e) Defense.—A good faith reliance on a court order under this chapter, a request pursuant to section 3125 of this title, a legislative authorization, or a statutory authorization is a complete defense against any civil or criminal action brought under this chapter or any other law.

(f) Communications Assistance Enforcement Orders.—Pursuant to section 2522, an order may be issued to enforce the assistance capability and capacity requirements under the Communications Assistance for Law Enforcement Act.

(Added Pub. L. 99–508, title III, §301(a), Oct. 21, 1986, 100 Stat. 1870; amended Pub. L. 100–690, title VII, §§7040, 7092(b), (d), Nov. 18, 1988, 102 Stat. 4399, 4411; Pub. L. 101–647, title XXXV, §3575, Nov. 29, 1990, 104 Stat. 4929; Pub. L. 103–414, title II, §201(b)(2), Oct. 25, 1994, 108 Stat. 4290; Pub. L. 107–56, title II, §216(c)(5), (6), Oct. 26, 2001, 115 Stat. 290.)

References in Text

The Communications Assistance for Law Enforcement Act, referred to in subsec. (f), is title I of Pub. L. 103–414, Oct. 25, 1994, 108 Stat. 4279, which is classified generally to subchapter I (§1001 et seq.) of chapter 9 of Title 47, Telecommunications. For complete classification of this Act to the Code, see Short Title note set out under section 1001 of Title 47 and Tables.

Amendments

2001—Subsec. (b). Pub. L. 107–56, §216(c)(6), inserted "or other facility" after "the appropriate line".

Subsec. (d). Pub. L. 107–56, §216(c)(5), struck out "the terms of" before "a court order".

1994—Subsec. (f). Pub. L. 103–414 added subsec. (f).

1990—Subsec. (b). Pub. L. 101–647 substituted "section 3123(b)" for "subsection 3123(b)".

1988—Subsec. (b). Pub. L. 100–690, §§7040, 7092(d), inserted ", pursuant to subsection 3123(b) or section 3125 of this title," after "shall be furnished" and "order" after last reference to "court".

Subsec. (d). Pub. L. 100–690, §7092(b)(1), inserted "or request pursuant to section 3125 of this title" after "this chapter".

Subsec. (e). Pub. L. 100–690, §7092(b)(2), inserted "under this chapter, a request pursuant to section 3125 of this title" after "court order".

Effective Date

Section effective 90 days after Oct. 21, 1986, and, in case of conduct pursuant to court order or extension, applicable only with respect to court orders and extensions made after such date, with special rule for State authorizations of interceptions, see section 302 of Pub. L. 99–508, set out as a note under section 3121 of this title.

Assistance to Law Enforcement Agencies

Pub. L. 107–56, title II, §222, Oct. 26, 2001, 115 Stat. 292, provided that: "Nothing in this Act [see Short Title of 2001 Amendment note set out under section 1 of this title] shall impose any additional technical obligation or requirement on a provider of a wire or electronic communication service or other person to furnish facilities or technical assistance. A provider of a wire or electronic communication service, landlord, custodian, or other person who furnishes facilities or technical assistance pursuant to section 216 [amending this section and sections 3121, 3123, and 3127 of this title] shall be reasonably compensated for such reasonable expenditures incurred in providing such facilities or assistance."

§3125. Emergency pen register and trap and trace device installation

(a) Notwithstanding any other provision of this chapter, any investigative or law enforcement officer, specially designated by the Attorney General, the Deputy Attorney General, the Associate Attorney General, any Assistant Attorney General, any acting Assistant Attorney General, or any Deputy Assistant Attorney General, or by the principal prosecuting attorney of any State or subdivision thereof acting pursuant to a statute of that State, who reasonably determines that—

(1) an emergency situation exists that involves—

(A) immediate danger of death or serious bodily injury to any person;

(B) conspiratorial activities characteristic of organized crime;

(C) an immediate threat to a national security interest; or

(D) an ongoing attack on a protected computer (as defined in section 1030) that constitutes a crime punishable by a term of imprisonment greater than one year;

that requires the installation and use of a pen register or a trap and trace device before an order authorizing such installation and use can, with due diligence, be obtained, and

(2) there are grounds upon which an order could be entered under this chapter to authorize such installation and use;

may have installed and use a pen register or trap and trace device if, within forty-eight hours after the installation has occurred, or begins to occur, an order approving the installation or use is issued in accordance with section 3123 of this title.

(b) In the absence of an authorizing order, such use shall immediately terminate when the information sought is obtained, when the application for the order is denied or when forty-eight hours have lapsed since the installation of the pen register or trap and trace device, whichever is earlier.

(c) The knowing installation or use by any investigative or law enforcement officer of a pen register or trap and trace device pursuant to subsection (a) without application for the authorizing order within forty-eight hours of the installation shall constitute a violation of this chapter.

(d) A provider of a wire or electronic service, landlord, custodian, or other person who furnished facilities or technical assistance pursuant to this section shall be reasonably compensated for such reasonable expenses incurred in providing such facilities and assistance.

(Added Pub. L. 100–690, title VII, §7092(a)(2), Nov. 18, 1988, 102 Stat. 4410; amended Pub. L. 103–322, title XXXIII, §330008(3), Sept. 13, 1994, 108 Stat. 2142; Pub. L. 104–294, title VI, §601(f)(5), Oct. 11, 1996, 110 Stat. 3499; Pub. L. 107–296, title II, §225(i), Nov. 25, 2002, 116 Stat. 2158.)

Prior Provisions

A prior section 3125 was renumbered section 3126 of this title.

Amendments

2002—Subsec. (a)(1)(C), (D). Pub. L. 107–296 added subpars. (C) and (D).

1996—Subsec. (a). Pub. L. 104–294 struck out closing quotation mark at end.

1994—Subsec. (a). Pub. L. 103–322, §330008(3)(A), (B), substituted "use;" for "use' " in par. (2) and directed that matter beginning with "may have installed" and ending with "section 3123 of this title" be realigned so that it is flush to the left margin, which was executed to text containing a period after "section 3123 of this title", to reflect the probable intent of Congress.

Subsec. (d). Pub. L. 103–322, §330008(3)(C), substituted "provider of" for "provider for".

Effective Date of 2002 Amendment

Amendment by Pub. L. 107–296 effective 60 days after Nov. 25, 2002, see section 4 of Pub. L. 107–296, set out as an Effective Date note under section 101 of Title 6, Domestic Security.

Effective Date

Section effective 90 days after Oct. 21, 1986, and, in case of conduct pursuant to court order or extension, applicable only with respect to court orders and extensions made after such date, with special rule for State authorizations of interceptions, see section 302 of Pub. L. 99–508, set out as a note under section 3121 of this title.

§3126. Reports concerning pen registers and trap and trace devices

The Attorney General shall annually report to Congress on the number of pen register orders and orders for trap and trace devices applied for by law enforcement agencies of the Department of Justice, which report shall include information concerning—
(1) the period of interceptions authorized by the order, and the number and duration of any extensions of the order;
(2) the offense specified in the order or application, or extension of an order;
(3) the number of investigations involved;
(4) the number and nature of the facilities affected; and
(5) the identity, including district, of the applying investigative or law enforcement agency making the application and the person authorizing the order.

(Added Pub. L. 99–508, title III, §301(a), Oct. 21, 1986, 100 Stat. 1871, §3125; renumbered §3126, Pub. L. 100–690, title VII, §7092(a)(1), Nov. 18, 1988, 102 Stat. 4410; amended Pub. L. 106–197, §3, May 2, 2000, 114 Stat. 247.)

Prior Provisions

A prior section 3126 was renumbered section 3127 of this title.

Amendments

2000—Pub. L. 106–197 substituted ", which report shall include information concerning—" and pars. (1) to (5) for period at end.
1988—Pub. L. 100–690 renumbered section 3125 of this title as this section.

Effective Date

Section effective 90 days after Oct. 21, 1986, and, in case of conduct pursuant to court order or extension, applicable only with respect to court orders and extensions made after such date, with special rule for State authorizations of interceptions, see section 302 of Pub. L. 99–508, set out as a note under section 3121 of this title.

Report on Use of DCS 1000 (Carnivore) To Implement Orders Under Section 3123

Pub. L. 107–273, div. A, title III, §305(a), Nov. 2, 2002, 116 Stat. 1782, provided that: "At the same time that the Attorney General submits to Congress the annual reports required by section 3126 of title 18, United States Code, that are respectively next due after the end of each of the fiscal years 2002 and 2003, the Attorney General shall also submit to the Chairmen and ranking minority members of the Committees on the Judiciary of the Senate and of the House of Representatives a report, covering the same respective time period, on the number of orders under section 3123 applied for by law enforcement agencies of the Department of Justice whose implementation involved the use of the DCS 1000 program (or any subsequent version of such program), which report shall include information concerning—
"(1) the period of interceptions authorized by the order, and the number and duration of any extensions of the order;
"(2) the offense specified in the order or application, or extension of an order;
"(3) the number of investigations involved;
"(4) the number and nature of the facilities affected;
"(5) the identity of the applying investigative or law enforcement agency making the application for an order; and

323

"(6) the specific persons authorizing the use of the DCS 1000 program (or any subsequent version of such program) in the implementation of such order."

§3127. Definitions for chapter

As used in this chapter—

(1) the terms "wire communication", "electronic communication", "electronic communication service", and "contents" have the meanings set forth for such terms in section 2510 of this title;

(2) the term "court of competent jurisdiction" means—

(A) any district court of the United States (including a magistrate judge of such a court) or any United States court of appeals that—

(i) has jurisdiction over the offense being investigated;

(ii) is in or for a district in which the provider of a wire or electronic communication service is located;

(iii) is in or for a district in which a landlord, custodian, or other person subject to subsections (a) or (b) of section 3124 of this title is located; or

(iv) is acting on a request for foreign assistance pursuant to section 3512 of this title; or

(B) a court of general criminal jurisdiction of a State authorized by the law of that State to enter orders authorizing the use of a pen register or a trap and trace device;

(3) the term "pen register" means a device or process which records or decodes dialing, routing, addressing, or signaling information transmitted by an instrument or facility from which a wire or electronic communication is transmitted, provided, however, that such information shall not include the contents of any communication, but such term does not include any device or process used by a provider or customer of a wire or electronic communication service for billing, or recording as an incident to billing, for communications services provided by such provider or any device or process used by a provider or customer of a wire communication service for cost accounting or other like purposes in the ordinary course of its business;

(4) the term "trap and trace device" means a device or process which captures the incoming electronic or other impulses which identify the originating number or other dialing, routing, addressing, and signaling information reasonably likely to identify the source of a wire or electronic communication, provided, however, that such information shall not include the contents of any communication;

(5) the term "attorney for the Government" has the meaning given such term for the purposes of the Federal Rules of Criminal Procedure; and

(6) the term "State" means a State, the District of Columbia, Puerto Rico, and any other possession or territory of the United States.

(Added Pub. L. 99–508, title III, §301(a), Oct. 21, 1986, 100 Stat. 1871, §3126; renumbered §3127, Pub. L. 100–690, title VII, §7092(a)(1), Nov. 18, 1988, 102 Stat. 4410; amended Pub. L. 107–56, title II, §216(c)(1)–(4), Oct. 26, 2001, 115 Stat. 290; Pub. L. 111–79, §2(3), Oct. 19, 2009, 123 Stat. 2087.)

References in Text

The Federal Rules of Criminal Procedure, referred to in par. (5), are set out in the Appendix to this title.

Amendments

2009—Par. (2)(A). Pub. L. 111–79 substituted "that—" and cls. (i) to (iv) for "having jurisdiction over the offense being investigated; or".

2001—Par. (1). Pub. L. 107–56, §216(c)(4), struck out "and" after " 'electronic communication'," and inserted ", and 'contents' " after " 'electronic communication service' ".

Par. (2)(A). Pub. L. 107–56, §216(c)(1), added subpar. (A) and struck out former subpar. (A) which read as follows: "a district court of the United States (including a magistrate judge of such a court) or a United States Court of Appeals; or".

Par. (3). Pub. L. 107–56, §216(c)(2), substituted "dialing, routing, addressing, or signaling information transmitted by an instrument or facility from which a wire or electronic communication is transmitted, provided, however, that such information shall not include the contents of any communication" for "electronic or other impulses which identify the numbers dialed or otherwise transmitted on the telephone line to which such device is attached" and inserted "or process" after "device" wherever appearing.

Par. (4). Pub. L. 107–56, §216(c)(3), inserted "or process" after "means a device" and substituted "or other dialing, routing, addressing, and signaling information reasonably likely to identify the source of a wire or electronic communication, provided, however, that such information shall not include the contents of any communication;" for "of an instrument or device from which a wire or electronic communication was transmitted;".

1988—Pub. L. 100–690 renumbered section 3126 of this title as this section.

Effective Date

Section effective 90 days after Oct. 21, 1986, and, in case of conduct pursuant to court order or extension, applicable only with respect to court orders and extensions made after such date, with special rule for State authorizations of interceptions, see section 302 of Pub. L. 99–508, set out as a note under section 3121 of this title.

CHAPTER 207 - RELEASE AND DETENTION PENDING JUDICIAL PROCEEDINGS

Amendments

1988—Pub. L. 100–690, title VII, §7084(b), Nov. 18, 1988, 102 Stat. 4408, added item 3151.

1984—Pub. L. 98–473, title II, §203(e), Oct. 12, 1984, 98 Stat. 1985, inserted "AND DETENTION PENDING JUDICIAL PROCEEDING" in chapter heading, added new items 3141 to 3150, and struck out former items 3141 to 3151 as follows: item 3141 "Power of courts and magistrates", item 3142 "Surrender by bail", item 3143 "Additional bail", item 3144 "Cases removed from State courts", item 3145 "Parties and witnesses—Rule", item 3146 "Release in noncapital cases prior to trial", item 3147 "Appeal from conditions of release", item 3148 "Release in capital cases or after conviction", item 3149 "Release of material witnesses", item 3150 "Penalties for failure to appear", item 3150a "Refund of forfeited bail", item 3151 "Contempt".

1982—Pub. L. 97–267, §6, Sept. 27, 1982, 96 Stat. 1138, struck out "agencies" after "services" in item 3152, substituted "and administration of pretrial services" for "of pretrial services agencies" in item 3153, "relating to pretrial services" for "of pretrial services agencies" in item 3154, and "Annual reports" for "Report to Congress" in item 3155.

Pub. L. 97–258, §2(d)(3)(A), Sept. 13, 1982, 96 Stat. 1058, added item 3150a.

1975—Pub. L. 93–619, title II, §202, Jan. 3, 1975, 88 Stat. 2089, added items 3153 to 3156, and in item 3152, substituted "Establishment of Pretrial Services Agencies" for "Definitions".

1966—Pub. L. 89–465, §§3(b), 5(e)(1), June 22, 1966, 80 Stat. 216, 217, substituted "RELEASE" for "BAIL" in chapter heading and "Release in noncapital cases prior to trial" for "Jumping Bail" in item 3146, and added items 3147 to 3152.

1954—Act Aug. 20, 1954, ch. 772, §2, 68 Stat. 748, added item 3146.

§3141. Release and detention authority generally

(a) Pending Trial.—A judicial officer authorized to order the arrest of a person under section 3041 of this title before whom an arrested person is brought shall order that such person be released or detained, pending judicial proceedings, under this chapter.

(b) Pending Sentence or Appeal.—A judicial officer of a court of original jurisdiction over an offense, or a judicial officer of a Federal appellate court, shall order that, pending imposition or execution of sentence, or pending appeal of conviction or sentence, a person be released or detained under this chapter.

(Added Pub. L. 98–473, title II, §203(a), Oct. 12, 1984, 98 Stat. 1976; amended Pub. L. 99–646, §55(a), (b), Nov. 10, 1986, 100 Stat. 3607.)

Prior Provisions

A prior section 3141, acts June 25, 1948, ch. 645, 62 Stat. 821; June 22, 1966, Pub. L. 89–465, §5(b), 80 Stat. 217, related to powers of courts and magistrates with respect to release on bail or otherwise, prior to repeal in the revision of this chapter by section 203(a) of Pub. L. 98–473.

Amendments

1986—Subsec. (a). Pub. L. 99–646, §55(a), (b), substituted "authorized to order the arrest of a person under section 3041 of this title before whom an arrested person is brought shall order that such person be released" for "who is authorized to order the arrest of a person pursuant to section 3041 of this title shall order that an arrested person who is brought before him be released" and "under this chapter" for "pursuant to the provisions of this chapter".

Subsec. (b). Pub. L. 99–646, §55(a), substituted "under this chapter" for "pursuant to the provisions of this chapter".

Effective Date of 1986 Amendment

Pub. L. 99–646, §55(j), Nov. 10, 1986, 100 Stat. 3611, provided that: "The amendments made by this section [amending this section and sections 3142 to 3144, 3146 to 3148, and 3156 of this title] shall take effect 30 days after the date of enactment of this Act [Nov. 10, 1986]."

Short Title of 2004 Amendment

Pub. L. 108–458, title VI, §6951, Dec. 17, 2004, 118 Stat. 3775, provided that: "This subtitle [subtitle K (§§6951, 6952) of title VI of Pub. L. 108–458, amending section 3142 of this title] may be cited as the 'Pretrial Detention of Terrorists Act of 2004'."

Short Title of 1990 Amendment

Pub. L. 101–647, title IX, §901, Nov. 29, 1990, 104 Stat. 4826, provided that: "This title [amending sections 3143 and 3145 of this title] may be cited as the 'Mandatory Detention for Offenders Convicted of Serious Crimes Act'."

Short Title of 1984 Amendment

Pub. L. 98–473, title II, §202, Oct. 12, 1984, 98 Stat. 1976, provided that: "This chapter [chapter I (§§202–210) of title II of Pub. L. 98–473, enacting sections 3062 and 3141 to 3150 of this title, amending sections 3041, 3042, 3154, 3156, 3731, 3772, and 4282 of this title and section 636 of Title 28, Judiciary and Judicial Procedure, repealing sections 3043 and 3141 to 3151 of this title, and amending rules 5, 15, 40, 46, and 54 of the Federal Rules of Criminal Procedure, set out in the Appendix to this title, and rule 9 of the Federal Rules of Appellate Procedure, set out in the Appendix to Title 28] may be cited as the 'Bail Reform Act of 1984'."

Short Title of 1982 Amendment

Pub. L. 97–267, §1, Sept. 27, 1982, 96 Stat. 1136, provided: "That this Act [amending sections 3152 to 3155 of this title and section 604 of Title 28, Judiciary and Judicial Procedure, and enacting provisions set out as notes under sections 3141 and 3152 of this title] may be cited as the 'Pretrial Services Act of 1982'."

Short Title

Pub. L. 89–465, §1, June 22, 1966, 80 Stat. 214, provided: "That this Act [enacting sections 3146 to 3152 of this title, amending sections 3041, 3141 to 3143, and 3568 of this title, and enacting provisions set out as a note below] may be cited as the 'Bail Reform Act of 1966'."

Purpose of Bail Reform Act of 1966

Pub. L. 89–465, §2, June 22, 1966, 80 Stat. 214, provided that: "The purpose of this Act [enacting sections 3146 to 3152 of this title, amending sections 3041, 3141 to 3143, and 3568 of this title and enacting provisions set out as a note above] is to revise the practices relating to bail to assure that all persons, regardless of their financial status, shall not needlessly be detained pending their appearance to answer charges, to testify, or pending appeal, when detention serves neither the ends of justice nor the public interest."

§3142. Release or detention of a defendant pending trial

(a) In General.—Upon the appearance before a judicial officer of a person charged with an offense, the judicial officer shall issue an order that, pending trial, the person be—
(1) released on personal recognizance or upon execution of an unsecured appearance bond, under subsection (b) of this section;
(2) released on a condition or combination of conditions under subsection (c) of this section;
(3) temporarily detained to permit revocation of conditional release, deportation, or exclusion under subsection (d) of this section; or
(4) detained under subsection (e) of this section.
(b) Release on Personal Recognizance or Unsecured Appearance Bond.—The judicial officer shall order the pretrial release of the person on personal recognizance, or upon execution of an unsecured appearance bond in an amount specified by the court, subject to the condition that the person not commit a Federal, State, or local crime during the period of release and subject to the condition that the person cooperate in the collection of a DNA sample from the person if the collection of such a sample is authorized pursuant to section 3 of the DNA Analysis Backlog Elimination Act of 2000 (42 U.S.C. 14135a),1 unless the judicial officer determines that such release will not reasonably assure the appearance of the person as required or will endanger the safety of any other person or the community.
(c) Release on Conditions.—(1) If the judicial officer determines that the release described in subsection (b) of this section will not reasonably assure the appearance of the person as required or will endanger the safety of any other person or the community, such judicial officer shall order the pretrial release of the person—
(A) subject to the condition that the person not commit a Federal, State, or local crime during the

period of release and subject to the condition that the person cooperate in the collection of a DNA sample from the person if the collection of such a sample is authorized pursuant to section 3 of the DNA Analysis Backlog Elimination Act of 2000 (42 U.S.C. 14135a); 1 and

(B) subject to the least restrictive further condition, or combination of conditions, that such judicial officer determines will reasonably assure the appearance of the person as required and the safety of any other person and the community, which may include the condition that the person—

(i) remain in the custody of a designated person, who agrees to assume supervision and to report any violation of a release condition to the court, if the designated person is able reasonably to assure the judicial officer that the person will appear as required and will not pose a danger to the safety of any other person or the community;

(ii) maintain employment, or, if unemployed, actively seek employment;

(iii) maintain or commence an educational program;

(iv) abide by specified restrictions on personal associations, place of abode, or travel;

(v) avoid all contact with an alleged victim of the crime and with a potential witness who may testify concerning the offense;

(vi) report on a regular basis to a designated law enforcement agency, pretrial services agency, or other agency;

(vii) comply with a specified curfew;

(viii) refrain from possessing a firearm, destructive device, or other dangerous weapon;

(ix) refrain from excessive use of alcohol, or any use of a narcotic drug or other controlled substance, as defined in section 102 of the Controlled Substances Act (21 U.S.C. 802), without a prescription by a licensed medical practitioner;

(x) undergo available medical, psychological, or psychiatric treatment, including treatment for drug or alcohol dependency, and remain in a specified institution if required for that purpose;

(xi) execute an agreement to forfeit upon failing to appear as required, property of a sufficient unencumbered value, including money, as is reasonably necessary to assure the appearance of the person as required, and shall provide the court with proof of ownership and the value of the property along with information regarding existing encumbrances as the judicial office may require;

(xii) execute a bail bond with solvent sureties; who will execute an agreement to forfeit in such amount as is reasonably necessary to assure appearance of the person as required and shall provide the court with information regarding the value of the assets and liabilities of the surety if other than an approved surety and the nature and extent of encumbrances against the surety's property; such surety shall have a net worth which shall have sufficient unencumbered value to pay the amount of the bail bond;

(xiii) return to custody for specified hours following release for employment, schooling, or other limited purposes; and

(xiv) satisfy any other condition that is reasonably necessary to assure the appearance of the person as required and to assure the safety of any other person and the community.

In any case that involves a minor victim under section 1201, 1591, 2241, 2242, 2244(a)(1), 2245, 2251, 2251A, 2252(a)(1), 2252(a)(2), 2252(a)(3), 2252A(a)(1), 2252A(a)(2), 2252A(a)(3), 2252A(a)(4), 2260, 2421, 2422, 2423, or 2425 of this title, or a failure to register offense under section 2250 of this title, any release order shall contain, at a minimum, a condition of electronic monitoring and each of the conditions specified at subparagraphs (iv), (v), (vi), (vii), and (viii).

(2) The judicial officer may not impose a financial condition that results in the pretrial detention of the person.

(3) The judicial officer may at any time amend the order to impose additional or different conditions of release.

(d) Temporary Detention To Permit Revocation of Conditional Release, Deportation, or Exclusion.—If the judicial officer determines that—

(1) such person—

(A) is, and was at the time the offense was committed, on—

(i) release pending trial for a felony under Federal, State, or local law;

(ii) release pending imposition or execution of sentence, appeal of sentence or conviction, or completion of sentence, for any offense under Federal, State, or local law; or

(iii) probation or parole for any offense under Federal, State, or local law; or

(B) is not a citizen of the United States or lawfully admitted for permanent residence, as defined in section 101(a)(20) of the Immigration and Nationality Act (8 U.S.C. 1101(a)(20)); and

(2) such person may flee or pose a danger to any other person or the community;

such judicial officer shall order the detention of such person, for a period of not more than ten days, excluding Saturdays, Sundays, and holidays, and direct the attorney for the Government to notify the appropriate court, probation or parole official, or State or local law enforcement official, or the appropriate official of the Immigration and Naturalization Service. If the official fails or declines to take such person into custody during that period, such person shall be treated in accordance with the other provisions of this section, notwithstanding the applicability of other provisions of law governing release pending trial or deportation or exclusion proceedings. If temporary detention is sought under paragraph (1)(B) of this subsection, such person has the burden of proving to the court such person's United States citizenship or lawful admission for permanent residence.

(e) Detention.—(1) If, after a hearing pursuant to the provisions of subsection (f) of this section, the judicial officer finds that no condition or combination of conditions will reasonably assure the appearance of the person as required and the safety of any other person and the community, such judicial officer shall order the detention of the person before trial.

(2) In a case described in subsection (f)(1) of this section, a rebuttable presumption arises that no condition or combination of conditions will reasonably assure the safety of any other person and the community if such judicial officer finds that—

(A) the person has been convicted of a Federal offense that is described in subsection (f)(1) of this section, or of a State or local offense that would have been an offense described in subsection (f)(1) of this section if a circumstance giving rise to Federal jurisdiction had existed;

(B) the offense described in subparagraph (A) was committed while the person was on release pending trial for a Federal, State, or local offense; and

(C) a period of not more than five years has elapsed since the date of conviction, or the release of the person from imprisonment, for the offense described in subparagraph (A), whichever is later.

(3) Subject to rebuttal by the person, it shall be presumed that no condition or combination of conditions will reasonably assure the appearance of the person as required and the safety of the community if the judicial officer finds that there is probable cause to believe that the person committed—

(A) an offense for which a maximum term of imprisonment of ten years or more is prescribed in the Controlled Substances Act (21 U.S.C. 801 et seq.), the Controlled Substances Import and Export Act (21 U.S.C. 951 et seq.), or chapter 705 of title 46;

(B) an offense under section 924(c), 956(a), or 2332b of this title;

(C) an offense listed in section 2332b(g)(5)(B) of title 18, United States Code, for which a maximum term of imprisonment of 10 years or more is prescribed;

(D) an offense under chapter 77 of this title for which a maximum term of imprisonment of 20 years or more is prescribed; or

(E) an offense involving a minor victim under section 1201, 1591, 2241, 2242, 2244(a)(1), 2245, 2251, 2251A, 2252(a)(1), 2252(a)(2), 2252(a)(3), 2252A(a)(1), 2252A(a)(2), 2252A(a)(3), 2252A(a)(4), 2260, 2421, 2422, 2423, or 2425 of this title.

(f) Detention Hearing.—The judicial officer shall hold a hearing to determine whether any condition or combination of conditions set forth in subsection (c) of this section will reasonably assure the appearance of such person as required and the safety of any other person and the community—

(1) upon motion of the attorney for the Government, in a case that involves—

(A) a crime of violence, a violation of section 1591, or an offense listed in section 2332b(g)(5)(B) for which a maximum term of imprisonment of 10 years or more is prescribed;

(B) an offense for which the maximum sentence is life imprisonment or death;

(C) an offense for which a maximum term of imprisonment of ten years or more is prescribed in the Controlled Substances Act (21 U.S.C. 801 et seq.), the Controlled Substances Import and Export Act (21 U.S.C. 951 et seq.), or chapter 705 of title 46;

(D) any felony if such person has been convicted of two or more offenses described in subparagraphs (A) through (C) of this paragraph, or two or more State or local offenses that would have been offenses described in subparagraphs (A) through (C) of this paragraph if a circumstance giving rise to Federal jurisdiction had existed, or a combination of such offenses; or

(E) any felony that is not otherwise a crime of violence that involves a minor victim or that involves the possession or use of a firearm or destructive device (as those terms are defined in section 921), or any other dangerous weapon, or involves a failure to register under section 2250 of title 18, United States Code; or

(2) upon motion of the attorney for the Government or upon the judicial officer's own motion in a case, that involves—

(A) a serious risk that such person will flee; or

(B) a serious risk that such person will obstruct or attempt to obstruct justice, or threaten, injure, or intimidate, or attempt to threaten, injure, or intimidate, a prospective witness or juror.

The hearing shall be held immediately upon the person's first appearance before the judicial officer unless that person, or the attorney for the Government, seeks a continuance. Except for good cause, a continuance on motion of such person may not exceed five days (not including any intermediate Saturday, Sunday, or legal holiday), and a continuance on motion of the attorney for the Government may not exceed three days (not including any intermediate Saturday, Sunday, or legal holiday). During a continuance, such person shall be detained, and the judicial officer, on motion of the attorney for the Government or sua sponte, may order that, while in custody, a person who appears to be a narcotics addict receive a medical examination to determine whether such person is an addict. At the hearing, such person has the right to be represented by counsel, and, if financially unable to obtain adequate representation, to have counsel appointed. The person shall be afforded an opportunity to testify, to present witnesses, to cross-examine witnesses who appear at the hearing, and to present information by proffer or otherwise. The rules concerning admissibility of evidence in criminal trials do not apply to the presentation and consideration of information at the hearing. The facts the judicial officer uses to support a finding pursuant to subsection (e) that no condition or combination of conditions will reasonably assure the safety of any other person and the community shall be supported by clear and convincing evidence. The person may be detained pending completion of the hearing. The hearing may be reopened, before or after a determination by the judicial officer, at any time before trial if the judicial officer finds that information exists that was not known to the movant at the time of the hearing and that has a material bearing on the issue whether there are conditions of release that will reasonably assure the appearance of such person as required and the safety of any other person and the community.

(g) Factors To Be Considered.—The judicial officer shall, in determining whether there are conditions of release that will reasonably assure the appearance of the person as required and the safety of any other person and the community, take into account the available information concerning—

(1) the nature and circumstances of the offense charged, including whether the offense is a crime of violence, a violation of section 1591, a Federal crime of terrorism, or involves a minor victim or a controlled substance, firearm, explosive, or destructive device;

(2) the weight of the evidence against the person;

(3) the history and characteristics of the person, including—

(A) the person's character, physical and mental condition, family ties, employment, financial resources, length of residence in the community, community ties, past conduct, history relating to drug or alcohol abuse, criminal history, and record concerning appearance at court proceedings; and

(B) whether, at the time of the current offense or arrest, the person was on probation, on parole, or on other release pending trial, sentencing, appeal, or completion of sentence for an offense under Federal, State, or local law; and

(4) the nature and seriousness of the danger to any person or the community that would be posed by the person's release. In considering the conditions of release described in subsection (c)(1)(B)(xi) or (c)(1)(B)(xii) of this section, the judicial officer may upon his own motion, or shall upon the motion of the Government, conduct an inquiry into the source of the property to be designated for potential forfeiture or offered as collateral to secure a bond, and shall decline to accept the designation, or the use as collateral, of property that, because of its source, will not reasonably assure the appearance of the person as required.

(h) Contents of Release Order.—In a release order issued under subsection (b) or (c) of this section, the judicial officer shall—

(1) include a written statement that sets forth all the conditions to which the release is subject, in a manner sufficiently clear and specific to serve as a guide for the person's conduct; and

(2) advise the person of—

(A) the penalties for violating a condition of release, including the penalties for committing an offense while on pretrial release;

(B) the consequences of violating a condition of release, including the immediate issuance of a warrant for the person's arrest; and

(C) sections 1503 of this title (relating to intimidation of witnesses, jurors, and officers of the court), 1510 (relating to obstruction of criminal investigations), 1512 (tampering with a witness, victim, or an informant), and 1513 (retaliating against a witness, victim, or an informant).

(i) Contents of Detention Order.—In a detention order issued under subsection (e) of this section, the judicial officer shall—

(1) include written findings of fact and a written statement of the reasons for the detention;

(2) direct that the person be committed to the custody of the Attorney General for confinement in a corrections facility separate, to the extent practicable, from persons awaiting or serving sentences or being held in custody pending appeal;

(3) direct that the person be afforded reasonable opportunity for private consultation with counsel; and

(4) direct that, on order of a court of the United States or on request of an attorney for the Government, the person in charge of the corrections facility in which the person is confined deliver the person to a United States marshal for the purpose of an appearance in connection with a court proceeding.

The judicial officer may, by subsequent order, permit the temporary release of the person, in the custody of a United States marshal or another appropriate person, to the extent that the judicial officer determines such release to be necessary for preparation of the person's defense or for another compelling reason.

(j) Presumption of Innocence.—Nothing in this section shall be construed as modifying or limiting the presumption of innocence.

(Added Pub. L. 98–473, title II, §203(a), Oct. 12, 1984, 98 Stat. 1976; amended Pub. L. 99–646, §§55(a), (c), 72, Nov. 10, 1986, 100 Stat. 3607, 3617; Pub. L. 100–690, title VII, §7073, Nov. 18, 1988, 102 Stat. 4405; Pub. L. 101–647, title X, §1001(b), title XXXVI, §§3622–3624, Nov. 29, 1990, 104 Stat. 4827, 4965; Pub. L. 104–132, title VII, §§702(d), 729, Apr. 24, 1996, 110 Stat. 1294, 1302; Pub. L. 108–21, title II, §203, Apr. 30, 2003, 117 Stat. 660; Pub. L. 108–458, title VI, §6952, Dec. 17, 2004, 118 Stat. 3775; Pub. L. 109–162, title X, §1004(b), Jan. 5, 2006, 119 Stat. 3085; Pub. L. 109–248, title II, §216, July 27, 2006, 120 Stat. 617; Pub. L. 109–304, §17(d)(7), Oct. 6, 2006, 120 Stat. 1707; Pub. L. 110–457, title II, §§222(a), 224(a), Dec. 23, 2008, 122 Stat. 5067, 5072.)

References in Text

Section 3 of the DNA Analysis Backlog Elimination Act of 2000, referred to in subsecs. (b) and (c)(1)(A), is section 3 of Pub. L. 106–546, which was classified to section 14135a of Title 42, The Public Health and Welfare, prior to editorial reclassification as section 40702 of Title 34, Crime Control and Law Enforcement.

The Controlled Substances Act, referred to in subsecs. (e) and (f)(1)(C), is title II of Pub. L. 91–513, Oct. 27, 1970, 84 Stat. 1242, as amended, which is classified principally to subchapter I (§801 et seq.) of chapter 13 of Title 21, Food and Drugs. For complete classification of this Act to the Code, see Short Title note set out under section 801 of Title 21 and Tables.

The Controlled Substances Import and Export Act, referred to in subsecs. (e) and (f)(1)(C), is title III of Pub. L. 91–513, Oct. 27, 1970, 84 Stat. 1285, as amended, which is classified principally to subchapter II (§951 et seq.) of chapter 13 of Title 21. For complete classification of this Act to the Code, see Short Title note set out under section 951 of Title 21 and Tables.

Prior Provisions

A prior section 3142, acts June 25, 1948, ch. 645, 62 Stat. 821; June 22, 1966, Pub. L. 89–465, §5(c), 80 Stat. 217, set forth provisions relating to surrender by bail, prior to repeal in the revision of this chapter by section 203(a) of Pub. L. 98–473.

Amendments

2008—Subsec. (e). Pub. L. 110–457, §222(a)(1)–(4), designated first through third sentences as pars. (1) to (3), respectively, and redesignated former pars. (1) to (3) as subpars. (A) to (C), respectively, of par. (2).

Subsec. (e)(2)(B), (C). Pub. L. 110–457, §222(a)(5), substituted "subparagraph (A)" for "paragraph (1) of this subsection".

Subsec. (e)(3). Pub. L. 110–457, §222(a)(6), substituted "committed—" for "committed", "46;" for "46,", "title;" for "title, or", and "10 years or more is prescribed;" for "10 years or more is prescribed or", inserted subpar. (A), (B), (C), and (E) designations, and added subpar. (D).

Subsecs. (f)(1)(A), (g)(1). Pub. L. 110–457, §224(a), substituted "violence, a violation of section 1591," for "violence,".

2006—Subsecs. (b), (c)(1)(A). Pub. L. 109–162 inserted "and subject to the condition that the person cooperate in the collection of a DNA sample from the person if the collection of such a sample is authorized pursuant to section 3 of the DNA Analysis Backlog Elimination Act of 2000 (42 U.S.C. 14135a)" after "period of release".

Subsec. (c)(1)(B). Pub. L. 109–248, §216(1), inserted concluding provisions.

Subsecs. (e), (f)(1)(C). Pub. L. 109–304 substituted "chapter 705 of title 46" for "the Maritime Drug Law Enforcement Act (46 U.S.C. App. 1901 et seq.)".

Subsec. (f)(1)(E). Pub. L. 109–248, §216(2), added subpar. (E).

Subsec. (g)(1). Pub. L. 109–248, §216(3), added par. (1) and struck out former par. (1) which read as follows: "the nature and circumstances of the offense charged, including whether the offense is a crime of violence, or an offense listed in section 2332b(g)(5)(B) for which a maximum term of imprisonment of 10 years or more is prescribed or involves a narcotic drug;".

2004—Subsec. (e). Pub. L. 108–458, §6952(1), in concluding provisions, inserted "or" before "the Maritime" and "or an offense listed in section 2332b(g)(5)(B) of title 18, United States Code, for which a maximum term of imprisonment of 10 years or more is prescribed" after "or 2332b of this title,".

Subsecs. (f)(1)(A), (g)(1). Pub. L. 108–458, §6952(2), inserted ", or an offense listed in section 2332b(g)(5)(B) for which a maximum term of imprisonment of 10 years or more is prescribed" after "violence".

2003—Subsec. (e). Pub. L. 108–21, in concluding provisions, substituted "1901 et seq.)," for "1901 et seq.), or" and "of this title, or an offense involving a minor victim under section 1201, 1591, 2241, 2242, 2244(a)(1), 2245, 2251, 2251A, 2252(a)(1), 2252(a)(2), 2252(a)(3), 2252A(a)(1), 2252A(a)(2), 2252A(a)(3), 2252A(a)(4), 2260, 2421, 2422, 2423, or 2425 of this title" for "of title 18 of the United States Code".

1996—Subsec. (e). Pub. L. 104–132, §702(d), inserted ", 956(a), or 2332b" after "section 924(c)" in concluding provisions.

Subsec. (f). Pub. L. 104–132, §729, in concluding provisions, inserted "(not including any

332

intermediate Saturday, Sunday, or legal holiday)" after "five days" and after "three days".

1990—Subsec. (c)(1)(B)(xi). Pub. L. 101–647, §3622, amended cl. (xi) generally. Prior to amendment, cl. (xi) read as follows: "execute an agreement to forfeit upon failing to appear as required, such designated property, including money, as is reasonably necessary to assure the appearance of the person as required, and post with the court such indicia of ownership of the property or such percentage of the money as the judicial officer may specify;".

Subsec. (c)(1)(B)(xii). Pub. L. 101–647, §3623, amended cl. (xii) generally. Prior to amendment, cl. (xii) read as follows: "execute a bail bond with solvent sureties in such amount as is reasonably necessary to assure the appearance of the person as required;".

Subsecs. (e), (f)(1)(C). Pub. L. 101–647, §1001(b), substituted "the Maritime Drug Law Enforcement Act (46 U.S.C. App. 1901 et seq.)" for "section 1 of the Act of September 15, 1980 (21 U.S.C. 955a)".

Subsec. (g)(4). Pub. L. 101–647, §3624, substituted "subsection (c)(1)(B)(xi) or (c)(1)(B)(xii)" for "subsection (c)(2)(K) or (c)(2)(L)".

1988—Subsec. (c)(3). Pub. L. 100–690 substituted "the order" for "order".

1986—Subsec. (a). Pub. L. 99–646, §55(a), (c)(1), in par. (1) struck out "his" after "released on" and substituted "under subsection (b) of this section" for "pursuant to the provisions of subsection (b)", in par. (2) substituted "under subsection (c) of this section" for "pursuant to the provisions of subsection (c)", in par. (3) substituted "under subsection (d) of this section" for "pursuant to provisions of subsection (d)", and in par. (4) substituted "under subsection (e) of this section" for "pursuant to provisions of subsection (e)".

Subsec. (b). Pub. L. 99–646, §55(c)(2), struck out "his" after "person on" and "period of".

Subsec. (c). Pub. L. 99–646, §55(c)(3), designated existing provision as par. (1) and redesignated former pars. (1) and (2) as subpars. (A) and (B), in provision preceding subpar. (A) substituted "subsection (b) of this section" for "subsection (b)" and "such judicial officer" for "he", in subpar. (B) redesignated subpars. (A) to (N) as cls. (i) to (xiv), in provision preceding cl. (i) substituted "such judicial officer" for "he", in cl. (i) substituted "assume supervision" for "supervise him", in cl. (iv) substituted "on personal" for "on his personal", in cl. (x) substituted "medical, psychological," for "medical", designated provision relating to the judicial officer not imposing a financial condition that results in the pretrial detention of a person as par. (2), and designated provision permitting the judicial officer to impose at any time additional or different conditions of release as par. (3), and in par. (3) struck out "his" after "amend".

Subsec. (d). Pub. L. 99–646, §55(c)(4), in pars. (1) and (2) substituted "such person" for "the person" and in concluding provisions substituted "such person" for "the person" in four places, "such judicial officer" for "he", "paragraph (1)(B) of this subsection" for "paragraph (1)(B)", and "such person's United States citizenship or lawful admission" for "that he is a citizen of the United States or is lawfully admitted".

Subsec. (e). Pub. L. 99–646, §55(c)(5), in introductory provisions inserted "of this section" after "subsection (f)" and substituted "such judicial officer" for "he", "before" for "prior to", "described in subsection (f)(1) of this section" for "described in (f)(1)", and "if such judicial officer" for "if the judge", in par. (1) inserted "of this section" after "subsection (f)(1)" in two places, and in pars. (2) and (3) inserted "of this section" after "paragraph (1)".

Subsec. (f). Pub. L. 99–646, §72, in par. (1)(D) substituted "any felony if the person has been convicted of two or more offenses" for "any felony committed after the person had been convicted of two or more prior offenses" and inserted ", or a combination of such offenses", in par. (2)(A) inserted "or" after "flee;", and in concluding provisions, inserted provision permitting the hearing to be reopened at any time before trial if the judicial officer finds that information exists that was unknown to the movant at the time of the hearing and that has a material bearing on whether there are conditions of release that will reasonably assure the appearance of the person as required and the safety of any other person and the community.

Pub. L. 99–646, §55(c)(6), substituted "such person" for "the person" wherever appearing, in introductory provision inserted "of this section" after "subsection (c)" and struck out "in a case" after "community", in par. (1) inserted "in a case" and in subpar. (D) of par. (1) inserted "of this paragraph" in two places, in par. (2) substituted "upon" for "Upon" and inserted "in a case", and in concluding provisions, substituted "sua sponte" for "on his own motion", "whether such person is an addict" for "whether he is an addict", and "financially" for "he is financially", and struck out "for him" after "appointed" and "on his own behalf" after "witnesses".

Subsec. (g). Pub. L. 99–646, §55(c)(7), in par. (3)(A) substituted "the person's" for "his", in par. (3)(B) substituted "the person" for "he", and in par. (4) inserted "of this section".

Subsec. (h). Pub. L. 99–646, §55(a), (c)(8), in introductory provision substituted "under" for "pursuant to the provisions of" and inserted "of this section" and in par. (2)(C) struck out "the provisions of" before "sections 1503".

Subsec. (i). Pub. L. 99–646, §55(a), (c)(9), in introductory provision substituted "under" for "pursuant to the provisions of" and inserted "of this section" and in par. (3) struck out "his" after "consultation with".

Effective Date of 1990 Amendment

Amendment by sections 3622 to 3624 of Pub. L. 101–647 effective 180 days after Nov. 29, 1990, see section 3631 of Pub. L. 101–647, set out as an Effective Date note under section 3001 of Title 28, Judiciary and Judicial Procedure.

Effective Date of 1986 Amendment

Amendment by Pub. L. 99–646 effective 30 days after Nov. 10, 1986, see section 55(j) of Pub. L. 99–646, set out as a note under section 3141 of this title.

Abolition of Immigration and Naturalization Service and Transfer of Functions

For abolition of Immigration and Naturalization Service, transfer of functions, and treatment of related references, see note set out under section 1551 of Title 8, Aliens and Nationality.

§3143. Release or detention of a defendant pending sentence or appeal

(a) Release or Detention Pending Sentence.—(1) Except as provided in paragraph (2), the judicial officer shall order that a person who has been found guilty of an offense and who is awaiting imposition or execution of sentence, other than a person for whom the applicable guideline promulgated pursuant to 28 U.S.C. 994 does not recommend a term of imprisonment, be detained, unless the judicial officer finds by clear and convincing evidence that the person is not likely to flee or pose a danger to the safety of any other person or the community if released under section 3142(b) or (c). If the judicial officer makes such a finding, such judicial officer shall order the release of the person in accordance with section 3142(b) or (c).

(2) The judicial officer shall order that a person who has been found guilty of an offense in a case described in subparagraph (A), (B), or (C) of subsection (f)(1) of section 3142 and is awaiting imposition or execution of sentence be detained unless—

(A)(i) the judicial officer finds there is a substantial likelihood that a motion for acquittal or new trial will be granted; or

(ii) an attorney for the Government has recommended that no sentence of imprisonment be imposed on the person; and

(B) the judicial officer finds by clear and convincing evidence that the person is not likely to flee or pose a danger to any other person or the community.

(b) Release or Detention Pending Appeal by the Defendant.—(1) Except as provided in paragraph (2), the judicial officer shall order that a person who has been found guilty of an offense and sentenced to a term of imprisonment, and who has filed an appeal or a petition for a writ of certiorari, be detained, unless the judicial officer finds—

(A) by clear and convincing evidence that the person is not likely to flee or pose a danger to the safety of any other person or the community if released under section 3142(b) or (c) of this title; and

(B) that the appeal is not for the purpose of delay and raises a substantial question of law or fact likely to result in—

(i) reversal,

(ii) an order for a new trial,

(iii) a sentence that does not include a term of imprisonment, or

(iv) a reduced sentence to a term of imprisonment less than the total of the time already served plus the expected duration of the appeal process.

If the judicial officer makes such findings, such judicial officer shall order the release of the person in accordance with section 3142(b) or (c) of this title, except that in the circumstance described in subparagraph (B)(iv) of this paragraph, the judicial officer shall order the detention terminated at the expiration of the likely reduced sentence.

(2) The judicial officer shall order that a person who has been found guilty of an offense in a case described in subparagraph (A), (B), or (C) of subsection (f)(1) of section 3142 and sentenced to a term of imprisonment, and who has filed an appeal or a petition for a writ of certiorari, be detained.

(c) Release or Detention Pending Appeal by the Government.—The judicial officer shall treat a defendant in a case in which an appeal has been taken by the United States under section 3731 of this title, in accordance with section 3142 of this title, unless the defendant is otherwise subject to a release or detention order. Except as provided in subsection (b) of this section, the judicial officer, in a case in which an appeal has been taken by the United States under section 3742, shall—

(1) if the person has been sentenced to a term of imprisonment, order that person detained; and

(2) in any other circumstance, release or detain the person under section 3142.

(Added Pub. L. 98–473, title II, §203(a), Oct. 12, 1984, 98 Stat. 1981; amended Pub. L. 98–473, title II, §223(f), Oct. 12, 1984, 98 Stat. 2028; Pub. L. 99–646, §§51(a), (b), 55(a), (d), Nov. 10, 1986, 100 Stat. 3605–3607, 3609; Pub. L. 100–690, title VII, §7091, Nov. 18, 1988, 102 Stat. 4410; Pub. L. 101–647, title IX, §902(a), (b), title X, §1001(a), Nov. 29, 1990, 104 Stat. 4826, 4827; Pub. L. 102–572, title VII, §703, Oct. 29, 1992, 106 Stat. 4515.)

Prior Provisions

A prior section 3143, acts June 25, 1948, ch. 645, 62 Stat. 821; June 22, 1966, Pub. L. 89–465, §5(d), 80 Stat. 217, related to additional bail, prior to repeal in the revision of this chapter by section 203(a) of Pub. L. 98–473.

Amendments

1992—Subsec. (b)(1). Pub. L. 102–572 substituted "subparagraph (B)(iv) of this paragraph" for "paragraph (b)(2)(D)".

1990—Subsec. (a). Pub. L. 101–647, §902(a), designated existing provisions as par. (1), substituted "Except as provided in paragraph (2), the judicial officer" for "The judicial officer", and added par. (2).

Subsec. (a)(1). Pub. L. 101–647, §1001(a), substituted "awaiting" for "waiting".

Subsec. (b). Pub. L. 101–647, §902(b), designated existing provisions as par. (1), substituted "Except as provided in paragraph (2), the judicial officer" for "The judicial officer", redesignated former pars. (1) and (2) as subpars. (A) and (B), redesignated former subpars. (A) to (D) as cls. (i) to (iv), respectively, of subpar. (B), and added par. (2).

1988—Subsec. (b). Pub. L. 100–690, §7091(2), inserted ", except that in the circumstance described in paragraph (b)(2)(D), the judicial officer shall order the detention terminated at the expiration of the likely reduced sentence" before period at end.

Subsec. (b)(2). Pub. L. 100–690, §7091(1), added par. (2) and struck out former par. (2) which read as follows: "that the appeal is not for purpose of delay and raises a substantial question of law or fact likely to result in reversal, an order for a new trial, or a sentence that does not include a term of imprisonment."

1986—Subsec. (a). Pub. L. 99–646, §55(d)(1), (2), (4), substituted "under" for "pursuant to" and "such judicial officer" for "he" and struck out "the provisions of" after "in accordance with".

Subsec. (b). Pub. L. 99–646, §55(d)(1)–(4), in par. (1) substituted "under" for "pursuant to" and inserted "of this title" after "(c)", and in concluding provision, substituted "such judicial officer" for "he", struck out "the provisions of" after "in accordance with", and inserted "of this title" after "(c)".

Subsec. (b)(2). Pub. L. 99–646, §51(a)(1), substituted "reversal," for "reversal or" and inserted ", or a sentence that does not include a term of imprisonment".

Subsec. (c). Pub. L. 99–646, §51(a)(2), inserted provision that, except as provided in subsec. (b), the judicial officer, in a case in which an appeal has been taken by the United States under section 3742, if the person has been sentenced to a term of imprisonment, order that person detained, and in any other circumstance, release or detain the person under section 3142.

Pub. L. 99–646, §55(a), (d)(2), (5), substituted "under section 3731" for "pursuant to the provisions of section 3731" and "with section 3142 of this title" for "with the provisions of section 3142".

Pub. L. 99–646, §51(b), provided that the amendment of subsec. (c) by section 223(f)(2) of Pub. L. 98–473 shall not take effect. See 1984 Amendment note below.

1984—Subsec. (a). Pub. L. 98–473, §223(f)(1), inserted provisions relating to applicable guideline under section 994 of title 28.

Subsec. (c). Pub. L. 98–473, §223(f)(2), which would have added a final sentence requiring a judge to treat a defendant in a case in which an appeal had been taken by the United States pursuant to the provisions of section 3742 in accordance with the provisions of (1) subsection (a) if the person had been sentenced to a term of imprisonment; or (2) section 3142 if the person had not been sentenced to a term of imprisonment did not become effective pursuant to section 51(b) of Pub. L. 99–646. See 1986 Amendment note above.

Effective Date of 1992 Amendment

Amendment by Pub. L. 102–572 effective Jan. 1, 1993, see section 1101 of Pub. L. 102–572, set out as a note under section 905 of Title 2, The Congress.

Effective Date of 1986 Amendment

Pub. L. 99–646, §51(c), Nov. 10, 1986, 100 Stat. 3606, provided that: "The amendment made by subsection (a)(2) [amending this section] shall take effect on the date of the taking of effect of section 3742 of title 18, United States Code [Nov. 1, 1987]."

Amendment by section 55(a), (d) of Pub. L. 99–646 effective 30 days after Nov. 10, 1986, see section 55(j) of Pub. L. 99–646, set out as a note under section 3141 of this title.

Effective Date of 1984 Amendment

Amendment by Pub. L. 98–473 effective Nov. 1, 1987, and applicable only to offenses committed after the taking effect of such amendment, see section 235(a)(1) of Pub. L. 98–473, set out as an Effective Date note under section 3551 of this title.

§3144. Release or detention of a material witness

If it appears from an affidavit filed by a party that the testimony of a person is material in a criminal proceeding, and if it is shown that it may become impracticable to secure the presence of the person by subpoena, a judicial officer may order the arrest of the person and treat the person in accordance with the provisions of section 3142 of this title. No material witness may be detained because of inability to comply with any condition of release if the testimony of such witness can adequately be secured by deposition, and if further detention is not necessary to prevent a failure of justice. Release of a material witness may be delayed for a reasonable period of time until the deposition of the witness can be taken pursuant to the Federal Rules of Criminal Procedure.

(Added Pub. L. 98–473, title II, §203(a), Oct. 12, 1984, 98 Stat. 1982; amended Pub. L. 99–646,

§55(e), Nov. 10, 1986, 100 Stat. 3609.)

References in Text
The Federal Rules of Criminal Procedure, referred to in text, are set out in the Appendix to this title.

Prior Provisions
A prior section 3144, act June 25, 1948, ch. 645, 62 Stat. 821, related to cases removed from State courts, prior to repeal in the revision of this chapter by section 203(a) of Pub. L. 98–473.

Amendments
1986—Pub. L. 99–646 substituted "subpoena" for "subpena" and inserted "of this title".

Effective Date of 1986 Amendment
Amendment by Pub. L. 99–646 effective 30 days after Nov. 10, 1986, see section 55(j) of Pub. L. 99–646, set out as a note under section 3141 of this title.

§3145. Review and appeal of a release or detention order
(a) Review of a Release Order.—If a person is ordered released by a magistrate judge, or by a person other than a judge of a court having original jurisdiction over the offense and other than a Federal appellate court—

(1) the attorney for the Government may file, with the court having original jurisdiction over the offense, a motion for revocation of the order or amendment of the conditions of release; and

(2) the person may file, with the court having original jurisdiction over the offense, a motion for amendment of the conditions of release.

The motion shall be determined promptly.

(b) Review of a Detention Order.—If a person is ordered detained by a magistrate judge, or by a person other than a judge of a court having original jurisdiction over the offense and other than a Federal appellate court, the person may file, with the court having original jurisdiction over the offense, a motion for revocation or amendment of the order. The motion shall be determined promptly.

(c) Appeal From a Release or Detention Order.—An appeal from a release or detention order, or from a decision denying revocation or amendment of such an order, is governed by the provisions of section 1291 of title 28 and section 3731 of this title. The appeal shall be determined promptly. A person subject to detention pursuant to section 3143(a)(2) or (b)(2), and who meets the conditions of release set forth in section 3143(a)(1) or (b)(1), may be ordered released, under appropriate conditions, by the judicial officer, if it is clearly shown that there are exceptional reasons why such person's detention would not be appropriate.

(Added Pub. L. 98–473, title II, §203(a), Oct. 12, 1984, 98 Stat. 1982; amended Pub. L. 101–647, title IX, §902(c), Nov. 29, 1990, 104 Stat. 4827; Pub. L. 101–650, title III, §321, Dec. 1, 1990, 104 Stat. 5117.)

Prior Provisions
A prior section 3145, act June 25, 1948, ch. 645, 62 Stat. 821, provided cross references to the Federal Rules of Criminal Procedure for rules covering parties and witnesses, prior to repeal in the revision of this chapter by section 203(a) of Pub. L. 98–473.

Amendments
1990—Subsec. (c). Pub. L. 101–647 inserted at end "A person subject to detention pursuant to section 3143(a)(2) or (b)(2), and who meets the conditions of release set forth in section 3143(a)(1) or (b)(1), may be ordered released, under appropriate conditions, by the judicial officer,

if it is clearly shown that there are exceptional reasons why such person's detention would not be appropriate."

Change of Name
Words "magistrate judge" substituted for "magistrate" in subsecs. (a) and (b) pursuant to section 321 of Pub. L. 101–650, set out as a note under section 631 of Title 28, Judiciary and Judicial Procedure.

§3146. Penalty for failure to appear
(a) Offense.—Whoever, having been released under this chapter knowingly—

(1) fails to appear before a court as required by the conditions of release; or

(2) fails to surrender for service of sentence pursuant to a court order;

shall be punished as provided in subsection (b) of this section.

(b) Punishment.—(1) The punishment for an offense under this section is—

(A) if the person was released in connection with a charge of, or while awaiting sentence, surrender for service of sentence, or appeal or certiorari after conviction for—

(i) an offense punishable by death, life imprisonment, or imprisonment for a term of 15 years or more, a fine under this title or imprisonment for not more than ten years, or both;

(ii) an offense punishable by imprisonment for a term of five years or more, a fine under this title or imprisonment for not more than five years, or both;

(iii) any other felony, a fine under this title or imprisonment for not more than two years, or both; or

(iv) a misdemeanor, a fine under this title or imprisonment for not more than one year, or both; and

(B) if the person was released for appearance as a material witness, a fine under this chapter or imprisonment for not more than one year, or both.

(2) A term of imprisonment imposed under this section shall be consecutive to the sentence of imprisonment for any other offense.

(c) Affirmative Defense.—It is an affirmative defense to a prosecution under this section that uncontrollable circumstances prevented the person from appearing or surrendering, and that the person did not contribute to the creation of such circumstances in reckless disregard of the requirement to appear or surrender, and that the person appeared or surrendered as soon as such circumstances ceased to exist.

(d) Declaration of Forfeiture.—If a person fails to appear before a court as required, and the person executed an appearance bond pursuant to section 3142(b) of this title or is subject to the release condition set forth in clause (xi) or (xii) of section 3142(c)(1)(B) of this title, the judicial officer may, regardless of whether the person has been charged with an offense under this section, declare any property designated pursuant to that section to be forfeited to the United States.

(Added Pub. L. 98–473, title II, §203(a), Oct. 12, 1984, 98 Stat. 1982; amended Pub. L. 99–646, §55(f), Nov. 10, 1986, 100 Stat. 3609; Pub. L. 103–322, title XXXIII, §330016(2)(K), Sept. 13, 1994, 108 Stat. 2148; Pub. L. 104–294, title VI, §601(a)(4), Oct. 11, 1996, 110 Stat. 3498.)

Prior Provisions
A prior section 3146, added Pub. L. 89–465, §3(a), June 22, 1966, 80 Stat. 214; amended Pub. L. 97–291, §8, Oct. 12, 1982, 96 Stat. 1257, related to release in noncapital cases prior to trial, prior to repeal in the revision of this chapter by section 203(a) of Pub. L. 98–473.

Another prior section 3146, act Aug. 20, 1954, ch. 772, §1, 68 Stat. 747, which prescribed penalties for jumping bail, was repealed by Pub. L. 89–465, §3(a), June 22, 1966, 80 Stat. 214, and covered by former sections 3150 and 3151 of this title.

Amendments
1996—Subsec. (b)(1)(A)(iv). Pub. L. 104–294 substituted "a fine under this title" for "a fined

under this title".

1994—Subsec. (b)(1)(A)(iv). Pub. L. 103–322 substituted "fined under this title" for "fine under this chapter".

1986—Subsec. (a). Pub. L. 99–646, §55(f)(1), added subsec. (a) and struck out former subsec. (a) which read as follows: "A person commits an offense if, after having been released pursuant to this chapter—

"(1) he knowingly fails to appear before a court as required by the conditions of his release; or

"(2) he knowingly fails to surrender for service of sentence pursuant to a court order."

Subsec. (b). Pub. L. 99–646, §55(f)(1), added subsec. (b) and struck out former subsec. (b) which was captioned "Grading", and which read as follows: "If the person was released—

"(1) in connection with a charge of, or while awaiting sentence, surrender for service of sentence, or appeal or certiorari after conviction, for—

"(A) an offense punishable by death, life imprisonment, or imprisonment for a term of fifteen years or more, he shall be fined not more than $25,000 or imprisoned for not more than ten years, or both;

"(B) an offense punishable by imprisonment for a term of five or more years, but less than fifteen years, he shall be fined not more than $10,000 or imprisoned for not more than five years, or both;

"(C) any other felony, he shall be fined not more than $5,000 or imprisoned for not more than two years, or both; or

"(D) a misdemeanor, he shall be fined not more than $2,000 or imprisoned for not more than one year, or both; or

"(2) for appearance as a material witness, he shall be fined not more than $1,000 or imprisoned for not more than one year, or both.

A term of imprisonment imposed pursuant to this section shall be consecutive to the sentence of imprisonment for any other offense."

Subsec. (c). Pub. L. 99–646, §55(f)(2), substituted "requirement to appear" for "requirement that he appear" and "the person appeared" for "he appeared".

Subsec. (d). Pub. L. 99–646, §55(f)(3), inserted "of this title" after "3142(b)" and substituted "clause (xi) or (xii) of section 3142(c)(1)(B) of this title" for "section 3142(c)(2)(K) or (c)(2)(L)".

Effective Date of 1986 Amendment

Amendment by Pub. L. 99–646 effective 30 days after Nov. 10, 1986, see section 55(j) of Pub. L. 99–646, set out as a note under section 3141 of this title.

§3147. Penalty for an offense committed while on release

A person convicted of an offense committed while released under this chapter shall be sentenced, in addition to the sentence prescribed for the offense, to—

(1) a term of imprisonment of not more than ten years if the offense is a felony; or

(2) a term of imprisonment of not more than one year if the offense is a misdemeanor.

A term of imprisonment imposed under this section shall be consecutive to any other sentence of imprisonment.

(Added Pub. L. 98–473, title II, §203(a), Oct. 12, 1984, 98 Stat. 1983; amended Pub. L. 98–473, title II, §223(g), Oct. 12, 1984, 98 Stat. 2028; Pub. L. 99–646, §55(g), Nov. 10, 1986, 100 Stat. 3610.)

Prior Provisions

A prior section 3147, added Pub. L. 89–465, §3(a), June 22, 1966, 80 Stat. 215, related to appeals from conditions of release, prior to repeal in the revision of this chapter by section 203(a) of Pub. L. 98–473.

Amendments

1986—Pub. L. 99–646 substituted "under" for "pursuant to" in two places and "for the offense," for "for the offense".

1984—Pub. L. 98–473, §223(g), struck out "not less than two years and" after "imprisonment of" in par. (1), and "not less than ninety days and" after "imprisonment of" in par. (2).

Effective Date of 1986 Amendment

Amendment by Pub. L. 99–646 effective 30 days after Nov. 10, 1986, see section 55(j) of Pub. L. 99–646, set out as a note under section 3141 of this title.

Effective Date of 1984 Amendment

Amendment by Pub. L. 98–473 effective Nov. 1, 1987, and applicable only to offenses committed after the taking effect of such amendment, see section 235(a)(1) of Pub. L. 98–473, set out as an Effective Date note under section 3551 of this title.

§3148. Sanctions for violation of a release condition

(a) Available Sanctions.—A person who has been released under section 3142 of this title, and who has violated a condition of his release, is subject to a revocation of release, an order of detention, and a prosecution for contempt of court.

(b) Revocation of Release.—The attorney for the Government may initiate a proceeding for revocation of an order of release by filing a motion with the district court. A judicial officer may issue a warrant for the arrest of a person charged with violating a condition of release, and the person shall be brought before a judicial officer in the district in which such person's arrest was ordered for a proceeding in accordance with this section. To the extent practicable, a person charged with violating the condition of release that such person not commit a Federal, State, or local crime during the period of release, shall be brought before the judicial officer who ordered the release and whose order is alleged to have been violated. The judicial officer shall enter an order of revocation and detention if, after a hearing, the judicial officer—

(1) finds that there is—

(A) probable cause to believe that the person has committed a Federal, State, or local crime while on release; or

(B) clear and convincing evidence that the person has violated any other condition of release; and

(2) finds that—

(A) based on the factors set forth in section 3142(g) of this title, there is no condition or combination of conditions of release that will assure that the person will not flee or pose a danger to the safety of any other person or the community; or

(B) the person is unlikely to abide by any condition or combination of conditions of release.

If there is probable cause to believe that, while on release, the person committed a Federal, State, or local felony, a rebuttable presumption arises that no condition or combination of conditions will assure that the person will not pose a danger to the safety of any other person or the community. If the judicial officer finds that there are conditions of release that will assure that the person will not flee or pose a danger to the safety of any other person or the community, and that the person will abide by such conditions, the judicial officer shall treat the person in accordance with the provisions of section 3142 of this title and may amend the conditions of release accordingly.

(c) Prosecution for Contempt.—The judicial officer may commence a prosecution for contempt, under section 401 of this title, if the person has violated a condition of release.

(Added Pub. L. 98–473, title II, §203(a), Oct. 12, 1984, 98 Stat. 1983; amended Pub. L. 99–646, §55(a), (h), Nov. 10, 1986, 100 Stat. 3607, 3610.)

Prior Provisions

A prior section 3148, added Pub. L. 89–465, §3(a), June 22, 1966, 80 Stat. 215; amended Pub. L. 91–452, title X, §1002, Oct. 12, 1970, 84 Stat. 952, related to release in capital cases or after conviction, prior to repeal in the revision of this chapter by section 203(a) of Pub. L. 98–473.

Amendments

1986—Subsec. (a). Pub. L. 99–646, §55(a), (h)(1), substituted "under section 3142 of this title" for "pursuant to the provisions of section 3142".

Subsec. (b). Pub. L. 99–646, §55(h)(2), in introductory provision, substituted "such person's arrest" for "his arrest", "condition of release that such person not commit" for "condition of his release that he not commit", and "period of release," for "period of release", in par. (1)(B) substituted "condition of release" for "condition of his release", in par. (2)(A) inserted "of this title" after "section 3142(g)", and in concluding provision, substituted "the judicial officer shall" for "he shall" and inserted "of this title" after "section 3142".

Subsec. (c). Pub. L. 99–646, §55(a), (h)(3), substituted "judicial officer" for "judge", "under section 401 of this title" for "pursuant to the provisions of section 401", and "condition of release" for "condition of his release".

Effective Date of 1986 Amendment

Amendment by Pub. L. 99–646 effective 30 days after Nov. 10, 1986, see section 55(j) of Pub. L. 99–646, set out as a note under section 3141 of this title.

§3149. Surrender of an offender by a surety

A person charged with an offense, who is released upon the execution of an appearance bond with a surety, may be arrested by the surety, and if so arrested, shall be delivered promptly to a United States marshal and brought before a judicial officer. The judicial officer shall determine in accordance with the provisions of section 3148(b) whether to revoke the release of the person, and may absolve the surety of responsibility to pay all or part of the bond in accordance with the provisions of Rule 46 of the Federal Rules of Criminal Procedure. The person so committed shall be held in official detention until released pursuant to this chapter or another provision of law.

(Added Pub. L. 98–473, title II, §203(a), Oct. 12, 1984, 98 Stat. 1984.)

Prior Provisions

A prior section 3149, added Pub. L. 89–465, §3(a), June 22, 1966, 80 Stat. 216, related to release of material witnesses, prior to repeal in the revision of this chapter by section 203(a) of Pub. L. 98–473.

§3150. Applicability to a case removed from a State court

The provisions of this chapter apply to a criminal case removed to a Federal court from a State court.

(Added Pub. L. 98–473, title II, §203(a), Oct. 12, 1984, 98 Stat. 1984.)

Prior Provisions

A prior section 3150, added Pub. L. 89–465, §3(a), June 22, 1966, 80 Stat. 216, related to penalties for failure to appear, prior to repeal in the revision of this chapter by section 203(a) of Pub. L. 98–473.

[§3150a. Repealed. Pub. L. 98–473, title II, §203(a), Oct. 12, 1984, 98 Stat. 1976]

Section, added Pub. L. 97–258, §2(d)(3)(B), Sept. 13, 1982, 96 Stat. 1059; amended Pub. L. 98–473, title II, §1410, Oct. 12, 1984, 98 Stat. 2178, related to refund of forfeited bail. Section 1410 of Pub. L. 98–473 was subsequently repealed by Pub. L. 99–646, §49, Nov. 10, 1986, 100 Stat. 3605.

§3151. Refund of forfeited bail

Appropriations available to refund money erroneously received and deposited in the Treasury are available to refund any part of forfeited bail deposited into the Treasury and ordered remitted under the Federal Rules of Criminal Procedure.

(Added Pub. L. 100–690, title VII, §7084(a), Nov. 18, 1988, 102 Stat. 4408.)

References in Text

The Federal Rules of Criminal Procedure, referred to in text, are set out in the Appendix to this title.

Prior Provisions

A prior section 3151, added Pub. L. 89–465, §3(a), June 22, 1966, 80 Stat. 216, related to contempt power of courts, prior to repeal by Pub. L. 98–473, title II, §203(a), Oct. 12, 1984, 98 Stat. 1976.

§3152. Establishment of pretrial services

(a) On and after the date of the enactment of the Pretrial Services Act of 1982, the Director of the Administrative Office of the United States Courts (hereinafter in this chapter referred to as the "Director") shall, under the supervision and direction of the Judicial Conference of the United States, provide directly, or by contract or otherwise (to such extent and in such amounts as are provided in appropriation Acts), for the establishment of pretrial services in each judicial district (other than the District of Columbia). Pretrial services established under this section shall be supervised by a chief probation officer appointed under section 3654 of this title or by a chief pretrial services officer selected under subsection (c) of this section.

(b) Beginning eighteen months after the date of the enactment of the Pretrial Services Act of 1982, if an appropriate United States district court and the circuit judicial council jointly recommend the establishment under this subsection of pretrial services in a particular district, pretrial services shall be established under the general authority of the Administrative Office of the United States Courts.

(c) The pretrial services established under subsection (b) of this section shall be supervised by a chief pretrial services officer appointed by the district court. The chief pretrial services officer appointed under this subsection shall be an individual other than one serving under authority of section 3602 of this title.

(Added Pub. L. 93–619, title II, §201, Jan. 3, 1975, 88 Stat. 2086; amended Pub. L. 97–267, §2, Sept. 27, 1982, 96 Stat. 1136; Pub. L. 110–406, §10, Oct. 13, 2008, 122 Stat. 4293.)

References in Text

The date of enactment of the Pretrial Services Act of 1982, referred to in subsecs. (a) and (b), is the date of enactment of Pub. L. 97–267, which was approved Sept. 27, 1982.

Prior Provisions

A prior section 3152, as added by Pub. L. 89–465, §3(a), June 22, 1966, 80 Stat. 216, defined the terms "judicial officer" and "offense", prior to repeal by Pub. L. 93–619, §201. See section 3156 of this title.

Amendments

2008—Subsec. (c). Pub. L. 110–406 added subsec. (c) and struck out former subsec. (c) which related to supervision of pretrial services.

1982—Pub. L. 97–267 struck out "agencies" after "services" in section catchline, divided previously unlettered text provisions into subsecs. (a), (b), and (c), and substituted revised provisions as so redesignated for provisions which required the Director of the Administrative Office of the United States Courts to establish, on a demonstration basis, in each of ten representative judicial districts (other than the District of Columbia), a pretrial services agency authorized to maintain effective supervision and control over, and to provide supportive services to, defendants released under this chapter such districts to be designated by the Chief Justice of the United States after consultation with the Attorney General, on the basis of such considerations as the number of criminal cases prosecuted annually in the district, the percentage of defendants in the district presently detained prior to trial, the incidence of crime charged against persons released pending trial under this chapter, and the availability of community resources to implement the conditions of release which may be imposed under this chapter.

Authorization of Appropriations

Pub. L. 97–267, §9, Sept. 27, 1982, 96 Stat. 1139, provided that:

"(a) There are authorized to be appropriated, for the fiscal year ending September 30, 1984, and each succeeding fiscal year thereafter, such sums as may be necessary to carry out the functions and powers of pretrial services established under section 3152(b) of title 18, United States Code.

"(b) There are authorized to be appropriated for the fiscal year ending September 30, 1983, and the fiscal year ending September 30, 1984, such sums as may be necessary to carry out the functions and powers of the pretrial services agencies established under section 3152 of title 18 of the United States Code in effect before the date of enactment of this Act [Sept. 27, 1982]."

Status of Pretrial Services Agencies in Effect Prior to September 27, 1982

Pub. L. 97–267, §8, Sept. 27, 1982, 96 Stat. 1139, provided that: "During the period beginning on the date of enactment of this Act [Sept. 27, 1982] and ending eighteen months after the date of the enactment of this Act, the pretrial services agencies established under section 3152 of title 18 of the United States Code in effect before the date of enactment of this Act may continue to operate, employ staff, provide pretrial services, and perform such functions and powers as are authorized under chapter 207 of title 18 of the United States Code [this chapter]."

§3153. Organization and administration of pretrial services

(a)(1) With the approval of the district court, the chief pretrial services officer in districts in which pretrial services are established under section 3152(b) of this title shall appoint such other personnel as may be required. The position requirements and rate of compensation of the chief pretrial services officer and such other personnel shall be established by the Director with the approval of the Judicial Conference of the United States, except that no such rate of compensation shall exceed the rate of basic pay in effect and then payable for grade GS–16 of the General Schedule under section 5332 of title 5, United States Code.

(2) The chief pretrial services officer in districts in which pretrial services are established under section 3152(b) of this title is authorized, subject to the general policy established by the Director and the approval of the district court, to procure temporary and intermittent services to the extent authorized by section 3109 of title 5, United States Code. The staff, other than clerical staff, may be drawn from law school students, graduate students, or such other available personnel.

(b) The chief probation officer in all districts in which pretrial services are established under section 3152(a) of this title shall designate personnel appointed under chapter 231 of this title to perform pretrial services under this chapter.

(c)(1) Except as provided in paragraph (2) of this subsection, information obtained in the course of performing pretrial services functions in relation to a particular accused shall be used only for the purposes of a bail determination and shall otherwise be confidential. Each pretrial services report shall be made available to the attorney for the accused and the attorney for the Government.

(2) The Director shall issue regulations establishing the policy for release of information made confidential by paragraph (1) of this subsection. Such regulations shall provide exceptions to the confidentiality requirements under paragraph (1) of this subsection to allow access to such information—

(A) by qualified persons for purposes of research related to the administration of criminal justice;

(B) by persons under contract under section 3154(4) of this title;

(C) by probation officers for the purpose of compiling presentence reports;

(D) insofar as such information is a pretrial diversion report, to the attorney for the accused and the attorney for the Government; and

(E) in certain limited cases, to law enforcement agencies for law enforcement purposes.

(3) Information made confidential under paragraph (1) of this subsection is not admissible on the issue of guilt in a criminal judicial proceeding unless such proceeding is a prosecution for a crime committed in the course of obtaining pretrial release or a prosecution for failure to appear for the criminal judicial proceeding with respect to which pretrial services were provided.

(Added Pub. L. 93–619, title II, §201, Jan. 3, 1975, 88 Stat. 2086; amended Pub. L. 97–287, §3, Sept. 27, 1982, 96 Stat. 1136.)

Amendments

1982—Pub. L. 97–267 substantially revised section by substituting provisions relating to the organization and administration of pretrial services for provisions relating to organization and administration of pretrial services agencies which vested the powers of five such agencies in the Division of Probation of the Administrative Office of the United States Courts and the powers of the remaining five agencies in Boards of Trustees, set forth requirements for membership and terms of office with respect to such Boards, and provided for appointment of Federal probation officers in agencies governed by the Division of Probation, and chief pretrial service officers in agencies governed by Boards of Trustees, which designated officers would be responsible for the direction and supervision of their respective agencies.

References in Other Laws to GS–16, 17, or 18 Pay Rates

References in laws to the rates of pay for GS–16, 17, or 18, or to maximum rates of pay under the General Schedule, to be considered references to rates payable under specified sections of Title 5, Government Organization and Employees, see section 529 [title I, §101(c)(1)] of Pub. L. 101–509, set out in a note under section 5376 of Title 5.

§3154. Functions and powers relating to pretrial services

Pretrial services functions shall include the following:

(1) Collect, verify, and report to the judicial officer, prior to the pretrial release hearing, information pertaining to the pretrial release of each individual charged with an offense, including information relating to any danger that the release of such person may pose to any other person or the community, and, where appropriate, include a recommendation as to whether such individual should be released or detained and, if release is recommended, recommend appropriate conditions of release; except that a district court may direct that information not be collected, verified, or reported under this paragraph on individuals charged with Class A misdemeanors as defined in section 3559(a)(6) of this title.

(2) Review and modify the reports and recommendations specified in paragraph (1) of this section for persons seeking release pursuant to section 3145 of this chapter.

(3) Supervise persons released into its custody under this chapter.

(4) Operate or contract for the operation of appropriate facilities for the custody or care of persons released under this chapter including residential halfway houses, addict and alcoholic treatment centers, and counseling services, and contract with any appropriate public or private agency or person, or expend funds, to monitor and provide treatment as well as nontreatment services to any such persons released in the community, including equipment and emergency housing, corrective and preventative guidance and training, and other services reasonably deemed necessary to protect the public and ensure that such persons appear in court as required.

(5) Inform the court and the United States attorney of all apparent violations of pretrial release conditions, arrests of persons released to the custody of providers of pretrial services or under the supervision of providers of pretrial services, and any danger that any such person may come to pose to any other person or the community, and recommend appropriate modifications of release

conditions.

(6) Serve as coordinator for other local agencies which serve or are eligible to serve as custodians under this chapter and advise the court as to the eligibility, availability, and capacity of such agencies.

(7) Assist persons released under this chapter in securing any necessary employment, medical, legal, or social services.

(8) Prepare, in cooperation with the United States marshal and the United States attorney such pretrial detention reports as are required by the provisions of the Federal Rules of Criminal Procedure relating to the supervision of detention pending trial.

(9) Develop and implement a system to monitor and evaluate bail activities, provide information to judicial officers on the results of bail decisions, and prepare periodic reports to assist in the improvement of the bail process.

(10) To the extent provided for in an agreement between a chief pretrial services officer in districts in which pretrial services are established under section 3152(b) of this title, or the chief probation officer in all other districts, and the United States attorney, collect, verify, and prepare reports for the United States attorney's office of information pertaining to the pretrial diversion of any individual who is or may be charged with an offense, and perform such other duties as may be required under any such agreement.

(11) Make contracts, to such extent and in such amounts as are provided in appropriation Acts, for the carrying out of any pretrial services functions.

(12)(A) As directed by the court and to the degree required by the regimen of care or treatment ordered by the court as a condition of release, keep informed as to the conduct and provide supervision of a person conditionally released under the provisions of section 4243 or 4246 of this title, and report such person's conduct and condition to the court ordering release and the Attorney General or his designee.

(B) Any violation of the conditions of release shall immediately be reported to the court and the Attorney General or his designee.

(13) If approved by the district court, be authorized to carry firearms under such rules and regulations as the Director of the Administrative Office of the United States Courts may prescribe.

(14) Perform, in a manner appropriate for juveniles, any of the functions identified in this section with respect to juveniles awaiting adjudication, trial, or disposition under chapter 403 of this title who are not detained.

(15) Perform such other functions as specified under this chapter.

(Added Pub. L. 93–619, title II, §201, Jan. 3, 1975, 88 Stat. 2087; amended Pub. L. 97–267, §4, Sept. 27, 1982, 96 Stat. 1137; Pub. L. 98–473, title II, §203(b), Oct. 12, 1984, 98 Stat. 1984; Pub. L. 101–647, title XXXV, §3576, Nov. 29, 1990, 104 Stat. 4929; Pub. L. 102–572, title VII, §701(b), title X, §1002, Oct. 29, 1992, 106 Stat. 4515, 4521; Pub. L. 104–317, title I, §101(b), Oct. 19, 1996, 110 Stat. 3848; Pub. L. 110–406, §15(a), Oct. 13, 2008, 122 Stat. 4294; Pub. L. 111–174, §5, May 27, 2010, 124 Stat. 1216.)

Amendments

2010—Pars. (14), (15). Pub. L. 111–174 added par. (14) and redesignated former par. (14) as (15).

2008—Par. (4). Pub. L. 110–406 inserted ", and contract with any appropriate public or private agency or person, or expend funds, to monitor and provide treatment as well as nontreatment services to any such persons released in the community, including equipment and emergency housing, corrective and preventative guidance and training, and other services reasonably deemed necessary to protect the public and ensure that such persons appear in court as required" before period at end.

1996—Pars. (13), (14). Pub. L. 104–317 added par. (13) and redesignated former par. (13) as (14).

1992—Par. (1). Pub. L. 102–572, §1002, inserted before period at end "; except that a district court may direct that information not be collected, verified, or reported under this paragraph on individuals charged with Class A misdemeanors as defined in section 3559(a)(6) of this title".

Pars. (12), (13). Pub. L. 102–572, §701(b), added par. (12) and redesignated former par. (12) as (13).

1990—Par. (1). Pub. L. 101–647 substituted "community, and, where appropriate, include a recommendation as to whether such individual should be released or detained and, if release is recommended, recommend appropriate conditions of release." for "community" and all that followed through end of par. (1).

1984—Par. (1). Pub. L. 98–473, §203(b)(1), which directed the amendment of par. (1), by striking out "and recommend appropriate release conditions for each such person" and inserting in lieu thereof "and, where appropriate, include a recommendation as to whether such individual should be released or detained and, if release is recommended, recommend appropriate conditions of release" could not be executed because such language did not appear. See 1990 Amendment note above.

Par. (2). Pub. L. 98–473, §203(b)(2), substituted "section 3145" for "section 3146(e) or section 3147".

1982—Pub. L. 97–267 substituted "relating to pretrial services" for "of pretrial services agencies" in section catchline, in par. (1) struck out provisions relating to agency files concerning the pretrial release of persons charged with an offense, the establishment of regulations concerning the release of such files, and the access to and admissibility of these files, in par. (4) struck out provision relating to the cooperation of the Administrative Office of the United States Courts and the approval of the Attorney General and provision not limiting this paragraph to those facilities listed thereunder, in par. (5) inserted provisions that pretrial services may provide the United States Attorney as well as the court with information described under this paragraph and that such information also includes any danger that a person released to the custody of pretrial services may come to pose to any other person or the community, in par. (9) substituted provisions that pretrial services shall develop and implement a system to monitor and evaluate bail activities, provide information on the result of bail decisions, and prepare periodic reports to assist the improvement of the bail process for provisions that pretrial services agencies would perform such other functions as the court might assign, and added pars. (10)–(12).

Effective Date of 1992 Amendment

Amendment by Pub. L. 102–572 effective Jan. 1, 1993, see section 1101 of Pub. L. 102–572, set out as a note under section 905 of Title 2, The Congress.

Demonstration Program for Drug Testing of Arrested Persons and Defendants on Probation or Supervised Release

Pub. L. 100–690, title VII, §7304, Nov. 18, 1988, 102 Stat. 4464, provided that:

"(a) Establishment.—The Director of the Administrative Office of the United States Courts shall establish a demonstration program of mandatory testing of criminal defendants.

"(b) Length of Program.—The demonstration program shall begin not later than January 1, 1989, and shall last two years.

"(c) Selection of Districts.—The Judicial Conference of the United States shall select 8 Federal judicial districts in which to carry out the demonstration program, so that the group selected represents a mix of districts on the basis of criminal caseload and the types of cases in that caseload.

"(d) Inclusion in Pretrial Services.—In each of the districts in which the demonstration program takes place, pretrial services under chapter 207 of title 18, United States Code, shall arrange for the drug testing of defendants in criminal cases. To the extent feasible, such testing shall be completed before the defendant makes the defendant's initial appearance in the case before a judicial officer. The results of such testing shall be included in the report to the judicial officer under section 3154 of title 18, United States Code.

"(e) Mandatory Condition of Probation and Supervised Release.—In each of the judicial districts in which the demonstration program is in effect, it shall be an additional, mandatory condition of probation, and an additional mandatory condition of supervised release for offenses occurring or completed on or after January 1, 1989, for any defendant convicted of a felony, that such defendant refrain from any illegal use of any controlled substance (as defined in section 102 of the Controlled Substances Act [21 U.S.C. 802]) and submit to periodic drug tests for use of controlled substances at least once every 60 days. The requirement that drug tests be administered at least once every 60 days may be suspended upon motion of the Director of the Administrative Office, or the Director's designee, if, after at least one year of probation or supervised release, the defendant has passed all drug tests administered pursuant to this section. No action may be taken against a defendant pursuant to a drug test administered in accordance with this subsection unless the drug test confirmation is a urine drug test confirmed using gas chromatography techniques or such test as the Secretary of Health and Human Services may determine to be of equivalent accuracy.

"(f) Report to Congress.—Not later than 90 days after the first year of the demonstration program and not later than 90 days after the end of the demonstration program, the Director of the Administrative Office of the United States Courts shall report to Congress on the effectiveness of the demonstration program and include in such report recommendations as to whether mandatory drug testing of defendants should be made more general and permanent."

§3155. Annual reports

Each chief pretrial services officer in districts in which pretrial services are established under section 3152(b) of this title, and each chief probation officer in all other districts, shall prepare an annual report to the chief judge of the district court concerning the administration and operation of pretrial services and shall ensure that case file, statistical, and other information concerning the work of pretrial services is provided to the Director. The Director shall be required to include in the Director's annual report to the Judicial Conference under section 604 of title 28 a report on the administration and operation of the pretrial services for the previous year.

(Added Pub. L. 93–619, title II, §201, Jan. 3, 1975, 88 Stat. 2088; amended Pub. L. 97–267, §5, Sept. 27, 1982, 96 Stat. 1138; Pub. L. 113–235, div. E, title III, §308, Dec. 16, 2014, 128 Stat. 2352.)

Amendments

2014—Pub. L. 113–235, in first sentence, struck out "and the Director" after "chief judge of the district court" and inserted at end "and shall ensure that case file, statistical, and other information concerning the work of pretrial services is provided to the Director".

1982—Pub. L. 97–267 substituted provisions that each pretrial services officer or chief probation officer shall prepare an annual report to the chief judge of the district court and to the Director concerning the administration and operation of pretrial services and that the Director must include in the Director's annual report to the Judicial Conference a report on the administration and operation of the pretrial services for the previous year for provisions relating to the Director's annual report to Congress, the contents of the Director's fourth annual report, and that on or before the expiration of the forty-eighth-month period following July 1, 1975, the Director would file a comprehensive report with Congress concerning the administration and operation of the amendments made by the Speedy Trial Act of 1974, including his views and recommendations with respect thereto.

§3156. Definitions

(a) As used in sections 3141–3150 of this chapter—

(1) the term "judicial officer" means, unless otherwise indicated, any person or court authorized pursuant to section 3041 of this title, or the Federal Rules of Criminal Procedure, to detain or release a person before trial or sentencing or pending appeal in a court of the United States, and any judge of the Superior Court of the District of Columbia;

(2) the term "offense" means any criminal offense, other than an offense triable by court-martial,

military commission, provost court, or other military tribunal, which is in violation of an Act of Congress and is triable in any court established by Act of Congress;

(3) the term "felony" means an offense punishable by a maximum term of imprisonment of more than one year;

(4) the term "crime of violence" means—

(A) an offense that has as an element of the offense the use, attempted use, or threatened use of physical force against the person or property of another;

(B) any other offense that is a felony and that, by its nature, involves a substantial risk that physical force against the person or property of another may be used in the course of committing the offense; or

(C) any felony under chapter 77, 109A, 110, or 117; and

(5) the term "State" includes a State of the United States, the District of Columbia, and any commonwealth, territory, or possession of the United States.

(b) As used in sections 3152–3155 of this chapter—

(1) the term "judicial officer" means, unless otherwise indicated, any person or court authorized pursuant to section 3041 of this title, or the Federal Rules of Criminal Procedure, to detain or release a person before trial or sentencing or pending appeal in a court of the United States, and

(2) the term "offense" means any Federal criminal offense which is in violation of any Act of Congress and is triable by any court established by Act of Congress (other than a Class B or C misdemeanor or an infraction, or an offense triable by court-martial, military commission, provost court, or other military tribunal).

(Added Pub. L. 93–619, title II, §201, Jan. 3, 1975, 88 Stat. 2088; amended Pub. L. 98–473, title II, §§203(c), 223(h), Oct. 12, 1984, 98 Stat. 1985, 2029; Pub. L. 99–646, §55(i), Nov. 10, 1986, 100 Stat. 3610; Pub. L. 103–322, title IV, §40501, Sept. 13, 1994, 108 Stat. 1945; Pub. L. 104–294, title VI, §607(i), Oct. 11, 1996, 110 Stat. 3512; Pub. L. 105–314, title VI, §601, Oct. 30, 1998, 112 Stat. 2982; Pub. L. 114–22, title I, §112, May 29, 2015, 129 Stat. 240.)

Amendments

2015—Subsec. (a)(4)(C). Pub. L. 114–22 inserted "77," after "chapter".

1998—Subsec. (a)(4)(C). Pub. L. 105–314 added subpar. (C) and struck out former subpar. (C) which read as follows: "any felony under chapter 109A or chapter 110; and".

1996—Subsec. (a)(5). Pub. L. 104–294 added par. (5).

1994—Subsec. (a)(4)(C). Pub. L. 103–322 added subpar. (C).

1986—Subsec. (a). Pub. L. 99–646 substituted "the term" for "The term" in pars. (1) to (4) and struck out "and" after "Congress;" in par. (2).

1984—Subsec. (a). Pub. L. 98–473, §203(c)(1), substituted "3141" for "3146" in provision preceding par. (1).

Subsec. (a)(1). Pub. L. 98–473, §203(c)(2), substituted "to detain or release" for "to bail or otherwise release" and struck out "and" after "District of Columbia;".

Subsec. (a)(3), (4). Pub. L. 98–473, §203(c)(3), (4), added pars. (3) and (4).

Subsec. (b)(1). Pub. L. 98–473, §203(c)(5), substituted "to detain or release" for "to bail or otherwise release".

Subsec. (b)(2). Pub. L. 98–473, §223(h), substituted "Class B or C misdemeanor or an infraction" for "petty offense as defined in section 1(3) of this title".

Effective Date of 1986 Amendment

Amendment by Pub. L. 99–646 effective 30 days after Nov. 10, 1986, see section 55(j) of Pub. L. 99–646, set out as a note under section 3141 of this title.

Effective Date of 1984 Amendment

Amendment by section 223(h) of Pub. L. 98–473 effective Nov. 1, 1987, and applicable only to offenses committed after the taking effect of such amendment, see section 235(a)(1) of Pub. L.

98–473, set out as an Effective Date note under section 3551 of this title.

CHAPTER 208 - SPEEDY TRIAL

Amendments

1979—Pub. L. 96–43, §11, Aug. 2, 1979, 93 Stat. 332, substituted "Persons detained or designated as being of high risk" for "Interim limits" in item 3164 and inserted "and implementation" in item 3174.

1975—Pub. L. 93–619, title I, §101, Jan. 3, 1975, 88 Stat. 2076, added chapter 208 and items 3161 to 3174.

§3161. Time limits and exclusions

(a) In any case involving a defendant charged with an offense, the appropriate judicial officer, at the earliest practicable time, shall, after consultation with the counsel for the defendant and the attorney for the Government, set the case for trial on a day certain, or list it for trial on a weekly or other short-term trial calendar at a place within the judicial district, so as to assure a speedy trial.

(b) Any information or indictment charging an individual with the commission of an offense shall be filed within thirty days from the date on which such individual was arrested or served with a summons in connection with such charges. If an individual has been charged with a felony in a district in which no grand jury has been in session during such thirty-day period, the period of time for filing of the indictment shall be extended an additional thirty days.

(c)(1) In any case in which a plea of not guilty is entered, the trial of a defendant charged in an information or indictment with the commission of an offense shall commence within seventy days from the filing date (and making public) of the information or indictment, or from the date the defendant has appeared before a judicial officer of the court in which such charge is pending, whichever date last occurs. If a defendant consents in writing to be tried before a magistrate judge on a complaint, the trial shall commence within seventy days from the date of such consent.

(2) Unless the defendant consents in writing to the contrary, the trial shall not commence less than thirty days from the date on which the defendant first appears through counsel or expressly waives counsel and elects to proceed pro se.

(d)(1) If any indictment or information is dismissed upon motion of the defendant, or any charge contained in a complaint filed against an individual is dismissed or otherwise dropped, and thereafter a complaint is filed against such defendant or individual charging him with the same offense or an offense based on the same conduct or arising from the same criminal episode, or an information or indictment is filed charging such defendant with the same offense or an offense based on the same conduct or arising from the same criminal episode, the provisions of subsections (b) and (c) of this section shall be applicable with respect to such subsequent complaint, indictment, or information, as the case may be.

(2) If the defendant is to be tried upon an indictment or information dismissed by a trial court and reinstated following an appeal, the trial shall commence within seventy days from the date the action occasioning the trial becomes final, except that the court retrying the case may extend the period for trial not to exceed one hundred and eighty days from the date the action occasioning the trial becomes final if the unavailability of witnesses or other factors resulting from the passage of time shall make trial within seventy days impractical. The periods of delay enumerated in section 3161(h) are excluded in computing the time limitations specified in this section. The sanctions of section 3162 apply to this subsection.

(e) If the defendant is to be tried again following a declaration by the trial judge of a mistrial or following an order of such judge for a new trial, the trial shall commence within seventy days from the date the action occasioning the retrial becomes final. If the defendant is to be tried again following an appeal or a collateral attack, the trial shall commence within seventy days from the date the action occasioning the retrial becomes final, except that the court retrying the case may extend the period for retrial not to exceed one hundred and eighty days from the date the action occasioning the retrial becomes final if unavailability of witnesses or other factors resulting from passage of time shall make trial within seventy days impractical. The periods of delay enumerated in section 3161(h) are excluded in computing the time limitations specified in this section. The sanctions of section 3162 apply to this subsection.

(f) Notwithstanding the provisions of subsection (b) of this section, for the first twelve-calendar-month period following the effective date of this section as set forth in section 3163(a) of this chapter the time limit imposed with respect to the period between arrest and indictment by subsection (b) of this section shall be sixty days, for the second such twelve-month period such time limit shall be forty-five days and for the third such period such time limit shall be thirty-five days.

(g) Notwithstanding the provisions of subsection (c) of this section, for the first twelve-calendar-month period following the effective date of this section as set forth in section 3163(b) of this chapter, the time limit with respect to the period between arraignment and trial imposed by subsection (c) of this section shall be one hundred and eighty days, for the second such twelve-month period such time limit shall be one hundred and twenty days, and for the third such period such time limit with respect to the period between arraignment and trial shall be eighty days.

(h) The following periods of delay shall be excluded in computing the time within which an information or an indictment must be filed, or in computing the time within which the trial of any such offense must commence:

(1) Any period of delay resulting from other proceedings concerning the defendant, including but not limited to—

(A) delay resulting from any proceeding, including any examinations, to determine the mental competency or physical capacity of the defendant;

(B) delay resulting from trial with respect to other charges against the defendant;

(C) delay resulting from any interlocutory appeal;

(D) delay resulting from any pretrial motion, from the filing of the motion through the conclusion of the hearing on, or other prompt disposition of, such motion;

(E) delay resulting from any proceeding relating to the transfer of a case or the removal of any defendant from another district under the Federal Rules of Criminal Procedure;

(F) delay resulting from transportation of any defendant from another district, or to and from places of examination or hospitalization, except that any time consumed in excess of ten days from the date an order of removal or an order directing such transportation, and the defendant's arrival at the destination shall be presumed to be unreasonable;

(G) delay resulting from consideration by the court of a proposed plea agreement to be entered into by the defendant and the attorney for the Government; and

(H) delay reasonably attributable to any period, not to exceed thirty days, during which any proceeding concerning the defendant is actually under advisement by the court.

(2) Any period of delay during which prosecution is deferred by the attorney for the Government pursuant to written agreement with the defendant, with the approval of the court, for the purpose of allowing the defendant to demonstrate his good conduct.

(3)(A) Any period of delay resulting from the absence or unavailability of the defendant or an essential witness.

(B) For purposes of subparagraph (A) of this paragraph, a defendant or an essential witness shall be considered absent when his whereabouts are unknown and, in addition, he is attempting to avoid apprehension or prosecution or his whereabouts cannot be determined by due diligence. For purposes of such subparagraph, a defendant or an essential witness shall be considered unavailable whenever his whereabouts are known but his presence for trial cannot be obtained by due diligence or he resists appearing at or being returned for trial.

(4) Any period of delay resulting from the fact that the defendant is mentally incompetent or physically unable to stand trial.

(5) If the information or indictment is dismissed upon motion of the attorney for the Government and thereafter a charge is filed against the defendant for the same offense, or any offense required to be joined with that offense, any period of delay from the date the charge was dismissed to the date the time limitation would commence to run as to the subsequent charge had there been no previous charge.

(6) A reasonable period of delay when the defendant is joined for trial with a codefendant as to whom the time for trial has not run and no motion for severance has been granted.

(7)(A) Any period of delay resulting from a continuance granted by any judge on his own motion or at the request of the defendant or his counsel or at the request of the attorney for the Government, if the judge granted such continuance on the basis of his findings that the ends of justice served by taking such action outweigh the best interest of the public and the defendant in a speedy trial. No such period of delay resulting from a continuance granted by the court in accordance with this paragraph shall be excludable under this subsection unless the court sets forth, in the record of the case, either orally or in writing, its reasons for finding that the ends of justice served by the granting of such continuance outweigh the best interests of the public and the defendant in a speedy trial.

(B) The factors, among others, which a judge shall consider in determining whether to grant a continuance under subparagraph (A) of this paragraph in any case are as follows:

(i) Whether the failure to grant such a continuance in the proceeding would be likely to make a continuation of such proceeding impossible, or result in a miscarriage of justice.

(ii) Whether the case is so unusual or so complex, due to the number of defendants, the nature of the prosecution, or the existence of novel questions of fact or law, that it is unreasonable to expect adequate preparation for pretrial proceedings or for the trial itself within the time limits established by this section.

(iii) Whether, in a case in which arrest precedes indictment, delay in the filing of the indictment is caused because the arrest occurs at a time such that it is unreasonable to expect return and filing of the indictment within the period specified in section 3161(b), or because the facts upon which the grand jury must base its determination are unusual or complex.

(iv) Whether the failure to grant such a continuance in a case which, taken as a whole, is not so unusual or so complex as to fall within clause (ii), would deny the defendant reasonable time to obtain counsel, would unreasonably deny the defendant or the Government continuity of counsel, or would deny counsel for the defendant or the attorney for the Government the reasonable time necessary for effective preparation, taking into account the exercise of due diligence.

(C) No continuance under subparagraph (A) of this paragraph shall be granted because of general congestion of the court's calendar, or lack of diligent preparation or failure to obtain available witnesses on the part of the attorney for the Government.

(8) Any period of delay, not to exceed one year, ordered by a district court upon an application of a party and a finding by a preponderance of the evidence that an official request, as defined in section 3292 of this title, has been made for evidence of any such offense and that it reasonably appears, or reasonably appeared at the time the request was made, that such evidence is, or was, in

such foreign country.

(i) If trial did not commence within the time limitation specified in section 3161 because the defendant had entered a plea of guilty or nolo contendere subsequently withdrawn to any or all charges in an indictment or information, the defendant shall be deemed indicted with respect to all charges therein contained within the meaning of section 3161, on the day the order permitting withdrawal of the plea becomes final.

(j)(1) If the attorney for the Government knows that a person charged with an offense is serving a term of imprisonment in any penal institution, he shall promptly—

(A) undertake to obtain the presence of the prisoner for trial; or

(B) cause a detainer to be filed with the person having custody of the prisoner and request him to so advise the prisoner and to advise the prisoner of his right to demand trial.

(2) If the person having custody of such prisoner receives a detainer, he shall promptly advise the prisoner of the charge and of the prisoner's right to demand trial. If at any time thereafter the prisoner informs the person having custody that he does demand trial, such person shall cause notice to that effect to be sent promptly to the attorney for the Government who caused the detainer to be filed.

(3) Upon receipt of such notice, the attorney for the Government shall promptly seek to obtain the presence of the prisoner for trial.

(4) When the person having custody of the prisoner receives from the attorney for the Government a properly supported request for temporary custody of such prisoner for trial, the prisoner shall be made available to that attorney for the Government (subject, in cases of interjurisdictional transfer, to any right of the prisoner to contest the legality of his delivery).

(k)(1) If the defendant is absent (as defined by subsection (h)(3)) on the day set for trial, and the defendant's subsequent appearance before the court on a bench warrant or other process or surrender to the court occurs more than 21 days after the day set for trial, the defendant shall be deemed to have first appeared before a judicial officer of the court in which the information or indictment is pending within the meaning of subsection (c) on the date of the defendant's subsequent appearance before the court.

(2) If the defendant is absent (as defined by subsection (h)(3)) on the day set for trial, and the defendant's subsequent appearance before the court on a bench warrant or other process or surrender to the court occurs not more than 21 days after the day set for trial, the time limit required by subsection (c), as extended by subsection (h), shall be further extended by 21 days.

(Added Pub. L. 93–619, title I, §101, Jan. 3, 1975, 88 Stat. 2076; amended Pub. L. 96–43, §§2–5, Aug. 2, 1979, 93 Stat. 327, 328; Pub. L. 98–473, title II, §1219, Oct. 12, 1984, 98 Stat. 2167; Pub. L. 100–690, title VI, §6476, Nov. 18, 1988, 102 Stat. 4380; Pub. L. 101–650, title III, §321, Dec. 1, 1990, 104 Stat. 5117; Pub. L. 110–406, §13, Oct. 13, 2008, 122 Stat. 4294.)

Amendments

2008—Subsec. (h)(1)(B) to (J). Pub. L. 110–406, §13(1), redesignated subpars. (D) to (J) as (B) to (H), respectively, and struck out former subpars. (B) and (C) which read as follows:

"(B) delay resulting from any proceeding, including any examination of the defendant, pursuant to section 2902 of title 28, United States Code;

"(C) delay resulting from deferral of prosecution pursuant to section 2902 of title 28, United States Code;".

Subsec. (h)(5) to (9). Pub. L. 110–406, §13(2), (3), redesignated pars. (6) to (9) as (5) to (8), respectively, and struck out former par. (5) which read as follows: "Any period of delay resulting from the treatment of the defendant pursuant to section 2902 of title 28, United States Code."

1988—Subsec. (k). Pub. L. 100–690 added subsec. (k).

1984—Subsec. (h)(8)(C). Pub. L. 98–473, §1219(1), substituted "subparagraph (A) of this paragraph" for "paragraph (8)(A) of this subsection".

Subsec. (h)(9). Pub. L. 98–473, §1219(2), added par. (9).

1979—Subsec. (c)(1). Pub. L. 96–43, §2, merged the ten day indictment-to-arraignment and the sixty day arraignment-to-trial limits into a single seventy day indictment-to-trial period.

Subsec. (c)(2). Pub. L. 96–43, §2, added par. (2).

Subsec. (d). Pub. L. 96–43, §3(a), designated existing provisions as par. (1) and added par. (2).

Subsec. (e). Pub. L. 96–43, §3(b), substituted "seventy days" for "sixty days" in three places and inserted provisions excluding the periods of delay enumerated in subsec. (h) of this section in computing the time limitations specified in this section and applying the sanctions of section 3162 of this title to this subsection.

Subsec. (h)(1). Pub. L. 96–43, §4, added to the listing of excludable delays, delays resulting from the deferral of prosecution under section 2902 of title 28, delays caused by consideration by the court of proposed plea agreements, and delays resulting from the transportation of a defendant from another district or for the purpose of examination or hospitalization, and expanded provisions relating to exclusions of periods of delay resulting from hearings on pretrial motions, examinations and hearings relating to the mental or physical condition of defendant, or the removal of a defendant from another district under the Federal Rules of Criminal Procedure.

Subsec. (h)(8)(B)(ii). Pub. L. 96–43, §5(a), expanded provisions authorizing the granting of continuances based on the complexity or unusual nature of a case to include delays in preparation of all phases of a case, including pretrial motion preparation.

Subsec. (h)(8)(B)(iii). Pub. L. 96–43, §5(b), inserted provision authorizing a continuance where the delay in filing the indictment is caused by the arrest taking place at such time that the return and filing of the indictment can not reasonably be expected within the period specified in section 3161(b) of this title.

Subsec. (h)(8)(B)(iv). Pub. L. 96–43, §5(c), added cl. (iv).

Change of Name

Words "magistrate judge" substituted for "magistrate" in subsec. (c)(1) pursuant to section 321 of Pub. L. 101–650, set out as a note under section 631 of Title 28, Judiciary and Judicial Procedure.

Effective Date of 1984 Amendment

Amendment by Pub. L. 98–473 effective 30 days after Oct. 12, 1984, see section 1220 of Pub. L. 98–473, set out as an Effective Date note under section 3505 of this title.

Short Title of 1979 Amendment

Pub. L. 96–43, §1, Aug. 2, 1979, 93 Stat. 327, provided: "That this Act [amending this section and sections 3163 to 3168, 3170 and 3174 of this title] may be cited as the 'Speedy Trial Act Amendments Act of 1979'."

Short Title

Pub. L. 93–619, §1, Jan. 3, 1975, 88 Stat. 2076, provided: "That this Act [enacting this chapter and sections 3153 to 3156 of this title, and amending section 3152 of this title, and section 604 of Title 28, Judiciary and Judicial Procedure] may be cited as the 'Speedy Trial Act of 1974'."

§3162. Sanctions

(a)(1) If, in the case of any individual against whom a complaint is filed charging such individual with an offense, no indictment or information is filed within the time limit required by section 3161(b) as extended by section 3161(h) of this chapter, such charge against that individual contained in such complaint shall be dismissed or otherwise dropped. In determining whether to dismiss the case with or without prejudice, the court shall consider, among others, each of the following factors: the seriousness of the offense; the facts and circumstances of the case which led to the dismissal; and the impact of a reprosecution on the administration of this chapter and on the administration of justice.

(2) If a defendant is not brought to trial within the time limit required by section 3161(c) as extended by section 3161(h), the information or indictment shall be dismissed on motion of the

defendant. The defendant shall have the burden of proof of supporting such motion but the Government shall have the burden of going forward with the evidence in connection with any exclusion of time under subparagraph 3161(h)(3). In determining whether to dismiss the case with or without prejudice, the court shall consider, among others, each of the following factors: the seriousness of the offense; the facts and circumstances of the case which led to the dismissal; and the impact of a reprosecution on the administration of this chapter and on the administration of justice. Failure of the defendant to move for dismissal prior to trial or entry of a plea of guilty or nolo contendere shall constitute a waiver of the right to dismissal under this section.

(b) In any case in which counsel for the defendant or the attorney for the Government (1) knowingly allows the case to be set for trial without disclosing the fact that a necessary witness would be unavailable for trial; (2) files a motion solely for the purpose of delay which he knows is totally frivolous and without merit; (3) makes a statement for the purpose of obtaining a continuance which he knows to be false and which is material to the granting of a continuance; or (4) otherwise willfully fails to proceed to trial without justification consistent with section 3161 of this chapter, the court may punish any such counsel or attorney, as follows:

(A) in the case of an appointed defense counsel, by reducing the amount of compensation that otherwise would have been paid to such counsel pursuant to section 3006A of this title in an amount not to exceed 25 per centum thereof;

(B) in the case of a counsel retained in connection with the defense of a defendant, by imposing on such counsel a fine of not to exceed 25 per centum of the compensation to which he is entitled in connection with his defense of such defendant;

(C) by imposing on any attorney for the Government a fine of not to exceed $250;

(D) by denying any such counsel or attorney for the Government the right to practice before the court considering such case for a period of not to exceed ninety days; or

(E) by filing a report with an appropriate disciplinary committee.

The authority to punish provided for by this subsection shall be in addition to any other authority or power available to such court.

(c) The court shall follow procedures established in the Federal Rules of Criminal Procedure in punishing any counsel or attorney for the Government pursuant to this section.

(Added Pub. L. 93–619, title I, §101, Jan. 3, 1975, 88 Stat. 2079.)

§3163. Effective dates

(a) The time limitation in section 3161(b) of this chapter—

(1) shall apply to all individuals who are arrested or served with a summons on or after the date of expiration of the twelve-calendar-month period following July 1, 1975; and

(2) shall commence to run on such date of expiration to all individuals who are arrested or served with a summons prior to the date of expiration of such twelve-calendar-month period, in connection with the commission of an offense, and with respect to which offense no information or indictment has been filed prior to such date of expiration.

(b) The time limitation in section 3161(c) of this chapter—

(1) shall apply to all offenses charged in informations or indictments filed on or after the date of expiration of the twelve-calendar-month period following July 1, 1975; and

(2) shall commence to run on such date of expiration as to all offenses charged in informations or indictments filed prior to that date.

(c) Subject to the provisions of section 3174(c), section 3162 of this chapter shall become effective and apply to all cases commenced by arrest or summons, and all informations or indictments filed, on or after July 1, 1980.

(Added Pub. L. 93–619, title I, §101, Jan. 3, 1975, 88 Stat. 2080; amended Pub. L. 96–43, §6, Aug. 2, 1979, 93 Stat. 328.)

Amendments

1979—Subsec. (c). Pub. L. 96–43 substituted provision that section 3162 of this title was to become effective and apply to all cases commenced by arrest or summons, and all informations and indictments filed, on or after July 1, 1980, subject to section 3174(c) of this title, for provision that such section was to become effective after the date of expiration of the fourth twelve-calendar-month period following July 1, 1975.

§3164. Persons detained or designated as being of high risk

(a) The trial or other disposition of cases involving—

(1) a detained person who is being held in detention solely because he is awaiting trial, and

(2) a released person who is awaiting trial and has been designated by the attorney for the Government as being of high risk,

shall be accorded priority.

(b) The trial of any person described in subsection (a)(1) or (a)(2) of this section shall commence not later than ninety days following the beginning of such continuous detention or designation of high risk by the attorney for the Government. The periods of delay enumerated in section 3161(h) are excluded in computing the time limitation specified in this section.

(c) Failure to commence trial of a detainee as specified in subsection (b), through no fault of the accused or his counsel, or failure to commence trial of a designated releasee as specified in subsection (b), through no fault of the attorney for the Government, shall result in the automatic review by the court of the conditions of release. No detainee, as defined in subsection (a), shall be held in custody pending trial after the expiration of such ninety-day period required for the commencement of his trial. A designated releasee, as defined in subsection (a), who is found by the court to have intentionally delayed the trial of his case shall be subject to an order of the court modifying his nonfinancial conditions of release under this title to insure that he shall appear at trial as required.

(Added Pub. L. 93–619, title I, §101, Jan. 3, 1975, 88 Stat. 2081; amended Pub. L. 96–43, §7, Aug. 2, 1979, 93 Stat. 329.)

Amendments

1979—Pub. L. 96–43, §7(1), substituted "Persons detained or designated as being of high risk" for "Interim limits" in section catchline.

Subsec. (a). Pub. L. 96–43, §7(2), struck out provisions limiting the trial priority to be accorded persons specified in cls. (1) and (2) of this subsection to the interim period commencing ninety days following July 1, 1975 and ending on the date immediately preceding the date on which the time limits provided for under section 3161(b) and (c) of this title become effective.

Subsec. (b). Pub. L. 96–43, §7(3), struck out provisions making trial priority provisions of this subsection applicable during an interim period only and requiring the trial of any person detained or designated by the government as being of high risk on or before the first day of such interim period to commence no later than ninety days following the first day of the period and inserted provision excluding the periods of delay specified in section 3161(h) of this title in computing the time limitation of this section.

§3165. District plans—generally

(a) Each district court shall conduct a continuing study of the administration of criminal justice in the district court and before United States magistrate judges of the district and shall prepare plans for the disposition of criminal cases in accordance with this chapter. Each such plan shall be formulated after consultation with, and after considering the recommendations of, the Federal Judicial Center and the planning group established for that district pursuant to section 3168. The plans shall be prepared in accordance with the schedule set forth in subsection (e) of this section.

(b) The planning and implementation process shall seek to accelerate the disposition of criminal cases in the district consistent with the time standards of this chapter and the objectives of effective law enforcement, fairness to accused persons, efficient judicial administration, and increased knowledge concerning the proper functioning of the criminal law. The process shall seek to avoid underenforcement, overenforcement and discriminatory enforcement of the law, prejudice to the prompt disposition of civil litigation, and undue pressure as well as undue delay in the trial of criminal cases.

(c) The plans prepared by each district court shall be submitted for approval to a reviewing panel consisting of the members of the judicial council of the circuit and either the chief judge of the district court whose plan is being reviewed or such other active judge of that court as the chief judge of that district court may designate. If approved by the reviewing panel, the plan shall be forwarded to the Administrative Office of the United States Courts, which office shall report annually on the operation of such plans to the Judicial Conference of the United States.

(d) The district court may modify the plan at any time with the approval of the reviewing panel. It shall modify the plan when directed to do so by the reviewing panel or the Judicial Conference of the United States. Modifications shall be reported to the Administrative Office of the United States Courts.

(e)(1) Prior to the expiration of the twelve-calendar-month period following July 1, 1975, each United States district court shall prepare and submit a plan in accordance with subsections (a) through (d) above to govern the trial or other disposition of offenses within the jurisdiction of such court during the second and third twelve-calendar-month periods following the effective date of subsection 3161(b) and subsection 3161(c).

(2) Prior to the expiration of the thirty-six calendar month period following July 1, 1975, each United States district court shall prepare and submit a plan in accordance with subsections (a) through (d) above to govern the trial or other disposition of offenses within the jurisdiction of such court during the fourth and fifth twelve-calendar-month periods following the effective date of subsection 3161(b) and subsection 3161(c).

(3) Not later than June 30, 1980, each United States district court with respect to which implementation has not been ordered under section 3174(c) shall prepare and submit a plan in accordance with subsections (a) through (d) to govern the trial or other disposition of offenses within the jurisdiction of such court during the sixth and subsequent twelve-calendar-month periods following the effective date of subsection 3161(b) and subsection 3161(c) in effect prior to the date of enactment of this paragraph.

(f) Plans adopted pursuant to this section shall, upon adoption, and recommendations of the district planning group shall, upon completion, become public documents.

(Added Pub. L. 93–619, title I, §101, Jan. 3, 1975, 88 Stat. 2081; amended Pub. L. 96–43, §8, Aug. 2, 1979, 93 Stat. 329; Pub. L. 101–647, title XXXV, §3577, Nov. 29, 1990, 104 Stat. 4929; Pub. L. 101–650, title III, §321, Dec. 1, 1990, 104 Stat. 5117.)

References in Text

For the effective date of subsection 3161(b) and subsection 3161(c) in effect prior to the date of enactment of this paragraph, referred to in subsec. (e), see section 3163(a) and (b) of this title. The date of enactment of par. (3) of subsec. (e) of this section is the date of enactment of Pub. L. 96–43, which was approved Aug. 2, 1979. Subsecs. (a) and (b) of section 3163 of this title were not amended by Pub. L. 96–43.

Amendments

1990—Subsec. (e)(2). Pub. L. 101–647 substituted "twelve-calendar-month" for "twelve-calendar month".

1979—Subsec. (e)(2). Pub. L. 96–43, §8(1), substituted "fifth twelve-calendar" for "subsequent twelve-calendar".

Subsec. (e)(3). Pub. L. 96–43, §8(2), added par. (3).

Change of Name

"United States magistrate judges" substituted for "United States magistrates" in subsec. (a) pursuant to section 321 of Pub. L. 101–650, set out as a note under section 631 of Title 28,

§3166. District plans—contents

(a) Each plan shall include a description of the time limits, procedural techniques, innovations, systems and other methods, including the development of reliable methods for gathering and monitoring information and statistics, by which the district court, the United States attorney, the Federal public defender, if any, and private attorneys experienced in the defense of criminal cases, have expedited or intend to expedite the trial or other disposition of criminal cases, consistent with the time limits and other objectives of this chapter.

(b) Each plan shall include information concerning the implementation of the time limits and other objectives of this chapter, including:

(1) the incidence of and reasons for, requests or allowances of extensions of time beyond statutory or district standards;

(2) the incidence of, and reasons for, periods of delay under section 3161(h) of this title;

(3) the incidence of, and reasons for, the invocation of sanctions for noncompliance with time standards, or the failure to invoke such sanctions, and the nature of the sanction, if any invoked for noncompliance;

(4) the new timetable set, or requested to be set, for an extension;

(5) the effect on criminal justice administration of the prevailing time limits and sanctions, including the effects on the prosecution, the defense, the courts, the correctional process, costs, transfers and appeals;

(6) the incidence and length of, reasons for, and remedies for detention prior to trial, and information required by the provisions of the Federal Rules of Criminal Procedure relating to the supervision of detention pending trial;

(7) the identity of cases which, because of their special characteristics, deserve separate or different time limits as a matter of statutory classifications;

(8) the incidence of, and reasons for each thirty-day extension under section 3161(b) with respect to an indictment in that district; and

(9) the impact of compliance with the time limits of subsections (b) and (c) of section 3161 upon the civil case calendar in the district.

(c) Each district plan required by section 3165 shall include information and statistics concerning the administration of criminal justice within the district, including, but not limited to:

(1) the time span between arrest and indictment, indictment and trial, and conviction and sentencing;

(2) the number of matters presented to the United States Attorney for prosecution, and the numbers of such matters prosecuted and not prosecuted;

(3) the number of matters transferred to other districts or to States for prosecution;

(4) the number of cases disposed of by trial and by plea;

(5) the rates of nolle prosequi, dismissal, acquittal, conviction, diversion, or other disposition;

(6) the extent of preadjudication detention and release, by numbers of defendants and days in custody or at liberty prior to disposition; and

(7)(A) the number of new civil cases filed in the twelve-calendar-month period preceding the submission of the plan;

(B) the number of civil cases pending at the close of such period; and

(C) the increase or decrease in the number of civil cases pending at the close of such period, compared to the number pending at the close of the previous twelve-calendar-month period, and the length of time each such case has been pending.

(d) Each plan shall further specify the rule changes, statutory amendments, and appropriations needed to effectuate further improvements in the administration of justice in the district which cannot be accomplished without such amendments or funds.

(e) Each plan shall include recommendations to the Administrative Office of the United States Courts for reporting forms, procedures, and time requirements. The Director of the Administrative

Office of the United States Courts, with the approval of the Judicial Conference of the United States, shall prescribe such forms and procedures and time requirements consistent with section 3170 after consideration of the recommendations contained in the district plan and the need to reflect both unique local conditions and uniform national reporting standards.

(f) Each plan may be accompanied by guidelines promulgated by the judicial council of the circuit for use by all district courts within that circuit to implement and secure compliance with this chapter.

(Added Pub. L. 93–619, title I, §101, Jan. 3, 1975, 88 Stat. 2082; amended Pub. L. 96–43, §9(a)–(c), Aug. 2, 1979, 93 Stat. 329; Pub. L. 101–647, title XXXV, §3578, Nov. 29, 1990, 104 Stat. 4929.)

Amendments

1990—Subsec. (b)(8). Pub. L. 101–647 substituted "extension" for "extention".

1979—Subsec. (b)(9). Pub. L. 96–43, §9(a), added par. (9).

Subsec. (c)(7). Pub. L. 96–43, §9(b), added par. (7).

Subsec. (f). Pub. L. 96–43, §9(c), added subsec. (f).

§3167. Reports to Congress

(a) The Administrative Office of the United States Courts, with the approval of the Judicial Conference, shall submit periodic reports to Congress detailing the plans submitted pursuant to section 3165. The reports shall be submitted within three months following the final dates for the submission of plans under section 3165(e) of this title.

(b) Such reports shall include recommendations for legislative changes or additional appropriations to achieve the time limits and objectives of this chapter. The report shall also contain pertinent information such as the state of the criminal docket at the time of the adoption of the plan; the extent of pretrial detention and release; and a description of the time limits, procedural techniques, innovations, systems, and other methods by which the trial or other disposition of criminal cases have been expedited or may be expedited in the districts. Such reports shall also include the following:

(1) The reasons why, in those cases not in compliance with the time limits of subsections (b) and (c) of section 3161, the provisions of section 3161(h) have not been adequate to accommodate reasonable periods of delay.

(2) The category of offenses, the number of defendants, and the number of counts involved in those cases which are not meeting the time limits specified in subsections (b) and (c) of section 3161.

(3) The additional judicial resources which would be necessary in order to achieve compliance with the time limits specified in subsections (b) and (c) of section 3161.

(4) The nature of the remedial measures which have been employed to improve conditions and practices in those districts with low compliance experience under this chapter or to promote the adoption of practices and procedures which have been successful in those districts with high compliance experience under this chapter.

(5) If a district has experienced difficulty in complying with this chapter, but an application for relief under section 3174 has not been made, the reason why such application has not been made.

(6) The impact of compliance with the time limits of subsections (b) and (c) of section 3161 upon the civil case calendar in each district as demonstrated by the information assembled and statistics compiled and submitted under sections 3166 and 3170.

(c) Not later than December 31, 1979, the Department of Justice shall prepare and submit to the Congress a report which sets forth the impact of the implementation of this chapter upon the office of the United States Attorney in each district and which shall also include—

(1) the reasons why, in those cases not in compliance, the provisions of section 3161(h) have not been adequate to accommodate reasonable periods of delay;

(2) the nature of the remedial measures which have been employed to improve conditions and

practices in the offices of the United States Attorneys in those districts with low compliance experience under this chapter or to promote the adoption of practices and procedures which have been successful in those districts with high compliance experience under this chapter;

(3) the additional resources for the offices of the United States Attorneys which would be necessary to achieve compliance with the time limits of subsections (b) and (c) of section 3161;

(4) suggested changes in the guidelines or other rules implementing this chapter or statutory amendments which the Department of Justice deems necessary to further improve the administration of justice and meet the objectives of this chapter; and

(5) the impact of compliance with the time limits of subsections (b) and (c) of section 3161 upon the litigation of civil cases by the offices of the United States Attorneys and the rule changes, statutory amendments, and resources necessary to assure that such litigation is not prejudiced by full compliance with this chapter.

(Added Pub. L. 93–619, title I, §101, Jan. 3, 1975, 88 Stat. 2083; amended Pub. L. 96–43, §9(e), Aug. 2, 1979, 93 Stat. 330.)

Amendments

1979—Subsec. (b). Pub. L. 96–43, §9(e)(1), inserted last sentence containing pars. (1) to (6). Subsec. (c). Pub. L. 96–43, §9(e)(2), added subsec. (c).

§3168. Planning process

(a) Within sixty days after July 1, 1975, each United States district court shall convene a planning group consisting at minimum of the Chief Judge, a United States magistrate judge, if any designated by the Chief Judge, the United States Attorney, the Clerk of the district court, the Federal Public Defender, if any, two private attorneys, one with substantial experience in the defense of criminal cases in the district and one with substantial experience in civil litigation in the district, the Chief United States Probation Officer for the district, and a person skilled in criminal justice research who shall act as reporter for the group. The group shall advise the district court with respect to the formulation of all district plans and shall submit its recommendations to the district court for each of the district plans required by section 3165. The group shall be responsible for the initial formulation of all district plans and of the reports required by this chapter and in aid thereof, it shall be entitled to the planning funds specified in section 3171.

(b) The planning group shall address itself to the need for reforms in the criminal justice system, including but not limited to changes in the grand jury system, the finality of criminal judgments, habeas corpus and collateral attacks, pretrial diversion, pretrial detention, excessive reach of Federal criminal law, simplification and improvement of pretrial and sentencing procedures, and appellate delay.

(c) Members of the planning group with the exception of the reporter shall receive no additional compensation for their services, but shall be reimbursed for travel, subsistence and other necessary expenses incurred by them in carrying out the duties of the advisory group in accordance with the provisions of title 5, United States Code, chapter 57. The reporter shall be compensated in accordance with section 3109 of title 5, United States Code, and notwithstanding other provisions of law he may be employed for any period of time during which his services are needed.

(Added Pub. L. 93–619, title I, §101, Jan. 3, 1975, 88 Stat. 2083; amended Pub. L. 96–43, §9(d), Aug. 2, 1979, 93 Stat. 330; Pub. L. 101–650, title III, §321, Dec. 1, 1990, 104 Stat. 5117.)

Amendments

1979—Subsec. (a). Pub. L. 96–43 substituted "two private attorneys, one with substantial experience in the defense of criminal cases in the district and one with substantial experience in civil litigation in the district" for "a private attorney experienced in the defense of criminal cases in the district".

Change of Name

"United States magistrate judge" substituted for "United States magistrate" in subsec. (a) pursuant to section 321 of Pub. L. 101–650, set out as a note under section 631 of Title 28, Judiciary and Judicial Procedure.

§3169. Federal Judicial Center

The Federal Judicial Center shall advise and consult with the planning groups and the district courts in connection with their duties under this chapter.

(Added Pub. L. 93–619, title I, §101, Jan. 3, 1975, 88 Stat. 2084.)

§3170. Speedy trial data

(a) To facilitate the planning process, the implementation of the time limits, and continuous and permanent compliance with the objectives of this chapter, the clerk of each district court shall assemble the information and compile the statistics described in sections 3166(b) and 3166(c) of this title. The clerk of each district court shall assemble such information and compile such statistics on such forms and under such regulations as the Administrative Office of the United States Courts shall prescribe with the approval of the Judicial Conference and after consultation with the Attorney General.

(b) The clerk of each district court is authorized to obtain the information required by sections 3166(b) and 3166(c) from all relevant sources including the United States Attorney, Federal Public Defender, private defense counsel appearing in criminal cases in the district, United States district court judges, and the chief Federal Probation Officer for the district. This subsection shall not be construed to require the release of any confidential or privileged information.

(c) The information and statistics compiled by the clerk pursuant to this section shall be made available to the district court, the planning group, the circuit council, and the Administrative Office of the United States Courts.

(Added Pub. L. 93–619, title I, §101, Jan. 3, 1975, 88 Stat. 2084; amended Pub. L. 96–43, §9(f), Aug. 2, 1979, 93 Stat. 331; Pub. L. 101–647, title XXXV, §3579, Nov. 29, 1990, 104 Stat. 4929.)

Amendments

1990—Subsecs. (a), (b). Pub. L. 101–647 substituted "sections 3166(b) and 3166(c)" for "sections 3166(b) and (c)".

1979—Subsec. (a). Pub. L. 96–43 inserted "continuous and permanent compliance with the" and substituted "described in" for "required by".

§3171. Planning appropriations

(a) There is authorized to be appropriated for the fiscal year ending June 30, 1975, to the Federal judiciary the sum of $2,500,000 to be allocated by the Administrative Office of the United States Courts to Federal judicial districts to carry out the initial phases of planning and implementation of speedy trial plans under this chapter. The funds so appropriated shall remain available until expended.

(b) No funds appropriated under this section may be expended in any district except by two-thirds vote of the planning group. Funds to the extent available may be expended for personnel, facilities, and any other purpose permitted by law.

(Added Pub. L. 93–619, title I, §101, Jan. 3, 1975, 88 Stat. 2084.)

§3172. Definitions

As used in this chapter—

(1) the terms "judge" or "judicial officer" mean, unless otherwise indicated, any United States magistrate judge, Federal district judge, and

(2) the term "offense" means any Federal criminal offense which is in violation of any Act of Congress and is triable by any court established by Act of Congress (other than a Class B or C misdemeanor or an infraction, or an offense triable by court-martial, military commission, provost

court, or other military tribunal).

(Added Pub. L. 93–619, title I, §101, Jan. 3, 1975, 88 Stat. 2085; amended Pub. L. 98–473, title II, §223(i), Oct. 12, 1984, 98 Stat. 2029; Pub. L. 101–650, title III, §321, Dec. 1, 1990, 104 Stat. 5117.)

Amendments

1984—Par. (2). Pub. L. 98–473 substituted "Class B or C misdemeanor or an infraction" for "petty offense as defined in section 1(3) of this title".

Change of Name

"United States magistrate judge" substituted for "United States magistrate" in par. (1) pursuant to section 321 of Pub. L. 101–650, set out as a note under section 631 of Title 28, Judiciary and Judicial Procedure.

Effective Date of 1984 Amendment

Amendment by Pub. L. 98–473 effective Nov. 1, 1987, and applicable only to offenses committed after the taking effect of such amendment, see section 235(a)(1) of Pub. L. 98–473, set out as an Effective Date note under section 3551 of this title.

§3173. Sixth amendment rights

No provision of this chapter shall be interpreted as a bar to any claim of denial of speedy trial as required by amendment VI of the Constitution.

(Added Pub. L. 93–619, title I, §101, Jan. 3, 1975, 88 Stat. 2085.)

§3174. Judicial emergency and implementation

(a) In the event that any district court is unable to comply with the time limits set forth in section 3161(c) due to the status of its court calendars, the chief judge, where the existing resources are being efficiently utilized, may, after seeking the recommendations of the planning group, apply to the judicial council of the circuit for a suspension of such time limits as provided in subsection (b). The judicial council of the circuit shall evaluate the capabilities of the district, the availability of visiting judges from within and without the circuit, and make any recommendations it deems appropriate to alleviate calendar congestion resulting from the lack of resources.

(b) If the judicial council of the circuit finds that no remedy for such congestion is reasonably available, such council may, upon application by the chief judge of a district, grant a suspension of the time limits in section 3161(c) in such district for a period of time not to exceed one year for the trial of cases for which indictments or informations are filed during such one-year period. During such period of suspension, the time limits from arrest to indictment, set forth in section 3161(b), shall not be reduced, nor shall the sanctions set forth in section 3162 be suspended; but such time limits from indictment to trial shall not be increased to exceed one hundred and eighty days. The time limits for the trial of cases of detained persons who are being detained solely because they are awaiting trial shall not be affected by the provisions of this section.

(c)(1) If, prior to July 1, 1980, the chief judge of any district concludes, with the concurrence of the planning group convened in the district, that the district is prepared to implement the provisions of section 3162 in their entirety, he may apply to the judicial council of the circuit in which the district is located to implement such provisions. Such application shall show the degree of compliance in the district with the time limits set forth in subsections (b) and (c) of section 3161 during the twelve-calendar-month period preceding the date of such application and shall contain a proposed order and schedule for such implementation, which includes the date on which the provisions of section 3162 are to become effective in the district, the effect such implementation will have upon such district's practices and procedures, and provision for adequate notice to all interested parties.

(2) After review of any such application, the judicial council of the circuit shall enter an order

implementing the provisions of section 3162 in their entirety in the district making application, or shall return such application to the chief judge of such district, together with an explanation setting forth such council's reasons for refusing to enter such order.

(d)(1) The approval of any application made pursuant to subsection (a) or (c) by a judicial council of a circuit shall be reported within ten days to the Director of the Administrative Office of the United States Courts, together with a copy of the application, a written report setting forth in sufficient detail the reasons for granting such application, and, in the case of an application made pursuant to subsection (a), a proposal for alleviating congestion in the district.

(2) The Director of the Administrative Office of the United States Courts shall not later than ten days after receipt transmit such report to the Congress and to the Judicial Conference of the United States. The judicial council of the circuit shall not grant a suspension to any district within six months following the expiration of a prior suspension without the consent of the Congress by Act of Congress. The limitation on granting a suspension made by this paragraph shall not apply with respect to any judicial district in which the prior suspension is in effect on the date of the enactment of the Speedy Trial Act Amendments Act of 1979.

(e) If the chief judge of the district court concludes that the need for suspension of time limits in such district under this section is of great urgency, he may order the limits suspended for a period not to exceed thirty days. Within ten days of entry of such order, the chief judge shall apply to the judicial council of the circuit for a suspension pursuant to subsection (a).

(Added Pub. L. 93–619, title I, §101, Jan. 3, 1975, 88 Stat. 2085; amended Pub. L. 96–43, §10, Aug. 2, 1979, 93 Stat. 331.)

References in Text

The date of enactment of the Speedy Trial Act Amendments Act of 1979, referred to in subsec. (d)(2), means the date of enactment of Pub. L. 96–43, which was approved Aug. 2, 1979.

Amendments

1979—Pub. L. 96–43, §10(6), inserted "and implementation" in section catchline.

Subsec. (a). Pub. L. 96–43, §10(1), inserted "as provided by subsection (b)".

Subsec. (b). Pub. L. 96–43, §10(2), (3), substituted provisions authorizing the circuit judicial council, upon application of the chief judge of a district, to grant a suspension of the time limits prescribed by section 3161(c) of this title for provisions requiring such circuit council to apply to the Judicial Council of the United States for a suspension of such time limits and substituted provision placing a one hundred and eighty day limit on any time increase from indictment to trial for provision placing such limit for any increase from arraignment to trial.

Subsec. (c). Pub. L. 96–43, §10(4), substituted provisions authorizing the chief judge of any district, with the approval of the planning group convened in such district, to apply to the circuit council to implement the provisions of section 3162 of this title at any time prior to the date the sanctions prescribed therein were to become effective, so long as there was concurrence that the district was prepared to fully implement the provisions of such section for provisions specifying the reporting requirements of this chapter, assuring involvement of the Congress in the suspension process, and guaranteeing that there be an interval of at least six months between consecutive suspension periods. See subsec. (d) of this section.

Subsecs. (d), (e). Pub. L. 96–43, §10(5), added subsecs. (d) and (e).

CHAPTER 209 - EXTRADITION

Amendments

1996—Pub. L. 104–294, title VI, §601(f)(9), (10), Oct. 11, 1996, 110 Stat. 3500, inserted comma after "District" in item 3182 and after "Territory" in item 3183.

1990—Pub. L. 101–623, §11(b), Nov. 21, 1990, 104 Stat. 3356, added item 3196.

§3181. Scope and limitation of chapter

(a) The provisions of this chapter relating to the surrender of persons who have committed crimes in foreign countries shall continue in force only during the existence of any treaty of extradition with such foreign government.

(b) The provisions of this chapter shall be construed to permit, in the exercise of comity, the surrender of persons, other than citizens, nationals, or permanent residents of the United States, who have committed crimes of violence against nationals of the United States in foreign countries without regard to the existence of any treaty of extradition with such foreign government if the Attorney General certifies, in writing, that—

(1) evidence has been presented by the foreign government that indicates that had the offenses been committed in the United States, they would constitute crimes of violence as defined under section 16 of this title; and

(2) the offenses charged are not of a political nature.

(c) As used in this section, the term "national of the United States" has the meaning given such term in section 101(a)(22) of the Immigration and Nationality Act (8 U.S.C. 1101(a)(22)).

(June 25, 1948, ch. 645, 62 Stat. 822; Pub. L. 104–132, title IV, §443(a), Apr. 24, 1996, 110 Stat. 1280.)

Historical and Revision Notes

Based on title 18, U.S.C., 1940 ed., §658 (R.S. §5274).

Minor changes were made in phraseology.

Amendments

1996—Pub. L. 104–132 designated existing provisions as subsec. (a) and added subsecs. (b) and (c).

Extradition Treaties Interpretation

Pub. L. 105–323, title II, Oct. 30, 1998, 112 Stat. 3033, provided that:

"SEC. 201. SHORT TITLE.

"This title may be cited as the 'Extradition Treaties Interpretation Act of 1998'.

"SEC. 202. FINDINGS.

"Congress finds that—

"(1) each year, several hundred children are kidnapped by a parent in violation of law, court order, or legally binding agreement and brought to, or taken from, the United States;

"(2) until the mid-1970's, parental abduction generally was not considered a criminal offense in the United States;

"(3) since the mid-1970's, United States criminal law has evolved such that parental abduction is now a criminal offense in each of the 50 States and the District of Columbia;

"(4) in enacting the International Parental Kidnapping Crime Act of 1993 (Public Law 103–173; 107 Stat. 1998; 18 U.S.C. 1204), Congress recognized the need to combat parental abduction by making the act of international parental kidnapping a Federal criminal offense;

"(5) many of the extradition treaties to which the United States is a party specifically list the offenses that are extraditable and use the word 'kidnapping', but it has been the practice of the United States not to consider the term to include parental abduction because these treaties were negotiated by the United States prior to the development in United States criminal law described in paragraphs (3) and (4);

"(6) the more modern extradition treaties to which the United States is a party contain dual criminality provisions, which provide for extradition where both parties make the offense a felony, and therefore it is the practice of the United States to consider such treaties to include parental abduction if the other foreign state party also considers the act of parental abduction to be a criminal offense; and

"(7) this circumstance has resulted in a disparity in United States extradition law which should be rectified to better protect the interests of children and their parents.

"SEC. 203. INTERPRETATION OF EXTRADITION TREATIES.

"For purposes of any extradition treaty to which the United States is a party, Congress authorizes the interpretation of the terms 'kidnaping' and 'kidnapping' to include parental kidnapping."

Judicial Assistance to International Tribunal for Yugoslavia and International Tribunal for Rwanda

Pub. L. 104–106, div. A, title XIII, §1342, Feb. 10, 1996, 110 Stat. 486, as amended by Pub. L. 111–117, div. F, title VII, §7034(t), Dec. 16, 2009, 123 Stat. 3364, provided that:

"(a) Surrender of Persons.—

"(1) Application of united states extradition laws.—Except as provided in paragraphs (2) and (3), the provisions of chapter 209 of title 18, United States Code, relating to the extradition of persons to a foreign country pursuant to a treaty or convention for extradition between the United States and a foreign government, shall apply in the same manner and extent to the surrender of persons, including United States citizens, to—

"(A) the International Tribunal for Yugoslavia, pursuant to the Agreement Between the United States and the International Tribunal for Yugoslavia; and

"(B) the International Tribunal for Rwanda, pursuant to the Agreement Between the United States and the International Tribunal for Rwanda.

"(2) Evidence on hearings.—For purposes of applying section 3190 of title 18, United States Code, in accordance with paragraph (1), the certification referred to in that section may be made by the principal diplomatic or consular officer of the United States resident in such foreign countries where the International Tribunal for Yugoslavia or the International Tribunal for Rwanda may be permanently or temporarily situated.

"(3) Payment of fees and costs.—(A) The provisions of the Agreement Between the United States and the International Tribunal for Yugoslavia and of the Agreement Between the United States and the International Tribunal for Rwanda shall apply in lieu of the provisions of section 3195 of title 18, United States Code, with respect to the payment of expenses arising from the surrender by the United States of a person to the International Tribunal for Yugoslavia or the International

Tribunal for Rwanda, respectively, or from any proceedings in the United States relating to such surrender.

"(B) The authority of subparagraph (A) may be exercised only to the extent and in the amounts provided in advance in appropriations Acts.

"(4) Nonapplicability of the federal rules.—The Federal Rules of Evidence [set out in the Appendix to Title 28, Judiciary and Judicial Procedure] and the Federal Rules of Criminal Procedure [set out in the Appendix to this title] do not apply to proceedings for the surrender of persons to the International Tribunal for Yugoslavia or the International Tribunal for Rwanda.

"(b) Assistance to Foreign and International Tribunals and to Litigants Before Such Tribunals.— [Amended section 1782 of Title 28, Judiciary and Judicial Procedure.]

"(c) Definitions.—For purposes of this section:

"(1) International tribunal for yugoslavia.—The term 'International Tribunal for Yugoslavia' means the International Tribunal for the Prosecution of Persons Responsible for Serious Violations of International Humanitarian Law in the Territory of the Former Yugoslavia, as established by United Nations Security Council Resolution 827 of May 25, 1993.

"(2) International tribunal for rwanda.—The term 'International Tribunal for Rwanda' means the International Tribunal for the Prosecution of Persons Responsible for Genocide and Other Serious Violations of International Humanitarian Law Committed in the Territory of Rwanda and Rwandan Citizens Responsible for Genocide and Other Such Violations Committed in the Territory of Neighboring States, as established by United Nations Security Council Resolution 955 of November 8, 1994.

"(3) Agreement between the united states and the international tribunal for yugoslavia.—The term 'Agreement Between the United States and the International Tribunal for Yugoslavia' means the Agreement on Surrender of Persons Between the Government of the United States and the International Tribunal for the Prosecution of Persons Responsible for Serious Violations of International Law in the Territory of the Former Yugoslavia, signed at The Hague, October 5, 1994, as amended.

"(4) Agreement between the united states and the international tribunal for rwanda.—The term 'Agreement between the United States and the International Tribunal for Rwanda' means the Agreement on Surrender of Persons Between the Government of the United States and the International Tribunal for the Prosecution of Persons Responsible for Genocide and Other Serious Violations of International Humanitarian Law Committed in the Territory of Rwanda and Rwandan Citizens Responsible for Genocide and Other Such Violations Committed in the Territory of Neighboring States, signed at The Hague, January 24, 1995."

Extradition and Mutual Legal Assistance Treaties and Model Comprehensive Antidrug Laws

Pub. L. 100–690, title IV, §4605, Nov. 18, 1988, 102 Stat. 4290, which directed greater emphasis on updating of extradition treaties and on negotiating mutual legal assistance treaties with major drug producing and drug-transit countries, and called for development of model treaties and anti-narcotics legislation, was repealed by Pub. L. 102–583, §6(e)(1), Nov. 2, 1992, 106 Stat. 4933.

Pub. L. 100–204, title VIII, §803, Dec. 22, 1987, 101 Stat. 1397, provided that: "The Secretary of State shall ensure that the Country Plan for the United States diplomatic mission in each major illicit drug producing country and in each major drug-transit country (as those terms are defined in section 481(i) of the Foreign Assistance Act of 1961 [22 U.S.C. 2291(i)]) includes, as an objective to be pursued by the mission—

"(1) negotiating an updated extradition treaty which ensures that drug traffickers can be extradited to the United States, or

"(2) if an existing treaty provides for such extradition, taking such steps as may be necessary to ensure that the treaty is effectively implemented."

Pub. L. 99–93, title I, §133, Aug. 16, 1985, 99 Stat. 420, provided that: "The Secretary of State, with the assistance of the National Drug Enforcement Policy Board, shall increase United States efforts to negotiate updated extradition treaties relating to narcotics offenses with each major drug-producing country, particularly those in Latin America."

EXTRADITION AGREEMENTS

The United States currently has bilateral extradition agreements with the following countries:

Country	Date signed	Entered into force	Citation
Albania	Mar. 1, 1933	Nov. 14, 1935	49 Stat. 3313.
Antigua and Barbuda	June 3, 1996	July 1, 1999	TIAS 99-701.1.
Argentina	June 10, 1997	June 15, 2000	TIAS 12866.
Australia	Dec. 22, 1931	Aug. 30, 1935	47 Stat. 2122.
	May 14, 1974	May 8, 1976	27 UST 957.
	Sept. 4, 1990	Dec. 21, 1992	1736 UNTS 344.
Austria	Jan. 8, 1998	Jan. 1, 2000	TIAS 12916.
	July 20, 2005	Feb. 1, 2010	TIAS 10-201.2.
Bahamas	Mar. 9, 1990	Sept. 22, 1994	TIAS.
Barbados	Feb. 28, 1996	Mar. 3, 2000	TIAS 00-303.
Belgium	Apr. 27, 1987	Sept. 1, 1997	TIAS 97-901.
	Dec. 16, 2004	Feb. 1, 2010	TIAS 10-201.
Belize	Mar. 30, 2000	Mar. 27, 2001	TIAS 13089.
Bolivia	June 27, 1995	Nov. 21, 1996	TIAS 96-112.
Brazil	Jan. 13, 1961	Dec. 17, 1964	15 UST 2093.
	June 18, 1962	Dec. 17, 1964	15 UST 2112.
Bulgaria	Mar. 19, 1924	June 24, 1924	43 Stat. 1886.
	June 8, 1934	Aug. 15, 1935	49 Stat. 3250.
	Sept. 19, 2007	May 21, 2009	TIAS 09-521.
Burma	Dec. 22, 1931	Nov. 1, 1941	47 Stat. 2122.
Canada	Dec. 3, 1971	Mar. 22, 1976	27 UST 983.
	June 28, July 9, 1974	Mar. 22, 1976	27 UST 1017.
	Jan. 11, 1988	Nov. 26, 1991	1853 UNTS 407.
	Jan. 12, 2001	Apr. 30, 2003	TIAS 03-430.
Chile	Apr. 17, 1900	June 26, 1902	32 Stat. 1850.
Colombia	Sept. 14, 1979	Mar. 4, 1982	TIAS.
Congo (Brazzaville)	Jan. 6, 1909Jan. 15, 1929Apr. 23, 1936	July 27, 1911May 19, 1929Sept. 24, 1936	37 Stat. 1526.46 Stat. 2276.50 Stat. 1117.
Costa Rica	Dec. 4, 1982	Oct. 11, 1991	TIAS.
Cuba	Apr. 6, 1904	Mar. 2, 1905	33 Stat. 2265.
	Dec. 6, 1904	Mar. 2, 1905	33 Stat. 2273.
	Jan. 14, 1926	June 18, 1926	44 Stat. 2392.
Cyprus	June 17, 1996	Sept. 14, 1999	TIAS 99-914.
	Jan. 20, 2006	Feb. 1, 2010	TIAS 10-201.4.
Czech Republic 1	July 2, 1925Apr. 29, 1935	Mar. 29, 1926Aug. 28, 1935	44 Stat. 2367.49 Stat. 3253.
	May 16, 2006	Feb. 1, 2010	TIAS 10-201.5.
Denmark	June 22, 1972	July 31, 1974	25 UST 1293.
	June 23, 2005	Feb. 1, 2010	TIAS 10-201.6.
Dominica	Oct. 10, 1996	May 25, 2000	TIAS 00-525.
Dominican Republic	June 19, 1909	Aug. 2, 1910	36 Stat. 2468.
Ecuador	June 28, 1872	Nov. 12, 1873	18 Stat. 199.
	Sept. 22, 1939	May 29, 1941	55 Stat. 1196.

Egypt	Aug. 11, 1874	Apr. 22, 1875	19 Stat. 572.
El Salvador	Apr. 18, 1911	July 10, 1911	37 Stat. 1516.
Estonia	Nov. 8, 1923	Nov. 15, 1924	43 Stat. 1849.
		Oct. 10, 1934	May 7, 1935	49 Stat. 3190.
		Feb. 8, 2006	Apr. 7, 2009	TIAS 09-407.
European Union	June 25, 2003	Feb. 1, 2010	TIAS 10-201.
Fiji	Dec. 22, 1931	June 24, 1935	47 Stat. 2122.
		July 14, 1972, Aug. 17, 1973	Aug. 17, 1973	24 UST 1965.
Finland	June 11, 1976	May 11, 1980	31 UST 944.
		Dec. 16, 2004	Feb. 1, 2010	TIAS 10-201.7.
France	Apr. 23, 1996	Feb. 1, 2002	TIAS 02-201.
		Sept. 30, 2004	Feb. 1, 2010	TIAS 10-201.8.
Gambia	Dec. 22, 1931	June 24, 1935	47 Stat. 2122.
Germany	June 20, 1978	Aug. 29, 1980	32 UST 1485.
		Oct. 21, 1986	Mar. 11, 1993	1909 UNTS 441.
		Apr. 18, 2006	Feb. 1, 2010	TIAS 10-201.9
Ghana	Dec. 22, 1931	June 24, 1935	47 Stat. 2122.
Greece	May 6, 1931	Nov. 1, 1932	47 Stat. 2185.
		Sept. 2, 1937	Sept. 2, 1937	51 Stat. 357.
		Jan. 18, 2006	Feb. 1, 2010	TIAS 10-201.10.
Grenada	May 30, 1996	Sept. 14, 1999	TIAS 99-914.1.
Guatemala	Feb. 27, 1903	Aug. 15, 1903	33 Stat. 2147.
		Feb. 20, 1940	Mar. 13, 1941	55 Stat. 1097.
Guyana	Dec. 22, 1931	June 24, 1935	47 Stat. 2122.
Haiti	Aug. 9, 1904	June 28, 1905	34 Stat. 2858.
Honduras	Jan. 15, 1909	July 10, 1912	37 Stat. 1616.
		Feb. 21, 1927	June 5, 1928	45 Stat. 2489.
Hong Kong	Dec. 20, 1996	Jan. 21, 1998	TIAS 98-121.
Hungary	Dec. 1, 1994	Mar. 18, 1997	TIAS 97-318.
		Nov. 15, 2005	Feb. 1, 2010	TIAS 10-201.11.
Iceland	Jan. 6, 1902	May 16, 1902	32 Stat. 1096.
		Nov. 6, 1905	Feb. 19, 1906	34 Stat. 2887.
India	June 25, 1997	July 21, 1999	TIAS 12873.
Iraq	June 7, 1934	Apr. 23, 1936	49 Stat. 3380.
Ireland	July 13, 1983	Dec. 15, 1984	TIAS 10813.
		July 14, 2005	Feb. 1, 2010	TIAS 10-201.12.
Israel	Dec. 10, 1962	Dec. 5, 1963	14 UST 1707.2
		July 6, 2005	Jan. 10, 2007	TIAS 07-110.
Italy	Oct. 13, 1983	Sept. 24, 1984	35 UST 3023.
		May 3, 2006	Feb. 1, 2010	TIAS 10-201.13.
Jamaica	June 14, 1983	July 7, 1991	TIAS.
Japan	Mar. 3, 1978	Mar. 26, 1980	31 UST 892.
Jordan	Mar. 28, 1995	July 29, 1995	TIAS.
Kenya	Dec. 22, 1931	June 24, 1935	47 Stat. 2122.
		May 14, Aug. 19, 1965	Aug. 19, 1965	16 UST 1866.
Kiribati	June 8, 1972	Jan. 21, 1977	28 UST 227.
Latvia	Oct. 16, 1923	Mar. 1, 1924	43 Stat. 1738.
		Oct. 10, 1934	Mar. 29, 1935	49 Stat. 3131.
		Dec. 7, 2005	Apr. 15, 2009	TIAS 09-415.
Lesotho	Dec. 22, 1931	June 24, 1935	47 Stat. 2122.
Liberia	Nov. 1, 1937	Nov. 21, 1939	54 Stat. 1733.
Liechtenstein	May 20, 1936	June 28, 1937	50 Stat. 1337.
Lithuania	Oct. 23, 2001	Mar. 31, 2003	TIAS 13166.

	June 15, 2005	Feb. 1, 2010	TIAS 10-201.14.
Luxembourg	Oct. 1, 1996	Feb. 1, 2002	TIAS 12804.
	Feb. 1, 2005	Feb. 1, 2010	TIAS 10-201.15.
Malawi	Dec. 22, 1931	June 24, 1935	47 Stat. 2122.
	Dec. 17, 1966, Jan. 6, Apr. 4, 1967	Apr. 4, 1967	18 UST 1822.
Malaysia	Aug. 3, 1995	June 2, 1997	TIAS 97-602.
Malta	Dec. 22, 1931	June 24, 1935	47 Stat. 2122.
	May 18, 2006	July 1, 2009	TIAS 09-701.
Marshall Islands	Apr. 30, 2003	May 1, 2004	TIAS 04-501.2.
Mauritius	Dec. 22, 1931	June 24, 1935	47 Stat. 2122.
Mexico	May 4, 1978	Jan. 25, 1980	31 UST 5059.
	Nov. 13, 1997	May 21, 2001	TIAS 12897.
Micronesia, Federated States of	May 14, 2003	June 25, 2004	TIAS 04-625.4.
Monaco	Feb. 15, 1939	Mar. 28, 1940	54 Stat. 1780.
Nauru	Dec. 22, 1931	Aug. 30, 1935	47 Stat. 2122.
Netherlands	June 24, 1980	Sept. 15, 1983	35 UST 1334.
	Sept. 29, 2004	Feb. 1, 2010	TIAS 10-201.16.
New Zealand	Jan. 12, 1970	Dec. 8, 1970	22 UST 1.
Nicaragua	Mar. 1, 1905	July 14, 1907	35 Stat. 1869.
Nigeria	Dec. 22, 1931	June 24, 1935	47 Stat. 2122.
Norway	June 9, 1977	Mar. 7, 1980	31 UST 5619.
Pakistan	Dec. 22, 1931	Mar. 9, 1942	47 Stat. 2122.
Panama	May 25, 1904	May 8, 1905	34 Stat. 2851.
Papua New Guinea	Dec. 22, 1931	Aug. 30, 1935	47 Stat. 2122.
	Feb. 2, 23, 1988	Feb. 23, 1988	TIAS.
Paraguay	Nov. 9, 1998	Mar. 9, 2001	TIAS 12995.
Peru	July 26, 2001	Aug. 25, 2003	TIAS 03-825.
Philippines	Nov. 13, 1994	Nov. 22, 1996	TIAS 96-1122.
Poland	July 10, 1996	Sept. 17, 1999	TIAS 99-917.
	June 9, 2006	Feb. 1, 2010	TIAS 10-201.17.
Portugal	May 7, 1908	Nov. 14, 1908	35 Stat. 2071.
	July 14, 2005	Feb. 1, 2010	TIAS 10-201.18.
Romania	July 23, 1924	Apr. 7, 1925	44 Stat. 2020.
	Nov. 10, 1936	July 27, 1937	50 Stat. 1349.
	Sept. 10, 2007	May 8, 2009	TIAS 09-508.
Saint Kitts and Nevis	Sept. 18, 1996	Feb. 23, 2000	TIAS 12805.
Saint Lucia	Apr. 18, 1996	Feb. 2, 2000	TIAS 00-202.
Saint Vincent and the Grenadines	Aug. 15, 1996	Sept. 8, 1999	TIAS 99-908.
San Marino	Jan. 10, 1906	July 8, 1908	35 Stat. 1971.
	Oct. 10, 1934	June 28, 1935	49 Stat. 3198.
Seychelles	Dec. 22, 1931	June 24, 1935	47 Stat. 2122.
Sierra Leone	Dec. 22, 1931	June 24, 1935	47 Stat. 2122.
Singapore	Dec. 22, 1931	June 24, 1935	47 Stat. 2122.
	Apr. 23, June 10, 1969	June 10, 1969	20 UST 2764.
Slovakia 1	July 2, 1925Apr. 29, 1935Feb. 6, 2006	Mar. 29, 1926Aug. 28, 1935Feb. 1, 2010
44 Stat. 2367.49 Stat. 3253.TIAS 10-201.19.
Slovenia 1	Oct. 17, 2005	Feb. 1, 2010	TIAS 10-201.20.
Solomon Islands	June 8, 1972	Jan. 21, 1977	28 UST 277.
South Africa	Sept. 16, 1999	June 25, 2001	TIAS 13060.
South Korea	June 9, 1998	Dec. 20, 1999	TIAS 12962.
Spain	May 29, 1970	June 16, 1971	22 UST 737.
	Jan. 25, 1975	June 2, 1978	29 UST 2283.
	Feb. 9, 1988	July 2, 1993	TIAS.

	Mar. 12, 1996	July 25, 1999	TIAS.
	Dec. 17, 2004	Feb. 1, 2010	TIAS 10-201.21.
Sri Lanka	Sept. 30, 1999	Jan. 12, 2001	TIAS 13066.
Suriname	June 2, 1887	July 11, 1889	26 Stat. 1481.
	Jan. 18, 1904	Aug. 28, 1904	33 Stat. 2257.
Swaziland	Dec. 22, 1931	June 24, 1935	47 Stat. 2122.
	May 13, July 28, 1970	July 28, 1970	21 UST 1930.
Sweden	Oct. 24, 1961	Dec. 3, 1963	14 UST 1845.
	Mar. 14, 1983	Sept. 24, 1984	35 UST 2501.
	Dec. 16, 2004	Feb. 1, 2010	TIAS 10-201.22.
Switzerland	Nov. 14, 1990	Sept. 10, 1997	TIAS 97-910.
Tanzania	Dec. 22, 1931	June 24, 1935	47 Stat. 2122.
	Nov. 30, Dec. 6, 1965	Dec. 6, 1965	16 UST 2066.
Thailand	Dec. 14, 1983	May 17, 1991	TIAS.
Tonga	Dec. 22, 1931	Aug. 1, 1966	47 Stat. 2122.
	Mar. 14, Apr. 13, 1977	Apr. 13, 1977	28 UST 5290.
Trinidad and Tobago	Mar. 4, 1996	Nov. 29, 1999	TIAS 99-1129.
Turkey	June 7, 1979	Jan. 1, 1981	32 UST 3111.
Tuvalu	June 8, 1972	Jan. 21, 1977	28 UST 227.
		Apr. 25, 1980	32 UST 1310.
United Kingdom	Mar. 31, 2003Dec. 16, 2004	Apr. 26, 2007Feb. 1, 2010	TIAS 07-426.TIAS 10-201.23.
Uruguay	Apr. 6, 1973	Apr. 11, 1984	35 UST 3197.
Venezuela	Jan. 19, 21, 1922	Apr. 14, 1923	43 Stat. 1698.
Yugoslavia 1	Oct. 25, 1901	June 12, 1902	32 Stat. 1890.
Zambia	Dec. 22, 1931	June 24, 1935	47 Stat. 2122.
Zimbabwe	July 25, 1997	Apr. 26, 2000	TIAS.

1 Status of agreements with successor states of Czechoslovakia and Yugoslavia is under review; inquire of the Treaty Office of the United States Department of State.
2 Typographical error corrected by diplomatic notes exchanged Apr. 4 and 11, 1967. See 18 UST 382, 383.

Convention on Extradition

The United States is a party to the Multilateral Convention on Extradition signed at Montevideo on Dec. 26, 1933, entered into force for the United States on Jan. 25, 1935. 49 Stat. 3111.
Other states which have become parties: Argentina, Chile, Colombia, Dominican Republic, Ecuador, El Salvador, Guatemala, Honduras, Mexico, Nicaragua, Panama.

§3182. Fugitives from State or Territory to State, District, or Territory

Whenever the executive authority of any State or Territory demands any person as a fugitive from justice, of the executive authority of any State, District, or Territory to which such person has fled, and produces a copy of an indictment found or an affidavit made before a magistrate of any State or Territory, charging the person demanded with having committed treason, felony, or other crime, certified as authentic by the governor or chief magistrate of the State or Territory from whence the person so charged has fled, the executive authority of the State, District, or Territory to which such person has fled shall cause him to be arrested and secured, and notify the executive authority making such demand, or the agent of such authority appointed to receive the fugitive, and shall cause the fugitive to be delivered to such agent when he shall appear. If no such agent appears within thirty days from the time of the arrest, the prisoner may be discharged.
(June 25, 1948, ch. 645, 62 Stat. 822; Pub. L. 104–294, title VI, §601(f)(9), Oct. 11, 1996, 110 Stat. 3500.)

Historical and Revision Notes

Based on title 18, U.S.C., 1940 ed., §662 (R.S. §5278).

Last sentence as to costs and expenses to be paid by the demanding authority was incorporated in section 3195 of this title.

Word "District" was inserted twice to make section equally applicable to fugitives found in the District of Columbia.

"Thirty days" was substituted for "six months" since, in view of modern conditions, the smaller time is ample for the demanding authority to act.

Minor changes were made in phraseology.

Amendments

1996—Pub. L. 104–294 inserted comma after "District" in section catchline and in two places in text.

§3183. Fugitives from State, Territory, or Possession into extraterritorial jurisdiction of United States

Whenever the executive authority of any State, Territory, District, or possession of the United States demands any American citizen or national as a fugitive from justice who has fled to a country in which the United States exercises extraterritorial jurisdiction, and produces a copy of an indictment found or an affidavit made before a magistrate of the demanding jurisdiction, charging the fugitive so demanded with having committed treason, felony, or other offense, certified as authentic by the Governor or chief magistrate of such demanding jurisdiction, or other person authorized to act, the officer or representative of the United States vested with judicial authority to whom the demand has been made shall cause such fugitive to be arrested and secured, and notify the executive authorities making such demand, or the agent of such authority appointed to receive the fugitive, and shall cause the fugitive to be delivered to such agent when he shall appear.

If no such agent shall appear within three months from the time of the arrest, the prisoner may be discharged.

The agent who receives the fugitive into his custody shall be empowered to transport him to the jurisdiction from which he has fled.

(June 25, 1948, ch. 645, 62 Stat. 822; Pub. L. 107–273, div. B, title IV, §4004(d), Nov. 2, 2002, 116 Stat. 1812.)

Historical and Revision Notes

Based on title 18, U.S.C., 1940 ed., §662c (Mar. 22, 1934, ch. 73, §2, 48 Stat. 455).

Said section 662c was incorporated in this section and sections 752 and 3195 of this title.

Provision as to costs or expenses to be paid by the demanding authority were incorporated in section 3196 of this title.

Reference to the Philippine Islands was deleted as obsolete in view of the independence of the Commonwealth of the Philippines effective July 4, 1946.

The attention of Congress is directed to the probability that this section may be of little, if any, possible use in view of present world conditions.

Minor changes were made in phraseology.

Amendments

2002—Pub. L. 107–273 struck out "or the Panama Canal Zone," after "possession of the United States" in first par.

§3184. Fugitives from foreign country to United States

Whenever there is a treaty or convention for extradition between the United States and any foreign government, or in cases arising under section 3181(b), any justice or judge of the United States, or any magistrate judge authorized so to do by a court of the United States, or any judge of a court of record of general jurisdiction of any State, may, upon complaint made under oath, charging any person found within his jurisdiction, with having committed within the jurisdiction of any such foreign government any of the crimes provided for by such treaty or convention, or provided for under section 3181(b), issue his warrant for the apprehension of the person so charged, that he may be brought before such justice, judge, or magistrate judge, to the end that the evidence of criminality may be heard and considered. Such complaint may be filed before and such warrant may be issued by a judge or magistrate judge of the United States District Court for the District of Columbia if the whereabouts within the United States of the person charged are not known or, if there is reason to believe the person will shortly enter the United States. If, on such hearing, he deems the evidence sufficient to sustain the charge under the provisions of the proper treaty or convention, or under section 3181(b), he shall certify the same, together with a copy of all the testimony taken before him, to the Secretary of State, that a warrant may issue upon the requisition of the proper authorities of such foreign government, for the surrender of such person, according to the stipulations of the treaty or convention; and he shall issue his warrant for the commitment of the person so charged to the proper jail, there to remain until such surrender shall be made. (June 25, 1948, ch. 645, 62 Stat. 822; Pub. L. 90–578, title III, §301(a)(3), Oct. 17, 1968, 82 Stat. 1115; Pub. L. 100–690, title VII, §7087, Nov. 18, 1988, 102 Stat. 4409; Pub. L. 101–647, title XVI, §1605, Nov. 29, 1990, 104 Stat. 4843; Pub. L. 101–650, title III, §321, Dec. 1, 1990, 104 Stat. 5117; Pub. L. 104–132, title IV, §443(b), Apr. 24, 1996, 110 Stat. 1281.)

Historical and Revision Notes
Based on title 18, U.S.C., 1940 ed., §651 (R.S. §5270; June 6, 1900, ch. 793, 31 Stat. 656). Minor changes of phraseology were made.

Amendments
1996—Pub. L. 104–132, in first sentence, inserted "or in cases arising under section 3181(b)," after "United States and any foreign government," and "or provided for under section 3181(b)," after "treaty or convention," and in third sentence, inserted "or under section 3181(b)," after "treaty or convention,".

1990—Pub. L. 101–647 inserted "or, if there is reason to believe the person will shortly enter the United States" after "are not known" in second sentence.

1988—Pub. L. 100–690 inserted after first sentence "Such complaint may be filed before and such warrant may be issued by a judge or magistrate of the United States District Court for the District of Columbia if the whereabouts within the United States of the person charged are not known."

1968—Pub. L. 90–578 substituted "magistrate" for "commissioner" in two places.

Change of Name
Words "magistrate judge" substituted for "magistrate" wherever appearing in text pursuant to section 321 of Pub. L. 101–650, set out as a note under section 631 of Title 28, Judiciary and Judicial Procedure.

Effective Date of 1968 Amendment
Amendment by Pub. L. 90–578 effective Oct. 17, 1968, except when a later effective date is applicable, which is the earlier of date when implementation of amendment by appointment of magistrates [now United States magistrate judges] and assumption of office takes place or third anniversary of enactment of Pub. L. 90–578 on Oct. 17, 1968, see section 403 of Pub. L. 90–578, set out as a note under section 631 of Title 28, Judiciary and Judicial Procedure.

§3185. Fugitives from country under control of United States into the United

States

Whenever any foreign country or territory, or any part thereof, is occupied by or under the control of the United States, any person who, having violated the criminal laws in force therein by the commission of any of the offenses enumerated below, departs or flees from justice therein to the United States, shall, when found therein, be liable to arrest and detention by the authorities of the United States, and on the written request or requisition of the military governor or other chief executive officer in control of such foreign country or territory shall be returned and surrendered as hereinafter provided to such authorities for trial under the laws in force in the place where such offense was committed.

(1) Murder and assault with intent to commit murder;

(2) Counterfeiting or altering money, or uttering or bringing into circulation counterfeit or altered money;

(3) Counterfeiting certificates or coupons of public indebtedness, bank notes, or other instruments of public credit, and the utterance or circulation of the same;

(4) Forgery or altering and uttering what is forged or altered;

(5) Embezzlement or criminal malversation of the public funds, committed by public officers, employees, or depositaries;

(6) Larceny or embezzlement of an amount not less than $100 in value;

(7) Robbery;

(8) Burglary, defined to be the breaking and entering by nighttime into the house of another person with intent to commit a felony therein;

(9) Breaking and entering the house or building of another, whether in the day or nighttime, with the intent to commit a felony therein;

(10) Entering, or breaking and entering the offices of the Government and public authorities, or the offices of banks, banking houses, savings banks, trust companies, insurance or other companies, with the intent to commit a felony therein;

(11) Perjury or the subornation of perjury;

(12) A felony under chapter 109A of this title;

(13) Arson;

(14) Piracy by the law of nations;

(15) Murder, assault with intent to kill, and manslaughter, committed on the high seas, on board a ship owned by or in control of citizens or residents of such foreign country or territory and not under the flag of the United States, or of some other government;

(16) Malicious destruction of or attempt to destroy railways, trams, vessels, bridges, dwellings, public edifices, or other buildings, when the act endangers human life.

This chapter, so far as applicable, shall govern proceedings authorized by this section. Such proceedings shall be had before a judge of the courts of the United States only, who shall hold such person on evidence establishing probable cause that he is guilty of the offense charged.

No return or surrender shall be made of any person charged with the commission of any offense of a political nature.

If so held, such person shall be returned and surrendered to the authorities in control of such foreign country or territory on the order of the Secretary of State of the United States, and such authorities shall secure to such a person a fair and impartial trial.

(June 25, 1948, ch. 645, 62 Stat. 823; May 24, 1949, ch. 139, §49, 63 Stat. 96; Pub. L. 99–646, §87(c)(6), Nov. 10, 1986, 100 Stat. 3623; Pub. L. 99–654, §3(a)(6), Nov. 14, 1986, 100 Stat. 3663.)

Historical and Revision Notes

1948 Act

Based on title 18, U.S.C., 1940 ed., §652 (R.S. §5270; June 6, 1900, ch. 793, 31 Stat. 656).

Reference to territory of the United States and the District of Columbia was omitted as covered by definitive section 5 of this title.

Changes were made in phraseology and arrangement.

1949 Act

This section [section 49] corrects typographical errors in section 3185 of title 18, U.S.C., by transferring to subdivision (3) the words, "indebtedness, bank notes, or other instruments of public", from subdivision (2) of such section where they had been erroneously included.

Amendments

1986—Par. (12). Pub. L. 99–646 and Pub. L. 99–654 amended par. (12) identically, substituting "A felony under chapter 109A of this title" for "Rape".

1949—Pars. (2), (3). Act May 24, 1949, transferred "indebtedness, bank notes, or other instruments of public" from par. (2) to par. (3).

Effective Date of 1986 Amendments

Amendments by Pub. L. 99–646 and Pub. L. 99–654 effective, respectively, 30 days after Nov. 10, 1986, and 30 days after Nov. 14, 1986, see section 87(e) of Pub. L. 99–646 and section 4 of Pub. L. 99–654, set out as an Effective Date note under section 2241 of this title.

§3186. Secretary of State to surrender fugitive

The Secretary of State may order the person committed under sections 3184 or 3185 of this title to be delivered to any authorized agent of such foreign government, to be tried for the offense of which charged.

Such agent may hold such person in custody, and take him to the territory of such foreign government, pursuant to such treaty.

A person so accused who escapes may be retaken in the same manner as any person accused of any offense.

(June 25, 1948, ch. 645, 62 Stat. 824.)

Historical and Revision Notes

Based on title 18, U.S.C., 1940 ed., §653 (R.S. §5272).

Changes were made in phraseology and surplusage was deleted.

§3187. Provisional arrest and detention within extraterritorial jurisdiction

The provisional arrest and detention of a fugitive, under sections 3042 and 3183 of this title, in advance of the presentation of formal proofs, may be obtained by telegraph upon the request of the authority competent to request the surrender of such fugitive addressed to the authority competent to grant such surrender. Such request shall be accompanied by an express statement that a warrant for the fugitive's arrest has been issued within the jurisdiction of the authority making such request charging the fugitive with the commission of the crime for which his extradition is sought to be obtained.

No person shall be held in custody under telegraphic request by virtue of this section for more than ninety days.

(June 25, 1948, ch. 645, 62 Stat. 824.)

Historical and Revision Notes

Based on title 18, U.S.C., 1940 ed., §662d (Mar. 22, 1934, ch. 73, §3, 48 Stat. 455).

Provision for expense to be borne by the demanding authority is incorporated in section 3195 of this title.

Changes were made in phraseology and arrangement.

§3188. Time of commitment pending extradition

Whenever any person who is committed for rendition to a foreign government to remain until delivered up in pursuance of a requisition, is not so delivered up and conveyed out of the United States within two calendar months after such commitment, over and above the time actually required to convey the prisoner from the jail to which he was committed, by the readiest way, out of the United States, any judge of the United States, or of any State, upon application made to him by or on behalf of the person so committed, and upon proof made to him that reasonable notice of the intention to make such application has been given to the Secretary of State, may order the person so committed to be discharged out of custody, unless sufficient cause is shown to such judge why such discharge ought not to be ordered.

(June 25, 1948, ch. 645, 62 Stat. 824.)

Historical and Revision Notes

Based on title 18, U.S.C., 1940 ed., §654 (R.S. §5273).
Changes in phraseology only were made.

§3189. Place and character of hearing

Hearings in cases of extradition under treaty stipulation or convention shall be held on land, publicly, and in a room or office easily accessible to the public.

(June 25, 1948, ch. 645, 62 Stat. 824.)

Historical and Revision Notes

Based on title 18, U.S.C., 1940 ed., §657 (Aug. 3, 1882, ch. 378, §1, 22 Stat. 215).
First word "All" was omitted as unnecessary.

§3190. Evidence on hearing

Depositions, warrants, or other papers or copies thereof offered in evidence upon the hearing of any extradition case shall be received and admitted as evidence on such hearing for all the purposes of such hearing if they shall be properly and legally authenticated so as to entitle them to be received for similar purposes by the tribunals of the foreign country from which the accused party shall have escaped, and the certificate of the principal diplomatic or consular officer of the United States resident in such foreign country shall be proof that the same, so offered, are authenticated in the manner required.

(June 25, 1948, ch. 645, 62 Stat. 824.)

Historical and Revision Notes

Based on title 18, U.S.C., 1940 ed., §655 (R.S. §5271; Aug. 3, 1882, ch. 378, §5, 22 Stat. 216).
Unnecessary words were deleted.

§3191. Witnesses for indigent fugitives

On the hearing of any case under a claim of extradition by a foreign government, upon affidavit being filed by the person charged setting forth that there are witnesses whose evidence is material to his defense, that he cannot safely go to trial without them, what he expects to prove by each of them, and that he is not possessed of sufficient means, and is actually unable to pay the fees of such witnesses, the judge or magistrate judge hearing the matter may order that such witnesses be subpenaed; and the costs incurred by the process, and the fees of witnesses, shall be paid in the same manner as in the case of witnesses subpenaed in behalf of the United States.

(June 25, 1948, ch. 645, 62 Stat. 825; Pub. L. 90–578, title III, §301(a)(3), Oct. 17, 1968, 82 Stat. 1115; Pub. L. 101 650, title III, §321, Dec. 1, 1990, 104 Stat. 5117.)

Historical and Revision Notes

Based on title 18, U.S.C., 1940 ed., §656 (Aug. 3, 1882, ch. 378, §3, 22 Stat. 215).
Words "that similar" after "manner" were omitted as unnecessary.

Amendments
1968—Pub. L. 90–578 substituted "magistrate" for "commissioner".

Change of Name
Words "magistrate judge" substituted for "magistrate" in text pursuant to section 321 of Pub. L. 101–650, set out as a note under section 631 of Title 28, Judiciary and Judicial Procedure.

Effective Date of 1968 Amendment
Amendment by Pub. L. 90–578 effective Oct. 17, 1968, except when a later effective date is applicable, which is the earlier of date when implementation of amendment by appointment of magistrates [now United States magistrate judges] and assumption of office takes place or third anniversary of enactment of Pub. L. 90–578 on Oct. 17, 1968, see section 403 of Pub. L. 90–578, set out as a note under section 631 of Title 28, Judiciary and Judicial Procedure.

§3192. Protection of accused
Whenever any person is delivered by any foreign government to an agent of the United States, for the purpose of being brought within the United States and tried for any offense of which he is duly accused, the President shall have power to take all necessary measures for the transportation and safekeeping of such accused person, and for his security against lawless violence, until the final conclusion of his trial for the offenses specified in the warrant of extradition, and until his final discharge from custody or imprisonment for or on account of such offenses, and for a reasonable time thereafter, and may employ such portion of the land or naval forces of the United States, or of the militia thereof, as may be necessary for the safe-keeping and protection of the accused.
(June 25, 1948, ch. 645, 62 Stat. 825.)

Historical and Revision Notes
Based on title 18, U.S.C., 1940 ed., §659 (R.S. §5275).
Words "crimes or" before "offenses" were omitted as unnecessary.

§3193. Receiving agent's authority over offenders
A duly appointed agent to receive, in behalf of the United States, the delivery, by a foreign government, of any person accused of crime committed within the United States, and to convey him to the place of his trial, shall have all the powers of a marshal of the United States, in the several districts through which it may be necessary for him to pass with such prisoner, so far as such power is requisite for the prisoner's safe-keeping.
(June 25, 1948, ch. 645, 62 Stat. 825.)

Historical and Revision Notes
Based on title 18, U.S.C., 1940 ed., §660 (R.S. §5276).
Words "jurisdiction of the" were omitted in view of the definition of United States in section 5 of this title.
Minor changes only were made in phraseology.

Ex. Ord. No. 11517. Issuance and Signature by Secretary of State of Warrants Appointing Agents To Return Fugitives From Justice Extradited to United States
Ex. Ord. No. 11517, Mar. 19, 1970, 35 F.R. 4937, provided:
WHEREAS the President of the United States, under section 3192 of Title 18, United States Code,

has been granted the power to take all necessary measures for the transportation, safekeeping and security against lawless violence of any person delivered by any foreign government to an agent of the United States for return to the United States for trial for any offense of which he is duly accused; and

WHEREAS fugitives from justice in the United States whose extradition from abroad has been requested by the Government of the United States and granted by a foreign government are to be returned in the custody of duly appointed agents in accordance with the provisions of section 3193 of Title 18, United States Code; and

WHEREAS such duly appointed agents under the provisions of the law mentioned above, being authorized to receive delivery of the fugitive in behalf of the United States and to convey him to the place of his trial, are given the powers of a marshal of the United States in the several districts of the United States through which it may be necessary for them to pass with such prisoner, so far as such power is requisite for the prisoner's safekeeping; and

WHEREAS such warrants serve as a certification to the foreign government delivering the fugitives to any other foreign country through which such agents may pass, and to authorities in the United States of the powers therein conferred upon the agents; and

WHEREAS it is desirable by delegation of functions heretofore performed by the President to simplify and thereby expedite the issuance of such warrants to agents in the interests of the prompt return of fugitives to the United States:

NOW, THEREFORE, by virtue of the authority vested in me by section 301 of Title 3 of the United States Code, and as President of the United States, it is ordered as follows:

Section 1. The Secretary of State is hereby designated and empowered to issue and sign all warrants appointing agents to receive, in behalf of the United States, the delivery in extradition by a foreign government of any person accused of a crime committed within the United States, and to convey such person to the place of his trial.

Sec. 2. Agents appointed in accordance with section 1 of this order shall have all the powers conferred in respect of such agents by applicable treaties of the United States and by section 3193 of Title 18, United States Code, or by any other provisions of United States law.

Sec. 3. Executive Order No. 10347, April 18, 1952, as amended by Executive Order No. 11354, May 23, 1967, is further amended by deleting numbered paragraph 4 and renumbering paragraphs 5 and 6 as paragraphs 4 and 5, respectively.

Richard Nixon.

§3194. Transportation of fugitive by receiving agent

Any agent appointed as provided in section 3182 of this title who receives the fugitive into his custody is empowered to transport him to the State or Territory from which he has fled.

(June 25, 1948, ch. 645, 62 Stat. 825.)

Historical and Revision Notes

Based on title 18, U.S.C., 1940 ed., §663 (R.S. §5279).

Last sentence of said section 663, relating to rescue of such fugitive, was omitted as covered by section 752 of this title, the punishment provision of which is based on later statutes. (See reviser's note under that section.)

Minor changes were made in phraseology.

§3195. Payment of fees and costs

All costs or expenses incurred in any extradition proceeding in apprehending, securing, and transmitting a fugitive shall be paid by the demanding authority.

All witness fees and costs of every nature in cases of international extradition, including the fees of the magistrate judge, shall be certified by the judge or magistrate judge before whom the hearing shall take place to the Secretary of State of the United States, and the same shall be paid out of appropriations to defray the expenses of the judiciary or the Department of Justice as the case may be.

The Attorney General shall certify to the Secretary of State the amounts to be paid to the United States on account of said fees and costs in extradition cases by the foreign government requesting the extradition, and the Secretary of State shall cause said amounts to be collected and transmitted to the Attorney General for deposit in the Treasury of the United States.

(June 25, 1948, ch. 645, 62 Stat. 825; Pub. L. 90–578, title III, §301(a)(3), Oct. 17, 1968, 82 Stat. 1115; Pub. L. 101–650, title III, §321, Dec. 1, 1990, 104 Stat. 5117.)

Historical and Revision Notes

Based on title 18, U.S.C., 1940 ed., §§662, 662c, 662d, 668 (R.S. §5278; Aug. 3, 1882, ch. 378, §4, 22 Stat. 216; June 28, 1902, ch. 1301, §1, 32 Stat. 475; Mar. 22, 1934, ch. 73, §§2, 3, 48 Stat. 455).

First paragraph of this section consolidates provisions as to costs and expenses from said sections 662, 662c, and 662d.

Minor changes were made in phraseology and surplusage was omitted.

Remaining provisions of said sections 662, 662c, and 662d of title 18, U.S.C., 1940 ed., are incorporated in sections 752, 3182, 3183, and 3187 of this title.

The words "or the Department of Justice as the case may be" were added at the end of the second paragraph in conformity with the appropriation acts of recent years. See for example act July 5, 1946, ch. 541, title II, 60 Stat. 460.

Amendments

1968—Pub. L. 90–578 substituted "magistrate" for "commissioner" in two places.

Change of Name

Words "magistrate judge" substituted for "magistrate" wherever appearing in text pursuant to section 321 of Pub. L. 101–650, set out as a note under section 631 of Title 28, Judiciary and Judicial Procedure.

Effective Date of 1968 Amendment

Amendment by Pub. L. 90–578 effective Oct. 17, 1968, except when a later effective date is applicable, which is the earlier of a date when implementation of amendment by appointment of magistrates [now United States magistrate judges] and assumption of office takes place or third anniversary of enactment of Pub. L. 90–578 on Oct. 17, 1968, see section 403 of Pub. L. 90–578, set out as a note under section 631 of Title 28, Judiciary and Judicial Procedure.

§3196. Extradition of United States citizens

If the applicable treaty or convention does not obligate the United States to extradite its citizens to a foreign country, the Secretary of State may, nevertheless, order the surrender to that country of a United States citizen whose extradition has been requested by that country if the other requirements of that treaty or convention are met.

(Added Pub. L. 101–623, §11(a), Nov. 21, 1990, 104 Stat. 3356.)

CHAPTER 211 - JURISDICTION AND VENUE

Amendments

1994—Pub. L. 103–322, title XXXII, §320909(b), Sept. 13, 1994, 108 Stat. 2127, added item 3239.

1984—Pub. L. 98–473, title II, §1204(b), Oct. 12, 1984, 98 Stat. 2152, struck out item 3239 "Threatening communications".

1978—Pub. L. 95–598, title III, §314(j)(2), Nov. 6, 1978, 92 Stat. 2678, added item 3244.

§3231. District courts

The district courts of the United States shall have original jurisdiction, exclusive of the courts of the States, of all offenses against the laws of the United States.

Nothing in this title shall be held to take away or impair the jurisdiction of the courts of the several States under the laws thereof.

(June 25, 1948, ch. 645, 62 Stat. 826.)

Historical and Revision Notes

Based on section 588d of title 12, U.S.C., 1940 ed., Banks and Banking; title 18, U.S.C., 1940 ed., §§546, 547 (Mar. 4, 1909, ch. 321, §§326, 340, 35 Stat. 1151, 1153; Mar. 3, 1911, ch. 231, §291, 36 Stat. 1167; May 18, 1934, ch. 304, §4, 48 Stat. 783).

This section was formed by combining sections 546 and 547 of title 18, U.S.C., 1940 ed., with section 588d of title 12, U.S.C., Banks and Banking, with no change of substance.

The language of said section 588d of title 12, U.S.C., 1940 ed., which related to bank robbery, or killing or kidnapping as an incident thereto (see section 2113, of this title), and which read "Jurisdiction over any offense defined by sections 588b and 588c of this title shall not be reserved exclusively to courts of the United States" was omitted as adequately covered by this section.

Senate Revision Amendment

The text of this section was changed by Senate amendment. See Senate Report No. 1620, amendment No. 10, 80th Cong.

§3232. District of offense—(Rule)

See Federal Rules of Criminal Procedure

Proceedings to be in district and division in which offense committed, Rule 18.

(June 25, 1948, ch. 645, 62 Stat. 826.)

§3233. Transfer within district—(Rule)

See Federal Rules of Criminal Procedure

Arraignment, plea, trial, sentence in district of more than one division, Rule 19.

(June 25, 1948, ch. 645, 62 Stat. 826.)

References in Text

Rule 19 of the Federal Rules of Criminal Procedure, referred to in text, was rescinded Feb. 28, 1966, eff. July 1, 1966.

§3234. Change of venue to another district—(Rule)

See Federal Rules of Criminal Procedure

Plea or disposal of case in district other than that in which defendant was arrested, Rule 20.
(June 25, 1948, ch. 645, 62 Stat. 826.)

§3235. Venue in capital cases

The trial of offenses punishable with death shall be had in the county where the offense was committed, where that can be done without great inconvenience.
(June 25, 1948, ch. 645, 62 Stat. 826.)

Historical and Revision Notes

Based on section 101 of title 28, U.S.C., 1940 ed., Judicial Code and Judiciary (Mar. 3, 1911, ch. 231, §40, 36 Stat. 1100).

§3236. Murder or manslaughter

In all cases of murder or manslaughter, the offense shall be deemed to have been committed at the place where the injury was inflicted, or the poison administered or other means employed which caused the death, without regard to the place where the death occurs.
(June 25, 1948, ch. 645, 62 Stat. 826.)

Historical and Revision Notes

Based on title 18, U.S.C., 1940 ed., §553 (Mar. 4, 1909, ch. 321, §336, 35 Stat. 1152).

§3237. Offenses begun in one district and completed in another

(a) Except as otherwise expressly provided by enactment of Congress, any offense against the United States begun in one district and completed in another, or committed in more than one district, may be inquired of and prosecuted in any district in which such offense was begun, continued, or completed.

Any offense involving the use of the mails, transportation in interstate or foreign commerce, or the importation of an object or person into the United States is a continuing offense and, except as otherwise expressly provided by enactment of Congress, may be inquired of and prosecuted in any district from, through, or into which such commerce, mail matter, or imported object or person moves.

(b) Notwithstanding subsection (a), where an offense is described in section 7203 of the Internal Revenue Code of 1986, or where venue for prosecution of an offense described in section 7201 or 7206(1), (2), or (5) of such Code (whether or not the offense is also described in another provision of law) is based solely on a mailing to the Internal Revenue Service, and prosecution is begun in a judicial district other than the judicial district in which the defendant resides, he may upon motion filed in the district in which the prosecution is begun, elect to be tried in the district in which he was residing at the time the alleged offense was committed: Provided, That the motion is filed within twenty days after arraignment of the defendant upon indictment or information.
(June 25, 1948, ch. 645, 62 Stat. 826; Pub. L. 85–595, Aug. 6, 1958, 72 Stat. 512; Pub. L. 89–713, §2, Nov. 2, 1966, 80 Stat. 1108; Pub. L. 98–369, div. A, title I, §162, July 18, 1984, 98 Stat. 697; Pub. L. 98–473, title II, §1204(a), Oct. 12, 1984, 98 Stat. 2152; Pub. L. 99–514, §2, Oct. 22, 1986, 100 Stat. 2095.)

Historical and Revision Notes

Based on section 103 of title 28, U.S.C., 1940 ed., Judicial Code and Judiciary (Mar. 3, 1911, ch. 231, §42, 36 Stat. 1100).

Section was completely rewritten to clarify legislative intent and in order to omit special venue provisions from many sections.

The phrase "committed in more than one district" may be comprehensive enough to include "begun in one district and completed in another", but the use of both expressions precludes any doubt as to legislative intent.

Rules 18–22 of the Federal Rules of Criminal Procedure are in accord with this section.

The last paragraph of the revised section was added to meet the situation created by the decision of the Supreme Court of the United States in United States v. Johnson, 1944, 65 S. Ct. 249, 89 L. Ed. 236, which turned on the absence of a special venue provision in the Dentures Act, section 1821 of this revision. The revised section removes all doubt as to the venue of continuing offenses and makes unnecessary special venue provisions except in cases where Congress desires to restrict the prosecution of offenses to particular districts as in section 1073 of this revision.

References in Text

Section 7203 of the Internal Revenue Code of 1986, referred to in subsec. (b), is classified to section 7203 of Title 26, Internal Revenue Code.

Section 7201 or 7206(1), (2), or (5) of such Code, referred to in subsec. (b), are classified respectively to sections 7201 and 7206(1), (2), (5) of Title 26.

Amendments

1986—Subsec. (b). Pub. L. 99–514 substituted "Internal Revenue Code of 1986" for "Internal Revenue Code of 1954".

1984—Subsec. (a). Pub. L. 98–473 inserted "or the importation of an object or person into the United States" and ", or imported object or person" in second par.

Subsec. (b). Pub. L. 98–369 substituted "venue for prosecution of an offense" for "an offense involves use of the mails and is an offense" and inserted "is based solely on a mailing to the Internal Revenue Service".

1966—Subsec. (b). Pub. L. 89–713 inserted reference to offenses described in section 7203 of the Internal Revenue Code of 1954.

1958—Pub. L. 85–595 designated existing provisions as subsec. (a) and added subsec. (b).

Effective Date of 1966 Amendment

Amendment by Pub. L. 89–713 effective Nov. 2, 1966, see section 6 of Pub. L. 89–713, set out as a note under section 6091 of Title 26, Internal Revenue Code.

§3238. Offenses not committed in any district

The trial of all offenses begun or committed upon the high seas, or elsewhere out of the jurisdiction of any particular State or district, shall be in the district in which the offender, or any one of two or more joint offenders, is arrested or is first brought; but if such offender or offenders are not so arrested or brought into any district, an indictment or information may be filed in the district of the last known residence of the offender or of any one of two or more joint offenders, or if no such residence is known the indictment or information may be filed in the District of Columbia.

(June 25, 1948, ch. 645, 62 Stat. 826; Pub. L. 88–27, May 23, 1963, 77 Stat. 48.)

Historical and Revision Notes

Based on section 102 of title 28, U.S.C., 1940 ed., Judicial Code and Judiciary (Mar. 3, 1911, ch.

231, §41, 36 Stat. 1100).

Words "begun or" were inserted to clarify scope of this section and section 3237 of this title. This section is similar to section 219 of title 22, U.S.C., 1940 ed., Foreign Relations and Intercourse, providing in part that unlawful issuance of passports may be prosecuted in the district where the offender may be arrested or in custody. Said provision is therefore omitted as covered by this section. The remaining provisions of said section 219 are incorporated in section 1541 of this title.

Amendments

1963—Pub. L. 88–27 authorized the trial of offenses not committed in any district in the district in which the offender, or any one of two or more joint offenders, is arrested; an indictment or information to be filed in the district of the last known residence of the offender or of any one of two or more joint offenders where the offender or offenders are not arrested or brought into any district; and an indictment or information to be filed in the District of Columbia where there is no knowledge of the residence of the offender or of any one of two or more joint offenders.

§3239. Optional venue for espionage and related offenses

The trial for any offense involving a violation, begun or committed upon the high seas or elsewhere out of the jurisdiction of any particular State or district, of—

(1) section 793, 794, 798, or section 1030(a)(1) of this title;

(2) section 601 of the National Security Act of 1947 (50 U.S.C. 421); 1 or

(3) section 4(b) or 4(c) of the Subversive Activities Control Act of 1950 (50 U.S.C. 783(b) or (c));

may be in the District of Columbia or in any other district authorized by law.

(Added Pub. L. 103–322, title XXXII, §320909(a), Sept. 13, 1994, 108 Stat. 2127.)

References in Text

The National Security Act of 1947, referred to in par. (2), is act July 26, 1947, ch. 343, 61 Stat. 495, which was formerly classified principally to chapter 15 (§401 et seq.) of Title 50, War and National Defense, prior to editorial reclassification in chapter 44 (§3001 et seq.) of Title 50. Section 601 of this Act is now classified to section 3121 of Title 50. For complete classification of this Act to the Code, see Tables.

Prior Provisions

A prior section 3239, act June 25, 1948, ch. 645, 62 Stat. 827, related to threatening communications, prior to repeal by Pub. L. 98–473, title II, §1204(b), Oct. 12, 1984, 98 Stat. 2152.

§3240. Creation of new district or division

Whenever any new district or division is established, or any county or territory is transferred from one district or division to another district or division, prosecutions for offenses committed within such district, division, county, or territory prior to such transfer, shall be commenced and proceeded with the same as if such new district or division had not been created, or such county or territory had not been transferred, unless the court, upon the application of the defendant, shall order the case to be removed to the new district or division for trial.

(June 25, 1948, ch. 645, 62 Stat. 827; May 24, 1949, ch. 139, §50, 63 Stat. 96.)

Historical and Revision Notes

1948 Act

Based on section 121 of title 28, U.S.C., 1940 ed., Judicial Code and Judiciary (Mar. 3, 1911, ch. 231, §59, 36 Stat. 1103).

Section 121 of title 28, U.S.C., 1940 ed., Judicial Code and Judiciary, was divided into two sections. Only the portion relating to venue in civil cases was left in title 28, U.S.C., 1940 ed., Judicial Code and Judiciary.

Minor changes of phraseology were made.

1949 Act

This section [section 50] strikes the second sentence of section 3240 of title 18, U.S.C., as unnecessary. Section "119" of title 28, U.S.C., referred to in such sentence, became section 1404 of title 28 upon its revision and enactment into positive law in 1948, but reference to the latter, in said section 3240 of title 18, U.S.C., is surplusage in view of rule 19 et seq. of the Federal Rules of Criminal Procedure and the remainder of such section 3240.

Amendments

1949—Act May 24, 1949, struck out "The transfer of such prosecutions shall be made in the manner provided in section 119 of Title 28".

§3241. Jurisdiction of offenses under certain sections

The District Court of the Virgin Islands shall have jurisdiction of offenses under the laws of the United States, not locally inapplicable, committed within the territorial jurisdiction of such courts, and jurisdiction, concurrently with the district courts of the United States, of offenses against the laws of the United States committed upon the high seas.

(June 25, 1948, ch. 645, 62 Stat. 827; Pub. L. 85–508, §12(i), July 7, 1958, 72 Stat. 348; Pub. L. 107–273, div. B, title IV, §4004(e), Nov. 2, 2002, 116 Stat. 1812.)

Historical and Revision Notes

Based on title 18, U.S.C., 1940 ed., §§39, 574; sections 23, 101, 1406 of title 48, U.S.C., 1940 ed., Territories and Insular Possessions; section 39 of title 50, U.S.C., 1940 ed., War and National Defense (June 6, 1900, ch. 786, §4, 31 Stat. 322; Aug. 24, 1912, ch. 387, §3, 37 Stat. 512; June 15, 1917, ch. 30, title XIII, §2, 40 Stat. 231; Mar. 2, 1921, ch. 110, 41 Stat. 1203; June 22, 1936, ch. 699, §28, 49 Stat. 1814).

Section consolidates portions of sections 39 and 574 of title 18, U.S.C., 1940 ed., with jurisdictional provisions of sections 23, 101, and 1406 of title 48, U.S.C., 1940 ed., and section 39 of title 50 U.S.C., 1940 ed., with changes of phraseology necessary to effect consolidation.

The revised section simplifies and clarifies the Federal jurisdiction of the district courts of the Territories and Possessions. The enumeration of sections in section 574 of title 18, U.S.C., 1940 ed., was omitted as incomplete and misleading and the general language of the revised section was made applicable to the Canal Zone.

The phrase "the several courts of the first instance in the Philippine Islands" in section 574 of title 18, U.S.C., 1940 ed., was omitted as obsolete in view of the independence of the Commonwealth of the Philippines effective July 4, 1946.

The last sentence of section 574 of title 18, U.S.C., 1940 ed., with reference to the powers of district attorneys was omitted as unnecessary and otherwise covered by sections 403 and 404 of title 22, U.S.C., 1940 ed., Foreign Relations and Intercourse.

Definition of United States in section 39 of title 18, U.S.C., 1940 ed., is incorporated in section 5 of this title.

Amendments

2002—Pub. L. 107–273 struck out "United States District Court for the Canal Zone and the" after "The".

1958—Pub. L. 85–508 struck out provisions which related to the District Court for the Territory of Alaska. See section 81A of Title 28, Judiciary and Judicial Procedure, which establishes a United States District Court for the State of Alaska.

Effective Date of 1958 Amendment

Amendment by Pub. L. 85–508 effective Jan. 3, 1959, on admission of Alaska into the Union pursuant to Proc. No. 3269, Jan. 3, 1959, 24 F.R. 81, 73 Stat. c16, as required by sections 1 and 8(c) of Pub. L. 85–508, see notes set out under section 81A of Title 28, Judiciary and Judicial Procedure, and preceding former section 21 of Title 48, Territories and Insular Possessions.

§3242. Indians committing certain offenses; acts on reservations

All Indians committing any offense listed in the first paragraph of and punishable under section 1153 (relating to offenses committed within Indian country) of this title shall be tried in the same courts and in the same manner as are all other persons committing such offense within the exclusive jurisdiction of the United States.

(June 25, 1948, ch. 645, 62 Stat. 827; May 24, 1949, ch. 139, §51, 63 Stat. 96; Pub. L. 89–707, §2, Nov. 2, 1966, 80 Stat. 1101; Pub. L. 94–297, §4, May 29, 1976, 90 Stat. 586.)

Historical and Revision Notes

1948 Act

Based on title 18, U.S.C., 1940 ed., §548 (Mar. 4, 1909, ch. 321, §328, 35 Stat. 1151; June 1932, ch. 284, 47 Stat. 337).

The provisions defining rape in accordance with the law of the State and prescribing imprisonment at the discretion of the court for rape by an Indian upon an Indian are now included in section 1153 of this title. (See also section 6 of this title.)

Section 549 of said title 18, relating to crimes in Indian reservations in South Dakota, was omitted as covered by section 1153 of this title. Accordingly the last sentence of said section 548, extending this section to prosecutions of Indians in South Dakota, was also omitted as unnecessary because this section is sufficient and applicable. Other provisions of said section 548 are incorporated in sections 1151 and 1153 of this title.

Minor changes were made in phraseology.

1949 Act

This section [section 51] conforms section 3242 of title 18, U.S.C., with sections 1151 and 1153 of such title, thus eliminating inconsistency and ambiguity with respect to the definition of Indian country.

Amendments

1976—Pub. L. 94–297 substituted provision setting out reference to offenses listed in first paragraph of and punishable under section 1153 of this title, for provision specifically enumerating the covered offenses.

1966—Pub. L. 89–707 added carnal knowledge and assault with intent to commit rape as offenses cognizable within the exclusive jurisdiction of the United States when committed on and within the Indian country.

1949—Act May 24, 1949, substituted "within the Indian country" for "within any Indian reservation, including rights-of-way running through the reservation,".

§3243. Jurisdiction of State of Kansas over offenses committed by or against Indians on Indian reservations

Jurisdiction is conferred on the State of Kansas over offenses committed by or against Indians on Indian reservations, including trust or restricted allotments, within the State of Kansas, to the same extent as its courts have jurisdiction over offenses committed elsewhere within the State in accordance with the laws of the State.

This section shall not deprive the courts of the United States of jurisdiction over offenses defined by the laws of the United States committed by or against Indians on Indian reservations. (June 25, 1948, ch. 645, 62 Stat. 827.)

Historical and Revision Notes

Based on section 217a of title 25, U.S.C., 1940 ed., Indians (June 8, 1940, ch. 276, 54 Stat. 249). The attention of Congress is directed to consideration of the question whether this section should be broadened and made applicable to all states rather than only to Kansas. Such change was not regarded as within the scope of this revision.

Changes were made in phraseology.

§3244. Jurisdiction of proceedings relating to transferred offenders

When a treaty is in effect between the United States and a foreign country providing for the transfer of convicted offenders—

(1) the country in which the offender was convicted shall have exclusive jurisdiction and competence over proceedings seeking to challenge, modify, or set aside convictions or sentences handed down by a court of such country;

(2) all proceedings instituted by or on behalf of an offender transferred from the United States to a foreign country seeking to challenge, modify, or set aside the conviction or sentence upon which the transfer was based shall be brought in the court which would have jurisdiction and competence if the offender had not been transferred;

(3) all proceedings instituted by or on behalf of an offender transferred to the United States pertaining to the manner of execution in the United States of the sentence imposed by a foreign court shall be brought in the United States district court for the district in which the offender is confined or in which supervision is exercised and shall name the Attorney General and the official having immediate custody or exercising immediate supervision of the offender as respondents. The Attorney General shall defend against such proceedings;

(4) all proceedings instituted by or on behalf of an offender seeking to challenge the validity or legality of the offender's transfer from the United States shall be brought in the United States district court of the district in which the proceedings to determine the validity of the offender's consent were held and shall name the Attorney General as respondent; and

(5) all proceedings instituted by or on behalf of an offender seeking to challenge the validity or legality of the offender's transfer to the United States shall be brought in the United States district court of the district in which the offender is confined or of the district in which supervision is exercised and shall name the Attorney General and the official having immediate custody or exercising immediate supervision of the offender as respondents. The Attorney General shall defend against such proceedings.

(Added Pub. L. 95–144, §3, Oct. 28, 1977, 91 Stat. 1220, title 28, §2256; renumbered Pub. L. 95–598, title III, §314(j)(1), Nov. 6, 1978, 92 Stat. 2677.)

Codification

Section was formerly classified to section 2256 of Title 28, Judiciary and Judicial Procedure.

Savings Provision

Amendment by section 314 of Pub. L. 95–598 not to affect the application of chapter 9 (§151 et seq.), chapter 96 (§1961 et seq.), or section 2516, 3057, or 3284 of this title to any act of any person (1) committed before Oct. 1, 1979, or (2) committed after Oct. 1, 1979, in connection with a case commenced before such date, see section 403(d) of Pub. L. 95–598, set out as a note preceding section 101 of Title 11, Bankruptcy.

CHAPTER 212 - MILITARY EXTRATERRITORIAL JURISDICTION

§3261. Criminal offenses committed by certain members of the Armed Forces and by persons employed by or accompanying the Armed Forces outside the United States

(a) Whoever engages in conduct outside the United States that would constitute an offense punishable by imprisonment for more than 1 year if the conduct had been engaged in within the special maritime and territorial jurisdiction of the United States—

(1) while employed by or accompanying the Armed Forces outside the United States; or

(2) while a member of the Armed Forces subject to chapter 47 of title 10 (the Uniform Code of Military Justice),

shall be punished as provided for that offense.

(b) No prosecution may be commenced against a person under this section if a foreign government, in accordance with jurisdiction recognized by the United States, has prosecuted or is prosecuting such person for the conduct constituting such offense, except upon the approval of the Attorney General or the Deputy Attorney General (or a person acting in either such capacity), which function of approval may not be delegated.

(c) Nothing in this chapter may be construed to deprive a court-martial, military commission, provost court, or other military tribunal of concurrent jurisdiction with respect to offenders or offenses that by statute or by the law of war may be tried by a court-martial, military commission, provost court, or other military tribunal.

(d) No prosecution may be commenced against a member of the Armed Forces subject to chapter 47 of title 10 (the Uniform Code of Military Justice) under this section unless—

(1) such member ceases to be subject to such chapter; or

(2) an indictment or information charges that the member committed the offense with one or more other defendants, at least one of whom is not subject to such chapter.

(Added Pub. L. 106–523, §2(a), Nov. 22, 2000, 114 Stat. 2488.)

Short Title of 2000 Amendment

Pub. L. 106–523, §1, Nov. 22, 2000, 114 Stat. 2488, provided that: "This Act [enacting this chapter] may be cited as the 'Military Extraterritorial Jurisdiction Act of 2000'."

§3262. Arrest and commitment

(a) The Secretary of Defense may designate and authorize any person serving in a law enforcement position in the Department of Defense to arrest, in accordance with applicable international agreements, outside the United States any person described in section 3261(a) if there is probable cause to believe that such person violated section 3261(a).

(b) Except as provided in sections 3263 and 3264, a person arrested under subsection (a) shall be delivered as soon as practicable to the custody of civilian law enforcement authorities of the United States for removal to the United States for judicial proceedings in relation to conduct

referred to in such subsection unless such person has had charges brought against him or her under chapter 47 of title 10 for such conduct.
(Added Pub. L. 106–523, §2(a), Nov. 22, 2000, 114 Stat. 2489.)

§3263. Delivery to authorities of foreign countries

(a) Any person designated and authorized under section 3262(a) may deliver a person described in section 3261(a) to the appropriate authorities of a foreign country in which such person is alleged to have violated section 3261(a) if—

(1) appropriate authorities of that country request the delivery of the person to such country for trial for such conduct as an offense under the laws of that country; and

(2) the delivery of such person to that country is authorized by a treaty or other international agreement to which the United States is a party.

(b) The Secretary of Defense, in consultation with the Secretary of State, shall determine which officials of a foreign country constitute appropriate authorities for purposes of this section.
(Added Pub. L. 106–523, §2(a), Nov. 22, 2000, 114 Stat. 2489.)

§3264. Limitation on removal

(a) Except as provided in subsection (b), and except for a person delivered to authorities of a foreign country under section 3263, a person arrested for or charged with a violation of section 3261(a) shall not be removed—

(1) to the United States; or

(2) to any foreign country other than a country in which such person is believed to have violated section 3261(a).

(b) The limitation in subsection (a) does not apply if—

(1) a Federal magistrate judge orders the person to be removed to the United States to be present at a detention hearing held pursuant to section 3142(f);

(2) a Federal magistrate judge orders the detention of the person before trial pursuant to section 3142(e), in which case the person shall be promptly removed to the United States for purposes of such detention;

(3) the person is entitled to, and does not waive, a preliminary examination under the Federal Rules of Criminal Procedure, in which case the person shall be removed to the United States in time for such examination;

(4) a Federal magistrate judge otherwise orders the person to be removed to the United States; or

(5) the Secretary of Defense determines that military necessity requires that the limitations in subsection (a) be waived, in which case the person shall be removed to the nearest United States military installation outside the United States adequate to detain the person and to facilitate the initial appearance described in section 3265(a).
(Added Pub. L. 106–523, §2(a), Nov. 22, 2000, 114 Stat. 2489.)

References in Text

The Federal Rules of Criminal Procedure, referred to in subsec. (b)(3), are set out in the Appendix to this title.

§3265. Initial proceedings

(a)(1) In the case of any person arrested for or charged with a violation of section 3261(a) who is not delivered to authorities of a foreign country under section 3263, the initial appearance of that person under the Federal Rules of Criminal Procedure—

(A) shall be conducted by a Federal magistrate judge; and

(B) may be carried out by telephony or such other means that enables voice communication among the participants, including any counsel representing the person.

(2) In conducting the initial appearance, the Federal magistrate judge shall also determine whether there is probable cause to believe that an offense under section 3261(a) was committed and that

the person committed it.

(3) If the Federal magistrate judge determines that probable cause exists that the person committed an offense under section 3261(a), and if no motion is made seeking the person's detention before trial, the Federal magistrate judge shall also determine at the initial appearance the conditions of the person's release before trial under chapter 207 of this title.

(b) In the case of any person described in subsection (a), any detention hearing of that person under section 3142(f)—

(1) shall be conducted by a Federal magistrate judge; and

(2) at the request of the person, may be carried out by telephony or such other means that enables voice communication among the participants, including any counsel representing the person.

(c)(1) If any initial proceeding under this section with respect to any such person is conducted while the person is outside the United States, and the person is entitled to have counsel appointed for purposes of such proceeding, the Federal magistrate judge may appoint as such counsel for purposes of such hearing a qualified military counsel.

(2) For purposes of this subsection, the term "qualified military counsel" means a judge advocate made available by the Secretary of Defense for purposes of such proceedings, who—

(A) is a graduate of an accredited law school or is a member of the bar of a Federal court or of the highest court of a State; and

(B) is certified as competent to perform such duties by the Judge Advocate General of the armed force of which he is a member.

(Added Pub. L. 106–523, §2(a), Nov. 22, 2000, 114 Stat. 2490.)

References in Text

The Federal Rules of Criminal Procedure, referred to in subsec. (a)(1), are set out in the Appendix to this title.

§3266. Regulations

(a) The Secretary of Defense, after consultation with the Secretary of State and the Attorney General, shall prescribe regulations governing the apprehension, detention, delivery, and removal of persons under this chapter and the facilitation of proceedings under section 3265. Such regulations shall be uniform throughout the Department of Defense.

(b)(1) The Secretary of Defense, after consultation with the Secretary of State and the Attorney General, shall prescribe regulations requiring that, to the maximum extent practicable, notice shall be provided to any person employed by or accompanying the Armed Forces outside the United States who is not a national of the United States that such person is potentially subject to the criminal jurisdiction of the United States under this chapter.

(2) A failure to provide notice in accordance with the regulations prescribed under paragraph (1) shall not defeat the jurisdiction of a court of the United States or provide a defense in any judicial proceeding arising under this chapter.

(c) The regulations prescribed under this section, and any amendments to those regulations, shall not take effect before the date that is 90 days after the date on which the Secretary of Defense submits a report containing those regulations or amendments (as the case may be) to the Committee on the Judiciary of the House of Representatives and the Committee on the Judiciary of the Senate.

(Added Pub. L. 106–523, §2(a), Nov. 22, 2000, 114 Stat. 2491.)

§3267. Definitions

As used in this chapter:

(1) The term "employed by the Armed Forces outside the United States" means—

(A) employed as—

(i) a civilian employee of—

(I) the Department of Defense (including a nonappropriated fund instrumentality of the

Department); or

(II) any other Federal agency, or any provisional authority, to the extent such employment relates to supporting the mission of the Department of Defense overseas;

(ii) a contractor (including a subcontractor at any tier) of—

(I) the Department of Defense (including a nonappropriated fund instrumentality of the Department); or

(II) any other Federal agency, or any provisional authority, to the extent such employment relates to supporting the mission of the Department of Defense overseas; or

(iii) an employee of a contractor (or subcontractor at any tier) of—

(I) the Department of Defense (including a nonappropriated fund instrumentality of the Department); or

(II) any other Federal agency, or any provisional authority, to the extent such employment relates to supporting the mission of the Department of Defense overseas;

(B) present or residing outside the United States in connection with such employment; and

(C) not a national of or ordinarily resident in the host nation.

(2) The term "accompanying the Armed Forces outside the United States" means—

(A) a dependent of—

(i) a member of the Armed Forces;

(ii) a civilian employee of the Department of Defense (including a nonappropriated fund instrumentality of the Department); or

(iii) a Department of Defense contractor (including a subcontractor at any tier) or an employee of a Department of Defense contractor (including a subcontractor at any tier);

(B) residing with such member, civilian employee, contractor, or contractor employee outside the United States; and

(C) not a national of or ordinarily resident in the host nation.

(3) The term "Armed Forces" has the meaning given the term "armed forces" in section 101(a)(4) of title 10.

(4) The terms "Judge Advocate General" and "judge advocate" have the meanings given such terms in section 801 of title 10.

(Added Pub. L. 106–523, §2(a), Nov. 22, 2000, 114 Stat. 2491; amended Pub. L. 108–375, div. A, title X, §1088, Oct. 28, 2004, 118 Stat. 2066.)

Amendments

2004—Par. (1)(A). Pub. L. 108–375 amended subpar. (A) generally. Prior to amendment, subpar. (A) read as follows: "employed as a civilian employee of the Department of Defense (including a nonappropriated fund instrumentality of the Department), as a Department of Defense contractor (including a subcontractor at any tier), or as an employee of a Department of Defense contractor (including a subcontractor at any tier);".

CHAPTER 212A - EXTRATERRITORIAL JURISDICTION OVER CERTAIN OFFENSES

Amendments

2016—Pub. L. 114–316, §2(a)(1), (b)(2), Dec. 16, 2016, 130 Stat. 1593, 1594, struck out

"TRAFFICKING IN PERSONS" before "OFFENSES" in chapter heading and added item 3273.

§3271. Trafficking in persons offenses committed by persons employed by or accompanying the Federal Government outside the United States

(a) Whoever, while employed by or accompanying the Federal Government outside the United States, engages in conduct outside the United States that would constitute an offense under chapter 77 or 117 of this title if the conduct had been engaged in within the United States or within the special maritime and territorial jurisdiction of the United States shall be punished as provided for that offense.

(b) No prosecution may be commenced against a person under this section if a foreign government, in accordance with jurisdiction recognized by the United States, has prosecuted or is prosecuting such person for the conduct constituting such offense, except upon the approval of the Attorney General or the Deputy Attorney General (or a person acting in either such capacity), which function of approval may not be delegated.

(Added Pub. L. 109–164, title I, §103(a)(1), Jan. 10, 2006, 119 Stat. 3562.)

§3272. Definitions

As used in this chapter:

(1) The term "employed by the Federal Government outside the United States" means—

(A) employed as a civilian employee of the Federal Government, as a Federal contractor (including a subcontractor at any tier), or as an employee of a Federal contractor (including a subcontractor at any tier);

(B) present or residing outside the United States in connection with such employment; and

(C) not a national of or ordinarily resident in the host nation.

(2) The term "accompanying the Federal Government outside the United States" means—

(A) a dependant of—

(i) a civilian employee of the Federal Government; or

(ii) a Federal contractor (including a subcontractor at any tier) or an employee of a Federal contractor (including a subcontractor at any tier);

(B) residing with such civilian employee, contractor, or contractor employee outside the United States; and

(C) not a national of or ordinarily resident in the host nation.

(Added Pub. L. 109–164, title I, §103(a)(1), Jan. 10, 2006, 119 Stat. 3562.)

§3273. Offenses committed by certain United States personnel stationed in Canada in furtherance of border security initiatives

(a) In General.—Whoever, while employed by the Department of Homeland Security or the Department of Justice and stationed or deployed in Canada pursuant to a treaty, executive agreement, or bilateral memorandum in furtherance of a border security initiative, engages in conduct (or conspires or attempts to engage in conduct) in Canada that would constitute an offense for which a person may be prosecuted in a court of the United States had the conduct been engaged in within the United States or within the special maritime and territorial jurisdiction of the United States shall be fined or imprisoned, or both, as provided for that offense.

(b) Definition.—In this section, the term "employed by the Department of Homeland Security or the Department of Justice" means—

(1) being employed as a civilian employee, a contractor (including a subcontractor at any tier), or an employee of a contractor (or a subcontractor at any tier) of the Department of Homeland Security or the Department of Justice;

(2) being present or residing in Canada in connection with such employment; and

(3) not being a national of or ordinarily resident in Canada.

(Added Pub. L. 114–316, §2(a)(2), Dec. 16, 2016, 130 Stat. 1593.)

Rule of Construction

Pub. L. 114–316, §2(c), Dec. 16, 2016, 130 Stat. 1594, provided that: "Nothing in this section [enacting this section] or the amendments made by this section shall be construed to infringe upon or otherwise affect the exercise of prosecutorial discretion by the Department of Justice in implementing this section and the amendments made by this section."

CHAPTER 213 - LIMITATIONS

Amendments

2010—Pub. L. 111–203, title X, §1079A(b)(2), July 21, 2010, 124 Stat. 2079, added item 3301.

2008—Pub. L. 110–340, §2(a)(3)(B), Oct. 3, 2008, 122 Stat. 3736, added item 3300.

2006—Pub. L. 109–248, title II, §211(2), July 27, 2006, 120 Stat. 616, added item 3299.

Pub. L. 109–162, title XI, §1182(b), Jan. 5, 2006, 119 Stat. 3126, added item 3298.

2004—Pub. L. 108–405, title II, §204(b), Oct. 30, 2004, 118 Stat. 2271, added item 3297.

2002—Pub. L. 107–273, div. B, title III, §3003(b), Nov. 2, 2002, 116 Stat. 1805, added item 3296.

1996—Pub. L. 104–132, title VII, §708(c)(2), Apr. 24, 1996, 110 Stat. 1297, added item 3295.

1994—Pub. L. 103–322, title XII, §120001(c), title XXXII, §320902(d)(2), title XXXIII, §330018(c), Sept. 13, 1994, 108 Stat. 2021, 2124, 2149, substituted "Child abuse offenses" for "Customs and slave trade violations" in item 3283 and added items 3286 and 3294.

1990—Pub. L. 101–647, title XII, §1207(b), Nov. 29, 1990, 104 Stat. 4832, struck out item 3286 "Seduction on vessel of United States".

1989—Pub. L. 101–73, title IX, §961(l)(2), Aug. 9, 1989, 103 Stat. 501, added item 3293.

1988—Pub. L. 100–690, title VII, §7081(c), Nov. 18, 1988, 102 Stat. 4407, substituted "Indictments and information dismissed after period of limitations" for "Reindictment where defect found after period of limitations" in item 3288 and "Indictments and information dismissed before period of limitations" for "Reindictment where defect found before period of limitations" in item 3289.

1984—Pub. L. 98–473, title II, §1218(b), Oct. 12, 1984, 98 Stat. 2167, added item 3292.

1951—Act June 30, 1951, ch. 194, §2, 65 Stat. 107, added item 3291.

§3281. Capital offenses

An indictment for any offense punishable by death may be found at any time without limitation. (June 25, 1948, ch. 645, 62 Stat. 827; Pub. L. 103–322, title XXXIII, §330004(16), Sept. 13, 1994, 108 Stat. 2142.)

Historical and Revision Notes

Based on title 18, U.S.C., 1940 ed., §§581a, 581b (Aug. 4, 1939, ch. 419, §§1, 2, 53 Stat. 1198). Sections 581a and 581b of title 18, U.S.C., 1940 ed., were consolidated into this section without change of substance.

Amendments

1994—Pub. L. 103–322 struck out before period at end "except for offenses barred by the provisions of law existing on August 4, 1939".

§3282. Offenses not capital

(a) In General.—Except as otherwise expressly provided by law, no person shall be prosecuted, tried, or punished for any offense, not capital, unless the indictment is found or the information is instituted within five years next after such offense shall have been committed.

(b) DNA Profile Indictment.—

(1) In general.—In any indictment for an offense under chapter 109A for which the identity of the accused is unknown, it shall be sufficient to describe the accused as an individual whose name is unknown, but who has a particular DNA profile.

(2) Exception.—Any indictment described under paragraph (1), which is found not later than 5 years after the offense under chapter 109A is committed, shall not be subject to—

(A) the limitations period described under subsection (a); and

(B) the provisions of chapter 208 until the individual is arrested or served with a summons in connection with the charges contained in the indictment.

(3) Defined term.—For purposes of this subsection, the term "DNA profile" means a set of DNA identification characteristics.

(June 25, 1948, ch. 645, 62 Stat. 828; Sept. 1, 1954, ch. 1214, §12(a), formerly §10(a), 68 Stat. 1145; renumbered Pub. L. 87–299, §1, Sept. 26, 1961, 75 Stat. 648; Pub. L. 108–21, title VI, §610(a), Apr. 30, 2003, 117 Stat. 692.)

Historical and Revision Notes

Based on section 746(g) of title 8, U.S.C., 1940 ed., Aliens and Nationality, and on title 18, U.S.C., 1940 ed., §582 (R.S. §1044; Apr. 13, 1876, ch. 56, 19 Stat. 32; Nov. 17, 1921, ch. 124, §1, 42 Stat. 220; Dec. 27, 1927, ch. 6, 45 Stat. 51; Oct. 14, 1940, ch. 876, title I, subchap. III, §346(g), 54 Stat. 1167).

Section 582 of title 18, U.S.C., 1940 ed., and section 746(g) of title 8, U.S.C., 1940 ed., Aliens and Nationality, were consolidated. "Except as otherwise expressly provided by law" was inserted to avoid enumeration of exceptive provisions.

The proviso contained in the act of 1927 "That nothing herein contained shall apply to any offense for which an indictment has been heretofore found or an information instituted, or to any proceedings under any such indictment or information," was omitted as no longer necessary.

In the consolidation of these sections the 5-year period of limitation for violations of the Nationality Code, provided for in said section 746(g) of title 8, U.S.C., 1940 ed., Aliens and Nationality, is reduced to 3 years. There seemed no sound basis for considering 3 years adequate in the case of heinous felonies and gross frauds against the United States but inadequate for misuse of a passport or false statement to a naturalization examiner.

Amendments

2003—Pub. L. 108–21 designated existing provisions as subsec. (a), inserted heading, and added subsec. (b).

1954—Act Sept. 1, 1954, changed the limitation period from three years to five years.

Effective Date of 1954 Amendment

Act Sept. 1, 1954, ch. 1214, §12(b), formerly section 10(b), 68 Stat. 1145, as renumbered by Pub. L. 87–299, §1, Sept. 26, 1961, 75 Stat. 648, provided that: "The amendment made by subsection (a) [amending this section] shall be effective with respect to offenses (1) committed on or after September 1, 1954, or (2) committed prior to such date, if on such date prosecution therefor is not barred by provisions of law in effect prior to such date."

Fugitives From Justice

Statutes of limitations as not extending to persons fleeing from justice, see section 3290 of this title.

Offenses Against Internal Security

Limitation period in connection with offenses against internal security, see section 783 of Title 50, War and National Defense.

Sections 792, 793, and 794 of This Title; Limitation Period

Limitation period in connection with sections 792, 793, and 794 of this title, see note set out under section 792.

§3283. Offenses against children

No statute of limitations that would otherwise preclude prosecution for an offense involving the sexual or physical abuse, or kidnaping, of a child under the age of 18 years shall preclude such prosecution during the life of the child, or for ten years after the offense, whichever is longer.

(June 25, 1948, ch. 645, 62 Stat. 828; Pub. L. 103–322, title XXXIII, §330018(a), Sept. 13, 1994, 108 Stat. 2149; Pub. L. 108–21, title II, §202, Apr. 30, 2003, 117 Stat. 660; Pub. L. 109–162, title XI, §1182(c), Jan. 5, 2006, 119 Stat. 3126.)

Historical and Revision Notes

Based on title 18, U.S.C., 1940 ed., §584 (R.S. §1046; July 5, 1884, ch. 225, §2, 23 Stat. 122). Words "customs laws" were substituted for "revenue laws," since different limitations are provided for internal revenue violations by section 3748 of title 26, U.S.C., 1940 ed., Internal Revenue Code.

This section was held to apply to offenses under the customs laws. Those offenses are within the term "revenue laws" but not within the term "internal revenue laws". United States v. Hirsch (1879, 100 U.S. 33, 25 L. Ed. 539), United States v. Shorey (1869, Fed. Cas. No. 16,282), and United States v. Platt (1840, Fed. Cas. No. 16,054a) applied this section in customs cases. Hence it appears that there was no proper basis for the complete elimination from section 584 of title 18, U.S.C., 1940 ed., of the reference to revenue laws.

Meaning of "revenue laws". United States v. Norton (1876, 91 U.S. 566, 23 L.Ed. 454), quoting Webster that "revenue" refers to "The income of a nation, derived from its taxes, duties, or other sources, for the payment of the national expenses." Quoting United States v. Mayo (1813, Fed. Cas. No. 15,755) that "revenue laws" meant such laws "as are made for the direct and avowed purpose of creating revenue or public funds for the service of the Government."

Definition of revenue. "Revenue" is the income of a State, and the revenue of the Post Office Department, being raised by a tax on mailable matter conveyed in the mail, and which is disbursed in the public service, is as much a part of the income of the government as moneys collected for duties on imports (United States v. Bromley, 53 U.S. 88, 99, 13 L. Ed. 905).

"Revenue" is the product or fruit of taxation. It matters not in what form the power of taxation may be exercised or to what subjects it may be applied, its exercise is intended to provide means for the support of the Government, and the means provided are necessarily to be regarded as the internal revenue. Duties upon imports are imposed for the same general object and, because they are so imposed, the money thus produced is considered revenue, not because it is derived from any particular source (United States v. Wright, 1870, Fed. Cas. No. 16,770).

"Revenue law" is defined as a law for direct object of imposing and collecting taxes, dues, imports, and excises for government and its purposes (In re Mendenhall, D.C. Mont. 1935, 10 F. Supp. 122).

Act Cong. March 2, 1799, ch. 22, 1 Stat. 627, regulating the collection of duties on imports, is a revenue law, within the meaning of act Cong. April 18, 1818, ch. 70, 3 Stat. 433, providing for the mode of suing for and recovering penalties and forfeitures for violations of the revenue laws of the United States (The Abigail, 1824, Fed. Cas. No. 18).

Changes were made in phraseology.

Amendments

2006—Pub. L. 109–162 inserted ", or for ten years after the offense, whichever is longer" after "of the child".

2003—Pub. L. 108–21 substituted "Offenses against children" for "Child abuse offenses" in section catchline and amended text generally. Prior to amendment, text read as follows: "No statute of limitations that would otherwise preclude prosecution for an offense involving the sexual or physical abuse of a child under the age of 18 years shall preclude such prosecution before the child reaches the age of 25 years."

1994—Pub. L. 103–322 substituted "Child abuse offenses" for "Customs and slave trade violations" as section catchline and amended text generally. Prior to amendment, text read as follows: "No person shall be prosecuted, tried or punished for any violation of the customs laws or the slave trade laws of the United States unless the indictment is found or the information is instituted within five years next after the commission of the offense."

§3284. Concealment of bankrupt's assets

The concealment of assets of a debtor in a case under title 11 shall be deemed to be a continuing offense until the debtor shall have been finally discharged or a discharge denied, and the period of limitations shall not begin to run until such final discharge or denial of discharge.

(June 25, 1948, ch. 645, 62 Stat. 828; Pub. L. 95–598, title III, §314(k), Nov. 6, 1978, 92 Stat. 2678.)

Historical and Revision Notes

Based on section 52(d) of title 11, U.S.C., 1940 ed., Bankruptcy (May 27, 1926, ch. 406, §11d, 44 Stat. 665; June 22, 1938, ch. 575, §1, 52 Stat. 856).

The 3-year-limitation provision was omitted as unnecessary in view of the general statute, section 3282 of this title.

The words "or a discharge denied" and "or denial of discharge" were added on the recommendation of the Department of Justice to supply an omission in existing law.

Other subsections of said section 52 of title 11, U.S.C., 1940 ed., are incorporated in sections 151–154 and 3057 of this title.

Other minor changes of phraseology were made.

Amendments

1978—Pub. L. 95–598 substituted "debtor in a case under title 11" for "bankrupt or other debtor".

Effective Date of 1978 Amendment

Amendment by Pub. L. 95–598 effective Oct. 1, 1979, see section 402(a) of Pub. L. 95–598, set out as an Effective Date note preceding section 101 of Title 11, Bankruptcy.

Savings Provision

Amendment by section 314 of Pub. L. 95–598 not to affect the application of chapter 9 (§151 et seq.), chapter 96 (§1961 et seq.), or section 2516, 3057, or 3284 of this title to any act of any person (1) committed before Oct. 1, 1979, or (2) committed after Oct. 1, 1979, in connection with a case commenced before such date, see section 403(d) of Pub. L. 95–598, set out as a note preceding section 101 of Title 11, Bankruptcy.

§3285. Criminal contempt

No proceeding for criminal contempt within section 402 of this title shall be instituted against any person, corporation or association unless begun within one year from the date of the act complained of; nor shall any such proceeding be a bar to any criminal prosecution for the same act.

(June 25, 1948, ch. 645, 62 Stat. 828.)

Historical and Revision Notes

Based on section 390 of title 28, U.S.C., 1940 ed., Judicial Code and Judiciary (Oct. 15, 1914, ch. 323, §25, 38 Stat. 740).

Word "criminal" was inserted before "contempt" in first line. Words "within section 402 of this title" were inserted after "contempt".

The correct meaning and narrow application of title 28, U.S.C., 1940 ed., §390, are preserved, as section 389 of that title is incorporated in sections 402 and 3691 of this title.

Words "corporation or association" were inserted after "person", thus embodying applicable definition of section 390a of title 28, U.S.C., 1940 ed. (See reviser's note under section 402 of this title.)

§3286. Extension of statute of limitation for certain terrorism offenses

(a) Eight-Year Limitation.—Notwithstanding section 3282, no person shall be prosecuted, tried, or punished for any noncapital offense involving a violation of any provision listed in section 2332b(g)(5)(B), or a violation of section 112, 351(e), 1361, or 1751(e) of this title, or section 46504, 46505, or 46506 of title 49, unless the indictment is found or the information is instituted within 8 years after the offense was committed. Notwithstanding the preceding sentence, offenses listed in section 3295 are subject to the statute of limitations set forth in that section.

(b) No Limitation.—Notwithstanding any other law, an indictment may be found or an information instituted at any time without limitation for any offense listed in section 2332b(g)(5)(B), if the commission of such offense resulted in, or created a forseeable 1 risk of, death or serious bodily injury to another person.

(Added Pub. L. 103–322, title XII, §120001(a), Sept. 13, 1994, 108 Stat. 2021; amended Pub. L. 104–132, title VII, §702(c), Apr. 24, 1996, 110 Stat. 1294; Pub. L. 104–294, title VI, §601(b)(1), Oct. 11, 1996, 110 Stat. 3498; Pub. L. 107–56, title VIII, §809(a), Oct. 26, 2001, 115 Stat. 379; Pub. L. 107–273, div. B, title IV, §4002(c)(1), Nov. 2, 2002, 116 Stat. 1808.)

Prior Provisions

A prior section 3286, act June 25, 1948, ch. 645, 62 Stat. 828, related to seduction on vessel of United States, prior to repeal by Pub. L. 101–647, title XII, §1207(b), Nov. 29, 1990, 104 Stat. 4832.

Amendments

2002—Pub. L. 107–273 repealed Pub. L. 104–294, §601(b)(1). See 1996 Amendment note below.

2001—Pub. L. 107–56 reenacted section catchline without change and amended text generally. Text read as follows: "Notwithstanding section 3282, no person shall be prosecuted, tried, or punished for any non-capital offense involving a violation of section 32 (aircraft destruction), section 37 (airport violence), section 112 (assaults upon diplomats), section 351 (crimes against Congressmen or Cabinet officers), section 1116 (crimes against diplomats), section 1203 (hostage taking), section 1361 (willful injury to government property), section 1751 (crimes against the President), section 2280 (maritime violence), section 2281 (maritime platform violence), section 2332 (terrorist acts abroad against United States nationals), section 2332a (use of weapons of mass destruction), 2332b (acts of terrorism transcending national boundaries), or section 2340A (torture) of this title or section 46502, 46504, 46505, or 46506 of title 49, unless the indictment is found or the information is instituted within 8 years after the offense was committed."

1996—Pub. L. 104–132, §702(c)(2)–(4), substituted "2332" for "2331", "2332a" for "2339", and "37" for "36". Pub. L. 104–294, §601(b)(1), which amended section identically, was repealed by Pub. L. 107–273.

Pub. L. 104–132, §702(c)(1), (5), inserted "2332b (acts of terrorism transcending national boundaries)," after "(use of weapons of mass destruction),", and substituted "any non-capital offense" for "any offense".

Effective Date of 2002 Amendment

Pub. L. 107–273, div. B, title IV, §4002(c)(1), Nov. 2, 2002, 116 Stat. 1808, provided that the amendment made by section 4002(c)(1) is effective Oct. 11, 1996.

Effective Date of 2001 Amendment

Pub. L. 107–56, title VIII, §809(b), Oct. 26, 2001, 115 Stat. 380, provided that: "The amendments made by this section [amending this section] shall apply to the prosecution of any offense committed before, on, or after the date of the enactment of this section [Oct. 26, 2001]."

Effective Date

Pub. L. 103–322, title XII, §120001(b), Sept. 13, 1994, 108 Stat. 2021, provided that: "The amendment made by subsection (a) [enacting this section] shall not apply to any offense committed more than 5 years prior to the date of enactment of this Act [Sept. 13, 1994]."

§3287. Wartime suspension of limitations

When the United States is at war or Congress has enacted a specific authorization for the use of the Armed Forces, as described in section 5(b) of the War Powers Resolution (50 U.S.C. 1544(b)), the running of any statute of limitations applicable to any offense (1) involving fraud or attempted fraud against the United States or any agency thereof in any manner, whether by conspiracy or not, or (2) committed in connection with the acquisition, care, handling, custody, control or disposition of any real or personal property of the United States, or (3) committed in connection with the negotiation, procurement, award, performance, payment for, interim financing, cancelation, or other termination or settlement, of any contract, subcontract, or purchase order which is connected with or related to the prosecution of the war or directly connected with or related to the authorized use of the Armed Forces, or with any disposition of termination inventory by any war contractor or Government agency, shall be suspended until 5 years after the termination of hostilities as proclaimed by a Presidential proclamation, with notice to Congress, or by a concurrent resolution of Congress.

Definitions of terms in section 103 1 of title 41 shall apply to similar terms used in this section. For purposes of applying such definitions in this section, the term "war" includes a specific authorization for the use of the Armed Forces, as described in section 5(b) of the War Powers Resolution (50 U.S.C. 1544(b)).

(June 25, 1948, ch. 645, 62 Stat. 828; Pub. L. 110–329, div. C, title VIII, §8117, Sept. 30, 2008, 122 Stat. 3647; Pub. L. 110–417, [div. A], title VIII, §855, Oct. 14, 2008, 122 Stat. 4545; Pub. L.

111–84, div. A, title X, §1073(c)(7), Oct. 28, 2009, 123 Stat. 2475.)

Historical and Revision Notes

Based on title 18, U.S.C., 1940 ed., §590a (Aug. 24, 1942, ch. 555, §1, 56 Stat. 747; July 1, 1944, ch. 358, §19(b), 58 Stat. 667; Oct. 3, 1944, ch. 479, §28, 58 Stat. 781).

The phrase "when the United States is at war" was inserted at the beginning of this section to make it permanent instead of temporary legislation, and to obviate the necessity of reenacting such legislation in the future. This permitted the elimination of references to dates and to the provision limiting the application of the section to transactions not yet fully barred. When the provisions of the War Contract Settlements Act of 1944, upon which this section is based, are considered in connection with said section 590a which it amends, it is obvious that no purpose can be served now by the provisions omitted.

Phrase (2), reading "or committed in connection with the acquisition, care, handling, custody, control or disposition of any real or personal property of the United States" was derived from section 28 of the Surplus Property Act of 1944 which amended said section 590a of title 18, U.S.C., 1940 ed. This act is temporary by its terms and relates only to offenses committed in the disposition of surplus property thereunder.

The revised section extends its provisions to all offenses involving the disposition of any property, real or personal, of the United States. This extension is more apparent than real since phrase (2), added as the result of said Act, was merely a more specific statement of offenses embraced in phrase (1) of this section.

The revised section is written in general terms as permanent legislation applicable whenever the United States is at war. (See, also, reviser's note under section 284 of this title.)

The last paragraph was added to obviate any possibility of doubt as to meaning of terms defined in section 103 of title 41, U.S.C., 1940 ed., Public Contracts.

Changes were made in phraseology.

References in Text

Section 103 of title 41, referred to in text, probably means section 3 of act July 1, 1944, ch. 358, 58 Stat. 650, which was classified to section 103 of former Title 41, Public Contracts, prior to repeal by Pub. L. 111–350, §7(b), Jan. 4, 2011, 124 Stat. 3855. For disposition of sections of former Title 41, see Disposition Table preceding section 101 of Title 41.

Amendments

2009—Pub. L. 111–84 repealed Pub. L. 110–417, §855. See 2008 Amendment note below.

2008—Pub. L. 110–417, §855, which amended this section identically to amendment by Pub. L. 110–329, was repealed by Pub. L. 111–84. See 2008 Amendment note below.

Pub. L. 110–329, in first par., inserted "or Congress has enacted a specific authorization for the use of the Armed Forces, as described in section 5(b) of the War Powers Resolution (50 U.S.C. 1544(b))," after "is at war" and "or directly connected with or related to the authorized use of the Armed Forces" after "prosecution of the war" and substituted "5 years" for "three years" and "proclaimed by a Presidential proclamation, with notice to Congress," for "proclaimed by the President", and, in second par., inserted last sentence.

Effective Date of 2009 Amendment

Pub. L. 111–84, div. A, title X, §1073(c), Oct. 28, 2009, 123 Stat. 2474, provided in part that the amendment made by section 1073(c)(7) of Pub. L. 111–84 is effective as of Oct. 14, 2008, and as if included in Pub. L. 110–417 as enacted.

§3288. Indictments and information dismissed after period of limitations

Whenever an indictment or information charging a felony is dismissed for any reason after the period prescribed by the applicable statute of limitations has expired, a new indictment may be returned in the appropriate jurisdiction within six calendar months of the date of the dismissal of the indictment or information, or, in the event of an appeal, within 60 days of the date the dismissal of the indictment or information becomes final, or, if no regular grand jury is in session in the appropriate jurisdiction when the indictment or information is dismissed, within six calendar months of the date when the next regular grand jury is convened, which new indictment shall not be barred by any statute of limitations. This section does not permit the filing of a new indictment or information where the reason for the dismissal was the failure to file the indictment or information within the period prescribed by the applicable statute of limitations, or some other reason that would bar a new prosecution.

(June 25, 1948, ch. 645, 62 Stat. 828; Pub. L. 88–139, §2, Oct. 16, 1963, 77 Stat. 248; Pub. L. 88–520, §1, Aug. 30, 1964, 78 Stat. 699; Pub. L. 100–690, title VII, §7081(a), Nov. 18, 1988, 102 Stat. 4407.)

Historical and Revision Notes

Based on title 18, U.S.C., 1940 ed., §§556a, 587, 589 (Apr. 30, 1934, ch. 170, §1, 48 Stat. 648; May 10, 1934, ch. 278, §§1, 3, 48 Stat. 772; July 10, 1940, ch. 567, 54 Stat. 747).

This section is a consolidation of sections 556a, 587, and 589 of title 18, U.S.C., 1940 ed., without change of substance. (See reviser's note under section 3289 of this title.)

Amendments

1988—Pub. L. 100–690, in section catchline, substituted "Indictments and information dismissed after period of limitations" for "Indictment where defect found after period of limitations", and in text, substituted "Whenever an indictment or information charging a felony is dismissed for any reason" for "Whenever an indictment is dismissed for any error, defect, or irregularity with respect to the grand jury, or an indictment or information filed after the defendant waives in open court prosecution by indictment is found otherwise defective or insufficient for any cause,", inserted ", or, in the event of an appeal, within 60 days of the date the dismissal of the indictment or information becomes final" after "dismissal of the indictment or information", and inserted provisions which prohibited filing of new indictment or information where reason for dismissal was failure to file within period prescribed or some other reason that would bar a new prosecution.

1964—Pub. L. 88–520 substituted "Indictment" for "Reindictment" in section catchline, included indictments or informations filed after the defendant waives in open court prosecution by indictment which are dismissed for any error, defect, or irregularity, or are otherwise found defective or insufficient, and substituted provisions authorizing the return of a new indictment in the appropriate jurisdiction within six calendar months of the date of the dismissal of the indictment or information, or, if no regular grand jury is in session when the indictment or information is dismissed, within six calendar months of the date when the next grand jury is convened, for provisions which authorized the return of a new indictment not later than the end of the next succeeding regular session of the court, following the session at which the indictment was found defective or insufficient, during which a grand jury shall be in session.

1963—Pub. L. 88–139 substituted "session" for "term" wherever appearing.

§3289. Indictments and information dismissed before period of limitations

Whenever an indictment or information charging a felony is dismissed for any reason before the period prescribed by the applicable statute of limitations has expired, and such period will expire within six calendar months of the date of the dismissal of the indictment or information, a new indictment may be returned in the appropriate jurisdiction within six calendar months of the expiration of the applicable statute of limitations, or, in the event of an appeal, within 60 days of the date the dismissal of the indictment or information becomes final, or, if no regular grand jury is in session in the appropriate jurisdiction at the expiration of the applicable statute of limitations, within six calendar months of the date when the next regular grand jury is convened, which new indictment shall not be barred by any statute of limitations. This section does not permit the filing of a new indictment or information where the reason for the dismissal was the failure to file the indictment or information within the period prescribed by the applicable statute of limitations, or some other reason that would bar a new prosecution.

(June 25, 1948, ch. 645, 62 Stat. 829; Pub. L. 88–139, §2, Oct. 16, 1963, 77 Stat. 248; Pub. L. 88–520, §2, Aug. 30, 1964, 78 Stat. 699; Pub. L. 100–690, title VII, §7081(b), Nov. 18, 1988, 102 Stat. 4407; Pub. L. 101–647, title XII, §1213, title XXV, §2595(b), title XXXV, §3580, Nov. 29, 1990, 104 Stat. 4833, 4907, 4929; Pub. L. 103–322, title XXXIII, §330011(q)(2), Sept. 13, 1994, 108 Stat. 2145.)

Historical and Revision Notes

Based on title 18, U.S.C., 1940 ed., §§556a, 588, 589 (Apr. 30, 1934, ch. 170, §1, 48 Stat. 648; May 10, 1934, ch. 278, §§2, 3, 48 Stat. 772).

Consolidation of sections 556a, 588, and 589 of title 18, U.S.C., 1940 ed., without change of substance. The provisions of said section 556a, with reference to time of filing motion, were omitted and numerous changes of phraseology were necessary to effect consolidation, particularly in view of rules 6(b) and 12(b)(2), (3), (5) of the Federal Rules of Criminal Procedure.

Words "regular or special" were omitted and "regular" inserted after "succeeding" to harmonize with section 3288 of this title.

Amendments

1994—Pub. L. 103–322, §330011(q)(2), repealed amendment by Pub. L. 101–647, §1213. See 1990 Amendment note below.

1990—Pub. L. 101–647, §3580, inserted a comma after "information" the second place it appeared.

Pub. L. 101–647, §2595(b), struck out "or, in the event of an appeal, within 60 days of the date the dismissal of the indictment or information becomes final," after "the date of the dismissal of the indictment or information" and inserted such language after "within six calendar months of the expiration of the applicable statute of limitations,".

Pub. L. 101–647, §1213, which directed the striking of "or, in the event of an appeal, within 60 days of the date the dismissal of the indictment or information becomes final," and the insertion of such language after "within six months of the expiration of the statute of limitations,", was repealed by Pub. L. 103–322, §330011(q)(2). See above.

1988—Pub. L. 100–690 in section catchline substituted "Indictments and information dismissed after period of limitations" for "Indictment where defect found before period of limitations", and in text, substituted "Whenever an indictment or information charging a felony is dismissed for any reason" for "Whenever an indictment is dismissed for any error, defect, or irregularity with respect to the grand jury, or an indictment or information filed after the defendant waives in open court prosecution by indictment is found otherwise defective or insufficient for any cause,", inserted "or, in the event of an appeal, within 60 days of the date the dismissal of the indictment or information becomes final" after "dismissal of the indictment or information", and inserted provisions which prohibited filing of new indictment or information where reason for dismissal was failure to file within period prescribed or some other reason that would bar a new prosecution.

1964—Pub. L. 88–520 substituted "Indictment" for "Reindictment" in section catchline, included indictments or informations filed after the defendant waives in open court prosecution by indictment which are dismissed for any error, defect, or irregularity, or are otherwise found defective or insufficient, and substituted provisions authorizing, where the period of the statute of limitations will expire within six calendar months of the date of the dismissal, the return of a new indictment within six calendar months of the expiration of the applicable statute of limitations, or, if no regular grand jury is in session at the expiration of the applicable statute of limitations, within six calendar months of the date when the next regular grand jury is convened, for provisions which authorized, where the period of the statute of limitations will expire before the end of the next regular session of the court to which such indictment was returned, the return of a new indictment not later than the end of the next succeeding regular session of the court following the session at which the indictment was found defective or insufficient, during which a grand jury shall be in session.

1963—Pub. L. 88–139 substituted "session" for "term" wherever appearing.

Effective Date of 1994 Amendment

Pub. L. 103–322, title XXXIII, §330011(q)(2), Sept. 13, 1994, 108 Stat. 2145, provided that the amendment made by that section is effective as of the date on which section 1213 of Pub. L. 101–647 took effect.

§3290. Fugitives from justice

No statute of limitations shall extend to any person fleeing from justice.

(June 25, 1948, ch. 645, 62 Stat. 829.)

Historical and Revision Notes

Based on Title 18, U.S.C., 1940 ed., §583 (R.S. §1045).

Said section 583 was rephrased and made applicable to all statutes of limitation and is merely declaratory of the generally accepted rule of law.

§3291. Nationality, citizenship and passports

No person shall be prosecuted, tried, or punished for violation of any provision of sections 1423 to 1428, inclusive, of chapter 69 and sections 1541 to 1544, inclusive, of chapter 75 of title 18 of the United States Code, or for conspiracy to violate any of such sections, unless the indictment is found or the information is instituted within ten years after the commission of the offense.

(Added June 30, 1951, ch. 194, §1, 65 Stat. 107; amended Pub. L. 103–322, title XXXIII, §330008(9), Sept. 13, 1994, 108 Stat. 2143.)

Amendments

1994—Pub. L. 103–322 substituted "violate any of such sections" for "violate any of the afore-mentioned sections".

§3292. Suspension of limitations to permit United States to obtain foreign evidence

(a)(1) Upon application of the United States, filed before return of an indictment, indicating that evidence of an offense is in a foreign country, the district court before which a grand jury is impaneled to investigate the offense shall suspend the running of the statute of limitations for the offense if the court finds by a preponderance of the evidence that an official request has been made for such evidence and that it reasonably appears, or reasonably appeared at the time the request was made, that such evidence is, or was, in such foreign country.

(2) The court shall rule upon such application not later than thirty days after the filing of the application.

(b) Except as provided in subsection (c) of this section, a period of suspension under this section shall begin on the date on which the official request is made and end on the date on which the foreign court or authority takes final action on the request.

(c) The total of all periods of suspension under this section with respect to an offense—

(1) shall not exceed three years; and

(2) shall not extend a period within which a criminal case must be initiated for more than six months if all foreign authorities take final action before such period would expire without regard to this section.

(d) As used in this section, the term "official request" means a letter rogatory, a request under a treaty or convention, or any other request for evidence made by a court of the United States or an authority of the United States having criminal law enforcement responsibility, to a court or other authority of a foreign country.

(Added Pub. L. 98–473, title II, §1218(a), Oct. 12, 1984, 98 Stat. 2167.)

Effective Date

Section effective 30 days after Oct. 12, 1984, see section 1220 of Pub. L. 98–473, set out as a note under section 3505 of this title.

§3293. Financial institution offenses

No person shall be prosecuted, tried, or punished for a violation of, or a conspiracy to violate—

(1) section 215, 656, 657, 1005, 1006, 1007, 1014, 1033, or 1344;

(2) section 1341 or 1343, if the offense affects a financial institution; or

(3) section 1963, to the extent that the racketeering activity involves a violation of section 1344;

unless the indictment is returned or the information is filed within 10 years after the commission of the offense.

(Added Pub. L. 101–73, title IX, §961(l)(1), Aug. 9, 1989, 103 Stat. 501; amended Pub. L. 101–647, title XXV, §2505(a), Nov. 29, 1990, 104 Stat. 4862; Pub. L. 103–322, title XXXII, §320604(b), title XXXIII, §330002(e), Sept. 13, 1994, 108 Stat. 2119, 2140.)

Amendments

1994—Par. (1). Pub. L. 103–322 struck out "1008," after "1007," and inserted "1033," after "1014,".

1990—Par. (3). Pub. L. 101–647 added par. (3).

Effective Date of 1990 Amendment

Pub. L. 101–647, title XXV, §2505(b), Nov. 29, 1990, 104 Stat. 4862, provided that: "The amendments made by subsection (a) [amending this section] shall apply to any offense committed before the date of the enactment of this section [Nov. 29, 1990], if the statute of limitations applicable to that offense had not run as of such date."

Effect of This Section on Offenses for Which Prior Period of Limitations Had Not Run

Pub. L. 101–73, title IX, §961(l)(3), Aug. 9, 1989, 103 Stat. 501, provided that: "The amendments made by this subsection [enacting this section] shall apply to an offense committed before the effective date of this section [Aug. 9, 1989], if the statute of limitations applicable to that offense under this chapter had not run as of such date."

§3294. Theft of major artwork

No person shall be prosecuted, tried, or punished for a violation of or conspiracy to violate section 668 unless the indictment is returned or the information is filed within 20 years after the commission of the offense.

(Added Pub. L. 103–322, title XXXII, §320902(b), Sept. 13, 1994, 108 Stat. 2124.)

§3295. Arson offenses

No person shall be prosecuted, tried, or punished for any non-capital offense under section 81 or subsection (f), (h), or (i) of section 844 unless the indictment is found or the information is instituted not later than 10 years after the date on which the offense was committed.

(Added Pub. L. 104–132, title VII, §708(c)(1), Apr. 24, 1996, 110 Stat. 1297.)

§3296. Counts dismissed pursuant to a plea agreement

(a) In General.—Notwithstanding any other provision of this chapter, any counts of an indictment or information that are dismissed pursuant to a plea agreement shall be reinstated by the District Court if—

(1) the counts sought to be reinstated were originally filed within the applicable limitations period;

(2) the counts were dismissed pursuant to a plea agreement approved by the District Court under which the defendant pled guilty to other charges;

(3) the guilty plea was subsequently vacated on the motion of the defendant; and

(4) the United States moves to reinstate the dismissed counts within 60 days of the date on which the order vacating the plea becomes final.

(b) Defenses; Objections.—Nothing in this section shall preclude the District Court from considering any defense or objection, other than statute of limitations, to the prosecution of the counts reinstated under subsection (a).

(Added Pub. L. 107–273, div. B, title III, §3003(a), Nov. 2, 2002, 116 Stat. 1805.)

§3297. Cases involving DNA evidence

In a case in which DNA testing implicates an identified person in the commission of a felony, no statute of limitations that would otherwise preclude prosecution of the offense shall preclude such prosecution until a period of time following the implication of the person by DNA testing has elapsed that is equal to the otherwise applicable limitation period.

(Added Pub. L. 108–405, title II, §204(a), Oct. 30, 2004, 118 Stat. 2271; amended Pub. L. 109–162, title X, §1005, Jan. 5, 2006, 119 Stat. 3086.)

Amendments

2006—Pub. L. 109–162 struck out "except for a felony offense under chapter 109A," before "no statute of limitations".

Effective Date

Pub. L. 108–405, title II, §204(c), Oct. 30, 2004, 118 Stat. 2271, provided that: "The amendments made by this section [enacting this section] shall apply to the prosecution of any offense committed before, on, or after the date of the enactment of this section [Oct. 30, 2004] if the applicable limitation period has not yet expired."

§3298. Trafficking-related offenses

No person shall be prosecuted, tried, or punished for any non-capital offense or conspiracy to commit a non-capital offense under section 1581 (Peonage; Obstructing Enforcement), 1583 (Enticement into Slavery), 1584 (Sale into Involuntary Servitude), 1589 (Forced Labor), 1590 (Trafficking with Respect to Peonage, Slavery, Involuntary Servitude, or Forced Labor), or 1592 (Unlawful Conduct with Respect to Documents in furtherance of Trafficking, Peonage, Slavery, Involuntary Servitude, or Forced Labor) of this title or under section 274(a) of the Immigration and Nationality Act unless the indictment is found or the information is instituted not later than 10 years after the commission of the offense.

(Added Pub. L. 109–162, title XI, §1182(a), Jan. 5, 2006, 119 Stat. 3126.)

References in Text

Section 274(a) of the Immigration and Nationality Act, referred to in text, is classified to section 1324(a) of Title 8, Aliens and Nationality.

§3299. Child abduction and sex offenses

Notwithstanding any other law, an indictment may be found or an information instituted at any time without limitation for any offense under section 1201 involving a minor victim, and for any felony under chapter 109A, 110 (except for section 1 2257 and 2257A), or 117, or section 1591.

(Added Pub. L. 109–248, title II, §211(1), July 27, 2006, 120 Stat. 616.)

§3300. Recruitment or use of child soldiers

No person may be prosecuted, tried, or punished for a violation of section 2442 unless the indictment or the information is filed not later than 10 years after the commission of the offense.

(Added Pub. L. 110–340, §2(a)(2), Oct. 3, 2008, 122 Stat. 3736.)

§3301. Securities fraud offenses

(a) Definition.—In this section, the term "securities fraud offense" means a violation of, or a conspiracy or an attempt to violate—

(1) section 1348;

(2) section 32(a) of the Securities Exchange Act of 1934 (15 U.S.C. 78ff(a));

(3) section 24 of the Securities Act of 1933 (15 U.S.C. 77x);

(4) section 217 of the Investment Advisers Act of 1940 (15 U.S.C. 80b–17);

(5) section 49 of the Investment Company Act of 1940 (15 U.S.C. 80a–48); or

(6) section 325 of the Trust Indenture Act of 1939 (15 U.S.C. 77yyy).

(b) Limitation.—No person shall be prosecuted, tried, or punished for a securities fraud offense, unless the indictment is found or the information is instituted within 6 years after the commission of the offense.

(Added Pub. L. 111–203, title X, §1079A(b)(1), July 21, 2010, 124 Stat. 2079.)

Effective Date

Section effective 1 day after July 21, 2010, except as otherwise provided, see section 4 of Pub. L. 111–203, set out as a note under section 5301 of Title 12, Banks and Banking.

CHAPTER 215 - GRAND JURY

Amendments

1989—Pub. L. 101–73, title IX, §964(b), Aug. 9, 1989, 103 Stat. 506, added item 3322 "Disclosure of certain matters occurring before grand jury" and struck out former items 3322 "Number; summoning—Rule", 3323 "Objections and motions—Rule", 3324 "Foreman and deputy; powers and duties; records—Rule", 3325 "Persons present at proceedings—Rule", 3326 "Secrecy of proceedings and disclosure—Rule", 3327 "Indictment; finding and return—Rule", and 3328 "Discharging jury and excusing juror—Rule".

§3321. Number of grand jurors; summoning additional jurors

Every grand jury impaneled before any district court shall consist of not less than sixteen nor more than twenty-three persons. If less than sixteen of the persons summoned attend, they shall be placed on the grand jury, and the court shall order the marshal to summon, either immediately or for a day fixed, from the body of the district, and not from the bystanders, a sufficient number of persons to complete the grand jury. Whenever a challenge to a grand juror is allowed, and there are not in attendance other jurors sufficient to complete the grand jury, the court shall make a like order to the marshal to summon a sufficient number of persons for that purpose.

(June 25, 1948, ch. 645, 62 Stat. 829.)

Historical and Revision Notes

Based on section 419 of title 28, U.S.C., 1940 ed., Judicial Code and Judiciary (Mar. 3, 1911, ch. 231, §282, 36 Stat. 1165).

The provisions of the first sentence are embodied in rule 6(a) of the Federal Rules of Criminal Procedure, but it has been retained because of its relation to the remainder of the text which is not covered by said rule.

§3322. Disclosure of certain matters occurring before grand jury

(a) A person who is privy to grand jury information—

(1) received in the course of duty as an attorney for the government; or

(2) disclosed under rule 6(e)(3)(A)(ii) of the Federal Rules of Criminal Procedure;

may disclose that information to an attorney for the government for use in enforcing section 951 of the Financial Institutions Reform, Recovery and Enforcement Act of 1989 or for use in connection with any civil forfeiture provision of Federal law.

(b)(1) Upon motion of an attorney for the government, a court may direct disclosure of matters occurring before a grand jury during an investigation of a banking law violation to identified personnel of a Federal or State financial institution regulatory agency—

(A) for use in relation to any matter within the jurisdiction of such regulatory agency; or

(B) to assist an attorney for the government to whom matters have been disclosed under subsection (a).

(2) A court may issue an order under paragraph (1) at any time during or after the completion of the investigation of the grand jury, upon a finding of a substantial need.

(c) A person to whom matter has been disclosed under this section shall not use such matter other than for the purpose for which such disclosure was authorized.

(d) As used in this section—

(1) the term "banking law violation" means a violation of, or a conspiracy to violate—

(A) section 215, 656, 657, 1005, 1006, 1007, 1014, 1344, 1956, or 1957;

(B) section 1341 or 1343 affecting a financial institution; or

(C) any provision of subchapter II of chapter 53 of title 31, United States Code;

(2) the term "attorney for the government" has the meaning given such term in the Federal Rules of Criminal Procedure; and

(3) the term "grand jury information" means matters occurring before a grand jury other than the deliberations of the grand jury or the vote of any grand juror.

(Added Pub. L. 101–73, title IX, §964(a), Aug. 9, 1989, 103 Stat. 505; amended Pub. L. 106–102, title VII, §740, Nov. 12, 1999, 113 Stat. 1480; Pub. L. 106–185, §10, Apr. 25, 2000, 114 Stat. 217; Pub. L. 107–273, div. C, title I, §11002, Nov. 2, 2002, 116 Stat. 1816.)

References in Text

Section 951 of the Financial Institutions Reform, Recovery and Enforcement Act of 1989, referred to in subsec. (a), is classified to section 1833a of Title 12, Banks and Banking.

The Federal Rules of Criminal Procedure, referred to in subsecs. (a)(2) and (d)(2), are set out in the Appendix to this title.

Prior Provisions

A prior section 3322, act June 25, 1948, ch. 645, 62 Stat. 829, related to the summoning of and number of grand jurors, prior to repeal by Pub. L. 101–73, §964(a). See Rule 6(a) of the Federal Rules of Criminal Procedure, set out in the Appendix to this title.

Amendments

2002—Subsec. (d)(1)(A). Pub. L. 107–273, §11002(1), substituted "1344, 1956, or 1957;" for "or 1344; or".

Subsec. (d)(1)(C). Pub. L. 107–273, §11002(2), (3), added subpar. (C).

2000—Subsec. (a). Pub. L. 106–185 struck out "concerning a banking law violation" after "grand jury information" in introductory provisions and substituted "any civil forfeiture provision of Federal law" for "civil forfeiture under section 981 of title 18, United States Code, of property described in section 981(a)(1)(C) of such title" in concluding provisions.

1999—Subsec. (b)(1). Pub. L. 106–102, §740(1), inserted "Federal or State" before "financial institution" in introductory provisions.

Subsec. (b)(2). Pub. L. 106–102, §740(2), inserted "at any time during or after the completion of the investigation of the grand jury," after "paragraph (1)".

Effective Date of 2000 Amendment

Amendment by Pub. L. 106–185 applicable to any forfeiture proceeding commenced on or after the date that is 120 days after Apr. 25, 2000, see section 21 of Pub. L. 106–185, set out as a note under section 1324 of Title 8, Aliens and Nationality.

[§§3323 to 3328. Repealed. Pub. L. 101–73, title IX, §964(a), Aug. 9, 1989, 103 Stat. 505]

Section 3323, act June 25, 1948, ch. 645, 62 Stat. 829, related to challenging the array of grand jurors or individual grand jurors and motions to dismiss. See Rule 6(b) of the Federal Rules of Criminal Procedure, set out in the Appendix to this title.

Section 3324, act June 25, 1948, ch. 645, 62 Stat. 829, related to the appointment of the grand jury foreman and deputy foreman, oaths, affirmations and indictments, and records of jurors concurring. See Rule 6(c) of the Federal Rules of Criminal Procedure, set out in the Appendix to this title.

Section 3325, act June 25, 1948, ch. 645, 62 Stat. 829, related to persons who may be present while the grand jury is in session, and exclusion while the jury is deliberating or voting. See Rule 6(d) of the Federal Rules of Criminal Procedure, set out in the Appendix to this title.

Section 3326, act June 25, 1948, ch. 645, 62 Stat. 829, related to disclosure of proceedings to government attorneys, disclosure by direction of the court or permission of the defendant, and secrecy of the indictment. See Rule 6(e) of the Federal Rules of Criminal Procedure, set out in the Appendix to this title.

Section 3327, act June 25, 1948, ch. 645, 62 Stat. 830, related to concurrence of 12 or more jurors in the indictment and return of the indictment to the judge in open court. See Rule 6(f) of the Federal Rules of Criminal Procedure, set out in the Appendix to this title.

Section 3328, act June 25, 1948, ch. 645, 62 Stat. 830, related to discharge of grand jury by court, limitation of service, and excusing jurors for cause. See Rule 6(g) of the Federal Rules of Criminal Procedure, set out in the Appendix to this title.

CHAPTER 216 - SPECIAL GRAND JURY

Amendments

1970—Pub. L. 91–452, title I, §101(a), Oct. 15, 1970, 84 Stat. 923, added chapter 216 and items 3331 to 3334.

National Commission on Individual Rights

Pub. L. 91–452, title XII, §§1201–1211, Oct. 15, 1970, 84 Stat. 960, 961, established the National Commission on Individual Rights to conduct a comprehensive study and review of Federal laws and practices relating to special grand juries authorized under chapter 216 of this title, dangerous special offender sentencing under section 3575 of this title, wiretapping and electronic surveillance, bail reform and preventive detention, no-knock search warrants, the accumulation of data on individuals by Federal agencies as authorized by law or acquired by executive action, and other practices which in its opinion might infringe upon the individual rights of the people of the United States. The Commission was required to make interim reports at least every two years and a final report to the President and Congress six years after Jan. 1, 1972, and was to cease to exist 60 days after submission of the final report.

§3331. Summoning and term

(a) In addition to such other grand juries as shall be called from time to time, each district court which is located in a judicial district containing more than four million inhabitants or in which the Attorney General, the Deputy Attorney General, the Associate Attorney General, or any designated Assistant Attorney General, certifies in writing to the chief judge of the district that in his judgment a special grand jury is necessary because of criminal activity in the district shall order a special grand jury to be summoned at least once in each period of eighteen months unless another special grand jury is then serving. The grand jury shall serve for a term of eighteen months unless an order for its discharge is entered earlier by the court upon a determination of the grand jury by majority vote that its business has been completed. If, at the end of such term or any extension thereof, the district court determines the business of the grand jury has not been completed, the court may enter an order extending such term for an additional period of six months. No special grand jury term so extended shall exceed thirty-six months, except as provided in subsection (e) of section 3333 of this chapter.

(b) If a district court within any judicial circuit fails to extend the term of a special grand jury or enters an order for the discharge of such grand jury before such grand jury determines that it has completed its business, the grand jury, upon the affirmative vote of a majority of its members, may apply to the chief judge of the circuit for an order for the continuance of the term of the grand jury. Upon the making of such an application by the grand jury, the term thereof shall continue until the entry upon such application by the chief judge of the circuit of an appropriate order. No special grand jury term so extended shall exceed thirty-six months, except as provided in subsection (e) of section 3333 of this chapter.

(Added Pub. L. 91–452, title I, §101(a), Oct. 15, 1970, 84 Stat. 923; amended Pub. L. 100–690, title VII, §7020(d), Nov. 18, 1988, 102 Stat. 4396.)

Amendments

1988—Subsec. (a). Pub. L. 100–690 inserted ", the Associate Attorney General" after "Deputy Attorney General".

§3332. Powers and duties

(a) It shall be the duty of each such grand jury impaneled within any judicial district to inquire into offenses against the criminal laws of the United States alleged to have been committed within that district. Such alleged offenses may be brought to the attention of the grand jury by the court or by any attorney appearing on behalf of the United States for the presentation of evidence. Any such attorney receiving information concerning such an alleged offense from any other person shall, if requested by such other person, inform the grand jury of such alleged offense, the identity of such other person, and such attorney's action or recommendation.

(b) Whenever the district court determines that the volume of business of the special grand jury exceeds the capacity of the grand jury to discharge its obligations, the district court may order an additional special grand jury for that district to be impaneled.

(Added Pub. L. 91–452, title I, §101(a), Oct. 15, 1970, 84 Stat. 924.)

References in Text

The criminal laws of the United States, referred to in subsec. (a), are classified generally to this title.

§3333. Reports

(a) A special grand jury impaneled by any district court, with the concurrence of a majority of its members, may, upon completion of its original term, or each extension thereof, submit to the court a report—

(1) concerning noncriminal misconduct, malfeasance, or misfeasance in office involving organized criminal activity by an appointed public officer or employee as the basis for a recommendation of removal or disciplinary action; or

(2) regarding organized crime conditions in the district.

(b) The court to which such report is submitted shall examine it and the minutes of the special grand jury and, except as otherwise provided in subsections (c) and (d) of this section, shall make an order accepting and filing such report as a public record only if the court is satisfied that it complies with the provisions of subsection (a) of this section and that—

(1) the report is based upon facts revealed in the course of an investigation authorized by subsection (a) of section 3332 and is supported by the preponderance of the evidence; and

(2) when the report is submitted pursuant to paragraph (1) of subsection (a) of this section, each person named therein and any reasonable number of witnesses in his behalf as designated by him to the foreman of the grand jury were afforded an opportunity to testify before the grand jury prior to the filing of such report, and when the report is submitted pursuant to paragraph (2) of subsection (a) of this section, it is not critical of an identified person.

(c)(1) An order accepting a report pursuant to paragraph (1) of subsection (a) of this section and the report shall be sealed by the court and shall not be filed as a public record or be subject to subpena or otherwise made public (i) until at least thirty-one days after a copy of the order and report are served upon each public officer or employee named therein and an answer has been filed or the time for filing an answer has expired, or (ii) if an appeal is taken, until all rights of review of the public officer or employee named therein have expired or terminated in an order accepting the report. No order accepting a report pursuant to paragraph (1) of subsection (a) of this section shall be entered until thirty days after the delivery of such report to the public officer or body pursuant to paragraph (3) of subsection (c) of this section. The court may issue such orders as it shall deem appropriate to prevent unauthorized publication of a report. Unauthorized publication may be punished as contempt of the court.

(2) Such public officer or employee may file with the clerk a verified answer to such a report not later than twenty days after service of the order and report upon him. Upon a showing of good cause, the court may grant such public officer or employee an extension of time within which to file such answer and may authorize such limited publication of the report as may be necessary to prepare such answer. Such an answer shall plainly and concisely state the facts and law constituting the defense of the public officer or employee to the charges in said report, and, except for those parts thereof which the court determines to have been inserted scandalously, prejudiciously, or unnecessarily, such answer shall become an appendix to the report.

(3) Upon the expiration of the time set forth in paragraph (1) of subsection (c) of this section, the United States attorney shall deliver a true copy of such report, and the appendix, if any, for appropriate action to each public officer or body having jurisdiction, responsibility, or authority over each public officer or employee named in the report.

(d) Upon the submission of a report pursuant to subsection (a) of this section, if the court finds that the filing of such report as a public record may prejudice fair consideration of a pending criminal matter, it shall order such report sealed and such report shall not be subject to subpena or public inspection during the pendency of such criminal matter, except upon order of the court.

(e) Whenever the court to which a report is submitted pursuant to paragraph (1) of subsection (a) of this section is not satisfied that the report complies with the provisions of subsection (b) of this section, it may direct that additional testimony be taken before the same grand jury, or it shall make an order sealing such report, and it shall not be filed as a public record or be subject to subpena or otherwise made public until the provisions of subsection (b) of this section are met. A special grand jury term may be extended by the district court beyond thirty-six months in order that such additional testimony may be taken or the provisions of subsection (b) of this section may be met.

(f) As used in this section, "public officer or employee" means any officer or employee of the United States, any State, the District of Columbia, the Commonwealth of Puerto Rico, any territory or possession of the United States, or any political subdivision, or any department, agency, or instrumentality thereof.

(Added Pub. L. 91–452, title I, §101(a), Oct. 15, 1970, 84 Stat. 924.)

§3334. General provisions

The provisions of chapter 215, title 18, United States Code, and the Federal Rules of Criminal Procedure applicable to regular grand juries shall apply to special grand juries to the extent not inconsistent with sections 3331, 3332, or 3333 of this chapter.

(Added Pub. L. 91–452, title I, §101(a), Oct. 15, 1970, 84 Stat. 926.)

CHAPTER 217 - INDICTMENT AND INFORMATION

§3361. Form and contents—(Rule)

See Federal Rules of Criminal Procedure

Contents and form; striking surplusage, Rule 7(a), (c), (d).

(June 25, 1948, ch. 645, 62 Stat. 830.)

§3362. Waiver of indictment and prosecution on information—(Rule)

See Federal Rules of Criminal Procedure

Waiver of indictment for offenses not punishable by death, Rule 7(b).

(June 25, 1948, ch. 645, 62 Stat. 830.)

§3363. Joinder of offenses—(Rule)

See Federal Rules of Criminal Procedure

Joinder of two or more offenses in same indictment, Rule 8(a).

Trial together of indictments or informations, Rule 13.

(June 25, 1948, ch. 645, 62 Stat. 830.)

§3364. Joinder of defendants—(Rule)

See Federal Rules of Criminal Procedure

Joinder of two or more defendants charged in same indictment, Rule 8(b).

Relief from prejudicial joinder, Rule 14.

(June 25, 1948, ch. 645, 62 Stat. 830.)

§3365. Amendment of information—(Rule)

See Federal Rules of Criminal Procedure

Amendment of information, time and conditions, Rule 7(e).
(June 25, 1948, ch. 645, 62 Stat. 830.)

§3366. Bill of particulars—(Rule)

See Federal Rules of Criminal Procedure

Bill of particulars for cause; motion after arraignment; time; amendment, Rule 7(f).
(June 25, 1948, ch. 645, 62 Stat. 830.)

§3367. Dismissal—(Rule)

See Federal Rules of Criminal Procedure

Dismissal filed by Attorney General or United States Attorney, Rule 48.
Dismissal on objection to array of grand jury or lack of legal qualification of individual grand juror, Rule 6(b)(2).
(June 25, 1948, ch. 645, 62 Stat. 830.)

CHAPTER 219 - TRIAL BY UNITED STATES MAGISTRATE JUDGES

| 3401. | Misdemeanors; application of probation laws. |
| 3402. | Rules of procedure, practice and appeal. |

Amendments

1979—Pub. L. 96–82, §7(c), Oct. 10, 1979, 93 Stat. 646, substituted "Misdemeanors" for "Minor offenses" in item 3401.
1968—Pub. L. 90–578, title III, §§301(c), 302(c), Oct. 17, 1968, 82 Stat. 1115, 1116, substituted "TRIAL BY UNITED STATES MAGISTRATES" for "TRIAL BY COMMISSIONERS" in chapter heading, and substituted "Minor offenses" for "Petty offenses" and struck out "fees" after "probation laws" in item 3401.

Change of Name

"UNITED STATES MAGISTRATE JUDGES" substituted for "UNITED STATES MAGISTRATES" in chapter heading pursuant to section 321 of Pub. L. 101–650, set out as a note under section 631 of Title 28, Judiciary and Judicial Procedure.

§3401. Misdemeanors; application of probation laws

(a) When specially designated to exercise such jurisdiction by the district court or courts he serves, any United States magistrate judge shall have jurisdiction to try persons accused of, and sentence persons convicted of, misdemeanors committed within that judicial district.
(b) Any person charged with a misdemeanor, other than a petty offense may elect, however, to be tried before a district judge for the district in which the offense was committed. The magistrate judge shall carefully explain to the defendant that he has a right to trial, judgment, and sentencing by a district judge and that he may have a right to trial by jury before a district judge or magistrate

judge. The magistrate judge may not proceed to try the case unless the defendant, after such explanation, expressly consents to be tried before the magistrate judge and expressly and specifically waives trial, judgment, and sentencing by a district judge. Any such consent and waiver shall be made in writing or orally on the record.

(c) A magistrate judge who exercises trial jurisdiction under this section, and before whom a person is convicted or pleads either guilty or nolo contendere, may, with the approval of a judge of the district court, direct the probation service of the court to conduct a presentence investigation on that person and render a report to the magistrate judge prior to the imposition of sentence.

(d) The probation laws shall be applicable to persons tried by a magistrate judge under this section, and such officer shall have power to grant probation and to revoke, modify, or reinstate the probation of any person granted probation by a magistrate judge.

(e) Proceedings before United States magistrate judges under this section shall be taken down by a court reporter or recorded by suitable sound recording equipment. For purposes of appeal a copy of the record of such proceedings shall be made available at the expense of the United States to a person who makes affidavit that he is unable to pay or give security therefor, and the expense of such copy shall be paid by the Director of the Administrative Office of the United States Courts.

(f) The district court may order that proceedings in any misdemeanor case be conducted before a district judge rather than a United States magistrate judge upon the court's own motion or, for good cause shown, upon petition by the attorney for the Government. Such petition should note the novelty, importance, or complexity of the case, or other pertinent factors, and be filed in accordance with regulations promulgated by the Attorney General.

(g) The magistrate judge may, in a petty offense case involving a juvenile, exercise all powers granted to the district court under chapter 403 of this title. The magistrate judge may, in the case of any misdemeanor, other than a petty offense, involving a juvenile in which consent to trial before a magistrate judge has been filed under subsection (b), exercise all powers granted to the district court under chapter 403 of this title. For purposes of this subsection, proceedings under chapter 403 of this title may be instituted against a juvenile by a violation notice or complaint, except that no such case may proceed unless the certification referred to in section 5032 of this title has been filed in open court at the arraignment.

(h) The magistrate judge shall have power to modify, revoke, or terminate supervised release of any person sentenced to a term of supervised release by a magistrate judge.

(i) A district judge may designate a magistrate judge to conduct hearings to modify, revoke, or terminate supervised release, including evidentiary hearings, and to submit to the judge proposed findings of fact and recommendations for such modification, revocation, or termination by the judge, including, in the case of revocation, a recommended disposition under section 3583(e) of this title. The magistrate judge shall file his or her proposed findings and recommendations.

(June 25, 1948, ch. 645, 62 Stat. 830; Pub. L. 85–508, §12(j), July 7, 1958, 72 Stat. 348; Pub. L. 90–578, title III, §302(a), Oct. 17, 1968, 82 Stat. 1115; Pub. L. 96–82, §7(a), (b), Oct. 10, 1979, 93 Stat. 645, 646; Pub. L. 98–473, title II, §223(j), Oct. 12, 1984, 98 Stat. 2029; Pub. L. 100–690, title VII, §7072(a), Nov. 18, 1988, 102 Stat. 4405; Pub. L. 101–650, title III, §321, Dec. 1, 1990, 104 Stat. 5117; Pub. L. 102–572, title I, §103, Oct. 29, 1992, 106 Stat. 4507; Pub. L. 104–317, title II, §202(a), Oct. 19, 1996, 110 Stat. 3848; Pub. L. 106–518, title II, §203(a), Nov. 13, 2000, 114 Stat. 2414.)

Historical and Revision Notes

Based on title 18, U.S.C., 1940 ed., §§576, 576b, 576c, 576d (Oct. 9, 1940, ch. 785, §§1, 3–5, 54 Stat. 1058, 1059).

The phrase "the commissioner shall have power to grant probation" was inserted in paragraph (c) in order to make clear the authority of the commissioner to grant probation without application to the District judge.

Four sections were consolidated herein with minor rearrangements and deletion of unnecessary words.

Amendments

2000—Subsec. (b). Pub. L. 106–518, §203(a)(1), struck out "that is a class B misdemeanor charging a motor vehicle offense, a class C misdemeanor, or an infraction," after "petty offense".

Subsec. (g). Pub. L. 106–518, §203(a)(2), substituted first sentence for former first sentence which read: "The magistrate judge may, in a petty offense case involving a juvenile, that is a class B misdemeanor charging a motor vehicle offense, a class C misdemeanor, or an infraction, exercise all powers granted to the district court under chapter 403 of this title.", substituted "the case of any misdemeanor, other than a petty offense," for "any other class B or C misdemeanor case" in second sentence, and struck out at end "No term of imprisonment shall be imposed by the magistrate in any such case."

1996—Subsec. (b). Pub. L. 104–317, §202(a)(1), inserted ", other than a petty offense that is a class B misdemeanor charging a motor vehicle offense, a class C misdemeanor, or an infraction," after "misdemeanor", substituted "tried before a district judge" for "tried before a judge of the district court" and "by a district judge" for "by a judge of the district court", substituted "magistrate judge" for "magistrate" in two places, and substituted "The magistrate judge may not proceed to try the case unless the defendant, after such explanation, expressly consents to be tried before the magistrate judge and expressly and specifically waives trial, judgment, and sentencing by a district judge. Any such consent and waiver shall be made in writing or orally on the record." for "The magistrate shall not proceed to try the case unless the defendant, after such explanation, files a written consent to be tried before the magistrate that specifically waives trial, judgment, and sentencing by a judge of the district court."

Subsec. (g). Pub. L. 104–317, §202(a)(2), substituted "The magistrate judge may, in a petty offense case involving a juvenile, that is a class B misdemeanor charging a motor vehicle offense, a class C misdemeanor, or an infraction, exercise all powers granted to the district court under chapter 403 of this title. The magistrate judge may, in any other class B or C misdemeanor case involving a juvenile in which consent to trial before a magistrate judge has been filed under subsection (b), exercise all powers granted to the district court under chapter 403 of this title." for "The magistrate may, in a Class B or C misdemeanor case, or infraction case, involving a juvenile in which consent to trial before a magistrate has been filed under subsection (b) of this section, exercise all powers granted to the district court under chapter 403 of this title."

1992—Subsec. (d). Pub. L. 102–572, §103(1), substituted "and to revoke, modify, or reinstate the probation of any person granted probation by a magistrate judge" for "and to revoke or reinstate the probation of any person granted probation by him".

Subsecs. (h), (i). Pub. L. 102–572, §103(2), added subsecs. (h) and (i).

1988—Subsec. (g). Amendment by Pub. L. 100–690 directing that "and section 4216" be struck out after "under chapter 402" in subsec. (g), was executed to subsec. (g) applicable to offenses committed prior to Nov. 1, 1987, as the probable intent of Congress, in view of the amendment by section 223(j) of Pub. L. 98–473. See 1984 Amendment notes below.

1984—Subsecs. (g), (h). Pub. L. 98–473, §223(j)(1), redesignated subsec. (h) as (g) and struck out former subsec. (g) which related to powers of magistrate in case involving youthful offender. Former subsec. (g), as amended by Pub. L. 100–690, read as follows: "The magistrate may, in a case involving a youth offender in which consent to trial before a magistrate has been filed under subsection (b) of this section, impose sentence and exercise the other powers granted to the district court under chapter 402 of this title, except that—

"(1) the magistrate may not sentence the youth offender to the custody of the Attorney General pursuant to such chapter for a period in excess of 1 year for conviction of a misdemeanor or 6 months for conviction of a petty offense;

"(2) such youth offender shall be released conditionally under supervision no later than 3 months before the expiration of the term imposed by the magistrate, and shall be discharged unconditionally on or before the expiration of the maximum sentence imposed; and

"(3) the magistrate may not suspend the imposition of sentence and place the youth offender on probation for a period in excess of 1 year for conviction of a misdemeanor or 6 months for conviction of a petty offense."

Pub. L. 98–473, §223(j)(2), which directed amendment of subsec. (h) by substituting reference to Class B or C misdemeanor case or an infraction case, for reference to petty offense case, was executed to subsec. (g) as the probable intent of Congress in view of redesignation of subsec. (h) as (g) by section 223(j)(1) of Pub. L. 98–473, see above.

1979—Pub. L. 96–82, §7(b), substituted "Misdemeanors" for "Minor offenses" in section catchline.

Subsec. (a). Pub. L. 96–82, §7(a)(1), substituted "any United States magistrate shall have jurisdiction to try persons accused of, and sentence persons convicted of, misdemeanors committed" for "and under such conditions as may be imposed by the terms of the special designation, any United States magistrate shall have jurisdiction to try persons accused of, and sentence persons convicted of, minor offenses committed".

Subsec. (b). Pub. L. 96–82, §7(a)(2), substituted reference to persons charged with misdemeanors for reference to persons charged with minor offenses, substituted reference to right to trial, judgment, and sentencing for reference to right to trial, and struck out provisions relating to the waiver of the right to a trial by jury.

Subsec. (f). Pub. L. 96–82, §7(a)(3), substituted provisions authorizing the district court to order misdemeanor proceedings to be conducted before a district court judge for provisions defining term "minor offenses".

Subsecs. (g), (h). Pub. L. 96–82, §7(a)(4), added subsecs. (g) and (h).

1968—Pub. L. 90–578 substituted "Minor offenses" for "Petty offenses" and struck out provision for "fees" in section catchline.

Subsec. (a). Pub. L. 90–578 provided for trial by a magistrate rather than a commissioner of minor offenses instead of petty offenses, under such conditions as may be imposed by the terms of the special designation, required imposition of sentence after conviction instead of sentencing of person committing the offense, and omitted provision for trial of offense committed in any place over which the Congress has exclusive power to legislate or over which the United States has concurrent jurisdiction.

Subsec. (b). Pub. L. 90–578 provided that the person be charged with a minor offense rather than a petty offense, prescribed trial in district court for the district in which the offense was committed, and required an explanation to be given of right to trial before a district court judge with right to jury trial before such judge and that the written consent to trial before the magistrate specifically waive trial before the district court judge and any right to a jury trial.

Subsec. (c). Pub. L. 90–578 substituted authorization for magistrate to conduct presentence investigation for prior provisions making probation laws applicable to persons tried by commissioners having power to grant probation, now incorporated in subsec. (d) of this section.

Subsec. (d). Pub. L. 90–578 incorporated existing provisions of former subsec. (c) of this section in provisions designated as subsec. (d), substituted "magistrate" for "commissioner", authorized revocation or reinstatement of probation by the officer granting the probation, and struck out former provision for receipt of fees provided by law for services as a commissioner.

Subsec. (e). Pub. L. 90–578 substituted requirement that proceedings before magistrates be taken down by a court reporter or recorded by sound recording equipment and provision for availability of a copy of the record of such proceedings for appeal purposes to be paid by the Director at Federal expense when a person is unable to pay or give security therefor for prior provisions making the section inapplicable to the District of Columbia and interpreting it as not repealing or limiting existing jurisdiction, power or authority of commissioners appointed in the several national parks.

Subsec. (f). Pub. L. 90–578 added subsec. (f).

1958—Subsec. (e). Pub. L. 85–508 struck out provisions which related to commissioners appointed for Alaska. See section 81A of Title 28, Judiciary and Judicial Procedure, which establishes a United States District Court for the State of Alaska.

Change of Name

"United States magistrate judge", "magistrate judge", and "magistrate judges" substituted for "United States magistrate", "magistrate", and "magistrates", respectively, in subsecs. (a), (c), (e), and (f), and "magistrate judge under" substituted for "magistrate under" in subsec. (d), pursuant to section 321 of Pub. L. 101–650, set out as a note under section 631 of Title 28, Judiciary and Judicial Procedure.

Effective Date of 1992 Amendment

Amendment by Pub. L. 102–572 effective Jan. 1, 1993, see section 1101 of Pub. L. 102–572, set out as a note under section 905 of Title 2, The Congress.

Effective Date of 1984 Amendment

Amendment by Pub. L. 98–473 effective Nov. 1, 1987, and applicable only to offenses committed after the taking effect of such amendment, see section 235(a)(1) of Pub. L. 98–473, set out as an Effective Date note under section 3551 of this title.

Effective Date of 1968 Amendment

Amendment by Pub. L. 90–578 effective Oct. 17, 1968, except when a later effective date is applicable, which is the earlier of date when implementation of amendment by appointment of magistrates [now United States magistrate judges] and assumption of office takes place or third anniversary of enactment of Pub. L. 90–578 on Oct. 17, 1968, see section 403 of Pub. L. 90–578, set out as a note under section 631 of Title 28, Judiciary and Judicial Procedure.

Effective Date of 1958 Amendment

Amendment by Pub. L. 85–508 effective Jan. 3, 1959, on admission of Alaska into the Union pursuant to Proc. No. 3269, Jan. 3, 1959, 24 F.R. 81, 73 Stat. c16, as required by sections 1 and 8(c) of Pub. L. 85–508, see notes set out under section 81A of Title 28, Judiciary and Judicial Procedure, and preceding former section 21 of Title 48, Territories and Insular Possessions.

§3402. Rules of procedure, practice and appeal 1

In all cases of conviction by a United States magistrate judge an appeal of right shall lie from the judgment of the magistrate judge to a judge of the district court of the district in which the offense was committed.

(June 25, 1948, ch. 645, 62 Stat. 831; Pub. L. 90–578, title III, §302(b), Oct. 17, 1968, 82 Stat. 1116; Pub. L. 100–702, title IV, §404(b)(2), Nov. 19, 1988, 102 Stat. 4651; Pub. L. 101–650, title III, §321, Dec. 1, 1990, 104 Stat. 5117.)

Historical and Revision Notes

Based on title 18 U.S.C., 1940 ed., §576a (Oct. 9, 1940, ch. 685, §2, 54 Stat. 1059).

Amendments

1988—Pub. L. 100–702 struck out second par. which read as follows: "The Supreme Court shall prescribe rules of procedure and practice for the trial of cases before magistrates and for taking and hearing of appeals to the judges of the district courts of the United States."

1968—Pub. L. 90–578 provided that the appeal shall be of right, substituted "a United States magistrate", "magistrate", and "magistrates" for "United States commissioners", "commissioner", and "commissioners", respectively, and provided that the appeals be to the judge of the district court and not to the district court and that the rules of the Supreme Court relate to appeals to the judges of the district courts rather than to the district courts.

Change of Name

"United States magistrate judge" and "magistrate judge" substituted for "United States magistrate" and "magistrate", respectively, in text pursuant to section 321 of Pub. L. 101–650, set out as a note under section 631 of Title 28, Judiciary and Judicial Procedure.

Effective Date of 1988 Amendment
Amendment by Pub. L. 100–702 effective Dec. 1, 1988, see section 407 of Pub. L. 100–702, set out as a note under section 2071 of Title 28, Judiciary and Judicial Procedure.

Effective Date of 1968 Amendment
Amendment by Pub. L. 90–578 effective Oct. 17, 1968, except when a later effective date is applicable, which is the earlier of date when implementation of amendment by appointment of magistrates [now United States magistrate judges] and assumption of office takes place or third anniversary of enactment of Pub. L. 90–578 on Oct. 17, 1968, see section 403 of Pub. L. 90–578, set out as a note under section 631 of title 28, Judiciary and Judicial Procedure.

CHAPTER 221 - ARRAIGNMENT, PLEAS AND TRIAL

§3431. Term of court; power of court unaffected by expiration—(Rule)

See Federal Rules of Criminal Procedure
Expiration of term without significance in criminal cases, Rule 45(c).
(June 25, 1948, ch. 645, 62 Stat. 831.)

References in Text
Rule 45(c) of the Federal Rules of Criminal Procedure, referred to in text, was rescinded Feb. 28, 1966, eff. July 1, 1966.

§3432. Indictment and list of jurors and witnesses for prisoner in capital cases

A person charged with treason or other capital offense shall at least three entire days before commencement of trial, excluding intermediate weekends and holidays, be furnished with a copy of the indictment and a list of the veniremen, and of the witnesses to be produced on the trial for proving the indictment, stating the place of abode of each venireman and witness, except that such list of the veniremen and witnesses need not be furnished if the court finds by a preponderance of the evidence that providing the list may jeopardize the life or safety of any person.

(June 25, 1948, ch. 645, 62 Stat. 831; Pub. L. 103–322, title VI, §60025, Sept. 13, 1994, 108 Stat. 1982; Pub. L. 111–16, §3(10), May 7, 2009, 123 Stat. 1608.)

Historical and Revision Notes

Based on title 18, U.S.C., 1940 ed., §562 (R.S. §1033).

Words "or other capital offense" inserted after "treason" and "jurors" substituted for "jury". The concluding sentence "When any person is indicted for any other capital offense, such copy of the indictment and list of the jurors and witnesses shall be delivered to him at least two entire days before the trial" was omitted. The change made by the revisers, permitting an additional day's preparation for trial in homicide, kidnapping, rape, and other capital cases seemed not unreasonable.

Words "shall be delivered to him", at end of section, were omitted as unnecessary.

Rule 10 of the Federal Rules of Criminal Procedure requires that the defendant in every case be given a copy of the indictment or information before he is called upon to plead. Thus there is no conflict between the rule and the revised section.

Minor changes in phraseology were made.

Amendments

2009—Pub. L. 111–16 inserted ", excluding intermediate weekends and holidays," after "commencement of trial".

1994—Pub. L. 103–322 inserted before period at end ", except that such list of the veniremen and witnesses need not be furnished if the court finds by a preponderance of the evidence that providing the list may jeopardize the life or safety of any person".

Effective Date of 2009 Amendment

Amendment by Pub. L. 111–16 effective Dec. 1, 2009, see section 7 of Pub. L. 111–16, set out as a note under section 109 of Title 11, Bankruptcy.

§3433. Arraignment—(Rule)

See Federal Rules of Criminal Procedure

Reading and furnishing copy of indictment to accused, Rule 10.

(June 25, 1948, ch. 645, 62 Stat. 831.)

§3434. Presence of defendant—(Rule)

See Federal Rules of Criminal Procedure

Right of defendant to be present generally; corporation; waiver, Rule 43.

(June 25, 1948, ch. 645, 62 Stat. 831.)

§3435. Receiver of stolen property triable before or after principal

A person charged with receiving or concealing stolen property may be tried either before or after the trial of the principal offender.

(June 25, 1948, ch. 645, 62 Stat. 831.)

Historical and Revision Notes

Based on title 18, U.S.C., 1940 ed., §§101, 467 (Mar. 4, 1909, ch. 321, §§48, 288, 35 Stat. 1098,

1145).

Other provisions of sections 101 and 467 of title 18, U.S.C., 1940 ed., were incorporated in sections 641 and 662 of this title.

Necessary changes were made in phraseology.

§3436. Consolidation of indictments or informations—(Rule)

See Federal Rules of Criminal Procedure

Two or more indictments or informations triable together, Rule 13.

(June 25, 1948, ch. 645, 62 Stat. 832.)

§3437. Severance—(Rule)

See Federal Rules of Criminal Procedure

Relief from prejudicial joinder of defendants or offenses, Rule 14.

(June 25, 1948, ch. 645, 62 Stat. 832.)

§3438. Pleas—(Rule)

See Federal Rules of Criminal Procedure

Plea of guilty, not guilty, or nolo contendere; acceptance by court; refusal to plead; corporation failing to appear, Rule 11.

Withdrawal of plea of guilty, Rule 32.

(June 25, 1948, ch. 645, 62 Stat. 832.)

§3439. Demurrers and special pleas in bar or abatement abolished; relief on motion—(Rule)

See Federal Rules of Criminal Procedure

Motion to dismiss or for appropriate relief substituted for demurrer or dilatory plea or motion to quash, Rule 12.

(June 25, 1948, ch. 645, 62 Stat. 832.)

§3440. Defenses and objections determined on motion—(Rule)

See Federal Rules of Criminal Procedure

Defenses or objections which may or must be raised before trial; time; hearing; effect of determination; limitations by law unaffected, Rule 12(b).

(June 25, 1948, ch. 645, 62 Stat. 832.)

§3441. Jury; number of jurors; waiver—(Rule)

See Federal Rules of Criminal Procedure

Jury trial, waiver, twelve jurors or less by written stipulation, trial by court on general or special findings, Rule 23.

(June 25, 1948, ch. 645, 62 Stat. 832.)

§3442. Jurors, examination, peremptory challenges; alternates—(Rule)

See Federal Rules of Criminal Procedure

Examination and peremptory challenges of trial jurors; alternate jurors, Rule 24.
(June 25, 1948, ch. 645, 62 Stat. 832.)

§3443. Instructions to jury—(Rule)

See Federal Rules of Criminal Procedure
Court's instructions to jury, written requests and copies, objections, Rule 30.
(June 25, 1948, ch. 645, 62 Stat. 832.)

§3444. Disability of judge—(Rule)

See Federal Rules of Criminal Procedure
Disability of judge after verdict or finding of guilt, Rule 25.
(June 25, 1948, ch. 645, 62 Stat. 832.)

§3445. Motion for judgment of acquittal—(Rule)

See Federal Rules of Criminal Procedure
Motions for directed verdict abolished.
Motions for judgment of acquittal adopted; court may reserve decision; renewal, Rule 29.
(June 25, 1948, ch. 645, 62 Stat. 832.)

§3446. New trial—(Rule)

See Federal Rules of Criminal Procedure
Granting of new trial, grounds, and motion, Rule 33.
(June 25, 1948, ch. 645, 62 Stat. 832.)

CHAPTER 223 - WITNESSES AND EVIDENCE

Amendments

2009—Pub. L. 111–79, §2(5), Oct. 19, 2009, 123 Stat. 2089, added item 3512.

2006—Pub. L. 109–177, title I, §115(1), Mar. 9, 2006, 120 Stat. 211, added item 3511.

2002—Pub. L. 107–273, div. B, title IV, §4002(c)(3)(B), Nov. 2, 2002, 116 Stat. 1809, struck out item 3503 "Depositions to preserve testimony".

2000—Pub. L. 106–544, §5(b)(2), (3), Dec. 19, 2000, 114 Stat. 2718, struck out "in Federal health care investigations" after "subpoenas" in item 3486 and struck out item 3486A "Administrative subpoenas in cases involving child abuse and child sexual exploitation".

1998—Pub. L. 105–314, title VI, §606(b), Oct. 30, 1998, 112 Stat. 2985, added items 3486 and 3486A and struck out former item 3486 "Authorized investigative demand procedures".

1997—Pub. L. 105–6, §2(b), Mar. 19, 1997, 111 Stat. 12, added item 3510.

1996—Pub. L. 104–294, title VI, §604(a)(4), Oct. 11, 1996, 110 Stat. 3506, substituted "victims' " for "Victims' " in item 3509.

Pub. L. 104–191, title II, §248(b), Aug. 21, 1996, 110 Stat. 2019, added item 3486.

1994—Pub. L. 103–322, title XXXIII, §330002(j), Sept. 13, 1994, 108 Stat. 2140, added item 3509.

1988—Pub. L. 100–690, title VI, §6484(b), Nov. 18, 1988, 102 Stat. 4384, added item 3508.

1984—Pub. L. 98–473, title II, §1217(b), Oct. 12, 1984, 98 Stat. 2166, added items 3505, 3506, and 3507.

1970—Pub. L. 91–452, title II, §228(b), title VI, §601(b), title VII, §702(b), Oct. 15, 1970, 84 Stat. 930, 935, 936, added items 3503 and 3504, and struck out item 3486 "Compelled testimony tending to incriminate witnesses; immunity".

1968—Pub. L. 90–351, title II, §701(b), June 19, 1968, 82 Stat. 211, added items 3501 and 3502.

1957—Pub. L. 85–269, Sept. 2, 1957, 71 Stat. 596, added item 3500.

1954—Act Aug. 20, 1954, ch. 769, §2, 68 Stat. 746, rephrased item 3486.

Protected Facilities for Housing Government Witnesses

Pub. L. 91–452, title V, §§501–504, Oct. 15, 1970, 84 Stat. 933, which authorized the Attorney General to provide for the security of Government witnesses and the families of Government witnesses in legal proceedings against any person alleged to have participated in an organized criminal activity, was repealed by Pub. L. 98–473, title II, §1209(b), Oct. 12, 1984, 98 Stat. 2163, effective Oct. 1, 1984.

§3481. Competency of accused

In trial of all persons charged with the commission of offenses against the United States and in all proceedings in courts martial and courts of inquiry in any State, District, Possession or Territory,

the person charged shall, at his own request, be a competent witness. His failure to make such request shall not create any presumption against him.
(June 25, 1948, ch. 645, 62 Stat. 833.)

Historical and Revision Notes

Based on section 632 of title 28, U.S.C., 1940 ed., Judicial Code and Judiciary, and section 1200, Art. 42(a), of Title 34, Navy. (Mar. 16, 1878, ch. 37, 20 Stat. 30).
Section was rewritten without change of substance.

Short Title of 1997 Amendment

Pub. L. 105–6, §1, Mar. 19, 1997, 111 Stat. 12, provided that: "This Act [enacting section 3510 of this title, amending section 3593 of this title, and enacting provisions set out as a note under section 3510 of this title] may be cited as the 'Victim Rights Clarification Act of 1997'."

§3482. Evidence and witnesses—(Rule)

See Federal Rules of Criminal Procedure

Competency and privileges of witnesses and admissibility of evidence governed by principles of common law, Rule 26.
(June 25, 1948, ch. 645, 62 Stat. 833.)

References in Text

Rule 26 of the Federal Rules of Criminal Procedure, referred to in text, was amended in 1972. The subject matter is covered by the Federal Rules of Evidence, set out in the Appendix to Title 28, Judiciary and Judicial Procedure.

§3483. Indigent defendants, process to produce evidence—(Rule)

See Federal Rules of Criminal Procedure

Subpoena for indigent defendants, motion, affidavit, costs, Rule 17(b).
(June 25, 1948, ch. 645, 62 Stat. 833.)

§3484. Subpoenas—(Rule)

See Federal Rules of Criminal Procedure

Form, contents and issuance of subpoena, Rule 17(a).
Service in United States, Rule 17(d), (e,1).
Service in foreign country, Rule 17(d), (e,2).
Indigent defendants, Rule 17(b).
On taking depositions, Rule 17(f).
Papers and documents, Rule 17(c).
Disobedience of subpoena as contempt of court, Rule 17(g).
(June 25, 1948, ch. 645, 62 Stat. 833.)

§3485. Expert witnesses—(Rule)

See Federal Rules of Criminal Procedure

Selection and appointment of expert witnesses by court or parties; compensation, Rule 28.
(June 25, 1948, ch. 645, 62 Stat. 833.)

References in Text

Rule 28 of the Federal Rules of Criminal Procedure, referred to in text, was amended in 1972. The subject matter of this reference is covered by Federal Rules of Evidence, set out in the Appendix to Title 28, Judiciary and Judicial Procedure.

§3486. Administrative subpoenas

(a) Authorization.—(1)(A) In any investigation of—

(i)(I) a Federal health care offense; or (II) a Federal offense involving the sexual exploitation or abuse of children, the Attorney General;

(ii) an unregistered sex offender conducted by the United States Marshals Service, the Director of the United States Marshals Service; or

(iii) an offense under section 871 or 879, or a threat against a person protected by the United States Secret Service under paragraph (5) or (6) of section 3056,1 if the Director of the Secret Service determines that the threat constituting the offense or the threat against the person protected is imminent, the Secretary of the Treasury,

may issue in writing and cause to be served a subpoena requiring the production and testimony described in subparagraph (B).

(B) Except as provided in subparagraph (C), a subpoena issued under subparagraph (A) may require—

(i) the production of any records or other things relevant to the investigation; and

(ii) testimony by the custodian of the things required to be produced concerning the production and authenticity of those things.

(C) A subpoena issued under subparagraph (A) with respect to a provider of electronic communication service or remote computing service, in an investigation of a Federal offense involving the sexual exploitation or abuse of children shall not extend beyond—

(i) requiring that provider to disclose the information specified in section 2703(c)(2), which may be relevant to an authorized law enforcement inquiry; or

(ii) requiring a custodian of the records of that provider to give testimony concerning the production and authentication of such records or information.

(D) As used in this paragraph—

(i) the term "Federal offense involving the sexual exploitation or abuse of children" means an offense under section 1201, 1591, 2241(c), 2242, 2243, 2251, 2251A, 2252, 2252A, 2260, 2421, 2422, or 2423, in which the victim is an individual who has not attained the age of 18 years; and

(ii) the term "sex offender" means an individual required to register under the Sex Offender Registration and Notification Act (42 U.S.C. 16901 et seq.).2

(2) A subpoena under this subsection shall describe the objects required to be produced and prescribe a return date within a reasonable period of time within which the objects can be assembled and made available.

(3) The production of records relating to a Federal health care offense shall not be required under this section at any place more than 500 miles distant from the place where the subpoena for the production of such records is served. The production of things in any other case may be required from any place within the United States or subject to the laws or jurisdiction of the United States.

(4) Witnesses subpoenaed under this section shall be paid the same fees and mileage that are paid witnesses in the courts of the United States.

(5) At any time before the return date specified in the summons, the person or entity summoned may, in the United States district court for the district in which that person or entity does business or resides, petition for an order modifying or setting aside the summons, or a prohibition of disclosure ordered by a court under paragraph (6).

(6)(A) A United States district court for the district in which the summons is or will be served, upon application of the United States, may issue an ex parte order that no person or entity disclose to any other person or entity (other than to an attorney in order to obtain legal advice) the existence of such summons for a period of up to 90 days.

(B) Such order may be issued on a showing that the things being sought may be relevant to the investigation and there is reason to believe that such disclosure may result in—

(i) endangerment to the life or physical safety of any person;

(ii) flight to avoid prosecution;

(iii) destruction of or tampering with evidence; or

(iv) intimidation of potential witnesses.

(C) An order under this paragraph may be renewed for additional periods of up to 90 days upon a showing that the circumstances described in subparagraph (B) continue to exist.

(7) A summons issued under this section shall not require the production of anything that would be protected from production under the standards applicable to a subpoena duces tecum issued by a court of the United States.

(8) If no case or proceeding arises from the production of records or other things pursuant to this section within a reasonable time after those records or things are produced, the agency to which those records or things were delivered shall, upon written demand made by the person producing those records or things, return them to that person, except where the production required was only of copies rather than originals.

(9) A subpoena issued under paragraph (1)(A)(i)(II) or (1)(A)(iii) may require production as soon as possible, but in no event less than 24 hours after service of the subpoena.

(10) As soon as practicable following the issuance of a subpoena under paragraph (1)(A)(iii), the Secretary of the Treasury shall notify the Attorney General of its issuance.

(b) Service.—A subpoena issued under this section may be served by any person who is at least 18 years of age and is designated in the subpoena to serve it. Service upon a natural person may be made by personal delivery of the subpoena to him. Service may be made upon a domestic or foreign corporation or upon a partnership or other unincorporated association which is subject to suit under a common name, by delivering the subpoena to an officer, to a managing or general agent, or to any other agent authorized by appointment or by law to receive service of process. The affidavit of the person serving the subpoena entered on a true copy thereof by the person serving it shall be proof of service.

(c) Enforcement.—In the case of contumacy by or refusal to obey a subpoena issued to any person, the Attorney General may invoke the aid of any court of the United States within the jurisdiction of which the investigation is carried on or of which the subpoenaed person is an inhabitant, or in which he carries on business or may be found, to compel compliance with the subpoena. The court may issue an order requiring the subpoenaed person to appear before the Attorney General to produce records, if so ordered, or to give testimony concerning the production and authentication of such records. Any failure to obey the order of the court may be punished by the court as a contempt thereof. All process in any such case may be served in any judicial district in which such person may be found.

(d) Immunity From Civil Liability.—Notwithstanding any Federal, State, or local law, any person, including officers, agents, and employees, receiving a subpoena under this section, who complies in good faith with the subpoena and thus produces the materials sought, shall not be liable in any court of any State or the United States to any customer or other person for such production or for nondisclosure of that production to the customer.

(e) Limitation on Use.—(1) Health information about an individual that is disclosed under this section may not be used in, or disclosed to any person for use in, any administrative, civil, or criminal action or investigation directed against the individual who is the subject of the information unless the action or investigation arises out of and is directly related to receipt of health care or payment for health care or action involving a fraudulent claim related to health; or if authorized by an appropriate order of a court of competent jurisdiction, granted after application showing good cause therefor.

(2) In assessing good cause, the court shall weigh the public interest and the need for disclosure against the injury to the patient, to the physician-patient relationship, and to the treatment services.

(3) Upon the granting of such order, the court, in determining the extent to which any disclosure of all or any part of any record is necessary, shall impose appropriate safeguards against

unauthorized disclosure.

(Added Pub. L. 104–191, title II, §248(a), Aug. 21, 1996, 110 Stat. 2018; amended Pub. L. 105–277, div. A, §101(b) [title I, §122], Oct. 21, 1998, 112 Stat. 2681–50, 2681–72; Pub. L. 105–314, title VI, §606(a)(1), Oct. 30, 1998, 112 Stat. 2984; Pub. L. 106–544, §5(a), (b)(1), (c), Dec. 19, 2000, 114 Stat. 2716, 2718; Pub. L. 108–21, title V, §509, Apr. 30, 2003, 117 Stat. 684; Pub. L. 110–457, title II, §224(b), Dec. 23, 2008, 122 Stat. 5072; Pub. L. 112–206, §4(a), Dec. 7, 2012, 126 Stat. 1492.)

References in Text

The Sex Offender Registration and Notification Act, referred to in subsec. (a)(1)(D)(ii), is title I of Pub. L. 109–248, July 27, 2006, 120 Stat. 590, which was classified principally to subchapter I (§16901 et seq.) of chapter 151 of Title 42, The Public Health and Welfare, prior to editorial reclassification as chapter 209 (§20901 et seq.) of Title 34, Crime Control and Law Enforcement. For complete classification of this Act to the Code, see Short Title of 2006 Act note set out under section 10101 of Title 34 and Tables.

Prior Provisions

A prior section 3486, acts June 25, 1948, ch. 645, 62 Stat. 833; Aug. 20, 1954, ch. 769, §1, 68 Stat. 745; Aug. 28, 1965, Pub. L. 89–141, §2, 79 Stat. 581, set forth procedure for granting of immunity to witnesses compelled to testify or produce evidence in course of any Congressional investigation, or case or proceeding before any grand jury or court of the United States, involving interference with or endangering of national security or defense of the United States, prior to repeal by Pub. L. 91–452, title II, §228(a), Oct. 15, 1970, 84 Stat. 930, effective on sixtieth day following Oct. 15, 1970. See section 6001 et seq. of this title.

Amendments

2012—Subsec. (a)(1)(A)(ii), (iii). Pub. L. 112–206, §4(a)(1)(A), added cl. (ii) and redesignated former cl. (ii) as (iii).

Subsec. (a)(1)(D). Pub. L. 112–206, §4(a)(1)(B), substituted "paragraph—" for "paragraph,", inserted cl. (i) designation before "the term", substituted "years; and" for "years.", and added cl. (ii).

Subsec. (a)(6)(A). Pub. L. 112–206, §4(a)(2)(A), substituted "United States" for "United State".

Subsec. (a)(9), (10). Pub. L. 112–206, §4(a)(2)(B), (C), substituted "(1)(A)(iii)" for "(1)(A)(ii)".

2008—Subsec. (a)(1)(D). Pub. L. 110–457 inserted "1591," after "1201,".

2003—Subsec. (a)(1)(C)(i). Pub. L. 108–21 substituted "the information specified in section 2703(c)(2)" for "the name, address, local and long distance telephone toll billing records, telephone number or other subscriber number or identity, and length of service of a subscriber to or customer of such service and the types of services the subscriber or customer utilized".

2000—Pub. L. 106–544, §5(b)(1), struck out "in Federal health care investigations" after "subpoenas" in section catchline.

Subsec. (a)(1). Pub. L. 106–544, §5(a)(1), amended par. (1) generally. Prior to amendment, par. (1) read as follows: "In any investigation relating to any act or activity involving a Federal health care offense, or any act or activity involving a Federal offense relating to the sexual exploitation or other abuse of children, the Attorney General or the Attorney General's designee may issue in writing and cause to be served a subpoena—

"(A) requiring the production of any records (including any books, papers, documents, electronic media, or other objects or tangible things), which may be relevant to an authorized law enforcement inquiry, that a person or legal entity may possess or have care, custody, or control; or

"(B) requiring a custodian of records to give testimony concerning the production and authentication of such records."

Subsec. (a)(3). Pub. L. 106–544, §5(a)(2), inserted "relating to a Federal health care offense" after "production of records" and inserted at end "The production of things in any other case may be required from any place within the United States or subject to the laws or jurisdiction of the United States."

Subsec. (a)(4). Pub. L. 106–544, §5(c)(1), substituted "subpoenaed" for "summoned".

Subsec. (a)(5) to (10). Pub. L. 106–544, §5(a)(3), added pars. (5) to (10).

Subsec. (d). Pub. L. 106–544, §5(c)(2), substituted "subpoena" for "summons" in two places.

1998—Pub. L. 105–314 substituted "Administrative subpoenas in Federal health care investigations" for "Authorized investigative demand procedures" in section catchline.

Subsec. (a)(1). Pub. L. 105–277 inserted "or any act or activity involving a Federal offense relating to the sexual exploitation or other abuse of children," after "health care offense," in introductory provisions.

Transfer of Functions

For transfer of the functions, personnel, assets, and obligations of the United States Secret Service, including the functions of the Secretary of the Treasury relating thereto, to the Secretary of Homeland Security, and for treatment of related references, see sections 381, 551(d), 552(d), and 557 of Title 6, Domestic Security, and the Department of Homeland Security Reorganization Plan of November 25, 2002, as modified, set out as a note under section 542 of Title 6.

[§3486A. Repealed. Pub. L. 106–544, §5(b)(3), Dec. 19, 2000, 114 Stat. 2718]

Section, added Pub. L. 105–314, title VI, §606(a)(2), Oct. 30, 1998, 112 Stat. 2984, related to administrative subpoenas in cases involving child abuse and child sexual exploitation.

§3487. Refusal to pay as evidence of embezzlement

The refusal of any person, whether in or out of office, charged with the safe-keeping, transfer, or disbursement of the public money to pay any draft, order, or warrant, drawn upon him by the Government Accountability Office, for any public money in his hands belonging to the United States, no matter in what capacity the same may have been received, or may be held, or to transfer or disburse any such money, promptly, upon the legal requirement of any authorized officer, shall be deemed, upon the trial of any indictment against such person for embezzlement, prima facie evidence of such embezzlement.

(June 25, 1948, ch. 645, 62 Stat. 833; Pub. L. 108–271, §8(b), July 7, 2004, 118 Stat. 814.)

Historical and Revision Notes

Based on title 18, U.S.C., 1940 ed., §180 (Mar. 4, 1909, ch. 321, §94, 35 Stat. 1106; June 10, 1921, ch. 18, §304, 42 Stat. 24).

"General Accounting Office" was substituted for "proper accounting officer of the Treasury".

Amendments

2004—Pub. L. 108–271 substituted "Government Accountability Office" for "General Accounting Office".

§3488. Intoxicating liquor in Indian country as evidence of unlawful introduction

The possession by a person of intoxicating liquors in Indian country where the introduction is prohibited by treaty or Federal statute shall be prima facie evidence of unlawful introduction.

(June 25, 1948, ch. 645, 62 Stat. 834.)

Historical and Revision Notes

Based on section 245 of title 25, U.S.C., 1940 ed., Indians (May 18, 1916, ch. 125, §1, 39 Stat. 124).

The only change made was the insertion of the word "Indian" before "country", to substitute specificity for generality. (See definition of "Indian country" in section 1151 of this title.)

§3489. Discovery and inspection—(Rule)

See Federal Rules of Criminal Procedure
Inspection of documents and papers taken from defendant, Rule 16.
(June 25, 1948, ch. 645, 62 Stat. 834.)

§3490. Official record or entry—(Rule)

See Federal Rules of Criminal Procedure
Proof of official record or entry as in civil actions, Rule 27.
(June 25, 1948, ch. 645, 62 Stat. 834.)

§3491. Foreign documents

Any book, paper, statement, record, account, writing, or other document, or any portion thereof, of whatever character and in whatever form, as well as any copy thereof equally with the original, which is not in the United States shall, when duly certified as provided in section 3494 of this title, be admissible in evidence in any criminal action or proceeding in any court of the United States if the court shall find, from all the testimony taken with respect to such foreign document pursuant to a commission executed under section 3492 of this title, that such document (or the original thereof in case such document is a copy) satisfies the authentication requirements of the Federal Rules of Evidence, unless in the event that the genuineness of such document is denied, any party to such criminal action or proceeding making such denial shall establish to the satisfaction of the court that such document is not genuine. Nothing contained herein shall be deemed to require authentication under the provisions of section 3494 of this title of any such foreign documents which may otherwise be properly authenticated by law.
(June 25, 1948, ch. 645, 62 Stat. 834; May 24, 1949, ch. 139, §52, 63 Stat. 96; Pub. L. 88–619, §2, Oct. 3, 1964, 78 Stat. 995; Pub. L. 94–149, §3, Dec. 12, 1975, 89 Stat. 806.)

Historical and Revision Notes

1948 Act
Based on section 695a of title 28, U.S.C., 1940 ed., Judicial Code and Judiciary (June 20, 1936, ch. 640, §2, 49 Stat. 1562.)

1949 Act
This section [section 52] corrects section 3491 of title 18, U.S.C., so that the references therein will be to the correct section numbers in title 28, U.S.C., as revised and enacted in 1948.

References in Text
The Federal Rules of Evidence, referred to in text, are set out in the Appendix to Title 28, Judiciary and Judicial Procedure.

Amendments
1975—Pub. L. 94–149 substituted "the authentication requirements of the Federal Rules of Evidence" for "the requirements of section 1732 of Title 28".
1964—Pub. L. 88–619 struck out "and section 1741 of Title 28" after "section 3494 of this title" in two places.
1949—Act May 24, 1949, substituted "section 1741" for "section 695e" and "section 1732" for "section 695" wherever appearing.

§3492. Commission to consular officers to authenticate foreign documents

(a) The testimony of any witness in a foreign country may be taken either on oral or written interrogatories, or on interrogatories partly oral and partly written, pursuant to a commission issued, as hereinafter provided, for the purpose of determining whether any foreign documents sought to be used in any criminal action or proceeding in any court of the United States are genuine, and whether the authentication requirements of the Federal Rules of Evidence are satisfied with respect to any such document (or the original thereof in case such document is a copy). Application for the issuance of a commission for such purpose may be made to the court in which such action or proceeding is pending by the United States or any other party thereto, after five days' notice in writing by the applicant party, or his attorney, to the opposite party, or his attorney of record, which notice shall state the names and addresses of witnesses whose testimony is to be taken and the time when it is desired to take such testimony. In granting such application the court shall issue a commission for the purpose of taking the testimony sought by the applicant addressed to any consular officer of the United States conveniently located for the purpose. In cases of testimony taken on oral or partly oral interrogatories, the court shall make provisions in the commission for the selection as hereinafter provided of foreign counsel to represent each party (except the United States) to the criminal action or proceeding in which the foreign documents in question are to be used, unless such party has, prior to the issuance of the commission, notified the court that he does not desire the selection of foreign counsel to represent him at the time of taking of such testimony. In cases of testimony taken on written interrogatories, such provision shall be made only upon the request of any such party prior to the issuance of such commission. Selection of foreign counsel shall be made by the party whom such foreign counsel is to represent within ten days prior to the taking of testimony or by the court from which the commission issued, upon the request of such party made within such time.

(b) Any consular officer to whom a commission is addressed to take testimony, who is interested in the outcome of the criminal action or proceeding in which the foreign documents in question are to be used or has participated in the prosecution of such action or proceeding, whether by investigations, preparation of evidence, or otherwise, may be disqualified on his own motion or on that of the United States or any other party to such criminal action or proceeding made to the court from which the commission issued at any time prior to the execution thereof. If after notice and hearing, the court grants the motion, it shall instruct the consular officer thus disqualified to send the commission to any other consular officer of the United States named by the court, and such other officer shall execute the commission according to its terms and shall for all purposes be deemed the officer to whom the commission is addressed.

(c) The provisions of this section and sections 3493–3496 of this title applicable to consular officers shall be applicable to diplomatic officers pursuant to such regulations as may be prescribed by the President. For purposes of this section and sections 3493 through 3496 of this title, the term "consular officers" includes any United States citizen who is designated to perform notarial functions pursuant to section 1750 of the Revised Statutes, as amended (22 U.S.C. 4221).

(June 25, 1948, ch. 645, 62 Stat. 834; May 24, 1949, ch. 139, §53, 63 Stat. 96; Pub. L. 94–149, §4, Dec. 12, 1975, 89 Stat. 806; Pub. L. 105–277, div. G, subdiv. B, title XXII, §2222(c)(2), Oct. 21, 1998, 112 Stat. 2681–818.)

Historical and Revision Notes

1948 Act

Based on section 695b of title 28, U.S.C., 1940 ed., Judicial Code and Judiciary (June 20, 1936, ch. 640, §3, 49 Stat. 1562).

1949 Act

This section [section 53] corrects section 3492(a) of title 18, U.S.C., so that the reference in the first sentence thereof will be to the correct section number in title 28, U.S.C., as revised and enacted in 1948.

References in Text
The Federal Rules of Evidence, referred to in subsec. (a), are set out in the Appendix to Title 28, Judiciary and Judicial Procedure.

Amendments
1998—Subsec. (c). Pub. L. 105–277 inserted at end "For purposes of this section and sections 3493 through 3496 of this title, the term 'consular officers' includes any United States citizen who is designated to perform notarial functions pursuant to section 1750 of the Revised Statutes, as amended (22 U.S.C. 4221)."

1975—Subsec. (a). Pub. L. 94–149 substituted "the authentication requirements of the Federal Rules of Evidence" for "the requirements of section 1732 of Title 28".

1949—Subsec. (a). Act May 24, 1949, substituted "section 1732" for "section 695".

§3493. Deposition to authenticate foreign documents
The consular officer to whom any commission authorized under section 3492 of this title is addressed shall take testimony in accordance with its terms. Every person whose testimony is taken shall be cautioned and sworn to testify the whole truth and carefully examined. His testimony shall be reduced to writing or typewriting by the consular officer taking the testimony, or by some person under his personal supervision, or by the witness himself, in the presence of the consular officer and by no other person, and shall, after it has been reduced to writing or typewriting, be subscribed by the witness. Every foreign document, with respect to which testimony is taken, shall be annexed to such testimony and subscribed by each witness who appears for the purpose of establishing the genuineness of such document. When counsel for all the parties attend the examination of any witness whose testimony is to be taken on written interrogatories, they may consent that oral interrogatories in addition to those accompanying the commission may be put to the witness. The consular officer taking any testimony shall require an interpreter to be present when his services are needed or are requested by any party or his attorney.
(June 25, 1948, ch. 645, 62 Stat. 835.)

Historical and Revision Notes
Based on section 695c of title 28, U.S.C., 1940 ed., Judicial Code and Judiciary (June 20, 1936, ch. 640, §4, 49 Stat. 1563).

§3494. Certification of genuineness of foreign document
If the consular officer executing any commission authorized under section 3492 of this title shall be satisfied, upon all the testimony taken, that a foreign document is genuine, he shall certify such document to be genuine under the seal of his office. Such certification shall include a statement that he is not subject to disqualification under the provisions of section 3492 of this title. He shall thereupon transmit, by mail, such foreign documents, together with the record of all testimony taken and the commission which has been executed, to the clerk of the court from which such commission issued, in the manner in which his official dispatches are transmitted to the Government. The clerk receiving any executed commission shall open it and shall make any foreign documents and record of testimony, transmitted with such commission, available for inspection by the parties to the criminal action or proceeding in which such documents are to be used, and said parties shall be furnished copies of such documents free of charge.
(June 25, 1948, ch. 645, 62 Stat. 835.)

Historical and Revision Notes

Based on section 695d of title 28, U.S.C., 1940 ed., Judicial Code and Judiciary (June 20, 1936, ch. 640, §5, 49 Stat. 1563).

§3495. Fees and expenses of consuls, counsel, interpreters and witnesses

(a) The consular fees prescribed under section 1201 of Title 22, for official services in connection with the taking of testimony under sections 3492–3494 of this title, and the fees of any witness whose testimony is taken shall be paid by the party who applied for the commission pursuant to which such testimony was taken. Every witness under section 3493 of this title shall be entitled to receive, for each day's attendance, fees prescribed under section 3496 of this title. Every foreign counsel selected pursuant to a commission issued on application of the United States, and every interpreter whose services are required by a consular officer under section 3493 of this title, shall be paid by the United States, such compensation, together with such personal and incidental expense upon verified statements filed with the consular officer, as he may allow. Compensation and expenses of foreign counsel selected pursuant to a commission issued on application of any party other than the United States shall be paid by the party whom such counsel represents and shall be allowed in the same manner.

(b) Whenever any party makes affidavit, prior to the issuance of a commission for the purpose of taking testimony, that he is not possessed of sufficient means and is actually unable to pay any fees and costs incurred under this section, such fees and costs shall, upon order of the court, be paid in the same manner as fees and costs are paid which are chargeable to the United States.

(c) Any appropriation available for the payment of fees and costs in the case of witnesses subpenaed in behalf of the United States in criminal cases shall be available for any fees or costs which the United States is required to pay under this section.

(June 25, 1948, ch. 645, 62 Stat. 836; May 24, 1949, ch. 139, §54, 63 Stat. 96.)

Historical and Revision Notes

1948 Act

Based on section 695f of title 28, U.S.C., 1940 ed., Judicial Code and Judiciary (June 20, 1936, ch. 640, §7, 49 Stat. 1564).

1949 Act

This section [section 54] corrects the reference in the first sentence of section 3495(a) of title 18, U.S.C., because the provisions which were formerly set out as section 127 of title 22, U.S.C., are now set out as section 1201 of such title.

References in Text

Section 1201 of Title 22, referred to in subsec. (a), was transferred to section 4219 of Title 22, Foreign Relations and Intercourse.

Amendments

1949—Subsec. (a). Act May 24, 1949, substituted "section 1201" for "section 127".

§3496. Regulations by President as to commissions, fees of witnesses, counsel and interpreters

The President is authorized to prescribe regulations governing the manner of executing and returning commissions by consular officers under the provisions of sections 3492–3494 of this title and schedules of fees allowable to witnesses, foreign counsel, and interpreters under section 3495 of this title.

(June 25, 1948, ch. 645, 62 Stat. 836.)

Historical and Revision Notes

Based on section 695g of title 28, U.S.C., 1940 ed., Judicial Code and Judiciary (June 20, 1936, ch. 640, §8, 49 Stat. 1564).

Ex. Ord. No. 10307. Delegation of Authority

Ex. Ord. No. 10307, Nov. 23, 1951, 16 F.R. 11907, provided:

By virtue of the authority vested in me by the act of August 8, 1950, 64 Stat. 419 (3 U.S.C. Supp. 301–303), I hereby delegate to the Secretary of State (1) the authority vested in the President by section 3496 of title 18 of the United States Code (62 Stat. 836) to prescribe regulations governing the manner of executing and returning commissions by consular officers under the provisions of sections 3492–3494 of the said title, and schedules of fees allowable to witnesses, foreign counsel, and interpreters under section 3495 of the said title, and (2) the authority vested in the President by section 3492(c) of title 18 of the United States Code (62 Stat. 835) to prescribe regulations making the provisions of sections 3492–3496 of the said title applicable to diplomatic officers.

Executive Order No. 8298 of December 4, 1939, entitled "Regulations Governing the Manner of Executing and Returning Commissions by Officers of the Foreign Service in Criminal Cases, and Schedule of Fees and Compensation in Such Cases", is hereby revoked.

§3497. Account as evidence of embezzlement

Upon the trial of any indictment against any person for embezzling public money it shall be sufficient evidence, prima facie, for the purpose of showing a balance against such person, to produce a transcript from the books and proceedings of the Government Accountability Office. (June 25, 1948, ch. 645, 62 Stat. 836; Pub. L. 108–271, §8(b), July 7, 2004, 118 Stat. 814.)

Historical and Revision Notes

Based on title 18, U.S.C., 1940 ed., §§179, 355; section 668 of title 28, U.S.C., 1940 ed., Judicial Code and Judiciary (R.S. §887; Mar. 4, 1909, ch. 321, §§93, 225, 35 Stat. 1105, 1133; June 10, 1921, ch. 18, §304, 42 Stat. 24).

This section is a consolidation of section 179 of title 18, U.S.C., 1940 ed., with similar provisions of section 355 of title 18, U.S.C., 1940 ed., and section 668 of title 28, U.S.C., 1940 ed., Judicial Code and Judiciary, with changes of phraseology only except that "General Accounting Office" was substituted for "Treasury Department".

Other provisions of said section 355 of title 18, U.S.C., 1940 ed., are incorporated in section 1711 of this title.

Words in second sentence of said section 355 of title 18, U.S.C., 1940 ed., which preceded the semicolon therein and which read "Any failure to produce or to pay over any such money or property, when required so to do as above provided, shall be taken to be prima facie evidence of such embezzlement" were omitted as surplusage, because such failure to produce or to pay over such money or property constitutes embezzlement. (See sections 653 and 1711 of this title.)

Amendments

2004—Pub. L. 108–271 substituted "Government Accountability Office" for "General Accounting Office".

§3498. Depositions—(Rule)

See Federal Rules of Criminal Procedure

Time, manner and conditions of taking depositions; costs; notice; use; objections; written interrogatories, Rule 15.

Subpoenas on taking depositions, Rule 17(f).

(June 25, 1948, ch. 645, 62 Stat. 836.)

§3499. Contempt of court by witness—(Rule)

See Federal Rules of Criminal Procedure

Disobedience of subpoena without excuse as contempt, Rule 17(g).
(June 25, 1948, ch. 645, 62 Stat. 836.)

§3500. Demands for production of statements and reports of witnesses

(a) In any criminal prosecution brought by the United States, no statement or report in the possession of the United States which was made by a Government witness or prospective Government witness (other than the defendant) shall be the subject of subpena, discovery, or inspection until said witness has testified on direct examination in the trial of the case.

(b) After a witness called by the United States has testified on direct examination, the court shall, on motion of the defendant, order the United States to produce any statement (as hereinafter defined) of the witness in the possession of the United States which relates to the subject matter as to which the witness has testified. If the entire contents of any such statement relate to the subject matter of the testimony of the witness, the court shall order it to be delivered directly to the defendant for his examination and use.

(c) If the United States claims that any statement ordered to be produced under this section contains matter which does not relate to the subject matter of the testimony of the witness, the court shall order the United States to deliver such statement for the inspection of the court in camera. Upon such delivery the court shall excise the portions of such statement which do not relate to the subject matter of the testimony of the witness. With such material excised, the court shall then direct delivery of such statement to the defendant for his use. If, pursuant to such procedure, any portion of such statement is withheld from the defendant and the defendant objects to such withholding, and the trial is continued to an adjudication of the guilt of the defendant, the entire text of such statement shall be preserved by the United States and, in the event the defendant appeals, shall be made available to the appellate court for the purpose of determining the correctness of the ruling of the trial judge. Whenever any statement is delivered to a defendant pursuant to this section, the court in its discretion, upon application of said defendant, may recess proceedings in the trial for such time as it may determine to be reasonably required for the examination of such statement by said defendant and his preparation for its use in the trial.

(d) If the United States elects not to comply with an order of the court under subsection (b) or (c) hereof to deliver to the defendant any such statement, or such portion thereof as the court may direct, the court shall strike from the record the testimony of the witness, and the trial shall proceed unless the court in its discretion shall determine that the interests of justice require that a mistrial be declared.

(e) The term "statement", as used in subsections (b), (c), and (d) of this section in relation to any witness called by the United States, means—

(1) a written statement made by said witness and signed or otherwise adopted or approved by him;

(2) a stenographic, mechanical, electrical, or other recording, or a transcription thereof, which is a substantially verbatim recital of an oral statement made by said witness and recorded contemporaneously with the making of such oral statement; or

(3) a statement, however taken or recorded, or a transcription thereof, if any, made by said witness to a grand jury.

(Added Pub. L. 85–269, Sept. 2, 1957, 71 Stat. 595; amended Pub. L. 91–452, title I, §102, Oct. 15, 1970, 84 Stat. 926.)

Amendments

1970—Subsec. (a). Pub. L. 91–452, §102(a), struck out "to an agent of the Government" after "(other than the defendant)".

Subsec. (d). Pub. L. 91–452, §102(b), substituted "subsection" for "paragraph".

Subsec. (e). Pub. L. 91–452, §102(c), (d), struck out "or" after "by him;" in par. (1), struck out "to an agent of the Government" after "said witness" in par. (2), and added par. (3).

§3501. Admissibility of confessions

(a) In any criminal prosecution brought by the United States or by the District of Columbia, a confession, as defined in subsection (e) hereof, shall be admissible in evidence if it is voluntarily given. Before such confession is received in evidence, the trial judge shall, out of the presence of the jury, determine any issue as to voluntariness. If the trial judge determines that the confession was voluntarily made it shall be admitted in evidence and the trial judge shall permit the jury to hear relevant evidence on the issue of voluntariness and shall instruct the jury to give such weight to the confession as the jury feels it deserves under all the circumstances.

(b) The trial judge in determining the issue of voluntariness shall take into consideration all the circumstances surrounding the giving of the confession, including (1) the time elapsing between arrest and arraignment of the defendant making the confession, if it was made after arrest and before arraignment, (2) whether such defendant knew the nature of the offense with which he was charged or of which he was suspected at the time of making the confession, (3) whether or not such defendant was advised or knew that he was not required to make any statement and that any such statement could be used against him, (4) whether or not such defendant had been advised prior to questioning of his right to the assistance of counsel; and (5) whether or not such defendant was without the assistance of counsel when questioned and when giving such confession.

The presence or absence of any of the above-mentioned factors to be taken into consideration by the judge need not be conclusive on the issue of voluntariness of the confession.

(c) In any criminal prosecution by the United States or by the District of Columbia, a confession made or given by a person who is a defendant therein, while such person was under arrest or other detention in the custody of any law-enforcement officer or law-enforcement agency, shall not be inadmissible solely because of delay in bringing such person before a magistrate judge or other officer empowered to commit persons charged with offenses against the laws of the United States or of the District of Columbia if such confession is found by the trial judge to have been made voluntarily and if the weight to be given the confession is left to the jury and if such confession was made or given by such person within six hours immediately following his arrest or other detention: Provided, That the time limitation contained in this subsection shall not apply in any case in which the delay in bringing such person before such magistrate judge or other officer beyond such six-hour period is found by the trial judge to be reasonable considering the means of transportation and the distance to be traveled to the nearest available such magistrate judge or other officer.

(d) Nothing contained in this section shall bar the admission in evidence of any confession made or given voluntarily by any person to any other person without interrogation by anyone, or at any time at which the person who made or gave such confession was not under arrest or other detention.

(e) As used in this section, the term "confession" means any confession of guilt of any criminal offense or any self-incriminating statement made or given orally or in writing.

(Added Pub. L. 90–351, title II, §701(a), June 19, 1968, 82 Stat. 210; amended Pub. L. 90–578, title III, §301(a)(3), Oct. 17, 1968, 82 Stat. 1115; Pub. L. 101–650, title III, §321, Dec. 1, 1990, 104 Stat. 5117.)

Constitutionality

For information regarding constitutionality of this section, as added by section 701(a) of Pub. L. 90–351, see Congressional Research Service, The Constitution of the United States of America: Analysis and Interpretation, Appendix 1, Acts of Congress Held Unconstitutional in Whole or in Part by the Supreme Court of the United States.

Amendments

1968—Subsec. (c). Pub. L. 90–578 substituted "magistrate" for "commissioner" wherever appearing.

Change of Name

Words "magistrate judge" substituted for "magistrate" wherever appearing in subsec. (c) pursuant to section 321 of Pub. L. 101–650, set out as a note under section 631 of Title 28, Judiciary and Judicial Procedure.

§3502. Admissibility in evidence of eye witness testimony

The testimony of a witness that he saw the accused commit or participate in the commission of the crime for which the accused is being tried shall be admissible in evidence in a criminal prosecution in any trial court ordained and established under article III of the Constitution of the United States.

(Added Pub. L. 90–351, title II, §701(a), June 19, 1968, 82 Stat. 211.)

[§3503. Repealed. Pub. L. 107–273, div. B, title IV, §4002(c)(3)(A), Nov. 2, 2002, 116 Stat. 1809]

Section, added Pub. L. 91–452, title VI, §601(a), Oct. 15, 1970, 84 Stat. 934, related to depositions to preserve testimony.

§3504. Litigation concerning sources of evidence

(a) In any trial, hearing, or other proceeding in or before any court, grand jury, department, officer, agency, regulatory body, or other authority of the United States—

(1) upon a claim by a party aggrieved that evidence is inadmissible because it is the primary product of an unlawful act or because it was obtained by the exploitation of an unlawful act, the opponent of the claim shall affirm or deny the occurrence of the alleged unlawful act;

(2) disclosure of information for a determination if evidence is inadmissible because it is the primary product of an unlawful act occurring prior to June 19, 1968, or because it was obtained by the exploitation of an unlawful act occurring prior to June 19, 1968, shall not be required unless such information may be relevant to a pending claim of such inadmissibility; and

(3) no claim shall be considered that evidence of an event is inadmissible on the ground that such evidence was obtained by the exploitation of an unlawful act occurring prior to June 19, 1968, if such event occurred more than five years after such allegedly unlawful act.

(b) As used in this section "unlawful act" means any act the use of any electronic, mechanical, or other device (as defined in section 2510(5) of this title) in violation of the Constitution or laws of the United States or any regulation or standard promulgated pursuant thereto.

(Added Pub. L. 91–452, title VII, §702(a), Oct. 15, 1970, 84 Stat. 935.)

Congressional Statement of Findings

Pub. L. 91–452, title VII, §701, Oct. 15, 1970, 84 Stat. 935, provided that: "The Congress finds that claims that evidence offered in proceedings was obtained by the exploitation of unlawful acts, and is therefore inadmissible in evidence, (1) often cannot reliably be determined when such claims concern evidence of events occurring years after the allegedly unlawful act, and (2) when the allegedly unlawful act has occurred more than five years prior to the event in question, there is virtually no likelihood that the evidence offered to prove the event has been obtained by the exploitation of that allegedly unlawful act."

Applicability to Proceedings

Pub. L. 91 452, title VII, §703, Oct. 15, 1970, 84 Stat. 936, provided that: "This title [enacting this section and provisions set as notes under this section] shall apply to all proceedings, regardless of when commenced, occurring after the date of its enactment [Oct. 15, 1970]. Paragraph (3) of subsection (a) of section 3504, chapter 223, title 18, United States Code, shall not apply to any proceeding in which all information to be relied upon to establish inadmissibility was possessed by the party making such claim and adduced in such proceeding prior to such enactment."

§3505. Foreign records of regularly conducted activity

(a)(1) In a criminal proceeding in a court of the United States, a foreign record of regularly conducted activity, or a copy of such record, shall not be excluded as evidence by the hearsay rule if a foreign certification attests that—

(A) such record was made, at or near the time of the occurrence of the matters set forth, by (or from information transmitted by) a person with knowledge of those matters;

(B) such record was kept in the course of a regularly conducted business activity;

(C) the business activity made such a record as a regular practice; and

(D) if such record is not the original, such record is a duplicate of the original;

unless the source of information or the method or circumstances of preparation indicate lack of trustworthiness.

(2) A foreign certification under this section shall authenticate such record or duplicate.

(b) At the arraignment or as soon after the arraignment as practicable, a party intending to offer in evidence under this section a foreign record of regularly conducted activity shall provide written notice of that intention to each other party. A motion opposing admission in evidence of such record shall be made by the opposing party and determined by the court before trial. Failure by a party to file such motion before trial shall constitute a waiver of objection to such record or duplicate, but the court for cause shown may grant relief from the waiver.

(c) As used in this section, the term—

(1) "foreign record of regularly conducted activity" means a memorandum, report, record, or data compilation, in any form, of acts, events, conditions, opinions, or diagnoses, maintained in a foreign country;

(2) "foreign certification" means a written declaration made and signed in a foreign country by the custodian of a foreign record of regularly conducted activity or another qualified person that, if falsely made, would subject the maker to criminal penalty under the laws of that country; and

(3) "business" includes business, institution, association, profession, occupation, and calling of every kind, whether or not conducted for profit.

(Added Pub. L. 98–473, title II, §1217(a), Oct. 12, 1984, 98 Stat. 2165.)

Effective Date

Pub. L. 98–473, title II, §1220, Oct. 12, 1984, 98 Stat. 2167, provided that: "This part [part K (§§1217–1220) of chapter XII of title II of Pub. L. 98–473, enacting this section and sections 3292, 3506, and 3507 of this title and amending section 3161 of this title] and the amendments made by this part shall take effect thirty days after the date of the enactment of this Act [Oct. 12, 1984]."

§3506. Service of papers filed in opposition to official request by United States to foreign government for criminal evidence

(a) Except as provided in subsection (b) of this section, any national or resident of the United States who submits, or causes to be submitted, a pleading or other document to a court or other authority in a foreign country in opposition to an official request for evidence of an offense shall serve such pleading or other document on the Attorney General at the time such pleading or other document is submitted.

(b) Any person who is a party to a criminal proceeding in a court of the United States who submits, or causes to be submitted, a pleading or other document to a court or other authority in a foreign country in opposition to an official request for evidence of an offense that is a subject of such proceeding shall serve such pleading or other document on the appropriate attorney for the Government, pursuant to the Federal Rules of Criminal Procedure, at the time such pleading or other document is submitted.

(c) As used in this section, the term "official request" means a letter rogatory, a request under a treaty or convention, or any other request for evidence made by a court of the United States or an authority of the United States having criminal law enforcement responsibility, to a court or other authority of a foreign country.

(Added Pub. L. 98–473, title II, §1217(a), Oct. 12, 1984, 98 Stat. 2166.)

Effective Date

Section effective 30 days after Oct. 12, 1984, see section 1220 of Pub. L. 98–473, set out as a note under section 3505 of this title.

§3507. Special master at foreign deposition

Upon application of a party to a criminal case, a United States district court before which the case is pending may, to the extent permitted by a foreign country, appoint a special master to carry out at a deposition taken in that country such duties as the court may direct, including presiding at the deposition or serving as an advisor on questions of United States law. Notwithstanding any other provision of law, a special master appointed under this section shall not decide questions of privilege under foreign law. The refusal of a court to appoint a special master under this section, or of the foreign country to permit a special master appointed under this section to carry out a duty at a deposition in that country, shall not affect the admissibility in evidence of a deposition taken under the provisions of the Federal Rules of Criminal Procedure.

(Added Pub. L. 98–473, title II, §1217(a), Oct. 12, 1984, 98 Stat. 2166.)

Effective Date

Section effective 30 days after Oct. 12, 1984, see section 1220 of Pub. L. 98–473, set out as a note under section 3505 of this title.

§3508. Custody and return of foreign witnesses

(a) When the testimony of a person who is serving a sentence, is in pretrial detention, or is otherwise being held in custody, in a foreign country, is needed in a State or Federal criminal proceeding, the Attorney General shall, when he deems it appropriate in the exercise of his discretion, have the authority to request the temporary transfer of that person to the United States for the purposes of giving such testimony, to transport such person to the United States in custody, to maintain the custody of such person while he is in the United States, and to return such person to the foreign country.

(b) Where the transfer to the United States of a person in custody for the purposes of giving testimony is provided for by treaty or convention, by this section, or both, that person shall be returned to the foreign country from which he is transferred. In no event shall the return of such person require any request for extradition or extradition proceedings, or proceedings under the immigration laws.

(c) Where there is a treaty or convention between the United States and the foreign country in which the witness is being held in custody which provides for the transfer, custody and return of such witnesses, the terms and conditions of that treaty shall apply. Where there is no such treaty or convention, the Attorney General may exercise the authority described in paragraph (a) if both the foreign country and the witness give their consent.

(Added Pub. L. 100–690, title VI, §6484(a), Nov. 18, 1988, 102 Stat. 4384.)

§3509. Child victims' and child witnesses' rights

(a) Definitions.—For purposes of this section—

(1) the term "adult attendant" means an adult described in subsection (i) who accompanies a child throughout the judicial process for the purpose of providing emotional support;

(2) the term "child" means a person who is under the age of 18, who is or is alleged to be—

(A) a victim of a crime of physical abuse, sexual abuse, or exploitation; or

(B) a witness to a crime committed against another person;

(3) the term "child abuse" means the physical or mental injury, sexual abuse or exploitation, or negligent treatment of a child;

(4) the term "physical injury" includes lacerations, fractured bones, burns, internal injuries, severe bruising or serious bodily harm;

(5) the term "mental injury" means harm to a child's psychological or intellectual functioning which may be exhibited by severe anxiety, depression, withdrawal or outward aggressive behavior, or a combination of those behaviors, which may be demonstrated by a change in behavior, emotional response, or cognition;

(6) the term "exploitation" means child pornography or child prostitution;

(7) the term "multidisciplinary child abuse team" means a professional unit composed of representatives from health, social service, law enforcement, and legal service agencies to coordinate the assistance needed to handle cases of child abuse;

(8) the term "sexual abuse" includes the employment, use, persuasion, inducement, enticement, or coercion of a child to engage in, or assist another person to engage in, sexually explicit conduct or the rape, molestation, prostitution, or other form of sexual exploitation of children, or incest with children;

(9) the term "sexually explicit conduct" means actual or simulated—

(A) sexual intercourse, including sexual contact in the manner of genital-genital, oral-genital, anal-genital, or oral-anal contact, whether between persons of the same or of opposite sex; sexual contact means the intentional touching, either directly or through clothing, of the genitalia, anus, groin, breast, inner thigh, or buttocks of any person with an intent to abuse, humiliate, harass, degrade, or arouse or gratify sexual desire of any person;

(B) bestiality;

(C) masturbation;

(D) lascivious exhibition of the genitals or pubic area of a person or animal; or

(E) sadistic or masochistic abuse;

(10) the term "sex crime" means an act of sexual abuse that is a criminal act;

(11) the term "negligent treatment" means the failure to provide, for reasons other than poverty, adequate food, clothing, shelter, or medical care so as to seriously endanger the physical health of the child; and

(12) the term "child abuse" does not include discipline administered by a parent or legal guardian to his or her child provided it is reasonable in manner and moderate in degree and otherwise does not constitute cruelty.

(b) Alternatives to Live In-Court Testimony.—

(1) Child's live testimony by 2-way closed circuit television.—

(A) In a proceeding involving an alleged offense against a child, the attorney for the Government, the child's attorney, or a guardian ad litem appointed under subsection (h) may apply for an order that the child's testimony be taken in a room outside the courtroom and be televised by 2-way closed circuit television. The person seeking such an order shall apply for such an order at least 7 days before the trial date, unless the court finds on the record that the need for such an order was not reasonably foreseeable.

(B) The court may order that the testimony of the child be taken by closed-circuit television as provided in subparagraph (A) if the court finds that the child is unable to testify in open court in the presence of the defendant, for any of the following reasons:

(i) The child is unable to testify because of fear.

(ii) There is a substantial likelihood, established by expert testimony, that the child would suffer emotional trauma from testifying.

(iii) The child suffers a mental or other infirmity.

(iv) Conduct by defendant or defense counsel causes the child to be unable to continue testifying.

(C) The court shall support a ruling on the child's inability to testify with findings on the record. In determining whether the impact on an individual child of one or more of the factors described in subparagraph (B) is so substantial as to justify an order under subparagraph (A), the court may question the minor in chambers, or at some other comfortable place other than the courtroom, on the record for a reasonable period of time with the child attendant, the prosecutor, the child's attorney, the guardian ad litem, and the defense counsel present.

(D) If the court orders the taking of testimony by television, the attorney for the Government and the attorney for the defendant not including an attorney pro se for a party shall be present in a room outside the courtroom with the child and the child shall be subjected to direct and cross-examination. The only other persons who may be permitted in the room with the child during the child's testimony are—

(i) the child's attorney or guardian ad litem appointed under subsection (h);

(ii) persons necessary to operate the closed-circuit television equipment;

(iii) a judicial officer, appointed by the court; and

(iv) other persons whose presence is determined by the court to be necessary to the welfare and well-being of the child, including an adult attendant.

The child's testimony shall be transmitted by closed circuit television into the courtroom for viewing and hearing by the defendant, jury, judge, and public. The defendant shall be provided with the means of private, contemporaneous communication with the defendant's attorney during the testimony. The closed circuit television transmission shall relay into the room in which the child is testifying the defendant's image, and the voice of the judge.

(2) Videotaped deposition of child.—(A) In a proceeding involving an alleged offense against a child, the attorney for the Government, the child's attorney, the child's parent or legal guardian, or the guardian ad litem appointed under subsection (h) may apply for an order that a deposition be taken of the child's testimony and that the deposition be recorded and preserved on videotape.

(B)(i) Upon timely receipt of an application described in subparagraph (A), the court shall make a preliminary finding regarding whether at the time of trial the child is likely to be unable to testify in open court in the physical presence of the defendant, jury, judge, and public for any of the following reasons:

(I) The child will be unable to testify because of fear.

(II) There is a substantial likelihood, established by expert testimony, that the child would suffer emotional trauma from testifying in open court.

(III) The child suffers a mental or other infirmity.

(IV) Conduct by defendant or defense counsel causes the child to be unable to continue testifying.

(ii) If the court finds that the child is likely to be unable to testify in open court for any of the reasons stated in clause (i), the court shall order that the child's deposition be taken and preserved by videotape.

(iii) The trial judge shall preside at the videotape deposition of a child and shall rule on all questions as if at trial. The only other persons who may be permitted to be present at the proceeding are—

(I) the attorney for the Government;

(II) the attorney for the defendant;

(III) the child's attorney or guardian ad litem appointed under subsection (h);

(IV) persons necessary to operate the videotape equipment;

(V) subject to clause (iv), the defendant; and

(VI) other persons whose presence is determined by the court to be necessary to the welfare and well-being of the child.

The defendant shall be afforded the rights applicable to defendants during trial, including the right to an attorney, the right to be confronted with the witness against the defendant, and the right to cross-examine the child.

(iv) If the preliminary finding of inability under clause (i) is based on evidence that the child is unable to testify in the physical presence of the defendant, the court may order that the defendant, including a defendant represented pro se, be excluded from the room in which the deposition is conducted. If the court orders that the defendant be excluded from the deposition room, the court shall order that 2-way closed circuit television equipment relay the defendant's image into the room in which the child is testifying, and the child's testimony into the room in which the defendant is viewing the proceeding, and that the defendant be provided with a means of private, contemporaneous communication with the defendant's attorney during the deposition.

(v) Handling of videotape.—The complete record of the examination of the child, including the image and voices of all persons who in any way participate in the examination, shall be made and preserved on video tape in addition to being stenographically recorded. The videotape shall be transmitted to the clerk of the court in which the action is pending and shall be made available for viewing to the prosecuting attorney, the defendant, and the defendant's attorney during ordinary business hours.

(C) If at the time of trial the court finds that the child is unable to testify as for a reason described in subparagraph (B)(i), the court may admit into evidence the child's videotaped deposition in lieu of the child's testifying at the trial. The court shall support a ruling under this subparagraph with findings on the record.

(D) Upon timely receipt of notice that new evidence has been discovered after the original videotaping and before or during trial, the court, for good cause shown, may order an additional videotaped deposition. The testimony of the child shall be restricted to the matters specified by the court as the basis for granting the order.

(E) In connection with the taking of a videotaped deposition under this paragraph, the court may enter a protective order for the purpose of protecting the privacy of the child.

(F) The videotape of a deposition taken under this paragraph shall be destroyed 5 years after the date on which the trial court entered its judgment, but not before a final judgment is entered on appeal including Supreme Court review. The videotape shall become part of the court record and be kept by the court until it is destroyed.

(c) Competency Examinations.—

(1) Effect of federal rules of evidence.—Nothing in this subsection shall be construed to abrogate rule 601 of the Federal Rules of Evidence.

(2) Presumption.—A child is presumed to be competent.

(3) Requirement of written motion.—A competency examination regarding a child witness may be conducted by the court only upon written motion and offer of proof of incompetency by a party.

(4) Requirement of compelling reasons.—A competency examination regarding a child may be conducted only if the court determines, on the record, that compelling reasons exist. A child's age alone is not a compelling reason.

(5) Persons permitted to be present.—The only persons who may be permitted to be present at a competency examination are—

(A) the judge;

(B) the attorney for the Government;

(C) the attorney for the defendant;

(D) a court reporter; and

(E) persons whose presence, in the opinion of the court, is necessary to the welfare and well-being of the child, including the child's attorney, guardian ad litem, or adult attendant.

(6) Not before jury.—A competency examination regarding a child witness shall be conducted out of the sight and hearing of a jury.

(7) Direct examination of child.—Examination of a child related to competency shall normally be conducted by the court on the basis of questions submitted by the attorney for the Government and the attorney for the defendant including a party acting as an attorney pro se. The court may permit an attorney but not a party acting as an attorney pro se to examine a child directly on competency if the court is satisfied that the child will not suffer emotional trauma as a result of the examination.

(8) Appropriate questions.—The questions asked at the competency examination of a child shall be appropriate to the age and developmental level of the child, shall not be related to the issues at trial, and shall focus on determining the child's ability to understand and answer simple questions.

(9) Psychological and psychiatric examinations.—Psychological and psychiatric examinations to assess the competency of a child witness shall not be ordered without a showing of compelling

need.

(d) Privacy Protection.—

(1) Confidentiality of information.—(A) A person acting in a capacity described in subparagraph (B) in connection with a criminal proceeding shall—

(i) keep all documents that disclose the name or any other information concerning a child in a secure place to which no person who does not have reason to know their contents has access; and

(ii) disclose documents described in clause (i) or the information in them that concerns a child only to persons who, by reason of their participation in the proceeding, have reason to know such information.

(B) Subparagraph (A) applies to—

(i) all employees of the Government connected with the case, including employees of the Department of Justice, any law enforcement agency involved in the case, and any person hired by the Government to provide assistance in the proceeding;

(ii) employees of the court;

(iii) the defendant and employees of the defendant, including the attorney for the defendant and persons hired by the defendant or the attorney for the defendant to provide assistance in the proceeding; and

(iv) members of the jury.

(2) Filing under seal.—All papers to be filed in court that disclose the name of or any other information concerning a child shall be filed under seal without necessity of obtaining a court order. The person who makes the filing shall submit to the clerk of the court—

(A) the complete paper to be kept under seal; and

(B) the paper with the portions of it that disclose the name of or other information concerning a child redacted, to be placed in the public record.

(3) Protective orders.—(A) On motion by any person the court may issue an order protecting a child from public disclosure of the name of or any other information concerning the child in the course of the proceedings, if the court determines that there is a significant possibility that such disclosure would be detrimental to the child.

(B) A protective order issued under subparagraph (A) may—

(i) provide that the testimony of a child witness, and the testimony of any other witness, when the attorney who calls the witness has reason to anticipate that the name of or any other information concerning a child may be divulged in the testimony, be taken in a closed courtroom; and

(ii) provide for any other measures that may be necessary to protect the privacy of the child.

(4) Disclosure of information.—This subsection does not prohibit disclosure of the name of or other information concerning a child to the defendant, the attorney for the defendant, a multidisciplinary child abuse team, a guardian ad litem, or an adult attendant, or to anyone to whom, in the opinion of the court, disclosure is necessary to the welfare and well-being of the child.

(e) Closing the Courtroom.—When a child testifies the court may order the exclusion from the courtroom of all persons, including members of the press, who do not have a direct interest in the case. Such an order may be made if the court determines on the record that requiring the child to testify in open court would cause substantial psychological harm to the child or would result in the child's inability to effectively communicate. Such an order shall be narrowly tailored to serve the Government's specific compelling interest.

(f) Victim Impact Statement.—In preparing the presentence report pursuant to rule 32(c) of the Federal Rules of Criminal Procedure, the probation officer shall request information from the multidisciplinary child abuse team and other appropriate sources to determine the impact of the offense on the child victim and any other children who may have been affected. A guardian ad litem appointed under subsection (h) shall make every effort to obtain and report information that accurately expresses the child's and the family's views concerning the child's victimization. A guardian ad litem shall use forms that permit the child to express the child's views concerning the personal consequences of the child's victimization, at a level and in a form of communication commensurate with the child's age and ability.

(g) Use of Multidisciplinary Child Abuse Teams.—

(1) In general.—A multidisciplinary child abuse team shall be used when it is feasible to do so. The court shall work with State and local governments that have established multidisciplinary child abuse teams designed to assist child victims and child witnesses, and the court and the attorney for the Government shall consult with the multidisciplinary child abuse team as appropriate.

(2) Role of multidisciplinary child abuse teams.—The role of the multidisciplinary child abuse team shall be to provide for a child services that the members of the team in their professional roles are capable of providing, including—

(A) medical diagnoses and evaluation services, including provision or interpretation of x-rays, laboratory tests, and related services, as needed, and documentation of findings;

(B) telephone consultation services in emergencies and in other situations;

(C) medical evaluations related to abuse or neglect;

(D) psychological and psychiatric diagnoses and evaluation services for the child, parent or parents, guardian or guardians, or other caregivers, or any other individual involved in a child victim or child witness case;

(E) expert medical, psychological, and related professional testimony;

(F) case service coordination and assistance, including the location of services available from public and private agencies in the community; and

(G) training services for judges, litigators, court officers and others that are involved in child victim and child witness cases, in handling child victims and child witnesses.

(h) Guardian Ad Litem.—

(1) In general.—The court may appoint, and provide reasonable compensation and payment of expenses for, a guardian ad litem for a child who was a victim of, or a witness to, a crime involving abuse or exploitation to protect the best interests of the child. In making the appointment, the court shall consider a prospective guardian's background in, and familiarity with, the judicial process, social service programs, and child abuse issues. The guardian ad litem shall not be a person who is or may be a witness in a proceeding involving the child for whom the guardian is appointed.

(2) Duties of guardian ad litem.—A guardian ad litem may attend all the depositions, hearings, and trial proceedings in which a child participates, and make recommendations to the court concerning the welfare of the child. The guardian ad litem may have access to all reports, evaluations and records, except attorney's work product, necessary to effectively advocate for the child. (The extent of access to grand jury materials is limited to the access routinely provided to victims and their representatives.) A guardian ad litem shall marshal and coordinate the delivery of resources and special services to the child. A guardian ad litem shall not be compelled to testify in any court action or proceeding concerning any information or opinion received from the child in the course of serving as a guardian ad litem.

(3) Immunities.—A guardian ad litem shall be presumed to be acting in good faith and shall be immune from civil and criminal liability for complying with the guardian's lawful duties described in paragraph (2).

(i) Adult Attendant.—A child testifying at or attending a judicial proceeding shall have the right to be accompanied by an adult attendant to provide emotional support to the child. The court, at its discretion, may allow the adult attendant to remain in close physical proximity to or in contact with the child while the child testifies. The court may allow the adult attendant to hold the child's hand or allow the child to sit on the adult attendant's lap throughout the course of the proceeding. An adult attendant shall not provide the child with an answer to any question directed to the child during the course of the child's testimony or otherwise prompt the child. The image of the child attendant, for the time the child is testifying or being deposed, shall be recorded on videotape.

(j) Speedy Trial.—In a proceeding in which a child is called to give testimony, on motion by the attorney for the Government or a guardian ad litem, or on its own motion, the court may designate the case as being of special public importance. In cases so designated, the court shall, consistent with these rules, expedite the proceeding and ensure that it takes precedence over any other. The court shall ensure a speedy trial in order to minimize the length of time the child must endure the stress of involvement with the criminal process. When deciding whether to grant a continuance, the court shall take into consideration the age of the child and the potential adverse impact the delay may have on the child's well-being. The court shall make written findings of fact and conclusions of law when granting a continuance in cases involving a child.

(k) Stay of Civil Action.—If, at any time that a cause of action for recovery of compensation for damage or injury to the person of a child exists, a criminal action is pending which arises out of the same occurrence and in which the child is the victim, the civil action shall be stayed until the end of all phases of the criminal action and any mention of the civil action during the criminal proceeding is prohibited. As used in this subsection, a criminal action is pending until its final adjudication in the trial court.

(l) Testimonial Aids.—The court may permit a child to use anatomical dolls, puppets, drawings, mannequins, or any other demonstrative device the court deems appropriate for the purpose of assisting a child in testifying.

(m) Prohibition on Reproduction of Child Pornography.—

(1) In any criminal proceeding, any property or material that constitutes child pornography (as defined by section 2256 of this title) shall remain in the care, custody, and control of either the Government or the court.

(2)(A) Notwithstanding Rule 16 of the Federal Rules of Criminal Procedure, a court shall deny, in any criminal proceeding, any request by the defendant to copy, photograph, duplicate, or otherwise reproduce any property or material that constitutes child pornography (as defined by section 2256 of this title), so long as the Government makes the property or material reasonably available to the defendant.

(B) For the purposes of subparagraph (A), property or material shall be deemed to be reasonably available to the defendant if the Government provides ample opportunity for inspection, viewing, and examination at a Government facility of the property or material by the defendant, his or her attorney, and any individual the defendant may seek to qualify to furnish expert testimony at trial.

(Added Pub. L. 101–647, title II, §225(a), Nov. 29, 1990, 104 Stat. 4798; amended Pub. L. 103–322, title XXXIII, §§330010(6), (7), 330011(e), 330018(b), Sept. 13, 1994, 108 Stat. 2143, 2145, 2149; Pub. L. 104–294, title VI, §605(h), Oct. 11, 1996, 110 Stat. 3510; Pub. L. 109–248, title V, §§504, 507, July 27, 2006, 120 Stat. 629, 631; Pub. L. 111–16, §3(11), May 7, 2009, 123 Stat. 1608.)

References in Text

The Federal Rules of Evidence, referred to in subsec. (c)(1), are set out in the Appendix to Title 28, Judiciary and Judicial Procedure.

The Federal Rules of Criminal Procedure, referred to in subsecs. (f) and (m)(2)(A), are set out in the Appendix to this title.

Amendments

2009—Subsec. (b)(1)(A). Pub. L. 111–16 substituted "7 days" for "5 days".

2006—Subsec. (h)(1). Pub. L. 109–248, §507, inserted ", and provide reasonable compensation and payment of expenses for," after "The court may appoint".

Subsec. (m). Pub. L. 109–248, §504, added subsec. (m).

1996—Subsec. (e). Pub. L. 104–294, §605(h)(1), substituted "serve the Government's" for "serve the government's".

Subsec. (h)(3). Pub. L. 104–294, §605(h)(2), substituted "in paragraph (2)" for "in subpart (2)".

1994—Pub. L. 103–322, §330011(e), made technical amendment to directory language of Pub. L. 101–647, §225(a), which enacted this section.

Pub. L. 103–322, §330010(7)(B), substituted "Government" for "government" in subsecs. (b)(1)(A), (D), (2)(A), and (c)(5)(B), in subsec. (d)(1)(B)(i) after "hired by the", and in subsec. (g)(1).

Pub. L. 103–322, §330010(7)(A), substituted "subsection" for "subdivision" in subsecs. (b)(1)(A), (D)(i), (2)(A), (B)(iii)(III), (c)(1), (d)(4), and (f).

Subsec. (a)(11) to (13). Pub. L. 103–322, §330010(6), redesignated pars. (12) and (13) as (11) and (12), respectively, and struck out former par. (11) which read as follows: "the term 'exploitation' means child pornography or child prostitution;".

Subsec. (k). Pub. L. 103–322, §330018(b), substituted heading for one which read "Extension of Child Statute of Limitations" and struck out first sentence which read as follows: "No statute of limitation that would otherwise preclude prosecution for an offense involving the sexual or physical abuse of a child under the age of 18 years shall preclude such prosecution before the child reaches the age of 25 years."

Effective Date of 2009 Amendment

Amendment by Pub. L. 111–16 effective Dec. 1, 2009, see section 7 of Pub. L. 111–16, set out as a note under section 109 of Title 11, Bankruptcy.

Effective Date of 1994 Amendment

Pub. L. 103–322, title XXXIII, §330011(e), Sept. 13, 1994, 108 Stat. 2145, provided that the amendment made by that section is effective as of the date on which section 225(a) of Pub. L. 101–647 took effect.

§3510. Rights of victims to attend and observe trial

(a) Non-Capital Cases.—Notwithstanding any statute, rule, or other provision of law, a United States district court shall not order any victim of an offense excluded from the trial of a defendant accused of that offense because such victim may, during the sentencing hearing, make a statement or present any information in relation to the sentence.

(b) Capital Cases.—Notwithstanding any statute, rule, or other provision of law, a United States district court shall not order any victim of an offense excluded from the trial of a defendant accused of that offense because such victim may, during the sentencing hearing, testify as to the effect of the offense on the victim and the victim's family or as to any other factor for which notice is required under section 3593(a).

(c) Definition.—As used in this section, the term "victim" includes all persons defined as victims in section 503(e)(2) of the Victims' Rights and Restitution Act of 1990.

(Added Pub. L. 105–6, §2(a), Mar. 19, 1997, 111 Stat. 12.)

References in Text

Section 503(e)(2) of the Victims' Rights and Restitution Act of 1990, referred to in subsec. (c), is classified to section 20141(e)(2) of Title 34, Crime Control and Law Enforcement.

Effective Date

Pub. L. 105–6, §2(d), Mar. 19, 1997, 111 Stat. 13, provided that: "The amendments made by this section [enacting this section and amending section 3593 of this title] shall apply in cases pending on the date of the enactment of this Act [Mar. 19, 1997]."

§3511. Judicial review of requests for information

(a) The recipient of a request for records, a report, or other information under section 2709(b) of this title, section 626(a) or (b) or 627(a) of the Fair Credit Reporting Act, section 1114(a)(5)(A) of the Right to Financial Privacy Act, or section 802(a) of the National Security Act of 1947 may, in the United States district court for the district in which that person or entity does business or resides, petition for an order modifying or setting aside the request. The court may modify or set aside the request if compliance would be unreasonable, oppressive, or otherwise unlawful.

(b) Nondisclosure.—

(1) In general.—

(A) Notice.—If a recipient of a request or order for a report, records, or other information under section 2709 of this title, section 626 or 627 of the Fair Credit Reporting Act (15 U.S.C. 1681u and 1681v), section 1114 of the Right to Financial Privacy Act of 1978 (12 U.S.C. 3414), or section 802 of the National Security Act of 1947 (50 U.S.C. 3162), wishes to have a court review a nondisclosure requirement imposed in connection with the request or order, the recipient may notify the Government or file a petition for judicial review in any court described in subsection (a).

(B) Application.—Not later than 30 days after the date of receipt of a notification under subparagraph (A), the Government shall apply for an order prohibiting the disclosure of the existence or contents of the relevant request or order. An application under this subparagraph may be filed in the district court of the United States for the judicial district in which the recipient of the order is doing business or in the district court of the United States for any judicial district within which the authorized investigation that is the basis for the request is being conducted. The applicable nondisclosure requirement shall remain in effect during the pendency of proceedings relating to the requirement.

(C) Consideration.—A district court of the United States that receives a petition under subparagraph (A) or an application under subparagraph (B) should rule expeditiously, and shall, subject to paragraph (3), issue a nondisclosure order that includes conditions appropriate to the circumstances.

(2) Application contents.—An application for a nondisclosure order or extension thereof or a response to a petition filed under paragraph (1) shall include a certification from the Attorney General, Deputy Attorney General, an Assistant Attorney General, or the Director of the Federal Bureau of Investigation, or a designee in a position not lower than Deputy Assistant Director at Bureau headquarters or a Special Agent in Charge in a Bureau field office designated by the Director, or in the case of a request by a department, agency, or instrumentality of the Federal Government other than the Department of Justice, the head or deputy head of the department, agency, or instrumentality, containing a statement of specific facts indicating that the absence of a prohibition of disclosure under this subsection may result in—

(A) a danger to the national security of the United States;

(B) interference with a criminal, counterterrorism, or counterintelligence investigation;

(C) interference with diplomatic relations; or

(D) danger to the life or physical safety of any person.

(3) Standard.—A district court of the United States shall issue a nondisclosure order or extension thereof under this subsection if the court determines that there is reason to believe that disclosure of the information subject to the nondisclosure requirement during the applicable time period may result in—

(A) a danger to the national security of the United States;

(B) interference with a criminal, counterterrorism, or counterintelligence investigation;

(C) interference with diplomatic relations; or

(D) danger to the life or physical safety of any person.

(c) In the case of a failure to comply with a request for records, a report, or other information made to any person or entity under section 2709(b) of this title, section 626(a) or (b) or 627(a) of the Fair Credit Reporting Act, section 1114(a)(5)(A) of the Right to Financial Privacy Act, or section 802(a) of the National Security Act of 1947, the Attorney General may invoke the aid of any district court of the United States within the jurisdiction in which the investigation is carried on or the person or entity resides, carries on business, or may be found, to compel compliance with the request. The court may issue an order requiring the person or entity to comply with the request. Any failure to obey the order of the court may be punished by the court as contempt thereof. Any process under this section may be served in any judicial district in which the person or entity may be found.

(d) In all proceedings under this section, subject to any right to an open hearing in a contempt proceeding, the court must close any hearing to the extent necessary to prevent an unauthorized disclosure of a request for records, a report, or other information made to any person or entity under section 2709(b) of this title, section 626(a) or (b) or 627(a) of the Fair Credit Reporting Act, section 1114(a)(5)(A) of the Right to Financial Privacy Act, or section 802(a) of the National Security Act of 1947. Petitions, filings, records, orders, and subpoenas must also be kept under seal to the extent and as long as necessary to prevent the unauthorized disclosure of a request for records, a report, or other information made to any person or entity under section 2709(b) of this title, section 626(a) or (b) or 627(a) of the Fair Credit Reporting Act, section 1114(a)(5)(A) of the Right to Financial Privacy Act, or section 802(a) of the National Security Act of 1947.

(e) In all proceedings under this section, the court shall, upon request of the government, review ex parte and in camera any government submission or portions thereof, which may include classified information.

(Added Pub. L. 109–177, title I, §115(2), Mar. 9, 2006, 120 Stat. 211; amended Pub. L. 114–23, title V, §502(g), June 2, 2015, 129 Stat. 288.)

References in Text

Sections 626(a), (b) and 627(a) of the Fair Credit Reporting Act, referred to in subsecs. (a), (c), and (d), are classified to sections 1681u(a), (b) and 1681v(a), respectively, of Title 15, Commerce and Trade.

Section 1114(a)(5)(A) of the Right to Financial Privacy Act, referred to in subsecs. (a), (c), and (d), probably means section 1114(a)(5)(A) of the Right to Financial Privacy Act of 1978, which is classified to section 3414(a)(5)(A) of Title 12, Banks and Banking.

Section 802(a) of the National Security Act of 1947, referred to in subsecs. (a), (c), and (d), is classified to section 3162(a) of Title 50, War and National Defense.

Amendments

2015—Subsec. (b). Pub. L. 114–23 added subsec. (b) and struck out former subsec. (b) which related to petitions for court orders modifying or setting aside a nondisclosure requirement imposed in connection with a request for records, reports, or other information.

Reports on National Security Letters

Pub. L. 109–177, title I, §118, Mar. 9, 2006, 120 Stat. 217, as amended by Pub. L. 114–23, title VI, §602(c), June 2, 2015, 129 Stat. 294, provided that:

"(a) Existing Reports.—Any report made to a committee of Congress regarding national security letters under section 2709(c)(1) of title 18, United States Code, section 626(d) or 627(c) of the Fair Credit Reporting Act (15 U.S.C. 1681u(d) or 1681v(c)), section 1114(a)(3) or 1114(a)(5)(D) of the Right to Financial Privacy Act [of 1978] (12 U.S.C. 3414(a)(3) or 3414(a)(5)(D)), or section 802(b) of the National Security Act of 1947 (50 U.S.C. 436(b) [now 50 U.S.C. 3162(b)]) shall also be made to the Committees on the Judiciary of the House of Representatives and the Senate.

"(b) Enhanced Oversight of Fair Credit Reporting Act Counterterrorism National Security Letter.—[Amended section 1681v of Title 15, Commerce and Trade.]

"(c) Report on Requests for National Security Letters.—

"(1) In general.—In April of each year, the Attorney General shall submit to Congress an aggregate report setting forth with respect to the preceding year the total number of requests made by the Department of Justice for information concerning different persons under—

"(A) section 2709 of title 18, United States Code (to access certain communication service provider records);

"(B) section 1114 of the Right to Financial Privacy Act [of 1978] (12 U.S.C. 3414) (to obtain financial institution customer records);

"(C) section 802 of the National Security Act of 1947 (50 U.S.C. 436) [now 50 U.S.C. 3162] (to obtain financial information, records, and consumer reports);

"(D) section 626 of the Fair Credit Reporting Act (15 U.S.C. 1681u) (to obtain certain financial information and consumer reports); and

"(E) section 627 of the Fair Credit Reporting Act (15 U.S.C. 1681v) (to obtain credit agency consumer records for counterterrorism investigations).

"(2) Content.—

"(A) In general.—Except as provided in subparagraph (B), each report required under this subsection shall include a good faith estimate of the total number of requests described in paragraph (1) requiring disclosure of information concerning—

"(i) United States persons; and

"(ii) persons who are not United States persons.

"(B) Exception.—With respect to the number of requests for subscriber information under section 2709 of title 18, United States Code, a report required under this subsection need not separate the number of requests into each of the categories described in subparagraph (A).

"(3) Unclassified form.—The report under this section shall be submitted in unclassified form.

"(d) National Security Letter Defined.—In this section, the term 'national security letter' means a request for information under one of the following provisions of law:

"(1) Section 2709(a) of title 18, United States Code (to access certain communication service provider records).

"(2) Section 1114(a)(5)(A) of the Right to Financial Privacy Act [of 1978] (12 U.S.C. 3414(a)(5)(A)) (to obtain financial institution customer records).

"(3) Section 802 of the National Security Act of 1947 (50 U.S.C. 436) [now 50 U.S.C. 3162] (to obtain financial information, records, and consumer reports).

"(4) Section 626 of the Fair Credit Reporting Act (15 U.S.C. 1681u) (to obtain certain financial information and consumer reports).

"(5) Section 627 of the Fair Credit Reporting Act (15 U.S.C. 1681v) (to obtain credit agency consumer records for counterterrorism investigations)."

§3512. Foreign requests for assistance in criminal investigations and prosecutions

(a) Execution of Request for Assistance.—

(1) In general.—Upon application, duly authorized by an appropriate official of the Department of Justice, of an attorney for the Government, a Federal judge may issue such orders as may be necessary to execute a request from a foreign authority for assistance in the investigation or prosecution of criminal offenses, or in proceedings related to the prosecution of criminal offenses, including proceedings regarding forfeiture, sentencing, and restitution.

(2) Scope of orders.—Any order issued by a Federal judge pursuant to paragraph (1) may include the issuance of—

(A) a search warrant, as provided under Rule 41 of the Federal Rules of Criminal Procedure;

(B) a warrant or order for contents of stored wire or electronic communications or for records related thereto, as provided under section 2703 of this title;

(C) an order for a pen register or trap and trace device as provided under section 3123 of this title; or

(D) an order requiring the appearance of a person for the purpose of providing testimony or a statement, or requiring the production of documents or other things, or both.

(b) Appointment of Persons To Take Testimony or Statements.—

(1) In general.—In response to an application for execution of a request from a foreign authority as described under subsection (a), a Federal judge may also issue an order appointing a person to direct the taking of testimony or statements or of the production of documents or other things, or both.

(2) Authority of appointed person.—Any person appointed under an order issued pursuant to paragraph (1) may—

(A) issue orders requiring the appearance of a person, or the production of documents or other things, or both;

(B) administer any necessary oath; and

(C) take testimony or statements and receive documents or other things.

(c) Filing of Requests.—Except as provided under subsection (d), an application for execution of a request from a foreign authority under this section may be filed—

(1) in the district in which a person who may be required to appear resides or is located or in which the documents or things to be produced are located;

(2) in cases in which the request seeks the appearance of persons or production of documents or things that may be located in multiple districts, in any one of the districts in which such a person, documents, or things may be located; or

(3) in any case, the district in which a related Federal criminal investigation or prosecution is being conducted, or in the District of Columbia.

(d) Search Warrant Limitation.—An application for execution of a request for a search warrant from a foreign authority under this section, other than an application for a warrant issued as provided under section 2703 of this title, shall be filed in the district in which the place or person to be searched is located.

(e) Search Warrant Standard.—A Federal judge may issue a search warrant under this section only if the foreign offense for which the evidence is sought involves conduct that, if committed in the United States, would be considered an offense punishable by imprisonment for more than one year under Federal or State law.

(f) Service of Order or Warrant.—Except as provided under subsection (d), an order or warrant issued pursuant to this section may be served or executed in any place in the United States.

(g) Rule of Construction.—Nothing in this section shall be construed to preclude any foreign authority or an interested person from obtaining assistance in a criminal investigation or prosecution pursuant to section 1782 of title 28, United States Code.

(h) Definitions.—As used in this section, the following definitions shall apply:

(1) Federal judge.—The terms "Federal judge" and "attorney for the Government" have the meaning given such terms for the purposes of the Federal Rules of Criminal Procedure.

(2) Foreign authority.—The term "foreign authority" means a foreign judicial authority, a foreign authority responsible for the investigation or prosecution of criminal offenses or for proceedings related to the prosecution of criminal offenses, or an authority designated as a competent authority or central authority for the purpose of making requests for assistance pursuant to an agreement or treaty with the United States regarding assistance in criminal matters.

(Added Pub. L. 111–79, §2(4), Oct. 19, 2009, 123 Stat. 2087.)

References in Text

The Federal Rules of Criminal Procedure, referred to in subsecs. (a)(2)(A) and (h)(1), are set out in the Appendix to this title.

CHAPTER 224 - PROTECTION OF WITNESSES

Amendments

1990—Pub. L. 101–647, title XXXV, §3581, Nov. 29, 1990, 104 Stat. 4929, substituted "State governments; reimbursement of expenses" for "State governments" in item 3526.

§3521. Witness relocation and protection

(a)(1) The Attorney General may provide for the relocation and other protection of a witness or a potential witness for the Federal Government or for a State government in an official proceeding concerning an organized criminal activity or other serious offense, if the Attorney General determines that an offense involving a crime of violence directed at the witness with respect to that proceeding, an offense set forth in chapter 73 of this title directed at the witness, or a State offense that is similar in nature to either such offense, is likely to be committed. The Attorney General may also provide for the relocation and other protection of the immediate family of, or a person otherwise closely associated with, such witness or potential witness if the family or person may also be endangered on account of the participation of the witness in the judicial proceeding.

(2) The Attorney General shall issue guidelines defining the types of cases for which the exercise of the authority of the Attorney General contained in paragraph (1) would be appropriate.

(3) The United States and its officers and employees shall not be subject to any civil liability on account of any decision to provide or not to provide protection under this chapter.

(b)(1) In connection with the protection under this chapter of a witness, a potential witness, or an immediate family member or close associate of a witness or potential witness, the Attorney General shall take such action as the Attorney General determines to be necessary to protect the person involved from bodily injury and otherwise to assure the health, safety, and welfare of that person, including the psychological well-being and social adjustment of that person, for as long as, in the judgment of the Attorney General, the danger to that person exists. The Attorney General may, by regulation—

(A) provide suitable documents to enable the person to establish a new identity or otherwise protect the person;

(B) provide housing for the person;

(C) provide for the transportation of household furniture and other personal property to a new residence of the person;

(D) provide to the person a payment to meet basic living expenses, in a sum established in accordance with regulations issued by the Attorney General, for such times as the Attorney General determines to be warranted;

(E) assist the person in obtaining employment;

(F) provide other services necessary to assist the person in becoming self-sustaining;

(G) disclose or refuse to disclose the identity or location of the person relocated or protected, or any other matter concerning the person or the program after weighing the danger such a disclosure would pose to the person, the detriment it would cause to the general effectiveness of the program, and the benefit it would afford to the public or to the person seeking the disclosure, except that the Attorney General shall, upon the request of State or local law enforcement officials or pursuant to a court order, without undue delay, disclose to such officials the identity, location, criminal records, and fingerprints relating to the person relocated or protected when the Attorney General knows or the request indicates that the person is under investigation for or has been arrested for or charged with an offense that is punishable by more than one year in prison or that is a crime of violence;

(H) protect the confidentiality of the identity and location of persons subject to registration requirements as convicted offenders under Federal or State law, including prescribing alternative procedures to those otherwise provided by Federal or State law for registration and tracking of such persons; and

(I) exempt procurement for services, materials, and supplies, and the renovation and construction of safe sites within existing buildings from other provisions of law as may be required to maintain the security of protective witnesses and the integrity of the Witness Security Program.

The Attorney General shall establish an accurate, efficient, and effective system of records concerning the criminal history of persons provided protection under this chapter in order to provide the information described in subparagraph (G).

(2) Deductions shall be made from any payment made to a person pursuant to paragraph (1)(D) to satisfy obligations of that person for family support payments pursuant to a State court order.

(3) Any person who, without the authorization of the Attorney General, knowingly discloses any information received from the Attorney General under paragraph (1)(G) shall be fined $5,000 or imprisoned five years, or both.

(c) Before providing protection to any person under this chapter, the Attorney General shall, to the extent practicable, obtain information relating to the suitability of the person for inclusion in the program, including the criminal history, if any, and a psychological evaluation of, the person. The Attorney General shall also make a written assessment in each case of the seriousness of the investigation or case in which the person's information or testimony has been or will be provided and the possible risk of danger to other persons and property in the community where the person is to be relocated and shall determine whether the need for that person's testimony outweighs the risk of danger to the public. In assessing whether a person should be provided protection under this chapter, the Attorney General shall consider the person's criminal record, alternatives to providing protection under this chapter, the possibility of securing similar testimony from other sources, the need for protecting the person, the relative importance of the person's testimony, results of psychological examinations, whether providing such protection will substantially infringe upon the relationship between a child who would be relocated in connection with such protection and that child's parent who would not be so relocated, and such other factors as the Attorney General considers appropriate. The Attorney General shall not provide protection to any person under this chapter if the risk of danger to the public, including the potential harm to innocent victims, outweighs the need for that person's testimony. This subsection shall not be construed to authorize the disclosure of the written assessment made pursuant to this subsection.

(d)(1) Before providing protection to any person under this chapter, the Attorney General shall enter into a memorandum of understanding with that person. Each such memorandum of understanding shall set forth the responsibilities of that person, including—

(A) the agreement of the person, if a witness or potential witness, to testify in and provide information to all appropriate law enforcement officials concerning all appropriate proceedings;

(B) the agreement of the person not to commit any crime;

(C) the agreement of the person to take all necessary steps to avoid detection by others of the facts concerning the protection provided to that person under this chapter;

(D) the agreement of the person to comply with legal obligations and civil judgments against that person;

(E) the agreement of the person to cooperate with all reasonable requests of officers and employees of the Government who are providing protection under this chapter;

(F) the agreement of the person to designate another person to act as agent for the service of process;

(G) the agreement of the person to make a sworn statement of all outstanding legal obligations, including obligations concerning child custody and visitation;

(H) the agreement of the person to disclose any probation or parole responsibilities, and if the person is on probation or parole under State law, to consent to Federal supervision in accordance with section 3522 of this title; and

(I) the agreement of the person to regularly inform the appropriate program official of the activities and current address of such person.

Each such memorandum of understanding shall also set forth the protection which the Attorney General has determined will be provided to the person under this chapter, and the procedures to be followed in the case of a breach of the memorandum of understanding, as such procedures are established by the Attorney General. Such procedures shall include a procedure for filing and resolution of grievances of persons provided protection under this chapter regarding the administration of the program. This procedure shall include the opportunity for resolution of a grievance by a person who was not involved in the case.

(2) The Attorney General shall enter into a separate memorandum of understanding pursuant to

this subsection with each person protected under this chapter who is eighteen years of age or older. The memorandum of understanding shall be signed by the Attorney General and the person protected.

(3) The Attorney General may delegate the responsibility initially to authorize protection under this chapter only to the Deputy Attorney General, to the Associate Attorney General, to any Assistant Attorney General in charge of the Criminal Division or National Security Division of the Department of Justice, to the Assistant Attorney General in charge of the Civil Rights Division of the Department of Justice (insofar as the delegation relates to a criminal civil rights case), and to one other officer or employee of the Department of Justice.

(e) If the Attorney General determines that harm to a person for whom protection may be provided under section 3521 of this title is imminent or that failure to provide immediate protection would otherwise seriously jeopardize an ongoing investigation, the Attorney General may provide temporary protection to such person under this chapter before making the written assessment and determination required by subsection (c) of this section or entering into the memorandum of understanding required by subsection (d) of this section. In such a case the Attorney General shall make such assessment and determination and enter into such memorandum of understanding without undue delay after the protection is initiated.

(f) The Attorney General may terminate the protection provided under this chapter to any person who substantially breaches the memorandum of understanding entered into between the Attorney General and that person pursuant to subsection (d), or who provides false information concerning the memorandum of understanding or the circumstances pursuant to which the person was provided protection under this chapter, including information with respect to the nature and circumstances concerning child custody and visitation. Before terminating such protection, the Attorney General shall send notice to the person involved of the termination of the protection provided under this chapter and the reasons for the termination. The decision of the Attorney General to terminate such protection shall not be subject to judicial review.

(Added Pub. L. 98–473, title II, §1208, Oct. 12, 1984, 98 Stat. 2153; amended Pub. L. 101–647, title XXXV, §3582, Nov. 29, 1990, 104 Stat. 4929; Pub. L. 105–119, title I, §115(a)(9), Nov. 26, 1997, 111 Stat. 2467; Pub. L. 109–177, title V, §506(a)(7), Mar. 9, 2006, 120 Stat. 248.)

Amendments

2006—Subsec. (d)(3). Pub. L. 109–177 substituted "to any Assistant Attorney General in charge of the Criminal Division or National Security Division of the Department of Justice" for "to the Assistant Attorney General in charge of the Criminal Division of the Department of Justice".

1997—Subsec. (b)(1)(H), (I). Pub. L. 105–119 added subpar. (H) and redesignated former subpar. (H) as (I).

1990—Subsec. (b)(1). Pub. L. 101–647, §3582(1), inserted "(G)" after "subparagraph" in last sentence.

Subsec. (d)(3). Pub. L. 101–647, §3582(2), inserted "the" before "Civil Rights Division".

Effective Date of 1997 Amendment

Pub. L. 105–119, title I, §115(c), Nov. 26, 1997, 111 Stat. 2467, provided that: "This section [amending this section, sections 3563, 3583, 4042, and 4209 of this title, and sections 14071 and 14072 of Title 42, The Public Health and Welfare, enacting provisions set out as notes under section 951 of Title 10, Armed Forces, and section 14039 of Title 42, and amending provisions set out as a note under section 14071 of Title 42] shall take effect on the date of the enactment of this Act [Nov. 26, 1997], except that—

"(1) subparagraphs (A), (B), and (C) of subsection (a)(8) [amending sections 3563, 3583, 4042, and 4209 of this title and enacting provisions set out as a note under section 951 of Title 10] shall take effect 1 year after the date of the enactment of this Act; and

"(2) States shall have 3 years from such date of enactment to implement amendments made by this Act [probably should be "this section"] which impose new requirements under the [former] Jacob

Wetterling Crimes Against Children and Sexually Violent Offender Registration Act [42 U.S.C. 14071 et seq.], and the Attorney General may grant an additional 2 years to a State that is making good faith efforts to implement these amendments."

Effective Date

Pub. L. 98–473, title II, §1210, Oct. 12, 1984, 98 Stat. 2163, provided that: "This subpart [subpart A (§§1207–1210) of part F of chapter XII of title II of Pub. L. 98–473, see Short Title note below] and the amendments made by this subpart shall take effect on October 1, 1984."

Short Title

Pub. L. 98–473, title II, §1207, Oct. 12, 1984, 98 Stat. 2153, provided that: "This subpart [subpart A (§§1207–1210) of part F of chapter XII of title II of Pub. L. 98–473, enacting this chapter, repealing provisions set out as a note preceding section 3481 of this title, and enacting provisions set out as a note under this section] may be cited as the 'Witness Security Reform Act of 1984'."

§3522. Probationers and parolees

(a) A probation officer may, upon the request of the Attorney General, supervise any person provided protection under this chapter who is on probation or parole under State law, if the State involved consents to such supervision. Any person so supervised shall be under Federal jurisdiction during the period of supervision and shall, during that period be subject to all laws of the United States which pertain to probationers or parolees, as the case may be.

(b) The failure by any person provided protection under this chapter who is supervised under subsection (a) to comply with the memorandum of understanding entered into by that person pursuant to section 3521(d) of this title shall be grounds for the revocation of probation or parole, as the case may be.

(c) The United States Parole Commission and the Chairman of the Commission shall have the same powers and duties with respect to a probationer or parolee transferred from State supervision pursuant to this section as they have with respect to an offender convicted in a court of the United States and paroled under chapter 311 1 of this title. The provisions of sections 4201 through 4204, 4205(a), (e), and (h), 4206 through 4215, and 4218 1 of this title shall apply following a revocation of probation or parole under this section.

(d) If a person provided protection under this chapter who is on probation or parole and is supervised under subsection (a) of this section has been ordered by the State court which imposed sentence on the person to pay a sum of money to the victim of the offense involved for damage caused by the offense, that penalty or award of damages may be enforced as though it were a civil judgment rendered by a United States district court. Proceedings to collect the moneys ordered to be paid may be instituted by the Attorney General in any United States district court. Moneys recovered pursuant to such proceedings shall be distributed to the victim.

(Added Pub. L. 98–473, title II, §1208, Oct. 12, 1984, 98 Stat. 2157; amended Pub. L. 99–646, §75, Nov. 10, 1986, 100 Stat. 3618; Pub. L. 100–690, title VII, §7072(b), Nov. 18, 1988, 102 Stat. 4405.)

References in Text

Chapter 311 of this title, referred to in subsec. (c), which consisted of sections 4201 to 4218 of this title, was repealed effective Nov. 1, 1987, by Pub. L. 98–473, title II, §§218(a)(5), 235(a)(1), (b)(1), Oct. 12, 1984, 98 Stat. 2027, 2031, 2032, subject to remaining effective for five years after Nov. 1, 1987, in certain circumstances.

Amendments

1988—Subsec. (c). Pub. L. 100–690 substituted "4215" for "4216".
1986—Subsec. (a). Pub. L. 99–646 substituted "probationers or parolees, as the case may be" for "parolees".

Effective Date

Section effective Oct. 1, 1984, see section 1210 of Pub. L. 98–473, set out as a note under section 3521 of this title.

§3523. Civil judgments

(a) If a person provided protection under this chapter is named as a defendant in a civil cause of action arising prior to or during the period in which the protection is provided, process in the civil proceeding may be served upon that person or an agent designated by that person for that purpose. The Attorney General shall make reasonable efforts to serve a copy of the process upon the person protected at the person's last known address. The Attorney General shall notify the plaintiff in the action whether such process has been served. If a judgment in such action is entered against that person the Attorney General shall determine whether the person has made reasonable efforts to comply with the judgment. The Attorney General shall take appropriate steps to urge the person to comply with the judgment. If the Attorney General determines that the person has not made reasonable efforts to comply with the judgment, the Attorney General may, after considering the danger to the person and upon the request of the person holding the judgment disclose the identity and location of the person to the plaintiff entitled to recovery pursuant to the judgment. Any such disclosure of the identity and location of the person shall be made upon the express condition that further disclosure by the plaintiff of such identity or location may be made only if essential to the plaintiff's efforts to recover under the judgment, and only to such additional persons as is necessary to effect the recovery. Any such disclosure or nondisclosure by the Attorney General shall not subject the United States and its officers or employees to any civil liability.

(b)(1) Any person who holds a judgment entered by a Federal or State court in his or her favor against a person provided protection under this chapter may, upon a decision by the Attorney General to deny disclosure of the current identity and location of such protected person, bring an action against the protected person in the United States district court in the district where the person holding the judgment (hereinafter in this subsection referred to as the "petitioner") resides. Such action shall be brought within one hundred and twenty days after the petitioner requested the Attorney General to disclose the identity and location of the protected person. The complaint in such action shall contain statements that the petitioner holds a valid judgment of a Federal or State court against a person provided protection under this chapter and that the petitioner sought to enforce the judgment by requesting the Attorney General to disclose the identity and location of the protected person.

(2) The petitioner in an action described in paragraph (1) shall notify the Attorney General of the action at the same time the action is brought. The Attorney General shall appear in the action and shall affirm or deny the statements in the complaint that the person against whom the judgment is allegedly held is provided protection under this chapter and that the petitioner requested the Attorney General to disclose the identity and location of the protected person for the purpose of enforcing the judgment.

(3) Upon a determination (A) that the petitioner holds a judgment entered by a Federal or State court and (B) that the Attorney General has declined to disclose to the petitioner the current identity and location of the protected person against whom the judgment was entered, the court shall appoint a guardian to act on behalf of the petitioner to enforce the judgment. The clerk of the court shall forthwith furnish the guardian with a copy of the order of appointment. The Attorney General shall disclose to the guardian the current identity and location of the protected person and any other information necessary to enable the guardian to carry out his or her duties under this subsection.

(4) It is the duty of the guardian to proceed with all reasonable diligence and dispatch to enforce the rights of the petitioner under the judgment. The guardian shall, however, endeavor to carry out such enforcement duties in a manner that maximizes, to the extent practicable, the safety and security of the protected person. In no event shall the guardian disclose the new identity or

location of the protected person without the permission of the Attorney General, except that such disclosure may be made to a Federal or State court in order to enforce the judgment. Any good faith disclosure made by the guardian in the performance of his or her duties under this subsection shall not create any civil liability against the United States or any of its officers or employees.

(5) Upon appointment, the guardian shall have the power to perform any act with respect to the judgment which the petitioner could perform, including the initiation of judicial enforcement actions in any Federal or State court or the assignment of such enforcement actions to a third party under applicable Federal or State law. The Federal Rules of Civil Procedure shall apply in any action brought under this subsection to enforce a Federal or State court judgment.

(6) The costs of any action brought under this subsection with respect to a judgment, including any enforcement action described in paragraph (5), and the compensation to be allowed to a guardian appointed in any such action shall be fixed by the court and shall be apportioned among the parties as follows: the petitioner shall be assessed in the amount the petitioner would have paid to collect on the judgment in an action not arising under the provisions of this subsection; the protected person shall be assessed the costs which are normally charged to debtors in similar actions and any other costs which are incurred as a result of an action brought under this subsection. In the event that the costs and compensation to the guardian are not met by the petitioner or by the protected person, the court may, in its discretion, enter judgment against the United States for costs and fees reasonably incurred as a result of the action brought under this subsection.

(7) No officer or employee of the Department of Justice shall in any way impede the efforts of a guardian appointed under this subsection to enforce the judgment with respect to which the guardian was appointed.

(c) The provisions of this section shall not apply to a court order to which section 3524 of this title applies.

(Added Pub. L. 98–473, title II, §1208, Oct. 12, 1984, 98 Stat. 2157.)

References in Text

The Federal Rules of Civil Procedure, referred to in subsec. (b)(5), are set out in the Appendix to Title 28, Judiciary and Judicial Procedure.

Effective Date

Section effective Oct. 1, 1984, see section 1210 of Pub. L. 98–473, set out as a note under section 3521 of this title.

§3524. Child custody arrangements

(a) The Attorney General may not relocate any child in connection with protection provided to a person under this chapter if it appears that a person other than that protected person has legal custody of that child.

(b) Before protection is provided under this chapter to any person (1) who is a parent of a child of whom that person has custody, and (2) who has obligations to another parent of that child with respect to custody or visitation of that child under a court order, the Attorney General shall obtain and examine a copy of such order for the purpose of assuring that compliance with the order can be achieved. If compliance with a visitation order cannot be achieved, the Attorney General may provide protection under this chapter to the person only if the parent being relocated initiates legal action to modify the existing court order under subsection (e)(1) of this section. The parent being relocated must agree in writing before being provided protection to abide by any ensuing court orders issued as a result of an action to modify.

(c) With respect to any person provided protection under this chapter (1) who is the parent of a child who is relocated in connection with such protection and (2) who has obligations to another parent of that child with respect to custody or visitation of that child under a State court order, the Attorney General shall, as soon as practicable after the person and child are so relocated, notify in writing the child's parent who is not so relocated that the child has been provided protection under this chapter. The notification shall also include statements that the rights of the parent not so relocated to visitation or custody, or both, under the court order shall not be infringed by the relocation of the child and the Department of Justice responsibility with respect thereto. The Department of Justice will pay all reasonable costs of transportation and security incurred in insuring that visitation can occur at a secure location as designated by the United States Marshals Service, but in no event shall it be obligated to pay such costs for visitation in excess of thirty days a year, or twelve in number a year. Additional visitation may be paid for, in the discretion of the Attorney General, by the Department of Justice in extraordinary circumstances. In the event that the unrelocated parent pays visitation costs, the Department of Justice may, in the discretion of the Attorney General, extend security arrangements associated with such visitation.

(d)(1) With respect to any person provided protection under this chapter (A) who is the parent of a child who is relocated in connection with such protection and (B) who has obligations to another parent of that child with respect to custody or visitation of that child under a court order, an action to modify that court order may be brought by any party to the court order in the District Court for the District of Columbia or in the district court for the district in which the child's parent resides who has not been relocated in connection with such protection.

(2) With respect to actions brought under paragraph (1), the district courts shall establish a procedure to provide a reasonable opportunity for the parties to the court order to mediate their dispute with respect to the order. The court shall provide a mediator for this purpose. If the dispute is mediated, the court shall issue an order in accordance with the resolution of the dispute.

(3) If, within sixty days after an action is brought under paragraph (1) to modify a court order, the dispute has not been mediated, any party to the court order may request arbitration of the dispute. In the case of such a request, the court shall appoint a master to act as arbitrator, who shall be experienced in domestic relations matters. Rule 53 of the Federal Rules of Civil Procedure shall apply to masters appointed under this paragraph. The court and the master shall, in determining the dispute, give substantial deference to the need for maintaining parent-child relationships, and any order issued by the court shall be in the best interests of the child. In actions to modify a court order brought under this subsection, the court and the master shall apply the law of the State in which the court order was issued or, in the case of the modification of a court order issued by a district court under this section, the law of the State in which the parent resides who was not relocated in connection with the protection provided under this chapter. The costs to the Government of carrying out a court order may be considered in an action brought under this subsection to modify that court order but shall not outweigh the relative interests of the parties themselves and the child.

(4) Until a court order is modified under this subsection, all parties to that court order shall comply with their obligations under that court order subject to the limitations set forth in subsection (c) of this section.

(5) With respect to any person provided protection under this chapter who is the parent of a child who is relocated in connection with such protection, the parent not relocated in connection with such protection may bring an action, in the District Court for the District of Columbia or in the district court for the district in which that parent resides, for violation by that protected person of a court order with respect to custody or visitation of that child. If the court finds that such a violation has occurred, the court may hold in contempt the protected person. Once held in contempt, the protected person shall have a maximum of sixty days, in the discretion of the Attorney General, to comply with the court order. If the protected person fails to comply with the order within the time specified by the Attorney General, the Attorney General shall disclose the new identity and address of the protected person to the other parent and terminate any financial assistance to the protected person unless otherwise directed by the court.

(6) The United States shall be required by the court to pay litigation costs, including reasonable attorneys' fees, incurred by a parent who prevails in enforcing a custody or visitation order; but shall retain the right to recover such costs from the protected person.

(e)(1) In any case in which the Attorney General determines that, as a result of the relocation of a person and a child of whom that person is a parent in connection with protection provided under this chapter, the implementation of a court order with respect to custody or visitation of that child would be substantially impossible, the Attorney General may bring, on behalf of the person provided protection under this chapter, an action to modify the court order. Such action may be brought in the district court for the district in which the parent resides who would not be or was not relocated in connection with the protection provided under this chapter. In an action brought under this paragraph, if the Attorney General establishes, by clear and convincing evidence, that implementation of the court order involved would be substantially impossible, the court may modify the court order but shall, subject to appropriate security considerations, provide an alternative as substantially equivalent to the original rights of the nonrelocating parent as feasible under the circumstances.

(2) With respect to any State court order in effect to which this section applies, and with respect to any district court order in effect which is issued under this section, if the parent who is not relocated in connection with protection provided under this chapter intentionally violates a reasonable security requirement imposed by the Attorney General with respect to the implementation of that court order, the Attorney General may bring an action in the district court for the district in which that parent resides to modify the court order. The court may modify the court order if the court finds such an intentional violation.

(3) The procedures for mediation and arbitration provided under subsection (d) of this section shall not apply to actions for modification brought under this subsection.

(f) In any case in which a person provided protection under this chapter is the parent of a child of whom that person has custody and has obligations to another parent of that child concerning custody and visitation of that child which are not imposed by court order, that person, or the parent not relocated in connection with such protection, may bring an action in the district court of the district in which that parent not relocated resides to obtain an order providing for custody or visitation, or both, of that child. In any such action, all the provisions of subsection (d) of this section shall apply.

(g) In any case in which an action under this section involves court orders from different States with respect to custody or visitation of the same child, the court shall resolve any conflicts by applying the rules of conflict of laws of the State in which the court is sitting.

(h)(1) Subject to paragraph (2), the costs of any action described in subsection (d), (e), or (f) of this section shall be paid by the United States.

(2) The Attorney General shall insure that any State court order in effect to which this section applies and any district court order in effect which is issued under this section are carried out. The Department of Justice shall pay all costs and fees described in subsections (c) and (d) of this section.

(i) As used in this section, the term "parent" includes any person who stands in the place of a parent by law.

(Added Pub. L. 98–473, title II, §1208, Oct. 12, 1984, 98 Stat. 2159.)

References in Text

The Federal Rules of Civil Procedure, referred to in subsec. (d)(3), are set out in the Appendix to Title 28, Judiciary and Judicial Procedure.

Effective Date

Section effective Oct. 1, 1984, see section 1210 of Pub. L. 98–473, set out as a note under section 3521 of this title.

§3525. Victims Compensation Fund

(a) The Attorney General may pay restitution to, or in the case of death, compensation for the death of any victim of a crime that causes or threatens death or serious bodily injury and that is committed by any person during a period in which that person is provided protection under this chapter.

(b) Not later than four months after the end of each fiscal year, the Attorney General shall transmit to the Congress a detailed report on payments made under this section for such year.

(c) There are authorized to be appropriated for the fiscal year 1985 and for each fiscal year thereafter, $1,000,000 for payments under this section.

(d) The Attorney General shall establish guidelines and procedures for making payments under this section. The payments to victims under this section shall be made for the types of expenses provided for in section 3579(b) 1 of this title, except that in the case of the death of the victim, an amount not to exceed $50,000 may be paid to the victim's estate. No payment may be made under this section to a victim unless the victim has sought restitution and compensation provided under Federal or State law or by civil action. Such payments may be made only to the extent the victim, or the victim's estate, has not otherwise received restitution and compensation, including insurance payments, for the crime involved. Payments may be made under this section to victims of crimes occurring on or after the date of the enactment of this chapter.1 In the case of a crime occurring before the date of the enactment of this chapter,1 a payment may be made under this section only in the case of the death of the victim, and then only in an amount not exceeding $25,000, and such a payment may be made notwithstanding the requirements of the third sentence of this subsection.

(e) Nothing in this section shall be construed to create a cause of action against the United States.

(Added Pub. L. 98–473, title II, §1208, Oct. 12, 1984, 98 Stat. 2162.)

References in Text

Section 3579(b) of this title, referred to in subsec. (d), was renumbered section 3663(b) of this title by Pub. L. 98–473, title II, §212(a)(1), Oct. 12, 1984, 98 Stat. 1987.

The date of the enactment of this chapter, referred to in subsec. (d), is the date of enactment of Pub. L. 98–473, which was approved Oct. 12, 1984.

Effective Date

Section effective Oct. 1, 1984, see section 1210 of Pub. L. 98–473, set out as a note under section 3521 of this title.

Restitution to Estate of Victims Killed Before October 12, 1984; Limitation

Pub. L. 99–180, title II, §200, Dec. 13, 1985, 99 Stat. 1142, provided: "That restitution of not to exceed $25,000 shall be paid to the estate of victims killed before October 12, 1984 as a result of crimes committed by persons who have been enrolled in the Federal witness protection program, if such crimes were committed within two years after protection was terminated, notwithstanding any limitations contained in part (a) of section 3525 of title 18 of the United States Code."

Similar Provisions

Similar provisions were contained in the following prior appropriation act:
Pub. L. 99–88, title I, §100, Aug. 15, 1985, 99 Stat. 303.

§3526. Cooperation of other Federal agencies and State governments; reimbursement of expenses

(a) Each Federal agency shall cooperate with the Attorney General in carrying out the provisions of this chapter and may provide, on a reimbursable basis, such personnel and services as the Attorney General may request in carrying out those provisions.

(b) In any case in which a State government requests the Attorney General to provide protection to any person under this chapter—

(1) the Attorney General may enter into an agreement with that State government in which that government agrees to reimburse the United States for expenses incurred in providing protection to that person under this chapter; and

(2) the Attorney General shall enter into an agreement with that State government in which that

government agrees to cooperate with the Attorney General in carrying out the provisions of this chapter with respect to all persons.
(Added Pub. L. 98–473, title II, §1208, Oct. 12, 1984, 98 Stat. 2162.)

Effective Date
Section effective Oct. 1, 1984, see section 1210 of Pub. L. 98–473, set out as a note under section 3521 of this title.

§3527. Additional authority of Attorney General
The Attorney General may enter into such contracts or other agreements as may be necessary to carry out this chapter. Any such contract or agreement which would result in the United States being obligated to make outlays may be entered into only to the extent and in such amount as may be provided in advance in an appropriation Act.
(Added Pub. L. 98–473, title II, §1208, Oct. 12, 1984, 98 Stat. 2163.)

Effective Date
Section effective Oct. 1, 1984, see section 1210 of Pub. L. 98–473, set out as a note under section 3521 of this title.

§3528. Definition
For purposes of this chapter, the term "State" means each of the several States, the District of Columbia, the Commonwealth of Puerto Rico, and any territory or possession of the United States.
(Added Pub. L. 98–473, title II, §1208, Oct. 12, 1984, 98 Stat. 2163.)

Effective Date
Section effective Oct. 1, 1984, see section 1210 of Pub. L. 98–473, set out as a note under section 3521 of this title.

CHAPTER 225 - VERDICT

§3531. Return; several defendants; conviction of less offense; poll of jury—(Rule)

See Federal Rules of Criminal Procedure
Verdict to be unanimous; return; several defendants; disagreement; conviction of less offense; poll of jury, Rule 31.
(June 25, 1948, ch. 645, 62 Stat. 837.)

§3532. Setting aside verdict of guilty; judgment notwithstanding verdict—(Rule)

See Federal Rules of Criminal Procedure
Setting aside verdict of guilty on motion for judgment of acquittal, entering of such judgment, or ordering new trial; absence of verdict, Rule 29(b).
(June 25, 1948, ch. 645, 62 Stat. 837.)

CHAPTER 227 - SENTENCES

Prior Provisions

A prior chapter 227 (§3561 et seq.) was repealed (except sections 3577 to 3580 which were renumbered sections 3661 to 3664, respectively), by Pub. L. 98–473, title II, §§212(a)(1), (2), 235(a)(1), Oct. 12, 1984, 98 Stat. 1987, 2031, as amended, effective Nov. 1, 1987, and applicable only to offenses committed after the taking effect of such repeal. See Effective Date note set out under section 3551 of this title.

Section 3561, act June 25, 1948, ch. 645, 62 Stat. 837, related to judgment form and entry—(Rule).

Section 3562, act June 25, 1948, ch. 645, 62 Stat. 837, related to sentence—(Rule).

Section 3563, act June 25, 1948, ch. 645, 62 Stat. 837, related to corruption of blood or forfeiture of estate.

Section 3564, act June 25, 1948, ch. 645, 62 Stat. 837, related to pillory and whipping.

Section 3565, acts June 25, 1948, ch. 645, 62 Stat. 837; Oct. 12, 1984, Pub. L. 98–473, title II, §§235(a)(1), 238(g)(1), (i), 98 Stat. 2031, 2039; Oct. 30, 1984, Pub. L. 98–596, §§2, 12(a)(7)(A), (9), (b), 98 Stat. 3134, 3139, 3140; Oct. 22, 1986, Pub. L. 99–514, §2, 100 Stat. 2095, related to collection and payment of fines and penalties.

Section 3566, act June 25, 1948, ch. 645, 62 Stat. 837, related to execution of death sentence.

Section 3567, act June 25, 1948, ch. 645, 62 Stat. 838, related to death sentence may prescribe dissection.

Section 3568, acts June 25, 1948, ch. 645, 62 Stat. 838; Sept. 2, 1960, Pub. L. 86–691, §1(a), 74 Stat. 738; June 22, 1966, Pub. L. 89–465, §4, 80 Stat. 217, related to effective date of sentence and credit for time in custody prior to the imposition of sentence.

Section 3569, acts June 25, 1948, ch. 645, 62 Stat. 838; Oct. 17, 1968, Pub. L. 90–578, title III, §301(a)(1), (3), 82 Stat. 1115; Oct. 12, 1984, Pub. L. 98–473, title II, §§235(a)(1), 238(h), (i), 98 Stat. 2031, 2039; Oct. 30, 1984, Pub. L. 98–596, §§3, 12(a)(8), (9), (b), 98 Stat. 3136, 3139, 3140, related to discharge of indigent prisoner.

Section 3570, act June 25, 1948, ch. 645, 62 Stat. 839, related to presidential remission as affecting unremitted part.

Section 3571, act June 25, 1948, ch. 645, 62 Stat. 839, related to clerical mistakes—(Rule).

Section 3572, act June 25, 1948, ch. 645, 62 Stat. 839, related to correction or reduction of sentence—(Rule).

Section 3573, act June 25, 1948, ch. 645, 62 Stat. 839, related to arrest or setting aside of judgment—(Rule).

Section 3574, act June 25, 1948, ch. 645, 62 Stat. 839, related to stay of execution and supersedeas—(Rule).

Section 3575, added Pub. L. 91–452, title X, §1001(a), Oct. 15, 1970, 84 Stat. 948, related to increased sentence for dangerous special offenders.

Section 3576, added Pub. L. 91–452, title X, §1001(a), Oct. 15, 1970, 84 Stat. 950, related to review of sentence.

Section 3577 renumbered section 3661 of this title.

Section 3578 renumbered section 3662 of this title.

Section 3579 renumbered section 3663 of this title.

Section 3580 renumbered section 3664 of this title.

SUBCHAPTER A—GENERAL PROVISIONS 1

3551.	Authorized sentences.
3552.	Presentence reports.
3553.	Imposition of a sentence.

Amendments

1994—Pub. L. 103–322, title XXXIII, §330010(3), Sept. 13, 1994, 108 Stat. 2143, transferred analysis for this subchapter to follow heading of this subchapter.

§3551. Authorized sentences

(a) In General.—Except as otherwise specifically provided, a defendant who has been found guilty of an offense described in any Federal statute, including sections 13 and 1153 of this title, other than an Act of Congress applicable exclusively in the District of Columbia or the Uniform Code of Military Justice, shall be sentenced in accordance with the provisions of this chapter so as to achieve the purposes set forth in subparagraphs (A) through (D) of section 3553(a)(2) to the extent that they are applicable in light of all the circumstances of the case.

(b) Individuals.—An individual found guilty of an offense shall be sentenced, in accordance with the provisions of section 3553, to—

(1) a term of probation as authorized by subchapter B;

(2) a fine as authorized by subchapter C; or

(3) a term of imprisonment as authorized by subchapter D.

A sentence to pay a fine may be imposed in addition to any other sentence. A sanction authorized by section 3554, 3555, or 3556 may be imposed in addition to the sentence required by this subsection.

(c) Organizations.—An organization found guilty of an offense shall be sentenced, in accordance with the provisions of section 3553, to—

(1) a term of probation as authorized by subchapter B; or

(2) a fine as authorized by subchapter C.

A sentence to pay a fine may be imposed in addition to a sentence to probation. A sanction authorized by section 3554, 3555, or 3556 may be imposed in addition to the sentence required by this subsection.

(Added Pub. L. 98–473, title II, §212(a)(2), Oct. 12, 1984, 98 Stat. 1988; amended Pub. L. 101–647, title XVI, §1602, Nov. 29, 1990, 104 Stat. 4843.)

References in Text

Acts of Congress applicable exclusively in the District of Columbia, referred to in subsec. (a), are classified generally to the District of Columbia Code.

The Uniform Code of Military Justice, referred to in subsec. (a), is classified generally to chapter 47 (§801 et seq.) of Title 10, Armed Forces.

Amendments

1990—Subsec. (a). Pub. L. 101–647 inserted "including sections 13 and 1153 of this title," after "any Federal statute,".

Effective Date; Savings Provision

Pub. L. 98–473, title II, §235, Oct. 12, 1984, 98 Stat. 2031, as amended by Pub. L. 99–217, §§2, 4, Dec. 26, 1985, 99 Stat. 1728; Pub. L. 99–646, §35, Nov. 10, 1986, 100 Stat. 3599; Pub. L. 100–182, §2, Dec. 7, 1987, 101 Stat. 1266; Pub. L. 104–232, §4, Oct. 2, 1996, 110 Stat. 3056, provided that:

"(a)(1) This chapter [chapter II (§§211–239) of title II of Pub. L. 98–473, see Tables for classification] shall take effect on the first day of the first calendar month beginning 36 months after the date of enactment [Oct. 12, 1984] and shall apply only to offenses committed after the taking effect of this chapter, except that—

"(A) the repeal of chapter 402 of title 18, United States Code, shall take effect on the date of enactment [Oct. 12, 1984];

"(B)(i) chapter 58 of title 28, United States Code, shall take effect on the date of enactment of this Act [Oct. 12, 1984] or October 1, 1983, whichever occurs later, and the United States Sentencing Commission shall submit the initial sentencing guidelines promulgated under section 994(a)(1) of title 28 to the Congress within 30 months of the effective date of such chapter 58; and

"(ii) the sentencing guidelines promulgated pursuant to section 994(a)(1) shall not go into effect until—

"(I) the United States Sentencing Commission has submitted the initial set of sentencing guidelines to the Congress pursuant to subparagraph (B)(i), along with a report stating the reasons for the Commission's recommendations;

"(II) the General Accounting Office [now Government Accountability Office] has undertaken a study of the guidelines, and their potential impact in comparison with the operation of the existing sentencing and parole release system, and has, within one hundred and fifty days of submission of the guidelines, reported to the Congress the results of its study; and

"(III) the day after the Congress has had six months after the date described in subclause (I) in which to examine the guidelines and consider the reports; and

"(IV) section 212(a)(2) [enacting chapters 227 and 229 of this title and repealing former chapters 227, 229, and 231 of this title] takes effect, in the case of the initial sentencing guidelines so promulgated.

"(2) For the purposes of section 992(a) of title 28, the terms of the first members of the United States Sentencing Commission shall not begin to run until the sentencing guidelines go into effect pursuant to paragraph (1)(B)(ii).

"(b)(1) The following provisions of law in effect on the day before the effective date of this Act shall remain in effect for five years after the effective date as to an individual who committed an offense or an act of juvenile delinquency before the effective date and as to a term of imprisonment during the period described in subsection (a)(1)(B):

"(A) Chapter 311 of title 18, United States Code.

"(B) Chapter 309 of title 18, United States Code.

"(C) Sections 4251 through 4255 of title 18, United States Code.

"(D) Sections 5041 and 5042 of title 18, United States Code.

"(E) Sections 5017 through 5020 of title 18, United States Code, as to a sentence imposed before the date of enactment [Oct. 12, 1984].

"(F) The maximum term of imprisonment in effect on the effective date for an offense committed before the effective date.

"(G) Any other law relating to a violation of a condition of release or to arrest authority with regard to a person who violates a condition of release.

"[(2) Repealed. Pub. L. 104–232, §4, Oct. 2, 1996, 110 Stat. 3056.]

"(3) The United States Parole Commission shall set a release date, for an individual who will be in its jurisdiction the day before the expiration of five years after the effective date of this Act, pursuant to section 4206 of title 18, United States Code. A release date set pursuant to this paragraph shall be set early enough to permit consideration of an appeal of the release date, in accordance with Parole Commission procedures, before the expiration of five years following the effective date of this Act.

"(4) Notwithstanding the other provisions of this subsection, all laws in effect on the day before the effective date of this Act pertaining to an individual who is—

"(A) released pursuant to a provision listed in paragraph (1); and

"(B)(i) subject to supervision on the day before the expiration of the five-year period following the effective date of this Act; or

"(ii) released on a date set pursuant to paragraph (3);

including laws pertaining to terms and conditions of release, revocation of release, provision of counsel, and payment of transportation costs, shall remain in effect as to the individual until the expiration of his sentence, except that the district court shall determine, in accord with the Federal Rules of Criminal Procedure, whether release should be revoked or the conditions of release amended for violation of a condition of release.

"(5) Notwithstanding the provisions of section 991 of title 28, United States Code, and sections 4351 and 5002 of title 18, United States Code, the Chairman of the United States Parole Commission or his designee shall be a member of the National Institute of Corrections, and the Chairman of the United States Parole Commission shall be a member of the Advisory Corrections Council and a nonvoting member of the United States Sentencing Commission, ex officio, until the expiration of the five-year period following the effective date of this Act. Notwithstanding the provisions of section 4351 of title 18, during the five-year period the National Institute of Corrections shall have seventeen members, including seven ex officio members. Notwithstanding the provisions of section 991 of title 28, during the five-year period the United States Sentencing Commission shall consist of nine members, including two ex officio, nonvoting members."

[Pub. L. 104–232, §3(b)(2), Oct. 2, 1996, 110 Stat. 3056, provided that: "Effective on the date the plan [alternative plan by Attorney General for transfer of United States Parole Commission's functions to another entity within Department of Justice pursuant to section 3 of Pub. L. 104–232, set out as a note under section 4201 of this title] takes effect, paragraphs (3) and (4) of section 235(b) of the Sentencing Reform Act of 1984 [Pub. L. 98–473, set out above] (98 Stat. 2032) are repealed."]

[Pub. L. 113–47, §2, Oct. 31, 2013, 127 Stat. 572, provided that: "For purposes of section 235(b) of the Sentencing Reform Act of 1984 (18 U.S.C. 3551 note; Public Law 98–473; 98 Stat. 2032), as such section relates to chapter 311 of title 18, United States Code, and the United States Parole Commission, each reference in such section to '26 years' or '26-year period' shall be deemed a reference to '31 years' or '31-year period', respectively."]

[Pub. L. 112–44, §2, Oct. 21, 2011, 125 Stat. 532, provided that: "For purposes of section 235(b) of the Sentencing Reform Act of 1984 (18 U.S.C. 3551 note; Public Law 98–473; 98 Stat. 2032), as such section relates to chapter 311 of title 18, United States Code, and the United States Parole Commission, each reference in such section to '24 years' or '24-year period' shall be deemed a reference to '26 years' or '26-year period', respectively."]

[Pub. L. 110–312, §2, Aug. 12, 2008, 122 Stat. 3013, provided that: "For purposes of section 235(b) of the Sentencing Reform Act of 1984 (18 U.S.C. 3551 note; Public Law 98–473; 98 Stat. 2032), as such section relates to chapter 311 of title 18, United States Code, and the United States Parole Commission, each reference in such section to '21 years' or '21-year period' shall be deemed a reference to '24 years' or '24-year period', respectively."]

[Pub. L. 109–76, §2, Sept. 29, 2005, 119 Stat. 2035, provided that: "For purposes of section 235(b) of the Sentencing Reform Act of 1984 [Pub. L. 98–473, set out above] (98 Stat. 2032) as such section relates to chapter 311 of title 18, United States Code, and the United States Parole Commission, each reference in such section to 'eighteen years' or 'eighteen-year period' shall be deemed a reference to '21 years' or '21-year period', respectively."]

[For purposes of section 235(b) of Pub. L. 98–473, set out above, as it relates to chapter 311 of this title and the Parole Commission, references to "fifteen years" or "fifteen-year period" are deemed to be references to "eighteen years" or "eighteen-year period", respectively, see section 11017(a) of Pub. L. 107–273, set out as a note under section 4202 of this title.]

[For purposes of section 235(b) of Pub. L. 98–473, set out above, as it relates to chapter 311 of this title and the Parole Commission, references to "ten years" or "ten-year period" are deemed to be references to "fifteen years" or "fifteen-year period", respectively, see section 2(a) of Pub. L. 104–232, set out as a note under section 4201 of this title.]

[Pub. L. 101–650, title III, §316, Dec. 1, 1990, 104 Stat. 5115, provided that: "For the purposes of section 235(b) of Public Law 98–473 [set out above] as it relates to chapter 311 of title 18, United States Code, and the United States Parole Commission, each reference in such section to 'five years' or a 'five-year period' shall be deemed a reference to 'ten years' or a 'ten-year period', respectively."]

Short Title of 2008 Amendment
Pub. L. 110–312, §1, Aug. 12, 2008, 122 Stat. 3013, provided that: "This Act [enacting provisions set out as a note under this section] may be cited as the 'United States Parole Commission Extension Act of 2008'."

Short Title of 2005 Amendment
Pub. L. 109–76, §1, Sept. 29, 2005, 119 Stat. 2035, provided that: "This Act [enacting provisions set out as a note under this section and enacting provisions listed in a table relating to sentencing guidelines set out as a note under section 994 of Title 28, Judiciary and Judicial Procedure] may be cited as the 'United States Parole Commission Extension and Sentencing Commission Authority Act of 2005'."

Short Title of 1996 Amendment
Pub. L. 104–132, title II, §201, Apr. 24, 1996, 110 Stat. 1227, provided that: "This subtitle [subtitle A (§§201–211) of title II of Pub. L. 104–132, enacting sections 3613A and 3663A of this title, amending sections 2248, 2259, 2264, 2327, 3013, 3556, 3563, 3572, 3611 to 3613, 3614, 3663, and 3664 of this title and Rule 32 of the Federal Rules of Criminal Procedure set out in the Appendix to this title, and enacting provisions set out as notes under this section, section 2248 of this title, and section 994 of Title 28, Judiciary and Judicial Procedure] may be cited as the 'Mandatory Victims Restitution Act of 1996'."

Short Title of 1987 Amendment
Pub. L. 100–182, §1, Dec. 7, 1987, 101 Stat. 1266, provided that: "This Act [amending sections 3006A, 3553, 3561, 3563, 3564, 3583, 3663, 3672, 3742, and 4106 of this title, section 994 of Title 28, Judiciary and Judicial Procedure, and sections 504 and 1111 of Title 29, Labor, enacting provisions set out as notes under sections 3006A and 3553 of this title, rule 35 of the Federal Rules of Criminal Procedure, set out in the Appendix to this title, and section 994 of Title 28, and amending provisions set out as a note under this section] may be cited as the 'Sentencing Act of 1987'."

Short Title of 1985 Amendment
Pub. L. 99–217, §1, Dec. 26, 1985, 99 Stat. 1728, provided that: "This Act [amending section 994 of Title 28, Judiciary and Judicial Procedure, and provisions set out as a note under this section] may be cited as the 'Sentencing Reform Amendments Act of 1985'."

Short Title
Pub. L. 98–473, title II, §211, Oct. 12, 1984, 98 Stat. 1987, provided that: "This chapter [chapter II (§§211–239) of title II of Pub. L. 98–473, see Tables for classification] may be cited as the 'Sentencing Reform Act of 1984'."

Mandatory Victim Restitution; Promulgation of Regulations by Attorney General
Pub. L. 104–132, title II, §209, Apr. 24, 1996, 110 Stat. 1240, provided that: "Not later than 90 days after the date of enactment of this subtitle [Apr. 24, 1996], the Attorney General shall promulgate guidelines, or amend existing guidelines, to carry out this subtitle [subtitle A (§§201–211) of title II of Pub. L. 104–132, see Short Title of 1996 Amendment note set out above] and the amendments made by this subtitle and to ensure that—

"(1) in all plea agreements negotiated by the United States, consideration is given to requesting that the defendant provide full restitution to all victims of all charges contained in the indictment

or information, without regard to the counts to which the defendant actually pleaded; and
"(2) orders of restitution made pursuant to the amendments made by this subtitle are enforced to the fullest extent of the law."

Sentencing of Nonviolent and Nonserious Offenders; Sense of Congress

Pub. L. 98–473, title II, §239, Oct. 12, 1984, 98 Stat. 2039, provided that:

"Since, due to an impending crisis in prison overcrowding, available Federal prison space must be treated as a scarce resource in the sentencing of criminal defendants;

"Since, sentencing decisions should be designed to ensure that prison resources are, first and foremost, reserved for those violent and serious criminal offenders who pose the most dangerous threat to society;

"Since, in cases of nonviolent and nonserious offenders, the interests of society as a whole as well as individual victims of crime can continue to be served through the imposition of alternative sentences, such as restitution and community service;

"Since, in the two years preceding the enactment of sentencing guidelines, Federal sentencing practice should ensure that scarce prison resources are available to house violent and serious criminal offenders by the increased use of restitution, community service, and other alternative sentences in cases of nonviolent and nonserious offenders: Now, therefore, be it

"Declared, That it is the sense of the Senate that in the two years preceding the enactment of the sentencing guidelines, Federal judges, in determining the particular sentence to be imposed, consider—

"(1) the nature and circumstances of the offense and the history and characteristics of the defendant;

"(2) the general appropriateness of imposing a sentence other than imprisonment in cases in which the defendant has not been convicted of a crime of violence or otherwise serious offense; and

"(3) the general appropriateness of imposing a sentence of imprisonment in cases in which the defendant has been convicted of a crime of violence or otherwise serious offense."

§3552. Presentence reports

(a) Presentence Investigation and Report by Probation Officer.—A United States probation officer shall make a presentence investigation of a defendant that is required pursuant to the provisions of Rule 32(c) of the Federal Rules of Criminal Procedure, and shall, before the imposition of sentence, report the results of the investigation to the court.

(b) Presentence Study and Report by Bureau of Prisons.—If the court, before or after its receipt of a report specified in subsection (a) or (c), desires more information than is otherwise available to it as a basis for determining the sentence to be imposed on a defendant found guilty of a misdemeanor or felony, it may order a study of the defendant. The study shall be conducted in the local community by qualified consultants unless the sentencing judge finds that there is a compelling reason for the study to be done by the Bureau of Prisons or there are no adequate professional resources available in the local community to perform the study. The period of the study shall be no more than sixty days. The order shall specify the additional information that the court needs before determining the sentence to be imposed. Such an order shall be treated for administrative purposes as a provisional sentence of imprisonment for the maximum term authorized by section 3581(b) for the offense committed. The study shall inquire into such matters as are specified by the court and any other matters that the Bureau of Prisons or the professional consultants believe are pertinent to the factors set forth in section 3553(a). The period of the study may, in the discretion of the court, be extended for an additional period of not more than sixty days. By the expiration of the period of the study, or by the expiration of any extension granted by the court, the United States marshal shall, if the defendant is in custody, return the defendant to the court for final sentencing. The Bureau of Prisons or the professional consultants shall provide the court with a written report of the pertinent results of the study and make to the court whatever recommendations the Bureau or the consultants believe will be helpful to a proper resolution of the case. The report shall include recommendations of the Bureau or the consultants concerning the guidelines and policy statements, promulgated by the Sentencing Commission pursuant to 28 U.S.C. 994(a), that they believe are applicable to the defendant's case. After receiving the report and the recommendations, the court shall proceed finally to sentence the defendant in accordance with the sentencing alternatives and procedures available under this chapter.

(c) Presentence Examination and Report by Psychiatric or Psychological Examiners.—If the court, before or after its receipt of a report specified in subsection (a) or (b) desires more information than is otherwise available to it as a basis for determining the mental condition of the defendant, the court may order the same psychiatric or psychological examination and report thereon as may be ordered under section 4244(b) of this title.

(d) Disclosure of Presentence Reports.—The court shall assure that a report filed pursuant to this section is disclosed to the defendant, the counsel for the defendant, and the attorney for the Government at least ten days prior to the date set for sentencing, unless this minimum period is waived by the defendant. The court shall provide a copy of the presentence report to the attorney for the Government to use in collecting an assessment, criminal fine, forfeiture or restitution imposed.

(Added Pub. L. 98–473, title II, §212(a)(2), Oct. 12, 1984, 98 Stat. 1988; amended Pub. L. 99–646, §7(a), Nov. 10, 1986, 100 Stat. 3593; Pub. L. 101–647, title XXXVI, §3625, Nov. 29, 1990, 104 Stat. 4965.)

Amendments

1990—Subsec. (d). Pub. L. 101–647 inserted at end "The court shall provide a copy of the presentence report to the attorney for the Government to use in collecting an assessment, criminal fine, forfeiture or restitution imposed."

1986—Subsec. (b). Pub. L. 99–646, §7(a)(1), (2), substituted "study shall be" for "study shall take" and inserted ", if the defendant is in custody," after "United States marshal shall".

Subsec. (c). Pub. L. 99–646, §7(a)(3), substituted "the court may order the same psychiatric or psychological examination and report thereon as may be ordered under section 4244(b) of this title" for "it may order that the defendant undergo a psychiatric or psychological examination and that the court be provided with a written report of the results of the examination pursuant to the provisions of section 4247".

Effective Date of 1990 Amendment

Amendment by Pub. L. 101–647 effective 180 days after Nov. 29, 1990, see section 3631 of Pub. L. 101–647, set out as an Effective Date note under section 3001 of Title 28, Judiciary and Judicial Procedure.

Effective Date of 1986 Amendment

Pub. L. 99–646, §7(b), Nov. 10, 1986, 100 Stat. 3593, provided that: "The amendments made by this section [amending this section] shall take effect on the date of the taking effect of section 3552 of title 18, United States Code [Nov. 1, 1987]."

Effective Date

Section effective Nov. 1, 1987, and applicable only to offenses committed after the taking effect of this section, see section 235(a)(1) of Pub. L. 98–473, set out as a note under section 3551 of this title.

Use of Certain Technology To Facilitate Criminal Conduct

Pub. L. 104–294, title V, §501, Oct. 11, 1996, 110 Stat. 3497, provided that:

"(a) Information.—The Administrative Office of the United States courts shall establish policies and procedures for the inclusion in all presentence reports of information that specifically identifies and describes any use of encryption or scrambling technology that would be relevant to an enhancement under section 3C1.1 (dealing with Obstructing or Impeding the Administration of Justice) of the Sentencing Guidelines or to offense conduct under the Sentencing Guidelines.

"(b) Compiling and Report.—The United States Sentencing Commission shall—

"(1) compile and analyze any information contained in documentation described in subsection (a) relating to the use of encryption or scrambling technology to facilitate or conceal criminal conduct; and

"(2) based on the information compiled and analyzed under paragraph (1), annually report to the Congress on the nature and extent of the use of encryption or scrambling technology to facilitate or conceal criminal conduct."

§3553. Imposition of a sentence

(a) Factors To Be Considered in Imposing a Sentence.—The court shall impose a sentence sufficient, but not greater than necessary, to comply with the purposes set forth in paragraph (2) of this subsection. The court, in determining the particular sentence to be imposed, shall consider—

(1) the nature and circumstances of the offense and the history and characteristics of the defendant;

(2) the need for the sentence imposed—

(A) to reflect the seriousness of the offense, to promote respect for the law, and to provide just punishment for the offense;

(B) to afford adequate deterrence to criminal conduct;

(C) to protect the public from further crimes of the defendant; and

(D) to provide the defendant with needed educational or vocational training, medical care, or other correctional treatment in the most effective manner;

(3) the kinds of sentences available;

(4) the kinds of sentence and the sentencing range established for—

(A) the applicable category of offense committed by the applicable category of defendant as set forth in the guidelines—

(i) issued by the Sentencing Commission pursuant to section 994(a)(1) of title 28, United States Code, subject to any amendments made to such guidelines by act of Congress (regardless of whether such amendments have yet to be incorporated by the Sentencing Commission into amendments issued under section 994(p) of title 28); and

(ii) that, except as provided in section 3742(g), are in effect on the date the defendant is sentenced; or

(B) in the case of a violation of probation or supervised release, the applicable guidelines or policy statements issued by the Sentencing Commission pursuant to section 994(a)(3) of title 28, United States Code, taking into account any amendments made to such guidelines or policy statements by act of Congress (regardless of whether such amendments have yet to be incorporated by the Sentencing Commission into amendments issued under section 994(p) of title 28);

(5) any pertinent policy statement—

(A) issued by the Sentencing Commission pursuant to section 994(a)(2) of title 28, United States Code, subject to any amendments made to such policy statement by act of Congress (regardless of whether such amendments have yet to be incorporated by the Sentencing Commission into amendments issued under section 994(p) of title 28); and

(B) that, except as provided in section 3742(g), is in effect on the date the defendant is sentenced.1

(6) the need to avoid unwarranted sentence disparities among defendants with similar records who have been found guilty of similar conduct; and

(7) the need to provide restitution to any victims of the offense.

(b) Application of Guidelines in Imposing a Sentence.—

(1) In general.—Except as provided in paragraph (2), the court shall impose a sentence of the kind, and within the range, referred to in subsection (a)(4) unless the court finds that there exists an aggravating or mitigating circumstance of a kind, or to a degree, not adequately taken into consideration by the Sentencing Commission in formulating the guidelines that should result in a

sentence different from that described. In determining whether a circumstance was adequately taken into consideration, the court shall consider only the sentencing guidelines, policy statements, and official commentary of the Sentencing Commission. In the absence of an applicable sentencing guideline, the court shall impose an appropriate sentence, having due regard for the purposes set forth in subsection (a)(2). In the absence of an applicable sentencing guideline in the case of an offense other than a petty offense, the court shall also have due regard for the relationship of the sentence imposed to sentences prescribed by guidelines applicable to similar offenses and offenders, and to the applicable policy statements of the Sentencing Commission.

(2) Child crimes and sexual offenses.—

(A) 2 Sentencing.—In sentencing a defendant convicted of an offense under section 1201 involving a minor victim, an offense under section 1591, or an offense under chapter 71, 109A, 110, or 117, the court shall impose a sentence of the kind, and within the range, referred to in subsection (a)(4) unless—

(i) the court finds that there exists an aggravating circumstance of a kind, or to a degree, not adequately taken into consideration by the Sentencing Commission in formulating the guidelines that should result in a sentence greater than that described;

(ii) the court finds that there exists a mitigating circumstance of a kind or to a degree, that—

(I) has been affirmatively and specifically identified as a permissible ground of downward departure in the sentencing guidelines or policy statements issued under section 994(a) of title 28, taking account of any amendments to such sentencing guidelines or policy statements by Congress;

(II) has not been taken into consideration by the Sentencing Commission in formulating the guidelines; and

(III) should result in a sentence different from that described; or

(iii) the court finds, on motion of the Government, that the defendant has provided substantial assistance in the investigation or prosecution of another person who has committed an offense and that this assistance established a mitigating circumstance of a kind, or to a degree, not adequately taken into consideration by the Sentencing Commission in formulating the guidelines that should result in a sentence lower than that described.

In determining whether a circumstance was adequately taken into consideration, the court shall consider only the sentencing guidelines, policy statements, and official commentary of the Sentencing Commission, together with any amendments thereto by act of Congress. In the absence of an applicable sentencing guideline, the court shall impose an appropriate sentence, having due regard for the purposes set forth in subsection (a)(2). In the absence of an applicable sentencing guideline in the case of an offense other than a petty offense, the court shall also have due regard for the relationship of the sentence imposed to sentences prescribed by guidelines applicable to similar offenses and offenders, and to the applicable policy statements of the Sentencing Commission, together with any amendments to such guidelines or policy statements by act of Congress.

(c) Statement of Reasons for Imposing a Sentence.—The court, at the time of sentencing, shall state in open court the reasons for its imposition of the particular sentence, and, if the sentence—

(1) is of the kind, and within the range, described in subsection (a)(4), and that range exceeds 24 months, the reason for imposing a sentence at a particular point within the range; or

(2) is not of the kind, or is outside the range, described in subsection (a)(4), the specific reason for the imposition of a sentence different from that described, which reasons must also be stated with specificity in a statement of reasons form issued under section 994(w)(1)(B) of title 28, except to the extent that the court relies upon statements received in camera in accordance with Federal Rule of Criminal Procedure 32. In the event that the court relies upon statements received in camera in accordance with Federal Rule of Criminal Procedure 32 the court shall state that such statements were so received and that it relied upon the content of such statements.

If the court does not order restitution, or orders only partial restitution, the court shall include in the statement the reason therefor. The court shall provide a transcription or other appropriate public record of the court's statement of reasons, together with the order of judgment and commitment, to the Probation System and to the Sentencing Commission,,3 and, if the sentence includes a term of imprisonment, to the Bureau of Prisons.

(d) Presentence Procedure for an Order of Notice.—Prior to imposing an order of notice pursuant to section 3555, the court shall give notice to the defendant and the Government that it is considering imposing such an order. Upon motion of the defendant or the Government, or on its own motion, the court shall—

(1) permit the defendant and the Government to submit affidavits and written memoranda addressing matters relevant to the imposition of such an order;

(2) afford counsel an opportunity in open court to address orally the appropriateness of the imposition of such an order; and

(3) include in its statement of reasons pursuant to subsection (c) specific reasons underlying its determinations regarding the nature of such an order.

Upon motion of the defendant or the Government, or on its own motion, the court may in its discretion employ any additional procedures that it concludes will not unduly complicate or prolong the sentencing process.

(e) Limited Authority To Impose a Sentence Below a Statutory Minimum.—Upon motion of the Government, the court shall have the authority to impose a sentence below a level established by statute as a minimum sentence so as to reflect a defendant's substantial assistance in the investigation or prosecution of another person who has committed an offense. Such sentence shall be imposed in accordance with the guidelines and policy statements issued by the Sentencing Commission pursuant to section 994 of title 28, United States Code.

(f) Limitation on Applicability of Statutory Minimums in Certain Cases.—Notwithstanding any other provision of law, in the case of an offense under section 401, 404, or 406 of the Controlled Substances Act (21 U.S.C. 841, 844, 846) or section 1010 or 1013 of the Controlled Substances Import and Export Act (21 U.S.C. 960, 963), the court shall impose a sentence pursuant to guidelines promulgated by the United States Sentencing Commission under section 994 of title 28 without regard to any statutory minimum sentence, if the court finds at sentencing, after the Government has been afforded the opportunity to make a recommendation, that—

(1) the defendant does not have more than 1 criminal history point, as determined under the sentencing guidelines;

(2) the defendant did not use violence or credible threats of violence or possess a firearm or other dangerous weapon (or induce another participant to do so) in connection with the offense;

(3) the offense did not result in death or serious bodily injury to any person;

(4) the defendant was not an organizer, leader, manager, or supervisor of others in the offense, as determined under the sentencing guidelines and was not engaged in a continuing criminal enterprise, as defined in section 408 of the Controlled Substances Act; and

(5) not later than the time of the sentencing hearing, the defendant has truthfully provided to the Government all information and evidence the defendant has concerning the offense or offenses that were part of the same course of conduct or of a common scheme or plan, but the fact that the defendant has no relevant or useful other information to provide or that the Government is already aware of the information shall not preclude a determination by the court that the defendant has complied with this requirement.

(Added Pub. L. 98–473, title II, §212(a)(2), Oct. 12, 1984, 98 Stat. 1989; amended Pub. L. 99–570, title I, §1007(a), Oct. 27, 1986, 100 Stat. 3207–7; Pub. L. 99–646, §§8(a), 9(a), 80(a), 81(a), Nov. 10, 1986, 100 Stat. 3593, 3619; Pub. L. 100–182, §§3, 16(a), 17, Dec. 7, 1987, 101 Stat. 1266, 1269, 1270; Pub. L. 100–690, title VII, §7102, Nov. 18, 1988, 102 Stat. 4416; Pub. L. 103–322, title VIII, §80001(a), title XXVIII, §280001, Sept. 13, 1994, 108 Stat. 1985, 2095; Pub. L. 104–294, title VI, §§601(b)(5), (6), (h), Oct. 11, 1996, 110 Stat. 3499, 3500; Pub. L. 107–273, div. B, title IV, §4002(a)(8), Nov. 2, 2002, 116 Stat. 1807; Pub. L. 108–21, title IV, §401(a), (c), (j)(5), Apr. 30, 2003, 117 Stat. 667, 669, 673; Pub. L. 111–174, §4, May 27, 2010, 124 Stat. 1216.)

References in Text

The Federal Rules of Criminal Procedure, referred to in subsec. (c)(2), are set out in the Appendix to this title.

Section 408 of the Controlled Substances Act, referred to in subsec. (f)(4), is classified to section 848 of Title 21, Food and Drugs.

Constitutionality

For information regarding constitutionality of certain provisions of this section, as amended by section 401(a)(1) of Pub. L. 108–21, see Congressional Research Service, The Constitution of the United States of America: Analysis and Interpretation, Appendix 1, Acts of Congress Held Unconstitutional in Whole or in Part by the Supreme Court of the United States.

Amendments

2010—Subsec. (c)(2). Pub. L. 111–174 substituted "a statement of reasons form issued under section 994(w)(1)(B) of title 28" for "the written order of judgment and commitment".

2003—Subsec. (a)(4)(A). Pub. L. 108–21, §401(j)(5)(A), amended subpar. (A) generally. Prior to amendment, subpar. (A) read as follows: "the applicable category of offense committed by the applicable category of defendant as set forth in the guidelines issued by the Sentencing Commission pursuant to section 994(a)(1) of title 28, United States Code, and that are in effect on the date the defendant is sentenced; or".

Subsec. (a)(4)(B). Pub. L. 108–21, §401(j)(5)(B), inserted before semicolon at end ", taking into account any amendments made to such guidelines or policy statements by act of Congress (regardless of whether such amendments have yet to be incorporated by the Sentencing Commission into amendments issued under section 994(p) of title 28)".

Subsec. (a)(5). Pub. L. 108–21, §401(j)(5)(C), amended par. (5) generally. Prior to amendment, par. (5) read as follows: "any pertinent policy statement issued by the Sentencing Commission pursuant to 28 U.S.C. 994(a)(2) that is in effect on the date the defendant is sentenced;".

Subsec. (b). Pub. L. 108–21, §401(a), designated existing provisions as par. (1), inserted par. heading, substituted "Except as provided in paragraph (2), the court" for "The court", and added par. (2) and concluding provisions.

Subsec. (c). Pub. L. 108–21, §401(c)(2), (3), in concluding provisions, inserted ", together with the order of judgment and commitment," after "the court's statement of reasons" and "and to the Sentencing Commission," after "to the Probation System".

Subsec. (c)(2). Pub. L. 108–21, §401(c)(1), substituted "described, which reasons must also be stated with specificity in the written order of judgment and commitment, except to the extent that the court relies upon statements received in camera in accordance with Federal Rule of Criminal Procedure 32. In the event that the court relies upon statements received in camera in accordance with Federal Rule of Criminal Procedure 32 the court shall state that such statements were so received and that it relied upon the content of such statements" for "described".

2002—Subsec. (e). Pub. L. 107–273 inserted "a" before "minimum sentence".

1996—Subsec. (f). Pub. L. 104–294, §601(h), amended directory language of Pub. L. 103–322, §80001(a). See 1994 Amendment note below.

Pub. L. 104–294, §601(b)(5), in introductory provisions, substituted "section 1010 or 1013 of the Controlled Substances Import and Export Act (21 U.S.C. 960, 963)" for "section 1010 or 1013 of the Controlled Substances Import and Export Act (21 U.S.C. 961, 963)".

Subsec. (f)(4). Pub. L. 104–294, §601(b)(6), substituted "section 408 of the Controlled Substances Act" for "21 U.S.C. 848".

1994—Subsec. (a)(4). Pub. L. 103–322, §280001, amended par. (4) generally. Prior to amendment, par. (4) read as follows: "the kinds of sentence and the sentencing range established for the applicable category of offense committed by the applicable category of defendant as set forth in the guidelines that are issued by the Sentencing Commission pursuant to 28 U.S.C. 994(a)(1) and that are in effect on the date the defendant is sentenced;".

Subsec. (f). Pub. L. 103–322, §80001(a), as amended by Pub. L. 104–294, §601(h), added subsec.

(f).

1988—Subsec. (c). Pub. L. 100–690 inserted "or other appropriate public record" after "transcription" in second sentence and struck out "clerk of the" before "court" in last sentence.

1987—Subsec. (b). Pub. L. 100–182, §3(1), (2), substituted "court finds that there exists an aggravating or mitigating circumstance of a kind, or to a degree, not adequately taken into consideration by the Sentencing Commission in formulating the guidelines that should result" for "court finds that an aggravating or mitigating circumstance exists that was not adequately taken into consideration by the Sentencing Commission in formulating the guidelines and that should result".

Pub. L. 100–182, §3(3), inserted after first sentence "In determining whether a circumstance was adequately taken into consideration, the court shall consider only the sentencing guidelines, policy statements, and official commentary of the Sentencing Commission."

Pub. L. 100–182, §16(a), substituted "In the absence of an applicable sentencing guideline, the court shall impose an appropriate sentence, having due regard for the purposes set forth in subsection (a)(2). In the absence of an applicable sentencing guideline in the case of an offense other than a petty offense, the court shall also have due regard for the relationship of the sentence imposed to sentences prescribed by guidelines applicable to similar offenses and offenders, and to the applicable policy statements of the Sentencing Commission." for "In the absence of an applicable sentencing guideline, the court shall impose an appropriate sentence, having due regard for the relationship of the sentence imposed to sentences prescribed by guidelines applicable to similar offenses and offenders, the applicable policy statements of the Sentencing Commission, and the purposes of sentencing set forth in subsection (a)(2)."

Subsec. (c)(1). Pub. L. 100–182, §17, inserted "and that range exceeds 24 months,".

1986—Subsec. (a)(7). Pub. L. 99–646, §81(a), added par. (7).

Subsec. (b). Pub. L. 99–646, §9(a), inserted provision relating to sentencing in the absence of applicable guidelines.

Subsec. (c). Pub. L. 99–646, §8(a), substituted "If the court does not order restitution, or orders only partial restitution" for "If the sentence does not include an order of restitution".

Subsec. (d). Pub. L. 99–646, §80(a), struck out "or restitution" after "notice" in heading, and struck out "or an order of restitution pursuant to section 3556," after "section 3555," in introductory text.

Subsec. (e). Pub. L. 99–570 added subsec. (e).

Effective Date of 1994 Amendment

Pub. L. 103–322, title VIII, §80001(c), Sept. 13, 1994, 108 Stat. 1986, provided that: "The amendment made by subsection (a) [amending this section] shall apply to all sentences imposed on or after the 10th day beginning after the date of enactment of this Act [Sept. 13, 1994]."

Effective Date of 1987 Amendment

Amendment by Pub. L. 100–182 applicable with respect to offenses committed after Dec. 7, 1987, see section 26 of Pub. L. 100–182, set out as a note under section 3006A of this title.

Effective Date of 1986 Amendments

Pub. L. 99–646, §8(c), Nov. 10, 1986, 100 Stat. 3593, provided that: "The amendments made by this section [amending this section and section 3663 of this title] shall take effect on the date of the taking effect of section 3553 of title 18, United States Code [Nov. 1, 1987]."

Pub. L. 99–646, §9(b), Nov. 10, 1986, 100 Stat. 3593, provided that: "The amendments made by this section [amending this section] shall take effect on the date of the taking effect of section 3553 of title 18, United States Code [Nov. 1, 1987]."

Pub. L. 99–646, §80(b), Nov. 10, 1986, 100 Stat. 3619, provided that: "The amendments made by this section [amending this section] shall take effect on the date of the taking effect of section 212(a)(2) of the Sentencing Reform Act of 1984 [section 212(a)(2) of Pub. L. 98–473, effective

Nov. 1, 1987]."

Pub. L. 99–646, §81(b), Nov. 10, 1986, 100 Stat. 3619, provided that: "The amendments made by this section [amending this section] shall take effect on the date of the taking effect of section 212(a)(2) of the Sentencing Reform Act of 1984 [section 212(a)(2) of Pub. L. 98–473, effective Nov. 1, 1987]."

Pub. L. 99–570, title I, §1007(b), Oct. 27, 1986, 100 Stat. 3207–7, provided that: "The amendment made by this section [amending this section] shall take effect on the date of the taking effect of section 3553 of title 18, United States Code [Nov. 1, 1987]."

Effective Date

Section effective Nov. 1, 1987, and applicable only to offenses committed after the taking effect of this section, see section 235(a)(1) of Pub. L. 98–473, set out as a note under section 3551 of this title.

Report by Attorney General

Pub. L. 108–21, title IV, §401(l), Apr. 30, 2003, 117 Stat. 674, provided that:

"(1) Defined term.—For purposes of this section [amending this section, section 3742 of this title, and section 994 of Title 28, Judiciary and Judicial Procedure, enacting provisions set out as a note under section 991 of Title 28, and enacting provisions listed in a table relating to sentencing guidelines set out under section 994 of Title 28], the term 'report described in paragraph (3)' means a report, submitted by the Attorney General, which states in detail the policies and procedures that the Department of Justice has adopted subsequent to the enactment of this Act [Apr. 30, 2003]—

"(A) to ensure that Department of Justice attorneys oppose sentencing adjustments, including downward departures, that are not supported by the facts and the law;

"(B) to ensure that Department of Justice attorneys in such cases make a sufficient record so as to permit the possibility of an appeal;

"(C) to delineate objective criteria, specified by the Attorney General, as to which such cases may warrant consideration of an appeal, either because of the nature or magnitude of the sentencing error, its prevalence in the district, or its prevalence with respect to a particular judge;

"(D) to ensure that Department of Justice attorneys promptly notify the designated Department of Justice component in Washington concerning such adverse sentencing decisions; and

"(E) to ensure the vigorous pursuit of appropriate and meritorious appeals of such adverse decisions.

"(2) Report required.—

"(A) In general.—Not later than 15 days after a district court's grant of a downward departure in any case, other than a case involving a downward departure for substantial assistance to authorities pursuant to section 5K1.1 of the United States Sentencing Guidelines, the Attorney General shall submit a report to the Committees on the Judiciary of the House of Representatives and the Senate containing the information described under subparagraph (B).

"(B) Contents.—The report submitted pursuant to subparagraph (A) shall set forth—

"(i) the case;

"(ii) the facts involved;

"(iii) the identity of the district court judge;

"(iv) the district court's stated reasons, whether or not the court provided the United States with advance notice of its intention to depart; and

"(v) the position of the parties with respect to the downward departure, whether or not the United States has filed, or intends to file, a motion for reconsideration.

"(C) Appeal of the departure.—Not later than 5 days after a decision by the Solicitor General regarding the authorization of an appeal of the departure, the Attorney General shall submit a report to the Committees on the Judiciary of the House of Representatives and the Senate that describes the decision of the Solicitor General and the basis for such decision.

"(3) Effective date.—Paragraph (2) shall take effect on the day that is 91 days after the date of enactment of this Act [Apr. 30, 2003], except that such paragraph shall not take effect if not more than 90 days after the date of enactment of this Act the Attorney General has submitted to the Judiciary Committees of the House of Representatives and the Senate the report described in paragraph (3)."

Authority To Lower a Sentence Below Statutory Minimum for Old Offenses

Pub. L. 100–182, §24, Dec. 7, 1987, 101 Stat. 1271, provided that: "Notwithstanding section 235 of the Comprehensive Crime Control Act of 1984 [section 235 of Pub. L. 98–473, set out as a note under section 3551 of this title]—

"(1) section 3553(e) of title 18, United States Code;

"(2) rule 35(b) of the Federal Rules of Criminal Procedure as amended by section 215(b) of such Act [set out in the Appendix to this title]; and

"(3) rule 35(b) as in effect before the taking effect of the initial set of guidelines promulgated by the United States Sentencing Commission pursuant to chapter 58 of title 28, United States Code, shall apply in the case of an offense committed before the taking effect of such guidelines."

§3554. Order of criminal forfeiture

The court, in imposing a sentence on a defendant who has been found guilty of an offense described in section 1962 of this title or in title II or III of the Comprehensive Drug Abuse Prevention and Control Act of 1970 shall order, in addition to the sentence that is imposed pursuant to the provisions of section 3551, that the defendant forfeit property to the United States in accordance with the provisions of section 1963 of this title or section 413 of the Comprehensive Drug Abuse and Control Act of 1970.

(Added Pub. L. 98–473, title II, §212(a)(2), Oct. 12, 1984, 98 Stat. 1990.)

References in Text

The Comprehensive Drug Abuse Prevention and Control Act of 1970, referred to in text, is Pub. L. 91–513, Oct. 27, 1970, 84 Stat. 1236, as amended. Title II of this Act, known as the Controlled Substances Act, is classified principally to subchapter I (§801 et seq.) of chapter 13 of Title 21, Food and Drugs. Title III of this Act, known as the Controlled Substances Import and Export Act, is classified principally to subchapter II (§951 et seq.) of chapter 13 of Title 21. Section 413 of this Act is classified to section 853 of Title 21. For complete classification of this Act to the Code, see Short Title note set out under sections 801 and 951 of Title 21 and Tables.

Effective Date

Section effective Nov. 1, 1987, and applicable only to offenses committed after the taking effect of this section, see section 235(a)(1) of Pub. L. 98–473, set out as a note under section 3551 of this title.

§3555. Order of notice to victims

The court, in imposing a sentence on a defendant who has been found guilty of an offense involving fraud or other intentionally deceptive practices, may order, in addition to the sentence that is imposed pursuant to the provisions of section 3551, that the defendant give reasonable notice and explanation of the conviction, in such form as the court may approve, to the victims of the offense. The notice may be ordered to be given by mail, by advertising in designated areas or through designated media, or by other appropriate means. In determining whether to require the defendant to give such notice, the court shall consider the factors set forth in section 3553(a) to the extent that they are applicable and shall consider the cost involved in giving the notice as it relates to the loss caused by the offense, and shall not require the defendant to bear the costs of notice in excess of $20,000.

(Added Pub. L. 98–473, title II, §212(a)(2), Oct. 12, 1984, 98 Stat. 1991.)

Effective Date

Section effective Nov. 1, 1987, and applicable only to offenses committed after the taking effect of this section, see section 235(a)(1) of Pub. L. 98–473, set out as a note under section 3551 of this title.

§3556. Order of restitution

The court, in imposing a sentence on a defendant who has been found guilty of an offense shall order restitution in accordance with section 3663A, and may order restitution in accordance with section 3663. The procedures under section 3664 shall apply to all orders of restitution under this section.

(Added Pub. L. 98–473, title II, §212(a)(2), Oct. 12, 1984, 98 Stat. 1991; amended Pub. L. 99–646, §20(b), Nov. 10, 1986, 100 Stat. 3596; Pub. L. 104–132, title II, §202, Apr. 24, 1996, 110 Stat. 1227.)

Amendments

1996—Pub. L. 104–132 substituted "shall order restitution" for "may order restitution" and "section 3663A, and may order restitution in accordance with section 3663. The procedures under section 3664 shall apply to all orders of restitution under this section" for "sections 3663 and 3664".

1986—Pub. L. 99–646 substituted "may order restitution in accordance with sections 3663 and 3664" for "under this title, or an offense under section 902(h), (i), (j), or (n) of the Federal Aviation Act of 1958 (49 U.S.C. 1472), may order, in addition to the sentence that is imposed pursuant to the provisions of section 3551, that the defendant make restitution to any victim of the offense in accordance with the provisions of sections 3663 and 3664".

Effective Date of 1996 Amendment

Amendment by Pub. L. 104–132 to be effective, to extent constitutionally permissible, for sentencing proceedings in cases in which defendant is convicted on or after Apr. 24, 1996, see section 211 of Pub. L. 104–132, set out as a note under section 2248 of this title.

Effective Date of 1986 Amendment

Pub. L. 99–646, §20(c), Nov. 10, 1986, 100 Stat. 3596, provided that: "The amendments made by this section [amending this section and section 3663 of this title] shall take effect on the date of the taking effect of section 212(a)(2) of the Sentencing Reform Act of 1984 [section 212(a)(2) of Pub. L. 98–473, effective Nov. 1, 1987]."

Effective Date

Section effective Nov. 1, 1987, and applicable only to offenses committed after the taking effect of this section, see section 235(a)(1) of Pub. L. 98–473, set out as a note under section 3551 of this title.

§3557. Review of a sentence

The review of a sentence imposed pursuant to section 3551 is governed by the provisions of section 3742.

(Added Pub. L. 98–473, title II, §212(a)(2), Oct. 12, 1984, 98 Stat. 1991.)

Effective Date

Section effective Nov. 1, 1987, and applicable only to offenses committed after the taking effect of this section, see section 235(a)(1) of Pub. L. 98–473, set out as a note under section 3551 of this title.

§3558. Implementation of a sentence

The implementation of a sentence imposed pursuant to section 3551 is governed by the provisions of chapter 229.

(Added Pub. L. 98–473, title II, §212(a)(2), Oct. 12, 1984, 98 Stat. 1991.)

Effective Date

Section effective Nov. 1, 1987, and applicable only to offenses committed after the taking effect of this section, see section 235(a)(1) of Pub. L. 98–473, set out as a note under section 3551 of this title.

§3559. Sentencing classification of offenses

(a) Classification.—An offense that is not specifically classified by a letter grade in the section defining it, is classified if the maximum term of imprisonment authorized is—

(1) life imprisonment, or if the maximum penalty is death, as a Class A felony;

(2) twenty-five years or more, as a Class B felony;

(3) less than twenty-five years but ten or more years, as a Class C felony;

(4) less than ten years but five or more years, as a Class D felony;

(5) less than five years but more than one year, as a Class E felony;

(6) one year or less but more than six months, as a Class A misdemeanor;

(7) six months or less but more than thirty days, as a Class B misdemeanor;

(8) thirty days or less but more than five days, as a Class C misdemeanor; or

(9) five days or less, or if no imprisonment is authorized, as an infraction.

(b) Effect of Classification.—Except as provided in subsection (c), an offense classified under subsection (a) carries all the incidents assigned to the applicable letter designation, except that the maximum term of imprisonment is the term authorized by the law describing the offense.

(c) Imprisonment of Certain Violent Felons.—

(1) Mandatory life imprisonment.—Notwithstanding any other provision of law, a person who is convicted in a court of the United States of a serious violent felony shall be sentenced to life imprisonment if—

(A) the person has been convicted (and those convictions have become final) on separate prior occasions in a court of the United States or of a State of—

(i) 2 or more serious violent felonies; or

(ii) one or more serious violent felonies and one or more serious drug offenses; and

(B) each serious violent felony or serious drug offense used as a basis for sentencing under this subsection, other than the first, was committed after the defendant's conviction of the preceding serious violent felony or serious drug offense.

(2) Definitions.—For purposes of this subsection—

(A) the term "assault with intent to commit rape" means an offense that has as its elements engaging in physical contact with another person or using or brandishing a weapon against another person with intent to commit aggravated sexual abuse or sexual abuse (as described in sections 2241 and 2242);

(B) the term "arson" means an offense that has as its elements maliciously damaging or destroying any building, inhabited structure, vehicle, vessel, or real property by means of fire or an explosive;

(C) the term "extortion" means an offense that has as its elements the extraction of anything of value from another person by threatening or placing that person in fear of injury to any person or kidnapping of any person;

(D) the term "firearms use" means an offense that has as its elements those described in section 924(c) or 929(a), if the firearm was brandished, discharged, or otherwise used as a weapon and the crime of violence or drug trafficking crime during and relation to which the firearm was used was subject to prosecution in a court of the United States or a court of a State, or both;

(E) the term "kidnapping" means an offense that has as its elements the abduction, restraining, confining, or carrying away of another person by force or threat of force;

(F) the term "serious violent felony" means—

(i) a Federal or State offense, by whatever designation and wherever committed, consisting of murder (as described in section 1111); manslaughter other than involuntary manslaughter (as described in section 1112); assault with intent to commit murder (as described in section 113(a)); assault with intent to commit rape; aggravated sexual abuse and sexual abuse (as described in sections 2241 and 2242); abusive sexual contact (as described in sections 2244(a)(1) and (a)(2)); kidnapping; aircraft piracy (as described in section 46502 of Title 49); robbery (as described in section 2111, 2113, or 2118); carjacking (as described in section 2119); extortion; arson; firearms use; firearms possession (as described in section 924(c)); or attempt, conspiracy, or solicitation to commit any of the above offenses; and

(ii) any other offense punishable by a maximum term of imprisonment of 10 years or more that has as an element the use, attempted use, or threatened use of physical force against the person of another or that, by its nature, involves a substantial risk that physical force against the person of another may be used in the course of committing the offense;

(G) the term "State" means a State of the United States, the District of Columbia, and a commonwealth, territory, or possession of the United States; and

(H) the term "serious drug offense" means—

(i) an offense that is punishable under section 401(b)(1)(A) or 408 of the Controlled Substances Act (21 U.S.C. 841(b)(1)(A), 848) or section 1010(b)(1)(A) of the Controlled Substances Import and Export Act (21 U.S.C. 960(b)(1)(A)); or

(ii) an offense under State law that, had the offense been prosecuted in a court of the United States, would have been punishable under section 401(b)(1)(A) or 408 of the Controlled Substances Act (21 U.S.C. 841(b)(1)(A), 848) or section 1010(b)(1)(A) of the Controlled Substances Import and Export Act (21 U.S.C. 960(b)(1)(A)).

(3) Nonqualifying felonies.—

(A) Robbery in certain cases.—Robbery, an attempt, conspiracy, or solicitation to commit robbery; or an offense described in paragraph (2)(F)(ii) shall not serve as a basis for sentencing under this subsection if the defendant establishes by clear and convincing evidence that—

(i) no firearm or other dangerous weapon was used in the offense and no threat of use of a firearm or other dangerous weapon was involved in the offense; and

(ii) the offense did not result in death or serious bodily injury (as defined in section 1365) to any person.

(B) Arson in certain cases.—Arson shall not serve as a basis for sentencing under this subsection if the defendant establishes by clear and convincing evidence that—

(i) the offense posed no threat to human life; and

(ii) the defendant reasonably believed the offense posed no threat to human life.

(4) Information filed by united states attorney.—The provisions of section 411(a) of the Controlled Substances Act (21 U.S.C. 851(a)) shall apply to the imposition of sentence under this subsection.

(5) Rule of construction.—This subsection shall not be construed to preclude imposition of the death penalty.

(6) Special provision for indian country.—No person subject to the criminal jurisdiction of an Indian tribal government shall be subject to this subsection for any offense for which Federal jurisdiction is solely predicated on Indian country (as defined in section 1151) and which occurs within the boundaries of such Indian country unless the governing body of the tribe has elected that this subsection have effect over land and persons subject to the criminal jurisdiction of the tribe.

(7) Resentencing upon overturning of prior conviction.—If the conviction for a serious violent felony or serious drug offense that was a basis for sentencing under this subsection is found, pursuant to any appropriate State or Federal procedure, to be unconstitutional or is vitiated on the explicit basis of innocence, or if the convicted person is pardoned on the explicit basis of innocence, the person serving a sentence imposed under this subsection shall be resentenced to any sentence that was available at the time of the original sentencing.

(d) Death or Imprisonment for Crimes Against Children.—

(1) In general.—Subject to paragraph (2) and notwithstanding any other provision of law, a person who is convicted of a Federal offense that is a serious violent felony (as defined in subsection (c)) or a violation of section 2422, 2423, or 2251 shall, unless the sentence of death is imposed, be sentenced to imprisonment for life, if—

(A) the victim of the offense has not attained the age of 14 years;

(B) the victim dies as a result of the offense; and

(C) the defendant, in the course of the offense, engages in conduct described in section 3591(a)(2).

(2) Exception.—With respect to a person convicted of a Federal offense described in paragraph (1), the court may impose any lesser sentence that is authorized by law to take into account any substantial assistance provided by the defendant in the investigation or prosecution of another person who has committed an offense, in accordance with the Federal Sentencing Guidelines and the policy statements of the Federal Sentencing Commission pursuant to section 994(p) of title 28, or for other good cause.

(e) Mandatory Life Imprisonment for Repeated Sex Offenses Against Children.—

(1) In general.—A person who is convicted of a Federal sex offense in which a minor is the victim shall be sentenced to life imprisonment if the person has a prior sex conviction in which a minor was the victim, unless the sentence of death is imposed.

(2) Definitions.—For the purposes of this subsection—

(A) the term "Federal sex offense" means an offense under section 1591 (relating to sex trafficking of children), 2241 (relating to aggravated sexual abuse), 2242 (relating to sexual abuse), 2244(a)(1) (relating to abusive sexual contact), 2245 (relating to sexual abuse resulting in death), 2251 (relating to sexual exploitation of children), 2251A (relating to selling or buying of children), 2422(b) (relating to coercion and enticement of a minor into prostitution), or 2423(a) (relating to transportation of minors);

(B) the term "State sex offense" means an offense under State law that is punishable by more than one year in prison and consists of conduct that would be a Federal sex offense if, to the extent or in the manner specified in the applicable provision of this title—

(i) the offense involved interstate or foreign commerce, or the use of the mails; or

(ii) the conduct occurred in any commonwealth, territory, or possession of the United States, within the special maritime and territorial jurisdiction of the United States, in a Federal prison, on any land or building owned by, leased to, or otherwise used by or under the control of the Government of the United States, or in the Indian country (as defined in section 1151);

(C) the term "prior sex conviction" means a conviction for which the sentence was imposed before the conduct occurred constituting the subsequent Federal sex offense, and which was for a Federal sex offense or a State sex offense;

(D) the term "minor" means an individual who has not attained the age of 17 years; and

(E) the term "State" has the meaning given that term in subsection (c)(2).

(3) Nonqualifying Felonies.—An offense described in section 2422(b) or 2423(a) shall not serve as a basis for sentencing under this subsection if the defendant establishes by clear and convincing evidence that—

(A) the sexual act or activity was consensual and not for the purpose of commercial or pecuniary gain;

(B) the sexual act or activity would not be punishable by more than one year in prison under the law of the State in which it occurred; or

(C) no sexual act or activity occurred.

(f) Mandatory Minimum Terms of Imprisonment for Violent Crimes Against Children.—A person who is convicted of a Federal offense that is a crime of violence against the person of an individual who has not attained the age of 18 years shall, unless a greater mandatory minimum sentence of imprisonment is otherwise provided by law and regardless of any maximum term of imprisonment otherwise provided for the offense—

(1) if the crime of violence is murder, be imprisoned for life or for any term of years not less than 30, except that such person shall be punished by death or life imprisonment if the circumstances

satisfy any of subparagraphs (A) through (D) of section 3591(a)(2) of this title;

(2) if the crime of violence is kidnapping (as defined in section 1201) or maiming (as defined in section 114), be imprisoned for life or any term of years not less than 25; and

(3) if the crime of violence results in serious bodily injury (as defined in section 1365), or if a dangerous weapon was used during and in relation to the crime of violence, be imprisoned for life or for any term of years not less than 10.

(g)(1) If a defendant who is convicted of a felony offense (other than offense of which an element is the false registration of a domain name) knowingly falsely registered a domain name and knowingly used that domain name in the course of that offense, the maximum imprisonment otherwise provided by law for that offense shall be doubled or increased by 7 years, whichever is less.

(2) As used in this section—

(A) the term "falsely registers" means registers in a manner that prevents the effective identification of or contact with the person who registers; and

(B) the term "domain name" has the meaning given that term is 1 section 45 of the Act entitled "An Act to provide for the registration and protection of trademarks used in commerce, to carry out the provisions of certain international conventions, and for other purposes" approved July 5, 1946 (commonly referred to as the "Trademark Act of 1946") (15 U.S.C. 1127).

(Added Pub. L. 98–473, title II, §212(a)(2), Oct. 12, 1984, 98 Stat. 1991; amended Pub. L. 100–185, §5, Dec. 11, 1987, 101 Stat. 1279; Pub. L. 100–690, title VII, §7041, Nov. 18, 1988, 102 Stat. 4399; Pub. L. 103–322, title VII, §70001, Sept. 13, 1994, 108 Stat. 1982; Pub. L. 105–314, title V, §501, Oct. 30, 1998, 112 Stat. 2980; Pub. L. 105–386, §1(b), Nov. 13, 1998, 112 Stat. 3470; Pub. L. 108–21, title I, §106(a), Apr. 30, 2003, 117 Stat. 654; Pub. L. 108–482, title II, §204(a), Dec. 23, 2004, 118 Stat. 3917; Pub. L. 109–248, title II, §§202, 206(c), July 27, 2006, 120 Stat. 612, 614.)

Amendments

2006—Subsec. (e)(2)(A). Pub. L. 109–248, §206(c), inserted "1591 (relating to sex trafficking of children)," after "under section".

Subsecs. (f), (g). Pub. L. 109–248, §202, added subsec. (f) and redesignated former subsec. (f) as (g).

2004—Subsec. (f). Pub. L. 108–482 added subsec. (f).

2003—Subsec. (e). Pub. L. 108–21 added subsec. (e).

1998—Subsec. (c)(2)(F)(i). Pub. L. 105–386 inserted "firearms possession (as described in section 924(c));" after "firearms use;".

Subsec. (d). Pub. L. 105–314 added subsec. (d).

1994—Subsec. (b). Pub. L. 103–322, §70001(1), substituted "Except as provided in subsection (c), an" for "An".

Subsec. (c). Pub. L. 103–322, §70001(2), added subsec. (c).

1988—Subsec. (a). Pub. L. 100–690, §7041(a)(1), substituted "classified if the maximum term of imprisonment authorized is—" for "classified—

"(1) if the maximum term of imprisonment authorized is—".

Subsec. (a)(1) to (9). Pub. L. 100–690, §7041(a)(2), (b), redesignated subpars. (A) to (I) as pars. (1) to (9), respectively, and substituted "twenty-five" for "twenty" in pars. (2) and (3).

1987—Subsec. (b). Pub. L. 100–185 substituted ", except that the maximum term of imprisonment is the term authorized by the law describing the offense." for "except that:

"(1) the maximum fine that may be imposed is the fine authorized by the statute describing the offense, or by this chapter, whichever is the greater; and

"(2) the maximum term of imprisonment is the term authorized by the statute describing the offense."

Effective Date

Section effective Nov. 1, 1987, and applicable only to offenses committed after the taking effect of this section, see section 235(a)(1) of Pub. L. 98–473, set out as a note under section 3551 of this title.

SUBCHAPTER B—PROBATION 1

Amendments

1994—Pub. L. 103–322, title XXXIII, §330010(3), Sept. 13, 1994, 108 Stat. 2143, transferred analysis for this subchapter to follow heading for this subchapter.

§3561. Sentence of probation

(a) In General.—A defendant who has been found guilty of an offense may be sentenced to a term of probation unless—

(1) the offense is a Class A or Class B felony and the defendant is an individual;

(2) the offense is an offense for which probation has been expressly precluded; or

(3) the defendant is sentenced at the same time to a term of imprisonment for the same or a different offense that is not a petty offense.

(b) Domestic Violence Offenders.—A defendant who has been convicted for the first time of a domestic violence crime shall be sentenced to a term of probation if not sentenced to a term of imprisonment. The term "domestic violence crime" means a crime of violence for which the defendant may be prosecuted in a court of the United States in which the victim or intended victim is the spouse, former spouse, intimate partner, former intimate partner, child, or former child of the defendant, or any other relative of the defendant.

(c) Authorized Terms.—The authorized terms of probation are—

(1) for a felony, not less than one nor more than five years;

(2) for a misdemeanor, not more than five years; and

(3) for an infraction, not more than one year.

(Added Pub. L. 98–473, title II, §212(a)(2), Oct. 12, 1984, 98 Stat. 1992; amended Pub. L. 99–646, §10(a), Nov. 10, 1986, 100 Stat. 3593; Pub. L. 100–182, §7, Dec. 7, 1987, 101 Stat. 1267; Pub. L. 103–322, title XXVIII, §280004, title XXXII, §320921(a), Sept. 13, 1994, 108 Stat. 2096, 2130; Pub. L. 104–294, title VI, §604(c)(1), Oct. 11, 1996, 110 Stat. 3509.)

Prior Provisions

For a prior section 3561, applicable to offenses committed prior to Nov. 1, 1987, see note set out preceding section 3551 of this title.

Amendments

1996—Subsec. (b). Pub. L. 104–294 struck out "or any relative defendant, child, or former child of the defendant," before "or any other relative of the defendant".

1994—Subsec. (a)(3). Pub. L. 103–322, §280004, inserted before period at end "that is not a petty offense".

Subsecs. (b), (c). Pub. L. 103–322, §320921(a), added subsec. (b) and redesignated former subsec. (b) as (c).

1987—Subsec. (a)(1). Pub. L. 100–182 inserted "and the defendant is an individual" after "Class B felony".

1986—Subsec. (a). Pub. L. 99–646 struck out at end "The liability of a defendant for any unexecuted fine or other punishment imposed as to which probation is granted shall be fully discharged by the fulfillment of the terms and conditions of probation."

Effective Date of 1996 Amendment
Amendment by Pub. L. 104–294 effective Sept. 13, 1994, see section 604(d) of Pub. L. 104–294, set out as a note under section 13 of this title.

Effective Date of 1987 Amendment
Amendment by Pub. L. 100–182 applicable with respect to offenses committed after Dec. 7, 1987, see section 26 of Pub. L. 100–182, set out as a note under section 3006A of this title.

Effective Date of 1986 Amendment
Pub. L. 99–646, §10(b), Nov. 10, 1986, 100 Stat. 3593, provided that: "The amendment made by this section [amending this section] shall take effect on the date of the taking effect of such section 3561(a) [Nov. 1, 1987]."

Effective Date
Section effective Nov. 1, 1987, and applicable only to offenses committed after the taking effect of this section, see section 235(a)(1) of Pub. L. 98–473, set out as a note under section 3551 of this title.

§3562. Imposition of a sentence of probation
(a) Factors To Be Considered in Imposing a Term of Probation.—The court, in determining whether to impose a term of probation, and, if a term of probation is to be imposed, in determining the length of the term and the conditions of probation, shall consider the factors set forth in section 3553(a) to the extent that they are applicable.

(b) Effect of Finality of Judgment.—Notwithstanding the fact that a sentence of probation can subsequently be—

(1) modified or revoked pursuant to the provisions of section 3564 or 3565;

(2) corrected pursuant to the provisions of rule 35 of the Federal Rules of Criminal Procedure and section 3742; or

(3) appealed and modified, if outside the guideline range, pursuant to the provisions of section 3742;

a judgment of conviction that includes such a sentence constitutes a final judgment for all other purposes.

(Added Pub. L. 98–473, title II, §212(a)(2), Oct. 12, 1984, 98 Stat. 1992; amended Pub. L. 101–647, title XXXV, §3583, Nov. 29, 1990, 104 Stat. 4930.)

References in Text
The Federal Rules of Criminal Procedure, referred to in subsec. (b)(2), are set out in the Appendix to this title.

Prior Provisions
For a prior section 3562, applicable to offenses committed prior to Nov. 1, 1987, see note set out preceding section 3551 of this title.

Amendments
1990—Subsec. (b)(2). Pub. L. 101–647 inserted "of the Federal Rules of Criminal Procedure" after "rule 35".

Effective Date

Section effective Nov. 1, 1987, and applicable only to offenses committed after the taking effect of this section, see section 235(a)(1) of Pub. L. 98–473, set out as a note under section 3551 of this title.

§3563. Conditions of probation

(a) Mandatory Conditions.—The court shall provide, as an explicit condition of a sentence of probation—

(1) for a felony, a misdemeanor, or an infraction, that the defendant not commit another Federal, State, or local crime during the term of probation;

(2) for a felony, that the defendant also abide by at least one condition set forth in subsection (b)(2) or (b)(12), unless the court has imposed a fine under this chapter, or unless the court finds on the record that extraordinary circumstances exist that would make such a condition plainly unreasonable, in which event the court shall impose one or more of the other conditions set forth under subsection (b);

(3) for a felony, a misdemeanor, or an infraction, that the defendant not unlawfully possess a controlled substance;

(4) for a domestic violence crime as defined in section 3561(b) by a defendant convicted of such an offense for the first time that the defendant attend a public, private, or private nonprofit offender rehabilitation program that has been approved by the court, in consultation with a State Coalition Against Domestic Violence or other appropriate experts, if an approved program is readily available within a 50-mile radius of the legal residence of the defendant;

(5) for a felony, a misdemeanor, or an infraction, that the defendant refrain from any unlawful use of a controlled substance and submit to one drug test within 15 days of release on probation and at least 2 periodic drug tests thereafter (as determined by the court) for use of a controlled substance, but the condition stated in this paragraph may be ameliorated or suspended by the court for any individual defendant if the defendant's presentence report or other reliable sentencing information indicates a low risk of future substance abuse by the defendant;

(6) that the defendant—

(A) make restitution in accordance with sections 2248, 2259, 2264, 2327, 3663, 3663A, and 3664; and

(B) pay the assessment imposed in accordance with section 3013;

(7) that the defendant will notify the court of any material change in the defendant's economic circumstances that might affect the defendant's ability to pay restitution, fines, or special assessments;

(8) for a person required to register under the Sex Offender Registration and Notification Act, that the person comply with the requirements of that Act; and

(9) that the defendant cooperate in the collection of a DNA sample from the defendant if the collection of such a sample is authorized pursuant to section 3 of the DNA Analysis Backlog Elimination Act of 2000.

If the court has imposed and ordered execution of a fine and placed the defendant on probation, payment of the fine or adherence to the court-established installment schedule shall be a condition of the probation.

(b) Discretionary Conditions.—The court may provide, as further conditions of a sentence of probation, to the extent that such conditions are reasonably related to the factors set forth in section 3553(a)(1) and (a)(2) and to the extent that such conditions involve only such deprivations of liberty or property as are reasonably necessary for the purposes indicated in section 3553(a)(2), that the defendant—

(1) support his dependents and meet other family responsibilities;

(2) make restitution to a victim of the offense under section 3556 (but not subject to the limitation of section 3663(a) or 3663A(c)(1)(A));

(3) give to the victims of the offense the notice ordered pursuant to the provisions of section 3555;

(4) work conscientiously at suitable employment or pursue conscientiously a course of study or

vocational training that will equip him for suitable employment;

(5) refrain, in the case of an individual, from engaging in a specified occupation, business, or profession bearing a reasonably direct relationship to the conduct constituting the offense, or engage in such a specified occupation, business, or profession only to a stated degree or under stated circumstances;

(6) refrain from frequenting specified kinds of places or from associating unnecessarily with specified persons;

(7) refrain from excessive use of alcohol, or any use of a narcotic drug or other controlled substance, as defined in section 102 of the Controlled Substances Act (21 U.S.C. 802), without a prescription by a licensed medical practitioner;

(8) refrain from possessing a firearm, destructive device, or other dangerous weapon;

(9) undergo available medical, psychiatric, or psychological treatment, including treatment for drug or alcohol dependency, as specified by the court, and remain in a specified institution if required for that purpose;

(10) remain in the custody of the Bureau of Prisons during nights, weekends, or other intervals of time, totaling no more than the lesser of one year or the term of imprisonment authorized for the offense, during the first year of the term of probation or supervised release;

(11) reside at, or participate in the program of, a community corrections facility (including a facility maintained or under contract to the Bureau of Prisons) for all or part of the term of probation;

(12) work in community service as directed by the court;

(13) reside in a specified place or area, or refrain from residing in a specified place or area;

(14) remain within the jurisdiction of the court, unless granted permission to leave by the court or a probation officer;

(15) report to a probation officer as directed by the court or the probation officer;

(16) permit a probation officer to visit him at his home or elsewhere as specified by the court;

(17) answer inquiries by a probation officer and notify the probation officer promptly of any change in address or employment;

(18) notify the probation officer promptly if arrested or questioned by a law enforcement officer;

(19) remain at his place of residence during nonworking hours and, if the court finds it appropriate, that compliance with this condition be monitored by telephonic or electronic signaling devices, except that a condition under this paragraph may be imposed only as an alternative to incarceration;

(20) comply with the terms of any court order or order of an administrative process pursuant to the law of a State, the District of Columbia, or any other possession or territory of the United States, requiring payments by the defendant for the support and maintenance of a child or of a child and the parent with whom the child is living;

(21) be ordered deported by a United States district court, or United States magistrate judge, pursuant to a stipulation entered into by the defendant and the United States under section 238(d)(5) of the Immigration and Nationality Act, except that, in the absence of a stipulation, the United States district court or a United States magistrate judge, may order deportation as a condition of probation, if, after notice and hearing pursuant to such section, the Attorney General demonstrates by clear and convincing evidence that the alien is deportable;

(22) satisfy such other conditions as the court may impose or; 1

(23) if required to register under the Sex Offender Registration and Notification Act, submit his person, and any property, house, residence, vehicle, papers, computer, other electronic communication or data storage devices or media, and effects to search at any time, with or without a warrant, by any law enforcement or probation officer with reasonable suspicion concerning a violation of a condition of probation or unlawful conduct by the person, and by any probation officer in the lawful discharge of the officer's supervision functions.

(c) Modifications of Conditions.—The court may modify, reduce, or enlarge the conditions of a sentence of probation at any time prior to the expiration or termination of the term of probation, pursuant to the provisions of the Federal Rules of Criminal Procedure relating to the modification of probation and the provisions applicable to the initial setting of the conditions of probation.

(d) Written Statement of Conditions.—The court shall direct that the probation officer provide the defendant with a written statement that sets forth all the conditions to which the sentence is subject, and that is sufficiently clear and specific to serve as a guide for the defendant's conduct and for such supervision as is required.

(e) Results of Drug Testing.—The results of a drug test administered in accordance with subsection (a)(5) shall be subject to confirmation only if the results are positive, the defendant is subject to possible imprisonment for such failure, and either the defendant denies the accuracy of such test or there is some other reason to question the results of the test. A defendant who tests positive may be detained pending verification of a positive drug test result. A drug test confirmation shall be a urine drug test confirmed using gas chromatography/mass spectrometry techniques or such test as the Director of the Administrative Office of the United States Courts after consultation with the Secretary of Health and Human Services may determine to be of equivalent accuracy. The court shall consider whether the availability of appropriate substance abuse treatment programs, or an individual's current or past participation in such programs, warrants an exception in accordance with United States Sentencing Commission guidelines from the rule of section 3565(b), when considering any action against a defendant who fails a drug test administered in accordance with subsection (a)(5).

(Added Pub. L. 98–473, title II, §212(a)(2), Oct. 12, 1984, 98 Stat. 1993; amended Pub. L. 99–646, §§11(a), 12(a), Nov. 10, 1986, 100 Stat. 3594; Pub. L. 100–182, §§10, 18, Dec. 7, 1987, 101 Stat. 1267, 1270; Pub. L. 100–690, title VII, §§7086, 7110, 7303(a)(1), 7305(a), Nov. 18, 1988, 102 Stat. 4408, 4419, 4464, 4465; Pub. L. 101–647, title XXXV, §3584, Nov. 29, 1990, 104 Stat. 4930; Pub. L. 102–521, §3, Oct. 25, 1992, 106 Stat. 3404; Pub. L. 103–322, title II, §20414(b), title XXVIII, §280002, title XXXII, §320921(b), Sept. 13, 1994, 108 Stat. 1830, 2096, 2130; Pub. L. 104–132, title II, §203, Apr. 24, 1996, 110 Stat. 1227; Pub. L. 104–208, div. C, title III, §§308(g)(10)(E), 374(b), Sept. 30, 1996, 110 Stat. 3009–625, 3009–647; Pub. L. 104–294, title VI, §601(k), Oct. 11, 1996, 110 Stat. 3501; Pub. L. 105–119, title I, §115(a)(8)(B)(i)–(iii), Nov. 26, 1997, 111 Stat. 2465; Pub. L. 106–546, §7(a), Dec. 19, 2000, 114 Stat. 2734; Pub. L. 107–273, div. B, title IV, §4002(c)(1), (e)(12), Nov. 2, 2002, 116 Stat. 1808, 1811; Pub. L. 109–248, title I, §141(d), title II, §210(a), July 27, 2006, 120 Stat. 603, 615; Pub. L. 110–406, §14(a), (c), Oct. 13, 2008, 122 Stat. 4294.)

References in Text

The Sex Offender Registration and Notification Act, referred to in subsecs. (a)(8) and (b)(23), is title I of Pub. L. 109–248, July 27, 2006, 120 Stat. 590, which was classified principally to subchapter I (§16901 et seq.) of chapter 151 of Title 42, The Public Health and Welfare, prior to editorial reclassification as chapter 209 (§20901 et seq.) of Title 34, Crime Control and Law Enforcement. For complete classification of this Act to the Code, see Short Title of 2006 Act note set out under section 10101 of Title 34 and Tables.

Section 3 of the DNA Analysis Backlog Elimination Act of 2000, referred to in subsec. (a)(9), is section 3 of Pub. L. 106–546, which is classified to section 40702 of Title 34, Crime Control and Law Enforcement.

Section 238(d)(5) of the Immigration and Nationality Act, referred to in subsec. (b)(21), is classified to section 1228(d)(5) of Title 8, Aliens and Nationality.

The Federal Rules of Criminal Procedure, referred to in subsec. (c), are set out in the Appendix to this title.

Prior Provisions

For a prior section 3563, applicable to offenses committed prior to Nov. 1, 1987, see note set out preceding section 3551 of this title.

Amendments

2008—Subsec. (a)(2). Pub. L. 110–406, §14(a), substituted "(b)(2) or (b)(12), unless the court has imposed a fine under this chapter, or" for "(b)(2), (b)(3), or (b)(13),".

Subsec. (b)(10). Pub. L. 110–406, §14(c), inserted "or supervised release" after "probation".

2006—Subsec. (a)(8). Pub. L. 109–248, §141(d), amended par. (8) generally. Prior to amendment, par. (8) read as follows: "for a person described in section 4042(c)(4), that the person report the address where the person will reside and any subsequent change of residence to the probation officer responsible for supervision, and that the person register in any State where the person resides, is employed, carries on a vocation, or is a student (as such terms are defined under section 170101(a)(3) of the Violent Crime Control and Law Enforcement Act of 1994); and".

Subsec. (b)(21). Pub. L. 109–248, §210(a)(1), which directed amendment of par. (21) by striking "or", was executed by striking "or" at the end of the par. to reflect the probable intent of Congress.

Subsec. (b)(22). Pub. L. 109–248, §210(a)(2), substituted "or;" for period at end.

Subsec. (b)(23). Pub. L. 109–248, §210(a)(3), added par. (23).

2002—Subsec. (a). Pub. L. 107–273, §4002(e)(12)(A), made technical correction to directory language of Pub. L. 105–119, §115(a)(8)(B)(i). See 1997 Amendment note below.

Subsec. (a)(3) to (5). Pub. L. 107–273, §4002(c)(1), repealed Pub. L. 104–294, §601(k)(1), (2). See 1996 Amendment notes below.

Subsec. (e). Pub. L. 107–273, §4002(e)(12)(B), made technical correction to directory language of Pub. L. 107–273, §115(a)(8)(B)(ii). See 1997 Amendment note below.

2000—Subsec. (a)(9). Pub. L. 106–546 added par. (9).

1997—Subsec. (a). Pub. L. 105–119, §115(a)(8)(B)(i), as amended by Pub. L. 107–273, §4002(e)(12)(A), struck out at end "The results of a drug test administered in accordance with paragraph (4) shall be subject to confirmation only if the results are positive, the defendant is subject to possible imprisonment for such failure, and either the defendant denies the accuracy of such test or there is some other reason to question the results of the test. A defendant who tests positive may be detained pending verification of a positive drug test result. A drug test confirmation shall be a urine drug test confirmed using gas chromatography/mass spectrometry techniques or such test as the Director of the Administrative Office of the United States Courts after consultation with the Secretary of Health and Human Services may determine to be of equivalent accuracy. The court shall consider whether the availability of appropriate substance abuse treatment programs, or an individual's current or past participation in such programs, warrants an exception in accordance with United States Sentencing Commission guidelines from the rule of section 3565(b), when considering any action against a defendant who fails a drug test administered in accordance with paragraph (4)." and inserted these provisions at the end of this section.

Subsec. (a)(6), (7). Pub. L. 105–119, §115(a)(8)(B)(iii)(I), made technical amendment to place pars. (6) and (7) in numerical order immediately after par. (5).

Subsec. (a)(8). Pub. L. 105–119, §115(a)(8)(B)(iii)(II)–(IV), added par. (8).

Subsec. (e). Pub. L. 105–119, §115(a)(8)(B)(ii), as amended by Pub. L. 107–273, §4002(e)(12)(B), designated provisions which were struck out from the concluding provisions of subsec. (a) and inserted at the end of this section by Pub. L. 105–119, §115(a)(8)(B)(i), as amended, as subsec. (e), inserted subsec. heading, and substituted "subsection (a)(5)" for "paragraph (4)" in two places.

1996—Subsec. (a)(3). Pub. L. 104–294, §601(k)(2)(A), which could not be executed due to prior amendment by Pub. L. 104–132, §203(1)(A), was repealed by Pub. L. 107–273, §4002(c)(1). See below.

Pub. L. 104–132, §203(1)(A), struck out "and" at end of par. (3).

Subsec. (a)(4), (5). Pub. L. 104–294, §601(k)(3), transferred pars. (4) and (5) to appear in numerical order.

Pub. L. 104–294, §601(k)(1), (2)(B), which could not be executed due to prior amendment by Pub. L. 104–132, §203(1)(B)–(D), was repealed by Pub. L. 107–273, §4002(c)(1). See below.

Pub. L. 104–132, §203(1)(B)–(D), redesignated second par. (4), relating to conditions of probation concerning drug use and testing, as (5), and substituted semicolon for period at end of pars. (4)

and (5).

Subsec. (a)(6), (7). Pub. L. 104–132, §203(1)(E), added pars. (6) and (7).

Subsec. (b)(2). Pub. L. 104–132, §203(2)(C), amended par. (2) generally. Prior to amendment, par. (2) read as follows: "make restitution to a victim of the offense under sections 3663 and 3664 (but not subject to the limitations of section 3663(a));".

Pub. L. 104–132, §203(2)(A), (B), redesignated par. (3) as (2) and struck out former par. (2) which read as follows: "pay a fine imposed pursuant to the provisions of subchapter C;".

Subsec. (b)(3) to (20). Pub. L. 104–132, §203(2)(B), redesignated pars. (4) to (21) as (3) to (20), respectively. Former par. (3) redesignated (2).

Subsec. (b)(21). Pub. L. 104–208, §374(b), added par. (21). Former par. (21) redesignated (22).

Pub. L. 104–208, §308(g)(10)(E), substituted "238(d)(5)" for "242A(d)(5)".

Pub. L. 104–132, §203(2)(B), redesignated par. (22) as (21). Former par. (21) redesignated (20).

Subsec. (b)(22). Pub. L. 104–208, §374(b), redesignated par. (21) as (22).

Pub. L. 104–132, §203(b)(2), redesignated par. (22) as (21).

1994—Subsec. (a). Pub. L. 103–322, §20414(b)(4), inserted at end of concluding provisions "The results of a drug test administered in accordance with paragraph (4) shall be subject to confirmation only if the results are positive, the defendant is subject to possible imprisonment for such failure, and either the defendant denies the accuracy of such test or there is some other reason to question the results of the test. A defendant who tests positive may be detained pending verification of a positive drug test result. A drug test confirmation shall be a urine drug test confirmed using gas chromatography/mass spectrometry techniques or such test as the Director of the Administrative Office of the United States Courts after consultation with the Secretary of Health and Human Services may determine to be of equivalent accuracy. The court shall consider whether the availability of appropriate substance abuse treatment programs, or an individual's current or past participation in such programs, warrants an exception in accordance with United States Sentencing Commission guidelines from the rule of section 3565(b), when considering any action against a defendant who fails a drug test administered in accordance with paragraph (4)."

Subsec. (a)(2). Pub. L. 103–322, §§20414(b)(1), 320921(b)(1), amended par. (2) identically, striking out "and" at end.

Subsec. (a)(3). Pub. L. 103–322, §280002, substituted "unlawfully possess a controlled substance" for "possess illegal controlled substances".

Pub. L. 103–322, §§20414(b)(2), 320921(b)(2), amended par. (3) identically, substituting "; and" for period at end.

Subsec. (a)(4). Pub. L. 103–322, §320921(b)(3), added par. (4) relating to attendance at a rehabilitation program in the case of conviction of a domestic violence crime.

Pub. L. 103–322, §20414(b)(3), added at end of subsec. (a) par. (4) relating to conditions of probation concerning drug use and testing.

1992—Subsec. (b)(21), (22). Pub. L. 102–521 added par. (21) and redesignated former par. (21) as (22).

1990—Subsec. (a). Pub. L. 101–647, §3584(1), substituted "defendant" for "defendent" in last sentence.

Subsec. (b)(3). Pub. L. 101–647, §3584(2), substituted "under sections 3663 and 3664" for "pursuant to the provisions of section 3663 and 3664" and "section 3663(a)" for "3663(a)".

1988—Subsec. (a)(2). Pub. L. 100–690, §7086, inserted ", unless the court finds on the record that extraordinary circumstances exist that would make such a condition plainly unreasonable, in which event the court shall impose one or more of the other conditions set forth under subsection (b)".

Subsec. (a)(3). Pub. L. 100–690, §7303(a)(1), added par. (3).

Subsec. (b)(3). Pub. L. 100–690, §7110, substituted "3663 and 3664 (but not subject to the limitations of 3663(a))" for "3556".

Subsec. (b)(20), (21). Pub. L. 100–690, §7305(a), added par. (20) and redesignated former par. (20) as (21).

1987—Subsec. (b)(12). Pub. L. 100–182, §18, inserted "(including a facility maintained or under contract to the Bureau of Prisons)" after "facility".

Subsec. (c). Pub. L. 100–182, §10, struck out comma after "The court may" and substituted "the modification of probation and" for "revocation or modification of probation".

1986—Subsec. (b)(11). Pub. L. 99–646, §11(a), struck out "in section 3581(b)" after "the offense".

Subsec. (c). Pub. L. 99–646, §12(a), struck out ", after a hearing" after "court may" and inserted "the provisions of the Federal Rules of Criminal Procedure relating to revocation or modification of probation" after "pursuant to".

Effective Date of 2002 Amendment

Pub. L. 107–273, div. B, title IV, §4002(c)(1), Nov. 2, 2002, 116 Stat. 1808, provided that the amendment made by section 4002(c)(1) is effective Oct. 11, 1996.

Pub. L. 107–273, div. B, title IV, §4002(e)(12), Nov. 2, 2002, 116 Stat. 1811, provided that the amendment made by section 4002(e)(12) is effective Nov. 26, 1997.

Effective Date of 1997 Amendment

Amendment by Pub. L. 105–119 effective 1 year after Nov. 26, 1997, see section 115(c)(1) of Pub. L. 105–119, set out as a note under section 3521 of this title.

Effective Date of 1996 Amendments

Amendment by section 308(g)(10)(E) of Pub. L. 104–208 effective, with certain transitional provisions, on the first day of the first month beginning more than 180 days after Sept. 30, 1996, see section 309 of Pub. L. 104–208, set out as a note under section 1101 of Title 8, Aliens and Nationality.

Amendment by Pub. L. 104–132 to be effective, to extent constitutionally permissible, for sentencing proceedings in cases in which defendant is convicted on or after Apr. 24, 1996, see section 211 of Pub. L. 104–132, set out as a note under section 2248 of this title.

Effective Date of 1988 Amendment

Pub. L. 100–690, title VII, §7303(d), Nov. 18, 1988, 102 Stat. 4464, provided that: "The amendments made by this section [amending this section and sections 3565, 3583, 4209, and 4214 of this title] shall apply with respect to persons whose probation, supervised release, or parole begins after December 31, 1988."

Effective Date of 1987 Amendment

Amendment by Pub. L. 100–182 applicable with respect to offenses committed after Dec. 7, 1987, see section 26 of Pub. L. 100–182, set out as a note under section 3006A of this title.

Effective Date of 1986 Amendment

Pub. L. 99–646, §11(b), Nov. 10, 1986, 100 Stat. 3594, provided that: "The amendment made by this section [amending this section] shall take effect on the date of the taking effect of such section 3563(b)(11) [Nov. 1, 1987]."

Pub. L. 99–646, §12(c)(1), Nov. 10, 1986, 100 Stat. 3594, provided that: "The amendments made by subsection (a) [amending this section] shall take effect on the date of the taking effect of such section 3563(c) [Nov. 1, 1987]."

Effective Date

Section effective Nov. 1, 1987, and applicable only to offenses committed after the taking effect of this section, see section 235(a)(1) of Pub. L. 98–473, set out as a note under section 3551 of this title.

§3564. Running of a term of probation

(a) Commencement.—A term of probation commences on the day that the sentence of probation is imposed, unless otherwise ordered by the court.

(b) Concurrence With Other Sentences.—Multiple terms of probation, whether imposed at the same time or at different times, run concurrently with each other. A term of probation runs concurrently with any Federal, State, or local term of probation, supervised release, or parole for another offense to which the defendant is subject or becomes subject during the term of probation. A term of probation does not run while the defendant is imprisoned in connection with a conviction for a Federal, State, or local crime unless the imprisonment is for a period of less than thirty consecutive days.

(c) Early Termination.—The court, after considering the factors set forth in section 3553(a) to the extent that they are applicable, may, pursuant to the provisions of the Federal Rules of Criminal Procedure relating to the modification of probation, terminate a term of probation previously ordered and discharge the defendant at any time in the case of a misdemeanor or an infraction or at any time after the expiration of one year of probation in the case of a felony, if it is satisfied that such action is warranted by the conduct of the defendant and the interest of justice.

(d) Extension.—The court may, after a hearing, extend a term of probation, if less than the maximum authorized term was previously imposed, at any time prior to the expiration or termination of the term of probation, pursuant to the provisions applicable to the initial setting of the term of probation.

(e) Subject to Revocation.—A sentence of probation remains conditional and subject to revocation until its expiration or termination.

(Added Pub. L. 98–473, title II, §212(a)(2), Oct. 12, 1984, 98 Stat. 1994; amended Pub. L. 99–646, §13(a), Nov. 10, 1986, 100 Stat. 3594; Pub. L. 100–182, §11, Dec. 7, 1987, 101 Stat. 1268.)

References in Text

The Federal Rules of Criminal Procedure, referred to in subsec. (c), are set out in the Appendix to this title.

Prior Provisions

For a prior section 3564, applicable to offenses committed prior to Nov. 1, 1987, see note set out preceding section 3551 of this title.

Amendments

1987—Subsec. (c). Pub. L. 100–182 inserted ", pursuant to the provisions of the Federal Rules of Criminal Procedure relating to the modification of probation," after "may".

1986—Subsec. (b). Pub. L. 99–646 substituted provision that the term of probation does not run while the defendant is imprisoned in connection with a conviction for a Federal, State, or local crime unless the imprisonment is for a period of less than thirty consecutive days, for provision that the term of probation does not run during any period in which the defendant is imprisoned for a period of at least thirty consecutive days in connection with a conviction for a Federal, State, or local crime.

Effective Date of 1987 Amendment

Amendment by Pub. L. 100–182 applicable with respect to offenses committed after Dec. 7, 1987, see section 26 of Pub. L. 100–182, set out as a note under section 3006A of this title.

Effective Date of 1986 Amendment

Pub. L. 99–646, §13(b), Nov. 10, 1986, 100 Stat. 3594, provided that: "The amendments made by this section [amending this section] shall take effect on the date of the taking effect of such section 3564 [Nov. 1, 1987]."

Section effective Nov. 1, 1987, and applicable only to offenses committed after the taking effect of this section, see section 235(a)(1) of Pub. L. 98–473, set out as a note under section 3551 of this title.

§3565. Revocation of probation

(a) Continuation or Revocation.—If the defendant violates a condition of probation at any time prior to the expiration or termination of the term of probation, the court may, after a hearing pursuant to Rule 32.1 of the Federal Rules of Criminal Procedure, and after considering the factors set forth in section 3553(a) to the extent that they are applicable—

(1) continue him on probation, with or without extending the term or modifying or enlarging the conditions; or

(2) revoke the sentence of probation and resentence the defendant under subchapter A.

(b) Mandatory Revocation for Possession of Controlled Substance or Firearm or Refusal To Comply With Drug Testing.—If the defendant—

(1) possesses a controlled substance in violation of the condition set forth in section 3563(a)(3);

(2) possesses a firearm, as such term is defined in section 921 of this title, in violation of Federal law, or otherwise violates a condition of probation prohibiting the defendant from possessing a firearm;

(3) refuses to comply with drug testing, thereby violating the condition imposed by section 3563(a)(4); 1 or

(4) as a part of drug testing, tests positive for illegal controlled substances more than 3 times over the course of 1 year;

the court shall revoke the sentence of probation and resentence the defendant under subchapter A to a sentence that includes a term of imprisonment.

(c) Delayed Revocation.—The power of the court to revoke a sentence of probation for violation of a condition of probation, and to impose another sentence, extends beyond the expiration of the term of probation for any period reasonably necessary for the adjudication of matters arising before its expiration if, prior to its expiration, a warrant or summons has been issued on the basis of an allegation of such a violation.

(Added Pub. L. 98–473, title II, §212(a)(2), Oct. 12, 1984, 98 Stat. 1995; amended Pub. L. 100–690, title VI, §6214, title VII, §7303(a)(2), Nov. 18, 1988, 102 Stat. 4361, 4464; Pub. L. 101–647, title XXXV, §3585, Nov. 29, 1990, 104 Stat. 4930; Pub. L. 103–322, title XI, §110506, Sept. 13, 1994, 108 Stat. 2017; Pub. L. 107–273, div. B, title II, §2103(a), Nov. 2, 2002, 116 Stat. 1793.)

References in Text

The Federal Rules of Criminal Procedure, referred to in subsec. (a), are set out in the Appendix to this title.

Section 3563(a)(4), referred to in subsec. (b)(3), probably means the par. (4) of section 3563(a) added by section 20414(b)(3) of Pub. L. 103–322, which was renumbered par. (5) by Pub. L. 104–132, title II, §203(1)(C), Apr. 24, 1996, 110 Stat. 1227.

Prior Provisions

For a prior section 3565, applicable to offenses committed prior to Nov. 1, 1987, see note set out preceding section 3551 of this title.

Amendments

2002—Subsec. (b)(4). Pub. L. 107–273 added par. (4).

1994—Subsec. (a). Pub. L. 103–322, §110506(a)(2), struck out concluding sentence which read as follows: "Notwithstanding any other provision of this section, if a defendant is found by the court to be in possession of a controlled substance, thereby violating the condition imposed by section 3563(a)(3), the court shall revoke the sentence of probation and sentence the defendant to not less than one-third of the original sentence."

Subsec. (a)(2). Pub. L. 103–322, §110506(a)(1), substituted "resentence the defendant under subchapter A" for "impose any other sentence that was available under subchapter A at the time of the initial sentencing".

Subsec. (b). Pub. L. 103–322, §110506(b), amended subsec. (b) generally. Prior to amendment, subsec. (b) read as follows:

"(b) Mandatory Revocation for Possession of a Firearm.—If the defendant is in actual possession of a firearm, as that term is defined in section 921 of this title, at any time prior to the expiration or termination of the term of probation, the court shall, after a hearing pursuant to Rule 32.1 of the Federal Rules of Criminal Procedure, revoke the sentence of probation and impose any other sentence that was available under subchapter A at the time of the initial sentencing."

1990—Subsec. (a)(1). Pub. L. 101–647 substituted "or modifying" for "of modifying".

1988—Subsec. (a). Pub. L. 100–690, §7303(a)(2), inserted at end "Notwithstanding any other provision of this section, if a defendant is found by the court to be in possession of a controlled substance, thereby violating the condition imposed by section 3563(a)(3), the court shall revoke the sentence of probation and sentence the defendant to not less than one-third of the original sentence."

Subsecs. (b), (c). Pub. L. 100–690, §6214, added subsec. (b) and redesignated former subsec. (b) as (c).

Effective Date of 1988 Amendment

Amendment by section 7303(a)(2) of Pub. L. 100–690 applicable with respect to persons whose probation, supervised release, or parole begins after Dec. 31, 1988, see section 7303(d) of Pub. L. 100–690, set out as a note under section 3563 of this title.

Effective Date

Section effective Nov. 1, 1987, and applicable only to offenses committed after the taking effect of this section, see section 235(a)(1) of Pub. L. 98–473, set out as a note under section 3551 of this title.

§3566. Implementation of a sentence of probation

The implementation of a sentence of probation is governed by the provisions of subchapter A of chapter 229.

(Added Pub. L. 98–473, title II, §212(a)(2), Oct. 12, 1984, 98 Stat. 1995.)

Prior Provisions

For prior sections 3566 to 3570, applicable to offenses committed prior to Nov. 1, 1987, see note set out preceding section 3551 of this title.

Effective Date

Section effective Nov. 1, 1987, and applicable only to offenses committed after the taking effect of this section, see section 235(a)(1) of Pub. L. 98–473, set out as a note under section 3551 of this title.

SUBCHAPTER C—FINES 1

3571.	Sentence of fine.
3572.	Imposition of a sentence of fine and related matters.
3573.	Petition of the Government for modification or remission.
3574.	Implementation of a sentence of fine.

Amendments

1994—Pub. L. 103–322, title XXXIII, §330010(3), Sept. 13, 1994, 108 Stat. 2143, transferred analysis for this subchapter to follow heading for this subchapter.

1990—Pub. L. 101–647, title XXXV, §3586(1), Nov. 29, 1990, 104 Stat. 4930, as amended, effective as of the date on which section 3586(1) of Pub. L. 101–647 took effect, by Pub. L. 103–322, title XXXIII, §330011(n), Sept. 13, 1994, 108 Stat. 2145, substituted "sentence of fine and related matters" for "sentence of fine" in item 3572.

Pub. L. 101–647, title XXXV, §3586(2), Nov. 29, 1990, 104 Stat. 4930, substituted "remission" for "revision" in item 3573.

1987—Pub. L. 100–185, §8(b), Dec. 11, 1987, 101 Stat. 1282, substituted "Petition of the Government for modification or revision" for "Modification or remission of fine" in item 3573.

§3571. Sentence of fine

(a) In General.—A defendant who has been found guilty of an offense may be sentenced to pay a fine.

(b) Fines for Individuals.—Except as provided in subsection (e) of this section, an individual who has been found guilty of an offense may be fined not more than the greatest of—

(1) the amount specified in the law setting forth the offense;

(2) the applicable amount under subsection (d) of this section;

(3) for a felony, not more than $250,000;

(4) for a misdemeanor resulting in death, not more than $250,000;

(5) for a Class A misdemeanor that does not result in death, not more than $100,000;

(6) for a Class B or C misdemeanor that does not result in death, not more than $5,000; or

(7) for an infraction, not more than $5,000.

(c) Fines for Organizations.—Except as provided in subsection (e) of this section, an organization that has been found guilty of an offense may be fined not more than the greatest of—

(1) the amount specified in the law setting forth the offense;

(2) the applicable amount under subsection (d) of this section;

(3) for a felony, not more than $500,000;

(4) for a misdemeanor resulting in death, not more than $500,000;

(5) for a Class A misdemeanor that does not result in death, not more than $200,000;

(6) for a Class B or C misdemeanor that does not result in death, not more than $10,000; and

(7) for an infraction, not more than $10,000.

(d) Alternative Fine Based on Gain or Loss.—If any person derives pecuniary gain from the offense, or if the offense results in pecuniary loss to a person other than the defendant, the defendant may be fined not more than the greater of twice the gross gain or twice the gross loss, unless imposition of a fine under this subsection would unduly complicate or prolong the sentencing process.

(e) Special Rule for Lower Fine Specified in Substantive Provision.—If a law setting forth an offense specifies no fine or a fine that is lower than the fine otherwise applicable under this section and such law, by specific reference, exempts the offense from the applicability of the fine otherwise applicable under this section, the defendant may not be fined more than the amount specified in the law setting forth the offense.

(Added Pub. L. 98–473, title II, §212(a)(2), Oct. 12, 1984, 98 Stat. 1995; amended Pub. L. 100–185, §6, Dec. 11, 1987, 101 Stat. 1280.)

Prior Provisions

For a prior section 3571, applicable to offenses committed prior to Nov. 1, 1987, see note set out preceding section 3551 of this title.

Amendments

1987—Pub. L. 100–185 amended section generally, revising and restating as subsecs. (a) to (e) provisions formerly contained in subsecs. (a) and (b).

Effective Date

Section effective Nov. 1, 1987, and applicable only to offenses committed after the taking effect of this section, see section 235(a)(1) of Pub. L. 98–473, set out as a note under section 3551 of this title.

§3572. Imposition of a sentence of fine and related matters

(a) Factors To Be Considered.—In determining whether to impose a fine, and the amount, time for payment, and method of payment of a fine, the court shall consider, in addition to the factors set forth in section 3553(a)—

(1) the defendant's income, earning capacity, and financial resources;

(2) the burden that the fine will impose upon the defendant, any person who is financially dependent on the defendant, or any other person (including a government) that would be responsible for the welfare of any person financially dependent on the defendant, relative to the burden that alternative punishments would impose;

(3) any pecuniary loss inflicted upon others as a result of the offense;

(4) whether restitution is ordered or made and the amount of such restitution;

(5) the need to deprive the defendant of illegally obtained gains from the offense;

(6) the expected costs to the government of any imprisonment, supervised release, or probation component of the sentence;

(7) whether the defendant can pass on to consumers or other persons the expense of the fine; and

(8) if the defendant is an organization, the size of the organization and any measure taken by the organization to discipline any officer, director, employee, or agent of the organization responsible for the offense and to prevent a recurrence of such an offense.

(b) Fine Not to Impair Ability to Make Restitution.—If, as a result of a conviction, the defendant has the obligation to make restitution to a victim of the offense, other than the United States, the court shall impose a fine or other monetary penalty only to the extent that such fine or penalty will not impair the ability of the defendant to make restitution.

(c) Effect of Finality of Judgment.—Notwithstanding the fact that a sentence to pay a fine can subsequently be—

(1) modified or remitted under section 3573;

(2) corrected under rule 35 of the Federal Rules of Criminal Procedure and section 3742; or

(3) appealed and modified under section 3742;

a judgment that includes such a sentence is a final judgment for all other purposes.

(d) Time, Method of Payment, and Related Items.—(1) A person sentenced to pay a fine or other monetary penalty, including restitution, shall make such payment immediately, unless, in the interest of justice, the court provides for payment on a date certain or in installments. If the court provides for payment in installments, the installments shall be in equal monthly payments over the period provided by the court, unless the court establishes another schedule.

(2) If the judgment, or, in the case of a restitution order, the order, permits other than immediate payment, the length of time over which scheduled payments will be made shall be set by the court, but shall be the shortest time in which full payment can reasonably be made.

(3) A judgment for a fine which permits payments in installments shall include a requirement that the defendant will notify the court of any material change in the defendant's economic circumstances that might affect the defendant's ability to pay the fine. Upon receipt of such notice the court may, on its own motion or the motion of any party, adjust the payment schedule, or require immediate payment in full, as the interests of justice require.

(e) Alternative Sentence Precluded.—At the time a defendant is sentenced to pay a fine, the court may not impose an alternative sentence to be carried out if the fine is not paid.

(f) Responsibility for Payment of Monetary Obligation Relating to Organization.—If a sentence includes a fine, special assessment, restitution or other monetary obligation (including interest) with respect to an organization, each individual authorized to make disbursements for the organization has a duty to pay the obligation from assets of the organization. If such an obligation is imposed on a director, officer, shareholder, employee, or agent of an organization, payments may not be made, directly or indirectly, from assets of the organization, unless the court finds that such payment is expressly permissible under applicable State law.

(g) Security for Stayed Fine.—If a sentence imposing a fine is stayed, the court shall, absent exceptional circumstances (as determined by the court)—

(1) require the defendant to deposit, in the registry of the district court, any amount of the fine that is due;

(2) require the defendant to provide a bond or other security to ensure payment of the fine; or

(3) restrain the defendant from transferring or dissipating assets.

(h) Delinquency.—A fine or payment of restitution is delinquent if a payment is more than 30 days late.

(i) Default.—A fine or payment of restitution is in default if a payment is delinquent for more than 90 days. Notwithstanding any installment schedule, when a fine or payment of restitution is in default, the entire amount of the fine or restitution is due within 30 days after notification of the default, subject to the provisions of section 3613A.

(Added Pub. L. 98–473, title II, §212(a)(2), Oct. 12, 1984, 98 Stat. 1995; amended Pub. L. 100–185, §7, Dec. 11, 1987, 101 Stat. 1280; Pub. L. 101–647, title XXXV, §3587, Nov. 29, 1990, 104 Stat. 4930; Pub. L. 103–322, title II, §20403(a), Sept. 13, 1994, 108 Stat. 1825; Pub. L. 104–132, title II, §207(b), Apr. 24, 1996, 110 Stat. 1236.)

References in Text

The Federal Rules of Criminal Procedure, referred to in subsec. (c)(2), are set out in the Appendix to this title.

Prior Provisions

For a prior section 3572, applicable to offenses committed prior to Nov. 1, 1987, see note set out preceding section 3551 of this title.

Amendments

1996—Subsec. (b). Pub. L. 104–132, §207(b)(1), inserted "other than the United States," after "offense,".

Subsec. (d). Pub. L. 104–132, §207(b)(2)(A), (B), substituted "(1) A person sentenced to pay a fine or other monetary penalty, including restitution," for "A person sentenced to pay a fine or other monetary penalty" and struck out at end "If the judgment permits other than immediate payment, the period provided for shall not exceed five years, excluding any period served by the defendant as imprisonment for the offense."

Subsec. (d)(2), (3). Pub. L. 104–132, §207(b)(2)(C), added pars. (2) and (3).

Subsec. (f). Pub. L. 104–132, §207(b)(3), inserted "restitution" after "special assessment,".

Subsec. (h). Pub. L. 104–132, §207(b)(4), inserted "or payment of restitution" after "A fine".

Subsec. (i). Pub. L. 104–132, §207(b)(5), inserted "or payment of restitution" after "A fine" in first sentence and amended second sentence generally. Prior to amendment, second sentence read as follows: "When a fine is in default, the entire amount of the fine is due within 30 days after notification of the default, notwithstanding any installment schedule."

1994—Subsec. (a)(6) to (8). Pub. L. 103–322 added par. (6) and redesignated former pars. (6) and (7) as (7) and (8), respectively.

1990—Subsec. (c)(2). Pub. L. 101–647 inserted "of the Federal Rules of Criminal Procedure" after "rule 35".

1987—Pub. L. 100–185 inserted "and related matters" in section catchline and amended text generally, revising and restating as subsecs. (a) to (i) provisions formerly contained in subsecs. (a) to (j).

Effective Date of 1996 Amendment

Amendment by Pub. L. 104–132 to be effective, to extent constitutionally permissible, for sentencing proceedings in cases in which defendant is convicted on or after Apr. 24, 1996, see section 211 of Pub. L. 104–132, set out as a note under section 2248 of this title.

Effective Date

Section effective Nov. 1, 1987, and applicable only to offenses committed after the taking effect of this section, see section 235(a)(1) of Pub. L. 98–473, set out as a note under section 3551 of this title.

§3573. Petition of the Government for modification or remission

Upon petition of the Government showing that reasonable efforts to collect a fine or assessment are not likely to be effective, the court may, in the interest of justice—

(1) remit all or part of the unpaid portion of the fine or special assessment, including interest and penalties;

(2) defer payment of the fine or special assessment to a date certain or pursuant to an installment schedule; or

(3) extend a date certain or an installment schedule previously ordered.

A petition under this subsection shall be filed in the court in which sentence was originally imposed, unless the court transfers jurisdiction to another court. This section shall apply to all fines and assessments irrespective of the date of imposition.

(Added Pub. L. 98–473, title II, §212(a)(2), Oct. 12, 1984, 98 Stat. 1997; amended Pub. L. 100–185, §8(a), Dec. 11, 1987, 101 Stat. 1282; Pub. L. 100–690, title VII, §7082(a), Nov. 18, 1988, 102 Stat. 4407.)

Prior Provisions

For a prior section 3573, applicable to offenses committed prior to Nov. 1, 1987, see note set out preceding section 3551 of this title.

Amendments

1988—Pub. L. 100–690 inserted at end "This section shall apply to all fines and assessments irrespective of the date of imposition."

1987—Pub. L. 100–185 substituted "Petition of the Government for modification or remission" for "Modification or remission of fine" in section catchline and amended text generally, revising and restating as a single paragraph with three numbered clauses provisions formerly contained in subsecs. (a) and (b).

Effective Date

Section effective Nov. 1, 1987, and applicable only to offenses committed after the taking effect of this section, see section 235(a)(1) of Pub. L. 98–473, set out as a note under section 3551 of this title.

§3574. Implementation of a sentence of fine

The implementation of a sentence to pay a fine is governed by the provisions of subchapter B of chapter 229.

(Added Pub. L. 98–473, title II, §212(a)(2), Oct. 12, 1984, 98 Stat. 1997.)

Prior Provisions

For prior sections 3574 to 3580, applicable to offenses committed prior to Nov. 1, 1987, see note set out preceding section 3551 of this title.

Effective Date

Section effective Nov. 1, 1987, and applicable only to offenses committed after the taking effect of this section, see section 235(a)(1) of Pub. L. 98–473, set out as a note under section 3551 of this title.

SUBCHAPTER D—IMPRISONMENT 1

Amendments

1994—Pub. L. 103–322, title XXXIII, §330010(3), Sept. 13, 1994, 108 Stat. 2143, transferred analysis of this subchapter to follow heading for this subchapter.

§3581. Sentence of imprisonment

(a) In General.—A defendant who has been found guilty of an offense may be sentenced to a term of imprisonment.

(b) Authorized Terms.—The authorized terms of imprisonment are—

(1) for a Class A felony, the duration of the defendant's life or any period of time;

(2) for a Class B felony, not more than twenty-five years;

(3) for a Class C felony, not more than twelve years;

(4) for a Class D felony, not more than six years;

(5) for a Class E felony, not more than three years;

(6) for a Class A misdemeanor, not more than one year;

(7) for a Class B misdemeanor, not more than six months;

(8) for a Class C misdemeanor, not more than thirty days; and

(9) for an infraction, not more than five days.

(Added Pub. L. 98–473, title II, §212(a)(2), Oct. 12, 1984, 98 Stat. 1998.)

Effective Date

Section effective Nov. 1, 1987, and applicable only to offenses committed after the taking effect of this section, see section 235(a)(1) of Pub. L. 98–473, set out as a note under section 3551 of this title.

§3582. Imposition of a sentence of imprisonment

(a) Factors To Be Considered in Imposing a Term of Imprisonment.—The court, in determining whether to impose a term of imprisonment, and, if a term of imprisonment is to be imposed, in determining the length of the term, shall consider the factors set forth in section 3553(a) to the extent that they are applicable, recognizing that imprisonment is not an appropriate means of promoting correction and rehabilitation. In determining whether to make a recommendation concerning the type of prison facility appropriate for the defendant, the court shall consider any pertinent policy statements issued by the Sentencing Commission pursuant to 28 U.S.C. 994(a)(2).

(b) Effect of Finality of Judgment.—Notwithstanding the fact that a sentence to imprisonment can subsequently be—

(1) modified pursuant to the provisions of subsection (c);

(2) corrected pursuant to the provisions of rule 35 of the Federal Rules of Criminal Procedure and section 3742; or

(3) appealed and modified, if outside the guideline range, pursuant to the provisions of section

3742;

a judgment of conviction that includes such a sentence constitutes a final judgment for all other purposes.

(c) Modification of an Imposed Term of Imprisonment.—The court may not modify a term of imprisonment once it has been imposed except that—

(1) in any case—

(A) the court, upon motion of the Director of the Bureau of Prisons, may reduce the term of imprisonment (and may impose a term of probation or supervised release with or without conditions that does not exceed the unserved portion of the original term of imprisonment), after considering the factors set forth in section 3553(a) to the extent that they are applicable, if it finds that—

(i) extraordinary and compelling reasons warrant such a reduction; or

(ii) the defendant is at least 70 years of age, has served at least 30 years in prison, pursuant to a sentence imposed under section 3559(c), for the offense or offenses for which the defendant is currently imprisoned, and a determination has been made by the Director of the Bureau of Prisons that the defendant is not a danger to the safety of any other person or the community, as provided under section 3142(g);

and that such a reduction is consistent with applicable policy statements issued by the Sentencing Commission; and

(B) the court may modify an imposed term of imprisonment to the extent otherwise expressly permitted by statute or by Rule 35 of the Federal Rules of Criminal Procedure; and

(2) in the case of a defendant who has been sentenced to a term of imprisonment based on a sentencing range that has subsequently been lowered by the Sentencing Commission pursuant to 28 U.S.C. 994(o), upon motion of the defendant or the Director of the Bureau of Prisons, or on its own motion, the court may reduce the term of imprisonment, after considering the factors set forth in section 3553(a) to the extent that they are applicable, if such a reduction is consistent with applicable policy statements issued by the Sentencing Commission.

(d) Inclusion of an Order To Limit Criminal Association of Organized Crime and Drug Offenders.—The court, in imposing a sentence to a term of imprisonment upon a defendant convicted of a felony set forth in chapter 95 (racketeering) or 96 (racketeer influenced and corrupt organizations) of this title or in the Comprehensive Drug Abuse Prevention and Control Act of 1970 (21 U.S.C. 801 et seq.), or at any time thereafter upon motion by the Director of the Bureau of Prisons or a United States attorney, may include as a part of the sentence an order that requires that the defendant not associate or communicate with a specified person, other than his attorney, upon a showing of probable cause to believe that association or communication with such person is for the purpose of enabling the defendant to control, manage, direct, finance, or otherwise participate in an illegal enterprise.

(Added Pub. L. 98–473, title II, §212(a)(2), Oct. 12, 1984, 98 Stat. 1998; amended Pub. L. 100–690, title VII, §7107, Nov. 18, 1988, 102 Stat. 4418; Pub. L. 101–647, title XXXV, §3588, Nov. 29, 1990, 104 Stat. 4930; Pub. L. 103–322, title VII, §70002, Sept. 13, 1994, 108 Stat. 1984; Pub. L. 104–294, title VI, §604(b)(3), Oct. 11, 1996, 110 Stat. 3506; Pub. L. 107–273, div. B, title III, §3006, Nov. 2, 2002, 116 Stat. 1806.)

References in Text

The Federal Rules of Criminal Procedure, referred to in subsec. (b)(2), are set out in the Appendix to this title.

The Comprehensive Drug Abuse Prevention and Control Act of 1970, referred to in subsec. (d), is Pub. L. 91–513, Oct. 27, 1970, 84 Stat. 1236, as amended, which is classified principally to chapter 13 (§801 et seq.) of Title 21, Food and Drugs. For complete classification of this Act to the Code, see Short Title note set out under section 801 of Title 21 and Tables.

Amendments

2002—Subsec. (c)(1)(A). Pub. L. 107–273 inserted "(and may impose a term of probation or supervised release with or without conditions that does not exceed the unserved portion of the original term of imprisonment)" after "may reduce the term of imprisonment" in introductory provisions.

1996—Subsec. (c)(1)(A)(i). Pub. L. 104–294 inserted "or" after semicolon at end.

1994—Subsec. (c)(1)(A). Pub. L. 103–322, inserted a dash after "if it finds that", designated "extraordinary and compelling reasons warrant such a reduction" as cl. (i), inserted a semicolon at end of cl. (i), realigned margins accordingly, and added cl. (ii) before concluding provisions.

1990—Subsec. (b)(2). Pub. L. 101–647 inserted "of the Federal Rules of Criminal Procedure" after "rule 35".

1988—Subsec. (c)(2). Pub. L. 100–690 substituted "994(o)" for "994(n)".

Effective Date of 1996 Amendment

Amendment by Pub. L. 104–294 effective Sept. 13, 1994, see section 604(d) of Pub. L. 104–294, set out as a note under section 13 of this title.

Effective Date

Section effective Nov. 1, 1987, and applicable only to offenses committed after the taking effect of this section, see section 235(a)(1) of Pub. L. 98–473, set out as a note under section 3551 of this title.

§3583. Inclusion of a term of supervised release after imprisonment

(a) In General.—The court, in imposing a sentence to a term of imprisonment for a felony or a misdemeanor, may include as a part of the sentence a requirement that the defendant be placed on a term of supervised release after imprisonment, except that the court shall include as a part of the sentence a requirement that the defendant be placed on a term of supervised release if such a term is required by statute or if the defendant has been convicted for the first time of a domestic violence crime as defined in section 3561(b).

(b) Authorized Terms of Supervised Release.—Except as otherwise provided, the authorized terms of supervised release are—

(1) for a Class A or Class B felony, not more than five years;

(2) for a Class C or Class D felony, not more than three years; and

(3) for a Class E felony, or for a misdemeanor (other than a petty offense), not more than one year.

(c) Factors To Be Considered in Including a Term of Supervised Release.—The court, in determining whether to include a term of supervised release, and, if a term of supervised release is to be included, in determining the length of the term and the conditions of supervised release, shall consider the factors set forth in section 3553(a)(1), (a)(2)(B), (a)(2)(C), (a)(2)(D), (a)(4), (a)(5), (a)(6), and (a)(7).

(d) Conditions of Supervised Release.—The court shall order, as an explicit condition of supervised release, that the defendant not commit another Federal, State, or local crime during the term of supervision, that the defendant make restitution in accordance with sections 3663 and 3663A, or any other statute authorizing a sentence of restitution, and that the defendant not unlawfully possess a controlled substance. The court shall order as an explicit condition of supervised release for a defendant convicted for the first time of a domestic violence crime as defined in section 3561(b) that the defendant attend a public, private, or private nonprofit offender rehabilitation program that has been approved by the court, in consultation with a State Coalition Against Domestic Violence or other appropriate experts, if an approved program is readily available within a 50-mile radius of the legal residence of the defendant. The court shall order, as an explicit condition of supervised release for a person required to register under the Sex Offender Registration and Notification Act, that the person comply with the requirements of that Act. The court shall order, as an explicit condition of supervised release, that the defendant cooperate in the collection of a DNA sample from the defendant, if the collection of such a sample is authorized pursuant to section 3 of the DNA Analysis Backlog Elimination Act of 2000. The court shall also order, as an explicit condition of supervised release, that the defendant refrain from any unlawful use of a controlled substance and submit to a drug test within 15 days of release on supervised release and at least 2 periodic drug tests thereafter (as determined by the court) for use of a controlled substance. The condition stated in the preceding sentence may be ameliorated or suspended by the court as provided in section 3563(a)(4).1 The results of a drug test administered in accordance with the preceding subsection shall be subject to confirmation only if the results are positive, the defendant is subject to possible imprisonment for such failure, and either the defendant denies the accuracy of such test or there is some other reason to question the results of the test. A drug test confirmation shall be a urine drug test confirmed using gas chromatography/mass spectrometry techniques or such test as the Director of the Administrative Office of the United States Courts after consultation with the Secretary of Health and Human Services may determine to be of equivalent accuracy. The court shall consider whether the availability of appropriate substance abuse treatment programs, or an individual's current or past participation in such programs, warrants an exception in accordance with United States Sentencing Commission guidelines from the rule of section 3583(g) when considering any action against a defendant who fails a drug test. The court may order, as a further condition of supervised release, to the extent that such condition—

(1) is reasonably related to the factors set forth in section 3553(a)(1), (a)(2)(B), (a)(2)(C), and (a)(2)(D);

(2) involves no greater deprivation of liberty than is reasonably necessary for the purposes set forth in section 3553(a)(2)(B), (a)(2)(C), and (a)(2)(D); and

(3) is consistent with any pertinent policy statements issued by the Sentencing Commission pursuant to 28 U.S.C. 994(a);

any condition set forth as a discretionary condition of probation in section 3563(b) and any other condition it considers to be appropriate, provided, however that a condition set forth in subsection 3563(b)(10) shall be imposed only for a violation of a condition of supervised release in accordance with section 3583(e)(2) and only when facilities are available. If an alien defendant is subject to deportation, the court may provide, as a condition of supervised release, that he be deported and remain outside the United States, and may order that he be delivered to a duly authorized immigration official for such deportation. The court may order, as an explicit condition of supervised release for a person who is a felon and required to register under the Sex Offender Registration and Notification Act, that the person submit his person, and any property, house, residence, vehicle, papers, computer, other electronic communications or data storage devices or media, and effects to search at any time, with or without a warrant, by any law enforcement or probation officer with reasonable suspicion concerning a violation of a condition of supervised release or unlawful conduct by the person, and by any probation officer in the lawful discharge of the officer's supervision functions.

(e) Modification of Conditions or Revocation.—The court may, after considering the factors set forth in section 3553(a)(1), (a)(2)(B), (a)(2)(C), (a)(2)(D), (a)(4), (a)(5), (a)(6), and (a)(7)—

(1) terminate a term of supervised release and discharge the defendant released at any time after the expiration of one year of supervised release, pursuant to the provisions of the Federal Rules of Criminal Procedure relating to the modification of probation, if it is satisfied that such action is warranted by the conduct of the defendant released and the interest of justice;

(2) extend a term of supervised release if less than the maximum authorized term was previously imposed, and may modify, reduce, or enlarge the conditions of supervised release, at any time prior to the expiration or termination of the term of supervised release, pursuant to the provisions of the Federal Rules of Criminal Procedure relating to the modification of probation and the provisions applicable to the initial setting of the terms and conditions of post-release supervision;

(3) revoke a term of supervised release, and require the defendant to serve in prison all or part of the term of supervised release authorized by statute for the offense that resulted in such term of supervised release without credit for time previously served on postrelease supervision, if the court, pursuant to the Federal Rules of Criminal Procedure applicable to revocation of probation or

supervised release, finds by a preponderance of the evidence that the defendant violated a condition of supervised release, except that a defendant whose term is revoked under this paragraph may not be required to serve on any such revocation more than 5 years in prison if the offense that resulted in the term of supervised release is a class A felony, more than 3 years in prison if such offense is a class B felony, more than 2 years in prison if such offense is a class C or D felony, or more than one year in any other case; or

(4) order the defendant to remain at his place of residence during nonworking hours and, if the court so directs, to have compliance monitored by telephone or electronic signaling devices, except that an order under this paragraph may be imposed only as an alternative to incarceration.

(f) Written Statement of Conditions.—The court shall direct that the probation officer provide the defendant with a written statement that sets forth all the conditions to which the term of supervised release is subject, and that is sufficiently clear and specific to serve as a guide for the defendant's conduct and for such supervision as is required.

(g) Mandatory Revocation for Possession of Controlled Substance or Firearm or for Refusal To Comply With Drug Testing.—If the defendant—

(1) possesses a controlled substance in violation of the condition set forth in subsection (d);

(2) possesses a firearm, as such term is defined in section 921 of this title, in violation of Federal law, or otherwise violates a condition of supervised release prohibiting the defendant from possessing a firearm;

(3) refuses to comply with drug testing imposed as a condition of supervised release; or

(4) as a part of drug testing, tests positive for illegal controlled substances more than 3 times over the course of 1 year;

the court shall revoke the term of supervised release and require the defendant to serve a term of imprisonment not to exceed the maximum term of imprisonment authorized under subsection (e)(3).

(h) Supervised Release Following Revocation.—When a term of supervised release is revoked and the defendant is required to serve a term of imprisonment, the court may include a requirement that the defendant be placed on a term of supervised release after imprisonment. The length of such a term of supervised release shall not exceed the term of supervised release authorized by statute for the offense that resulted in the original term of supervised release, less any term of imprisonment that was imposed upon revocation of supervised release.

(i) Delayed Revocation.—The power of the court to revoke a term of supervised release for violation of a condition of supervised release, and to order the defendant to serve a term of imprisonment and, subject to the limitations in subsection (h), a further term of supervised release, extends beyond the expiration of the term of supervised release for any period reasonably necessary for the adjudication of matters arising before its expiration if, before its expiration, a warrant or summons has been issued on the basis of an allegation of such a violation.

(j) Supervised Release Terms for Terrorism Predicates.—Notwithstanding subsection (b), the authorized term of supervised release for any offense listed in section 2332b(g)(5)(B) is any term of years or life.

(k) Notwithstanding subsection (b), the authorized term of supervised release for any offense under section 1201 involving a minor victim, and for any offense under section 1591, 1594(c), 2241, 2242, 2243, 2244, 2245, 2250, 2251, 2251A, 2252, 2252A, 2260, 2421, 2422, 2423, or 2425, is any term of years not less than 5, or life. If a defendant required to register under the Sex Offender Registration and Notification Act commits any criminal offense under chapter 109A, 110, or 117, or section 1201 or 1591, for which imprisonment for a term longer than 1 year can be imposed, the court shall revoke the term of supervised release and require the defendant to serve a term of imprisonment under subsection (e)(3) without regard to the exception contained therein. Such term shall be not less than 5 years.

(Added Pub. L. 98–473, title II, §212(a)(2), Oct. 12, 1984, 98 Stat. 1999; amended Pub. L. 99–570, title I, §1006(a)(1)–(3), Oct. 27, 1986, 100 Stat. 3207–6; Pub. L. 99–646, §14(a), Nov. 10, 1986, 100 Stat. 3594; Pub. L. 100–182, §§8, 9, 12, 25, Dec. 7, 1987, 101 Stat. 1267, 1268, 1272; Pub. L. 100–690, title VII, §§7108, 7303(b), 7305(b), Nov. 18, 1988, 102 Stat. 4418, 4464, 4465;

Pub. L. 101–647, title XXXV, §3589, Nov. 29, 1990, 104 Stat. 4930; Pub. L. 103–322, title II, §20414(c), title XI, §110505, title XXXII, §320921(c), Sept. 13, 1994, 108 Stat. 1831, 2016, 2130; Pub. L. 105–119, title I, §115(a)(8)(B)(iv), Nov. 26, 1997, 111 Stat. 2466; Pub. L. 106–546, §7(b), Dec. 19, 2000, 114 Stat. 2734; Pub. L. 107–56, title VIII, §812, Oct. 26, 2001, 115 Stat. 382; Pub. L. 107–273, div. B, title II, §2103(b), title III, §3007, Nov. 2, 2002, 116 Stat. 1793, 1806; Pub. L. 108–21, title I, §101, Apr. 30, 2003, 117 Stat. 651; Pub. L. 109–177, title II, §212, Mar. 9, 2006, 120 Stat. 230; Pub. L. 109–248, title I, §141(e), title II, §210(b), July 27, 2006, 120 Stat. 603, 615; Pub. L. 110–406, §14(b), Oct. 13, 2008, 122 Stat. 4294; Pub. L. 114–22, title I, §114(d), May 29, 2015, 129 Stat. 242; Pub. L. 114–324, §2(a), Dec. 16, 2016, 130 Stat. 1948.)

References in Text

The Sex Offender Registration and Notification Act, referred to in subsecs. (d) and (k), is title I of Pub. L. 109–248, July 27, 2006, 120 Stat. 590, which was classified principally to subchapter I (§16901 et seq.) of chapter 151 of Title 42, The Public Health and Welfare, prior to editorial reclassification as chapter 209 (§20901 et seq.) of Title 34, Crime Control and Law Enforcement. For complete classification of this Act to the Code, see Short Title of 2006 Act note set out under section 10101 of Title 34 and Tables.

Section 3 of the DNA Analysis Backlog Elimination Act of 2000, referred to in subsec. (d), is section 3 of Pub. L. 106–546, which is classified to section 40702 of Title 34, Crime Control and Law Enforcement.

Section 3563(a)(4), referred to in subsec. (d), probably means the par. (4) of section 3563(a) added by section 20414(b)(3) of Pub. L. 103–322, which was renumbered par. (5) by Pub. L. 104–132, title II, §203(1)(C), Apr. 24, 1996, 110 Stat. 1227.

The Federal Rules of Criminal Procedure, referred to in subsec. (e)(1), (2), (3), are set out in the Appendix to this title.

Amendments

2016—Subsec. (d). Pub. L. 114–324 inserted ", that the defendant make restitution in accordance with sections 3663 and 3663A, or any other statute authorizing a sentence of restitution," after "supervision" in first sentence.

2015—Subsec. (k). Pub. L. 114–22, which directed amendment of subsec. (k) by inserting "1594(c)," after "1591,", was executed by making the insertion after "1591," the first place appearing to reflect the probable intent of Congress.

2008—Subsec. (d). Pub. L. 110–406 substituted "section 3563(b) and any other condition it considers to be appropriate, provided, however that a condition set forth in subsection 3563(b)(10) shall be imposed only for a violation of a condition of supervised release in accordance with section 3583(e)(2) and only when facilities are available." for "section 3563(b)(1) through (b)(10) and (b)(12) through (b)(20), and any other condition it considers to be appropriate." in concluding provisions.

2006—Subsec. (d). Pub. L. 109–248, §§141(e)(1), 210(b), substituted "required to register under the Sex Offender Registration and Notification Act, that the person comply with the requirements of that Act." for "described in section 4042(c)(4), that the person report the address where the person will reside and any subsequent change of residence to the probation officer responsible for supervision, and that the person register in any State where the person resides, is employed, carries on a vocation, or is a student (as such terms are defined under section 170101(a)(3) of the Violent Crime Control and Law Enforcement Act of 1994)." in third sentence of introductory provisions and inserted "The court may order, as an explicit condition of supervised release for a person who is a felon and required to register under the Sex Offender Registration and Notification Act, that the person submit his person, and any property, house, residence, vehicle, papers, computer, other electronic communications or data storage devices or media, and effects to search at any time, with or without a warrant, by any law enforcement or probation officer with reasonable suspicion concerning a violation of a condition of supervised release or unlawful conduct by the person, and by any probation officer in the lawful discharge of the officer's supervision functions." at end of concluding provisions.

Subsec. (j). Pub. L. 109–177 struck out ", the commission of which resulted in, or created a foreseeable risk of, death or serious bodily injury to another person," before "is any term of years or life."

Subsec. (k). Pub. L. 109–248, §141(e)(2), substituted "2243, 2244, 2245, 2250" for "2244(a)(1), 2244(a)(2)", inserted "not less than 5," after "any term of years", and inserted "If a defendant required to register under the Sex Offender Registration and Notification Act commits any criminal offense under chapter 109A, 110, or 117, or section 1201 or 1591, for which imprisonment for a term longer than 1 year can be imposed, the court shall revoke the term of supervised release and require the defendant to serve a term of imprisonment under subsection (e)(3) without regard to the exception contained therein. Such term shall be not less than 5 years." at end.

2003—Subsec. (e)(3). Pub. L. 108–21, §101(1), inserted "on any such revocation" after "required to serve".

Subsec. (h). Pub. L. 108–21, §101(2), struck out "that is less than the maximum term of imprisonment authorized under subsection (e)(3)" after "required to serve a term of imprisonment".

Subsec. (k). Pub. L. 108–21, §101(3), added subsec. (k).

2002—Subsecs. (c), (e). Pub. L. 107–273, §3007, substituted "(a)(6), and (a)(7)" for "and (a)(6)".

Subsec. (g)(4). Pub. L. 107–273, §2103(b), added par. (4).

2001—Subsec. (j). Pub. L. 107–56 added subsec. (j).

2000—Subsec. (d). Pub. L. 106–546 inserted "The court shall order, as an explicit condition of supervised release, that the defendant cooperate in the collection of a DNA sample from the defendant, if the collection of such a sample is authorized pursuant to section 3 of the DNA Analysis Backlog Elimination Act of 2000." before "The court shall also order,".

1997—Subsec. (d). Pub. L. 105–119 inserted after second sentence "The court shall order, as an explicit condition of supervised release for a person described in section 4042(c)(4), that the person report the address where the person will reside and any subsequent change of residence to the probation officer responsible for supervision, and that the person register in any State where the person resides, is employed, carries on a vocation, or is a student (as such terms are defined under section 170101(a)(3) of the Violent Crime Control and Law Enforcement Act of 1994)."

1994—Subsec. (a). Pub. L. 103–322, §320921(c)(1), inserted before period at end "or if the defendant has been convicted for the first time of a domestic violence crime as defined in section 3561(b)".

Subsec. (d). Pub. L. 103–322, §320921(c)(2), inserted after first sentence "The court shall order as an explicit condition of supervised release for a defendant convicted for the first time of a domestic violence crime as defined in section 3561(b) that the defendant attend a public, private, or private nonprofit offender rehabilitation program that has been approved by the court, in consultation with a State Coalition Against Domestic Violence or other appropriate experts, if an approved program is readily available within a 50-mile radius of the legal residence of the defendant."

Pub. L. 103–322, §20414(c), inserted after first sentence "The court shall also order, as an explicit condition of supervised release, that the defendant refrain from any unlawful use of a controlled substance and submit to a drug test within 15 days of release on supervised release and at least 2 periodic drug tests thereafter (as determined by the court) for use of a controlled substance. The condition stated in the preceding sentence may be ameliorated or suspended by the court as provided in section 3563(a)(4). The results of a drug test administered in accordance with the preceding subsection shall be subject to confirmation only if the results are positive, the defendant is subject to possible imprisonment for such failure, and either the defendant denies the accuracy of such test or there is some other reason to question the results of the test. A drug test confirmation shall be a urine drug test confirmed using gas chromatography/mass spectrometry techniques or such test as the Director of the Administrative Office of the United States Courts after consultation with the Secretary of Health and Human Services may determine to be of equivalent accuracy. The court shall consider whether the availability of appropriate substance abuse treatment programs, or an individual's current or past participation in such programs, warrants an exception in accordance with United States Sentencing Commission guidelines from the rule of section 3583(g) when considering any action against a defendant who fails a drug test." Pub. L. 103–322, §110505(1), substituted "unlawfully possess a controlled substance" for "possess illegal controlled substances" in first sentence.

Subsec. (e)(1). Pub. L. 103–322, §110505(2)(A), substituted "defendant" for "person" in two places.

Subsec. (e)(3). Pub. L. 103–322, §110505(2)(B), amended par. (3) generally. Prior to amendment, par. (3) read as follows: "revoke a term of supervised release, and require the person to serve in prison all or part of the term of supervised release without credit for time previously served on postrelease supervision, if it finds by a preponderance of the evidence that the person violated a condition of supervised release, pursuant to the provisions of the Federal Rules of Criminal Procedure that are applicable to probation revocation and to the provisions of applicable policy statements issued by the Sentencing Commission, except that a person whose term is revoked under this paragraph may not be required to serve more than 3 years in prison if the offense for which the person was convicted was a Class B felony, or more than 2 years in prison if the offense was a Class C or D felony; or".

Subsec. (e)(4). Pub. L. 103–322, §110505(2)(A), substituted "defendant" for "person".

Subsecs. (g) to (i). Pub. L. 103–322, §110505(3), added subsecs. (g) to (i) and struck out former subsec. (g) which read as follows:

"(g) Possession of Controlled Substances.—If the defendant is found by the court to be in the possession of a controlled substance, the court shall terminate the term of supervised release and require the defendant to serve in prison not less than one-third of the term of supervised release."

1990—Subsec. (d)(2). Pub. L. 101–647, §3589(1), inserted a comma after "3553(a)(2)(B)".

Subsec. (e)(2) to (5). Pub. L. 101–647, §3589(2)(A)–(C), struck out "or" at end of par. (2), substituted "; or" for period at end of par. (3), and redesignated par. (5) as (4).

1988—Subsec. (d). Pub. L. 100–690, §7303(b)(1), inserted "and that the defendant not possess illegal controlled substances" before period at end of first sentence.

Pub. L. 100–690, §7305(b)(1), substituted "(b)(20)" for "(b)(19)" in concluding provisions.

Subsec. (d)(1). Pub. L. 100–690, §7108(a)(1), inserted "(a)(2)(C)," after "(a)(2)(B),".

Subsec. (d)(2). Pub. L. 100–690, §7108(a)(2), which directed that "(a)(2)(C)," be inserted after "(a)(2)(B)," was executed by inserting "(a)(2)(C)," after "(a)(2)(B)" as the probable intent of Congress, because no comma appeared after "(a)(2)(B)".

Subsec. (e). Pub. L. 100–690, §7108(b)(1), inserted "(a)(2)(C)," after "(a)(2)(B)," in introductory provisions.

Subsec. (e)(2). Pub. L. 100–690, §7108(b)(2), inserted "or" after "supervision;".

Subsec. (e)(3). Pub. L. 100–690, §7305(b)(2)(A), which directed amendment of par. (3) by striking "or" at the end could not be executed because of the intervening amendment by Pub. L. 100–690, §7108(b)(3), (4). See below.

Pub. L. 100–690, §7108(b)(3), (4), redesignated par. (4) as (3) and struck out former par. (3) which read as follows: "treat a violation of a condition of a term of supervised release as contempt of court pursuant to section 401(3) of this title; or".

Subsec. (e)(4). Pub. L. 100–690, §7305(b)(2)(B), which directed amendment of par. (4) by striking the period at the end and inserting "; or" could not be executed because subsec. (e) did not contain a par. (4) after the intervening amendment by Pub. L. 100–690, §7108(b)(4). See below.

Pub. L. 100–690, §7108(b)(4), redesignated par. (4) as (3).

Subsec. (e)(5). Pub. L. 100–690, §7305(b)(2)(C), added par. (5).

Subsec. (g). Pub. L. 100–690, §7303(b)(2), added subsec. (g).

1987—Subsec. (b)(1). Pub. L. 100–182, §8(1), substituted "five years" for "three years".

Subsec. (b)(2). Pub. L. 100–182, §8(2), substituted "three years" for "two years".

Subsec. (b)(3). Pub. L. 100–182, §8(3), inserted "(other than a petty offense)" after "misdemeanor".

Subsec. (c). Pub. L. 100–182, §9, inserted "(a)(2)(C),".

Subsec. (e)(1). Pub. L. 100–182, §12(1), inserted "pursuant to the provisions of the Federal Rules of Criminal Procedure relating to the modification of probation,".

Subsec. (e)(2). Pub. L. 100–182, §12(2), struck out "after a hearing," before "extend a term" and inserted "the provisions of the Federal Rules of Criminal Procedure relating to the modification of probation and" after "pursuant to".

Subsec. (e)(4). Pub. L. 100–182, §25, inserted ", except that a person whose term is revoked under this paragraph may not be required to serve more than 3 years in prison if the offense for which the person was convicted was a Class B felony, or more than 2 years in prison if the offense was a Class C or D felony" before "Commission" at end.

1986—Subsec. (a). Pub. L. 99–570, §1006(a)(1), inserted ", except that the court shall include as a part of the sentence a requirement that the defendant be placed on a term of supervised release if such a term is required by statute".

Subsec. (b). Pub. L. 99–570, §1006(a)(2), substituted "Except as otherwise provided, the" for "The".

Subsec. (e). Pub. L. 99–570, §1006(a)(3)(A), and Pub. L. 99–646, §14(a)(1), amended section catchline identically, substituting "conditions or revocation" for "term or conditions".

Subsec. (e)(1). Pub. L. 99–646, §14(a)(2), struck out "previously ordered" before "and discharge".

Subsec. (e)(4). Pub. L. 99–570, §224(a)(3)(B)–(D), added par. (4).

Effective Date of 1997 Amendment

Amendment by Pub. L. 105–119 effective 1 year after Nov. 26, 1997, see section 115(c)(1) of Pub. L. 105–119, set out as a note under section 3521 of this title.

Effective Date of 1988 Amendment

Amendment by section 7303(b) of Pub. L. 100–690 applicable with respect to persons whose probation, supervised release, or parole begins after Dec. 31, 1988, see section 7303(d) of Pub. L. 100–690, set out as a note under section 3563 of this title.

Effective Date of 1987 Amendment

Amendment by Pub. L. 100–182 applicable with respect to offenses committed after Dec. 7, 1987, see section 26 of Pub. L. 100–182, set out as a note under section 3006A of this title.

Effective Date of 1986 Amendments

Pub. L. 99–646, §14(b), Nov. 10, 1986, 100 Stat. 3594, provided that: "The amendments made by this section [amending this section] shall take effect on the date of the taking effect of section 3583 of title 18, United States Code [Nov. 1, 1987]."

Pub. L. 99–570, title I, §1006(a)(4), Oct. 27, 1986, 100 Stat. 3207–7, provided that: "The amendments made by this subsection [amending this section] shall take effect on the date of the taking effect of section 3583 of title 18, United States Code [Nov. 1, 1987]."

Effective Date

Section effective Nov. 1, 1987, and applicable only to offenses committed after the taking effect of this section, see section 235(a)(1) of Pub. L. 98–473, set out as a note under section 3551 of this title.

§3584. Multiple sentences of imprisonment

(a) Imposition of Concurrent or Consecutive Terms.—If multiple terms of imprisonment are imposed on a defendant at the same time, or if a term of imprisonment is imposed on a defendant who is already subject to an undischarged term of imprisonment, the terms may run concurrently or consecutively, except that the terms may not run consecutively for an attempt and for another offense that was the sole objective of the attempt. Multiple terms of imprisonment imposed at the same time run concurrently unless the court orders or the statute mandates that the terms are to run consecutively. Multiple terms of imprisonment imposed at different times run consecutively unless the court orders that the terms are to run concurrently.

(b) Factors To Be Considered in Imposing Concurrent or Consecutive Terms.—The court, in determining whether the terms imposed are to be ordered to run concurrently or consecutively, shall consider, as to each offense for which a term of imprisonment is being imposed, the factors set forth in section 3553(a).

(c) Treatment of Multiple Sentence as an Aggregate.—Multiple terms of imprisonment ordered to run consecutively or concurrently shall be treated for administrative purposes as a single, aggregate term of imprisonment.

(Added Pub. L. 98–473, title II, §212(a)(2), Oct. 12, 1984, 98 Stat. 2000.)

Effective Date

Section effective Nov. 1, 1987, and applicable only to offenses committed after the taking effect of this section, see section 235(a)(1) of Pub. L. 98–473, set out as a note under section 3551 of this title.

§3585. Calculation of a term of imprisonment

(a) Commencement of Sentence.—A sentence to a term of imprisonment commences on the date the defendant is received in custody awaiting transportation to, or arrives voluntarily to commence service of sentence at, the official detention facility at which the sentence is to be served.

(b) Credit for Prior Custody.—A defendant shall be given credit toward the service of a term of imprisonment for any time he has spent in official detention prior to the date the sentence commences—

(1) as a result of the offense for which the sentence was imposed; or

(2) as a result of any other charge for which the defendant was arrested after the commission of the offense for which the sentence was imposed;

that has not been credited against another sentence.

(Added Pub. L. 98–473, title II, §212(a)(2), Oct. 12, 1984, 98 Stat. 2001.)

Effective Date

Section effective Nov. 1, 1987, and applicable only to offenses committed after the taking effect of this section, see section 235(a)(1) of Pub. L. 98–473, set out as a note under section 3551 of this title.

§3586. Implementation of a sentence of imprisonment

The implementation of a sentence of imprisonment is governed by the provisions of subchapter C of chapter 229 and, if the sentence includes a term of supervised release, by the provisions of subchapter A of chapter 229.

(Added Pub. L. 98–473, title II, §212(a)(2), Oct. 12, 1984, 98 Stat. 2001.)

Effective Date

Section effective Nov. 1, 1987, and applicable only to offenses committed after the taking effect of this section, see section 235(a)(1) of Pub. L. 98–473, set out as a note under section 3551 of this title.

CHAPTER 228 - DEATH SENTENCE

Prior Provisions

A prior chapter 228 (§§3591 to 3599) relating to imposition, payment, and collection of fines was added by Pub. L. 98–473, title II, §238(a), Oct. 12, 1984, 98 Stat. 2034, effective pursuant to section 235(a)(1) of Pub. L. 98–473 the first day of the first calendar month beginning twenty-four months after Oct. 12, 1984. Pub. L. 98–596, §12(a)(1), Oct. 30, 1984, 98 Stat. 3139, repealed chapter 228 applicable pursuant to section 12(b) of Pub. L. 98–596 on and after the date of enactment of Pub. L. 98–473 (Oct. 12, 1984). Section 238(i) of Pub. L. 98–473 which repealed section 238 of Pub. L. 98–473 on the same date established by section 235(a)(1) of Pub. L. 98–473 was repealed by section 12(a)(9) of Pub. L. 98–596.

Amendments

2006—Pub. L. 109–177, title II, §222(b), Mar. 9, 2006, 120 Stat. 232, which directed amendment of the "table of sections of the bill" by adding item 3599 after item 3598, was executed by adding item 3599 to the table of sections for this chapter to reflect the probable intent of Congress.

§3591. Sentence of death

(a) A defendant who has been found guilty of—

(1) an offense described in section 794 or section 2381; or

(2) any other offense for which a sentence of death is provided, if the defendant, as determined beyond a reasonable doubt at the hearing under section 3593—

(A) intentionally killed the victim;

(B) intentionally inflicted serious bodily injury that resulted in the death of the victim;

(C) intentionally participated in an act, contemplating that the life of a person would be taken or intending that lethal force would be used in connection with a person, other than one of the participants in the offense, and the victim died as a direct result of the act; or

(D) intentionally and specifically engaged in an act of violence, knowing that the act created a grave risk of death to a person, other than one of the participants in the offense, such that participation in the act constituted a reckless disregard for human life and the victim died as a direct result of the act,

shall be sentenced to death if, after consideration of the factors set forth in section 3592 in the course of a hearing held pursuant to section 3593, it is determined that imposition of a sentence of death is justified, except that no person may be sentenced to death who was less than 18 years of age at the time of the offense.

(b) A defendant who has been found guilty of—

(1) an offense referred to in section 408(c)(1) of the Controlled Substances Act (21 U.S.C. 848(c)(1)), committed as part of a continuing criminal enterprise offense under the conditions described in subsection (b) of that section which involved not less than twice the quantity of controlled substance described in subsection (b)(2)(A) or twice the gross receipts described in subsection (b)(2)(B); or

(2) an offense referred to in section 408(c)(1) of the Controlled Substances Act (21 U.S.C. 848(c)(1)), committed as part of a continuing criminal enterprise offense under that section, where

the defendant is a principal administrator, organizer, or leader of such an enterprise, and the defendant, in order to obstruct the investigation or prosecution of the enterprise or an offense involved in the enterprise, attempts to kill or knowingly directs, advises, authorizes, or assists another to attempt to kill any public officer, juror, witness, or members of the family or household of such a person,

shall be sentenced to death if, after consideration of the factors set forth in section 3592 in the course of a hearing held pursuant to section 3593, it is determined that imposition of a sentence of death is justified, except that no person may be sentenced to death who was less than 18 years of age at the time of the offense.

(Added Pub. L. 103–322, title VI, §60002(a), Sept. 13, 1994, 108 Stat. 1959.)

Short Title

Pub. L. 103–322, title VI, §60001, Sept. 13, 1994, 108 Stat. 1959, provided that: "This title [enacting this chapter and sections 36, 37, 1118 to 1121, 2245, 2280, 2281, and 2332a of this title, amending sections 34, 241, 242, 245, 247, 794, 844, 924, 930, 1091, 1111, 1114, 1116, 1117, 1201, 1203, 1503, 1512, 1513, 1716, 1958, 1959, 1992, 2113, 2119, 2251, 2332, 2340A, 3005, and 3432 of this title and section 1324 of Title 8, Aliens and Nationality, renumbering former section 2245 of this title as 2246, repealing section 46503 of Title 49, Transportation, and enacting provisions set out as notes under this section and sections 36, 37, and 2280 of this title] may be cited as the 'Federal Death Penalty Act of 1994'."

Applicability to Uniform Code of Military Justice

Pub. L. 103–322, title VI, §60004, Sept. 13, 1994, 108 Stat. 1970, provided that: "Chapter 228 of title 18, United States Code, as added by this title, shall not apply to prosecutions under the Uniform Code of Military Justice (10 U.S.C. 801)."

§3592. Mitigating and aggravating factors to be considered in determining whether a sentence of death is justified

(a) Mitigating Factors.—In determining whether a sentence of death is to be imposed on a defendant, the finder of fact shall consider any mitigating factor, including the following:

(1) Impaired capacity.—The defendant's capacity to appreciate the wrongfulness of the defendant's conduct or to conform conduct to the requirements of law was significantly impaired, regardless of whether the capacity was so impaired as to constitute a defense to the charge.

(2) Duress.—The defendant was under unusual and substantial duress, regardless of whether the duress was of such a degree as to constitute a defense to the charge.

(3) Minor participation.—The defendant is punishable as a principal in the offense, which was committed by another, but the defendant's participation was relatively minor, regardless of whether the participation was so minor as to constitute a defense to the charge.

(4) Equally culpable defendants.—Another defendant or defendants, equally culpable in the crime, will not be punished by death.

(5) No prior criminal record.—The defendant did not have a significant prior history of other criminal conduct.

(6) Disturbance.—The defendant committed the offense under severe mental or emotional disturbance.

(7) Victim's consent.—The victim consented to the criminal conduct that resulted in the victim's death.

(8) Other factors.—Other factors in the defendant's background, record, or character or any other circumstance of the offense that mitigate against imposition of the death sentence.

(b) Aggravating Factors for Espionage and Treason.—In determining whether a sentence of death is justified for an offense described in section 3591(a)(1), the jury, or if there is no jury, the court, shall consider each of the following aggravating factors for which notice has been given and determine which, if any, exist:

(1) Prior espionage or treason offense.—The defendant has previously been convicted of another offense involving espionage or treason for which a sentence of either life imprisonment or death was authorized by law.

(2) Grave risk to national security.—In the commission of the offense the defendant knowingly created a grave risk of substantial danger to the national security.

(3) Grave risk of death.—In the commission of the offense the defendant knowingly created a grave risk of death to another person.

The jury, or if there is no jury, the court, may consider whether any other aggravating factor for which notice has been given exists.

(c) Aggravating Factors for Homicide.—In determining whether a sentence of death is justified for an offense described in section 3591(a)(2), the jury, or if there is no jury, the court, shall consider each of the following aggravating factors for which notice has been given and determine which, if any, exist:

(1) Death during commission of another crime.—The death, or injury resulting in death, occurred during the commission or attempted commission of, or during the immediate flight from the commission of, an offense under section 32 (destruction of aircraft or aircraft facilities), section 33 (destruction of motor vehicles or motor vehicle facilities), section 37 (violence at international airports), section 351 (violence against Members of Congress, Cabinet officers, or Supreme Court Justices), an offense under section 751 (prisoners in custody of institution or officer), section 794 (gathering or delivering defense information to aid foreign government), section 844(d) (transportation of explosives in interstate commerce for certain purposes), section 844(f) (destruction of Government property by explosives), section 1118 (prisoners serving life term), section 1201 (kidnapping), section 844(i) (destruction of property affecting interstate commerce by explosives), section 1116 (killing or attempted killing of diplomats), section 1203 (hostage taking), section 1992 1 (wrecking trains), section 2245 (offenses resulting in death), section 2280 (maritime violence), section 2281 (maritime platform violence), section 2332 (terrorist acts abroad against United States nationals), section 2332a (use of weapons of mass destruction), or section 2381 (treason) of this title, or section 46502 of title 49, United States Code (aircraft piracy).

(2) Previous conviction of violent felony involving firearm.—For any offense, other than an offense for which a sentence of death is sought on the basis of section 924(c), the defendant has previously been convicted of a Federal or State offense punishable by a term of imprisonment of more than 1 year, involving the use or attempted or threatened use of a firearm (as defined in section 921) against another person.

(3) Previous conviction of offense for which a sentence of death or life imprisonment was authorized.—The defendant has previously been convicted of another Federal or State offense resulting in the death of a person, for which a sentence of life imprisonment or a sentence of death was authorized by statute.

(4) Previous conviction of other serious offenses.—The defendant has previously been convicted of 2 or more Federal or State offenses, punishable by a term of imprisonment of more than 1 year, committed on different occasions, involving the infliction of, or attempted infliction of, serious bodily injury or death upon another person.

(5) Grave risk of death to additional persons.—The defendant, in the commission of the offense, or in escaping apprehension for the violation of the offense, knowingly created a grave risk of death to 1 or more persons in addition to the victim of the offense.

(6) Heinous, cruel, or depraved manner of committing offense.—The defendant committed the offense in an especially heinous, cruel, or depraved manner in that it involved torture or serious physical abuse to the victim.

(7) Procurement of offense by payment.—The defendant procured the commission of the offense by payment, or promise of payment, of anything of pecuniary value.

(8) Pecuniary gain.—The defendant committed the offense as consideration for the receipt, or in the expectation of the receipt, of anything of pecuniary value.

(9) Substantial planning and premeditation.—The defendant committed the offense after substantial planning and premeditation to cause the death of a person or commit an act of

terrorism.

(10) Conviction for two felony drug offenses.—The defendant has previously been convicted of 2 or more State or Federal offenses punishable by a term of imprisonment of more than one year, committed on different occasions, involving the distribution of a controlled substance.

(11) Vulnerability of victim.—The victim was particularly vulnerable due to old age, youth, or infirmity.

(12) Conviction for serious federal drug offenses.—The defendant had previously been convicted of violating title II or III of the Comprehensive Drug Abuse Prevention and Control Act of 1970 for which a sentence of 5 or more years may be imposed or had previously been convicted of engaging in a continuing criminal enterprise.

(13) Continuing criminal enterprise involving drug sales to minors.—The defendant committed the offense in the course of engaging in a continuing criminal enterprise in violation of section 408(c) of the Controlled Substances Act (21 U.S.C. 848(c)), and that violation involved the distribution of drugs to persons under the age of 21 in violation of section 418 of that Act (21 U.S.C. 859).

(14) High public officials.—The defendant committed the offense against—

(A) the President of the United States, the President-elect, the Vice President, the Vice President-elect, the Vice President-designate, or, if there is no Vice President, the officer next in order of succession to the office of the President of the United States, or any person who is acting as President under the Constitution and laws of the United States;

(B) a chief of state, head of government, or the political equivalent, of a foreign nation;

(C) a foreign official listed in section 1116(b)(3)(A), if the official is in the United States on official business; or

(D) a Federal public servant who is a judge, a law enforcement officer, or an employee of a United States penal or correctional institution—

(i) while he or she is engaged in the performance of his or her official duties;

(ii) because of the performance of his or her official duties; or

(iii) because of his or her status as a public servant.

For purposes of this subparagraph, a "law enforcement officer" is a public servant authorized by law or by a Government agency or Congress to conduct or engage in the prevention, investigation, or prosecution or adjudication of an offense, and includes those engaged in corrections, parole, or probation functions.

(15) Prior conviction of sexual assault or child molestation.—In the case of an offense under chapter 109A (sexual abuse) or chapter 110 (sexual abuse of children), the defendant has previously been convicted of a crime of sexual assault or crime of child molestation.

(16) Multiple killings or attempted killings.—The defendant intentionally killed or attempted to kill more than one person in a single criminal episode.

The jury, or if there is no jury, the court, may consider whether any other aggravating factor for which notice has been given exists.

(d) Aggravating Factors for Drug Offense Death Penalty.—In determining whether a sentence of death is justified for an offense described in section 3591(b), the jury, or if there is no jury, the court, shall consider each of the following aggravating factors for which notice has been given and determine which, if any, exist:

(1) Previous conviction of offense for which a sentence of death or life imprisonment was authorized.—The defendant has previously been convicted of another Federal or State offense resulting in the death of a person, for which a sentence of life imprisonment or death was authorized by statute.

(2) Previous conviction of other serious offenses.—The defendant has previously been convicted of two or more Federal or State offenses, each punishable by a term of imprisonment of more than one year, committed on different occasions, involving the importation, manufacture, or distribution of a controlled substance (as defined in section 102 of the Controlled Substances Act (21 U.S.C. 802)) or the infliction of, or attempted infliction of, serious bodily injury or death upon another person.

(3) Previous serious drug felony conviction.—The defendant has previously been convicted of another Federal or State offense involving the manufacture, distribution, importation, or possession of a controlled substance (as defined in section 102 of the Controlled Substances Act (21 U.S.C. 802)) for which a sentence of five or more years of imprisonment was authorized by statute.

(4) Use of firearm.—In committing the offense, or in furtherance of a continuing criminal enterprise of which the offense was a part, the defendant used a firearm or knowingly directed, advised, authorized, or assisted another to use a firearm to threaten, intimidate, assault, or injure a person.

(5) Distribution to persons under 21.—The offense, or a continuing criminal enterprise of which the offense was a part, involved conduct proscribed by section 418 of the Controlled Substances Act (21 U.S.C. 859) which was committed directly by the defendant.

(6) Distribution near schools.—The offense, or a continuing criminal enterprise of which the offense was a part, involved conduct proscribed by section 419 of the Controlled Substances Act (21 U.S.C. 860) which was committed directly by the defendant.

(7) Using minors in trafficking.—The offense, or a continuing criminal enterprise of which the offense was a part, involved conduct proscribed by section 420 of the Controlled Substances Act (21 U.S.C. 861) which was committed directly by the defendant.

(8) Lethal adulterant.—The offense involved the importation, manufacture, or distribution of a controlled substance (as defined in section 102 of the Controlled Substances Act (21 U.S.C. 802)), mixed with a potentially lethal adulterant, and the defendant was aware of the presence of the adulterant.

The jury, or if there is no jury, the court, may consider whether any other aggravating factor for which notice has been given exists.

(Added and amended Pub. L. 103–322, title VI, §60002(a), title XXXIII, §330021(1), Sept. 13, 1994, 108 Stat. 1960, 2150; Pub. L. 104–132, title VII, §728, Apr. 24, 1996, 110 Stat. 1302; Pub. L. 104–294, title VI, §§601(b)(7), 604(b)(35), Oct. 11, 1996, 110 Stat. 3499, 3508; Pub. L. 107–273, div. B, title IV, §4002(e)(2), Nov. 2, 2002, 116 Stat. 1810; Pub. L. 109–248, title II, §206(a)(4), July 27, 2006, 120 Stat. 614.)

References in Text

Section 1992 of this title, referred to in subsec. (c)(1), was repealed and a new section 1992 enacted by Pub. L. 109–177, title I, §110(a), Mar. 9, 2006, 120 Stat. 205, and, as so enacted, section 1992 no longer relates only to the crime of wrecking trains.

The Comprehensive Drug Abuse Prevention and Control Act of 1970, referred to in subsec. (c)(12), is Pub. L. 91–513, Oct. 27, 1970, 84 Stat. 1236, as amended. Title II of the Act, known as the Controlled Substances Act, is classified principally to subchapter I (§801 et seq.) of chapter 13 of Title 21, Food and Drugs. Title III of the Act, known as the Controlled Substances Import and Export Act, is classified principally to subchapter II (§951 et seq.) of chapter 13 of Title 21. For complete classification of this Act to the Code, see Short Title note set out under sections 801 and 951 of Title 21 and Tables.

Amendments

2006—Subsec. (c)(1). Pub. L. 109–248 inserted "section 2245 (offenses resulting in death)," after "section 1992 (wrecking trains),".

2002—Subsec. (c)(1). Pub. L. 107–273 substituted "section 37" for "section 36".

1996—Subsec. (c)(1). Pub. L. 104–294, §601(b)(7), substituted "section 2332a (use of weapons of mass destruction)" for "section 2339 (use of weapons of mass destruction)".

Subsec. (c)(12). Pub. L. 104–294, §604(b)(35), substituted "Comprehensive Drug Abuse Prevention and Control Act of 1970" for "Controlled Substances Act".

Subsec. (c)(16). Pub. L. 104–132 added par. (16).

1994—Subsec. (c)(1). Pub. L. 103–322, §330021(1), substituted "kidnapping" for "kidnaping".

Effective Date of 1996 Amendment

Amendment by section 604(b)(35) of Pub. L. 104–294 effective Sept. 13, 1994, see section 604(d) of Pub. L. 104–294, set out as a note under section 13 of this title.

§3593. Special hearing to determine whether a sentence of death is justified

(a) Notice by the Government.—If, in a case involving an offense described in section 3591, the attorney for the government believes that the circumstances of the offense are such that a sentence of death is justified under this chapter, the attorney shall, a reasonable time before the trial or before acceptance by the court of a plea of guilty, sign and file with the court, and serve on the defendant, a notice—

(1) stating that the government believes that the circumstances of the offense are such that, if the defendant is convicted, a sentence of death is justified under this chapter and that the government will seek the sentence of death; and

(2) setting forth the aggravating factor or factors that the government, if the defendant is convicted, proposes to prove as justifying a sentence of death.

The factors for which notice is provided under this subsection may include factors concerning the effect of the offense on the victim and the victim's family, and may include oral testimony, a victim impact statement that identifies the victim of the offense and the extent and scope of the injury and loss suffered by the victim and the victim's family, and any other relevant information. The court may permit the attorney for the government to amend the notice upon a showing of good cause.

(b) Hearing Before a Court or Jury.—If the attorney for the government has filed a notice as required under subsection (a) and the defendant is found guilty of or pleads guilty to an offense described in section 3591, the judge who presided at the trial or before whom the guilty plea was entered, or another judge if that judge is unavailable, shall conduct a separate sentencing hearing to determine the punishment to be imposed. The hearing shall be conducted—

(1) before the jury that determined the defendant's guilt;

(2) before a jury impaneled for the purpose of the hearing if—

(A) the defendant was convicted upon a plea of guilty;

(B) the defendant was convicted after a trial before the court sitting without a jury;

(C) the jury that determined the defendant's guilt was discharged for good cause; or

(D) after initial imposition of a sentence under this section, reconsideration of the sentence under this section is necessary; or

(3) before the court alone, upon the motion of the defendant and with the approval of the attorney for the government.

A jury impaneled pursuant to paragraph (2) shall consist of 12 members, unless, at any time before the conclusion of the hearing, the parties stipulate, with the approval of the court, that it shall consist of a lesser number.

(c) Proof of Mitigating and Aggravating Factors.—Notwithstanding rule 32 of the Federal Rules of Criminal Procedure, when a defendant is found guilty or pleads guilty to an offense under section 3591, no presentence report shall be prepared. At the sentencing hearing, information may be presented as to any matter relevant to the sentence, including any mitigating or aggravating factor permitted or required to be considered under section 3592. Information presented may include the trial transcript and exhibits if the hearing is held before a jury or judge not present during the trial, or at the trial judge's discretion. The defendant may present any information relevant to a mitigating factor. The government may present any information relevant to an aggravating factor for which notice has been provided under subsection (a). Information is admissible regardless of its admissibility under the rules governing admission of evidence at criminal trials except that information may be excluded if its probative value is outweighed by the danger of creating unfair prejudice, confusing the issues, or misleading the jury. For the purposes of the preceding sentence, the fact that a victim, as defined in section 3510, attended or observed the trial shall not be construed to pose a danger of creating unfair prejudice, confusing the issues, or misleading the jury. The government and the defendant shall be permitted to rebut any information received at the hearing, and shall be given fair opportunity to present argument as to the adequacy of the information to establish the existence of any aggravating or mitigating factor, and as to the appropriateness in the case of imposing a sentence of death. The government shall open the argument. The defendant shall be permitted to reply. The government shall then be permitted to reply in rebuttal. The burden of establishing the existence of any aggravating factor is on the government, and is not satisfied unless the existence of such a factor is established beyond a reasonable doubt. The burden of establishing the existence of any mitigating factor is on the defendant, and is not satisfied unless the existence of such a factor is established by a preponderance of the information.

(d) Return of Special Findings.—The jury, or if there is no jury, the court, shall consider all the information received during the hearing. It shall return special findings identifying any aggravating factor or factors set forth in section 3592 found to exist and any other aggravating factor for which notice has been provided under subsection (a) found to exist. A finding with respect to a mitigating factor may be made by 1 or more members of the jury, and any member of the jury who finds the existence of a mitigating factor may consider such factor established for purposes of this section regardless of the number of jurors who concur that the factor has been established. A finding with respect to any aggravating factor must be unanimous. If no aggravating factor set forth in section 3592 is found to exist, the court shall impose a sentence other than death authorized by law.

(e) Return of a Finding Concerning a Sentence of Death.—If, in the case of—

(1) an offense described in section 3591(a)(1), an aggravating factor required to be considered under section 3592(b) is found to exist;

(2) an offense described in section 3591(a)(2), an aggravating factor required to be considered under section 3592(c) is found to exist; or

(3) an offense described in section 3591(b), an aggravating factor required to be considered under section 3592(d) is found to exist,

the jury, or if there is no jury, the court, shall consider whether all the aggravating factor or factors found to exist sufficiently outweigh all the mitigating factor or factors found to exist to justify a sentence of death, or, in the absence of a mitigating factor, whether the aggravating factor or factors alone are sufficient to justify a sentence of death. Based upon this consideration, the jury by unanimous vote, or if there is no jury, the court, shall recommend whether the defendant should be sentenced to death, to life imprisonment without possibility of release or some other lesser sentence.

(f) Special Precaution To Ensure Against Discrimination.—In a hearing held before a jury, the court, prior to the return of a finding under subsection (e), shall instruct the jury that, in considering whether a sentence of death is justified, it shall not consider the race, color, religious beliefs, national origin, or sex of the defendant or of any victim and that the jury is not to recommend a sentence of death unless it has concluded that it would recommend a sentence of death for the crime in question no matter what the race, color, religious beliefs, national origin, or sex of the defendant or of any victim may be. The jury, upon return of a finding under subsection (e), shall also return to the court a certificate, signed by each juror, that consideration of the race, color, religious beliefs, national origin, or sex of the defendant or any victim was not involved in reaching his or her individual decision and that the individual juror would have made the same recommendation regarding a sentence for the crime in question no matter what the race, color, religious beliefs, national origin, or sex of the defendant or any victim may be.

(Added Pub. L. 103–322, title VI, §60002(a), Sept. 13, 1994, 108 Stat. 1964; amended Pub. L. 105–6, §2(c), Mar. 19, 1997, 111 Stat. 12; Pub. L. 107–273, div. B, title IV, §4002(e)(8), Nov. 2, 2002, 116 Stat. 1810.)

References in Text

The Federal Rules of Criminal Procedure, referred to in subsec. (c), are set out in the Appendix to this title.

Amendments

2002—Subsec. (c). Pub. L. 107–273 substituted "rule 32" for "rule 32(c)" in first sentence.

1997—Subsec. (c). Pub. L. 105–6 inserted "For the purposes of the preceding sentence, the fact that a victim, as defined in section 3510, attended or observed the trial shall not be construed to pose a danger of creating unfair prejudice, confusing the issues, or misleading the jury."

Effective Date of 1997 Amendment

Amendment by Pub. L. 105–6 applicable to cases pending on Mar. 19, 1997, see section 2(d) of Pub. L. 105–6, set out as an Effective Date note under section 3510 of this title.

§3594. Imposition of a sentence of death

Upon a recommendation under section 3593(e) that the defendant should be sentenced to death or life imprisonment without possibility of release, the court shall sentence the defendant accordingly. Otherwise, the court shall impose any lesser sentence that is authorized by law. Notwithstanding any other law, if the maximum term of imprisonment for the offense is life imprisonment, the court may impose a sentence of life imprisonment without possibility of release.

(Added Pub. L. 103–322, title VI, §60002(a), Sept. 13, 1994, 108 Stat. 1966.)

§3595. Review of a sentence of death

(a) Appeal.—In a case in which a sentence of death is imposed, the sentence shall be subject to review by the court of appeals upon appeal by the defendant. Notice of appeal must be filed within the time specified for the filing of a notice of appeal. An appeal under this section may be consolidated with an appeal of the judgment of conviction and shall have priority over all other cases.

(b) Review.—The court of appeals shall review the entire record in the case, including—

(1) the evidence submitted during the trial;

(2) the information submitted during the sentencing hearing;

(3) the procedures employed in the sentencing hearing; and

(4) the special findings returned under section 3593(d).

(c) Decision and Disposition.—

(1) The court of appeals shall address all substantive and procedural issues raised on the appeal of a sentence of death, and shall consider whether the sentence of death was imposed under the influence of passion, prejudice, or any other arbitrary factor and whether the evidence supports the special finding of the existence of an aggravating factor required to be considered under section 3592.

(2) Whenever the court of appeals finds that—

(A) the sentence of death was imposed under the influence of passion, prejudice, or any other arbitrary factor;

(B) the admissible evidence and information adduced does not support the special finding of the existence of the required aggravating factor; or

(C) the proceedings involved any other legal error requiring reversal of the sentence that was properly preserved for appeal under the rules of criminal procedure,

the court shall remand the case for reconsideration under section 3593 or imposition of a sentence other than death. The court of appeals shall not reverse or vacate a sentence of death on account of any error which can be harmless, including any erroneous special finding of an aggravating factor, where the Government establishes beyond a reasonable doubt that the error was harmless.

(3) The court of appeals shall state in writing the reasons for its disposition of an appeal of a sentence of death under this section.

(Added Pub. L. 103–322, title VI, §60002(a), Sept. 13, 1994, 108 Stat. 1967.)

§3596. Implementation of a sentence of death

(a) In General.—A person who has been sentenced to death pursuant to this chapter shall be committed to the custody of the Attorney General until exhaustion of the procedures for appeal of the judgment of conviction and for review of the sentence. When the sentence is to be implemented, the Attorney General shall release the person sentenced to death to the custody of a United States marshal, who shall supervise implementation of the sentence in the manner prescribed by the law of the State in which the sentence is imposed. If the law of the State does not provide for implementation of a sentence of death, the court shall designate another State, the law of which does provide for the implementation of a sentence of death, and the sentence shall be implemented in the latter State in the manner prescribed by such law.

(b) Pregnant Woman.—A sentence of death shall not be carried out upon a woman while she is pregnant.

(c) Mental Capacity.—A sentence of death shall not be carried out upon a person who is mentally retarded. A sentence of death shall not be carried out upon a person who, as a result of mental disability, lacks the mental capacity to understand the death penalty and why it was imposed on that person.

(Added Pub. L. 103–322, title VI, §60002(a), Sept. 13, 1994, 108 Stat. 1967.)

§3597. Use of State facilities

(a) In General.—A United States marshal charged with supervising the implementation of a sentence of death may use appropriate State or local facilities for the purpose, may use the services of an appropriate State or local official or of a person such an official employs for the purpose, and shall pay the costs thereof in an amount approved by the Attorney General.

(b) Excuse of an Employee on Moral or Religious Grounds.—No employee of any State department of corrections, the United States Department of Justice, the Federal Bureau of Prisons, or the United States Marshals Service, and no employee providing services to that department, bureau, or service under contract shall be required, as a condition of that employment or contractual obligation, to be in attendance at or to participate in any prosecution or execution under this section if such participation is contrary to the moral or religious convictions of the employee. In this subsection, "participation in executions" includes personal preparation of the condemned individual and the apparatus used for execution and supervision of the activities of other personnel in carrying out such activities.

(Added Pub. L. 103–322, title VI, §60002(a), Sept. 13, 1994, 108 Stat. 1968.)

§3598. Special provisions for Indian country

Notwithstanding sections 1152 and 1153, no person subject to the criminal jurisdiction of an Indian tribal government shall be subject to a capital sentence under this chapter for any offense the Federal jurisdiction for which is predicated solely on Indian country (as defined in section 1151 of this title) and which has occurred within the boundaries of Indian country, unless the governing body of the tribe has elected that this chapter have effect over land and persons subject to its criminal jurisdiction.

(Added Pub. L. 103–322, title VI, §60002(a), Sept. 13, 1994, 108 Stat. 1968.)

§3599. Counsel for financially unable defendants

(a)(1) Notwithstanding any other provision of law to the contrary, in every criminal action in which a defendant is charged with a crime which may be punishable by death, a defendant who is or becomes financially unable to obtain adequate representation or investigative, expert, or other reasonably necessary services at any time either—

(A) before judgment; or

(B) after the entry of a judgment imposing a sentence of death but before the execution of that judgment;

shall be entitled to the appointment of one or more attorneys and the furnishing of such other services in accordance with subsections (b) through (f).

(2) In any post conviction proceeding under section 2254 or 2255 of title 28, United States Code, seeking to vacate or set aside a death sentence, any defendant who is or becomes financially unable to obtain adequate representation or investigative, expert, or other reasonably necessary services shall be entitled to the appointment of one or more attorneys and the furnishing of such other services in accordance with subsections (b) through (f).

(b) If the appointment is made before judgment, at least one attorney so appointed must have been admitted to practice in the court in which the prosecution is to be tried for not less than five years, and must have had not less than three years experience in the actual trial of felony prosecutions in that court.

(c) If the appointment is made after judgment, at least one attorney so appointed must have been admitted to practice in the court of appeals for not less than five years, and must have had not less than three years experience in the handling of appeals in that court in felony cases.

(d) With respect to subsections (b) and (c), the court, for good cause, may appoint another attorney whose background, knowledge, or experience would otherwise enable him or her to properly represent the defendant, with due consideration to the seriousness of the possible penalty and to the unique and complex nature of the litigation.

(e) Unless replaced by similarly qualified counsel upon the attorney's own motion or upon motion of the defendant, each attorney so appointed shall represent the defendant throughout every subsequent stage of available judicial proceedings, including pretrial proceedings, trial, sentencing, motions for new trial, appeals, applications for writ of certiorari to the Supreme Court of the United States, and all available post-conviction process, together with applications for stays of execution and other appropriate motions and procedures, and shall also represent the defendant in such competency proceedings and proceedings for executive or other clemency as may be available to the defendant.

(f) Upon a finding that investigative, expert, or other services are reasonably necessary for the representation of the defendant, whether in connection with issues relating to guilt or the sentence, the court may authorize the defendant's attorneys to obtain such services on behalf of the defendant and, if so authorized, shall order the payment of fees and expenses therefor under subsection (g). No ex parte proceeding, communication, or request may be considered pursuant to this section unless a proper showing is made concerning the need for confidentiality. Any such proceeding, communication, or request shall be transcribed and made a part of the record available for appellate review.

(g)(1) Compensation shall be paid to attorneys appointed under this subsection 1 at a rate of not more than $125 per hour for in-court and out-of-court time. The Judicial Conference is authorized to raise the maximum for hourly payment specified in the 2 paragraph up to the aggregate of the overall average percentages of the adjustments in the rates of pay for the General Schedule made pursuant to section 5305 3 of title 5 on or after such date. After the rates are raised under the preceding sentence, such hourly range may be raised at intervals of not less than one year, up to the aggregate of the overall average percentages of such adjustments made since the last raise under this paragraph.

(2) Fees and expenses paid for investigative, expert, and other reasonably necessary services authorized under subsection (f) shall not exceed $7,500 in any case, unless payment in excess of that limit is certified by the court, or by the United States magistrate judge, if the services were rendered in connection with the case disposed of entirely before such magistrate judge, as necessary to provide fair compensation for services of an unusual character or duration, and the amount of the excess payment is approved by the chief judge of the circuit. The chief judge of the circuit may delegate such approval authority to an active or senior circuit judge.

(3) The amounts paid under this paragraph 4 for services in any case shall be disclosed to the public, after the disposition of the petition.

(Added Pub. L. 109–177, title II, §222(a), Mar. 9, 2006, 120 Stat. 231; amended Pub. L. 110–406,

Amendments
2008—Subsec. (g)(2). Pub. L. 110–406 inserted "or senior" after "active" in second sentence.

CHAPTER 228A - POST-CONVICTION DNA TESTING

| 3600. | DNA testing. |
| 3600A. | Preservation of biological evidence. |

§3600. DNA testing
(a) In General.—Upon a written motion by an individual sentenced to imprisonment or death pursuant to a conviction for a Federal offense (referred to in this section as the "applicant"), the court that entered the judgment of conviction shall order DNA testing of specific evidence if the court finds that all of the following apply:

(1) The applicant asserts, under penalty of perjury, that the applicant is actually innocent of—

(A) the Federal offense for which the applicant is sentenced to imprisonment or death; or

(B) another Federal or State offense, if—

(i) evidence of such offense was admitted during a Federal sentencing hearing and exoneration of such offense would entitle the applicant to a reduced sentence or new sentencing hearing; and

(ii) in the case of a State offense—

(I) the applicant demonstrates that there is no adequate remedy under State law to permit DNA testing of the specified evidence relating to the State offense; and

(II) to the extent available, the applicant has exhausted all remedies available under State law for requesting DNA testing of specified evidence relating to the State offense.

(2) The specific evidence to be tested was secured in relation to the investigation or prosecution of the Federal or State offense referenced in the applicant's assertion under paragraph (1).

(3) The specific evidence to be tested—

(A) was not previously subjected to DNA testing and the applicant did not knowingly fail to request DNA testing of that evidence in a prior motion for postconviction DNA testing; or

(B) was previously subjected to DNA testing and the applicant is requesting DNA testing using a new method or technology that is substantially more probative than the prior DNA testing.

(4) The specific evidence to be tested is in the possession of the Government and has been subject to a chain of custody and retained under conditions sufficient to ensure that such evidence has not been substituted, contaminated, tampered with, replaced, or altered in any respect material to the proposed DNA testing.

(5) The proposed DNA testing is reasonable in scope, uses scientifically sound methods, and is consistent with accepted forensic practices.

(6) The applicant identifies a theory of defense that—

(A) is not inconsistent with an affirmative defense presented at trial; and

(B) would establish the actual innocence of the applicant of the Federal or State offense referenced in the applicant's assertion under paragraph (1).

(7) If the applicant was convicted following a trial, the identity of the perpetrator was at issue in the trial.

(8) The proposed DNA testing of the specific evidence may produce new material evidence that would—

(A) support the theory of defense referenced in paragraph (6); and

(B) raise a reasonable probability that the applicant did not commit the offense.

(9) The applicant certifies that the applicant will provide a DNA sample for purposes of

comparison.

(10) The motion is made in a timely fashion, subject to the following conditions:

(A) There shall be a rebuttable presumption of timeliness if the motion is made within 60 months of enactment of the Justice For All Act of 2004 or within 36 months of conviction, whichever comes later. Such presumption may be rebutted upon a showing—

(i) that the applicant's motion for a DNA test is based solely upon information used in a previously denied motion; or

(ii) of clear and convincing evidence that the applicant's filing is done solely to cause delay or harass.

(B) There shall be a rebuttable presumption against timeliness for any motion not satisfying subparagraph (A) above. Such presumption may be rebutted upon the court's finding—

(i) that the applicant was or is incompetent and such incompetence substantially contributed to the delay in the applicant's motion for a DNA test;

(ii) the evidence to be tested is newly discovered DNA evidence;

(iii) that the applicant's motion is not based solely upon the applicant's own assertion of innocence and, after considering all relevant facts and circumstances surrounding the motion, a denial would result in a manifest injustice; or

(iv) upon good cause shown.

(C) For purposes of this paragraph—

(i) the term "incompetence" has the meaning as defined in section 4241 of title 18, United States Code;

(ii) the term "manifest" means that which is unmistakable, clear, plain, or indisputable and requires that the opposite conclusion be clearly evident.

(b) Notice to the Government; Preservation Order; Appointment of Counsel.—

(1) Notice.—Upon the receipt of a motion filed under subsection (a), the court shall—

(A) notify the Government;

(B) allow the Government a reasonable time period to respond to the motion; and

(C) order the Government to—

(i) prepare an inventory of the evidence related to the case; and

(ii) issue a copy of the inventory to the court, the applicant, and the Government.

(2) Preservation order.—To the extent necessary to carry out proceedings under this section, the court shall direct the Government to preserve the specific evidence relating to a motion under subsection (a).

(3) Appointment of counsel.—The court may appoint counsel for an indigent applicant under this section in the same manner as in a proceeding under section 3006A(a)(2)(B).

(c) Testing Procedures.—

(1) In general.—The court shall direct that any DNA testing ordered under this section be carried out by the Federal Bureau of Investigation.

(2) Exception.—Notwithstanding paragraph (1), the court may order DNA testing by another qualified laboratory if the court makes all necessary orders to ensure the integrity of the specific evidence and the reliability of the testing process and test results.

(3) Costs.—The costs of any DNA testing ordered under this section shall be paid—

(A) by the applicant; or

(B) in the case of an applicant who is indigent, by the Government.

(d) Time Limitation in Capital Cases.—In any case in which the applicant is sentenced to death—

(1) any DNA testing ordered under this section shall be completed not later than 60 days after the date on which the Government responds to the motion filed under subsection (a); and

(2) not later than 120 days after the date on which the DNA testing ordered under this section is completed, the court shall order any post-testing procedures under subsection (f) or (g), as appropriate.

(e) Reporting of Test Results.—

(1) Results.—

(A) In general.—The results of any DNA testing ordered under this section shall be simultaneously disclosed to the court, the applicant, and the Government.

(B) Results exclude applicant.—

(i) In general.—If a DNA profile is obtained through testing that excludes the applicant as the source and the DNA complies with the Federal Bureau of Investigation's requirements for the uploading of crime scene profiles to the National DNA Index System (referred to in this subsection as "NDIS"), the court shall order that the law enforcement entity with direct or conveyed statutory jurisdiction that has access to the NDIS submit the DNA profile obtained from probative biological material from crime scene evidence to determine whether the DNA profile matches a profile of a known individual or a profile from an unsolved crime.

(ii) NDIS search.—The results of a search under clause (i) shall be simultaneously disclosed to the court, the applicant, and the Government.

(2) NDIS.—The Government shall submit any test results relating to the DNA of the applicant to NDIS.

(3) Retention of dna sample.—

(A) Entry into ndis.—If the DNA test results obtained under this section are inconclusive or show that the applicant was the source of the DNA evidence, the DNA sample of the applicant may be retained in NDIS.

(B) Match with other offense.—If the DNA test results obtained under this section exclude the applicant as the source of the DNA evidence, and a comparison of the DNA sample of the applicant results in a match between the DNA sample of the applicant and another offense, the Attorney General shall notify the appropriate agency and preserve the DNA sample of the applicant.

(C) No match.—If the DNA test results obtained under this section exclude the applicant as the source of the DNA evidence, and a comparison of the DNA sample of the applicant does not result in a match between the DNA sample of the applicant and another offense, the Attorney General shall destroy the DNA sample of the applicant and ensure that such information is not retained in NDIS if there is no other legal authority to retain the DNA sample of the applicant in NDIS.

(f) Post-Testing Procedures; Inconclusive and Inculpatory Results.—

(1) Inconclusive results.—If DNA test results obtained under this section are inconclusive, the court may order further testing, if appropriate, or may deny the applicant relief.

(2) Inculpatory results.—If DNA test results obtained under this section show that the applicant was the source of the DNA evidence, the court shall—

(A) deny the applicant relief; and

(B) on motion of the Government—

(i) make a determination whether the applicant's assertion of actual innocence was false, and, if the court makes such a finding, the court may hold the applicant in contempt;

(ii) assess against the applicant the cost of any DNA testing carried out under this section;

(iii) forward the finding to the Director of the Bureau of Prisons, who, upon receipt of such a finding, may deny, wholly or in part, the good conduct credit authorized under section 3632 on the basis of that finding;

(iv) if the applicant is subject to the jurisdiction of the United States Parole Commission, forward the finding to the Commission so that the Commission may deny parole on the basis of that finding; and

(v) if the DNA test results relate to a State offense, forward the finding to any appropriate State official.

(3) Sentence.—In any prosecution of an applicant under chapter 79 for false assertions or other conduct in proceedings under this section, the court, upon conviction of the applicant, shall sentence the applicant to a term of imprisonment of not less than 3 years, which shall run consecutively to any other term of imprisonment the applicant is serving.

(g) Post-Testing Procedures; Motion for New Trial or Resentencing.—

(1) In general.—Notwithstanding any law that would bar a motion under this paragraph as untimely, if DNA test results obtained under this section exclude the applicant as the source of the DNA evidence, the applicant may file a motion for a new trial or resentencing, as appropriate. The

court shall establish a reasonable schedule for the applicant to file such a motion and for the Government to respond to the motion.

(2) Standard for granting motion for new trial or resentencing.—The court shall grant the motion of the applicant for a new trial or resentencing, as appropriate, if the DNA test results, when considered with all other evidence in the case (regardless of whether such evidence was introduced at trial), establish by compelling evidence that a new trial would result in an acquittal of—

(A) in the case of a motion for a new trial, the Federal offense for which the applicant is sentenced to imprisonment or death; and

(B) in the case of a motion for resentencing, another Federal or State offense, if evidence of such offense was admitted during a Federal sentencing hearing and exoneration of such offense would entitle the applicant to a reduced sentence or a new sentencing proceeding.

(h) Other Laws Unaffected.—

(1) Post-conviction relief.—Nothing in this section shall affect the circumstances under which a person may obtain DNA testing or post-conviction relief under any other law.

(2) Habeas corpus.—Nothing in this section shall provide a basis for relief in any Federal habeas corpus proceeding.

(3) Not a motion under section 2255.—A motion under this section shall not be considered to be a motion under section 2255 for purposes of determining whether the motion or any other motion is a second or successive motion under section 2255.

(Added Pub. L. 108–405, title IV, §411(a)(1), Oct. 30, 2004, 118 Stat. 2279; amended Pub. L. 114–324, §11(a), Dec. 16, 2016, 130 Stat. 1956.)

References in Text

Enactment of the Justice For All Act of 2004, referred to in subsec. (a)(10)(A), is the enactment of Pub. L. 108–405, which was approved Oct. 30, 2004.

Amendments

2016—Subsec. (a). Pub. L. 114–324, §11(a)(1), substituted "sentenced to" for "under a sentence of" in introductory provisions.

Subsec. (a)(1)(A). Pub. L. 114–324, §11(a)(1), substituted "sentenced to" for "under a sentence of".

Subsec. (a)(1)(B)(i). Pub. L. 114–324, §11(a)(2)(A), struck out "death" after "Federal".

Subsec. (a)(3)(A). Pub. L. 114–324, §11(a)(2)(B), struck out dash after "the applicant did not" and cl. (ii) designation before "knowingly fail" and struck out cl. (i) which read as follows: "knowingly and voluntarily waive the right to request DNA testing of that evidence in a court proceeding after the date of enactment of the Innocence Protection Act of 2004; or".

Subsec. (b)(1)(C). Pub. L. 114–324, §11(a)(3), added subpar. (C).

Subsec. (e)(1). Pub. L. 114–324, §11(a)(4)(A), amended par. (1) generally. Prior to amendment, text read as follows: "The results of any DNA testing ordered under this section shall be simultaneously disclosed to the court, the applicant, and the Government."

Subsec. (e)(2). Pub. L. 114–324, §11(a)(4)(B), substituted "to NDIS" for "to the National DNA Index System (referred to in this subsection as 'NDIS')".

Subsec. (g)(2)(A). Pub. L. 114–324, §11(a)(1), substituted "sentenced to" for "under a sentence of".

Subsec. (g)(2)(B). Pub. L. 114–324, §11(a)(5), struck out "death" after "during a Federal".

Effective Date

Pub. L. 108–405, title IV, §411(c), Oct. 30, 2004, 118 Stat. 2284, provided that: "This section [enacting this chapter and provisions set out as a note under this section] and the amendments made by this section shall take effect on the date of enactment of this Act [Oct. 30, 2004] and shall apply with respect to any offense committed, and to any judgment of conviction entered, before, on, or after that date of enactment."

Short Title of 2004 Amendment

Pub. L. 108–405, title IV, §401, Oct. 30, 2004, 118 Stat. 2278, provided that: "This title [enacting this chapter and sections 14136e and 14163 to 14163e of Title 42, The Public Health and Welfare, amending section 2513 of Title 28, Judiciary and Judicial Procedure, and enacting provisions set out as notes under this section and section 14136 of Title 42] may be cited as the 'Innocence Protection Act of 2004'."

System for Reporting Motions

Pub. L. 108–405, title IV, §411(b), Oct. 30, 2004, 118 Stat. 2284, provided that:

"(1) Establishment.—The Attorney General shall establish a system for reporting and tracking motions filed in accordance with section 3600 of title 18, United States Code.

"(2) Operation.—In operating the system established under paragraph (1), the Federal courts shall provide to the Attorney General any requested assistance in operating such a system and in ensuring the accuracy and completeness of information included in that system.

"(3) Report.—Not later than 2 years after the date of enactment of this Act [Oct. 30, 2004], the Attorney General shall submit a report to Congress that contains—

"(A) a list of motions filed under section 3600 of title 18, United States Code, as added by this title;

"(B) whether DNA testing was ordered pursuant to such a motion;

"(C) whether the applicant obtained relief on the basis of DNA test results; and

"(D) whether further proceedings occurred following a granting of relief and the outcome of such proceedings.

"(4) Additional information.—The report required to be submitted under paragraph (3) may include any other information the Attorney General determines to be relevant in assessing the operation, utility, or costs of section 3600 of title 18, United States Code, as added by this title, and any recommendations the Attorney General may have relating to future legislative action concerning that section."

§3600A. Preservation of biological evidence

(a) In General.—Notwithstanding any other provision of law, the Government shall preserve biological evidence that was secured in the investigation or prosecution of a Federal offense, if a defendant is sentenced to imprisonment for such offense.

(b) Defined Term.—For purposes of this section, the term "biological evidence" means—

(1) a sexual assault forensic examination kit; or

(2) semen, blood, saliva, hair, skin tissue, or other identified biological material.

(c) Applicability.—Subsection (a) shall not apply if—

(1) after a conviction becomes final and the defendant has exhausted all opportunities for direct review of the conviction, the defendant is notified that the biological evidence may be destroyed and the defendant does not file a motion under section 3600 within 180 days of receipt of the notice;

(2)(A) the evidence must be returned to its rightful owner, or is of such a size, bulk, or physical character as to render retention impracticable; and

(B) the Government takes reasonable measures to remove and preserve portions of the material evidence sufficient to permit future DNA testing; or

(3) the biological evidence has already been subjected to DNA testing under section 3600 and the results included the defendant as the source of such evidence.

(d) Other Preservation Requirement.—Nothing in this section shall preempt or supersede any statute, regulation, court order, or other provision of law that may require evidence, including biological evidence, to be preserved.

(e) Regulations.—Not later than 180 days after the date of enactment of the Innocence Protection Act of 2004, the Attorney General shall promulgate regulations to implement and enforce this section, including appropriate disciplinary sanctions to ensure that employees comply with such regulations.

(f) Criminal Penalty.—Whoever knowingly and intentionally destroys, alters, or tampers with biological evidence that is required to be preserved under this section with the intent to prevent that evidence from being subjected to DNA testing or prevent the production or use of that evidence in an official proceeding, shall be fined under this title, imprisoned for not more than 5 years, or both.

(g) Habeas Corpus.—Nothing in this section shall provide a basis for relief in any Federal habeas corpus proceeding.

(Added Pub. L. 108–405, title IV, §411(a)(1), Oct. 30, 2004, 118 Stat. 2283; amended Pub. L. 114–324, §11(b), Dec. 16, 2016, 130 Stat. 1957.)

References in Text

The date of enactment of the Innocence Protection Act of 2004, referred to in subsec. (e), is the date of enactment of Pub. L. 108–405, which was approved Oct. 30, 2004.

Amendments

2016—Subsec. (a). Pub. L. 114–324, §11(b)(1), substituted "sentenced to" for "under a sentence of".

Subsec. (c). Pub. L. 114–324, §11(b)(2), redesignated pars. (3) to (5) as (1) to (3), respectively, and struck out former pars. (1) and (2) which read as follows:

"(1) a court has denied a request or motion for DNA testing of the biological evidence by the defendant under section 3600, and no appeal is pending;

"(2) the defendant knowingly and voluntarily waived the right to request DNA testing of the biological evidence in a court proceeding conducted after the date of enactment of the Innocence Protection Act of 2004;".

CHAPTER 229 - POSTSENTENCE ADMINISTRATION

Prior Provisions

A prior chapter 229 (§3611 et seq.) was repealed (except sections 3611, 3612, 3615, 3617 to 3620 which were renumbered sections 3665 to 3671, respectively), by Pub. L. 98–473, title II, §§212(a)(1), (2), 235(a)(1), Oct. 12, 1984, 98 Stat. 1987, 2031, as amended, effective Nov. 1, 1987, and applicable only to offenses committed after the taking effect of such repeal. See Effective Date note set out under section 3551 of this title.

Section 3611 renumbered section 3665 of this title.

Section 3612 renumbered section 3666 of this title.

Section 3613, act June 25, 1948, ch. 645, 62 Stat. 840, related to fines for setting grass and timber fires.

Section 3614, act June 25, 1948, ch. 645, 62 Stat. 840, related to fine for seduction.

Section 3615 renumbered section 3667 of this title.

Section 3616, act June 25, 1948, ch. 645, 62 Stat. 840, authorized use of confiscated vehicles by narcotics agents and payment of costs of acquisition, maintenance, repair, and operation thereof, prior to repeal by Pub. L. 91–513, title III, §1101(b)(2)(A), Oct. 27, 1970, 84 Stat. 1292.

Section 3617 renumbered section 3668 of this title.

Section 3618 renumbered section 3669 of this title.

Section 3619 renumbered section 3670 of this title.

Section 3620 renumbered section 3671 of this title.

Section 3621, added Pub. L. 98–596, §6(a), Oct. 30, 1984, 98 Stat. 3136, related to criminal default on fine.

Section 3622, added Pub. L. 98–596, §6(a), Oct. 30, 1984, 98 Stat. 3136, related to factors relating to imposition of fines.

Section 3623, added Pub. L. 98–596, §6(a), Oct. 30, 1984, 98 Stat. 3137, related to alternative fines.

Section 3624, added Pub. L. 98–596, §6(a), Oct. 30, 1984, 98 Stat. 3138, related to security for stayed fine.

SUBCHAPTER A—PROBATION 1

Amendments

1994—Pub. L. 103–322, title II, §20414(a)(2), title XXXIII, §330010(3), Sept. 13, 1994, 108 Stat. 1830, 2143, transferred analysis of this subchapter to follow heading for this subchapter and added item 3608.

1990—Pub. L. 101–647, title XXXV, §3590, Nov. 29, 1990, 104 Stat. 4930, substituted "possessors" for "possessor" in item 3607.

§3601. Supervision of probation

A person who has been sentenced to probation pursuant to the provisions of subchapter B of chapter 227, or placed on probation pursuant to the provisions of chapter 403, or placed on supervised release pursuant to the provisions of section 3583, shall, during the term imposed, be supervised by a probation officer to the degree warranted by the conditions specified by the sentencing court.

(Added Pub. L. 98–473, title II, §212(a)(2), Oct. 12, 1984, 98 Stat. 2001.)

Effective Date

Section effective Nov. 1, 1987, and applicable only to offenses committed after the taking effect of this section, see section 235(a)(1) of Pub. L. 98–473, set out as a note under section 3551 of this title.

Short Title of 1996 Amendment

Pub. L. 104–134, title I, §101[(a)] [title VIII, §801], Apr. 26, 1996, 110 Stat. 1321, 1321–66; renumbered title I, Pub. L. 104–140, §1(a), May 2, 1996, 110 Stat. 1327, provided that: "This title [enacting sections 1915A and 1932 of Title 28, Judiciary and Judicial Procedure, amending sections 3624 and 3626 of this title, section 523 of Title 11, Bankruptcy, sections 1346 and 1915 of Title 28, and sections 1997a to 1997c, 1997e, 1997f, and 1997h of Title 42, The Public Health and Welfare, enacting provisions set out as notes under section 3626 of this title, and repealing provisions set out as a note under section 3626 of this title] may be cited as the 'Prison Litigation Reform Act of 1995'."

Post Incarceration Vocational and Remedial Educational Opportunities for Inmates

Pub. L. 107–273, div. B, title II, §2411, Nov. 2, 2002, 116 Stat. 1799, provided that:

"(a) Federal Reentry Center Demonstration.—

"(1) Authority and establishment of demonstration project.—The Attorney General, in consultation with the Director of the Administrative Office of the United States Courts, shall establish the Federal Reentry Center Demonstration project. The project shall involve appropriate prisoners from the Federal prison population and shall utilize community corrections facilities, home confinement, and a coordinated response by Federal agencies to assist participating prisoners in preparing for and adjusting to reentry into the community.

"(2) Project elements.—The project authorized by paragraph (1) shall include the following core elements:

"(A) A Reentry Review Team for each prisoner, consisting of a representative from the Bureau of Prisons, the United States Probation System, the United States Parole Commission, and the relevant community corrections facility, who shall initially meet with the prisoner to develop a reentry plan tailored to the needs of the prisoner.

"(B) A system of graduated levels of supervision with the community corrections facility to promote community safety, provide incentives for prisoners to complete the reentry plan, including victim restitution, and provide a reasonable method for imposing sanctions for a prisoner's violation of the conditions of participation in the project.

"(C) Substance abuse treatment and aftercare, mental and medical health treatment and aftercare, vocational and educational training, life skills instruction, conflict resolution skills training, batterer intervention programs, assistance obtaining suitable affordable housing, and other programming to promote effective reintegration into the community as needed.

"(3) Probation officers.—From funds made available to carry out this section, the Director of the Administrative Office of the United States Courts shall assign 1 or more probation officers from each participating judicial district to the Reentry Demonstration project. Such officers shall be assigned to and stationed at the community corrections facility and shall serve on the Reentry Review Teams.

"(4) Project duration.—The Reentry Center Demonstration project shall begin not later than 6 months following the availability of funds to carry out this subsection, and shall last 3 years.

"(b) Definitions.—In this section, the term 'appropriate prisoner' shall mean a person who is considered by prison authorities—

"(1) to pose a medium to high risk of committing a criminal act upon reentering the community; and

"(2) to lack the skills and family support network that facilitate successful reintegration into the community.

"(c) Authorization of Appropriations.—To carry out this section, there are authorized to be appropriated, to remain available until expended—

"(1) to the Federal Bureau of Prisons—

"(A) $1,375,000 for fiscal year 2003;

"(B) $1,110,000 for fiscal year 2004;

"(C) $1,130,000 for fiscal year 2005;

"(D) $1,155,000 for fiscal year 2006; and

"(E) $1,230,000 for fiscal year 2007; and

"(2) to the Federal Judiciary—

"(A) $3,380,000 for fiscal year 2003;

"(B) $3,540,000 for fiscal year 2004;

"(C) $3,720,000 for fiscal year 2005;

"(D) $3,910,000 for fiscal year 2006; and

"(E) $4,100,000 for fiscal year 2007."

§3602. Appointment of probation officers

(a) Appointment.—A district court of the United States shall appoint qualified persons to serve, with or without compensation, as probation officers within the jurisdiction and under the direction of the court making the appointment. A person appointed as a probation officer in one district may serve in another district with the consent of the appointing court and the court in the other district. The appointing court may, for cause, remove a probation officer appointed to serve with compensation, and may, in its discretion, remove a probation officer appointed to serve without compensation.

(b) Record of Appointment.—The order of appointment shall be entered on the records of the court, a copy of the order shall be delivered to the officer appointed, and a copy shall be sent to the Director of the Administrative Office of the United States Courts.

(c) Chief Probation Officer.—If the court appoints more than one probation officer, one may be designated by the court as chief probation officer and shall direct the work of all probation officers serving in the judicial district.

(Added Pub. L. 98–473, title II, §212(a)(2), Oct. 12, 1984, 98 Stat. 2001; amended Pub. L. 114–113, div. E, title III, §307, Dec. 18, 2015, 129 Stat. 2443.)

Amendments

2015—Subsec. (a). Pub. L. 114–113 inserted "A person appointed as a probation officer in one district may serve in another district with the consent of the appointing court and the court in the other district." after first sentence and "appointing" before "court may, for cause, remove".

Effective Date

Section effective Nov. 1, 1987, and applicable only to offenses committed after the taking effect of this section, see section 235(a)(1) of Pub. L. 98–473, set out as a note under section 3551 of this title.

§3603. Duties of probation officers

A probation officer shall—

(1) instruct a probationer or a person on supervised release, who is under his supervision, as to the conditions specified by the sentencing court, and provide him with a written statement clearly setting forth all such conditions;

(2) keep informed, to the degree required by the conditions specified by the sentencing court, as to the conduct and condition of a probationer or a person on supervised release, who is under his supervision, and report his conduct and condition to the sentencing court;

(3) use all suitable methods, not inconsistent with the conditions specified by the court, to aid a probationer or a person on supervised release who is under his supervision, and to bring about improvements in his conduct and condition;

(4) be responsible for the supervision of any probationer or a person on supervised release who is known to be within the judicial district;

(5) keep a record of his work, and make such reports to the Director of the Administrative Office of the United States Courts as the Director may require;

(6) upon request of the Attorney General or his designee, assist in the supervision of and furnish information about, a person within the custody of the Attorney General while on work release, furlough, or other authorized release from his regular place of confinement, or while in prerelease custody pursuant to the provisions of section 3624(c);

(7) keep informed concerning the conduct, condition, and compliance with any condition of probation, including the payment of a fine or restitution of each probationer under his supervision and report thereon to the court placing such person on probation and report to the court any failure of a probationer under his supervision to pay a fine in default within thirty days after notification that it is in default so that the court may determine whether probation should be revoked;

(8)(A) when directed by the court, and to the degree required by the regimen of care or treatment ordered by the court as a condition of release, keep informed as to the conduct and provide supervision of a person conditionally released under the provisions of section 4243 or 4246 of this title, and report such person's conduct and condition to the court ordering release and to the Attorney General or his designee; and

(B) immediately report any violation of the conditions of release to the court and the Attorney General or his designee;

(9) if approved by the district court, be authorized to carry firearms under such rules and regulations as the Director of the Administrative Office of the United States Courts may prescribe; and

(10) perform any other duty that the court may designate.

(Added Pub. L. 98–473, title II, §212(a)(2), Oct. 12, 1984, 98 Stat. 2002; amended Pub. L. 99–646, §15(a), Nov. 10, 1986, 100 Stat. 3595; Pub. L. 102–572, title VII, §701(a), Oct. 29, 1992, 106 Stat. 4514; Pub. L. 104–317, title I, §101(a), Oct. 19, 1996, 110 Stat. 3848.)

Amendments

1996—Pars. (9), (10). Pub. L. 104–317 added par. (9) and redesignated former par. (9) as (10).
1992—Pars. (8), (9). Pub. L. 102–572 added par. (8) and redesignated former par. (8) as (9).
1986—Pub. L. 99–646 redesignated pars. (a) to (h) as (1) to (8), respectively, and in par. (6) substituted "assist in the supervision of" for "supervise" and inserted a comma after "about".

Effective Date of 1992 Amendment

Amendment by Pub. L. 102–572 effective Jan. 1, 1993, see section 1101 of Pub. L. 102–572, set out as a note under section 905 of Title 2, The Congress.

Effective Date of 1986 Amendment

Pub. L. 99–646, §15(b), Nov. 10, 1986, 100 Stat. 3595, provided that: "The amendments made by this section [amending this section] shall take effect on the date of the taking effect of section 3603 of title 18, United States Code [Nov. 1, 1987]."

Effective Date

Section effective Nov. 1, 1987, and applicable only to offenses committed after the taking effect of this section, see section 235(a)(1) of Pub. L. 98–473, set out as a note under section 3551 of this title.

§3604. Transportation of a probationer

A court, after imposing a sentence of probation, may direct a United States marshal to furnish the probationer with—

(a) transportation to the place to which he is required to proceed as a condition of his probation; and

(b) money, not to exceed such amount as the Attorney General may prescribe, for subsistence expenses while traveling to his destination.

(Added Pub. L. 98–473, title II, §212(a)(2), Oct. 12, 1984, 98 Stat. 2002.)

Effective Date

Section effective Nov. 1, 1987, and applicable only to offenses committed after the taking effect of this section, see section 235(a)(1) of Pub. L. 98–473, set out as a note under section 3551 of this title.

§3605. Transfer of jurisdiction over a probationer

A court, after imposing a sentence, may transfer jurisdiction over a probationer or person on supervised release to the district court for any other district to which the person is required to proceed as a condition of his probation or release, or is permitted to proceed, with the concurrence of such court. A later transfer of jurisdiction may be made in the same manner. A court to which jurisdiction is transferred under this section is authorized to exercise all powers over the probationer or releasee that are permitted by this subchapter or subchapter B or D of chapter 227. (Added Pub. L. 98–473, title II, §212(a)(2), Oct. 12, 1984, 98 Stat. 2003.)

Effective Date

Section effective Nov. 1, 1987, and applicable only to offenses committed after the taking effect of this section, see section 235(a)(1) of Pub. L. 98–473, set out as a note under section 3551 of this title.

§3606. Arrest and return of a probationer

If there is probable cause to believe that a probationer or a person on supervised release has violated a condition of his probation or release, he may be arrested, and, upon arrest, shall be taken without unnecessary delay before the court having jurisdiction over him. A probation officer may make such an arrest wherever the probationer or releasee is found, and may make the arrest without a warrant. The court having supervision of the probationer or releasee, or, if there is no such court, the court last having supervision of the probationer or releasee, may issue a warrant for the arrest of a probationer or releasee for violation of a condition of release, and a probation officer or United States marshal may execute the warrant in the district in which the warrant was issued or in any district in which the probationer or releasee is found. (Added Pub. L. 98–473, title II, §212(a)(2), Oct. 12, 1984, 98 Stat. 2003.)

Effective Date

Section effective Nov. 1, 1987, and applicable only to offenses committed after the taking effect of this section, see section 235(a)(1) of Pub. L. 98–473, set out as a note under section 3551 of this title.

§3607. Special probation and expungement procedures for drug possessors

(a) Pre-judgment Probation.—If a person found guilty of an offense described in section 404 of the Controlled Substances Act (21 U.S.C. 844)—
(1) has not, prior to the commission of such offense, been convicted of violating a Federal or State law relating to controlled substances; and
(2) has not previously been the subject of a disposition under this subsection;
the court may, with the consent of such person, place him on probation for a term of not more than one year without entering a judgment of conviction. At any time before the expiration of the term of probation, if the person has not violated a condition of his probation, the court may, without entering a judgment of conviction, dismiss the proceedings against the person and discharge him from probation. At the expiration of the term of probation, if the person has not violated a condition of his probation, the court shall, without entering a judgment of conviction, dismiss the proceedings against the person and discharge him from probation. If the person violates a condition of his probation, the court shall proceed in accordance with the provisions of section 3565.
(b) Record of Disposition.—A nonpublic record of a disposition under subsection (a), or a conviction that is the subject of an expungement order under subsection (c), shall be retained by the Department of Justice solely for the purpose of use by the courts in determining in any subsequent proceeding whether a person qualifies for the disposition provided in subsection (a) or the expungement provided in subsection (c). A disposition under subsection (a), or a conviction that is the subject of an expungement order under subsection (c), shall not be considered a conviction for the purpose of a disqualification or a disability imposed by law upon conviction of a crime, or for any other purpose.
(c) Expungement of Record of Disposition.—If the case against a person found guilty of an offense under section 404 of the Controlled Substances Act (21 U.S.C. 844) is the subject of a disposition under subsection (a), and the person was less than twenty-one years old at the time of

the offense, the court shall enter an expungement order upon the application of such person. The expungement order shall direct that there be expunged from all official records, except the nonpublic records referred to in subsection (b), all references to his arrest for the offense, the institution of criminal proceedings against him, and the results thereof. The effect of the order shall be to restore such person, in the contemplation of the law, to the status he occupied before such arrest or institution of criminal proceedings. A person concerning whom such an order has been entered shall not be held thereafter under any provision of law to be guilty of perjury, false swearing, or making a false statement by reason of his failure to recite or acknowledge such arrests or institution of criminal proceedings, or the results thereof, in response to an inquiry made of him for any purpose.

(Added Pub. L. 98–473, title II, §212(a)(2), Oct. 12, 1984, 98 Stat. 2003.)

Effective Date

Section effective Nov. 1, 1987, and applicable only to offenses committed after the taking effect of this section, see section 235(a)(1) of Pub. L. 98–473, set out as a note under section 3551 of this title.

§3608. Drug testing of Federal offenders on post-conviction release

The Director of the Administrative Office of the United States Courts, in consultation with the Attorney General and the Secretary of Health and Human Services, shall, subject to the availability of appropriations, establish a program of drug testing of Federal offenders on post-conviction release. The program shall include such standards and guidelines as the Director may determine necessary to ensure the reliability and accuracy of the drug testing programs. In each judicial district the chief probation officer shall arrange for the drug testing of defendants on post-conviction release pursuant to a conviction for a felony or other offense described in section 3563(a)(4).1

(Added Pub. L. 103–322, title II, §20414(a)(1), Sept. 13, 1994, 108 Stat. 1830.)

References in Text

Section 3563(a)(4), referred to in text, probably means the par. (4) of section 3563(a) added by section 20414(b)(3) of Pub. L. 103–322, which was renumbered par. (5) by Pub. L. 104–132, title II, §203(1)(C), Apr. 24, 1996, 110 Stat. 1227.

SUBCHAPTER B—FINES 1

3611.	Payment of a fine or restitution.
3612.	Collection of an unpaid fine or restitution.
3613.	Civil remedies for satisfaction of an unpaid fine.
3613A.	Effect of default.
3614.	Resentencing upon failure to pay a fine or restitution.
3615.	Criminal default.

Amendments

1996—Pub. L. 104–132, title II, §207(d), Apr. 24, 1996, 110 Stat. 1240, amended table of sections generally, inserting "or restitution" after "fine" in items 3611, 3612, and 3614, reenacting items 3613 and 3615 without change, and adding item 3613A.

1994—Pub. L. 103–322, title XXXIII, §330010(3), Sept. 13, 1994, 108 Stat. 2143, transferred analysis of this subchapter to follow heading for this subchapter.

§3611. Payment of a fine or restitution

A person who is sentenced to pay a fine, assessment, or restitution, shall pay the fine, assessment, or restitution (including any interest or penalty), as specified by the Director of the Administrative

Office of the United States Courts. Such Director may specify that such payment be made to the clerk of the court or in the manner provided for under section 604(a)(18) of title 28, United States Code.

(Added Pub. L. 98–473, title II, §212(a)(2), Oct. 12, 1984, 98 Stat. 2004; amended Pub. L. 100–185, §10(a), Dec. 11, 1987, 101 Stat. 1283; Pub. L. 101–647, title XXXV, §3591, Nov. 29, 1990, 104 Stat. 4931; Pub. L. 104–132, title II, §207(c)(1), Apr. 24, 1996, 110 Stat. 1237.)

Prior Provisions

For a prior section 3611, applicable to offenses committed prior to Nov. 1, 1987, see note set out preceding section 3601 of this title.

Amendments

1996—Pub. L. 104–132 substituted "Payment of a fine or restitution" for "Payment of a fine" in section catchline and ", assessment, or restitution, shall pay the fine, assessment, or restitution" for "or assessment shall pay the fine or assessment" in text.

1990—Pub. L. 101–647 substituted "604(a)(18)" for "604(a)(17)".

1987—Pub. L. 100–185 amended section generally. Prior to amendment, section read as follows: "A person who has been sentenced to pay a fine pursuant to the provisions of subchapter C of chapter 227 shall pay the fine immediately, or by the time and method specified by the sentencing court, to the clerk of the court. The clerk shall forward the payment to the United States Treasury."

Effective Date of 1996 Amendment

Amendment by Pub. L. 104–132 to be effective, to extent constitutionally permissible, for sentencing proceedings in cases in which defendant is convicted on or after Apr. 24, 1996, see section 211 of Pub. L. 104–132, set out as a note under section 2248 of this title.

Effective Date of 1987 Amendment

Pub. L. 100–185, §10(b), Dec. 11, 1987, 101 Stat. 1283, provided that: "The amendment made by this section [amending this section] shall apply with respect to any fine imposed after October 31, 1988. Such amendment shall also apply with respect to any fine imposed on or before October 31, 1988, if the fine remains uncollected as of February 1, 1989, unless the Director of the Administrative Office of the United States Courts determines further delay is necessary. If the Director so determines, the amendment made by this section shall apply with respect to any such fine imposed on or before October 31, 1988, if the fine remains uncollected as of May 1, 1989."

Effective Date

Section effective Nov. 1, 1987, and applicable only to offenses committed after the taking effect of this section, see section 235(a)(1) of Pub. L. 98–473, set out as a note under section 3551 of this title.

Receipt of Fines—Interim Provisions

Pub. L. 100–185, §9, Dec. 11, 1987, 101 Stat. 1282, provided that:

"(a) November 1, 1987, to April 30, 1988.—Notwithstanding section 3611 of title 18, United States Code, a person who, during the period beginning on November 1, 1987, and ending on April 30, 1988, is sentenced to pay a fine or assessment shall pay the fine or assessment (including any interest or penalty) to the clerk of the court, with respect to an offense committed on or before December 31, 1984, and to the Attorney General, with respect to an offense committed after December 31, 1984.

"(b) May 1, 1988, to October 31, 1988.—(1) Notwithstanding section 3611 of title 18, United States Code, a person who during the period beginning on May 1, 1988, and ending on October 31, 1988, is sentenced to pay a fine or assessment shall pay the fine or assessment in accordance with this subsection.

"(2) In a case initiated by citation or violation notice, such person shall pay the fine or assessment (including any interest or penalty), as specified by the Director of the Administrative Office of the United States Courts. Such Director may specify that such payment be made to the clerk of the court or in the manner provided for under section 604(a)(17) of title 28, United States Code.

"(3) In any other case, such person shall pay the fine or assessment (including any interest or penalty) to the clerk of the court, with respect to an offense committed on or before December 31, 1984, and to the Attorney General, with respect to an offense committed after December 31, 1984."

§3612. Collection of unpaid fine or restitution

(a) Notification of Receipt and Related Matters.—The clerk or the person designated under section 604(a)(18) of title 28 shall notify the Attorney General of each receipt of a payment with respect to which a certification is made under subsection (b), together with other appropriate information relating to such payment. The notification shall be provided—

(1) in such manner as may be agreed upon by the Attorney General and the Director of the Administrative Office of the United States Courts; and

(2) within 15 days after the receipt or at such other time as may be determined jointly by the Attorney General and the Director of the Administrative Office of the United States Courts.

If the fifteenth day under paragraph (2) is a Saturday, Sunday, or legal public holiday, the clerk, or the person designated under section 604(a)(18) of title 28, shall provide notification not later than the next day that is not a Saturday, Sunday, or legal public holiday.

(b) Information to be Included in Judgment; Judgment to be Transmitted to Attorney General.—

(1) A judgment or order imposing, modifying, or remitting a fine or restitution order of more than $100 shall include—

(A) the name, social security account number, mailing address, and residence address of the defendant;

(B) the docket number of the case;

(C) the original amount of the fine or restitution order and the amount that is due and unpaid;

(D) the schedule of payments (if other than immediate payment is permitted under section 3572(d));

(E) a description of any modification or remission;

(F) if other than immediate payment is permitted, a requirement that, until the fine or restitution order is paid in full, the defendant notify the Attorney General of any change in the mailing address or residence address of the defendant not later than thirty days after the change occurs; and

(G) in the case of a restitution order, information sufficient to identify each victim to whom restitution is owed. It shall be the responsibility of each victim to notify the Attorney General, or the appropriate entity of the court, by means of a form to be provided by the Attorney General or the court, of any change in the victim's mailing address while restitution is still owed the victim. The confidentiality of any information relating to a victim shall be maintained.

(2) Not later than ten days after entry of the judgment or order, the court shall transmit a certified copy of the judgment or order to the Attorney General.

(c) Responsibility for Collection.—The Attorney General shall be responsible for collection of an unpaid fine or restitution concerning which a certification has been issued as provided in subsection (b). An order of restitution, pursuant to section 3556, does not create any right of action against the United States by the person to whom restitution is ordered to be paid. Any money received from a defendant shall be disbursed so that each of the following obligations is paid in full in the following sequence:

(1) A penalty assessment under section 3013 of title 18, United States Code.

(2) Restitution of all victims.

(3) All other fines, penalties, costs, and other payments required under the sentence.

(d) Notification of Delinquency.—Within ten working days after a fine or restitution is determined to be delinquent as provided in section 3572(h), the Attorney General shall notify the person whose fine or restitution is delinquent, to inform the person of the delinquency.

(e) Notification of Default.—Within ten working days after a fine or restitution is determined to be in default as provided in section 3572(i), the Attorney General shall notify the person defaulting to inform the person that the fine or restitution is in default and the entire unpaid balance, including interest and penalties, is due within thirty days.

(f) Interest on Fines and restitution.—

(1) In general.—The defendant shall pay interest on any fine or restitution of more than $2,500, unless the fine is paid in full before the fifteenth day after the date of the judgment. If that day is a Saturday, Sunday, or legal public holiday, the defendant shall be liable for interest beginning with the next day that is not a Saturday, Sunday, or legal public holiday.

(2) Computation.—Interest on a fine shall be computed—

(A) daily (from the first day on which the defendant is liable for interest under paragraph (1)); and

(B) at a rate equal to the weekly average 1-year constant maturity Treasury yield, as published by the Board of Governors of the Federal Reserve System, for the calendar week preceding the first day on which the defendant is liable for interest under paragraph (1).

(3) Modification of interest by court.—If the court determines that the defendant does not have the ability to pay interest under this subsection, the court may—

(A) waive the requirement for interest;

(B) limit the total of interest payable to a specific dollar amount; or

(C) limit the length of the period during which interest accrues.

(g) Penalty for Delinquent Fine.—If a fine or restitution becomes delinquent, the defendant shall pay, as a penalty, an amount equal to 10 percent of the principal amount that is delinquent. If a fine or restitution becomes in default, the defendant shall pay, as a penalty, an additional amount equal to 15 percent of the principal amount that is in default.

(h) Waiver of Interest or Penalty by Attorney General.—The Attorney General may waive all or part of any interest or penalty under this section or any interest or penalty relating to a fine imposed under any prior law if, as determined by the Attorney General, reasonable efforts to collect the interest or penalty are not likely to be effective.

(i) Application of Payments.—Payments relating to fines and restitution shall be applied in the following order: (1) to principal; (2) to costs; (3) to interest; and (4) to penalties.

(j) Evaluation of Offices of the United States Attorney and Department Components.—

(1) In general.—The Attorney General shall, as part of the regular evaluation process, evaluate each office of the United States attorney and each component of the Department of Justice on the performance of the office or the component, as the case may be, in seeking and recovering restitution for victims under each provision of this title and the Controlled Substances Act (21 U.S.C. 801 et seq.) that authorizes restitution.

(2) Requirement.—Following an evaluation under paragraph (1), each office of the United States attorney and each component of the Department of Justice shall work to improve the practices of the office or component, as the case may be, with respect to seeking and recovering restitution for victims under each provision of this title and the Controlled Substances Act (21 U.S.C. 801 et seq.) that authorizes restitution.

(k) GAO Reports.—

(1) Report.—Not later than 1 year after the date of enactment of this subsection, the Comptroller General of the United States shall prepare and submit to the Committee on the Judiciary of the House of Representatives and the Committee on the Judiciary of the Senate a report on restitution sought by the Attorney General under each provision of this title and the Controlled Substances Act (21 U.S.C. 801 et seq.) that authorizes restitution during the 3-year period preceding the report.

(2) Contents.—The report required under paragraph (1) shall include statistically valid estimates of—

(A) the number of cases in which a defendant was convicted and the Attorney General could seek restitution under this title or the Controlled Substances Act (21 U.S.C. 801 et seq.);

(B) the number of cases in which the Attorney General sought restitution;

(C) of the cases in which the Attorney General sought restitution, the number of times restitution was ordered by the district courts of the United States;

(D) the amount of restitution ordered by the district courts of the United States;

(E) the amount of restitution collected pursuant to the restitution orders described in subparagraph (D);

(F) the percentage of restitution orders for which the full amount of restitution has not been collected; and

(G) any other measurement the Comptroller General determines would assist in evaluating how to improve the restitution process in Federal criminal cases.

(3) Recommendations.—The report required under paragraph (1) shall include recommendations on the best practices for—

(A) requesting restitution in cases in which restitution may be sought under each provision of this title and the Controlled Substances Act (21 U.S.C. 801 et seq.) that authorizes restitution;

(B) obtaining restitution orders from the district courts of the United States; and

(C) collecting restitution ordered by the district courts of the United States.

(4) Report.—Not later than 3 years after the date on which the report required under paragraph (1) is submitted, the Comptroller General of the United States shall prepare and submit to the Committee on the Judiciary of the House of Representatives and the Committee on the Judiciary of the Senate a report on the implementation by the Attorney General of the best practices recommended under paragraph (3).

(Added Pub. L. 98–473, title II, §212(a)(2), Oct. 12, 1984, 98 Stat. 2004; amended Pub. L. 100–185, §11, Dec. 11, 1987, 101 Stat. 1283; Pub. L. 100–690, title VII, §7082(c), (d), Nov. 18, 1988, 102 Stat. 4408; Pub. L. 101–647, title XXXV, §3592, Nov. 29, 1990, 104 Stat. 4931; Pub. L. 104–132, title II, §207(c)(2), Apr. 24, 1996, 110 Stat. 1237; Pub. L. 106–554, §1(a)(7) [title III, §307(b)], Dec. 21, 2000, 114 Stat. 2763, 2763A–635; Pub. L. 107–273, div. B, title IV, §4002(b)(15), Nov. 2, 2002, 116 Stat. 1808; Pub. L. 114–324, §18, Dec. 16, 2016, 130 Stat. 1962.)

References in Text

The Controlled Substances Act, referred to in subsecs. (j) and (k), is title II of Pub. L. 91–513, Oct. 27, 1970, 84 Stat. 1242, which is classified principally to subchapter I (§801 et seq.) of chapter 13 of Title 21, Food and Drugs. For complete classification of this Act to the Code, see Short Title note set out under section 801 of Title 21 and Tables.

The date of enactment of this subsection, referred to in subsec. (k)(1), is the date of enactment of Pub. L. 114–324, which was approved Dec. 16, 2016.

Prior Provisions

For a prior section 3612, applicable to offenses committed prior to Nov. 1, 1987, see note set out preceding section 3601 of this title.

Amendments

2016—Subsecs. (j), (k). Pub. L. 114–324 added subsecs. (j) and (k).

2002—Subsec. (f)(2)(B). Pub. L. 107–273 substituted "preceding the first day" for "preceding. the first day".

2000—Subsec. (f)(2)(B). Pub. L. 106–554 substituted "the weekly average 1-year constant maturity Treasury yield, as published by the Board of Governors of the Federal Reserve System, for the calendar week preceding." for "the coupon issue yield equivalent (as determined by the Secretary of the Treasury) of the average accepted auction price for the last auction of fifty-two week United States Treasury bills settled before".

1996—Pub. L. 104–132, §207(c)(2)(A), substituted "Collection of unpaid fine or restitution" for "Collection of an unpaid fine" in section catchline.

Subsec. (b)(1). Pub. L. 104–132, §207(c)(2)(B)(i), inserted "or restitution order" after "fine" in introductory provisions.

Subsec. (b)(1)(C). Pub. L. 104–132, §207(c)(2)(B)(ii), inserted "or restitution order" after "fine".

Subsec. (b)(1)(E). Pub. L. 104–132, §207(c)(2)(B)(iii), struck out "and" at end.

Subsec. (b)(1)(F). Pub. L. 104–132, §207(c)(2)(B)(iv), inserted "or restitution order" after "fine" and substituted "; and" for period at end.

Subsec. (b)(1)(G). Pub. L. 104–132, §207(c)(2)(B)(v), added subpar. (G).

Subsec. (c). Pub. L. 104–132, §207(c)(2)(C), inserted "or restitution" after "unpaid fine" in first sentence and inserted at end "Any money received from a defendant shall be disbursed so that each of the following obligations is paid in full in the following sequence:

"(1) A penalty assessment under section 3013 of title 18, United States Code.

"(2) Restitution of all victims.

"(3) All other fines, penalties, costs, and other payments required under the sentence."

Subsec. (d). Pub. L. 104–132, §207(c)(2)(D)(ii), which directed substitution of "or restitution is delinquent, to inform the person of the delinquency" for "is delinquent, to inform him that the fine is delinquent", was executed by making the substitution for "is delinquent to inform him that the fine is delinquent" to reflect the probable intent of Congress.

Pub. L. 104–132, §207(c)(2)(D)(i), inserted "or restitution" after "Within ten working days after a fine".

Subsec. (e). Pub. L. 104–132, §207(c)(2)(E), inserted "or restitution" after "days after a fine" and substituted "the person that the fine or restitution is in default" for "him that the fine is in default".

Subsec. (f). Pub. L. 104–132, §207(c)(2)(F)(i), which directed amendment of heading by inserting "and restitution" after "on fines", was executed by inserting the material after "on fines" to reflect the probable intent of Congress.

Subsec. (f)(1). Pub. L. 104–132, §207(c)(2)(F)(ii), inserted "or restitution" after "any fine".

Subsec. (g). Pub. L. 104–132, §207(c)(2)(G), inserted "or restitution" after "fine" in two places.

Subsec. (i). Pub. L. 104–132, §207(c)(2)(H), inserted "and restitution" after "fines".

1990—Subsec. (a). Pub. L. 101–647 substituted "604(a)(18)" for "604(a)(17)" wherever appearing.

1988—Subsec. (d). Pub. L. 100–690, §7082(d), struck out ", by certified mail," after "fine is delinquent".

Subsec. (e). Pub. L. 100–690, §7082(d), struck out ", by certified mail," after "the person defaulting".

Subsec. (h). Pub. L. 100–690, §7082(c), inserted "or any interest or penalty relating to a fine imposed under any prior law" after "under this section".

1987—Subsec. (a). Pub. L. 100–185, §11(a), substituted "Notification of receipt and related matters" for "Disposition of payment" in heading and amended text generally. Prior to amendment, text read as follows: "The clerk shall forward each fine payment to the United States Treasury and shall notify the Attorney General of its receipt within ten working days."

Subsec. (b). Pub. L. 100–185, §11(b), substituted "Information to be included in judgment; judgment to be transmitted to Attorney General" for "Certification of imposition" in heading and amended text generally. Prior to amendment, text read as follows: "If a fine exceeding $100 is imposed, modified, or remitted, the sentencing court shall incorporate in the order imposing, remitting, or modifying such fine, and promptly certify to the Attorney General—

"(1) the name of the person fined;

"(2) his current address;

"(3) the docket number of the case;

"(4) the amount of the fine imposed;

"(5) any installment schedule;

"(6) the nature of any modification or remission of the fine or installment schedule; and

"(7) the amount of the fine that is due and unpaid."

Subsec. (d). Pub. L. 100–185, §11(c)(1), substituted "section 3572(h)" for "section 3572(i)".

Subsec. (e). Pub. L. 100–185, §11(c)(2), substituted "section 3572(i)" for "section 3572(j)".

Subsec. (f). Pub. L. 100–185, §11(d), amended subsec. (f) generally, substituting provisions relating to interest on fines, computation of interest, and modification of interest by court, for provisions relating to interest and monetary penalties for delinquent fines.

Subsecs. (g) to (i). Pub. L. 100–185, §11(e), added subsecs. (g) to (i).

Effective Date of 1996 Amendment

Amendment by Pub. L. 104–132 to be effective, to extent constitutionally permissible, for sentencing proceedings in cases in which defendant is convicted on or after Apr. 24, 1996, see section 211 of Pub. L. 104–132, set out as a note under section 2248 of this title.

Effective Date

Section effective Nov. 1, 1987, and applicable only to offenses committed after the taking effect of this section, see section 235(a)(1) of Pub. L. 98–473, set out as a note under section 3551 of this title.

Collection of Outstanding Fines

Pub. L. 98–473, title II, §237, Oct. 12, 1984, 98 Stat. 2033, provided that:

"(a)(1) Except as provided in paragraph (2), for each criminal fine for which the unpaid balance exceeds $100 as of the effective date of this Act [see section 235 of Pub. L. 98–473, as amended, set out as a note under section 3551 of this title], the Attorney General shall, within one hundred and twenty days, notify the person by certified mail of his obligation, within thirty days after notification, to—

"(A) pay the fine in full;

"(B) specify, and demonstrate compliance with, an installment schedule established by a court before enactment of the amendments made by this Act [Oct. 12, 1984], specifying the dates on which designated partial payments will be made; or

"(C) establish with the concurrence of the Attorney General, a new installment schedule of a duration not exceeding two years, except in special circumstances, and specifying the dates on which designated partial payments will be made.

"(2) This subsection shall not apply in cases in which—

"(A) the Attorney General believes the likelihood of collection is remote; or

"(B) criminal fines have been stayed pending appeal.

"(b) The Attorney General shall, within one hundred and eighty days after the effective date of this Act, declare all fines for which this obligation is unfulfilled to be in criminal default, subject to the civil and criminal remedies established by amendments made by this Act [see Short Title note set out under section 3551 of this title]. No interest or monetary penalties shall be charged on any fines subject to this section.

"(c) Not later than one year following the effective date of this Act, the Attorney General shall include in the annual crime report steps taken to implement this Act and the progress achieved in criminal fine collection, including collection data for each judicial district."

§3613. Civil remedies for satisfaction of an unpaid fine

(a) Enforcement.—The United States may enforce a judgment imposing a fine in accordance with the practices and procedures for the enforcement of a civil judgment under Federal law or State law. Notwithstanding any other Federal law (including section 207 of the Social Security Act), a judgment imposing a fine may be enforced against all property or rights to property of the person fined, except that—

(1) property exempt from levy for taxes pursuant to section 6334(a)(1), (2), (3), (4), (5), (6), (7), (8), (10), and (12) of the Internal Revenue Code of 1986 shall be exempt from enforcement of the judgment under Federal law;

(2) section 3014 of chapter 176 of title 28 shall not apply to enforcement under Federal law; and

(3) the provisions of section 303 of the Consumer Credit Protection Act (15 U.S.C. 1673) shall apply to enforcement of the judgment under Federal law or State law.

(b) Termination of Liability.—The liability to pay a fine shall terminate the later of 20 years from the entry of judgment or 20 years after the release from imprisonment of the person fined, or upon the death of the individual fined. The liability to pay restitution shall terminate on the date that is the later of 20 years from the entry of judgment or 20 years after the release from imprisonment of the person ordered to pay restitution. In the event of the death of the person ordered to pay restitution, the individual's estate will be held responsible for any unpaid balance of the restitution amount, and the lien provided in subsection (c) of this section shall continue until the estate receives a written release of that liability.

(c) Lien.—A fine imposed pursuant to the provisions of subchapter C of chapter 227 of this title, or an order of restitution made pursuant to sections 1 2248, 2259, 2264, 2327, 3663, 3663A, or 3664 of this title, is a lien in favor of the United States on all property and rights to property of the person fined as if the liability of the person fined were a liability for a tax assessed under the Internal Revenue Code of 1986. The lien arises on the entry of judgment and continues for 20 years or until the liability is satisfied, remitted, set aside, or is terminated under subsection (b).

(d) Effect of Filing Notice of Lien.—Upon filing of a notice of lien in the manner in which a notice of tax lien would be filed under section 6323(f)(1) and (2) of the Internal Revenue Code of 1986, the lien shall be valid against any purchaser, holder of a security interest, mechanic's lienor or judgment lien creditor, except with respect to properties or transactions specified in subsection (b), (c), or (d) of section 6323 of the Internal Revenue Code of 1986 for which a notice of tax lien properly filed on the same date would not be valid. The notice of lien shall be considered a notice of lien for taxes payable to the United States for the purpose of any State or local law providing for the filing of a notice of a tax lien. A notice of lien that is registered, recorded, docketed, or indexed in accordance with the rules and requirements relating to judgments of the courts of the State where the notice of lien is registered, recorded, docketed, or indexed shall be considered for all purposes as the filing prescribed by this section. The provisions of section 3201(e) of chapter 176 of title 28 shall apply to liens filed as prescribed by this section.

(e) Discharge of Debt Inapplicable.—No discharge of debts in a proceeding pursuant to any chapter of title 11, United States Code, shall discharge liability to pay a fine pursuant to this section, and a lien filed as prescribed by this section shall not be voided in a bankruptcy proceeding.

(f) Applicability to Order of Restitution.—In accordance with section 3664(m)(1)(A) of this title, all provisions of this section are available to the United States for the enforcement of an order of restitution.

(Added Pub. L. 98–473, title II, §212(a)(2), Oct. 12, 1984, 98 Stat. 2005; amended Pub. L. 99–514, §2, Oct. 22, 1986, 100 Stat. 2095; Pub. L. 101–647, title XXXV, §3593, Nov. 29, 1990, 104 Stat. 4931; Pub. L. 104–132, title II, §207(c)(3), Apr. 24, 1996, 110 Stat. 1238; Pub. L. 114–324, §2(b), Dec. 16, 2016, 130 Stat. 1948.)

References in Text

Section 207 of the Social Security Act, referred to in subsec. (a), is classified to section 407 of Title 42, The Public Health and Welfare.

The Internal Revenue Code of 1986, referred to in subsecs. (a)(1), (c), and (d), is classified generally to Title 26, Internal Revenue Code.

Prior Provisions

For a prior section 3613, applicable to offenses committed prior to Nov. 1, 1987, see note set out preceding section 3601 of this title.

Amendments

2016—Subsec. (b). Pub. L. 114–324 inserted at end "The liability to pay restitution shall terminate on the date that is the later of 20 years from the entry of judgment or 20 years after the release from imprisonment of the person ordered to pay restitution. In the event of the death of the person ordered to pay restitution, the individual's estate will be held responsible for any unpaid balance of the restitution amount, and the lien provided in subsection (c) of this section shall continue until the estate receives a written release of that liability."

1996—Pub. L. 104–132 amended section generally, reenacting section catchline without change and substituting, in subsec. (a), provisions relating to enforcement for provisions relating to lien, in subsec. (b), provisions relating to termination of liability for provisions relating to expiration of lien, in subsec. (c), provisions relating to lien for provisions relating to application of other lien provisions, in subsec. (d), provisions relating to effect of filing notice of lien for provisions relating to effect of notice of lien, in subsec. (e), provisions relating to inapplicability of bankruptcy discharges of debt for provisions relating to alternative enforcement, and in subsec. (f), provisions relating to applicability to order of restitution for provisions relating to inapplicability of bankruptcy discharges of debt.

1990—Subsec. (c). Pub. L. 101–647, which directed amendment of "Section 3613(c)" by striking the period before the closing quotation marks and inserting a period after such marks, without identifying a Code title or Act for section 3613, was executed by substituting "construed to mean 'fine'." for "construed to mean 'fine.' " in subsec. (c) of this section to reflect the probable intent of Congress.

1986—Subsecs. (b) to (d). Pub. L. 99–514 substituted "Internal Revenue Code of 1986" for "Internal Revenue Code of 1954" wherever appearing.

Effective Date of 1996 Amendment

Amendment by Pub. L. 104–132 to be effective, to extent constitutionally permissible, for sentencing proceedings in cases in which defendant is convicted on or after Apr. 24, 1996, see section 211 of Pub. L. 104–132, set out as a note under section 2248 of this title.

Effective Date

Section effective Nov. 1, 1987, and applicable only to offenses committed after the taking effect of this section, see section 235(a)(1) of Pub. L. 98–473, set out as a note under section 3551 of this title.

§3613A. Effect of default

(a)(1) Upon a finding that the defendant is in default on a payment of a fine or restitution, the court may, pursuant to section 3565, revoke probation or a term of supervised release, modify the terms or conditions of probation or a term of supervised release, resentence a defendant pursuant to section 3614, hold the defendant in contempt of court, enter a restraining order or injunction, order the sale of property of the defendant, accept a performance bond, enter or adjust a payment schedule, or take any other action necessary to obtain compliance with the order of a fine or restitution.

(2) In determining what action to take, the court shall consider the defendant's employment status, earning ability, financial resources, the willfulness in failing to comply with the fine or restitution order, and any other circumstances that may have a bearing on the defendant's ability or failure to comply with the order of a fine or restitution.

(b)(1) Any hearing held pursuant to this section may be conducted by a magistrate judge, subject to de novo review by the court.

(2) To the extent practicable, in a hearing held pursuant to this section involving a defendant who is confined in any jail, prison, or other correctional facility, proceedings in which the prisoner's participation is required or permitted shall be conducted by telephone, video conference, or other communications technology without removing the prisoner from the facility in which the prisoner is confined.

(Added Pub. L. 104–132, title II, §207(c)(4), Apr. 24, 1996, 110 Stat. 1239.)

Effective Date

Section to be effective, to extent constitutionally permissible, for sentencing proceedings in cases in which the defendant is convicted on or after Apr. 24, 1996, see section 211 of Pub. L. 104–132, set out as an Effective Date of 1996 Amendment note under section 2248 of this title.

§3614. Resentencing upon failure to pay a fine or restitution

(a) Resentencing.—Subject to the provisions of subsection (b), if a defendant knowingly fails to pay a delinquent fine or restitution the court may resentence the defendant to any sentence which might originally have been imposed.

(b) Imprisonment.—The defendant may be sentenced to a term of imprisonment under subsection (a) only if the court determines that—

(1) the defendant willfully refused to pay the delinquent fine or had failed to make sufficient bona fide efforts to pay the fine; or

(2) in light of the nature of the offense and the characteristics of the person, alternatives to imprisonment are not adequate to serve the purposes of punishment and deterrence.

(c) Effect of Indigency.—In no event shall a defendant be incarcerated under this section solely on the basis of inability to make payments because the defendant is indigent.

(Added Pub. L. 98–473, title II, §212(a)(2), Oct. 12, 1984, 98 Stat. 2006; amended Pub. L. 104–132, title II, §207(c)(5), Apr. 24, 1996, 110 Stat. 1240.)

Prior Provisions

For a prior section 3614, applicable to offenses committed prior to Nov. 1, 1987, see note set out preceding section 3601 of this title.

Amendments

1996—Pub. L. 104–232, §207(c)(5)(A), inserted "or restitution" after "fine" in section catchline.
Subsec. (a). Pub. L. 104–232, §207(c)(5)(B), inserted "or restitution" after "fine".
Subsec. (c). Pub. L. 104–232, §207(c)(5)(C), added subsec. (c).

Effective Date of 1996 Amendment

Amendment by Pub. L. 104–132 to be effective, to extent constitutionally permissible, for sentencing proceedings in cases in which defendant is convicted on or after Apr. 24, 1996, see section 211 of Pub. L. 104–132, set out as a note under section 2248 of this title.

Effective Date

Section effective Nov. 1, 1987, and applicable only to offenses committed after the taking effect of this section, see section 235(a)(1) of Pub. L. 98–473, set out as a note under section 3551 of this title.

§3615. Criminal default

Whoever, having been sentenced to pay a fine, willfully fails to pay the fine, shall be fined not more than twice the amount of the unpaid balance of the fine or $10,000, whichever is greater, imprisoned not more than one year, or both.

(Added Pub. L. 98–473, title II, §212(a)(2), Oct. 12, 1984, 98 Stat. 2006.)

Prior Provisions

For prior sections 3615 to 3620, applicable to offenses committed prior to Nov. 1, 1987, see note set out preceding section 3601 of this title.

Effective Date

Section effective Nov. 1, 1987, and applicable only to offenses committed after the taking effect of this section, see section 235(a)(1) of Pub. L. 98–473, set out as a note under section 3551 of this title.

SUBCHAPTER C—IMPRISONMENT 1

Amendments

1996—Pub. L. 104–134, title I, §101[(a)] [title VIII, §802(c)], Apr. 26, 1996, 110 Stat. 1321, 1321–70; renumbered title I, Pub. L. 104–140, §1(a), May 2, 1996, 110 Stat. 1327, which directed that table of sections at beginning of subchapter C of this chapter be amended generally to read "3626. Appropriate remedies with respect to prison conditions.", was executed by making amendment in item 3626 to reflect the probable intent of Congress. Prior to amendment, item 3626 read as follows: "3626. Appropriate remedies with respect to prison crowding."

1994—Pub. L. 103–322, title II, §20409(c), title XXXIII, §330010(3), Sept. 13, 1994, 108 Stat. 1828, 2143, transferred analysis of this subchapter to follow heading for this subchapter and added item 3626.

§3621. Imprisonment of a convicted person

(a) Commitment to Custody of Bureau of Prisons.—A person who has been sentenced to a term of imprisonment pursuant to the provisions of subchapter D of chapter 227 shall be committed to the custody of the Bureau of Prisons until the expiration of the term imposed, or until earlier released for satisfactory behavior pursuant to the provisions of section 3624.

(b) Place of Imprisonment.—The Bureau of Prisons shall designate the place of the prisoner's imprisonment. The Bureau may designate any available penal or correctional facility that meets minimum standards of health and habitability established by the Bureau, whether maintained by the Federal Government or otherwise and whether within or without the judicial district in which the person was convicted, that the Bureau determines to be appropriate and suitable, considering—

(1) the resources of the facility contemplated;

(2) the nature and circumstances of the offense;

(3) the history and characteristics of the prisoner;

(4) any statement by the court that imposed the sentence—

(A) concerning the purposes for which the sentence to imprisonment was determined to be warranted; or

(B) recommending a type of penal or correctional facility as appropriate; and

(5) any pertinent policy statement issued by the Sentencing Commission pursuant to section 994(a)(2) of title 28.

In designating the place of imprisonment or making transfers under this subsection, there shall be no favoritism given to prisoners of high social or economic status. The Bureau may at any time, having regard for the same matters, direct the transfer of a prisoner from one penal or correctional facility to another. The Bureau shall make available appropriate substance abuse treatment for each prisoner the Bureau determines has a treatable condition of substance addiction or abuse. Any order, recommendation, or request by a sentencing court that a convicted person serve a term of imprisonment in a community corrections facility shall have no binding effect on the authority of the Bureau under this section to determine or change the place of imprisonment of that person.

(c) Delivery of Order of Commitment.—When a prisoner, pursuant to a court order, is placed in the custody of a person in charge of a penal or correctional facility, a copy of the order shall be delivered to such person as evidence of this authority to hold the prisoner, and the original order, with the return endorsed thereon, shall be returned to the court that issued it.

(d) Delivery of Prisoner for Court Appearances.—The United States marshal shall, without charge, bring a prisoner into court or return him to a prison facility on order of a court of the United States or on written request of an attorney for the Government.

(e) Substance Abuse Treatment.—

(1) Phase-in.—In order to carry out the requirement of the last sentence of subsection (b) of this section, that every prisoner with a substance abuse problem have the opportunity to participate in appropriate substance abuse treatment, the Bureau of Prisons shall, subject to the availability of appropriations, provide residential substance abuse treatment (and make arrangements for appropriate aftercare)—

(A) for not less than 50 percent of eligible prisoners by the end of fiscal year 1995, with priority for such treatment accorded based on an eligible prisoner's proximity to release date;

(B) for not less than 75 percent of eligible prisoners by the end of fiscal year 1996, with priority for such treatment accorded based on an eligible prisoner's proximity to release date; and

(C) for all eligible prisoners by the end of fiscal year 1997 and thereafter, with priority for such treatment accorded based on an eligible prisoner's proximity to release date.

(2) Incentive for prisoners' successful completion of treatment program.—

(A) Generally.—Any prisoner who, in the judgment of the Director of the Bureau of Prisons, has successfully completed a program of residential substance abuse treatment provided under paragraph (1) of this subsection, shall remain in the custody of the Bureau under such conditions as the Bureau deems appropriate. If the conditions of confinement are different from those the prisoner would have experienced absent the successful completion of the treatment, the Bureau shall periodically test the prisoner for substance abuse and discontinue such conditions on determining that substance abuse has recurred.

(B) Period of custody.—The period a prisoner convicted of a nonviolent offense remains in custody after successfully completing a treatment program may be reduced by the Bureau of Prisons, but such reduction may not be more than one year from the term the prisoner must otherwise serve.

(3) Report.—The Bureau of Prisons shall transmit to the Committees on the Judiciary of the Senate and the House of Representatives on January 1, 1995, and on January 1 of each year thereafter, a report. Such report shall contain—

(A) a detailed quantitative and qualitative description of each substance abuse treatment program, residential or not, operated by the Bureau;

(B) a full explanation of how eligibility for such programs is determined, with complete information on what proportion of prisoners with substance abuse problems are eligible; and

(C) a complete statement of to what extent the Bureau has achieved compliance with the requirements of this title.

(4) Authorization of appropriations.—There are authorized to carry out this subsection such sums as may be necessary for each of fiscal years 2007 through 2011.

(5) Definitions.—As used in this subsection—

(A) the term "residential substance abuse treatment" means a course of individual and group activities and treatment, lasting at least 6 months, in residential treatment facilities set apart from the general prison population (which may include the use of pharmocotherapies,1 where appropriate, that may extend beyond the 6-month period);

(B) the term "eligible prisoner" means a prisoner who is—

(i) determined by the Bureau of Prisons to have a substance abuse problem; and

(ii) willing to participate in a residential substance abuse treatment program; and

(C) the term "aftercare" means placement, case management and monitoring of the participant in a community-based substance abuse treatment program when the participant leaves the custody of the Bureau of Prisons.

(6) Coordination of federal assistance.—The Bureau of Prisons shall consult with the Department of Health and Human Services concerning substance abuse treatment and related services and the incorporation of applicable components of existing comprehensive approaches including relapse prevention and aftercare services.

(f) Sex Offender Management.—

(1) In general.—The Bureau of Prisons shall make available appropriate treatment to sex offenders who are in need of and suitable for treatment, as follows:

(A) Sex offender management programs.—The Bureau of Prisons shall establish non-residential sex offender management programs to provide appropriate treatment, monitoring, and supervision of sex offenders and to provide aftercare during pre-release custody.

(B) Residential sex offender treatment programs.—The Bureau of Prisons shall establish residential sex offender treatment programs to provide treatment to sex offenders who volunteer for such programs and are deemed by the Bureau of Prisons to be in need of and suitable for residential treatment.

(2) Regions.—At least 1 sex offender management program under paragraph (1)(A), and at least one residential sex offender treatment program under paragraph (1)(B), shall be established in each region within the Bureau of Prisons.

(3) Authorization of appropriations.—There are authorized to be appropriated to the Bureau of Prisons for each fiscal year such sums as may be necessary to carry out this subsection.

(g) Continued Access to Medical Care.—

(1) In general.—In order to ensure a minimum standard of health and habitability, the Bureau of Prisons should ensure that each prisoner in a community confinement facility has access to necessary medical care, mental health care, and medicine through partnerships with local health service providers and transition planning.

(2) Definition.—In this subsection, the term "community confinement" has the meaning given that term in the application notes under section 5F1.1 of the Federal Sentencing Guidelines Manual, as in effect on the date of the enactment of the Second Chance Act of 2007.

(Added Pub. L. 98–473, title II, §212(a)(2), Oct. 12, 1984, 98 Stat. 2007; amended Pub. L. 101–647, title XXIX, §2903, Nov. 29, 1990, 104 Stat. 4913; Pub. L. 103–322, title II, §20401, title III, §32001, Sept. 13, 1994, 108 Stat. 1824, 1896; Pub. L. 109–162, title XI, §1146, Jan. 5, 2006, 119 Stat. 3112; Pub. L. 109–248, title VI, §622, July 27, 2006, 120 Stat. 634; Pub. L. 110–199, title II, §§231(f), 251(b), 252, Apr. 9, 2008, 122 Stat. 687, 693.)

References in Text

The date of the enactment of the Second Chance Act of 2007, referred to in subsec. (g)(2), is the date of enactment of Pub. L. 110–199, which was approved Apr. 9, 2008.

Prior Provisions

For a prior section 3621, applicable to offenses committed prior to Nov. 1, 1987, see note set out preceding section 3601 of this title.

Amendments

2008—Subsec. (b). Pub. L. 110–199, §251(b), inserted "Any order, recommendation, or request by a sentencing court that a convicted person serve a term of imprisonment in a community corrections facility shall have no binding effect on the authority of the Bureau under this section to determine or change the place of imprisonment of that person." at end of concluding provisions.

Subsec. (e)(5)(A). Pub. L. 110–199, §252, substituted "means a course of individual and group activities and treatment, lasting at least 6 months, in residential treatment facilities set apart from the general prison population (which may include the use of pharmocotherapies, where appropriate, that may extend beyond the 6-month period);" for "means a course of individual and group activities, lasting between 6 and 12 months, in residential treatment facilities set apart from the general prison population—

"(i) directed at the substance abuse problems of the prisoner;

"(ii) intended to develop the prisoner's cognitive, behavioral, social, vocational, and other skills so as to solve the prisoner's substance abuse and related problems; and

"(iii) which may include the use of pharmacoptherapies, if appropriate, that may extend beyond the treatment period;".

Subsec. (g). Pub. L. 110–199, §231(f), added subsec. (g).

2006—Subsec. (e)(4). Pub. L. 109–162, §1146(1), added par. (4) and struck out heading and text of former par. (4). Text read as follows: "There are authorized to be appropriated to carry out this subsection—

"(A) $13,500,000 for fiscal year 1996;

"(B) $18,900,000 for fiscal year 1997;

"(C) $25,200,000 for fiscal year 1998;

"(D) $27,000,000 for fiscal year 1999; and

"(E) $27,900,000 for fiscal year 2000."

Subsec. (e)(5)(A)(iii). Pub. L. 109–162, §1146(2), added cl. (iii).

Subsec. (f). Pub. L. 109–248 added subsec. (f).

1994—Subsec. (b). Pub. L. 103–322, §32001(1), struck out ", to the extent practicable," after "The Bureau shall" in concluding provisions.

Pub. L. 103–322, §20401, inserted "In designating the place of imprisonment or making transfers under this subsection, there shall be no favoritism given to prisoners of high social or economic status." after subsec. (b)(5).

Subsec. (e). Pub. L. 103–322, §32001(2), added subsec. (e).

1990—Subsec. (b). Pub. L. 101–647 inserted at end "The Bureau shall, to the extent practicable, make available appropriate substance abuse treatment for each prisoner the Bureau determines has a treatable condition of substance addiction or abuse."

Effective Date

Section effective Nov. 1, 1987, and applicable only to offenses committed after the taking effect of this section, see section 235(a)(1) of Pub. L. 98–473, set out as a note under section 3551 of this title.

Construction of 2008 Amendment

For construction of amendments by Pub. L. 110–199 and requirements for grants made under such amendments, see section 60504 of Title 34, Crime Control and Law Enforcement.

§3622. Temporary release of a prisoner

The Bureau of Prisons may release a prisoner from the place of his imprisonment for a limited period if such release appears to be consistent with the purpose for which the sentence was imposed and any pertinent policy statement issued by the Sentencing Commission pursuant to 28 U.S.C. 994(a)(2), if such release otherwise appears to be consistent with the public interest and if there is reasonable cause to believe that a prisoner will honor the trust to be imposed in him, by authorizing him, under prescribed conditions, to—

(a) visit a designated place for a period not to exceed thirty days, and then return to the same or another facility, for the purpose of—

(1) visiting a relative who is dying;

(2) attending a funeral of a relative;

(3) obtaining medical treatment not otherwise available;

(4) contacting a prospective employer;

(5) establishing or reestablishing family or community ties; or

(6) engaging in any other significant activity consistent with the public interest;

(b) participate in a training or educational program in the community while continuing in official detention at the prison facility; or

(c) work at paid employment in the community while continuing in official detention at the penal or correctional facility if—

(1) the rates of pay and other conditions of employment will not be less than those paid or provided for work of a similar nature in the community; and

(2) the prisoner agrees to pay to the Bureau such costs incident to official detention as the Bureau finds appropriate and reasonable under all the circumstances, such costs to be collected by the Bureau and deposited in the Treasury to the credit of the appropriation available for such costs at the time such collections are made.

(Added Pub. L. 98–473, title II, §212(a)(2), Oct. 12, 1984, 98 Stat. 2007.)

Prior Provisions

For a prior section 3622, applicable to offenses committed prior to Nov. 1, 1987, see note set out preceding section 3601 of this title.

Effective Date

Section effective Nov. 1, 1987, and applicable only to offenses committed after the taking effect of this section, see section 235(a)(1) of Pub. L. 98–473, set out as a note under section 3551 of this title.

Ex. Ord. No. 11755. Prison Labor

Ex. Ord. No. 11755, Dec. 29, 1973, 39 F.R. 779, as amended by Ex. Ord. No. 12608, Sept. 9, 1987, 52 F.R. 34617; Ex. Ord. No. 12943, Dec. 13, 1994, 59 F.R. 64553, provided:

The development of the occupational and educational skills of prison inmates is essential to their rehabilitation and to their ability to make an effective return to free society. Meaningful employment serves to develop those skills. It is also true, however, that care must be exercised to avoid either the exploitation of convict labor or any unfair competition between convict labor and free labor in the production of goods and services.

Under sections 3621 and 3622 of title 18, United States Code, the Bureau of Prisons is empowered to authorize Federal prisoners to work at paid employment in the community during their terms of imprisonment under conditions that protect against both the exploitation of convict labor and unfair competition with free labor.

Several states and other jurisdictions have similar laws or regulations under which individuals confined for violations of the laws of those places may be authorized to work at paid employment in the community.

Executive Order No. 325A, which was originally issued by President Theodore Roosevelt in 1905, prohibits the employment, in the performance of Federal contracts, of any person who is serving a sentence of imprisonment at hard labor imposed by a court of a State, territory, or municipality.

I have now determined that Executive Order No. 325A should be replaced with a new Executive Order which would permit the employment of non-Federal prison inmates in the performance of Federal contracts under terms and conditions that are comparable to those now applicable to inmates of Federal prisons.

NOW, THEREFORE, pursuant to the authority vested in me as President of the United States, it is hereby ordered as follows:

Section 1. (a) All contracts involving the use of appropriated funds which shall hereafter be entered into by any department or agency of the executive branch for performance in any State, the District of Columbia, the Commonwealth of Puerto Rico, the Virgin Islands, Guam, American Samoa, the Commonwealth of the Northern Mariana Islands, or the Trust Territory of the Pacific Islands shall, unless otherwise provided by law, contain a stipulation forbidding in the performance of such contracts, the employment of persons undergoing sentences of imprisonment which have been imposed by any court of a State, the District of Columbia, the Commonwealth of Puerto Rico, the Virgin Islands, Guam, American Samoa, the Commonwealth of the Northern Mariana Islands, or the Trust Territory of the Pacific Islands. This limitation, however, shall not prohibit the employment by a contractor in the performance of such contracts of persons on parole or probation to work at paid employment during the term of their sentence or persons who have been pardoned or who have served their terms. Nor shall it prohibit the employment by a contractor in the performance of such contracts of persons confined for violation of the laws of any of the States, the District of Columbia, the Commonwealth of Puerto Rico, the Virgin Islands, Guam, American Samoa, the Commonwealth of the Northern Mariana Islands, or the Trust Territory of the Pacific Islands who are authorized to work at paid employment in the community under the laws of such jurisdiction, if

(1)(A) The worker is paid or is in an approved work training program on a voluntary basis;
(B) Representatives of local union central bodies or similar labor union organizations have been consulted;
(C) Such paid employment will not result in the displacement of employed workers, or be applied in skills, crafts, or trades in which there is a surplus of available gainful labor in the locality, or impair existing contracts for services; and
(D) The rates of pay and other conditions of employment will not be less than those paid or provided for work of a similar nature in the locality in which the work is being performed; and
(2) The Attorney General has certified that the work-release laws or regulations of the jurisdiction involved are in conformity with the requirements of this order.
(b) After notice and opportunity for hearing, the Attorney General shall revoke any such certification under section 1(a)(2) if he finds that the work-release program of the jurisdiction involved is not being conducted in conformity with the requirements of this order or with its intent or purposes.
(c) The provisions of this order do not apply to purchases made under the micropurchase authority contained in section 32 of the Office of Federal Procurement Policy Act, as amended [now 41 U.S.C. 1902].
Sec. 2. The Federal Procurement Regulations, the Armed Services Procurement Regulations, and to the extent necessary, any supplemental or comparable regulations issued by any agency of the executive branch shall be revised to reflect the policy prescribed by this order.
Sec. 3. Executive Order No. 325A is hereby superseded.
Sec. 4. This order shall be effective as of January 1, 1974.

§3623. Transfer of a prisoner to State authority

The Director of the Bureau of Prisons shall order that a prisoner who has been charged in an indictment or information with, or convicted of, a State felony, be transferred to an official detention facility within such State prior to his release from a Federal prison facility if—
(1) the transfer has been requested by the Governor or other executive authority of the State;
(2) the State has presented to the Director a certified copy of the indictment, information, or judgment of conviction; and
(3) the Director finds that the transfer would be in the public interest.
If more than one request is presented with respect to a prisoner, the Director shall determine which request should receive preference. The expenses of such transfer shall be borne by the State requesting the transfer.
(Added Pub. L. 98–473, title II, §212(a)(2), Oct. 12, 1984, 98 Stat. 2008.)

Prior Provisions

For a prior section 3623, applicable to offenses committed prior to Nov. 1, 1987, see note set out preceding section 3601 of this title.

Effective Date

Section effective Nov. 1, 1987, and applicable only to offenses committed after the taking effect of this section, see section 235(a)(1) of Pub. L. 98–473, set out as a note under section 3551 of this title.

§3624. Release of a prisoner

(a) Date of Release.—A prisoner shall be released by the Bureau of Prisons on the date of the expiration of the prisoner's term of imprisonment, less any time credited toward the service of the prisoner's sentence as provided in subsection (b). If the date for a prisoner's release falls on a Saturday, a Sunday, or a legal holiday at the place of confinement, the prisoner may be released by the Bureau on the last preceding weekday.

(b) Credit Toward Service of Sentence for Satisfactory Behavior.—(1) Subject to paragraph (2), a prisoner who is serving a term of imprisonment of more than 1 year 1 other than a term of imprisonment for the duration of the prisoner's life, may receive credit toward the service of the prisoner's sentence, beyond the time served, of up to 54 days at the end of each year of the prisoner's term of imprisonment, beginning at the end of the first year of the term, subject to determination by the Bureau of Prisons that, during that year, the prisoner has displayed exemplary compliance with institutional disciplinary regulations. Subject to paragraph (2), if the Bureau determines that, during that year, the prisoner has not satisfactorily complied with such institutional regulations, the prisoner shall receive no such credit toward service of the prisoner's sentence or shall receive such lesser credit as the Bureau determines to be appropriate. In awarding credit under this section, the Bureau shall consider whether the prisoner, during the relevant period, has earned, or is making satisfactory progress toward earning, a high school diploma or an equivalent degree. Credit that has not been earned may not later be granted. Subject to paragraph (2), credit for the last year or portion of a year of the term of imprisonment shall be prorated and credited within the last six weeks of the sentence.

(2) Notwithstanding any other law, credit awarded under this subsection after the date of enactment of the Prison Litigation Reform Act shall vest on the date the prisoner is released from custody.

(3) The Attorney General shall ensure that the Bureau of Prisons has in effect an optional General Educational Development program for inmates who have not earned a high school diploma or its equivalent.

(4) Exemptions to the General Educational Development requirement may be made as deemed appropriate by the Director of the Federal Bureau of Prisons.

(c) Prerelease Custody.—

(1) In general.—The Director of the Bureau of Prisons shall, to the extent practicable, ensure that a prisoner serving a term of imprisonment spends a portion of the final months of that term (not to exceed 12 months), under conditions that will afford that prisoner a reasonable opportunity to adjust to and prepare for the reentry of that prisoner into the community. Such conditions may include a community correctional facility.

(2) Home confinement authority.—The authority under this subsection may be used to place a prisoner in home confinement for the shorter of 10 percent of the term of imprisonment of that prisoner or 6 months.

(3) Assistance.—The United States Probation System shall, to the extent practicable, offer assistance to a prisoner during prerelease custody under this subsection.

(4) No limitations.—Nothing in this subsection shall be construed to limit or restrict the authority of the Director of the Bureau of Prisons under section 3621.

(5) Reporting.—Not later than 1 year after the date of the enactment of the Second Chance Act of 2007 (and every year thereafter), the Director of the Bureau of Prisons shall transmit to the Committee on the Judiciary of the Senate and the Committee on the Judiciary of the House of Representatives a report describing the Bureau's utilization of community corrections facilities. Each report under this paragraph shall set forth the number and percentage of Federal prisoners placed in community corrections facilities during the preceding year, the average length of such placements, trends in such utilization, the reasons some prisoners are not placed in community corrections facilities, and any other information that may be useful to the committees in determining if the Bureau is utilizing community corrections facilities in an effective manner.

(6) Issuance of regulations.—The Director of the Bureau of Prisons shall issue regulations pursuant to this subsection not later than 90 days after the date of the enactment of the Second Chance Act of 2007, which shall ensure that placement in a community correctional facility by the Bureau of Prisons is—

(A) conducted in a manner consistent with section 3621(b) of this title;

(B) determined on an individual basis; and

(C) of sufficient duration to provide the greatest likelihood of successful reintegration into the community.

(d) Allotment of Clothing, Funds, and Transportation.—Upon the release of a prisoner on the expiration of the prisoner's term of imprisonment, the Bureau of Prisons shall furnish the prisoner with—

(1) suitable clothing;

(2) an amount of money, not more than $500, determined by the Director to be consistent with the needs of the offender and the public interest, unless the Director determines that the financial position of the offender is such that no sum should be furnished; and

(3) transportation to the place of the prisoner's conviction, to the prisoner's bona fide residence within the United States, or to such other place within the United States as may be authorized by the Director.

(e) Supervision After Release.—A prisoner whose sentence includes a term of supervised release after imprisonment shall be released by the Bureau of Prisons to the supervision of a probation officer who shall, during the term imposed, supervise the person released to the degree warranted by the conditions specified by the sentencing court. The term of supervised release commences on the day the person is released from imprisonment and runs concurrently with any Federal, State, or local term of probation or supervised release or parole for another offense to which the person is subject or becomes subject during the term of supervised release. A term of supervised release does not run during any period in which the person is imprisoned in connection with a conviction for a Federal, State, or local crime unless the imprisonment is for a period of less than 30 consecutive days. Upon the release of a prisoner by the Bureau of Prisons to supervised release, the Bureau of Prisons shall notify such prisoner, verbally and in writing, of the requirement that the prisoner adhere to an installment schedule, not to exceed 2 years except in special circumstances, to pay for any fine imposed for the offense committed by such prisoner, and of the consequences of failure to pay such fines under sections 3611 through 3614 of this title.

(f) Mandatory Functional Literacy Requirement.—

(1) The Attorney General shall direct the Bureau of Prisons to have in effect a mandatory functional literacy program for all mentally capable inmates who are not functionally literate in each Federal correctional institution within 6 months from the date of the enactment of this Act.

(2) Each mandatory functional literacy program shall include a requirement that each inmate participate in such program for a mandatory period sufficient to provide the inmate with an adequate opportunity to achieve functional literacy, and appropriate incentives which lead to successful completion of such programs shall be developed and implemented.

(3) As used in this section, the term "functional literacy" means—

(A) an eighth grade equivalence in reading and mathematics on a nationally recognized standardized test;

(B) functional competency or literacy on a nationally recognized criterion-referenced test; or

(C) a combination of subparagraphs (A) and (B).

(4) Non-English speaking inmates shall be required to participate in an English-As-A-Second-Language program until they function at the equivalence of the eighth grade on a nationally recognized educational achievement test.

(5) The Chief Executive Officer of each institution shall have authority to grant waivers for good cause as determined and documented on an individual basis.

(Added Pub. L. 98–473, title II, §212(a)(2), Oct. 12, 1984, 98 Stat. 2008; amended Pub. L. 99–646, §§16(a), 17(a), Nov. 10, 1986, 100 Stat. 3595; Pub. L. 101–647, title XXIX, §§2902(a), 2904, Nov. 29, 1990, 104 Stat. 4913; Pub. L. 103–322, title II, §§20405, 20412, Sept. 13, 1994, 108 Stat. 1825, 1828; Pub. L. 104–66, title I, §1091(c), Dec. 21, 1995, 109 Stat. 722; Pub. L. 104–134, title I, §101[(a)] [title VIII, §809(c)], Apr. 26, 1996, 110 Stat. 1321, 1321–76; renumbered title I, Pub. L. 104–140, §1(a), May 2, 1996, 110 Stat. 1327; Pub. L. 110–177, title V, §505, Jan. 7, 2008, 121 Stat. 2542; Pub. L. 110–199, title II, §251(a), Apr. 9, 2008, 122 Stat. 692.)

References in Text

The date of enactment of the Prison Litigation Reform Act, referred to in subsec. (b)(2), probably means the date of enactment of the Prison Litigation Reform Act of 1995, section 101[(a)] [title VIII] of Pub. L. 104–134, which was approved Apr. 26, 1996.

The date of the enactment of the Second Chance Act of 2007, referred to in subsec. (c)(5), (6), is the date of enactment of Pub. L. 110–199, which was approved Apr. 9, 2008.

The date of the enactment of this Act, referred to in subsec. (f)(1), probably means the date of enactment of Pub. L. 101–647, which enacted subsec. (f) and was approved Nov. 29, 1990.

Prior Provisions

For a prior section 3624, applicable to offenses committed prior to Nov. 1, 1987, see note set out preceding section 3601 of this title.

Amendments

2008—Subsec. (c). Pub. L. 110–199 amended subsec. (c) generally. Prior to amendment, text read as follows: "The Bureau of Prisons shall, to the extent practicable, assure that a prisoner serving a term of imprisonment spends a reasonable part, not to exceed six months, of the last 10 per centum of the term to be served under conditions that will afford the prisoner a reasonable opportunity to adjust to and prepare for the prisoner's re-entry into the community. The authority provided by this subsection may be used to place a prisoner in home confinement. The United States Probation System shall, to the extent practicable, offer assistance to a prisoner during such pre-release custody."

Subsec. (e). Pub. L. 110–177 substituted "Upon the release of a prisoner by the Bureau of Prisons to supervised release, the Bureau of Prisons shall notify such prisoner, verbally and in writing, of the requirement that the prisoner adhere to an installment schedule, not to exceed 2 years except in special circumstances, to pay for any fine imposed for the offense committed by such prisoner, and of the consequences of failure to pay such fines under sections 3611 through 3614 of this title." for "No prisoner shall be released on supervision unless such prisoner agrees to adhere to an installment schedule, not to exceed two years except in special circumstances, to pay for any fine imposed for the offense committed by such prisoner."

1996—Subsec. (b)(1). Pub. L. 104–134, §101[(a)] [title VIII, §809(c)(1)(A)], struck out at beginning "A prisoner (other than a prisoner serving a sentence for a crime of violence) who is serving a term of imprisonment of more than one year, other than a term of imprisonment for the duration of the prisoner's life, shall receive credit toward the service of the prisoner's sentence, beyond the time served, of fifty-four days at the end of each year of the prisoner's term of imprisonment, beginning at the end of the first year of the term, unless the Bureau of Prisons determines that, during that year, the prisoner has not satisfactorily complied with such institutional disciplinary regulations as have been approved by the Attorney General and issued to the prisoner."

Pub. L. 104–134, §101[(a)] [title VIII, §809(c)(1)(B)], in second sentence substituted "Subject to paragraph (2), a prisoner" for "A prisoner", struck out "for a crime of violence," after "1 year", and struck out "such" after "compliance with".

Pub. L. 104–134, §101[(a)] [title VIII, §809(c)(1)(C)], in third sentence substituted "Subject to paragraph (2), if the Bureau" for "If the Bureau".

Pub. L. 104–134, §101[(a)] [title VIII, §809(c)(1)(D)], in fourth sentence substituted "In awarding credit under this section, the Bureau shall consider whether the prisoner, during the relevant period, has earned, or is making satisfactory progress toward earning, a high school diploma or an equivalent degree." for "The Bureau's determination shall be made within fifteen days after the end of each year of the sentence."

Pub. L. 104–134, §101[(a)] [title VIII, §809(c)(1)(E)], in sixth sentence substituted "Subject to paragraph (2), credit for the last" for "Credit for the last".

Subsec. (b)(2). Pub. L. 104–134, §101[(a)] [title VIII, §809(c)(2)], amended par. (2) generally.

Prior to amendment, par. (2) read as follows: "Credit toward a prisoner's service of sentence shall not be vested unless the prisoner has earned or is making satisfactory progress toward a high school diploma or an equivalent degree."

1995—Subsec. (f)(6). Pub. L. 104–66 struck out par. (6) which read as follows: "A report shall be provided to Congress on an annual basis summarizing the results of this program, including the number of inmate participants, the number successfully completing the program, the number who do not successfully complete the program, and the reasons for failure to successfully complete the program."

1994—Subsec. (a). Pub. L. 103–322, §20405(2), substituted "the prisoner's" for "his" after "the expiration of" and "toward the service of".

Subsec. (b). Pub. L. 103–322, §20412(1), (2), designated existing provisions as par. (1), substituted "Credit that has not been earned may not later be granted." for "Such credit toward service of sentence vests at the time that it is received. Credit that has vested may not later be withdrawn, and credit that has not been earned may not later be granted.", and added pars. (2) to (4).

Pub. L. 103–322, §20405, inserted "(other than a prisoner serving a sentence for a crime of violence)" after "A prisoner" in first sentence, substituted "the prisoner" for "he" before "has not satisfactorily complied with" in first sentence and before "shall receive no such credit toward" in third sentence and "the prisoner's" for "his" wherever appearing in first and third sentences, and inserted after first sentence "A prisoner who is serving a term of imprisonment of more than 1 year for a crime of violence, other than a term of imprisonment for the duration of the prisoner's life, may receive credit toward the service of the prisoner's sentence, beyond the time served, of up to 54 days at the end of each year of the prisoner's term of imprisonment, beginning at the end of the first year of the term, subject to determination by the Bureau of Prisons that, during that year, the prisoner has displayed exemplary compliance with such institutional disciplinary regulations."

Subsec. (c). Pub. L. 103–322, §20405(2), substituted "the prisoner's re-entry" for "his re-entry".

Subsec. (d). Pub. L. 103–322, §20405(2), (3), substituted "the prisoner" for "him" in introductory provisions and "the prisoner's" for "his" wherever appearing in introductory provisions and par. (3).

1990—Subsec. (c). Pub. L. 101–647, §2902(a), inserted after first sentence "The authority provided by this subsection may be used to place a prisoner in home confinement."

Subsec. (f). Pub. L. 101–647, §2904, added subsec. (f).

1986—Subsec. (b). Pub. L. 99–646, §16(a), substituted "beginning at the end of" for "beginning after".

Subsec. (e). Pub. L. 99–646, §17(a), substituted "imprisonment and runs concurrently" for "imprisonment. The term runs concurrently" and "supervised released. A term of supervised release does not run" for "supervised release, except that it does not run", struck out ", other than during limited intervals as a condition of probation or supervised release," after "person is imprisoned", and inserted "unless the imprisonment is for a period of less than 30 consecutive days" before the period at end of third sentence.

Effective Date of 1990 Amendment

Pub. L. 101–647, title XXIX, §2902(b), Nov. 29, 1990, 104 Stat. 4913, provided that: "Section 3624(c) of title 18, United States Code, as amended by this section, shall apply with respect to all inmates, regardless of the date of their offense."

Effective Date of 1986 Amendment

Pub. L. 99–646, §16(b), Nov. 10, 1986, 100 Stat. 3595, provided that: "The amendment made by this section [amending this section] shall take effect on the date of the taking effect of such section 3624 [Nov. 1, 1987]."

Pub. L. 99–646, §17(b), Nov. 10, 1986, 100 Stat. 3595, provided that: "The amendment made by this section [amending this section] shall take effect on the date of the taking effect of such section

3624 [Nov. 1, 1987]."

Effective Date
Section effective Nov. 1, 1987, and applicable only to offenses committed after the taking effect of this section, see section 235(a)(1) of Pub. L. 98–473, set out as a note under section 3551 of this title.

Construction of 2008 Amendment
For construction of amendments by Pub. L. 110–199 and requirements for grants made under such amendments, see section 60504 of Title 34, Crime Control and Law Enforcement.

§3625. Inapplicability of the Administrative Procedure Act
The provisions of sections 554 and 555 and 701 through 706 of title 5, United States Code, do not apply to the making of any determination, decision, or order under this subchapter.
(Added Pub. L. 98–473, title II, §212(a)(2), Oct. 12, 1984, 98 Stat. 2010.)

Effective Date
Section effective Nov. 1, 1987, and applicable only to offenses committed after the taking effect of this section, see section 235(a)(1) of Pub. L. 98–473, set out as a note under section 3551 of this title.

§3626. Appropriate remedies with respect to prison conditions
(a) Requirements for Relief.—
(1) Prospective relief.—(A) Prospective relief in any civil action with respect to prison conditions shall extend no further than necessary to correct the violation of the Federal right of a particular plaintiff or plaintiffs. The court shall not grant or approve any prospective relief unless the court finds that such relief is narrowly drawn, extends no further than necessary to correct the violation of the Federal right, and is the least intrusive means necessary to correct the violation of the Federal right. The court shall give substantial weight to any adverse impact on public safety or the operation of a criminal justice system caused by the relief.
(B) The court shall not order any prospective relief that requires or permits a government official to exceed his or her authority under State or local law or otherwise violates State or local law, unless—
(i) Federal law requires such relief to be ordered in violation of State or local law;
(ii) the relief is necessary to correct the violation of a Federal right; and
(iii) no other relief will correct the violation of the Federal right.
(C) Nothing in this section shall be construed to authorize the courts, in exercising their remedial powers, to order the construction of prisons or the raising of taxes, or to repeal or detract from otherwise applicable limitations on the remedial powers of the courts.
(2) Preliminary injunctive relief.—In any civil action with respect to prison conditions, to the extent otherwise authorized by law, the court may enter a temporary restraining order or an order for preliminary injunctive relief. Preliminary injunctive relief must be narrowly drawn, extend no further than necessary to correct the harm the court finds requires preliminary relief, and be the least intrusive means necessary to correct that harm. The court shall give substantial weight to any adverse impact on public safety or the operation of a criminal justice system caused by the preliminary relief and shall respect the principles of comity set out in paragraph (1)(B) in tailoring any preliminary relief. Preliminary injunctive relief shall automatically expire on the date that is 90 days after its entry, unless the court makes the findings required under subsection (a)(1) for the entry of prospective relief and makes the order final before the expiration of the 90-day period.
(3) Prisoner release order.—(A) In any civil action with respect to prison conditions, no court shall enter a prisoner release order unless—
(i) a court has previously entered an order for less intrusive relief that has failed to remedy the

deprivation of the Federal right sought to be remedied through the prisoner release order; and (ii) the defendant has had a reasonable amount of time to comply with the previous court orders.

(B) In any civil action in Federal court with respect to prison conditions, a prisoner release order shall be entered only by a three-judge court in accordance with section 2284 of title 28, if the requirements of subparagraph (E) have been met.

(C) A party seeking a prisoner release order in Federal court shall file with any request for such relief, a request for a three-judge court and materials sufficient to demonstrate that the requirements of subparagraph (A) have been met.

(D) If the requirements under subparagraph (A) have been met, a Federal judge before whom a civil action with respect to prison conditions is pending who believes that a prison release order should be considered may sua sponte request the convening of a three-judge court to determine whether a prisoner release order should be entered.

(E) The three-judge court shall enter a prisoner release order only if the court finds by clear and convincing evidence that—

(i) crowding is the primary cause of the violation of a Federal right; and

(ii) no other relief will remedy the violation of the Federal right.

(F) Any State or local official including a legislator or unit of government whose jurisdiction or function includes the appropriation of funds for the construction, operation, or maintenance of prison facilities, or the prosecution or custody of persons who may be released from, or not admitted to, a prison as a result of a prisoner release order shall have standing to oppose the imposition or continuation in effect of such relief and to seek termination of such relief, and shall have the right to intervene in any proceeding relating to such relief.

(b) Termination of Relief.—

(1) Termination of prospective relief.—(A) In any civil action with respect to prison conditions in which prospective relief is ordered, such relief shall be terminable upon the motion of any party or intervener—

(i) 2 years after the date the court granted or approved the prospective relief;

(ii) 1 year after the date the court has entered an order denying termination of prospective relief under this paragraph; or

(iii) in the case of an order issued on or before the date of enactment of the Prison Litigation Reform Act, 2 years after such date of enactment.

(B) Nothing in this section shall prevent the parties from agreeing to terminate or modify relief before the relief is terminated under subparagraph (A).

(2) Immediate termination of prospective relief.—In any civil action with respect to prison conditions, a defendant or intervener shall be entitled to the immediate termination of any prospective relief if the relief was approved or granted in the absence of a finding by the court that the relief is narrowly drawn, extends no further than necessary to correct the violation of the Federal right, and is the least intrusive means necessary to correct the violation of the Federal right.

(3) Limitation.—Prospective relief shall not terminate if the court makes written findings based on the record that prospective relief remains necessary to correct a current and ongoing violation of the Federal right, extends no further than necessary to correct the violation of the Federal right, and that the prospective relief is narrowly drawn and the least intrusive means to correct the violation.

(4) Termination or modification of relief.—Nothing in this section shall prevent any party or intervener from seeking modification or termination before the relief is terminable under paragraph (1) or (2), to the extent that modification or termination would otherwise be legally permissible.

(c) Settlements.—

(1) Consent decrees.—In any civil action with respect to prison conditions, the court shall not enter or approve a consent decree unless it complies with the limitations on relief set forth in subsection (a).

(2) Private settlement agreements.—(A) Nothing in this section shall preclude parties from

entering into a private settlement agreement that does not comply with the limitations on relief set forth in subsection (a), if the terms of that agreement are not subject to court enforcement other than the reinstatement of the civil proceeding that the agreement settled.

(B) Nothing in this section shall preclude any party claiming that a private settlement agreement has been breached from seeking in State court any remedy available under State law.

(d) State Law Remedies.—The limitations on remedies in this section shall not apply to relief entered by a State court based solely upon claims arising under State law.

(e) Procedure for Motions Affecting Prospective Relief.—

(1) Generally.—The court shall promptly rule on any motion to modify or terminate prospective relief in a civil action with respect to prison conditions. Mandamus shall lie to remedy any failure to issue a prompt ruling on such a motion.

(2) Automatic stay.—Any motion to modify or terminate prospective relief made under subsection (b) shall operate as a stay during the period—

(A)(i) beginning on the 30th day after such motion is filed, in the case of a motion made under paragraph (1) or (2) of subsection (b); or

(ii) beginning on the 180th day after such motion is filed, in the case of a motion made under any other law; and

(B) ending on the date the court enters a final order ruling on the motion.

(3) Postponement of automatic stay.—The court may postpone the effective date of an automatic stay specified in subsection (e)(2)(A) for not more than 60 days for good cause. No postponement shall be permissible because of general congestion of the court's calendar.

(4) Order blocking the automatic stay.—Any order staying, suspending, delaying, or barring the operation of the automatic stay described in paragraph (2) (other than an order to postpone the effective date of the automatic stay under paragraph (3)) shall be treated as an order refusing to dissolve or modify an injunction and shall be appealable pursuant to section 1292(a)(1) of title 28, United States Code, regardless of how the order is styled or whether the order is termed a preliminary or a final ruling.

(f) Special Masters.—

(1) In general.—(A) In any civil action in a Federal court with respect to prison conditions, the court may appoint a special master who shall be disinterested and objective and who will give due regard to the public safety, to conduct hearings on the record and prepare proposed findings of fact.

(B) The court shall appoint a special master under this subsection during the remedial phase of the action only upon a finding that the remedial phase will be sufficiently complex to warrant the appointment.

(2) Appointment.—(A) If the court determines that the appointment of a special master is necessary, the court shall request that the defendant institution and the plaintiff each submit a list of not more than 5 persons to serve as a special master.

(B) Each party shall have the opportunity to remove up to 3 persons from the opposing party's list.

(C) The court shall select the master from the persons remaining on the list after the operation of subparagraph (B).

(3) Interlocutory appeal.—Any party shall have the right to an interlocutory appeal of the judge's selection of the special master under this subsection, on the ground of partiality.

(4) Compensation.—The compensation to be allowed to a special master under this section shall be based on an hourly rate not greater than the hourly rate established under section 3006A for payment of court-appointed counsel, plus costs reasonably incurred by the special master. Such compensation and costs shall be paid with funds appropriated to the Judiciary.

(5) Regular review of appointment.—In any civil action with respect to prison conditions in which a special master is appointed under this subsection, the court shall review the appointment of the special master every 6 months to determine whether the services of the special master continue to be required under paragraph (1). In no event shall the appointment of a special master extend beyond the termination of the relief.

(6) Limitations on powers and duties.—A special master appointed under this subsection—

(A) may be authorized by a court to conduct hearings and prepare proposed findings of fact, which shall be made on the record;

(B) shall not make any findings or communications ex parte;

(C) may be authorized by a court to assist in the development of remedial plans; and

(D) may be removed at any time, but shall be relieved of the appointment upon the termination of relief.

(g) Definitions.—As used in this section—

(1) the term "consent decree" means any relief entered by the court that is based in whole or in part upon the consent or acquiescence of the parties but does not include private settlements;

(2) the term "civil action with respect to prison conditions" means any civil proceeding arising under Federal law with respect to the conditions of confinement or the effects of actions by government officials on the lives of persons confined in prison, but does not include habeas corpus proceedings challenging the fact or duration of confinement in prison;

(3) the term "prisoner" means any person subject to incarceration, detention, or admission to any facility who is accused of, convicted of, sentenced for, or adjudicated delinquent for, violations of criminal law or the terms and conditions of parole, probation, pretrial release, or diversionary program;

(4) the term "prisoner release order" includes any order, including a temporary restraining order or preliminary injunctive relief, that has the purpose or effect of reducing or limiting the prison population, or that directs the release from or nonadmission of prisoners to a prison;

(5) the term "prison" means any Federal, State, or local facility that incarcerates or detains juveniles or adults accused of, convicted of, sentenced for, or adjudicated delinquent for, violations of criminal law;

(6) the term "private settlement agreement" means an agreement entered into among the parties that is not subject to judicial enforcement other than the reinstatement of the civil proceeding that the agreement settled;

(7) the term "prospective relief" means all relief other than compensatory monetary damages;

(8) the term "special master" means any person appointed by a Federal court pursuant to Rule 53 of the Federal Rules of Civil Procedure or pursuant to any inherent power of the court to exercise the powers of a master, regardless of the title or description given by the court; and

(9) the term "relief" means all relief in any form that may be granted or approved by the court, and includes consent decrees but does not include private settlement agreements.

(Added Pub. L. 103–322, title II, §20409(a), Sept. 13, 1994, 108 Stat. 1827; amended Pub. L. 104–134, title I, §101[(a)] [title VIII, §802(a)], Apr. 26, 1996, 110 Stat. 1321, 1321–66; renumbered title I, Pub. L. 104–140, §1(a), May 2, 1996, 110 Stat. 1327; Pub. L. 105–119, title I, §123(a), Nov. 26, 1997, 111 Stat. 2470.)

References in Text

The date of enactment of the Prison Litigation Reform Act, referred to in subsec. (b)(1)(A)(iii), probably means the date of enactment of the Prison Litigation Reform Act of 1995, section 101[(a)] [title VIII] of Pub. L. 104–134, which was approved Apr. 26, 1996.

The Federal Rules of Civil Procedure, referred to in subsec. (g)(8), are set out in the Appendix to Title 28, Judiciary and Judicial Procedure.

Amendments

1997—Subsec. (a)(1)(B)(i). Pub. L. 105–119, §123(a)(1)(A), substituted "requires" for "permits".

Subsec. (a)(3)(A). Pub. L. 105–119, §123(a)(1)(B)(i), substituted "no court shall enter a prisoner release order unless" for "no prisoner release order shall be entered unless".

Subsec. (a)(3)(F). Pub. L. 105–119, §123(a)(1)(B)(ii), inserted "including a legislator" after "local official" and substituted "prison facilities" for "program facilities".

Subsec. (b)(3). Pub. L. 105–119, §123(a)(2), substituted "current and ongoing" for "current or ongoing".

Subsec. (e)(1). Pub. L. 105–119, §123(a)(3)(A), inserted at end "Mandamus shall lie to remedy any failure to issue a prompt ruling on such a motion."

Subsec. (e)(2). Pub. L. 105–119, §123(a)(3)(B), substituted "Any motion to modify or terminate prospective relief made under subsection (b) shall operate as a stay" for "Any prospective relief subject to a pending motion shall be automatically stayed".

Subsec. (e)(3), (4). Pub. L. 105–119, §123(a)(3)(C), added pars. (3) and (4).

1996—Pub. L. 104–134 amended section generally, substituting provisions relating to appropriate remedies with respect to prison conditions for former provisions relating to appropriate remedies with respect to prison crowding.

Effective Date of 1997 Amendment

Pub. L. 105–119, title I, §123(b), Nov. 26, 1997, 111 Stat. 2471, provided that: "The amendments made by this Act [probably should be "section", amending this section] shall take effect upon the date of the enactment of this Act [Nov. 26, 1997] and shall apply to pending cases."

Effective Date of 1996 Amendment

Pub. L. 104–134, title I, §101[(a)] [title VIII, §802(b)(1)], Apr. 26, 1996, 110 Stat. 1321, 1321–70, provided that: "Section 3626 of title 18, United States Code, as amended by this section, shall apply with respect to all prospective relief whether such relief was originally granted or approved before, on, or after the date of the enactment of this title [Apr. 26, 1996]."

Effective and Termination Dates

Pub. L. 103–322, title II, §20409(b), Sept. 13, 1994, 108 Stat. 1828, which provided that this section applied to all court orders outstanding on Sept. 13, 1994, and Pub. L. 103–322, title II, §20409(d), Sept. 13, 1994, 108 Stat. 1828, which provided for the repeal of this section 5 years after Sept. 13, 1994, were repealed by Pub. L. 104–134, title I, §101[(a)] [title VIII, §802(b)(2)], Apr. 26, 1996, 110 Stat. 1321, 1321–70; renumbered title I, Pub. L. 104–140, §1(a), May 2, 1996, 110 Stat. 1327.

Severability

Pub. L. 104–134, title I, §101[(a)] [title VIII, §810], Apr. 26, 1996, 110 Stat. 1321, 1321–77, provided that: "If any provision of this title [see Short Title of 1996 Amendment note set out under section 3601 of this title], an amendment made by this title, or the application of such provision or amendment to any person or circumstance is held to be unconstitutional, the remainder of this title, the amendments made by this title, and the application of the provisions of such to any person or circumstance shall not be affected thereby."

Special Masters Appointed Prior to April 26, 1996; Prohibition on Use of Funds

Pub. L. 104–208, div. A, title I, §101(a) [title III, §306], Sept. 30, 1996, 110 Stat. 3009, 3009–45, provided that: "None of the funds available to the Judiciary in fiscal years 1996 and 1997 and hereafter shall be available for expenses authorized pursuant to section 802(a) of title VIII of section 101(a) of title I of the Omnibus Consolidated Rescissions and Appropriations Act of 1996, Public Law 104–134 [amending this section], for costs related to the appointment of Special Masters prior to April 26, 1996."

Payment of Damage Award in Satisfaction of Pending Restitution Orders

Pub. L. 104–134, title I, §101[(a)] [title VIII, §807], Apr. 26, 1996, 110 Stat. 1321, 1321–75, provided that: "Any compensatory damages awarded to a prisoner in connection with a civil action brought against any Federal, State, or local jail, prison, or correctional facility or against any official or agent of such jail, prison, or correctional facility, shall be paid directly to satisfy any outstanding restitution orders pending against the prisoner. The remainder of any such award after full payment of all pending restitution orders shall be forwarded to the prisoner."

Notice to Crime Victims of Pending Damage Award

Pub. L. 104–134, title I, §101[(a)] [title VIII, §808], Apr. 26, 1996, 110 Stat. 1321, 1321–76, provided that: "Prior to payment of any compensatory damages awarded to a prisoner in connection with a civil action brought against any Federal, State, or local jail, prison, or correctional facility or against any official or agent of such jail, prison, or correctional facility, reasonable efforts shall be made to notify the victims of the crime for which the prisoner was convicted and incarcerated concerning the pending payment of any such compensatory damages."

[CHAPTER 231 - REPEALED]

[§§3651 to 3656. Repealed or Renumbered. Pub. L. 98–473, title II, §212(a)(1), (2), Oct. 12, 1984, 98 Stat. 1987]

Section 3651, acts June 25, 1948, ch. 645, 62 Stat. 842; June 20, 1958, Pub. L. 85–463, §1, 72 Stat. 216; Aug. 23, 1958, Pub. L. 85–741, 72 Stat. 834; Oct. 22, 1970, Pub. L. 91–492, §1, 84 Stat. 1090; May 11, 1972, Pub. L. 92–293, §1, 86 Stat. 136; Oct. 27, 1978, Pub. L. 95–537, §2, 92 Stat. 2038; Oct. 12, 1984, Pub. L. 98–473, title II, §§235(a)(1), 238(b), (c), (i), 98 Stat. 2031, 2038, 2039; Oct. 30, 1984, Pub. L. 98–596, §§4, 12(a)(2), (3), (9), (b), 98 Stat. 3136, 3139, 3140, related to suspension of sentence and probation.

Section 3652, act June 25, 1948, ch. 645, 62 Stat. 842, related to probation—(Rule).

Section 3653, acts June 25, 1948, ch. 645, 62 Stat. 842; May 24, 1949, ch. 139, §56, 63 Stat. 96, related to report of probation officer and arrest of probationer.

Section 3654, acts June 25, 1948, ch. 645, 62 Stat. 843; Aug. 2, 1949, ch. 383, §2, 63 Stat. 491, related to appointment and removal of probation officers.

Section 3655, acts June 25, 1948, ch. 645, 62 Stat. 843; Mar. 15, 1976, Pub. L. 94–233, §14, 90 Stat. 233; Oct. 12, 1984, Pub. L. 98–473, title II, §§235(a)(1), 238(d), (i), 98 Stat. 2031, 2038, 2039; Oct. 30, 1984, Pub. L. 98–596, §§5, 12(a)(4), (9), (b), 98 Stat. 3136, 3139, 3140, related to duties of probation officers.

Section 3656 renumbered section 3672 of this title.

Effective Date of Repeal

Repeal effective Nov. 1, 1987, and applicable only to offenses committed after the taking effect of such repeal, see section 235(a)(1) of Pub. L. 98–473, set out as an Effective Date note under section 3551 of this title.

CHAPTER 232 - MISCELLANEOUS SENTENCING PROVISIONS

Amendments

1996—Pub. L. 104–132, title II, §§204(b), 206(b), Apr. 24, 1996, 110 Stat. 1229, 1236, added item 3663A and substituted "issuance and enforcement of order of restitution" for "issuing order of restitution" in item 3664.

1990—Pub. L. 101–647, title XXXV, §3594, Nov. 29, 1990, 104 Stat. 4931, substituted "Conveyances" for "Conveyance" in item 3669.

1984—Pub. L. 98–473, title II, §§212(a)(5), 235(a)(1), Oct. 12, 1984, 98 Stat. 2010, 2031, as amended, added chapter heading and analysis of sections for chapter 232 consisting of items 3661 to 3673, effective Nov. 1, 1987.

Effective Date

Pub. L. 98–473, title II, §§212(a)(1), (3)–(5), 235(a)(1), Oct. 12, 1984, 98 Stat. 1987, 2010, 2031, as amended, enacted heading, analysis, and section 3673 of this chapter (§§3661 to 3673), provided that sections 3577, 3578, 3579, 3580, 3611, 3612, 3615, 3617, 3618, 3619, 3620, and 3656 of this title are renumbered as sections 3661, 3662, 3663, 3664, 3665, 3666, 3667, 3668, 3669, 3670, 3671, and 3672, respectively, of this chapter, and amended section 3663 of this chapter, effective Nov. 1, 1987, and applicable only to offenses committed after the taking effect of this chapter. Section 235 of Pub. L. 98–473, as amended, relating to effective dates, is set out as a note under section 3551 of this title.

§3661. Use of information for sentencing

No limitation shall be placed on the information concerning the background, character, and conduct of a person convicted of an offense which a court of the United States may receive and consider for the purpose of imposing an appropriate sentence.

(Added Pub. L. 91–452, title X, §1001(a), Oct. 15, 1970, 84 Stat. 951, §3577; renumbered §3661, Pub. L. 98–473, title II, §212(a)(1), Oct. 12, 1984, 98 Stat. 1987.)

Short Title of 1990 Amendment

Pub. L. 101–421, §1, Oct. 12, 1990, 104 Stat. 909, provided that: "This Act [amending provisions set out as a note under section 3672 of this title] may be cited as the 'Drug and Alcohol Dependent Offenders Treatment Act of 1989'."

Short Title of 1986 Amendment

Pub. L. 99–570, title I, §1861(a), Oct. 27, 1986, 100 Stat. 3207–53, provided that: "This section [amending sections 3672 and 4255 of this title, enacting provisions set out as a note under section 3672 of this title, and amending provisions set out as a note under section 4255 of this title] may be cited as the 'Drug and Alcohol Dependent Offenders Treatment Act of 1986'."

§3662. Conviction records

(a) The Attorney General of the United States is authorized to establish in the Department of Justice a repository for records of convictions and determinations of the validity of such convictions.

(b) Upon the conviction thereafter of a defendant in a court of the United States, the District of

Columbia, the Commonwealth of Puerto Rico, a territory or possession of the United States, any political subdivision, or any department, agency, or instrumentality thereof for an offense punishable in such court by death or imprisonment in excess of one year, or a judicial determination of the validity of such conviction on collateral review, the court shall cause a certified record of the conviction or determination to be made to the repository in such form and containing such information as the Attorney General of the United States shall by regulation prescribe.

(c) Records maintained in the repository shall not be public records. Certified copies thereof—

(1) may be furnished for law enforcement purposes on request of a court or law enforcement or corrections officer of the United States, the District of Columbia, the Commonwealth of Puerto Rico, a territory or possession of the United States, any political subdivision, or any department, agency, or instrumentality thereof;

(2) may be furnished for law enforcement purposes on request of a court or law enforcement or corrections officer of a State, any political subdivision, or any department, agency, or instrumentality thereof, if a statute of such State requires that, upon the conviction of a defendant in a court of the State or any political subdivision thereof for an offense punishable in such court by death or imprisonment in excess of one year, or a judicial determination of the validity of such conviction on collateral review, the court cause a certified record of the conviction or determination to be made to the repository in such form and containing such information as the Attorney General of the United States shall by regulation prescribe; and

(3) shall be prima facie evidence in any court of the United States, the District of Columbia, the Commonwealth of Puerto Rico, a territory or possession of the United States, any political subdivision, or any department, agency, or instrumentality thereof, that the convictions occurred and whether they have been judicially determined to be invalid on collateral review.

(d) The Attorney General of the United States shall give reasonable public notice, and afford to interested parties opportunity for hearing, prior to prescribing regulations under this section.

(Added Pub. L. 91–452, title X, §1001(a), Oct. 15, 1970, 84 Stat. 951, §3578; renumbered §3662, Pub. L. 98–473, title II, §212(a)(1), Oct. 12, 1984, 98 Stat. 1987.)

§3663. Order of restitution

(a)(1)(A) The court, when sentencing a defendant convicted of an offense under this title, section 401, 408(a), 409, 416, 420, or 422(a) of the Controlled Substances Act (21 U.S.C. 841, 848(a), 849, 856, 861, 863) (but in no case shall a participant in an offense under such sections be considered a victim of such offense under this section), or section 5124, 46312, 46502, or 46504 of title 49, other than an offense described in section 3663A(c), may order, in addition to or, in the case of a misdemeanor, in lieu of any other penalty authorized by law, that the defendant make restitution to any victim of such offense, or if the victim is deceased, to the victim's estate. The court may also order, if agreed to by the parties in a plea agreement, restitution to persons other than the victim of the offense.

(B)(i) The court, in determining whether to order restitution under this section, shall consider—

(I) the amount of the loss sustained by each victim as a result of the offense; and

(II) the financial resources of the defendant, the financial needs and earning ability of the defendant and the defendant's dependents, and such other factors as the court deems appropriate.

(ii) To the extent that the court determines that the complication and prolongation of the sentencing process resulting from the fashioning of an order of restitution under this section outweighs the need to provide restitution to any victims, the court may decline to make such an order.

(2) For the purposes of this section, the term "victim" means a person directly and proximately harmed as a result of the commission of an offense for which restitution may be ordered including, in the case of an offense that involves as an element a scheme, conspiracy, or pattern of criminal activity, any person directly harmed by the defendant's criminal conduct in the course of the scheme, conspiracy, or pattern. In the case of a victim who is under 18 years of age, incompetent,

incapacitated, or deceased, the legal guardian of the victim or representative of the victim's estate, another family member, or any other person appointed as suitable by the court, may assume the victim's rights under this section, but in no event shall the defendant be named as such representative or guardian.

(3) The court may also order restitution in any criminal case to the extent agreed to by the parties in a plea agreement.

(b) The order may require that such defendant—

(1) in the case of an offense resulting in damage to or loss or destruction of property of a victim of the offense—

(A) return the property to the owner of the property or someone designated by the owner; or

(B) if return of the property under subparagraph (A) is impossible, impractical, or inadequate, pay an amount equal to the greater of—

(i) the value of the property on the date of the damage, loss, or destruction, or

(ii) the value of the property on the date of sentencing,

less the value (as of the date the property is returned) of any part of the property that is returned;

(2) in the case of an offense resulting in bodily injury to a victim including an offense under chapter 109A or chapter 110—

(A) pay an amount equal to the cost of necessary medical and related professional services and devices relating to physical, psychiatric, and psychological care, including nonmedical care and treatment rendered in accordance with a method of healing recognized by the law of the place of treatment;

(B) pay an amount equal to the cost of necessary physical and occupational therapy and rehabilitation; and

(C) reimburse the victim for income lost by such victim as a result of such offense;

(3) in the case of an offense resulting in bodily injury also results in the death of a victim, pay an amount equal to the cost of necessary funeral and related services;

(4) in any case, reimburse the victim for lost income and necessary child care, transportation, and other expenses related to participation in the investigation or prosecution of the offense or attendance at proceedings related to the offense;

(5) in any case, if the victim (or if the victim is deceased, the victim's estate) consents, make restitution in services in lieu of money, or make restitution to a person or organization designated by the victim or the estate; and

(6) in the case of an offense under sections 1028(a)(7) or 1028A(a) of this title, pay an amount equal to the value of the time reasonably spent by the victim in an attempt to remediate the intended or actual harm incurred by the victim from the offense.

(c)(1) Notwithstanding any other provision of law (but subject to the provisions of subsections (a)(1)(B)(i)(II) and (ii),1 when sentencing a defendant convicted of an offense described in section 401, 408(a), 409, 416, 420, or 422(a) of the Controlled Substances Act (21 U.S.C. 841, 848(a), 849, 856, 861, 863), in which there is no identifiable victim, the court may order that the defendant make restitution in accordance with this subsection.

(2)(A) An order of restitution under this subsection shall be based on the amount of public harm caused by the offense, as determined by the court in accordance with guidelines promulgated by the United States Sentencing Commission.

(B) In no case shall the amount of restitution ordered under this subsection exceed the amount of the fine which may be ordered for the offense charged in the case.

(3) Restitution under this subsection shall be distributed as follows:

(A) 65 percent of the total amount of restitution shall be paid to the State entity designated to administer crime victim assistance in the State in which the crime occurred.

(B) 35 percent of the total amount of restitution shall be paid to the State entity designated to receive Federal substance abuse block grant funds.

(4) The court shall not make an award under this subsection if it appears likely that such award would interfere with a forfeiture under chapter 46 or chapter 96 of this title or under the Controlled Substances Act (21 U.S.C. 801 et seq.).

(5) Notwithstanding section 3612(c) or any other provision of law, a penalty assessment under section 3013 or a fine under subchapter C of chapter 227 shall take precedence over an order of restitution under this subsection.

(6) Requests for community restitution under this subsection may be considered in all plea agreements negotiated by the United States.

(7)(A) The United States Sentencing Commission shall promulgate guidelines to assist courts in determining the amount of restitution that may be ordered under this subsection.

(B) No restitution shall be ordered under this subsection until such time as the Sentencing Commission promulgates guidelines pursuant to this paragraph.

(d) An order of restitution made pursuant to this section shall be issued and enforced in accordance with section 3664.

(Added Pub. L. 97–291, §5(a), Oct. 12, 1982, 96 Stat. 1253, §3579; renumbered §3663 and amended Pub. L. 98–473, title II, §212(a)(1), (3), Oct. 12, 1984, 98 Stat. 1987, 2010; Pub. L. 98–596, §9, Oct. 30, 1984, 98 Stat. 3138; Pub. L. 99–646, §§8(b), 20(a), 77(a), 78(a), 79(a), Nov. 10, 1986, 100 Stat. 3593, 3596, 3618, 3619; Pub. L. 100–182, §13, Dec. 7, 1987, 101 Stat. 1268; Pub. L. 100–185, §12, Dec. 11, 1987, 101 Stat. 1285; Pub. L. 100–690, title VII, §7042, Nov. 18, 1988, 102 Stat. 4399; Pub. L. 101–647, title XXV, §2509, title XXXV, §3595, Nov. 29, 1990, 104 Stat. 4863, 4931; Pub. L. 103–272, §5(e)(12), July 5, 1994, 108 Stat. 1374; Pub. L. 103–322, title IV, §§40504, 40505, Sept. 13, 1994, 108 Stat. 1947; Pub. L. 104–132, title II, §205(a), Apr. 24, 1996, 110 Stat. 1229; Pub. L. 104–294, title VI, §§601(r)(1), (2), 605(l), Oct. 11, 1996, 110 Stat. 3502, 3510; Pub. L. 106–310, div. B, title XXXVI, §3613(c), Oct. 17, 2000, 114 Stat. 1230; Pub. L. 109–59, title VII, §7128(b), Aug. 10, 2005, 119 Stat. 1910; Pub. L. 110–326, title II, §202, Sept. 26, 2008, 122 Stat. 3561.)

References in Text

The Controlled Substances Act, referred to in subsec. (c)(4), is title II of Pub. L. 91–513, Oct. 27, 1970, 84 Stat. 1242, as amended, which is classified principally to subchapter I (§801 et seq.) of chapter 13 of Title 21, Food and Drugs. For complete classification of this Act to the Code, see Short Title note set out under section 801 of Title 21 and Tables.

Amendments

2008—Subsec. (b)(6). Pub. L. 110–326 added par. (6).

2005—Subsec. (a)(1)(A). Pub. L. 109–59 inserted "5124," before "46312,".

2000—Subsec. (c)(2)(B). Pub. L. 106–310 inserted "which may be" after "fine".

1996—Subsec. (a)(1). Pub. L. 104–132, §205(a)(1)(A)–(E), substituted "(a)(1)(A) The court" for "(a)(1) The court", inserted ", section 401, 408(a), 409, 416, 420, or 422(a) of the Controlled Substances Act (21 U.S.C. 841, 848(a), 849, 856, 861, 863) (but in no case shall a participant in an offense under such sections be considered a victim of such offense under this section)," before "or section 46312,", "other than an offense described in section 3663A(c)," after "title 49", and ", or if the victim is deceased, to the victim's estate" before period at end, and added subpar. (B).

Subsec. (a)(1)(A). Pub. L. 104–294, §601(r)(1), inserted at end "The court may also order, if agreed to by the parties in a plea agreement, restitution to persons other than the victim of the offense."

Subsec. (a)(2). Pub. L. 104–132, §205(a)(1)(F), as amended by Pub. L. 104–294, §605(l), amended par. (2) generally. Prior to amendment, par. (2) read as follows: "For the purposes of restitution, a victim of an offense that involves as an element a scheme, a conspiracy, or a pattern of criminal activity means any person directly harmed by the defendant's criminal conduct in the course of the scheme, conspiracy, or pattern."

Subsec. (c). Pub. L. 104–132, §205(a)(2), (3), added subsec. (c) and struck out former subsec. (c) which read as follows: "If the court decides to order restitution under this section, the court shall, if the victim is deceased, order that the restitution be made to the victim's estate."

Subsec. (c)(4). Pub. L. 104–294, §601(r)(2), inserted "or chapter 96" after "under chapter 46".

Subsec. (d). Pub. L. 104–132, §205(a)(2), (3), added subsec. (d) and struck out former subsec. (d) which read as follows: "To the extent that the court determines that the complication and prolongation of the sentencing process resulting from the fashioning of an order of restitution under this section outweighs the need to provide restitution to any victims, the court may decline to make such an order."

Subsecs. (e) to (i). Pub. L. 104–132, §205(a)(2), struck out subsecs. (e) to (i), relating to provisions for restitution to persons who had compensated victims for their loss as well as offsets for restitution received by victims against amounts later recovered as compensatory damages, court orders that defendant make restitution in specified time period or in specified installments, payment of restitution as condition of probation or of supervised release, enforcement of restitution orders by United States or by victim, and supervision, termination, or restoration of eligibility for Federal benefits of persons delinquent in making restitution, respectively.

1994—Subsec. (a)(1). Pub. L. 103–272 substituted "section 46312, 46502, or 46504 of title 49" for "under subsection (h), (i), (j), or (n) of section 902 of the Federal Aviation Act of 1958 (49 U.S.C. 1472)".

Subsec. (b)(2). Pub. L. 103–322, §40504(1), in introductory provisions, inserted "including an offense under chapter 109A or chapter 110" after "victim".

Subsec. (b)(3) to (5). Pub. L. 103–322, §40504(2)–(4), struck out "and" at end of par. (3), added par. (4), and redesignated former par. (4) as (5).

Subsec. (i). Pub. L. 103–322, §40505, added subsec. (i).

1990—Subsec. (a). Pub. L. 101–647, §2509, designated existing provisions as par. (1) and added pars. (2) and (3).

Subsec. (f)(4). Pub. L. 101–647, §3595, substituted "604(a)(18)" for "604(a)(17)".

1988—Subsec. (h). Pub. L. 100–690 amended subsec. (h) generally. Prior to amendment, subsec. (h) read as follows: "An order of restitution may be enforced by the United States in the manner provided in sections 3812 and 3813 or in the same manner as a judgment in a civil action, and by the victim named in the order to receive the restitution in the same manner as a judgment in a civil action."

1987—Subsec. (f)(4). Pub. L. 100–185 inserted "or the person designated under section 604(a)(17) of title 28" after "Attorney General".

Subsec. (g). Pub. L. 100–182 substituted "revoke probation or a term of supervised release," for "revoke probation," in two places and inserted "probation or" after "modify the term or conditions of" in two places.

1986—Subsec. (a). Pub. L. 99–646, §20(a), which directed that subsec. (a)(1) be amended by inserting ", in the case of a misdemeanor," after "in addition to or", was executed to subsec. (a) to reflect the probable intent of Congress and the prior amendment to subsec. (a) by Pub. L. 99–646, §8(b), below.

Pub. L. 99–646, §8(b), struck out par. (1) designation, and struck out par. (2) which read as follows: "If the court does not order restitution, or orders only partial restitution, under this section, the court shall state on the record the reasons therefor."

Subsec. (a)(1). Pub. L. 99–646, §79(a), substituted "such offense" for "the offense".

Subsec. (d). Pub. L. 99–646, §77(a), amended subsec. (d) generally. Prior to amendment, subsec. (d) read as follows: "The court shall impose an order of restitution to the extent that such order is as fair as possible to the victim and the imposition of such order will not unduly complicate or prolong the sentencing process."

Subsec. (h). Pub. L. 99–646, §78(a), substituted "in the manner provided for the collection of fines and penalties by section 3565 or by a victim" for "or a victim".

1984—Pub. L. 98–473, §212(a)(1), renumbered section 3579 of this title as this section.

Subsec. (c). Pub. L. 98–596, §9(1), substituted "court" for "Court" after "If the".

Subsec. (f)(4). Pub. L. 98–596, §9(2), added par. (4).

Subsec. (g). Pub. L. 98–473, §212(a)(3)(A), amended subsec. (g) generally. Prior to amendment, subsec. (g) read as follows: "If such defendant is placed on probation or paroled under this title, any restitution ordered under this section shall be a condition of such probation or parole. The court may revoke probation and the Parole Commission may revoke parole if the defendant fails to comply with such order. In determining whether to revoke probation or parole, the court or Parole Commission shall consider the defendant's employment status, earning ability, financial resources, the willfulness of the defendant's failure to pay, and any other special circumstances that may have a bearing on the defendant's ability to pay."

Subsec. (h). Pub. L. 98–473, §212(a)(3)(B), amended subsec. (h) generally. Prior to amendment, subsec. (h) read as follows: "An order of restitution may be enforced by the United States in the manner provided for the collection of fines and penalties by section 3565 or by a victim named in the order to receive the restitution in the same manner as a judgment in a civil action."

Effective Date of 1996 Amendment

Amendment by Pub. L. 104–132 to be effective, to extent constitutionally permissible, for sentencing proceedings in cases in which defendant is convicted on or after Apr. 24, 1996, see section 211 of Pub. L. 104–132, set out as a note under section 2248 of this title.

Effective Date of 1987 Amendment

Amendment by Pub. L. 100–182 applicable with respect to offenses committed after Dec. 7, 1987, see section 26 of Pub. L. 100–182, set out as a note under section 3006A of this title.

Effective Date of 1986 Amendment

Amendment by section 8(b) of Pub. L. 99–646 effective Nov. 1, 1987, see section 8(c) of Pub. L. 99–646, set out as a note under section 3553 of this title.

Amendment by section 20(a) of Pub. L. 99–646 effective Nov. 1, 1987, see section 20(c) of Pub. L. 99–646, set out as a note under section 3556 of this title.

Pub. L. 99–646, §77(b), Nov. 10, 1986, 100 Stat. 3618, provided that: "The amendment made by this section [amending this section] shall take effect on the 30th day after the date of the enactment of this Act [Nov. 10, 1986]."

Pub. L. 99–646, §78(b), Nov. 10, 1986, 100 Stat. 3618, provided that: "The amendment made by this section [amending this section] shall take effect on the 30th day after the date of the enactment of this Act [Nov. 10, 1986]."

Pub. L. 99–646, §79(b), Nov. 10, 1986, 100 Stat. 3619, provided that: "The amendment made by this section [amending this section] shall take effect on the date of the enactment of this Act [Nov. 10, 1986]."

Effective Date of 1984 Amendments

Amendment by Pub. L. 98–596 applicable to offenses committed after Dec. 31, 1984, see section 10 of Pub. L. 98–596.

Amendment by section 212(a)(3) of Pub. L. 98–473 effective Nov. 1, 1987, and applicable only to offenses committed after the taking effect of such amendment, see section 235(a)(1) of Pub. L. 98–473, set out as an Effective Date note under section 3551 of this title.

Effective Date

Section effective with respect to offenses occurring after Jan. 1, 1983, see section 9(b)(2) of Pub. L. 97–291, set out as a note under section 1512 of this title.

Profit by a Criminal From Sale of His Story

Pub. L. 97–291, §7, Oct. 12, 1982, 96 Stat. 1257, required the Attorney General to report, by Oct. 12, 1982, to Congress regarding any laws that are necessary to ensure that no Federal felon derives any profit from the sale of the recollections, thoughts, and feelings of such felon with regards to the offense committed by the felon until any victim of the offense receives restitution.

§3663A. Mandatory restitution to victims of certain crimes

(a)(1) Notwithstanding any other provision of law, when sentencing a defendant convicted of an offense described in subsection (c), the court shall order, in addition to, or in the case of a misdemeanor, in addition to or in lieu of, any other penalty authorized by law, that the defendant make restitution to the victim of the offense or, if the victim is deceased, to the victim's estate.

(2) For the purposes of this section, the term "victim" means a person directly and proximately harmed as a result of the commission of an offense for which restitution may be ordered including, in the case of an offense that involves as an element a scheme, conspiracy, or pattern of criminal activity, any person directly harmed by the defendant's criminal conduct in the course of the scheme, conspiracy, or pattern. In the case of a victim who is under 18 years of age, incompetent, incapacitated, or deceased, the legal guardian of the victim or representative of the victim's estate, another family member, or any other person appointed as suitable by the court, may assume the victim's rights under this section, but in no event shall the defendant be named as such representative or guardian.

(3) The court shall also order, if agreed to by the parties in a plea agreement, restitution to persons other than the victim of the offense.

(b) The order of restitution shall require that such defendant—

(1) in the case of an offense resulting in damage to or loss or destruction of property of a victim of the offense—

(A) return the property to the owner of the property or someone designated by the owner; or

(B) if return of the property under subparagraph (A) is impossible, impracticable, or inadequate, pay an amount equal to—

(i) the greater of—

(I) the value of the property on the date of the damage, loss, or destruction; or

(II) the value of the property on the date of sentencing, less

(ii) the value (as of the date the property is returned) of any part of the property that is returned;

(2) in the case of an offense resulting in bodily injury to a victim—

(A) pay an amount equal to the cost of necessary medical and related professional services and devices relating to physical, psychiatric, and psychological care, including nonmedical care and treatment rendered in accordance with a method of healing recognized by the law of the place of treatment;

(B) pay an amount equal to the cost of necessary physical and occupational therapy and rehabilitation; and

(C) reimburse the victim for income lost by such victim as a result of such offense;

(3) in the case of an offense resulting in bodily injury that results in the death of the victim, pay an amount equal to the cost of necessary funeral and related services; and

(4) in any case, reimburse the victim for lost income and necessary child care, transportation, and other expenses incurred during participation in the investigation or prosecution of the offense or attendance at proceedings related to the offense.

(c)(1) This section shall apply in all sentencing proceedings for convictions of, or plea agreements relating to charges for, any offense—

(A) that is—

(i) a crime of violence, as defined in section 16;

(ii) an offense against property under this title, or under section 416(a) of the Controlled Substances Act (21 U.S.C. 856(a)), including any offense committed by fraud or deceit;

(iii) an offense described in section 1365 (relating to tampering with consumer products); or

(iv) an offense under section 670 (relating to theft of medical products); and

(B) in which an identifiable victim or victims has suffered a physical injury or pecuniary loss.

(2) In the case of a plea agreement that does not result in a conviction for an offense described in paragraph (1), this section shall apply only if the plea specifically states that an offense listed under such paragraph gave rise to the plea agreement.

(3) This section shall not apply in the case of an offense described in paragraph (1)(A)(ii) if the

court finds, from facts on the record, that—

(A) the number of identifiable victims is so large as to make restitution impracticable; or

(B) determining complex issues of fact related to the cause or amount of the victim's losses would complicate or prolong the sentencing process to a degree that the need to provide restitution to any victim is outweighed by the burden on the sentencing process.

(d) An order of restitution under this section shall be issued and enforced in accordance with section 3664.

(Added Pub. L. 104–132, title II, §204(a), Apr. 24, 1996, 110 Stat. 1227; amended Pub. L. 106–310, div. B, title XXXVI, §3613(d), Oct. 17, 2000, 114 Stat. 1230; Pub. L. 112–186, §6, Oct. 5, 2012, 126 Stat. 1430.)

Amendments

2012—Subsec. (c)(1)(A)(iv). Pub. L. 112–186 added cl. (iv).

2000—Subsec. (c)(1)(A)(ii). Pub. L. 106–310 inserted "or under section 416(a) of the Controlled Substances Act (21 U.S.C. 856(a))," after "under this title,".

Effective Date

Section to be effective, to extent constitutionally permissible, for sentencing proceedings in cases in which defendant is convicted on or after Apr. 24, 1996, see section 211 of Pub. L. 104–132, set out as an Effective Date of 1996 Amendment note under section 2248 of this title.

§3664. Procedure for issuance and enforcement of order of restitution

(a) For orders of restitution under this title, the court shall order the probation officer to obtain and include in its presentence report, or in a separate report, as the court may direct, information sufficient for the court to exercise its discretion in fashioning a restitution order. The report shall include, to the extent practicable, a complete accounting of the losses to each victim, any restitution owed pursuant to a plea agreement, and information relating to the economic circumstances of each defendant. If the number or identity of victims cannot be reasonably ascertained, or other circumstances exist that make this requirement clearly impracticable, the probation officer shall so inform the court.

(b) The court shall disclose to both the defendant and the attorney for the Government all portions of the presentence or other report pertaining to the matters described in subsection (a) of this section.

(c) The provisions of this chapter, chapter 227, and Rule 32(c) of the Federal Rules of Criminal Procedure shall be the only rules applicable to proceedings under this section.

(d)(1) Upon the request of the probation officer, but not later than 60 days prior to the date initially set for sentencing, the attorney for the Government, after consulting, to the extent practicable, with all identified victims, shall promptly provide the probation officer with a listing of the amounts subject to restitution.

(2) The probation officer shall, prior to submitting the presentence report under subsection (a), to the extent practicable—

(A) provide notice to all identified victims of—

(i) the offense or offenses of which the defendant was convicted;

(ii) the amounts subject to restitution submitted to the probation officer;

(iii) the opportunity of the victim to submit information to the probation officer concerning the amount of the victim's losses;

(iv) the scheduled date, time, and place of the sentencing hearing;

(v) the availability of a lien in favor of the victim pursuant to subsection (m)(1)(B); and

(vi) the opportunity of the victim to file with the probation officer a separate affidavit relating to the amount of the victim's losses subject to restitution; and

(B) provide the victim with an affidavit form to submit pursuant to subparagraph (A)(vi).

(3) Each defendant shall prepare and file with the probation officer an affidavit fully describing

the financial resources of the defendant, including a complete listing of all assets owned or controlled by the defendant as of the date on which the defendant was arrested, the financial needs and earning ability of the defendant and the defendant's dependents, and such other information that the court requires relating to such other factors as the court deems appropriate.

(4) After reviewing the report of the probation officer, the court may require additional documentation or hear testimony. The privacy of any records filed, or testimony heard, pursuant to this section shall be maintained to the greatest extent possible, and such records may be filed or testimony heard in camera.

(5) If the victim's losses are not ascertainable by the date that is 10 days prior to sentencing, the attorney for the Government or the probation officer shall so inform the court, and the court shall set a date for the final determination of the victim's losses, not to exceed 90 days after sentencing. If the victim subsequently discovers further losses, the victim shall have 60 days after discovery of those losses in which to petition the court for an amended restitution order. Such order may be granted only upon a showing of good cause for the failure to include such losses in the initial claim for restitutionary relief.

(6) The court may refer any issue arising in connection with a proposed order of restitution to a magistrate judge or special master for proposed findings of fact and recommendations as to disposition, subject to a de novo determination of the issue by the court.

(e) Any dispute as to the proper amount or type of restitution shall be resolved by the court by the preponderance of the evidence. The burden of demonstrating the amount of the loss sustained by a victim as a result of the offense shall be on the attorney for the Government. The burden of demonstrating the financial resources of the defendant and the financial needs of the defendant's dependents, shall be on the defendant. The burden of demonstrating such other matters as the court deems appropriate shall be upon the party designated by the court as justice requires.

(f)(1)(A) In each order of restitution, the court shall order restitution to each victim in the full amount of each victim's losses as determined by the court and without consideration of the economic circumstances of the defendant.

(B) In no case shall the fact that a victim has received or is entitled to receive compensation with respect to a loss from insurance or any other source be considered in determining the amount of restitution.

(2) Upon determination of the amount of restitution owed to each victim, the court shall, pursuant to section 3572, specify in the restitution order the manner in which, and the schedule according to which, the restitution is to be paid, in consideration of—

(A) the financial resources and other assets of the defendant, including whether any of these assets are jointly controlled;

(B) projected earnings and other income of the defendant; and

(C) any financial obligations of the defendant; including obligations to dependents.

(3)(A) A restitution order may direct the defendant to make a single, lump-sum payment, partial payments at specified intervals, in-kind payments, or a combination of payments at specified intervals and in-kind payments.

(B) A restitution order may direct the defendant to make nominal periodic payments if the court finds from facts on the record that the economic circumstances of the defendant do not allow the payment of any amount of a restitution order, and do not allow for the payment of the full amount of a restitution order in the foreseeable future under any reasonable schedule of payments.

(4) An in-kind payment described in paragraph (3) may be in the form of—

(A) return of property;

(B) replacement of property; or

(C) if the victim agrees, services rendered to the victim or a person or organization other than the victim.

(g)(1) No victim shall be required to participate in any phase of a restitution order.

(2) A victim may at any time assign the victim's interest in restitution payments to the Crime Victims Fund in the Treasury without in any way impairing the obligation of the defendant to make such payments.

(h) If the court finds that more than 1 defendant has contributed to the loss of a victim, the court may make each defendant liable for payment of the full amount of restitution or may apportion liability among the defendants to reflect the level of contribution to the victim's loss and economic circumstances of each defendant.

(i) If the court finds that more than 1 victim has sustained a loss requiring restitution by a defendant, the court may provide for a different payment schedule for each victim based on the type and amount of each victim's loss and accounting for the economic circumstances of each victim. In any case in which the United States is a victim, the court shall ensure that all other victims receive full restitution before the United States receives any restitution.

(j)(1) If a victim has received compensation from insurance or any other source with respect to a loss, the court shall order that restitution be paid to the person who provided or is obligated to provide the compensation, but the restitution order shall provide that all restitution of victims required by the order be paid to the victims before any restitution is paid to such a provider of compensation.

(2) Any amount paid to a victim under an order of restitution shall be reduced by any amount later recovered as compensatory damages for the same loss by the victim in—

(A) any Federal civil proceeding; and

(B) any State civil proceeding, to the extent provided by the law of the State.

(k) A restitution order shall provide that the defendant shall notify the court and the Attorney General of any material change in the defendant's economic circumstances that might affect the defendant's ability to pay restitution. The court may also accept notification of a material change in the defendant's economic circumstances from the United States or from the victim. The Attorney General shall certify to the court that the victim or victims owed restitution by the defendant have been notified of the change in circumstances. Upon receipt of the notification, the court may, on its own motion, or the motion of any party, including the victim, adjust the payment schedule, or require immediate payment in full, as the interests of justice require.

(l) A conviction of a defendant for an offense involving the act giving rise to an order of restitution shall estop the defendant from denying the essential allegations of that offense in any subsequent Federal civil proceeding or State civil proceeding, to the extent consistent with State law, brought by the victim.

(m)(1)(A)(i) An order of restitution may be enforced by the United States in the manner provided for in subchapter C of chapter 227 and subchapter B of chapter 229 of this title; or

(ii) by all other available and reasonable means.

(B) At the request of a victim named in a restitution order, the clerk of the court shall issue an abstract of judgment certifying that a judgment has been entered in favor of such victim in the amount specified in the restitution order. Upon registering, recording, docketing, or indexing such abstract in accordance with the rules and requirements relating to judgments of the court of the State where the district court is located, the abstract of judgment shall be a lien on the property of the defendant located in such State in the same manner and to the same extent and under the same conditions as a judgment of a court of general jurisdiction in that State.

(2) An order of in-kind restitution in the form of services shall be enforced by the probation officer.

(n) If a person obligated to provide restitution, or pay a fine, receives substantial resources from any source, including inheritance, settlement, or other judgment, during a period of incarceration, such person shall be required to apply the value of such resources to any restitution or fine still owed.

(o) A sentence that imposes an order of restitution is a final judgment notwithstanding the fact that—

(1) such a sentence can subsequently be—

(A) corrected under Rule 35 of the Federal Rules of Criminal Procedure and section 3742 of chapter 235 of this title;

(B) appealed and modified under section 3742;

(C) amended under subsection (d)(5); or

(D) adjusted under section 3664(k), 3572, or 3613A; or

(2) the defendant may be resentenced under section 3565 or 3614.

(p) Nothing in this section or sections 2248, 2259, 2264, 2327, 3663, and 3663A and arising out of the application of such sections, shall be construed to create a cause of action not otherwise authorized in favor of any person against the United States or any officer or employee of the United States.

(Added Pub. L. 97–291, §5(a), Oct. 12, 1982, 96 Stat. 1255, §3580; renumbered §3664, Pub. L. 98–473, title II, §212(a)(1), Oct. 12, 1984, 98 Stat. 1987; amended Pub. L. 101–647, title XXXV, §3596, Nov. 29, 1990, 104 Stat. 4931; Pub. L. 104–132, title II, §206(a), Apr. 24, 1996, 110 Stat. 1232; Pub. L. 107–273, div. B, title IV, §4002(e)(1), Nov. 2, 2002, 116 Stat. 1810.)

References in Text

The Federal Rules of Criminal Procedure, referred to in subsecs. (c) and (o)(1)(A), are set out in the Appendix to this title.

Amendments

2002—Subsec. (o)(1)(C). Pub. L. 107–273 substituted "subsection (d)(5)" for "section 3664(d)(3)".

1996—Pub. L. 104–132 amended section generally, substituting provisions relating to procedure for issuance and enforcement of orders of restitution for provisions relating to procedure for issuing orders of restitution.

1990—Subsec. (a). Pub. L. 101–647 substituted "3663" for "3579".

Effective Date of 1996 Amendment

Amendment by Pub. L. 104–132 to be effective, to extent constitutionally permissible, for sentencing proceedings in cases in which defendant is convicted on or after Apr. 24, 1996, see section 211 of Pub. L. 104–132, set out as a note under section 2248 of this title.

Effective Date

Section effective with respect to offenses occurring after Jan. 1, 1983, see section 9(b)(2) of Pub. L. 97–291, set out as a note under section 1512 of this title.

§3665. Firearms possessed by convicted felons

A judgment of conviction for transporting a stolen motor vehicle in interstate or foreign commerce or for committing or attempting to commit a felony in violation of any law of the United States involving the use of threats, force, or violence or perpetrated in whole or in part by the use of firearms, may, in addition to the penalty provided by law for such offense, order the confiscation and disposal of firearms and ammunition found in the possession or under the immediate control of the defendant at the time of his arrest.

The court may direct the delivery of such firearms or ammunition to the law-enforcement agency which apprehended such person, for its use or for any other disposition in its discretion.

(June 25, 1948, ch. 645, 62 Stat. 839, §3611; renumbered §3665, Pub. L. 98–473, title II, §212(a)(1), Oct. 12, 1984, 98 Stat. 1987.)

Historical and Revision Notes

Based on title 18, U.S.C., 1940 ed., §645 (June 13, 1939, ch. 197, 53 Stat. 814).

The condensation and simplification of this section clarifies its intent to confiscate the firearms taken from persons convicted of crimes of violence without any real change of substance.

§3666. Bribe moneys

Moneys received or tendered in evidence in any United States Court, or before any officer thereof, which have been paid to or received by any official as a bribe, shall, after the final disposition of the case, proceeding or investigation, be deposited in the registry of the court to be disposed of in accordance with the order of the court, to be subject, however, to the provisions of section 2042 of Title 28.

(June 25, 1948, ch. 645, 62 Stat. 840, §3612; May 24, 1949, ch. 139, §55, 63 Stat. 96; renumbered §3666, Pub. L. 98–473, title II, §212(a)(1), Oct. 12, 1984, 98 Stat. 1987.)

Historical and Revision Notes

1948 Act
Based on title 18, U.S.C., 1940 ed., §570 (Jan. 7, 1925, ch. 33, 43 Stat. 726).
Changes were made in phraseology.

1949 Act
This section [section 55] corrects section 3612 of title 18, U.S.C., so that the reference in such section will be to the correct section number in title 28, U.S.C., as revised and enacted in 1948.

Amendments
1949—Act May 24, 1949, substituted "section 2042" for "section 852".

§3667. Liquors and related property; definitions

All liquor involved in any violation of sections 1261–1265 of this title, the containers of such liquor, and every vehicle or vessel used in the transportation thereof, shall be seized and forfeited and such property or its proceeds disposed of in accordance with the laws relating to seizures, forfeitures, and dispositions of property or proceeds, for violation of the internal-revenue laws. As used in this section, "vessel" includes every description of watercraft used, or capable of being used, as a means of transportation in water or in water and air; "vehicle" includes animals and every description of carriage or other contrivance used, or capable of being used, as a means of transportation on land or through the air.

(June 25, 1948, ch. 645, 62 Stat. 840, §3615; renumbered §3667, Pub. L. 98–473, title II, §212(a)(1), Oct. 12, 1984, 98 Stat. 1987.)

Historical and Revision Notes

Based on sections 222 and 224 of title 27, U.S.C., 1940 ed., Intoxicating Liquors (June 25, 1936, ch. 815, §§2, 4, 49 Stat. 1928).

Section consolidates sections 222 and 224 of title 27, U.S.C., 1940 ed., with changes in phraseology and arrangement necessary to effect the consolidation. Said section 222 is also incorporated in section 1262 of this title.

Definition of "State" in section 222 of title 27 U.S.C., 1940 ed., as meaning and including "every State, Territory, and Possession of the United States," was omitted because the words "Territory, District," and so forth, appear after "State" in sections 1262, 1265, of this title, which are the only sections in chapter 59, constituting sections 1261–1265 of this title, to which such definition would have been applicable.

Changes made in phraseology.

§3668. Remission or mitigation of forfeitures under liquor laws; possession pending trial

(a) Jurisdiction of court
Whenever, in any proceeding in court for the forfeiture, under the internal-revenue laws, of any vehicle or aircraft seized for a violation of the internal-revenue laws relating to liquors, such forfeiture is decreed, the court shall have exclusive jurisdiction to remit or mitigate the forfeiture.

(b) Conditions precedent to remission or mitigation

In any such proceeding the court shall not allow the claim of any claimant for remission or mitigation unless and until he proves (1) that he has an interest in such vehicle or aircraft, as owner or otherwise, which he acquired in good faith, (2) that he had at no time any knowledge or reason to believe that it was being or would be used in the violation of laws of the United States or of any State relating to liquor, and (3) if it appears that the interest asserted by the claimant arises out of or is in any way subject to any contract or agreement under which any person having a record or reputation for violating laws of the United States or of any State relating to liquor has a right with respect to such vehicle or aircraft, that, before such claimant acquired his interest, or such other person acquired his right under such contract or agreement, whichever occurred later, the claimant, his officer or agent, was informed in answer to his inquiry, at the headquarters of the sheriff, chief of police, principal Federal internal-revenue officer engaged in the enforcement of the liquor laws, or other principal local or Federal law-enforcement officer of the locality in which such other person acquired his right under such contract or agreement, of the locality in which such other person then resided, and of each locality in which the claimant has made any other inquiry as to the character or financial standing of such other person, that such other person had no such record or reputation.

(c) Claimants first entitled to delivery

Upon the request of any claimant whose claim for remission or mitigation is allowed and whose interest is first in the order of priority among such claims allowed in such proceeding and is of an amount in excess of, or equal to, the appraised value of such vehicle or aircraft, the court shall order its return to him; and, upon the joint request of any two or more claimants whose claims are allowed and whose interests are not subject to any prior or intervening interests claimed and allowed in such proceedings, and are of a total amount in excess of, or equal to, the appraised value of such vehicle or aircraft, the court shall order its return to such of the joint requesting claimants as is designated in such request. Such return shall be made only upon payment of all expenses incident to the seizure and forfeiture incurred by the United States. In all other cases the court shall order disposition of such vehicle or aircraft as provided in section 1306 of title 40, and if such disposition be by public sale, payment from the proceeds thereof, after satisfaction of all such expenses, of any such claim in its order of priority among the claims allowed in such proceedings.

(d) Delivery on bond pending trial

In any proceeding in court for the forfeiture under the internal-revenue laws of any vehicle or aircraft seized for a violation of the internal-revenue laws relating to liquor, the court shall order delivery thereof to any claimant who shall establish his right to the immediate possession thereof, and shall execute, with one or more sureties approved by the court, and deliver to the court, a bond to the United States for the payment of a sum equal to the appraised value of such vehicle or aircraft. Such bond shall be conditioned to return such vehicle or aircraft at the time of the trial and to pay the difference between the appraised value of such vehicle or aircraft as of the time it shall have been so released on bond and the appraised value thereof as of the time of trial; and conditioned further that, if the vehicle or aircraft be not returned at the time of trial, the bond shall stand in lieu of, and be forfeited in the same manner as, such vehicle or aircraft. Notwithstanding this subsection or any other provisions of law relating to the delivery of possession on bond of vehicles or aircraft sought to be forfeited under the internal-revenue laws, the court may, in its discretion and upon good cause shown by the United States, refuse to order such delivery of possession.

(June 25, 1948, ch. 645, 62 Stat. 840, §3617; renumbered §3668, Pub. L. 98–473, title II, §212(a)(1), Oct. 12, 1984, 98 Stat. 1987; amended Pub. L. 107–217, §3(d), Aug. 21, 2002, 116 Stat. 1299.)

Historical and Revision Notes

Based on title 18, U.S.C., 1940 ed., §646 (Aug. 27, 1935, ch. 740, §204, 49 Stat. 878).

A minor change was made in phraseology.

Amendments
2002—Subsec. (c). Pub. L. 107–217 substituted "section 1306 of title 40" for "sections 304f–304m of Title 40".

§3669. Conveyances carrying liquor
Any conveyance, whether used by the owner or another in introducing or attempting to introduce intoxicants into the Indian country, or into other places where the introduction is prohibited by treaty or enactment of Congress, shall be subject to seizure, libel, and forfeiture.

(June 25, 1948, ch. 645, 62 Stat. 841, §3618; renumbered §3669, Pub. L. 98–473, title II, §212(a)(1), Oct. 12, 1984, 98 Stat. 1987.)

Historical and Revision Notes
Based on section 247 of title 25, U.S.C., 1940 ed., Indians (Mar. 2, 1917, ch. 146, §1, 39 Stat. 970).

Words "Automobiles or any other vehicles or" at beginning of section were omitted, and "any conveyance" substituted to remove possible ambiguity as to scope of section.

Words at conclusion of section "provided in section 246 of this title" added nothing and were therefore omitted. (See also rule 41 of the Federal Rules of Criminal Procedure.)

Minor changes were made in arrangement and phraseology.

§3670. Disposition of conveyances seized for violation of the Indian liquor laws
The provisions of section 3668 of this title shall apply to any conveyances seized, proceeded against by libel, or forfeited under the provisions of section 3113 or 3669 of this title for having been used in introducing or attempting to introduce intoxicants into the Indian country or into other places where such introduction is prohibited by treaty or enactment of Congress.

(Added Oct. 24, 1951, ch. 546, §2, 65 Stat. 609, §3619; renumbered §3670 and amended Pub. L. 98–473, title II, §§212(a)(1), 223(k), Oct. 12, 1984, 98 Stat. 1987, 2029.)

Amendments
1984—Pub. L. 98–473 renumbered section 3619 of this title as this section and substituted "3668" for "3617" and "3669" for "3618".

Effective Date of 1984 Amendment
Amendment by section 223(k) of Pub. L. 98–473 effective Nov. 1, 1987, and applicable only to offenses committed after the taking effect of such amendment, see section 235(a)(1) of Pub. L. 98–473, set out as an Effective Date note under section 3551 of this title.

§3671. Vessels carrying explosives and steerage passengers
The amount of any fine imposed upon the master of a steamship or other vessel under the provisions of section 2278 of this title shall be a lien upon such vessel, and such vessel may be libeled therefor in the district court of the United States for any district in which such vessel shall arrive or from which it shall depart.

(Added Sept. 3, 1954, ch. 1263, §36, 68 Stat. 1239, §3620; renumbered §3671, Pub. L. 98–473, title II, §212(a)(1), Oct. 12, 1984, 98 Stat. 1987.)

§3672. Duties of Director of Administrative Office of the United States Courts
The Director of the Administrative Office of the United States Courts, or his authorized agent,

shall investigate the work of the probation officers and make recommendations concerning the same to the respective judges and shall have access to the records of all probation officers.

He shall collect for publication statistical and other information concerning the work of the probation officers.

He shall prescribe record forms and statistics to be kept by the probation officers and shall formulate general rules for the proper conduct of the probation work.

He shall endeavor by all suitable means to promote the efficient administration of the probation system and the enforcement of the probation laws in all United States courts.

He shall, under the supervision and direction of the Judicial Conference of the United States, fix the salaries of probation officers and shall provide for their necessary expenses including clerical service and travel expenses.

He shall incorporate in his annual report a statement concerning the operation of the probation system in such courts.

He shall have the authority to contract with any appropriate public or private agency or person for the detection of and care in the community of an offender who is an alcohol-dependent person, an addict or a drug-dependent person, or a person suffering from a psychiatric disorder within the meaning of section 2 of the Public Health Service Act. This authority shall include the authority to provide equipment and supplies; testing; medical, educational, social, psychological and vocational services; corrective and preventative guidance and training; and other rehabilitative services designed to protect the public and benefit the alcohol-dependent person, addict or drug-dependent person, or a person suffering from a psychiatric disorder by eliminating his dependence on alcohol or addicting drugs, by controlling his dependence and his susceptibility to addiction, or by treating his psychiatric disorder. He may negotiate and award contracts identified in this paragraph without regard to section 6101(b) to (d) of title 41. He also shall have the authority to expend funds or to contract with any appropriate public or private agency or person to monitor and provide services to any offender in the community authorized by this Act, including treatment, equipment and emergency housing, corrective and preventative guidance and training, and other rehabilitative services designed to protect the public and promote the successful reentry of the offender into the community.

He shall pay for presentence studies and reports by qualified consultants and presentence examinations and reports by psychiatric or psychological examiners ordered by the court under subsection (b) or (c) of section 3552, except for studies conducted by the Bureau of Prisons. Whenever the court finds that funds are available for payment by or on behalf of a person furnished such services, training, or guidance, the court may direct that such funds be paid to the Director. Any moneys collected under this paragraph shall be used to reimburse the appropriations obligated and disbursed in payment for such services, training, or guidance.

(June 25, 1948, ch. 645, 62 Stat. 843, §3656; May 24, 1949, ch. 139, §57, 63 Stat. 97; renumbered §3672, Pub. L. 98–473, title II, §212(a)(1), Oct. 12, 1984, 98 Stat. 1987; Pub. L. 99–570, title I, §1861(b)(1), Oct. 27, 1986, 100 Stat. 3207–53; Pub. L. 99–646, §18(a), Nov. 10, 1986, 100 Stat. 3595; Pub. L. 100–182, §20, Dec. 7, 1987, 101 Stat. 1270; Pub. L. 110–199, title II, §253, Apr. 9, 2008, 122 Stat. 693; Pub. L. 110–406, §15(b), Oct. 13, 2008, 122 Stat. 4294; Pub. L. 111–350, §5(d)(1), Jan. 4, 2011, 124 Stat. 3847.)

Historical and Revision Notes

1948 Act

Based on title 18, U.S.C., 1940 ed., §728 (Mar. 4, 1925, ch. 521, §4(a), as added June 6, 1930, ch. 406, §2, 46 Stat. 503).

The only change made in this section was the substitution of the "Director of the Administrative Office of the United States Courts" for "Attorney General". (See reviser's note under section 3654 of this title.)

1949 Act
This amendment [see section 57] conforms the language of section 3656 of title 18, U.S.C., to that of title 28, U.S.C., section 604(a).

References in Text
Section 2 of the Public Health Service Act, referred to in the seventh undesignated par., is classified to section 201 of Title 42, The Public Health and Welfare.

This Act, referred to in the seventh undesignated par., probably means Pub. L. 110–199, Apr. 9, 2008, 122 Stat. 657, known as the Second Chance Act of 2007: Community Safety Through Recidivism Prevention and also as the Second Chance Act of 2007. For complete classification of this Act to the Code, see Short Title of 2008 Act note set out under section 10101 of Title 34, Crime Control and Law Enforcement, and Tables.

Amendments
2011—Pub. L. 111–350 substituted "section 6101(b) to (d) of title 41" for "section 3709 of the Revised Statutes of the United States" in seventh undesignated par.

2008—Pub. L. 110–406, §15(b)(2), which directed insertion of "to expend funds or" after "He shall also have the authority" in fourth sentence of seventh undesignated par., was executed by making the insertion after "He also shall have the authority" to reflect the probable intent of Congress.

Pub. L. 110–406, §15(b)(1), substituted "negotiate and award contracts identified in this paragraph" for "negotiate and award such contracts" in third sentence of seventh undesignated par.

Pub. L. 110–199 inserted last sentence of seventh undesignated par.

1987—Pub. L. 100–182, §20(1), amended seventh undesignated par. generally. Prior to amendment, seventh undesignated par. read as follows: "He shall have the authority to contract with any appropriate public or private agency or person for the detection of and care in the community of an offender who is an alcohol-dependent person, or an addict or a drug-dependent person within the meaning of section 2 of the Public Health Service Act (42 U.S.C. 201). This authority shall include the authority to provide equipment and supplies; testing; medical, educational, social, psychological, and vocational services; corrective and preventive guidance and training; and other rehabilitative services designed to protect the public and benefit the alcohol-dependent person, addict, or drug-dependent person by eliminating his dependence on alcohol or addicting drugs, or by controlling his dependence and his susceptibility to addiction. He may negotiate and award such contracts without regard to section 3709 of the Revised Statutes (41 U.S.C. 5)."

Pub. L. 100–182, §20(2), added ninth undesignated par.: "Whenever the court finds that funds are available for payment by or on behalf of a person furnished such services, training, or guidance, the court may direct that such funds be paid to the Director. Any moneys collected under this paragraph shall be used to reimburse the appropriations obligated and disbursed in payment for such services, training, or guidance."

1986—Pub. L. 99–570 and Pub. L. 99–646 added substantially identical seventh and eighth undesignated pars. containing provision relating to authority to contract with any appropriate public or private agency or person for the detection of and care in the community of an offender who is an alcohol-dependent person, an addict, or a drug-dependent person and provision relating to payment for presentence studies and reports by qualified consultants and presentence examinations and reports by psychiatric and psychological examiners ordered by the court under section 3552(b) or (c).

1949—Act May 24, 1949, inserted in fifth par. of section "and direction" after "supervision".

Effective Date of 1987 Amendment
Amendment by Pub. L. 100–182 applicable with respect to offenses committed after Dec. 7, 1987, see section 26 of Pub. L. 100–182, set out as a note under section 3006A of this title.

Effective Date of 1986 Amendments

Pub. L. 99–646, §18(b), Nov. 10, 1986, 100 Stat. 3596, provided that: "The amendment made by this section [amending this section] shall take effect on the date of the taking effect of such redesignation [section 3656 of this title renumbered section 3672 effective Nov. 1, 1987]."

Pub. L. 99–570, title I, §1861(b)(2), Oct. 27, 1986, 100 Stat. 3207–53, provided that: "The amendment made by this section [probably should be "subsection", amending this section] shall take effect on the date of the taking effect of such redesignation [section 3656 of this title renumbered section 3672 effective Nov. 1, 1987]."

Construction of 2008 Amendment

For construction of amendments by Pub. L. 110–199 and requirements for grants made under such amendments, see section 60504 of Title 34, Crime Control and Law Enforcement.

Authorization of Appropriations

Pub. L. 95–537, §4(a), Oct. 27, 1978, 92 Stat. 2038, as amended by Pub. L. 98–236, §2, Mar. 20, 1984, 98 Stat. 66; Pub. L. 99–570, title I, §1861(d), Oct. 27, 1986, 100 Stat. 3207–53; Pub. L. 100–690, title VI, §6291, Nov. 18, 1988, 102 Stat. 4369; Pub. L. 101–421, §2, Oct. 12, 1990, 104 Stat. 909, authorized appropriations to carry out the purposes of Pub. L. 95–537 and the seventh par. of this section for the fiscal year ending Sept. 30, 1980, to the fiscal year ending Sept. 30, 1992.

Increase in Compensation Rates

Increase in compensation rates fixed under this section, see note under section 603 of Title 28, Judiciary and Judicial Procedure.

§3673. Definitions for sentencing provisions

As used in chapters 227 and 229—

(1) the term "found guilty" includes acceptance by a court of a plea of guilty or nolo contendere;

(2) the term "commission of an offense" includes the attempted commission of an offense, the consummation of an offense, and any immediate flight after the commission of an offense; and

(3) the term "law enforcement officer" means a public servant authorized by law or by a government agency to engage in or supervise the prevention, detection, investigation, or prosecution of an offense.

(Added Pub. L. 98–473, title II, §212(a)(4), Oct. 12, 1984, 98 Stat. 2010; amended Pub. L. 99–646, §2(a), Nov. 10, 1986, 100 Stat. 3592.)

Amendments

1986—Pub. L. 99–646 redesignated pars. (a) to (c) as (1) to (3), respectively, and inserted "the term" after "(1)", "(2)", and "(3)".

Effective Date of 1986 Amendment

Pub. L. 99–646, §2(b), Nov. 10, 1986, 100 Stat. 3592, provided that: "The amendments made by this section [amending this section] shall take effect on the date of the taking effect of section 3673 of title 18, United States Code [Nov. 1, 1987]."

Effective Date

Section effective Nov. 1, 1987, and applicable only to offenses committed after the taking effect of this section, see section 235(a)(1) of Pub. L. 98–473, set out as a note under section 3551 of this title.

CHAPTER 232A - SPECIAL FORFEITURE OF COLLATERAL PROFITS OF CRIME

Amendments

1986—Pub. L. 99–646, §41(b), (c), Nov. 10, 1986, 100 Stat. 3600, renumbered chapter 232 (relating to special forfeiture of collateral profits of crime) as chapter 232A, and renumbered items 3671 and 3672 as items 3681 and 3682, respectively.

§3681. Order of special forfeiture

(a) Upon the motion of the United States attorney made at any time after conviction of a defendant for an offense under section 794 of this title or for an offense against the United States resulting in physical harm to an individual, and after notice to any interested party, the court shall, if the court determines that the interest of justice or an order of restitution under this title so requires, order such defendant to forfeit all or any part of proceeds received or to be received by that defendant, or a transferee of that defendant, from a contract relating to a depiction of such crime in a movie, book, newspaper, magazine, radio or television production, or live entertainment of any kind, or an expression of that defendant's thoughts, opinions, or emotions regarding such crime.

(b) An order issued under subsection (a) of this section shall require that the person with whom the defendant contracts pay to the Attorney General any proceeds due the defendant under such contract.

(c)(1) Proceeds paid to the Attorney General under this section shall be retained in escrow in the Crime Victims Fund in the Treasury by the Attorney General for five years after the date of an order under this section, but during that five year period may—

(A) be levied upon to satisfy—

(i) a money judgment rendered by a United States district court in favor of a victim of an offense for which such defendant has been convicted, or a legal representative of such victim; and

(ii) a fine imposed by a court of the United States; and

(B) if ordered by the court in the interest of justice, be used to—

(i) satisfy a money judgment rendered in any court in favor of a victim of any offense for which such defendant has been convicted, or a legal representative of such victim; and

(ii) pay for legal representation of the defendant in matters arising from the offense for which such defendant has been convicted, but no more than 20 percent of the total proceeds may be so used.

(2) The court shall direct the disposition of all such proceeds in the possession of the Attorney General at the end of such five years and may require that all or any part of such proceeds be released from escrow and paid into the Crime Victims Fund in the Treasury.

(d) As used in this section, the term "interested party" includes the defendant and any transferee of proceeds due the defendant under the contract, the person with whom the defendant has contracted, and any person physically harmed as a result of the offense for which the defendant has been convicted.

(Added Pub. L. 98–473, title II, §1406(a), Oct. 12, 1984, 98 Stat. 2175, §3671; amended Pub. L. 99–399, title XIII, §1306(c), Aug. 27, 1986, 100 Stat. 899; renumbered §3681 and amended Pub. L. 99–646, §§40, 41(a), Nov. 10, 1986, 100 Stat. 3600.)

Amendments

1986—Subsec. (a). Pub. L. 99–646, §40, struck out "chapter 227 or 231 of" after "restitution under".

Pub. L. 99–399 inserted "an offense under section 794 of this title or for".

Effective Date

Chapter effective 30 days after Oct. 12, 1984, see section 1409(a) of Pub. L. 98–473, set out as a note under section 20101 of Title 34, Crime Control and Law Enforcement.

§3682. Notice to victims of order of special forfeiture

The United States attorney shall, within thirty days after the imposition of an order under this chapter and at such other times as the Attorney General may require, publish in a newspaper of general circulation in the district in which the offense for which a defendant was convicted occurred, a notice that states—

(1) the name of, and other identifying information about, the defendant;

(2) the offense for which the defendant was convicted; and

(3) that the court has ordered a special forfeiture of certain proceeds that may be used to satisfy a judgment obtained against the defendant by a victim of an offense for which the defendant has been convicted.

(Added Pub. L. 98–473, title II, §1406(a), Oct. 12, 1984, 98 Stat. 2176, §3672; renumbered §3682, Pub. L. 99–646, §41(a), Nov. 10, 1986, 100 Stat. 3600.)

CHAPTER 233 - CONTEMPTS

§3691. Jury trial of criminal contempts

Whenever a contempt charged shall consist in willful disobedience of any lawful writ, process, order, rule, decree, or command of any district court of the United States by doing or omitting any act or thing in violation thereof, and the act or thing done or omitted also constitutes a criminal offense under any Act of Congress, or under the laws of any state in which it was done or omitted, the accused, upon demand therefor, shall be entitled to trial by a jury, which shall conform as near as may be to the practice in other criminal cases.

This section shall not apply to contempts committed in the presence of the court, or so near thereto as to obstruct the administration of justice, nor to contempts committed in disobedience of any lawful writ, process, order, rule, decree, or command entered in any suit or action brought or prosecuted in the name of, or on behalf of, the United States.

(June 25, 1948, ch. 645, 62 Stat. 844.)

Historical and Revision Notes

Based on sections 386, 389 of title 28, U.S.C., 1940 ed., Judicial Code and Judiciary (Oct. 15, 1914, ch. 323, §§21, 24, 38 Stat. 738, 739).

The first paragraph of this section is completely rewritten from section 386 of title 28, U.S.C., 1940 ed., Judicial Code and Judiciary, omitting everything covered and superseded by rules 23 and 42 of the Federal Rules of Criminal Procedure.

The second paragraph of this section is derived from section 389 of title 28, U.S.C., 1940 ed., Judicial Code and Judiciary, omitting directions as to the trial of other contempts which are now covered by rule 42 of the Federal Rules of Criminal Procedure.

Minor changes were made in phraseology.

§3692. Jury trial for contempt in labor dispute cases

In all cases of contempt arising under the laws of the United States governing the issuance of injunctions or restraining orders in any case involving or growing out of a labor dispute, the accused shall enjoy the right to a speedy and public trial by an impartial jury of the State and district wherein the contempt shall have been committed.

This section shall not apply to contempts committed in the presence of the court or so near thereto as to interfere directly with the administration of justice nor to the misbehavior, misconduct, or disobedience of any officer of the court in respect to the writs, orders or process of the court. (June 25, 1948, ch. 645, 62 Stat. 844.)

Historical and Revision Notes

Based on section 111 of Title 29, U.S.C., 1940 ed., Labor (Mar. 23, 1932, ch. 90, §11, 47 Stat. 72).

The phrase "or the District of Columbia arising under the laws of the United States governing the issuance of injunctions or restraining orders in any case involving or growing out of a labor dispute" was inserted and the reference to specific sections of the Norris-LaGuardia Act (sections 101–115 of Title 29, U.S.C., 1940 ed.) were eliminated.

Taft-Hartley Injunctions

Former section 111 of Title 29, Labor, upon which this section is based, as inapplicable to injunctions issued under the Taft-Hartley Act, see section 178 of Title 29.

§3693. Summary disposition or jury trial; notice—(Rule)

See Federal Rules of Criminal Procedure

Summary punishment; certificate of judge; order; notice; jury trial; bail; disqualification of judge, Rule 42.
(June 25, 1948, ch. 645, 62 Stat. 844.)

CHAPTER 235 - APPEAL

Amendments

1984—Pub. L. 98–473, title II, §213(b), Oct. 12, 1984, 98 Stat. 2013, added item 3742.

§3731. Appeal by United States

In a criminal case an appeal by the United States shall lie to a court of appeals from a decision, judgment, or order of a district court dismissing an indictment or information or granting a new trial after verdict or judgment, as to any one or more counts, or any part thereof, except that no appeal shall lie where the double jeopardy clause of the United States Constitution prohibits further prosecution.

An appeal by the United States shall lie to a court of appeals from a decision or order of a district court suppressing or excluding evidence or requiring the return of seized property in a criminal proceeding, not made after the defendant has been put in jeopardy and before the verdict or finding on an indictment or information, if the United States attorney certifies to the district court that the appeal is not taken for purpose of delay and that the evidence is a substantial proof of a fact material in the proceeding.

An appeal by the United States shall lie to a court of appeals from a decision or order, entered by a district court of the United States, granting the release of a person charged with or convicted of an offense, or denying a motion for revocation of, or modification of the conditions of, a decision or order granting release.

The appeal in all such cases shall be taken within thirty days after the decision, judgment or order has been rendered and shall be diligently prosecuted.

The provisions of this section shall be liberally construed to effectuate its purposes.

(June 25, 1948, ch. 645, 62 Stat. 844; May 24, 1949, ch. 139, §58, 63 Stat. 97; Pub. L. 90–351, title VIII, §1301, June 19, 1968, 82 Stat. 237; Pub. L. 91–644, title III, §14(a), Jan. 2, 1971, 84 Stat. 1890; Pub. L. 98–473, title II, §§205, 1206, Oct. 12, 1984, 98 Stat. 1986, 2153; Pub. L. 99–646, §32, Nov. 10, 1986, 100 Stat. 3598; Pub. L. 103–322, title XXXIII, §330008(4), Sept. 13, 1994, 108 Stat. 2142; Pub. L. 107–273, div. B, title III, §3004, Nov. 2, 2002, 116 Stat. 1805.)

Historical and Revision Notes

1948 Act

Based on title 18, U.S.C., 1940 ed., §682 (Mar. 2, 1907, ch. 2564, 34 Stat. 1246; Mar. 3, 1911, ch. 231, §291, 36 Stat. 1167; Jan. 31, 1928, ch. 14, §1, 45 Stat. 54; May 9, 1942, ch. 295, §1, 56 Stat. 271).

The word "dismissing" was substituted for "sustaining a motion to dismiss" in two places for conciseness and clarity, there being no difference in effect of a decision of dismissal whether made on motion or by the court sua sponte.

Minor changes were made to conform to Rule 12 of the Federal Rules of Criminal Procedure. The final sentence authorizing promulgation of rules is omitted as redundant.

1949 Act

This section [section 58] corrects a typographical error in the second paragraph of section 3731 of title 18, U.S.C., and conforms the language of the fifth, tenth, and eleventh paragraphs of such section 3731 with the changed nomenclature of title 28, U.S.C., Judiciary and Judicial Procedure. See sections 41, 43, and 451 of the latter title.

Amendments

2002—First par. Pub. L. 107–273 inserted ", or any part thereof" after "as to any one or more counts".

1994—Second par. Pub. L. 103–322 substituted "order of a district court" for "order of a district courts".

1986—Fifth par. Pub. L. 99–646 struck out fifth par. which read as follows: "Pending the prosecution and determination of the appeal in the foregoing instances, the defendant shall be released in accordance with chapter 207 of this title."

1984—First par. Pub. L. 98–473, §1206, inserted "or granting a new trial after verdict or judgment," after "indictment or information".

Third par. Pub. L. 98–473, §205, inserted third par. relating to appeals from a decision or order, entered by a district court of the United States, granting the release of a person charged with or convicted of an offense, or denying a motion for revocation of, or modification of the conditions of, a decision or order granting release.

1971—First par. Pub. L. 91–644, §14(a)(1), enacted provision for appeal to a court of appeals from decision, judgment, or order of district court dismissing an indictment or information as to any one or more counts, except that no appeal shall lie where double jeopardy prohibits further prosecution.

Second par. Pub. L. 91–644, §14(a)(1), enacted provision for appeal to a court of appeals from decision or order of district court suppressing or excluding evidence or requiring the return of seized property in a criminal proceeding, not made after the defendant has been put in jeopardy and before the verdict or finding on an indictment or information, if the United States attorney certifies to the district court that the appeal is not taken for purpose of delay and that the evidence is a substantial proof of a fact material in the proceeding.

Such first and second pars. superseded former first eight pars. Pars. one through four had provided for appeal from district courts to Supreme Court from decision or judgment setting aside, or dismissing any indictment or information, or any count thereof and from decision arresting judgment of conviction for insufficiency of indictment or information, where such decision or judgment was based upon invalidity or construction of the statute upon which the indictment or information was founded and for an appeal from decision or judgment sustaining a motion in bar, where defendant had not been put in jeopardy. Pars. five through eight provided for appeal from district courts to a court of appeals where there were no provisions for direct appeal to Supreme Court from decision or judgment setting aside, or dismissing any indictment or information, or any count thereof and from decision arresting a judgment of conviction, and from an order, granting a motion for return of seized property or a motion to suppress evidence, made before trial of a person charged with violation of a Federal law, if the United States attorney certified to the judge who granted the motion that the appeal was not taken for purpose of delay and that the evidence was a substantial proof of the charge pending against the defendant.

Third par. Pub. L. 91–644, §14(a)(2), authorized within third par., formerly ninth, an appeal within thirty days after order has been rendered.

Fourth par. Pub. L. 91–644, §14(a), in revising the provisions, had the effect of designating former tenth par. as fourth par.

Fifth par. Pub. L. 91–644, §14(a)(3), substituted as a fifth par. provision for liberal construction of this section for prior eleventh par. provision respecting remand of case by Supreme Court to court of appeals that should have been taken to such court and treatment of the court's jurisdiction to hear and determine the case as if the appeal were so taken in the first instance and for prior twelfth par. provision respecting certification of case to Supreme Court that should have been taken directly to such Court and treatment of the Court's jurisdiction to hear and determine the case as if the appeal were taken directly to such Court.

1968—Pub. L. 90–351 inserted eighth par. providing for an appeal by the United States from decisions sustaining motions to suppress evidence and substituted in tenth par. "defendant shall be released in accordance with chapter 207 of this title" for "defendant shall be admitted to bail on his own recognizance", respectively.

1949—Act May 24, 1949, substituted "invalidity" for "validity" after "upon the" in second par., and conformed language of fifth, tenth, and eleventh pars. to the changed nomenclature of the courts.

Savings Provision

Pub. L. 91–644, title III, §14(b), Jan. 2, 1971, 84 Stat. 1890, provided that: "The amendments made by this section [amending this section] shall not apply with respect to any criminal case begun in any district court before the effective date of this section [Jan. 2, 1971]."

§3732. Taking of appeal; notice; time—(Rule)

See Federal Rules of Criminal Procedure

Taking appeal; notice, contents, signing; time, Rule 37(a).

(June 25, 1948, ch. 645, 62 Stat. 845.)

References in Text

Rule 37 of the Federal Rules of Criminal Procedure was abrogated Dec. 4, 1967, eff. July 1, 1968, and is covered by Rule 3, Federal Rules of Appellate Procedure, set out in the Appendix to Title 28, Judiciary and Judicial Procedure.

§3733. Assignment of errors—(Rule)

See Federal Rules of Criminal Procedure

Assignments of error on appeal abolished, Rule 37(a)(1).
Necessity of specific objection in order to assign error in instructions, Rule 30.
(June 25, 1948, ch. 645, 62 Stat. 845.)

References in Text

Rule 37 of the Federal Rules of Criminal Procedure was abrogated Dec. 4, 1947, eff. July 1, 1968, and is covered by Rule 3, Federal Rules of Appellate Procedure, set out in the Appendix to Title 28, Judiciary and Judicial Procedure.

§3734. Bill of exceptions abolished—(Rule)

See Federal Rules of Criminal Procedure

Exceptions abolished, Rule 51.
Bill of exceptions not required, Rule 37(a)(1).
(June 25, 1948, ch. 645, 62 Stat. 845.)

References in Text

Rule 37 of the Federal Rules of Criminal Procedure was abrogated Dec. 4, 1967, eff. July 1, 1968, and is covered by Rule 3, Federal Rules of Appellate Procedure, set out in the Appendix to Title 28, Judiciary and Judicial Procedure.

§3735. Bail on appeal or certiorari—(Rule)

See Federal Rules of Criminal Procedure

Bail on appeal or certiorari; application, Rules 38(c) and 46(a)(2).
(June 25, 1948, ch. 645, 62 Stat. 845.)

References in Text

Rule 38(c) of the Federal Rules of Criminal Procedure was abrogated Dec. 4, 1967, eff. July 1, 1968, and is covered by rule 9, Federal Rules of Appellate Procedure, set out in the Appendix to Title 28, Judiciary and Judicial Procedure.
Rule 46 was amended as part of the Bail Reform Act in 1966 and in 1972, and some provisions originally contained in Rule 46 are covered by this chapter, see Notes of Advisory Committee on Rules and Amendment notes under Rule 46, this Appendix.

§3736. Certiorari—(Rule)

See Federal Rules of Criminal Procedure

Petition to Supreme Court, time, Rule 37(b).
(June 25, 1948, ch. 645, 62 Stat. 845.)

Rule 37 of the Federal Rules of Criminal Procedure was abrogated Dec. 4, 1967, eff. July 1, 1968. Provisions of such former rule for certiorari are covered by rule 19 et seq. of the Rules of the United States Supreme Court.

§3737. Record—(Rule)

See Federal Rules of Criminal Procedure
Preparation, form; typewritten record, Rule 39(b).
Exceptions abolished, Rule 51.
Bill of exceptions unnecessary, Rule 37(a)(1).
(June 25, 1948, ch. 645, 62 Stat. 846.)

References in Text
Rules 37 and 39 of the Federal Rules of Criminal Procedure were abrogated Dec. 4, 1967, eff. July 1, 1968, and are covered by Rule 10, Federal Rules of Appellate Procedure, set out in the Appendix to Title 28, Judiciary and Judicial Procedure.

§3738. Docketing appeal and record—(Rule)

See Federal Rules of Criminal Procedure
Filing record on appeal and docketing proceeding; time, Rule 39(c).
(June 25, 1948, ch. 645, 62 Stat. 846.)

References in Text
Rule 39 of the Federal Rules of Criminal Procedure was abrogated Dec. 4, 1967, eff. July 1, 1968, and is covered by Rules 10 to 12, Federal Rules of Appellate Procedure, set out in the Appendix to Title 28, Judiciary and Judicial Procedure.

§3739. Supervision—(Rule)

See Federal Rules of Criminal Procedure
Control and supervision in appellate court, Rule 39(a).
(June 25, 1948, ch. 645, 62 Stat. 846.)

References in Text
Rule 39 of the Federal Rules of Criminal Procedure was abrogated Dec. 4, 1967, eff. July 1, 1968, and is covered by Rule 27, Federal Rules of Appellate Procedure, set out in the Appendix to Title 28, Judiciary and Judicial Procedure.

§3740. Argument—(Rule)

See Federal Rules of Criminal Procedure
Setting appeal for argument; preference to criminal appeals, Rule 39(d).
(June 25, 1948, ch. 645, 62 Stat. 846.)

References in Text
Rule 39 of the Federal Rules of Criminal Procedure was abrogated Dec. 4, 1967, eff. July 1, 1968, and is covered by Rule 34, Federal Rules of Appellate Procedure, set out in the Appendix to Title

28, Judiciary and Judicial Procedure.

§3741. Harmless error and plain error—(Rule)

See Federal Rules of Criminal Procedure
Error or defect as affecting substantial rights, Rule 52.
Defects in indictment, Rule 7.
Waiver of error, Rules 12(b)(2) and 30.
(June 25, 1948, ch. 645, 62 Stat. 846.)

§3742. Review of a sentence
(a) Appeal by a Defendant.—A defendant may file a notice of appeal in the district court for review of an otherwise final sentence if the sentence—
(1) was imposed in violation of law;
(2) was imposed as a result of an incorrect application of the sentencing guidelines; or
(3) is greater than the sentence specified in the applicable guideline range to the extent that the sentence includes a greater fine or term of imprisonment, probation, or supervised release than the maximum established in the guideline range, or includes a more limiting condition of probation or supervised release under section 3563(b)(6) or (b)(11) 1 than the maximum established in the guideline range; or
(4) was imposed for an offense for which there is no sentencing guideline and is plainly unreasonable.
(b) Appeal by the Government.—The Government may file a notice of appeal in the district court for review of an otherwise final sentence if the sentence—
(1) was imposed in violation of law;
(2) was imposed as a result of an incorrect application of the sentencing guidelines;
(3) is less than the sentence specified in the applicable guideline range to the extent that the sentence includes a lesser fine or term of imprisonment, probation, or supervised release than the minimum established in the guideline range, or includes a less limiting condition of probation or supervised release under section 3563(b)(6) or (b)(11) 1 than the minimum established in the guideline range; or
(4) was imposed for an offense for which there is no sentencing guideline and is plainly unreasonable.
The Government may not further prosecute such appeal without the personal approval of the Attorney General, the Solicitor General, or a deputy solicitor general designated by the Solicitor General.
(c) Plea Agreements.—In the case of a plea agreement that includes a specific sentence under rule 11(e)(1)(C) of the Federal Rules of Criminal Procedure—
(1) a defendant may not file a notice of appeal under paragraph (3) or (4) of subsection (a) unless the sentence imposed is greater than the sentence set forth in such agreement; and
(2) the Government may not file a notice of appeal under paragraph (3) or (4) of subsection (b) unless the sentence imposed is less than the sentence set forth in such agreement.
(d) Record on Review.—If a notice of appeal is filed in the district court pursuant to subsection (a) or (b), the clerk shall certify to the court of appeals—
(1) that portion of the record in the case that is designated as pertinent by either of the parties;
(2) the presentence report; and
(3) the information submitted during the sentencing proceeding.
(e) Consideration.—Upon review of the record, the court of appeals shall determine whether the sentence—
(1) was imposed in violation of law;
(2) was imposed as a result of an incorrect application of the sentencing guidelines;
(3) is outside the applicable guideline range, and

(A) the district court failed to provide the written statement of reasons required by section 3553(c);

(B) the sentence departs from the applicable guideline range based on a factor that—

(i) does not advance the objectives set forth in section 3553(a)(2); or

(ii) is not authorized under section 3553(b); or

(iii) is not justified by the facts of the case; or

(C) the sentence departs to an unreasonable degree from the applicable guidelines range, having regard for the factors to be considered in imposing a sentence, as set forth in section 3553(a) of this title and the reasons for the imposition of the particular sentence, as stated by the district court pursuant to the provisions of section 3553(c); or

(4) was imposed for an offense for which there is no applicable sentencing guideline and is plainly unreasonable.

The court of appeals shall give due regard to the opportunity of the district court to judge the credibility of the witnesses, and shall accept the findings of fact of the district court unless they are clearly erroneous and, except with respect to determinations under subsection (3)(A) or (3)(B), shall give due deference to the district court's application of the guidelines to the facts. With respect to determinations under subsection (3)(A) or (3)(B), the court of appeals shall review de novo the district court's application of the guidelines to the facts.

(f) Decision and Disposition.—If the court of appeals determines that—

(1) the sentence was imposed in violation of law or imposed as a result of an incorrect application of the sentencing guidelines, the court shall remand the case for further sentencing proceedings with such instructions as the court considers appropriate;

(2) the sentence is outside the applicable guideline range and the district court failed to provide the required statement of reasons in the order of judgment and commitment, or the departure is based on an impermissible factor, or is to an unreasonable degree, or the sentence was imposed for an offense for which there is no applicable sentencing guideline and is plainly unreasonable, it shall state specific reasons for its conclusions and—

(A) if it determines that the sentence is too high and the appeal has been filed under subsection (a), it shall set aside the sentence and remand the case for further sentencing proceedings with such instructions as the court considers appropriate, subject to subsection (g);

(B) if it determines that the sentence is too low and the appeal has been filed under subsection (b), it shall set aside the sentence and remand the case for further sentencing proceedings with such instructions as the court considers appropriate, subject to subsection (g);

(3) the sentence is not described in paragraph (1) or (2), it shall affirm the sentence.

(g) Sentencing Upon Remand.—A district court to which a case is remanded pursuant to subsection (f)(1) or (f)(2) shall resentence a defendant in accordance with section 3553 and with such instructions as may have been given by the court of appeals, except that—

(1) In determining the range referred to in subsection 3553(a)(4), the court shall apply the guidelines issued by the Sentencing Commission pursuant to section 994(a)(1) of title 28, United States Code, and that were in effect on the date of the previous sentencing of the defendant prior to the appeal, together with any amendments thereto by any act of Congress that was in effect on such date; and

(2) The court shall not impose a sentence outside the applicable guidelines range except upon a ground that—

(A) was specifically and affirmatively included in the written statement of reasons required by section 3553(c) in connection with the previous sentencing of the defendant prior to the appeal; and

(B) was held by the court of appeals, in remanding the case, to be a permissible ground of departure.

(h) Application to a Sentence by a Magistrate Judge.—An appeal of an otherwise final sentence imposed by a United States magistrate judge may be taken to a judge of the district court, and this section shall apply (except for the requirement of approval by the Attorney General or the Solicitor General in the case of a Government appeal) as though the appeal were to a court of appeals from a sentence imposed by a district court.

(i) Guideline Not Expressed as a Range.—For the purpose of this section, the term "guideline range" includes a guideline range having the same upper and lower limits.

(j) Definitions.—For purposes of this section—

(1) a factor is a "permissible" ground of departure if it—

(A) advances the objectives set forth in section 3553(a)(2); and

(B) is authorized under section 3553(b); and

(C) is justified by the facts of the case; and

(2) a factor is an "impermissible" ground of departure if it is not a permissible factor within the meaning of subsection (j)(1).

(Added Pub. L. 98–473, title II, §213(a), Oct. 12, 1984, 98 Stat. 2011; amended Pub. L. 99–646, §73(a), Nov. 10, 1986, 100 Stat. 3617; Pub. L. 100–182, §§4–6, Dec. 7, 1987, 101 Stat. 1266, 1267; Pub. L. 100–690, title VII, §7103(a), Nov. 18, 1988, 102 Stat. 4416; Pub. L. 101–647, title XXXV, §§3501, 3503, Nov. 29, 1990, 104 Stat. 4921; Pub. L. 101–650, title III, §321, Dec. 1, 1990, 104 Stat. 5117; Pub. L. 103–322, title XXXIII, §330002(k), Sept. 13, 1994, 108 Stat. 2140; Pub. L. 108–21, title IV, §401(d)–(f), Apr. 30, 2003, 117 Stat. 670, 671.)

References in Text

Section 3563(b)(6) or (b)(11), referred to in subsecs. (a)(3) and (b)(3), was renumbered section 3563(b)(5) or (b)(10) by Pub. L. 104–132, title II, §203(2)(B), Apr. 24, 1996, 110 Stat. 1227. The Federal Rules of Criminal Procedure, referred to in subsec. (c), are set out in the Appendix of this title.

Constitutionality

For information regarding constitutionality of certain provisions of this section, as added and amended by section 401(d)(2), (e) of Pub. L. 108–21, see Congressional Research Service, The Constitution of the United States of America: Analysis and Interpretation, Appendix 1, Acts of Congress Held Unconstitutional in Whole or in Part by the Supreme Court of the United States.

Amendments

2003—Subsec. (e). Pub. L. 108–21, §401(d)(2), in concluding provisions, substituted ", except with respect to determinations under subsection (3)(A) or (3)(B), shall give due deference to the district court's application of the guidelines to the facts. With respect to determinations under subsection (3)(A) or (3)(B), the court of appeals shall review de novo the district court's application of the guidelines to the facts" for "shall give due deference to the district court's application of the guidelines to the facts".

Subsec. (e)(3). Pub. L. 108–21, §401(d)(1), amended par. (3) generally. Prior to amendment, par. (3) read as follows: "is outside the applicable guideline range, and is unreasonable, having regard for—

"(A) the factors to be considered in imposing a sentence, as set forth in chapter 227 of this title; and

"(B) the reasons for the imposition of the particular sentence, as stated by the district court pursuant to the provisions of section 3553(c); or".

Subsec. (f). Pub. L. 108–21, §401(d)(3)(A), struck out "the sentence" before dash at end of introductory provisions.

Subsec. (f)(1). Pub. L. 108–21, §401(d)(3)(B), inserted "the sentence" before "was imposed".

Subsec. (f)(2). Pub. L. 108–21, §401(d)(3)(C), amended par. (2) generally. Prior to amendment, par. (2) read as follows: "is outside the applicable guideline range and is unreasonable or was imposed for an offense for which there is no applicable sentencing guideline and is plainly unreasonable, it shall state specific reasons for its conclusions and—

"(A) if it determines that the sentence is too high and the appeal has been filed under subsection (a), it shall set aside the sentence and remand the case for further sentencing proceedings with such instructions as the court considers appropriate;

"(B) if it determines that the sentence is too low and the appeal has been filed under subsection (b), it shall set aside the sentence and remand the case for further sentencing proceedings with such instructions as the court considers appropriate;".

Subsec. (f)(3). Pub. L. 108–21, §401(d)(3)(D), inserted "the sentence" before "is not described".

Subsecs. (g) to (i). Pub. L. 108–21, §401(e), added subsec. (g) and redesignated former subsecs. (g) and (h) as (h) and (i), respectively.

Subsec. (j). Pub. L. 108–21, §401(f), added subsec. (j).

1994—Subsec. (b). Pub. L. 103–322 struck out comma after "Government" in introductory provisions.

1990—Subsec. (b). Pub. L. 101–647, §3501, struck out ", with the personal approval of the Attorney General or the Solicitor General" after "The Government" in introductory provisions and inserted at end "The Government may not further prosecute such appeal without the personal approval of the Attorney General, the Solicitor General, or a deputy solicitor general designated by the Solicitor General."

Subsec. (g). Pub. L. 101–647, §3503, inserted "(except for the requirement of approval by the Attorney General or the Solicitor General in the case of a Government appeal)" after "and this section shall apply".

1988—Subsec. (a)(2). Pub. L. 100–690, §7103(a)(1), struck out "issued by the Sentencing Commission pursuant to 28 U.S.C. 994(a)" after "guidelines".

Subsec. (a)(3). Pub. L. 100–690, §7103(a)(2), added par. (3) and struck out former par. (3) which read as follows: "was imposed for an offense for which a sentencing guideline has been issued by the Sentencing Commission pursuant to 28 U.S.C. 994(a)(1), and the sentence is greater than—

"(A) the sentence specified in the applicable guideline to the extent that the sentence includes a greater fine or term of imprisonment or term of supervised release than the maximum established in the guideline, or includes a more limiting condition of probation or supervised release under section 3563(b)(6) or (b)(11) than the maximum established in the guideline; and

"(B) the sentence specified in a plea agreement, if any, under Rule 11(e)(1)(B) or (e)(1)(C) of the Federal Rules of Criminal Procedure; or".

Subsec. (a)(4). Pub. L. 100–690, §7103(a)(4), added par. (4) and struck out former par. (4) which read as follows: "was imposed for an offense for which no sentencing guideline has been issued by the Sentencing Commission pursuant to 28 U.S.C. 994(a)(1) and is plainly unreasonable or greater than the sentence specified in a plea agreement under Rule 11(e)(1)(B) or (e)(1)(C) of the Federal Rules of Criminal Procedure."

Subsec. (b). Pub. L. 100–690, §7103(a)(5), inserted ", with the personal approval of the Attorney General or the Solicitor General," after "The Government" in introductory provisions, and struck out concluding provisions which read as follows: "and the Attorney General or the Solicitor General personally approves the filing of the notice of appeal."

Subsec. (b)(2). Pub. L. 100–690, §7103(a)(1), struck out "issued by the Sentencing Commission pursuant to 28 U.S.C. 994(a)" after "guidelines".

Subsec. (b)(3). Pub. L. 100–690, §7103(a)(3), added par. (3) and struck out former par. (3) which read as follows: "was imposed for an offense for which a sentencing guideline has been issued by the Sentencing Commission pursuant to 28 U.S.C. 994(a)(1), and the sentence is less than—

"(A) the sentence specified in the applicable guideline to the extent that the sentence includes a lesser fine or term of imprisonment or term of supervised release than the minimum established in the guideline, or includes a less limiting condition of probation or supervised release under section 3563(b)(6) or (b)(11) than the minimum established in the guideline; and

"(B) the sentence specified in a plea agreement, if any, under Rule 11(e)(1)(B) or (e)(1)(C) of the Federal Rules of Criminal Procedure; or".

Subsec. (b)(4). Pub. L. 100–690, §7103(a)(5)(A), added par. (4) and struck out former par. (4) which read as follows: "was imposed for an offense for which no sentencing guideline has been issued by the Sentencing Commission pursuant to 28 U.S.C. 994(a)(1) and is plainly unreasonable or less than the sentence specified in a plea agreement under Rule 11(e)(1)(B) or (e)(1)(C) of the Federal Rules of Criminal Procedure;".

Subsec. (c). Pub. L. 100–690, §7103(a)(8), added subsec. (c). Former subsec. (c) redesignated (d).

Subsec. (d). Pub. L. 100–690, §7103(a)(8), redesignated former subsec. (c) as (d). Former subsec. (d) redesignated (e).

Pub. L. 100–690, §7103(a)(6), (7), substituted "applicable guideline range" for "range of the applicable sentencing guideline" in par. (3) and inserted "and shall give due deference to the district court's application of the guidelines to the facts" after "are clearly erroneous" in concluding provisions.

Subsec. (e). Pub. L. 100–690, §7103(a)(8), redesignated former subsec. (d) as (e). Former subsec. (e) redesignated (f).

Subsec. (e)(2). Pub. L. 100–690, §7103(a)(6), substituted "applicable guideline range" for "range of the applicable sentencing guideline".

Subsecs. (f), (g). Pub. L. 100–690, §7103(a)(8), redesignated former subsecs. (e) and (f) as (f) and (g), respectively.

Subsec. (h). Pub. L. 100–690, §7103(a)(9), added subsec. (h).

1987—Subsec. (a)(4). Pub. L. 100–182, §5(1), substituted "and is plainly unreasonable or greater than the sentence specified in a plea agreement under" for "and is greater than the sentence specified in a plea agreement, if any, under".

Subsec. (b)(4). Pub. L. 100–182, §5(2), substituted "and is plainly unreasonable or less than the sentence specified in a plea agreement under" for "and is less than the sentence specified in a plea agreement, if any, under".

Subsec. (d)(4). Pub. L. 100–182, §5(3), added par. (4).

Subsec. (e)(2). Pub. L. 100–182, §5(4), inserted "or was imposed for an offense for which there is no applicable sentencing guideline and is plainly unreasonable" in introductory provisions.

Subsec. (e)(2)(A), (B). Pub. L. 100–182, §5(5), substituted "and" for "the court shall" before "remand".

Subsec. (e)(3). Pub. L. 100–182, §6, amended par. (3) generally. Prior to amendment, par. (3) read as follows: "was not imposed in violation of law or imposed as a result of an incorrect application of the sentencing guidelines, and is not unreasonable, it shall affirm the sentence."

Subsec. (f). Pub. L. 100–182, §4, added subsec. (f).

1986—Subsec. (e)(1). Pub. L. 99–646, §73(a)(1), substituted provision directing the court to remand the case for further sentencing proceedings with such instructions as the court considers appropriate, for provision directing the court to remand the case for further sentencing proceedings or correct the sentence.

Subsec. (e)(2)(A). Pub. L. 99–646, §73(a)(2), substituted provision directing the court to remand the case for further sentencing proceedings with such instructions as the court considers appropriate for provision directing the court to remand the case for imposition of a lesser sentence, remand the case for further sentencing proceedings, or impose a lesser sentence.

Subsec. (e)(2)(B). Pub. L. 99–646, §73(a)(2), substituted provision directing the court to remand the case for further sentencing proceedings with such instructions as the court considers appropriate, for provision directing the court to remand the case for imposition of a greater sentence, remand the case for further sentencing proceedings, or impose a greater sentence.

Change of Name

Words "Magistrate Judge" and "United States magistrate judge" substituted for "Magistrate" and "United States magistrate", respectively, in subsec. (g) pursuant to section 321 of Pub. L. 101–650, set out as a note under section 631 of Title 28, Judiciary and Judicial Procedure.

Effective Date of 1987 Amendment

Amendment by Pub. L. 100–182 applicable with respect to offenses committed after Dec. 7, 1987, see section 26 of Pub. L. 100–182, set out as a note under section 3006A of this title.

Effective Date

Section effective Nov. 1, 1987, and applicable only to offenses committed after the taking effect of this section, see section 235(a)(1) of Pub. L. 98–473, set out as a note under section 3551 of this title.

CHAPTER 237 - CRIME VICTIMS' RIGHTS

| 3771. | Crime victims' rights. |

Prior Provisions

A prior chapter 237, consisting of sections 3771 and 3772, related to criminal procedure, prior to repeal by Pub. L. 100–702, title IV, §§404(a), 407, Nov. 19, 1988, 102 Stat. 4651, 4652, effective Dec. 1, 1988. See sections 2071 to 2074 of Title 28, Judiciary and Judicial Procedure.

§3771. Crime victims' rights

(a) Rights of Crime Victims.—A crime victim has the following rights:

(1) The right to be reasonably protected from the accused.

(2) The right to reasonable, accurate, and timely notice of any public court proceeding, or any parole proceeding, involving the crime or of any release or escape of the accused.

(3) The right not to be excluded from any such public court proceeding, unless the court, after receiving clear and convincing evidence, determines that testimony by the victim would be materially altered if the victim heard other testimony at that proceeding.

(4) The right to be reasonably heard at any public proceeding in the district court involving release, plea, sentencing, or any parole proceeding.

(5) The reasonable right to confer with the attorney for the Government in the case.

(6) The right to full and timely restitution as provided in law.

(7) The right to proceedings free from unreasonable delay.

(8) The right to be treated with fairness and with respect for the victim's dignity and privacy.

(9) The right to be informed in a timely manner of any plea bargain or deferred prosecution agreement.

(10) The right to be informed of the rights under this section and the services described in section 503(c) of the Victims' Rights and Restitution Act of 1990 (42 U.S.C. 10607(c)) 1 and provided contact information for the Office of the Victims' Rights Ombudsman of the Department of Justice.

(b) Rights Afforded.—

(1) In general.—In any court proceeding involving an offense against a crime victim, the court shall ensure that the crime victim is afforded the rights described in subsection (a). Before making a determination described in subsection (a)(3), the court shall make every effort to permit the fullest attendance possible by the victim and shall consider reasonable alternatives to the exclusion of the victim from the criminal proceeding. The reasons for any decision denying relief under this chapter shall be clearly stated on the record.

(2) Habeas corpus proceedings.—

(A) In general.—In a Federal habeas corpus proceeding arising out of a State conviction, the court shall ensure that a crime victim is afforded the rights described in paragraphs (3), (4), (7), and (8) of subsection (a).

(B) Enforcement.—

(i) In general.—These rights may be enforced by the crime victim or the crime victim's lawful representative in the manner described in paragraphs (1) and (3) of subsection (d).

(ii) Multiple victims.—In a case involving multiple victims, subsection (d)(2) shall also apply.

(C) Limitation.—This paragraph relates to the duties of a court in relation to the rights of a crime victim in Federal habeas corpus proceedings arising out of a State conviction, and does not give rise to any obligation or requirement applicable to personnel of any agency of the Executive

Branch of the Federal Government.

(D) Definition.—For purposes of this paragraph, the term "crime victim" means the person against whom the State offense is committed or, if that person is killed or incapacitated, that person's family member or other lawful representative.

(c) Best Efforts To Accord Rights.—

(1) Government.—Officers and employees of the Department of Justice and other departments and agencies of the United States engaged in the detection, investigation, or prosecution of crime shall make their best efforts to see that crime victims are notified of, and accorded, the rights described in subsection (a).

(2) Advice of attorney.—The prosecutor shall advise the crime victim that the crime victim can seek the advice of an attorney with respect to the rights described in subsection (a).

(3) Notice.—Notice of release otherwise required pursuant to this chapter shall not be given if such notice may endanger the safety of any person.

(d) Enforcement and Limitations.—

(1) Rights.—The crime victim or the crime victim's lawful representative, and the attorney for the Government may assert the rights described in subsection (a). A person accused of the crime may not obtain any form of relief under this chapter.

(2) Multiple crime victims.—In a case where the court finds that the number of crime victims makes it impracticable to accord all of the crime victims the rights described in subsection (a), the court shall fashion a reasonable procedure to give effect to this chapter that does not unduly complicate or prolong the proceedings.

(3) Motion for relief and writ of mandamus.—The rights described in subsection (a) shall be asserted in the district court in which a defendant is being prosecuted for the crime or, if no prosecution is underway, in the district court in the district in which the crime occurred. The district court shall take up and decide any motion asserting a victim's right forthwith. If the district court denies the relief sought, the movant may petition the court of appeals for a writ of mandamus. The court of appeals may issue the writ on the order of a single judge pursuant to circuit rule or the Federal Rules of Appellate Procedure. The court of appeals shall take up and decide such application forthwith within 72 hours after the petition has been filed, unless the litigants, with the approval of the court, have stipulated to a different time period for consideration. In deciding such application, the court of appeals shall apply ordinary standards of appellate review. In no event shall proceedings be stayed or subject to a continuance of more than five days for purposes of enforcing this chapter. If the court of appeals denies the relief sought, the reasons for the denial shall be clearly stated on the record in a written opinion.

(4) Error.—In any appeal in a criminal case, the Government may assert as error the district court's denial of any crime victim's right in the proceeding to which the appeal relates.

(5) Limitation on relief.—In no case shall a failure to afford a right under this chapter provide grounds for a new trial. A victim may make a motion to re-open a plea or sentence only if—

(A) the victim has asserted the right to be heard before or during the proceeding at issue and such right was denied;

(B) the victim petitions the court of appeals for a writ of mandamus within 14 days; and

(C) in the case of a plea, the accused has not pled to the highest offense charged.

This paragraph does not affect the victim's right to restitution as provided in title 18, United States Code.

(6) No cause of action.—Nothing in this chapter shall be construed to authorize a cause of action for damages or to create, to enlarge, or to imply any duty or obligation to any victim or other person for the breach of which the United States or any of its officers or employees could be held liable in damages. Nothing in this chapter shall be construed to impair the prosecutorial discretion of the Attorney General or any officer under his direction.

(e) Definitions.—For the purposes of this chapter:

(1) Court of appeals.—The term "court of appeals" means—

(A) the United States court of appeals for the judicial district in which a defendant is being prosecuted; or

(B) for a prosecution in the Superior Court of the District of Columbia, the District of Columbia Court of Appeals.

(2) Crime victim.—

(A) In general.—The term "crime victim" means a person directly and proximately harmed as a result of the commission of a Federal offense or an offense in the District of Columbia.

(B) Minors and certain other victims.—In the case of a crime victim who is under 18 years of age, incompetent, incapacitated, or deceased, the legal guardians of the crime victim or the representatives of the crime victim's estate, family members, or any other persons appointed as suitable by the court, may assume the crime victim's rights under this chapter, but in no event shall the defendant be named as such guardian or representative.

(3) District court; court.—The terms "district court" and "court" include the Superior Court of the District of Columbia.

(f) Procedures To Promote Compliance.—

(1) Regulations.—Not later than 1 year after the date of enactment of this chapter, the Attorney General of the United States shall promulgate regulations to enforce the rights of crime victims and to ensure compliance by responsible officials with the obligations described in law respecting crime victims.

(2) Contents.—The regulations promulgated under paragraph (1) shall—

(A) designate an administrative authority within the Department of Justice to receive and investigate complaints relating to the provision or violation of the rights of a crime victim;

(B) require a course of training for employees and offices of the Department of Justice that fail to comply with provisions of Federal law pertaining to the treatment of crime victims, and otherwise assist such employees and offices in responding more effectively to the needs of crime victims;

(C) contain disciplinary sanctions, including suspension or termination from employment, for employees of the Department of Justice who willfully or wantonly fail to comply with provisions of Federal law pertaining to the treatment of crime victims; and

(D) provide that the Attorney General, or the designee of the Attorney General, shall be the final arbiter of the complaint, and that there shall be no judicial review of the final decision of the Attorney General by a complainant.

(Added Pub. L. 108–405, title I, §102(a), Oct. 30, 2004, 118 Stat. 2261; amended Pub. L. 109–248, title II, §212, July 27, 2006, 120 Stat. 616; Pub. L. 111–16, §3(12), May 7, 2009, 123 Stat. 1608; Pub. L. 114–22, title I, §113(a), (c)(1), May 29, 2015, 129 Stat. 240, 241.)

References in Text

Section 503(c) of the Victims' Rights and Restitution Act of 1990, referred to in subsec. (a)(10), is section 503(c) of title V of Pub. L. 101–647, which was classified to section 10607(c) of Title 42, The Public Health and Welfare, prior to editorial reclassification as section 20141(c) of Title 34, Crime Control and Law Enforcement.

The Federal Rules of Appellate Procedure, referred to in subsec. (d)(3), are set out in the Appendix to Title 28, Judiciary and Judicial Procedure.

The date of enactment of this chapter, referred to in subsec. (f)(1), is the date of enactment of Pub. L. 108–405, which was approved Oct. 30, 2004.

Prior Provisions

A prior section 3771, acts June 25, 1948, ch. 645, 62 Stat. 846; May 24, 1949, ch. 139, §59, 63 Stat. 98; May 10, 1950, ch. 174, §1, 64 Stat. 158; July 7, 1958, Pub. L. 85–508, §12(k), 72 Stat. 348; Mar. 18, 1959, Pub. L. 86–3, §14(g), 73 Stat. 11; Oct. 17, 1968, Pub. L. 90–578, title III, §301(a)(2), 82 Stat. 1115, related to procedure to and including verdict, prior to repeal by Pub. L. 100–702, title IV, §§404(a), 407, Nov. 19, 1988, 102 Stat. 4651, 4652, effective Dec. 1, 1988.

Amendments

2015—Subsec. (a)(9), (10). Pub. L. 114–22, §113(a)(1), added pars. (9) and (10).

Subsec. (d)(3). Pub. L. 114–22, §113(c)(1), inserted "In deciding such application, the court of appeals shall apply ordinary standards of appellate review." before "In no event shall".

Pub. L. 114–22, §113(a)(2), inserted ", unless the litigants, with the approval of the court, have stipulated to a different time period for consideration" after "after the petition has been filed".

Subsec. (e). Pub. L. 114–22, §113(a)(3), substituted "For the purposes of this chapter:" for "For the purposes of this chapter, the term", designated remainder of existing provisions as par. (2) and inserted par. heading, in par. (2), inserted subpar. (A) designation, heading, and "The term" before " 'crime victim' means" and inserted subpar. (B) designation and heading before "In the case", and added pars. (1) and (3).

2009—Subsec. (d)(5)(B). Pub. L. 111–16 substituted "14 days" for "10 days".

2006—Subsec. (b). Pub. L. 109–248 designated existing provisions as par. (1), inserted heading, and added par. (2).

Effective Date of 2015 Amendment

Pub. L. 114–22, title I, §113(c)(2), May 29, 2015, 129 Stat. 241, provided that: "The amendment made by paragraph (1) [amending this section] shall apply with respect to any petition for a writ of mandamus filed under section 3771(d)(3) of title 18, United States Code, that is pending on the date of enactment of this Act [May 29, 2015]."

Effective Date of 2009 Amendment

Amendment by Pub. L. 111–16 effective Dec. 1, 2009, see section 7 of Pub. L. 111–16, set out as a note under section 109 of Title 11, Bankruptcy.

Short Title of 2004 Amendment

Pub. L. 108–405, title I, §101, Oct. 30, 2004, 118 Stat. 2261, provided that: "This title [enacting this chapter and sections 10603d and 10603e of Title 42, The Public Health and Welfare, repealing section 10606 of Title 42, and enacting provisions set out as a note under this section] may be cited as the 'Scott Campbell, Stephanie Roper, Wendy Preston, Louarna Gillis, and Nila Lynn Crime Victims' Rights Act'."

Reports on Assertion of Crime Victims' Rights in Criminal Cases

Pub. L. 108–405, title I, §104(a), Oct. 30, 2004, 118 Stat. 2265, provided that: "Not later than 1 year after the date of enactment of this Act [Oct. 30, 2004] and annually thereafter, the Administrative Office of the United States Courts, for each Federal court, shall report to Congress the number of times that a right established in chapter 237 of title 18, United States Code, is asserted in a criminal case and the relief requested is denied and, with respect to each such denial, the reason for such denial, as well as the number of times a mandamus action is brought pursuant to chapter 237 of title 18, and the result reached."

CHAPTER 238 - SEXUAL ASSAULT SURVIVORS' RIGHTS

| 3772. | Sexual assault survivors' rights. |

§3772. Sexual assault survivors' rights

(a) Rights of Sexual Assault Survivors.—In addition to those rights provided in section 3771, a sexual assault survivor has the following rights:

(1) The right not to be prevented from, or charged for, receiving a medical forensic examination.

(2) The right to—

(A) subject to paragraph (3), have a sexual assault evidence collection kit or its probative contents preserved, without charge, for the duration of the maximum applicable statute of limitations or 20 years, whichever is shorter;

(B) be informed of any result of a sexual assault evidence collection kit, including a DNA profile match, toxicology report, or other information collected as part of a medical forensic examination, if such disclosure would not impede or compromise an ongoing investigation; and

(C) be informed in writing of policies governing the collection and preservation of a sexual assault evidence collection kit.

(3) The right to—

(A) upon written request, receive written notification from the appropriate official with custody not later than 60 days before the date of the intended destruction or disposal; and

(B) upon written request, be granted further preservation of the kit or its probative contents.

(4) The right to be informed of the rights under this subsection.

(b) Applicability.—Subsections (b) through (f) of section 3771 shall apply to sexual assault survivors.

(c) Definition of Sexual Assault.—In this section, the term "sexual assault" means any nonconsensual sexual act proscribed by Federal, tribal, or State law, including when the victim lacks capacity to consent.

(d) Funding.—This section, other than paragraphs (2)(A) and (3)(B) of subsection (a), shall be carried out using funds made available under section 1402(d)(3)(A)(i) of the Victims of Crime Act of 1984 (42 U.S.C. 10601(d)(3)(A)(i)).1 No additional funds are authorized to be appropriated to carry out this section.

(Added Pub. L. 114–236, §2(a), Oct. 7, 2016, 130 Stat. 966.)

References in Text

Section 1402(d)(3)(A)(i) of the Victims of Crime Act of 1984, referred to in subsec. (d), is section 1402(d)(3)(A)(i) of chapter XIV of title II of Pub. L. 98–473, which was classified to section 10601(d)(3)(A)(i) of Title 42, The Public Health and Welfare, prior to editorial reclassification as section 20101(d)(3)(A)(i) of Title 34, Crime Control and Law Enforcement.

Prior Provisions

A prior section 3772, acts June 25, 1948, ch. 645, 62 Stat. 846; May 24, 1949, ch. 139, §60, 63 Stat. 98; July 7, 1958, Pub. L. 85–508, §12(l), 72 Stat. 348; Mar. 18, 1959, Pub. L. 86–3, §14(h), 73 Stat. 11; Oct. 12, 1984, Pub. L. 98–473, title II, §206, 98 Stat. 1986, related to procedure after verdict, prior to repeal by Pub. L. 100–702, title IV, §§404(a), 407, Nov. 19, 1988, 102 Stat. 4651, 4652, effective Dec. 1, 1988.

Amendments

1990—Pub. L. 101–647, title XXXV, §3597, Nov. 29, 1990, 104 Stat. 4931, added items 306 and 319.

1984—Pub. L. 98–473, title II, §218(d), Oct. 12, 1984, 98 Stat. 2027, in items 309, 311, and 314 substituted "Repealed" for "Good time allowances", "Parole", and "Narcotic addicts", respectively. Pub. L. 98–473, title II, §403(b), Oct. 12, 1984, 98 Stat. 2067, substituted "Offenders with mental disease or defect" for "Mental defectives" in item 313.

1966—Pub. L. 89–793, title VI, §603, Nov. 8, 1966, 80 Stat. 1450, added item 314.

CHAPTER 301 - GENERAL PROVISIONS

Amendments

1998—Pub. L. 105–370, §2(b), Nov. 12, 1998, 112 Stat. 3375, added item 4014.

1988—Pub. L. 100–690, title VII, §7608(d)(2), Nov. 18, 1988, 102 Stat. 4517, added item 4013.

1984—Pub. L. 98–473, title II, §1109(e), Oct. 12, 1984, 98 Stat. 2148, added item 4012.

1971—Pub. L. 92–128, §1(c), Sept. 25, 1971, 85 Stat. 347, substituted "Limitation on detention; control of prisons" for "Control by Attorney General" in item 4001.

1966—Pub. L. 89–554, §3(e), Sept. 6, 1966, 80 Stat. 610, added items 4010 and 4011.

§4001. Limitation on detention; control of prisons

(a) No citizen shall be imprisoned or otherwise detained by the United States except pursuant to an Act of Congress.

(b)(1) The control and management of Federal penal and correctional institutions, except military or naval institutions, shall be vested in the Attorney General, who shall promulgate rules for the government thereof, and appoint all necessary officers and employees in accordance with the civil-service laws, the Classification Act, as amended, and the applicable regulations.

(2) The Attorney General may establish and conduct industries, farms, and other activities and classify the inmates; and provide for their proper government, discipline, treatment, care, rehabilitation, and reformation.

(June 25, 1948, ch. 645, 62 Stat. 847; Pub. L. 92–128, §1(a), (b), Sept. 25, 1971, 85 Stat. 347.)

Historical and Revision Notes

Based on title 18, U.S.C., 1934 ed., §§741 and 753e (Mar. 3, 1891, ch. 529, §§1, 4, 26 Stat. 839; May 14, 1930, ch. 274, §6, 46 Stat. 326).

This section consolidates said sections 741 and 753e with such changes of language as were necessary to effect consolidation.

"The Classification Act, as amended," was inserted more clearly to express the existing procedure for appointment of officers and employees as noted in letter of the Director of Bureau of Prisons, June 19, 1944.

References in Text

The Classification Act, as amended, referred to in subsec. (b)(1), originally was the Classification Act of 1923, Mar. 4, 1923, ch. 265, 42 Stat. 1488, which was repealed by section 1202 of the Classification Act of 1949, Oct. 28, 1949, ch. 782, 63 Stat. 972. Section 1106(a) of the 1949 Act provided that references in other laws to the Classification Act of 1923 shall be held and considered to mean the Classification Act of 1949. The Classification Act of 1949 was in turn repealed by Pub. L. 89–554, §8(a), Sept. 6, 1966, 80 Stat. 632, and reenacted by the first section thereof as chapter 51 and subchapter III of chapter 53 of Title 5.

Amendments

1971—Pub. L. 92–128, §1(b), substituted "Limitation on detention; control of prisons" for "Control by Attorney General" in section catchline.

Subsec. (a). Pub. L. 92–128, §1(a), added subsec. (a).

Subsec. (b). Pub. L. 92–128, §1(a), designated existing first and second pars. as pars. (1) and (2) of subsec. (b).

Short Title of 2000 Amendment

Pub. L. 106–294, §1, Oct. 12, 2000, 114 Stat. 1038, provided that: "This Act [enacting section 4048 of this title and amending section 4013 of this title] may be cited as the 'Federal Prisoner Health Care Copayment Act of 2000'."

Short Title of 1998 Amendment

Pub. L. 105–370, §1, Nov. 12, 1998, 112 Stat. 3374, provided that: "This Act [enacting section 4014 of this title and provisions set out as a note under section 4042 of this title] may be cited as the 'Correction Officers Health and Safety Act of 1998'."

Federal Law Enforcement Death in Custody Reporting Requirement

Pub. L. 113–242, §3, Dec. 18, 2014, 128 Stat. 2861, provided that:

"(a) In General.—For each fiscal year (beginning after the date that is 120 days after the date of the enactment of this Act [Dec. 18, 2014]), the head of each Federal law enforcement agency shall submit to the Attorney General a report (in such form and manner specified by the Attorney General) that contains information regarding the death of any person who is—

"(1) detained, under arrest, or is in the process of being arrested by any officer of such Federal law enforcement agency (or by any State or local law enforcement officer while participating in and for purposes of a Federal law enforcement operation, task force, or any other Federal law enforcement capacity carried out by such Federal law enforcement agency); or

"(2) en route to be incarcerated or detained, or is incarcerated or detained at—

"(A) any facility (including any immigration or juvenile facility) pursuant to a contract with such Federal law enforcement agency;

"(B) any State or local government facility used by such Federal law enforcement agency; or

"(C) any Federal correctional facility or Federal pre-trial detention facility located within the United States.

"(b) Information Required.—Each report required by this section shall include, at a minimum, the information required by section 2(b) [34 U.S.C. 60105(b)].

"(c) Study and Report.—Information reported under subsection (a) shall be analyzed and included in the study and report required by section 2(f) [34 U.S.C. 60105(f)]."

Placement of Certain Persons in Privately Operated Prisons

Pub. L. 106–553, §1(a)(2) [title I, §114, formerly §115], Dec. 21, 2000, 114 Stat. 2762, 2762A–68; renumbered §114, Pub. L. 106–554, §1(a)(4) [div. A, §213(a)(2)], Dec. 21, 2000, 114 Stat. 2763, 2763A–179, provided that: "Beginning in fiscal year 2001 and thereafter, funds appropriated to the Federal Prison System may be used to place in privately operated prisons only such persons sentenced to incarceration under the District of Columbia Code as the Director, Bureau of Prisons, may determine to be appropriate for such placement consistent with Federal classification standards, after consideration of all relevant factors, including the threat of danger to public safety."

Fee To Recover Cost of Incarceration

Pub. L. 102–395, title I, §111(a), Oct. 6, 1992, 106 Stat. 1842, provided that:

"(1) For fiscal year 1993 and thereafter the Attorney General shall establish and collect a fee to cover the costs of confinement from any person convicted in a United States District Court and committed to the Attorney General's custody.

"(2) Such fee shall be equivalent to the average cost of one year of incarceration, and the Attorney General shall credit or rebate a prorated portion of the fee with respect to any such person incarcerated for 334 days or fewer in a given fiscal year.

"(3) The calculation of the number of days of incarceration in a given fiscal year for the purpose of such fee shall include time served prior to conviction.

"(4) The Attorney General shall not collect such fee from any person with respect to whom a fine was imposed or waived by a judge of a United States District Court pursuant to section 5E1.2(f) and (i) of the United States Sentencing Guidelines, or any successor provisions.

"(5) In cases in which the Attorney General has authority to collect the fee, the Attorney General shall have discretion to waive the fee or impose a lesser fee if the person under confinement establishes that (1) he or she is not able and, even with the use of a reasonable installment schedule, is not likely to become able to pay all or part of the fee, or (2) imposition of a fine would unduly burden the defendant's dependents.

"(6) For fiscal year 1993 only, fees collected in accordance with this section shall be deposited as offsetting receipts to the Treasury.

"(7) For fiscal year 1994 and thereafter, fees collected in accordance with this section shall be deposited as offsetting collections to the appropriation Federal Prison System, 'Salaries and expenses', and shall be available, inter alia, to enhance alcohol and drug abuse prevention programs."

Use of Inactive Department of Defense Facilities as Prisons

Pub. L. 95–624, §9, Nov. 9, 1978, 92 Stat. 3463, provided that: "The Attorney General shall consult with the Secretary of Defense in order to develop a plan to assure that such suitable facilities as the Department of Defense operates which are not in active use shall be made available for operation by the Department of Justice for the confinement of United States prisoners. Such plan shall provide for the return to the management of the Department of Defense of any such facility upon a finding by the Secretary of Defense that such return is necessary to the operation of the Department."

§4002. Federal prisoners in State institutions; employment

For the purpose of providing suitable quarters for the safekeeping, care, and subsistence of all persons held under authority of any enactment of Congress, the Attorney General may contract, for a period not exceeding three years, with the proper authorities of any State, Territory, or political subdivision thereof, for the imprisonment, subsistence, care, and proper employment of such persons.

Such Federal prisoners shall be employed only in the manufacture of articles for, the production of supplies for, the construction of public works for, and the maintenance and care of the institutions of, the State or political subdivision in which they are imprisoned.

The rates to be paid for the care and custody of said persons shall take into consideration the character of the quarters furnished, sanitary conditions, and quality of subsistence and may be such as will permit and encourage the proper authorities to provide reasonably decent, sanitary, and healthful quarters and subsistence for such persons.

(June 25, 1948, ch. 645, 62 Stat. 847; Pub. L. 95–624, §8, Nov. 9, 1978, 92 Stat. 3463.)

Historical and Revision Notes

Based on title 18, U.S.C., 1940 ed., §753b, (May 14, 1930, ch. 274, §3, 46 Stat. 325).

Changes were made in phraseology. The first sentence was incorporated in section 4042 of this title.

Amendments

1978—Pub. L. 95–624 substituted "Attorney General" for "Director of the Bureau of Prisons".

§4003. Federal institutions in States without appropriate facilities

If by reason of the refusal or inability of the authorities having control of any jail, workhouse, penal, correctional, or other suitable institution of any State or Territory, or political subdivision thereof, to enter into a contract for the imprisonment, subsistence, care, or proper employment of United States prisoners, or if there are no suitable or sufficient facilities available at reasonable cost, the Attorney General may select a site either within or convenient to the State, Territory, or judicial district concerned and cause to be erected thereon a house of detention, workhouse, jail, prison-industries project, or camp, or other place of confinement, which shall be used for the detention of persons held under authority of any Act of Congress, and of such other persons as in the opinion of the Attorney General are proper subjects for confinement in such institutions. (June 25, 1948, ch. 645, 62 Stat. 848.)

Historical and Revision Notes

Based on title 18, U.S.C., 1940 ed., §753c (May 14, 1930, ch. 274, §4, 46 Stat. 326).
Words "with or without hard labor" were omitted as unnecessary in view of omission of "hard labor" as part of the punishment. (See reviser's note under section 1 of this title.)
The phrase "held under authority of any Act of Congress," was substituted for the following "held as material witnesses, persons awaiting trial, persons sentenced to imprisonment and awaiting transfer to other institutions, persons held for violation of the immigration laws or awaiting deportation, and for the confinement of persons convicted of offenses against the United States and sentenced to imprisonment".
Minor changes in arrangement and phraseology were made.

§4004. Oaths and acknowledgments

The wardens and superintendents, associate wardens and superintendents, chief clerks, and record clerks, of Federal penal or correctional institutions, may administer oaths to and take acknowledgments of officers, employees, and inmates of such institutions, but shall not demand or accept any fee or compensation therefor. (June 25, 1948, ch. 645, 62 Stat. 848; July 7, 1955, ch. 282, 69 Stat. 282; Pub. L. 98–473, title II, §223(l), Oct. 12, 1984, 98 Stat. 2029.)

Historical and Revision Notes

Based on title 18, U.S.C., 1940 ed., §754 (Feb. 11, 1938, ch. 24, §§1, 2, 52 Stat. 28).
Section was extended to include superintendents and associate superintendents.
Minor changes were made in phraseology. Words "the authority conferred by" were omitted as surplusage.

Amendments

1984—Pub. L. 98–473 substituted "and record clerks" for "record clerks, and parole officers".
1955—Act July 7, 1955, permitted chief clerks, record clerks, and parole officers to administer oaths and take acknowledgments.

Effective Date of 1984 Amendment

Amendment by Pub. L. 98–473 effective Nov. 1, 1987, and applicable only to offenses committed after the taking effect of such amendment, see section 235(a)(1) of Pub. L. 98–473, set out as an Effective Date note under section 3551 of this title.

§4005. Medical relief; expenses

(a) Upon request of the Attorney General and to the extent consistent with the Assisted Suicide Funding Restriction Act of 1997, the Federal Security Administrator shall detail regular and reserve commissioned officers of the Public Health Service, pharmacists, acting assistant surgeons, and other employees of the Public Health Service to the Department of Justice for the purpose of supervising and furnishing medical, psychiatric, and other technical and scientific services to the Federal penal and correctional institutions.

(b) The compensation, allowances, and expenses of the personnel detailed under this section may be paid from applicable appropriations of the Public Health Service in accordance with the law and regulations governing the personnel of the Public Health Service, such appropriations to be reimbursed from applicable appropriations of the Department of Justice; or the Attorney General may make allotments of funds and transfer of credit to the Public Health Service in such amounts as are available and necessary, for payment of compensation, allowances, and expenses of personnel so detailed, in accordance with the law and regulations governing the personnel of the Public Health Service.

(June 25, 1948, ch. 645, 62 Stat. 848; Pub. L. 105–12, §9(k), Apr. 30, 1997, 111 Stat. 28.)

Historical and Revision Notes

Based on title 18, U.S.C., 1940 ed., §§751, 752 (May 13, 1930, ch. 256, §§1, 2, 46 Stat. 273; Reorg. Plan No. I, §§201, 205, 4 F.R. 2728, 2729, 53 Stat. 1424, 1425).

Section consolidates sections 751 and 752 of title 18, U.S.C., 1940 ed., as subsections (a) and (b), respectively.

"Federal Security Administrator" was substituted for "Federal Security Agency."

Functions of the Secretary of the Treasury were transferred to the Federal Security Administrator by Reorg. Plan No. I, §205, 4 F.R. 2729, 53 Stat. 1425. (See note under section 133t of title 5, U.S.C., 1940 ed., Executive Departments and Government Officers and Employees.)

The first part of said section 751, which read "Authorized medical relief under the Department of Justice in Federal penal and correctional institutions shall be supervised and furnished by personnel of the Public Health Service, and" was omitted as surplusage, considering the remainder of the text.

Minor changes of phraseology were made.

References in Text

The Assisted Suicide Funding Restriction Act of 1997, referred to in subsec. (a), is Pub. L. 105–12, Apr. 30, 1997, 111 Stat. 23, which is classified principally to chapter 138 (§14401 et seq.) of Title 42, The Public Health and Welfare. For complete classification of this Act to the Code, see Short Title note set out under section 14401 of Title 42 and Tables.

Amendments

1997—Subsec. (a). Pub. L. 105–12 inserted "and to the extent consistent with the Assisted Suicide Funding Restriction Act of 1997" after "Upon request of the Attorney General".

Effective Date of 1997 Amendment

Amendment by Pub. L. 105–12 effective Apr. 30, 1997, and applicable to Federal payments made pursuant to obligations incurred after Apr. 30, 1997, for items and services provided on or after such date, subject to also being applicable with respect to contracts entered into, renewed, or extended after Apr. 30, 1997, as well as contracts entered into before Apr. 30, 1997, to the extent permitted under such contracts, see section 11 of Pub. L. 105–12, set out as an Effective Date note under section 14401 of Title 42, The Public Health and Welfare.

Transfer of Functions

Functions of Federal Security Administrator transferred to Secretary of Health, Education, and Welfare, and office of Federal Security Administrator abolished by sections 5 and 8 of Reorg. Plan No. 1 of 1953, as amended, eff. Apr. 11, 1953, 18 F.R. 2053, 67 Stat. 631, set out in the Appendix to Title 5, Government Organization and Employees.

Functions of Public Health Service, Surgeon General of Public Health Service, and all other officers and employees of Public Health Service, and functions of all agencies of or in Public Health Service transferred to Secretary of Health, Education, and Welfare by Reorg. Plan No. 3 of 1966, eff. June 25, 1966, 31 F.R. 8855, 80 Stat. 1610, set out in the Appendix to Title 5. Secretary of Health, Education, and Welfare redesignated Secretary of Health and Human Services by Pub. L. 96–88, title V, §509(b), Oct. 17, 1979, 93 Stat. 695, which is classified to section 3508(b) of Title 20, Education.

§4006. Subsistence for prisoners

(a) In General.—The Attorney General or the Secretary of Homeland Security, as applicable, shall allow and pay only the reasonable and actual cost of the subsistence of prisoners in the custody of any marshal of the United States, and shall prescribe such regulations for the government of the marshals as will enable him to determine the actual and reasonable expenses incurred.
(b) Health Care Items and Services.—
(1) In general.—Payment for costs incurred for the provision of health care items and services for individuals in the custody of the United States Marshals Service, the Federal Bureau of Investigation and the Department of Homeland Security shall be the amount billed, not to exceed the amount that would be paid for the provision of similar health care items and services under the Medicare program under title XVIII of the Social Security Act.
(2) Full and final payment.—Any payment for a health care item or service made pursuant to this subsection, shall be deemed to be full and final payment.
(June 25, 1948, ch. 645, 62 Stat. 848; Pub. L. 106–113, div. B, §1000(a)(1) [title I, §114], Nov. 29, 1999, 113 Stat. 1535, 1501A–20; Pub. L. 106–553, §1(a)(2) [title VI, §626], Dec. 21, 2000, 114 Stat. 2762, 2762A–108; Pub. L. 109–162, title XI, §1157, Jan. 5, 2006, 119 Stat. 3114.)

Historical and Revision Notes

Based on title 18, U.S.C., 1940 ed., §703 (R.S. §5545; Mar. 2, 1911, ch. 192, 36 Stat. 1003). The provisions relating to the Washington Asylum and Jail are now included in the District of Columbia Code. (See D.C. Code, 1940 ed., §24–421.)
Changes of phraseology were made.

References in Text

The Social Security Act, referred to in subsec. (b)(1), is act Aug. 14, 1935, ch. 531, 49 Stat. 620, as amended. Title XVIII of the Act is classified generally to subchapter XVIII (§1395 et seq.) of chapter 7 of Title 42, The Public Health and Welfare. For complete classification of this Act to the Code, see section 1305 of Title 42 and Tables.

Amendments

2006—Subsec. (a). Pub. L. 109–162, §1157(1), inserted "or the Secretary of Homeland Security, as applicable," after "The Attorney General".
Subsec. (b)(1). Pub. L. 109–162, §1157(2), substituted "the Department of Homeland Security" for "the Immigration and Naturalization Service", "shall be the amount billed, not to exceed the amount" for "shall not exceed the lesser of the amount", and "items and services under the Medicare program" for "items and services under—
"(A) the Medicare program"
and struck out subpar. (B) which read as follows: "the Medicaid program under title XIX of such Act of the State in which the services were provided."
2000—Subsec. (b)(1). Pub. L. 106–553 inserted ", the Federal Bureau of Investigation" after "United States Marshals Service".
1999—Pub. L. 106–113 designated existing provisions as subsec. (a), inserted heading, and added subsec. (b).

§4007. Expenses of prisoners

The expenses attendant upon the confinement of persons arrested or committed under the laws of the United States, as well as upon the execution of any sentence of a court thereof respecting them, shall be paid out of the Treasury of the United States in the manner provided by law.
(June 25, 1948, ch. 645, 62 Stat. 848.)

Historical and Revision Notes

Based on title 18, U.S.C., 1940 ed., §701 (R.S. §5536).

Provision authorizing expenses for transportation was omitted as covered by similar provision in section 4008 of this title.

Minor changes of phraseology were made.

Payment of Costs of Incarceration by Federal Prisoners

Pub. L. 100–690, title VII, §7301, Nov. 18, 1988, 102 Stat. 4463, provided that: "Not later than 1 year after the date of enactment of this section [Nov. 18, 1988], the United States Sentencing Commission shall study the feasibility of requiring prisoners incarcerated in Federal correctional institutions to pay some or all of the costs incident to the prisoner's confinement, including, but not limited to, the costs of food, housing, and shelter. The study shall review measures which would allow prisoners unable to pay such costs to work at paid employment within the community, during incarceration or after release, in order to pay the costs incident to the prisoner's confinement."

§4008. Transportation expenses

Prisoners shall be transported by agents designated by the Attorney General or his authorized representative.

The reasonable expense of transportation, necessary subsistence, and hire and transportation of guards and agents shall be paid by the Attorney General from such appropriation for the Department of Justice as he shall direct.

Upon conviction by a consular court or court martial the prisoner shall be transported from the court to the place of confinement by agents of the Department of State, the Army, Navy, or Air Force, as the case may be, the expense to be paid out of the Treasury of the United States in the manner provided by law.

(June 25, 1948, ch. 645, 62 Stat. 849; May 24, 1949, ch. 139, §61, 63 Stat. 98.)

Historical and Revision Notes

1948 Act

Based on title 18, U.S.C., 1940 ed., §753g (May 14, 1930, ch. 274, §8, 46 Stat. 327).

The second paragraph was originally a proviso.

Minor changes of phraseology were made.

1949 Act

This section [section 61] corrects the third paragraph of section 4008 of title 18, U.S.C., by redesignating the "War Department" as the "Department of the Army", to conform to such redesignation by act of July 26, 1947 (ch. 343, title II, §205(a), 61 Stat. 501), and by inserting a reference to the Department of the Air Force, in view of the creation of such Department by the same act.

Amendments

1949—Act May 24, 1949, substituted "the Army, Navy, or Air Force" for "War, or the Navy".

§4009. Appropriations for sites and buildings

The Attorney General may authorize the use of a sum not to exceed $100,000 in each instance, payable from any unexpended balance of the appropriation "Support of United States prisoners" for the purpose of leasing or acquiring a site, preparation of plans, and erection of necessary buildings under section 4003 of this title.

If in any instance it shall be impossible or impracticable to secure a proper site and erect the necessary buildings within the above limitation the Attorney General may authorize the use of a sum not to exceed $10,000 in each instance, payable from any unexpended balance of the appropriation "Support of United States prisoners" for the purpose of securing options and making preliminary surveys or sketches.

Upon selection of an appropriate site the Attorney General shall submit to Congress an estimate of the cost of purchasing same and of remodeling, constructing, and equipping the necessary buildings thereon.

(June 25, 1948, ch. 645, 62 Stat. 849.)

Historical and Revision Notes

Based on title 18, U.S.C., 1940 ed., §753d (May 14, 1930, ch. 274, §5, 46 Stat. 326). Minor changes of phraseology were made.

§4010. Acquisition of additional land

The Attorney General may, when authorized by law, acquire land adjacent to or in the vicinity of a Federal penal or correctional institution if he considers the additional land essential to the protection of the health or safety of the inmates of the institution.

(Added Pub. L. 89–554, §3(f), Sept. 6, 1966, 80 Stat. 610.)

Historical and Revision Notes

Derivation	U.S. Code	Revised Statutes and Statutes at Large
	5 U.S.C. 341f.	July 28, 1950, ch. 503, §7, 64 Stat. 381.
		Sept. 16, 1959, Pub. L. 86–286, 73 Stat. 567.

The reference to an appropriation law is omitted as covered by the words "when authorized by law".

§4011. Disposition of cash collections for meals, laundry, etc.

Collections in cash for meals, laundry, barber service, uniform equipment, and other items for which payment is made originally from appropriations for the maintenance and operation of Federal penal and correctional institutions, may be deposited in the Treasury to the credit of the appropriation currently available for those items when the collection is made.

(Added Pub. L. 89–554, §3(f), Sept. 6, 1966, 80 Stat. 610.)

Historical and Revision Notes

Derivation	U.S. Code	Revised Statutes and Statutes at Large
	5 U.S.C. 341g.	July 28, 1950, ch. 503, §8, 64 Stat. 381.

§4012. Summary seizure and forfeiture of prison contraband

An officer or employee of the Bureau of Prisons may, pursuant to rules and regulations of the Director of the Bureau of Prisons, summarily seize any object introduced into a Federal penal or correctional facility or possessed by an inmate of such a facility in violation of a rule, regulation or order promulgated by the Director, and such object shall be forfeited to the United States.

(Added Pub. L. 98–473, title II, §1109(d), Oct. 12, 1984, 98 Stat. 2148.)

§4013. Support of United States prisoners in non-Federal institutions

(a) The Attorney General, in support of United States prisoners in non-Federal institutions, is authorized to make payments from funds appropriated for Federal prisoner detention for—

(1) necessary clothing;

(2) medical care and necessary guard hire; and

(3) the housing, care, and security of persons held in custody of a United States marshal pursuant to Federal law under agreements with State or local units of government or contracts with private entities.

(b) The Attorney General, in support of Federal prisoner detainees in non-Federal institutions, is authorized to make payments, from funds appropriated for State and local law enforcement assistance, for entering into contracts or cooperative agreements with any State, territory, or political subdivision thereof, for the necessary construction, physical renovation, acquisition of equipment, supplies, or materials required to establish acceptable conditions of confinement and detention services in any State or local jurisdiction which agrees to provide guaranteed bed space for Federal detainees within that correctional system, in accordance with regulations which are issued by the Attorney General and are comparable to the regulations issued under section 4006 of this title, except that—

(1) amounts made available for purposes of this paragraph shall not exceed the average per-inmate cost of constructing similar confinement facilities for the Federal prison population,

(2) the availability of such federally assisted facility shall be assured for housing Federal prisoners, and

(3) the per diem rate charged for housing such Federal prisoners shall not exceed allowable costs or other conditions specified in the contract or cooperative agreement.

(c)(1) The United States Marshals Service may designate districts that need additional support from private detention entities under subsection (a)(3) based on—

(A) the number of Federal detainees in the district; and

(B) the availability of appropriate Federal, State, and local government detention facilities.

(2) In order to be eligible for a contract for the housing, care, and security of persons held in custody of the United States Marshals pursuant to Federal law and funding under subsection (a)(3), a private entity shall—

(A) be located in a district that has been designated as needing additional Federal detention facilities pursuant to paragraph (1);

(B) meet the standards of the American Correctional Association;

(C) comply with all applicable State and local laws and regulations;

(D) have approved fire, security, escape, and riot plans; and

(E) comply with any other regulations that the Marshals Service deems appropriate.

(3) The United States Marshals Service shall provide an opportunity for public comment on a contract under subsection (a)(3).

(d) Health Care Fees For Federal Prisoners in Non-Federal Institutions.—

(1) In general.—Notwithstanding amounts paid under subsection (a)(3), a State or local government may assess and collect a reasonable fee from the trust fund account (or institutional equivalent) of a Federal prisoner for health care services, if—

(A) the prisoner is confined in a non-Federal institution pursuant to an agreement between the Federal Government and the State or local government;

(B) the fee—

(i) is authorized under State law; and

(ii) does not exceed the amount collected from State or local prisoners for the same services; and

(C) the services—

(i) are provided within or outside of the institution by a person who is licensed or certified under State law to provide health care services and who is operating within the scope of such license;

(ii) constitute a health care visit within the meaning of section 4048(a)(4) of this title; and

587

(iii) are not preventative health care services, emergency services, prenatal care, diagnosis or treatment of chronic infectious diseases, mental health care, or substance abuse treatment.

(2) No refusal of treatment for financial reasons.—Nothing in this subsection may be construed to permit any refusal of treatment to a prisoner on the basis that—

(A) the account of the prisoner is insolvent; or

(B) the prisoner is otherwise unable to pay a fee assessed under this subsection.

(3) Notice to prisoners of law.—Each person who is or becomes a prisoner shall be provided with written and oral notices of the provisions of this subsection and the applicability of this subsection to the prisoner. Notwithstanding any other provision of this subsection, a fee under this section may not be assessed against, or collected from, such person—

(A) until the expiration of the 30-day period beginning on the date on which each prisoner in the prison system is provided with such notices; and

(B) for services provided before the expiration of such period.

(4) Notice to prisoners of state or local implementation.—The implementation of this subsection by the State or local government, and any amendment to that implementation, shall not take effect until the expiration of the 30-day period beginning on the date on which each prisoner in the prison system is provided with written and oral notices of the provisions of that implementation (or amendment, as the case may be). A fee under this subsection may not be assessed against, or collected from, a prisoner pursuant to such implementation (or amendments, as the case may be) for services provided before the expiration of such period.

(5) Notice before public comment period.—Before the beginning of any period a proposed implementation under this subsection is open to public comment, written and oral notice of the provisions of that proposed implementation shall be provided to groups that advocate on behalf of Federal prisoners and to each prisoner subject to such proposed implementation.

(6) Comprehensive hiv/aids services required.—Any State or local government assessing or collecting a fee under this subsection shall provide comprehensive coverage for services relating to human immunodeficiency virus (HIV) and acquired immune deficiency syndrome (AIDS) to each Federal prisoner in the custody of such State or local government when medically appropriate. The State or local government may not assess or collect a fee under this subsection for providing such coverage.

(Added Pub. L. 100–690, title VII, §7608(d)(1), Nov. 18, 1988, 102 Stat. 4516; amended Pub. L. 101–647, title XVII, §1701, title XXXV, §3599, Nov. 29, 1990, 104 Stat. 4843, 4931; Pub. L. 103–322, title XXXIII, §330011(o), Sept. 13, 1994, 108 Stat. 2145; Pub. L. 106–294, §3, Oct. 12, 2000, 114 Stat. 1040; Pub. L. 107–273, div. A, title III, §302(2), Nov. 2, 2002, 116 Stat. 1781.)

Amendments

2002—Subsec. (a). Pub. L. 107–273, §302(2)(A), in introductory provisions, substituted "Federal prisoner detention" for "the support of United States prisoners", inserted "and" at end of par. (2), substituted period for "; and" at end of par. (3), and in introductory provisions of par. (4), inserted "The Attorney General, in support of Federal prisoner detainees in non-Federal institutions, is authorized to make payments, from funds appropriated for State and local law enforcement assistance, for" before "entering".

Subsecs. (a)(4), (b). Pub. L. 107–273, §302(2)(B)(ii), redesignated par. (4) of subsec. (a) as subsec. (b) and subpars. (A) to (C) as pars. (1) to (3), respectively. Former subsec. (b) redesignated (c).

Subsecs. (c), (d). Pub. L. 107–273, §302(2)(B)(i), redesignated subsecs. (b) and (c) as (c) and (d), respectively.

2000—Subsec. (c). Pub. L. 106–294 added subsec. (c).

1994—Pub. L. 103–322, §330011(o), repealed Pub. L. 101–647, §3599. See 1990 Amendment note below.

1990—Subsec. (a). Pub. L. 101–647, §3599, which struck out "(a)" at beginning of text, was repealed by Pub. L. 103–322, §330011(o).

Subsec. (b). Pub. L. 101–647, §1701, added subsec. (b).

Effective Date of 1994 Amendment

Pub. L. 103–322, title XXXIII, §330011(o), Sept. 13, 1994, 108 Stat. 2145, provided that the amendment made by section 330011(o) is effective Nov. 29, 1990.

Contracts for Space or Facilities

Pub. L. 106–553, §1(a)(2) [title I, §118, formerly §119], Dec. 21, 2000, 114 Stat. 2762, 2762A–69; renumbered §118, Pub. L. 106–554, §1(a)(4) [div. A, §213(a)(2)], Dec. 21, 2000, 114 Stat. 2763, 2763A–179, provided that: "Notwithstanding any other provision of law, including section 4(d) of the Service Contract Act of 1965 ([former] 41 U.S.C. 353(d)) [now 41 U.S.C. 6707(d)], the Attorney General hereafter may enter into contracts and other agreements, of any reasonable duration, for detention or incarceration space or facilities, including related services, on any reasonable basis."

Justice Prisoner and Alien Transportation System Fund, United States Marshals Service

Pub. L. 106–553, §1(a)(2) [title I], Dec. 21, 2000, 114 Stat. 2762, 2762A–55, provided in part that: "Beginning in fiscal year 2000 and thereafter, payment shall be made from the Justice Prisoner and Alien Transportation System Fund for necessary expenses related to the scheduling and transportation of United States prisoners and illegal and criminal aliens in the custody of the United States Marshals Service, as authorized in 18 U.S.C. 4013, including, without limitation, salaries and expenses, operations, and the acquisition, lease, and maintenance of aircraft and support facilities: Provided, That the Fund shall be reimbursed or credited with advance payments from amounts available to the Department of Justice, other Federal agencies, and other sources at rates that will recover the expenses of Fund operations, including, without limitation, accrual of annual leave and depreciation of plant and equipment of the Fund: Provided further, That proceeds from the disposal of Fund aircraft shall be credited to the Fund: Provided further, That amounts in the Fund shall be available without fiscal year limitation, and may be used for operating equipment lease agreements that do not exceed 10 years."

Similar provisions were contained in the following prior appropriations act:

Pub. L. 106–113, div. B, §1000(a)(1) [title I], Nov. 29, 1999, 113 Stat. 1535, 1501A–7.

Pub. L. 105–277, div. A, §101(b) [title I], Oct. 21, 1998, 112 Stat. 2681–50, 2681–54, provided that: "There is hereby established a Justice Prisoner and Alien Transportation System Fund for the payment of necessary expenses related to the scheduling and transportation of United States prisoners and illegal and criminal aliens in the custody of the United States Marshals Service, as authorized in 18 U.S.C. 4013, including, without limitation, salaries and expenses, operations, and the acquisition, lease, and maintenance of aircraft and support facilities: Provided, That the Fund shall be reimbursed or credited with advance payments from amounts available to the Department of Justice, other Federal agencies, and other sources at rates that will recover the expenses of Fund operations, including, without limitation, accrual of annual leave and depreciation of plant and equipment of the Fund: Provided further, That proceeds from the disposal of Fund aircraft shall be credited to the Fund: Provided further, That amounts in the Fund shall be available without fiscal year limitation, and may be used for operating equipment lease agreements that do not exceed 5 years."

§4014. Testing for human immunodeficiency virus

(a) The Attorney General shall cause each individual convicted of a Federal offense who is sentenced to incarceration for a period of 6 months or more to be tested for the presence of the human immunodeficiency virus, as appropriate, after the commencement of that incarceration, if such individual is determined to be at risk for infection with such virus in accordance with the guidelines issued by the Bureau of Prisons relating to infectious disease management.

(b) If the Attorney General has a well-founded reason to believe that a person sentenced to a term of imprisonment for a Federal offense, or ordered detained before trial under section 3142(e), may have intentionally or unintentionally transmitted the human immunodeficiency virus to any officer or employee of the United States, or to any person lawfully present in a correctional facility who is not incarcerated there, the Attorney General shall—

(1) cause the person who may have transmitted the virus to be tested promptly for the presence of such virus and communicate the test results to the person tested; and

(2) consistent with the guidelines issued by the Bureau of Prisons relating to infectious disease management, inform any person (in, as appropriate, confidential consultation with the person's physician) who may have been exposed to such virus, of the potential risk involved and, if warranted by the circumstances, that prophylactic or other treatment should be considered.

(c) If the results of a test under subsection (a) or (b) indicate the presence of the human immunodeficiency virus, the Attorney General shall provide appropriate access for counselling, health care, and support services to the affected officer, employee, or other person, and to the person tested.

(d) The results of a test under this section are inadmissible against the person tested in any Federal or State civil or criminal case or proceeding.

(e) Not later than 1 year after the date of the enactment of this section, the Attorney General shall issue rules to implement this section. Such rules shall require that the results of any test are communicated only to the person tested, and, if the results of the test indicate the presence of the virus, to correctional facility personnel consistent with guidelines issued by the Bureau of Prisons. Such rules shall also provide for procedures designed to protect the privacy of a person requesting that the test be performed and the privacy of the person tested.

(Added Pub. L. 105–370, §2(a), Nov. 12, 1998, 112 Stat. 3374.)

References in Text

The date of the enactment of this section, referred to in subsec. (e), is the date of enactment of Pub. L. 105–370, which was approved Nov. 12, 1998.

CHAPTER 303 - BUREAU OF PRISONS

Amendments

2016—Pub. L. 114–133, §2(b), Mar. 9, 2016, 130 Stat. 297, added item 4049.

2000—Pub. L. 106–294, §2(b), Oct. 12, 2000, 114 Stat. 1040, added item 4048.

1994—Pub. L. 103–322, title II, §20402(b), Sept. 13, 1994, 108 Stat. 1825, added item 4047.

1990—Pub. L. 101–647, title XXX, §3001(b), Nov. 29, 1990, 104 Stat. 4915, added item 4046.

1986—Pub. L. 99–646, §67(b), Nov. 10, 1986, 100 Stat. 3616, added items 4044 and 4045.

1982—Pub. L. 97–258, §2(d)(4)(A), Sept. 13, 1982, 96 Stat. 1059, added item 4043.

§4041. Bureau of Prisons; director and employees

The Bureau of Prisons shall be in charge of a director appointed by and serving directly under the Attorney General. The Attorney General may appoint such additional officers and employees as he deems necessary.

(June 25, 1948, ch. 645, 62 Stat. 849; Pub. L. 107–273, div. A, title III, §302(1), Nov. 2, 2002, 116 Stat. 1781.)

Historical and Revision Notes

Based on title 18, U.S.C., 1940 ed., §753 (May 14, 1930, ch. 274, §1, 46 Stat. 325).

The entire second sentence was omitted as executed. All powers and authority originally vested in the former Superintendent of Prisons are now possessed by the Bureau of Prisons.

Minor changes of phraseology were made.

Amendments

2002—Pub. L. 107–273 struck out "at a salary of $10,000 a year" after "under the Attorney General".

Compensation of Director

Compensation of Director, see section 5315 of Title 5, Government Organization and Employees.

§4042. Duties of Bureau of Prisons

(a) In General.—The Bureau of Prisons, under the direction of the Attorney General, shall—

(1) have charge of the management and regulation of all Federal penal and correctional institutions;

(2) provide suitable quarters and provide for the safekeeping, care, and subsistence of all persons charged with or convicted of offenses against the United States, or held as witnesses or otherwise;

(3) provide for the protection, instruction, and discipline of all persons charged with or convicted of offenses against the United States;

(4) provide technical assistance to State, tribal, and local governments in the improvement of their correctional systems;

(5) provide notice of release of prisoners in accordance with subsections (b) and (c);

(D) [1] establish prerelease planning procedures that help prisoners—

(i) apply for Federal and State benefits upon release (including Social Security Cards, Social Security benefits, and veterans' benefits); and

(ii) secure such identification and benefits prior to release, subject to any limitations in law; and

(E) [2] establish reentry planning procedures that include providing Federal prisoners with information in the following areas:

(i) Health and nutrition.

(ii) Employment.

(iii) Literacy and education.

(iv) Personal finance and consumer skills.

(v) Community resources.

(vi) Personal growth and development.

(vii) Release requirements and procedures.

(b) Notice of Release of Prisoners.—(1) At least 5 days prior to the date on which a prisoner described in paragraph (3) is to be released on supervised release, or, in the case of a prisoner on supervised release, at least 5 days prior to the date on which the prisoner changes residence to a new jurisdiction, written notice of the release or change of residence shall be provided to the chief law enforcement officers of each State, tribal, and local jurisdiction in which the prisoner will reside. Notice prior to release shall be provided by the Director of the Bureau of Prisons. Notice concerning a change of residence following release shall be provided by the probation officer responsible for the supervision of the released prisoner, or in a manner specified by the Director of the Administrative Office of the United States Courts. The notice requirements under this subsection do not apply in relation to a prisoner being protected under chapter 224.

(2) A notice under paragraph (1) shall disclose—

(A) the prisoner's name;

(B) the prisoner's criminal history, including a description of the offense of which the prisoner was convicted; and

(C) any restrictions on conduct or other conditions to the release of the prisoner that are imposed by law, the sentencing court, or the Bureau of Prisons or any other Federal agency.

(3) A prisoner is described in this paragraph if the prisoner was convicted of—

(A) a drug trafficking crime, as that term is defined in section 924(c)(2); or

(B) a crime of violence (as defined in section 924(c)(3)).

(c) Notice of Sex Offender Release.—(1) In the case of a person described in paragraph (3), or any other person in a category specified by the Attorney General, who is released from prison or sentenced to probation, notice shall be provided to—

(A) the chief law enforcement officer of each State, tribal, and local jurisdiction in which the person will reside; and

(B) a State, tribal, or local agency responsible for the receipt or maintenance of sex offender registration information in the State, tribal, or local jurisdiction in which the person will reside. The notice requirements under this subsection do not apply in relation to a person being protected under chapter 224.

(2) Notice provided under paragraph (1) shall include the information described in subsection (b)(2), the place where the person will reside, and the information that the person shall register as required by the Sex Offender Registration and Notification Act. For a person who is released from the custody of the Bureau of Prisons whose expected place of residence following release is known to the Bureau of Prisons, notice shall be provided at least 5 days prior to release by the Director of the Bureau of Prisons. For a person who is sentenced to probation, notice shall be provided promptly by the probation officer responsible for the supervision of the person, or in a manner specified by the Director of the Administrative Office of the United States Courts. Notice concerning a subsequent change of residence by a person described in paragraph (3) during any period of probation, supervised release, or parole shall also be provided to the agencies and officers specified in paragraph (1) by the probation officer responsible for the supervision of the person, or in a manner specified by the Director of the Administrative Office of the United States Courts.

(3) The Director of the Bureau of Prisons shall inform a person who is released from prison and required to register under the Sex Offender Registration and Notification Act of the requirements of that Act as they apply to that person and the same information shall be provided to a person sentenced to probation by the probation officer responsible for supervision of that person.

[(4) Repealed. Pub. L. 109–248, title I, §141(h), July 27, 2006, 120 Stat. 604.]

(5) The United States and its agencies, officers, and employees shall be immune from liability based on good faith conduct in carrying out this subsection and subsection (b).

(d) Application of Section.—This section shall not apply to military or naval penal or correctional institutions or the persons confined therein.

(June 25, 1948, ch. 645, 62 Stat. 849; Pub. L. 90–371, July 1, 1968, 82 Stat. 280; Pub. L. 103–322, title II, §20417, Sept. 13, 1994, 108 Stat. 1834; Pub. L. 105–119, title I, §115(a)(8)(A), Nov. 26, 1997, 111 Stat. 2464; Pub. L. 109–248, title I, §141(f)–(h), July 27, 2006, 120 Stat. 603, 604; Pub. L. 110–199, title II, §231(d)(1), Apr. 9, 2008, 122 Stat. 685; Pub. L. 111–211, title II, §261(a), July 29, 2010, 124 Stat. 2299.)

Historical and Revision Notes

Based on title 18, U.S.C., 1940 ed., §§753a, 753b, (May 14, 1930, ch. 274, §§2, 3, 46 Stat. 325). Because of similarity in the provisions, the first sentence of section 753b of title 18, U.S.C., 1940 ed., was consolidated with section 753a of title 18, U.S.C., 1940 ed., to form this section.

Minor changes were made in phraseology.

The remainder of said section 753b of title 18, U.S.C., 1940 ed., is incorporated in section 4002 of this title.

References in Text

The Sex Offender Registration and Notification Act, referred to in subsec. (c)(2), (3), is title I of Pub. L. 109–248, July 27, 2006, 120 Stat. 590, which was classified principally to subchapter I (§16901 et seq.) of chapter 151 of Title 42, The Public Health and Welfare, prior to editorial reclassification as chapter 209 (§20901 et seq.) of Title 34, Crime Control and Law Enforcement. For complete classification of this Act to the Code, see Short Title of 2006 Act note set out under section 10101 of Title 34 and Tables.

Amendments

2010—Subsec. (a)(4). Pub. L. 111–211, §261(a)(1), inserted ", tribal," after "State".

Subsec. (b)(1). Pub. L. 111–211, §261(a)(2), substituted "officers of each State, tribal, and local jurisdiction" for "officer of the State and of the local jurisdiction".

Subsec. (c)(1)(A). Pub. L. 111–211, §261(a)(3)(A), substituted "officer of each State, tribal, and local jurisdiction" for "officer of the State and of the local jurisdiction".

Subsec. (c)(1)(B). Pub. L. 111–211, §261(a)(3)(B), inserted ", tribal," after "State" in two places.

2008—Subsec. (a)(D), (E). Pub. L. 110–199 added pars. (D) and (E).

2006—Subsec. (c)(1). Pub. L. 109–248, §141(g)(1), substituted "paragraph (3), or any other person in a category specified by the Attorney General," for "paragraph (4)" in introductory provisions.

Subsec. (c)(2). Pub. L. 109–248, §141(g)(2), substituted "shall register as required by the Sex Offender Registration and Notification Act" for "shall be subject to a registration requirement as a sex offender" in first sentence and "paragraph (3)" for "paragraph (4)" in fourth sentence.

Subsec. (c)(3). Pub. L. 109–248, §141(f), amended par. (3) generally. Prior to amendment, par. (3) read as follows: "The Director of the Bureau of Prisons shall inform a person described in paragraph (4) who is released from prison that the person shall be subject to a registration requirement as a sex offender in any State in which the person resides, is employed, carries on a vocation, or is a student (as such terms are defined for purposes of section 170101(a)(3) of the Violent Crime Control and Law Enforcement Act of 1994), and the same information shall be provided to a person described in paragraph (4) who is sentenced to probation by the probation officer responsible for supervision of the person or in a manner specified by the Director of the Administrative Office of the United States Courts."

Subsec. (c)(4). Pub. L. 109–248, §141(h), struck out par. (4) which read as follows: "A person is described in this paragraph if the person was convicted of any of the following offenses (including such an offense prosecuted pursuant to section 1152 or 1153):

"(A) An offense under section 1201 involving a minor victim.

"(B) An offense under chapter 109A.

"(C) An offense under chapter 110.

"(D) An offense under chapter 117.

"(E) Any other offense designated by the Attorney General as a sexual offense for purposes of this subsection."

1997—Subsec. (a)(5). Pub. L. 105–119, §115(a)(8)(A)(i), substituted "subsections (b) and (c)" for "subsection (b)".

Subsec. (b)(4). Pub. L. 105–119, §115(a)(8)(A)(ii), struck out par. (4) which read as follows: "The notice provided under this section shall be used solely for law enforcement purposes."

Subsecs. (c), (d). Pub. L. 105–119, §115(a)(8)(A)(iv), added subsec. (c) and redesignated former subsec. (c) as (d).

1994—Pub. L. 103–322 designated first par. of existing provisions as subsec. (a) and inserted heading, substituted "provide" for "Provide" and "; and" for period at end of par. (4), added par.

(5) and subsec. (b), and designated second sentence of existing provisions as subsec. (c) and inserted heading.

1968—Pub. L. 90–371 added cl. (4).

Effective Date of 1997 Amendment

Amendment by Pub. L. 105–119 effective 1 year after Nov. 26, 1997, see section 115(c)(1) of Pub. L. 105–119, set out as a note under section 3521 of this title.

Construction of 2008 Amendment

For construction of amendments by Pub. L. 110–199 and requirements for grants made under such amendments, see section 60504 of Title 34, Crime Control and Law Enforcement.

Amenities or Personal Comforts

Pub. L. 107–77, title VI, §611, Nov. 28, 2001, 115 Stat. 800, provided that: "Hereafter, none of the funds appropriated or otherwise made available to the Bureau of Prisons shall be used to provide the following amenities or personal comforts in the Federal prison system—

"(1) in-cell television viewing except for prisoners who are segregated from the general prison population for their own safety;

"(2) the viewing of R, X, and NC–17 rated movies, through whatever medium presented;

"(3) any instruction (live or through broadcasts) or training equipment for boxing, wrestling, judo, karate, or other martial art, or any bodybuilding or weightlifting equipment of any sort;

"(4) possession of in-cell coffee pots, hot plates or heating elements; or

"(5) the use or possession of any electric or electronic musical instrument."

Similar provisions were contained in the following appropriation acts:

Pub. L. 106–553, §1(a)(2) [title VI, §611], Dec. 21, 2000, 114 Stat. 2762, 2762A–105.

Pub. L. 106–113, div. B, §1000(a)(1) [title VI, §612], Nov. 29, 1999, 113 Stat. 1535, 1501A–54.

Pub. L. 105–277, div. A, §101(b) [title VI, §611], Oct. 21, 1998, 112 Stat. 2681–50, 2681–113.

Pub. L. 105–119, title VI, §611, Nov. 26, 1997, 111 Stat. 2517.

Pub. L. 104–208, div. A, title I, §101(a) [title VI, §611], Sept. 30, 1996, 110 Stat. 3009, 3009–66.

Pub. L. 104–134, title I, §101[(a)] [title VI, §611], Apr. 26, 1996, 110 Stat. 1321, 1321–64; renumbered title I, Pub. L. 104–140, §1(a), May 2, 1996, 110 Stat. 1327.

Sexually Explicit Commercially Published Material

Pub. L. 107–77, title VI, §614, Nov. 28, 2001, 115 Stat. 801, provided that: "Hereafter, none of the funds appropriated or otherwise made available to the Federal Bureau of Prisons may be used to distribute or make available any commercially published information or material to a prisoner when it is made known to the Federal official having authority to obligate or expend such funds that such information or material is sexually explicit or features nudity."

Similar provisions were contained in the following appropriation acts:

Pub. L. 106–553, §1(a)(2) [title VI, §614], Dec. 21, 2000, 114 Stat. 2762, 2762A–106.

Pub. L. 106–113, div. B, §1000(a)(1) [title VI, §615], Nov. 29, 1999, 113 Stat. 1535, 1501A–54.

Pub. L. 105–277, div. A, §101(b) [title VI, §614], Oct. 21, 1998, 112 Stat. 2681–50, 2681–113.

Pub. L. 105–119, title VI, §614, Nov. 26, 1997, 111 Stat. 2518.

Pub. L. 104–208, div. A, title I, §101(a) [title VI, §614], Sept. 30, 1996, 110 Stat. 3009, 3009–66.

Reimbursement for Certain Expenses Outside of Federal Institutions

Pub. L. 106–553, §1(a)(2) [title I], Dec. 21, 2000, 114 Stat. 2762, 2762A–55, provided in part: "That hereafter amounts appropriated for Federal Prisoner Detention shall be available to reimburse the Federal Bureau of Prisons for salaries and expenses of transporting, guarding and providing medical care outside of Federal penal and correctional institutions to prisoners awaiting trial or sentencing."

Guidelines for States Regarding Infectious Diseases in Correctional Institutions

Pub. L. 105–370, §2(c), Nov. 12, 1998, 112 Stat. 3375, which required the Attorney General to provide to States proposed guidelines related to infectious diseases in correctional institutions, was editorially reclassified as a note under section 60101 of Title 34, Crime Control and Law Enforcement.

Prisoner Access

Pub. L. 105–314, title VIII, §801, Oct. 30, 1998, 112 Stat. 2990, provided that: "Notwithstanding any other provision of law, no agency, officer, or employee of the United States shall implement, or provide any financial assistance to, any Federal program or Federal activity in which a Federal prisoner is allowed access to any electronic communication service or remote computing service without the supervision of an official of the Federal Government."

Application to Prisoners to Which Prior Law Applies

Pub. L. 103–322, title II, §20404, Sept. 13, 1994, 108 Stat. 1825, provided that: "In the case of a prisoner convicted of an offense committed prior to November 1, 1987, the reference to supervised release in section 4042(b) of title 18, United States Code, shall be deemed to be a reference to probation or parole."

Cost Savings Measures

Pub. L. 101–647, title XXIX, §2907, Nov. 29, 1990, 104 Stat. 4915, provided that: "The Director of the Federal Bureau of Prisons (referred to as the 'Director') shall, to the extent practicable, take such measures as are appropriate to cut costs of construction. Such measures may include reducing expenditures for amenities including, for example, color television or pool tables."

Administration of Confinement Facilities Located on Military Installations by Bureau of Prisons

Pub. L. 100–690, title VII, §7302, Nov. 18, 1988, 102 Stat. 4463, provided that: "In conjunction with the Department of Defense and the Commission on Alternative Utilization of Military Facilities as established in the National Defense Authorization Act of Fiscal Year 1989 [see section 2819 of Pub. L. 100–456, 104 Stat. 1820, formerly set out as a note under section 2391 of Title 10, Armed Forces], the Bureau of Prisons shall be responsible for—

"(1) administering Bureau of Prisons confinement facilities for civilian nonviolent prisoners located on military installations in cooperation with the Secretary of Defense, with an emphasis on placing women inmates in such facilities, or in similar minimum security confinement facilities not located on military installations, so that the percentage of eligible women equals the percentage of eligible men housed in such or similar minimum security confinement facilities (i.e., prison camps);

"(2) establishing and regulating drug treatment programs for inmates held in such facilities in coordination and cooperation with the National Institute on Drug Abuse; and

"(3) establishing and managing work programs in accordance with guidelines under the Bureau of Prisons for persons held in such facilities and in cooperation with the installation commander."

Limiting the Use of Restrictive Housing by the Federal Government

Memorandum of President of the United States, Mar. 1, 2016, 81 F.R. 11997, provided:
Memorandum for the Heads of Executive Departments and Agencies
A growing body of evidence suggests that the overuse of solitary confinement and other forms of restrictive housing in U.S. correctional systems undermines public safety and is contrary to our Nation's values.
In July 2015, as part of my Administration's ongoing efforts to pursue reforms that make the

criminal justice system more fair and effective, I directed the Attorney General to undertake a comprehensive review of the overuse of solitary confinement across American prisons. Since that time, senior officials at the Department of Justice (DOJ) have met regularly to study the issue and develop strategies for reducing the use of this practice nationwide.

Those efforts gave rise to a final report transmitted to me on January 25, 2016 (DOJ Report and Recommendations Concerning the Use of Restrictive Housing) (the "DOJ Report"), that sets forth specific policy recommendations for DOJ with respect to the Federal Bureau of Prisons and other DOJ entities as well as more general guiding principles for all correctional systems.

As the DOJ Report makes clear, although occasions exist when correctional officials have no choice but to segregate inmates from the general population, this action has the potential to cause serious, long-lasting harm. The DOJ Report accordingly emphasizes the responsibility of Government to ensure that this practice is limited, applied with constraints, and used only as a measure of last resort.

Given the urgency and importance of this issue, it is critical that DOJ accelerate efforts to reduce the number of Federal inmates and detainees held in restrictive housing and that Federal correctional and detention systems be models for facilities across the United States. Therefore, by the authority vested in me as President by the Constitution and the laws of the United States of America, and to address the overuse of solitary confinement in correctional and detention systems throughout the United States, I hereby direct as follows:

Section 1. Implementation of the DOJ Report. (a) DOJ shall promptly undertake to revise its regulations and policies, consistent with the direction of the Attorney General, to implement the policy recommendations in the DOJ Report concerning the use of restrictive housing. DOJ shall provide me with an update on the status of these efforts not later than 180 days after the date of this memorandum.

(b) Other executive departments and agencies (agencies) that impose restrictive housing shall review the DOJ Report to determine whether corresponding changes at their facilities should be made in light of the policy recommendations and guiding principles in the DOJ Report. These other agencies shall report back to me not later than 180 days after the date of this memorandum on how they plan to address their use of restrictive housing.

Sec. 2. General Provisions. (a) This memorandum shall be implemented consistent with applicable law and subject to the availability of appropriations.

(b) Nothing in this memorandum shall be construed to impair or otherwise affect:

(i) the authority granted by law to an executive department, agency, or the head thereof; or

(ii) the functions of the Director of the Office of Management and Budget relating to budgetary, administrative, or legislative proposals.

(c) This memorandum is not intended to, and does not, create any right or benefit, substantive or procedural, enforceable at law or in equity by any party against the United States, its departments, agencies, or entities, its officers, employees, or agents, or any other person.

Sec. 3. Publication. The Attorney General is authorized and directed to publish this memorandum in the Federal Register.

Barack Obama.

§4043. Acceptance of gifts and bequests to the Commissary Funds, Federal Prisons

The Attorney General may accept gifts or bequests of money for credit to the "Commissary Funds, Federal Prisons". A gift or bequest under this section is a gift or bequest to or for the use of the United States under the Internal Revenue Code of 1986 (26 U.S.C. 1 et seq.).

(Added Pub. L. 97–258, §2(d)(4)(B), Sept. 13, 1982, 96 Stat. 1059; amended Pub. L. 99–514, §2, Oct. 22, 1986, 100 Stat. 2095.)

Historical and Revision Notes
| Revised Section | Source (U.S. Code) | Source (Statutes at Large) |

| 4043 | 31:725s–4. | May 15, 1952, ch. 289, §2, 66 Stat. 72; July 9, 1952, ch. 600, 66 Stat. 479. |

Amendments

1986—Pub. L. 99–514 substituted "Internal Revenue Code of 1986" for "Internal Revenue Code of 1954".

Expenditures; Inmate Telephone System

Pub. L. 105–277, div. A, §101(b) [title I, §108], Oct. 21, 1998, 112 Stat. 2681–50, 2681–67, provided that: "For fiscal year 1999 and thereafter, the Director of the Bureau of Prisons may make expenditures out of the Commissary Fund of the Federal Prison System, regardless of whether any such expenditure is security-related, for programs, goods, and services for the benefit of inmates (to the extent the provision of those programs, goods, or services to inmates is not otherwise prohibited by law), including—

"(1) the installation, operation, and maintenance of the Inmate Telephone System;

"(2) the payment of all the equipment purchased or leased in connection with the Inmate Telephone System; and

"(3) the salaries, benefits, and other expenses of personnel who install, operate, and maintain the Inmate Telephone System."

Deposit or Investment of Excess Amounts in Federal Prison Commissary Fund

Section 108 of H.R. 2076, One Hundred Fourth Congress, as passed by the House of Representatives on Dec. 6, 1995, and as enacted into law by Pub. L. 104–91, title I, §101(a), Jan. 6, 1996, 110 Stat. 11, as amended by Pub. L. 104–99, title II, §211, Jan. 26, 1996, 110 Stat. 37, provided that: "For fiscal year 1996 and each fiscal year thereafter, amounts in the Federal Prison System's Commissary Fund, Federal Prisons, which are not currently needed for operations, shall be kept on deposit or invested in obligations of, or guaranteed by, the United States and all earnings on such investment shall be deposited in the Commissary Fund."

Similar provisions were contained in the following prior appropriation act:

Pub. L. 103–317, title I, §107, Aug. 26, 1994, 108 Stat. 1735.

§4044. Donations on behalf of the Bureau of Prisons

The Attorney General may, in accordance with rules prescribed by the Attorney General, accept in the name of the Department of Justice any form of devise, bequest, gift or donation of money or property for use by the Bureau of Prisons or Federal Prison Industries. The Attorney General may take all appropriate steps to secure possession of such property and may sell, assign, transfer, or convey such property other than money.

(Added Pub. L. 99–646, §67(a), Nov. 10, 1986, 100 Stat. 3616.)

§4045. Authority to conduct autopsies

A chief executive officer of a Federal penal or correctional facility may, pursuant to rules prescribed by the Director, order an autopsy and related scientific or medical tests to be performed on the body of a deceased inmate of the facility in the event of homicide, suicide, fatal illness or accident, or unexplained death, when it is determined that such autopsy or test is necessary to detect a crime, maintain discipline, protect the health or safety of other inmates, remedy official misconduct, or defend the United States or its employees from civil liability arising from the administration of the facility. To the extent consistent with the needs of the autopsy or of specific scientific or medical tests, provisions of State and local law protecting religious beliefs with respect to such autopsies shall be observed. Such officer may also order an autopsy or post-mortem operation, including removal of tissue for transplanting, to be performed on the body of a deceased inmate of the facility, with the written consent of a person authorized to permit such an autopsy or post-mortem operation under the law of the State in which the facility is located. (Added Pub. L. 99–646, §67(a), Nov. 10, 1986, 100 Stat. 3616.)

§4046. Shock incarceration program

(a) The Bureau of Prisons may place in a shock incarceration program any person who is sentenced to a term of imprisonment of more than 12, but not more than 30, months, if such person consents to that placement.

(b) For such initial portion of the term of imprisonment as the Bureau of Prisons may determine, not to exceed 6 months, an inmate in the shock incarceration program shall be required to—

(1) adhere to a highly regimented schedule that provides the strict discipline, physical training, hard labor, drill, and ceremony characteristic of military basic training; and

(2) participate in appropriate job training and educational programs (including literacy programs) and drug, alcohol, and other counseling programs.

(c) An inmate who in the judgment of the Director of the Bureau of Prisons has successfully completed the required period of shock incarceration shall remain in the custody of the Bureau for such period (not to exceed the remainder of the prison term otherwise required by law to be served by that inmate), and under such conditions, as the Bureau deems appropriate.

(Added Pub. L. 101–647, title XXX, §3001(a), Nov. 29, 1990, 104 Stat. 4915.)

Authorization of Appropriations

Pub. L. 101–647, title XXX, §3002, Nov. 29, 1990, 104 Stat. 4915, provided that: "There are authorized to be appropriated for fiscal year 1990 and each fiscal year thereafter such sums as may be necessary to carry out the shock incarceration program established under the amendments made by this Act [see Tables for classification]".

§4047. Prison impact assessments

(a) Any submission of legislation by the Judicial or Executive branch which could increase or decrease the number of persons incarcerated in Federal penal institutions shall be accompanied by a prison impact statement (as defined in subsection (b)).

(b) The Attorney General shall, in consultation with the Sentencing Commission and the Administrative Office of the United States Courts, prepare and furnish prison impact assessments under subsection (c) of this section, and in response to requests from Congress for information relating to a pending measure or matter that might affect the number of defendants processed through the Federal criminal justice system. A prison impact assessment on pending legislation must be supplied within 21 days of any request. A prison impact assessment shall include—

(1) projections of the impact on prison, probation, and post prison supervision populations;

(2) an estimate of the fiscal impact of such population changes on Federal expenditures, including those for construction and operation of correctional facilities for the current fiscal year and 5 succeeding fiscal years;

(3) an analysis of any other significant factor affecting the cost of the measure and its impact on the operations of components of the criminal justice system; and

(4) a statement of the methodologies and assumptions utilized in preparing the assessment.

(c) The Attorney General shall prepare and transmit to the Congress, by March 1 of each year, a prison impact assessment reflecting the cumulative effect of all relevant changes in the law taking effect during the preceding calendar year.

(Added Pub. L. 103–322, title II, §20402(a), Sept. 13, 1994, 108 Stat. 1824.)

§4048. Fees for health care services for prisoners

(a) Definitions.—In this section—

(1) the term "account" means the trust fund account (or institutional equivalent) of a prisoner;

(2) the term "Director" means the Director of the Bureau of Prisons;

(3) the term "health care provider" means any person who is—

(A) authorized by the Director to provide health care services; and

(B) operating within the scope of such authorization;

(4) the term "health care visit"—

(A) means a visit, as determined by the Director, by a prisoner to an institutional or noninstitutional health care provider; and

(B) does not include a visit initiated by a prisoner—

(i) pursuant to a staff referral; or

(ii) to obtain staff-approved follow-up treatment for a chronic condition; and

(5) the term "prisoner" means—

(A) any individual who is incarcerated in an institution under the jurisdiction of the Bureau of Prisons; or

(B) any other individual, as designated by the Director, who has been charged with or convicted of an offense against the United States.

(b) Fees for Health Care Services.—

(1) In general.—The Director, in accordance with this section and with such regulations as the Director shall promulgate to carry out this section, may assess and collect a fee for health care services provided in connection with each health care visit requested by a prisoner.

(2) Exclusion.—The Director may not assess or collect a fee under this section for preventative health care services, emergency services, prenatal care, diagnosis or treatment of chronic infectious diseases, mental health care, or substance abuse treatment, as determined by the Director.

(c) Persons Subject to Fee.—Each fee assessed under this section shall be collected by the Director from the account of—

(1) the prisoner receiving health care services in connection with a health care visit described in subsection (b)(1); or

(2) in the case of health care services provided in connection with a health care visit described in subsection (b)(1) that results from an injury inflicted on a prisoner by another prisoner, the prisoner who inflicted the injury, as determined by the Director.

(d) Amount of Fee.—Any fee assessed and collected under this section shall be in an amount of not less than $1.

(e) No Consent Required.—Notwithstanding any other provision of law, the consent of a prisoner shall not be required for the collection of a fee from the account of the prisoner under this section. However, each such prisoner shall be given a reasonable opportunity to dispute the amount of the fee or whether the prisoner qualifies under an exclusion under this section.

(f) No Refusal of Treatment For Financial Reasons.—Nothing in this section may be construed to permit any refusal of treatment to a prisoner on the basis that—

(1) the account of the prisoner is insolvent; or

(2) the prisoner is otherwise unable to pay a fee assessed under this section.

(g) Use of Amounts.—

(1) Restitution of specific victims.—Amounts collected by the Director under this section from a prisoner subject to an order of restitution issued pursuant to section 3663 or 3663A shall be paid to victims in accordance with the order of restitution.

(2) Allocation of other amounts.—Of amounts collected by the Director under this section from prisoners not subject to an order of restitution issued pursuant to section 3663 or 3663A—

(A) 75 percent shall be deposited in the Crime Victims Fund established under section 1402 of the Victims of Crime Act of 1984 (42 U.S.C. 10601); 1 and

(B) 25 percent shall be available to the Attorney General for administrative expenses incurred in carrying out this section.

(h) Notice to Prisoners of Law.—Each person who is or becomes a prisoner shall be provided with written and oral notices of the provisions of this section and the applicability of this section to the prisoner. Notwithstanding any other provision of this section, a fee under this section may not be assessed against, or collected from, such person—

(1) until the expiration of the 30-day period beginning on the date on which each prisoner in the prison system is provided with such notices; and

(2) for services provided before the expiration of such period.

(i) Notice to Prisoners of Regulations.—The regulations promulgated by the Director under subsection (b)(1), and any amendments to those regulations, shall not take effect until the expiration of the 30-day period beginning on the date on which each prisoner in the prison system is provided with written and oral notices of the provisions of those regulations (or amendments, as the case may be). A fee under this section may not be assessed against, or collected from, a prisoner pursuant to such regulations (or amendments, as the case may be) for services provided before the expiration of such period.

(j) Notice Before Public Comment Period.—Before the beginning of any period a proposed regulation under this section is open to public comment, the Director shall provide written and oral notice of the provisions of that proposed regulation to groups that advocate on behalf of Federal prisoners and to each prisoner subject to such proposed regulation.

(k) Reports to Congress.—Not later than 1 year after the date of the enactment of the Federal Prisoner Health Care Copayment Act of 2000, and annually thereafter, the Director shall transmit to Congress a report, which shall include—

(1) a description of the amounts collected under this section during the preceding 12-month period;

(2) an analysis of the effects of the implementation of this section, if any, on the nature and extent of heath care visits by prisoners;

(3) an itemization of the cost of implementing and administering the program;

(4) a description of current inmate health status indicators as compared to the year prior to enactment; and

(5) a description of the quality of health care services provided to inmates during the preceding 12-month period, as compared with the quality of those services provided during the 12-month period ending on the date of the enactment of such Act.

(l) Comprehensive HIV/AIDS Services Required.—The Bureau of Prisons shall provide comprehensive coverage for services relating to human immunodeficiency virus (HIV) and acquired immune deficiency syndrome (AIDS) to each Federal prisoner in the custody of the Bureau of Prisons when medically appropriate. The Bureau of Prisons may not assess or collect a fee under this section for providing such coverage.

(Added Pub. L. 106–294, §2(a), Oct. 12, 2000, 114 Stat. 1038.)

References in Text

Section 1402 of the Victims of Crime Act of 1984, referred to in subsec. (g)(2)(A), is section 1402 of chapter XIV of title II of Pub. L. 98–473, which was classified to section 10601 of Title 42, The Public Health and Welfare, prior to editorial reclassification as section 20101 of Title 34, Crime Control and Law Enforcement.

The date of the enactment of the Federal Prisoner Health Care Copayment Act of 2000, referred to in subsec. (k), is the date of enactment of Pub. L. 106–294, which was approved Oct. 12, 2000.

§4049. Officers and employees of the Bureau of Prisons authorized to carry oleoresin capsicum spray

(a) In General.—The Director of the Bureau of Prisons shall issue, on a routine basis, oleoresin capsicum spray to—

(1) any officer or employee of the Bureau of Prisons who—

(A) is employed in a prison that is not a minimum or low security prison; and

(B) may respond to an emergency situation in such a prison; and

(2) to such additional officers and employees of prisons as the Director determines appropriate, in accordance with this section.

(b) Training Requirement.—

(1) In general.—In order for an officer or employee of the Bureau of Prisons, including a correctional officer, to be eligible to receive and carry oleoresin capsicum spray pursuant to this section, the officer or employee shall complete a training course before being issued such spray, and annually thereafter, on the use of oleoresin capsicum spray.

(2) Transferability of training.—An officer or employee of the Bureau of Prisons who completes a training course pursuant to paragraph (1) and subsequently transfers to employment at a different prison, shall not be required to complete an additional training course solely due such transfer.

(3) Training conducted during regular employment.—An officer or employee of the Bureau of Prisons who completes a training course required under paragraph (1) shall do so during the course of that officer or employee's regular employment, and shall be compensated at the same rate that the officer or employee would be compensated for conducting the officer or employee's regular duties.

(c) Use of Oleoresin Capsicum Spray.—Officers and employees of the Bureau of Prisons issued oleoresin capsicum spray pursuant to subsection (a) may use such spray to reduce acts of violence—

(1) committed by prisoners against themselves, other prisoners, prison visitors, and officers and employees of the Bureau of Prisons; and

(2) committed by prison visitors against themselves, prisoners, other visitors, and officers and employees of the Bureau of Prisons.

(Added Pub. L. 114–133, §2(a), Mar. 9, 2016, 130 Stat. 296.)

CHAPTER 305 - COMMITMENT AND TRANSFER

Amendments

1996—Pub. L. 104–294, title VI, §601(f)(14), Oct. 11, 1996, 110 Stat. 3500, substituted "centers;" for "centers," in item 4082.

1984—Pub. L. 98–473, title II, §218(e), Oct. 12, 1984, 98 Stat. 2027, substituted "Repealed" for "Copy of commitment delivered with prisoner" in item 4084, and "Repealed" for "Transfer for state offense; expense" in item 4085.

1965—Pub. L. 89–176, §2, Sept. 10, 1965, 79 Stat. 675, substituted "residential treatment centers, extension of limits of confinement; work furlough" for "transfer" in item 4082.

§4081. Classification and treatment of prisoners

The Federal penal and correctional institutions shall be so planned and limited in size as to facilitate the development of an integrated system which will assure the proper classification and segregation of Federal prisoners according to the nature of the offenses committed, the character and mental condition of the prisoners, and such other factors as should be considered in providing an individualized system of discipline, care, and treatment of the persons committed to such institutions.

(June 25, 1948, ch. 645, 62 Stat. 850.)

Historical and Revision Notes

Based on title 18, U.S.C., 1940 ed., §907 (May 27, 1930, ch. 339, §7, 46 Stat. 390).

Language of section is so changed as to make one policy for all institutions, thus clarifying the manifest intent of Congress.

Minor changes were made in phraseology.

§4082. Commitment to Attorney General; residential treatment centers; extension of limits of confinement; work furlough

(a) The willful failure of a prisoner to remain within the extended limits of his confinement, or to return within the time prescribed to an institution or facility designated by the Attorney General, shall be deemed an escape from the custody of the Attorney General punishable as provided in chapter 35 of this title.

(b)(1) The Attorney General shall, upon the request of the head of any law enforcement agency of a State or of a unit of local government in a State, make available as expeditiously as possible to such agency, with respect to prisoners who have been convicted of felony offenses against the United States and who are confined at a facility which is a residential community treatment center located in the geographical area in which such agency has jurisdiction, the following information maintained by the Bureau of Prisons (to the extent that the Bureau of Prisons maintains such information)—

(A) the names of such prisoners;

(B) the community treatment center addresses of such prisoners;

(C) the dates of birth of such prisoners;

(D) the Federal Bureau of Investigation numbers assigned to such prisoners;

(E) photographs and fingerprints of such prisoners; and

(F) the nature of the offenses against the United States of which each such prisoner has been convicted and the factual circumstances relating to such offenses.

(2) Any law enforcement agency which receives information under this subsection shall not disseminate such information outside of such agency.

(c) As used in this section—

the term "facility" shall include a residential community treatment center; and

the term "relative" shall mean a spouse, child (including stepchild, adopted child or child as to whom the prisoner, though not a natural parent, has acted in the place of a parent), parent (including a person who, though not a natural parent, has acted in the place of a parent), brother, or sister.

(June 25, 1948, ch. 645, 62 Stat. 850; Pub. L. 89–176, §1, Sept. 10, 1965, 79 Stat. 674; Pub. L. 93–209, Dec. 28, 1973, 87 Stat. 907; Pub. L. 98–473, title II, §218(a), Oct. 12, 1984, 98 Stat. 2027; Pub. L. 99–646, §57(a), Nov. 10, 1986, 100 Stat. 3611.)

Historical and Revision Notes

Based on title 18, U.S.C., 1940 ed., §753f (May 14, 1930, ch. 274, §7, 46 Stat. 326; June 14, 1941, ch. 204, 55 Stat. 252; Oct. 21, 1941, ch. 453, 55 Stat. 743).

Words "by the juvenile court of the District of Columbia, as well as to those committed by any court of the United States," at end of section were omitted as unnecessary, and word "all" inserted before "persons", without change of meaning.

Provision against penitentiary imprisonment for a term of 1 year or less without consent of defendant was incorporated in section 4083 of this title.

The phrase "if in his judgment it shall be for the well-being of the prisoner or relieve overcrowded or unhealthful conditions in the institution where such person is confined or for other reasons", was omitted as unnecessary.

Changes were made in phraseology.

This section supersedes section 705 of title 18, U.S.C., 1940 ed., providing for execution of sentences in houses of correction or reformation; and section 748 of title 18, U.S.C., 1940 ed., providing for confinement of prisoners in United States Disciplinary Barracks.

Amendments

1986—Subsecs. (f), (g). Pub. L. 99–646 added subsec. (f) and redesignated former subsec. (f) as (g).

1984—Pub. L. 98 473 struck out subsecs. (a) to (c) and (e) and redesignated subsecs. (d), (f), and (g) as (a), (b), and (c), respectively. Prior to amendment subsecs. (a) to (c) and (e) read as follows:

"(a) A person convicted of an offense against the United States shall be committed, for such term of imprisonment as the court may direct, to the custody of the Attorney General of the United States, who shall designate the place of confinement where the sentence shall be served.

"(b) The Attorney General may designate as a place of confinement any available, suitable, and appropriate institution or facility, whether maintained by the Federal Government or otherwise, and whether within or without the judicial district in which the person was convicted, and may at any time transfer a person from one place of confinement to another.

"(c) The Attorney General may extend the limits of the place of confinement of a prisoner as to whom there is reasonable cause to believe he will honor his trust, by authorizing him, under prescribed conditions, to—

"(1) visit a specifically designated place or places for a period not to exceed thirty days and return to the same or another institution or facility. An extension of limits may be granted to permit a visit to a dying relative, attendance at the funeral of a relative, the obtaining of medical services not otherwise available, the contacting of prospective employers, the establishment or reestablishment of family and community ties or for any other significant reason consistent with the public interest; or

"(2) work at paid employment or participate in a training program in the community on a voluntary basis while continuing as a prisoner of the institution or facility to which he is committed, provided that—

"(i) representatives of local union central bodies or similar labor union organizations are consulted;

"(ii) such paid employment will not result in the displacement of employed workers, or be applied in skills, crafts, or trades in which there is a surplus of available gainful labor in the locality, or impair existing contracts for services; and

"(iii) the rates of pay and other conditions of employment will not be less than those paid or provided for work of similar nature in the locality in which the work is to be performed.

A prisoner authorized to work at paid employment in the community under this subsection may be required to pay, and the Attorney General is authorized to collect, such costs incident to the prisoner's confinement as the Attorney General deems appropriate and reasonable. Collections shall be deposited in the Treasury of the United States as miscellaneous receipts.

"(e) The authority conferred upon the Attorney General by this section shall extend to all persons committed to the National Training School for Boys."

1973—Subsec. (c)(1). Pub. L. 93–209 provided for extension of limits to permit establishment or reestablishment of family and community ties and struck out "only" after "may be granted".

1965—Subsec. (a). Pub. L. 89–176 designated as subsec. (a) first unnumbered par. and struck out "or his authorized representative" after "Attorney General of the United States".

Subsec. (b). Pub. L. 89–176 designated as subsec. (b) second and third unnumbered par., inserted "or facility" after "appropriate institution", substituted "may at any time transfer a person from one place of confinement to another" for "may order any inmate transferred from one institution to another", and made minor changes in language.

Subsecs. (c), (d). Pub. L. 89–176 added subsecs. (c) and (d).

Subsec. (e). Pub. L. 89–176 designated as subsec. (e) fourth and last unnumbered pars.

Subsec. (f). Pub. L. 89–176 added subsec. (f).

Effective Date of 1984 Amendment

Amendment by Pub. L. 98–473 effective Nov. 1, 1987, and applicable only to offenses committed after the taking effect of such amendment, see section 235(a)(1) of Pub. L. 98–473, set out as an Effective Date note under section 3551 of this title.

§4083. Penitentiary imprisonment; consent

Persons convicted of offenses against the United States or by courts-martial punishable by imprisonment for more than one year may be confined in any United States penitentiary. A sentence for an offense punishable by imprisonment for one year or less shall not be served in a penitentiary without the consent of the defendant.

(June 25, 1948, ch. 645, 62 Stat. 850; Pub. L. 86–256, Sept. 14, 1959, 73 Stat. 518.)

Historical and Revision Notes

Based on title 18, U.S.C., 1940 ed., §§753f, 762 (Mar. 2, 1895, ch. 189, §1, 28 Stat. 957; June 10, 1896, ch. 400, §1, 29 Stat. 380; May 14, 1930, ch. 274, §7, 46 Stat. 326; June 14, 1941, ch. 204, 55 Stat. 252; Oct. 21, 1941, ch. 453, 55 Stat. 743).

Said section 762 was condensed and simplified and extended to all penitentiaries instead of to Leavenworth only, since the section is merely declaratory of existing law. (See section 1 of this title classifying offenses and notes thereunder.)

The second paragraph is derived from said section 753f of title 18, U.S.C., 1940 ed.

Minor changes of phraseology were made.

Amendments

1959—Pub. L. 86–256 substituted "punishable by imprisonment for" for "and sentenced to terms of imprisonment of" in first sentence.

[§§4084, 4085. Repealed. Pub. L. 98–473, title II, §218(a)(3), Oct. 12, 1984, 98 Stat. 2027]

Section 4084, act June 25, 1948, ch. 645, 62 Stat. 850, related to delivery of prisoner with copy of commitment.

Section 4085, act June 25, 1948, ch. 645, 62 Stat. 850, related to authority, expense, etc., respecting transfer of Federal prisoner for State offense.

Effective Date of Repeal

Repeal effective Nov. 1, 1987, and applicable only to offenses committed after the taking effect of such repeal, see section 235(a)(1) of Pub. L. 98–473, set out as an Effective Date note under section 3551 of this title.

§4086. Temporary safe-keeping of federal offenders by marshals

United States marshals shall provide for the safe-keeping of any person arrested, or held under authority of any enactment of Congress pending commitment to an institution.

(June 25, 1948, ch. 645, 62 Stat. 851.)

Historical and Revision Notes

Based on title 18, U.S.C., 1940 ed., §§691, 692, (R.S. §§5537, 5538).

Said section 691 of title 18, U.S.C., 1940 ed., is superseded by sections 753b and 753c of title 18, U.S.C., 1940 ed., which are incorporated in sections 4002, 4003 and 4042 of this title.

This section is rewritten to retain the intent of section 692 of title 18, U.S.C., 1940 ed., which was to insure a safekeeping of United States prisoners until their commitment or confinement in Federal penal institutions. The language conforms with that of said sections 692 and 753b.

Minor changes were made in phraseology.

CHAPTER 306 - TRANSFER TO OR FROM FOREIGN COUNTRIES

Amendments

1988—Pub. L. 100–690, title VII, §7101(c), Nov. 18, 1988, 102 Stat. 4415, added item 4106A.

§4100. Scope and limitation of chapter

(a) The provisions of this chapter relating to the transfer of offenders shall be applicable only when a treaty providing for such a transfer is in force, and shall only be applicable to transfers of offenders to and from a foreign country pursuant to such a treaty. A sentence imposed by a foreign country upon an offender who is subsequently transferred to the United States pursuant to a treaty shall be subject to being fully executed in the United States even though the treaty under which the offender was transferred is no longer in force.

(b) An offender may be transferred from the United States pursuant to this chapter only to a country of which the offender is a citizen or national. Only an offender who is a citizen or national of the United States may be transferred to the United States. An offender may be transferred to or from the United States only with the offender's consent, and only if the offense for which the offender was sentenced satisfies the requirement of double criminality as defined in this chapter. Once an offender's consent to transfer has been verified by a verifying officer, that consent shall be irrevocable. If at the time of transfer the offender is under eighteen years of age, or is deemed by the verifying officer to be mentally incompetent or otherwise incapable of knowingly and voluntarily consenting to the transfer, the transfer shall not be accomplished unless consent to the transfer be given by a parent or guardian, guardian ad litem, or by an appropriate court of the sentencing country. The appointment of a guardian ad litem shall be independent of the appointment of counsel under section 4109 of this title.

(c) An offender shall not be transferred to or from the United States if a proceeding by way of appeal or of collateral attack upon the conviction or sentence be pending.

(d) The United States upon receiving notice from the country which imposed the sentence that the offender has been granted a pardon, commutation, or amnesty, or that there has been an ameliorating modification or a revocation of the sentence shall give the offender the benefit of the action taken by the sentencing country.

(Added Pub. L. 95–144, §1, Oct. 28, 1977, 91 Stat. 1212; amended Pub. L. 100–690, title VII,

§7101(e), Nov. 18, 1988, 102 Stat. 4416.)

Amendments

1988—Subsec. (b). Pub. L. 100–690 inserted ", or is deemed by the verifying officer to be mentally incompetent or otherwise incapable of knowingly and voluntarily consenting to the transfer," after "under eighteen years of age", ", guardian ad litem," after "guardian", and "The appointment of a guardian ad litem shall be independent of the appointment of counsel under section 4109 of this title."

Authorization of Appropriations

Pub. L. 95–144, §5(a), Oct. 28, 1977, 91 Stat. 1221, provided that: "There is authorized to be appropriated such funds as may be required to carry out the purposes of this Act [which enacted this chapter and sections 955 of Title 10, Armed Forces, and 2256 of Title 28, Judiciary and Judicial Procedure, amended section 636 of Title 28, and enacted provisions set out as notes under sections 3006A, 4100, and 4102 of this title]".

Prisoner Transfer Treaties

Pub. L. 104–208, div. C, title III, §330, Sept. 30, 1996, 110 Stat. 3009–631, provided that:
"(a) Negotiations With Other Countries.—(1) Congress advises the President to begin to negotiate and renegotiate, not later than 90 days after the date of enactment of this Act [Sept. 30, 1996], bilateral prisoner transfer treaties, providing for the incarceration, in the country of the alien's nationality, of any alien who—
"(A) is a national of a country that is party to such a treaty; and
"(B) has been convicted of a criminal offense under Federal or State law and who—
"(i) is not in lawful immigration status in the United States, or
"(ii) on the basis of conviction for a criminal offense under Federal or State law, or on any other basis, is subject to deportation or removal under the Immigration and Nationality Act [8 U.S.C. 1101 et seq.],
for the duration of the prison term to which the alien was sentenced for the offense referred to in subparagraph (B). Any such agreement may provide for the release of such alien pursuant to parole procedures of that country.
"(2) In entering into negotiations under paragraph (1), the President may consider providing for appropriate compensation, subject to the availability of appropriations, in cases where the United States is able to independently verify the adequacy of the sites where aliens will be imprisoned and the length of time the alien is actually incarcerated in the foreign country under such a treaty.
"(b) Sense of Congress.—It is the sense of the Congress that—
"(1) the focus of negotiations for such agreements should be—
"(A) to expedite the transfer of aliens unlawfully in the United States who are (or are about to be) incarcerated in United States prisons,
"(B) to ensure that a transferred prisoner serves the balance of the sentence imposed by the United States courts,
"(C) to eliminate any requirement of prisoner consent to such a transfer, and
"(D) to allow the Federal Government or the States to keep their original prison sentences in force so that transferred prisoners who return to the United States prior to the completion of their original United States sentences can be returned to custody for the balance of their prisons [sic] sentences;
"(2) the Secretary of State should give priority to concluding an agreement with any country for which the President determines that the number of aliens described in subsection (a) who are nationals of that country in the United States represents a significant percentage of all such aliens in the United States; and
"(3) no new treaty providing for the transfer of aliens from Federal, State, or local incarceration facilities to a foreign incarceration facility should permit the alien to refuse the transfer.

"(c) Prisoner Consent.—Notwithstanding any other provision of law, except as required by treaty, the transfer of an alien from a Federal, State, or local incarceration facility under an agreement of the type referred to in subsection (a) shall not require consent of the alien.

"(d) Annual Report.—Not later than 90 days after the date of the enactment of this Act [Sept. 30, 1996], and annually thereafter, the Attorney General shall submit a report to the Committees on the Judiciary of the House of Representatives and of the Senate stating whether each prisoner transfer treaty to which the United States is a party has been effective in the preceding 12 months in bringing about the return of deportable incarcerated aliens to the country of which they are nationals and in ensuring that they serve the balance of their sentences.

"(e) Training Foreign Law Enforcement Personnel.—(1) Subject to paragraph (2), the President shall direct the Border Patrol Academy and the Customs Service Academy to enroll for training an appropriate number of foreign law enforcement personnel, and shall make appointments of foreign law enforcement personnel to such academies, as necessary to further the following United States law enforcement goals:

"(A) Preventing of drug smuggling and other cross-border criminal activity.

"(B) Preventing illegal immigration.

"(C) Preventing the illegal entry of goods into the United States (including goods the sale of which is illegal in the United States, the entry of which would cause a quota to be exceeded, or the appropriate duty or tariff for which has not been paid).

"(2) The appointments described in paragraph (1) shall be made only to the extent there is capacity in such academies beyond what is required to train United States citizens needed in the Border Patrol and Customs Service, and only of personnel from a country with which the prisoner transfer treaty has been stated to be effective in the most recent report referred to in subsection (d).

"(f) Authorization of Appropriations.—There are authorized to be appropriated such sums as may be necessary to carry out this section."

[For transfer of functions, personnel, assets, and liabilities of the United States Customs Service of the Department of the Treasury, including functions of the Secretary of the Treasury relating thereto, to the Secretary of Homeland Security, and for treatment of related references, see sections 203(1), 551(d), 552(d), and 557 of Title 6, Domestic Security, and the Department of Homeland Security Reorganization Plan of November 25, 2002, as modified, set out as a note under section 542 of Title 6. For establishment of U.S. Customs and Border Protection in the Department of Homeland Security, treated as if included in Pub. L. 107–296 as of Nov. 25, 2002, see section 211 of Title 6, as amended generally by Pub. L. 114–125, and section 802(b) of Pub. L. 114–125, set out as a note under section 211 of Title 6.]

§4101. Definitions

As used in this chapter the term—

(a) "double criminality" means that at the time of transfer of an offender the offense for which he has been sentenced is still an offense in the transferring country and is also an offense in the receiving country. With regard to a country which has a federal form of government, an act shall be deemed to be an offense in that country if it is an offense under the federal laws or the laws of any state or province thereof;

(b) "imprisonment" means a penalty imposed by a court under which the individual is confined to an institution;

(c) "juvenile" means—

(1) a person who is under eighteen years of age; or

(2) for the purpose of proceedings and disposition under chapter 403 of this title because of an act of juvenile delinquency, a person who is under twenty-one years of age;

(d) "juvenile delinquency" means—

(1) a violation of the laws of the United States or a State thereof or of a foreign country committed by a juvenile which would have been a crime if committed by an adult; or

(2) noncriminal acts committed by a juvenile for which supervision or treatment by juvenile

authorities of the United States, a State thereof, or of the foreign country concerned is authorized;

(e) "offender" means a person who has been convicted of an offense or who has been adjudged to have committed an act of juvenile delinquency;

(f) "parole" means any form of release of an offender from imprisonment to the community by a releasing authority prior to the expiration of his sentence, subject to conditions imposed by the releasing authority and to its supervision, including a term of supervised release pursuant to section 3583;

(g) "probation" means any form of a sentence under which the offender is permitted to remain at liberty under supervision and subject to conditions for the breach of which a penalty of imprisonment may be ordered executed;

(h) "sentence" means not only the penalty imposed but also the judgment of conviction in a criminal case or a judgment of acquittal in the same proceeding, or the adjudication of delinquency in a juvenile delinquency proceeding or dismissal of allegations of delinquency in the same proceedings;

(i) "State" means any State of the United States, the District of Columbia, the Commonwealth of Puerto Rico, and any territory or possession of the United States;

(j) "transfer" means a transfer of an individual for the purpose of the execution in one country of a sentence imposed by the courts of another country; and

(k) "treaty" means a treaty under which an offender sentenced in the courts of one country may be transferred to the country of which he is a citizen or national for the purpose of serving the sentence.

(Added Pub. L. 95–144, §1, Oct. 28, 1977, 91 Stat. 1213; amended Pub. L. 98–473, title II, §223(m)(1), Oct. 12, 1984, 98 Stat. 2029.)

Amendments

1984—Subsec. (f). Pub. L. 98–473 inserted "including a term of supervised release pursuant to section 3583" after "supervision".

Subsec. (g). Pub. L. 98–473 substituted "under which" for "to a penalty of imprisonment the execution of which is suspended" and "a" for "the suspended" before "penalty".

Effective Date of 1984 Amendment

Amendment by Pub. L. 98–473 effective Nov. 1, 1987, and applicable only to offenses committed after the taking effect of such amendment, see section 235(a)(1) of Pub. L. 98–473, set out as an Effective Date note under section 3551 of this title.

§4102. Authority of the Attorney General

The Attorney General is authorized—

(1) to act on behalf of the United States as the authority referred to in a treaty;

(2) to receive custody of offenders under a sentence of imprisonment, on parole, or on probation who are citizens or nationals of the United States transferred from foreign countries and as appropriate confine them in penal or correctional institutions, or assign them to the parole or probation authorities for supervision;

(3) to transfer offenders under a sentence of imprisonment, on parole, or on probation to the foreign countries of which they are citizens or nationals;

(4) to make regulations for the proper implementation of such treaties in accordance with this chapter and to make regulations to implement this chapter;

(5) to render to foreign countries and to receive from them the certifications and reports required to be made under such treaties;

(6) to make arrangements by agreement with the States for the transfer of offenders in their custody who are citizens or nationals of foreign countries to the foreign countries of which they are citizens or nationals and for the confinement, where appropriate, in State institutions of offenders transferred to the United States;

(7) to make agreements and establish regulations for the transportation through the territory of the United States of offenders convicted in a foreign country who are being transported to a third country for the execution of their sentences, the expenses of which shall be paid by the country requesting the transportation;

(8) to make agreements with the appropriate authorities of a foreign country and to issue regulations for the transfer and treatment of juveniles who are transferred pursuant to treaty, the expenses of which shall be paid by the country of which the juvenile is a citizen or national;

(9) in concert with the Secretary of Health, Education, and Welfare, to make arrangements with the appropriate authorities of a foreign country and to issue regulations for the transfer and treatment of individuals who are accused of an offense but who have been determined to be mentally ill; the expenses of which shall be paid by the country of which such person is a citizen or national;

(10) to designate agents to receive, on behalf of the United States, the delivery by a foreign government of any citizen or national of the United States being transferred to the United States for the purpose of serving a sentence imposed by the courts of the foreign country, and to convey him to the place designated by the Attorney General. Such agent shall have all the powers of a marshal of the United States in the several districts through which it may be necessary for him to pass with the offender, so far as such power is requisite for the offender's transfer and safekeeping; within the territory of a foreign country such agent shall have such powers as the authorities of the foreign country may accord him;

(11) to delegate the authority conferred by this chapter to officers of the Department of Justice.
(Added Pub. L. 95–144, §1, Oct. 28, 1977, 91 Stat. 1214.)

Change of Name
Secretary and Department of Health, Education, and Welfare redesignated Secretary and Department of Health and Human Services by Pub. L. 96–88, title V, §509(b), Oct. 17, 1979, 93 Stat. 695, which is classified to section 3508(b) of Title 20, Education.

Certification by Attorney General to Secretary of State for Reimbursement of Expenses Incurred Under Transfer Treaty
Pub. L. 95–144, §5(b), Oct. 28, 1977, 91 Stat. 1221, provided that: "The Attorney General shall certify to the Secretary of State the expenses of the United States related to the return of an offender to the foreign country of which the offender is a citizen or national for which the United States is entitled to seek reimbursement from that country under a treaty providing for transfer and reimbursement."

§4103. Applicability of United States laws
All laws of the United States, as appropriate, pertaining to prisoners, probationers, parolees, and juvenile offenders shall be applicable to offenders transferred to the United States, unless a treaty or this chapter provides otherwise.
(Added Pub. L. 95–144, §1, Oct. 28, 1977, 91 Stat. 1215.)

§4104. Transfer of offenders on probation
(a) Prior to consenting to the transfer to the United States of an offender who is on probation, the Attorney General shall determine that the appropriate United States district court is willing to undertake the supervision of the offender.

(b) Upon the receipt of an offender on probation from the authorities of a foreign country, the Attorney General shall cause the offender to be brought before the United States district court which is to exercise supervision over the offender.

(c) The court shall place the offender under supervision of the probation officer of the court. The offender shall be supervised by a probation officer, under such conditions as are deemed appropriate by the court as though probation had been imposed by the United States district court.

(d) The probation may be revoked in accordance with section 3565 of this title and the applicable provisions of the Federal Rules of Criminal Procedure. A violation of the conditions of probation shall constitute grounds for revocation. If probation is revoked the suspended sentence imposed by the sentencing court shall be executed.

(e) The provisions of sections 4105 and 4106 of this title shall be applicable following a revocation of probation.

(f) Prior to consenting to the transfer from the United States of an offender who is on probation, the Attorney General shall obtain the assent of the court exercising jurisdiction over the probationer.

(Added Pub. L. 95–144, §1, Oct. 28, 1977, 91 Stat. 1215; amended Pub. L. 107–273, div. B, title IV, §4002(e)(6), Nov. 2, 2002, 116 Stat. 1810.)

Amendments

2002—Subsec. (d). Pub. L. 107–273 substituted "section 3565 of this title and the applicable provisions of" for "section 3653 of this title and rule 32(f) of".

§4105. Transfer of offenders serving sentence of imprisonment

(a) Except as provided elsewhere in this section, an offender serving a sentence of imprisonment in a foreign country transferred to the custody of the Attorney General shall remain in the custody of the Attorney General under the same conditions and for the same period of time as an offender who had been committed to the custody of the Attorney General by a court of the United States for the period of time imposed by the sentencing court.

(b) The transferred offender shall be given credit toward service of the sentence for any days, prior to the date of commencement of the sentence, spent in custody in connection with the offense or acts for which the sentence was imposed.

(c)(1) The transferred offender shall be entitled to all credits for good time, for labor, or any other credit toward the service of the sentence which had been given by the transferring country for time served as of the time of the transfer. Subsequent to the transfer, the offender shall in addition be entitled to credits toward service of sentence for satisfactory behavior, computed on the basis of the time remaining to be served at the time of the transfer and at the rate provided in section 3624(b) of this title for a sentence of the length of the total sentence imposed and certified by the foreign authorities. These credits shall be combined to provide a release date for the offender pursuant to section 3624(a) of this title.

(2) If the country from which the offender is transferred does not give credit for good time, the basis of computing the deduction from the sentence shall be the sentence imposed by the sentencing court and certified to be served upon transfer, at the rate provided in section 3624(b) of this title.

(3) Credit toward service of sentence may be withheld as provided in section 3624(b) of this title.

(4) Any sentence for an offense against the United States, imposed while the transferred offender is serving the sentence of imprisonment imposed in a foreign country, shall be aggregated with the foreign sentence, in the same manner as if the foreign sentence was one imposed by a United States district court for an offense against the United States.

(Added Pub. L. 95–144, §1, Oct. 28, 1977, 91 Stat. 1215; amended Pub. L. 98–473, title II, §223(m)(2), Oct. 12, 1984, 98 Stat. 2029.)

Amendments

1984—Subsec. (c)(1). Pub. L. 98–473 substituted "toward service of sentence for satisfactory behavior" for "for good time", "3624(b)" for "4161", and "3624(a)" for "4164".

Subsec. (c)(2). Pub. L. 98–473 substituted "3624(b)" for "4161".

Subsec. (c)(3), (4). Pub. L. 98–473 redesignated par. (4) as (3) and amended it generally, and struck out former par. (3). Prior to redesignation and amendment, former pars. (3) and (4) read as follows:

"(3) A transferred offender may earn extra good time deductions, as authorized in section 4162 of this title, from the time of transfer.

"(4) All credits toward service of the sentence, other than the credit for time in custody before sentencing, may be forfeited as provided in section 4165 of this title and may be restored by the Attorney General as provided in section 4166 of this title."

Subsec. (c)(5). Pub. L. 98–473 redesignated par. (5) as (4).

Effective Date of 1984 Amendment

Amendment by Pub. L. 98–473 effective Nov. 1, 1987, and applicable only to offenses committed after the taking effect of such amendment, see section 235(a)(1) of Pub. L. 98–473, set out as an Effective Date note under section 3551 of this title.

§4106. Transfer of offenders on parole; parole of offenders transferred

(a) Upon the receipt of an offender who is on parole from the authorities of a foreign country, the Attorney General shall assign the offender to the United States Parole Commission for supervision.

(b) The United States Parole Commission and the Chairman of the Commission shall have the same powers and duties with reference to an offender transferred to the United States to serve a sentence of imprisonment or who at the time of transfer is on parole as they have with reference to an offender convicted in a court of the United States except as otherwise provided in this chapter or in the pertinent treaty. Sections 4201 through 4204; 4205(d), (e), and (h); 4206 through 4215; and 4218 1 of this title shall be applicable.

(c) An offender transferred to the United States to serve a sentence of imprisonment may be released on parole at such time as the Parole Commission may determine.

(d) This section shall apply only to offenses committed before November 1, 1987, and the Parole Commission's performance of its responsibilities under this section shall be subject to section 235 of the Comprehensive Crime Control Act of 1984.

(Added Pub. L. 95–144, §1, Oct. 28, 1977, 91 Stat. 1216; amended Pub. L. 98–473, title II, §223(m)(3), Oct. 12, 1984, 98 Stat. 2029; Pub. L. 100–182, §14, Dec. 7, 1987, 101 Stat. 1268; Pub. L. 100–690, title VII, §7072(c), Nov. 18, 1988, 102 Stat. 4405.)

References in Text

Sections 4201 through 4204; 4205(d), (e), and (h); 4206 through 4215; and 4218 of this title, referred to in subsec. (b), were repealed effective Nov. 1, 1987, by Pub. L. 98–473, title II, §§218(a)(5), 235(a)(1), (b)(1), Oct. 12, 1984, 98 Stat. 2027, 2031, 2032, subject to remaining effective for five years after Nov. 1, 1987, in certain circumstances.

Section 235 of the Comprehensive Crime Control Act of 1984, referred to in subsec. (d), is set out as an Effective Date note under section 3551 of this title.

Amendments

1988—Subsec. (b). Pub. L. 100–690 substituted "4215" for "4216".

1987—Pub. L. 100–182 amended section generally. Prior to amendment, section read as follows:

"(a) Upon the receipt of an offender who is on parole from the authorities of a foreign country, the Attorney General shall assign the offender to the United States Probation System for supervision.

"(b) An offender transferred to the United States to serve a sentence of imprisonment shall be released pursuant to section 3624(a) of this title after serving the period of time specified in the applicable sentencing guideline promulgated pursuant to 28 U.S.C. 994(a)(1). He shall be released to serve a term of supervised release for any term specified in the applicable guideline. The provisions of section 3742 of this title apply to a sentence to a term of imprisonment under this subsection, and the United States court of appeals for the district in which the offender is imprisoned after transfer to the United States has jurisdiction to review the period of imprisonment as though it had been imposed by the United States district court."

1984—Subsec. (a). Pub. L. 98–473 substituted "Probation System" for "Parole Commission".
Subsec. (b). Pub. L. 98–473 amended subsec. (b) generally. Prior to amendment, subsec. (b) read as follows: "The United States Parole Commission and the Chairman of the Commission shall have the same powers and duties with reference to an offender transferred to the United States to serve a sentence of imprisonment or who at the time of transfer is on parole as they have with reference to an offender convicted in a court of the United States except as otherwise provided in this chapter or in the pertinent treaty. Sections 4201 through 4204; 4205(d), (e), and (h); 4206 through 4216; and 4218 of this title shall be applicable."
Subsec. (c). Pub. L. 98–473 struck out subsec. (c) which read as follows: "An offender transferred to the United States to serve a sentence of imprisonment may be released on parole at such time as the Parole Commission may determine."

Effective Date of 1984 Amendment
Amendment by Pub. L. 98–473 effective Nov. 1, 1987, and applicable only to offenses committed after the taking effect of such amendment, see section 235(a)(1) of Pub. L. 98–473, set out as an Effective Date note under section 3551 of this title.

§4106A. Transfer of offenders on parole; parole of offenders transferred
(a) Upon the receipt of an offender who is on parole from the authorities of a foreign country, the Attorney General shall assign the offender to the United States Parole Commission for supervision.
(b)(1)(A) The United States Parole Commission shall, without unnecessary delay, determine a release date and a period and conditions of supervised release for an offender transferred to the United States to serve a sentence of imprisonment, as though the offender were convicted in a United States district court of a similar offense.
(B) In making such determination, the United States Parole Commission shall consider—
(i) any recommendation of the United States Probation Service, including any recommendation as to the applicable guideline range; and
(ii) any documents provided by the transferring country;
relating to that offender.
(C) The combined periods of imprisonment and supervised release that result from such determination shall not exceed the term of imprisonment imposed by the foreign court on that offender.
(D) The duties conferred on a United States probation officer with respect to a defendant by section 3552 of this title shall, with respect to an offender so transferred, be carried out by the United States Probation Service.
(2)(A) A determination by the United States Parole Commission under this subsection may be appealed to the United States court of appeals for the circuit in which the offender is imprisoned at the time of the determination of such Commission. Notice of appeal must be filed not later than 45 days after receipt of notice of such determination.
(B) The court of appeals shall decide and dispose of the appeal in accordance with section 3742 of this title as though the determination appealed had been a sentence imposed by a United States district court.
(3) During the supervised release of an offender under this subsection, the United States district court for the district in which the offender resides shall supervise the offender.
(c) This section shall apply only to offenses committed on or after November 1, 1987.
(Added Pub. L. 100–690, title VII, §7101(a), Nov. 18, 1988, 102 Stat. 4415; amended Pub. L. 101–647, title XXXV, §§3599B, 3599C, Nov. 29, 1990, 104 Stat. 4931, 4932.)

Amendments
1990—Pub. L. 101–647, §3599B, inserted "of" before second reference to "offenders" in section catchline.

Subsec. (b)(1)(C). Pub. L. 101–647, §3599C, inserted period at end.

§4107. Verification of consent of offender to transfer from the United States

(a) Prior to the transfer of an offender from the United States, the fact that the offender consents to such transfer and that such consent is voluntary and with full knowledge of the consequences thereof shall be verified by a United States magistrate judge or a judge as defined in section 451 of title 28, United States Code.

(b) The verifying officer shall inquire of the offender whether he understands and agrees that the transfer will be subject to the following conditions:

(1) only the appropriate courts in the United States may modify or set aside the conviction or sentence, and any proceedings seeking such action may only be brought in such courts;

(2) the sentence shall be carried out according to the laws of the country to which he is to be transferred and that those laws are subject to change;

(3) if a court in the country to which he is transferred should determine upon a proceeding initiated by him or on his behalf that his transfer was not accomplished in accordance with the treaty or laws of that country, he may be returned to the United States for the purpose of completing the sentence if the United States requests his return; and

(4) his consent to transfer, once verified by the verifying officer, is irrevocable.

(c) The verifying officer, before determining that an offender's consent is voluntary and given with full knowledge of the consequences, shall advise the offender of his right to consult with counsel as provided by this chapter. If the offender wishes to consult with counsel before giving his consent, he shall be advised that the proceedings will be continued until he has had an opportunity to consult with counsel.

(d) The verifying officer shall make the necessary inquiries to determine that the offender's consent is voluntary and not the result of any promises, threats, or other improper inducements, and that the offender accepts the transfer subject to the conditions set forth in subsection (b). The consent and acceptance shall be on an appropriate form prescribed by the Attorney General.

(e) The proceedings shall be taken down by a reporter or recorded by suitable sound recording equipment. The Attorney General shall maintain custody of the records.

(Added Pub. L. 95–144, §1, Oct. 28, 1977, 91 Stat. 1216; amended Pub. L. 101–650, title III, §321, Dec. 1, 1990, 104 Stat. 5117.)

Change of Name

"United States magistrate judge" substituted for "United States magistrate" in subsec. (a) pursuant to section 321 of Pub. L. 101–650, set out as a note under section 631 of Title 28, Judiciary and Judicial Procedure.

§4108. Verification of consent of offender to transfer to the United States

(a) Prior to the transfer of an offender to the United States, the fact that the offender consents to such transfer and that such consent is voluntary and with full knowledge of the consequences thereof, shall be verified in the country in which the sentence was imposed by a United States magistrate judge, or by a citizen specifically designated by a judge of the United States as defined in section 451 of title 28, United States Code. The designation of a citizen who is an employee or officer of a department or agency of the United States shall be with the approval of the head of that department or agency.

(b) The verifying officer shall inquire of the offender whether he understands and agrees that the transfer will be subject to the following conditions:

(1) only the country in which he was convicted and sentenced can modify or set aside the conviction or sentence, and any proceedings seeking such action may only be brought in that country;

(2) the sentence shall be carried out according to the laws of the United States and that those laws are subject to change;

(3) if a United States court should determine upon a proceeding initiated by him or on his behalf that his transfer was not accomplished in accordance with the treaty or laws of the United States, he may be returned to the country which imposed the sentence for the purpose of completing the sentence if that country requests his return; and

(4) his consent to transfer, once verified by the verifying officer, is irrevocable.

(c) The verifying officer, before determining that an offender's consent is voluntary and given with full knowledge of the consequences, shall advise the offender of his right to consult with counsel as provided by this chapter. If the offender wishes to consult with counsel before giving his consent, he shall be advised that the proceedings will be continued until he has had an opportunity to consult with counsel.

(d) The verifying officer shall make the necessary inquiries to determine that the offender's consent is voluntary and not the result of any promises, threats, or other improper inducements, and that the offender accepts the transfer subject to the conditions set forth in subsection (b). The consent and acceptance shall be on an appropriate form prescribed by the Attorney General.

(e) The proceedings shall be taken down by a reporter or recorded by suitable sound recording equipment. The Attorney General shall maintain custody of the records.

(Added Pub. L. 95–144, §1, Oct. 28, 1977, 91 Stat. 1217; amended Pub. L. 98–473, title II, §223(m)(4), Oct. 12, 1984, 98 Stat. 2030; Pub. L. 100–690, title VII, §7101(b), Nov. 18, 1988, 102 Stat. 4415; Pub. L. 101–650, title III, §321, Dec. 1, 1990, 104 Stat. 5117.)

Amendments

1988—Subsec. (a). Pub. L. 100–690 struck out "including any term of imprisonment or term of supervised release specified in the applicable sentencing guideline promulgated pursuant to 28 U.S.C. 944(a)(1)," after "consequences thereof,".

1984—Subsec. (a). Pub. L. 98–473 inserted ", including any term of imprisonment or term of supervised release specified in the applicable sentencing guideline promulgated pursuant to 28 U.S.C. 994(a)(1)," after "consequences thereof".

Change of Name

"United States magistrate judge" substituted for "United States magistrate" in subsec. (a) pursuant to section 321 of Pub. L. 101–650, set out as a note under section 631 of Title 28, Judiciary and Judicial Procedure.

Effective Date of 1984 Amendment

Amendment by Pub. L. 98–473 effective Nov. 1, 1987, and applicable only to offenses committed after the taking effect of such amendment, see section 235(a)(1) of Pub. L. 98–473, set out as an Effective Date note under section 3551 of this title.

§4109. Right to counsel, appointment of counsel

(a) In proceedings to verify consent of an offender for transfer, the offender shall have the right to advice of counsel. If the offender is financially unable to obtain counsel—

(1) counsel for proceedings conducted under section 4107 shall be appointed in accordance with section 3006A of this title. Such appointment shall be considered an appointment in a misdemeanor case for purposes of compensation under the Act; 1

(2) counsel for proceedings conducted under section 4108 shall be appointed by the verifying officer pursuant to such regulations as may be prescribed by the Director of the Administrative Office of the United States Courts. The Secretary of State shall make payments of fees and expenses of the appointed counsel, in amounts approved by the verifying officer, which shall not exceed the amounts authorized under section 3006A of this title for representation in a misdemeanor case. Payment in excess of the maximum amount authorized may be made for extended or complex representation whenever the verifying officer certifies that the amount of the excess payment is necessary to provide fair compensation, and the payment is approved by the

chief judge of the United States court of appeals for the appropriate circuit. Counsel from other agencies in any branch of the Government may be appointed: Provided, That in such cases the Secretary of State shall pay counsel directly, or reimburse the employing agency for travel and transportation expenses. Notwithstanding section 3324(a) and (b) of title 31, the Secretary may make advance payments of travel and transportation expenses to counsel appointed under this subsection.

(b) Guardians ad litem appointed by the verifying officer under section 4100 of this title to represent offenders who are financially unable to provide for compensation and travel expenses of the guardian ad litem shall be compensated and reimbursed under subsection (a)(1) of this section.

(c) The offender shall have the right to advice of counsel in proceedings before the United States Parole Commission under section 4106A of this title and in an appeal from a determination of such Commission under such section. If the offender is financially unable to obtain counsel, counsel for such proceedings and appeal shall be appointed under section 3006A of this title.

(Added Pub. L. 95–144, §1, Oct. 28, 1977, 91 Stat. 1218; amended Pub. L. 97–258, §3(e)(2), Sept. 13, 1982, 96 Stat. 1064; Pub. L. 100–690, title VII, §7101(d), Nov. 18, 1988, 102 Stat. 4416; Pub. L. 101–647, title XXXV, §3598, Nov. 29, 1990, 104 Stat. 4931.)

Amendments

1990—Subsec. (a). Pub. L. 101–647 substituted "section 3006A of this title" for "the Criminal Justice Act (18 U.S.C. 3006A)" in par. (1) and for "the Criminal Justice Act (18 U.S.C. 3006(a))" in par. (2).

1988—Pub. L. 100–690 designated existing provisions as subsec. (a) and added subsecs. (b) and (c).

1982—Par. (2). Pub. L. 97–258 substituted "section 3324(a) and (b) of title 31" for "section 3648 of the Revised Statutes as amended (31 U.S.C. 529)".

§4110. Transfer of juveniles

An offender transferred to the United States because of an act which would have been an act of juvenile delinquency had it been committed in the United States or any State thereof shall be subject to the provisions of chapter 403 of this title except as otherwise provided in the relevant treaty or in an agreement pursuant to such treaty between the Attorney General and the authority of the foreign country.

(Added Pub. L. 95–144, §1, Oct. 28, 1977, 91 Stat. 1218.)

§4111. Prosecution barred by foreign conviction

An offender transferred to the United States shall not be detained, prosecuted, tried, or sentenced by the United States, or any State thereof for any offense the prosecution of which would have been barred if the sentence upon which the transfer was based had been by a court of the jurisdiction seeking to prosecute the transferred offender, or if prosecution would have been barred by the laws of the jurisdiction seeking to prosecute the transferred offender if the sentence on which the transfer was based had been issued by a court of the United States or by a court of another State.

(Added Pub. L. 95–144, §1, Oct. 28, 1977, 91 Stat. 1218.)

§4112. Loss of rights, disqualification

An offender transferred to the United States to serve a sentence imposed by a foreign court shall not incur any loss of civil, political, or civic rights nor incur any disqualification other than those which under the laws of the United States or of the State in which the issue arises would result from the fact of the conviction in the foreign country.

(Added Pub. L. 95–144, §1, Oct. 28, 1977, 91 Stat. 1218.)

§4113. Status of alien offender transferred to a foreign country

(a) An alien who is deportable from the United States but who has been granted voluntary departure pursuant to section 240B of the Immigration and Nationality Act and who is transferred to a foreign country pursuant to this chapter shall be deemed for all purposes to have voluntarily departed from this country.

(b) An alien who is the subject of an order of removal from the United States pursuant to section 240 of the Immigration and Nationality Act who is transferred to a foreign country pursuant to this chapter shall be deemed for all purposes to have been removed from this country.

(c) An alien who is the subject of an order of removal from the United States pursuant to section 240 of the Immigration and Nationality Act, who is transferred to a foreign country pursuant to this chapter shall be deemed for all purposes to have been excluded from admission and removed from the United States.

(Added Pub. L. 95–144, §1, Oct. 28, 1977, 91 Stat. 1219; amended Pub. L. 104–208, div. C, title III, §308(d)(4)(U), (e)(1)(Q), (2)(I), (g)(3)(B), (5)(A)(iv), Sept. 30, 1996, 110 Stat. 3009–619, 3009–620, 3009–622, 3009–623.)

References in Text

Section 240B of the Immigration and Nationality Act, referred to in subsec. (a), is classified to section 1229c of Title 8, Aliens and Nationality.

Section 240 of the Immigration and Nationality Act, referred to in subsecs. (b) and (c), is classified to section 1229a of Title 8.

Amendments

1996—Subsec. (a). Pub. L. 104–208, §308(g)(5)(A)(iv)(I), substituted "section 240B of the Immigration and Nationality Act" for "section 1252(b) or section 1254(e) of title 8, United States Code,".

Subsec. (b). Pub. L. 104–208, §308(g)(5)(A)(iv)(II), substituted "section 240 of the Immigration and Nationality Act" for "section 1252 of title 8, United States Code,".

Pub. L. 104–208, §308(e)(1)(Q), (2)(I), substituted "removal" for "deportation" and "removed" for "deported".

Subsec. (c). Pub. L. 104–208, §308(g)(3)(B), substituted "240 of the Immigration and Nationality Act" for "1226 of title 8, United States Code".

Pub. L. 104–208, §308(d)(4)(U), (e)(2)(I), substituted "removal" for "exclusion and deportation" and "removed" for "deported".

Effective Date of 1997 Amendment

Amendment by Pub. L. 104–208 effective, with certain transitional provisions, on the first day of the first month beginning more than 180 days after Sept. 30, 1996, see section 309 of Pub. L. 104–208, set out as a note under section 1101 of Title 8, Aliens and Nationality.

§4114. Return of transferred offenders

(a) Upon a final decision by the courts of the United States that the transfer of the offender to the United States was not in accordance with the treaty or the laws of the United States and ordering the offender released from serving the sentence in the United States the offender may be returned to the country from which he was transferred to complete the sentence if the country in which the sentence was imposed requests his return. The Attorney General shall notify the appropriate authority of the country which imposed the sentence, within ten days, of a final decision of a court of the United States ordering the offender released. The notification shall specify the time within which the sentencing country must request the return of the offender which shall be no longer than thirty days.

(b) Upon receiving a request from the sentencing country that the offender ordered released be returned for the completion of his sentence, the Attorney General may file a complaint for the return of the offender with any justice or judge of the United States or any authorized magistrate judge within whose jurisdiction the offender is found. The complaint shall be upon oath and supported by affidavits establishing that the offender was convicted and sentenced by the courts of the country to which his return is requested; the offender was transferred to the United States for the execution of his sentence; the offender was ordered released by a court of the United States before he had completed his sentence because the transfer of the offender was not in accordance with the treaty or the laws of the United States; and that the sentencing country has requested that he be returned for the completion of the sentence. There shall be attached to the complaint a copy of the sentence of the sentencing court and of the decision of the court which ordered the offender released.

A summons or a warrant shall be issued by the justice, judge or magistrate judge ordering the offender to appear or to be brought before the issuing authority. If the justice, judge, or magistrate judge finds that the person before him is the offender described in the complaint and that the facts alleged in the complaint are true, he shall issue a warrant for commitment of the offender to the custody of the Attorney General until surrender shall be made. The findings and a copy of all the testimony taken before him and of all documents introduced before him shall be transmitted to the Secretary of State, that a Return Warrant may issue upon the requisition of the proper authorities of the sentencing country, for the surrender of offender.

(c) A complaint referred to in subsection (b) must be filed within sixty days from the date on which the decision ordering the release of the offender becomes final.

(d) An offender returned under this section shall be subject to the jurisdiction of the country to which he is returned for all purposes.

(e) The return of an offender shall be conditioned upon the offender being given credit toward service of the sentence for the time spent in the custody of or under the supervision of the United States.

(f) Sections 3186, 3188 through 3191, and 3195 of this title shall be applicable to the return of an offender under this section. However, an offender returned under this section shall not be deemed to have been extradited for any purpose.

(g) An offender whose return is sought pursuant to this section may be admitted to bail or be released on his own recognizance at any stage of the proceedings.

(Added Pub. L. 95–144, §1, Oct. 28, 1977, 91 Stat. 1219; amended Pub. L. 101–650, title III, §321, Dec. 1, 1990, 104 Stat. 5117.)

Change of Name

Words "magistrate judge" substituted for "magistrate" wherever appearing in subsec. (b) pursuant to section 321 of Pub. L. 101–650, set out as a note under section 631 of Title 28, Judiciary and Judicial Procedure.

§4115. Execution of sentences imposing an obligation to make restitution or reparations

If in a sentence issued in a penal proceeding of a transferring country an offender transferred to the United States has been ordered to pay a sum of money to the victim of the offense for damage caused by the offense, that penalty or award of damages may be enforced as though it were a civil judgment rendered by a United States district court. Proceedings to collect the moneys ordered to be paid may be instituted by the Attorney General in any United States district court. Moneys recovered pursuant to such proceedings shall be transmitted through diplomatic channels to the treaty authority of the transferring country for distribution to the victim.

(Added Pub. L. 95–144, §1, Oct. 28, 1977, 91 Stat. 1220.)

CHAPTER 307 - EMPLOYMENT

Amendments

1990—Pub. L. 101–647, title XXXV, §3599A, Nov. 29, 1990, 104 Stat. 4931, substituted "Fund" for "fund" in item 4126.

1988—Pub. L. 100–690, title VII, §7093(b), Nov. 18, 1988, 102 Stat. 4412, added item 4129.

§4121. Federal Prison Industries; board of directors

"Federal Prison Industries", a government corporation of the District of Columbia, shall be administered by a board of six directors, appointed by the President to serve at the will of the President without compensation.

The directors shall be representatives of (1) industry, (2) labor, (3) agriculture, (4) retailers and consumers, (5) the Secretary of Defense, and (6) the Attorney General, respectively.

(June 25, 1948, ch. 645, 62 Stat. 851; May 24, 1949, ch. 139, §62, 63 Stat. 98.)

Historical and Revision Notes

1948 Act

Based on title 18, U.S.C., 1940 ed., §§744i, 744j (June 23, 1934, ch. 736, §§1, 2, 48 Stat. 1211). Section consolidates sections 744i and 744j of title 18, U.S.C., 1940 ed. The former was rewritten omitting unnecessary recital as to policy and expressing the original language of the two sections more logically.

Changes were made in transportation and phraseology.

1949 Act

This section [section 62] incorporates in section 4121 of title 18, U.S.C., with changes in phraseology, the provisions of section 3 of act of June 29, 1948 (ch. 719, 62 Stat. 1100), which was enacted subsequent to the enactment of the revision of title 18 and which provided for appointment of an additional member of the board of directors of the Federal Prison Industries, as a representative of the Secretary of Defense.

Amendments

1949—Act May 24, 1949, made a representative of the Secretary of Defense a member of the board of directors.

Transfer of Functions

Federal Prison Industries, Inc. (together with its Board of Directors), and its functions transferred to Department of Justice to be administered under general direction and supervision of Attorney General, by Reorg. Plan No. II of 1939, §3(a), eff. July 1, 1939, 4 F.R. 2731, 53 Stat. 1431, set out in the Appendix to Title 5, Government Organization and Employees. See, also, Reorg. Plan No. 2 of 1950, §1, eff. May 1, 1950, 15 F.R. 3173, 64 Stat. 1261, and section 509 of Title 28, Judiciary and Judicial Procedure.

Mandatory Work Requirement for All Prisoners

Pub. L. 101–647, title XXIX, §2905, Nov. 29, 1990, 104 Stat. 4914, provided that:

"(a) In General.—(1) It is the policy of the Federal Government that convicted inmates confined in Federal prisons, jails, and other detention facilities shall work. The type of work in which they will be involved shall be dictated by appropriate security considerations and by the health of the prisoner involved.

"(2) A Federal prisoner may be excused from the requirement to work only as necessitated by—

"(A) security considerations;

"(B) disciplinary action;

"(C) medical certification of disability such as would make it impracticable for prison officials to arrange useful work for the prisoner to perform; or

"(D) a need for the prisoner to work less than a full work schedule in order to participate in literacy training, drug rehabilitation, or similar programs in addition to the work program."

Closure of McNeil Island Penitentiary; Report on Status of Federal Prison Industries

Pub. L. 95–624, §10, Nov. 9, 1978, 92 Stat. 3463, provided that:

"(a) On or before September 1, 1979, the Attorney General shall submit to the Congress—

"(1) a plan to assure the closure of the United States Penitentiary on McNeil Island, Steilacoom, Washington, on or before January 1, 1982; and

"(2) a report on the status of the Federal Prison Industries.

"(b) The report made under this section shall include a long-range plan for the improvement of meaningful employment training, and the methods which could be undertaken to employ a greater number of United States prisoners in the program. Such report may include recommendations for legislation."

§4122. Administration of Federal Prison Industries

(a) Federal Prison Industries shall determine in what manner and to what extent industrial operations shall be carried on in Federal penal and correctional institutions for the production of commodities for consumption in such institutions or for sale to the departments or agencies of the United States, but not for sale to the public in competition with private enterprise.

(b)(1) Its board of directors shall provide employment for the greatest number of those inmates in the United States penal and correctional institutions who are eligible to work as is reasonably possible, diversify, so far as practicable, prison industrial operations and so operate the prison shops that no single private industry shall be forced to bear an undue burden of competition from the products of the prison workshops, and to reduce to a minimum competition with private industry or free labor.

(2) Federal Prison Industries shall conduct its operations so as to produce products on an economic basis, but shall avoid capturing more than a reasonable share of the market among Federal departments, agencies, and institutions for any specific product. Federal Prison Industries shall concentrate on providing to the Federal Government only those products which permit employment of the greatest number of those inmates who are eligible to work as is reasonably possible.

(3) Federal Prison Industries shall diversify its products so that its sales are distributed among its industries as broadly as possible.

(4) Any decision by Federal Prison Industries to produce a new product or to significantly expand the production of an existing product shall be made by the board of directors of the corporation. Before the board of directors makes a final decision, the corporation shall do the following:

(A) The corporation shall prepare a detailed written analysis of the probable impact on industry and free labor of the plans for new production or expanded production. In such written analysis the corporation shall, at a minimum, identify and consider—

(i) the number of vendors currently meeting the requirements of the Federal Government for the product;

(ii) the proportion of the Federal Government market for the product currently served by small businesses, small disadvantaged businesses, or businesses operating in labor surplus areas;

(iii) the size of the Federal Government and non-Federal Government markets for the product;

(iv) the projected growth in the Federal Government demand for the product; and

(v) the projected ability of the Federal Government market to sustain both Federal Prison Industries and private vendors.

(B) The corporation shall announce in a publication designed to most effectively provide notice to potentially affected private vendors the plans to produce any new product or to significantly expand production of an existing product. The announcement shall also indicate that the analysis prepared under subparagraph (A) is available through the corporation and shall invite comments from private industry regarding the new production or expanded production.

(C) The corporation shall directly advise those affected trade associations that the corporation can reasonably identify the plans for new production or expanded production, and the corporation shall invite such trade associations to submit comments on those plans.

(D) The corporation shall provide to the board of directors—

(i) the analysis prepared under subparagraph (A) on the proposal to produce a new product or to significantly expand the production of an existing product,

(ii) comments submitted to the corporation on the proposal, and

(iii) the corporation's recommendations for action on the proposal in light of such comments.

In addition, the board of directors, before making a final decision under this paragraph on a proposal, shall, upon the request of an established trade association or other interested representatives of private industry, provide a reasonable opportunity to such trade association or other representatives to present comments directly to the board of directors on the proposal.

(5) Federal Prison Industries shall publish in the manner specified in paragraph (4)(B) the final decision of the board with respect to the production of a new product or the significant expansion of the production of an existing product.

(6) Federal Prison Industries shall publish, after the end of each 6-month period, a list of sales by the corporation for that 6-month period. Such list shall be made available to all interested parties.

(c) Its board of directors may provide for the vocational training of qualified inmates without regard to their industrial or other assignments.

(d)(1) The provisions of this chapter shall apply to the industrial employment and training of prisoners convicted by general courts-martial and confined in any institution under the jurisdiction of any department or agency comprising the Department of Defense, to the extent and under terms and conditions agreed upon by the Secretary of Defense, the Attorney General and the Board of Directors of Federal Prison Industries.

(2) Any department or agency of the Department of Defense may, without exchange of funds, transfer to Federal Prison Industries any property or equipment suitable for use in performing the functions and duties covered by agreement entered into under paragraph (1) of this subsection.

(e)(1) The provisions of this chapter shall apply to the industrial employment and training of prisoners confined in any penal or correctional institution under the direction of the Commissioner of the District of Columbia to the extent and under terms and conditions agreed upon by the Commissioner, the Attorney General, and the Board of Directors of Federal Prison Industries.

(2) The Commissioner of the District of Columbia may, without exchange of funds, transfer to the Federal Prison Industries any property or equipment suitable for use in performing the functions and duties covered by an agreement entered into under subsection (e)(1) of this section.

(3) Nothing in this chapter shall be construed to affect the provisions of the Act approved October 3, 1964 (D.C. Code, sections 24–451 et seq.), entitled "An Act to establish in the Treasury a correctional industries fund for the government of the District of Columbia, and for other purposes."

(June 25, 1948, ch. 645, 62 Stat. 851; May 24, 1949, ch. 139, §63, 63 Stat. 98; Oct. 31, 1951, ch. 655, §31, 65 Stat. 722; Pub. L. 90–226, title VIII, §802, Dec. 27, 1967, 81 Stat. 741; Pub. L. 100–690, title VII, §7096, Nov. 18, 1988, 102 Stat. 4413.)

Historical and Revision Notes

1948 Act

Based on title 18, U.S.C., 1940 ed., §§744a, 744c, 744k (May 27, 1930, ch. 340, §§1, 3, 46 Stat. 391; June 23, 1934, ch. 736, §3, 48 Stat. 1211).

Section consolidates sections 744a, part of 744c, and 744k of title 18, U.S.C., 1940 ed., with such changes of phraseology as were necessary to effect the consolidation.

Provisions in section 744k of title 18, U.S.C., 1940 ed., for transfer of duties to the corporation was omitted as executed.

Other provisions of said section 744c of title 18, U.S.C., 1940 ed., form section 4123 of this title. Changes were made in phraseology.

1949 Act

Subsection (c) of section 4122 of title 18, U.S.C., as added by this amendment [see section 63], incorporates provisions of act of May 11, 1948 (ch. 276, 62 Stat. 230), which was not incorporated in title 18 when the revision was enacted. The remainder of such act is incorporated in section 4126 of such title by another section of this bill.

Subsections (d) and (e) of such section 4122, added by this amendment [see section 63], incorporate, with changes in phraseology, the provisions of sections 1 and 2 of act of June 29, 1948 (ch. 719, 62 Stat. 1100), extending the functions and duties of Federal Prisons Industries, Incorporated, to military disciplinary barracks. Section 3 of such act is incorporated in section 4121 of such title by another section of this bill, and section 4 of such act is classified to section 1621a of title 50, U.S.C., Appendix, War and National Defense.

References in Text

The Act approved October 3, 1964 (D.C. Code, sections 24–451 et seq.), entitled "An Act to establish in the Treasury a correctional institution industries fund for the government of the District of Columbia, and for other purposes", referred to in subsec. (e)(3), is Pub. L. 88–622, Oct. 3, 1964, 78 Stat. 1000.

Amendments

1988—Subsec. (b). Pub. L. 100–690 designated existing provisions as par. (1), substituted "the greatest number of those inmates in the United States penal and correctional institutions who are eligible to work as is reasonably possible" for "all physically fit inmates in the United States penal and correctional institutions", and added pars. (2) to (6).

1967—Subsec. (d). Pub. L. 90–226, §802(1), (2), designated existing provisions of subsec. (d) as par. (1) thereof, designated existing provisions of subsec. (e) as par. (2) of subsec. (d), and substituted reference to par. (1) of this subsection for reference to subsec. (d) of this section.

Subsec. (e). Pub. L. 90–226, §802(3), added subsec. (e). Former subsec. (e) redesignated (d)(2).

1951—Subsecs. (d), (e). Act Oct. 31, 1951, substituted "Department of Defense" for "National Military Establishment".

1949—Act May 24, 1949, designated existing first two pars. as subsecs. (a) and (b), respectively, and added subsecs. (c) to (e).

Transfer of Functions

Office of Commissioner of District of Columbia, as established by Reorg. Plan No. 3 of 1967, abolished as of noon Jan. 2, 1975, by Pub. L. 93–198, title VII, §711, Dec. 24, 1973, 87 Stat. 818, and replaced by Office of Mayor of District of Columbia by section 421 of Pub. L. 93–198.

Utilization of Surplus Property

Act June 29, 1948, ch. 719, §4, 62 Stat. 1100, provided that: "For its own use in the industrial employment and training of prisoners and not for transfer or disposition, transfers of surplus property under the Surplus Property Act of 1944 [former sections 1611 to 1646 of the former Appendix to Title 50, War and National Defense], may be made to Federal Prison Industries, Incorporated, without reimbursement or transfer of funds."

§4123. New industries

Any industry established under this chapter shall be so operated as not to curtail the production of any existing arsenal, navy yard, or other Government workshop.

Such forms of employment shall be provided as will give the inmates of all Federal penal and correctional institutions a maximum opportunity to acquire a knowledge and skill in trades and occupations which will provide them with a means of earning a livelihood upon release.

The industries may be either within the precincts of any penal or correctional institution or in any convenient locality where an existing property may be obtained by lease, purchase, or otherwise.

(June 25, 1948, ch. 645, 62 Stat. 851.)

Historical and Revision Notes

Based on title 18, U.S.C., 1940 ed., §744c (May 27, 1930, ch. 340, §3, 46 Stat. 391).

A part of said section 744c of title 18, U.S.C., 1940 ed., is incorporated in section 4122 of this title.

References to the Attorney General were omitted because section 744k of title 18, U.S.C., 1940 ed., as originally enacted, provided for the transfer to Federal Prison Industries of the powers and duties then vested in the Attorney General.

References to "this chapter" were substituted for "this section" since the general authority to establish and supervise prison industries is contained in this chapter.

Minor changes of phraseology were made.

§4124. Purchase of prison-made products by Federal departments

(a) The several Federal departments and agencies and all other Government institutions of the United States shall purchase at not to exceed current market prices, such products of the industries authorized by this chapter as meet their requirements and may be available.

(b) Disputes as to the price, quality, character, or suitability of such products shall be arbitrated by a board consisting of the Attorney General, the Administrator of General Services, and the President, or their representatives. Their decision shall be final and binding upon all parties.

(c) Each Federal department, agency, and institution subject to the requirements of subsection (a) shall separately report acquisitions of products and services from Federal Prison Industries to the Federal Procurement Data System (as referred to in section 1122(a)(4) of title 41) in the same manner as it reports other acquisitions. Each report published by the Federal Procurement Data System that contains the information collected by the System shall include a statement to accompany the information reported by the department, agency, or institution under the preceding sentence as follows: "Under current law, sales by Federal Prison Industries are considered intragovernmental transfers. The purpose of reporting sales by Federal Prison Industries is to provide a complete overview of acquisitions by the Federal Government during the reporting period.".

(d) Within 90 days after the date of the enactment of this subsection, Federal Prison Industries shall publish a catalog of all products and services which it offers for sale. This catalog shall be updated periodically to the extent necessary to ensure that the information in the catalog is complete and accurate.

(June 25, 1948, ch. 645, 62 Stat. 851; Oct. 31, 1951, ch. 655, §32, 65 Stat. 723; Pub. L. 98–216, §3(b)(2), Feb. 14, 1984, 98 Stat. 6; Pub. L. 101–647, title XXIX, §2901, Nov. 29, 1990, 104 Stat. 4912; Pub. L. 102–564, title III, §303(b), Oct. 28, 1992, 106 Stat. 4262; Pub. L. 104–316, title I, §109(b), Oct. 19, 1996, 110 Stat. 3832; Pub. L. 111–350, §5(d)(2), Jan. 4, 2011, 124 Stat. 3847.)

Historical and Revision Notes

Based on title 18, U.S.C., 1940 ed., §744g (May 27, 1930, ch. 340, §7, 46 Stat. 392).

The revised section substituted the Director of the Bureau of Federal Supply of the Treasury Department for the General Supply Committee, the functions of the latter having been transferred to the Procurement Division of the Treasury Department by Executive Order No. 6166, §1, June 10, 1933, and the name of that unit having been changed to Bureau of Federal Supply by order of the Secretary of the Treasury effective January 1, 1947, 11 Federal Register No. 13,638. The Bureau of the Budget was substituted for the Bureau of Efficiency which was abolished by Act of March 3, 1933, ch. 212, §17, 47 Stat. 1519, without transferring its functions elsewhere. However, the Bureau of the Budget performs similar duties and its Director logically should serve on the arbitration board.

Reference to authority for appropriations was omitted and words "by this chapter" substituted therefor.

The word "agencies" was substituted for "independent establishments" to avoid any possibility of ambiguity. See definition of "agency" in section 6 of this title.

References in Text

The date of the enactment of this subsection, referred to in subsec. (d), is the date of enactment of Pub. L. 101–647, which was approved Nov. 29, 1990.

Amendments

2011—Subsec. (c). Pub. L. 111–350 substituted "section 1122(a)(4) of title 41" for "section 6(d)(4) of the Office of Federal Procurement Policy Act".

1996—Subsec. (b). Pub. L. 104–316 substituted "Attorney General" for "Comptroller General of the United States".

1992—Subsec. (c). Pub. L. 102–564 substituted "acquisitions of products and services from Federal Prison Industries to the Federal Procurement Data System (as referred to in section 6(d)(4) of the Office of Federal Procurement Policy Act) in the same manner as it reports other acquisitions" for "to the General Services Administration all of its acquisitions of products and services from Federal Prison Industries, and that reported information shall be entered in the Federal Procurement Data System referred to in section 6(d)(4) of the Office of Federal Procurement Policy Act".

1990—Pub. L. 101–647 designated first and second pars. as subsecs. (a) and (b), respectively, and added subsecs. (c) and (d).

1984—Pub. L. 98–216 substituted "President" for "Director of the Bureau of the Budget" in second par.

1951—Act Oct. 31, 1951, substituted "Administrator of General Services" for "Director of the Bureau of Federal Supply, Department of the Treasury" in second par.

Agency Purchase of Federal Prison Industries Products or Services

Pub. L. 108–447, div. H, title VI, §637, Dec. 8, 2004, 118 Stat. 3281, provided that: "None of the funds made available under this or any other Act for fiscal year 2005 and each fiscal year thereafter shall be expended for the purchase of a product or service offered by Federal Prison Industries, Inc., unless the agency making such purchase determines that such offered product or service provides the best value to the buying agency pursuant to governmentwide procurement regulations, issued pursuant to section 25(c)(1) of the Office of Federal Procurement Act ([former] 41 U.S.C. 421(c)(1)) [now 41 U.S.C. 1303(a)(1)] that impose procedures, standards, and limitations of section 2410n of title 10, United States Code."

Similar provisions were contained in the following prior appropriations act:

Pub. L. 108–199, div. F, title VI, §637, Jan. 23, 2004, 118 Stat. 358.

Purchases by Central Intelligence Agency of Products of Federal Prison Industries

Pub. L. 108–177, title IV, §404, Dec. 13, 2003, 117 Stat. 2632, as amended by Pub. L. 108–458, title I, §1071(g)(3)(C), Dec. 17, 2004, 118 Stat. 3692, provided that: "Notwithstanding section 4124 of title 18, United States Code, purchases by the Central Intelligence Agency from Federal Prison Industries shall be made only if the Director of the Central Intelligence Agency determines that the product or service to be purchased from Federal Prison Industries best meets the needs of the Agency."

§4125. Public works; prison camps

(a) The Attorney General may make available to the heads of the several departments the services of United States prisoners under terms, conditions, and rates mutually agreed upon, for constructing or repairing roads, clearing, maintaining and reforesting public lands, building levees, and constructing or repairing any other public ways or works financed wholly or in major part by funds appropriated by Congress.

(b) The Attorney General may establish, equip, and maintain camps upon sites selected by him elsewhere than upon Indian reservations, and designate such camps as places for confinement of persons convicted of an offense against the laws of the United States.

(c) The expenses of transferring and maintaining prisoners at such camps and of operating such camps shall be paid from the appropriation "Support of United States prisoners", which may, in the discretion of the Attorney General, be reimbursed for such expenses.

(d) As part of the expense of operating such camps the Attorney General is authorized to provide for the payment to the inmates or their dependents such pecuniary earnings as he may deem proper, under such rules and regulations as he may prescribe.

(e) All other laws of the United States relating to the imprisonment, transfer, control, discipline, escape, release of, or in any way affecting prisoners, shall apply to prisoners transferred to such camps.

(June 25, 1948, ch. 645, 62 Stat. 852.)

Historical and Revision Notes

Based on title 18, U.S.C., 1940 ed., §§744b, 851, 853, 854, 855 (Feb. 26, 1929, ch. 336, §§1, 3, 4, 5, 45 Stat. 1318; May 27, 1930, ch. 340, §2, 46 Stat. 391).

Section consolidates section 744b of title 18, U.S.C., 1940 ed., with those portions of sections 851, 853–855 of title 18, U.S.C., 1940 ed., which may not have been superseded by section 744b of said title.

Section 851 of title 18, U.S.C., 1940 ed., was superseded except for the proviso which formed the basis for the added words "elsewhere than upon Indian reservations".

Section 855 of title 18, U.S.C., 1940 ed., was superseded by section 744b of title 18, U.S.C., 1940 ed., except as to the specific mention in section 855 of said title of expense for maintenance and operation of camps. Hence a reference to operation was added in subsection (c) of this section.

Section 854 of title 18, U.S.C., 1940 ed., was added as a part of subsection (c).

Section 853 of title 18, U.S.C., 1940 ed., was added as subsection (d) of this section, although its retention may be unnecessary.

The phrase "the cost of which is borne exclusively by the United States" which followed the words "constructing or repairing roads" was omitted as inconsistent with the later phrase "constructing or repairing any other public ways or works financed wholly or in major part by funds appropriated from the Treasury of the United States."

The provision for transfer of prisoners was omitted as duplicitous of a similar provision in section 4082 of this title.

Other changes of phraseology were made.

§4126. Prison Industries Fund; use and settlement of accounts

(a) All moneys under the control of Federal Prison Industries, or received from the sale of the products or by-products of such Industries, or for the services of federal prisoners, shall be deposited or covered into the Treasury of the United States to the credit of the Prison Industries Fund and withdrawn therefrom only pursuant to accountable warrants or certificates of settlement issued by the Government Accountability Office.

(b) All valid claims and obligations payable out of said fund shall be assumed by the corporation.

(c) The corporation, in accordance with the laws generally applicable to the expenditures of the several departments, agencies, and establishments of the Government, is authorized to employ the fund, and any earnings that may accrue to the corporation—

(1) as operating capital in performing the duties imposed by this chapter;

(2) in the lease, purchase, other acquisition, repair, alteration, erection, and maintenance of industrial buildings and equipment;

(3) in the vocational training of inmates without regard to their industrial or other assignments;

(4) in paying, under rules and regulations promulgated by the Attorney General, compensation to inmates employed in any industry, or performing outstanding services in institutional operations, and compensation to inmates or their dependents for injuries suffered in any industry or in any work activity in connection with the maintenance or operation of the institution in which the inmates are confined.

In no event may compensation for such injuries be paid in an amount greater than that provided in chapter 81 of title 5.

(d) Accounts of all receipts and disbursements of the corporation shall be rendered to the Government Accountability Office for settlement and adjustment, as required by the Comptroller General.

(e) Such accounting shall include all fiscal transactions of the corporation, whether involving appropriated moneys, capital, or receipts from other sources.

(f) Funds available to the corporation may be used for the lease, purchase, other acquisition, repair, alteration, erection, or maintenance of facilities only to the extent such facilities are necessary for the industrial operations of the corporation under this chapter. Such funds may not be used for the construction or acquisition of penal or correctional institutions, including camps described in section 4125.

(June 25, 1948, ch. 645, 62 Stat. 852; May 24, 1949, ch. 139, §64, 63 Stat. 99; Pub. L. 87–317, Sept. 26, 1961, 75 Stat. 681; Pub. L. 100–690, title VII, §7094, Nov. 18, 1988, 102 Stat. 4412; Pub. L. 108–271, §8(b), July 7, 2004, 118 Stat. 814.)

Historical and Revision Notes

1948 Act

Based on title 18, U.S.C., 1940 ed., §§744d, 744e, 744f, 744l (May 27, 1930, ch. 340, §§4–6, 46 Stat. 391, 392; June 23, 1934, ch. 736, §4, 48 Stat. 1211).

This section is a restatement of section 744l of title 18, U.S.C., 1940 ed., with which sections 744d and 744f and the first sentence of section 744e of title 18, U.S.C., 1940 ed., are consolidated, in view of the fact that those provisions have been superseded by section 744l of title 18, U.S.C., 1940 ed., in connection with other provisions of the act of June 23, 1934, ch. 736, 48 Stat. 1211. The first sentence of section 744l of title 18, U.S.C., 1940 ed., authorizing replacement of the prison industries working capital fund by the prison industries fund was omitted, as executed. That provision superseded section 744d of title 18, U.S.C., 1940 ed., which authorized creation of the prison industries working capital fund and the first sentence of section 744e of title 18, U.S.C., 1940 ed., directing that certain funds should be credited to the consolidated prison industries working capital fund.

The phrase "or received from the sale of the products or by-products of such Industries, or for the services of Federal prisoners," was inserted to make the first paragraph of this section complete, and required the Federal Prison Industries to account for all moneys under its control.

The words "in the repair, alteration, erection and maintenance of industrial buildings and equipment" and "under rules and regulations promulgated by the Attorney General in paying compensation to inmates employed in any industry, or performing outstanding services in industrial operations" were inserted in part to conform to administrative construction, and in part to provide greater flexibility in the operation of Prison Industries. Much friction was caused by the inability of Prison Industries to compensate inmates whose services in operating the utilities of the institution were most necessary but which were uncompensated while those prisoners who worked in the Industries received compensation. This inequitable situation is corrected by the revised section.

The words "in performing the duties imposed by this chapter" were substituted for the words "for the purposes enumerated in sections 744a–744h of this title," since the provisions with regard to prison industries now appear in this chapter. The general provisions as to use of the fund supersede the more specific provisions of section 744f of said title (enacted earlier).

A reference to the Federal Employees' Compensation Act as appeared in the 1934 act was substituted for the reference to specific sections of title 5. The word "law" was substituted for the reference to sections in title 31 since translation of the reference in the 1934 act was not practicable.

Remaining provisions of said section 744e of title 18, U.S.C., 1940 ed., relating to authorization of appropriations, were omitted as unnecessary.

Other changes in phraseology were made.

1949 Act

This section [section 64] incorporates in section 4126 of title 18, U.S.C., provisions of act of May 11, 1948 (ch. 276, 62 Stat. 230), which was not incorporated in title 18 when the revision was enacted. The remainder of such act is incorporated in section 4122 of such title by another section of this bill.

Amendments

2004—Subsecs. (a), (d). Pub. L. 108–271 substituted "Government Accountability Office" for "General Accounting Office".

1988—Subsecs. (a), (b). Pub. L. 100–690, §7094(1), designated first and second pars. as subsecs. (a) and (b), respectively.

Subsec. (c). Pub. L. 100–690, §7094(1), (2), designated third par. as subsec. (c) and amended subsec. (c) generally. Prior to amendment, subsec. (c) read as follows: "The corporation, in accordance with the laws generally applicable to the expenditures of the several departments and establishments of the government, is authorized to employ the fund, and any earnings that may accrue to the corporation, as operating capital in performing the duties imposed by this chapter; in the repair, alteration, erection and maintenance of industrial buildings and equipment; in the vocational training of inmates without regard to their industrial or other assignments; in paying, under rules and regulations promulgated by the Attorney General, compensation to inmates employed in any industry, or performing outstanding services in institutional operations, and compensation to inmates or their dependents for injuries suffered in any industry or in any work activity in connection with the maintenance or operation of the institution where confined. In no event shall compensation be paid in a greater amount than that provided in the Federal Employees' Compensation Act."

Subsecs. (d), (e). Pub. L. 100–690, §7094(1), designated fourth and fifth pars. as subsecs. (d) and (e), respectively.

Subsec. (f). Pub. L. 100–690, §7094(3), added subsec. (f).

1961—Pub. L. 87–317 authorized compensation for injuries to inmates incurred while working in connection with the maintenance or operation of the institution where confined.

1949—Act May 24, 1949, inserted "in the vocational training of inmates without regard to their industrial or other assignments;" after second semicolon in third par.

§4127. Prison Industries report to Congress

The board of directors of Federal Prison Industries shall submit an annual report to the Congress on the conduct of the business of the corporation during each fiscal year, and on the condition of its funds during such fiscal year. Such report shall include a statement of the amount of obligations issued under section 4129(a)(1) during such fiscal year, and an estimate of the amount of obligations that will be so issued in the following fiscal year.

(June 25, 1948, ch. 645, 62 Stat. 852; Pub. L. 100–690, title VII, §7095, Nov. 18, 1988, 102 Stat. 4413.)

Historical and Revision Notes

Based on title 18, U.S.C., 1940 ed., §744m (June 23, 1934, ch. 736, §5, 48 Stat. 1212).
Words "of Federal Prison Industries" were inserted after "board of directors".
Minor changes were made in phraseology.

Amendments

1988—Pub. L. 100–690 amended section generally. Prior to amendment, section read as follows:
"The board of directors of Federal Prison Industries shall make annual reports to Congress on the conduct of the business of the corporation and on the condition of its funds."

Termination of Reporting Requirements

For termination, effective May 15, 2000, of reporting provisions in this section, see section 3003 of Pub. L. 104–66, as amended, set out as a note under section 1113 of Title 31, Money and Finance, and page 117 of House Document No. 103–7.

§4128. Enforcement by Attorney General

In the event of any failure of Federal Prison Industries to act, the Attorney General shall not be limited in carrying out the duties conferred upon him by law.

(June 25, 1948, ch. 645, 62 Stat. 853.)

Historical and Revision Notes

Based on title 18, U.S.C., 1940 ed., §744n (June 23, 1934, ch. 736, §6, 48 Stat. 1212).
Phrase relating to section being "supplemental" to sections 744i–744h of title 18, U.S.C., 1940 ed., is omitted as unnecessary.
Retention of remainder of section is essential to insure authority of Attorney General to require performance of duties of Prison Industries. (See sections 4001 and 4003 of this title.) This is also consistent with 1939 Reorganization Plan No. II, §3(a), transferring the corporation to the Department of Justice "under the general direction and supervision of the Attorney General". (See section 133t of title 5, U.S.C., 1940 ed., Executive Departments and Government Officers and Employees.)
Words "Federal Prison Industries" were substituted for "the corporation".

§4129. Authority to borrow and invest

(a)(1) As approved by the board of directors, Federal Prison Industries, to such extent and in such amounts as are provided in appropriations Acts, is authorized to issue its obligations to the Secretary of the Treasury, and the Secretary of the Treasury, in the Secretary's discretion, may purchase or agree to purchase any such obligations, except that the aggregate amount of obligations issued by Federal Prison Industries under this paragraph that are outstanding at any time may not exceed 25 percent of the net worth of the corporation. For purchases of such obligations by the Secretary of the Treasury, the Secretary is authorized to use as a public debt transaction the proceeds of the sale of any securities issued under chapter 31 of title 31 after the date of the enactment of this section, and the purposes for which securities may be issued under that chapter are extended to include such purchases. Each purchase of obligations by the Secretary of the Treasury under this subsection shall be upon such terms and conditions as to yield a return at a rate not less than a rate determined by the Secretary of the Treasury, taking into consideration the current average yield on outstanding marketable obligations of the United States of comparable maturity. For purposes of the first sentence of this paragraph, the net worth of Federal Prison Industries is the amount by which its assets (including capital) exceed its liabilities.

(2) The Secretary of the Treasury may sell, upon such terms and conditions and at such price or prices as the Secretary shall determine, any of the obligations acquired by the Secretary under this subsection. All purchases and sales by the Secretary of the Treasury of such obligations under this subsection shall be treated as public debt transactions of the United States.

(b) Federal Prison Industries may request the Secretary of the Treasury to invest excess moneys from the Prison Industries Fund. Such investments shall be in public debt securities with maturities suitable to the needs of the corporation as determined by the board of directors, and bearing interest at rates determined by the Secretary of the Treasury, taking into consideration current market yields on outstanding marketable obligations of the United States of comparable maturities.

(Added Pub. L. 100–690, title VII, §7093(a), Nov. 18, 1988, 102 Stat. 4411.)

References in Text

The date of the enactment of this section, referred to in subsec. (a)(1), is the date of enactment of Pub. L. 100–690 which was approved Nov. 18, 1988.

[CHAPTER 309 - REPEALED]

[§§4161 to 4166. Repealed. Pub. L. 98–473, title II, §218(a)(4), Oct. 12, 1984, 98 Stat. 2027]

Section 4161, acts June 25, 1948, ch. 645, 62 Stat. 853; Sept. 14, 1959, Pub. L. 86–259, 73 Stat. 546, related to computation of reduction of time of sentence generally.

Section 4162, act June 25, 1948, ch. 645, 62 Stat. 853, related to deduction from sentence for industrial good time.

Section 4163, acts June 25, 1948, ch. 645, 62 Stat. 853; Sept. 19, 1962, Pub. L. 87–665, 76 Stat. 552, related to discharge of prisoner.

Section 4164, acts June 25, 1948, ch. 645, 62 Stat. 853; June 29, 1951, ch. 176, 65 Stat. 98, related to released prisoner as parolee.

Section 4165, act June 25, 1948, ch. 645, 62 Stat. 854, related to forfeiture of good time for offense.

Section 4166, act June 25, 1948, ch. 645, 62 Stat. 854, related to restoration of forfeited commutation.

Effective Date of Repeal

Repeal effective Nov. 1, 1987, and applicable only to offenses committed after the taking effect of such repeal, with sections to remain in effect for five years as to an individual who committed as offense or an act of juvenile delinquency before Nov. 1, 1987, and as to a term of imprisonment during the period described in section 235(a)(1)(B) of Pub. L. 98–473, see section 235(a)(1), (b)(1)(B) of Pub. L. 98–473, set out as an Effective Date note under section 3551 of this title.

[CHAPTER 311 - REPEALED]

Codification

A prior chapter 311, consisting of sections 4201–4210, act June 25, 1948, ch. 645, 62 Stat. 854, 855, as amended, was repealed by section 2 of Pub. L. 94–233 as part of the general revision of this chapter by Pub. L. 94–233.

[§§4201 to 4218. Repealed. Pub. L. 98–473, title II, §218(a)(5), Oct. 12, 1984, 98 Stat. 2027]

Effective Date of Repeal; Chapter To Remain in Effect for Twenty-Six Years After Nov. 1, 1987

Pub. L. 98–473, title II, §235(a)(1), Oct. 12, 1984, 98 Stat. 2031, set out as an Effective Date note under section 3551 of this title, provided that the repeal of this chapter is effective Nov. 1, 1987, and applicable only to offenses committed after the taking effect of such repeal. Pub. L. 98–473, title II, §235(b)(1)(A), Oct. 12, 1984, 98 Stat. 2032, provided that the provisions of this chapter in effect before Nov. 1, 1987, shall remain in effect for five years after Nov. 1, 1987, as to an individual who committed an offense or an act of juvenile delinquency before Nov. 1, 1987, and as to a term of imprisonment during the period described in section 235(a)(1)(B) of Pub. L. 98–473. Pub. L. 101–650, title III, §316, Dec. 1, 1990, 104 Stat. 5115, extended the period that this chapter remains in effect after Nov. 1, 1987, from five years to ten years. Pub. L. 104–232, §2(a), Oct. 2, 1996, 110 Stat. 3055, extended the period that this chapter remains in effect after Nov. 1, 1987, from ten years to fifteen years. Pub. L. 107–273, div. C, title I, §11017(a), Nov. 2, 2002, 116 Stat. 1824, extended the period that this chapter remains in effect after Nov. 1, 1987, from fifteen years to eighteen years. Pub. L. 109–76, §2, Sept. 29, 2005, 119 Stat. 2035, extended the period that this chapter remains in effect after Nov. 1, 1987, from eighteen years to twenty-one years. Pub. L. 110–312, §2, Aug. 12, 2008, 122 Stat. 3013, extended the period that this chapter remains in effect after Nov. 1, 1987, from twenty-one years to twenty-four years. Pub. L. 112–44, §2, Oct. 21, 2011, 125 Stat. 532, extended the period that this chapter remains in effect after Nov. 1, 1987, from twenty-four years to twenty-six years. The provisions of this chapter as in effect prior to repeal, and as amended subsequent to repeal, read as follows:

§4201. Definitions

As used in this chapter—

(1) "Commission" means the United States Parole Commission;

(2) "Commissioner" means any member of the United States Parole Commission;

(3) "Director" means the Director of the Bureau of Prisons;

(4) "Eligible prisoner" means any Federal prisoner who is eligible for parole pursuant to this title or any other law including any Federal prisoner whose parole has been revoked and who is not otherwise ineligible for parole;

(5) "Parolee" means any eligible prisoner who has been released on parole or deemed as if released on parole under section 4164 or section 4205(f); and

(6) "Rules and regulations" means rules and regulations promulgated by the Commission pursuant to section 4203 and section 553 of title 5, United States Code.

(Added Pub. L. 94–233, §2, Mar. 15, 1976, 90 Stat. 219.)

§4202. Parole Commission created

There is hereby established, as an independent agency in the Department of Justice, a United States Parole Commission which shall be comprised of nine members appointed by the President, by and with the advice and consent of the Senate. The President shall designate from among the

Commissioners one to serve as Chairman. The term of office of a Commissioner shall be six years, except that the term of a person appointed as a Commissioner to fill a vacancy shall expire six years from the date upon which such person was appointed and qualified. Upon the expiration of a term of office of a Commissioner, the Commissioner shall continue to act until a successor has been appointed and qualified, except that no Commissioner may serve in excess of twelve years. Commissioners shall be compensated at the highest rate now or hereafter prescribed for grade 18 of the General Schedule pay rates (5 U.S.C. 5332).

(Added Pub. L. 94–233, §2, Mar. 15, 1976, 90 Stat. 219.)

United States Parole Commission Extension

Pub. L. 107–273, div. C, title I, §11017, Nov. 2, 2002, 116 Stat. 1824, provided that:

"(a) Extension of the Parole Commission.—For purposes of section 235(b) of the Sentencing Reform Act of 1984 [Pub. L. 98–473, set out as a note under section 3551 of this title] (98 Stat. 2032) as such section relates to chapter 311 of title 18, United States Code, and the Parole Commission, each reference in such section to 'fifteen years' or 'fifteen-year period' shall be deemed to be a reference to 'eighteen years' or 'eighteen-year period', respectively.

"(b) Study by Attorney General.—The Attorney General, not later than 60 days after the enactment of this Act [Nov. 2, 2002], should establish a committee within the Department of Justice to evaluate the merits and feasibility of transferring the United States Parole Commission's functions regarding the supervised release of District of Columbia offenders to another entity or entities outside the Department of Justice. This committee should consult with the District of Columbia Superior Court and the District of Columbia Court Services and Offender Supervision Agency, and should report its findings and recommendations to the Attorney General. The Attorney General, in turn, should submit to Congress, not later than 18 months after the enactment of this Act, a long-term plan for the most effective and cost-efficient assignment of responsibilities relating to the supervised release of District of Columbia offenders.

"(c) Service as Commissioner.—Notwithstanding subsection (a), the final clause of the fourth sentence of section 4202 of title 18, United States Code, which begins 'except that', shall not apply to a person serving as a Commissioner of the United States Parole Commission when this Act takes effect [Nov. 2, 2002]."

Parole Commission Phaseout

Pub. L. 104–232, §§1–3, Oct. 2, 1996, 110 Stat. 3055, 3056, as amended by Pub. L. 105–33, title XI, §11231(d), Aug. 5, 1997, 111 Stat. 745, provided that:

"SECTION 1. SHORT TITLE.

"This Act [enacting and amending provisions set out as notes under section 3551 of this title] may be cited as the 'Parole Commission Phaseout Act of 1996'.

"SEC. 2. EXTENSION OF PAROLE COMMISSION.

"(a) In General.—For purposes of section 235(b) of the Sentencing Reform Act of 1984 [Pub. L. 98–473, set out as a note under section 3551 of this title] (98 Stat. 2032) as it related to chapter 311 of title 18, United States Code, and the Parole Commission, each reference in such section to 'ten years' or 'ten-year period' shall be deemed to be a reference to 'fifteen years' or 'fifteen-year period', respectively.

"(b) Powers and Duties of Parole Commission.—Notwithstanding section 4203 of title 18, United States Code, the United States Parole Commission may perform its functions with any quorum of Commissioners, or Commissioner, as the Commission may prescribe by regulation.

"(c) The United States Parole Commission shall have no more than five members.

"SEC. 3. REPORTS BY THE ATTORNEY GENERAL.

"(a) In General.—Beginning in the year 1998, the Attorney General shall report to the Congress not later than May 1 of each year through the year 2002 on the status of the United States Parole Commission. Unless the Attorney General, in such report, certifies that the continuation of the Commission is the most effective and cost-efficient manner for carrying out the Commission's functions, the Attorney General shall include in such report an alternative plan for a transfer of the Commission's functions to another entity.

"(b) Transfer Within the Department of Justice.—

"(1) Effect of plan.—If the Attorney General includes such a plan in the report, and that plan provides for the transfer of the Commission's functions and powers to another entity within the Department of Justice, such plan shall take effect according to its terms on November 1 of that year in which the report is made, unless Congress by law provides otherwise. In the event such plan takes effect, all laws pertaining to the authority and jurisdiction of the Commission with respect to individual offenders shall remain in effect notwithstanding the expiration of the period specified in section 2 of this Act.

"(2) Conditional repeal.—Effective on the date such plan takes effect, paragraphs (3) and (4) of section 235(b) of the Sentencing Reform Act of 1984 [Pub. L. 98–473, set out as a note under section 3551 of this title] (98 Stat. 2032) are repealed."

References in Other Laws to GS–16, 17, or 18 Pay Rates

References in laws to the rates of pay for GS–16, 17, or 18, or to maximum rates of pay under the General Schedule, to be considered references to rates payable under specified sections of Title 5, Government Organization and Employees, see section 529 [title I, §101(c)(1)] of Pub. L. 101–509, set out in a note under section 5376 of Title 5.

Extension of Term of Commissioner

Pub. L. 98–473, title II, §235(b)(2), Oct. 12, 1984, 98 Stat. 2032, which provided that notwithstanding the provisions of section 4202 of this title as in effect on the day before Nov. 1, 1987 [set out above], the term of office of a Commissioner who is in office on Nov. 1, 1987, is extended to the end of the five-year period after Nov. 1, 1987, was repealed by Pub. L. 104–232, §4, Oct. 2, 1996, 110 Stat. 3056. Pub. L. 101–650, title III, §316, Dec. 1, 1990, 104 Stat. 5115, further extended the term of office of a Commissioner to a ten-year period after Nov. 1, 1987.

§4203. Powers and duties of the Commission

(a) The Commission shall meet at least quarterly, and by majority vote shall—

(1) promulgate rules and regulations establishing guidelines for the powers enumerated in subsection (b) of this section and such other rules and regulations as are necessary to carry out a national parole policy and the purposes of this chapter;

(2) create such regions as are necessary to carry out the provisions of this chapter; and

(3) ratify, revise, or deny any request for regular, supplemental, or deficiency appropriations, prior to the submission of the requests to the Office of Management and Budget by the Chairman, which requests shall be separate from those of any other agency of the Department of Justice.

(b) The Commission, by majority vote, and pursuant to the procedures set out in this chapter, shall have the power to—

(1) grant or deny an application or recommendation to parole any eligible prisoner;

(2) impose reasonable conditions on an order granting parole;

(3) modify or revoke an order paroling any eligible prisoner; and

(4) request probation officers and other individuals, organizations, and public or private agencies to perform such duties with respect to any parolee as the Commission deems necessary for maintaining proper supervision of and assistance to such parolees; and so as to assure that no probation officers, individuals, organizations, or agencies shall bear excessive caseloads.

(c) The Commission, by majority vote, and pursuant to rules and regulations—

(1) may delegate to any Commissioner or commissioners powers enumerated in subsection (b) of this section;

(2) may delegate to hearing examiners any powers necessary to conduct hearings and proceedings, take sworn testimony, obtain and make a record of pertinent information, make findings of probable cause and issue subpenas for witnesses or evidence in parole revocation proceedings, and recommend disposition of any matters enumerated in subsection (b) of this section, except that any such findings or recommendations shall be based upon the concurrence of not less than two hearing examiners;

(3) may delegate authority to conduct hearings held pursuant to section 4214 to any officer or employee of the executive or judicial branch of Federal or State government; and

(4) may review, or may delegate to the National Appeals Board the power to review, any decision made pursuant to subparagraph (1) of this subsection except that any such decision so reviewed must be reaffirmed, modified or reversed within thirty days of the date the decision is rendered, and, in case of such review, the individual to whom the decision applies shall be informed in writing of the Commission's actions with respect thereto and the reasons for such actions.

(d) Except as otherwise provided by law, any action taken by the Commission pursuant to subsection (a) of this section shall be taken by a majority vote of all individuals currently holding office as members of the Commission which shall maintain and make available for public inspection a record of the final vote of each member on statements of policy and interpretations adopted by it. In so acting, each Commissioner shall have equal responsibility and authority, shall have full access to all information relating to the performance of such duties and responsibilities, and shall have one vote.

(e)(1) The Commission shall, upon the request of the head of any law enforcement agency of a State or of a unit of local government in a State, make available as expeditiously as possible to such agency, with respect to individuals who are under the jurisdiction of the Commission, who have been convicted of felony offenses against the United States, and who reside, are employed, or are supervised in the geographical area in which such agency has jurisdiction, the following information maintained by the Commission (to the extent that the Commission maintains such information)—

(A) the names of such individuals;

(B) the addresses of such individuals;

(C) the dates of birth of such individuals;

(D) the Federal Bureau of Investigation numbers assigned to such individuals;

(E) photographs and fingerprints of such individuals; and

(F) the nature of the offenses against the United States of which each such individual has been convicted and the factual circumstances relating to such offense.

(2) Any law enforcement agency which receives information under this subsection shall not disseminate such information outside of such agency.

(Added Pub. L. 94–233, §2, Mar. 15, 1976, 90 Stat. 220; amended Pub. L. 99–646, §57(b), (c), Nov. 10, 1986, 100 Stat. 3611, 3612.)

§4204. Powers and duties of the Chairman

(a) The Chairman shall—

(1) convene and preside at meetings of the Commission pursuant to section 4203 and such additional meetings of the Commission as the Chairman may call or as may be requested in writing by at least three Commissioners;

(2) appoint, fix the compensation of, assign, and supervise all personnel employed by the Commission except that—

(A) the appointment of any hearing examiner shall be subject to approval of the Commission within the first year of such hearing examiner's employment; and

(B) regional Commissioners shall appoint and supervise such personnel employed regularly and full time in their respective regions as are compensated at a rate up to and including grade 9 of the General Schedule pay rates (5 U.S.C. 5332);

(3) assign duties among officers and employees of the Commission, including Commissioners, so

as to balance the workload and provide for orderly administration;

(4) direct the preparation of requests for appropriations for the Commission, and the use of funds made available to the Commission;

(5) designate not fewer than three Commissioners to serve on the National Appeals Board of whom one shall be so designated to serve as vice chairman of the Commission (who shall act as Chairman of the Commission in the absence or disability of the Chairman or in the event of the vacancy of the Chairmanship), and designate, for each such region established pursuant to section 4203, one Commissioner to serve as regional Commissioner in each such region; except that in each such designation the Chairman shall consider years of service, personal preference and fitness, and no such designation shall take effect unless concurred in by the President, or his designee;

(6) serve as spokesman for the Commission and report annually to each House of Congress on the activities of the Commission; and

(7) exercise such other powers and duties and perform such other functions as may be necessary to carry out the purposes of this chapter or as may be provided under any other provision of law.

(b) The Chairman shall have the power to—

(1) without regard to section 3324(a) and (b) of title 31, enter into and perform such contracts, leases, cooperative agreements, and other transactions as may be necessary in the conduct of the functions of the Commission, with any public agency, or with any person, firm, association, corporation, educational institution, or nonprofit organization;

(2) accept voluntary and uncompensated services, notwithstanding the provisions of section 1342 of title 31;

(3) procure for the Commission temporary and intermittent services to the same extent as is authorized by section 3109(b) of title 5, United States Code;

(4) collect systematically the data obtained from studies, research, and the empirical experience of public and private agencies concerning the parole process;

(5) carry out programs of research concerning the parole process to develop classification systems which describe types of offenders, and to develop theories and practices which can be applied to the different types of offenders;

(6) publish data concerning the parole process;

(7) devise and conduct, in various geographical locations, seminars, workshops and training programs providing continuing studies and instruction for personnel of Federal, State and local agencies and private and public organizations working with parolees and connected with the parole process; and

(8) utilize the services, equipment, personnel, information, facilities, and instrumentalities with or without reimbursement therefor of other Federal, State, local, and private agencies with their consent.

(c) In carrying out his functions under this section, the Chairman shall be governed by the national parole policies promulgated by the Commission.

(Added Pub. L. 94–233, §2, Mar. 15, 1976, 90 Stat. 221; amended Pub. L. 97–258, §3(e)(3), (4), Sept. 13, 1982, 96 Stat. 1064; Pub. L. 99–646, §58(a), Nov. 10, 1986, 100 Stat. 3612.)

Ex. Ord. No. 11919. Delegation of Presidential Authority To Concur in Designations of Commissioners

Ex. Ord. No. 11919, June 9, 1976, 41 F.R. 23663, provided:

By virtue of the authority vested in me by section 301 of title 3, United States Code, and section 4204(a)(5) of title 18, United States Code, as enacted by the Parole Commission and Reorganization Act (Public Law 94–233), and as President of the United States of America, it is hereby ordered that the Attorney General shall serve as the President's designee for purposes of concurring in designations of Commissioners of the United States Parole Commission to serve on the National Appeals Board, as vice chairman of the Commission, and as regional Commissioner.

Gerald R. Ford.

§4205. Time of eligibility for release on parole

(a) Whenever confined and serving a definite term or terms of more than one year, a prisoner shall be eligible for release on parole after serving one-third of such term or terms or after serving ten years of a life sentence or of a sentence of over thirty years, except to the extent otherwise provided by law.

(b) Upon entering a judgment of conviction, the court having jurisdiction to impose sentence, when in its opinion the ends of justice and best interest of the public require that the defendant be sentenced to imprisonment for a term exceeding one year, may (1) designate in the sentence of imprisonment imposed a minimum term at the expiration of which the prisoner shall become eligible for parole, which term may be less than but shall not be more than one-third of the maximum sentence imposed by the court, or (2) the court may fix the maximum sentence of imprisonment to be served in which event the court may specify that the prisoner may be released on parole at such time as the Commission may determine.

(c) If the court desires more detailed information as a basis for determining the sentence to be imposed, the court may commit the defendant to the custody of the Attorney General, which commitment shall be deemed to be for the maximum sentence of imprisonment prescribed by law, for a study as described in subsection (d) of this section. The results of such study, together with any recommendations which the Director of the Bureau of Prisons believes would be helpful in determining the disposition of the case, shall be furnished to the court within three months unless the court grants time, not to exceed an additional three months, for further study. After receiving such reports and recommendations, the court may in its discretion: (1) place the offender on probation as authorized by section 3651; or (2) affirm the sentence of imprisonment originally imposed, or reduce the sentence of imprisonment, and commit the offender under any applicable provision of law. The term of the sentence shall run from the date of original commitment under this section.

(d) Upon commitment of a prisoner sentenced to imprisonment under the provisions of subsections (a) or (b) of this section, the Director, under such regulations as the Attorney General may prescribe, shall cause a complete study to be made of the prisoner and shall furnish to the Commission a summary report together with any recommendations which in his opinion would be helpful in determining the suitability of the prisoner for parole. This report may include but shall not be limited to data regarding the prisoner's previous delinquency or criminal experience, pertinent circumstances of his social background, his capabilities, his mental and physical health, and such other factors as may be considered pertinent. The Commission may make such other investigation as it may deem necessary.

(e) Upon request of the Commission, it shall be the duty of the various probation officers and government bureaus and agencies to furnish the Commission information available to such officer, bureau, or agency, concerning any eligible prisoner or parolee and whenever not incompatible with the public interest, their views and recommendation with respect to any matter within the jurisdiction of the Commission.

(f) Any prisoner sentenced to imprisonment for a term or terms of not less than six months but not more than one year shall be released at the expiration of such sentence less good time deductions provided by law, unless the court which imposed sentence, shall, at the time of sentencing, provide for the prisoner's release as if on parole after service of one-third of such term or terms notwithstanding the provisions of section 4164. This subsection shall not prevent delivery of any person released on parole to the authorities of any State otherwise entitled to his custody.

(g) At any time upon motion of the Bureau of Prisons, the court may reduce any minimum term to the time the defendant has served. The court shall have jurisdiction to act upon the application at any time and no hearing shall be required.

(h) Nothing in this chapter shall be construed to provide that any prisoner shall be eligible for release on parole if such prisoner is ineligible for such release under any other provision of law.

(Added Pub. L. 94–233, §2, Mar. 15, 1976, 90 Stat. 222.)

§4206. Parole determination criteria

(a) If an eligible prisoner has substantially observed the rules of the institution or institutions to which he has been confined, and if the Commission, upon consideration of the nature and circumstances of the offense and the history and characteristics of the prisoner, determines:

(1) that release would not depreciate the seriousness of his offense or promote disrespect for the law; and

(2) that release would not jeopardize the public welfare;

subject to the provisions of subsections (b) and (c) of this section, and pursuant to guidelines promulgated by the Commission pursuant to section 4203(a)(1), such prisoner shall be released.

(b) The Commission shall furnish the eligible prisoner with a written notice of its determination not later than twenty-one days, excluding holidays, after the date of the parole determination proceeding. If parole is denied such notice shall state with particularity the reasons for such denial.

(c) The Commission may grant or deny release on parole notwithstanding the guidelines referred to in subsection (a) of this section if it determines there is good cause for so doing: Provided, That the prisoner is furnished written notice stating with particularity the reasons for its determination, including a summary of the information relied upon.

(d) Any prisoner, serving a sentence of five years or longer, who is not earlier released under this section or any other applicable provision of law, shall be released on parole after having served two-thirds of each consecutive term or terms, or after serving thirty years of each consecutive term or terms of more than forty-five years including any life term, whichever is earlier: Provided, however, That the Commission shall not release such prisoner if it determines that he has seriously or frequently violated institution rules and regulations or that there is a reasonable probability that he will commit any Federal, State, or local crime.

(Added Pub. L. 94–233, §2, Mar. 15, 1976, 90 Stat. 223.)

§4207. Information considered

In making a determination under this chapter (relating to release on parole) the Commission shall consider, if available and relevant:

(1) reports and recommendations which the staff of the facility in which such prisoner is confined may make;

(2) official reports of the prisoner's prior criminal record, including a report or record of earlier probation and parole experiences;

(3) presentence investigation reports;

(4) recommendations regarding the prisoner's parole made at the time of sentencing by the sentencing judge;

(5) a statement, which may be presented orally or otherwise, by any victim of the offense for which the prisoner is imprisoned about the financial, social, psychological, and emotional harm done to, or loss suffered by such victim; and

(5)[(6)] reports of physical, mental, or psychiatric examination of the offender.

There shall also be taken into consideration such additional relevant information concerning the prisoner (including information submitted by the prisoner) as may be reasonably available.

(Added Pub. L. 94–233, §2, Mar. 15, 1976, 90 Stat. 224; amended Pub. L. 98–473, title II, §1408(a), Oct. 12, 1984, 98 Stat. 2177.)

§4208. Parole determination proceeding; time

(a) In making a determination under this chapter (relating to parole) the Commission shall conduct a parole determination proceeding unless it determines on the basis of the prisoner's record that the prisoner will be released on parole. Whenever feasible, the initial parole determination proceeding for a prisoner eligible for parole pursuant to subsections (a) and (b)(1) of section 4205 shall be held not later than thirty days before the date of such eligibility for parole. Whenever feasible, the initial parole determination proceeding for a prisoner eligible for parole pursuant to subsection (b)(2) of section 4205 or released on parole and whose parole has been revoked shall be held not later than one hundred and twenty days following such prisoner's imprisonment or reimprisonment in a Federal institution, as the case may be. An eligible prisoner may knowingly and intelligently waive any proceeding.

(b) At least thirty days prior to any parole determination proceeding, the prisoner shall be provided with (1) written notice of the time and place of the proceeding, and (2) reasonable access to a report or other document to be used by the Commission in making its determination. A prisoner may waive such notice, except that if notice is not waived the proceeding shall be held during the next regularly scheduled proceedings by the Commission at the institution in which the prisoner is confined.

(c) Subparagraph (2) of subsection (b) shall not apply to—

(1) diagnostic opinions which, if made known to the eligible prisoner, could lead to a serious disruption of his institutional program;

(2) any document which reveals sources of information obtained upon a promise of confidentiality; or

(3) any other information which, if disclosed, might result in harm, physical or otherwise, to any person.

If any document is deemed by either the Commission, the Bureau of Prisons, or any other agency to fall within the exclusionary provisions of subparagraphs (1), (2), or (3) of this subsection, then it shall become the duty of the Commission, the Bureau, or such other agency, as the case may be, to summarize the basic contents of the material withheld, bearing in mind the need for confidentiality or the impact on the inmate, or both, and furnish such summary to the inmate.

(d)(1) During the period prior to the parole determination proceeding as provided in subsection (b) of this section, a prisoner may consult, as provided by the director, with a representative as referred to in subparagraph (2) of this subsection, and by mail or otherwise with any person concerning such proceeding.

(2) The prisoner shall, if he chooses, be represented at the parole determination proceeding by a representative who qualifies under rules and regulations promulgated by the Commission. Such rules shall not exclude attorneys as a class.

(e) The prisoner shall be allowed to appear and testify on his own behalf at the parole determination proceeding.

(f) A full and complete record of every proceeding shall be retained by the Commission. Upon request, the Commission shall make available to any eligible prisoner such record as the Commission may retain of the proceeding.

(g) If parole is denied, a personal conference to explain the reasons for such denial shall be held, if feasible, between the prisoner and a representative of the Commission at the conclusion of the proceeding. When feasible, the conference shall include advice to the prisoner as to what steps may be taken to enhance his chance of being released at a subsequent proceeding.

(h) In any case in which release on parole is not granted, subsequent parole determination proceedings shall be held not less frequently than:

(1) eighteen months in the case of a prisoner with a term or terms of more than one year but less than seven years; and

(2) twenty-four months in the case of a prisoner with a term or terms of seven years or longer.

(Added Pub. L. 94–233, §2, Mar. 15, 1976, 90 Stat. 224; amended Pub. L. 99–646, §58(b), Nov. 10, 1986, 100 Stat. 3612.)

§4209. Conditions of parole

(a) In every case, the Commission shall impose as conditions of parole that the parolee not commit another Federal, State, or local crime, that the parolee not possess illegal controlled substances.[sic] and, if a fine was imposed, that the parolee make a diligent effort to pay the fine in accordance with the judgment. In every case, the Commission shall impose as a condition of parole for a person required to register under the Sex Offender Registration and Notification Act

that the person comply with the requirements of that Act. In every case, the Commission shall impose as a condition of parole that the parolee cooperate in the collection of a DNA sample from the parolee, if the collection of such a sample is authorized pursuant to section 3 or section 4 of the DNA Analysis Backlog Elimination Act of 2000 or section 1565 of title 10. In every case, the Commission shall also impose as a condition of parole that the parolee pass a drug test prior to release and refrain from any unlawful use of a controlled substance and submit to at least 2 periodic drug tests (as determined by the Commission) for use of a controlled substance. The condition stated in the preceding sentence may be ameliorated or suspended by the Commission for any individual parolee if it determines that there is good cause for doing so. The results of a drug test administered in accordance with the provisions of the preceding sentence shall be subject to confirmation only if the results are positive, the defendant is subject to possible imprisonment for such failure, and either the defendant denies the accuracy of such test or there is some other reason to question the results of the test. A drug test confirmation shall be a urine drug test confirmed using gas chromatography/mass spectrometry techniques or such test as the Director of the Administrative Office of the United States Courts after consultation with the Secretary of Health and Human Services may determine to be of equivalent accuracy. The Commission shall consider whether the availability of appropriate substance abuse treatment programs, or an individual's current or past participation in such programs, warrants an exception in accordance with United States Sentencing Commission guidelines from the rule of section 4214(f) when considering any action against a defendant who fails a drug test. The Commission may impose or modify other conditions of parole to the extent that such conditions are reasonably related to—
(1) the nature and circumstances of the offense; and
(2) the history and characteristics of the parolee;
and may provide for such supervision and other limitations as are reasonable to protect the public welfare.
(b) The conditions of parole should be sufficiently specific to serve as a guide to supervision and conduct, and upon release on parole the parolee shall be given a certificate setting forth the conditions of his parole. An effort shall be made to make certain that the parolee understands the conditions of his parole.
(c) Release on parole or release as if on parole (or probation, or supervised release where applicable) may as a condition of such release require—
(1) a parolee to reside in or participate in the program of a residential community treatment center, or both, for all or part of the period of such parole; or
(2) a parolee to remain at his place of residence during nonworking hours and, if the Commission so directs, to have compliance with this condition monitored by telephone or electronic signaling devices, except that a condition under this paragraph may be imposed only as an alternative to incarceration.
A parolee residing in a residential community treatment center pursuant to paragraph (1) of this subsection may be required to pay such costs incident to such residence as the Commission deems appropriate.
(d)(1) The Commission may modify conditions of parole pursuant to this section on its own motion, or on the motion of a United States probation officer supervising a parolee: Provided, That the parolee receives notice of such action and has ten days after receipt of such notice to express his views on the proposed modification. Following such ten-day period, the Commission shall have twenty-one days, exclusive of holidays, to act upon such motion or application. Notwithstanding any other provision of this paragraph, the Commission may modify conditions of parole, without regard to such ten-day period, on any such motion if the Commission determines that the immediate modification of conditions of parole is required to prevent harm to the parolee or to the public.
(2) A parolee may petition the Commission on his own behalf for a modification of conditions pursuant to this section.
(3) The provisions of this subsection shall not apply to modifications of parole conditions pursuant to a revocation proceeding under section 4214.

(Added Pub. L. 94–233, §2, Mar. 15, 1976, 90 Stat. 225; amended Pub. L. 98–473, title II, §§235(a)(1), 238(e), (i), Oct. 12, 1984, 98 Stat. 2031, 2039; Pub. L. 98–596, §§7, 12(a)(5), (9), (b), Oct. 30, 1984, 98 Stat. 3138, 3139, 3140; Pub. L. 99–646, §58(c), Nov. 10, 1986, 100 Stat. 3612; Pub. L. 100–690, title VII, §§7303(c)(1), (2), 7305(c), Nov. 18, 1988, 102 Stat. 4464, 4466; Pub. L. 103–322, title II, §20414(d), Sept. 13, 1994, 108 Stat. 1832; Pub. L. 105–119, title I, §115(a)(8)(B)(v), Nov. 26, 1997, 111 Stat. 2466; Pub. L. 106–546, §7(c), Dec. 19, 2000, 114 Stat. 2734; Pub. L. 109–248, title I, §141(j), July 27, 2006, 120 Stat. 604.)

References in Text

The Sex Offender Registration and Notification Act, referred to in subsec. (a), is title I of Pub. L. 109–248, July 27, 2006, 120 Stat. 590, which was classified principally to subchapter I (§16901 et seq.) of chapter 151 of Title 42, The Public Health and Welfare, prior to editorial reclassification as chapter 209 (§20901 et seq.) of Title 34, Crime Control and Law Enforcement. For complete classification of this Act to the Code, see Short Title of 2006 Act note set out under section 10101 of Title 34 and Tables.

Sections 3 and 4 of the DNA Analysis Backlog Elimination Act of 2000, referred to in subsec. (a), are sections 3 and 4 of Pub. L. 106–546, which are classified to sections 40702 and 40703, respectively, of Title 34, Crime Control and Law Enforcement.

Codification

Pub. L. 98–473, §§235(a)(1), 238(e), (i), and Pub. L. 98–596, §12(a)(5), (9), (b), amended section as follows: Section 238(e) of Pub. L. 98–473 amended provisions of subsec. (a) preceding par. (1) effective pursuant to section 235(a)(1) of Pub. L. 98–473 the first day of the first calendar month beginning twenty-four months after Oct. 12, 1984. Section 12(a)(5) of Pub. L. 98–596 amended provisions of subsec. (a) preceding par. (1) to read as they had before amendment by Pub. L. 98–473, applicable pursuant to section 12(b) of Pub. L. 98–596 on and after the date of enactment of Pub. L. 98–473 (Oct. 12, 1984). Section 238(i) of Pub. L. 98–473 which repealed section 238 of Pub. L. 98–473 on the same date established by section 235(a)(1) of Pub. L. 98–473 was repealed by section 12(a)(9) of Pub. L. 98–596. The cumulative effect of the amendments resulted in no change in this section.

Effective Date of 1997 Amendment

Amendment by Pub. L. 105–119 effective 1 year after Nov. 26, 1997, see section 115(c)(1) of Pub. L. 105–119, set out as a note under section 3521 of this title.

Effective Date of 1988 Amendment

Amendment by section 7303(c)(1), (2) of Pub. L. 100–690 applicable with respect to persons whose probation, supervised release, or parole begins after Dec. 31, 1988, see section 7303(d) of Pub. L. 100–690, set out as a note under section 3563 of this title.

§4210. Jurisdiction of Commission

(a) A parolee shall remain in the legal custody and under the control of the Attorney General, until the expiration of the maximum term or terms for which such parolee was sentenced.

(b) Except as otherwise provided in this section, the jurisdiction of the Commission over the parolee shall terminate no later than the date of the expiration of the maximum term or terms for which he was sentenced, except that—

(1) such jurisdiction shall terminate at an earlier date to the extent provided under section 4164 (relating to mandatory release) or section 4211 (relating to early termination of parole supervision), and

(2) in the case of a parolee who has been convicted of any criminal offense committed subsequent to his release on parole, and such offense is punishable by a term of imprisonment, detention or incarceration in any penal facility, the Commission shall determine, in accordance with the

provisions of section 4214(b) or (c), whether all or any part of the unexpired term being served at the time of parole shall run concurrently or consecutively with the sentence imposed for the new offense, but in no case shall such service together with such time as the parolee has previously served in connection with the offense for which he was paroled, be longer than the maximum term for which he was sentenced in connection with such offense.

(c) In the case of any parolee found to have intentionally refused or failed to respond to any reasonable request, order, summons, or warrant of the Commission or any member or agent thereof, the jurisdiction of the Commission may be extended for the period during which the parolee so refused or failed to respond.

(d) The parole of any parolee shall run concurrently with the period of parole or probation under any other Federal, State, or local sentence.

(e) Upon the termination of the jurisdiction of the Commission over any parolee, the Commission shall issue a certificate of discharge to such parolee and to such other agencies as it may determine.

(Added Pub. L. 94–233, §2, Mar. 15, 1976, 90 Stat. 226; amended Pub. L. 99–646, §58(d), (e), Nov. 10, 1986, 100 Stat. 3612.)

§4211. Early termination of parole

(a) Upon its own motion or upon request of the parolee, the Commission may terminate supervision over a parolee prior to the termination of jurisdiction under section 4210.

(b) Two years after each parolee's release on parole, and at least annually thereafter, the Commission shall review the status of the parolee to determine the need for continued supervision. In calculating such two-year period there shall not be included any period of release on parole prior to the most recent such release, nor any period served in confinement on any other sentence.

(c)(1) Five years after each parolee's release on parole, the Commission shall terminate supervision over such parolee unless it is determined, after a hearing conducted in accordance with the procedures prescribed in section 4214(a)(2), that such supervision should not be terminated because there is a likelihood that the parolee will engaged in conduct violating any criminal law.

(2) If supervision is not terminated under subparagraph (1) of this subsection the parolee may request a hearing annually thereafter, and a hearing, with procedures as provided in subparagraph (1) of this subsection shall be conducted with respect to such termination of supervision not less frequently than biennially.

(3) In calculating the five-year period referred to in subparagraph (1), there shall not be included any period of release on parole prior to the most recent such release, nor any period served in confinement on any other sentence.

(Added Pub. L. 94–233, §2, Mar. 15, 1976, 90 Stat. 227.)

§4212. Aliens

When an alien prisoner subject to deportation becomes eligible for parole, the Commission may authorize the release of such prisoner on condition that such person be deported and remain outside the United States.

Such prisoner when his parole becomes effective, shall be delivered to the duly authorized immigration official for deportation.

(Added Pub. L. 94–233, §2, Mar. 15, 1976, 90 Stat. 227.)

§4213. Summons to appear or warrant for retaking of parolee

(a) If any parolee is alleged to have violated his parole, the Commission may—

(1) summon such parolee to appear at a hearing conducted pursuant to section 4214; or

(2) issue a warrant and retake the parolee as provided in this section.

(b) Any summons or warrant issued under this section shall be issued by the Commission as soon as practicable after discovery of the alleged violation, except when delay is deemed necessary. Imprisonment in an institution shall not be deemed grounds for delay of such issuance, except that, in the case of any parolee charged with a criminal offense, issuance of a summons or warrant may be suspended pending disposition of the charge.

(c) Any summons or warrant issued pursuant to this section shall provide the parolee with written notice of—

(1) the conditions of parole he is alleged to have violated as provided under section 4209;

(2) his rights under this chapter; and

(3) the possible action which may be taken by the Commission.

(d) Any officer of any Federal penal or correctional institution, or any Federal officer authorized to serve criminal process within the United States, to whom a warrant issued under this section is delivered, shall execute such warrant by taking such parolee and returning him to the custody of the regional commissioner, or to the custody of the Attorney General, if the Commission shall so direct.

(Added Pub. L. 94–233, §2, Mar. 15, 1976, 90 Stat. 227.)

§4214. Revocation of parole

(a)(1) Except as provided in subsections (b) and (c), any alleged parole violator summoned or retaken under section 4213 shall be accorded the opportunity to have—

(A) a preliminary hearing at or reasonably near the place of the alleged parole violation or arrest, without unnecessary delay, to determine if there is probable cause to believe that he has violated a condition of his parole; and upon a finding of probable cause a digest shall be prepared by the Commission setting forth in writing the factors considered and the reasons for the decision, a copy of which shall be given to the parolee within a reasonable period of time; except that after a finding of probable cause the Commission may restore any parolee to parole supervision if:

(i) continuation of revocation proceedings is not warranted; or

(ii) incarceration of the parolee pending further revocation proceedings is not warranted by the alleged frequency or seriousness of such violation or violations;

(iii) the parolee is not likely to fail to appear for further proceedings; and

(iv) the parolee does not constitute a danger to himself or others.

(B) upon a finding of probable cause under subparagraph (1)(A), a revocation hearing at or reasonably near the place of the alleged parole violation or arrest within sixty days of such determination of probable cause except that a revocation hearing may be held at the same time and place set for the preliminary hearing.

(2) Hearings held pursuant to subparagraph (1) of this subsection shall be conducted by the Commission in accordance with the following procedures:

(A) notice to the parolee of the conditions of parole alleged to have been violated, and the time, place, and purposes of the scheduled hearing;

(B) opportunity for the parolee to be represented by an attorney (retained by the parolee, or if he is financially unable to retain counsel, counsel shall be provided pursuant to section 3006A) or, if he so chooses, a representative as provided by rules and regulations, unless the parolee knowingly and intelligently waives such representation.

(C) opportunity for the parolee to appear and testify, and present witnesses and relevant evidence on his own behalf; and

(D) opportunity for the parolee to be apprised of the evidence against him and, if he so requests, to confront and cross-examine adverse witnesses, unless the Commission specifically finds substantial reason for not so allowing.

For the purposes of subparagraph (1) of this subsection, the Commission may subpena witnesses and evidence, and pay witness fees as established for the courts of the United States. If a person refuses to obey such a subpena, the Commission may petition a court of the United States for the judicial district in which such parole proceeding is being conducted, or in which such person may be found, to request such person to attend, testify, and produce evidence. The court may issue an order requiring such person to appear before the Commission, when the court finds such information, thing, or testimony directly related to a matter with respect to which the Commission is empowered to make a determination under this section. Failure to obey such an order is punishable by such court as a contempt. All process in such a case may be served in the judicial district in which such a parole proceeding is being conducted, or in which such person may be found.

(b)(1) Conviction for any criminal offense committed subsequent to release on parole shall constitute probable cause for purposes of subsection (a) of this section. In cases in which a parolee has been convicted of such an offense and is serving a new sentence in an institution, a parole revocation warrant or summons issued pursuant to section 4213 may be placed against him as a detainer. Such detainer shall be reviewed by the Commission within one hundred and eighty days of notification to the Commission of placement. The parolee shall receive notice of the pending review, have an opportunity to submit a written application containing information relative to the disposition of the detainer, and, unless waived, shall have counsel as provided in subsection (a)(2)(B) of this section to assist him in the preparation of such application.

(2) If the Commission determines that additional information is needed to review a detainer, a dispositional hearing may be held at the institution where the parolee is confined. The parolee shall have notice of such hearing, be allowed to appear and testify on his own behalf, and, unless waived, shall have counsel as provided in subsection (a)(2)(B) of this section.

(3) Following the disposition review, the Commission may:

(A) let the detainer stand; or

(B) withdraw the detainer.

(c) Any alleged parole violator who is summoned or retaken by warrant under section 4213 who knowingly and intelligently waives his right to a hearing under subsection (a) of this section, or who knowingly and intelligently admits violation at a preliminary hearing held pursuant to subsection (a)(1)(A) of this section, or who is retaken pursuant to subsection (b) of this section, shall receive a revocation hearing within ninety days of the date of retaking. The Commission may conduct such hearing at the institution to which he has been returned, and the alleged parole violator shall have notice of such hearing, be allowed to appear and testify on his own behalf, and, unless waived, shall have counsel or another representative as provided in subsection (a)(2)(B) of this section.

(d) Whenever a parolee is summoned or retaken pursuant to section 4213, and the Commission finds pursuant to the procedures of this section and by a preponderance of the evidence that the parolee has violated a condition of his parole the Commission may take any of the following actions:

(1) restore the parolee to supervision;

(2) reprimand the parolee;

(3) modify the parolee's conditions of the parole;

(4) refer the parolee to a residential community treatment center for all or part of the remainder of his original sentence; or

(5) formally revoke parole or release as if on parole pursuant to this title.

The Commission may take any such action provided it has taken into consideration whether or not the parolee has been convicted of any Federal, State, or local crime subsequent to his release on parole, and the seriousness thereof, or whether such action is warranted by the frequency or seriousness of the parolee's violation of any other condition or conditions of his parole.

(e) The Commission shall furnish the parolee with a written notice of its determination not later than twenty-one days, excluding holidays, after the date of the revocation hearing. If parole is revoked, a digest shall be prepared by the Commission setting forth in writing the factors considered and reasons for such action, a copy of which shall be given to the parolee.

(f) Notwithstanding any other provision of this section, a parolee who is found by the Commission to be in possession of a controlled substance shall have his parole revoked.

(Added Pub. L. 94–233, §2, Mar. 15, 1976, 90 Stat. 228; amended Pub. L. 98–473, title II, §§235(a)(1), 238(f), (i), Oct. 12, 1984, 98 Stat. 2031, 2039; Pub. L. 98–596, §12(a)(6), (9), (b), Oct. 30, 1984, 98 Stat. 3139, 3140; Pub. L. 99–646, §58(f), Nov. 10, 1986, 100 Stat. 3612; Pub. L. 100–690, title VII, §7303(c)(3), Nov. 18, 1988, 102 Stat. 4464.)

Codification

Pub. L. 98–473, §§235(a)(1), 238(f), (i), and Pub. L. 98–596, §12(a)(6), (9), (b), amended section as follows: Section 238(f) of Pub. L. 98–473 amended par. (1) effective pursuant to section 235(a)(1) of Pub. L. 98–473 the first day of the first calendar month beginning twenty-four months after Oct. 12, 1984. Section 12(a)(6) of Pub. L. 98–596 amended par. (1) to read as it had before amendment by Pub. L. 98–473, applicable pursuant to section 12(b) of Pub. L. 98–596 on and after the date of enactment of Pub. L. 98–473 (Oct. 12, 1984). Section 238(i) of Pub. L. 98–473 which repealed section 238 of Pub. L. 98–473 on the same date established by section 235(a)(1) of Pub. L. 98–473 was repealed by section 12(a)(9) of Pub. L. 98–596. The cumulative effect of the amendments resulted in no change in this section.

Effective Date of 1988 Amendment

Amendment by section 7303(c)(3) of Pub. L. 100–690 applicable with respect to persons whose probation, supervised release, or parole begins after Dec. 31, 1988, see section 7303(d) of Pub. L. 100–690, set out as a note under section 3563 of this title.

§4215. Appeal

(a) Whenever parole release is denied under section 4206, parole conditions are imposed or modified under section 4209, parole discharge is denied under section 4211(c), or parole is modified or revoked under section 4214, the individual to whom any such decision applies may appeal such decision by submitting a written application to the National Appeal [Appeals] Board not later than thirty days following the date on which the decision is rendered.

(b) The National Appeals Board, upon receipt of the appellant's papers, must act pursuant to rules and regulations within sixty days to reaffirm, modify, or reverse the decision and shall inform the appellant in writing of the decision and the reasons therefor.

(c) The National Appeals Board may review any decision of a regional commissioner upon the written request of the Attorney General filed not later than thirty days following the decision and, by majority vote, shall reaffirm, modify, or reverse the decision within sixty days of the receipt of the Attorney General's request. The Board shall inform the Attorney General and the individual to whom the decision applies in writing of its decision and the reasons therefor.

(Added Pub. L. 94–233, §2, Mar. 15, 1976, 90 Stat. 230; amended Pub. L. 98–473, title II, §1408(c), Oct. 12, 1984, 98 Stat. 2178.)

[§4216. Repealed. Pub. L. 99–646, §3(a), Nov. 10, 1986, 100 Stat. 3592]

[§4217. Repealed. Pub. L. 99–646, §58(g)(1), Nov. 10, 1986, 100 Stat. 3612, as amended by Pub. L. 100–690, title VII, §7014, Nov. 18, 1988, 102 Stat. 4395]

§4218. Applicability of Administrative Procedure Act

(a) For purposes of the provisions of chapter 5 of title 5, United States Code, other than sections 554, 555, 556, and 557, the Commission is an "agency" as defined in such chapter.

(b) For purposes of subsection (a) of this section, section 553(b)(3)(A) of title 5, United States Code, relating to rulemaking, shall be deemed not to include the phrase "general statements of policy".

(c) To the extent that actions of the Commission pursuant to section 4203(a)(1) are not in accord with the provisions of section 553 of title 5, United States Code, they shall be reviewable in accordance with the provisions of sections 701 through 706 of title 5, United States Code.

(d) Actions of the Commission pursuant to paragraphs (1), (2), and (3) of section 4203(b) shall be considered actions committed to agency discretion for purposes of section 701(a)(2) of title 5, United States Code.

(Added Pub. L. 94–233, §2, Mar. 15, 1976, 90 Stat. 231.)

CHAPTER 313 - OFFENDERS WITH MENTAL DISEASE OR DEFECT

Amendments

2006—Pub. L. 109–248, title III, §302(1), July 27, 2006, 120 Stat. 619, inserted "or to undergo postrelease proceedings" after "trial" in item 4241 and added item 4248.

1984—Pub. L. 98–473, title II, §403(a), Oct. 12, 1984, 98 Stat. 2057, substituted "OFFENDERS WITH MENTAL DISEASE OR DEFECT" for "MENTAL DEFECTIVES" in chapter heading, "Determination of mental competency to stand trial" for "Examination and transfer to hospital" in item 4241, "Determination of the existence of insanity at the time of the offense" for "Retransfer upon recovery" in item 4242, "Hospitalization of a person found not guilty only by reason of insanity" for "Delivery to state authorities on expiration of sentence" in item 4243, "Hospitalization of a convicted person suffering from mental disease or defect" for "Mental competency after arrest and before trial" in item 4244, "Hospitalization of an imprisoned person suffering from mental disease or defect" for "Mental incompetency undisclosed at trial" in item 4245, "Hospitalization of a person due for release but suffering from mental disease or defect" for "Procedure upon finding of mental incompetency" in item 4246, and "General provisions for chapter" for "Alternate procedure on expiration of sentence" in item 4247, and struck out item 4248 "Termination of custody by release or transfer".

1951—Act Oct. 31, 1951, ch. 655, §33, 65 Stat. 723, inserted "on expiration of sentence" in item 4243.

1949—Act Sept. 7, 1949, ch. 535, §2, 63 Stat. 688, added items 4244 to 4248.

§4241. Determination of mental competency to stand trial to undergo postrelease proceedings 1

(a) Motion To Determine Competency of Defendant.—At any time after the commencement of a prosecution for an offense and prior to the sentencing of the defendant, or at any time after the commencement of probation or supervised release and prior to the completion of the sentence, the defendant or the attorney for the Government may file a motion for a hearing to determine the mental competency of the defendant. The court shall grant the motion, or shall order such a hearing on its own motion, if there is reasonable cause to believe that the defendant may presently be suffering from a mental disease or defect rendering him mentally incompetent to the extent that he is unable to understand the nature and consequences of the proceedings against him or to assist properly in his defense.

(b) Psychiatric or Psychological Examination and Report.—Prior to the date of the hearing, the court may order that a psychiatric or psychological examination of the defendant be conducted, and that a psychiatric or psychological report be filed with the court, pursuant to the provisions of section 4247(b) and (c).

(c) Hearing.—The hearing shall be conducted pursuant to the provisions of section 4247(d).

(d) Determination and Disposition.—If, after the hearing, the court finds by a preponderance of the evidence that the defendant is presently suffering from a mental disease or defect rendering him mentally incompetent to the extent that he is unable to understand the nature and consequences of the proceedings against him or to assist properly in his defense, the court shall commit the defendant to the custody of the Attorney General. The Attorney General shall hospitalize the defendant for treatment in a suitable facility—

(1) for such a reasonable period of time, not to exceed four months, as is necessary to determine whether there is a substantial probability that in the foreseeable future he will attain the capacity to permit the proceedings to go forward; and

(2) for an additional reasonable period of time until—

(A) his mental condition is so improved that trial may proceed, if the court finds that there is a substantial probability that within such additional period of time he will attain the capacity to permit the proceedings to go forward; or

(B) the pending charges against him are disposed of according to law;

whichever is earlier.

If, at the end of the time period specified, it is determined that the defendant's mental condition has not so improved as to permit the proceedings to go forward, the defendant is subject to the provisions of sections 4246 and 4248.

(e) Discharge.—When the director of the facility in which a defendant is hospitalized pursuant to subsection (d) determines that the defendant has recovered to such an extent that he is able to understand the nature and consequences of the proceedings against him and to assist properly in his defense, he shall promptly file a certificate to that effect with the clerk of the court that ordered the commitment. The clerk shall send a copy of the certificate to the defendant's counsel and to the attorney for the Government. The court shall hold a hearing, conducted pursuant to the provisions of section 4247(d), to determine the competency of the defendant. If, after the hearing, the court finds by a preponderance of the evidence that the defendant has recovered to such an extent that he is able to understand the nature and consequences of the proceedings against him and to assist properly in his defense, the court shall order his immediate discharge from the facility in which he is hospitalized and shall set the date for trial or other proceedings. Upon discharge, the defendant is subject to the provisions of chapters 207 and 227.

(f) Admissibility of Finding of Competency.—A finding by the court that the defendant is mentally competent to stand trial shall not prejudice the defendant in raising the issue of his insanity as a defense to the offense charged, and shall not be admissible as evidence in a trial for the offense charged.

(June 25, 1948, ch. 645, 62 Stat. 855; Pub. L. 98–473, title II, §403(a), Oct. 12, 1984, 98 Stat. 2057; Pub. L. 109–248, title III, §302(2), July 27, 2006, 120 Stat. 619.)

Historical and Revision Notes

Based on title 18, U.S.C., 1940 ed., §876 (May 13, 1930, ch. 254, §6, 46 Stat. 271).

Changes were made in phraseology and surplusage omitted.

Amendments

2006—Pub. L. 109–248, §302(2)(A), inserted "to undergo postrelease proceedings" after "trial" in section catchline.

Subsec. (a). Pub. L. 109–248, §302(2)(B), inserted "or at any time after the commencement of probation or supervised release and prior to the completion of the sentence," after "sentencing of the defendant,".

Subsec. (d). Pub. L. 109–248, §302(2)(C), substituted "proceedings to go forward" for "trial to proceed" wherever appearing and "sections 4246 and 4248" for "section 4246" in concluding provisions.

Subsec. (e). Pub. L. 109–248, §302(2)(D), inserted "or other proceedings" after "trial" and substituted "chapters 207 and 227" for "chapter 207".

1984—Pub. L. 98–473 amended section generally, substituting "Determination of mental competency to stand trial" for "Examination and transfer to hospital" in section catchline, and substituting provisions relating to motion, report, hearing, etc., for determination of competency of defendant, for provisions relating to boards of examiners for examination of inmates of Federal penal and correctional institutions and transfer of such inmates to hospitals.

Short Title of 1984 Amendment

Pub. L. 98–473, title II, §401, Oct. 12, 1984, 98 Stat. 2057, provided that: "This chapter [chapter IV (§§401–406) of title II of Pub. L. 98–473, enacting section 20 of this title and amending this chapter, section 3006A of this title, and rule 12.2 of the Federal Rules of Criminal Procedure and rule 704 of the Federal Rules of Evidence set out in the Appendix to this title] may be sited [cited] as the 'Insanity Defense Reform Act of 1984'."

§4242. Determination of the existence of insanity at the time of the offense

(a) Motion for Pretrial Psychiatric or Psychological Examination.—Upon the filing of a notice, as provided in Rule 12.2 of the Federal Rules of Criminal Procedure, that the defendant intends to rely on the defense of insanity, the court, upon motion of the attorney for the Government, shall order that a psychiatric or psychological examination of the defendant be conducted, and that a psychiatric or psychological report be filed with the court, pursuant to the provisions of section 4247(b) and (c).

(b) Special Verdict.—If the issue of insanity is raised by notice as provided in Rule 12.2 of the Federal Rules of Criminal Procedure on motion of the defendant or of the attorney for the Government, or on the court's own motion, the jury shall be instructed to find, or, in the event of a nonjury trial, the court shall find the defendant—

(1) guilty;

(2) not guilty; or

(3) not guilty only by reason of insanity.

(June 25, 1948, ch. 645, 62 Stat. 855; Pub. L. 98–473, title II, §403(a), Oct. 12, 1984, 98 Stat. 2059.)

Historical and Revision Notes

Based on title 18, U.S.C., 1940 ed., §877 (May 13, 1930, ch. 254, §7, 46 Stat. 272).

Minor change was made in phraseology.

Amendments

1984—Pub. L. 98–473 amended section generally, substituting "Determination of the existence of insanity at the time of the offense" for "Retransfer upon recovery" in section catchline, and substituting provisions relating to motion for pretrial psychiatric or psychological examination, and special verdict, for provisions relating to retransfer to a penal or correctional institution upon recovery of an inmate of the United States hospital for defective delinquents.

§4243. Hospitalization of a person found not guilty only by reason of insanity

(a) Determination of Present Mental Condition of Acquitted Person.—If a person is found not guilty only by reason of insanity at the time of the offense charged, he shall be committed to a suitable facility until such time as he is eligible for release pursuant to subsection (e).

(b) Psychiatric or Psychological Examination and Report.—Prior to the date of the hearing, pursuant to subsection (c), the court shall order that a psychiatric or psychological examination of the defendant be conducted, and that a psychiatric or psychological report be filed with the court, pursuant to the provisions of section 4247(b) and (c).

(c) Hearing.—A hearing shall be conducted pursuant to the provisions of section 4247(d) and shall take place not later than forty days following the special verdict.

(d) Burden of Proof.—In a hearing pursuant to subsection (c) of this section, a person found not guilty only by reason of insanity of an offense involving bodily injury to, or serious damage to the property of, another person, or involving a substantial risk of such injury or damage, has the burden of proving by clear and convincing evidence that his release would not create a substantial risk of bodily injury to another person or serious damage of property of another due to a present mental disease or defect. With respect to any other offense, the person has the burden of such proof by a preponderance of the evidence.

(e) Determination and Disposition.—If, after the hearing, the court fails to find by the standard specified in subsection (d) of this section that the person's release would not create a substantial risk of bodily injury to another person or serious damage of property of another due to a present mental disease or defect, the court shall commit the person to the custody of the Attorney General. The Attorney General shall release the person to the appropriate official of the State in which the person is domiciled or was tried if such State will assume responsibility for his custody, care, and treatment. The Attorney General shall make all reasonable efforts to cause such a State to assume such responsibility. If, notwithstanding such efforts, neither such State will assume such responsibility, the Attorney General shall hospitalize the person for treatment in a suitable facility until—

(1) such a State will assume such responsibility; or

(2) the person's mental condition is such that his release, or his conditional release under a prescribed regimen of medical, psychiatric, or psychological care or treatment, would not create a substantial risk of bodily injury to another person or serious damage to property of another; whichever is earlier. The Attorney General shall continue periodically to exert all reasonable efforts to cause such a State to assume such responsibility for the person's custody, care, and treatment.

(f) Discharge.—When the director of the facility in which an acquitted person is hospitalized pursuant to subsection (e) determines that the person has recovered from his mental disease or defect to such an extent that his release, or his conditional release under a prescribed regimen of medical, psychiatric, or psychological care or treatment, would no longer create a substantial risk of bodily injury to another person or serious damage to property of another, he shall promptly file a certificate to that effect with the clerk of the court that ordered the commitment. The clerk shall send a copy of the certificate to the person's counsel and to the attorney for the Government. The court shall order the discharge of the acquitted person or, on the motion of the attorney for the Government or on its own motion, shall hold a hearing, conducted pursuant to the provisions of section 4247(d), to determine whether he should be released. If, after the hearing, the court finds by the standard specified in subsection (d) that the person has recovered from his mental disease or defect to such an extent that—

(1) his release would no longer create a substantial risk of bodily injury to another person or serious damage to property of another, the court shall order that he be immediately discharged; or

(2) his conditional release under a prescribed regimen of medical, psychiatric, or psychological care or treatment would no longer create a substantial risk of bodily injury to another person or serious damage to property of another, the court shall—

(A) order that he be conditionally discharged under a prescribed regimen of medical, psychiatric, or psychological care or treatment that has been prepared for him, that has been certified to the court as appropriate by the director of the facility in which he is committed, and that has been found by the court to be appropriate; and

(B) order, as an explicit condition of release, that he comply with the prescribed regimen of medical, psychiatric, or psychological care or treatment.

The court at any time may, after a hearing employing the same criteria, modify or eliminate the regimen of medical, psychiatric, or psychological care or treatment.

(g) Revocation of Conditional Discharge.—The director of a medical facility responsible for administering a regimen imposed on an acquitted person conditionally discharged under subsection (f) shall notify the Attorney General and the court having jurisdiction over the person of any failure of the person to comply with the regimen. Upon such notice, or upon other probable cause to believe that the person has failed to comply with the prescribed regimen of medical, psychiatric, or psychological care or treatment, the person may be arrested, and, upon arrest, shall be taken without unnecessary delay before the court having jurisdiction over him. The court shall, after a hearing, determine whether the person should be remanded to a suitable facility on the ground that, in light of his failure to comply with the prescribed regimen of medical, psychiatric, or psychological care or treatment, his continued release would create a substantial risk of bodily injury to another person or serious damage to property of another.

(h) Limitations on Furloughs.—An individual who is hospitalized under subsection (e) of this section after being found not guilty only by reason of insanity of an offense for which subsection (d) of this section creates a burden of proof of clear and convincing evidence, may leave temporarily the premises of the facility in which that individual is hospitalized only—

(1) with the approval of the committing court, upon notice to the attorney for the Government and such individual, and after opportunity for a hearing;

(2) in an emergency; or

(3) when accompanied by a Federal law enforcement officer (as defined in section 115 of this title).

(i) Certain Persons Found Not Guilty by Reason of Insanity in the District of Columbia.—

(1) Transfer to custody of the attorney general.—Notwithstanding section 301(h) of title 24 of the District of Columbia Code, and notwithstanding subsection 4247(j) of this title, all persons who have been committed to a hospital for the mentally ill pursuant to section 301(d)(1) of title 24 of the District of Columbia Code, and for whom the United States has continuing financial responsibility, may be transferred to the custody of the Attorney General, who shall hospitalize the person for treatment in a suitable facility.

(2) Application.—

(A) In general.—The Attorney General may establish custody over such persons by filing an application in the United States District Court for the District of Columbia, demonstrating that the person to be transferred is a person described in this subsection.

(B) Notice.—The Attorney General shall, by any means reasonably designed to do so, provide written notice of the proposed transfer of custody to such person or such person's guardian, legal representative, or other lawful agent. The person to be transferred shall be afforded an opportunity, not to exceed 15 days, to respond to the proposed transfer of custody, and may, at the court's discretion, be afforded a hearing on the proposed transfer of custody. Such hearing, if granted, shall be limited to a determination of whether the constitutional rights of such person would be violated by the proposed transfer of custody.

(C) Order.—Upon application of the Attorney General, the court shall order the person transferred to the custody of the Attorney General, unless, pursuant to a hearing under this paragraph, the court finds that the proposed transfer would violate a right of such person under the United States Constitution.

(D) Effect.—Nothing in this paragraph shall be construed to—

(i) create in any person a liberty interest in being granted a hearing or notice on any matter;

(ii) create in favor of any person a cause of action against the United States or any officer or employee of the United States; or

(iii) limit in any manner or degree the ability of the Attorney General to move, transfer, or otherwise manage any person committed to the custody of the Attorney General.

(3) Construction with other sections.—Subsections (f) and (g) and section 4247 shall apply to any person transferred to the custody of the Attorney General pursuant to this subsection.

(June 25, 1948, ch. 645, 62 Stat. 855; Pub. L. 98–473, title II, §403(a), Oct. 12, 1984, 98 Stat. 2059; Pub. L. 100–690, title VII, §7043, Nov. 18, 1988, 102 Stat. 4400; Pub. L. 104–294, title III, §301(a), Oct. 11, 1996, 110 Stat. 3494.)

Historical and Revision Notes

Based on title 18, U.S.C., 1940 ed., §878 (May 13, 1930, ch. 254, §8, 46 Stat. 272).

Changes were made in translations and phraseology, and unnecessary words omitted.

Amendments

1996—Subsec. (i). Pub. L. 104–294 added subsec. (i).

1988—Subsec. (h). Pub. L. 100–690 added subsec. (h).

1984—Pub. L. 98–473 amended section generally, substituting "Hospitalization of a person found not guilty only by reason of insanity" for "Delivery to state authorities on expiration of sentence" in section catchline, and substituting provisions relating to determination of present mental condition of acquitted person, examination and report, hearing, etc., for provisions relating to duties of the superintendent of the United States hospital for defective delinquents regarding delivery to state authorities on expiration of sentence of any insane person.

Severability

Pub. L. 104–294, title III, §301(d), Oct. 11, 1996, 110 Stat. 3495, provided that: "If any provision of this section [amending this section and enacting provisions set out as notes below], an amendment made by this section, or the application of such provision or amendment to any person or circumstance is held to be unconstitutional, the remainder of this section and the amendments made by this section shall not be affected thereby."

Transfer of Records

Pub. L. 104–294, title III, §301(b), Oct. 11, 1996, 110 Stat. 3495, provided that: "Notwithstanding any provision of the District of Columbia Code or any other provision of law, the District of Columbia and St. Elizabeth's Hospital—

"(1) not later than 30 days after the date of enactment of this Act [Oct. 11, 1996], shall provide to the Attorney General copies of all records in the custody or control of the District or the Hospital on such date of enactment pertaining to persons described in section 4243(i) of title 18, United States Code (as added by subsection (a));

"(2) not later than 30 days after the creation of any records by employees, agents, or contractors of the District of Columbia or of St. Elizabeth's Hospital pertaining to persons described in section 4243(i) of title 18, United States Code, provide to the Attorney General copies of all such records created after the date of enactment of this Act;

"(3) shall not prevent or impede any employee, agent, or contractor of the District of Columbia or of St. Elizabeth's Hospital who has obtained knowledge of the persons described in section 4243(i) of title 18, United States Code, in the employee's professional capacity from providing that knowledge to the Attorney General, nor shall civil or criminal liability attach to such employees, agents, or contractors who provide such knowledge; and

"(4) shall not prevent or impede interviews of persons described in section 4243(i) of title 18, United States Code, by representatives of the Attorney General, if such persons voluntarily consent to such interviews."

Clarification of Effect on Certain Testimonial Privileges

Pub. L. 104–294, title III, §301(c), Oct. 11, 1996, 110 Stat. 3495, provided that: "The amendments made by this section [amending this section and enacting provisions set out as notes above] shall not be construed to affect in any manner any doctor-patient or psychotherapist-patient testimonial privilege that may be otherwise applicable to persons found not guilty by reason of insanity and affected by this section."

§4244. Hospitalization of a convicted person suffering from mental disease or defect

(a) Motion To Determine Present Mental Condition of Convicted Defendant.—A defendant found guilty of an offense, or the attorney for the Government, may, within ten days after the defendant is found guilty, and prior to the time the defendant is sentenced, file a motion for a hearing on the present mental condition of the defendant if the motion is supported by substantial information indicating that the defendant may presently be suffering from a mental disease or defect for the treatment of which he is in need of custody for care or treatment in a suitable facility. The court shall grant the motion, or at any time prior to the sentencing of the defendant shall order such a hearing on its own motion, if it is of the opinion that there is reasonable cause to believe that the defendant may presently be suffering from a mental disease or defect for the treatment of which he is in need of custody for care or treatment in a suitable facility.

(b) Psychiatric or Psychological Examination and Report.—Prior to the date of the hearing, the court may order that a psychiatric or psychological examination of the defendant be conducted, and that a psychiatric or psychological report be filed with the court, pursuant to the provisions of section 4247(b) and (c). In addition to the information required to be included in the psychiatric or psychological report pursuant to the provisions of section 4247(c), if the report includes an opinion by the examiners that the defendant is presently suffering from a mental disease or defect but that it is not such as to require his custody for care or treatment in a suitable facility, the report shall also include an opinion by the examiner concerning the sentencing alternatives that could best accord the defendant the kind of treatment he does need.

(c) Hearing.—The hearing shall be conducted pursuant to the provisions of section 4247(d).

(d) Determination and Disposition.—If, after the hearing, the court finds by a preponderance of the evidence that the defendant is presently suffering from a mental disease or defect and that he should, in lieu of being sentenced to imprisonment, be committed to a suitable facility for care or treatment, the court shall commit the defendant to the custody of the Attorney General. The Attorney General shall hospitalize the defendant for care or treatment in a suitable facility. Such a commitment constitutes a provisional sentence of imprisonment to the maximum term authorized by law for the offense for which the defendant was found guilty.

(e) Discharge.—When the director of the facility in which the defendant is hospitalized pursuant to subsection (d) determines that the defendant has recovered from his mental disease or defect to such an extent that he is no longer in need of custody for care or treatment in such a facility, he shall promptly file a certificate to that effect with the clerk of the court that ordered the commitment. The clerk shall send a copy of the certificate to the defendant's counsel and to the attorney for the Government. If, at the time of the filing of the certificate, the provisional sentence imposed pursuant to subsection (d) has not expired, the court shall proceed finally to sentencing and may modify the provisional sentence.

(Added Sept. 7, 1949, ch. 535, §1, 63 Stat. 686; amended Pub. L. 98–473, title II, §403(a), Oct. 12, 1984, 98 Stat. 2061.)

Amendments

1984—Pub. L. 98–473 amended section generally, substituting "Hospitalization of a convicted person suffering from mental disease or defect" for "Mental incompetency after arrest and before trial" in section catchline, and substituting provisions relating to motion, examination and report, hearing, etc., to determine present mental condition of convicted defendant, for provisions relating to motion, examination, etc., to determine the mental competency of a person after arrest and before trial.

Separability

Act Sept. 7, 1949, ch. 535, §4, 63 Stat. 688, provided that: "If any provision of Title 18, United States Code, sections 4244 to 4248, inclusive, or the application thereof to any person or circumstance shall be held invalid, the remainder of the said sections and the application of such provision to persons or circumstances other than those as to which it is held invalid shall not be affected thereby."

Use of Appropriations

Act Sept. 7, 1949, ch. 535, §3, 63 Stat. 688, provided that: "The Attorney General may authorize the use of any unexpended balance of the appropriation for 'Support of United States prisoners' for carrying out the purposes of Title 18, United States Code, sections 4244 to 4248, inclusive, or in payment of any expenses incidental thereto and not provided for by other specific appropriations."

§4245. Hospitalization of an imprisoned person suffering from mental disease or defect

(a) Motion To Determine Present Mental Condition of Imprisoned Person.—If a person serving a sentence of imprisonment objects either in writing or through his attorney to being transferred to a suitable facility for care or treatment, an attorney for the Government, at the request of the director of the facility in which the person is imprisoned, may file a motion with the court for the district in which the facility is located for a hearing on the present mental condition of the person. The court shall grant the motion if there is reasonable cause to believe that the person may presently be suffering from a mental disease or defect for the treatment of which he is in need of custody for care or treatment in a suitable facility. A motion filed under this subsection shall stay the transfer of the person pending completion of procedures contained in this section.

(b) Psychiatric or Psychological Examination and Report.—Prior to the date of the hearing, the court may order that a psychiatric or psychological examination of the person may be conducted, and that a psychiatric or psychological report be filed with the court, pursuant to the provisions of section 4247(b) and (c).

(c) Hearing.—The hearing shall be conducted pursuant to the provisions of section 4247(d).

(d) Determination and Disposition.—If, after the hearing, the court finds by a preponderance of the evidence that the person is presently suffering from a mental disease or defect for the treatment of which he is in need of custody for care or treatment in a suitable facility, the court shall commit the person to the custody of the Attorney General. The Attorney General shall hospitalize the person for treatment in a suitable facility until he is no longer in need of such custody for care or treatment or until the expiration of the sentence of imprisonment, whichever occurs earlier.

(e) Discharge.—When the director of the facility in which the person is hospitalized pursuant to subsection (d) determines that the person has recovered from his mental disease or defect to such an extent that he is no longer in need of custody for care or treatment in such a facility, he shall promptly file a certificate to that effect with the clerk of the court that ordered the commitment. The clerk shall send a copy of the certificate to the person's counsel and to the attorney for the Government. If, at the time of the filing of the certificate, the term of imprisonment imposed upon the person has not expired, the court shall order that the person be reimprisoned until the expiration of his sentence of imprisonment.

(Added Sept. 7, 1949, ch. 535, §1, 63 Stat. 687; amended Pub. L. 98–473, title II, §403(a), Oct. 12, 1984, 98 Stat. 2062.)

Amendments

1984—Pub. L. 98–473 amended section generally, substituting "Hospitalization of an imprisoned person suffering from mental disease or defect" for "Mental incompetency undisclosed at trial" in section catchline, and substituting provisions relating to motion, examination and report, hearing, etc., to determine present mental condition of imprisoned person, for provisions relating to procedures and authorities regarding mental incompetency undisclosed at trial.

§4246. Hospitalization of a person due for release but suffering from mental disease or defect

(a) Institution of Proceeding.—If the director of a facility in which a person is hospitalized certifies that a person in the custody of the Bureau of Prisons whose sentence is about to expire, or who has been committed to the custody of the Attorney General pursuant to section 4241(d), or against whom all criminal charges have been dismissed solely for reasons related to the mental condition of the person, is presently suffering from a mental disease or defect as a result of which his release would create a substantial risk of bodily injury to another person or serious damage to property of another, and that suitable arrangements for State custody and care of the person are not available, he shall transmit the certificate to the clerk of the court for the district in which the person is confined. The clerk shall send a copy of the certificate to the person, and to the attorney for the Government, and, if the person was committed pursuant to section 4241(d), to the clerk of the court that ordered the commitment. The court shall order a hearing to determine whether the person is presently suffering from a mental disease or defect as a result of which his release would create a substantial risk of bodily injury to another person or serious damage to property of another. A certificate filed under this subsection shall stay the release of the person pending completion of procedures contained in this section.

(b) Psychiatric or Psychological Examination and Report.—Prior to the date of the hearing, the court may order that a psychiatric or psychological examination of the defendant be conducted, and that a psychiatric or psychological report be filed with the court, pursuant to the provisions of section 4247(b) and (c).

(c) Hearing.—The hearing shall be conducted pursuant to the provisions of section 4247(d).

(d) Determination and Disposition.—If, after the hearing, the court finds by clear and convincing evidence that the person is presently suffering from a mental disease or defect as a result of which his release would create a substantial risk of bodily injury to another person or serious damage to property of another, the court shall commit the person to the custody of the Attorney General. The Attorney General shall release the person to the appropriate official of the State in which the person is domiciled or was tried if such State will assume responsibility for his custody, care, and treatment. The Attorney General shall make all reasonable efforts to cause such a State to assume such responsibility. If, notwithstanding such efforts, neither such State will assume such responsibility, the Attorney General shall hospitalize the person for treatment in a suitable facility, until—

(1) such a State will assume such responsibility; or

(2) the person's mental condition is such that his release, or his conditional release under a prescribed regimen of medical, psychiatric, or psychological care or treatment would not create a substantial risk of bodily injury to another person or serious damage to property of another; whichever is earlier. The Attorney General shall continue periodically to exert all reasonable efforts to cause such a State to assume such responsibility for the person's custody, care, and treatment.

(e) Discharge.—When the director of the facility in which a person is hospitalized pursuant to subsection (d) determines that the person has recovered from his mental disease or defect to such an extent that his release would no longer create a substantial risk of bodily injury to another person or serious damage to property of another, he shall promptly file a certificate to that effect with the clerk of the court that ordered the commitment. The clerk shall send a copy of the certificate to the person's counsel and to the attorney for the Government. The court shall order the discharge of the person or, on the motion of the attorney for the Government or on its own motion, shall hold a hearing, conducted pursuant to the provisions of section 4247(d), to determine whether he should be released. If, after the hearing, the court finds by a preponderance of the evidence that the person has recovered from his mental disease or defect to such an extent that—

(1) his release would no longer create a substantial risk of bodily injury to another person or serious damage to property of another, the court shall order that he be immediately discharged; or

(2) his conditional release under a prescribed regimen of medical, psychiatric, or psychological care or treatment would no longer create a substantial risk of bodily injury to another person or serious damage to property of another, the court shall—

(A) order that he be conditionally discharged under a prescribed regimen of medical, psychiatric, or psychological care or treatment that has been prepared for him, that has been certified to the court as appropriate by the director of the facility in which he is committed, and that has been found by the court to be appropriate; and

(B) order, as an explicit condition of release, that he comply with the prescribed regimen of medical, psychiatric, or psychological care or treatment.

The court at any time may, after a hearing employing the same criteria, modify or eliminate the regimen of medical, psychiatric, or psychological care or treatment.

(f) Revocation of Conditional Discharge.—The director of a medical facility responsible for administering a regimen imposed on a person conditionally discharged under subsection (e) shall notify the Attorney General and the court having jurisdiction over the person of any failure of the person to comply with the regimen. Upon such notice, or upon other probable cause to believe that the person has failed to comply with the prescribed regimen of medical, psychiatric, or psychological care or treatment, the person may be arrested, and, upon arrest, shall be taken without unnecessary delay before the court having jurisdiction over him. The court shall, after a hearing, determine whether the person should be remanded to a suitable facility on the ground that, in light of his failure to comply with the prescribed regimen of medical, psychiatric, or psychological care or treatment, his continued release would create a substantial risk of bodily injury to another person or serious damage to property of another.

(g) Release to State of Certain Other Persons.—If the director of a facility in which a person is hospitalized pursuant to this chapter certifies to the Attorney General that a person, against whom all charges have been dismissed for reasons not related to the mental condition of the person, is presently suffering from a mental disease or defect as a result of which his release would create a substantial risk of bodily injury to another person or serious damage to property of another, the Attorney General shall release the person to the appropriate official of the State in which the person is domiciled or was tried for the purpose of institution of State proceedings for civil commitment. If neither such State will assume such responsibility, the Attorney General shall release the person upon receipt of notice from the State that it will not assume such responsibility, but not later than ten days after certification by the director of the facility.

(h) Definition.—As used in this chapter the term "State" includes the District of Columbia.

(Added Sept. 7, 1949, ch. 535, §1, 63 Stat. 687; amended Pub. L. 98–473, title II, §403(a), Oct. 12, 1984, 98 Stat. 2062; Pub. L. 101–647, title XXXV, §3599D, Nov. 29, 1990, 104 Stat. 4932; Pub. L. 105–33, title XI, §11204(1), Aug. 5, 1997, 111 Stat. 739.)

Amendments

1997—Subsec. (a). Pub. L. 105–33, §11204(1)(A), inserted "in the custody of the Bureau of Prisons" after "certifies that a person".

Subsec. (h). Pub. L. 105–33, §11204(1)(B), added subsec. (h).

1990—Subsec. (g). Pub. L. 101–647 substituted "chapter" for "subchapter".

1984—Pub. L. 98–473 amended section generally, substituting "Hospitalization of a person due for release but suffering from mental disease or defect" for "Procedure upon finding of mental incompetency" in section catchline, and substituting provisions relating to proceedings, examination and report, hearing, etc., regarding hospitalization of a person due for release but suffering from mental disease or defect, for provisions relating to powers of the trial court with respect to finding of mental incompetency of accused.

Effective Date of 1997 Amendment

Pub. L. 105–33, title XI, §11721, Aug. 5, 1997, 111 Stat. 786, provided that: "Except as otherwise provided in this title [enacting section 138 of former Title 40, Public Buildings, Property, and Works, amending this section, section 4247 of this title, section 1063 of Title 20, Education, section 225b of Title 24, Hospitals and Asylums, sections 6103 and 7213 of Title 26, Internal Revenue Code, sections 715 and 6501 of Title 31, Money and Finance, sections 71f and 138 of former Title 40, and sections 13723 and 14407 of Title 42, The Public Health and Welfare, enacting provisions set out as a note under section 6103 of Title 26, and amending provisions set out as a note under section 4201 of this title], the provisions of this title shall take effect on the later of October 1, 1997, or the day the District of Columbia Financial Responsibility and Management Assistance Authority certifies that the financial plan and budget for the District government for fiscal year 1998 meet the requirements of section 201(c)(1) of the District of

Columbia Financial Responsibility and Management Assistance Act of 1995 [Pub. L. 104–8, 109 Stat. 108], as amended by this title [so certified Sept. 8, 1997]."

§4247. General provisions for chapter

(a) Definitions.—As used in this chapter—

(1) "rehabilitation program" includes—

(A) basic educational training that will assist the individual in understanding the society to which he will return and that will assist him in understanding the magnitude of his offense and its impact on society;

(B) vocational training that will assist the individual in contributing to, and in participating in, the society to which he will return;

(C) drug, alcohol, and sex offender treatment programs, and other treatment programs that will assist the individual in overcoming a psychological or physical dependence or any condition that makes the individual dangerous to others; and

(D) organized physical sports and recreation programs;

(2) "suitable facility" means a facility that is suitable to provide care or treatment given the nature of the offense and the characteristics of the defendant;

(3) "State" includes the District of Columbia;

(4) "bodily injury" includes sexual abuse;

(5) "sexually dangerous person" means a person who has engaged or attempted to engage in sexually violent conduct or child molestation and who is sexually dangerous to others; and

(6) "sexually dangerous to others" with respect 1 a person, means that the person suffers from a serious mental illness, abnormality, or disorder as a result of which he would have serious difficulty in refraining from sexually violent conduct or child molestation if released.

(b) Psychiatric or Psychological Examination.—A psychiatric or psychological examination ordered pursuant to this chapter shall be conducted by a licensed or certified psychiatrist or psychologist, or, if the court finds it appropriate, by more than one such examiner. Each examiner shall be designated by the court, except that if the examination is ordered under section 4245, 4246, or 4248, upon the request of the defendant an additional examiner may be selected by the defendant. For the purposes of an examination pursuant to an order under section 4241, 4244, or 4245, the court may commit the person to be examined for a reasonable period, but not to exceed thirty days, and under section 4242, 4243, 4246, or 4248, for a reasonable period, but not to exceed forty-five days, to the custody of the Attorney General for placement in a suitable facility. Unless impracticable, the psychiatric or psychological examination shall be conducted in the suitable facility closest to the court. The director of the facility may apply for a reasonable extension, but not to exceed fifteen days under section 4241, 4244, or 4245, and not to exceed thirty days under section 4242, 4243, 4246, or 4248, upon a showing of good cause that the additional time is necessary to observe and evaluate the defendant.

(c) Psychiatric or Psychological Reports.—A psychiatric or psychological report ordered pursuant to this chapter shall be prepared by the examiner designated to conduct the psychiatric or psychological examination, shall be filed with the court with copies provided to the counsel for the person examined and to the attorney for the Government, and shall include—

(1) the person's history and present symptoms;

(2) a description of the psychiatric, psychological, and medical tests that were employed and their results;

(3) the examiner's findings; and

(4) the examiner's opinions as to diagnosis, prognosis, and—

(A) if the examination is ordered under section 4241, whether the person is suffering from a mental disease or defect rendering him mentally incompetent to the extent that he is unable to understand the nature and consequences of the proceedings against him or to assist properly in his defense;

(B) if the examination is ordered under section 4242, whether the person was insane at the time of the offense charged;

(C) if the examination is ordered under section 4243 or 4246, whether the person is suffering from a mental disease or defect as a result of which his release would create a substantial risk of bodily injury to another person or serious damage to property of another;

(D) if the examination is ordered under section 4248, whether the person is a sexually dangerous person;

(E) if the examination is ordered under section 4244 or 4245, whether the person is suffering from a mental disease or defect as a result of which he is in need of custody for care or treatment in a suitable facility; or

(F) if the examination is ordered as a part of a presentence investigation, any recommendation the examiner may have as to how the mental condition of the defendant should affect the sentence.

(d) Hearing.—At a hearing ordered pursuant to this chapter the person whose mental condition is the subject of the hearing shall be represented by counsel and, if he is financially unable to obtain adequate representation, counsel shall be appointed for him pursuant to section 3006A. The person shall be afforded an opportunity to testify, to present evidence, to subpoena witnesses on his behalf, and to confront and cross-examine witnesses who appear at the hearing.

(e) Periodic Report and Information Requirements.—(1) The director of the facility in which a person is committed pursuant to—

(A) section 4241 shall prepare semiannual reports; or

(B) section 4243, 4244, 4245, 4246, or 4248 shall prepare annual reports concerning the mental condition of the person and containing recommendations concerning the need for his continued commitment. The reports shall be submitted to the court that ordered the person's commitment to the facility and copies of the reports shall be submitted to such other persons as the court may direct. A copy of each such report concerning a person committed after the beginning of a prosecution of that person for violation of section 871, 879, or 1751 of this title shall be submitted to the Director of the United States Secret Service. Except with the prior approval of the court, the Secret Service shall not use or disclose the information in these copies for any purpose other than carrying out protective duties under section 3056(a) of this title.

(2) The director of the facility in which a person is committed pursuant to section 4241, 4243, 4244, 4245, 4246, or 4248 shall inform such person of any rehabilitation programs that are available for persons committed in that facility.

(f) Videotape Record.—Upon written request of defense counsel, the court may order a videotape record made of the defendant's testimony or interview upon which the periodic report is based pursuant to subsection (e). Such videotape record shall be submitted to the court along with the periodic report.

(g) Habeas Corpus Unimpaired.—Nothing contained in section 4243, 4246, or 4248 precludes a person who is committed under either of such sections from establishing by writ of habeas corpus the illegality of his detention.

(h) Discharge.—Regardless of whether the director of the facility in which a person is committed has filed a certificate pursuant to the provisions of subsection (e) of section 4241, 4244, 4245, 4246, or 4248, or subsection (f) of section 4243, counsel for the person or his legal guardian may, at any time during such person's commitment, file with the court that ordered the commitment a motion for a hearing to determine whether the person should be discharged from such facility, but no such motion may be filed within one hundred and eighty days of a court determination that the person should continue to be committed. A copy of the motion shall be sent to the director of the facility in which the person is committed and to the attorney for the Government.

(i) Authority and Responsibility of the Attorney General.—The Attorney General—

(A) may contract with a State, a political subdivision, a locality, or a private agency for the confinement, hospitalization, care, or treatment of, or the provision of services to, a person committed to his custody pursuant to this chapter;

(B) may apply for the civil commitment, pursuant to State law, of a person committed to his custody pursuant to section 4243, 4246, or 4248;

(C) shall, before placing a person in a facility pursuant to the provisions of section 4241, 4243,

4244, 4245, 4246, or 4248, consider the suitability of the facility's rehabilitation programs in meeting the needs of the person; and

(D) shall consult with the Secretary of the Department of Health and Human Services in the general implementation of the provisions of this chapter and in the establishment of standards for facilities used in the implementation of this chapter.

(j) Sections 4241, 4242, 4243, and 4244 do not apply to a prosecution under an Act of Congress applicable exclusively to the District of Columbia or the Uniform Code of Military Justice.

(Added Sept. 7, 1949, ch. 535, §1, 63 Stat. 687; amended Pub. L. 98–473, title II, §403(a), Oct. 12, 1984, 98 Stat. 2065; Pub. L. 100–690, title VII, §§7044, 7047(a), Nov. 18, 1988, 102 Stat. 4400, 4401; Pub. L. 103–322, title XXXIII, §330003(d), Sept. 13, 1994, 108 Stat. 2141; Pub. L. 105–33, title XI, §11204(2), (3), Aug. 5, 1997, 111 Stat. 739; Pub. L. 109–248, title III, §302(3), July 27, 2006, 120 Stat. 619.)

References in Text

Acts of Congress applicable exclusively to the District of Columbia, referred to in subsec. (j), are classified generally to the District of Columbia Code.

The Uniform Code of Military Justice, referred to in subsec. (j), is classified generally to chapter 47 (§801 et seq.) of Title 10, Armed Forces.

Amendments

2006—Pub. L. 109–248, §302(3)(A), substituted ", 4246, or 4248" for ", or 4246" wherever appearing.

Subsec. (a)(1)(C). Pub. L. 109–248, §302(3)(C)(i), amended subpar. (C) generally. Prior to amendment, subpar. (C) read as follows: "drug, alcohol, and other treatment programs that will assist the individual in overcoming his psychological or physical dependence; and".

Subsec. (a)(4) to (6). Pub. L. 109–248, §302(3)(C)(ii)–(iv), added pars. (4) to (6).

Subsec. (b). Pub. L. 109–248, §302(3)(D), substituted "4245, 4246, or 4248" for "4245 or 4246".

Subsec. (c)(4)(D) to (F). Pub. L. 109–248, §302(3)(E), added subpar. (D) and redesignated former subpars. (D) and (E) as (E) and (F), respectively.

Subsec. (e). Pub. L. 109–248, §302(3)(F), substituted "committed" for "hospitalized" wherever appearing and "continued commitment" for "continued hospitalization" in par. (1)(B).

Subsec. (g). Pub. L. 109–248, §302(3)(B), substituted "4243, 4246, or 4248" for "4243 or 4246".

Subsec. (h). Pub. L. 109–248, §302(3)(F), substituted "committed" for "hospitalized" wherever appearing and "person's commitment" for "person's hospitalization".

Subsec. (i)(B). Pub. L. 109–248, §302(3)(B), substituted "4243, 4246, or 4248" for "4243 or 4246".

1997—Subsec. (a)(3). Pub. L. 105–33, §11024(2)(C), added par. (3).

Subsec. (j). Pub. L. 105–33, §11024(3), substituted "Sections 4241, 4242, 4243, and 4244 do" for "This chapter does".

1994—Subsec. (h). Pub. L. 103–322 substituted "subsection (e) of section 4241, 4244, 4245, or 4246, or subsection (f) of section 4243," for "subsection (e) of section 4241, 4243, 4244, 4245, or 4246,".

1988—Subsec. (b). Pub. L. 100–690, §7047(a), substituted "psychologist" for "clinical psychologist" in first sentence.

Subsec. (e)(1)(B). Pub. L. 100–690, §7044, inserted at end "A copy of each such report concerning a person hospitalized after the beginning of a prosecution of that person for violation of section 871, 879, or 1751 of this title shall be submitted to the Director of the United States Secret Service. Except with the prior approval of the court, the Secret Service shall not use or disclose the information in these copies for any purpose other than carrying out protective duties under section 3056(a) of this title."

1984—Pub. L. 98–473 amended section generally, substituting "General provisions for chapter" for "Alternate procedure of expiration of sentence" in section catchline, and substituting provisions relating to definitions, examinations, reports, etc., as applicable to chapter, for provisions relating to powers and duties regarding alternate procedure on expiration of sentence of prisoner.

Effective Date of 1997 Amendment

Amendment by Pub. L. 105–33 effective Oct. 1, 1997, except as otherwise provided in title XI of Pub. L. 105–33, see section 11721 of Pub. L. 105–33, set out as a note under section 4246 of this title.

Transfer of Functions

For transfer of the functions, personnel, assets, and obligations of the United States Secret Service, including the functions of the Secretary of the Treasury relating thereto, to the Secretary of Homeland Security, and for treatment of related references, see sections 381, 551(d), 552(d), and 557 of Title 6, Domestic Security, and the Department of Homeland Security Reorganization Plan of November 25, 2002, as modified, set out as a note under section 542 of Title 6.

§4248. Civil commitment of a sexually dangerous person

(a) Institution of Proceedings.—In relation to a person who is in the custody of the Bureau of Prisons, or who has been committed to the custody of the Attorney General pursuant to section 4241(d), or against whom all criminal charges have been dismissed solely for reasons relating to the mental condition of the person, the Attorney General or any individual authorized by the Attorney General or the Director of the Bureau of Prisons may certify that the person is a sexually dangerous person, and transmit the certificate to the clerk of the court for the district in which the person is confined. The clerk shall send a copy of the certificate to the person, and to the attorney for the Government, and, if the person was committed pursuant to section 4241(d), to the clerk of the court that ordered the commitment. The court shall order a hearing to determine whether the person is a sexually dangerous person. A certificate filed under this subsection shall stay the release of the person pending completion of procedures contained in this section.

(b) Psychiatric or Psychological Examination and Report.—Prior to the date of the hearing, the court may order that a psychiatric or psychological examination of the defendant be conducted, and that a psychiatric or psychological report be filed with the court, pursuant to the provisions of section 4247(b) and (c).

(c) Hearing.—The hearing shall be conducted pursuant to the provisions of section 4247(d).

(d) Determination and Disposition.—If, after the hearing, the court finds by clear and convincing evidence that the person is a sexually dangerous person, the court shall commit the person to the custody of the Attorney General. The Attorney General shall release the person to the appropriate official of the State in which the person is domiciled or was tried if such State will assume responsibility for his custody, care, and treatment. The Attorney General shall make all reasonable efforts to cause such a State to assume such responsibility. If, notwithstanding such efforts, neither such State will assume such responsibility, the Attorney General shall place the person for treatment in a suitable facility, until—

(1) such a State will assume such responsibility; or

(2) the person's condition is such that he is no longer sexually dangerous to others, or will not be sexually dangerous to others if released under a prescribed regimen of medical, psychiatric, or psychological care or treatment;

whichever is earlier.

(e) Discharge.—When the Director of the facility in which a person is placed pursuant to subsection (d) determines that the person's condition is such that he is no longer sexually dangerous to others, or will not be sexually dangerous to others if released under a prescribed regimen of medical, psychiatric, or psychological care or treatment, he shall promptly file a certificate to that effect with the clerk of the court that ordered the commitment. The clerk shall send a copy of the certificate to the person's counsel and to the attorney for the Government. The court shall order the discharge of the person or, on motion of the attorney for the Government or on its own motion, shall hold a hearing, conducted pursuant to the provisions of section 4247(d), to determine whether he should be released. If, after the hearing, the court finds by a preponderance of the evidence that the person's condition is such that—

(1) he will not be sexually dangerous to others if released unconditionally, the court shall order that he be immediately discharged; or

(2) he will not be sexually dangerous to others if released under a prescribed regimen of medical, psychiatric, or psychological care or treatment, the court shall—

(A) order that he be conditionally discharged under a prescribed regimen of medical, psychiatric, or psychological care or treatment that has been prepared for him, that has been certified to the court as appropriate by the Director of the facility in which he is committed, and that has been found by the court to be appropriate; and

(B) order, as an explicit condition of release, that he comply with the prescribed regimen of medical, psychiatric, or psychological care or treatment.

The court at any time may, after a hearing employing the same criteria, modify or eliminate the regimen of medical, psychiatric, or psychological care or treatment.

(f) Revocation of Conditional Discharge.—The director of a facility responsible for administering a regimen imposed on a person conditionally discharged under subsection (e) shall notify the Attorney General and the court having jurisdiction over the person of any failure of the person to comply with the regimen. Upon such notice, or upon other probable cause to believe that the person has failed to comply with the prescribed regimen of medical, psychiatric, or psychological care or treatment, the person may be arrested, and, upon arrest, shall be taken without unnecessary delay before the court having jurisdiction over him. The court shall, after a hearing, determine whether the person should be remanded to a suitable facility on the ground that he is sexually dangerous to others in light of his failure to comply with the prescribed regimen of medical, psychiatric, or psychological care or treatment.

(g) Release to State of Certain Other Persons.—If the director of the facility in which a person is hospitalized or placed pursuant to this chapter certifies to the Attorney General that a person, against whom all charges have been dismissed for reasons not related to the mental condition of the person, is a sexually dangerous person, the Attorney General shall release the person to the appropriate official of the State in which the person is domiciled or was tried for the purpose of institution of State proceedings for civil commitment. If neither such State will assume such responsibility, the Attorney General shall release the person upon receipt of notice from the State that it will not assume such responsibility, but not later than 10 days after certification by the director of the facility.

(Added Pub. L. 109–248, title III, §302(4), July 27, 2006, 120 Stat. 620.)

Prior Provisions

A prior section 4248, act Sept. 7, 1949, ch. 535, §1, 63 Stat. 688, related to the termination of custody by release or transfer, prior to its omission in the general amendment of this chapter by Pub. L. 98–473, title II, §403(a), Oct. 12, 1984, 98 Stat. 2057.

[CHAPTER 314 - REPEALED]

[§§4251 to 4255. Repealed. Pub. L. 98–473, title II, §218(a)(6), Oct. 12, 1984, 98 Stat. 2027]

Section 4251, added Pub. L. 89–793, title II, §201, Nov. 8, 1966, 80 Stat. 1442; amended Pub. L. 91–513, title III, §1102(s), Oct. 27, 1970, 84 Stat. 1294; Pub. L. 92–420, §3, Sept. 16, 1972, 86 Stat. 677, defined terms for purposes of this chapter.

Section 4252, added Pub. L. 89–793, title II, §201, Nov. 8, 1966, 80 Stat. 1443, related to examination to determine if offender is an addict and likely to be rehabilitated through treatment.
Section 4253, added Pub. L. 89–793, title II, §201, Nov. 8, 1966, 80 Stat. 1443, related to commitment for treatment.
Section 4254, added Pub. L. 89–793, title II, §201, Nov. 8, 1966, 80 Stat. 1443, related to conditional release.
Section 4255, added Pub. L. 89–793, title II, §201, Nov. 8, 1966, 80 Stat. 1443; amended Pub. L. 95–537, §3, Oct. 27, 1978, 92 Stat. 2038; Pub. L. 99–570, §1861(c), Oct. 27, 1986, 100 Stat. 3207–53; Pub. L. 99–646, §19, Nov. 10, 1986, 100 Stat. 3596, related to supervision in the community.

Effective Date of Repeal
Repeal effective Nov. 1, 1987, and applicable only to offenses committed after the taking effect of such repeal, with sections to remain in effect for five years as to an individual who committed an offense or an act of juvenile delinquency before Nov. 1, 1987, and as to a term of imprisonment during the period described in section 235(a)(1)(B) of Pub. L. 98–473, see section 235(a)(1), (b)(1)(C) of Pub. L. 98–473, set out as an Effective Date note under section 3551 of this title.

CHAPTER 315 - DISCHARGE AND RELEASE PAYMENTS

Amendments
1984—Pub. L. 98–473, title II, §218(f), Oct. 12, 1984, 98 Stat. 2027, in items 4281, 4283, and 4284, substituted "Repealed" for "Discharge from prison", "Probation", and "Advances for rehabilitation", respectively.
1978—Pub. L. 95–503, §2, Oct. 24, 1978, 92 Stat. 1704, added item 4285.
1952—Act May 15, 1952, ch. 289, §3, 66 Stat. 73, added item 4284.

[§4281. Repealed. Pub. L. 98–473, title II, §218(a)(7), Oct. 12, 1984, 98 Stat. 2027]
Section, acts June 25, 1948, ch. 645, 62 Stat. 856; Sept. 19, 1962, Pub. L. 87–672, 76 Stat. 557, related to discharge from prison of a convicted person.

Effective Date of Repeal
Repeal effective Nov. 1, 1987, and applicable only to offenses committed after the taking effect of such repeal, see section 235(a)(1) of Pub. L. 98–473, set out as an Effective Date note under section 3551 of this title.

§4282. Arrested but unconvicted persons
On the release from custody of a person arrested on a charge of violating any law of the United States or of the Territory of Alaska, but not indicted nor informed against, or indicted or informed against but not convicted, and detained pursuant to chapter 207, or a person held as a material witness, the court in its discretion may direct the United States marshal for the district wherein he

is released, pursuant to regulations promulgated by the Attorney General, to furnish the person so released with transportation and subsistence to the place of his arrest, or, at his election, to the place of his bona fide residence if such cost is not greater than to the place of arrest.

(June 25, 1948, ch. 645, 62 Stat. 856; Pub. L. 98–473, title II, §207, Oct. 12, 1984, 98 Stat. 1986.)

Historical and Revision Notes

Based on title 18, U.S.C., 1940 ed., §746a (July 3, 1926, ch. 795, §2, as added June 21, 1941, ch. 212, 55 Stat. 254).

The phrase "informed against" was inserted in two places in view of the fact that under the Federal Rules of Criminal Procedure the use of informations may be expected to increase. See Rule 7(b). The section was extended to cover a person held as a material witness and unable to make bail. His predicament obviously calls for the relief afforded by the revised section.

Changes were made in phraseology and surplusage omitted.

Amendments

1984—Pub. L. 98–473 substituted "and detained pursuant to chapter 207" for "and not admitted to bail" and struck out "and unable to make bail" after "held as a material witness".

Admission of Alaska as State

Admission of Alaska into the Union was accomplished Jan. 3, 1959, on issuance of Proc. No. 3269, Jan. 3, 1959, 24 F.R. 81, 73 Stat. c16, as required by sections 1 and 8(c) of Pub. L. 85–508, July 7, 1958, 72 Stat. 339, set out as notes preceding section 21 of Title 48, Territories and Insular Possessions.

[§§4283, 4284. Repealed. Pub. L. 98–473, title II, §218(a)(7), Oct. 12, 1984, 98 Stat. 2027]

Section 4283, act June 25, 1948, ch. 645, 62 Stat. 856, related to furnishing transportation when placing a defendant on probation.

Section 4284, added May 15, 1952, ch. 289, §1, 66 Stat. 72; amended Sept. 13, 1982, Pub. L. 97–258, §3(e)(5), 96 Stat. 1064, related to advances for rehabilitation.

Effective Date of Repeal

Repeal effective Nov. 1, 1987, and applicable only to offenses committed after the taking effect of such repeal, see section 235(a)(1) of Pub. L. 98–473, set out as an Effective Date note under section 3551 of this title.

§4285. Persons released pending further judicial proceedings

Any judge or magistrate judge of the United States, when ordering a person released under chapter 207 on a condition of his subsequent appearance before that court, any division of that court, or any court of the United States in another judicial district in which criminal proceedings are pending, may, when the interests of justice would be served thereby and the United States judge or magistrate judge is satisfied, after appropriate inquiry, that the defendant is financially unable to provide the necessary transportation to appear before the required court on his own, direct the United States marshal to arrange for that person's means of noncustodial transportation or furnish the fare for such transportation to the place where his appearance is required, and in addition may direct the United States marshal to furnish that person with an amount of money for subsistence expenses to his destination, not to exceed the amount authorized as a per diem allowance for travel under section 5702(a) of title 5, United States Code. When so ordered, such expenses shall be paid by the marshal out of funds authorized by the Attorney General for such expenses.

(Added Pub. L. 95–503, §1, Oct. 24, 1978, 92 Stat. 1704; amended Pub. L. 101–647, title XXXV, §3599E, Nov. 29, 1990, 104 Stat. 4932; Pub. L. 101–650, title III, §321, Dec. 1, 1990, 104 Stat.

5117.)

Amendments
1990—Pub. L. 101–647 substituted "exceed" for "exced" after "not to".

Change of Name
Words "magistrate judge" substituted for "magistrate" wherever appearing in text pursuant to section 321 of Pub. L. 101–650, set out as a note under section 631 of Title 28, Judiciary and Judicial Procedure.

Effective Date
Pub. L. 95–503, §3, Oct. 24, 1978, 92 Stat. 1704, provided that: "The amendments made by this Act [enacting this section] shall take effect on October 1, 1978."

CHAPTER 317 - INSTITUTIONS FOR WOMEN

| 4321. | Board of Advisers. |

§4321. Board of Advisers
Four citizens of the United States of prominence and distinction, appointed by the President to serve without compensation, for terms of four years, together with the Attorney General of the United States, the Director of the Bureau of Prisons and the warden of the Federal Reformatory for Women, shall constitute a Board of Advisers of said Federal Reformatory for Women, which shall recommend ways and means for the discipline and training of the inmates, to fit them for suitable employment upon their discharge.

Any person chosen to fill a vacancy shall be appointed only for the unexpired term of the citizen whom he shall succeed.

(June 25, 1948, ch. 645, 62 Stat. 856; Pub. L. 98–473, title II, §223(n), Oct. 12, 1984, 98 Stat. 2030.)

Historical and Revision Notes
Based on title 18, U.S.C., 1940 ed., §816 (June 7, 1924, ch. 287, §7, 43 Stat. 474; May 14, 1930, ch. 274, §1, 46 Stat. 325).

The provisions relating to the appointment of the board in the first instance were omitted as executed.

"Warden" was substituted for "superintendent" and "Federal Reformatory for Women" for "United States Industrial Institution for Women" to conform to existing administrative usage.

Minor changes were made in translation, phraseology, and arrangement.

Amendments
1984—Pub. L. 98–473 struck out "parole or" before "discharge" at end of first par.

Effective Date of 1984 Amendment
Amendment by Pub. L. 98–473 effective Nov. 1, 1987, and applicable only to offenses committed after the taking effect of such amendment, see section 235(a)(1) of Pub. L. 98–473, set out as an Effective Date note under section 3551 of this title.

CHAPTER 319 - NATIONAL INSTITUTE OF CORRECTIONS

Amendments

1974—Pub. L. 93–415, title V, §521, Sept. 7, 1974, 88 Stat. 1139, added chapter heading.

§4351. Establishment; Advisory Board; appointment of members; compensation; officers; committees; delegation of powers; Director, appointment and powers 1

(a) There is hereby established within the Bureau of Prisons a National Institute of Corrections.

(b) The overall policy and operations of the National Institute of Corrections shall be under the supervision of an Advisory Board. The Board shall consist of sixteen members. The following six individuals shall serve as members of the Commission ex officio: the Director of the Federal Bureau of Prisons or his designee, the Director of the Bureau of Justice Assistance or his designee, Chairman of the United States Sentencing Commission or his designee, the Director of the Federal Judicial Center or his designee, the Associate Administrator for the Office of Juvenile Justice and Delinquency Prevention 2 or his designee, and the Assistant Secretary for Human Development of the Department of Health, Education, and Welfare or his designee.

(c) The remaining ten members of the Board shall be selected as follows:

(1) Five shall be appointed initially by the Attorney General of the United States for staggered terms; one member shall serve for one year, one member for two years, and three members for three years. Upon the expiration of each member's term, the Attorney General shall appoint successors who will each serve for a term of three years. Each member selected shall be qualified as a practitioner (Federal, State, or local) in the field of corrections, probation, or parole.

(2) Five shall be appointed initially by the Attorney General of the United States for staggered terms, one member shall serve for one year, three members for two years, and one member for three years. Upon the expiration of each member's term the Attorney General shall appoint successors who will each serve for a term of three years. Each member selected shall be from the private sector, such as business, labor, and education, having demonstrated an active interest in corrections, probation, or parole.

(d) The members of the Board shall not, by reason of such membership, be deemed officers or employees of the United States. Members of the Commission who are full-time officers or employees of the United States shall serve without additional compensation, but shall be reimbursed for travel, subsistence, and other necessary expenses incurred in the performance of the duties vested in the Board. Other members of the Board shall, while attending meetings of the Board or while engaged in duties related to such meetings or in other activities of the Commission pursuant to this title, be entitled to receive compensation at the rate not to exceed the daily equivalent of the rate authorized for GS–18 by section 5332 of title 5, United States Code, including traveltime, and while away from their homes or regular places of business may be allowed travel expenses, including per diem in lieu of subsistence equal to that authorized by section 5703 of title 5, United States Code, for persons in the Government service employed intermittently.

(e) The Board shall elect a chairman from among its members who shall serve for a term of one year. The members of the Board shall also elect one or more members as a vice-chairman.

(f) The Board is authorized to appoint, without regard to the civil service laws, technical, or other advisory committees to advise the Institute with respect to the administration of this title as it deems appropriate. Members of these committees not otherwise employed by the United States, while engaged in advising the Institute or attending meetings of the committees, shall be entitled to receive compensation at the rate fixed by the Board but not to exceed the daily equivalent of the rate authorized for GS–18 by section 5332 of title 5, United States Code, and while away from their homes or regular places of business may be allowed travel expenses, including per diem in lieu of subsistence equal to that authorized by section 5703 of title 5, United States Code, for persons in the Government service employed intermittently.

(g) The Board is authorized to delegate its powers under this title to such persons as it deems appropriate.

(h) The Institute shall be under the supervision of an officer to be known as the Director, who shall be appointed by the Attorney General after consultation with the Board. The Director shall have authority to supervise the organization, employees, enrollees, financial affairs, and all other operations of the Institute and may employ such staff, faculty, and administrative personnel, subject to the civil service and classification laws, as are necessary to the functioning of the Institute. The Director shall have the power to acquire and hold real and personal property for the Institute and may receive gifts, donations, and trusts on behalf of the Institute. The Director shall also have the power to appoint such technical or other advisory councils comprised of consultants to guide and advise the Board. The Director is authorized to delegate his powers under this title to such persons as he deems appropriate.

(Added Pub. L. 93–415, title V, §521, Sept. 7, 1974, 88 Stat. 1139; amended Pub. L. 95–115, §8(a), Oct. 3, 1977, 91 Stat. 1060; Pub. L. 98–473, title II, §223(o), Oct. 12, 1984, 98 Stat. 2030; Pub. L. 103–322, title XXXIII, §330001(i), Sept. 13, 1994, 108 Stat. 2140.)

References in Text

The Office of Juvenile Justice and Delinquency Prevention, referred to in subsec. (b), as originally created by section 11111 of Title 34, Crime Control and Law Enforcement, was headed by an Associate Administrator. However, section 11111 of Title 34, as amended by Pub. L. 98–473, establishes the Office of Juvenile Justice and Delinquency Prevention, headed by an Administrator.

Amendments

1994—Subsec. (b). Pub. L. 103–322 substituted "Director of the Bureau of Justice Assistance" for "Administrator of the Law Enforcement Assistance Administration".

1984—Subsec. (b). Pub. L. 98–473 substituted "Sentencing Commission" for "Parole Board".

1977—Subsec. (b). Pub. L. 95–115 substituted "Associate" for "Deputy Assistant" and "Office of" for "National Institute for".

Change of Name

Department of Health, Education, and Welfare redesignated Department of Health and Human Services by Pub. L. 96–88, title V, §509(b), Oct. 17, 1979, 93 Stat. 695, which is classified to section 3508(b) of Title 20, Education.

Effective Date of 1984 Amendment

Amendment by Pub. L. 98–473 effective Nov. 1, 1987, and applicable only to offenses committed after the taking effect of such amendment, see section 235(a)(1) of Pub. L. 98–473, set out as an Effective Date note under section 3551 of this title.

Effective Date of 1977 Amendment

Amendment by Pub. L. 95–115 effective Oct. 1, 1977, see section 263(c) of Pub. L. 93–415, as added by Pub. L. 95–115, formerly set out as a note under section 11101 of Title 34, Crime Control and Law Enforcement.

Transfer of Functions

Effective Aug. 1, 2000, all functions of Director of Bureau of Justice Assistance, other than those enumerated in section 10142(3) through (6) of Title 34, Crime Control and Law Enforcement, transferred to Assistant Attorney General for Office of Justice Programs, see section 1000(a)(1) [title I, §108(b)] of Pub. L. 106–113, set out as a note under section 10141 of Title 34.

References in Other Laws to GS–16, 17, or 18 Pay Rates

References in laws to the rates of pay for GS–16, 17, or 18, or to maximum rates of pay under the General Schedule, to be considered references to rates payable under specified sections of Title 5, Government Organization and Employees, see section 529 [title I, §101(c)(1)] of Pub. L. 101–509, set out in a note under section 5376 of Title 5.

Termination of Advisory Boards

Advisory boards established after Jan. 5, 1973, to terminate not later than the expiration of the 2-year period beginning on the date of their establishment, unless, in the case of a board established by the President or an officer of the Federal Government, such board is renewed by appropriate action prior to the expiration of such 2-year period, or in the case of a board established by the Congress, its duration is otherwise provided for by law. See sections 3(2) and 14 of Pub. L. 92–463, Oct. 6, 1972, 86 Stat. 770, 776, set out in the Appendix to Title 5, Government Organization and Employees.

Exceptions to Membership Requirements During Five-Year Period

For exceptions to the membership requirements set forth in this section, which exceptions are applicable for five-year period following Nov. 1, 1987, see section 235(b)(5) of Pub. L. 98–473, set out as an Effective Date note under section 3551 of this title.

§4352. Authority of Institute; time; records of recipients; access; scope of section 1

(a) In addition to the other powers, express and implied, the National Institute of Corrections shall have authority—

(1) to receive from or make grants to and enter into contracts with Federal, State, tribal, and general units of local government, public and private agencies, educational institutions, organizations, and individuals to carry out the purposes of this chapter;

(2) to serve as a clearinghouse and information center for the collection, preparation, and dissemination of information on corrections, including, but not limited to, programs for prevention of crime and recidivism, training of corrections personnel, and rehabilitation and treatment of criminal and juvenile offenders;

(3) to assist and serve in a consulting capacity to Federal, State, tribal, and local courts, departments, and agencies in the development, maintenance, and coordination of programs, facilities, and services, training, treatment, and rehabilitation with respect to criminal and juvenile offenders;

(4) to encourage and assist Federal, State, tribal, and local government programs and services, and programs and services of other public and private agencies, institutions, and organizations in their efforts to develop and implement improved corrections programs;

(5) to devise and conduct, in various geographical locations, seminars, workshops, and training programs for law enforcement officers, judges, and judicial personnel, probation and parole personnel, correctional personnel, welfare workers, and other persons, including lay ex-offenders, and paraprofessional personnel, connected with the treatment and rehabilitation of criminal and juvenile offenders;

(6) to develop technical training teams to aid in the development of seminars, workshops, and training programs within the several States and tribal communities, and with the State, tribal, and

local agencies which work with prisoners, parolees, probationers, and other offenders;

(7) to conduct, encourage, and coordinate research relating to corrections, including the causes, prevention, diagnosis, and treatment of criminal offenders;

(8) to formulate and disseminate correctional policy, goals, standards, and recommendations for Federal, State, tribal, and local correctional agencies, organizations, institutions, and personnel;

(9) to conduct evaluation programs which study the effectiveness of new approaches, techniques, systems, programs, and devices employed to improve the corrections system;

(10) to receive from any Federal department or agency such statistics, data, program reports, and other material as the Institute deems necessary to carry out its functions. Each such department or agency is authorized to cooperate with the Institute and shall, to the maximum extent practicable, consult with and furnish information to the Institute;

(11) to arrange with and reimburse the heads of Federal departments and agencies for the use of personnel, facilities, or equipment of such departments and agencies;

(12) to confer with and avail itself of the assistance, services, records, and facilities of State, tribal, and local governments or other public or private agencies, organizations, or individuals;

(13) to enter into contracts with public or private agencies, organizations, or individuals, for the performance of any of the functions of the Institute; and

(14) to procure the services of experts and consultants in accordance with section 3109 of title 5 of the United States Code, at rates of compensation not to exceed the daily equivalent of the rate authorized for GS–18 by section 5332 of title 5 of the United States Code.

[(b) Repealed. Pub. L. 97–375, title I, §109(a), Dec. 21, 1982, 96 Stat. 1820.]

(c) Each recipient of assistance under this chapter shall keep such records as the Institute shall prescribe, including records which fully disclose the amount and disposition by such recipient of the proceeds of such assistance, the total cost of the project or undertaking in connection with which such assistance is given or used, and the amount of that portion of the cost of the project or undertaking supplied by other sources, and such other records as will facilitate an effective audit.

(d) The Institute, and the Comptroller General of the United States, or any of their duly authorized representatives, shall have access for purposes of audit and examinations to any books, documents, papers, and records of the recipients that are pertinent to the grants received under this chapter.

(e) The provision of this section shall apply to all recipients of assistance under this title, whether by direct grant or contract from the Institute or by subgrant or subcontract from primary grantees or contractors of the Institute.

(Added Pub. L. 93–415, title V, §521, Sept. 7, 1974, 88 Stat. 1140; amended Pub. L. 97–375, title I, §109(a), Dec. 21, 1982, 96 Stat. 1820; Pub. L. 101–647, title XXXV, §3599F, Nov. 29, 1990, 104 Stat. 4932; Pub. L. 111–211, title II, §261(b), July 29, 2010, 124 Stat. 2299.)

Amendments

2010—Subsec. (a)(1), (3), (4). Pub. L. 111–211, §261(b)(1), inserted "tribal," after "State,".

Subsec. (a)(6). Pub. L. 111–211, §261(b)(2), inserted "and tribal communities," after "States" and ", tribal," after "State".

Subsec. (a)(8). Pub. L. 111–211, §261(b)(1), inserted "tribal," after "State,".

Subsec. (a)(12). Pub. L. 111–211, §261(b)(3), inserted ", tribal," after "State".

1990—Subsec. (c). Pub. L. 101–647 substituted "this chapter shall" for "this shall".

1982—Subsec. (b). Pub. L. 97–375 struck out subsec. (b) which directed the Institute to submit an annual report to the President and Congress, including a comprehensive and detailed report of the Institute's operations, activities, financial condition and accomplishments under this title, and which might include such recommendations related to corrections as the Institute deemed appropriate.

Inclusion of National Institute of Corrections in Federal Prison System Salaries and Expenses Budget

Pub. L. 104–208, div. A, title I, §101(a), [title I], Sept. 30, 1996, 110 Stat. 3009, 3009–11, provided in part: "That the National Institute of Corrections hereafter shall be included in the FPS Salaries and Expenses budget, in the Contract Confinement program and shall continue to perform its current functions under 18 U.S.C. 4351, et seq., with the exception of its grant program and shall collect reimbursement for services whenever possible".

References in Other Laws to GS–16, 17, or 18 Pay Rates

References in laws to the rates of pay for GS–16, 17, or 18, or to maximum rates of pay under the General Schedule, to be considered references to rates payable under specified sections of Title 5, Government Organization and Employees, see section 529 [title I, §101(c)(1)] of Pub. L. 101–509, set out in a note under section 5376 of Title 5.

National Training Center for Prison Drug Rehabilitation Program Personnel

Pub. L. 100–690, title VI, §6292, Nov. 18, 1988, 102 Stat. 4369, which provided that the Director of the National Institute of Corrections, in consultation with persons with expertise in the field of community-based drug rehabilitation, was to establish and operate, at any suitable location, a national training center for training Federal, State, and local prison or jail officials to conduct drug rehabilitation programs for criminals convicted of drug-related crimes and for drug-dependent criminals, was editorially reclassified as section 10426 of Title 34, Crime Control and Law Enforcement.

[§4353. Repealed. Pub. L. 107–273, div. A, title III, §301(a), Nov. 2, 2002, 116 Stat. 1780]

Section, added Pub. L. 93–415, title V, §521, Sept. 7, 1974, 88 Stat. 1141, authorized appropriations to carry out purposes of this chapter.

Amendments

1984—Pub. L. 98–473, title II, §218(g), Oct. 12, 1984, 98 Stat. 2027, in item for chapter 402 substituted "Repealed" for "Federal Youth Corrections Act".
1950—Act Sept. 30, 1950, ch. 1115, §5(a), 64 Stat. 1090, added item for chapter 402.

CHAPTER 401 - GENERAL PROVISIONS

Amendments

1996—Pub. L. 104–134, title I, §101[(a)] [title VI, §614(a)(2)], Apr. 26, 1996, 110 Stat. 1321, 1321–65; renumbered title I, Pub. L. 104–140, §1(a), May 2, 1996, 110 Stat. 1327, struck out item 5002 "Advisory Corrections Council".
1952—Act May 9, 1952, ch. 253, §2, 66 Stat. 68, added item 5003.
1950—Act Sept. 30, 1950, ch. 1115, §5(b), 64 Stat. 1090, added item 5002.

§5001. Surrender to State authorities; expenses

Whenever any person under twenty-one years of age has been arrested, charged with the commission of an offense punishable in any court of the United States or of the District of Columbia, and, after investigation by the Department of Justice, it appears that such person has committed an offense or is a delinquent under the laws of any State or of the District of Columbia which can and will assume jurisdiction over such juvenile and will take him into custody and deal with him according to the laws of such State or of the District of Columbia, and that it will be to the best interest of the United States and of the juvenile offender, the United States attorney of the district in which such person has been arrested may forego his prosecution and surrender him as herein provided, unless such surrender is precluded under section 5032 of this title.

The United States marshal of such district upon written order of the United States attorney shall convey such person to such State or the District of Columbia, or, if already therein, to any other part thereof and deliver him into the custody of the proper authority thereof.

Before any person is conveyed from one State to another or from or to the District of Columbia under this section, he shall signify his willingness to be so returned, or there shall be presented to the United States attorney a demand from the executive authority of such State or the District of Columbia, to which the prisoner is to be returned, supported by indictment or affidavit as prescribed by section 3182 of this title.

The expense incident to the transportation of any such person, as herein authorized, shall be paid from the appropriation "Salaries, Fees, and Expenses, United States Marshals."

(June 25, 1948, ch. 645, 62 Stat. 857; Pub. L. 100–690, title VI, §6467(b), Nov. 18, 1988, 102 Stat. 4376.)

Historical and Revision Notes

Based on title 18, U.S.C., 1940 ed., §662a (June 11, 1932, ch. 243, 47 Stat. 301).

Language preceding "Whenever" was omitted as unnecessary, and "the District of Columbia" was inserted after "State".

Changes were made in phraseology and surplusage eliminated.

Amendments

1988—Pub. L. 100–690 inserted ", unless such surrender is precluded under section 5032 of this title" before period at end of first par.

[§5002. Repealed. Pub. L. 104–134, title I, §101[(a)] [title VI, §614(a)(1)], Apr. 26, 1996, 110 Stat. 1321, 1321–65; renumbered title I, Pub. L. 104–140, §1(a), May 2, 1996, 110 Stat. 1327]

Section, added act Sept. 30, 1950, ch. 1115, §4, 64 Stat. 1090; amended Oct. 12, 1984, Pub. L. 98–473, title II, §223(p), 98 Stat. 2030, provided for creation of Advisory Corrections Council.

Effective Date of Repeal

Pub. L. 104–134, title I, §101[(a)] [title VI, §614(b)], Apr. 26, 1996, 110 Stat. 1321, 1321–65, provided that: "This section [repealing this section] shall take effect 30 days after the date of the enactment of this Act [Apr. 26, 1996]."

§5003. Custody of State offenders

(a)(1) The Director of the Bureau of Prisons when proper and adequate facilities and personnel are available may contract with proper officials of a State or territory, for the custody, care, subsistence, education, treatment, and training of persons convicted of criminal offenses in the courts of such State or territory.

(2) Any such contract shall provide—

(A) for reimbursing the United States in full for all costs or expenses involved;

(B) for receiving in exchange persons convicted of criminal offenses in the courts of the United States, to serve their sentence in appropriate institutions or facilities of the State or territory by designation as provided in section 4082(b) 1 of this title, this exchange to be made according to formulas or conditions which may be negotiated in the contract; or

(C) for compensating the United States by means of a combination of monetary payment and of receipt of persons convicted of criminal offenses in the courts of the United States, according to formulas or conditions which may be negotiated in the contract.

(3) No such contract shall provide for the receipt of more State or territory prisoners by the United States than are transferred to that State or territory by such contract.

(b) Funds received under such contract may be deposited in the Treasury to the credit of the appropriation or appropriations from which the payments for such service were originally made.

(c) Unless otherwise specifically provided in the contract, a person committed to the Attorney General hereunder shall be subject to all the provisions of law and regulations applicable to persons committed for violations of laws of the United States not inconsistent with the sentence imposed.

(d) The term "State" as used in this section includes any State, territory, or possession of the United States, and the Canal Zone.

(Added May 9, 1952, ch. 253, §1, 66 Stat. 68; amended Pub. L. 89–267, §1, Oct. 19, 1965, 79 Stat. 990; Pub. L. 99–646, §66, Nov. 10, 1986, 100 Stat. 3615.)

References in Text

Section 4082(b) of this title, referred to in subsec. (a)(2)(B), was repealed, and section 4082(f) was redesignated section 4082(b), by Pub. L. 98–473, title II, §218(a), Oct. 12, 1984, 98 Stat. 2027. For definition of Canal Zone, referred to in subsec. (d), see section 3602(b) of Title 22, Foreign Relations and Intercourse.

Amendments

1986—Subsec. (a). Pub. L. 99–646 amended subsec. (a) generally. Prior to amendment, subsec. (a) read as follows: "The Attorney General, when the Director shall certify that proper and adequate treatment facilities and personnel are available, is hereby authorized to contract with the proper officials of a State or Territory for the custody, care, subsistence, education, treatment, and training of persons convicted of criminal offenses in the courts of such State or Territory: Provided, That any such contract shall provide for reimbursing the United States in full for all costs or other expenses involved."

1965—Subsec. (d). Pub. L. 89–267 added subsec. (d).

[CHAPTER 402 - REPEALED]

[§§5005, 5006. Repealed. Pub. L. 98–473, title II, §218(a)(8), Oct. 12, 1984, 98 Stat. 2027]

Section 5005, added act Sept. 30, 1950, ch. 1115, §2, 64 Stat. 1086; amended Mar. 15, 1976, Pub. L. 94–233, §3, 90 Stat. 231, related to the making of youth correction decisions by United States Parole Commission.

Section 5006, added act Sept. 30, 1950, ch. 1115, §2, 64 Stat. 1086; amended Mar. 15, 1976, Pub. L. 94–233, §4, 90 Stat. 231, defined terms for the purpose of this chapter.

Effective Date of Repeal

Repeal effective Oct. 12, 1984, see section 235(a)(1)(A) of Pub. L. 98–473, set out as an Effective Date note under section 3551 of this title.

[§§5007 to 5009. Repealed Pub. L. 94–233, §5, Mar. 15, 1976, 90 Stat. 231]

Section 5007, added act Sept. 30, 1950, ch. 1115, §2, 64 Stat. 1086, provided for meetings and duties of members of Youth Correction Division.

Section 5008, added act Sept. 30, 1950, ch. 1115, §2, 64 Stat. 1086, provided for appointment of officers and employees by Attorney General.

Section 5009, added act Sept. 30, 1950, ch. 1115, §2, 64 Stat. 1086, provided for adoption and promulgation of rules governing procedure by Youth Correction Division.

Effective Date of Repeal

Repeal effective on 60th day following Mar. 15, 1976, see section 16(b) of Pub. L. 94–233, set out as an Effective Date note under section 4201 of this title.

[§§5010 to 5026. Repealed. Pub. L. 98–473, title II, §218(a)(8), Oct. 12, 1984, 98 Stat. 2027]

Section 5010, added act Sept. 30, 1950, ch. 1115, §2, 64 Stat. 1087; amended Mar. 15, 1976, Pub. L. 94–233, §9, 90 Stat. 232, provided for imposition of a suspended sentence or sentence to custody of the Attorney General in the case of youth offenders.

Section 5011, added act Sept. 30, 1950, ch. 1115, §2, 64 Stat. 1087, provided for treatment of youth offenders.

Section 5012, added act Sept. 30, 1950, ch. 1115, §2, 64 Stat. 1087, provided for Director's certification of the availability of proper and adequate treatment facilities for youth offenders.

Section 5013, added act Sept. 30, 1950, ch. 1115, §2, 64 Stat. 1087, authorized Director of Bureau of Prisons to contract for maintenance of youth offenders.

Section 5014, added act Sept. 30, 1950, ch. 1115, §2, 64 Stat. 1087; amended July 17, 1970, Pub. L. 91–339, §1, 84 Stat. 437; Mar. 15, 1976, Pub. L. 94–233, §6, 90 Stat. 231, related to classification studies and reports.

Section 5015, added act Sept. 30, 1950, ch. 1115, §2, 64 Stat. 1088; amended Mar. 15, 1976, Pub. L. 94–233, §9, 90 Stat. 232, related to powers of Director as to placement of youth offenders.

Section 5016, added act Sept. 30, 1950, ch. 1115, §2, 64 Stat. 1088; amended Mar. 15, 1976, Pub. L. 94–233, §9, 90 Stat. 232, related to periodic reports which the Director was required to make on all committed youth offenders.

Section 5017, added act Sept. 30, 1950, ch. 1115, §2, 64 Stat. 1088; amended Mar. 15, 1976, Pub. L. 94–233, §7, 9, 90 Stat. 232, related to release of youth offenders.

Section 5018, added act Sept. 30, 1950, ch. 1115, §2, 64 Stat. 1089; amended Mar. 15, 1976, Pub. L. 94–233, §9, 90 Stat. 232, related to revocation of Commission orders.

Section 5019, added act Sept. 30, 1950, ch. 1115, §2, 64 Stat. 1089; amended Mar. 15, 1976, Pub. L. 94–233, §9, 90 Stat. 232, related to supervision of released youth offenders.

Section 5020, added act Sept. 30, 1950, ch. 1115, §2, 64 Stat. 1089; amended July 17, 1970, Pub. L. 91–339, §2, 84 Stat. 437; Mar. 15, 1976, Pub. L. 94–233, §8, 90 Stat. 232, related to apprehension of released youth offenders.

Section 5021, added act Sept. 30, 1950, ch. 1115, §2, 64 Stat. 1089; amended Oct. 3, 1961, Pub. L. 87–336, 75 Stat. 750; Mar. 15, 1976, Pub. L. 94–233, §9, 90 Stat. 232, related to issuance of certificates setting aside convictions of youth offenders.

Section 5022, added act Sept. 30, 1950, ch. 1115, §2, 64 Stat. 1089, provided that this chapter would not apply to offenses committed before its enactment (Sept. 30, 1950).

Section 5023, added act Sept. 30, 1950, ch. 1115, §2, 64 Stat. 1089; amended Apr. 8, 1952, ch. 163, §1, 66 Stat. 45, related to relationship between this chapter and Probation and Juvenile Delinquency Acts.

Section 5024, added act Sept. 30, 1950, ch. 1115, §2, 64 Stat. 1089; amended Apr. 8, 1952, ch. 163, §2, 66 Stat. 45; June 25, 1959, Pub. L. 86–70, §17(a), 73 Stat. 144; July 12, 1960, Pub. L. 86–624, §13(b), 74 Stat. 413; Dec. 27, 1967, Pub. L. 90–226, title VIII, §801(a), 81 Stat. 741, provided that this chapter was applicable to States of the United States and to District of Columbia.

Section 5025, added act Apr. 8, 1952, ch. 163, §3(a), 66 Stat. 46; amended Dec. 27, 1967, Pub. L. 90–226, title VIII, §801(b), 81 Stat. 741, related to applicability of this chapter to District of Columbia.

Section 5026, added act Apr. 8, 1952, ch. 163, §3(a), 66 Stat. 46, provided that this chapter did not affect parole of other offenders.

Effective Date of Repeal

Repeal effective Oct. 12, 1984, with sections 5017 to 5020 to remain in effect for five years as to an individual who committed an offense or an act of juvenile delinquency before Nov. 1, 1987, and as to a term of imprisonment during the period described in section 235(a)(1)(B) of Pub. L. 98–473, see section 235(a)(1)(A), (b)(1)(E) of Pub. L. 98–473, set out as an Effective Date note under section 3551 of this title.

CHAPTER 403 - JUVENILE DELINQUENCY

Amendments

1990—Pub. L. 101–647, title XXXV, §3599H, Nov. 29, 1990, 104 Stat. 4932, substituted "probation" for "Probation" in item 5042.

1984—Pub. L. 98–473, title II, §214(d), Oct. 12, 1984, 98 Stat. 2014, substituted "Repealed" for "Parole" in item 5041, and "Revocation of Probation" for "Revocation of parole or probation" in item 5042.

1974—Pub. L. 93–415, title V, §513, Sept. 7, 1974, 88 Stat. 1138, substituted "Delinquency proceedings in district courts; transfer for criminal prosecution." for "Proceeding against juvenile delinquent." in item 5032; "Custody prior to appearance before magistrate." for "Jurisdiction; written consent; jury trial precluded." in item 5033; "Duties of magistrate." for "Probation; commitment to custody of Attorney General; support." in item 5034; "Detention prior to disposition." for "Arrest, detention and bail." in item 5035; "Speedy trial." for "Contracts for support; payment." in item 5036; "Dispositional hearing." for "Parole." in item 5037; and added items 5038 to 5042.

Change of Name

Words "magistrate judge" substituted for "magistrate" in items 5033 and 5034 pursuant to section 321 of Pub. L. 101–650, set out as a note under section 631 of Title 28, Judiciary and Judicial Procedure.

§5031. Definitions

For the purposes of this chapter, a "juvenile" is a person who has not attained his eighteenth birthday, or for the purpose of proceedings and disposition under this chapter for an alleged act of juvenile delinquency, a person who has not attained his twenty-first birthday, and "juvenile delinquency" is the violation of a law of the United States committed by a person prior to his eighteenth birthday which would have been a crime if committed by an adult or a violation by such a person of section 922(x).

(June 25, 1948, ch. 645, 62 Stat. 857; Pub. L. 93–415, title V, §501, Sept. 7, 1974, 88 Stat. 1133; Pub. L. 103–322, title XI, §110201(c)(1), Sept. 13, 1994, 108 Stat. 2012.)

Historical and Revision Notes

Based on title 18, U.S.C., 1940 ed., §921 (June 16, 1938, ch. 486, §1, 52 Stat. 764).

The phrase "who has not attained his eighteenth birthday" was substituted for "seventeen years of age or under" as more clearly reflecting congressional intent and administrative construction. The necessity of a definite fixing of the age of the juvenile was emphasized by Hon. Arthur J. Tuttle, United States district judge, Detroit, Mich., in a letter to the Committee on Revision of the Laws dated June 24, 1944. Words "an offense against the" was changed to "the violation of a" without change of substance.

Minor change was made in translation of section references to "this chapter".

Codification

Another section 501 of title V of Pub. L. 93–415, as added by Pub. L. 107–273, div. C, title II, §12222(a), Nov. 2, 2002, 116 Stat. 1894, is set out as a note under section 10101 of Title 34, Crime Control and Law Enforcement.

Another section 501 of title V of Pub. L. 93–415, as added by Pub. L. 102–586, §5(a), Nov. 4, 1992, 106 Stat. 5027, was set out as a note under section 5601 of Title 42, The Public Health and Welfare, prior to the general amendment of that title V by Pub. L. 107–273.

Amendments

1994—Pub. L. 103–322 inserted before period at end "or a violation by such a person of section 922(x)".

1974—Pub. L. 93–415 amended section generally, inserting "or for the purpose of proceedings and disposition under this chapter for an alleged act of juvenile delinquency, a person who has not attained his twenty-first birthday" after "eighteenth birthday," and substituting "committed by a person prior to his eighteenth birthday which would have been a crime if committed by an adult", for "committed by a juvenile and not punishable by death or life imprisonment."

§5032. Delinquency proceedings in district courts; transfer for criminal prosecution

A juvenile alleged to have committed an act of juvenile delinquency, other than a violation of law committed within the special maritime and territorial jurisdiction of the United States for which the maximum authorized term of imprisonment does not exceed six months, shall not be proceeded against in any court of the United States unless the Attorney General, after investigation, certifies to the appropriate district court of the United States that (1) the juvenile court or other appropriate court of a State does not have jurisdiction or refuses to assume jurisdiction over said juvenile with respect to such alleged act of juvenile delinquency, (2) the State does not have available programs and services adequate for the needs of juveniles, or (3) the offense charged is a crime of violence that is a felony or an offense described in section 401 of the Controlled Substances Act (21 U.S.C. 841), or section 1002(a), 1003, 1005, 1009, or 1010(b)(1), (2), or (3) of the Controlled Substances Import and Export Act (21 U.S.C. 952(a), 953, 955, 959, 960(b)(1), (2), (3)), section 922(x) or section 924(b), (g), or (h) of this title, and that there is a substantial Federal interest in the case or the offense to warrant the exercise of Federal jurisdiction.

If the Attorney General does not so certify, such juvenile shall be surrendered to the appropriate legal authorities of such State. For purposes of this section, the term "State" includes a State of the United States, the District of Columbia, and any commonwealth, territory, or possession of the United States.

If an alleged juvenile delinquent is not surrendered to the authorities of a State pursuant to this section, any proceedings against him shall be in an appropriate district court of the United States. For such purposes, the court may be convened at any time and place within the district, in chambers or otherwise. The Attorney General shall proceed by information or as authorized under section 3401(g) of this title, and no criminal prosecution shall be instituted for the alleged act of juvenile delinquency except as provided below.

A juvenile who is alleged to have committed an act of juvenile delinquency and who is not surrendered to State authorities shall be proceeded against under this chapter unless he has requested in writing upon advice of counsel to be proceeded against as an adult, except that, with respect to a juvenile fifteen years and older alleged to have committed an act after his fifteenth birthday which if committed by an adult would be a felony that is a crime of violence or an offense described in section 401 of the Controlled Substances Act (21 U.S.C. 841), or section 1002(a), 1005, or 1009 of the Controlled Substances Import and Export Act (21 U.S.C. 952(a), 955, 959), or section 922(x) of this title, or in section 924(b), (g), or (h) of this title, criminal prosecution on the basis of the alleged act may be begun by motion to transfer of the Attorney General in the appropriate district court of the United States, if such court finds, after hearing, such transfer would be in the interest of justice. In the application of the preceding sentence, if the crime of violence is an offense under section 113(a), 113(b), 113(c), 1111, 1113, or, if the juvenile possessed a firearm during the offense, section 2111, 2113, 2241(a), or 2241(c), "thirteen" shall be substituted for "fifteen" and "thirteenth" shall be substituted for "fifteenth". Notwithstanding sections 1152 and 1153, no person subject to the criminal jurisdiction of an Indian tribal government shall be subject to the preceding sentence for any offense the Federal jurisdiction for which is predicated solely on Indian country (as defined in section 1151), and which has occurred within the boundaries of such Indian country, unless the governing body of the tribe has elected that the preceding sentence have effect over land and persons subject to its criminal jurisdiction. However, a juvenile who is alleged to have committed an act after his sixteenth birthday which if committed by an adult would be a felony offense that has as an element thereof the use, attempted use, or threatened use of physical force against the person of another, or that, by its very nature, involves a substantial risk that physical force against the person of another may be used in committing the offense, or would be an offense described in section 32, 81, 844(d), (e), (f), (h), (i) or 2275 of this title, subsection (b)(1)(A), (B), or (C), (d), or (e) of section 401 of the Controlled Substances Act, or section 1002(a), 1003, 1009, or 1010(b)(1), (2), or (3) of the Controlled Substances Import and Export Act (21 U.S.C. 952(a), 953, 959, 960(b)(1), (2), (3)), and who has previously been found guilty of an act which if committed by an adult would have been one of the offenses set forth in this paragraph or an offense in violation of a State felony statute that would have been such an offense if a circumstance giving rise to Federal jurisdiction had existed, shall be transferred to the appropriate district court of the United States for criminal prosecution.

Evidence of the following factors shall be considered, and findings with regard to each factor shall be made in the record, in assessing whether a transfer would be in the interest of justice: the age and social background of the juvenile; the nature of the alleged offense; the extent and nature of the juvenile's prior delinquency record; the juvenile's present intellectual development and psychological maturity; the nature of past treatment efforts and the juvenile's response to such efforts; the availability of programs designed to treat the juvenile's behavioral problems. In considering the nature of the offense, as required by this paragraph, the court shall consider the extent to which the juvenile played a leadership role in an organization, or otherwise influenced other persons to take part in criminal activities, involving the use or distribution of controlled substances or firearms. Such a factor, if found to exist, shall weigh in favor of a transfer to adult status, but the absence of this factor shall not preclude such a transfer.

Reasonable notice of the transfer hearing shall be given to the juvenile, his parents, guardian, or custodian and to his counsel. The juvenile shall be assisted by counsel during the transfer hearing, and at every other critical stage of the proceedings.

Once a juvenile has entered a plea of guilty or the proceeding has reached the stage that evidence has begun to be taken with respect to a crime or an alleged act of juvenile delinquency subsequent criminal prosecution or juvenile proceedings based upon such alleged act of delinquency shall be barred.

Statements made by a juvenile prior to or during a transfer hearing under this section shall not be admissible at subsequent criminal prosecutions.

Whenever a juvenile transferred to district court under this section is not convicted of the crime upon which the transfer was based or another crime which would have warranted transfer had the juvenile been initially charged with that crime, further proceedings concerning the juvenile shall be conducted pursuant to the provisions of this chapter.

A juvenile shall not be transferred to adult prosecution nor shall a hearing be held under section 5037 (disposition after a finding of juvenile delinquency) until any prior juvenile court records of such juvenile have been received by the court, or the clerk of the juvenile court has certified in writing that the juvenile has no prior record, or that the juvenile's record is unavailable and why it is unavailable.

Whenever a juvenile is adjudged delinquent pursuant to the provisions of this chapter, the specific acts which the juvenile has been found to have committed shall be described as part of the official record of the proceedings and part of the juvenile's official record.

(June 25, 1948, ch. 645, 62 Stat. 857; Pub. L. 93–415, title V, §502, Sept. 7, 1974, 88 Stat. 1134; Pub. L. 98–473, title II, §1201, Oct. 12, 1984, 98 Stat. 2149; Pub. L. 100–690, title VI, §6467(a), Nov. 18, 1988, 102 Stat. 4375; Pub. L. 101–647, title XII, §1205(n), title XXXV, §3599G, Nov. 29, 1990, 104 Stat. 4831, 4932; Pub. L. 103–322, title XI, §110201(c)(2), title XIV, §§140001, 140002, title XV, §150002, Sept. 13, 1994, 108 Stat. 2012, 2031, 2035; Pub. L. 104–294, title VI, §601(c)(1), (g)(1), Oct. 11, 1996, 110 Stat. 3499, 3500.)

Historical and Revision Notes

Based on title 18, U.S.C., 1940 ed., §922 (June 16, 1938, ch. 486, §2, 52 Stat. 765).

The final sentence of said section 922 of title 18, U.S.C., 1940 ed., was incorporated in section 5033 of this title.

Changes were made in arrangement and phraseology.

Codification

Another section 502 of title V of Pub. L. 93–415, as added by Pub. L. 107–273, div. C, title II, §12222(a), Nov. 2, 2002, 116 Stat. 1894, is classified to section 11311 of Title 34, Crime Control and Law Enforcement.

Another section 502 of title V of Pub. L. 93–415, as added by Pub. L. 102–586, §5(a), Nov. 4, 1992, 106 Stat. 5027, was classified to section 5781 of Title 42, The Public Health and Welfare, prior to the general amendment of that title V by Pub. L. 107–273.

Amendments

1996—Pub. L. 104–294, in first par., inserted "section 922(x)" before "or section 924(b)" and struck out "or (x)" after "or (h)", and in third par., inserted "or as authorized under section 3401(g) of this title" after "shall proceed by information".

1994—Pub. L. 103–322, §150002(1), substituted "924(b), (g), or (h)" for "922(p)" in first par.

Pub. L. 103–322, §110201(c)(2)(A), inserted "or (x)" after "922(p)" in first par.

Pub. L. 103–322, §140001, in fourth par., substituted ". In the application of the preceding sentence, if the crime of violence is an offense under section 113(a), 113(b), 113(c), 1111, 1113, or, if the juvenile possessed a firearm during the offense, section 2111, 2113, 2241(a), or 2241(c), 'thirteen' shall be substituted for 'fifteen' and 'thirteenth' shall be substituted for 'fifteenth'. Notwithstanding sections 1152 and 1153, no person subject to the criminal jurisdiction of an Indian tribal government shall be subject to the preceding sentence for any offense the Federal jurisdiction for which is predicated solely on Indian country (as defined in section 1151), and which has occurred within the boundaries of such Indian country, unless the governing body of the tribe has elected that the preceding sentence have effect over land and persons subject to its criminal jurisdiction. However" for "; however".

Pub. L. 103–322, §§110201(c)(2)(B), 150002(2), inserted "or section 922(x) of this title, or in section 924(b), (g), or (h) of this title," before "criminal prosecution on the basis" in fourth par.

Pub. L. 103–322, §150002(3), inserted at end of fifth par. "In considering the nature of the offense, as required by this paragraph, the court shall consider the extent to which the juvenile played a leadership role in an organization, or otherwise influenced other persons to take part in criminal activities, involving the use or distribution of controlled substances or firearms. Such a factor, if found to exist, shall weigh in favor of a transfer to adult status, but the absence of this factor shall not preclude such a transfer."

Pub. L. 103–322, §140002, substituted "A juvenile shall not be transferred to adult prosecution nor shall a hearing be held under section 5037 (disposition after a finding of juvenile delinquency) until" for "Any proceedings against a juvenile under this chapter or as an adult shall not be commenced until" in tenth par.

1990—Pub. L. 101–647 inserted definition of "State" at end of second par., struck out "or the District of Columbia" after "to the authorities of a State" in third par., and substituted "offenses set forth in this paragraph" for "offenses set forth in this subsection" in fourth par.

1988—Pub. L. 100–690, §6467(a)(1), substituted "section 401 of the Controlled Substances Act (21 U.S.C. 841), or section 1002(a), 1003, 1005, 1009, or 1010(b)(1), (2), or (3) of the Controlled Substances Import and Export Act (21 U.S.C. 952(a), 953, 955, 959, 960(b)(1), (2), (3)), or section 922(p) of this title," for "section 841, 952(a), 955, or 959 of title 21," in first par.

Pub. L. 100–690, §6467(a)(2), substituted "section 401 of the Controlled Substances Act (21 U.S.C. 841), or section 1002(a), 1005, or 1009 of the Controlled Substances Import and Export Act (21 U.S.C. 952(a), 955, 959)," for "section 841, 952(a), 955, or 959 of title 21," and inserted "subsection (b)(1)(A), (B), or (C), (d), or (e) of section 401 of the Controlled Substances Act, or section 1002(a), 1003, 1009, or 1010(b)(1), (2), or (3) of the Controlled Substances Import and Export Act (21 U.S.C. 952(a), 953, 959, 960(b)(1), (2), (3))," after "2275 of this title," in fourth par.

1984—Pub. L. 98–473, §1201(a), amended first par. generally, inserting ", other than a violation of law committed within the special maritime and territorial jurisdiction of the United States for which the maximum authorized term of imprisonment does not exceed six months," before "shall not be proceeded", inserting "(1)" before "the juvenile court", striking out "(1)" before "does not have", inserting "the State" after "(2)", and inserting ", or (3) the offense charged is a crime of violence that is a felony, or an offense described in section 841, 952(a), 955, or 959 of title 21, and that there is a substantial Federal interest in the case or the offense to warrant the exercise of Federal jurisdiction."

Pub. L. 98–473, §1201(b)(1), which directed the amendment of fourth par. by substituting "that is a crime of violence or an offense described in section 841, 952(a), 955, or 959 of title 21" for "punishable by a maximum penalty of ten years imprisonment or more, life imprisonment or death" was executed by substituting the quoted wording for "punishable by a maximum penalty of ten years imprisonment or more, life imprisonment, or death" as the probable intent of Congress.

Pub. L. 98–473, §1201(b)(2), substituted "fifteen" for "sixteen" and "fifteenth" for "sixteenth" in fourth par.

Pub. L. 98–473, §1201(b)(3), inserted provision at end of fourth par., relating to transfer of a juvenile who is alleged to have committed certain acts after his sixteenth birthday to the appropriate district court of the United States for criminal prosecution.

Pub. L. 98–473, §1201(c), added three pars. at end of section relating to juveniles not convicted of crimes in district court, reception of prior juveniles court records by the court, and description of the specific act of delinquency for the record.

1974—Pub. L. 93–415 amended section generally, substituting "Delinquency proceedings in district courts; transfer for criminal prosecution", for "Proceedings against juvenile delinquent" in section catchline, inserting provisions relating to certification to, and procedures in, district courts, transfer upon motion by Attorney General with respect to a juvenile sixteen years and older, factors considered in transfer, notice of transfer, barring of subsequent criminal or juvenile delinquency proceedings upon entering plea of guilty or upon taking of evidence, and admissibility of statements by a juvenile in subsequent criminal prosecution, and substituting provision relating to consent upon advice of counsel for treatment as an adult, for provision requiring consent for treatment as a juvenile.

§5033. Custody prior to appearance before magistrate judge

Whenever a juvenile is taken into custody for an alleged act of juvenile delinquency, the arresting officer shall immediately advise such juvenile of his legal rights, in language comprehensive to a juvenile, and shall immediately notify the Attorney General and the juvenile's parents, guardian, or custodian of such custody. The arresting officer shall also notify the parents, guardian, or custodian of the rights of the juvenile and of the nature of the alleged offense.

The juvenile shall be taken before a magistrate judge forthwith. In no event shall the juvenile be detained for longer than a reasonable period of time before being brought before a magistrate judge.

(June 25, 1948, ch. 645, 62 Stat. 857; Pub. L. 93–415, title V, §503, Sept. 7, 1974, 88 Stat. 1135; Pub. L. 101–650, title III, §321, Dec. 1, 1990, 104 Stat. 5117.)

Historical and Revision Notes

Based on title 18, U.S.C., 1940 ed., §§922, 923 (June 16, 1938, ch. 486, §§2, 3, 52 Stat. 765). This section consolidates said section 923, and the final sentence of said section 922, of title 18, U.S.C., 1940 ed., with such changes of phraseology as were necessary to effect the consolidation. This revised section and section 5032 of this title were rewritten to make clear the legislative intent that a juvenile delinquency proceeding shall result in the adjudication of a status rather than the conviction of a crime.

The other provisions of said section 922 are incorporated in section 5032 of this title.

Codification

Another section 503 of title V of Pub. L. 93–415, as added by Pub. L. 107–273, div. C, title II, §12222(a), Nov. 2, 2002, 116 Stat. 1894, is classified to section 11312 of Title 34, Crime Control and Law Enforcement.

Another section 503 of title V of Pub. L. 93–415, as added by Pub. L. 102–586, §5(a), Nov. 4, 1992, 106 Stat. 5027, was classified to section 5782 of Title 42, The Public Health and Welfare, prior to the general amendment of that title V by Pub. L. 107–273.

Amendments

1974—Pub. L. 93–415 amended section generally, substituting "Custody prior to appearance before magistrate", for "Jurisdiction; written consent; jury trial precluded" in section catchline, and substituting provisions relating to advice of rights by arresting officer, notification of Attorney General, parents, guardian or custodian, and appearance before magistrate, for provisions relating to jurisdiction of district courts, jury, consent by juvenile, and apprisal of rights by Judge of District Court.

Change of Name

Words "magistrate judge" substituted for "magistrate" in catchline and wherever appearing in text pursuant to section 321 of Pub. L. 101–650, set out as a note under section 631 of Title 28, Judiciary and Judicial Procedure.

§5034. Duties of magistrate judge

The magistrate judge shall insure that the juvenile is represented by counsel before proceeding with critical stages of the proceedings. Counsel shall be assigned to represent a juvenile when the juvenile and his parents, guardian, or custodian are financially unable to obtain adequate representation. In cases where the juvenile and his parents, guardian, or custodian are financially able to obtain adequate representation but have not retained counsel, the magistrate judge may assign counsel and order the payment of reasonable attorney's fees or may direct the juvenile, his parents, guardian, or custodian to retain private counsel within a specified period of time.

The magistrate judge may appoint a guardian ad litem if a parent or guardian of the juvenile is not present, or if the magistrate judge has reason to believe that the parents or guardian will not cooperate with the juvenile in preparing for trial, or that the interests of the parents or guardian and those of the juvenile are adverse.

If the juvenile has not been discharged before his initial appearance before the magistrate judge, the magistrate judge shall release the juvenile to his parents, guardian, custodian, or other responsible party (including, but not limited to, the director of a shelter-care facility) upon their promise to bring such juvenile before the appropriate court when requested by such court unless the magistrate judge determines, after hearing, at which the juvenile is represented by counsel, that the detention of such juvenile is required to secure his timely appearance before the appropriate court or to insure his safety or that of others.

(June 25, 1948, ch. 645, 62 Stat. 858; Pub. L. 87–428, Mar. 31, 1962, 76 Stat. 52; Pub. L. 93–415, title V, §504, Sept. 7, 1974, 88 Stat. 1135; Pub. L. 100–690, title VII, §7045, Nov. 18, 1988, 102 Stat. 4400; Pub. L. 101–650, title III, §321, Dec. 1, 1990, 104 Stat. 5117.)

Historical and Revision Notes

Based on title 18, U.S.C., 1940 ed., §924 (June 16, 1938, ch. 486, §4, 52 Stat. 765).

The words "foster homes" were inserted to remove any doubt as to the authority to commit to such foster homes in accordance with past and present administrative practice.

The reference to particular sections dealing with probation was omitted as unnecessary.

Changes were made in phraseology and arrangement.

Codification

Another section 504 of title V of Pub. L. 93–415, as added by Pub. L. 107–273, div. C, title II, §12222(a), Nov. 2, 2002, 116 Stat. 1895, is classified to section 11313 of Title 34, Crime Control and Law Enforcement.

Another section 504 of title V of Pub. L. 93–415, as added by Pub. L. 102–586, §5(a), Nov. 4, 1992, 106 Stat. 5027, was classified to section 5783 of Title 42, The Public Health and Welfare, prior to the general amendment of that title V by Pub. L. 107–273.

Amendments

1988—Pub. L. 100–690 substituted "facility) upon" for "facility upon" in last par.

1974—Pub. L. 93–415 amended section generally, substituting "Duties of magistrate", for "Probation; commitment to custody of Attorney General; support" in section catchline, and substituting provisions relating to procedure before, and duties of, magistrate, for provisions relating to probation, commitment to custody of Attorney General, duties of Attorney General, and procedures aiding court in determining whether to place juvenile on probation or commit him to custody of Attorney General.

1962—Pub. L. 87–428 added fourth par. authorizing commitment of a juvenile delinquent to the custody of the Attorney General for observation and study.

Change of Name

Words "magistrate judge" substituted for "magistrate" in catchline and wherever appearing in text pursuant to section 321 of Pub. L. 101–650, set out as a note under section 631 of Title 28, Judiciary and Judicial Procedure.

§5035. Detention prior to disposition

A juvenile alleged to be delinquent may be detained only in a juvenile facility or such other suitable place as the Attorney General may designate. Whenever possible, detention shall be in a foster home or community based facility located in or near his home community. The Attorney General shall not cause any juvenile alleged to be delinquent to be detained or confined in any institution in which the juvenile has regular contact with adult persons convicted of a crime or awaiting trial on criminal charges. Insofar as possible, alleged delinquents shall be kept separate from adjudicated delinquents. Every juvenile in custody shall be provided with adequate food, heat, light, sanitary facilities, bedding, clothing, recreation, education, and medical care, including necessary psychiatric, psychological, or other care and treatment.

(June 25, 1948, ch. 645, 62 Stat. 858; Pub. L. 93–415, title V, §505, Sept. 7, 1974, 88 Stat. 1135.)

Historical and Revision Notes

Based on title 18, U.S.C., 1940 ed., §925 (June 16, 1938, ch. 486, §5, 52, Stat. 765).
Minor changes were made in arrangement and phraseology.

Codification

Another section 505 of Pub. L. 93–415, as added by Pub. L. 107–273, div. C, title II, §12222(a), Nov. 2, 2002, 116 Stat. 1896, was classified to section 5784 of Title 42, The Public Health and Welfare, prior to being omitted from the Code.

Another section 505 of title V of Pub. L. 93–415, as added by Pub. L. 102–586, §5(a), Nov. 4, 1992, 106 Stat. 5028, was classified to section 5784 of Title 42, The Public Health and Welfare, prior to the general amendment of that title V by Pub. L. 107–273.

Amendments

1974—Pub. L. 93–415 amended section generally, substituting "Detention prior to disposition", for "Arrest, detention and bail" in section catchline, striking out provisions relating to discretionary power of arresting officer or marshal to confine juvenile in jail, provisions relating to bail and default of bail, and inserting provisions relating to mandatory separation of juvenile from adjudicated delinquents, and provisions relating to the physical conditions of confining facility.

§5036. Speedy trial

If an alleged delinquent who is in detention pending trial is not brought to trial within thirty days from the date upon which such detention was begun, the information shall be dismissed on motion of the alleged delinquent or at the direction of the court, unless the Attorney General shows that additional delay was caused by the juvenile or his counsel, or consented to by the juvenile and his counsel, or would be in the interest of justice in the particular case. Delays attributable solely to court calendar congestion may not be considered in the interest of justice. Except in extraordinary circumstances, an information dismissed under this section may not be reinstituted.

(June 25, 1948, ch. 645, 62 Stat. 858; Pub. L. 93–415, title V, §506, Sept. 7, 1974, 88 Stat. 1136.)

Historical and Revision Notes

Based on title 18, U.S.C., 1940 ed., §926 (June 16, 1938, ch. 486, §6, 52 Stat. 766).
The words "foster homes" were inserted to remove any doubt as to the authority to commit to such foster homes in accordance with past and present administrative practice.

Codification

Another section 506 of title V of Pub. L. 93–415, as added by Pub. L. 102–586, §5(a), Nov. 4, 1992, 106 Stat. 5029, was classified to section 5785 of Title 42, The Public Health and Welfare, prior to the general amendment of that title V by Pub. L. 107–273.

Amendments

1974—Pub. L. 93–415 amended section generally, substituting "Speedy trial" for "Contracts for support; payment" in section catchline, and substituting provisions relating to dismissal of information due to delay, for provisions relating to contracts with public or private agencies for custody and care of juvenile delinquents.

§5037. Dispositional hearing

(a) If the court finds a juvenile to be a juvenile delinquent, the court shall hold a disposition hearing concerning the appropriate disposition no later than twenty court days after the juvenile delinquency hearing unless the court has ordered further study pursuant to subsection (d). After the disposition hearing, and after considering any pertinent policy statements promulgated by the Sentencing Commission pursuant to 28 U.S.C. 994, the court may suspend the findings of juvenile delinquency, place him on probation, or commit him to official detention which may include a term of juvenile delinquent supervision to follow detention. In addition, the court may enter an order of restitution pursuant to section 3556. With respect to release or detention pending an appeal or a petition for a writ of certiorari after disposition, the court shall proceed pursuant to the provisions of chapter 207.

(b) The term for which probation may be ordered for a juvenile found to be a juvenile delinquent may not extend—

(1) in the case of a juvenile who is less than eighteen years old, beyond the lesser of—

(A) the date when the juvenile becomes twenty-one years old; or

(B) the maximum term that would be authorized by section 3561(c) if the juvenile had been tried and convicted as an adult; or

(2) in the case of a juvenile who is between eighteen and twenty-one years old, beyond the lesser of—

(A) three years; or

(B) the maximum term that would be authorized by section 3561(c) if the juvenile had been tried and convicted as an adult.

The provisions dealing with probation set forth in sections 3563 and 3564 are applicable to an order placing a juvenile on probation. If the juvenile violates a condition of probation at any time prior to the expiration or termination of the term of probation, the court may, after a dispositional hearing and after considering any pertinent policy statements promulgated by the Sentencing Commission pursuant to section 994 of title 28, revoke the term of probation and order a term of official detention. The term of official detention authorized upon revocation of probation shall not exceed the terms authorized in section 5037(c)(2)(A) and (B). The application of sections 5037(c)(2)(A) and (B) shall be determined based upon the age of the juvenile at the time of the disposition of the revocation proceeding. If a juvenile is over the age of 21 years old at the time of the revocation proceeding, the mandatory revocation provisions of section 3565(b) are applicable. A disposition of a juvenile who is over the age of 21 years shall be in accordance with the provisions of section 5037(c)(2), except that in the case of a juvenile who if convicted as an adult would be convicted of a Class A, B, or C felony, no term of official detention may continue beyond the juvenile's 26th birthday, and in any other case, no term of official detention may continue beyond the juvenile's 24th birthday. A term of official detention may include a term of juvenile delinquent supervision.

(c) The term for which official detention may be ordered for a juvenile found to be a juvenile delinquent may not extend—

(1) in the case of a juvenile who is less than eighteen years old, beyond the lesser of—

(A) the date when the juvenile becomes twenty-one years old;

(B) the maximum of the guideline range, pursuant to section 994 of title 28, applicable to an otherwise similarly situated adult defendant unless the court finds an aggravating factor to warrant an upward departure from the otherwise applicable guideline range; or

(C) the maximum term of imprisonment that would be authorized if the juvenile had been tried and convicted as an adult; or

(2) in the case of a juvenile who is between eighteen and twenty-one years old—

(A) who if convicted as an adult would be convicted of a Class A, B, or C felony, beyond the lesser of—

(i) five years; or

(ii) the maximum of the guideline range, pursuant to section 994 of title 28, applicable to an otherwise similarly situated adult defendant unless the court finds an aggravating factor to warrant an upward departure from the otherwise applicable guideline range; or

(B) in any other case beyond the lesser of—

(i) three years;

(ii) the maximum of the guideline range, pursuant to section 994 of title 28, applicable to an otherwise similarly situated adult defendant unless the court finds an aggravating factor to warrant an upward departure from the otherwise applicable guideline range; or

(iii) the maximum term of imprisonment that would be authorized if the juvenile had been tried and convicted as an adult.

Section 3624 is applicable to an order placing a juvenile under detention.

(d)(1) The court, in ordering a term of official detention, may include the requirement that the juvenile be placed on a term of juvenile delinquent supervision after official detention.

(2) The term of juvenile delinquent supervision that may be ordered for a juvenile found to be a juvenile delinquent may not extend—

(A) in the case of a juvenile who is less than 18 years old, a term that extends beyond the date when the juvenile becomes 21 years old; or

(B) in the case of a juvenile who is between 18 and 21 years old, a term that extends beyond the maximum term of official detention set forth in section 5037(c)(2)(A) and (B), less the term of official detention ordered.

(3) The provisions dealing with probation set forth in sections 3563 and 3564 are applicable to an order placing a juvenile on juvenile delinquent supervision.

(4) The court may modify, reduce, or enlarge the conditions of juvenile delinquent supervision at any time prior to the expiration or termination of the term of supervision after a dispositional hearing and after consideration of the provisions of section 3563 regarding the initial setting of the conditions of probation.

(5) If the juvenile violates a condition of juvenile delinquent supervision at any time prior to the expiration or termination of the term of supervision, the court may, after a dispositional hearing and after considering any pertinent policy statements promulgated by the Sentencing Commission pursuant to section 994 of title 18,1 revoke the term of supervision and order a term of official detention. The term of official detention which is authorized upon revocation of juvenile delinquent supervision shall not exceed the term authorized in section 5037(c)(2)(A) and (B), less any term of official detention previously ordered. The application of sections 5037(c)(2)(A) and (B) shall be determined based upon the age of the juvenile at the time of the disposition of the revocation proceeding. If a juvenile is over the age of 21 years old at the time of the revocation proceeding, the mandatory revocation provisions of section 3565(b) are applicable. A disposition of a juvenile who is over the age of 21 years old shall be in accordance with the provisions of section 5037(c)(2), except that in the case of a juvenile who if convicted as an adult would be convicted of a Class A, B, or C felony, no term of official detention may continue beyond the juvenile's 26th birthday, and in any other case, no term of official detention may continue beyond the juvenile's 24th birthday.

(6) When a term of juvenile delinquent supervision is revoked and the juvenile is committed to official detention, the court may include a requirement that the juvenile be placed on a term of juvenile delinquent supervision. Any term of juvenile delinquent supervision ordered following revocation for a juvenile who is over the age of 21 years old at the time of the revocation proceeding shall be in accordance with the provisions of section 5037(d)(1), except that in the case of a juvenile who if convicted as an adult would be convicted of a Class A, B, or C felony, no term of juvenile delinquent supervision may continue beyond the juvenile's 26th birthday, and in any other case, no term of juvenile delinquent supervision may continue beyond the juvenile's 24th birthday.

(e) If the court desires more detailed information concerning an alleged or adjudicated delinquent, it may commit him, after notice and hearing at which the juvenile is represented by counsel, to the custody of the Attorney General for observation and study by an appropriate agency. Such observation and study shall be conducted on an out-patient basis, unless the court determines that inpatient observation and study are necessary to obtain the desired information. In the case of an alleged juvenile delinquent, inpatient study may be ordered only with the consent of the juvenile and his attorney. The agency shall make a complete study of the alleged or adjudicated delinquent to ascertain his personal traits, his capabilities, his background, any previous delinquency or criminal experience, any mental or physical defect, and any other relevant factors. The Attorney General shall submit to the court and the attorneys for the juvenile and the Government the results of the study within thirty days after the commitment of the juvenile, unless the court grants additional time.

(June 25, 1948, ch. 645, 62 Stat. 858; Pub. L. 93–415, title V, §507, Sept. 7, 1974, 88 Stat. 1136; Pub. L. 98–473, title II, §214(a), Oct. 12, 1984, 98 Stat. 2013; Pub. L. 99–646, §21(a), Nov. 10, 1986, 100 Stat. 3596; Pub. L. 104–294, title VI, §604(b)(40), Oct. 11, 1996, 110 Stat. 3509; Pub. L. 107–273, div. C, title II, §12301, Nov. 2, 2002, 116 Stat. 1896.)

Historical and Revision Notes

Based on title 18, U.S.C., 1940 ed., §927 (June 16, 1938, ch. 486, §7, 52 Stat. 766).
Reference to section establishing the Board of Parole was omitted as unnecessary.
Minor changes were made in phraseology.

Amendments

2002—Subsec. (a). Pub. L. 107–273, §12301(1), in second sentence, struck out "enter an order of restitution pursuant to section 3556," after "findings of juvenile delinquency," and inserted "which may include a term of juvenile delinquent supervision to follow detention" after "official detention", and inserted after second sentence "In addition, the court may enter an order of restitution pursuant to section 3556."
Subsec. (b). Pub. L. 107–273, §12301(2), added concluding provisions and struck out former concluding provisions which read as follows: "The provisions dealing with probation set forth in sections 3563, 3564, and 3565 are applicable to an order placing a juvenile on probation."
Subsec. (c)(1)(B), (C). Pub. L. 107–273, §12301(3), added subpar. (B) and redesignated former subpar. (B) as (C).
Subsec. (c)(2)(A). Pub. L. 107–273, §12301(4), substituted "the lesser of—
"(i) five years; or
"(ii) the maximum of the guideline range, pursuant to section 994 of title 28, applicable to an otherwise similarly situated adult defendant unless the court finds an aggravating factor to warrant an upward departure from the otherwise applicable guideline range; or"
for "five years; or".
Subsec. (c)(2)(B)(ii), (iii). Pub. L. 107–273, §12301(5), added cl. (ii) and redesignated former cl. (ii) as (iii).
Subsecs. (d), (e). Pub. L. 107–273, §12301(6), (7), added subsec. (d) and redesignated former subsec. (d) as (e).
1996—Subsec. (b)(1)(B), (2)(B). Pub. L. 104–294 substituted "section 3561(c)" for "section 3561(b)".
1986—Subsec. (a). Pub. L. 99–646, §21(a)(1), substituted "subsection (d)" for "subsection (e)".
Subsec. (c). Pub. L. 99–646, §21(a)(2)–(4), struck out "by section 3581(b)" after "would be authorized" in pars. (1)(B) and (2)(B)(ii), and inserted provision that section 3624 is applicable to an order placing a juvenile under detention.
1984—Pub. L. 98–473 substituted subsecs. (a) to (c) for former subsecs. (a) and (b) and redesignated former subsec. (c) as (d). Prior to amendment, subsecs. (a) and (b) read as follows:
"(a) If a juvenile is adjudicated delinquent, a separate dispositional hearing shall be held no later than twenty court days after trial unless the court has ordered further study in accordance with

subsection (c). Copies of the presentence report shall be provided to the attorneys for both the juvenile and the Government a reasonable time in advance of the hearing.

"(b) The court may suspend the adjudication of delinquency or the disposition of the delinquent on such conditions as it deems proper, place him on probation, or commit him to the custody of the Attorney General. Probation, commitment, or commitment in accordance with subsection (c) shall not extend beyond the juvenile's twenty-first birthday or the maximum term which could have been imposed on an adult convicted of the same offense, whichever is sooner, unless the juvenile has attained his nineteenth birthday at the time of disposition, in which case probation, commitment, or commitment in accordance with subsection (c) shall not exceed the lesser of two years or the maximum term which could have been imposed on an adult convicted of the same offense."

1974—Pub. L. 93–415 amended section generally, substituting "Dispositional hearing" for "Parole" in section catchline and striking out provisions relating to parole.

Effective Date of 1996 Amendment

Amendment by Pub. L. 104–294 effective Sept. 13, 1994, see section 604(d) of Pub. L. 104–294, set out as a note under section 13 of this title.

Effective Date of 1986 Amendment

Pub. L. 99–646, §21(b), Nov. 10, 1986, 100 Stat. 3597, provided that: "The amendments made by this section [amending this section] shall take effect on the date the amendments made by such section 214 [of Pub. L. 98–473] take effect [Nov. 1, 1987]."

Effective Date of 1984 Amendment

Amendment by Pub. L. 98–473 effective Nov. 1, 1987, and applicable only to offenses committed after the taking effect of such amendment, see section 235(a)(1) of Pub. L. 98–473, set out as an Effective Date note under section 3551 of this title.

§5038. Use of juvenile records

(a) Throughout and upon the completion of the juvenile delinquency proceeding, the records shall be safeguarded from disclosure to unauthorized persons. The records shall be released to the extent necessary to meet the following circumstances:

(1) inquiries received from another court of law;

(2) inquiries from an agency preparing a presentence report for another court;

(3) inquiries from law enforcement agencies where the request for information is related to the investigation of a crime or a position within that agency;

(4) inquiries, in writing, from the director of a treatment agency or the director of a facility to which the juvenile has been committed by the court;

(5) inquiries from an agency considering the person for a position immediately and directly affecting the national security; and

(6) inquiries from any victim of such juvenile delinquency, or if the victim is deceased from the immediate family of such victim, related to the final disposition of such juvenile by the court in accordance with section 5037.

Unless otherwise authorized by this section, information about the juvenile record may not be released when the request for information is related to an application for employment, license, bonding, or any civil right or privilege. Responses to such inquiries shall not be different from responses made about persons who have never been involved in a delinquency proceeding.

(b) District courts exercising jurisdiction over any juvenile shall inform the juvenile, and his parent or guardian, in writing in clear and nontechnical language, of rights relating to his juvenile record.

(c) During the course of any juvenile delinquency proceeding, all information and records relating to the proceeding, which are obtained or prepared in the discharge of an official duty by an employee of the court or an employee of any other governmental agency, shall not be disclosed directly or indirectly to anyone other than the judge, counsel for the juvenile and the Government, or others entitled under this section to receive juvenile records.

(d) Whenever a juvenile is found guilty of committing an act which if committed by an adult would be a felony that is a crime of violence or an offense described in section 401 of the Controlled Substances Act or section 1001(a), 1005, or 1009 of the Controlled Substances Import and Export Act, such juvenile shall be fingerprinted and photographed. Except a juvenile described in subsection (f), fingerprints and photographs of a juvenile who is not prosecuted as an adult shall be made available only in accordance with the provisions of subsection (a) of this section. Fingerprints and photographs of a juvenile who is prosecuted as an adult shall be made available in the manner applicable to adult defendants.

(e) Unless a juvenile who is taken into custody is prosecuted as an adult neither the name nor picture of any juvenile shall be made public in connection with a juvenile delinquency proceeding.

(f) Whenever a juvenile has on two separate occasions been found guilty of committing an act which if committed by an adult would be a felony crime of violence or an offense described in section 401 of the Controlled Substances Act or section 1001(a), 1005, or 1009 of the Controlled Substances Import and Export Act, or whenever a juvenile has been found guilty of committing an act after his 13th birthday which if committed by an adult would be an offense described in the second sentence of the fourth paragraph of section 5032 of this title, the court shall transmit to the Federal Bureau of Investigation the information concerning the adjudications, including name, date of adjudication, court, offenses, and sentence, along with the notation that the matters were juvenile adjudications.

(Added Pub. L. 93–415, title V, §508, Sept. 7, 1974, 88 Stat. 1137; amended Pub. L. 95–115, §8(b), Oct. 3, 1977, 91 Stat. 1060; Pub. L. 98–473, title II, §1202, Oct. 12, 1984, 98 Stat. 2150; Pub. L. 103–322, title XIV, §140005, Sept. 13, 1994, 108 Stat. 2032; Pub. L. 104–294, title VI, §601(f)(16), (o), Oct. 11, 1996, 110 Stat. 3500, 3502.)

References in Text

Section 401 of the Controlled Substances Act, referred to in subsecs. (d) and (f), is classified to section 841 of Title 21, Food and Drugs.

Sections 1001(a), 1005, or 1009 of the Controlled Substances Import and Export Act, referred to in subsecs. (d) and (f), are classified to sections 951(a), 955, and 959, respectively, of Title 21.

Amendments

1996—Subsec. (d). Pub. L. 104–294, §601(f)(16), substituted "section 401 of the Controlled Substances Act or section 1001(a), 1005, or 1009 of the Controlled Substances Import and Export Act" for "section 841, 952(a), 955, or 959 of title 21".

Subsec. (f). Pub. L. 104–294 substituted "section 401 of the Controlled Substances Act or section 1001(a), 1005, or 1009 of the Controlled Substances Import and Export Act" for "section 841, 952(a), 955, or 959 of title 21", "juvenile has been found guilty" for "juvenille has been found guilty", and "the Federal Bureau of Investigation" for "the Federal Bureau of Investigation, Identification Division,".

1994—Subsec. (f). Pub. L. 103–322 inserted "or whenever a juvenille has been found guilty of committing an act after his 13th birthday which if committed by an adult would be an offense described in the second sentence of the fourth paragraph of section 5032 of this title," after "title 21,".

1984—Pub. L. 98–473 amended section generally, striking out in subsec. (a) provisions that, upon completion of any delinquency proceedings the court shall order the entire record and file to be sealed, substituting a new subsec. (d) for a former subsec. (d) which provided that unless a juvenile is prosecuted as an adult neither fingerprints nor photographs shall be taken without the consent of the judge and the juveniles name and picture shall not be made available to any public medium of communication and adding subsecs. (e) and (f).

1977—Subsec. (a)(6). Pub. L. 95–115 added par. (6).

Effective Date of 1977 Amendment

Amendment by Pub. L. 95–115 effective Oct. 1, 1977, see section 263(c) of Pub. L. 93–415, as added by Pub. L. 95–115, formerly set out as a note under section 11101 of Title 34, Crime Control and Law Enforcement.

§5039. Commitment

No juvenile committed, whether pursuant to an adjudication of delinquency or conviction for an offense, to the custody of the Attorney General may be placed or retained in an adult jail or correctional institution in which he has regular contact with adults incarcerated because they have been convicted of a crime or are awaiting trial on criminal charges.

Every juvenile who has been committed shall be provided with adequate food, heat, light, sanitary facilities, bedding, clothing, recreation, counseling, education, training, and medical care including necessary psychiatric, psychological, or other care and treatment.

Whenever possible, the Attorney General shall commit a juvenile to a foster home or community-based facility located in or near his home community.

(Added Pub. L. 93–415, title V, §509, Sept. 7, 1974, 88 Stat. 1138; amended Pub. L. 103–322, title XIV, §140003, Sept. 13, 1994, 108 Stat. 2032.)

Amendments

1994—Pub. L. 103–322 inserted ", whether pursuant to an adjudication of delinquency or conviction for an offense," after "committed" in first par.

§5040. Support

The Attorney General may contract with any public or private agency or individual and such community-based facilities as halfway houses and foster homes for the observation and study and the custody and care of juveniles in his custody. For these purposes, the Attorney General may promulgate such regulations as are necessary and may use the appropriation for "support of United States prisoners" or such other appropriations as he may designate.

(Added Pub. L. 93–415, title V, §510, Sept. 7, 1974, 88 Stat. 1138.)

[§5041. Repealed. Pub. L. 98–473, title II, §214(b), Oct. 12, 1984, 98 Stat. 2014]

Section, added Pub. L. 93–415, title V, §511, Sept. 7, 1974, 88 Stat. 1138; amended Pub. L. 94–233, §11, Mar. 15, 1976, 90 Stat. 233, related to parole for juvenile delinquents.

Effective Date of Repeal

Repeal effective Nov. 1, 1987, and applicable only to offenses committed after the taking effect of such repeal, with section to remain in effect for five years as to an individual who committed an offense or an act of juvenile delinquency before Nov. 1, 1987, and as to a term of imprisonment during the period described in section 235(a)(1)(B) of Pub. L. 98–473, see section 235(a)(1), (b)(1)(D) of Pub. L. 98–473, set out as an Effective Date note under section 3551 of this title.

§5042. Revocation of probation

Any juvenile probationer shall be accorded notice and a hearing with counsel before his probation can be revoked.

(Added Pub. L. 93–415, title V, §512, Sept. 7, 1974, 88 Stat. 1138; amended Pub. L. 98–473, title II, §214(c), Oct. 12, 1984, 98 Stat. 2014.)

Amendments

1984—Pub. L. 98–473 struck out "parole or" before "probation" in section catchline and text, and struck out "parolee or" before "probationer" in text.

Effective Date of 1984 Amendment

Amendment by Pub. L. 98–473 effective Nov. 1, 1987, and applicable only to offenses committed after the taking effect of such amendment, with section as in effect prior to such amendment to remain in effect for five years as and individual who committed an offense or an act of juvenile delinquency before Nov. 1, 1987, and as to a term of imprisonment during the period described in section 235(a)(1)(B) of Pub. L. 98–473, see section 235(a)(1), (b)(1)(D) of Pub. L. 98–473, set out as an Effective Date note under section 3551 of this title.

CHAPTER 601 - IMMUNITY OF WITNESSES

Amendments

1994—Pub. L. 103–322, title XXXIII, §330013(1), Sept. 13, 1994, 108 Stat. 2146, added heading for chapter 601.
1970—Pub. L. 91–452, title II, §201(a), Oct. 15, 1970, 84 Stat. 926, added part V and items 6001 to 6005.

§6001. Definitions

As used in this chapter—
(1) "agency of the United States" means any executive department as defined in section 101 of title 5, United States Code, a military department as defined in section 102 of title 5, United States Code, the Nuclear Regulatory Commission, the Board of Governors of the Federal Reserve System, the China Trade Act registrar appointed under 53 Stat. 1432 (15 U.S.C. sec. 143), the Commodity Futures Trading Commission, the Federal Communications Commission, the Federal Deposit Insurance Corporation, the Federal Maritime Commission, the Federal Power Commission, the Federal Trade Commission, the Surface Transportation Board, the National Labor Relations Board, the National Transportation Safety Board, the Railroad Retirement Board, an arbitration board established under 48 Stat. 1193 (45 U.S.C. sec. 157), the Securities and Exchange Commission, or a board established under 49 Stat. 31 (15 U.S.C. sec. 715d);
(2) "other information" includes any book, paper, document, record, recording, or other material;
(3) "proceeding before an agency of the United States" means any proceeding before such an agency with respect to which it is authorized to issue subpenas and to take testimony or receive other information from witnesses under oath; and
(4) "court of the United States" means any of the following courts: the Supreme Court of the United States, a United States court of appeals, a United States district court established under chapter 5, title 28, United States Code, a United States bankruptcy court established under chapter 6, title 28, United States Code, the District of Columbia Court of Appeals, the Superior Court of the District of Columbia, the District Court of Guam, the District Court of the Virgin Islands, the United States Court of Federal Claims, the Tax Court of the United States, the Court of International Trade, and the Court of Appeals for the Armed Forces.
(Added Pub. L. 91–452, title II, §201(a), Oct. 15, 1970, 84 Stat. 926; amended Pub. L. 95–405, §25, Sept. 30, 1978, 92 Stat. 877; Pub. L. 95–598, title III, §314(l), Nov. 6, 1978, 92 Stat. 2678;

Pub. L. 96–417, title VI, §601(1), Oct. 10, 1980, 94 Stat. 1744; Pub. L. 97–164, title I, §164(1), Apr. 2, 1982, 96 Stat. 50; Pub. L. 102–550, title XV, §1543, Oct. 28, 1992, 106 Stat. 4069; Pub. L. 102–572, title IX, §902(b)(1), Oct. 29, 1992, 106 Stat. 4516; Pub. L. 103–272, §4(d), July 5, 1994, 108 Stat. 1361; Pub. L. 103–322, title XXXIII, §330013(2), (3), Sept. 13, 1994, 108 Stat. 2146; Pub. L. 103–337, div. A, title IX, §924(d)(1)(B), Oct. 5, 1994, 108 Stat. 2832; Pub. L. 104–88, title III, §303(2), Dec. 29, 1995, 109 Stat. 943.)

Amendments

1995—Par. (1). Pub. L. 104–88 substituted "Surface Transportation Board" for "Interstate Commerce Commission".

1994—Pub. L. 103–322, §330013(3), substituted "chapter" for "part" in introductory provisions. Par. (1). Pub. L. 103–322, §330013(2), substituted "Nuclear Regulatory Commission" for "Atomic Energy Commission" and struck out "the Subversive Activities Control Board," after "Securities and Exchange Commission,".

Pub. L. 103–272 struck out "the Civil Aeronautics Board," before "the Commodity Futures".

Par. (4). Pub. L. 103–337 substituted "Court of Appeals for the Armed Forces" for "Court of Military Appeals".

1992—Par. (1). Pub. L. 102–550 inserted "the Board of Governors of the Federal Reserve System," after "the Atomic Energy Commission,".

Par. (4). Pub. L. 102–572 substituted "United States Court of Federal Claims" for "United States Claims Court".

1982—Par. (4). Pub. L. 97–164 substituted "the United States Claims Court" for "the United States Court of Claims, the United States Court of Customs and Patent Appeals".

1980—Par. (4). Pub. L. 96–417 redesignated the Customs Court as the Court of International Trade.

1978—Par. (1). Pub. L. 95–405 inserted "the Commodity Futures Trading Commission," after "Civil Aeronautics Board,".

Par. (4). Pub. L. 95–598 inserted "a United States bankruptcy court established under chapter 6, title 28, United States Code," after "title 28, United States Code,".

Effective Date of 1995 Amendment

Amendment by Pub. L. 104–88 effective Jan. 1, 1996, see section 2 of Pub. L. 104–88, set out as an Effective Date note under section 1301 of Title 49, Transportation.

Effective Date of 1992 Amendment

Amendment by Pub. L. 102–572 effective Oct. 29, 1992, see section 911 of Pub. L. 102–572, set out as a note under section 171 of Title 28, Judiciary and Judicial Procedure.

Effective Date of 1982 Amendment

Amendment by Pub. L. 97–164 effective Oct. 1, 1982, see section 402 of Pub. L. 97–164, set out as a note under section 171 of Title 28, Judiciary and Judicial Procedure.

Effective Date of 1980 Amendment

Amendment by Pub. L. 96–417 effective Nov. 1, 1980, and applicable with respect to civil actions pending on or commenced on or after such date, see section 701(a) of Pub. L. 96–417, set out as a note under section 251 of Title 28, Judiciary and Judicial Procedure.

Effective Date of 1978 Amendments

Amendment by Pub. L. 95–598 effective Oct. 1, 1979, see section 402(a) of Pub. L. 95–598, set out as an Effective Date note preceding section 101 of Title 11, Bankruptcy.

Amendment by Pub. L. 95–405 effective Oct. 1, 1978, see section 28 of Pub. L. 95–405, set out as a note under section 2 of Title 7, Agriculture.

Effective Date; Savings Provision

Pub. L. 91–452, title II, §260, Oct. 15, 1970, 84 Stat. 931, provided that: "The provisions of part V of title 18, United States Code, added by title II of this Act [this part], and the amendments and repeals made by title II of this Act [sections 835, 895, 1406, 1954, 2424, 2514 and 3486 of this title, sections 15, 87f(f), 135c, 499m(f), and 2115 of Title 7, Agriculture, section 25 of former Title 11, Bankruptcy, section 1820 of Title 12, Banks and Banking, sections 32, 33, 49, 77v, 78u(d), 79r(e), 80a–41, 80b–9, 155, 717m, 1271, and 1714 of Title 15, Commerce and Trade, section 825f of Title 16, Conservation, section 1333 of Title 19, Customs Duties, section 373 of Title 21, Food and Drugs, sections 4874 and 7493 of Title 26, Internal Revenue Code, section 161(3) of Title 29, Labor, section 506 of Title 33, Navigation and Navigable waters, sections 405(f) and 2201 of Title 42, The Public Health and Welfare, sections 157 and 362 of Title 45, Railroads, sections 827 and 1124 of former Title 46, Shipping, section 409(l) of Title 47, Telecommunications, sections 9, 43, 46, 47, 48, 916, 1017, and 1484 of former Title 49, Transportation, sections 792 and 4555 of Title 50, War and National Defense, and former sections 643a, 1152, and 2026 of the former Appendix to Title 50], shall take effect on the sixtieth day following the date of the enactment of this Act [Oct. 15, 1970]. No amendment to or repeal of any provision of law under title II of this Act shall affect any immunity to which any individual is entitled under such provision by reason of any testimony or other information given before such day."

Savings Provision

Amendment by section 314 of Pub. L. 95–598 not to affect the application of chapter 9 (§151 et seq.), chapter 96 (§1961 et seq.), or section 2516, 3057, or 3284 of this title to any act of any person (1) committed before Oct. 1, 1979, or (2) committed after Oct. 1, 1979, in connection with a case commenced before such date, see section 403(d) of Pub. L. 95–598, set out as a note preceding section 101 of Title 11, Bankruptcy.

Amendment or Repeal of Inconsistent Provisions

Section 259 of Pub. L. 91–452 provided that: "In addition to the provisions of law specifically amended or specifically repealed by this title [see Effective Date note above], any other provision of law inconsistent with the provisions of part V of title 18, United States Code (adding by title II of this Act) [this part], is to that extent amended or repealed."

Termination of Federal Power Commission

The Federal Power Commission, referred to in par. (1) was terminated and the functions, personnel, property, funds, etc., thereof were transferred to the Secretary of Energy (except for certain functions which were transferred to the Federal Energy Regulatory Commission) by sections 7151(b), 7171(a), 7172(a), 7291, and 7293 of Title 42, The Public Health and Welfare.

§6002. Immunity generally

Whenever a witness refuses, on the basis of his privilege against self-incrimination, to testify or provide other information in a proceeding before or ancillary to—

(1) a court or grand jury of the United States,

(2) an agency of the United States, or

(3) either House of Congress, a joint committee of the two Houses, or a committee or a subcommittee of either House,

and the person presiding over the proceeding communicates to the witness an order issued under this title, the witness may not refuse to comply with the order on the basis of his privilege against self-incrimination; but no testimony or other information compelled under the order (or any information directly or indirectly derived from such testimony or other information) may be used against the witness in any criminal case, except a prosecution for perjury, giving a false statement, or otherwise failing to comply with the order.

(Added Pub. L. 91–452, title II, §201(a), Oct. 15, 1970, 84 Stat. 927; amended Pub. L. 103–322, title XXXIII, §330013(4), Sept. 13, 1994, 108 Stat. 2146.)

Amendments

1994—Pub. L. 103–322 substituted "under this title" for "under this part" in concluding provisions.

§6003. Court and grand jury proceedings

(a) In the case of any individual who has been or may be called to testify or provide other information at any proceeding before or ancillary to a court of the United States or a grand jury of the United States, the United States district court for the judicial district in which the proceeding is or may be held shall issue, in accordance with subsection (b) of this section, upon the request of the United States attorney for such district, an order requiring such individual to give testimony or provide other information which he refuses to give or provide on the basis of his privilege against self-incrimination, such order to become effective as provided in section 6002 of this title.

(b) A United States attorney may, with the approval of the Attorney General, the Deputy Attorney General, the Associate Attorney General, or any designated Assistant Attorney General or Deputy Assistant Attorney General, request an order under subsection (a) of this section when in his judgment—

(1) the testimony or other information from such individual may be necessary to the public interest; and

(2) such individual has refused or is likely to refuse to testify or provide other information on the basis of his privilege against self-incrimination.

(Added Pub. L. 91–452, title II, §201(a), Oct. 15, 1970, 84 Stat. 927; amended Pub. L. 100–690, title VII, §7020(e), Nov. 18, 1988, 102 Stat. 4396; Pub. L. 103–322, title XXXIII, §330013(4), Sept. 13, 1994, 108 Stat. 2146.)

Amendments

1994—Subsec. (a). Pub. L. 103–322 substituted "title" for "part" before period at end.
1988—Subsec. (b). Pub. L. 100–690 inserted ", the Associate Attorney General" after "Deputy Attorney General", and "or Deputy Assistant Attorney General" after "Assistant Attorney General".

§6004. Certain administrative proceedings

(a) In the case of any individual who has been or who may be called to testify or provide other information at any proceeding before an agency of the United States, the agency may, with the approval of the Attorney General, issue, in accordance with subsection (b) of this section, an order requiring the individual to give testimony or provide other information which he refuses to give or provide on the basis of his privilege against self-incrimination, such order to become effective as provided in section 6002 of this title.

(b) An agency of the United States may issue an order under subsection (a) of this section only if in its judgment—

(1) the testimony or other information from such individual may be necessary to the public interest; and

(2) such individual has refused or is likely to refuse to testify or provide other information on the basis of his privilege against self-incrimination.

(Added Pub. L. 91–452, title II, §201(a), Oct. 15, 1970, 84 Stat. 927; amended Pub. L. 103–322, title XXXIII, §330013(4), Sept. 13, 1994, 108 Stat. 2146.)

Amendments

§6005. Congressional proceedings

(a) In the case of any individual who has been or may be called to testify or provide other information at any proceeding before or ancillary to either House of Congress, or any committee, or any subcommittee of either House, or any joint committee of the two Houses, a United States district court shall issue, in accordance with subsection (b) of this section, upon the request of a duly authorized representative of the House of Congress or the committee concerned, an order requiring such individual to give testimony or provide other information which he refuses to give or provide on the basis of his privilege against self-incrimination, such order to become effective as provided in section 6002 of this title.

(b) Before issuing an order under subsection (a) of this section, a United States district court shall find that—

(1) in the case of a proceeding before or ancillary to either House of Congress, the request for such an order has been approved by an affirmative vote of a majority of the Members present of that House;

(2) in the case of a proceeding before or ancillary to a committee or a subcommittee of either House of Congress or a joint committee of both Houses, the request for such an order has been approved by an affirmative vote of two-thirds of the members of the full committee; and

(3) ten days or more prior to the day on which the request for such an order was made, the Attorney General was served with notice of an intention to request the order.

(c) Upon application of the Attorney General, the United States district court shall defer the issuance of any order under subsection (a) of this section for such period, not longer than twenty days from the date of the request for such order, as the Attorney General may specify.

(Added Pub. L. 91–452, title II, §201(a), Oct. 15, 1970, 84 Stat. 928; amended Pub. L. 103–322, title XXXIII, §330013(4), Sept. 13, 1994, 108 Stat. 2146; Pub. L. 104–292, §5, Oct. 11, 1996, 110 Stat. 3460; Pub. L. 104–294, title VI, §605(o), Oct. 11, 1996, 110 Stat. 3510.)

Amendments

1996—Subsec. (a). Pub. L. 104–292, §5(1), inserted "or ancillary to" after "any proceeding before".

Subsec. (b)(1), (2). Pub. L. 104–292, §5(2)(A), inserted "or ancillary to" after "a proceeding before".

Subsec. (b)(3). Pub. L. 104–292, §5(2)(B), and Pub. L. 104–294, amended par. (3) identically, inserting period at end.

1994—Subsec. (a). Pub. L. 103–322 substituted "title" for "part" before period at end.

Made in the USA
Monee, IL
06 September 2023

42283307R00378